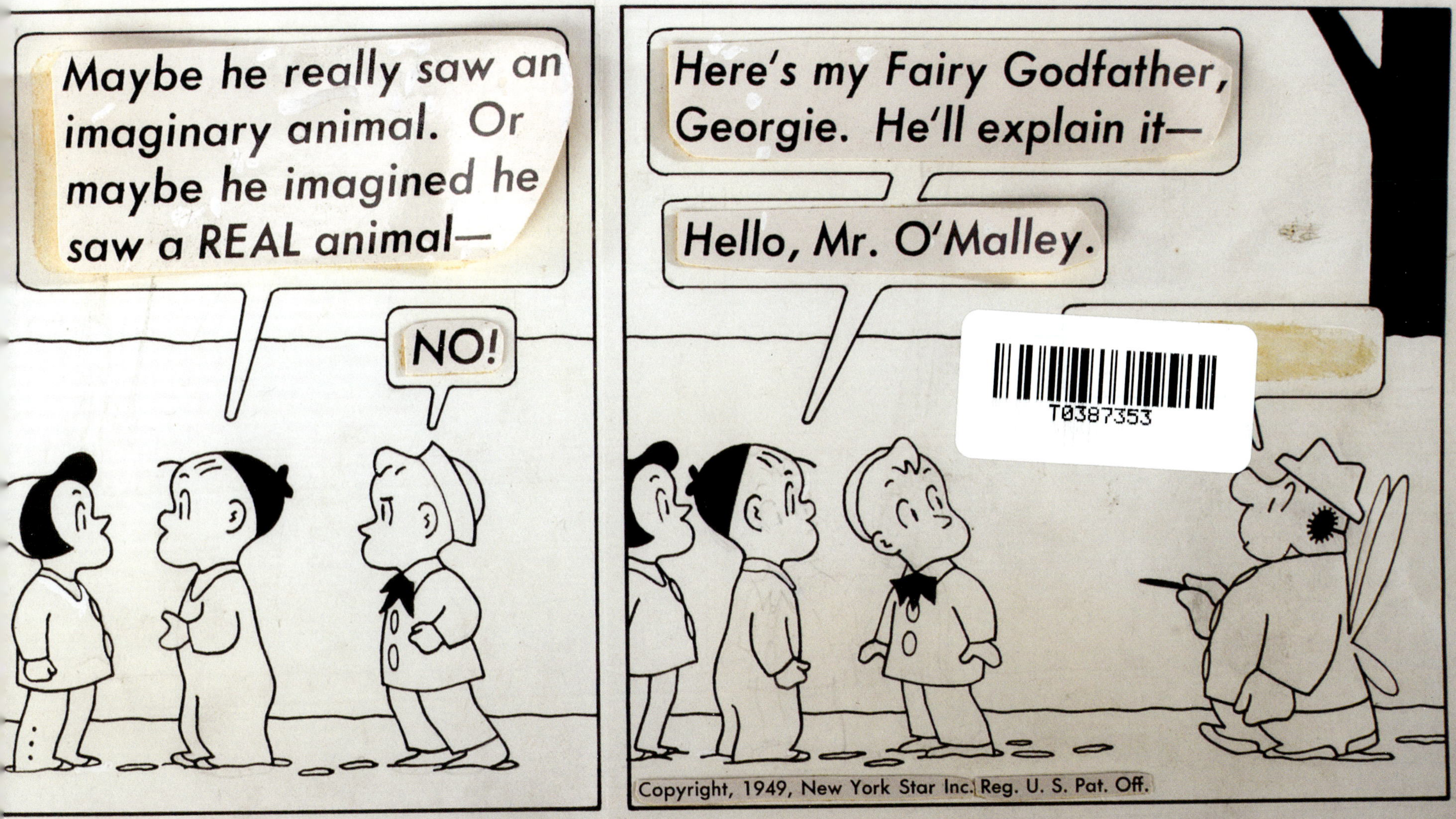
Maybe he really saw an imaginary animal. Or maybe he imagined he saw a REAL animal—
NO!
Here's my Fairy Godfather, Georgie. He'll explain it—
Hello, Mr. O'Malley.
Copyright, 1949, New York Star Inc. Reg. U. S. Pat. Off.

Barnaby

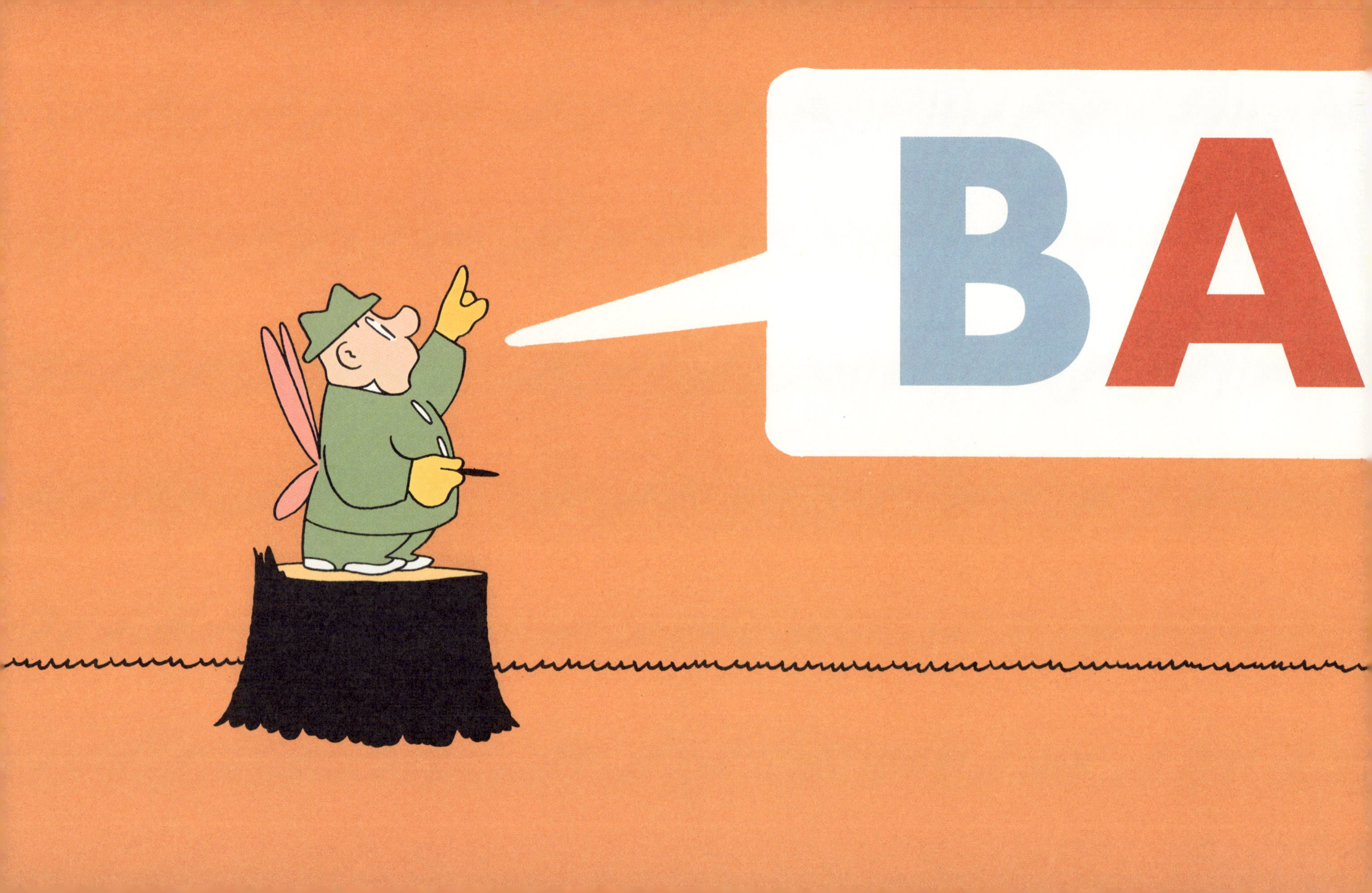
BA

RNABY

BY CROCKETT JOHNSON · VOLUME FIVE: 1950–1952
FANTAGRAPHICS BOOKS, INC. SEATTLE, WASHINGTON

Editors: Philip Nel & Eric Reynolds
Series Designer: Daniel Clowes
Production: Paul Baresh
Art Restoration: Paul Baresh & Ben Horak
Promotion: Tucker Stone
Marketing: Jennifer Chan
VP / Associate Publisher: Eric Reynolds
President / Publisher: Gary Groth

FANTAGRAPHICS BOOKS INC.
7563 Lake City Way NE
Seattle, Washington, 98115
www.fantagraphics.com

ISBN 979-8-8750-0046-1
Library of Congress Control Number 2024941968

First printing: February 2025
Printed in China

CONTENTS

Foreword by Ron Howard 6

O'Malley and the Long Goodbye by Susan Kirtley 11

Barnaby by Crockett Johnson (2 January 1950 – 2 February 1952)..17

Fantastic Companion by Crockett Johnson 346

Afterword: The End? by Philip Nel 351

**The Elves, Leprechauns, Gnomes and Little Men's Chowder and Marching Society:
A Handy Pocket Guide** by Philip Nel 375

Credits / Thank You 391

Errata for Barnaby Volumes One through Four..392

FOREWORD

By Ron Howard

When I was four or five years old, Dad took an acting workshop with a man named Sherman Marks, who also happened to be a television director. While Mom looked after my brother Clint, Dad invited me to tag along and observe.

Evidently, Sherman Marks was also observing me. When he got a job in 1959 to direct a pilot for an NBC comedy series, he asked for Dad's permission to have me audition for it.

Mr. O'Malley was based on a 1940s comic strip called *Barnaby* by Crockett Johnson, creator of *Harold and the Purple Crayon*. Barnaby was a five-year-old boy who, in a subversive inversion of traditional children's stories, had not a fairy godmother but a fairy god*father*. This fairy godfather, Mr. O'Malley, was a cantankerous little man who wore a porkpie hat, smoked cigars, and was borne aloft, just barely, by a set of four dinky little wings: a little bit like Clarence the Angel in *It's a Wonderful Life*, but more gruff. Barnaby was the only person who could actually see and speak with Mr. O'Malley, whose alleged existence exasperated Barnaby's parents. They took their son to a series of psychologists to dissuade him of his delusions.

I passed the audition and got the role as Barnaby. On paper, it sounds like a difficult concept for a five-year-old actor to grasp: a boy with an imaginary friend and parents who disbelieve him. But Dad broke things down for me, walking me through

General Electric Theater, Ron Howard, Bert Lahr ("Barnaby and Mr. O'Malley," Season 8, Episode 14, aired December 20, 1959). Image courtesy of the Everett Collection, Inc.

the character's logic. With Gig Young in *The Twilight Zone*, I didn't understand that I was participating in a parable about a hardened city slicker who has lost touch with his hometown values. Dad just said, "You have no idea what this man is talking about, and you think he's crazy." That was all I needed to know. In *Barnaby*, Dad said, Barnaby believes Mr. O'Malley *is* real and should be treated as such. When his parents say there's no such thing as a fairy godfather — well, Barnaby's parents are just wrong.

I didn't think of the *Barnaby and Mr. O'Malley* job as any kind of big deal until I learned that the actor playing Mr. O'Malley was the man who played the Cowardly Lion in *The Wizard of Oz*: Bert Lahr. That was a big *whoa*. In person, Lahr was simultaneously bigger than life and kind of a disappointment. He had a huge, bulbous nose and a commanding presence, but no particular affinity for his costar, me. He wasn't rude, just transactional, exuding no warmth. And he seemed impossibly old, though I just looked up the dates, and guess what? He was slightly younger than I am now.

Once again, I was working opposite a profuse perspirer — Bert Lahr sweated like a faucet was on. His sweat smelled like the cigarettes that he chain-smoked. Curiously enough, he couldn't stand cigars, so the prop department rigged up a fake cigar that could fit a cigarette inside it for Mr. O'Malley. God, the secondhand smoke I inhaled as a kid! Between Lahr, my mom, my grandparents, and the *Andy Griffith* cast and crew, it's a wonder that I don't have severe lung issues.

What made up for the Cowardly Lion's indifference was O'Malley's invisible sidekick, a leprechaun named McSnoyd, played by Mel Blanc, the voice of Bugs Bunny, Donald Duck, Porky Pig, Sylvester the Cat, Tweety Bird, Foghorn Leghorn, and Elmer Fudd. When Dad told me who the balding man with the mustache was, I zoomed up to him, eager to shake his hand. Blanc was clearly used to awestruck kids like me and obligingly performed a highlight reel of his characters, saliva flying everywhere as I delighted in his repertoire.

And to Lahr's credit, he was amazing once the cameras were rolling. He provided my first exposure to an entertainer for whom the command "Action!" is

like the flick of a switch. He rose to the occasion and transformed into the character, bringing a completely different energy to his performance than he did to his off-camera interactions with the cast and crew.

Barnaby and Mr. O'Malley was good television and I felt like I was part of something special. Right before my eyes was a sight that I, at least, found entertaining and hilarious: Lahr floating into the frame with little pink wings on his back and Blanc off to the side, bringing his voice wizardry to the leprechaun character.

ABOVE: Bert Lahr as Mr. O'Malley and Ronny Howard as Barnaby. Still from the Howard family's film of "Barnaby and Mr. O'Malley" (1959). The show aired in color, but the Howard family's print is in black-and-white. Courtesy of the Howard family.

What I didn't yet understand was the relationship between the scenes that we were shooting beneath those hot lights and a living, breathing audience of viewers. I made no connection between my own passionate viewing of *Superman*, *The Lone Ranger*, *Popeye*, the *Heckle and Jeckle* cartoons, and Laurel and Hardy comedy shorts and the work that I was doing. As for prime time, it was past my bedtime — I didn't see myself on TV until *The Andy Griffith Show*, which my parents occasionally allowed me to stay up to watch on Monday nights. I was not aware that the camera was a portal, and that people outside the studio were actually watching my performances, until I started hearing shouts of "Hey, Opie!" when I walked down the street.

The *Mr. O'Malley* pilot got its shot at winning over America when it aired one evening on *General Electric Theater*, yet another popular anthology TV series of the era. The program's host was a former movie star who was now in a career doldrum, reduced to being a television presenter. Give the guy credit, though: he liked what he saw in me. At the broadcast's conclusion, Ronald Reagan ad-libbed the line "And special thanks to little Ronny Howard, who did a wonderful job as Barnaby."

My performance caught the eye of a major TV producer named Sheldon Leonard, the cocreator of the long-running hit sitcom *The Danny Thomas Show*. Leonard's great gift was tailoring a TV show to a specific actor's skill set. For Thomas, a successful nightclub comedian, he created a series in which Thomas played a family man who was also... a successful nightclub comedian. Leonard also helped Carl Reiner mold *The Dick Van Dyke Show* so that it played to Van Dyke's strengths as an expressive actor with an elastic face and physical-comedy chops.

When Leonard saw me play Barnaby, he was building yet another program around a seasoned actor-comedian: in this case, a folksy guy from North Carolina named Andy Griffith.

Adapted from The Boys: A Memoir of Hollywood and Family *by Clint Howard and Ron Howard (HarperCollins, 2021).*

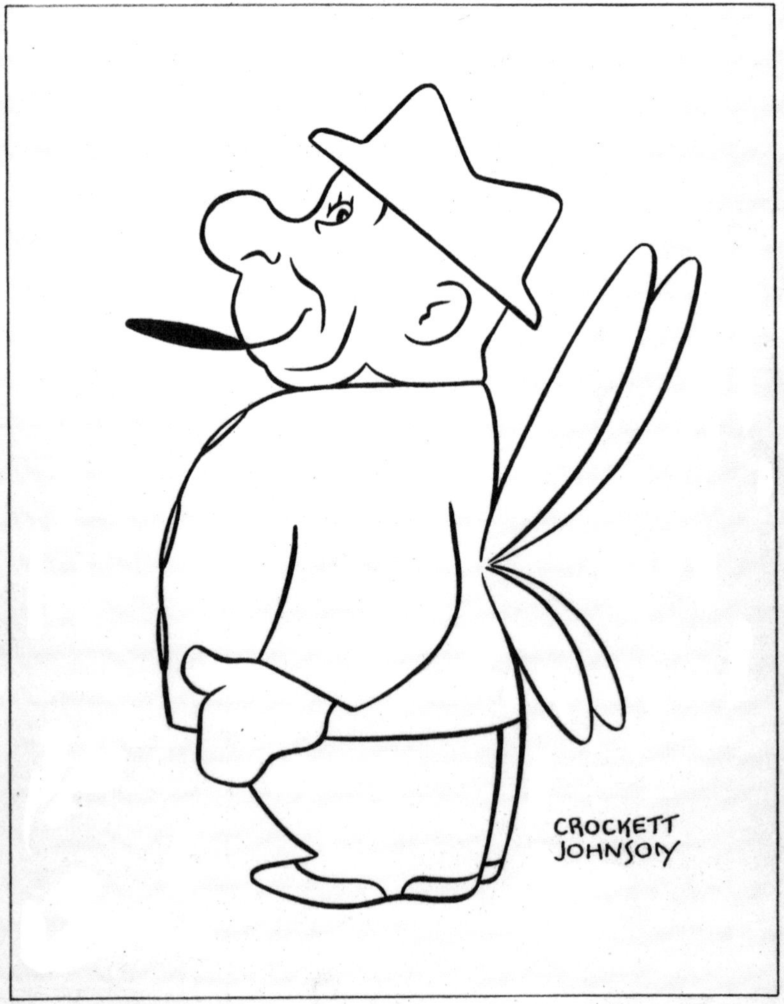
CROCKETT
JOHNSON

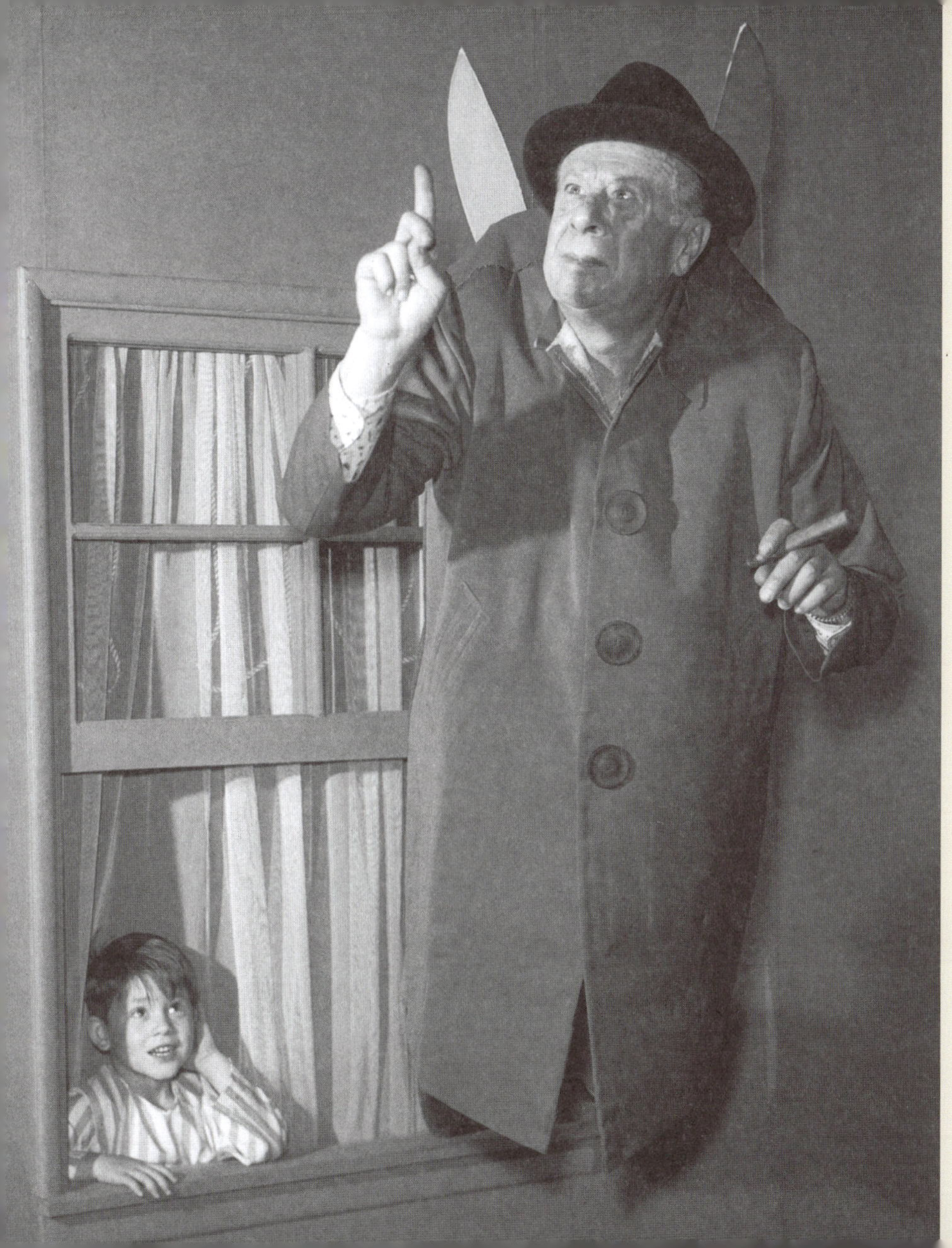

OPPOSITE: *Crockett Johnson, drawing of Bert Lahr as Mr. O'Malley. 1959. Image courtesy of the Ruth Krauss Foundation.*

LEFT: *General Electric Theater, Ron Howard, Bert Lahr ("Barnaby and Mr. O'Malley," Season 8, Episode 14, aired December 20, 1959). Image courtesy of the Everett Collection, Inc.*

RIGHT: *Advertisement for Barnaby and Mr. O'Malley, 20 December 1959.*

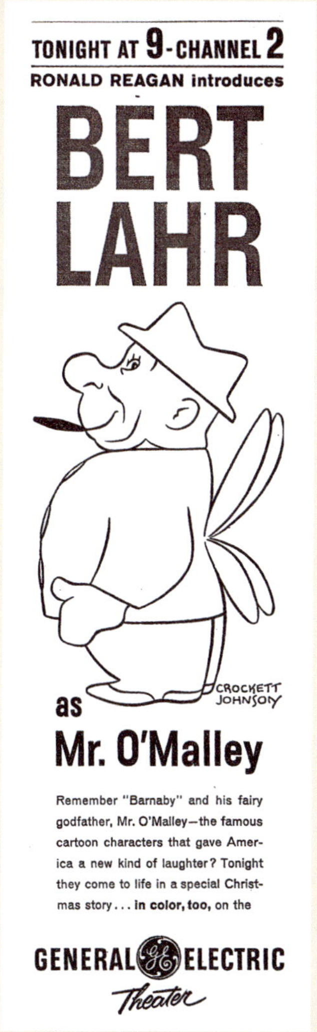

TONIGHT AT 9-CHANNEL 2
RONALD REAGAN introduces
BERT LAHR
CROCKETT JOHNSON
as
Mr. O'Malley
Remember "Barnaby" and his fairy godfather, Mr. O'Malley—the famous cartoon characters that gave America a new kind of laughter? Tonight they come to life in a special Christmas story... in color, too, on the
GENERAL ELECTRIC Theater

O'MALLEY AND THE LONG GOODBYE

By Susan Kirtley

Barnaby began with a boy's fervent wish on a special star, so it seems particularly appropriate that the comic strip should end much as it began. On April 21st, 1942 a young boy, drawn with simple elegance by Crockett Johnson, looked out his bedroom window in search of a star and wished for a fairy godmother. To the delight of his readers, Barnaby received instead the incorrigible Jackeen J. O'Malley, a cigar-smoking, delightfully pompous fairy godfather who arrived in a flurry of wings and bluster to guide the boy through a series of charming misadventures for the next decade. Happily, readers were able to share in this journey until 1952, when Mr. O'Malley flew out Barnaby's window and off the comics pages at the beckoning of another child's wish on a magical star.

During these ten years of comical escapades the world had changed a great deal. When *Barnaby* began the United States was embroiled in World War II and citizens were fully immersed in planting victory gardens, buying bonds, and building military equipment. Ten years later that war was over, and the country had entered a new military conflict, the Korean War, and a new period of prosperity. Much had also changed for creator Crockett Johnson. When *Barnaby* started, Johnson wrote and drew the strip on his own, imbuing it with his distinctive style and wit, but by

1944 he brought in Howard Sparber to do the inking. In 1945 Ted Ferro took over writing with Jack Morley doing the art (Nel 90) so that Johnson could pursue other *Barnaby*-related projects, such as radio broadcasts, a stage play, and a possible film, in addition to pursuing other creative endeavors, such as drafting illustrations for books like the acclaimed *The Carrot Seed*, written by his wife Ruth Krauss.

But Johnson simply couldn't leave Barnaby behind. He returned to writing the strip in 1947, with Morley continuing as the artist. In 1948, the color Sunday strips ended and a few years after that, Johnson decided it was finally time to let Barnaby and Mr. O'Malley go, allowing the author to enter the next stage of his career, this one marked primarily by another curious little boy, Harold, who in 1955 began a series of adventures with his purple crayon. Yet despite Johnson's success writing the Harold books, Barnaby — much like his magical godfather Mr. O'Malley — seemed to hover around Johnson, who returned to the characters over and over in subsequent years. Perhaps it is not surprising that Mr. O'Malley simply couldn't leave the party gracefully, and in 1960 the strip restarted from the beginning with Warren Sattler helping with the art as Johnson revised the older plotlines. The experiment lasted for only two years. In 1962 Johnson recycled the original ending and concluded the strip once more.

All of this history offers evidence that it isn't easy to say farewell to those we love, and *Barnaby*'s bittersweet and somewhat extended conclusion merits a closer look. Over the course of several weeks in early 1952, Johnson took a great deal of time building up to that final goodbye, allowing the audience (and the creator) time to revisit the characters and scenes that made the series special, celebrating the joy of friends and past adventures while grieving the end of the journey. On January 3rd, 1952 Barnaby's father broaches the subject of an impending and inevitable separation between boy and fairy godfather, informing his son, "Things ARE going to be different around here, son. That 'Mr. O'Malley' of yours is going away... You're going to be older. You'll be six soon... And big boys don't have imaginary Fairy Godfathers, do they?" When confronted with this objectionable notion, Mr. O'Malley seizes upon a loophole so that he might stay with his young charge, explaining on January 7th that "if you don't have your sixth birthday I won't have to go away."

Mr. O'Malley encourages Barnaby to hold a town meeting and consult with a panel of "fair-minded people who are not particularly in favor of growing up," since the choice of whether to mature is such a momentous decision. Barnaby enlists his mother to assist with the event, which she understands as a birthday party with cake, ice cream, and all of his young friends, rather than a gathering of "invisible" companions to debate the merits of entering adulthood. Over several days leading up to the birthday, Barnaby and O'Malley visit favorite characters under the pretense of inviting them to the town meeting/birthday party, giving Barnaby, and the audience, the chance to say a lengthy last goodbye. The duo seek out Gus the Ghost, who reprimands O'Malley, telling him to stop being "maudlin" and "disgraceful," and Lancelot McSnoyd, who teases the fairy godfather, chiding, "Can't you never loin, O'Malley?" Throughout these encounters Barnaby demonstrates more and more independence from his godfather. On January 18th, O'Malley, in a delightful turn of apophasis, declares that he won't advise Barnaby "on so vital a matter," before attempting to do just that when Barnaby suddenly interrupts his mentor and strides away, declaring, "All right, Mr. O'Malley. If you

say so, I won't ask you. I'll decide myself." Poor Mr. O'Malley looks on in wonder, emitting an unbelieving, "Eh?"

Mr. O'Malley continues to ponder the fate of his young charge when he happens upon Barnaby doing math on a chalkboard, "practicing numbers... For when I go to school" on January 22nd, 1952. This moment feels significant, as his dog Gorgon looks on with a slightly worried expression, and Mr. O'Malley warns Barnaby, "Such petty triumphs of logic tend to lure one into growing up, Barnaby. Be careful." The almost-six-year old ignores them both, exclaiming in delight at his calculations. Mr. O'Malley is no longer leading the way; Barnaby is moving forward into a world of ideas and "petty logic."

On January 24th, in one of the saddest days of the series, Barnaby continues his mathematical calculations while the normally loquacious Gorgon the dog abruptly stops speaking. In the first panel, Mr. O'Malley stands to the left side of the scene, his hand outstretched as he tries to convince Barnaby not to grow up, but to the right, Barnaby stands at the chalkboard, his back to the viewer, his head turning to address Gorgon. Barnaby asks, "Gorgon, do you know what three and three is?" Gorgon, looking up at his owner, posits, "Sure. A lot." The humorous retort is countered by Mr. O'Malley, who argues, "Things will change! Your talking dog —." Oblivious, Barnaby continues his calculations: "Look. One, two, three, four, five, SIX — It's six, wouldn't you say?" Yet now, even though the boy and his dog are in almost exactly the same position, the square speech balloon floating above Gorgon is entirely empty. The blank space functions as a glaring absence: Gorgon can no longer speak. In the third panel Gorgon scampers away, the vacant balloon hovering ominously over his worried countenance as Barnaby and Mr. O'Malley watch with concern. O'Malley decries, "He never WILL say, m'boy. He'll never speak again! See? You ARE growing up! This is a sign!" But Barnaby can

OPPOSITE LEFT: Crockett Johnson, script for Barnaby of 28 January 1952.

OPPOSITE RIGHT: Crockett Johnson, script for Barnaby of 29 January 1952. Images courtesy of the Smithsonian Institution.

BARNABY MON JAN 28

Arch of living room

Mom and
Pop holding a lighted
cake with six candles
stand partly in at left

Kids
Albert, pointing off right

Let's all go into the dining room and cut the cake--Now where's Barnaby? M

At the window. His Fairy Godfather is outside in the yard. A

Other shot of
living room

Mom dragging
Barnaby away
from window

Come, Barnaby. You have to blow out the candles-- M

But then I'll be six years old! And Mr. O'Malley, my Fairy Godfather, won't be able to come in--EVER! B

Front yard

O'malley standing
against tree

Corner of house
in background

BARNABY TUES JAN 29

Dining room

Table laden with buffet dishes,
Cake with smoking candles
Barnaby near it, surrounded by
Kids (Not Albert)
Mom
Pop } Partly in at left

Good! Barnaby blew out all the candles! M

All six! P

Where's the ice cream? Kid

Sauce pan to right
Kids packed in and off left
Barnaby pushing out of pack
toward right
Jane at right

I'm six years old now, Jane. So I guess Mr. O'Malley, my Fairy Godfather went away. Did he? B

He's not in the yard anymore. J

Pan more to right
Jane and Kids (left)
Barnaby
Albert in at right, pointing
off to right

Barnaby!...Your Fairy Godfather and an invisible Leprechaun and a Ghost are in the front hall! A

Huh? B

only respond with a solemn "Gosh." Barnaby can do math all by himself, gaining independence and intellect, but he has lost something extraordinarily precious. The connection with whimsy and belief in magic is fading, as suddenly as the text in Gorgon's speech balloon, and we readers feel bereft for the absence.

Barnaby's path feels inexorable, and, eventually, the day of the birthday party dawns. The guests arrive, the candles are blown out and Barnaby turns six, but a dejected Mr. O'Malley has just enough magic for one last goodbye, bringing along Gus the Ghost and the Invisible Leprechaun. Although Barnaby entreats Mr. O'Malley to stay and enjoy the party, his Fairy Godfather, tears streaming down his cheeks, walks to the door, explaining, "I must be going. You're six years old now, you see — Your Fairy Godfather understands... Well, good bye, Barnaby." And, without an embrace or further ado, Mr. O'Malley flies off as Barnaby waves farewell.

If that sequence wasn't emotional enough, Barnaby truly marks the end of his fanciful childhood in the following day's episode, calling back to the opening sequence of the series. When *Barnaby* first began, the young child was pictured resting in bed and looking out his bedroom window, wishing on the brightest star for "a couple of good Fairy Godmothers," at which point Mr. O'Malley came rocketing through the window, exclaiming "Cushlamochree! Broke my magic wand! You wished for a Godparent who could grant wishes? Lucky boy! Your wish is granted! I'm your Fairy Godfather." The penultimate *Barnaby* echoes the first strips textually and symbolically, with the now six-year-old Barnaby back in his room, poised at the threshold between the wakefulness of day and the dreams of nighttime. This time Barnaby has left the sanctity of his bed to stand on a stool beside the window, for he has noticed a "funny star in the sky," reminiscent of the one he wished on when Mr. O'Malley initially arrived. The star has reappeared, the symbol of wishes imagined and fulfilled, but Barnaby knows it isn't for him,

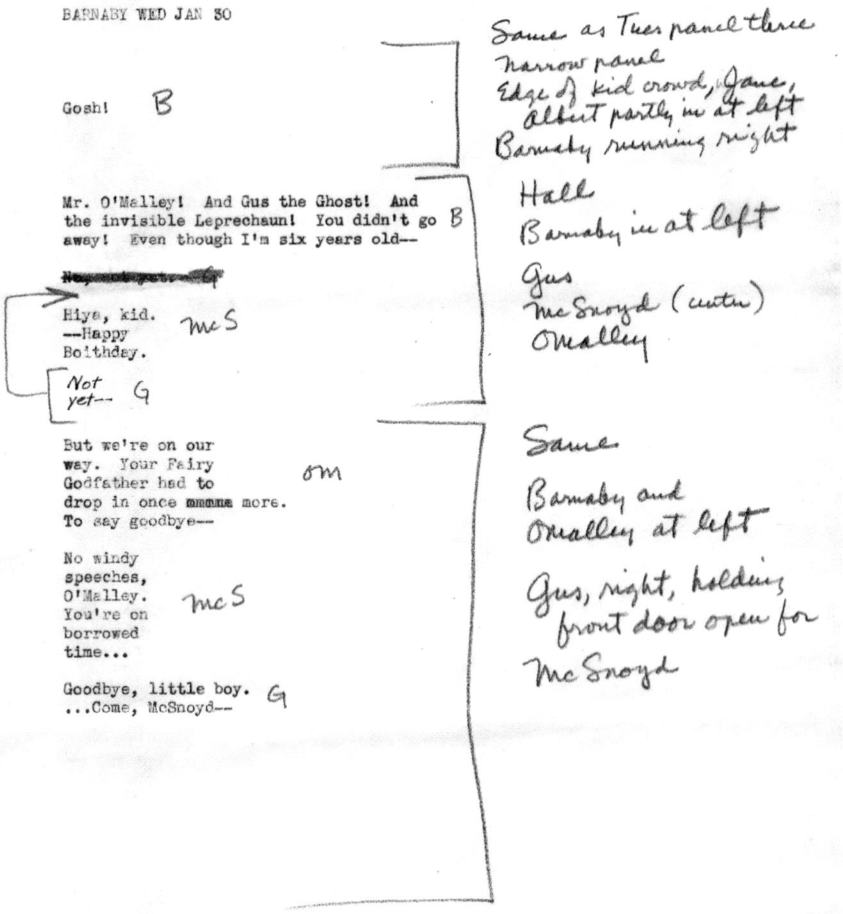
BARNABY WED JAN 30

Gosh! B

Same as Tues panel three
Narrow panel
Edge of kid crowd, Jane, Albert partly in at left
Barnaby running right

Mr. O'Malley! And Gus the Ghost! And the invisible Leprechaun! You didn't go away! Even though I'm six years old-- B

Hiya, kid. --Happy Boithday. McS

Not yet-- G

Hall
Barnaby in at left
Gus
McSnoyd (center)
OMalley

But we're on our way. Your Fairy Godfather had to drop in once more. To say goodbye-- OM

No windy speeches, O'Malley. You're on borrowed time... McS

Goodbye, little boy. ...Come, McSnoyd-- G

Same
Barnaby and
OMalley at left
Gus, right, holding front door open for
McSnoyd

LEFT: Crockett Johnson, script for Barnaby *of 30 January 1952. Image courtesy of the Smithsonian Institution.*

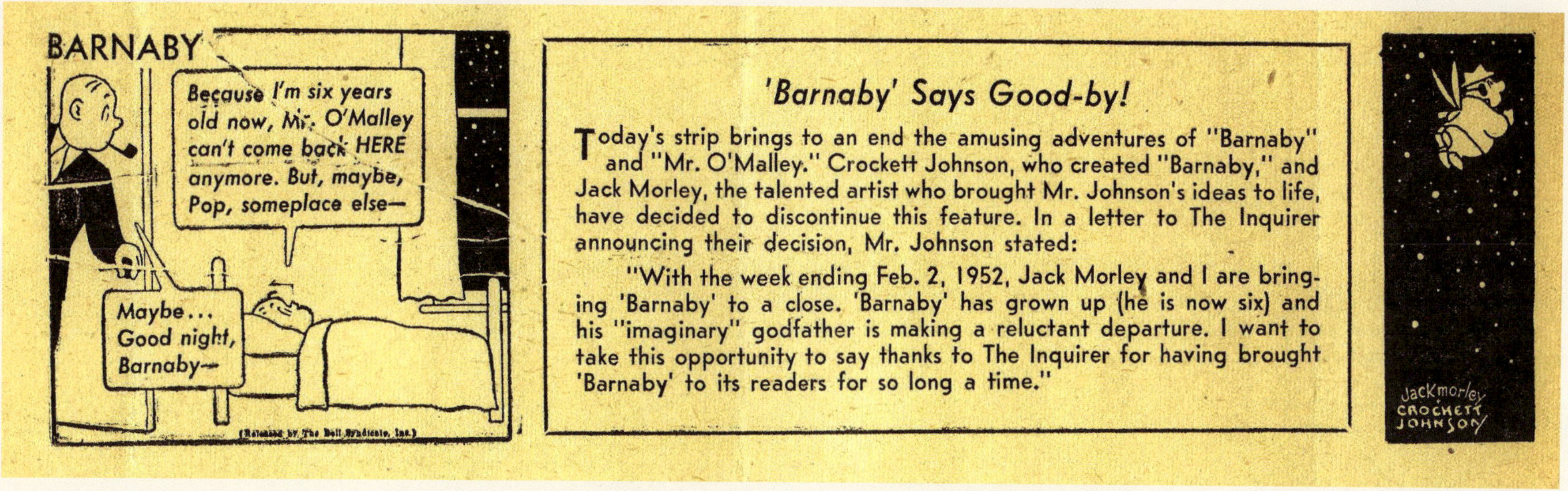

BARNABY

Because I'm six years old now, Mr. O'Malley can't come back HERE anymore. But, maybe, Pop, someplace else—

Maybe... Good night, Barnaby—

(Released by The Bell Syndicate, Inc.)

'Barnaby' Says Good-by!

Today's strip brings to an end the amusing adventures of "Barnaby" and "Mr. O'Malley." Crockett Johnson, who created "Barnaby," and Jack Morley, the talented artist who brought Mr. Johnson's ideas to life, have decided to discontinue this feature. In a letter to The Inquirer announcing their decision, Mr. Johnson stated:

"With the week ending Feb. 2, 1952, Jack Morley and I are bringing 'Barnaby' to a close. 'Barnaby' has grown up (he is now six) and his "imaginary" godfather is making a reluctant departure. I want to take this opportunity to say thanks to The Inquirer for having brought 'Barnaby' to its readers for so long a time."

Jack Morley
CROCKETT JOHNSON

responding to his father, "It was only a shooting star," and choosing to the shut the window himself. Barnaby asserts his autonomy from his father and from childhood whimsy, dismissing the star and physically closing off the opportunity for fantasy.

This moment feels poignant as Barnaby seems to fully relinquish the fanciful notions of childhood, but Johnson continues the narrative one more day, concluding with a promise that magic — even chaotic, buoyant, cigar-smoking magic — endures. In the very last strip Barnaby rests in bed, gazing out the closed window with his father poised to shut the door and say goodnight. As he looks out at the stars Barnaby wonders, "Because I'm six years old now, Mr. O'Malley can't come back HERE anymore, but maybe, Pop, somewhere else —" His father responds with a doubtful, "Maybe... Good night, Barnaby —." In those ellipses and dashes there is much unsaid, doubt but also desire — maybe magic *can* persevere. Despite his

newfound maturation, Barnaby gestures to a belief that, perhaps, fantasy survives.

The second panel is a thin one comprised of a black night and a sprinkling of stars. It stands at the threshold, a division between five-years-old and six, one child and the next, an empty space of stars and wonder. At the other end of the expanse there are two more panels, in which Mr. O'Malley crawls awkwardly through another boy's window and once more exclaims, "Cushlamochree! You wished for a Fairy Godparent? Lucky boy! Your wish is granted!... O'Malley's the name." The drawing makes it clear that this is a new boy with dark hair (as opposed to the bald Barnaby) in a new bedroom with dark bedcoverings, but Mr. O'Malley remains exuberant and unchanged and ready to begin the cycle anew.

ABOVE: The Philadelphia Inquirer's version of the final Barnaby strip, 2 February 1952. Image courtesy of the Smithsonian Institution.

Curiously, *The Philadelphia Inquirer* found this ending too ambiguous. Believing its readers would be confused by the turn, the paper instead altered the last strip, adding after Johnson's first panel a new large panel filled with text, explaining: "'Barnaby' Says Good-by! Today's strip brings to and end the amusing adventures of 'Barnaby' and 'Mr. O'Malley.' Crockett Johnson, who created "Barnaby," and Jack Morley, the talented artist who brought Mr. Johnson's ideas to life, have decided to discontinue the feature." This disclaimer makes it unequivocal that the strip has reached its conclusion, and furthermore, that this decision comes from the creators, and not the newspaper itself. However, this lengthy explanation only allows for a very narrow third and final panel, depicting O'Malley flying off into the starry night sky, and deprives audiences of the circular narrative finale, in which Mr. O'Malley meets another child.

Endings are hard enough as it is, but I shudder to think of the readers of the time who were subjected to this truncated finale, unaware that Mr. O'Malley continued his shenanigans *ad infinitum*. For Mr. O'Malley did live on, with his new young charge in his world, but also in Johnson's and, of course, in ours. Even as Johnson found novel inspiration with Harold, Mr. O'Malley circled around his psyche, and still makes himself known today, nudging at the window and demanding entrance in various guises and venues. Barnaby and Mr. O'Malley and all their friends live on in the minds of the readers, and now, they live on in another generation through this reprinted collection. Like Barnaby and Crockett Johnson, our lives are all the better for knowing that magic and mayhem and Mr. O'Malley endure.

RIGHT: E.B. Thompson, letter to Crockett Johnson, 4 February 1952. Image courtesy of the Smithsonian Institution.

The Philadelphia Inquirer
EDITORIAL ROOMS

February 4, 1952

Mr. Crockett Johnson
74 Rowayton Avenue
Rowayton, Conn.

Dear Mr. Johnson:

We took the liberty of making some changes in your final "Barnaby" strip and enclosed herewith is a proof of the one we printed last Saturday.

I felt that a strip of this sort would write "finis" in such a manner that we would not be deluged with letters and calls. It has proved effective and it occurred to me that you and Jack Morley might be interested in seeing it.

With best wishes, I am

Sincerely yours,

E. B. THOMPSON
Managing Editor - Features

EBT/ahr

Barnaby

2 JANUARY 1950 – 2 FEBRUARY 1952

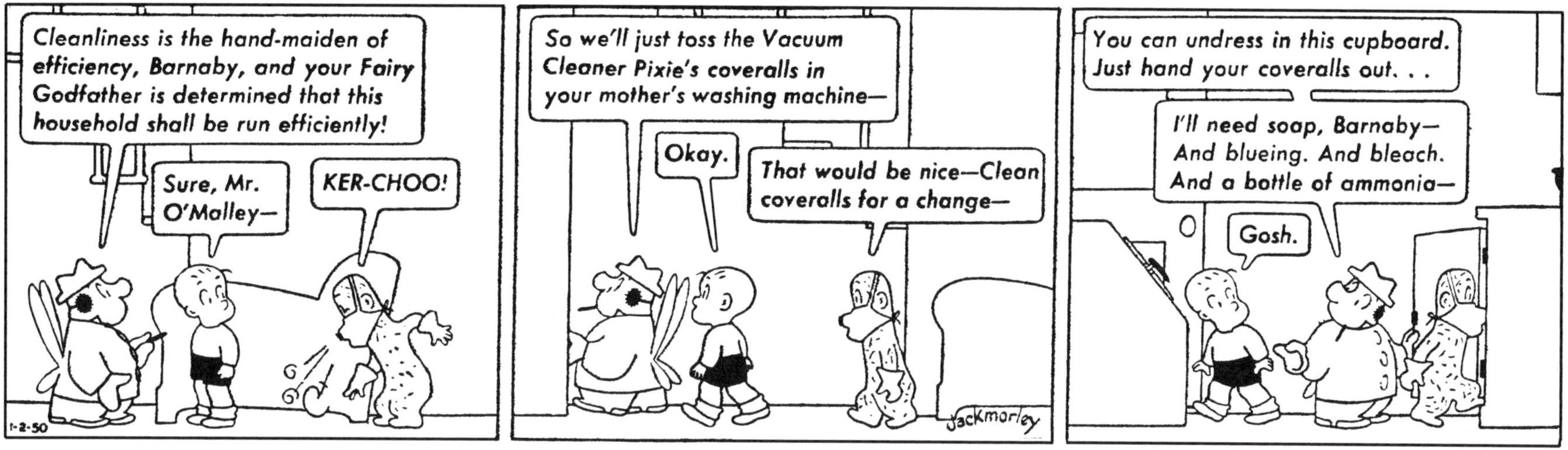
Cleanliness is the hand-maiden of efficiency, Barnaby, and your Fairy Godfather is determined that this household shall be run efficiently!
Sure, Mr. O'Malley—
KER-CHOO!
1-2-50
So we'll just toss the Vacuum Cleaner Pixie's coveralls in your mother's washing machine—
Okay.
That would be nice—Clean coveralls for a change—
Jackmorley
You can undress in this cupboard. Just hand your coveralls out. . .
I'll need soap, Barnaby— And blueing. And bleach. And a bottle of ammonia—
Gosh.

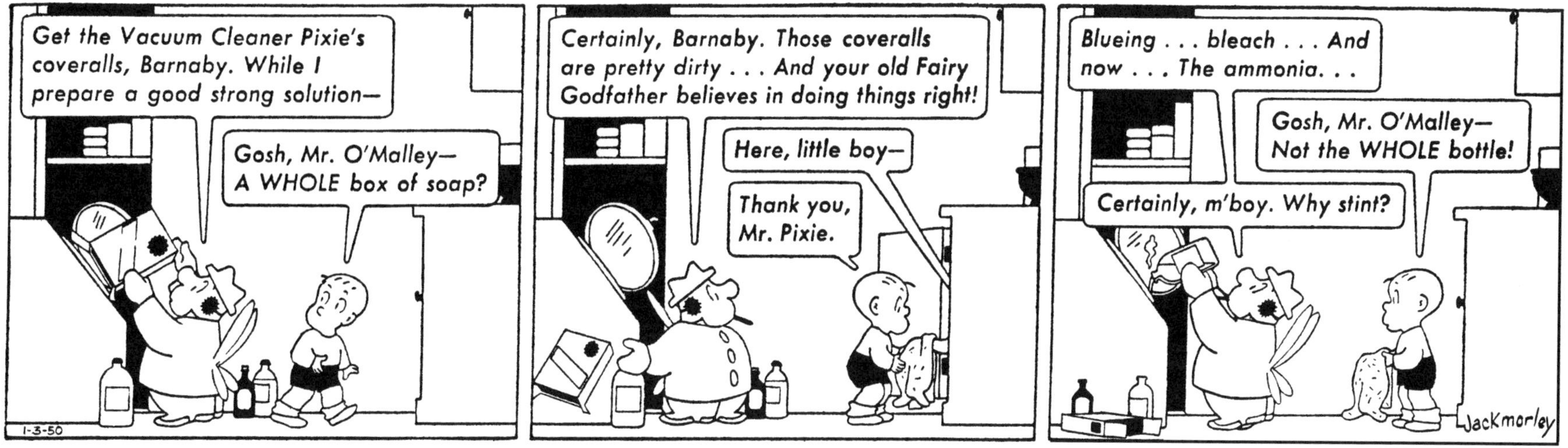
Get the Vacuum Cleaner Pixie's coveralls, Barnaby. While I prepare a good strong solution—
Gosh, Mr. O'Malley— A WHOLE box of soap?
1-3-50
Certainly, Barnaby. Those coveralls are pretty dirty . . . And your old Fairy Godfather believes in doing things right!
Here, little boy—
Thank you, Mr. Pixie.
Blueing . . . bleach . . . And now . . . The ammonia. . .
Gosh, Mr. O'Malley— Not the WHOLE bottle!
Certainly, m'boy. Why stint?
Jackmorley

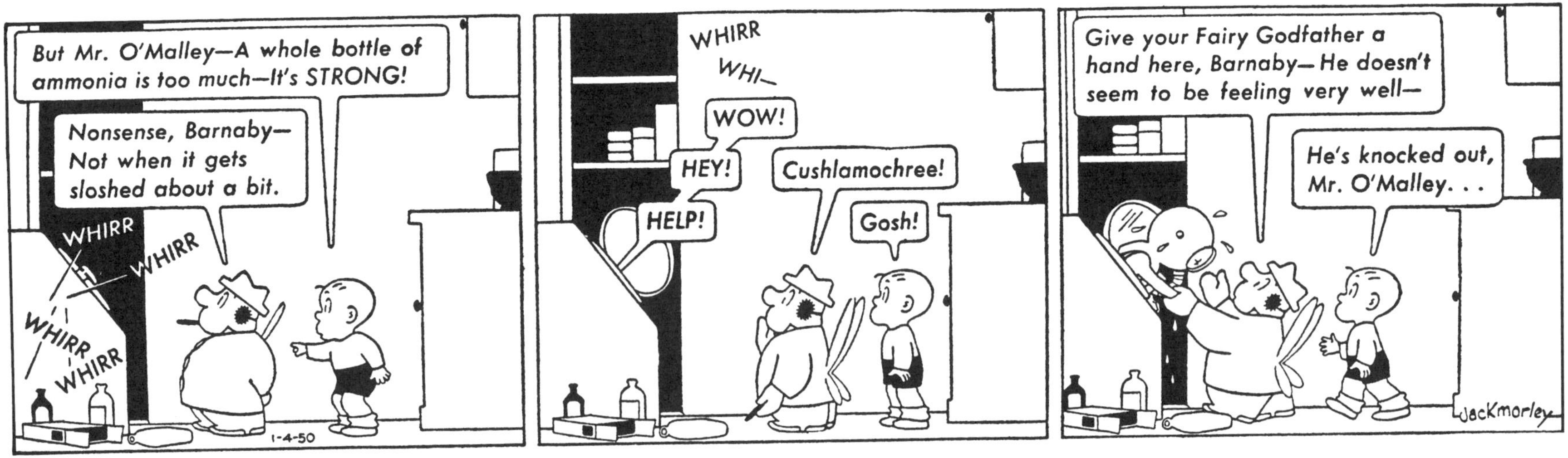
But Mr. O'Malley—A whole bottle of ammonia is too much—It's STRONG!
Nonsense, Barnaby— Not when it gets sloshed about a bit.
WHIRR
WHIRR
WHIRR
WHIRR
1-4-50
WHIRR
WHI—
WOW!
HEY!
HELP!
Cushlamochree!
Gosh!
Give your Fairy Godfather a hand here, Barnaby— He doesn't seem to be feeling very well—
He's knocked out, Mr. O'Malley. . .
JackMorley

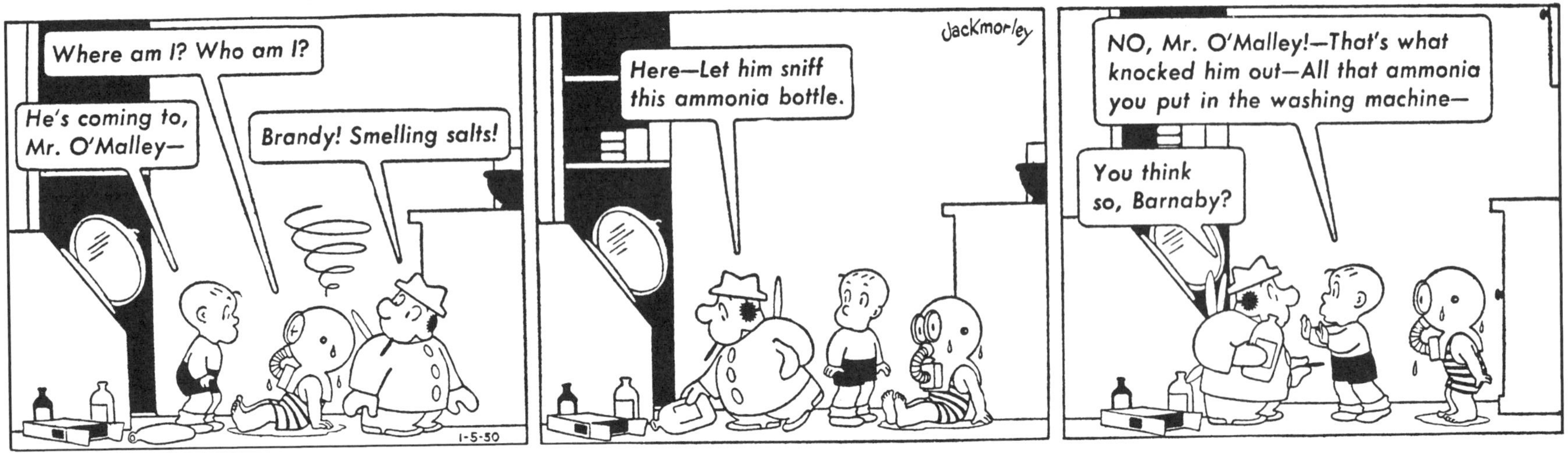
Where am I? Who am I?
He's coming to, Mr. O'Malley—
Brandy! Smelling salts!
1-5-50
JackMorley
Here—Let him sniff this ammonia bottle.
NO, Mr. O'Malley!—That's what knocked him out—All that ammonia you put in the washing machine—
You think so, Barnaby?

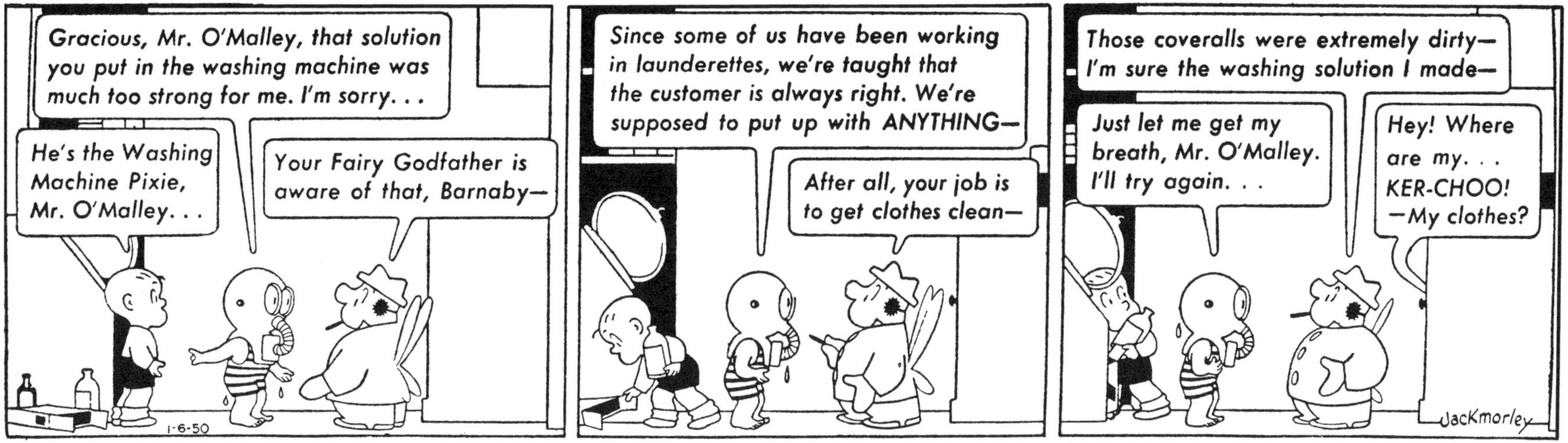
Gracious, Mr. O'Malley, that solution you put in the washing machine was much too strong for me. I'm sorry. . .
He's the Washing Machine Pixie, Mr. O'Malley. . .
Your Fairy Godfather is aware of that, Barnaby—
1-6-50
Since some of us have been working in launderettes, we're taught that the customer is always right. We're supposed to put up with ANYTHING—
After all, your job is to get clothes clean—
Those coveralls were extremely dirty— I'm sure the washing solution I made—
Just let me get my breath, Mr. O'Malley. I'll try again. . .
Hey! Where are my. . . KER-CHOO! —My clothes?
JacKmorley

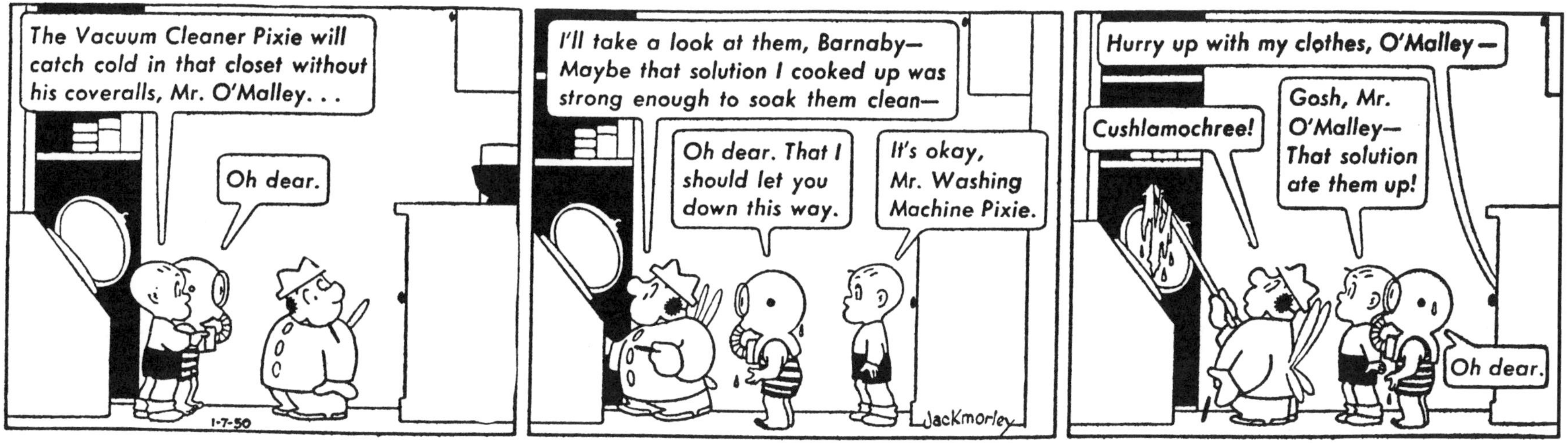
The Vacuum Cleaner Pixie will catch cold in that closet without his coveralls, Mr. O'Malley. . .
Oh dear.
1-7-50
I'll take a look at them, Barnaby— Maybe that solution I cooked up was strong enough to soak them clean—
Oh dear. That I should let you down this way.
It's okay, Mr. Washing Machine Pixie.
JacKmorley
Hurry up with my clothes, O'Malley—
Cushlamochree!
Gosh, Mr. O'Malley— That solution ate them up!
Oh dear.

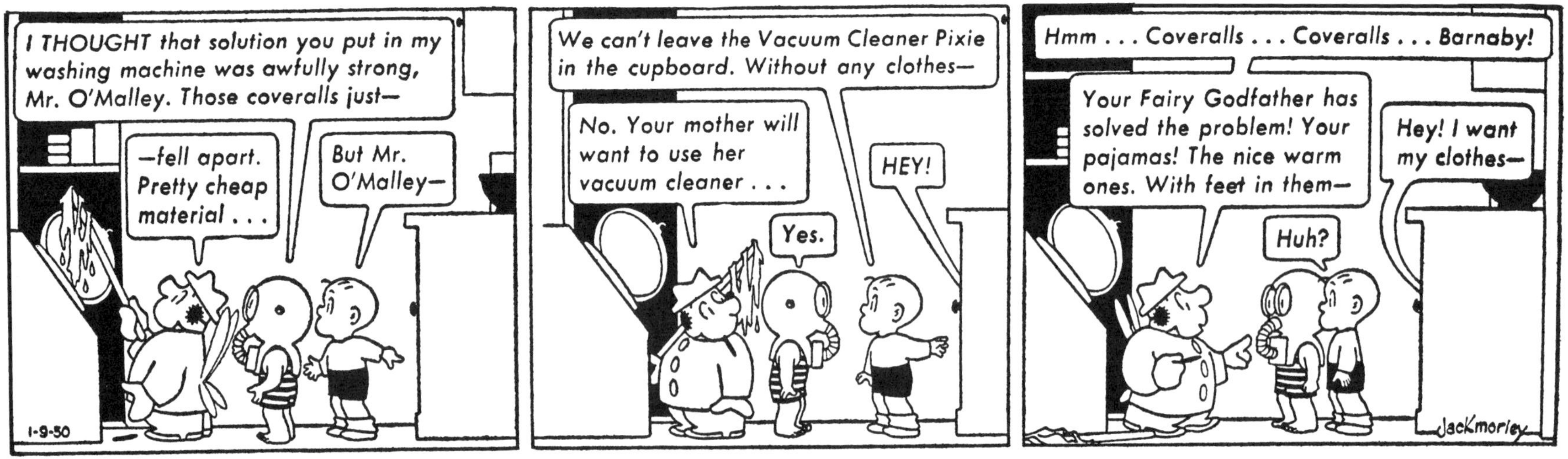
I THOUGHT that solution you put in my washing machine was awfully strong, Mr. O'Malley. Those coveralls just—
—fell apart. Pretty cheap material . . .
But Mr. O'Malley—
1-9-50
We can't leave the Vacuum Cleaner Pixie in the cupboard. Without any clothes—
No. Your mother will want to use her vacuum cleaner . . .
HEY!
Yes.
Hmm . . . Coveralls . . . Coveralls . . . Barnaby!
Your Fairy Godfather has solved the problem! Your pajamas! The nice warm ones. With feet in them—
Hey! I want my clothes—
Huh?
JacKmorley

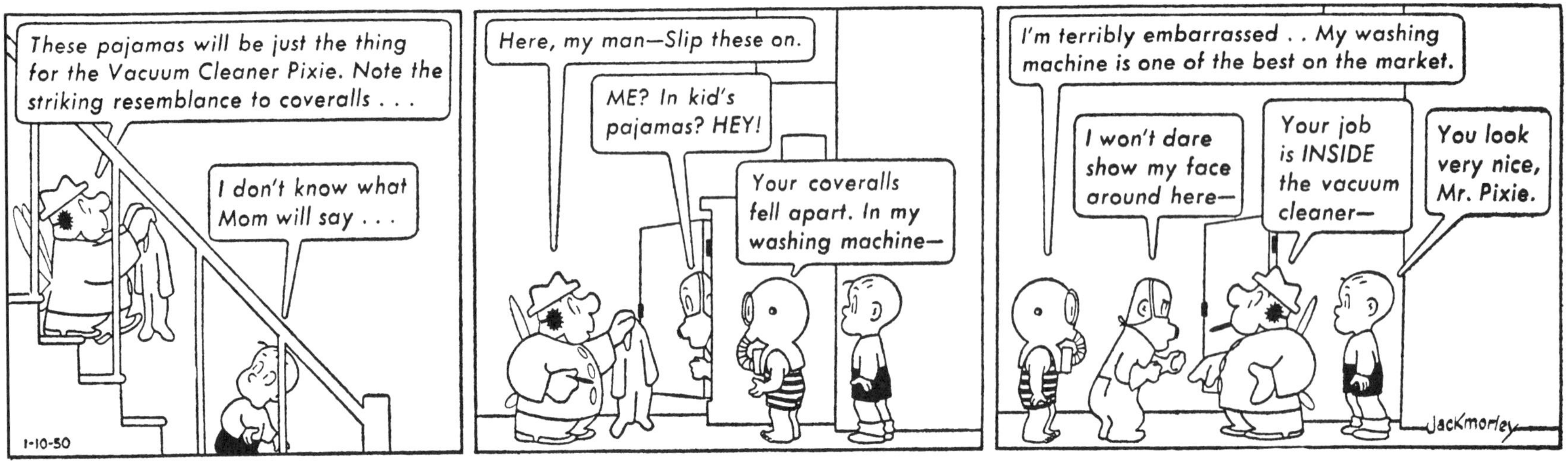
These pajamas will be just the thing for the Vacuum Cleaner Pixie. Note the striking resemblance to coveralls . . .
I don't know what Mom will say . . .
1-10-50
Here, my man—Slip these on.
ME? In kid's pajamas? HEY!
Your coveralls fell apart. In my washing machine—
I'm terribly embarrassed . . My washing machine is one of the best on the market.
I won't dare show my face around here—
Your job is INSIDE the vacuum cleaner—
You look very nice, Mr. Pixie.
JacKmorley

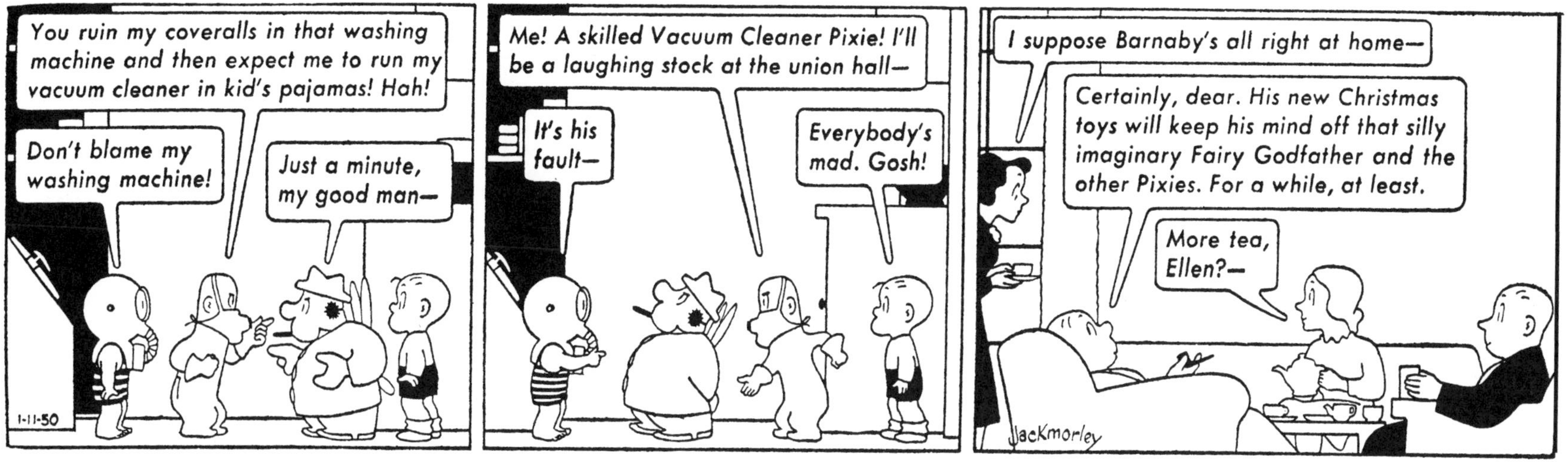
You ruin my coveralls in that washing machine and then expect me to run my vacuum cleaner in kid's pajamas! Hah!
Don't blame my washing machine!
Just a minute, my good man—
1-11-50
Me! A skilled Vacuum Cleaner Pixie! I'll be a laughing stock at the union hall—
It's his fault—
Everybody's mad. Gosh!
I suppose Barnaby's all right at home—
Certainly, dear. His new Christmas toys will keep his mind off that silly imaginary Fairy Godfather and the other Pixies. For a while, at least.
More tea, Ellen?—
JackMorley

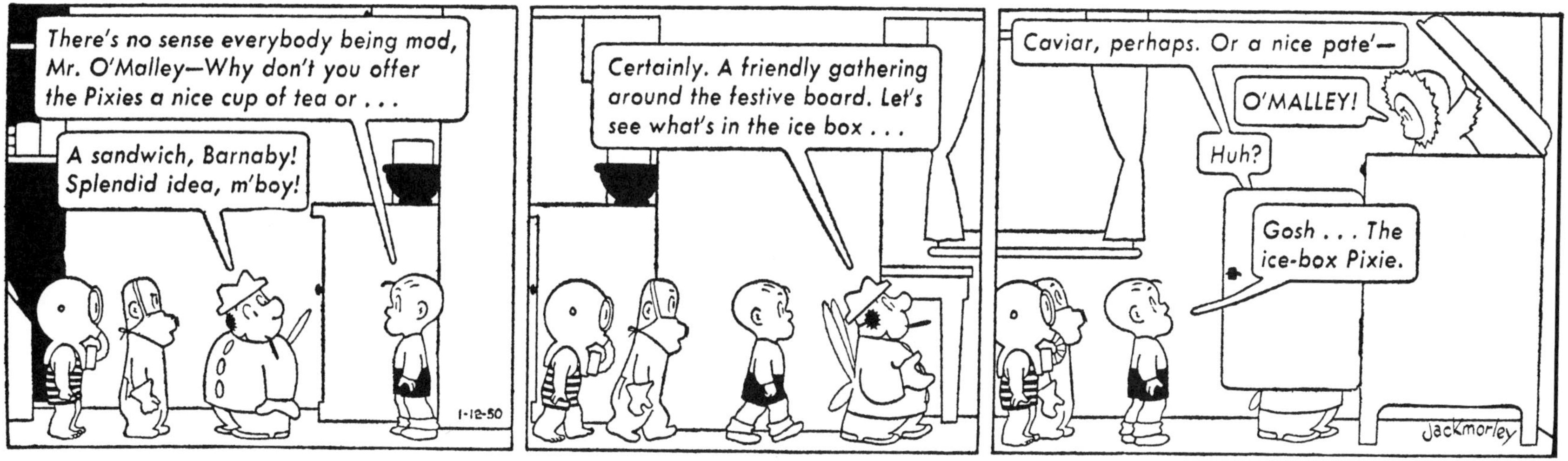
There's no sense everybody being mad, Mr. O'Malley—Why don't you offer the Pixies a nice cup of tea or . . .
A sandwich, Barnaby! Splendid idea, m'boy!
1-12-50
Certainly. A friendly gathering around the festive board. Let's see what's in the ice box . . .
Caviar, perhaps. Or a nice pate'—
O'MALLEY!
Huh?
Gosh . . . The ice-box Pixie.
JackMorley

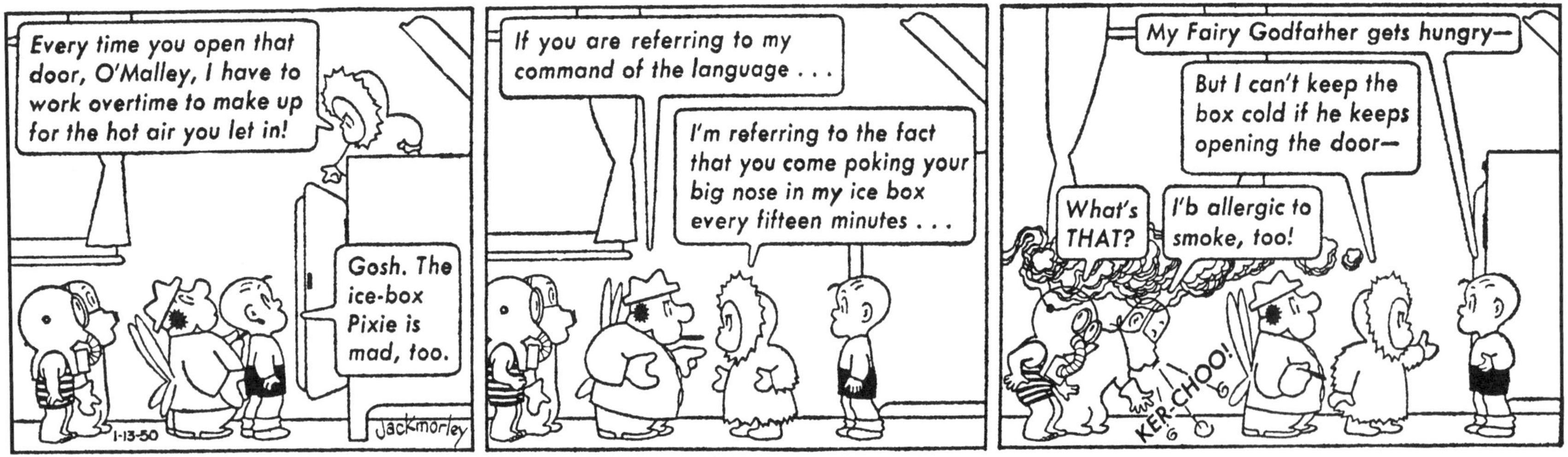
Every time you open that door, O'Malley, I have to work overtime to make up for the hot air you let in!
Gosh. The ice-box Pixie is mad, too.
1-13-50
JACKMORLEY
If you are referring to my command of the language . . .
I'm referring to the fact that you come poking your big nose in my ice box every fifteen minutes . . .
My Fairy Godfather gets hungry—
But I can't keep the box cold if he keeps opening the door—
What's THAT?
I'b allergic to smoke, too!
KER-CHOO!

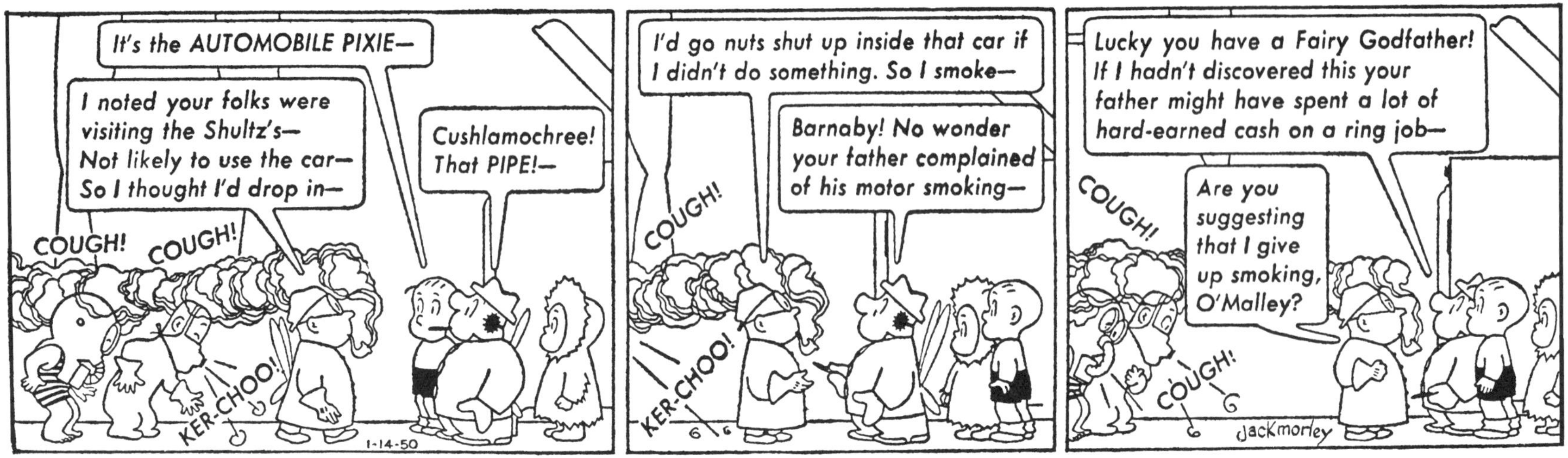
It's the AUTOMOBILE PIXIE—
I noted your folks were visiting the Shultz's— Not likely to use the car— So I thought I'd drop in—
Cushlamochree! That PIPE!—
COUGH! COUGH!
KER-CHOO!
1-14-50
I'd go nuts shut up inside that car if I didn't do something. So I smoke—
Barnaby! No wonder your father complained of his motor smoking—
COUGH!
KER-CHOO!
Lucky you have a Fairy Godfather! If I hadn't discovered this your father might have spent a lot of hard-earned cash on a ring job—
Are you suggesting that I give up smoking, O'Malley?
COUGH!
COUGH!
JACKMORLEY

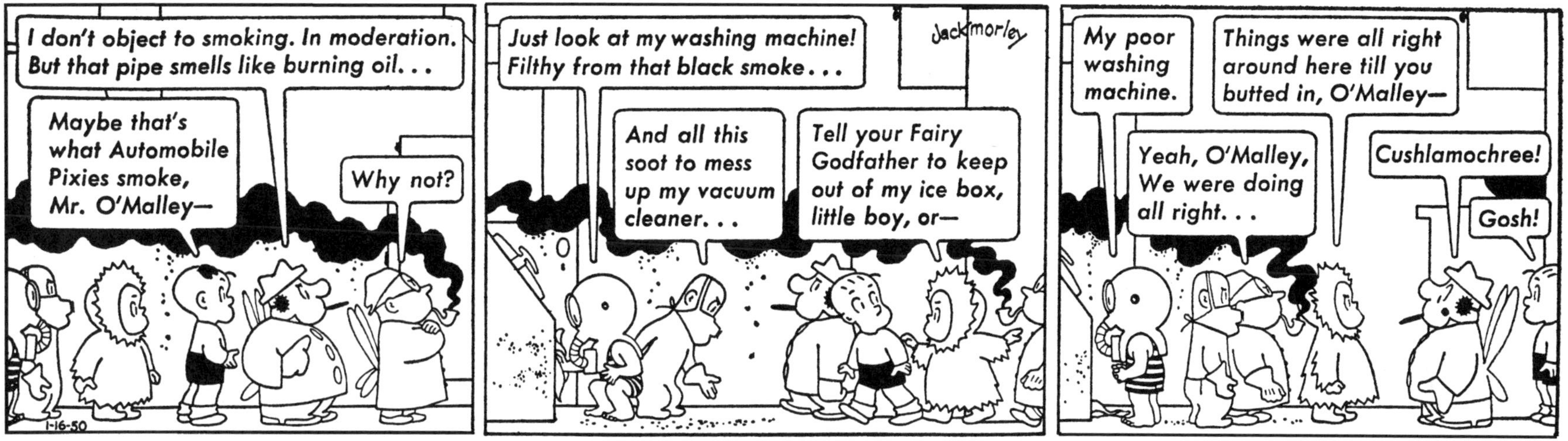
I don't object to smoking. In moderation. But that pipe smells like burning oil. . .
Maybe that's what Automobile Pixies smoke, Mr. O'Malley—
Why not?
1-16-50
Just look at my washing machine! Filthy from that black smoke. . .
Jack Morley
And all this soot to mess up my vacuum cleaner. . .
Tell your Fairy Godfather to keep out of my ice box, little boy, or—
My poor washing machine.
Things were all right around here till you butted in, O'Malley—
Yeah, O'Malley, We were doing all right. . .
Cushlamochree!
Gosh!

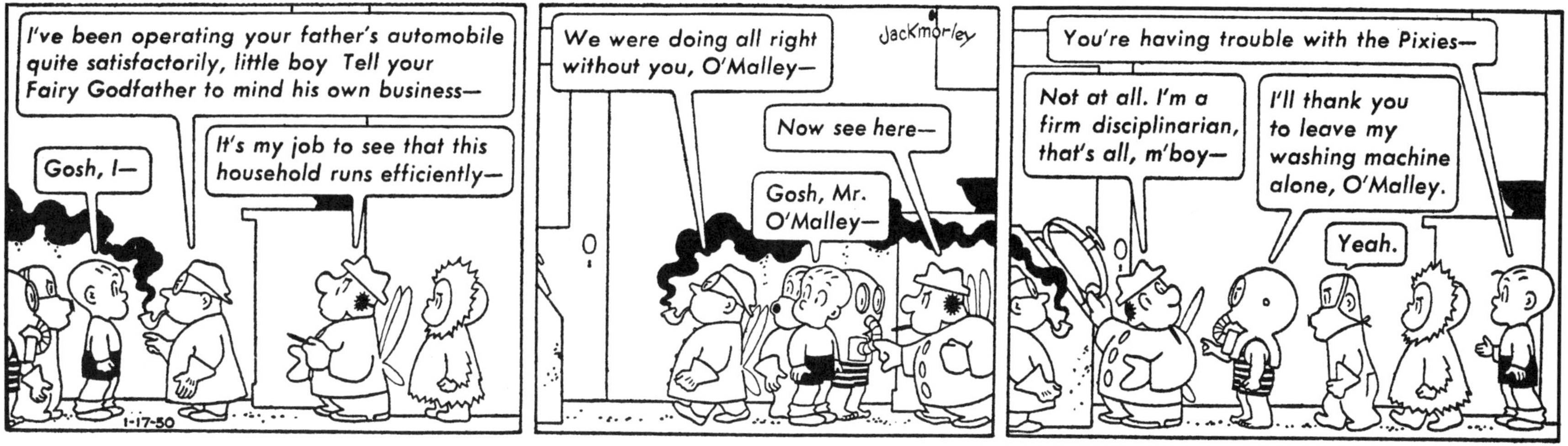
I've been operating your father's automobile quite satisfactorily, little boy Tell your Fairy Godfather to mind his own business—
Gosh, I—
It's my job to see that this household runs efficiently—
1-17-50
We were doing all right without you, O'Malley—
Jack Morley
Now see here—
Gosh, Mr. O'Malley—
You're having trouble with the Pixies—
Not at all. I'm a firm disciplinarian, that's all, m'boy—
I'll thank you to leave my washing machine alone, O'Malley.
Yeah.

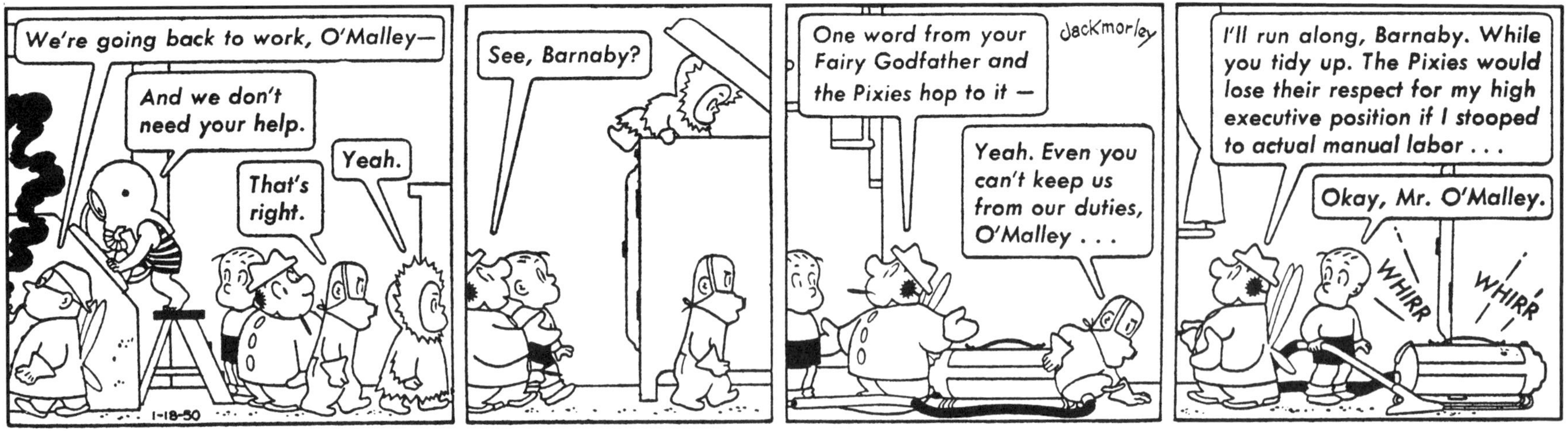
We're going back to work, O'Malley—
And we don't need your help.
That's right.
Yeah.
1-18-50
See, Barnaby?
One word from your Fairy Godfather and the Pixies hop to it —
JackMorley
Yeah. Even you can't keep us from our duties, O'Malley . . .
I'll run along, Barnaby. While you tidy up. The Pixies would lose their respect for my high executive position if I stooped to actual manual labor . . .
Okay, Mr. O'Malley.
WHIRR
WHIRR

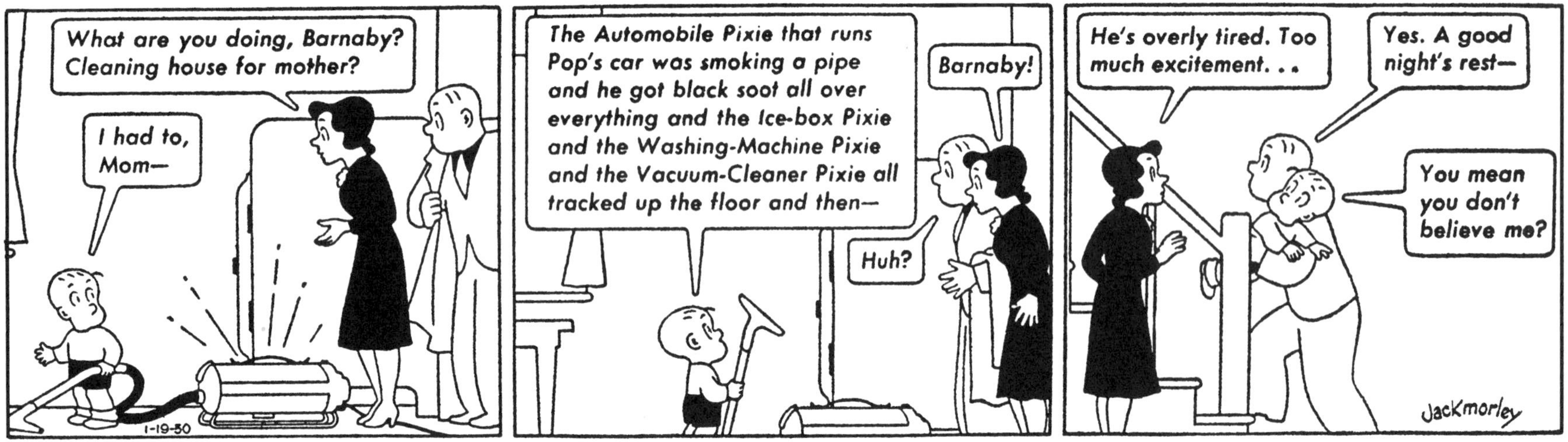
What are you doing, Barnaby? Cleaning house for mother?
I had to, Mom—
1-19-50
The Automobile Pixie that runs Pop's car was smoking a pipe and he got black soot all over everything and the Ice-box Pixie and the Washing-Machine Pixie and the Vacuum-Cleaner Pixie all tracked up the floor and then—
Barnaby!
Huh?
He's overly tired. Too much excitement. . .
Yes. A good night's rest—
You mean you don't believe me?
JackMorley

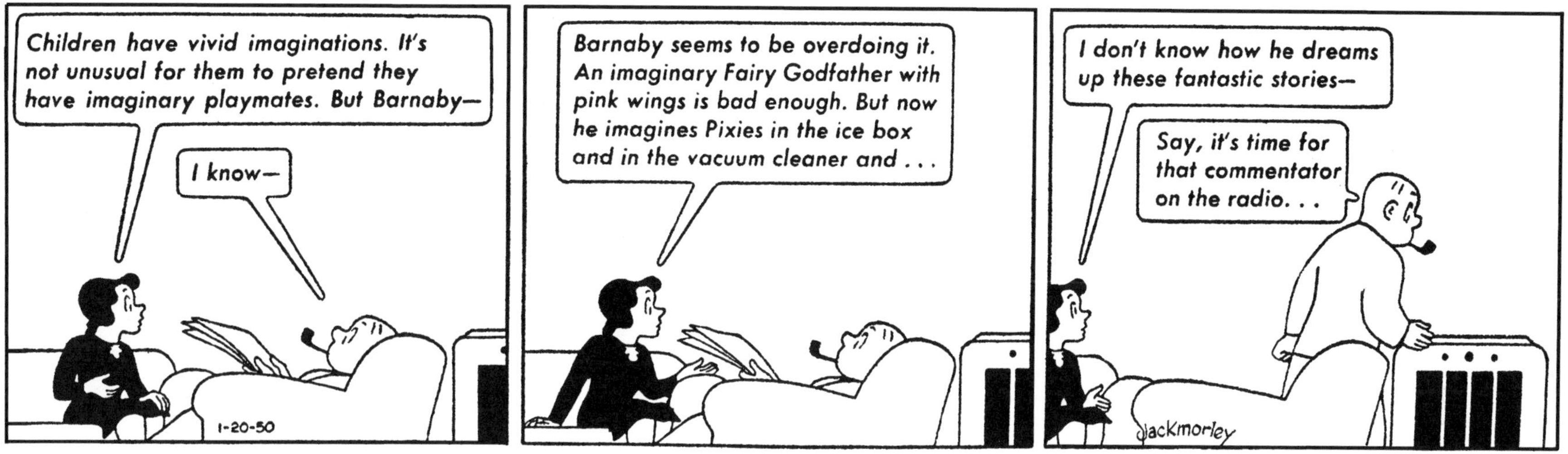

Children have vivid imaginations. It's not unusual for them to pretend they have imaginary playmates. But Barnaby—
I know—
1-20-50
Barnaby seems to be overdoing it. An imaginary Fairy Godfather with pink wings is bad enough. But now he imagines Pixies in the ice box and in the vacuum cleaner and . . .
I don't know how he dreams up these fantastic stories—
Say, it's time for that commentator on the radio. . .
JackMorley

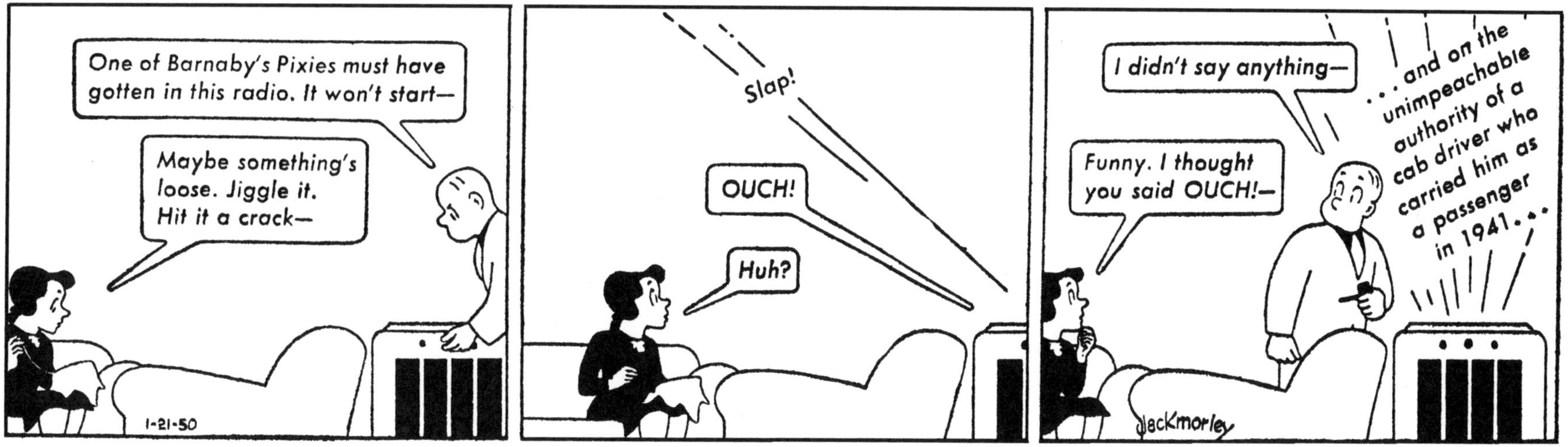

One of Barnaby's Pixies must have gotten in this radio. It won't start—
Maybe something's loose. Jiggle it. Hit it a crack—
1-21-50
Slap!
OUCH!
Huh?
I didn't say anything—
Funny. I thought you said OUCH!—
. . . and on the unimpeachable authority of a cab driver who carried him as a passenger in 1941. . .
JackMorley

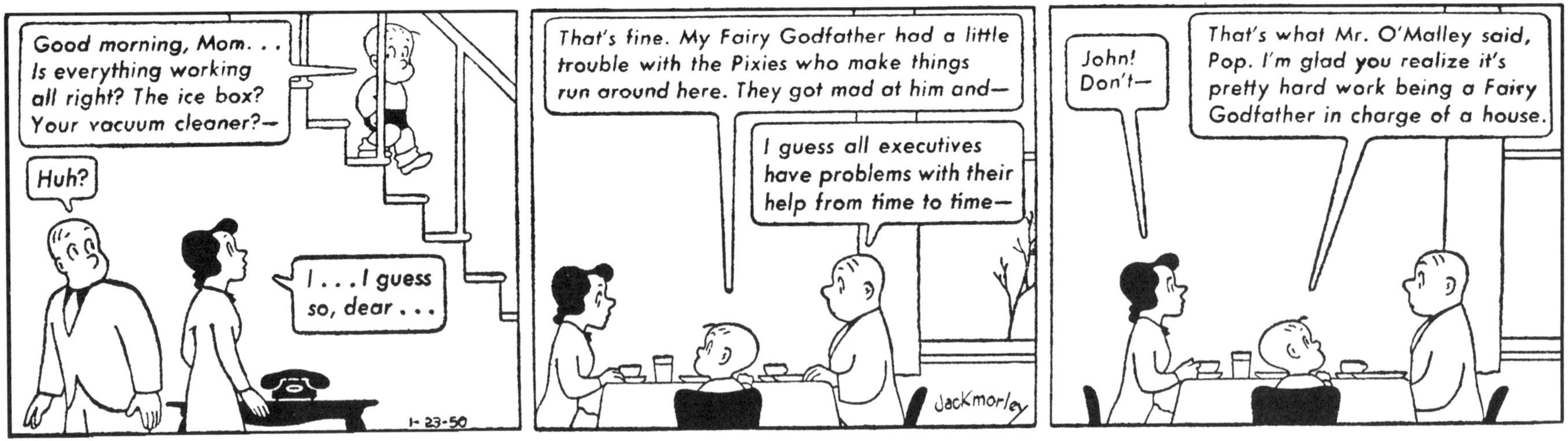
Good morning, Mom. . . Is everything working all right? The ice box? Your vacuum cleaner?—
Huh?
I . . . I guess so, dear . . .
1-23-50
That's fine. My Fairy Godfather had a little trouble with the Pixies who make things run around here. They got mad at him and—
I guess all executives have problems with their help from time to time—
JacKmorley
John! Don't—
That's what Mr. O'Malley said, Pop. I'm glad you realize it's pretty hard work being a Fairy Godfather in charge of a house.

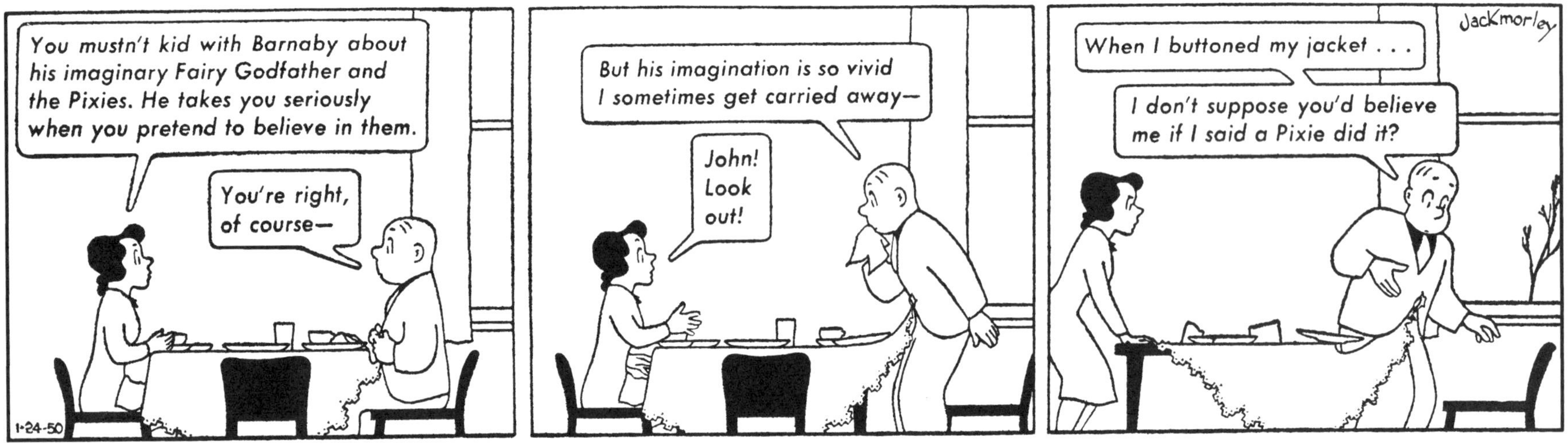
You mustn't kid with Barnaby about his imaginary Fairy Godfather and the Pixies. He takes you seriously when you pretend to believe in them.
You're right, of course—
1-24-50
But his imagination is so vivid I sometimes get carried away—
John! Look out!
JacKmorley
When I buttoned my jacket . . .
I don't suppose you'd believe me if I said a Pixie did it?

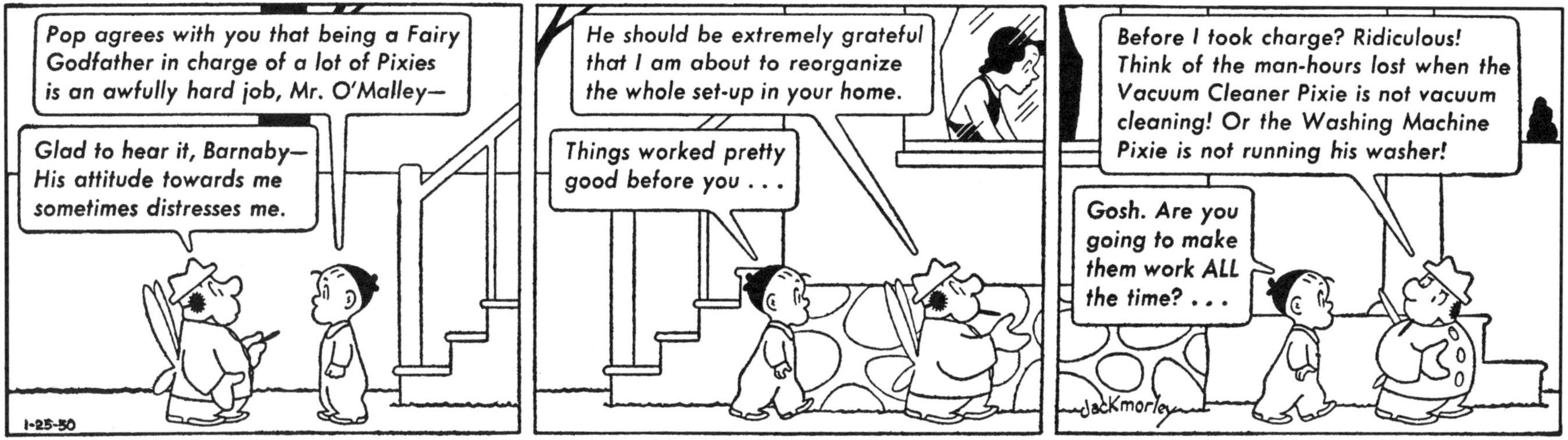

Pop agrees with you that being a Fairy Godfather in charge of a lot of Pixies is an awfully hard job, Mr. O'Malley—
Glad to hear it, Barnaby— His attitude towards me sometimes distresses me.
1-25-50
He should be extremely grateful that I am about to reorganize the whole set-up in your home.
Things worked pretty good before you . . .
Before I took charge? Ridiculous! Think of the man-hours lost when the Vacuum Cleaner Pixie is not vacuum cleaning! Or the Washing Machine Pixie is not running his washer!
Gosh. Are you going to make them work ALL the time? . . .
JackMorley

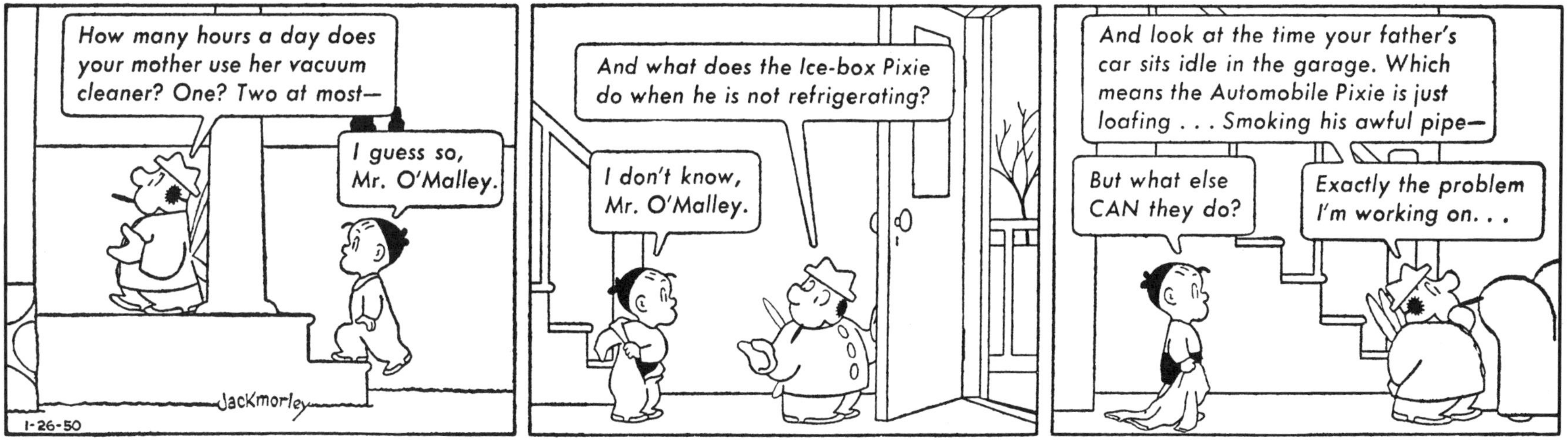

How many hours a day does your mother use her vacuum cleaner? One? Two at most—
I guess so, Mr. O'Malley.
1-26-50
JackMorley
And what does the Ice-box Pixie do when he is not refrigerating?
I don't know, Mr. O'Malley.
And look at the time your father's car sits idle in the garage. Which means the Automobile Pixie is just loafing . . . Smoking his awful pipe—
But what else CAN they do?
Exactly the problem I'm working on. . .

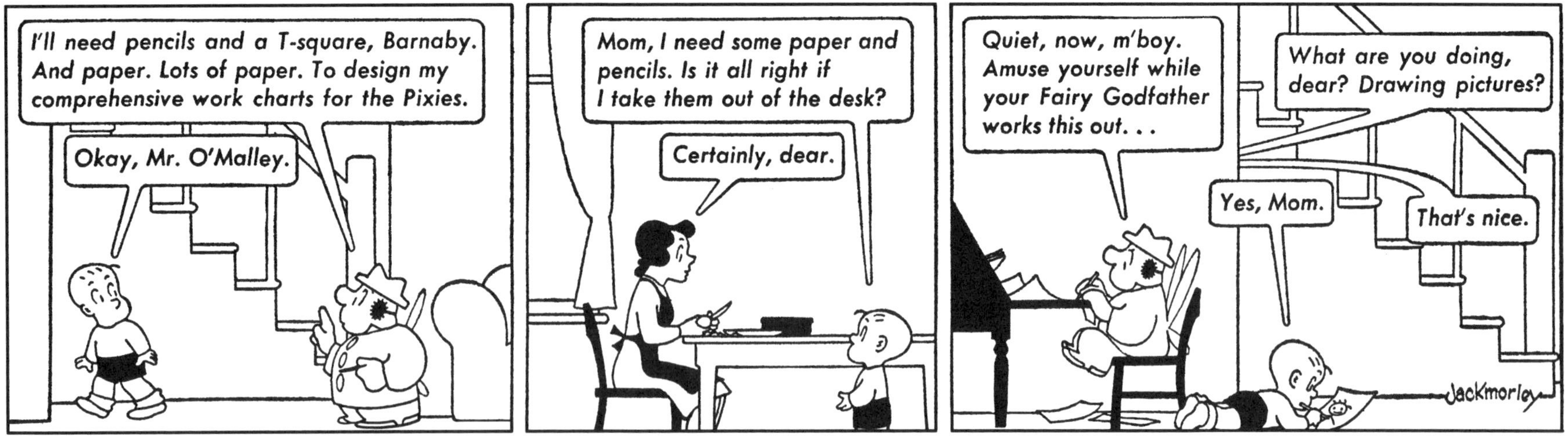
I'll need pencils and a T-square, Barnaby. And paper. Lots of paper. To design my comprehensive work charts for the Pixies.
Okay, Mr. O'Malley.
Mom, I need some paper and pencils. Is it all right if I take them out of the desk?
Certainly, dear.
Quiet, now, m'boy. Amuse yourself while your Fairy Godfather works this out. . .
What are you doing, dear? Drawing pictures?
Yes, Mom.
That's nice.
Jackmorley

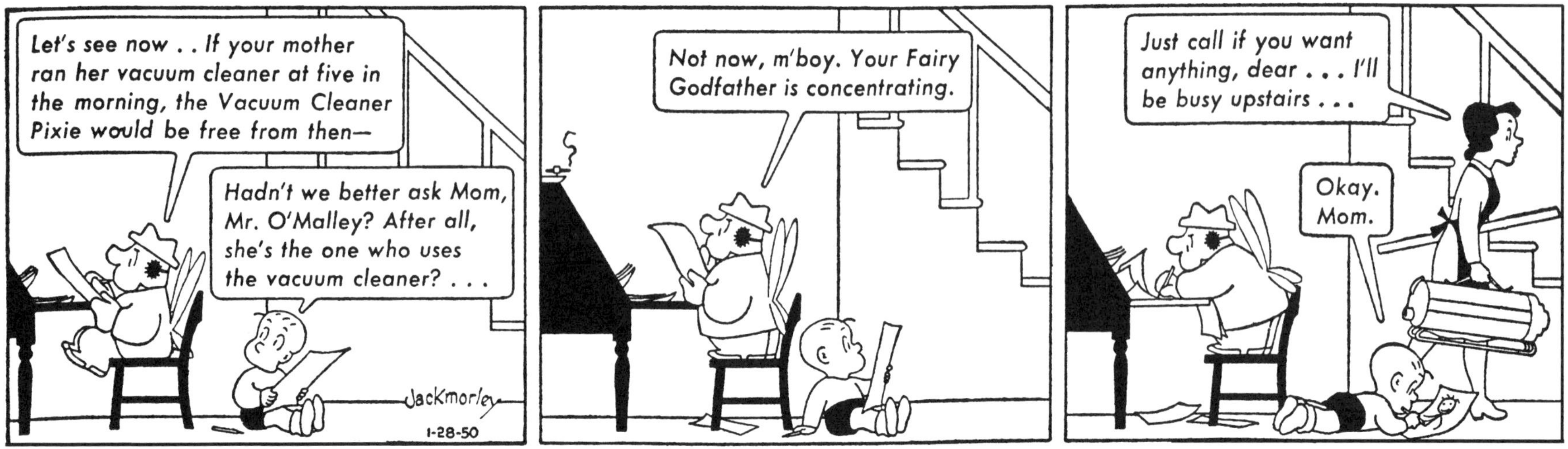
Let's see now . . If your mother ran her vacuum cleaner at five in the morning, the Vacuum Cleaner Pixie would be free from then—
Hadn't we better ask Mom, Mr. O'Malley? After all, she's the one who uses the vacuum cleaner? . . .
Jackmorley
1-28-50
Not now, m'boy. Your Fairy Godfather is concentrating.
Just call if you want anything, dear . . . I'll be busy upstairs . . .
Okay. Mom.

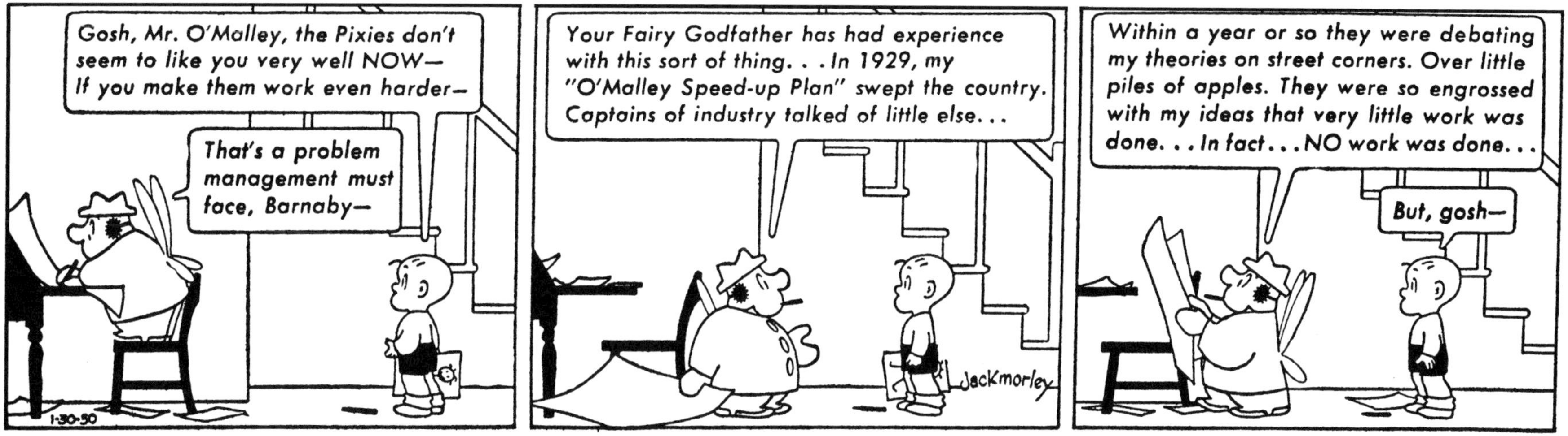
Gosh, Mr. O'Malley, the Pixies don't seem to like you very well NOW— If you make them work even harder—
That's a problem management must face, Barnaby—
1-30-50
Your Fairy Godfather has had experience with this sort of thing. . . In 1929, my "O'Malley Speed-up Plan" swept the country. Captains of industry talked of little else. . .
Jackmorley
Within a year or so they were debating my theories on street corners. Over little piles of apples. They were so engrossed with my ideas that very little work was done. . . In fact. . . NO work was done. . .
But, gosh—

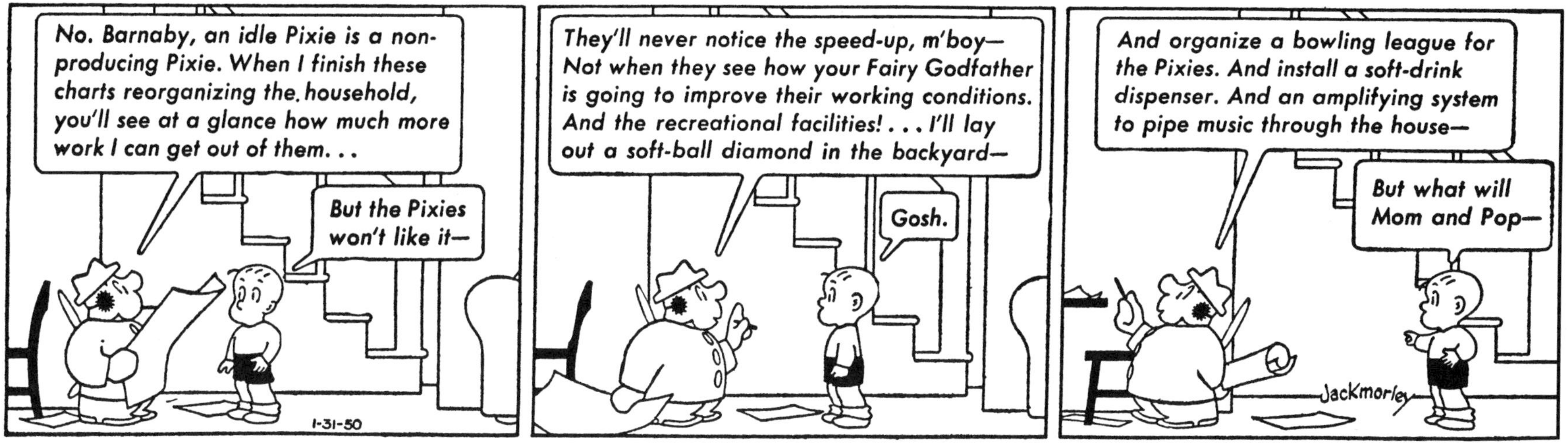
No. Barnaby, an idle Pixie is a non-producing Pixie. When I finish these charts reorganizing the household, you'll see at a glance how much more work I can get out of them. . .
But the Pixies won't like it—
1-31-50
They'll never notice the speed-up, m'boy— Not when they see how your Fairy Godfather is going to improve their working conditions. And the recreational facilities! . . . I'll lay out a soft-ball diamond in the backyard—
Gosh.
And organize a bowling league for the Pixies. And install a soft-drink dispenser. And an amplifying system to pipe music through the house—
But what will Mom and Pop—
Jackmorley

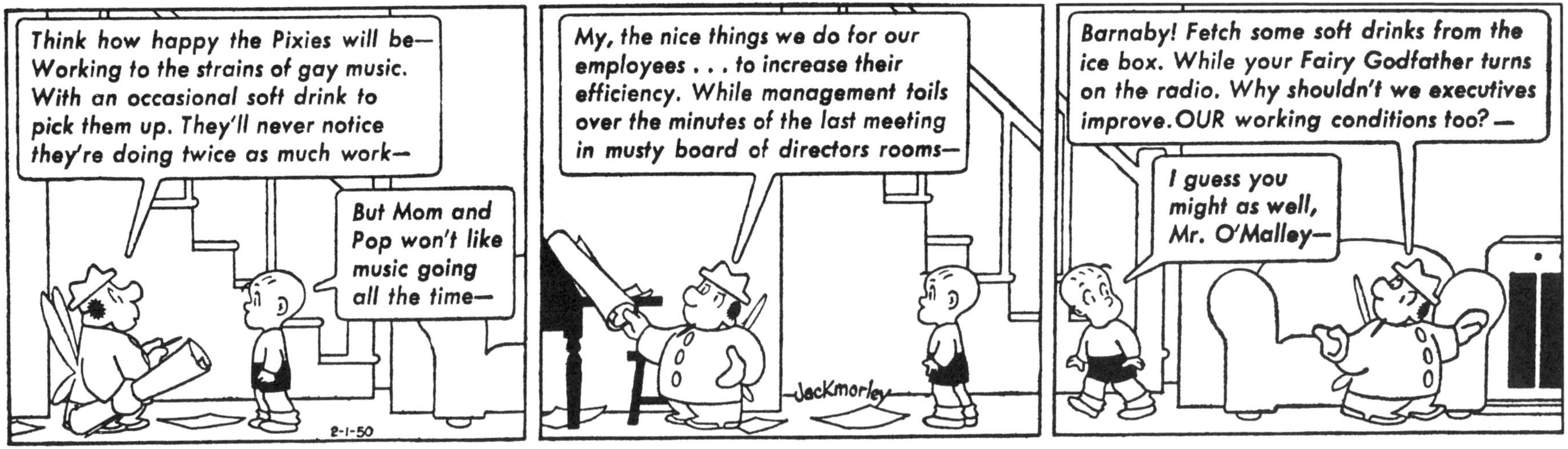
Think how happy the Pixies will be— Working to the strains of gay music. With an occasional soft drink to pick them up. They'll never notice they're doing twice as much work—
But Mom and Pop won't like music going all the time—
2-1-50
My, the nice things we do for our employees . . . to increase their efficiency. While management toils over the minutes of the last meeting in musty board of directors rooms—
Jackmorley
Barnaby! Fetch some soft drinks from the ice box. While your Fairy Godfather turns on the radio. Why shouldn't we executives improve. OUR working conditions too?—
I guess you might as well, Mr. O'Malley—

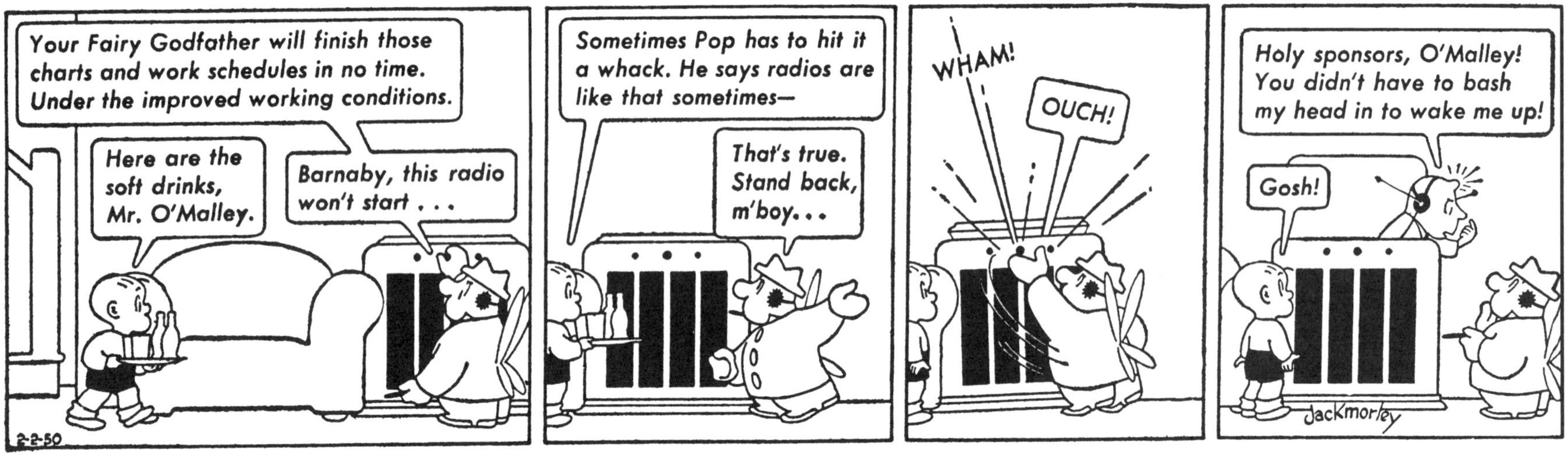
Your Fairy Godfather will finish those charts and work schedules in no time. Under the improved working conditions.
Here are the soft drinks, Mr. O'Malley.
Barnaby, this radio won't start . . .
2-2-50
Sometimes Pop has to hit it a whack. He says radios are like that sometimes—
That's true. Stand back, m'boy. . .
WHAM!
OUCH!
Holy sponsors, O'Malley! You didn't have to bash my head in to wake me up!
Gosh!
Jackmorley

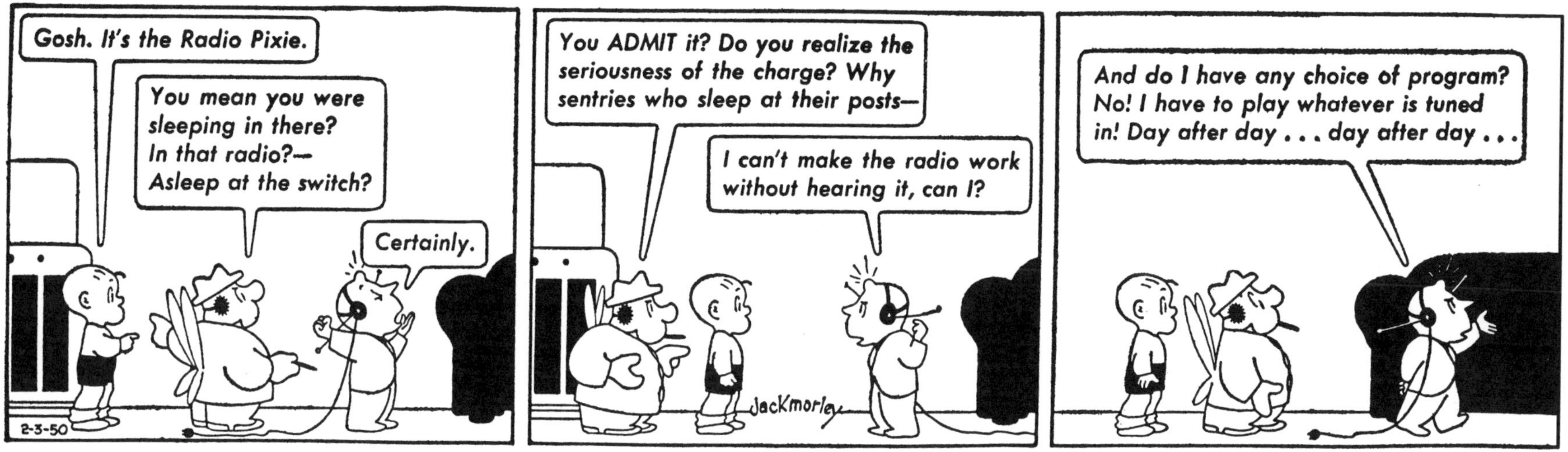
Gosh. It's the Radio Pixie.
You mean you were sleeping in there? In that radio?— Asleep at the switch?
Certainly.
2-3-50
You ADMIT it? Do you realize the seriousness of the charge? Why sentries who sleep at their posts—
I can't make the radio work without hearing it, can I?
JackMorley
And do I have any choice of program? No! I have to play whatever is tuned in! Day after day . . . day after day . . .

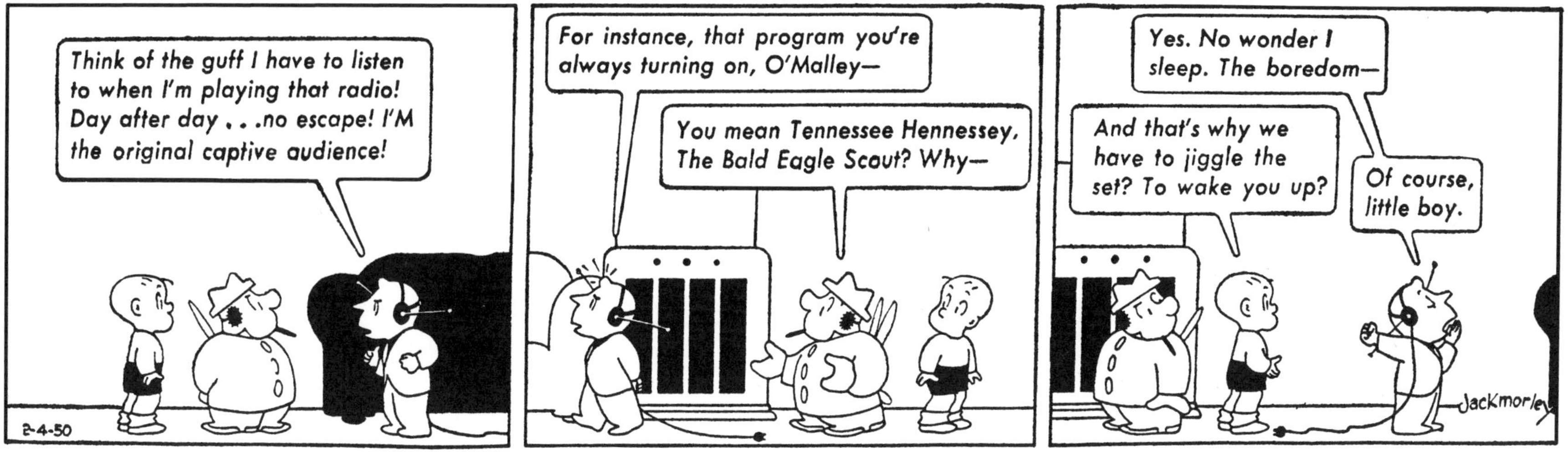
Think of the guff I have to listen to when I'm playing that radio! Day after day . . .no escape! I'M the original captive audience!
2-4-50
For instance, that program you're always turning on, O'Malley—
You mean Tennessee Hennessey, The Bald Eagle Scout? Why—
Yes. No wonder I sleep. The boredom—
And that's why we have to jiggle the set? To wake you up?
Of course, little boy.
JackMorley

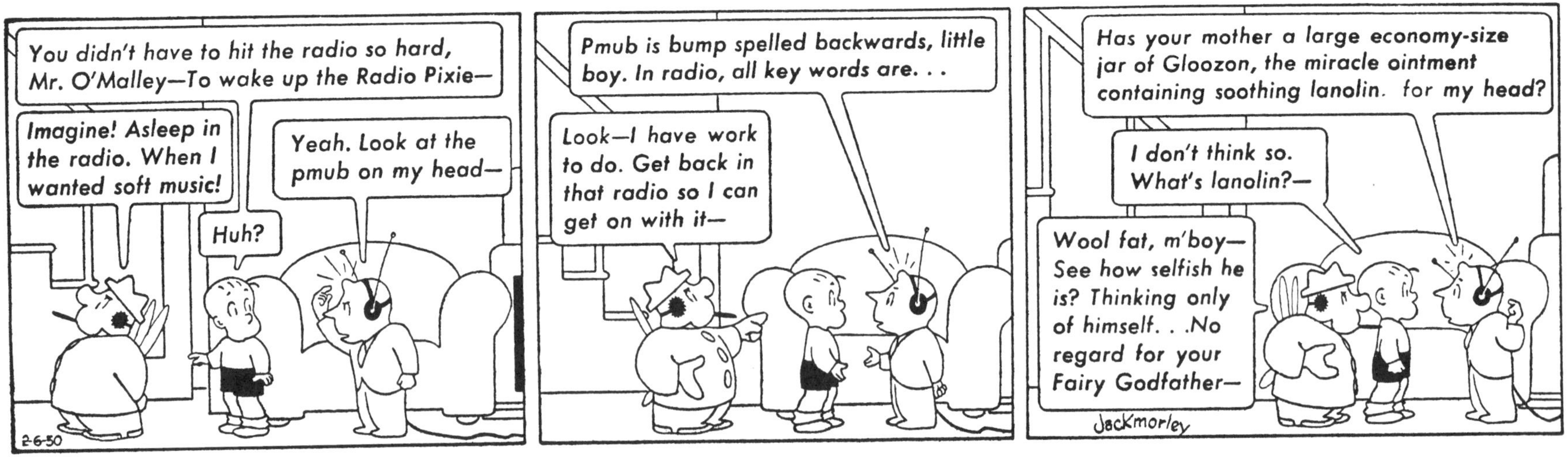
You didn't have to hit the radio so hard, Mr. O'Malley—To wake up the Radio Pixie—
Imagine! Asleep in the radio. When I wanted soft music!
Huh?
Yeah. Look at the pmub on my head—
2-6-50
Pmub is bump spelled backwards, little boy. In radio, all key words are. . .
Look—I have work to do. Get back in that radio so I can get on with it—
Has your mother a large economy-size jar of Gloozon, the miracle ointment containing soothing lanolin. for my head?
I don't think so. What's lanolin?—
Wool fat, m'boy—See how selfish he is? Thinking only of himself. . .No regard for your Fairy Godfather—
JackMorley

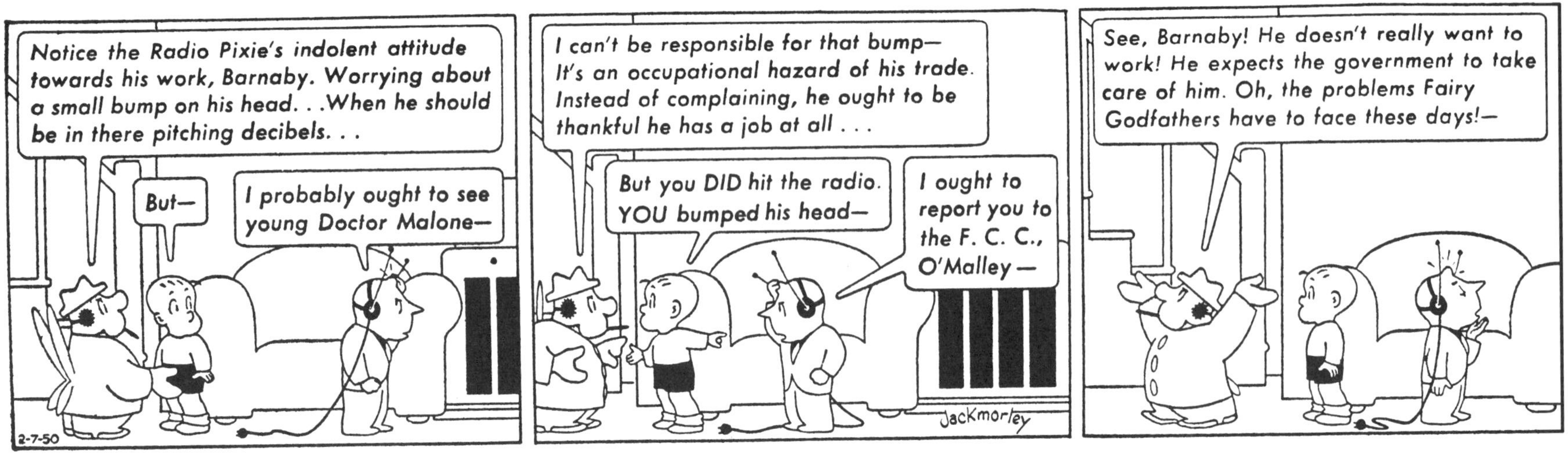
Notice the Radio Pixie's indolent attitude towards his work, Barnaby. Worrying about a small bump on his head. . .When he should be in there pitching decibels. . .
But—
I probably ought to see young Doctor Malone—
2-7-50
I can't be responsible for that bump—It's an occupational hazard of his trade. Instead of complaining, he ought to be thankful he has a job at all . . .
But you DID hit the radio. YOU bumped his head—
I ought to report you to the F. C. C., O'Malley —
JackMorley
See, Barnaby! He doesn't really want to work! He expects the government to take care of him. Oh, the problems Fairy Godfathers have to face these days!—

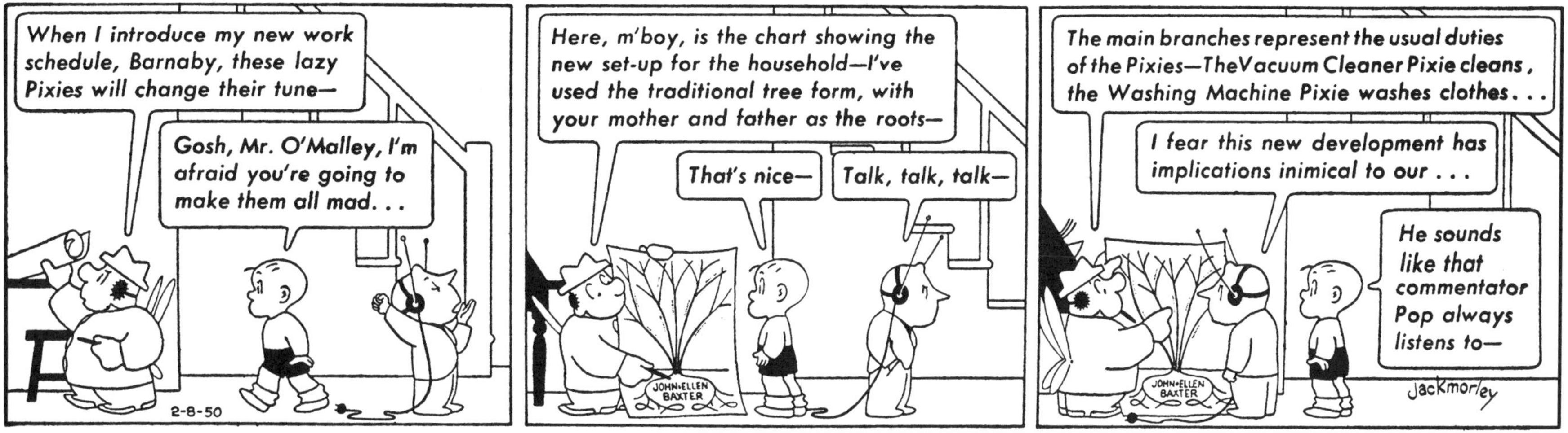
When I introduce my new work schedule, Barnaby, these lazy Pixies will change their tune—
Gosh, Mr. O'Malley, I'm afraid you're going to make them all mad. . .
2-8-50
Here, m'boy, is the chart showing the new set-up for the household—I've used the traditional tree form, with your mother and father as the roots—
That's nice—
Talk, talk, talk—
JOHN+ELLEN BAXTER
The main branches represent the usual duties of the Pixies—The Vacuum Cleaner Pixie cleans, the Washing Machine Pixie washes clothes. . .
I fear this new development has implications inimical to our . . .
He sounds like that commentator Pop always listens to—
JOHN+ELLEN BAXTER
Jackmorley

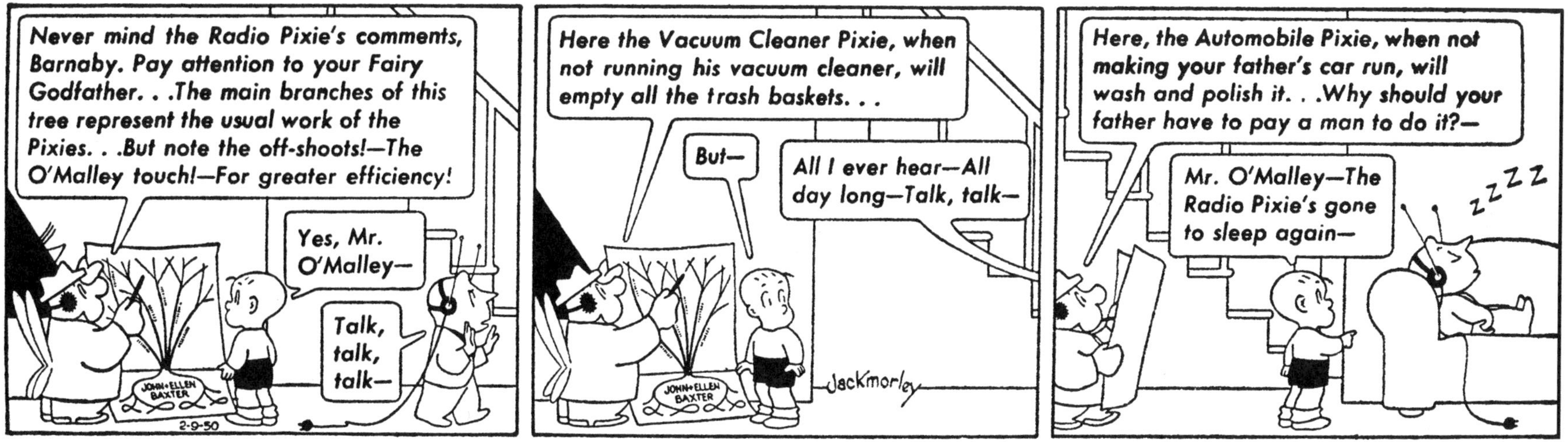
Never mind the Radio Pixie's comments, Barnaby. Pay attention to your Fairy Godfather. . .The main branches of this tree represent the usual work of the Pixies. . .But note the off-shoots!—The O'Malley touch!—For greater efficiency!
Yes, Mr. O'Malley—
Talk, talk, talk—
JOHN+ELLEN BAXTER
2-9-50
Here the Vacuum Cleaner Pixie, when not running his vacuum cleaner, will empty all the trash baskets. . .
But—
All I ever hear—All day long—Talk, talk—
JOHN+ELLEN BAXTER
Jackmorley
Here, the Automobile Pixie, when not making your father's car run, will wash and polish it. . .Why should your father have to pay a man to do it?—
Mr. O'Malley—The Radio Pixie's gone to sleep again—
ZZZZ

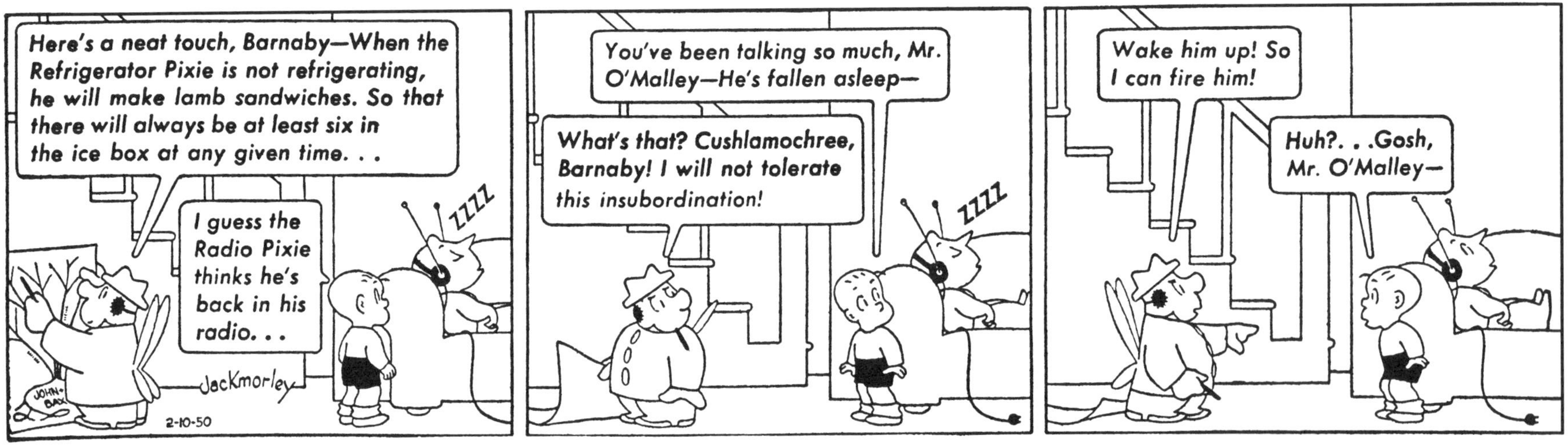
Here's a neat touch, Barnaby—When the Refrigerator Pixie is not refrigerating, he will make lamb sandwiches. So that there will always be at least six in the ice box at any given time. . .
I guess the Radio Pixie thinks he's back in his radio. . .
ZZZZ
2-10-50
You've been talking so much, Mr. O'Malley—He's fallen asleep—
What's that? Cushlamochree, Barnaby! I will not tolerate this insubordination!
ZZZZ
Wake him up! So I can fire him!
Huh?. . .Gosh, Mr. O'Malley—

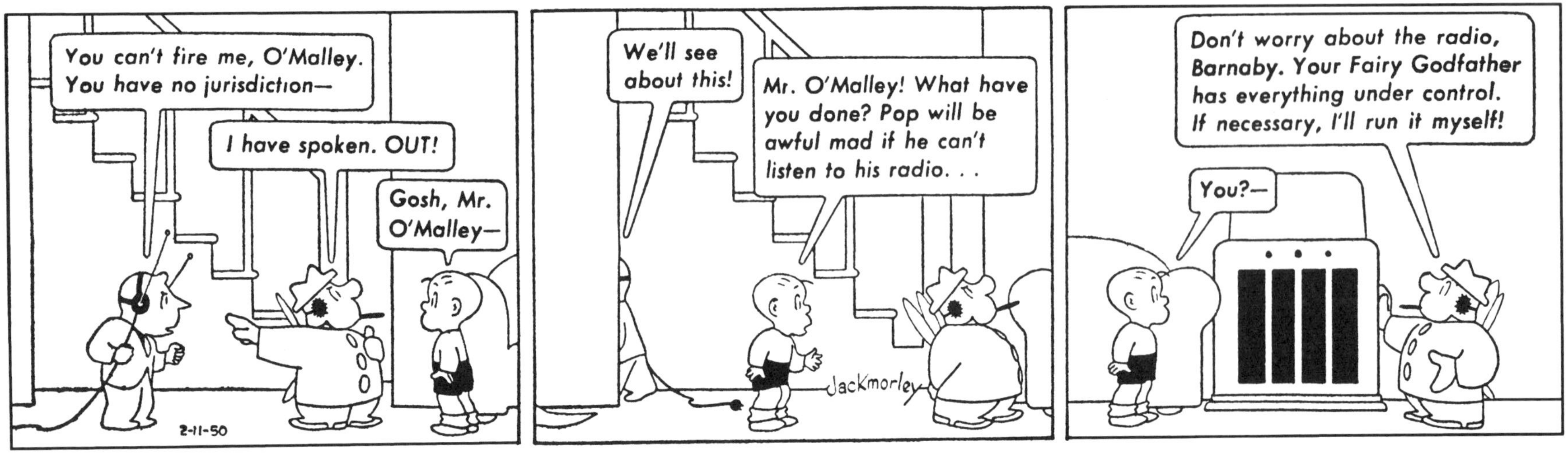
You can't fire me, O'Malley. You have no jurisdiction—
I have spoken. OUT!
Gosh, Mr. O'Malley—
2-11-50
We'll see about this!
Mr. O'Malley! What have you done? Pop will be awful mad if he can't listen to his radio. . .
Don't worry about the radio, Barnaby. Your Fairy Godfather has everything under control. If necessary, I'll run it myself!
You?—

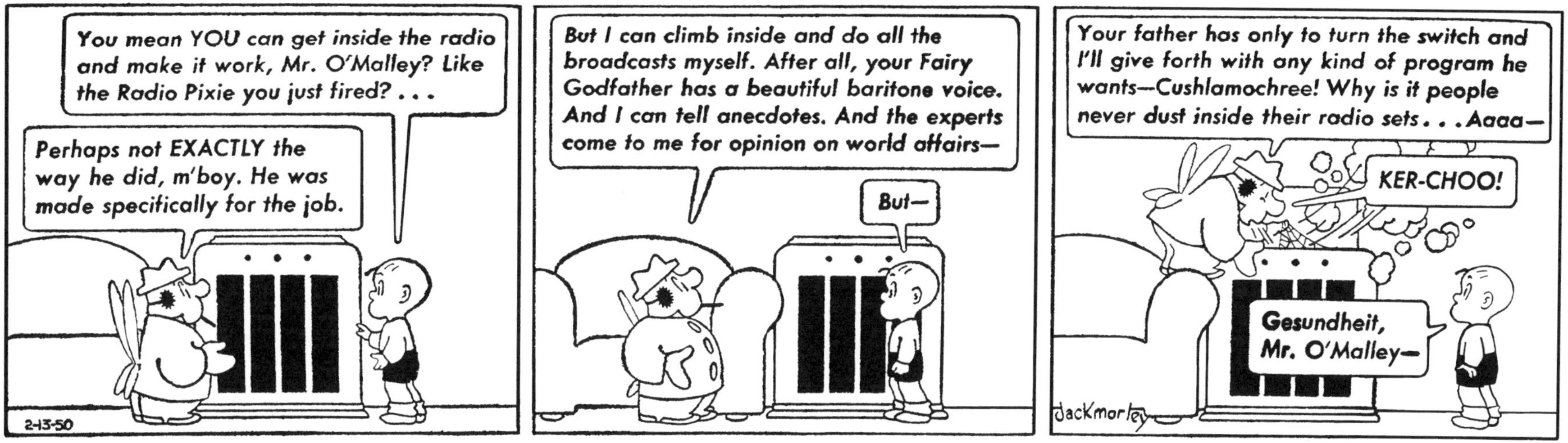
You mean YOU can get inside the radio and make it work, Mr. O'Malley? Like the Radio Pixie you just fired? . . .
Perhaps not EXACTLY the way he did, m'boy. He was made specifically for the job.
2-13-50
But I can climb inside and do all the broadcasts myself. After all, your Fairy Godfather has a beautiful baritone voice. And I can tell anecdotes. And the experts come to me for opinion on world affairs—
But—
Your father has only to turn the switch and I'll give forth with any kind of program he wants—Cushlamochree! Why is it people never dust inside their radio sets . . . Aaaa—
KER-CHOO!
Gesundheit, Mr. O'Malley—
JackMorley

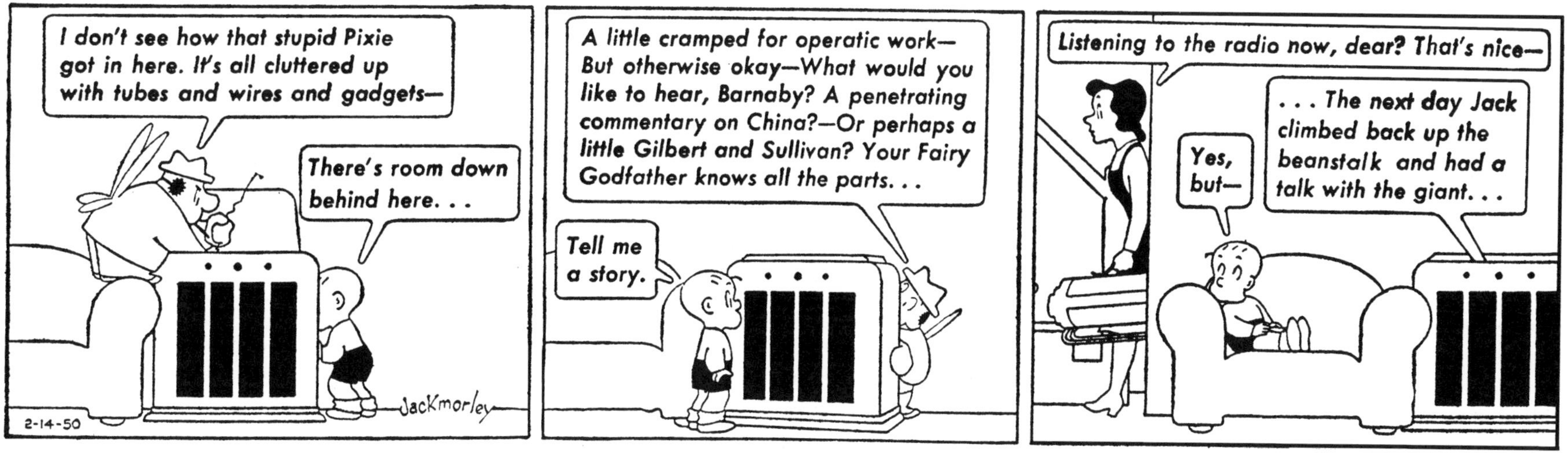
I don't see how that stupid Pixie got in here. It's all cluttered up with tubes and wires and gadgets—
There's room down behind here. . .
2-14-50
JackMorley
A little cramped for operatic work— But otherwise okay—What would you like to hear, Barnaby? A penetrating commentary on China?—Or perhaps a little Gilbert and Sullivan? Your Fairy Godfather knows all the parts. . .
Tell me a story.
Listening to the radio now, dear? That's nice—
Yes, but—
. . . The next day Jack climbed back up the beanstalk and had a talk with the giant. . .

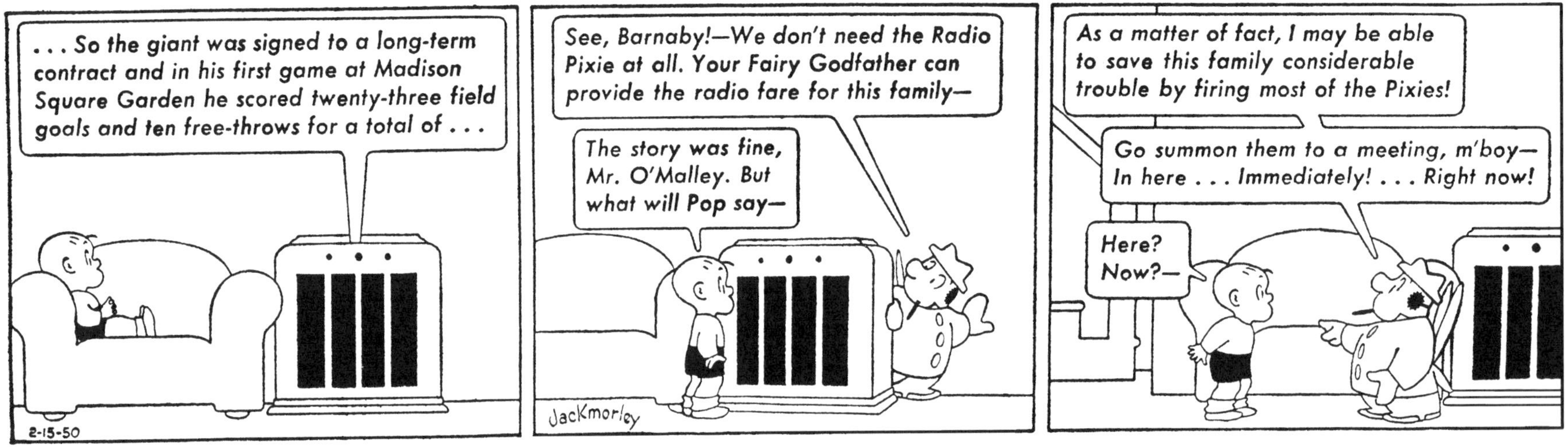

. . . So the giant was signed to a long-term contract and in his first game at Madison Square Garden he scored twenty-three field goals and ten free-throws for a total of . . .
2-15-50
See, Barnaby!—We don't need the Radio Pixie at all. Your Fairy Godfather can provide the radio fare for this family—
The story was fine, Mr. O'Malley. But what will Pop say—
JacKmorley
As a matter of fact, I may be able to save this family considerable trouble by firing most of the Pixies!
Go summon them to a meeting, m'boy—In here . . . Immediately! . . . Right now!
Here? Now?—

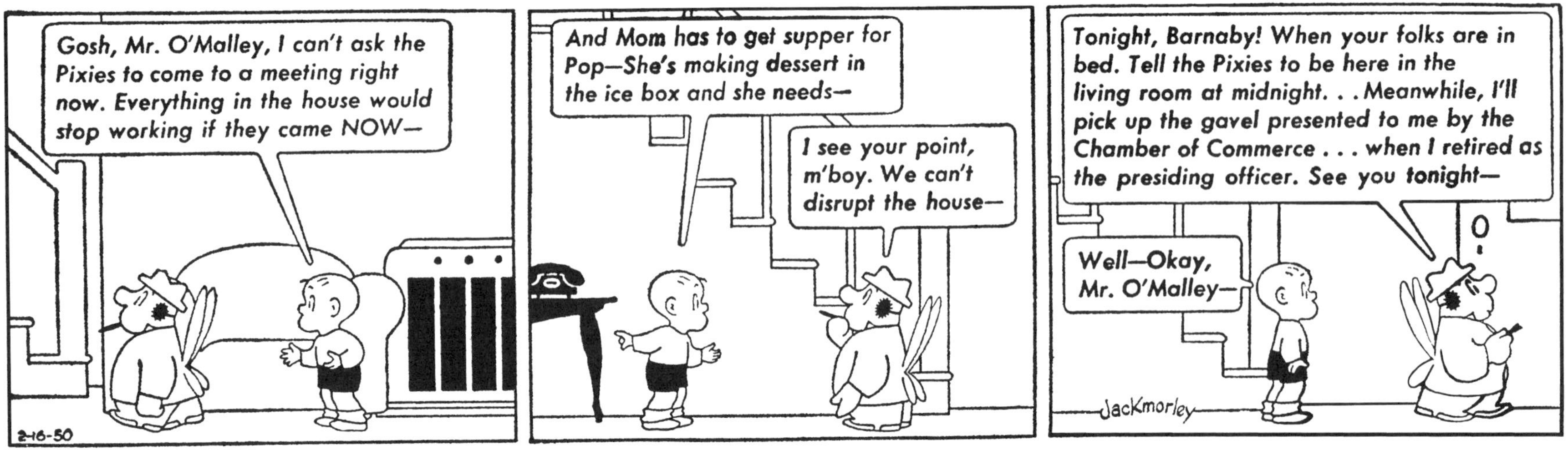

Gosh, Mr. O'Malley, I can't ask the Pixies to come to a meeting right now. Everything in the house would stop working if they came NOW—
2-16-50
And Mom has to get supper for Pop—She's making dessert in the ice box and she needs—
I see your point, m'boy. We can't disrupt the house—
Tonight, Barnaby! When your folks are in bed. Tell the Pixies to be here in the living room at midnight. . . Meanwhile, I'll pick up the gavel presented to me by the Chamber of Commerce . . . when I retired as the presiding officer. See you tonight—
Well—Okay, Mr. O'Malley—
JacKmorley

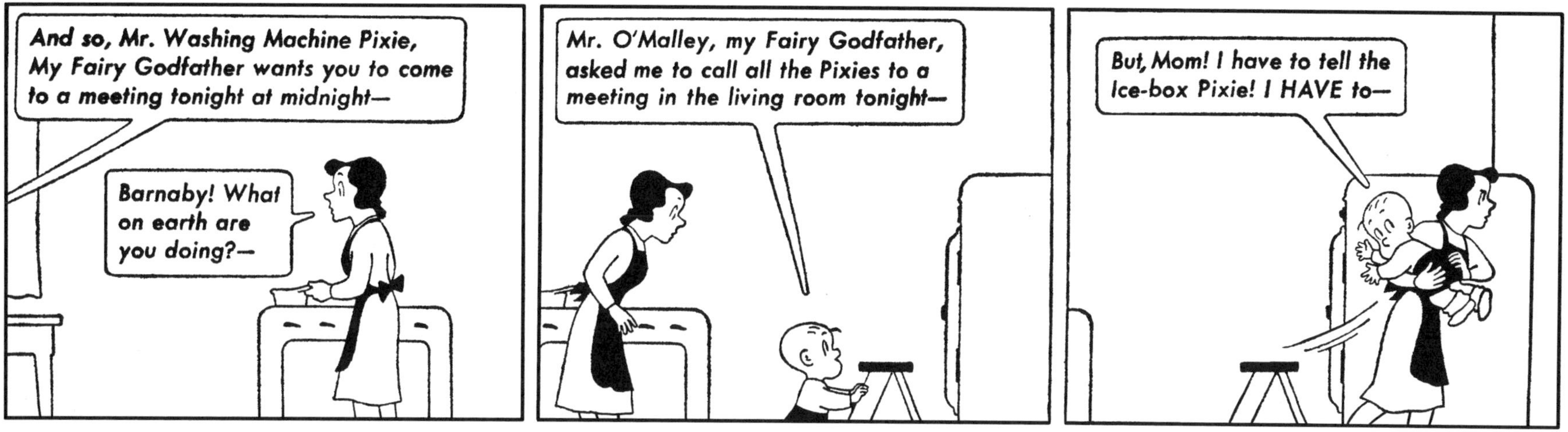
And so, Mr. Washing Machine Pixie, My Fairy Godfather wants you to come to a meeting tonight at midnight—
Barnaby! What on earth are you doing?—
Mr. O'Malley, my Fairy Godfather, asked me to call all the Pixies to a meeting in the living room tonight—
But, Mom! I have to tell the Ice-box Pixie! I HAVE to—

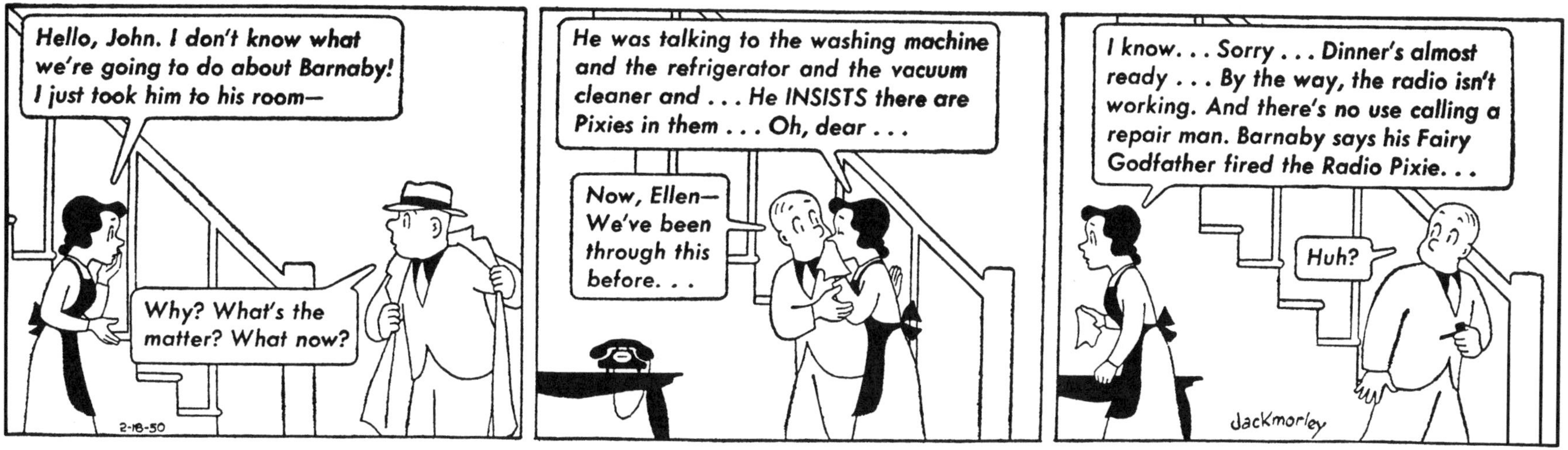
Hello, John. I don't know what we're going to do about Barnaby! I just took him to his room—
Why? What's the matter? What now?
2-18-50
He was talking to the washing machine and the refrigerator and the vacuum cleaner and . . . He INSISTS there are Pixies in them . . . Oh, dear . . .
Now, Ellen— We've been through this before. . .
I know. . . Sorry . . . Dinner's almost ready . . . By the way, the radio isn't working. And there's no use calling a repair man. Barnaby says his Fairy Godfather fired the Radio Pixie. . .
Huh?
Jack Morley

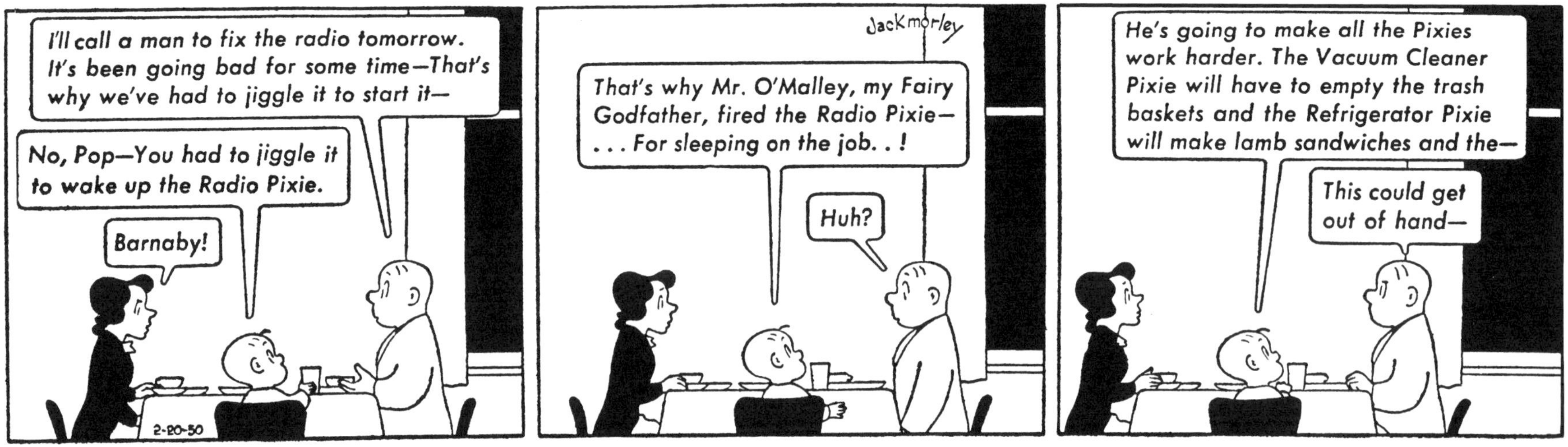
I'll call a man to fix the radio tomorrow. It's been going bad for some time—That's why we've had to jiggle it to start it—
No, Pop—You had to jiggle it to wake up the Radio Pixie.
Barnaby!
2-20-50
Jack Morley
That's why Mr. O'Malley, my Fairy Godfather, fired the Radio Pixie— . . . For sleeping on the job. . !
Huh?
He's going to make all the Pixies work harder. The Vacuum Cleaner Pixie will have to empty the trash baskets and the Refrigerator Pixie will make lamb sandwiches and the—
This could get out of hand—

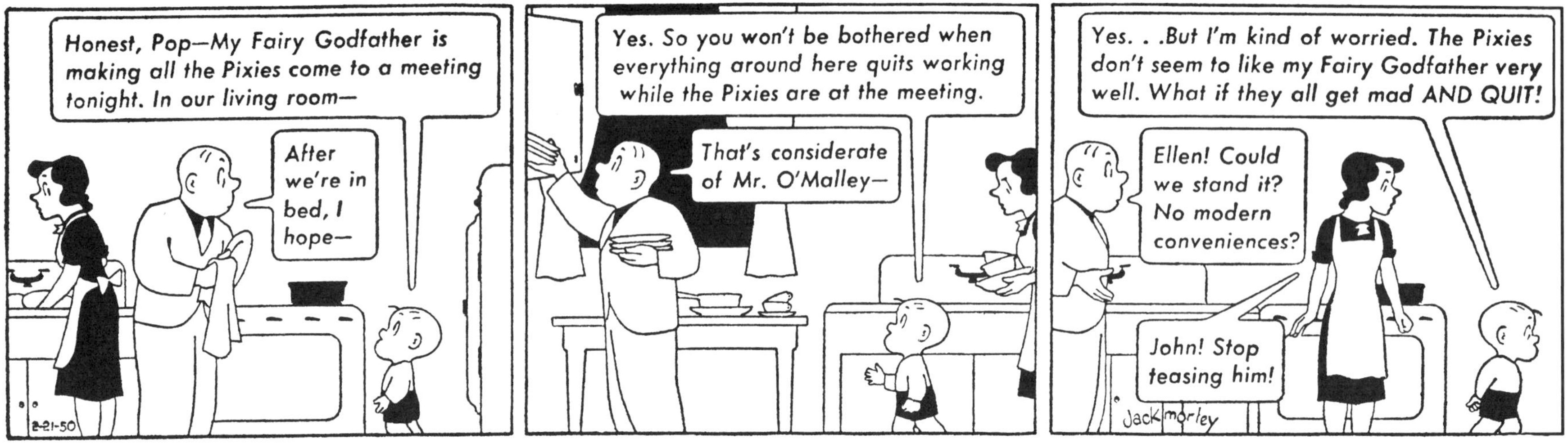
Honest, Pop—My Fairy Godfather is making all the Pixies come to a meeting tonight. In our living room—
After we're in bed, I hope—
2-21-50
Yes. So you won't be bothered when everything around here quits working while the Pixies are at the meeting.
That's considerate of Mr. O'Malley—
Yes. . .But I'm kind of worried. The Pixies don't seem to like my Fairy Godfather very well. What if they all get mad AND QUIT!
Ellen! Could we stand it? No modern conveniences?
John! Stop teasing him!
Jack Morley

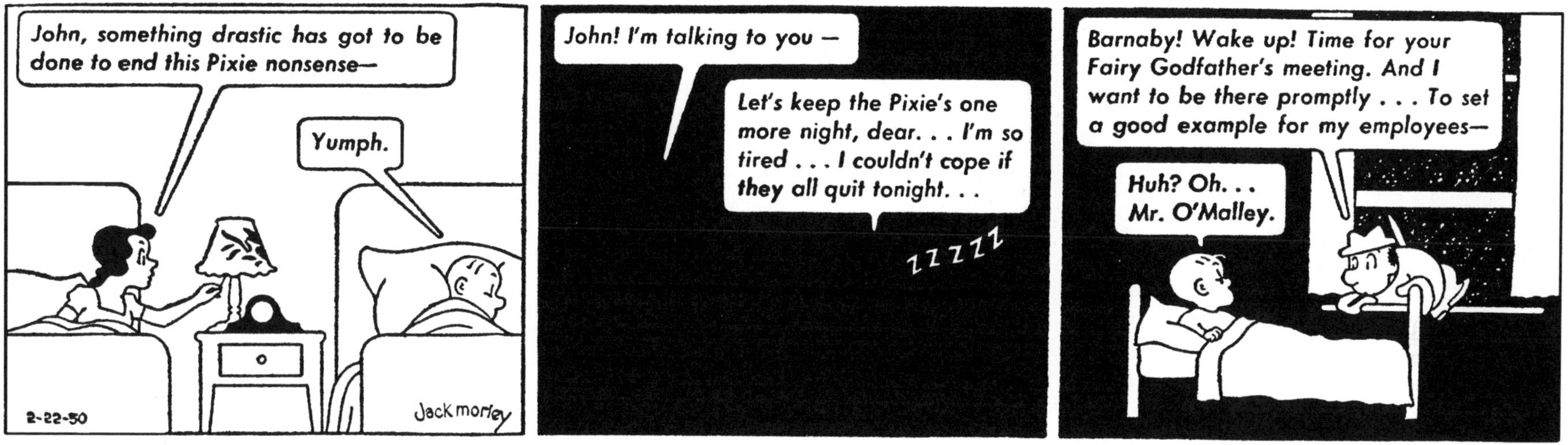
John, something drastic has got to be done to end this Pixie nonsense—
Yumph.
2-22-50
Jackmorley
John! I'm talking to you —
Let's keep the Pixie's one more night, dear. . . I'm so tired . . . I couldn't cope if they all quit tonight. . .
ZZZZZ
Barnaby! Wake up! Time for your Fairy Godfather's meeting. And I want to be there promptly . . . To set a good example for my employees—
Huh? Oh. . . Mr. O'Malley.

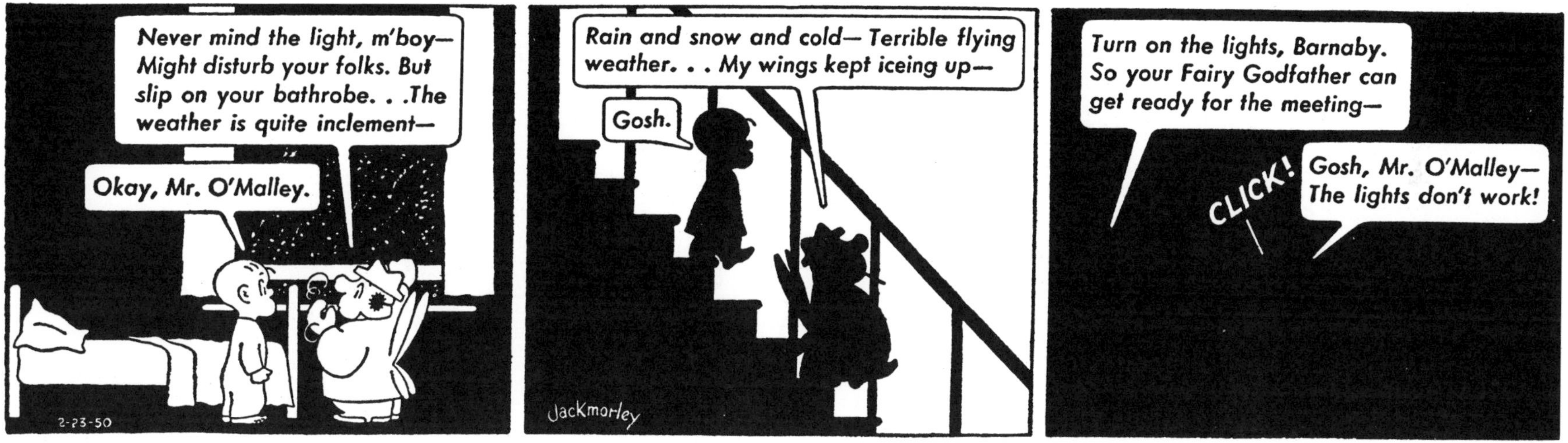
Never mind the light, m'boy— Might disturb your folks. But slip on your bathrobe. . .The weather is quite inclement—
Okay, Mr. O'Malley.
2-23-50
Rain and snow and cold— Terrible flying weather. . . My wings kept iceing up—
Gosh.
Jackmorley
Turn on the lights, Barnaby. So your Fairy Godfather can get ready for the meeting—
CLICK!
Gosh, Mr. O'Malley— The lights don't work!

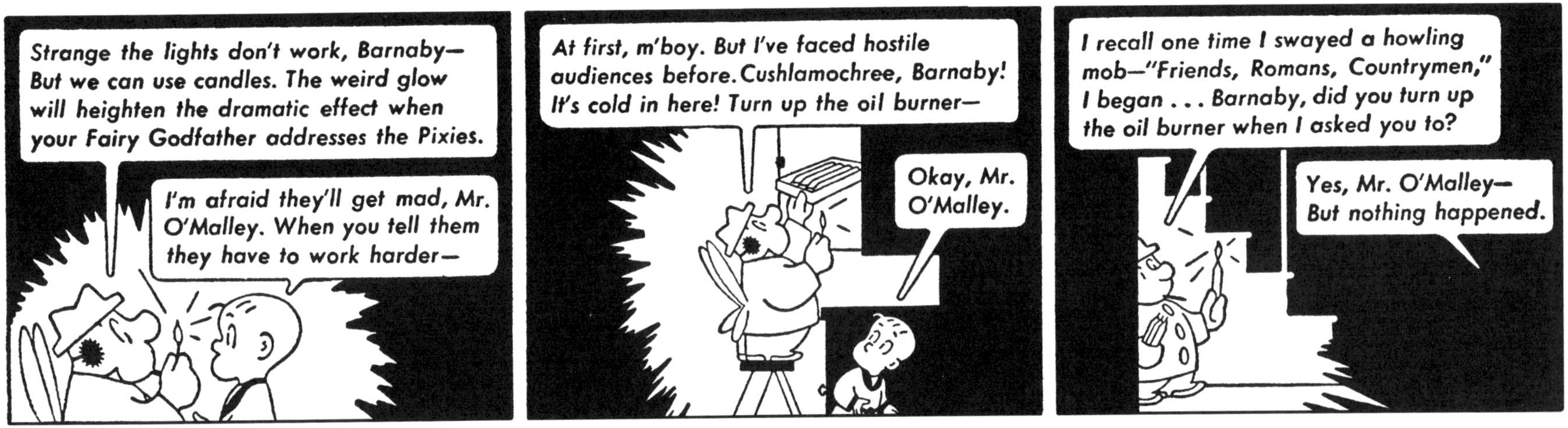
Strange the lights don't work, Barnaby—But we can use candles. The weird glow will heighten the dramatic effect when your Fairy Godfather addresses the Pixies.
I'm afraid they'll get mad, Mr. O'Malley. When you tell them they have to work harder—
At first, m'boy. But I've faced hostile audiences before. Cushlamochree, Barnaby! It's cold in here! Turn up the oil burner—
Okay, Mr. O'Malley.
I recall one time I swayed a howling mob—"Friends, Romans, Countrymen," I began . . . Barnaby, did you turn up the oil burner when I asked you to?
Yes, Mr. O'Malley—But nothing happened.

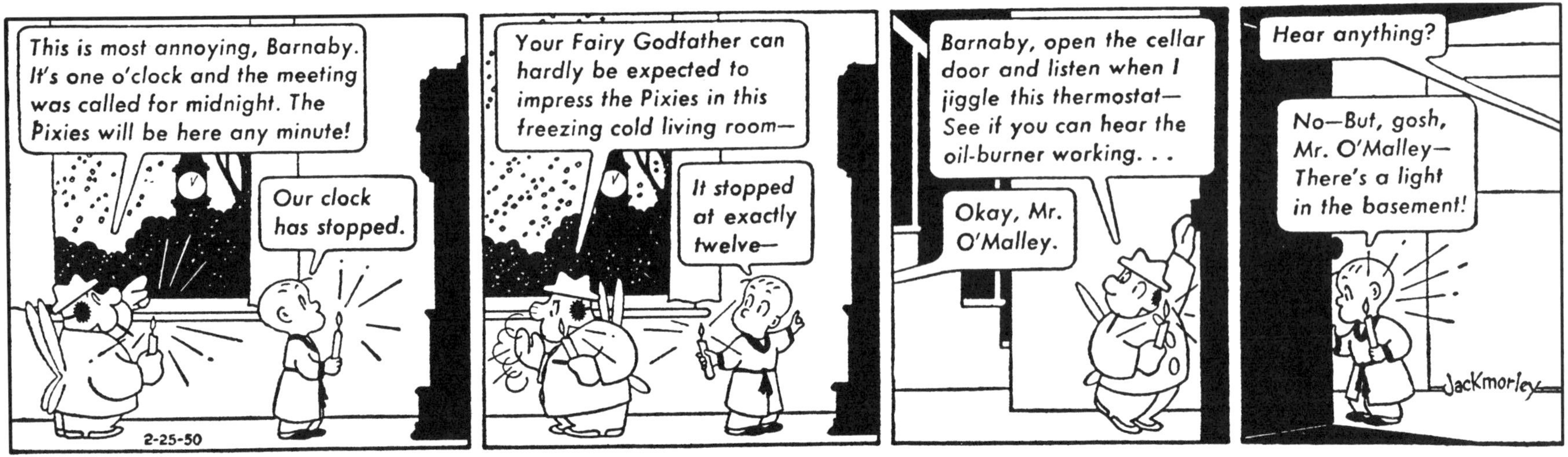
This is most annoying, Barnaby. It's one o'clock and the meeting was called for midnight. The Pixies will be here any minute!
Our clock has stopped.
2-25-50
Your Fairy Godfather can hardly be expected to impress the Pixies in this freezing cold living room—
It stopped at exactly twelve—
Barnaby, open the cellar door and listen when I jiggle this thermostat—See if you can hear the oil-burner working. . .
Okay, Mr. O'Malley.
Hear anything?
No—But, gosh, Mr. O'Malley—There's a light in the basement!
JacKmorley

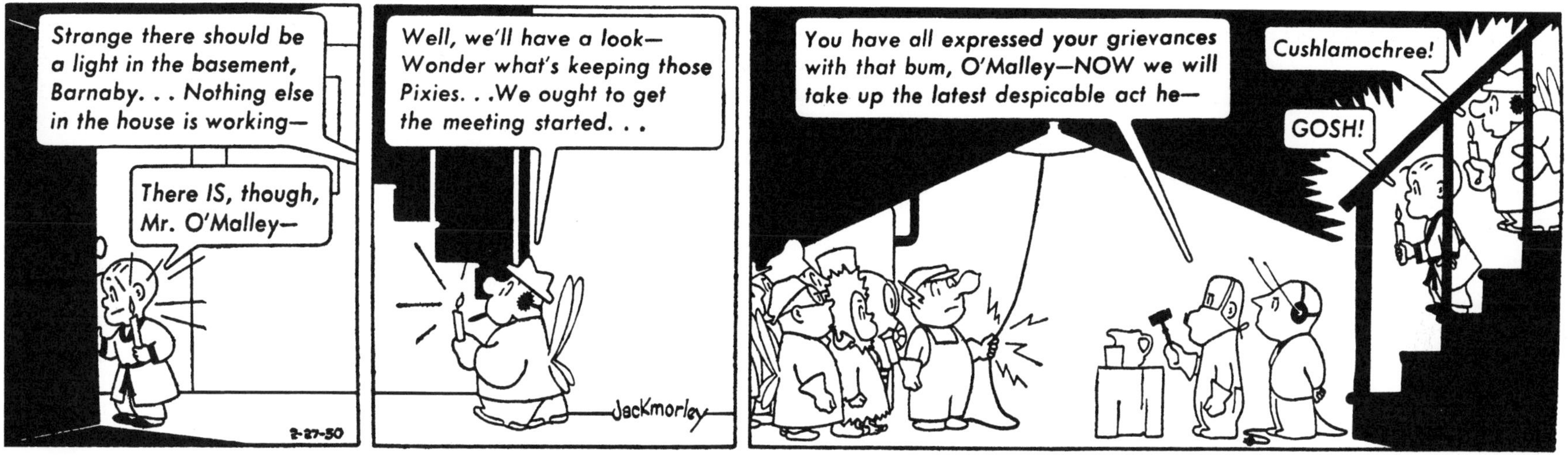
Strange there should be a light in the basement, Barnaby. . . Nothing else in the house is working—
There IS, though, Mr. O'Malley—
Well, we'll have a look— Wonder what's keeping those Pixies. . .We ought to get the meeting started. . .
Jackmorley
2-27-50
You have all expressed your grievances with that bum, O'Malley—NOW we will take up the latest despicable act he—
Cushlamochree!
GOSH!

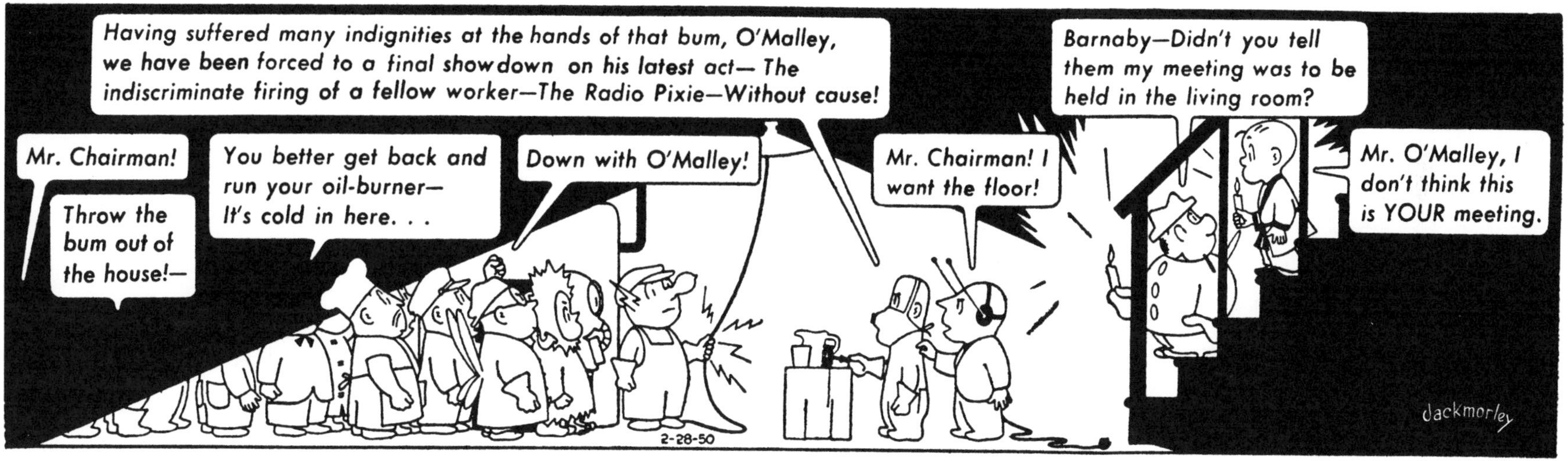
Having suffered many indignities at the hands of that bum, O'Malley, we have been forced to a final showdown on his latest act— The indiscriminate firing of a fellow worker—The Radio Pixie—Without cause!
Mr. Chairman!
Throw the bum out of the house!—
You better get back and run your oil-burner— It's cold in here. . .
Down with O'Malley!
Mr. Chairman! I want the floor!
Barnaby—Didn't you tell them my meeting was to be held in the living room?
Mr. O'Malley, I don't think this is YOUR meeting.
Jackmorley
2-28-50

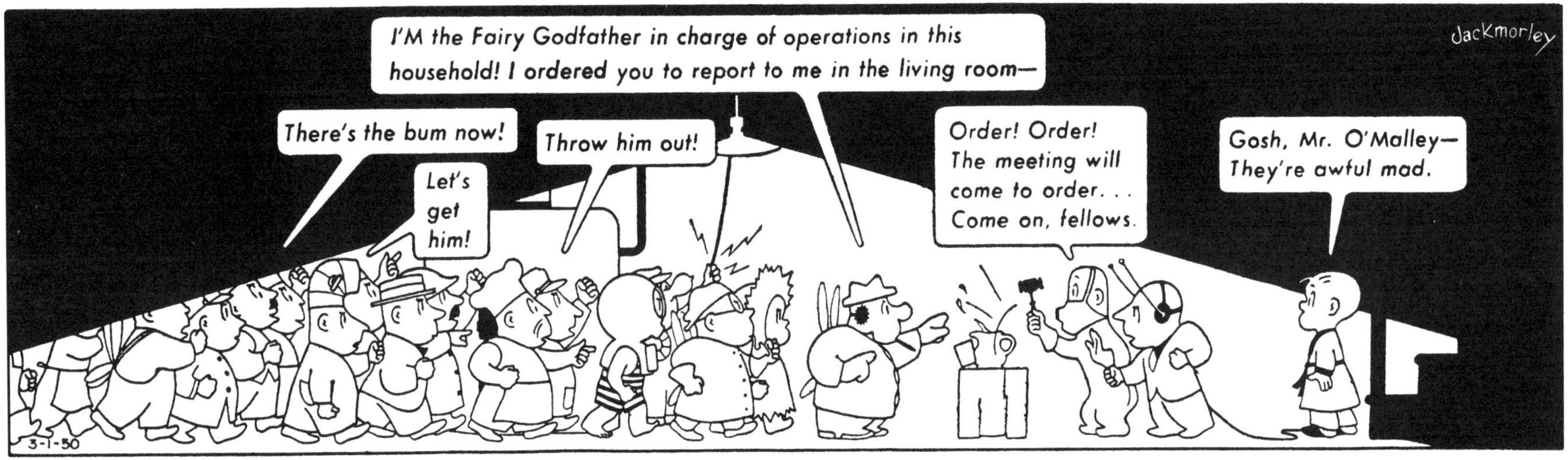

JacKmorley
I'M the Fairy Godfather in charge of operations in this household! I ordered you to report to me in the living room—
There's the bum now!
Let's get him!
Throw him out!
Order! Order! The meeting will come to order. . . Come on, fellows.
Gosh, Mr. O'Malley— They're awful mad.
3-1-50

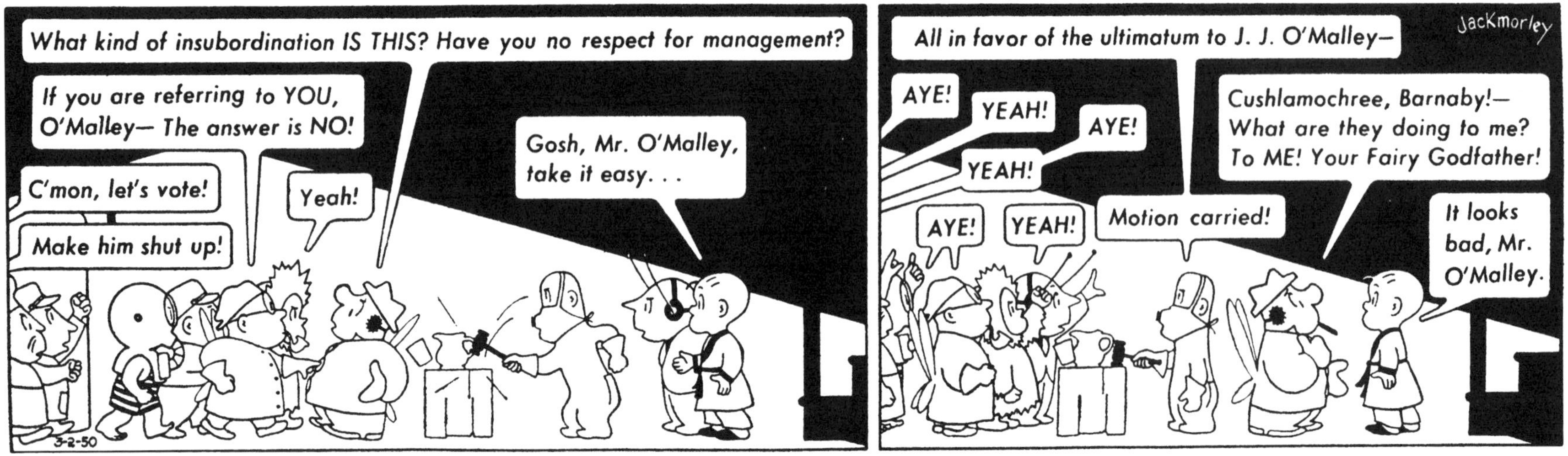

What kind of insubordination IS THIS? Have you no respect for management?
If you are referring to YOU, O'Malley— The answer is NO!
C'mon, let's vote!
Make him shut up!
Yeah!
Gosh, Mr. O'Malley, take it easy. . .
3-2-50
JacKmorley
All in favor of the ultimatum to J. J. O'Malley—
AYE!
YEAH!
AYE!
YEAH!
AYE!
YEAH!
Motion carried!
Cushlamochree, Barnaby!— What are they doing to me? To ME! Your Fairy Godfather!
It looks bad, Mr. O'Malley.

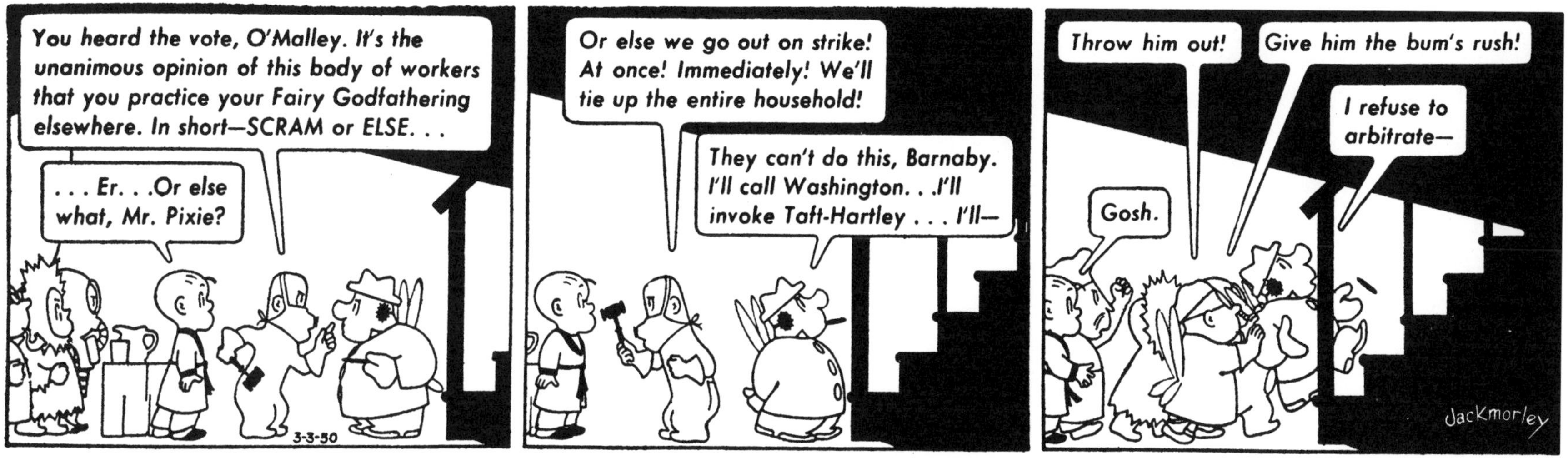
You heard the vote, O'Malley. It's the unanimous opinion of this body of workers that you practice your Fairy Godfathering elsewhere. In short—SCRAM or ELSE. . .
. . . Er. . .Or else what, Mr. Pixie?
3-3-50
Or else we go out on strike! At once! Immediately! We'll tie up the entire household!
They can't do this, Barnaby. I'll call Washington. . .I'll invoke Taft-Hartley . . . I'll—
Throw him out!
Give him the bum's rush!
I refuse to arbitrate—
Gosh.
JacKmorley

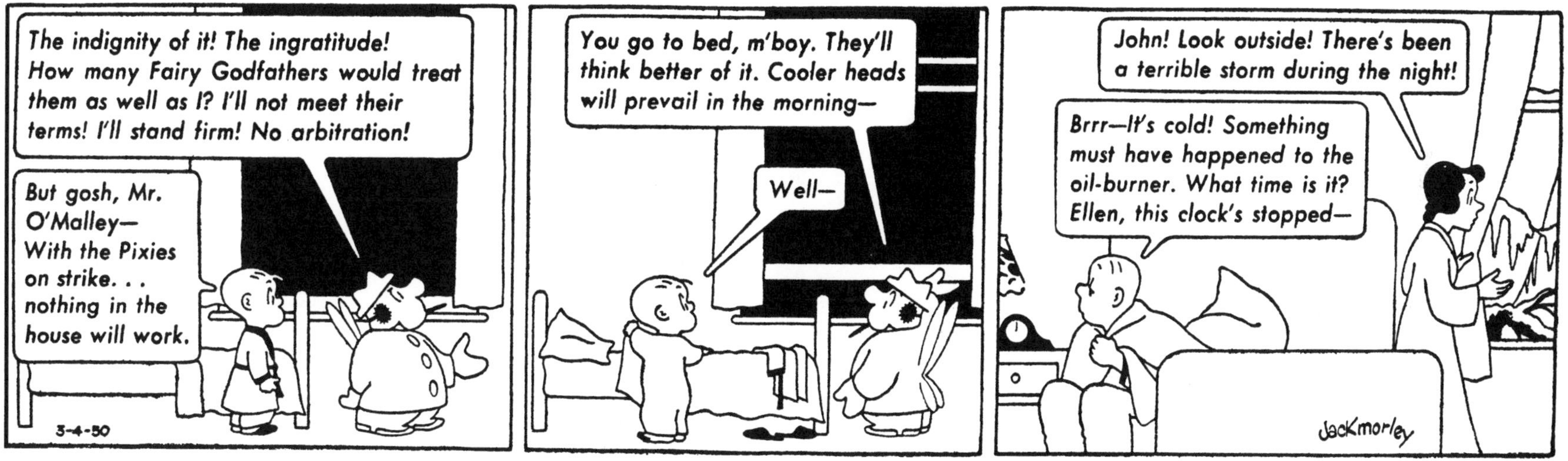
The indignity of it! The ingratitude! How many Fairy Godfathers would treat them as well as I? I'll not meet their terms! I'll stand firm! No arbitration!
But gosh, Mr. O'Malley— With the Pixies on strike. . . nothing in the house will work.
3-4-50
You go to bed, m'boy. They'll think better of it. Cooler heads will prevail in the morning—
Well—
John! Look outside! There's been a terrible storm during the night!
Brrr—It's cold! Something must have happened to the oil-burner. What time is it? Ellen, this clock's stopped—
JacKmorley

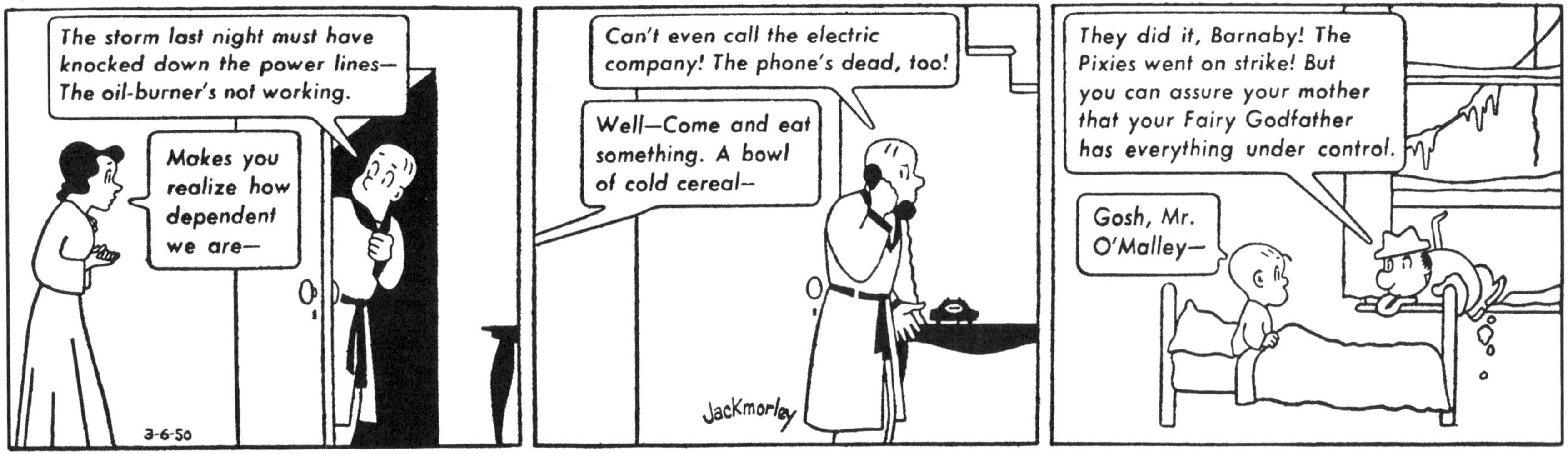
The storm last night must have knocked down the power lines— The oil-burner's not working.
Makes you realize how dependent we are—
3-6-50
Can't even call the electric company! The phone's dead, too!
Well—Come and eat something. A bowl of cold cereal—
JacKmorley
They did it, Barnaby! The Pixies went on strike! But you can assure your mother that your Fairy Godfather has everything under control.
Gosh, Mr. O'Malley—

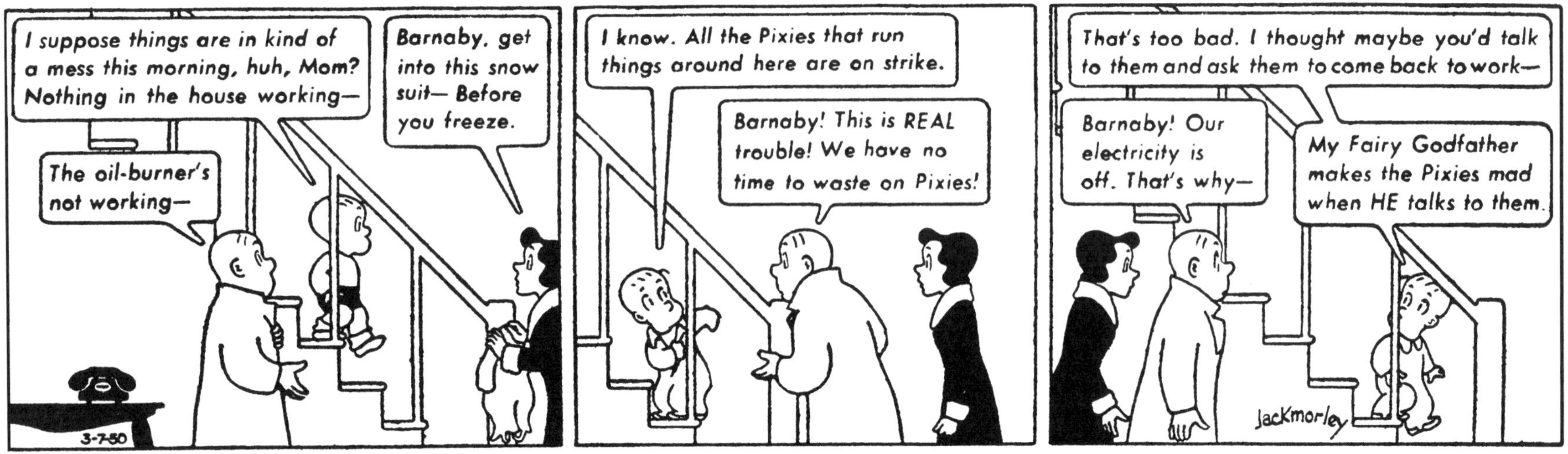
I suppose things are in kind of a mess this morning, huh, Mom? Nothing in the house working—
The oil-burner's not working—
Barnaby, get into this snow suit— Before you freeze.
3-7-50
I know. All the Pixies that run things around here are on strike.
Barnaby! This is REAL trouble! We have no time to waste on Pixies!
That's too bad. I thought maybe you'd talk to them and ask them to come back to work—
Barnaby! Our electricity is off. That's why—
My Fairy Godfather makes the Pixies mad when HE talks to them.
JacKmorley

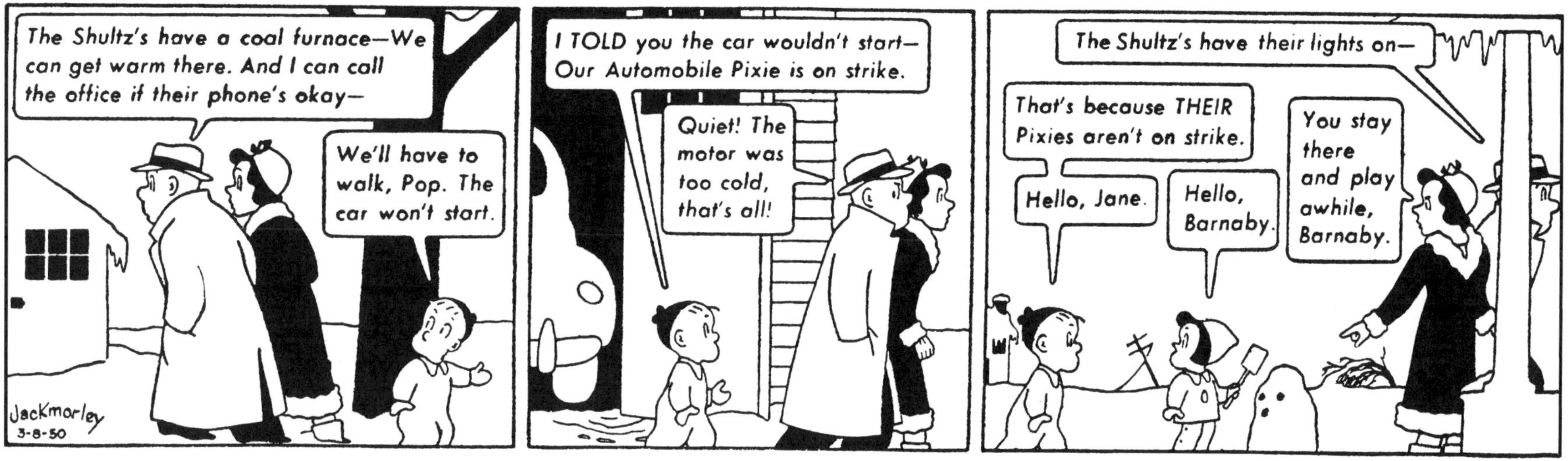

The Shultz's have a coal furnace—We can get warm there. And I can call the office if their phone's okay—
We'll have to walk, Pop. The car won't start.
Jackmorley
3-8-50
I TOLD you the car wouldn't start—Our Automobile Pixie is on strike.
Quiet! The motor was too cold, that's all!
The Shultz's have their lights on—
That's because THEIR Pixies aren't on strike.
You stay there and play awhile, Barnaby.
Hello, Jane.
Hello, Barnaby.

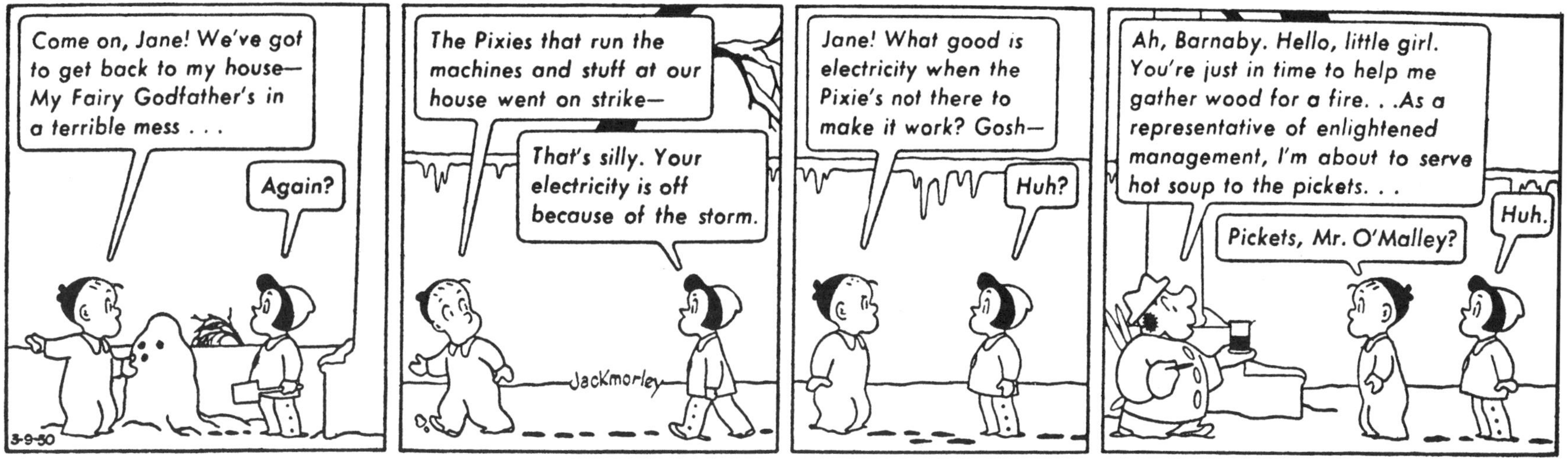

Come on, Jane! We've got to get back to my house—My Fairy Godfather's in a terrible mess . . .
Again?
3-9-50
The Pixies that run the machines and stuff at our house went on strike—
That's silly. Your electricity is off because of the storm.
Jackmorley
Jane! What good is electricity when the Pixie's not there to make it work? Gosh—
Huh?
Ah, Barnaby. Hello, little girl. You're just in time to help me gather wood for a fire. . .As a representative of enlightened management, I'm about to serve hot soup to the pickets. . .
Pickets, Mr. O'Malley?
Huh.

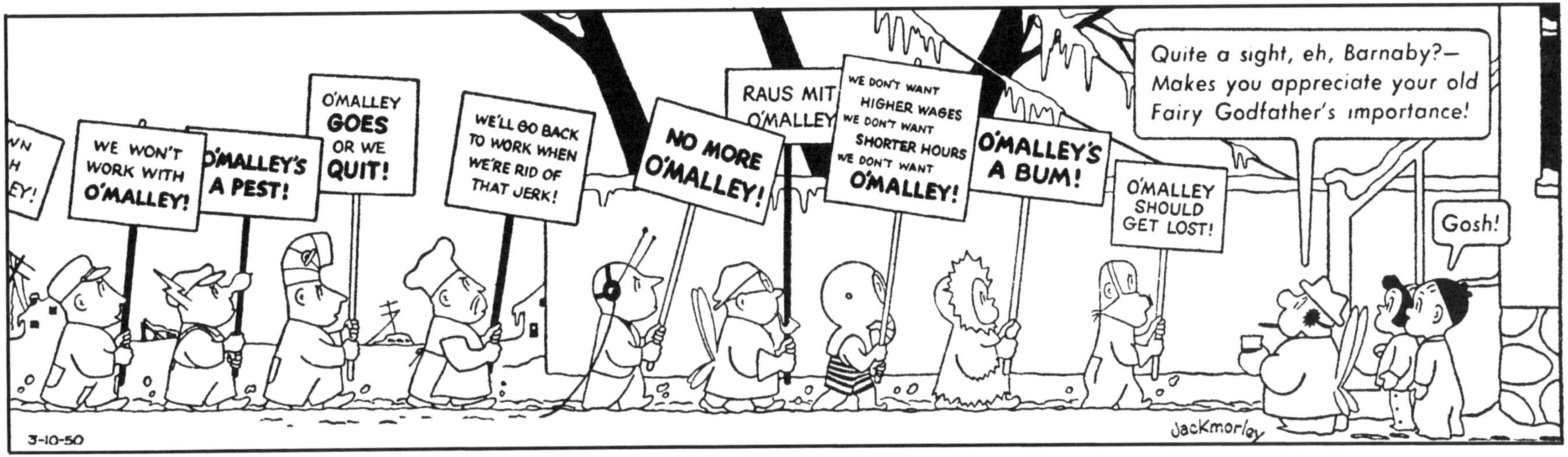
WE WON'T WORK WITH O'MALLEY!
O'MALLEY'S A PEST!
O'MALLEY GOES OR WE QUIT!
WE'LL GO BACK TO WORK WHEN WE'RE RID OF THAT JERK!
NO MORE O'MALLEY!
RAUS MIT O'MALLEY
WE DON'T WANT HIGHER WAGES WE DON'T WANT SHORTER HOURS WE DON'T WANT O'MALLEY!
O'MALLEY'S A BUM!
O'MALLEY SHOULD GET LOST!
Quite a sight, eh, Barnaby?— Makes you appreciate your old Fairy Godfather's importance!
Gosh!
3-10-50
JacKmorley

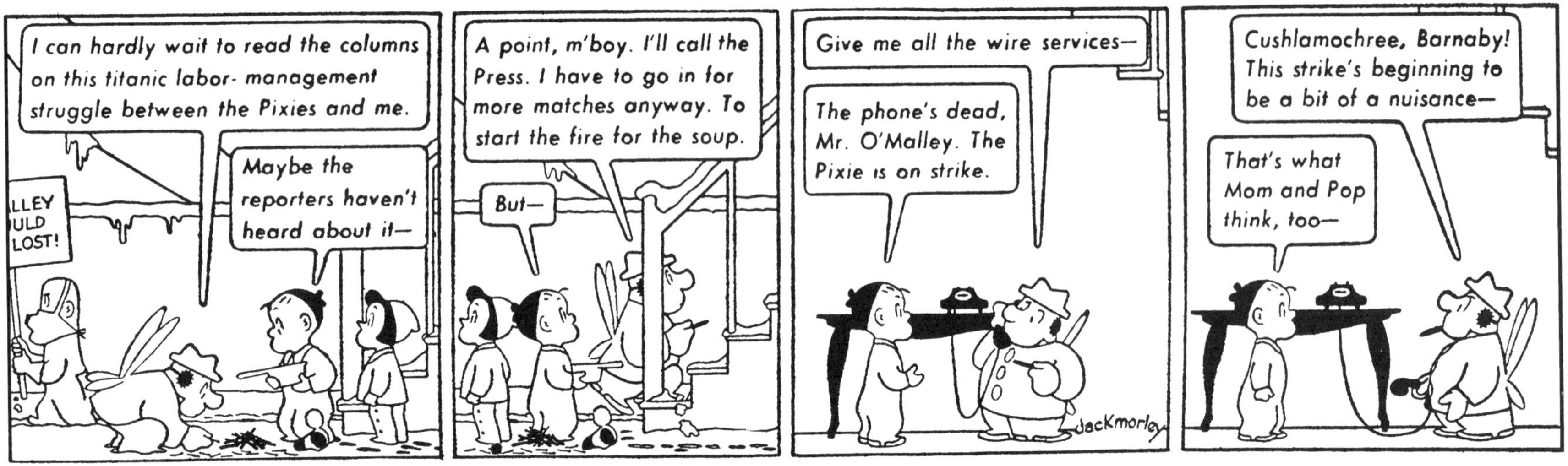
I can hardly wait to read the columns on this titanic labor- management struggle between the Pixies and me.
Maybe the reporters haven't heard about it—
A point, m'boy. I'll call the Press. I have to go in for more matches anyway. To start the fire for the soup.
But—
Give me all the wire services—
The phone's dead, Mr. O'Malley. The Pixie is on strike.
JacKmorley
Cushlamochree, Barnaby! This strike's beginning to be a bit of a nuisance—
That's what Mom and Pop think, too—

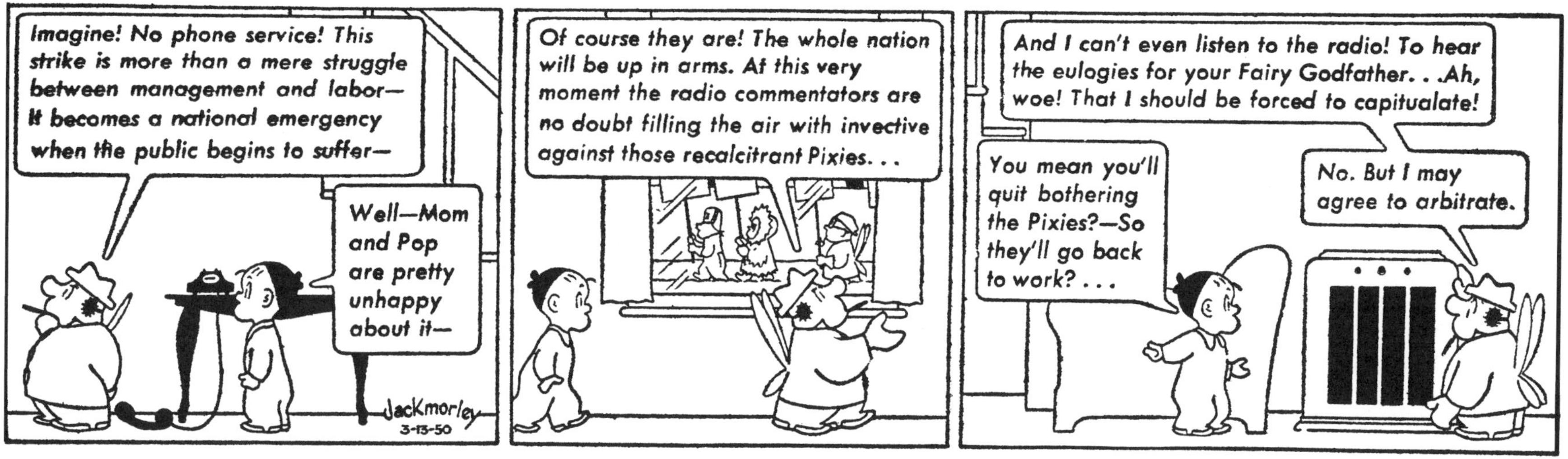
Imagine! No phone service! This strike is more than a mere struggle between management and labor— It becomes a national emergency when the public begins to suffer—
Well—Mom and Pop are pretty unhappy about it—
JackMorley 3-13-50
Of course they are! The whole nation will be up in arms. At this very moment the radio commentators are no doubt filling the air with invective against those recalcitrant Pixies. . .
And I can't even listen to the radio! To hear the eulogies for your Fairy Godfather. . .Ah, woe! That I should be forced to capitulate!
You mean you'll quit bothering the Pixies?—So they'll go back to work? . . .
No. But I may agree to arbitrate.

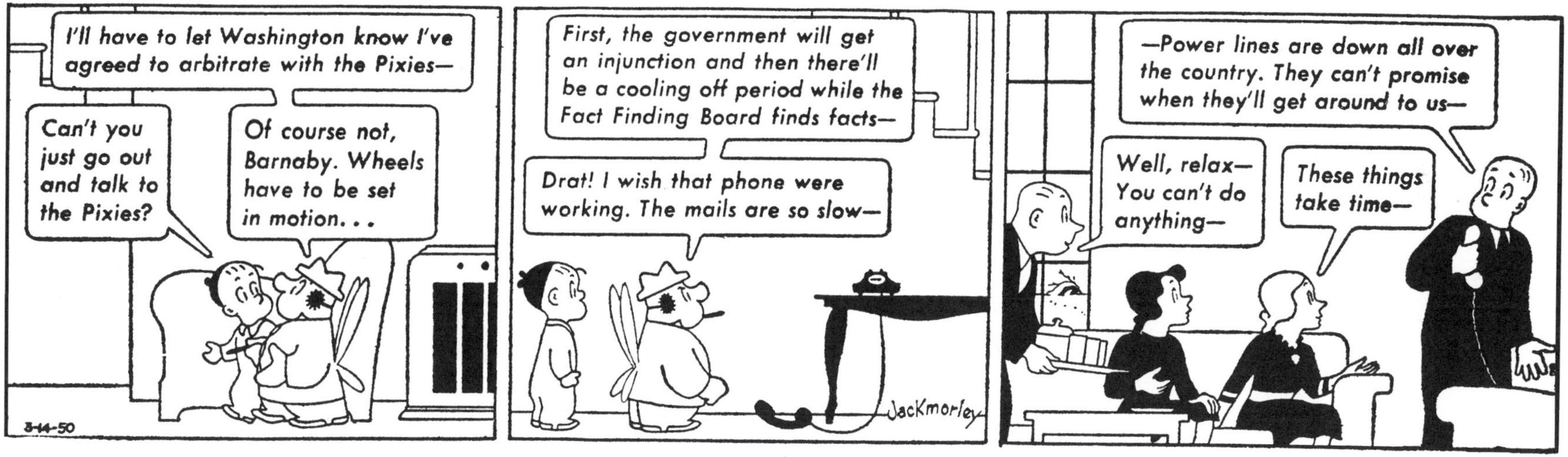
I'll have to let Washington know I've agreed to arbitrate with the Pixies—
Can't you just go out and talk to the Pixies?
Of course not, Barnaby. Wheels have to be set in motion. . .
3-14-50
First, the government will get an injunction and then there'll be a cooling off period while the Fact Finding Board finds facts—
Drat! I wish that phone were working. The mails are so slow—
JackMorley
—Power lines are down all over the country. They can't promise when they'll get around to us—
Well, relax— You can't do anything—
These things take time—

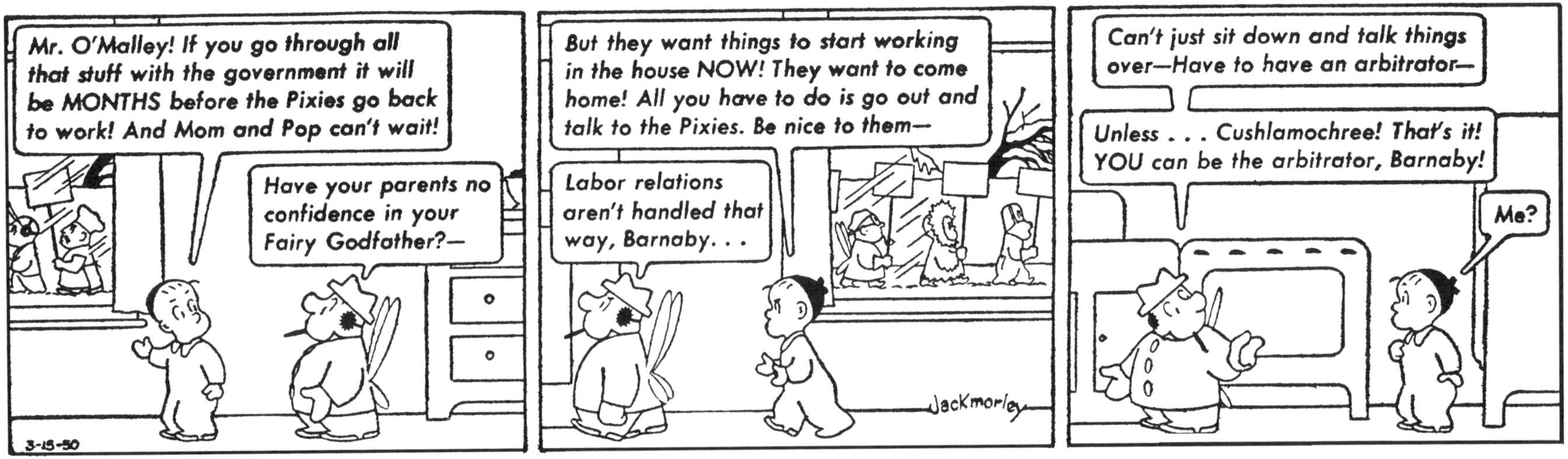
Mr. O'Malley! If you go through all that stuff with the government it will be MONTHS before the Pixies go back to work! And Mom and Pop can't wait!
Have your parents no confidence in your Fairy Godfather?—
3-15-50
But they want things to start working in the house NOW! They want to come home! All you have to do is go out and talk to the Pixies. Be nice to them—
Labor relations aren't handled that way, Barnaby. . .
JackMorley
Can't just sit down and talk things over—Have to have an arbitrator—
Unless . . . Cushlamochree! That's it! YOU can be the arbitrator, Barnaby!
Me?

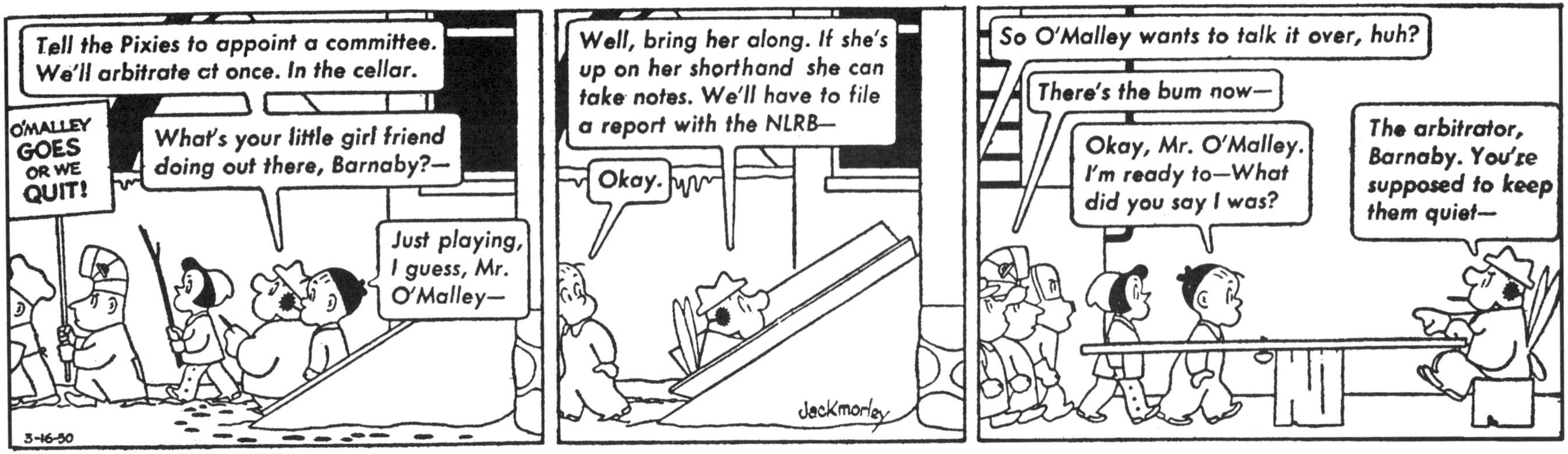
Tell the Pixies to appoint a committee. We'll arbitrate at once. In the cellar.
O'MALLEY GOES OR WE QUIT!
What's your little girl friend doing out there, Barnaby?—
Just playing, I guess, Mr. O'Malley—
3-16-50
Well, bring her along. If she's up on her shorthand she can take notes. We'll have to file a report with the NLRB—
Okay.
JackMorley
So O'Malley wants to talk it over, huh?
There's the bum now—
Okay, Mr. O'Malley. I'm ready to—What did you say I was?
The arbitrator, Barnaby. You're supposed to keep them quiet—

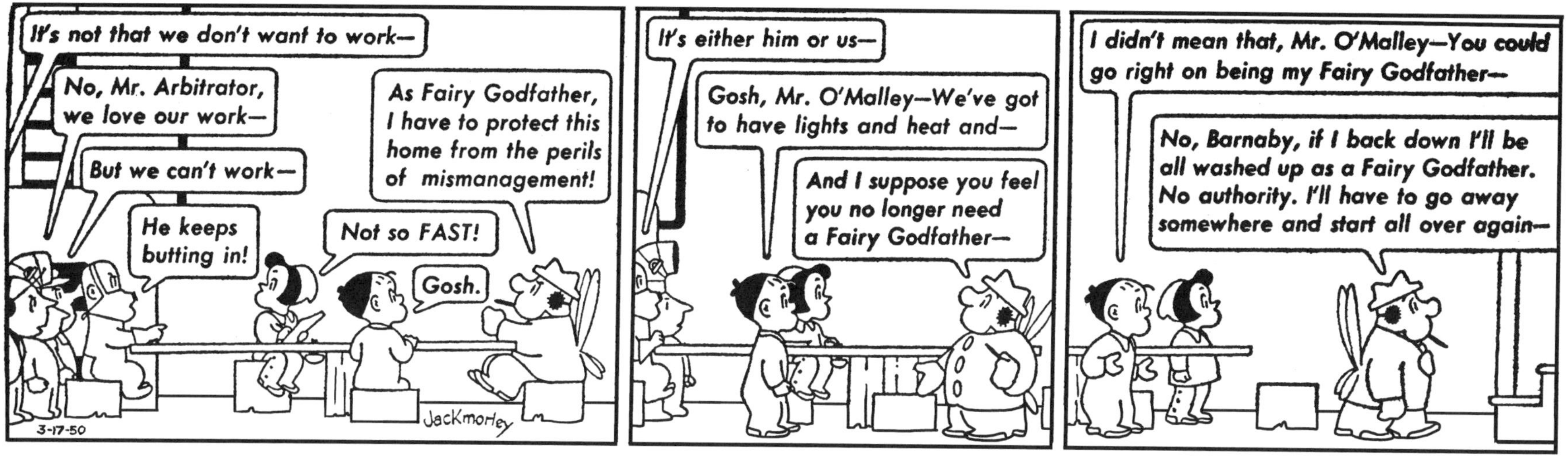
It's not that we don't want to work—
No, Mr. Arbitrator, we love our work—
But we can't work—
He keeps butting in!
Not so FAST!
As Fairy Godfather, I have to protect this home from the perils of mismanagement!
Gosh.
3-17-50
JackmorHey
It's either him or us—
Gosh, Mr. O'Malley—We've got to have lights and heat and—
And I suppose you feel you no longer need a Fairy Godfather—
I didn't mean that, Mr. O'Malley—You could go right on being my Fairy Godfather—
No, Barnaby, if I back down I'll be all washed up as a Fairy Godfather. No authority. I'll have to go away somewhere and start all over again—

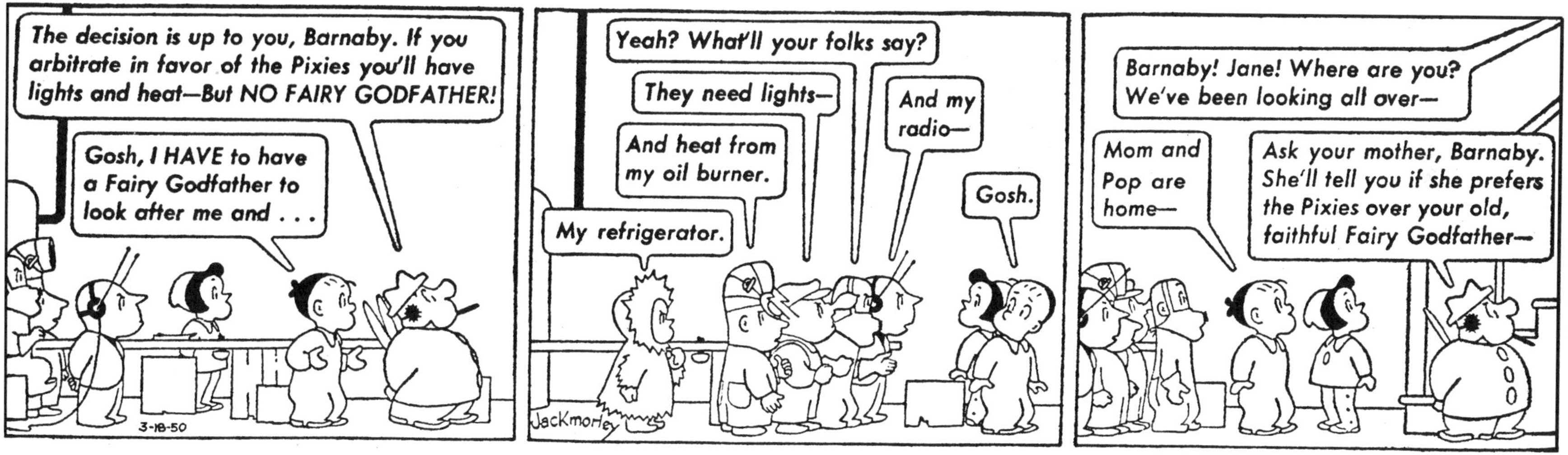
The decision is up to you, Barnaby. If you arbitrate in favor of the Pixies you'll have lights and heat—But NO FAIRY GODFATHER!
Gosh, I HAVE to have a Fairy Godfather to look after me and . . .
3-18-50
Yeah? What'll your folks say?
They need lights—
And my radio—
And heat from my oil burner.
Gosh.
My refrigerator.
JackmorHey
Barnaby! Jane! Where are you? We've been looking all over—
Mom and Pop are home—
Ask your mother, Barnaby. She'll tell you if she prefers the Pixies over your old, faithful Fairy Godfather—

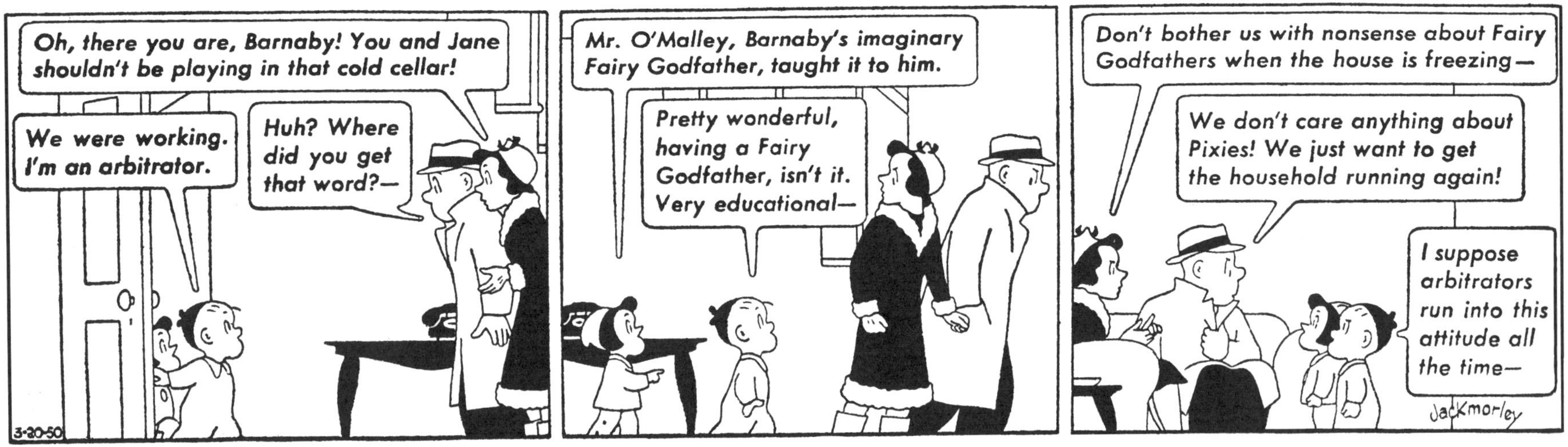
Oh, there you are, Barnaby! You and Jane shouldn't be playing in that cold cellar!
We were working. I'm an arbitrator.
Huh? Where did you get that word?—
3-20-50
Mr. O'Malley, Barnaby's imaginary Fairy Godfather, taught it to him.
Pretty wonderful, having a Fairy Godfather, isn't it. Very educational—
Don't bother us with nonsense about Fairy Godfathers when the house is freezing—
We don't care anything about Pixies! We just want to get the household running again!
I suppose arbitrators run into this attitude all the time—
Jackmorley

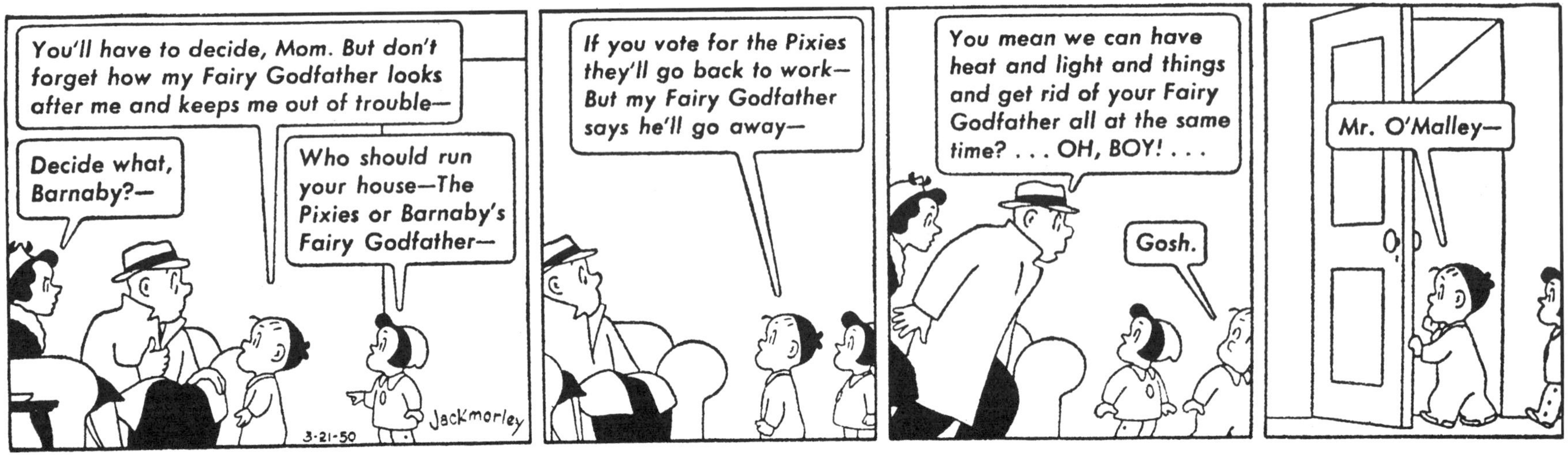
You'll have to decide, Mom. But don't forget how my Fairy Godfather looks after me and keeps me out of trouble—
Decide what, Barnaby?—
Who should run your house—The Pixies or Barnaby's Fairy Godfather—
3-21-50
Jackmorley
If you vote for the Pixies they'll go back to work— But my Fairy Godfather says he'll go away—
You mean we can have heat and light and things and get rid of your Fairy Godfather all at the same time? . . . OH, BOY! . . .
Gosh.
Mr. O'Malley—

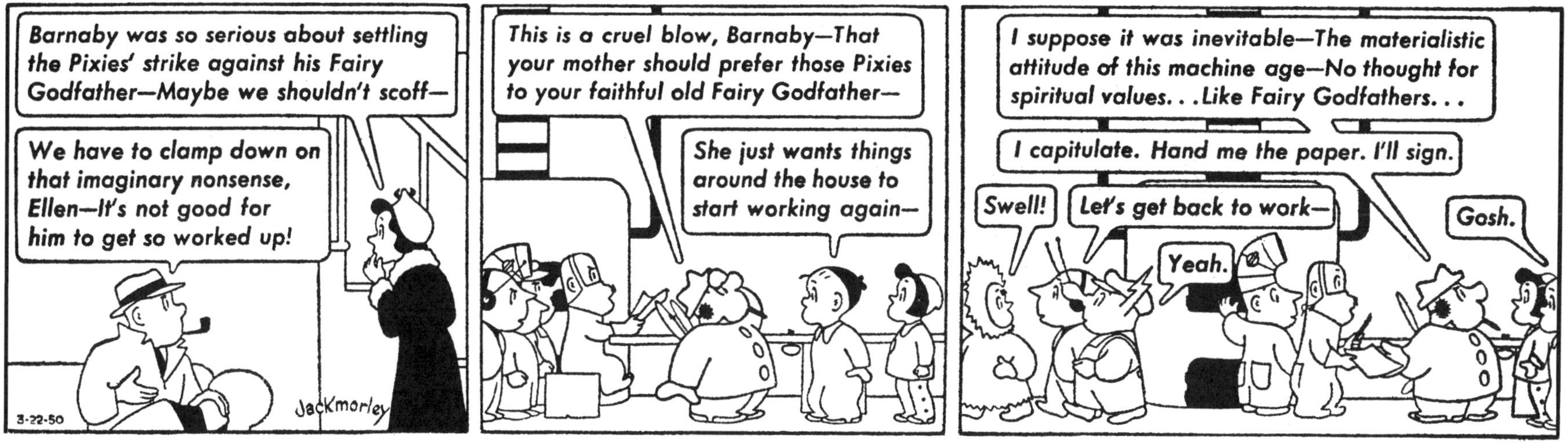
Barnaby was so serious about settling the Pixies' strike against his Fairy Godfather—Maybe we shouldn't scoff—
We have to clamp down on that imaginary nonsense, Ellen—It's not good for him to get so worked up!
3-22-50
JacKmorley
This is a cruel blow, Barnaby—That your mother should prefer those Pixies to your faithful old Fairy Godfather—
She just wants things around the house to start working again—
I suppose it was inevitable—The materialistic attitude of this machine age—No thought for spiritual values. . .Like Fairy Godfathers. . .
I capitulate. Hand me the paper. I'll sign.
Swell!
Let's get back to work—
Yeah.
Gosh.

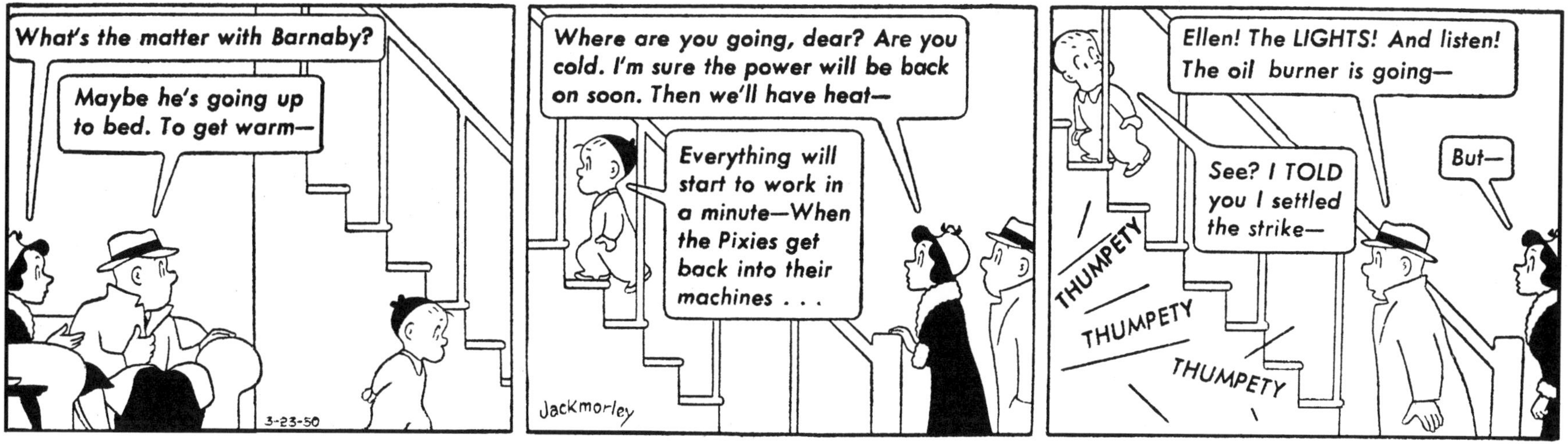
What's the matter with Barnaby?
Maybe he's going up to bed. To get warm—
3-23-50
Where are you going, dear? Are you cold. I'm sure the power will be back on soon. Then we'll have heat—
Everything will start to work in a minute—When the Pixies get back into their machines . . .
JacKmorley
Ellen! The LIGHTS! And listen! The oil burner is going—
See? I TOLD you I settled the strike—
But—
THUMPETY
THUMPETY
THUMPETY

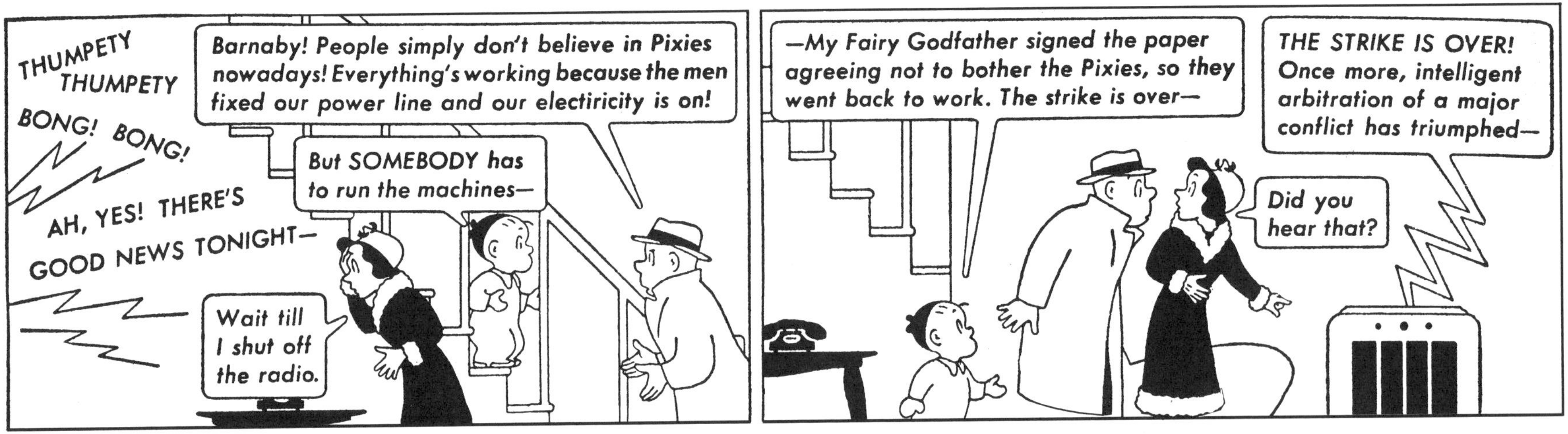
THUMPETY THUMPETY
BONG! BONG!
AH, YES! THERE'S GOOD NEWS TONIGHT—
Barnaby! People simply don't believe in Pixies nowadays! Everything's working because the men fixed our power line and our electiricity is on!
But SOMEBODY has to run the machines—
Wait till I shut off the radio.
—My Fairy Godfather signed the paper agreeing not to bother the Pixies, so they went back to work. The strike is over—
THE STRIKE IS OVER! Once more, intelligent arbitration of a major conflict has triumphed—
Did you hear that?

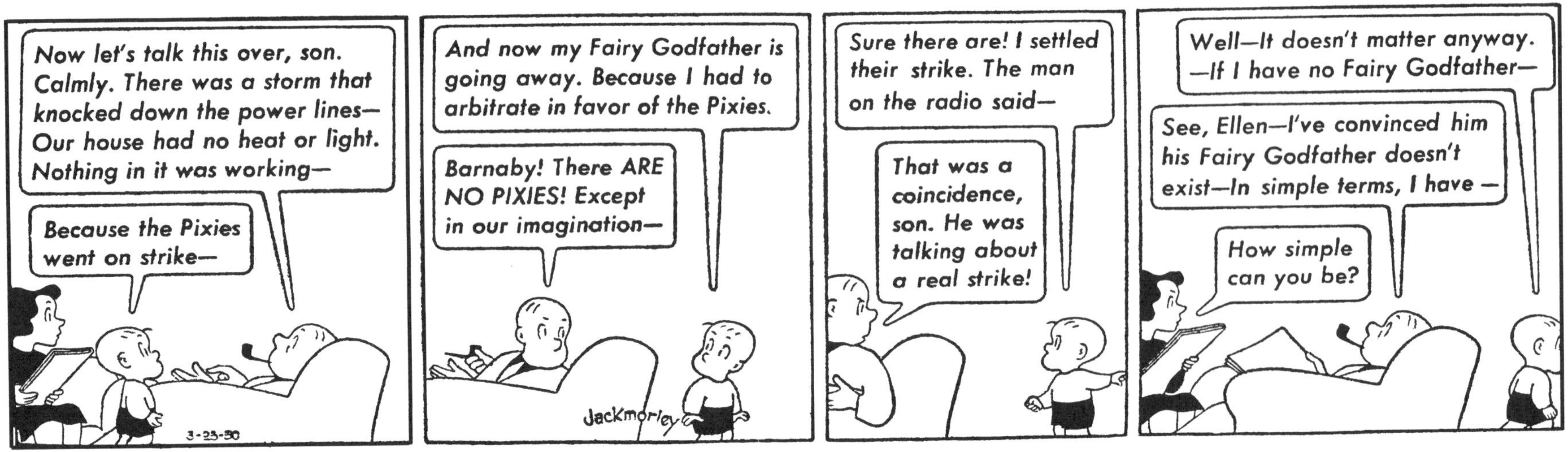
Now let's talk this over, son. Calmly. There was a storm that knocked down the power lines— Our house had no heat or light. Nothing in it was working—
Because the Pixies went on strike—
3-23-50
And now my Fairy Godfather is going away. Because I had to arbitrate in favor of the Pixies.
Barnaby! There ARE NO PIXIES! Except in our imagination—
Jackmorley
Sure there are! I settled their strike. The man on the radio said—
That was a coincidence, son. He was talking about a real strike!
Well—It doesn't matter anyway. —If I have no Fairy Godfather—
See, Ellen—I've convinced him his Fairy Godfather doesn't exist—In simple terms, I have —
How simple can you be?

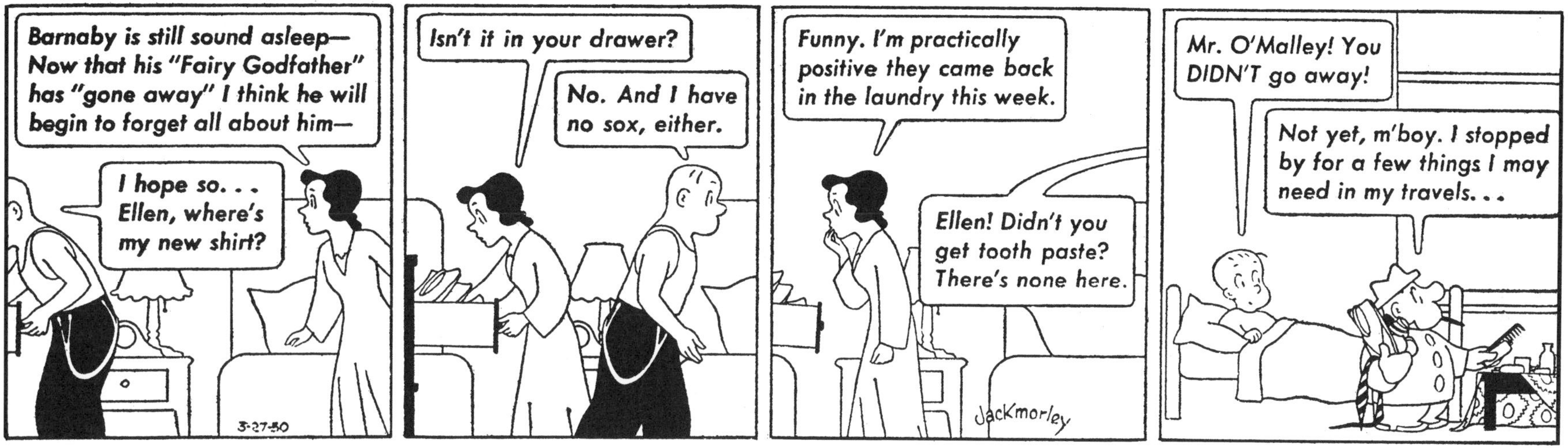
Barnaby is still sound asleep— Now that his "Fairy Godfather" has "gone away" I think he will begin to forget all about him—
I hope so. . . Ellen, where's my new shirt?
Isn't it in your drawer?
No. And I have no sox, either.
Funny. I'm practically positive they came back in the laundry this week.
Ellen! Didn't you get tooth paste? There's none here.
Mr. O'Malley! You DIDN'T go away!
Not yet, m'boy. I stopped by for a few things I may need in my travels. . .

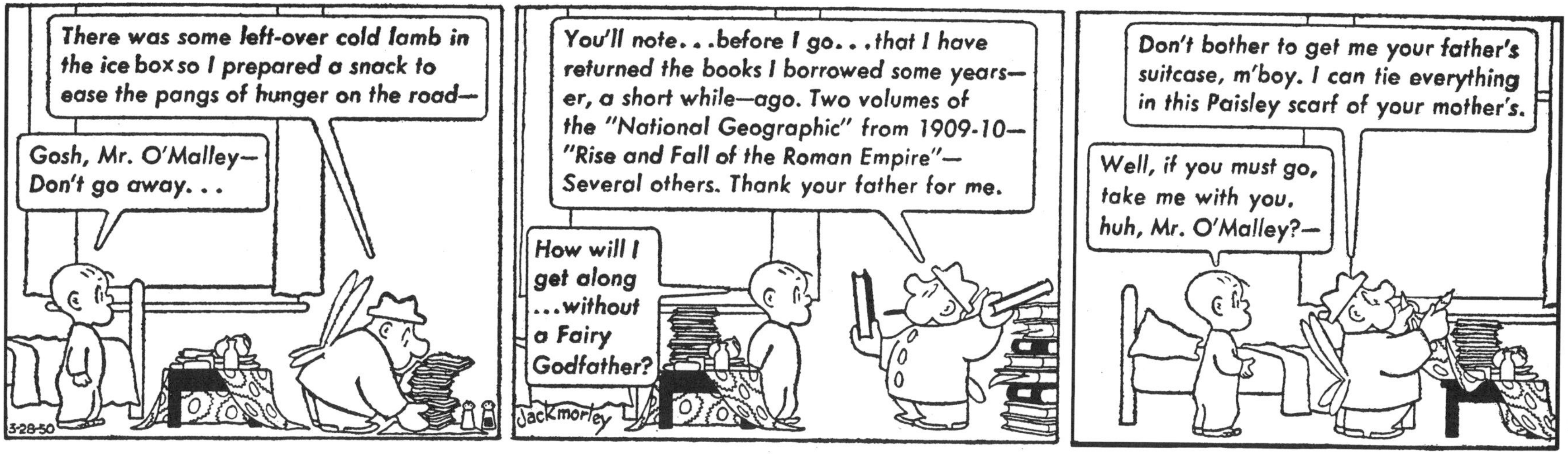
There was some left-over cold lamb in the ice box so I prepared a snack to ease the pangs of hunger on the road—
Gosh, Mr. O'Malley— Don't go away. . .
You'll note. . .before I go. . .that I have returned the books I borrowed some years— er, a short while—ago. Two volumes of the "National Geographic" from 1909-10— "Rise and Fall of the Roman Empire"— Several others. Thank your father for me.
How will I get along . . .without a Fairy Godfather?
Don't bother to get me your father's suitcase, m'boy. I can tie everything in this Paisley scarf of your mother's.
Well, if you must go, take me with you, huh, Mr. O'Malley?—

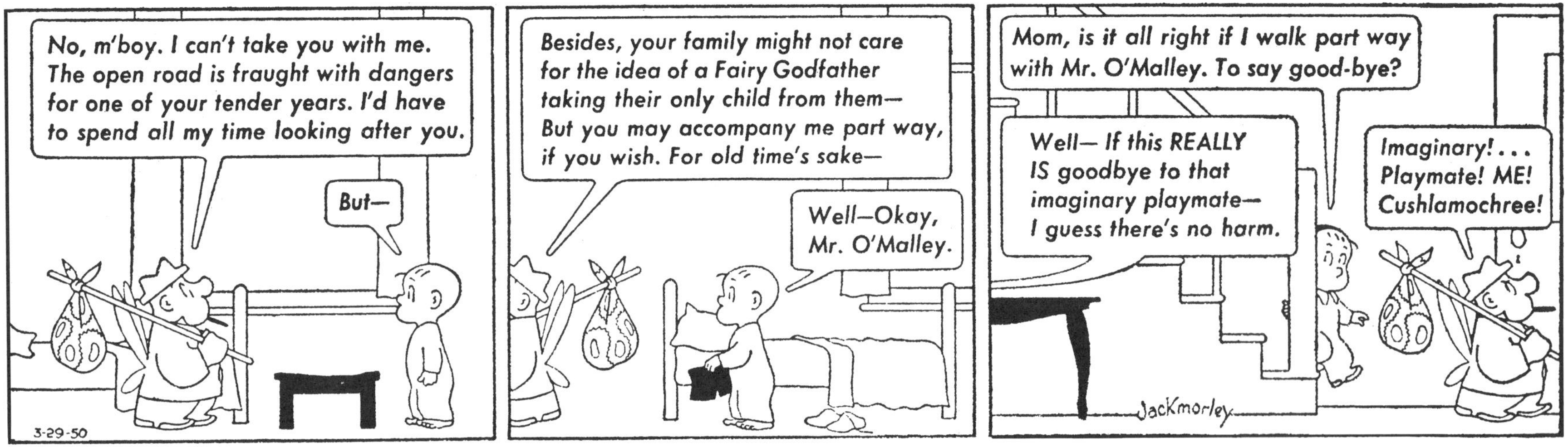
No, m'boy. I can't take you with me. The open road is fraught with dangers for one of your tender years. I'd have to spend all my time looking after you.
But—
Besides, your family might not care for the idea of a Fairy Godfather taking their only child from them— But you may accompany me part way, if you wish. For old time's sake—
Well—Okay, Mr. O'Malley.
Mom, is it all right if I walk part way with Mr. O'Malley. To say good-bye?
Well— If this REALLY IS goodbye to that imaginary playmate— I guess there's no harm.
Imaginary! . . . Playmate! ME! Cushlamochree!
3-29-50
JackMorley

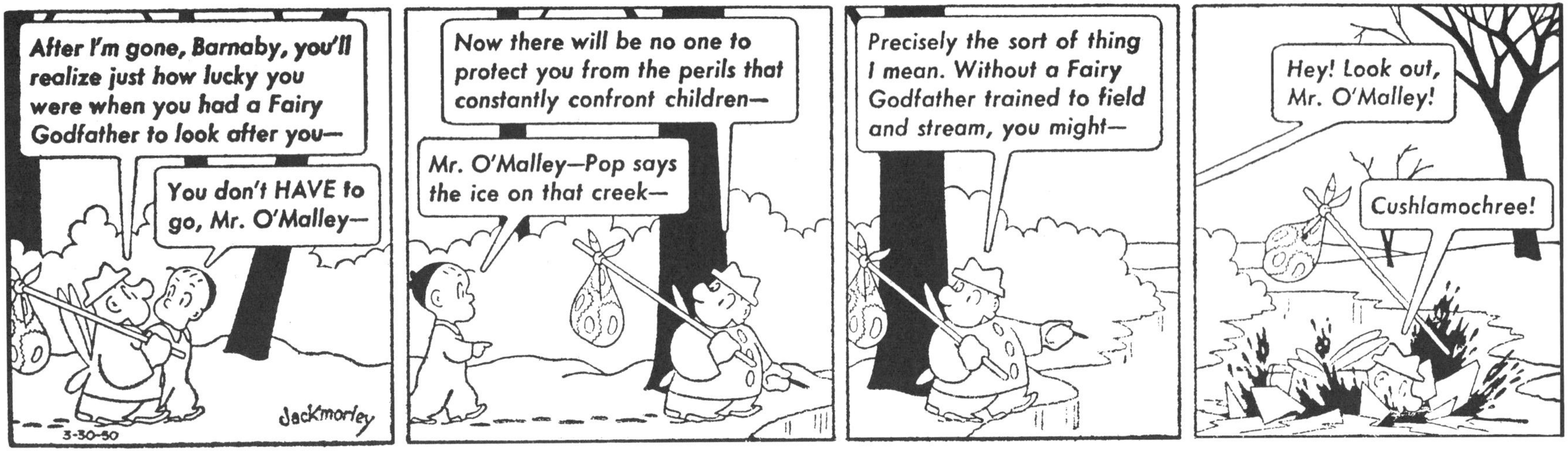
After I'm gone, Barnaby, you'll realize just how lucky you were when you had a Fairy Godfather to look after you—
You don't HAVE to go, Mr. O'Malley—
3-30-50
JackMorley
Now there will be no one to protect you from the perils that constantly confront children—
Mr. O'Malley—Pop says the ice on that creek—
Precisely the sort of thing I mean. Without a Fairy Godfather trained to field and stream, you might—
Hey! Look out, Mr. O'Malley!
Cushlamochree!

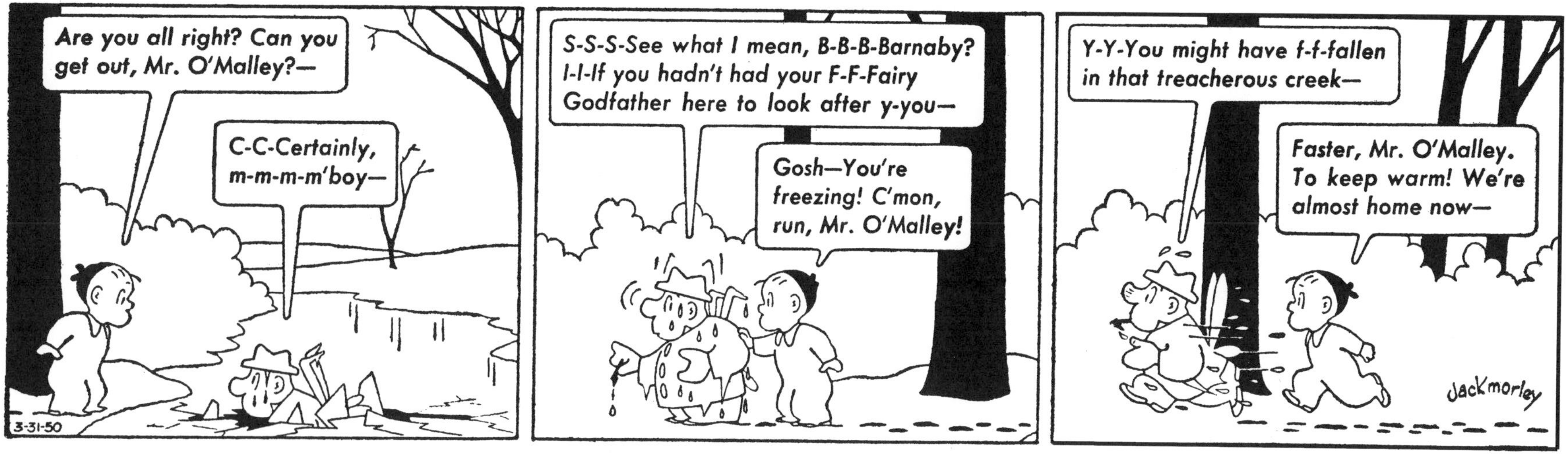
Are you all right? Can you get out, Mr. O'Malley?—
C-C-Certainly, m-m-m-m'boy—
3-31-50
S-S-S-See what I mean, B-B-B-Barnaby? I-I-If you hadn't had your F-F-Fairy Godfather here to look after y-you—
Gosh—You're freezing! C'mon, run, Mr. O'Malley!
Y-Y-You might have f-f-fallen in that treacherous creek—
Faster, Mr. O'Malley. To keep warm! We're almost home now—
JackMorley

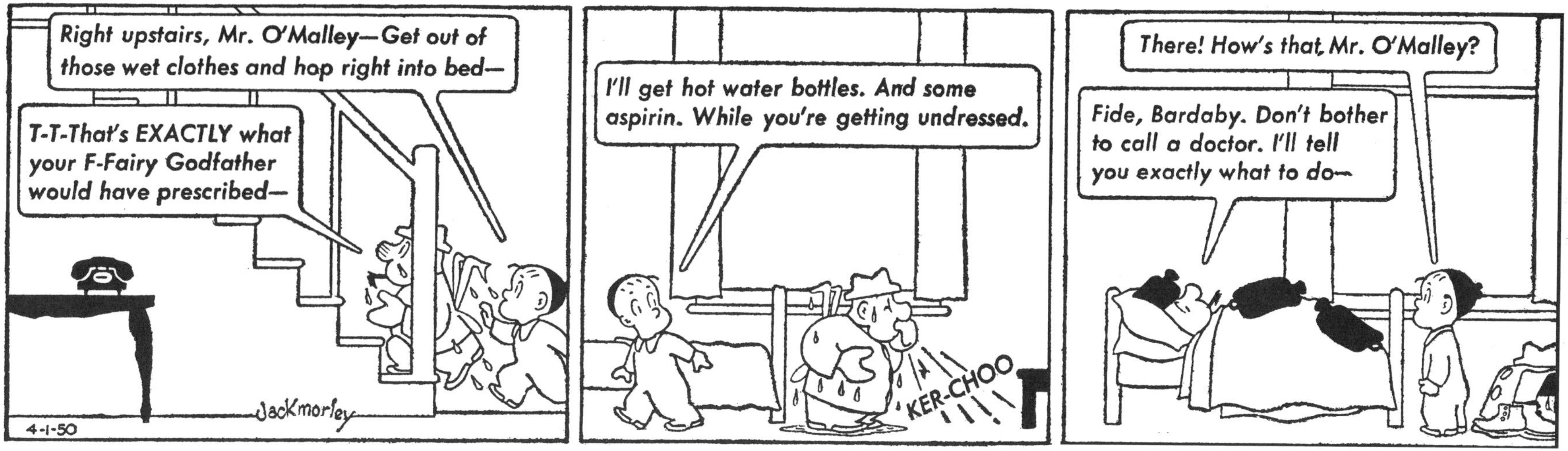
Right upstairs, Mr. O'Malley—Get out of those wet clothes and hop right into bed—
T-T-That's EXACTLY what your F-Fairy Godfather would have prescribed—
JackMorley
4-1-50
I'll get hot water bottles. And some aspirin. While you're getting undressed.
KER-CHOO
There! How's that, Mr. O'Malley?
Fide, Bardaby. Don't bother to call a doctor. I'll tell you exactly what to do—

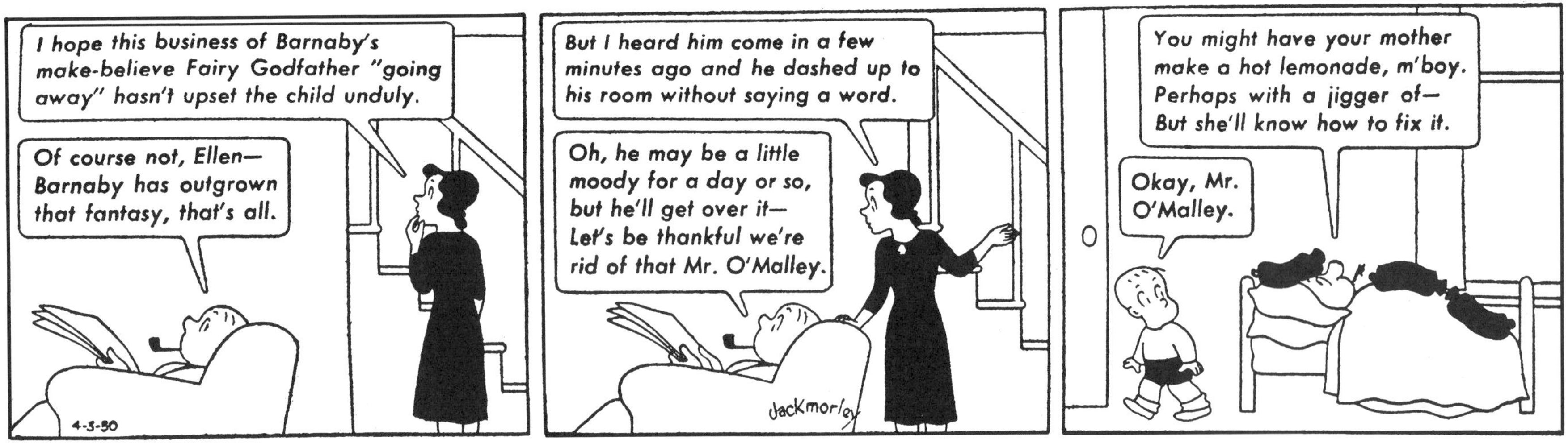
I hope this business of Barnaby's make-believe Fairy Godfather "going away" hasn't upset the child unduly.
Of course not, Ellen— Barnaby has outgrown that fantasy, that's all.
4-3-50
But I heard him come in a few minutes ago and he dashed up to his room without saying a word.
Oh, he may be a little moody for a day or so, but he'll get over it— Let's be thankful we're rid of that Mr. O'Malley.
JackMorley
You might have your mother make a hot lemonade, m'boy. Perhaps with a jigger of— But she'll know how to fix it.
Okay, Mr. O'Malley.

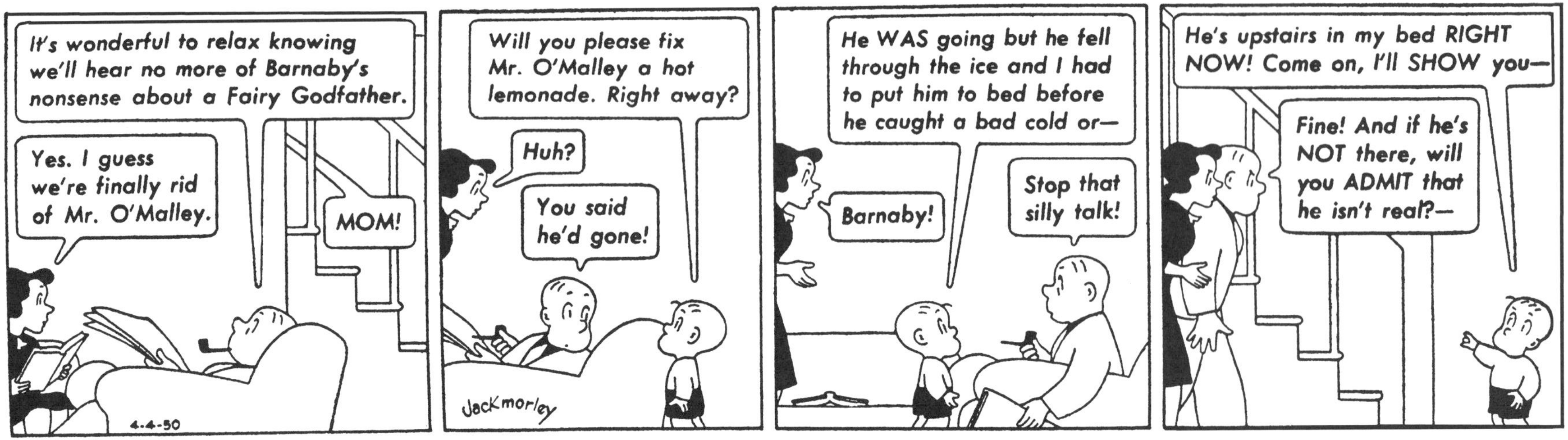
It's wonderful to relax knowing we'll hear no more of Barnaby's nonsense about a Fairy Godfather.
Yes. I guess we're finally rid of Mr. O'Malley.
MOM!
4-4-50
Will you please fix Mr. O'Malley a hot lemonade. Right away?
Huh?
You said he'd gone!
JackMorley
He WAS going but he fell through the ice and I had to put him to bed before he caught a bad cold or—
Barnaby!
Stop that silly talk!
He's upstairs in my bed RIGHT NOW! Come on, I'll SHOW you—
Fine! And if he's NOT there, will you ADMIT that he isn't real?—

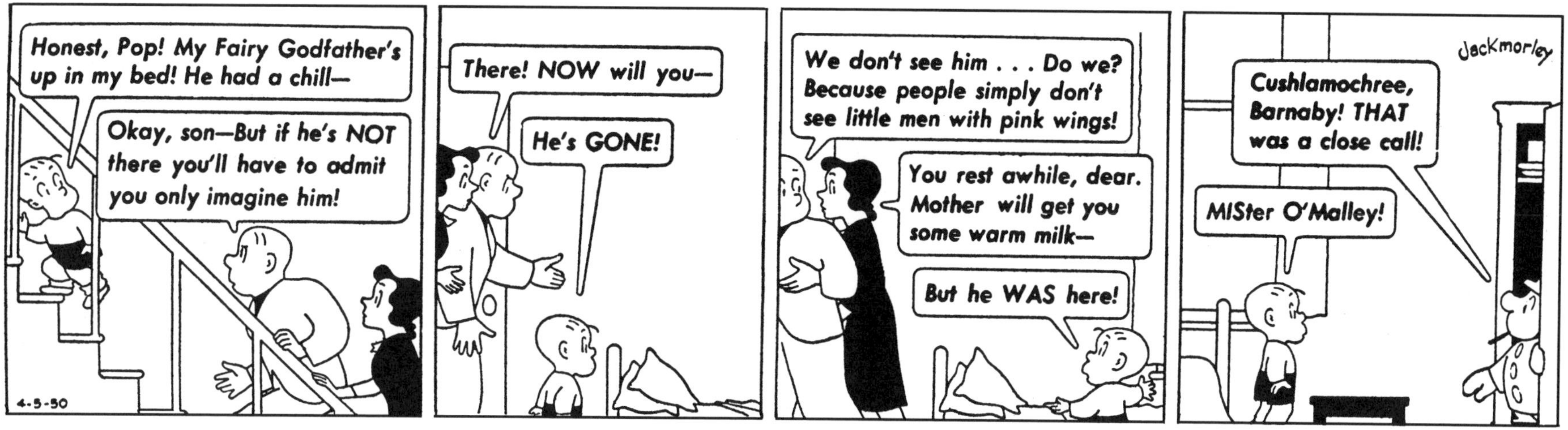
Honest, Pop! My Fairy Godfather's up in my bed! He had a chill—
Okay, son—But if he's NOT there you'll have to admit you only imagine him!
4-5-50
There! NOW will you—
He's GONE!
We don't see him . . . Do we? Because people simply don't see little men with pink wings!
You rest awhile, dear. Mother will get you some warm milk—
But he WAS here!
JackMorley
Cushlamochree, Barnaby! THAT was a close call!
MISter O'Malley!

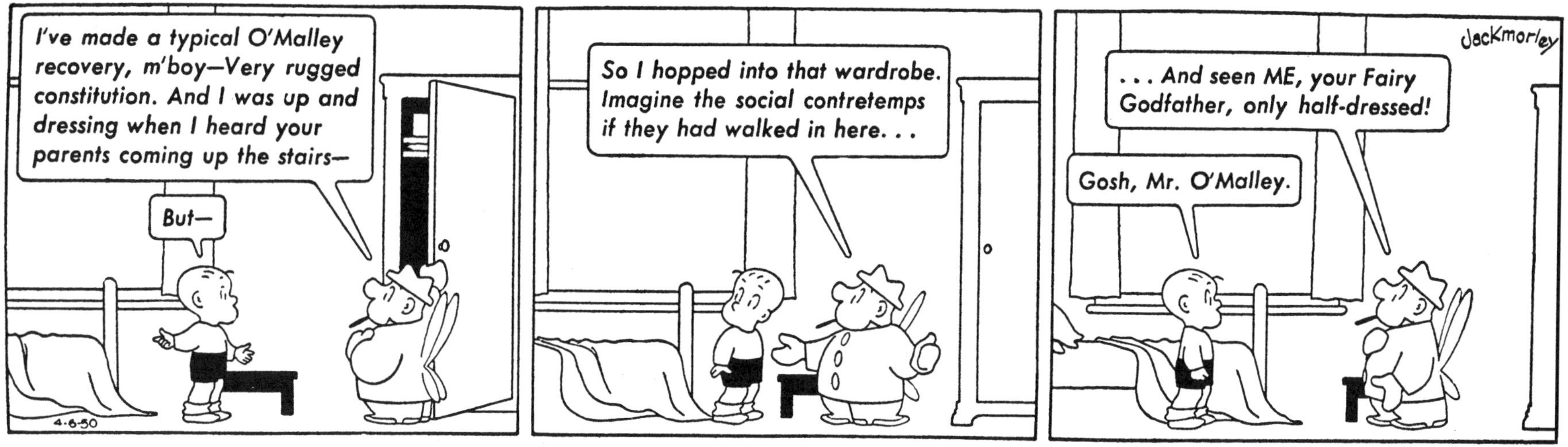
I've made a typical O'Malley recovery, m'boy—Very rugged constitution. And I was up and dressing when I heard your parents coming up the stairs—
But—
4-6-50
So I hopped into that wardrobe. Imagine the social contretemps if they had walked in here. . .
JackMorley
. . . And seen ME, your Fairy Godfather, only half-dressed!
Gosh, Mr. O'Malley.

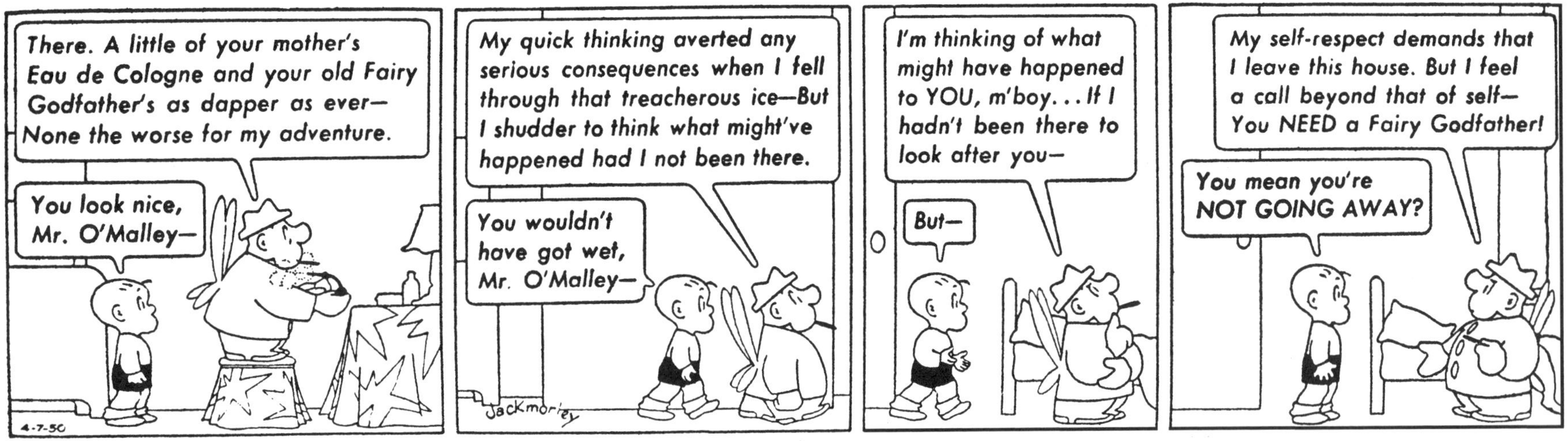
There. A little of your mother's Eau de Cologne and your old Fairy Godfather's as dapper as ever— None the worse for my adventure.
You look nice, Mr. O'Malley—
4-7-50
My quick thinking averted any serious consequences when I fell through that treacherous ice—But I shudder to think what might've happened had I not been there.
You wouldn't have got wet, Mr. O'Malley—
Jackmorley
I'm thinking of what might have happened to YOU, m'boy. . . If I hadn't been there to look after you—
But—
My self-respect demands that I leave this house. But I feel a call beyond that of self— You NEED a Fairy Godfather!
You mean you're NOT GOING AWAY?

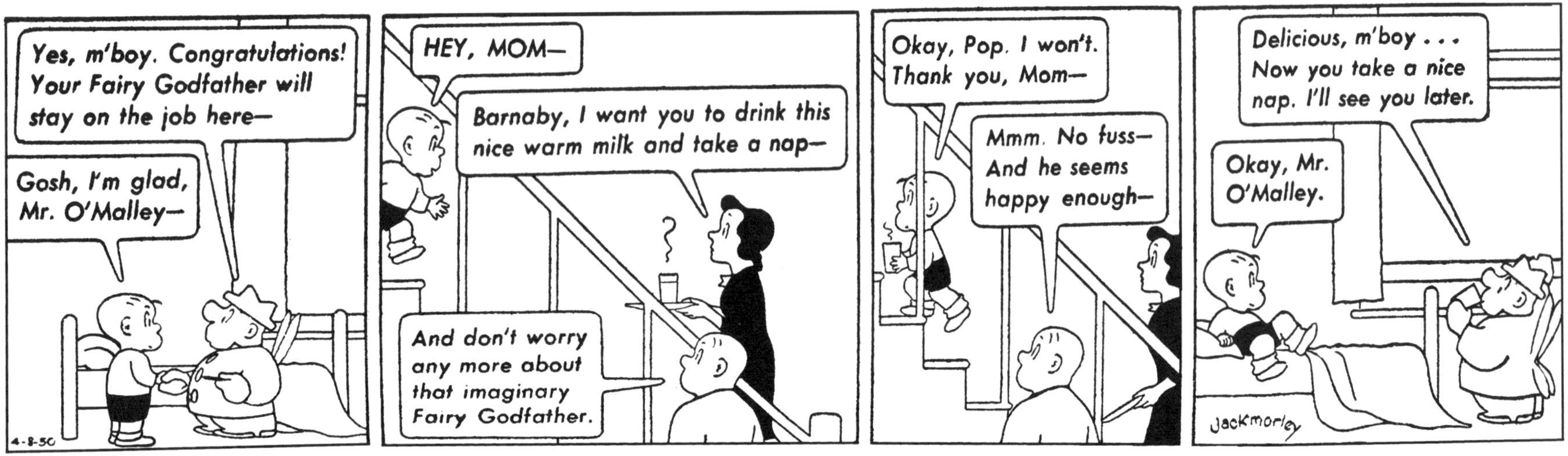
Yes, m'boy. Congratulations! Your Fairy Godfather will stay on the job here—
Gosh, I'm glad, Mr. O'Malley—
4-8-50
HEY, MOM—
Barnaby, I want you to drink this nice warm milk and take a nap—
And don't worry any more about that imaginary Fairy Godfather.
Okay, Pop. I won't. Thank you, Mom—
Mmm. No fuss— And he seems happy enough—
Delicious, m'boy . . . Now you take a nice nap. I'll see you later.
Okay, Mr. O'Malley.
Jackmorley

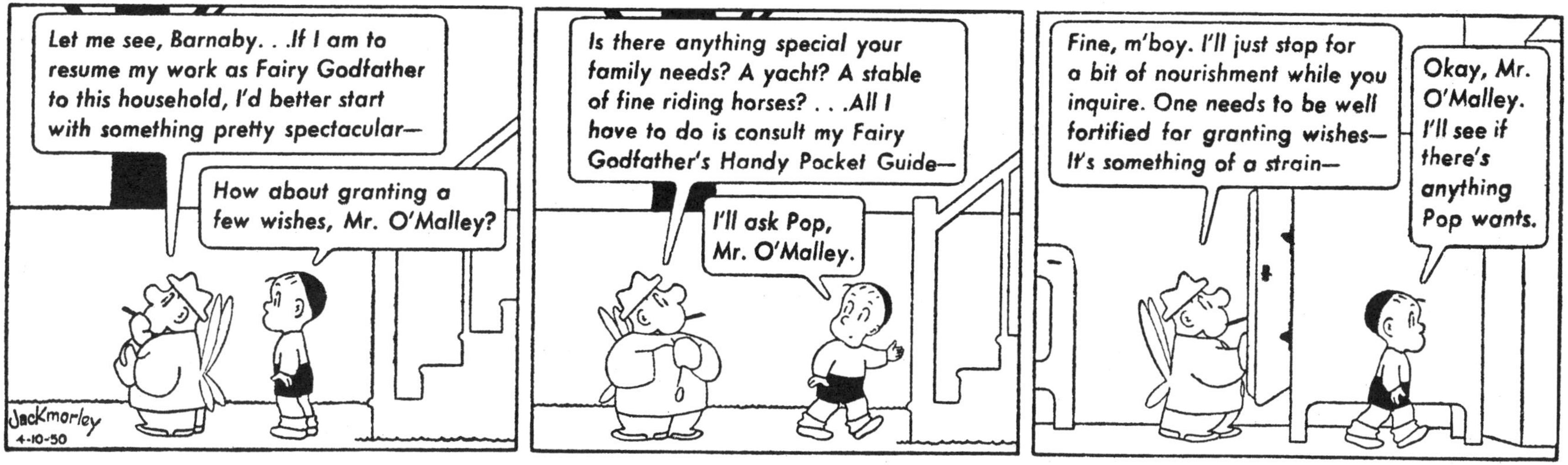
Let me see, Barnaby. . .If I am to resume my work as Fairy Godfather to this household, I'd better start with something pretty spectacular—
How about granting a few wishes, Mr. O'Malley?
Jackmorley
4-10-50
Is there anything special your family needs? A yacht? A stable of fine riding horses? . . .All I have to do is consult my Fairy Godfather's Handy Pocket Guide—
I'll ask Pop, Mr. O'Malley.
Fine, m'boy. I'll just stop for a bit of nourishment while you inquire. One needs to be well fortified for granting wishes—It's something of a strain—
Okay, Mr. O'Malley. I'll see if there's anything Pop wants.

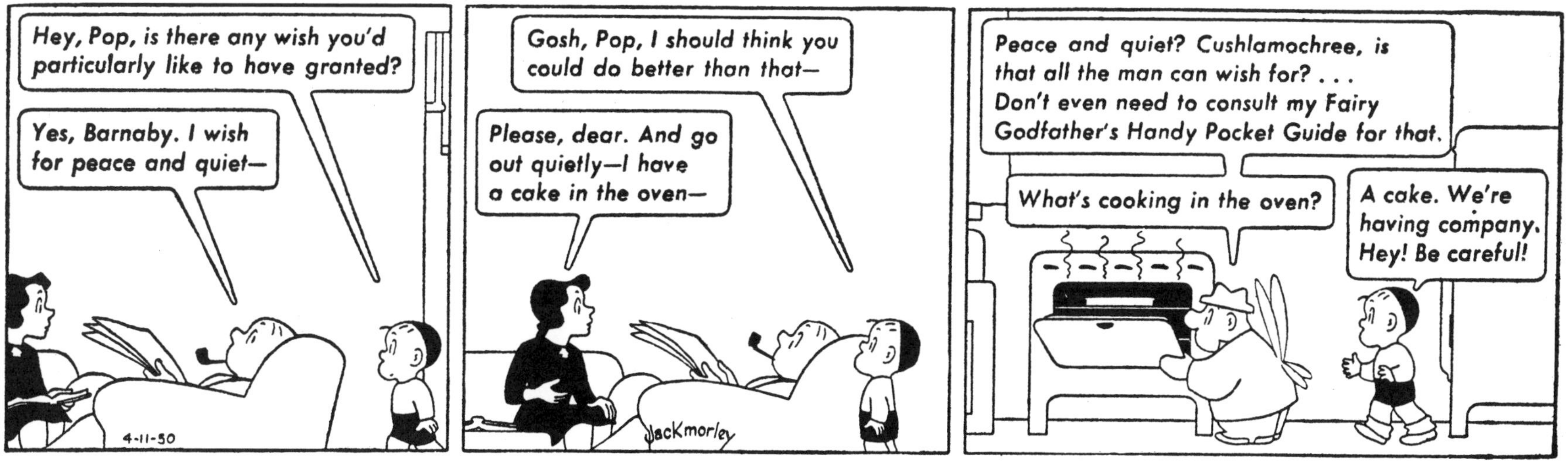
Hey, Pop, is there any wish you'd particularly like to have granted?
Yes, Barnaby. I wish for peace and quiet—
4-11-50
Gosh, Pop, I should think you could do better than that—
Please, dear. And go out quietly—I have a cake in the oven—
Jackmorley
Peace and quiet? Cushlamochree, is that all the man can wish for? . . . Don't even need to consult my Fairy Godfather's Handy Pocket Guide for that.
What's cooking in the oven?
A cake. We're having company. Hey! Be careful!

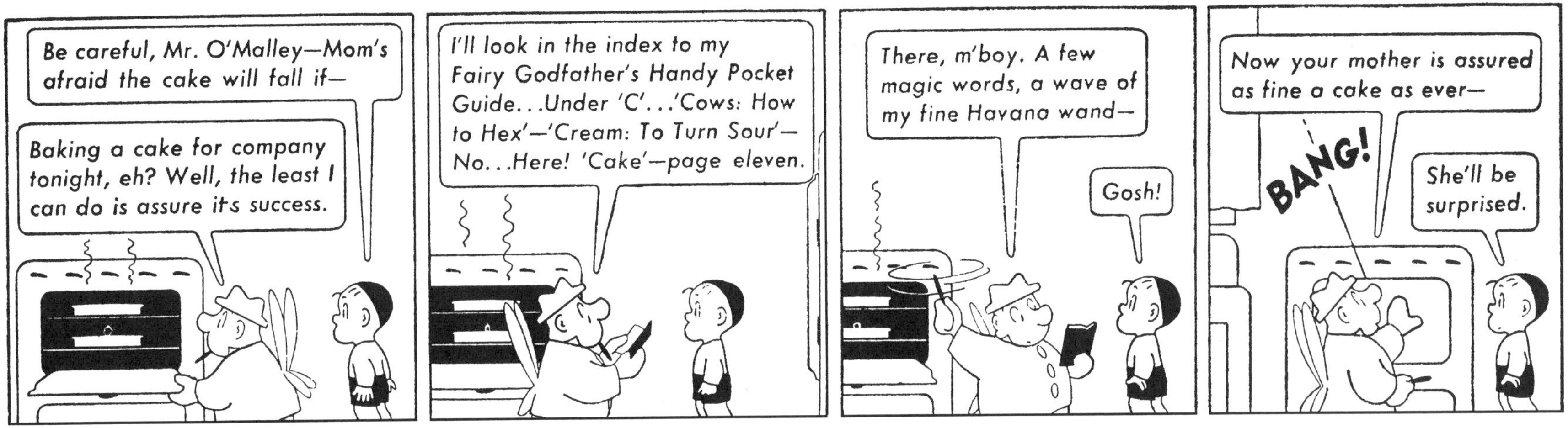
Be careful, Mr. O'Malley—Mom's afraid the cake will fall if—
Baking a cake for company tonight, eh? Well, the least I can do is assure its success.
I'll look in the index to my Fairy Godfather's Handy Pocket Guide...Under 'C'...'Cows: How to Hex'—'Cream: To Turn Sour'—No...Here! 'Cake'—page eleven.
There, m'boy. A few magic words, a wave of my fine Havana wand—
Gosh!
Now your mother is assured as fine a cake as ever—
BANG!
She'll be surprised.

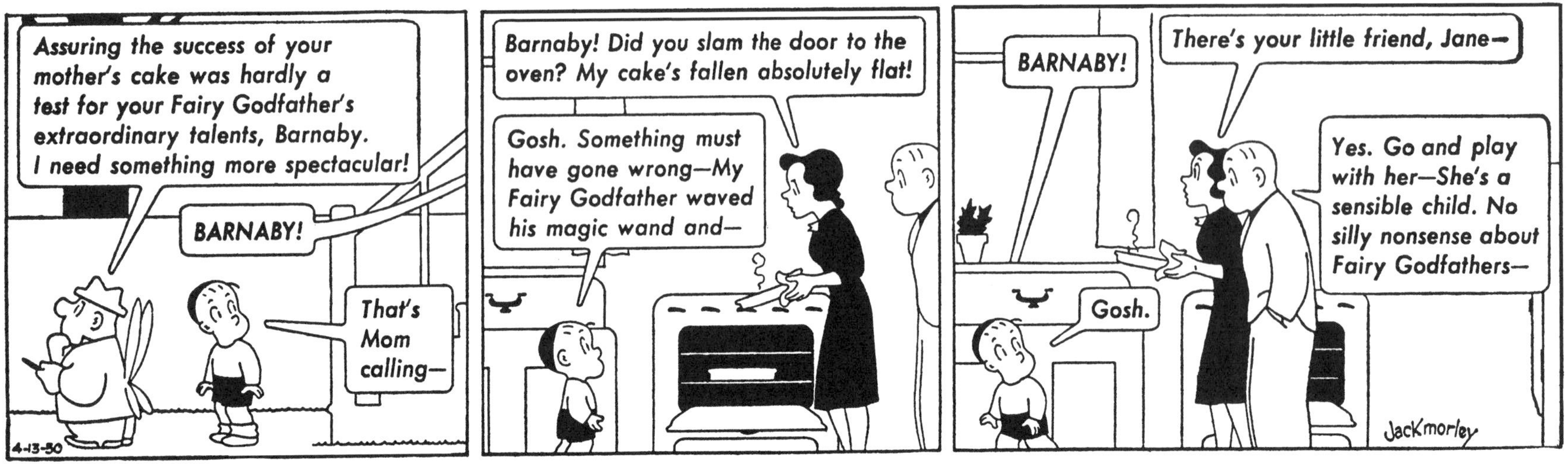
Assuring the success of your mother's cake was hardly a test for your Fairy Godfather's extraordinary talents, Barnaby. I need something more spectacular!
BARNABY!
That's Mom calling—
4-13-50
Barnaby! Did you slam the door to the oven? My cake's fallen absolutely flat!
Gosh. Something must have gone wrong—My Fairy Godfather waved his magic wand and—
BARNABY!
There's your little friend, Jane—
Yes. Go and play with her—She's a sensible child. No silly nonsense about Fairy Godfathers—
Gosh.
JackMorley

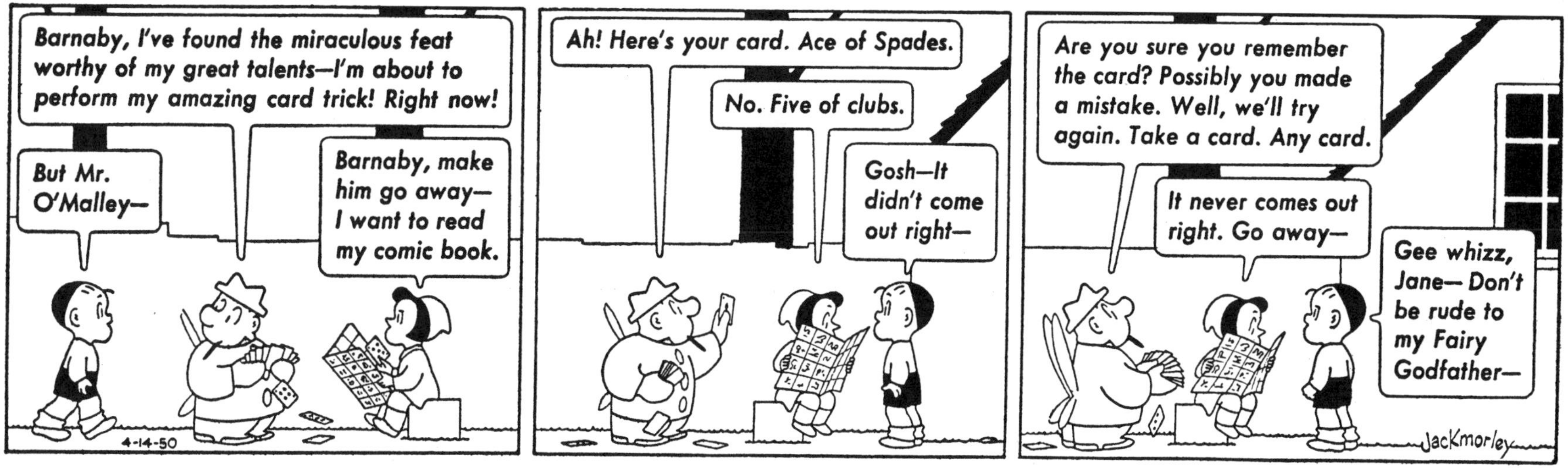
Barnaby, I've found the miraculous feat worthy of my great talents—I'm about to perform my amazing card trick! Right now!
But Mr. O'Malley—
Barnaby, make him go away— I want to read my comic book.
4-14-50
Ah! Here's your card. Ace of Spades.
No. Five of clubs.
Gosh—It didn't come out right—
Are you sure you remember the card? Possibly you made a mistake. Well, we'll try again. Take a card. Any card.
It never comes out right. Go away—
Gee whizz, Jane— Don't be rude to my Fairy Godfather—
JacKmorley

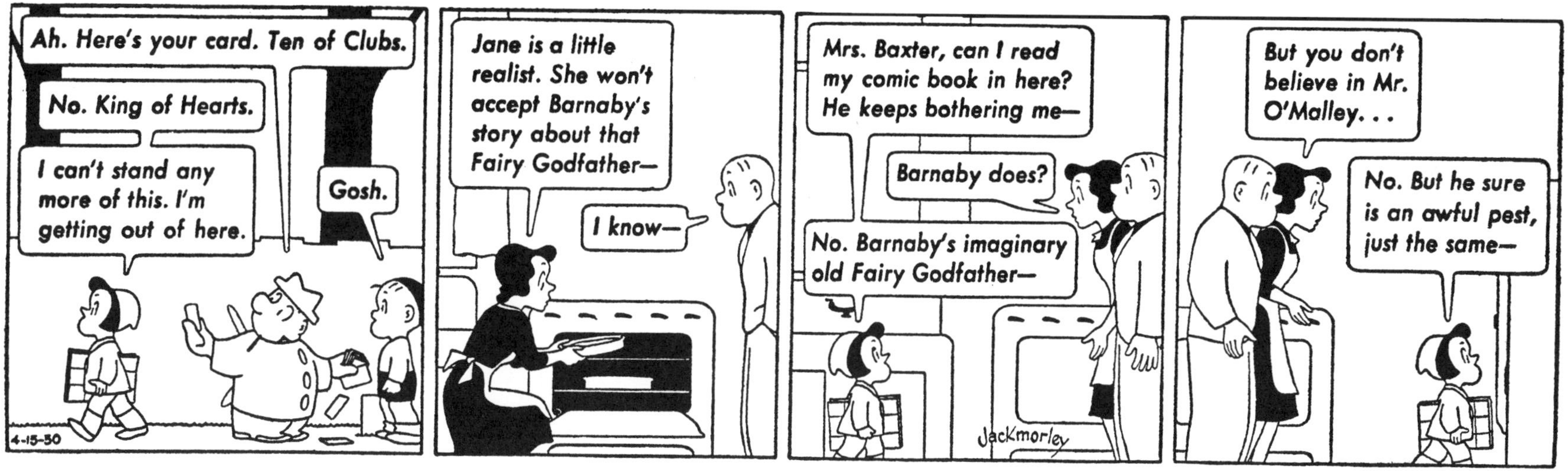
Ah. Here's your card. Ten of Clubs.
No. King of Hearts.
I can't stand any more of this. I'm getting out of here.
Gosh.
4-15-50
Jane is a little realist. She won't accept Barnaby's story about that Fairy Godfather—
I know—
Mrs. Baxter, can I read my comic book in here? He keeps bothering me—
Barnaby does?
No. Barnaby's imaginary old Fairy Godfather—
JacKmorley
But you don't believe in Mr. O'Malley. . .
No. But he sure is an awful pest, just the same—

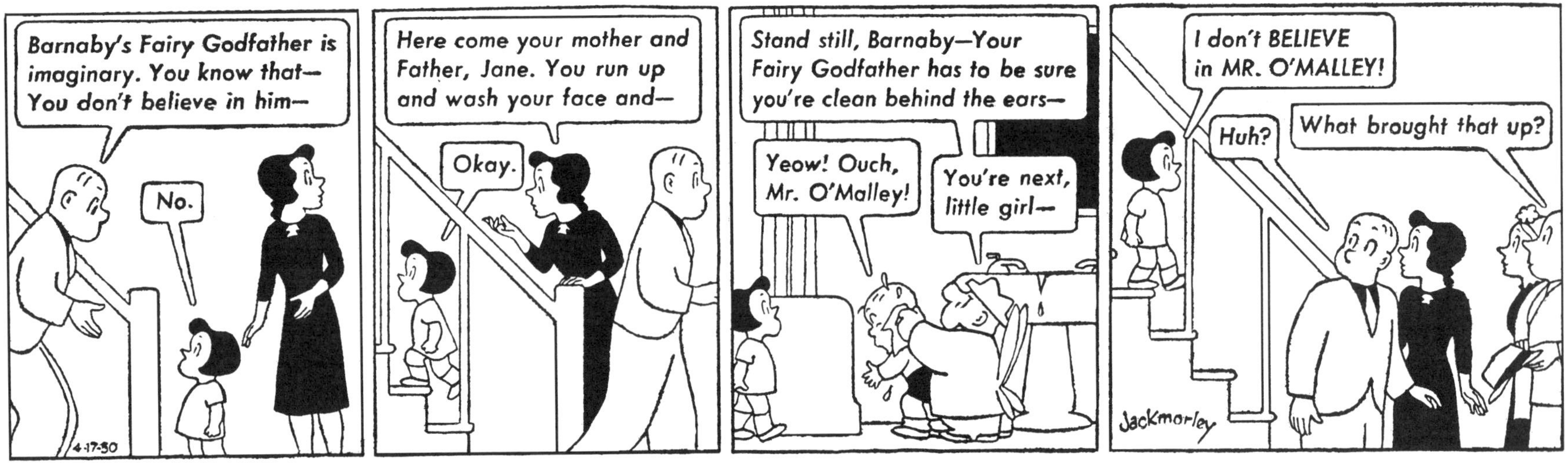
Barnaby's Fairy Godfather is imaginary. You know that— You don't believe in him—
No.
4-17-50
Here come your mother and Father, Jane. You run up and wash your face and—
Okay.
Stand still, Barnaby—Your Fairy Godfather has to be sure you're clean behind the ears—
Yeow! Ouch, Mr. O'Malley!
You're next, little girl—
I don't BELIEVE in MR. O'MALLEY!
Huh?
What brought that up?
JACKMORLEY

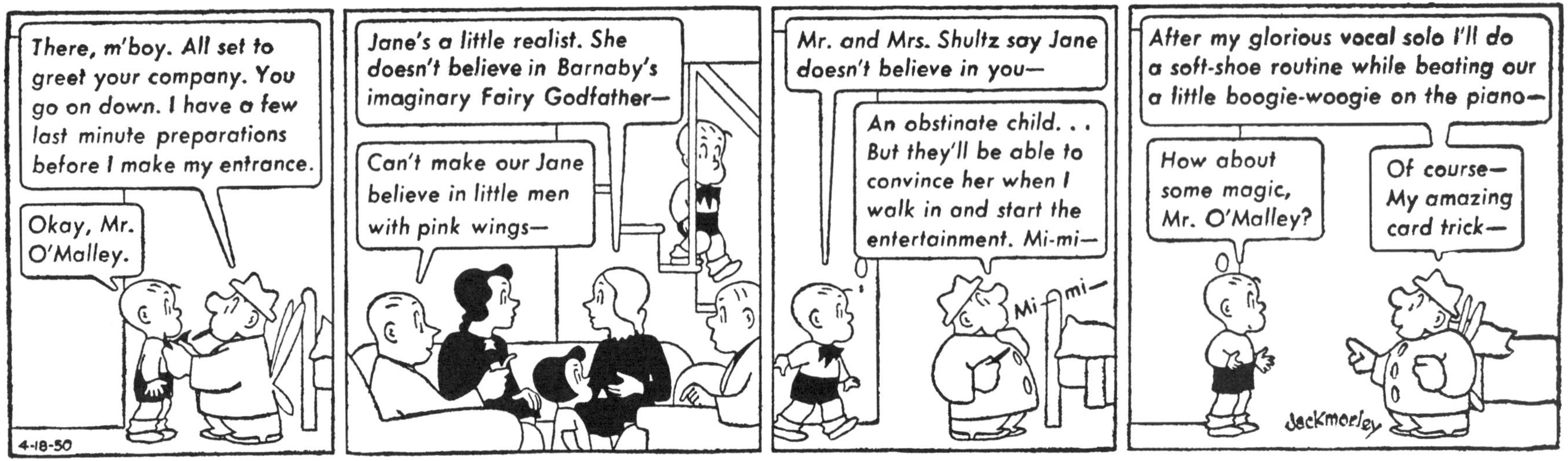
There, m'boy. All set to greet your company. You go on down. I have a few last minute preparations before I make my entrance.
Okay, Mr. O'Malley.
4-18-50
Jane's a little realist. She doesn't believe in Barnaby's imaginary Fairy Godfather—
Can't make our Jane believe in little men with pink wings—
Mr. and Mrs. Shultz say Jane doesn't believe in you—
An obstinate child. . . But they'll be able to convince her when I walk in and start the entertainment. Mi-mi—
Mi—mi—
After my glorious vocal solo I'll do a soft-shoe routine while beating our a little boogie-woogie on the piano—
How about some magic, Mr. O'Malley?
Of course— My amazing card trick—
JACKMORLEY

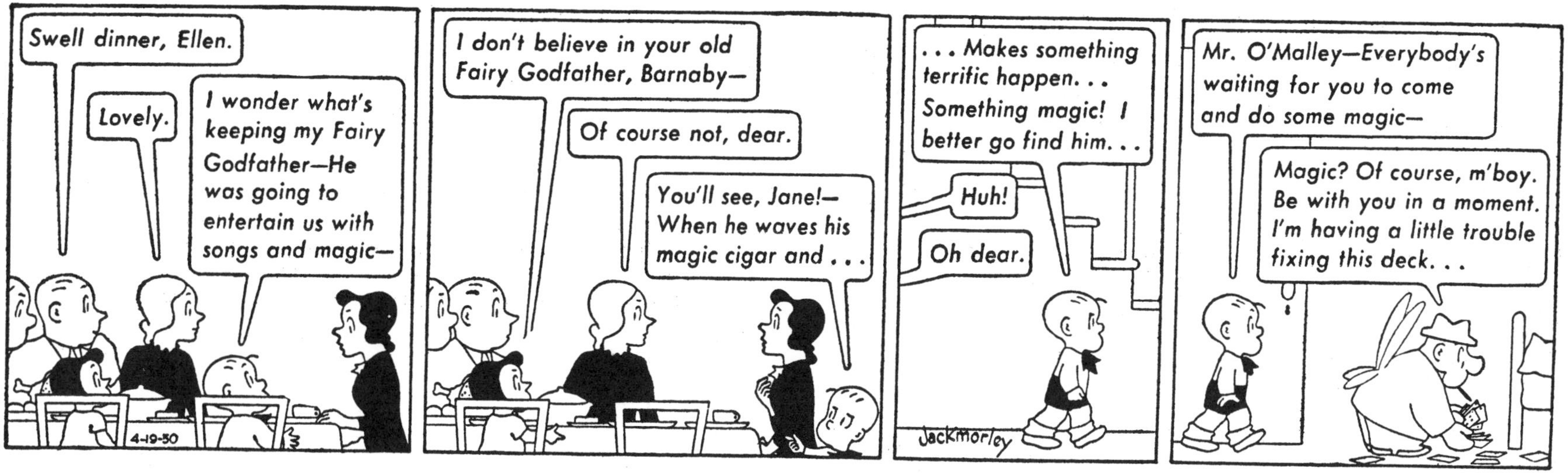
Swell dinner, Ellen.
Lovely.
I wonder what's keeping my Fairy Godfather—He was going to entertain us with songs and magic—
4-19-50
I don't believe in your old Fairy Godfather, Barnaby—
Of course not, dear.
You'll see, Jane!— When he waves his magic cigar and . . .
. . . Makes something terrific happen. . . Something magic! I better go find him. . .
Huh!
Oh dear.
Jackmorley
Mr. O'Malley—Everybody's waiting for you to come and do some magic—
Magic? Of course, m'boy. Be with you in a moment. I'm having a little trouble fixing this deck. . .

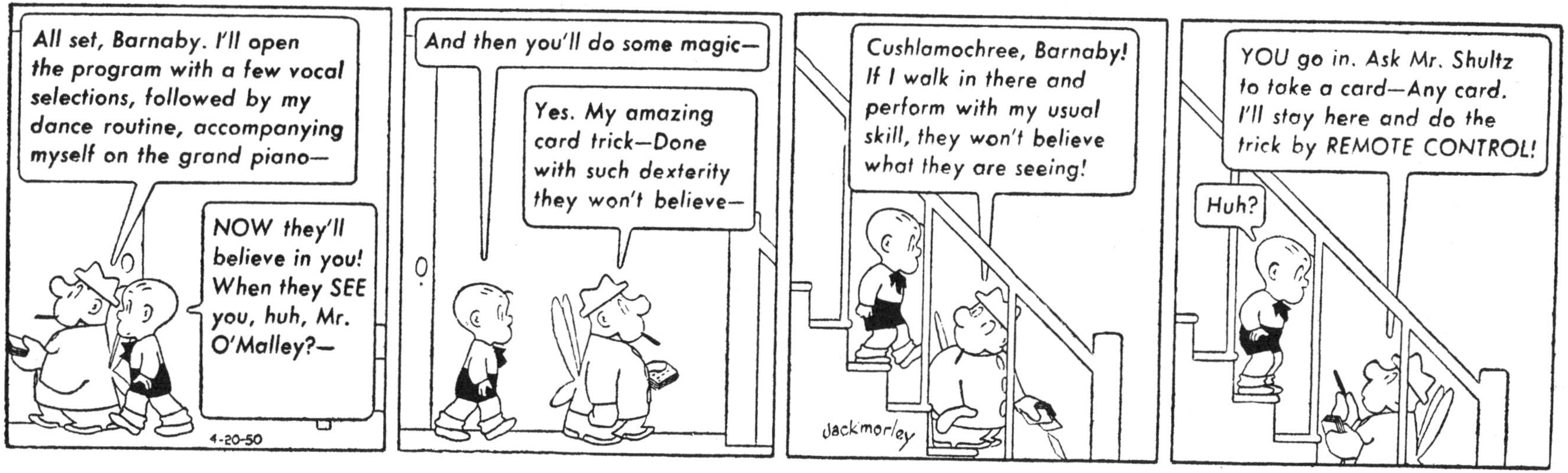
All set, Barnaby. I'll open the program with a few vocal selections, followed by my dance routine, accompanying myself on the grand piano—
NOW they'll believe in you! When they SEE you, huh, Mr. O'Malley?—
4-20-50
And then you'll do some magic—
Yes. My amazing card trick—Done with such dexterity they won't believe—
Cushlamochree, Barnaby! If I walk in there and perform with my usual skill, they won't believe what they are seeing!
Jackmorley
YOU go in. Ask Mr. Shultz to take a card—Any card. I'll stay here and do the trick by REMOTE CONTROL!
Huh?

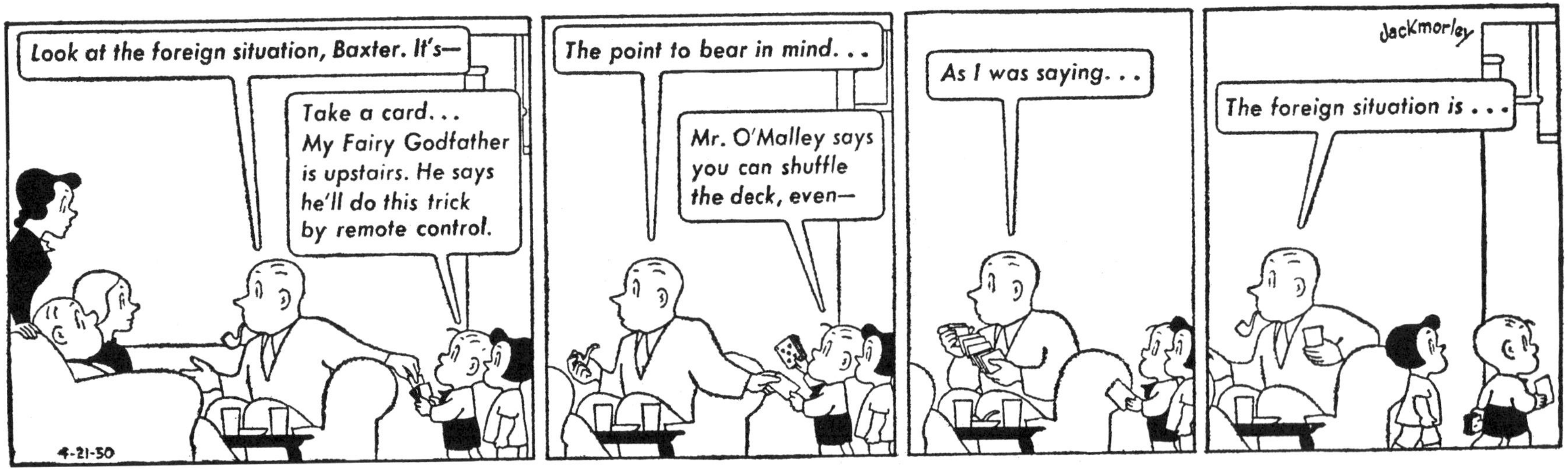
Look at the foreign situation, Baxter. It's—
Take a card... My Fairy Godfather is upstairs. He says he'll do this trick by remote control.
4-21-50
The point to bear in mind...
Mr. O'Malley says you can shuffle the deck, even—
As I was saying...
JackMorley
The foreign situation is ...

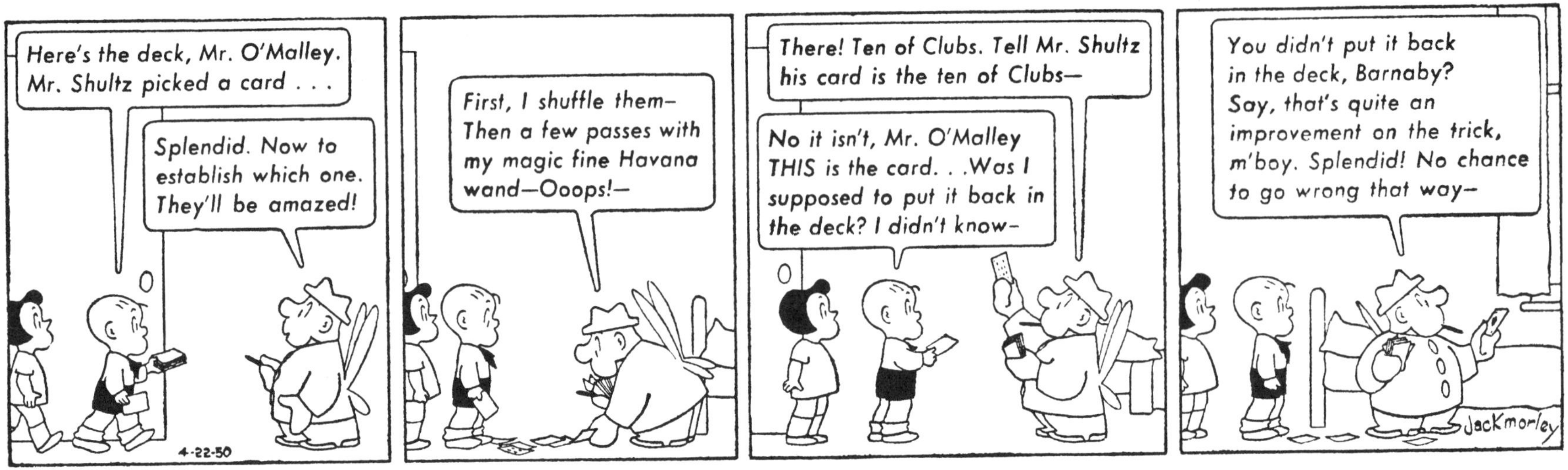
Here's the deck, Mr. O'Malley. Mr. Shultz picked a card . . .
Splendid. Now to establish which one. They'll be amazed!
4-22-50
First, I shuffle them— Then a few passes with my magic fine Havana wand—Ooops!—
There! Ten of Clubs. Tell Mr. Shultz his card is the ten of Clubs—
No it isn't, Mr. O'Malley THIS is the card. . .Was I supposed to put it back in the deck? I didn't know—
You didn't put it back in the deck, Barnaby? Say, that's quite an improvement on the trick, m'boy. Splendid! No chance to go wrong that way—
JackMorley

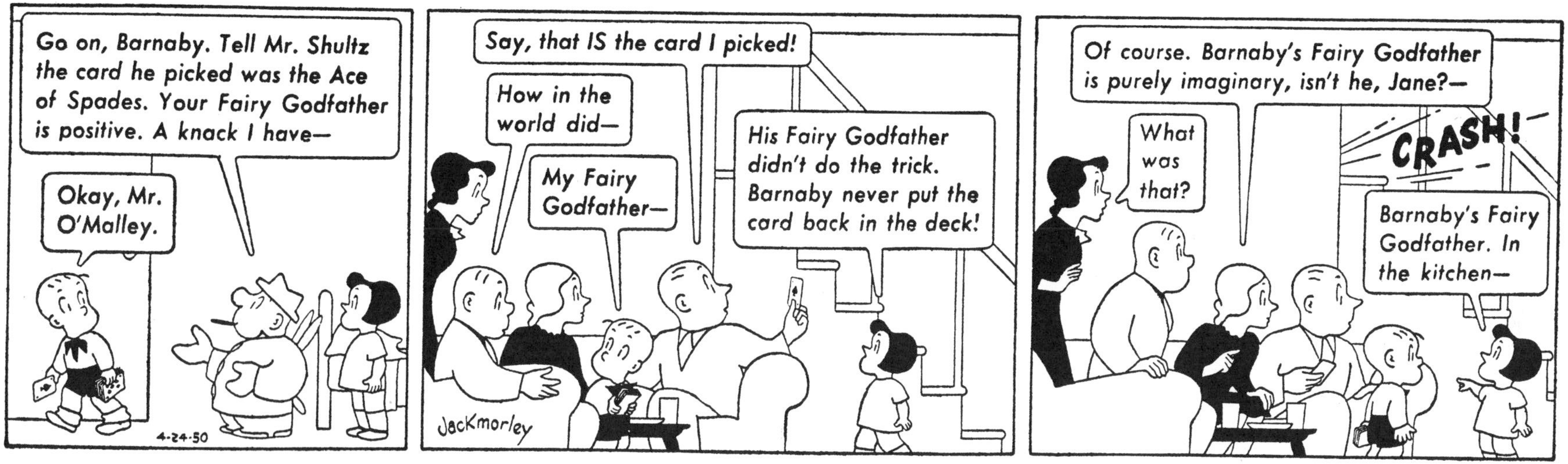
Go on, Barnaby. Tell Mr. Shultz the card he picked was the Ace of Spades. Your Fairy Godfather is positive. A knack I have—
Okay, Mr. O'Malley.
4-24-50
Say, that IS the card I picked!
How in the world did—
My Fairy Godfather—
His Fairy Godfather didn't do the trick. Barnaby never put the card back in the deck!
JacKmorley
Of course. Barnaby's Fairy Godfather is purely imaginary, isn't he, Jane?—
What was that?
CRASH!
Barnaby's Fairy Godfather. In the kitchen—

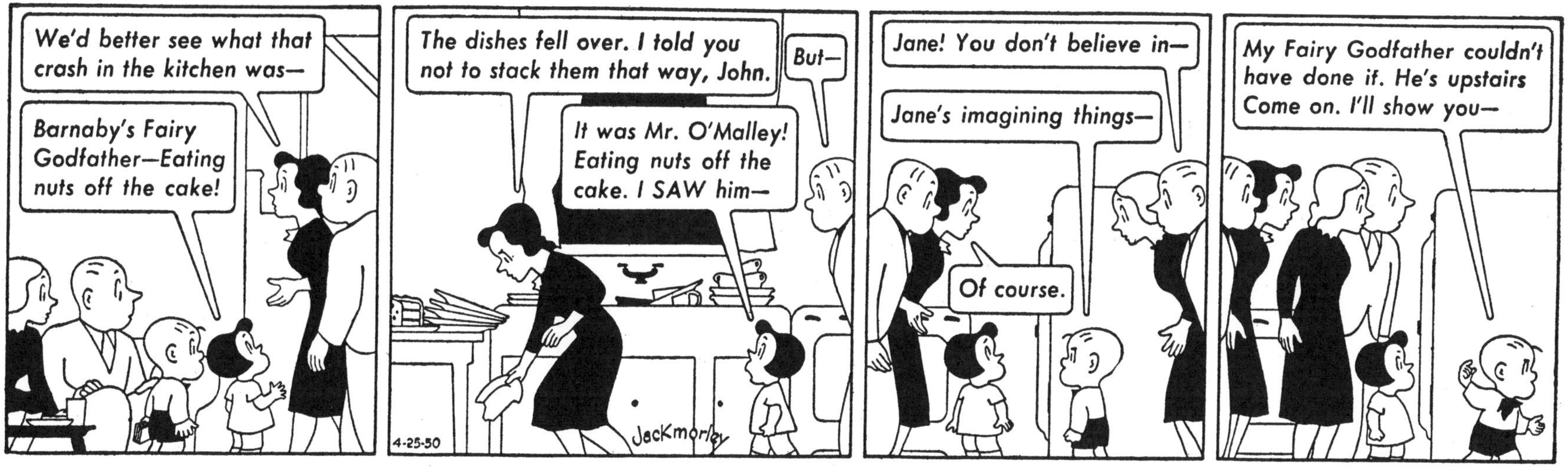
We'd better see what that crash in the kitchen was—
Barnaby's Fairy Godfather—Eating nuts off the cake!
The dishes fell over. I told you not to stack them that way, John.
But—
It was Mr. O'Malley! Eating nuts off the cake. I SAW him—
4-25-50
JacKmorley
Jane! You don't believe in—
Jane's imagining things—
Of course.
My Fairy Godfather couldn't have done it. He's upstairs Come on. I'll show you—

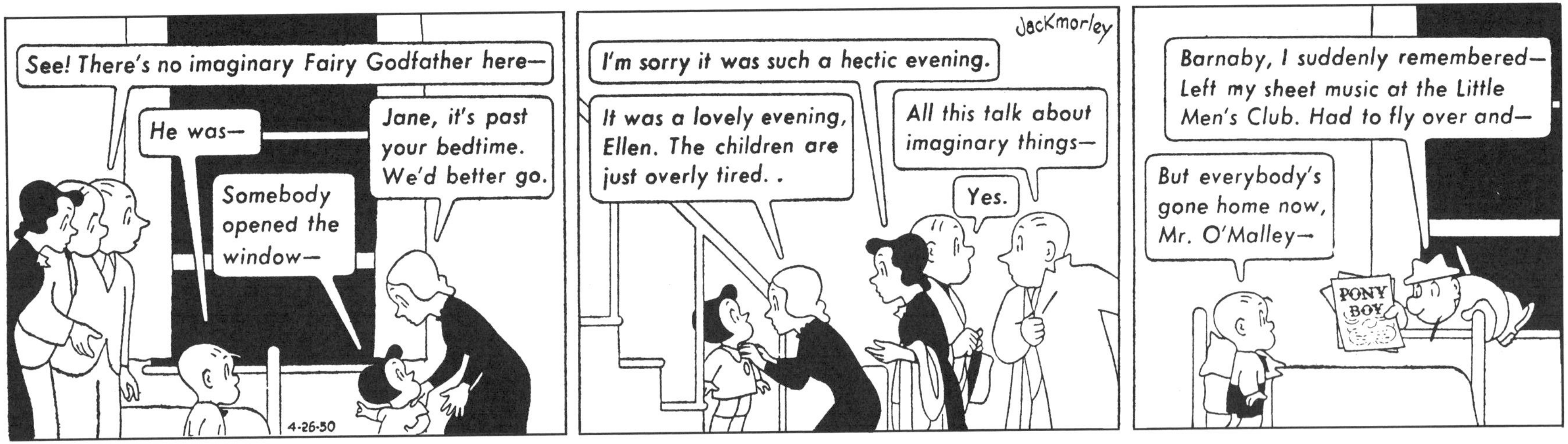
See! There's no imaginary Fairy Godfather here—
He was—
Somebody opened the window—
Jane, it's past your bedtime. We'd better go.
4-26-50
JackMorley
I'm sorry it was such a hectic evening.
It was a lovely evening, Ellen. The children are just overly tired. .
All this talk about imaginary things—
Yes.
Barnaby, I suddenly remembered— Left my sheet music at the Little Men's Club. Had to fly over and—
But everybody's gone home now, Mr. O'Malley—
PONY BOY

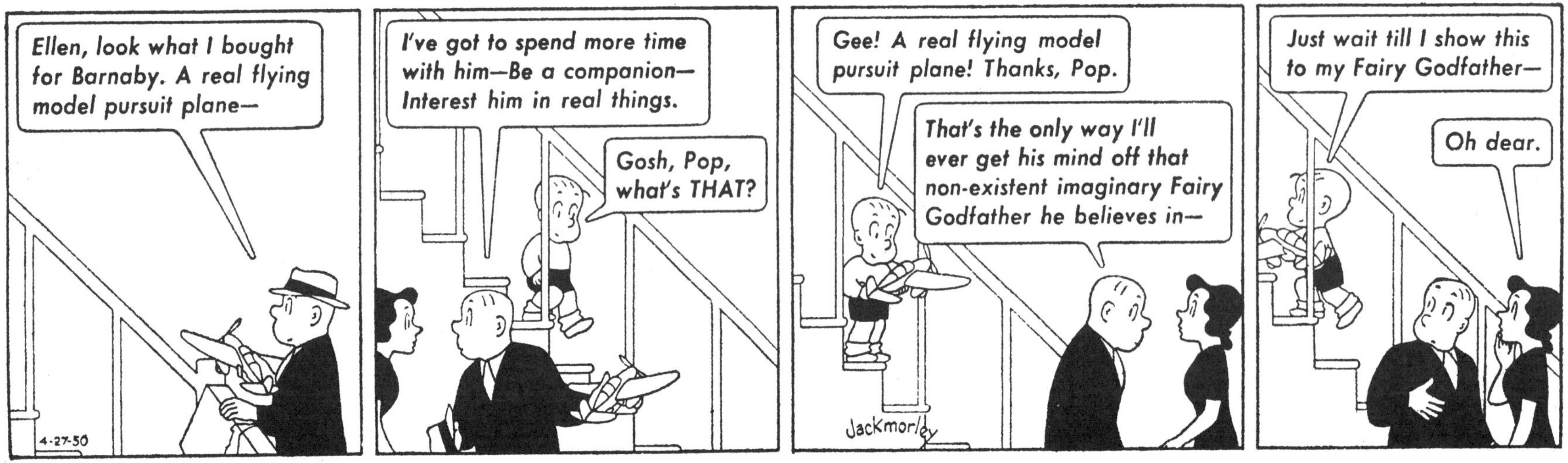
Ellen, look what I bought for Barnaby. A real flying model pursuit plane—
4-27-50
I've got to spend more time with him—Be a companion— Interest him in real things.
Gosh, Pop, what's THAT?
Gee! A real flying model pursuit plane! Thanks, Pop.
That's the only way I'll ever get his mind off that non-existent imaginary Fairy Godfather he believes in—
JackMorley
Just wait till I show this to my Fairy Godfather—
Oh dear.

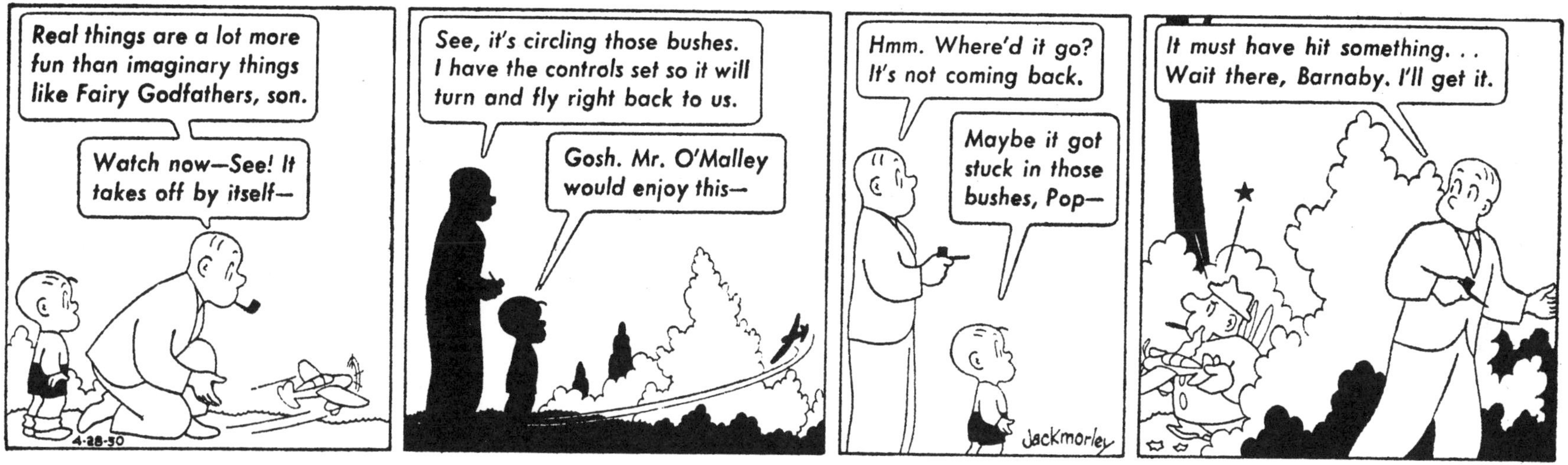
Real things are a lot more fun than imaginary things like Fairy Godfathers, son.
Watch now—See! It takes off by itself—
4-28-50
See, it's circling those bushes. I have the controls set so it will turn and fly right back to us.
Gosh. Mr. O'Malley would enjoy this—
Hmm. Where'd it go? It's not coming back.
Maybe it got stuck in those bushes, Pop—
JACKMORLEY
It must have hit something. . . Wait there, Barnaby. I'll get it.

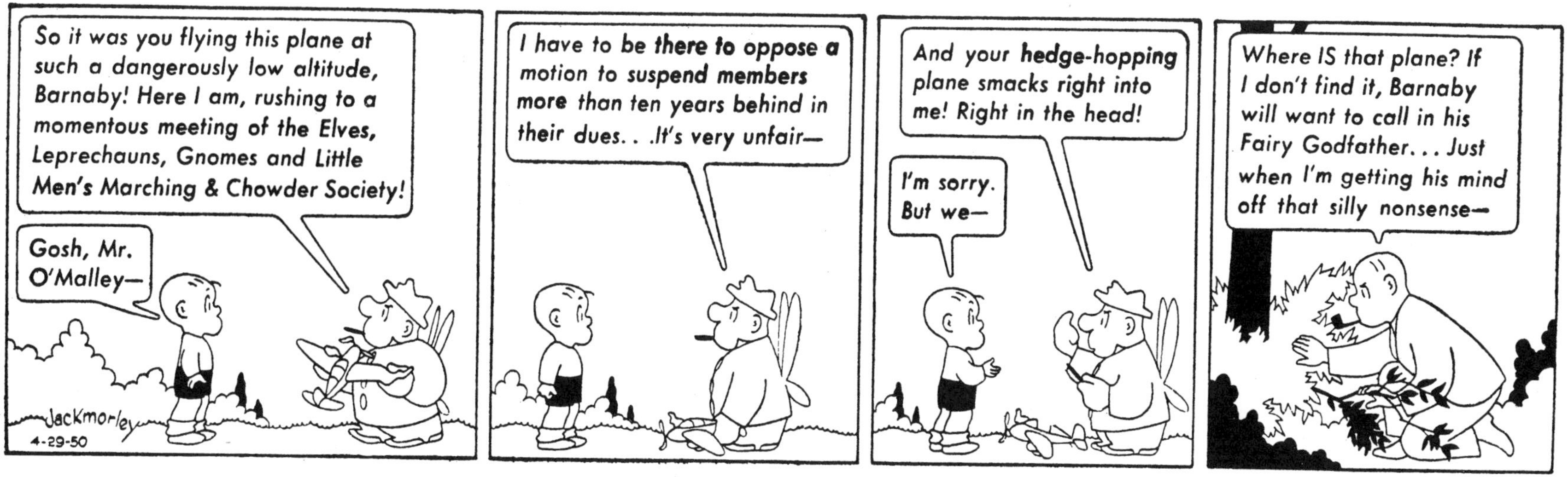
So it was you flying this plane at such a dangerously low altitude, Barnaby! Here I am, rushing to a momentous meeting of the Elves, Leprechauns, Gnomes and Little Men's Marching & Chowder Society!
Gosh, Mr. O'Malley—
JACKMORLEY
4-29-50
I have to be there to oppose a motion to suspend members more than ten years behind in their dues. . .It's very unfair—
And your hedge-hopping plane smacks right into me! Right in the head!
I'm sorry. But we—
Where IS that plane? If I don't find it, Barnaby will want to call in his Fairy Godfather. . . Just when I'm getting his mind off that silly nonsense—

April 28 – 29

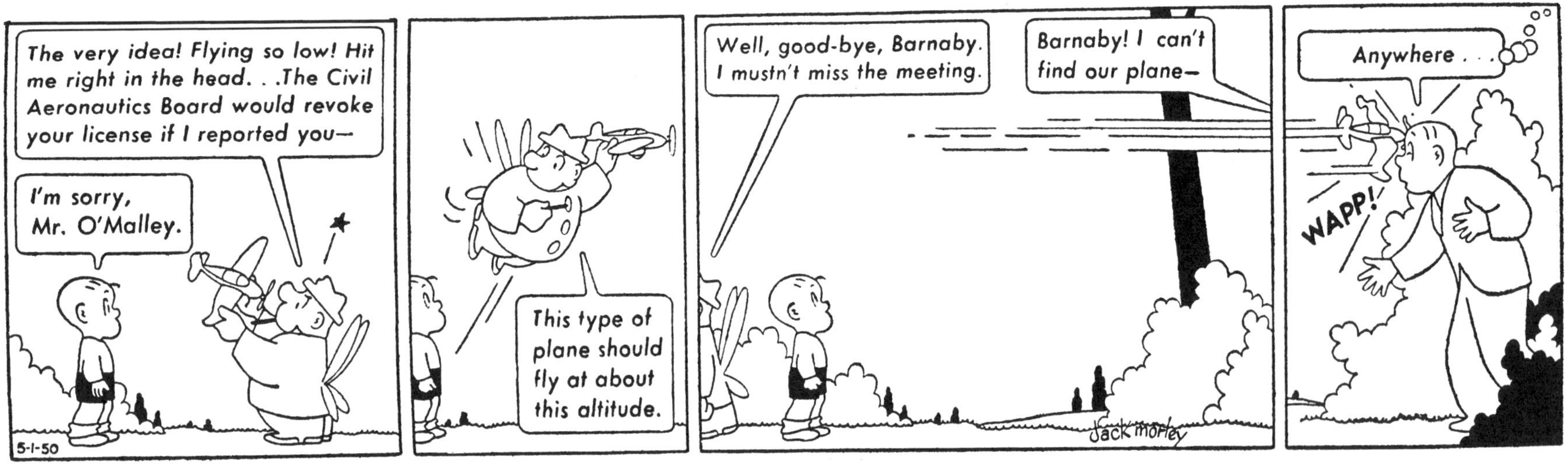
The very idea! Flying so low! Hit me right in the head. . .The Civil Aeronautics Board would revoke your license if I reported you—
I'm sorry, Mr. O'Malley.
5-1-50
This type of plane should fly at about this altitude.
Well, good-bye, Barnaby. I mustn't miss the meeting.
Barnaby! I can't find our plane—
Jack morley
Anywhere . . .
WAPP!

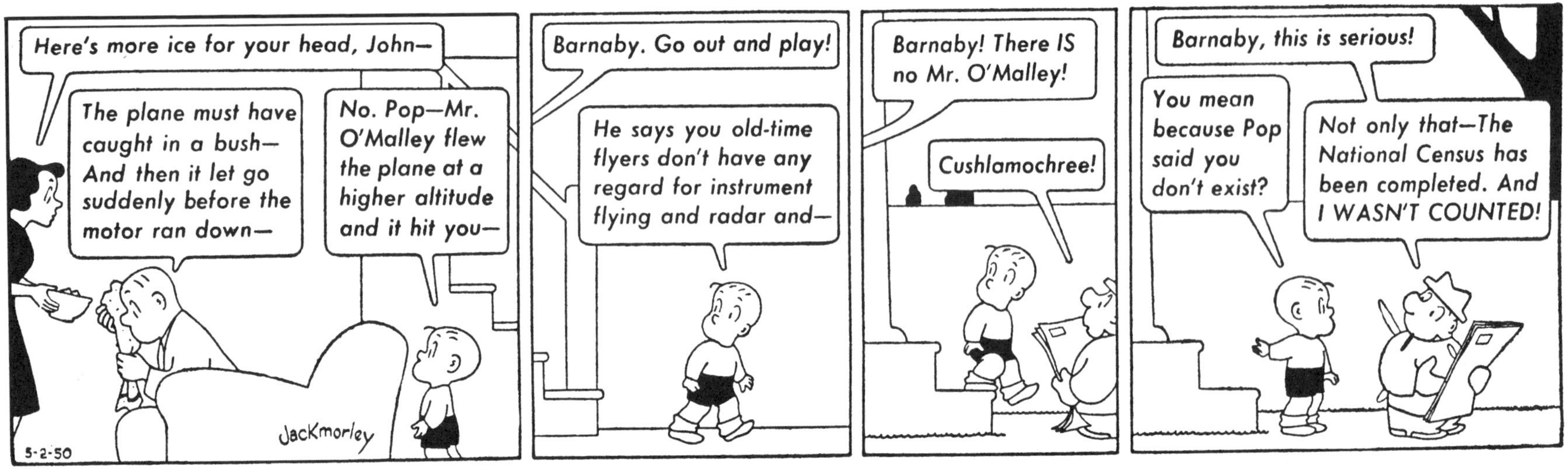
Here's more ice for your head, John—
The plane must have caught in a bush— And then it let go suddenly before the motor ran down—
No. Pop—Mr. O'Malley flew the plane at a higher altitude and it hit you—
JackMorley
5-2-50
Barnaby. Go out and play!
He says you old-time flyers don't have any regard for instrument flying and radar and—
Barnaby! There IS no Mr. O'Malley!
Cushlamochree!
Barnaby, this is serious!
You mean because Pop said you don't exist?
Not only that—The National Census has been completed. And I WASN'T COUNTED!

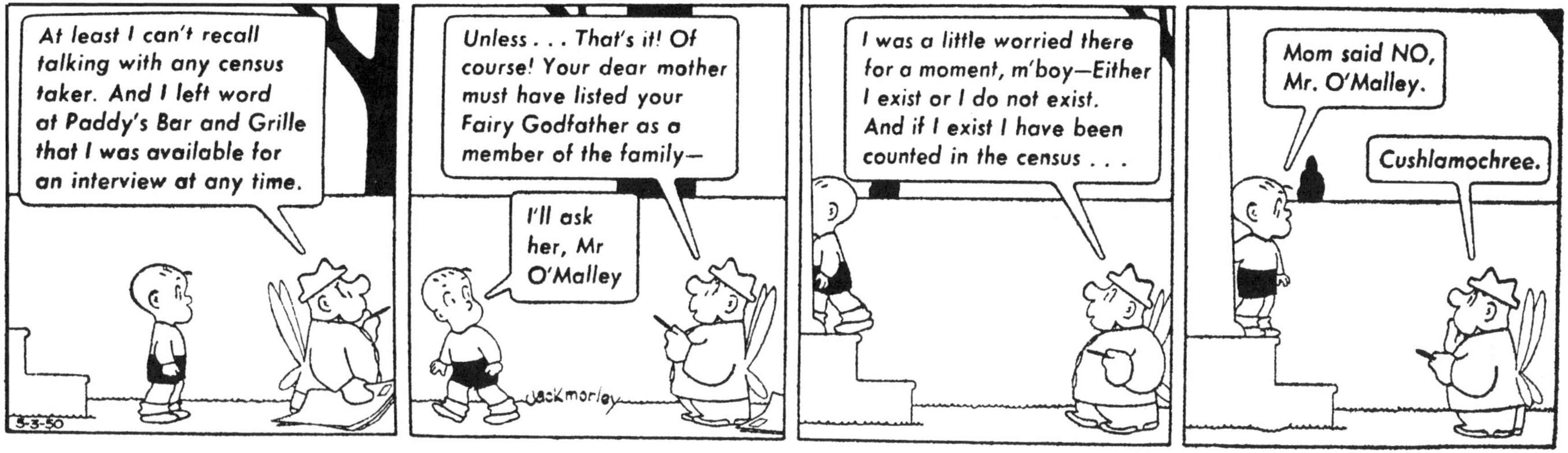
At least I can't recall talking with any census taker. And I left word at Paddy's Bar and Grille that I was available for an interview at any time.
5-3-50
Unless . . . That's it! Of course! Your dear mother must have listed your Fairy Godfather as a member of the family—
I'll ask her, Mr O'Malley
Jackmorley
I was a little worried there for a moment, m'boy—Either I exist or I do not exist. And if I exist I have been counted in the census . . .
Mom said NO, Mr. O'Malley.
Cushlamochree.

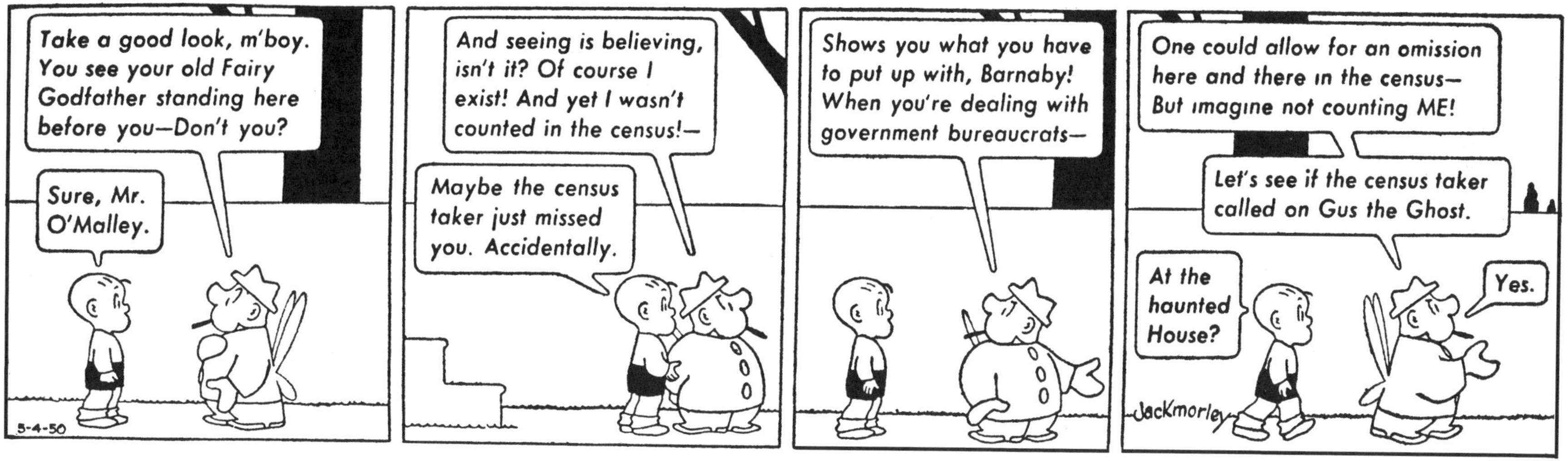
Take a good look, m'boy. You see your old Fairy Godfather standing here before you—Don't you?
Sure, Mr. O'Malley.
5-4-50
And seeing is believing, isn't it? Of course I exist! And yet I wasn't counted in the census!—
Maybe the census taker just missed you. Accidentally.
Shows you what you have to put up with, Barnaby! When you're dealing with government bureaucrats—
One could allow for an omission here and there in the census—But imagine not counting ME!
Let's see if the census taker called on Gus the Ghost.
At the haunted House?
Yes.
Jackmorley

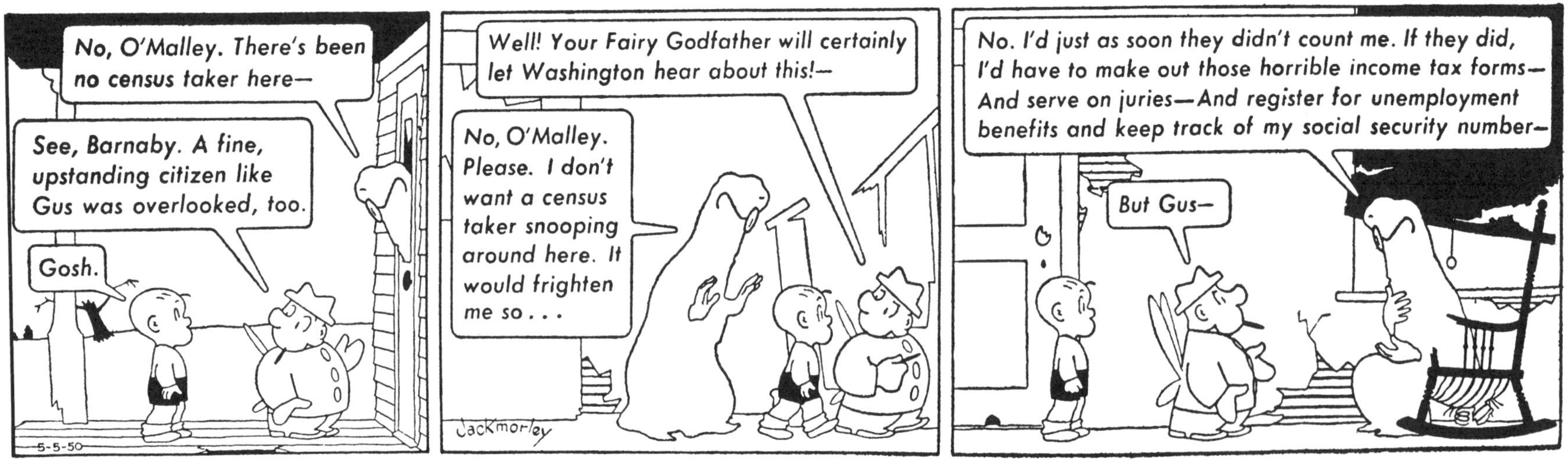
No, O'Malley. There's been no census taker here—
See, Barnaby. A fine, upstanding citizen like Gus was overlooked, too.
Gosh.
5-5-50
Well! Your Fairy Godfather will certainly let Washington hear about this!—
No, O'Malley. Please. I don't want a census taker snooping around here. It would frighten me so . . .
Jackmorley
No. I'd just as soon they didn't count me. If they did, I'd have to make out those horrible income tax forms—And serve on juries—And register for unemployment benefits and keep track of my social security number—
But Gus—

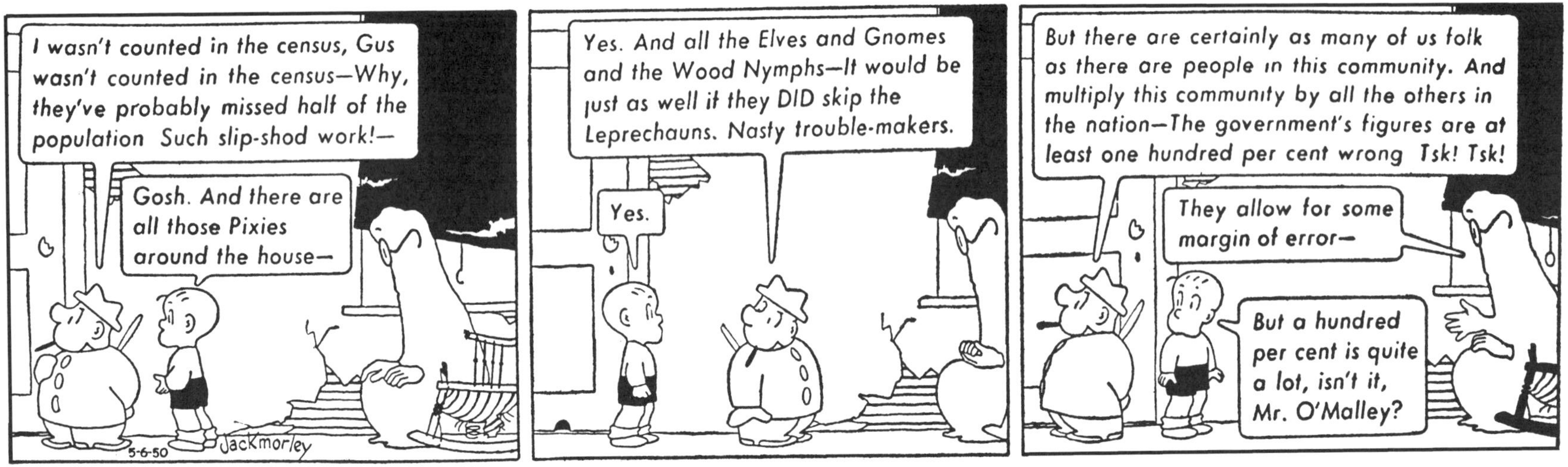
I wasn't counted in the census, Gus wasn't counted in the census—Why, they've probably missed half of the population Such slip-shod work!—
Gosh. And there are all those Pixies around the house—
5-6-50
Jackmorley
Yes. And all the Elves and Gnomes and the Wood Nymphs—It would be just as well if they DID skip the Leprechauns. Nasty trouble-makers.
Yes.
But there are certainly as many of us folk as there are people in this community. And multiply this community by all the others in the nation—The government's figures are at least one hundred per cent wrong Tsk! Tsk!
They allow for some margin of error—
But a hundred per cent is quite a lot, isn't it, Mr. O'Malley?

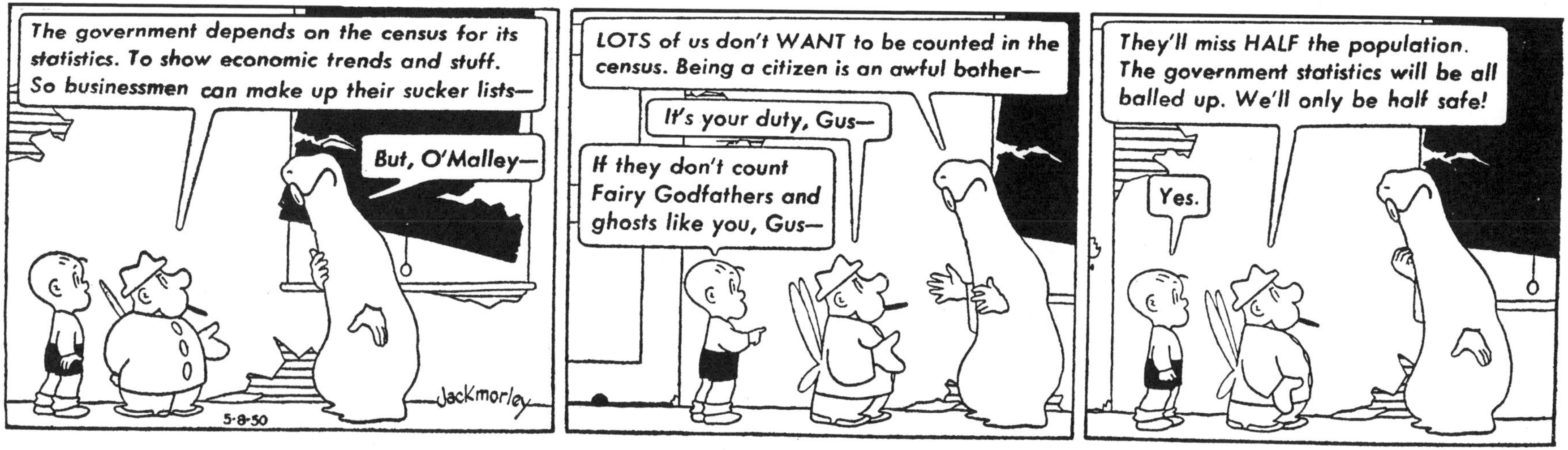
The government depends on the census for its statistics. To show economic trends and stuff. So businessmen can make up their sucker lists—
But, O'Malley—
5-8-50
Jackmorley
LOTS of us don't WANT to be counted in the census. Being a citizen is an awful bother—
It's your duty, Gus—
If they don't count Fairy Godfathers and ghosts like you, Gus—
They'll miss HALF the population. The government statistics will be all balled up. We'll only be half safe!
Yes.

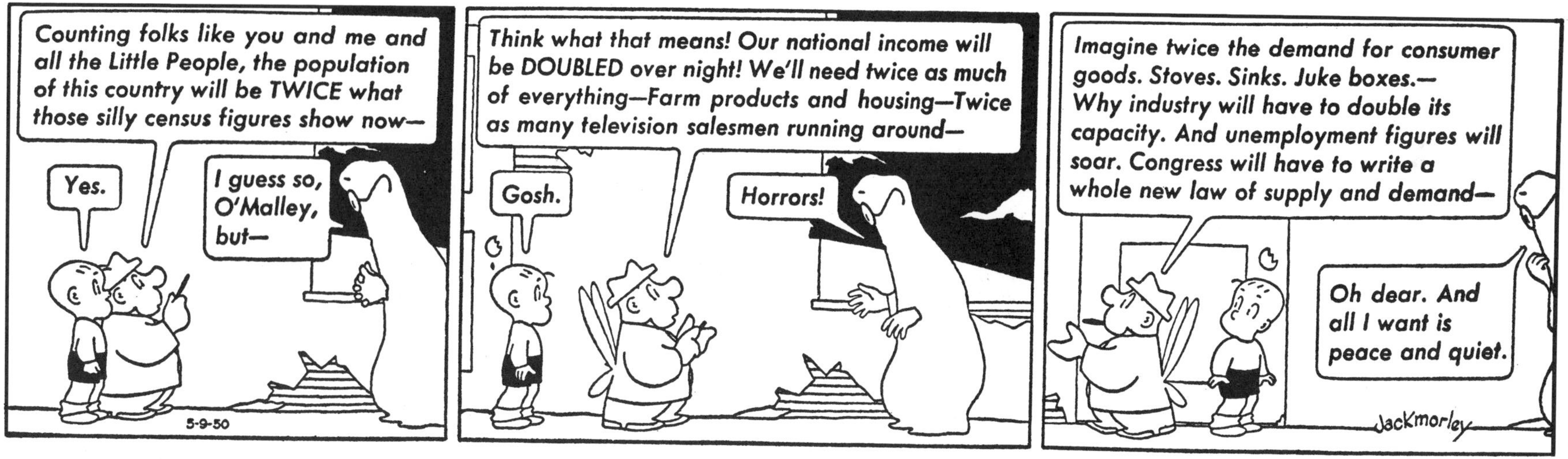
Counting folks like you and me and all the Little People, the population of this country will be TWICE what those silly census figures show now—
Yes.
I guess so, O'Malley, but—
5-9-50
Think what that means! Our national income will be DOUBLED over night! We'll need twice as much of everything—Farm products and housing—Twice as many television salesmen running around—
Gosh.
Horrors!
Imagine twice the demand for consumer goods. Stoves. Sinks. Juke boxes.— Why industry will have to double its capacity. And unemployment figures will soar. Congress will have to write a whole new law of supply and demand—
Oh dear. And all I want is peace and quiet.
Jackmorley

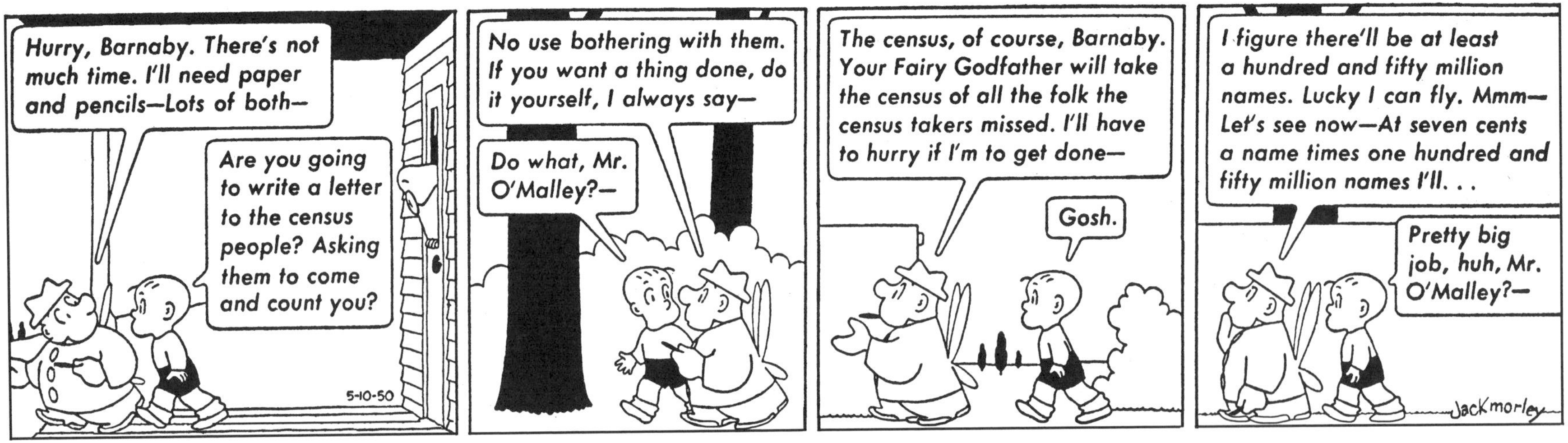
Hurry, Barnaby. There's not much time. I'll need paper and pencils—Lots of both—
Are you going to write a letter to the census people? Asking them to come and count you?
5-10-50
No use bothering with them. If you want a thing done, do it yourself, I always say—
Do what, Mr. O'Malley?—
The census, of course, Barnaby. Your Fairy Godfather will take the census of all the folk the census takers missed. I'll have to hurry if I'm to get done—
Gosh.
I figure there'll be at least a hundred and fifty million names. Lucky I can fly. Mmm— Let's see now—At seven cents a name times one hundred and fifty million names I'll. . .
Pretty big job, huh, Mr. O'Malley?—
JackMorley

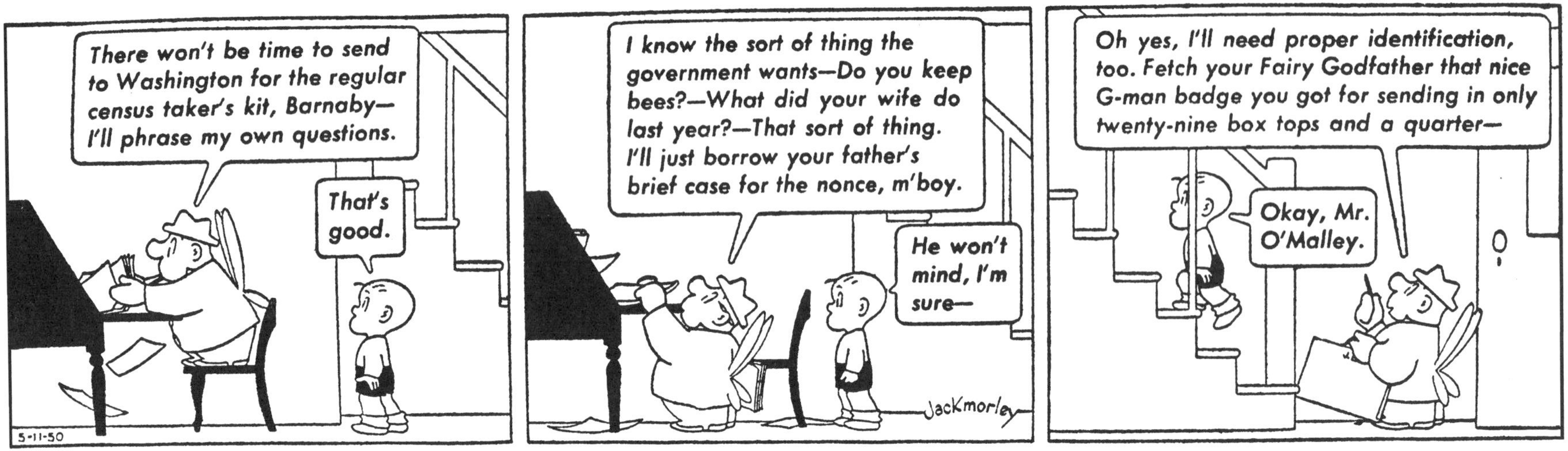
There won't be time to send to Washington for the regular census taker's kit, Barnaby— I'll phrase my own questions.
That's good.
5-11-50
I know the sort of thing the government wants—Do you keep bees?—What did your wife do last year?—That sort of thing. I'll just borrow your father's brief case for the nonce, m'boy.
He won't mind, I'm sure—
JackMorley
Oh yes, I'll need proper identification, too. Fetch your Fairy Godfather that nice G-man badge you got for sending in only twenty-nine box tops and a quarter—
Okay, Mr. O'Malley.

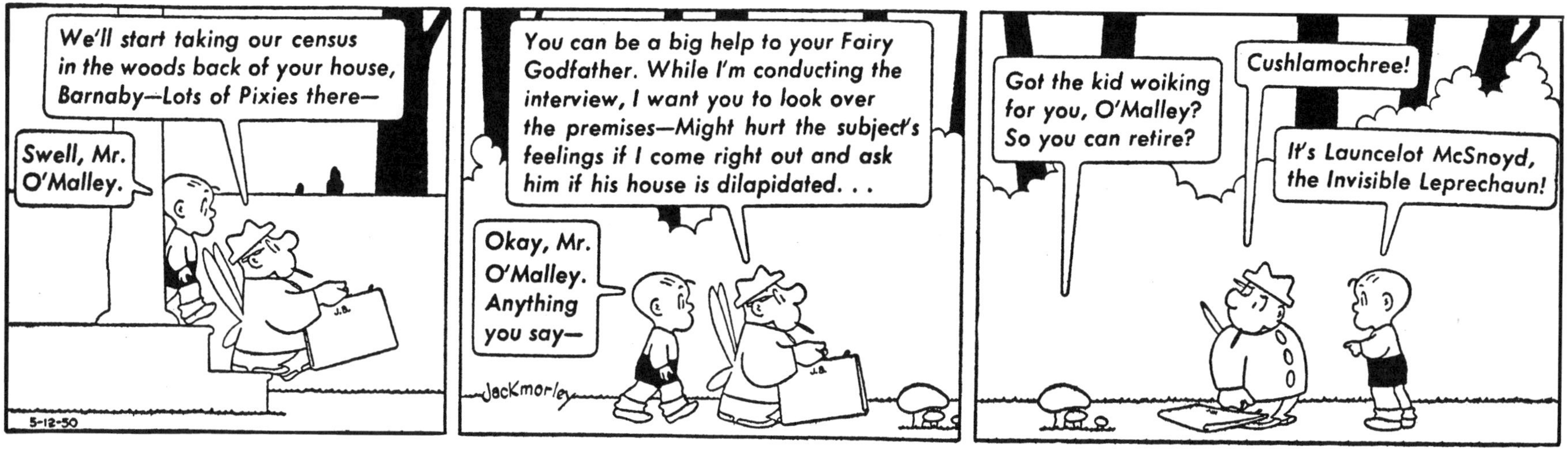
We'll start taking our census in the woods back of your house, Barnaby—Lots of Pixies there—
Swell, Mr. O'Malley.
5-12-50
You can be a big help to your Fairy Godfather. While I'm conducting the interview, I want you to look over the premises—Might hurt the subject's feelings if I come right out and ask him if his house is dilapidated. . .
Okay, Mr. O'Malley. Anything you say—
JackMorley
Got the kid woiking for you, O'Malley? So you can retire?
Cushlamochree!
It's Launcelot McSnoyd, the Invisible Leprechaun!

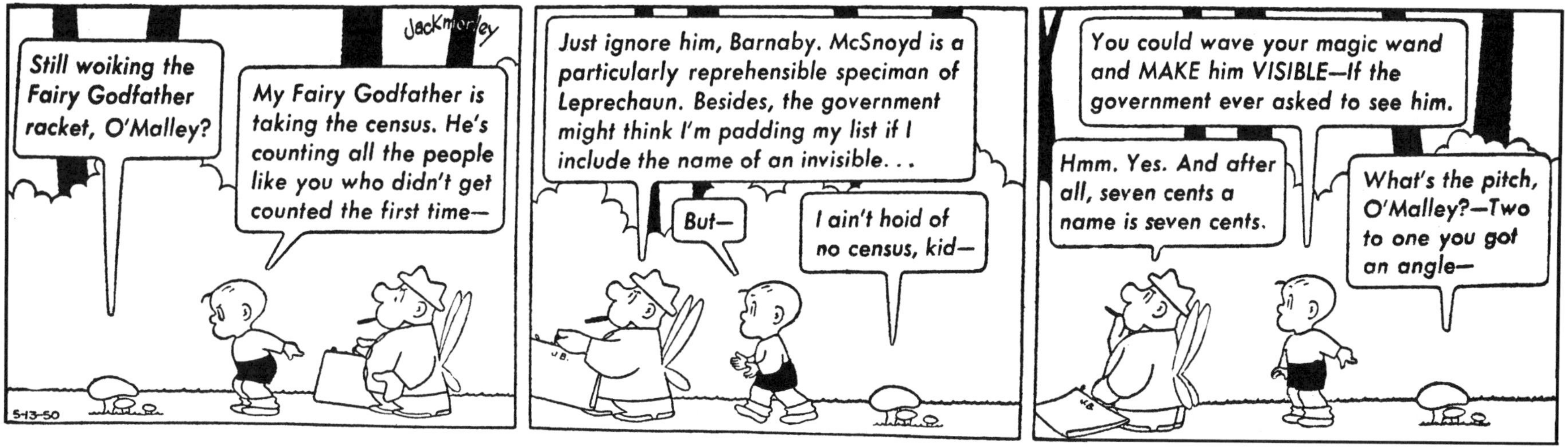
Still woiking the Fairy Godfather racket, O'Malley?
My Fairy Godfather is taking the census. He's counting all the people like you who didn't get counted the first time—
5-13-50
Just ignore him, Barnaby. McSnoyd is a particularly reprehensible speciman of Leprechaun. Besides, the government might think I'm padding my list if I include the name of an invisible. . .
But—
I ain't hoid of no census, kid—
You could wave your magic wand and MAKE him VISIBLE—If the government ever asked to see him.
Hmm. Yes. And after all, seven cents a name is seven cents.
What's the pitch, O'Malley?—Two to one you got an angle—

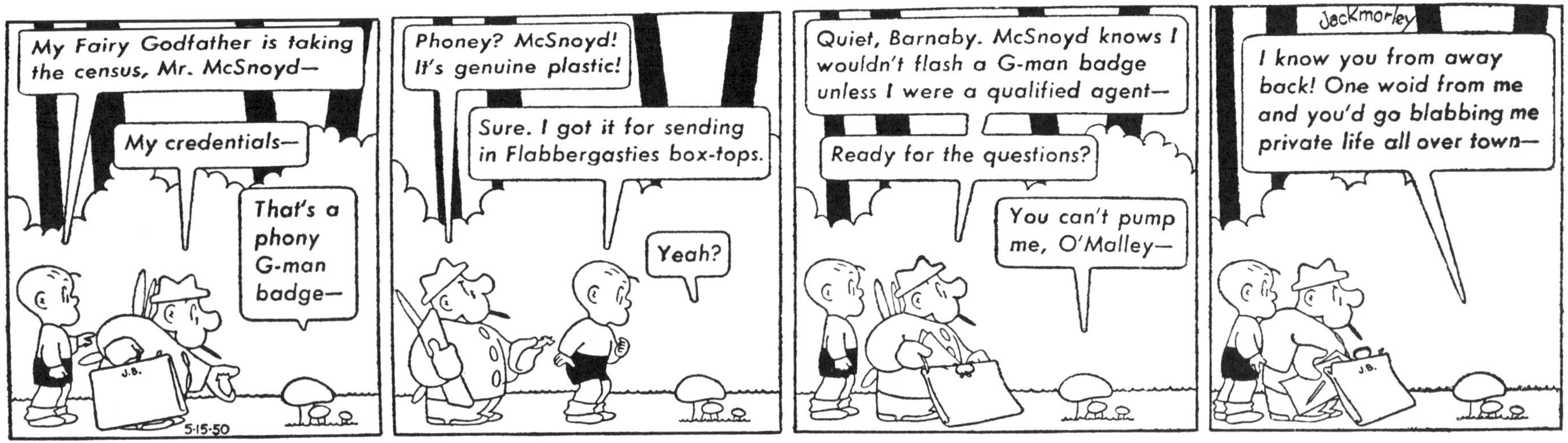
My Fairy Godfather is taking the census, Mr. McSnoyd—
My credentials—
That's a phony G-man badge—
J.B.
5-15-50
Phoney? McSnoyd! It's genuine plastic!
Sure. I got it for sending in Flabbergasties box-tops.
Yeah?
Quiet, Barnaby. McSnoyd knows I wouldn't flash a G-man badge unless I were a qualified agent—
Ready for the questions?
You can't pump me, O'Malley—
Jackmorley
I know you from away back! One woid from me and you'd go blabbing me private life all over town—
J.B.

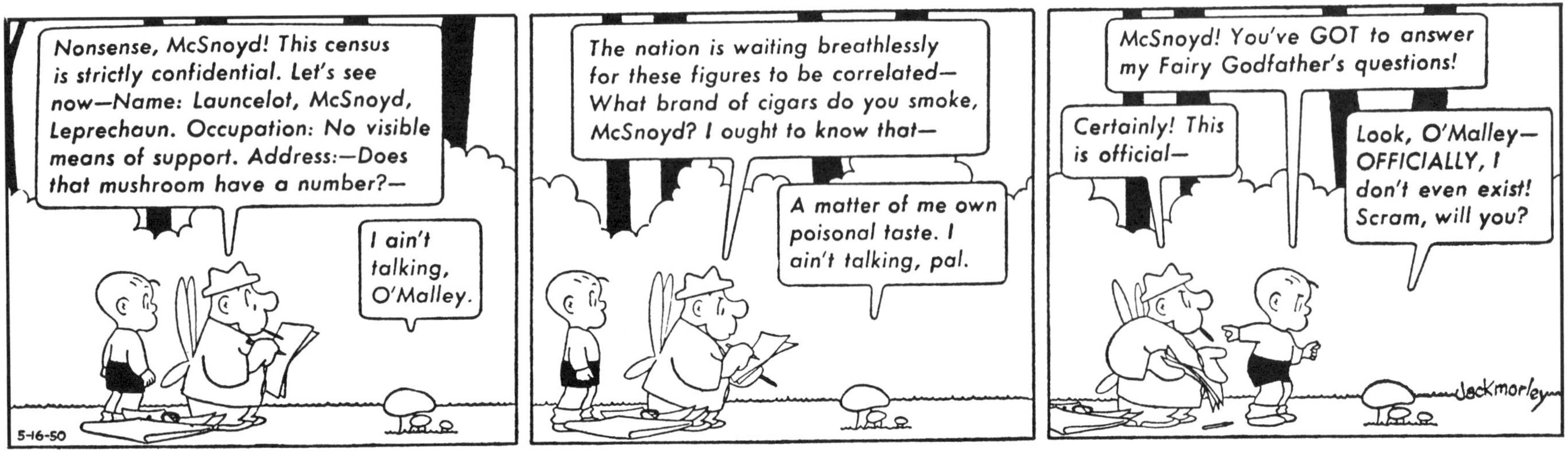
Nonsense, McSnoyd! This census is strictly confidential. Let's see now—Name: Launcelot, McSnoyd, Leprechaun. Occupation: No visible means of support. Address:—Does that mushroom have a number?—
I ain't talking, O'Malley.
5-16-50
The nation is waiting breathlessly for these figures to be correlated—What brand of cigars do you smoke, McSnoyd? I ought to know that—
A matter of me own poisonal taste. I ain't talking, pal.
McSnoyd! You've GOT to answer my Fairy Godfather's questions!
Certainly! This is official—
Look, O'Malley—OFFICIALLY, I don't even exist! Scram, will you?
Jackmorley

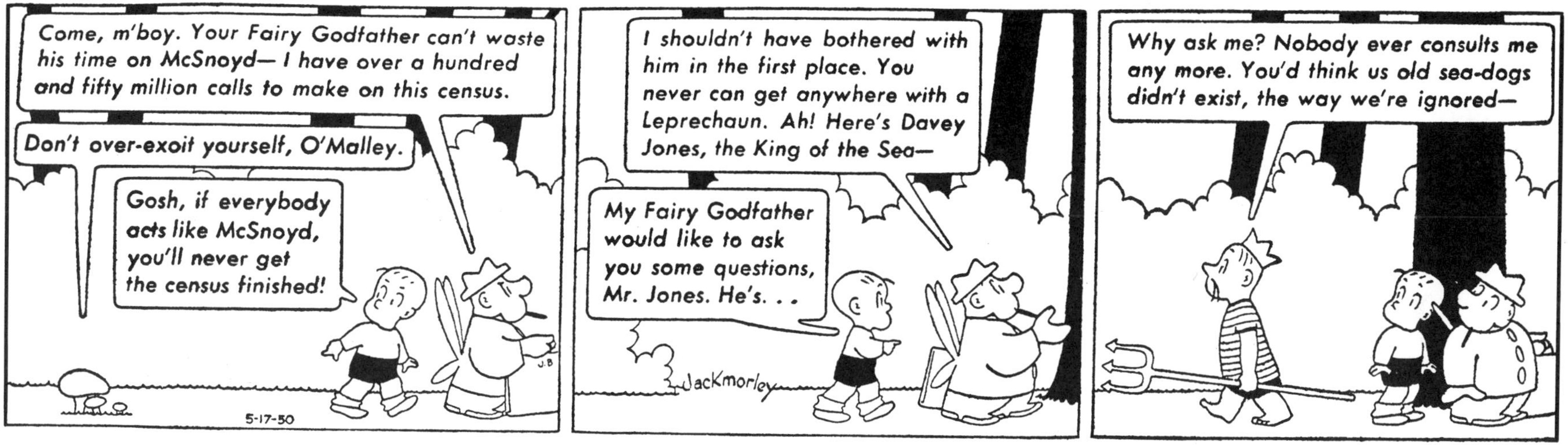
Come, m'boy. Your Fairy Godfather can't waste his time on McSnoyd— I have over a hundred and fifty million calls to make on this census.
Don't over-exoit yourself, O'Malley.
Gosh, if everybody acts like McSnoyd, you'll never get the census finished!
5-17-50
I shouldn't have bothered with him in the first place. You never can get anywhere with a Leprechaun. Ah! Here's Davey Jones, the King of the Sea—
My Fairy Godfather would like to ask you some questions, Mr. Jones. He's. . .
Why ask me? Nobody ever consults me any more. You'd think us old sea-dogs didn't exist, the way we're ignored—

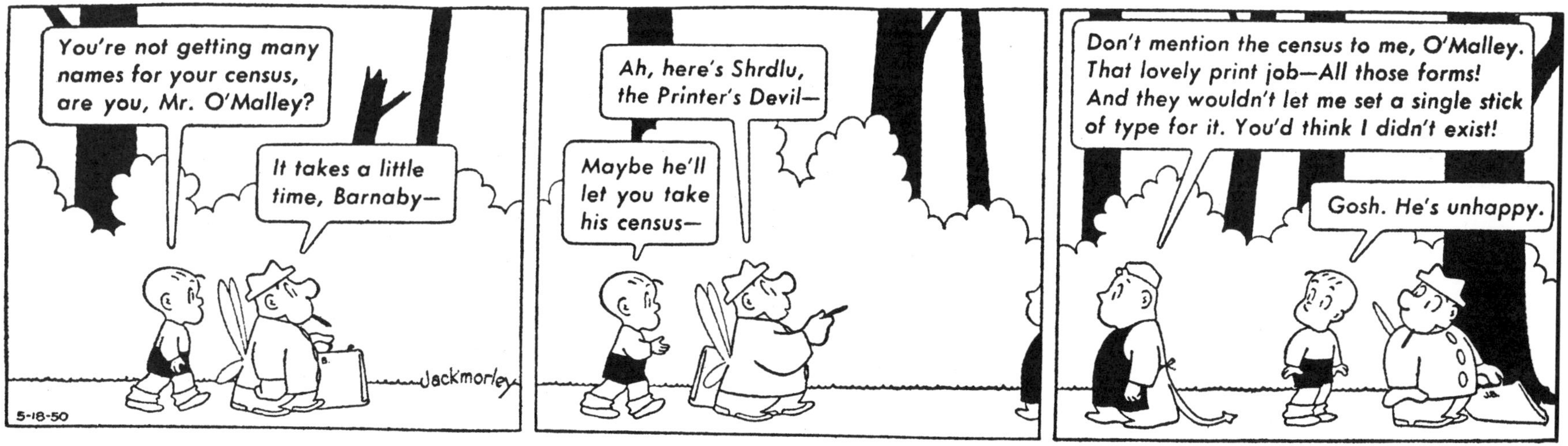
You're not getting many names for your census, are you, Mr. O'Malley?
It takes a little time, Barnaby—
5-18-50
Ah, here's Shrdlu, the Printer's Devil—
Maybe he'll let you take his census—
Don't mention the census to me, O'Malley. That lovely print job—All those forms! And they wouldn't let me set a single stick of type for it. You'd think I didn't exist!
Gosh. He's unhappy.

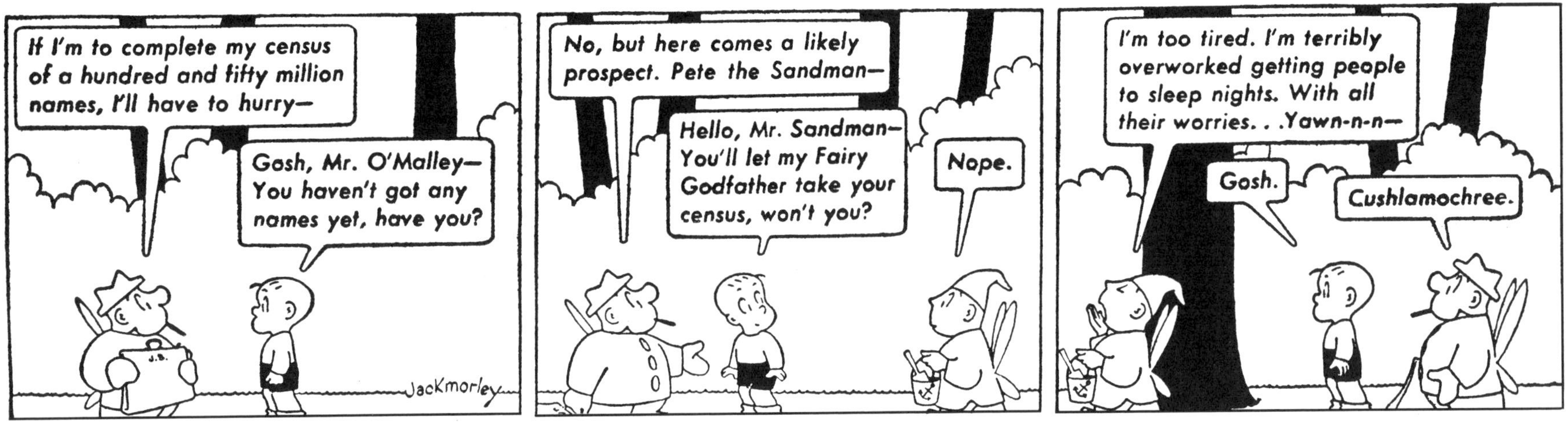

If I'm to complete my census of a hundred and fifty million names, I'll have to hurry—
Gosh, Mr. O'Malley— You haven't got any names yet, have you?
No, but here comes a likely prospect. Pete the Sandman—
Hello, Mr. Sandman— You'll let my Fairy Godfather take your census, won't you?
Nope.
I'm too tired. I'm terribly overworked getting people to sleep nights. With all their worries. . .Yawn-n-n—
Gosh.
Cushlamochree.
J.B.
Jackmorley

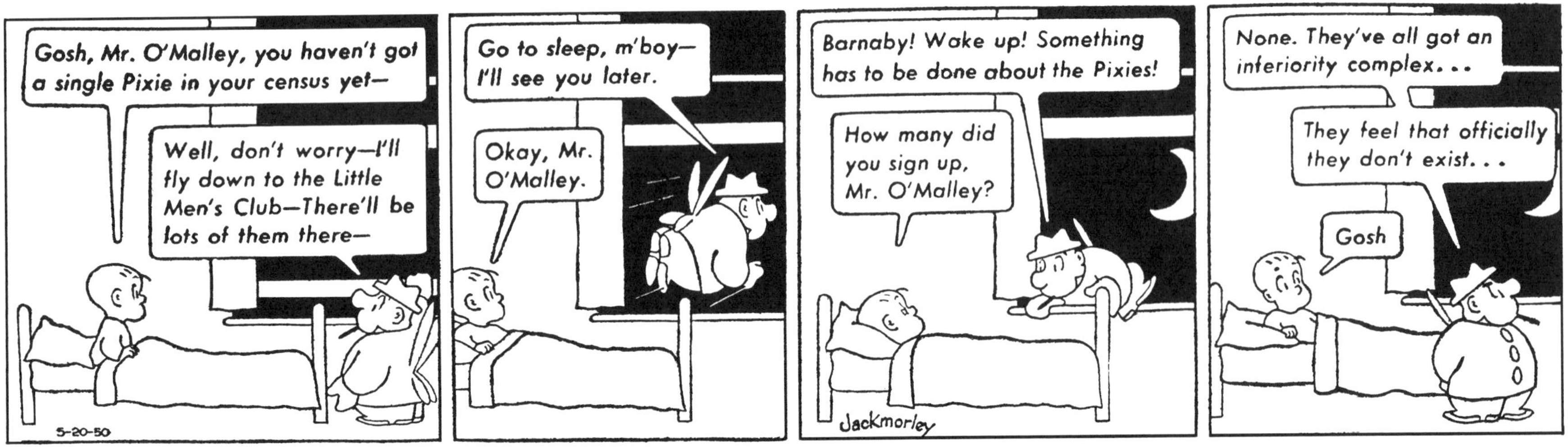

Gosh, Mr. O'Malley, you haven't got a single Pixie in your census yet—
Well, don't worry—I'll fly down to the Little Men's Club—There'll be lots of them there—
Go to sleep, m'boy— I'll see you later.
Okay, Mr. O'Malley.
Barnaby! Wake up! Something has to be done about the Pixies!
How many did you sign up, Mr. O'Malley?
None. They've all got an inferiority complex. . .
They feel that officially they don't exist. . .
Gosh
5-20-50
Jackmorley

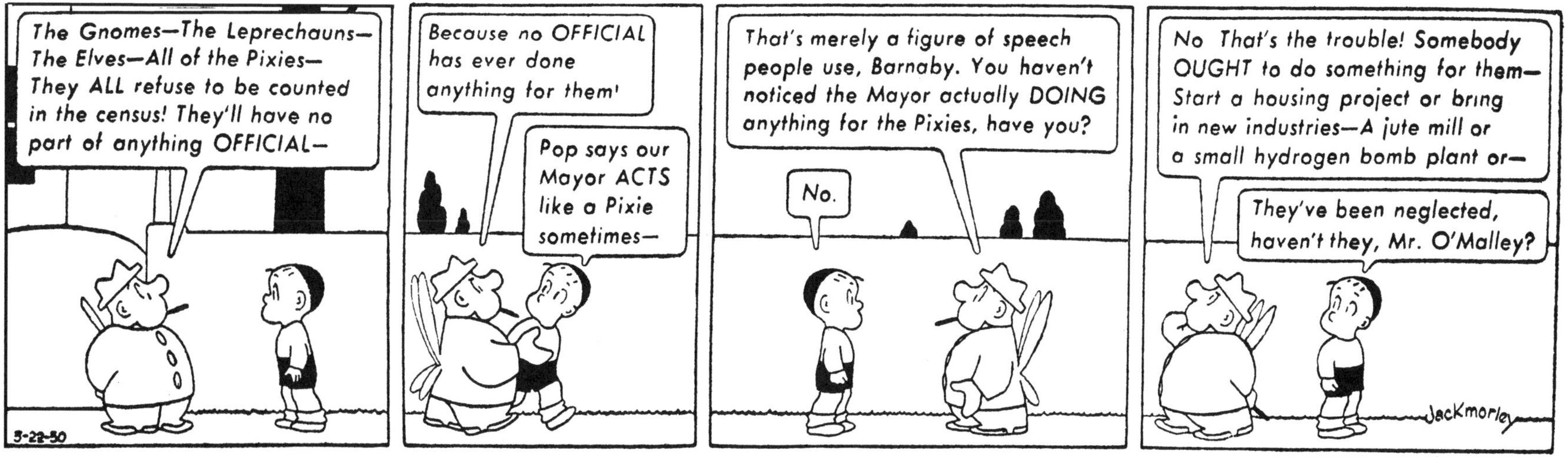
The Gnomes—The Leprechauns—The Elves—All of the Pixies—They ALL refuse to be counted in the census! They'll have no part of anything OFFICIAL—
Because no OFFICIAL has ever done anything for them!
Pop says our Mayor ACTS like a Pixie sometimes—
That's merely a figure of speech people use, Barnaby. You haven't noticed the Mayor actually DOING anything for the Pixies, have you?
No.
No That's the trouble! Somebody OUGHT to do something for them—Start a housing project or bring in new industries—A jute mill or a small hydrogen bomb plant or—
They've been neglected, haven't they, Mr. O'Malley?
JackMorley
5-22-50

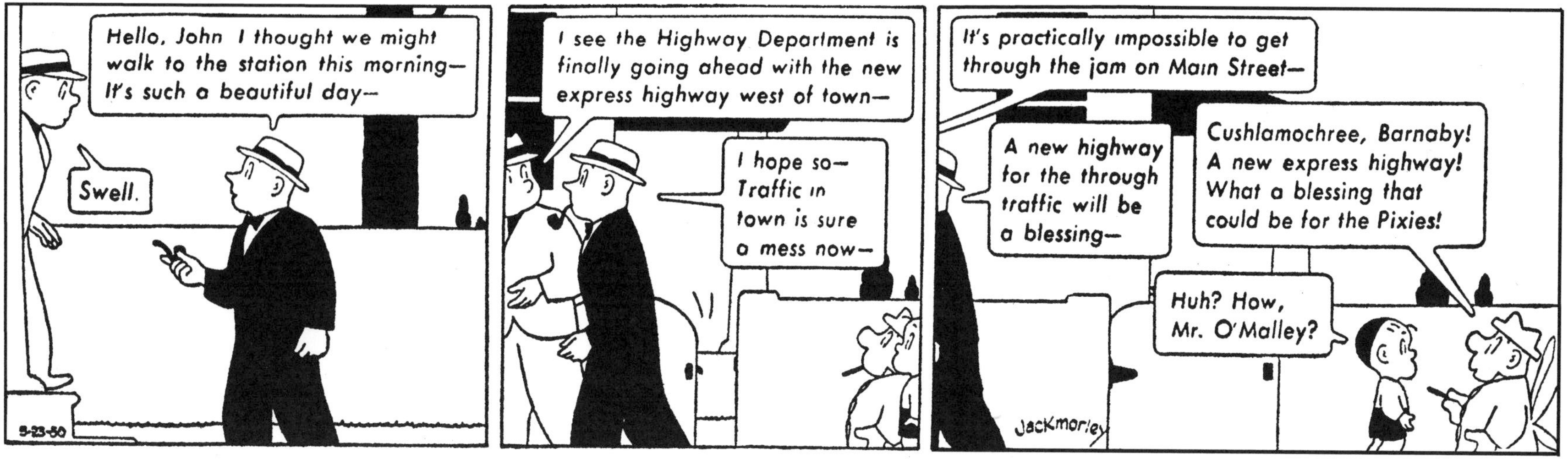
Hello, John I thought we might walk to the station this morning—It's such a beautiful day—
Swell.
I see the Highway Department is finally going ahead with the new express highway west of town—
I hope so—Traffic in town is sure a mess now—
It's practically impossible to get through the jam on Main Street—
A new highway for the through traffic will be a blessing—
Cushlamochree, Barnaby! A new express highway! What a blessing that could be for the Pixies!
Huh? How, Mr. O'Malley?
JackMorley
5-23-50

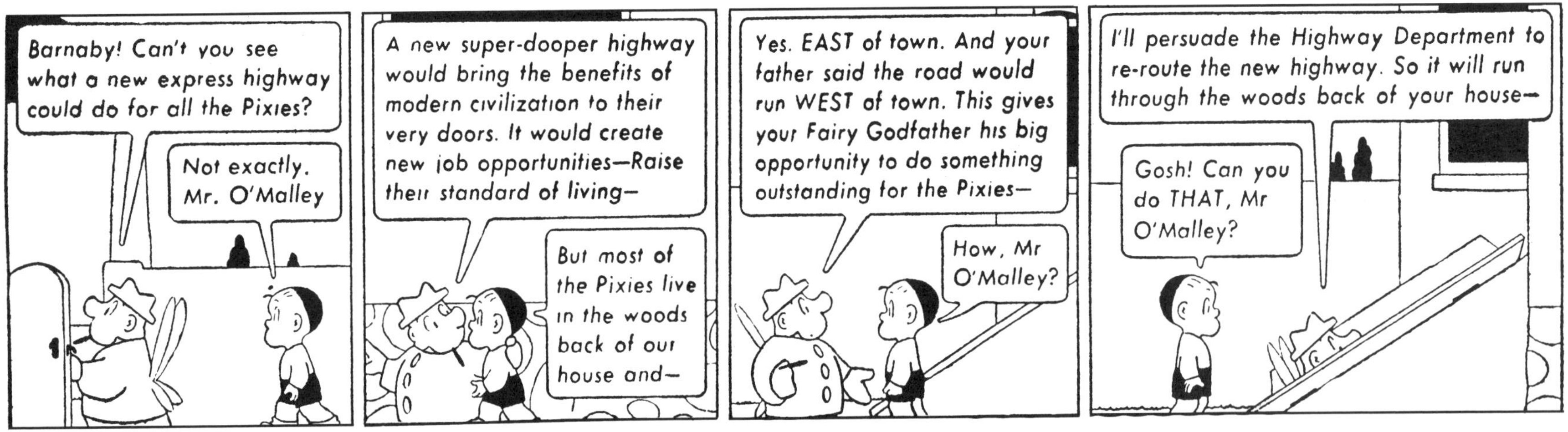
Barnaby! Can't you see what a new express highway could do for all the Pixies?
Not exactly. Mr. O'Malley
A new super-dooper highway would bring the benefits of modern civilization to their very doors. It would create new job opportunities—Raise their standard of living—
But most of the Pixies live in the woods back of our house and—
Yes. EAST of town. And your father said the road would run WEST of town. This gives your Fairy Godfather his big opportunity to do something outstanding for the Pixies—
How, Mr O'Malley?
I'll persuade the Highway Department to re-route the new highway. So it will run through the woods back of your house—
Gosh! Can you do THAT, Mr O'Malley?

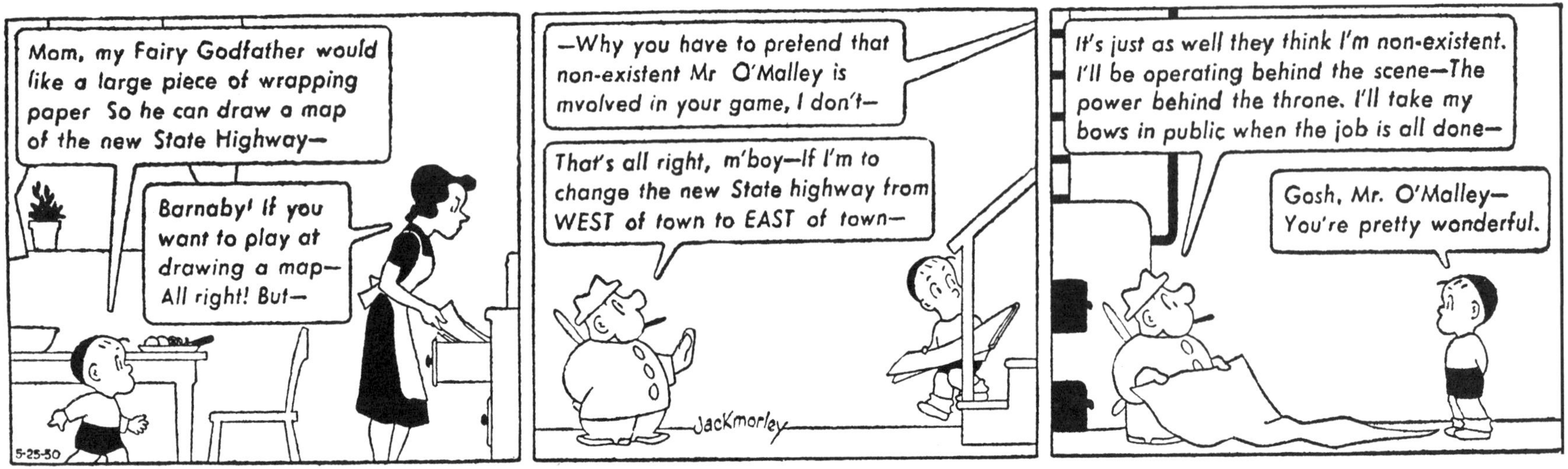
Mom, my Fairy Godfather would like a large piece of wrapping paper So he can draw a map of the new State Highway—
Barnaby! If you want to play at drawing a map— All right! But—
5-25-50
—Why you have to pretend that non-existent Mr O'Malley is involved in your game, I don't—
That's all right, m'boy—If I'm to change the new State highway from WEST of town to EAST of town—
JackMorley
It's just as well they think I'm non-existent. I'll be operating behind the scene—The power behind the throne. I'll take my bows in public when the job is all done—
Gosh, Mr. O'Malley— You're pretty wonderful.

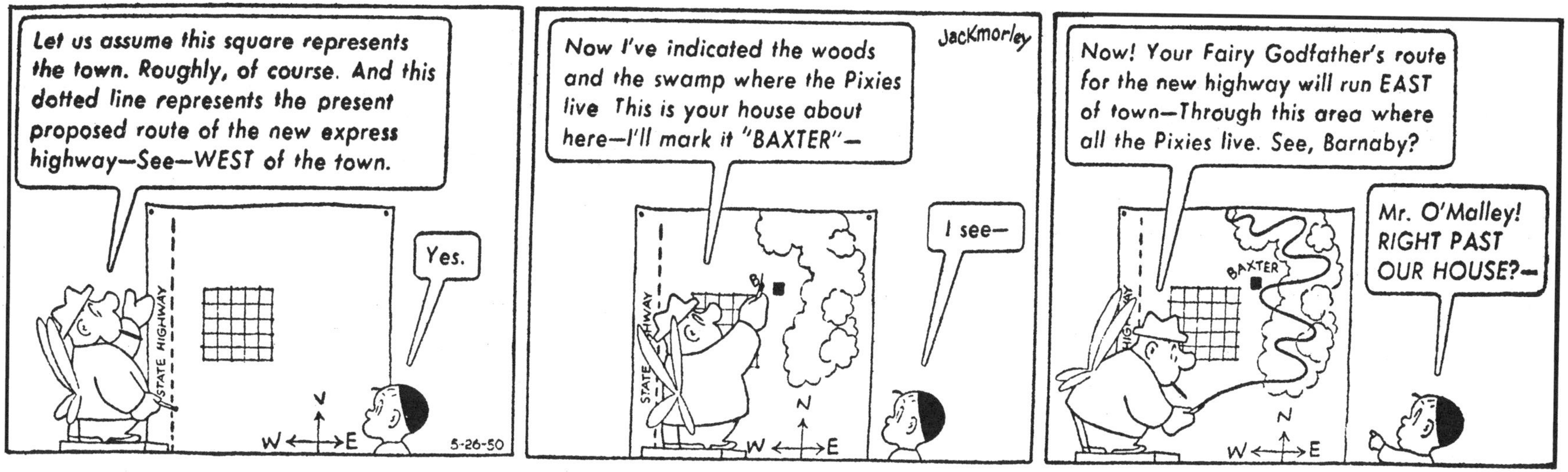
Let us assume this square represents the town. Roughly, of course. And this dotted line represents the present proposed route of the new express highway—See—WEST of the town.
Yes.
STATE HIGHWAY
W
E
5-26-50
JacKmorley
Now I've indicated the woods and the swamp where the Pixies live This is your house about here—I'll mark it "BAXTER"—
I see—
N
W
E
Now! Your Fairy Godfather's route for the new highway will run EAST of town—Through this area where all the Pixies live. See, Barnaby?
Mr. O'Malley! RIGHT PAST OUR HOUSE?—
BAXTER
N
W
E

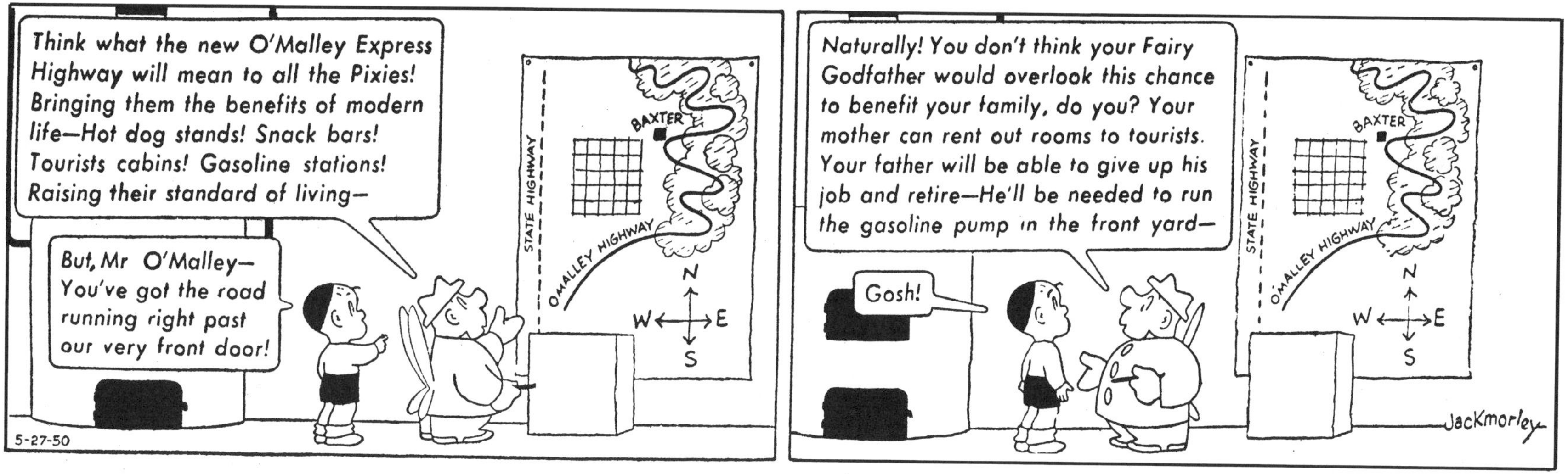
Think what the new O'Malley Express Highway will mean to all the Pixies! Bringing them the benefits of modern life—Hot dog stands! Snack bars! Tourists cabins! Gasoline stations! Raising their standard of living—
But, Mr O'Malley— You've got the road running right past our very front door!
STATE HIGHWAY
BAXTER
O'MALLEY HIGHWAY
N
W
E
S
5-27-50
Naturally! You don't think your Fairy Godfather would overlook this chance to benefit your family, do you? Your mother can rent out rooms to tourists. Your father will be able to give up his job and retire—He'll be needed to run the gasoline pump in the front yard—
Gosh!
STATE HIGHWAY
BAXTER
O'MALLEY HIGHWAY
N
W
E
S
JacKmorley

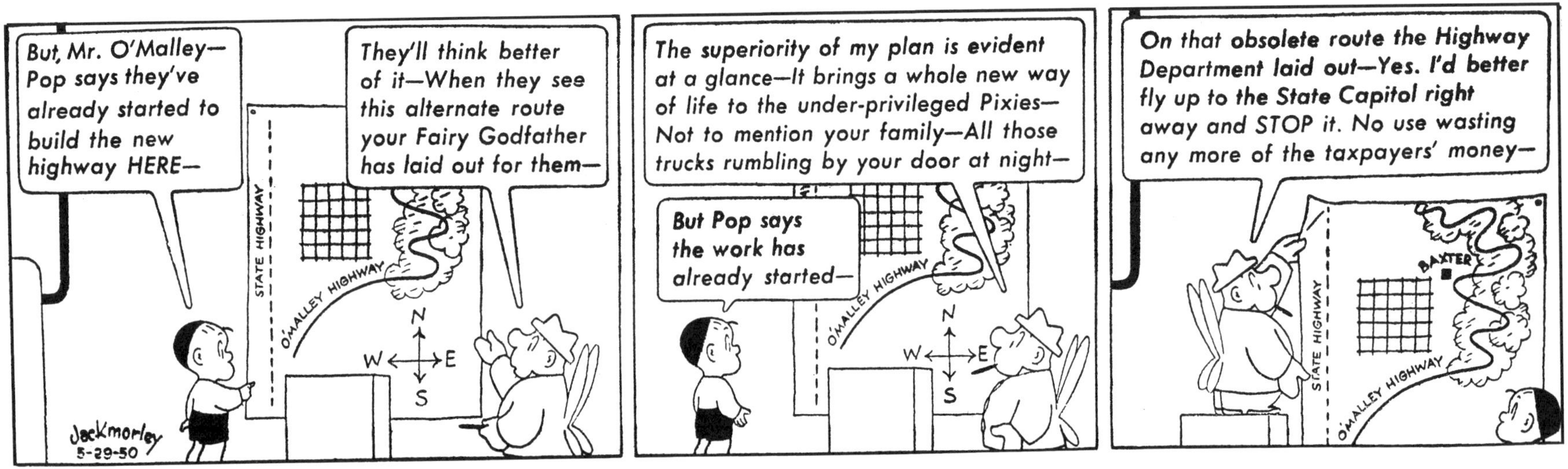
But, Mr. O'Malley— Pop says they've already started to build the new highway HERE—
They'll think better of it—When they see this alternate route your Fairy Godfather has laid out for them—
STATE HIGHWAY
O'MALLEY HIGHWAY
N
W
E
S
Jackmorley
5-29-50
The superiority of my plan is evident at a glance—It brings a whole new way of life to the under-privileged Pixies—Not to mention your family—All those trucks rumbling by your door at night—
But Pop says the work has already started—
On that obsolete route the Highway Department laid out—Yes. I'd better fly up to the State Capitol right away and STOP it. No use wasting any more of the taxpayers' money—
BAXTER
STATE HIGHWAY
O'MALLEY HIGHWAY

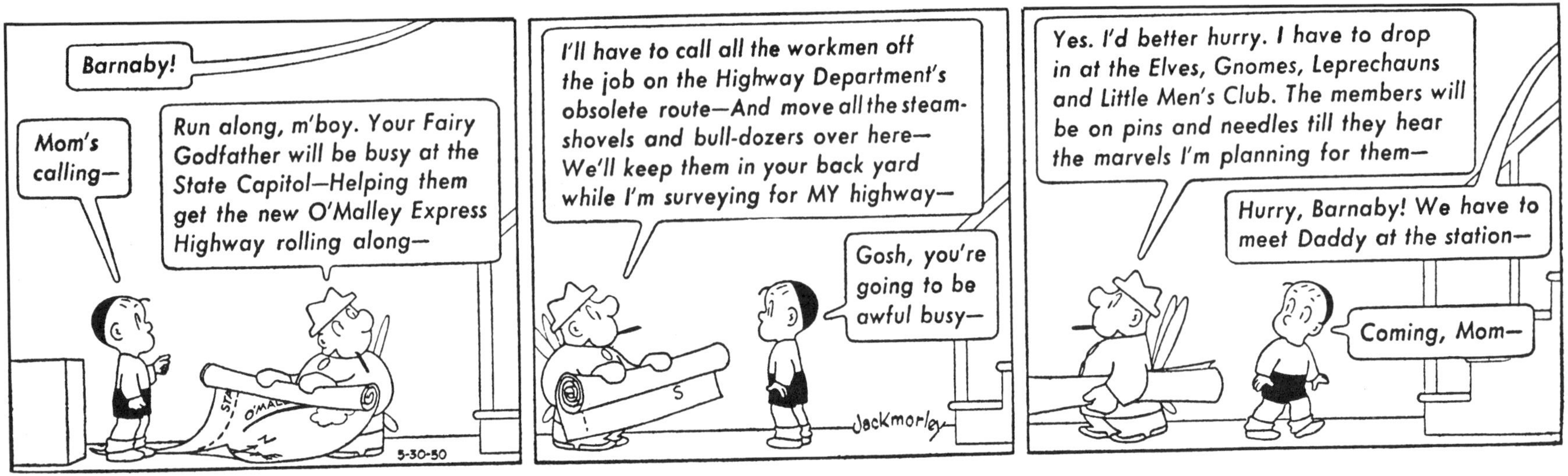
Barnaby!
Mom's calling—
Run along, m'boy. Your Fairy Godfather will be busy at the State Capitol—Helping them get the new O'Malley Express Highway rolling along—
5-30-50
I'll have to call all the workmen off the job on the Highway Department's obsolete route—And move all the steam-shovels and bull-dozers over here—We'll keep them in your back yard while I'm surveying for MY highway—
Gosh, you're going to be awful busy—
Jackmorley
Yes. I'd better hurry. I have to drop in at the Elves, Gnomes, Leprechauns and Little Men's Club. The members will be on pins and needles till they hear the marvels I'm planning for them—
Hurry, Barnaby! We have to meet Daddy at the station—
Coming, Mom—

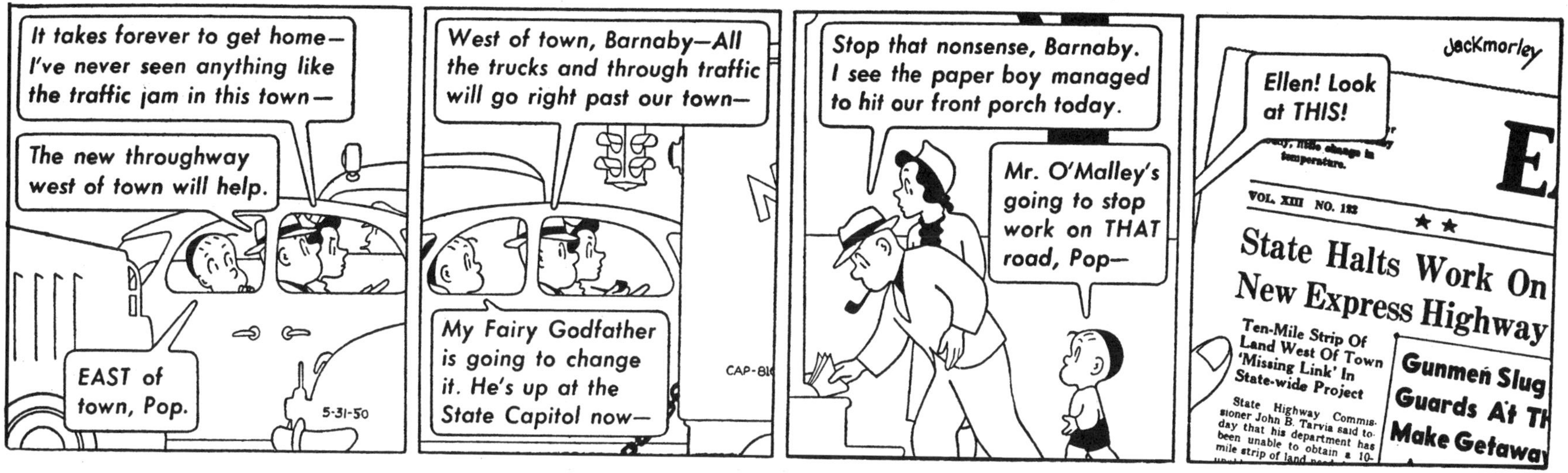
It takes forever to get home—I've never seen anything like the traffic jam in this town—
The new throughway west of town will help.
EAST of town, Pop.
5-31-50
West of town, Barnaby—All the trucks and through traffic will go right past our town—
My Fairy Godfather is going to change it. He's up at the State Capitol now—
Stop that nonsense, Barnaby. I see the paper boy managed to hit our front porch today.
Mr. O'Malley's going to stop work on THAT road, Pop—
JacKmorley
Ellen! Look at THIS!
State Halts Work On New Express Highway
Ten-Mile Strip Of Land West Of Town 'Missing Link' In State-wide Project
State Highway Commissioner John B. Tarvia said today that his department has been unable to obtain a 10-mile strip of land
Gunmen Slug
Guards At
Make Getaway

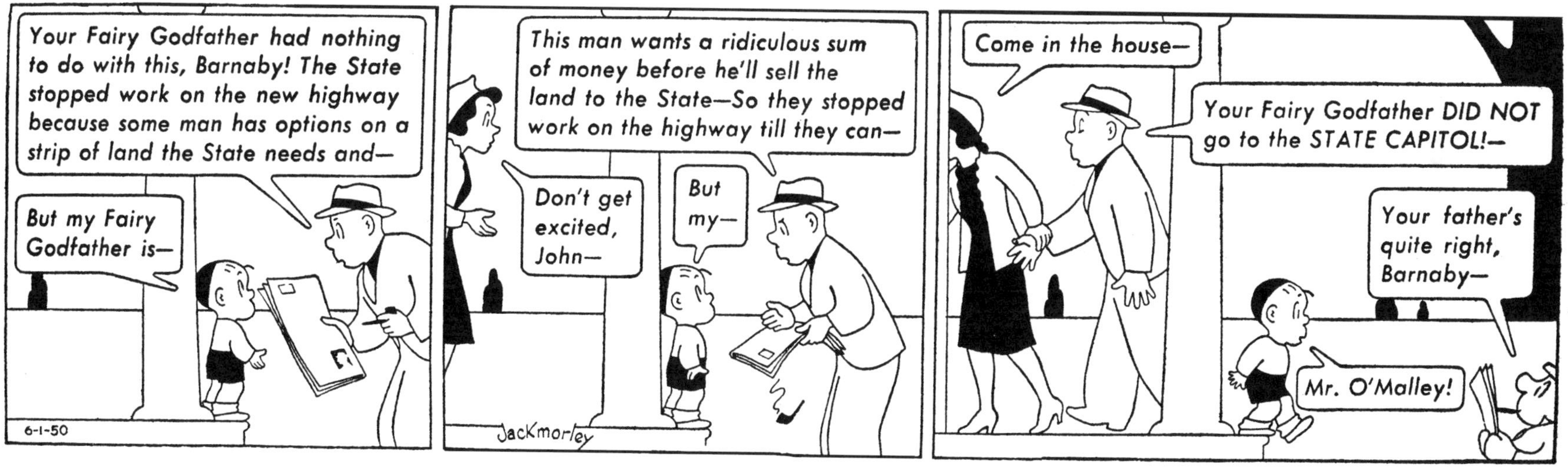
Your Fairy Godfather had nothing to do with this, Barnaby! The State stopped work on the new highway because some man has options on a strip of land the State needs and—
But my Fairy Godfather is—
6-1-50
This man wants a ridiculous sum of money before he'll sell the land to the State—So they stopped work on the highway till they can—
Don't get excited, John—
But my—
JacKmorley
Come in the house—
Your Fairy Godfather DID NOT go to the STATE CAPITOL!—
Your father's quite right, Barnaby—
Mr. O'Malley!

May 31 – June 1

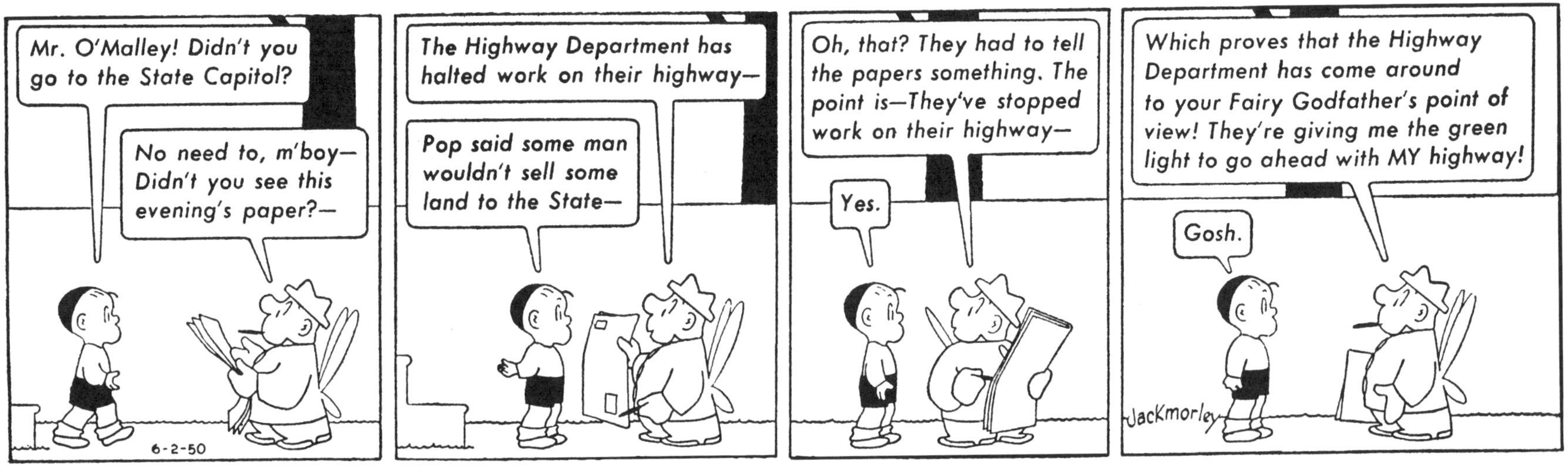
Mr. O'Malley! Didn't you go to the State Capitol?
No need to, m'boy— Didn't you see this evening's paper?—
6-2-50
The Highway Department has halted work on their highway—
Pop said some man wouldn't sell some land to the State—
Oh, that? They had to tell the papers something. The point is—They've stopped work on their highway—
Yes.
Which proves that the Highway Department has come around to your Fairy Godfather's point of view! They're giving me the green light to go ahead with MY highway!
Gosh.
JackMorley

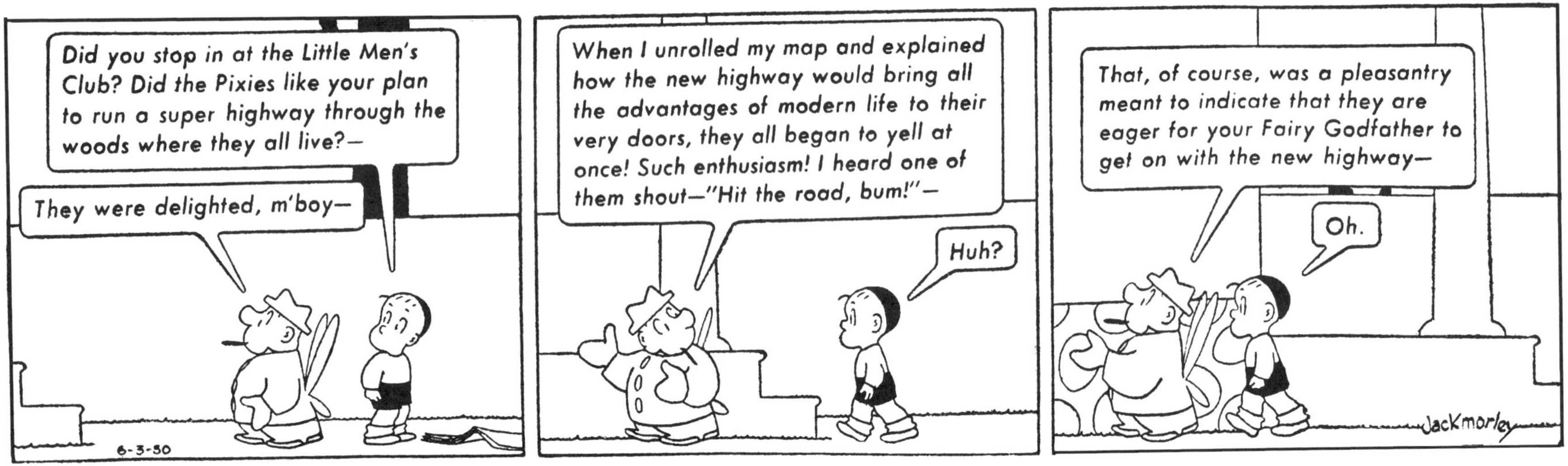
Did you stop in at the Little Men's Club? Did the Pixies like your plan to run a super highway through the woods where they all live?—
They were delighted, m'boy—
6-3-50
When I unrolled my map and explained how the new highway would bring all the advantages of modern life to their very doors, they all began to yell at once! Such enthusiasm! I heard one of them shout—"Hit the road, bum!"—
Huh?
That, of course, was a pleasantry meant to indicate that they are eager for your Fairy Godfather to get on with the new highway—
Oh.
JackMorley

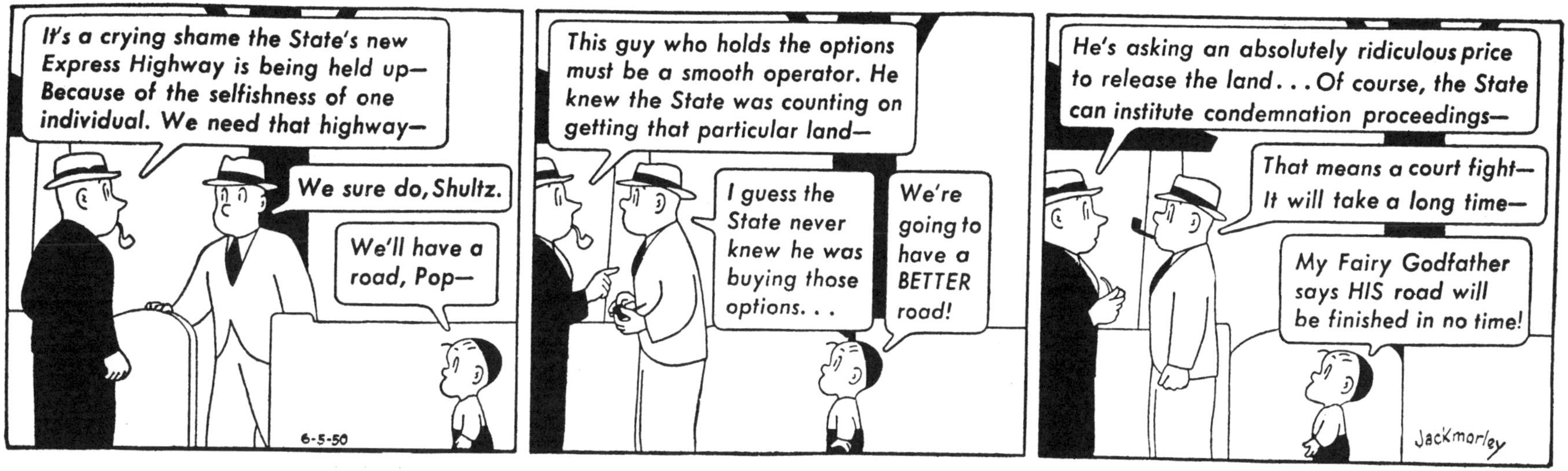
It's a crying shame the State's new Express Highway is being held up— Because of the selfishness of one individual. We need that highway—
We sure do, Shultz.
We'll have a road, Pop—
6-5-50
This guy who holds the options must be a smooth operator. He knew the State was counting on getting that particular land—
I guess the State never knew he was buying those options. . .
We're going to have a BETTER road!
He's asking an absolutely ridiculous price to release the land. . . Of course, the State can institute condemnation proceedings—
That means a court fight— It will take a long time—
My Fairy Godfather says HIS road will be finished in no time!
JackMorley

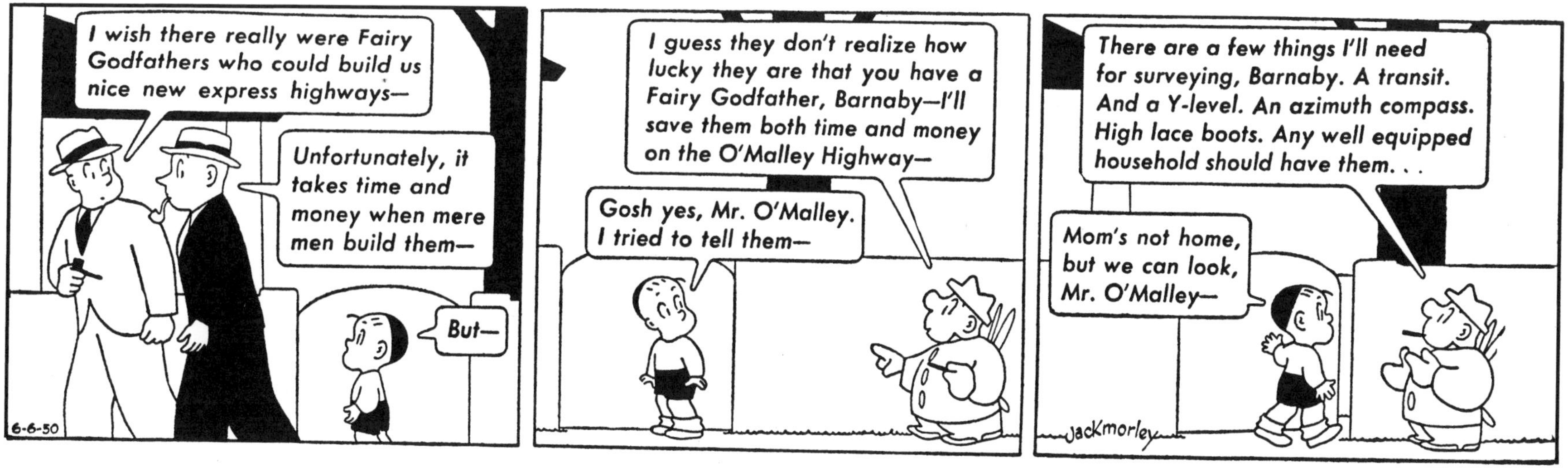
I wish there really were Fairy Godfathers who could build us nice new express highways—
Unfortunately, it takes time and money when mere men build them—
But—
6-6-50
I guess they don't realize how lucky they are that you have a Fairy Godfather, Barnaby—I'll save them both time and money on the O'Malley Highway—
Gosh yes, Mr. O'Malley. I tried to tell them—
There are a few things I'll need for surveying, Barnaby. A transit. And a Y-level. An azimuth compass. High lace boots. Any well equipped household should have them. . .
Mom's not home, but we can look, Mr. O'Malley—
JackMorley

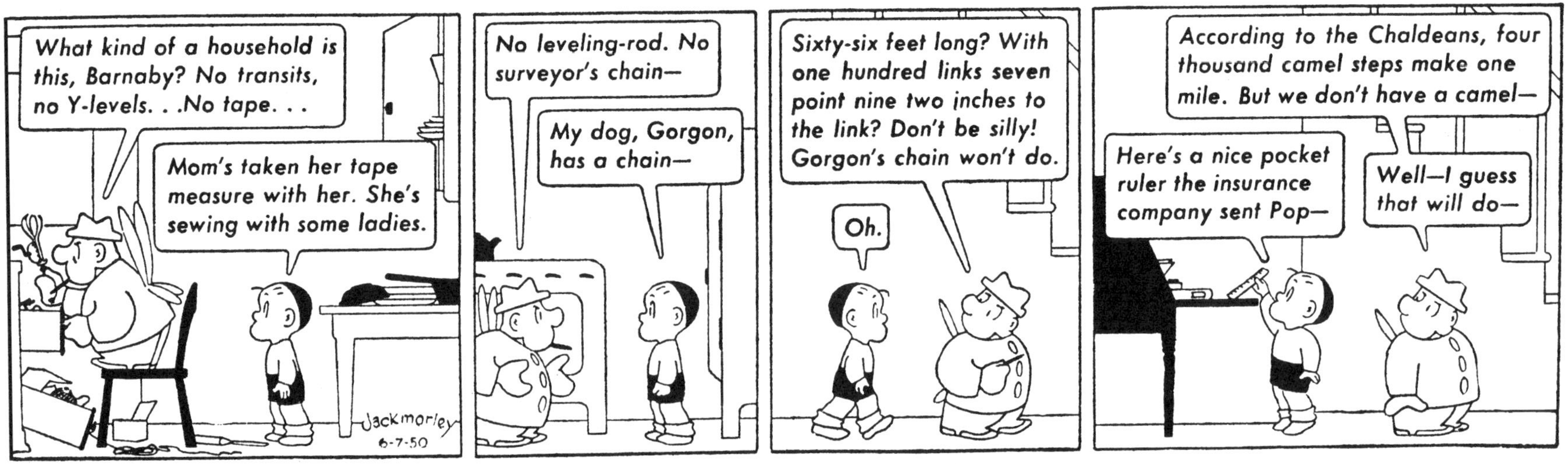
What kind of a household is this, Barnaby? No transits, no Y-levels. . .No tape. . .
Mom's taken her tape measure with her. She's sewing with some ladies.
Jackmorley
6-7-50
No leveling-rod. No surveyor's chain—
My dog, Gorgon, has a chain—
Sixty-six feet long? With one hundred links seven point nine two inches to the link? Don't be silly! Gorgon's chain won't do.
Oh.
According to the Chaldeans, four thousand camel steps make one mile. But we don't have a camel—
Here's a nice pocket ruler the insurance company sent Pop—
Well—I guess that will do—

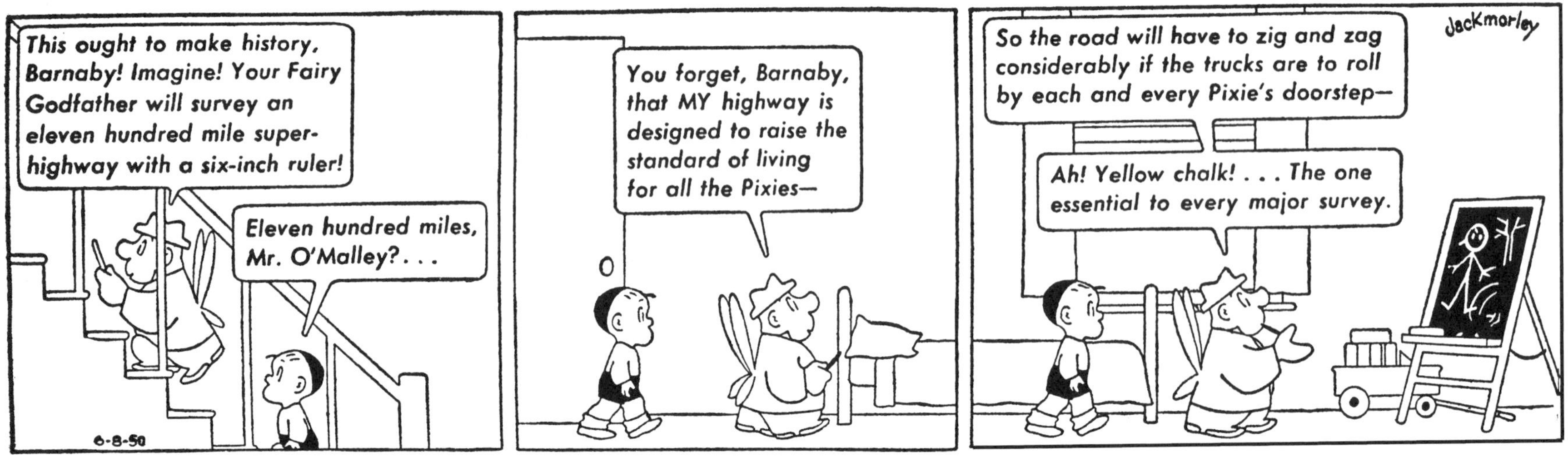
This ought to make history, Barnaby! Imagine! Your Fairy Godfather will survey an eleven hundred mile super-highway with a six-inch ruler!
Eleven hundred miles, Mr. O'Malley?. . .
6-8-50
You forget, Barnaby, that MY highway is designed to raise the standard of living for all the Pixies—
Jackmorley
So the road will have to zig and zag considerably if the trucks are to roll by each and every Pixie's doorstep—
Ah! Yellow chalk! . . . The one essential to every major survey.

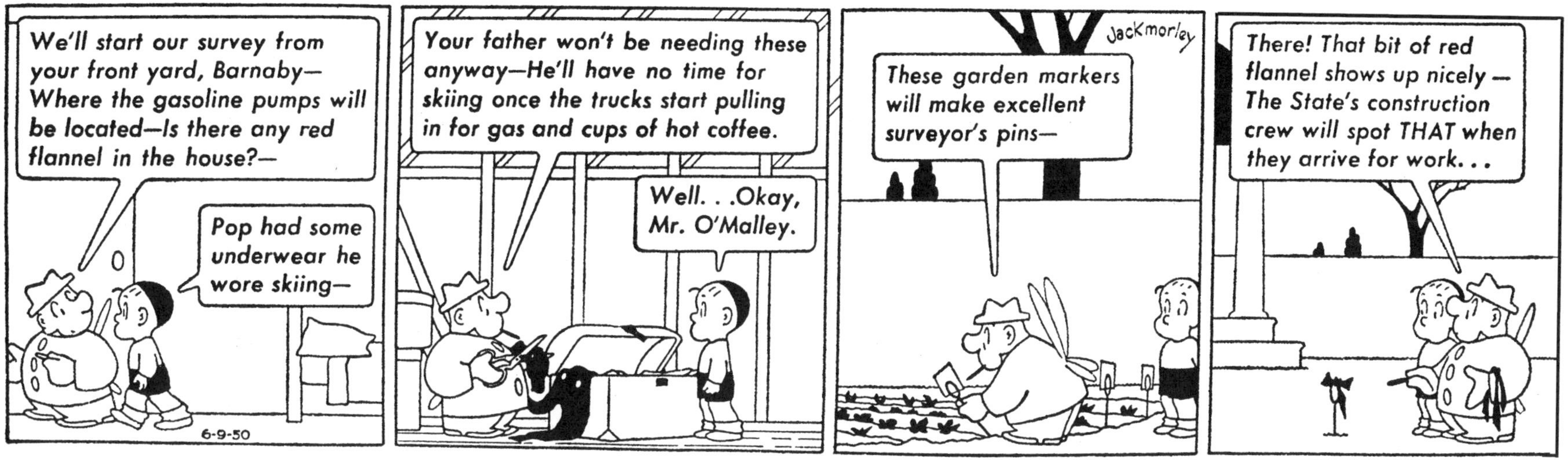
We'll start our survey from your front yard, Barnaby—Where the gasoline pumps will be located—Is there any red flannel in the house?—
Pop had some underwear he wore skiing—
6-9-50
Your father won't be needing these anyway—He'll have no time for skiing once the trucks start pulling in for gas and cups of hot coffee.
Well. . .Okay, Mr. O'Malley.
Jackmorley
These garden markers will make excellent surveyor's pins—
There! That bit of red flannel shows up nicely—The State's construction crew will spot THAT when they arrive for work. . .

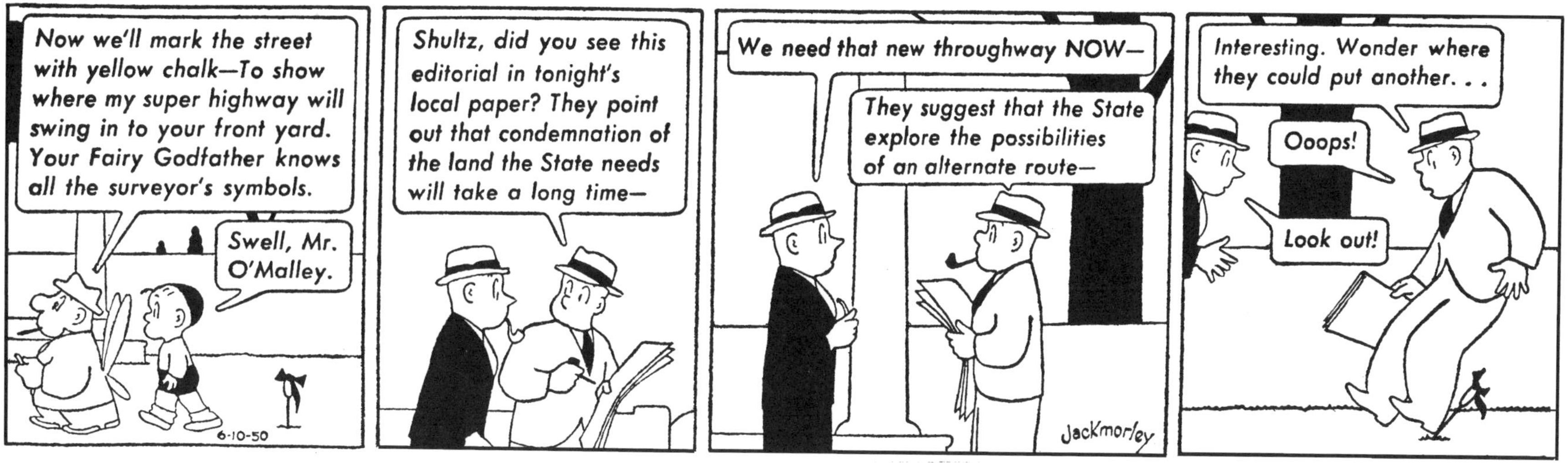
Now we'll mark the street with yellow chalk—To show where my super highway will swing in to your front yard. Your Fairy Godfather knows all the surveyor's symbols.
Swell, Mr. O'Malley.
6-10-50
Shultz, did you see this editorial in tonight's local paper? They point out that condemnation of the land the State needs will take a long time—
We need that new throughway NOW—
They suggest that the State explore the possibilities of an alternate route—
Jackmorley
Interesting. Wonder where they could put another. . .
Ooops!
Look out!

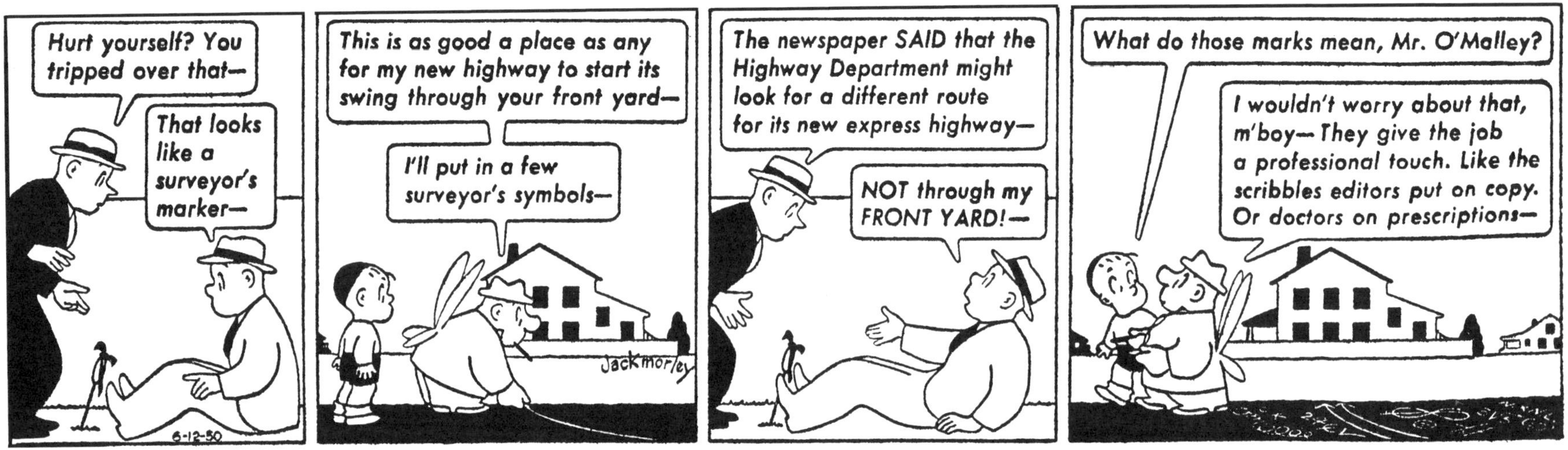
Hurt yourself? You tripped over that—
That looks like a surveyor's marker—
6-12-50
This is as good a place as any for my new highway to start its swing through your front yard—
I'll put in a few surveyor's symbols—
Jack morley
The newspaper SAID that the Highway Department might look for a different route for its new express highway—
NOT through my FRONT YARD!—
What do those marks mean, Mr. O'Malley?
I wouldn't worry about that, m'boy— They give the job a professional touch. Like the scribbles editors put on copy. Or doctors on prescriptions—

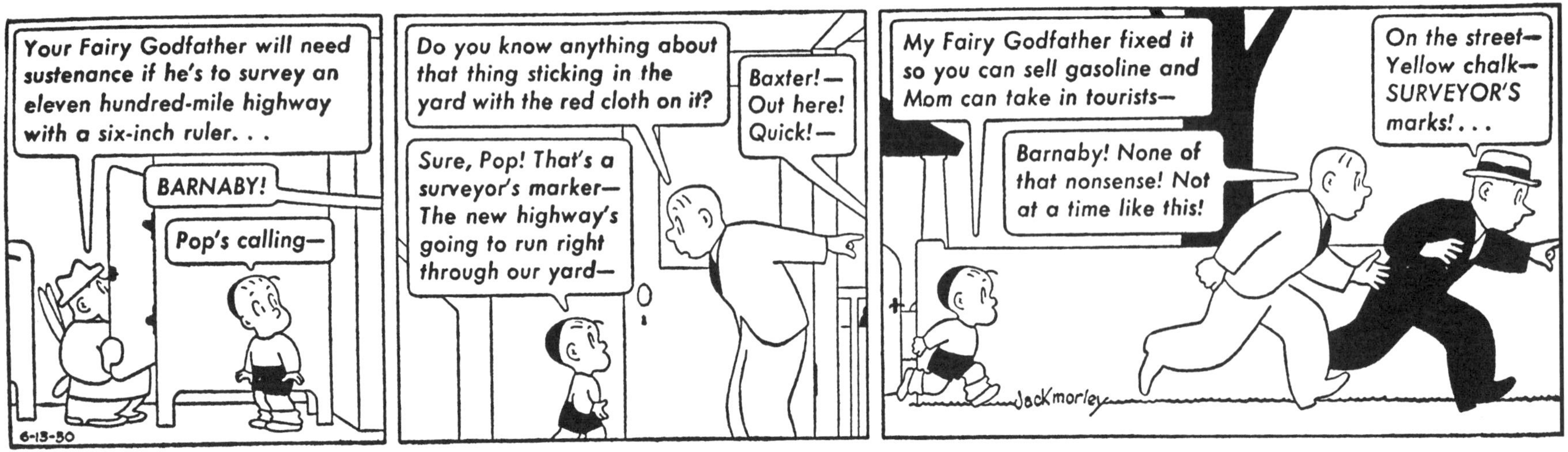
Your Fairy Godfather will need sustenance if he's to survey an eleven hundred-mile highway with a six-inch ruler. . .
BARNABY!
Pop's calling—
6-13-50
Do you know anything about that thing sticking in the yard with the red cloth on it?
Sure, Pop! That's a surveyor's marker— The new highway's going to run right through our yard—
Baxter!— Out here! Quick!—
My Fairy Godfather fixed it so you can sell gasoline and Mom can take in tourists—
Barnaby! None of that nonsense! Not at a time like this!
On the street— Yellow chalk— SURVEYOR'S marks! . . .
Jack morley

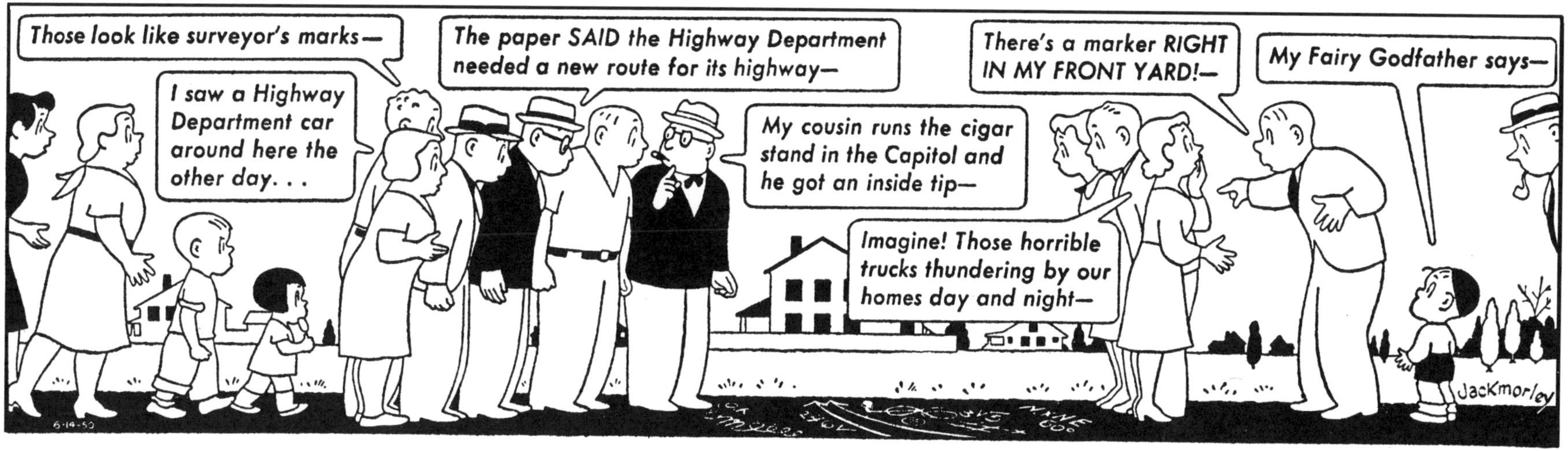
Those look like surveyor's marks—
I saw a Highway Department car around here the other day. . .
The paper SAID the Highway Department needed a new route for its highway—
My cousin runs the cigar stand in the Capitol and he got an inside tip—
There's a marker RIGHT IN MY FRONT YARD!—
Imagine! Those horrible trucks thundering by our homes day and night—
My Fairy Godfather says—
6-14-50
JACKMORLEY

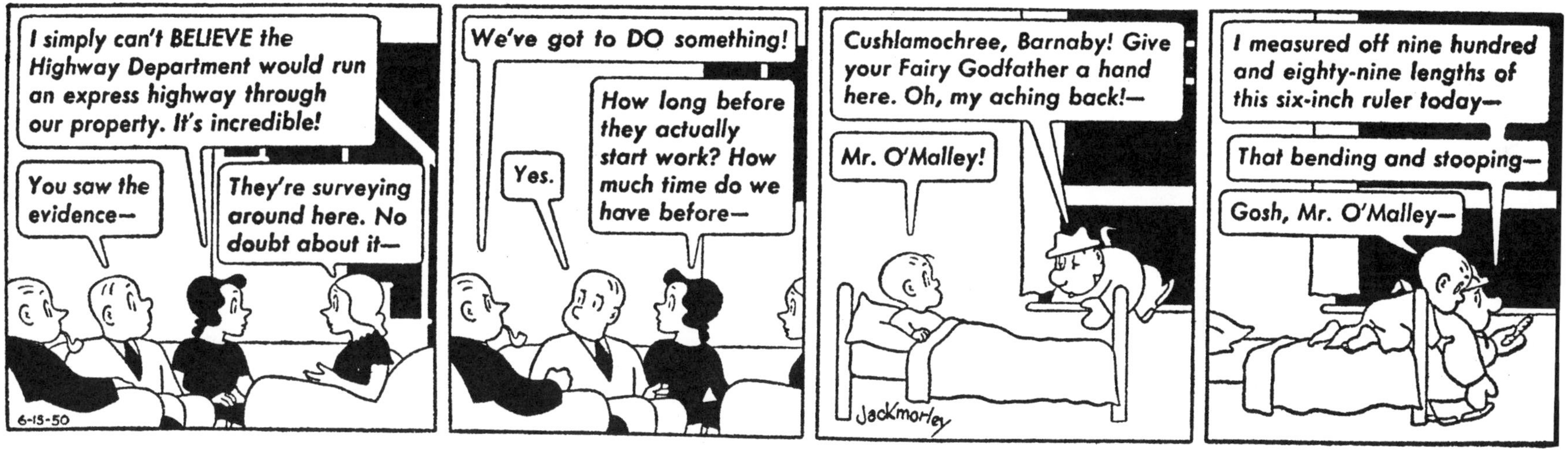
I simply can't BELIEVE the Highway Department would run an express highway through our property. It's incredible!
You saw the evidence—
They're surveying around here. No doubt about it—
6-15-50
We've got to DO something!
Yes.
How long before they actually start work? How much time do we have before—
Cushlamochree, Barnaby! Give your Fairy Godfather a hand here. Oh, my aching back!—
Mr. O'Malley!
JACKMORLEY
I measured off nine hundred and eighty-nine lengths of this six-inch ruler today—
That bending and stooping—
Gosh, Mr. O'Malley—

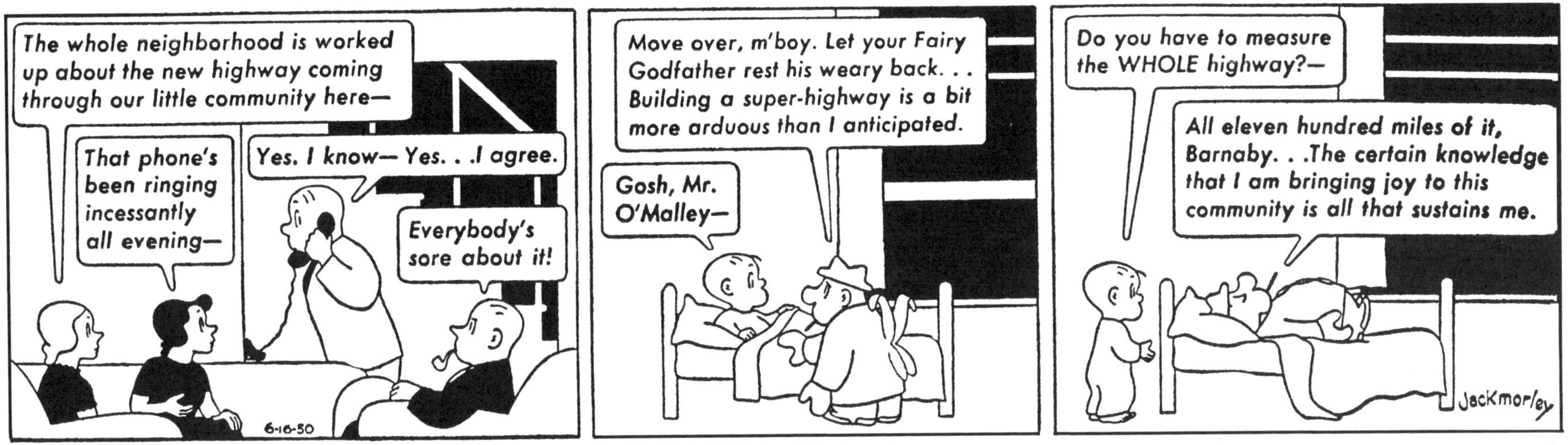
The whole neighborhood is worked up about the new highway coming through our little community here—
That phone's been ringing incessantly all evening—
Yes. I know— Yes. . .I agree.
Everybody's sore about it!
6-16-50
Move over, m'boy. Let your Fairy Godfather rest his weary back. . . Building a super-highway is a bit more arduous than I anticipated.
Gosh, Mr. O'Malley—
Do you have to measure the WHOLE highway?—
All eleven hundred miles of it, Barnaby. . .The certain knowledge that I am bringing joy to this community is all that sustains me.
JackMorley

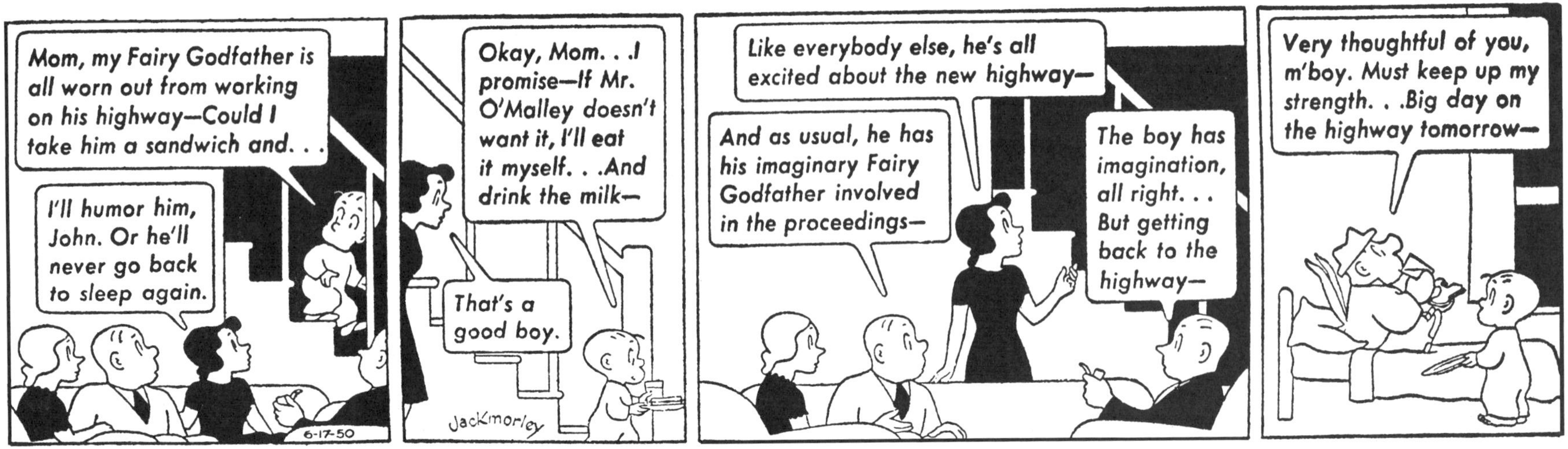
Mom, my Fairy Godfather is all worn out from working on his highway—Could I take him a sandwich and. . .
I'll humor him, John. Or he'll never go back to sleep again.
6-17-50
Okay, Mom. . .I promise—If Mr. O'Malley doesn't want it, I'll eat it myself. . .And drink the milk—
That's a good boy.
JackMorley
Like everybody else, he's all excited about the new highway—
And as usual, he has his imaginary Fairy Godfather involved in the proceedings—
The boy has imagination, all right. . . But getting back to the highway—
Very thoughtful of you, m'boy. Must keep up my strength. . .Big day on the highway tomorrow—

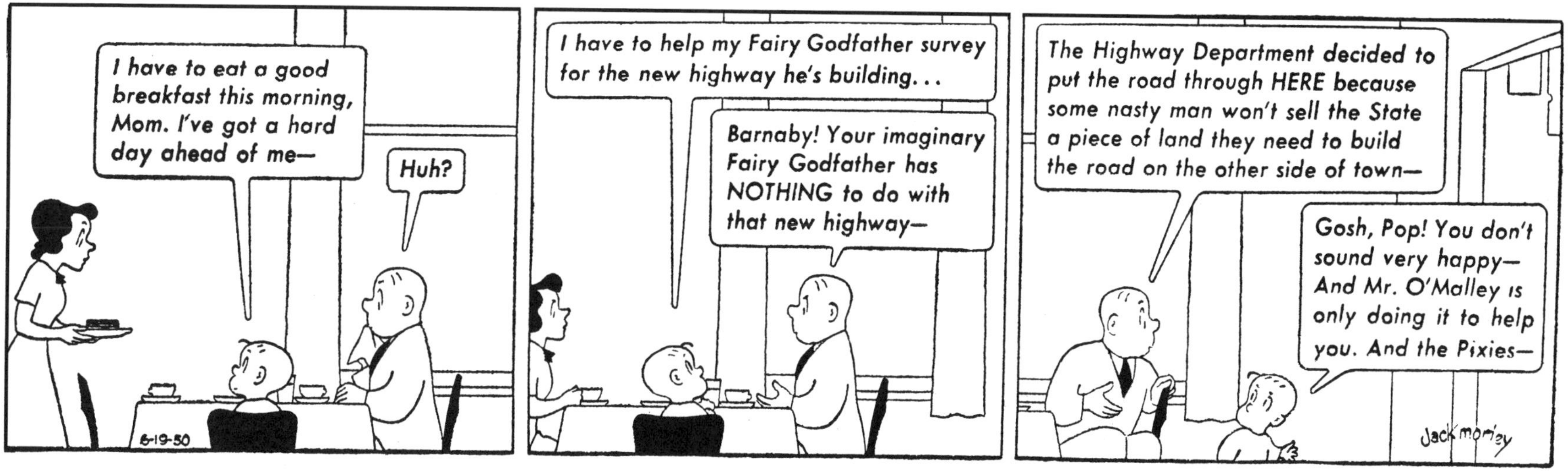
I have to eat a good breakfast this morning, Mom. I've got a hard day ahead of me—
Huh?
6-19-50
I have to help my Fairy Godfather survey for the new highway he's building...
Barnaby! Your imaginary Fairy Godfather has NOTHING to do with that new highway—
The Highway Department decided to put the road through HERE because some nasty man won't sell the State a piece of land they need to build the road on the other side of town—
Gosh, Pop! You don't sound very happy— And Mr. O'Malley is only doing it to help you. And the Pixies—
Jackmorley

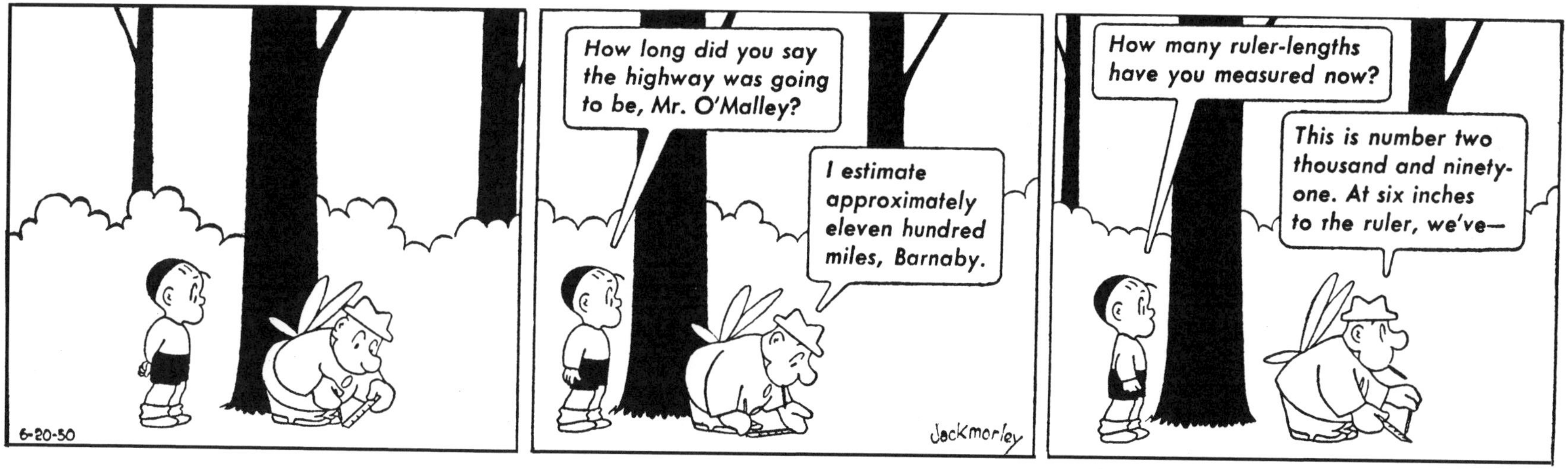
6-20-50
How long did you say the highway was going to be, Mr. O'Malley?
I estimate approximately eleven hundred miles, Barnaby.
Jackmorley
How many ruler-lengths have you measured now?
This is number two thousand and ninety-one. At six inches to the ruler, we've—

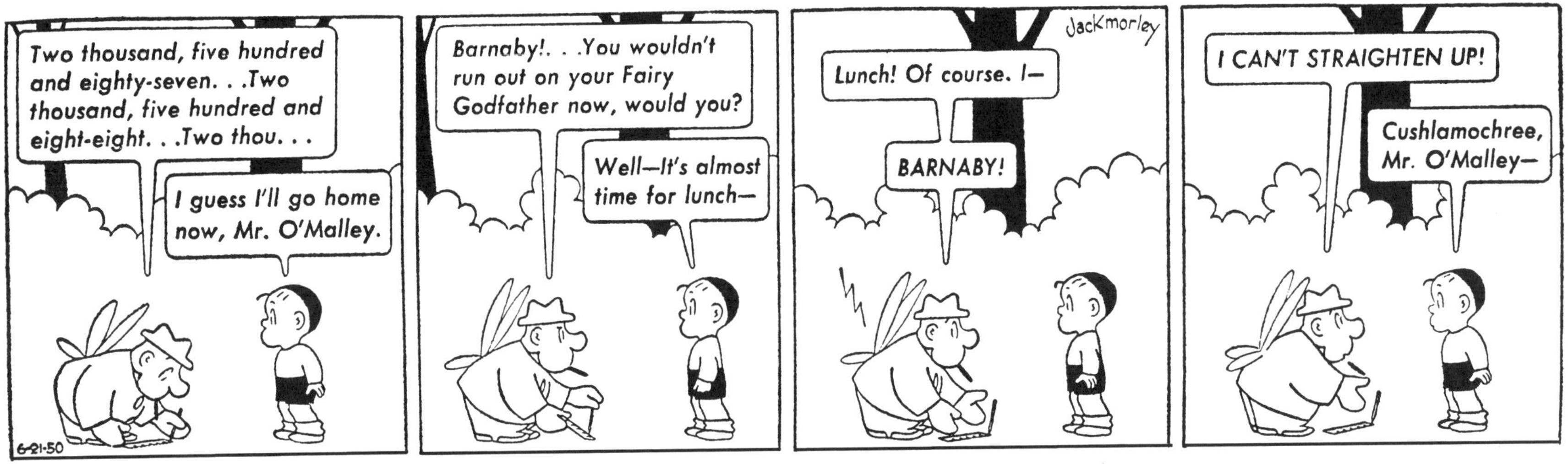
Two thousand, five hundred and eighty-seven. . .Two thousand, five hundred and eight-eight. . .Two thou. . .
I guess I'll go home now, Mr. O'Malley.
6-21-50
Barnaby!. . .You wouldn't run out on your Fairy Godfather now, would you?
Well—It's almost time for lunch—
Jackmorley
Lunch! Of course. I—
BARNABY!
I CAN'T STRAIGHTEN UP!
Cushlamochree, Mr. O'Malley—

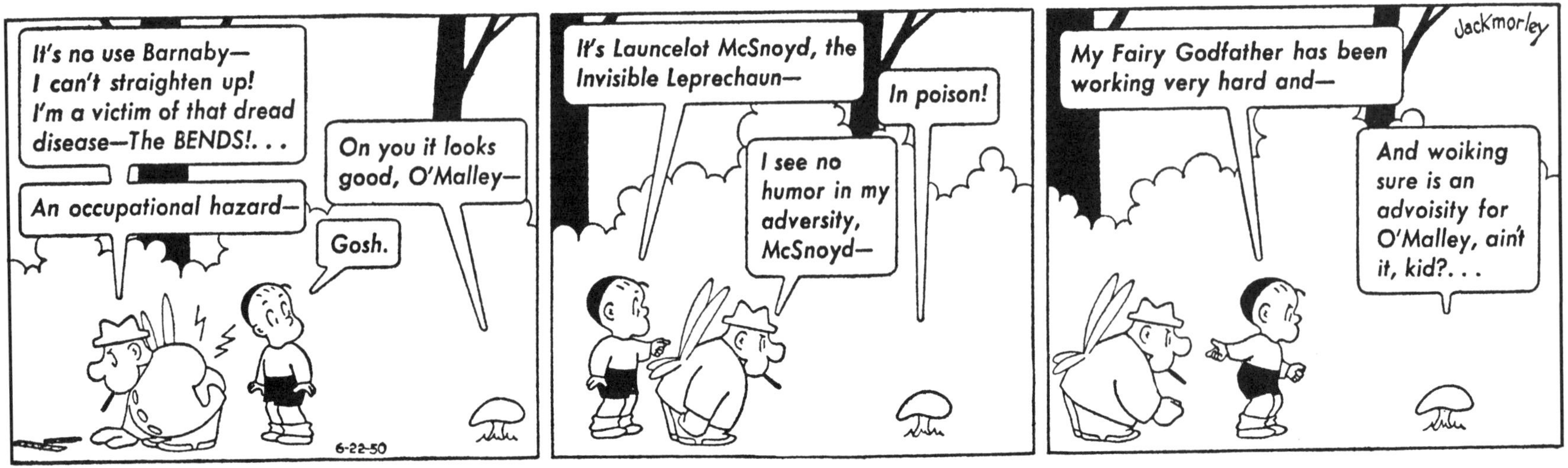
It's no use Barnaby—
I can't straighten up!
I'm a victim of that dread disease—The BENDS!. . .
An occupational hazard—
On you it looks good, O'Malley—
Gosh.
6-22-50
It's Launcelot McSnoyd, the Invisible Leprechaun—
In poison!
I see no humor in my adversity, McSnoyd—
Jackmorley
My Fairy Godfather has been working very hard and—
And woiking sure is an advoisity for O'Malley, ain't it, kid?. . .

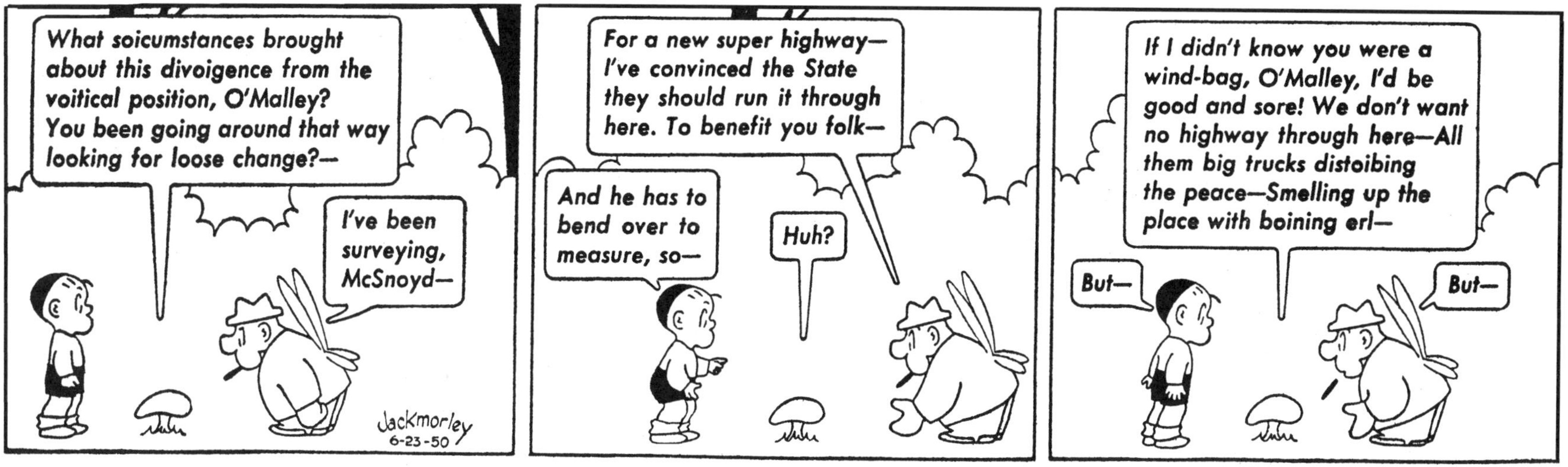
What soicumstances brought about this divoigence from the voitical position, O'Malley? You been going around that way looking for loose change?—
I've been surveying, McSnoyd—
Jackmorley
6-23-50
For a new super highway— I've convinced the State they should run it through here. To benefit you folk—
And he has to bend over to measure, so—
Huh?
If I didn't know you were a wind-bag, O'Malley, I'd be good and sore! We don't want no highway through here—All them big trucks distoibing the peace—Smelling up the place with boining erl—
But—
But—

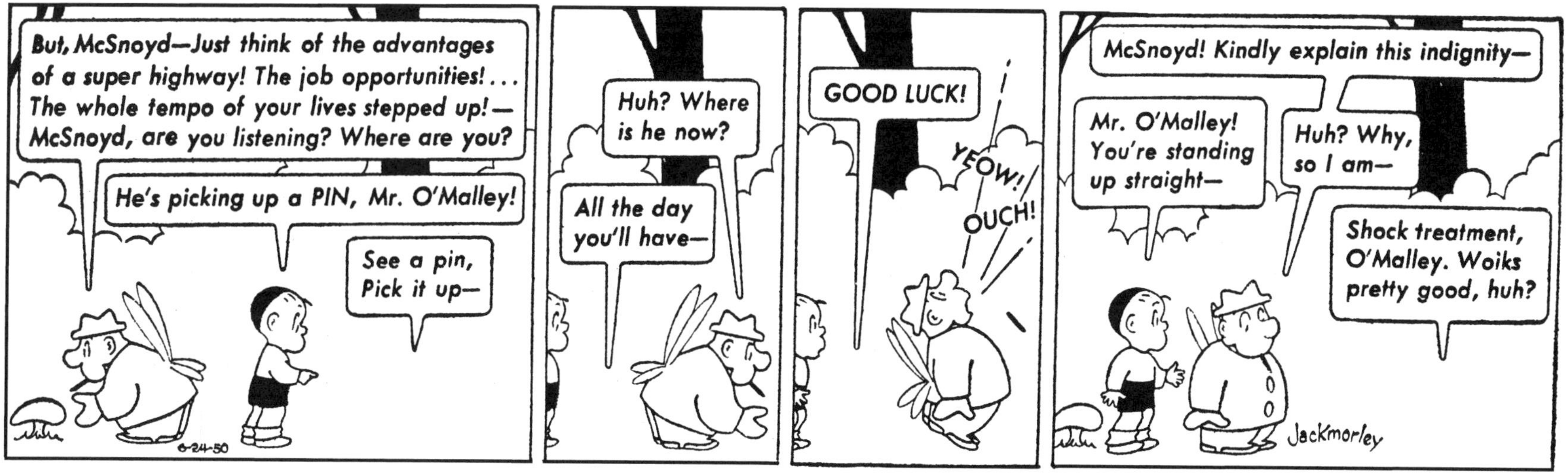
But, McSnoyd—Just think of the advantages of a super highway! The job opportunities! . . . The whole tempo of your lives stepped up!— —McSnoyd, are you listening? Where are you?
He's picking up a PIN, Mr. O'Malley!
See a pin, Pick it up—
6-24-50
Huh? Where is he now?
All the day you'll have—
GOOD LUCK!
YEOW!
OUCH!
McSnoyd! Kindly explain this indignity—
Mr. O'Malley! You're standing up straight—
Huh? Why, so I am—
Shock treatment, O'Malley. Woiks pretty good, huh?
Jackmorley

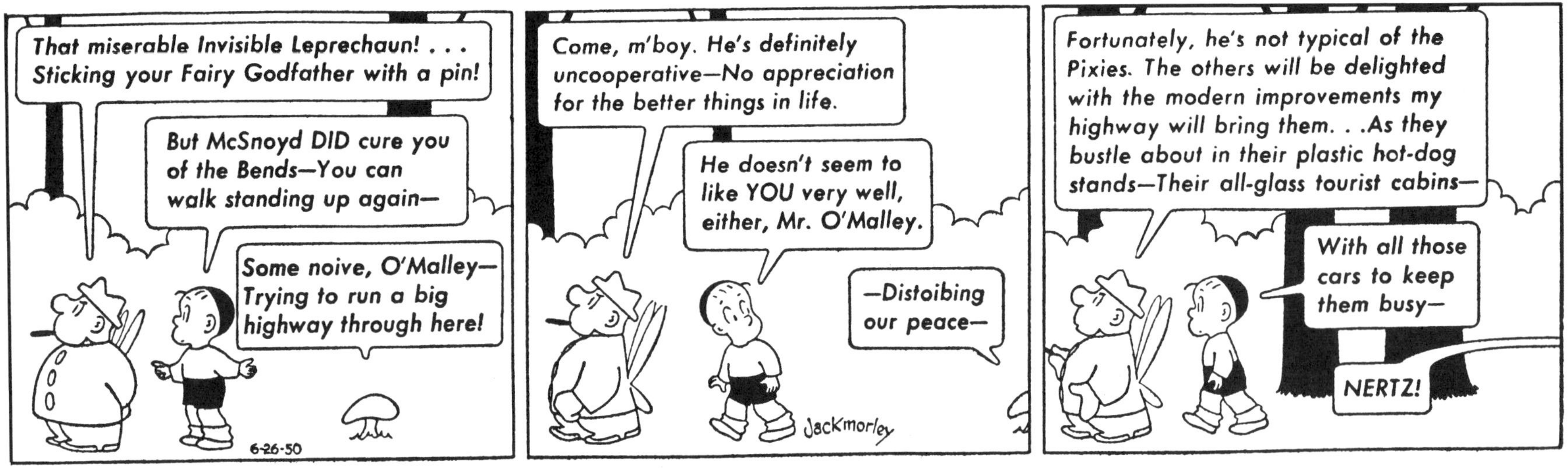
That miserable Invisible Leprechaun! . . . Sticking your Fairy Godfather with a pin!
But McSnoyd DID cure you of the Bends—You can walk standing up again—
Some noive, O'Malley—Trying to run a big highway through here!
6-26-50
Come, m'boy. He's definitely uncooperative—No appreciation for the better things in life.
He doesn't seem to like YOU very well, either, Mr. O'Malley.
—Distoibing our peace—
Jackmorley
Fortunately, he's not typical of the Pixies. The others will be delighted with the modern improvements my highway will bring them. . .As they bustle about in their plastic hot-dog stands—Their all-glass tourist cabins—
With all those cars to keep them busy—
NERTZ!

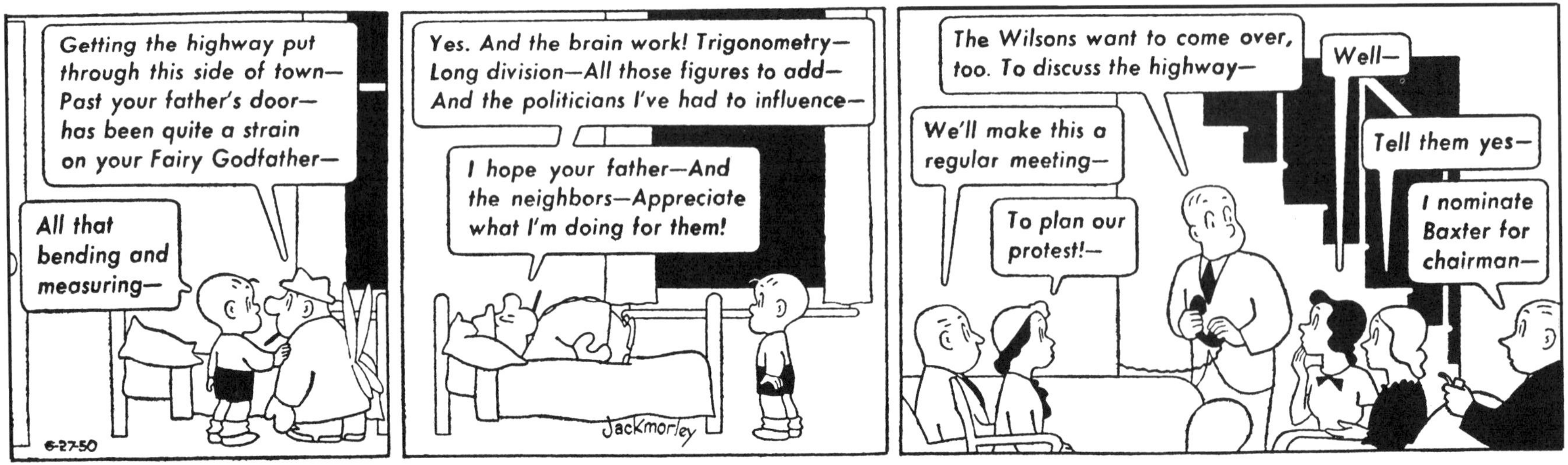
Getting the highway put through this side of town—Past your father's door—has been quite a strain on your Fairy Godfather—
All that bending and measuring—
6-27-50
Yes. And the brain work! Trigonometry—Long division—All those figures to add—And the politicians I've had to influence—
I hope your father—And the neighbors—Appreciate what I'm doing for them!
Jackmorley
The Wilsons want to come over, too. To discuss the highway—
We'll make this a regular meeting—
To plan our protest!—
Well—
Tell them yes—
I nominate Baxter for chairman—

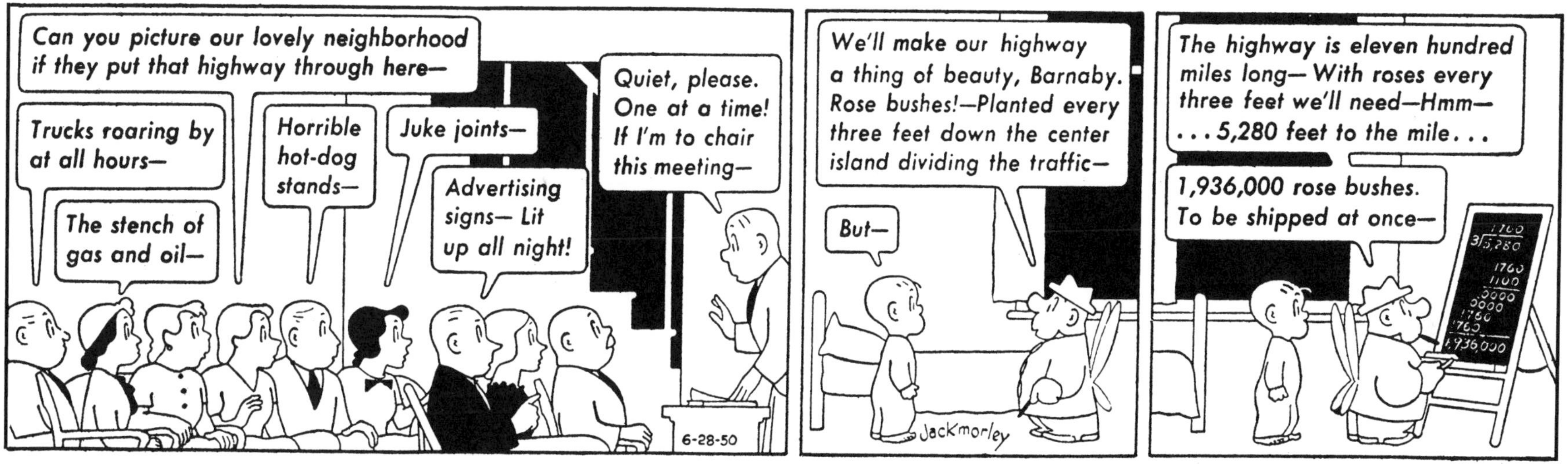
Can you picture our lovely neighborhood if they put that highway through here—
Trucks roaring by at all hours—
The stench of gas and oil—
Horrible hot-dog stands—
Juke joints—
Advertising signs— Lit up all night!
Quiet, please. One at a time! If I'm to chair this meeting—
6-28-50
We'll make our highway a thing of beauty, Barnaby. Rose bushes!—Planted every three feet down the center island dividing the traffic—
But—
JackMorley
The highway is eleven hundred miles long— With roses every three feet we'll need—Hmm— . . . 5,280 feet to the mile . . .
1,936,000 rose bushes. To be shipped at once—

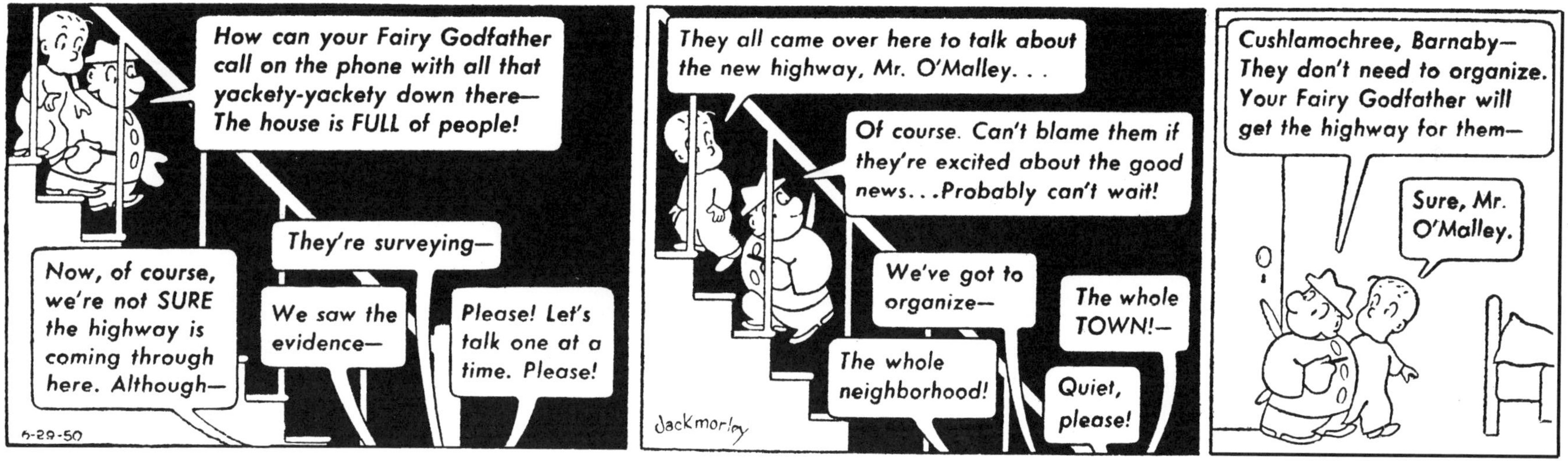
How can your Fairy Godfather call on the phone with all that yackety-yackety down there— The house is FULL of people!
Now, of course, we're not SURE the highway is coming through here. Although—
They're surveying—
We saw the evidence—
Please! Let's talk one at a time. Please!
6-29-50
They all came over here to talk about the new highway, Mr. O'Malley. . .
Of course. Can't blame them if they're excited about the good news. . .Probably can't wait!
We've got to organize—
The whole TOWN!—
The whole neighborhood!
Quiet, please!
JackMorley
Cushlamochree, Barnaby— They don't need to organize. Your Fairy Godfather will get the highway for them—
Sure, Mr. O'Malley.

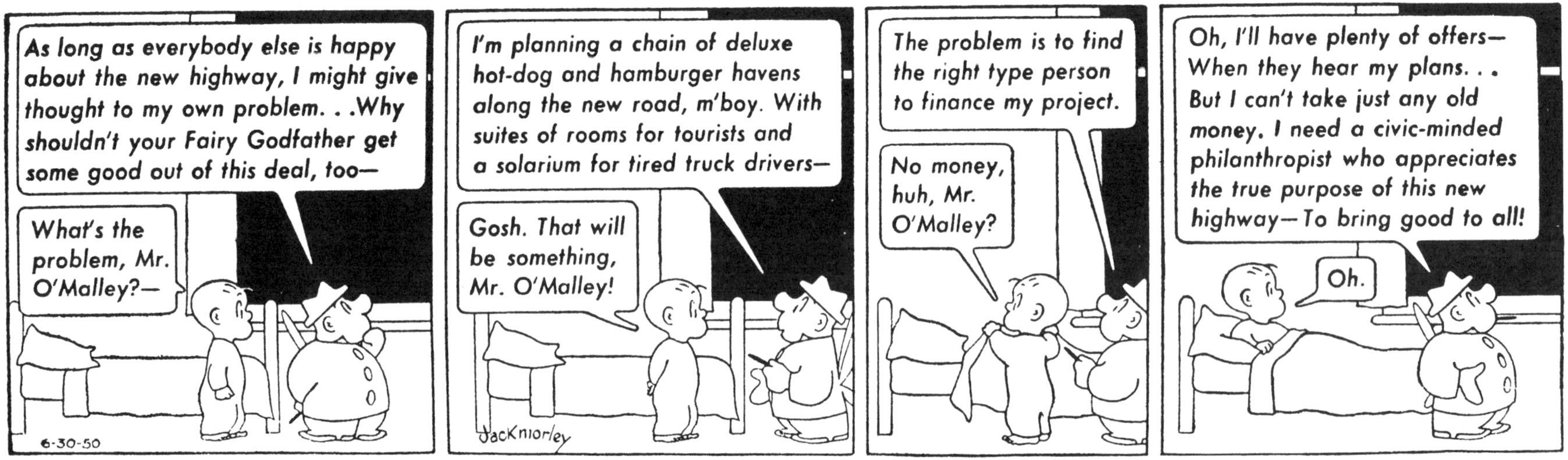
As long as everybody else is happy about the new highway, I might give thought to my own problem. . .Why shouldn't your Fairy Godfather get some good out of this deal, too—
What's the problem, Mr. O'Malley?—
6-30-50
I'm planning a chain of deluxe hot-dog and hamburger havens along the new road, m'boy. With suites of rooms for tourists and a solarium for tired truck drivers—
Gosh. That will be something, Mr. O'Malley!
JackMorley
The problem is to find the right type person to finance my project.
No money, huh, Mr. O'Malley?
Oh, I'll have plenty of offers— When they hear my plans. . . But I can't take just any old money. I need a civic-minded philanthropist who appreciates the true purpose of this new highway—To bring good to all!
Oh.

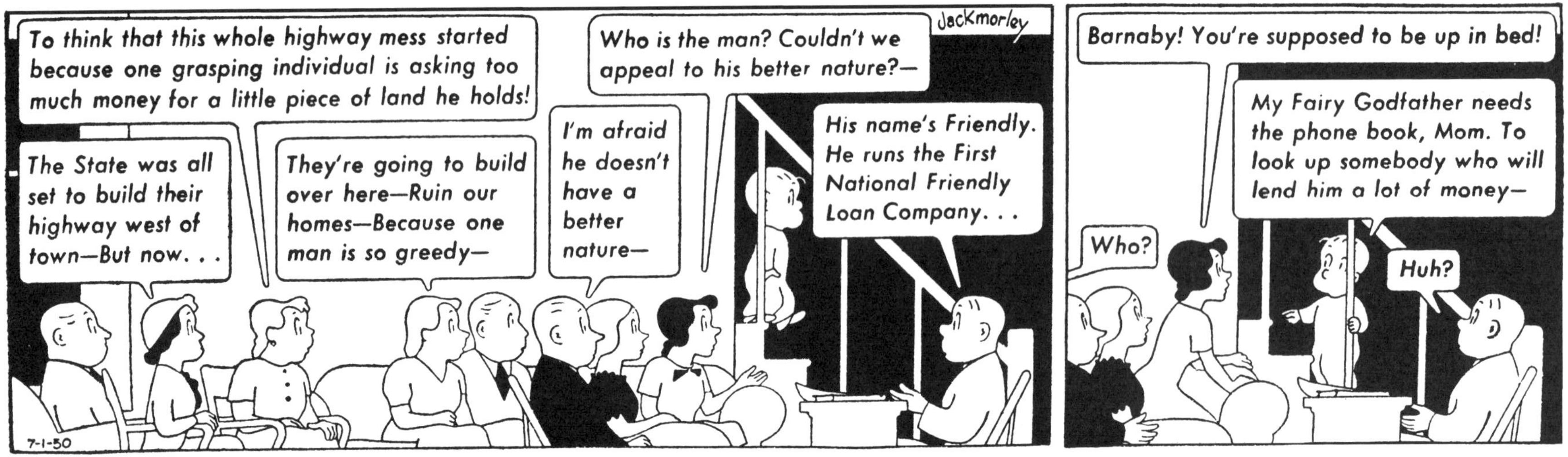
To think that this whole highway mess started because one grasping individual is asking too much money for a little piece of land he holds!
The State was all set to build their highway west of town—But now. . .
They're going to build over here—Ruin our homes—Because one man is so greedy—
I'm afraid he doesn't have a better nature—
Who is the man? Couldn't we appeal to his better nature?—
His name's Friendly. He runs the First National Friendly Loan Company. . .
JackMorley
7-1-50
Barnaby! You're supposed to be up in bed!
My Fairy Godfather needs the phone book, Mom. To look up somebody who will lend him a lot of money—
Who?
Huh?

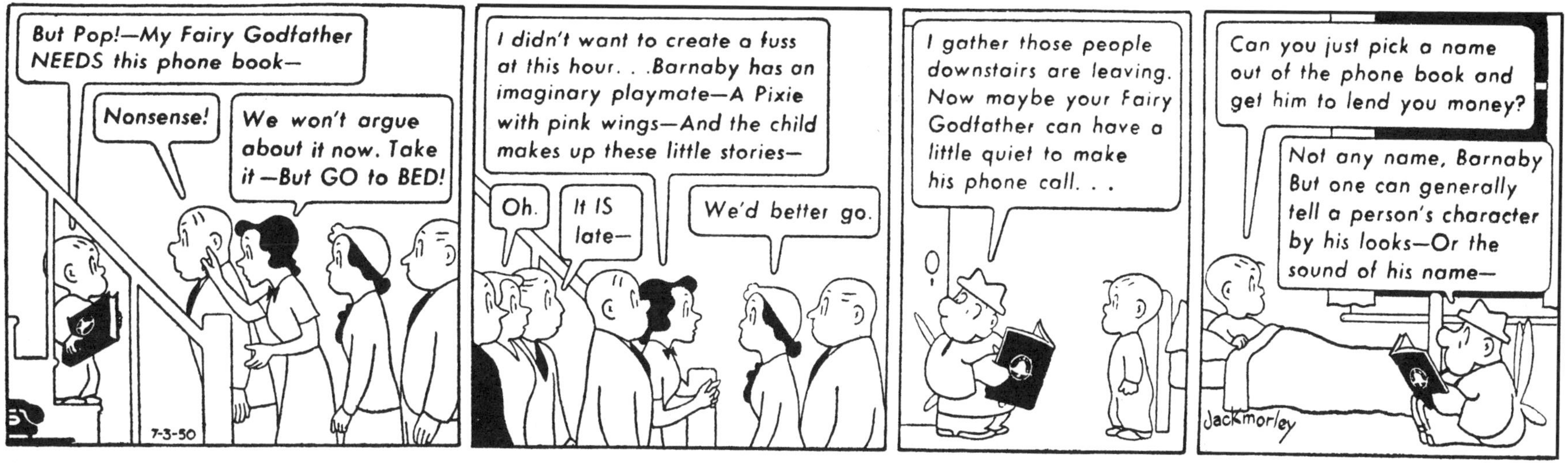
But Pop!—My Fairy Godfather NEEDS this phone book—
Nonsense!
We won't argue about it now. Take it—But GO to BED!
7-3-50
I didn't want to create a fuss at this hour. . .Barnaby has an imaginary playmate—A Pixie with pink wings—And the child makes up these little stories—
Oh.
It IS late—
We'd better go.
I gather those people downstairs are leaving. Now maybe your Fairy Godfather can have a little quiet to make his phone call. . .
Can you just pick a name out of the phone book and get him to lend you money?
Not any name, Barnaby But one can generally tell a person's character by his looks—Or the sound of his name—
Jackmorley

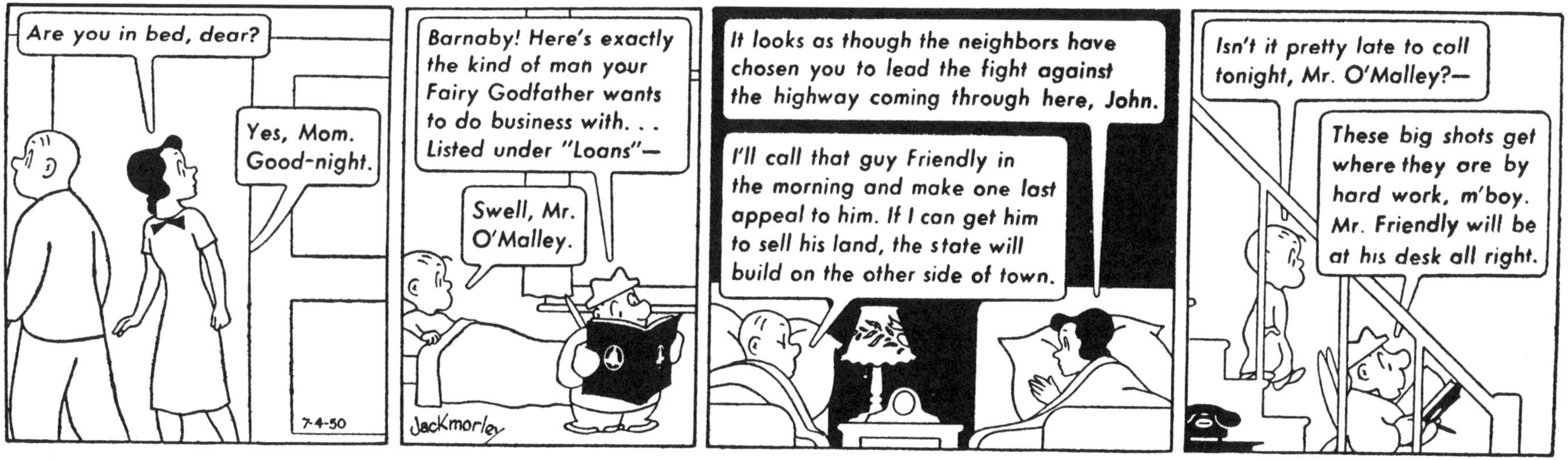
Are you in bed, dear?
Yes, Mom. Good-night.
7-4-50
Barnaby! Here's exactly the kind of man your Fairy Godfather wants to do business with. . . Listed under "Loans"—
Swell, Mr. O'Malley.
Jackmorley
It looks as though the neighbors have chosen you to lead the fight against the highway coming through here, John.
I'll call that guy Friendly in the morning and make one last appeal to him. If I can get him to sell his land, the state will build on the other side of town.
Isn't it pretty late to call tonight, Mr. O'Malley?—
These big shots get where they are by hard work, m'boy. Mr. Friendly will be at his desk all right.

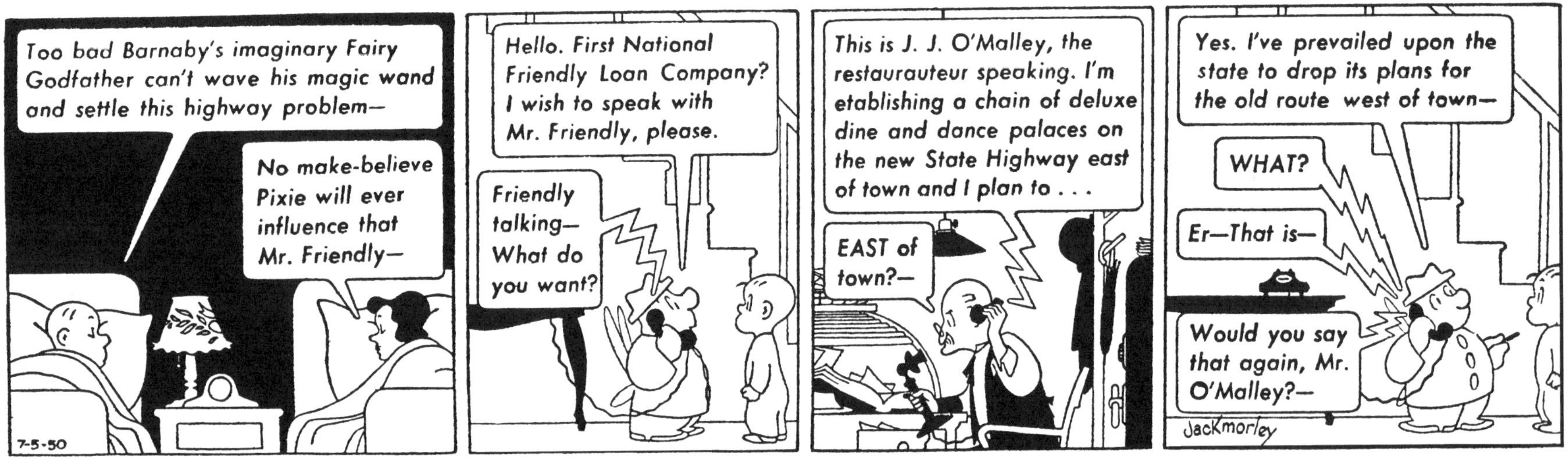
Too bad Barnaby's imaginary Fairy Godfather can't wave his magic wand and settle this highway problem—
No make-believe Pixie will ever influence that Mr. Friendly—
7-5-50
Hello. First National Friendly Loan Company? I wish to speak with Mr. Friendly, please.
Friendly talking— What do you want?
This is J. J. O'Malley, the restaurauteur speaking. I'm etablishing a chain of deluxe dine and dance palaces on the new State Highway east of town and I plan to . . .
EAST of town?—
Yes. I've prevailed upon the state to drop its plans for the old route west of town—
WHAT?
Er—That is—
Would you say that again, Mr. O'Malley?—
JacKmorley

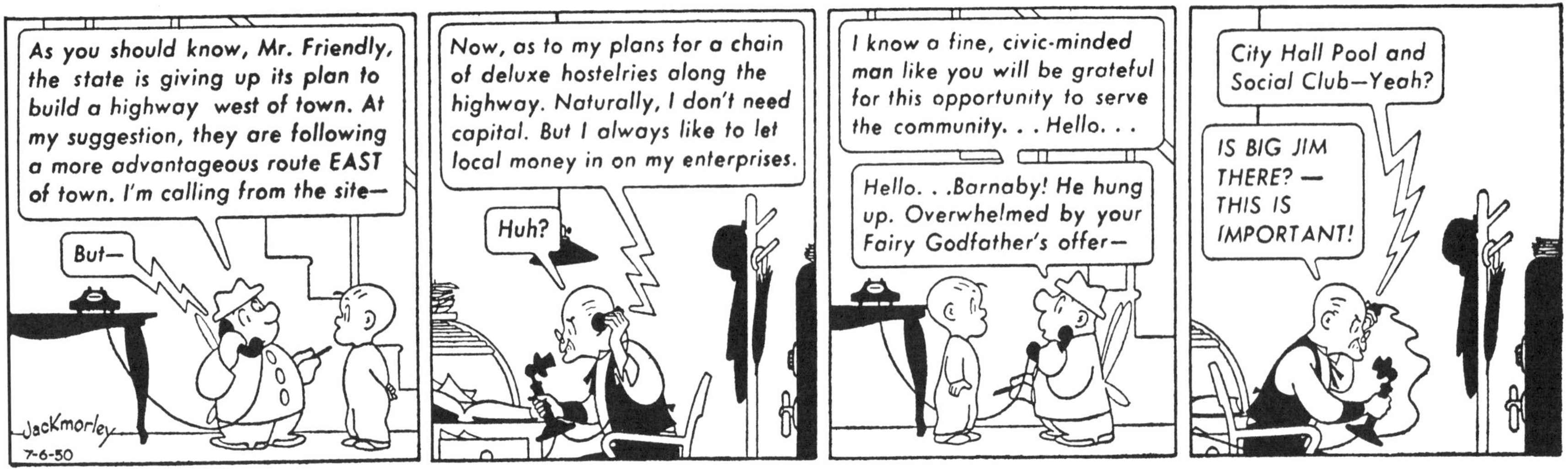
As you should know, Mr. Friendly, the state is giving up its plan to build a highway west of town. At my suggestion, they are following a more advantageous route EAST of town. I'm calling from the site—
But—
JacKmorley
7-6-50
Now, as to my plans for a chain of deluxe hostelries along the highway. Naturally, I don't need capital. But I always like to let local money in on my enterprises.
Huh?
I know a fine, civic-minded man like you will be grateful for this opportunity to serve the community. . . Hello. . .
Hello. . .Barnaby! He hung up. Overwhelmed by your Fairy Godfather's offer—
City Hall Pool and Social Club—Yeah?
IS BIG JIM THERE? — THIS IS IMPORTANT!

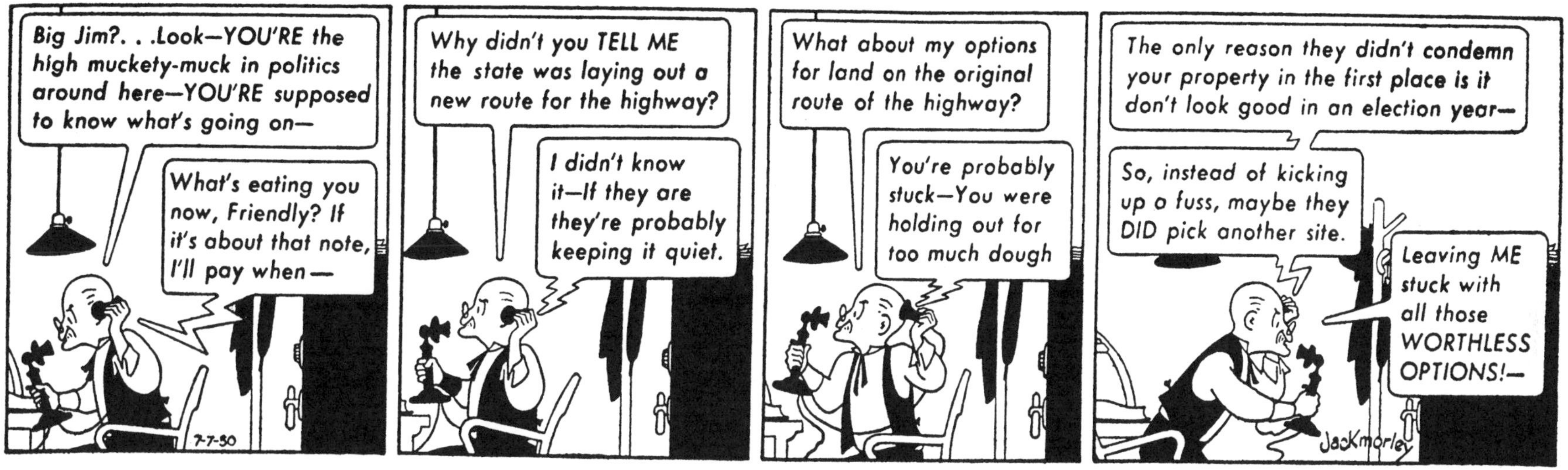

Big Jim?. . .Look—YOU'RE the high muckety-muck in politics around here—YOU'RE supposed to know what's going on—
What's eating you now, Friendly? If it's about that note, I'll pay when—
7-7-50
Why didn't you TELL ME the state was laying out a new route for the highway?
I didn't know it—If they are they're probably keeping it quiet.
What about my options for land on the original route of the highway?
You're probably stuck—You were holding out for too much dough
The only reason they didn't condemn your property in the first place is it don't look good in an election year—
So, instead of kicking up a fuss, maybe they DID pick another site.
Leaving ME stuck with all those WORTHLESS OPTIONS!—
JackMorley

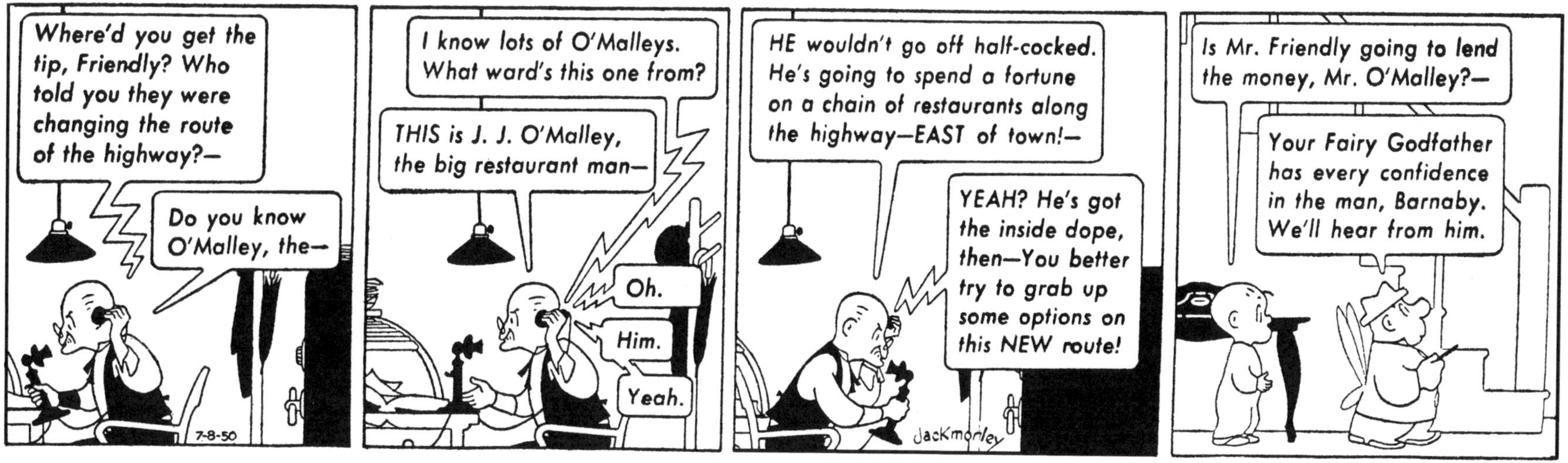

Where'd you get the tip, Friendly? Who told you they were changing the route of the highway?—
Do you know O'Malley, the—
7-8-50
I know lots of O'Malleys. What ward's this one from?
THIS is J. J. O'Malley, the big restaurant man—
Oh.
Him.
Yeah.
HE wouldn't go off half-cocked. He's going to spend a fortune on a chain of restaurants along the highway—EAST of town!—
YEAH? He's got the inside dope, then—You better try to grab up some options on this NEW route!
JackMorley
Is Mr. Friendly going to lend the money, Mr. O'Malley?—
Your Fairy Godfather has every confidence in the man, Barnaby. We'll hear from him.

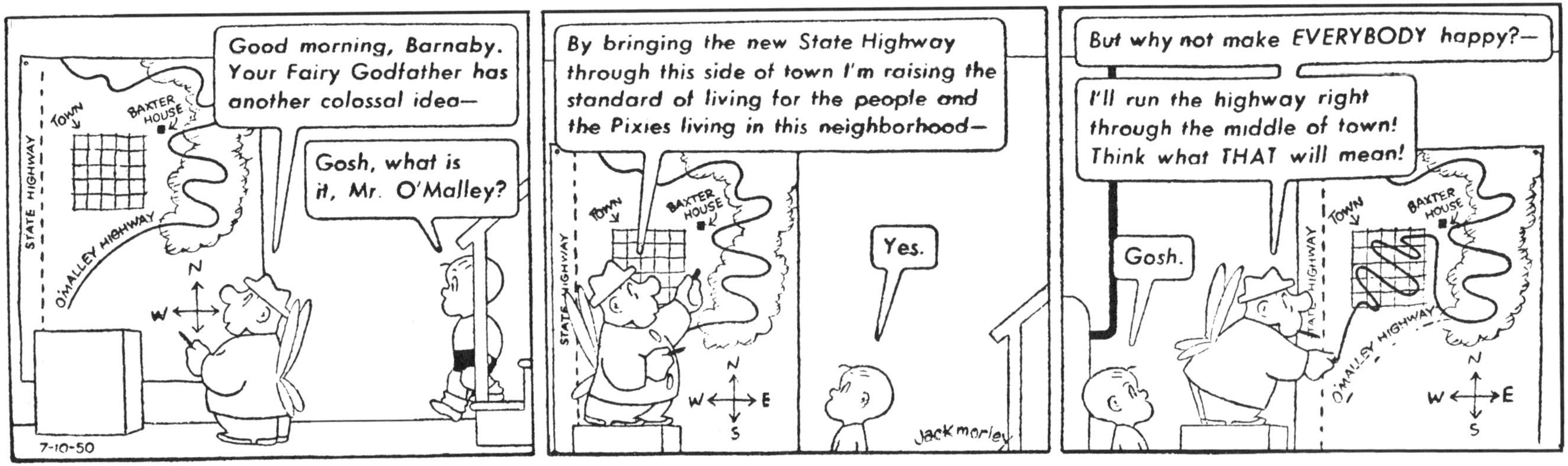
Good morning, Barnaby. Your Fairy Godfather has another colossal idea—
Gosh, what is it, Mr. O'Malley?
By bringing the new State Highway through this side of town I'm raising the standard of living for the people and the Pixies living in this neighborhood—
Yes.
But why not make EVERYBODY happy?—
I'll run the highway right through the middle of town! Think what THAT will mean!
Gosh.
STATE HIGHWAY
TOWN
BAXTER HOUSE
O'MALLEY HIGHWAY
N
W
E
S
7-10-50
Jack Morley

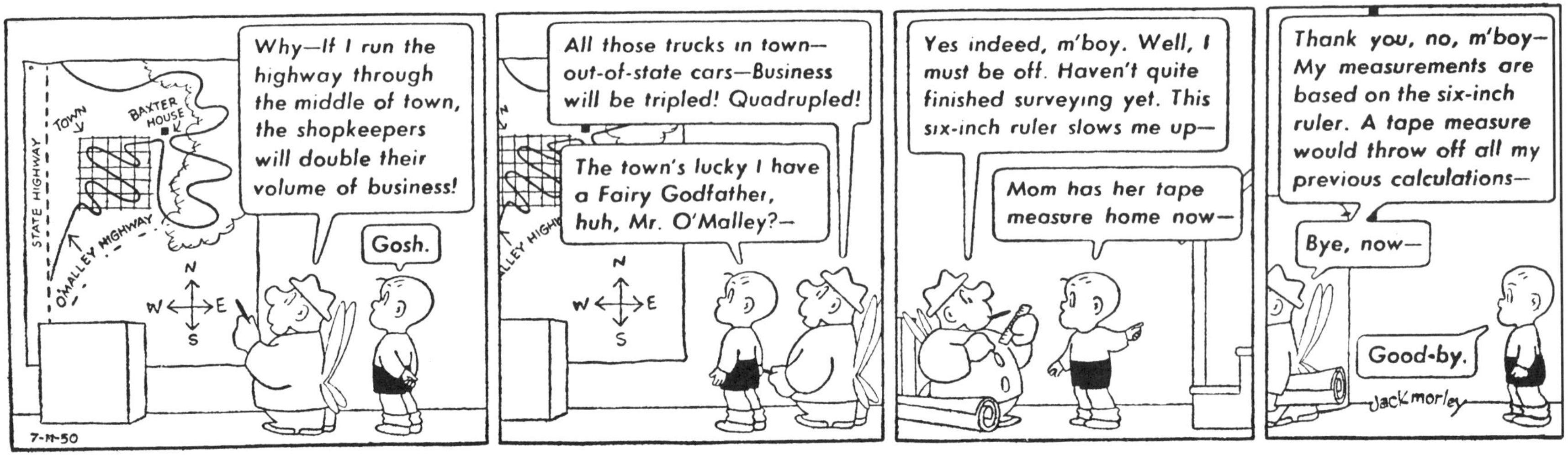
Why—If I run the highway through the middle of town, the shopkeepers will double their volume of business!
Gosh.
All those trucks in town—out-of-state cars—Business will be tripled! Quadrupled!
The town's lucky I have a Fairy Godfather, huh, Mr. O'Malley?—
Yes indeed, m'boy. Well, I must be off. Haven't quite finished surveying yet. This six-inch ruler slows me up—
Mom has her tape measure home now—
Thank you, no, m'boy—My measurements are based on the six-inch ruler. A tape measure would throw off all my previous calculations—
Bye, now—
Good-by.
STATE HIGHWAY
TOWN
BAXTER HOUSE
O'MALLEY HIGHWAY
N
W
E
S
7-11-50
Jack Morley

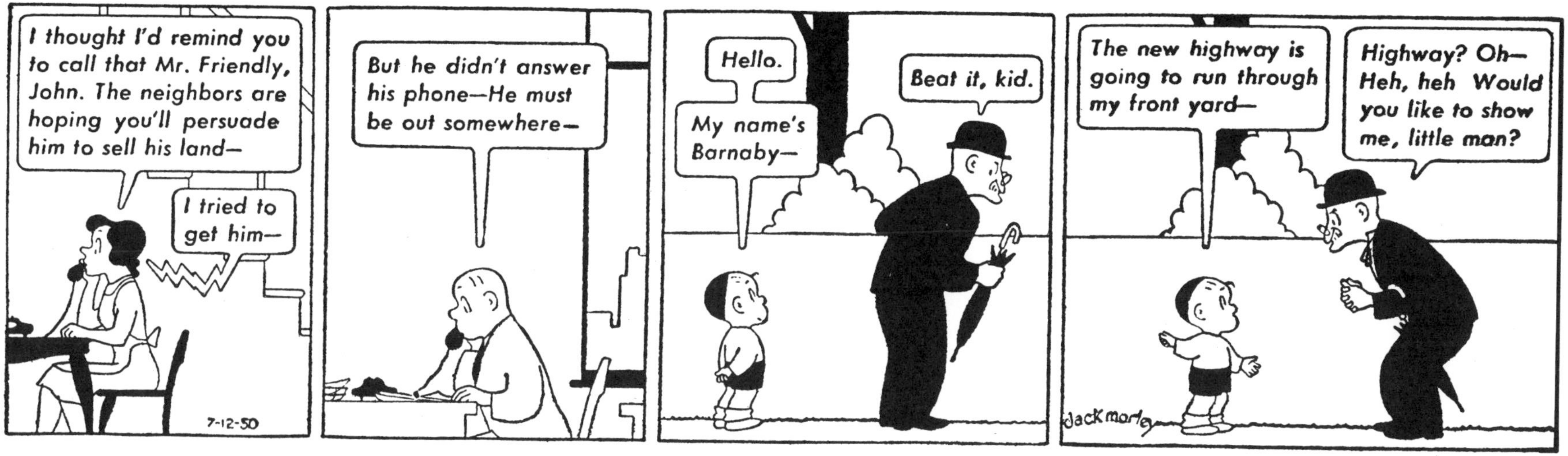
I thought I'd remind you to call that Mr. Friendly, John. The neighbors are hoping you'll persuade him to sell his land—
I tried to get him—
7-12-50
But he didn't answer his phone—He must be out somewhere—
Hello.
My name's Barnaby—
Beat it, kid.
The new highway is going to run through my front yard—
Highway? Oh—Heh, heh Would you like to show me, little man?
Jack Morley

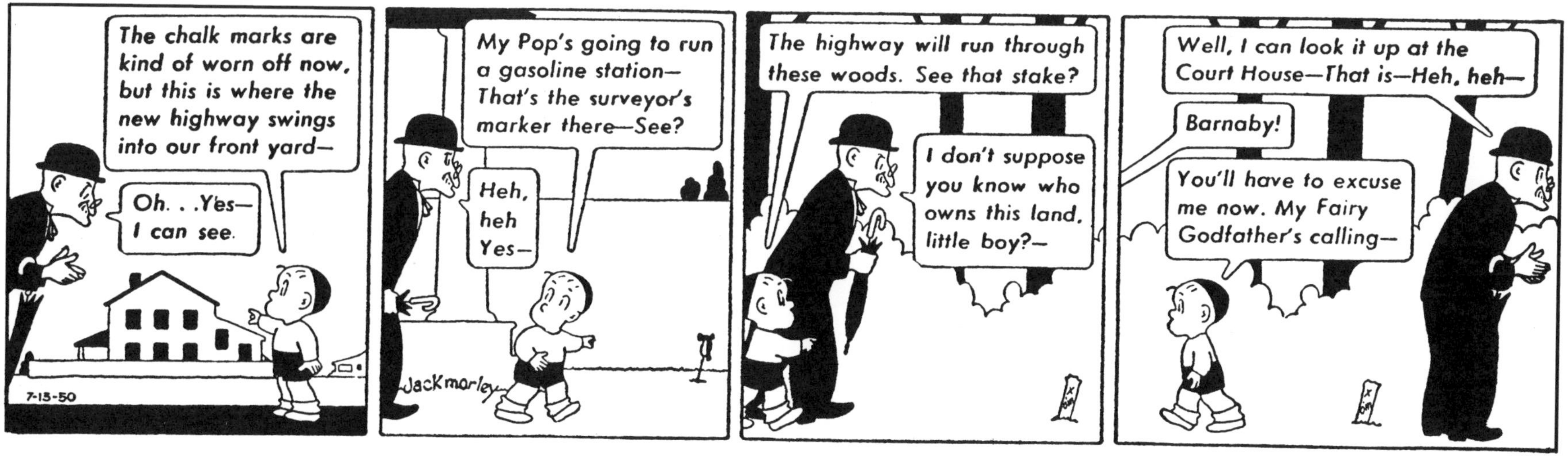
The chalk marks are kind of worn off now, but this is where the new highway swings into our front yard—
Oh. . .Yes—I can see.
7-13-50
My Pop's going to run a gasoline station—That's the surveyor's marker there—See?
Heh, heh Yes—
Jack Morley
The highway will run through these woods. See that stake?
I don't suppose you know who owns this land, little boy?—
Well, I can look it up at the Court House—That is—Heh, heh—
Barnaby!
You'll have to excuse me now. My Fairy Godfather's calling—

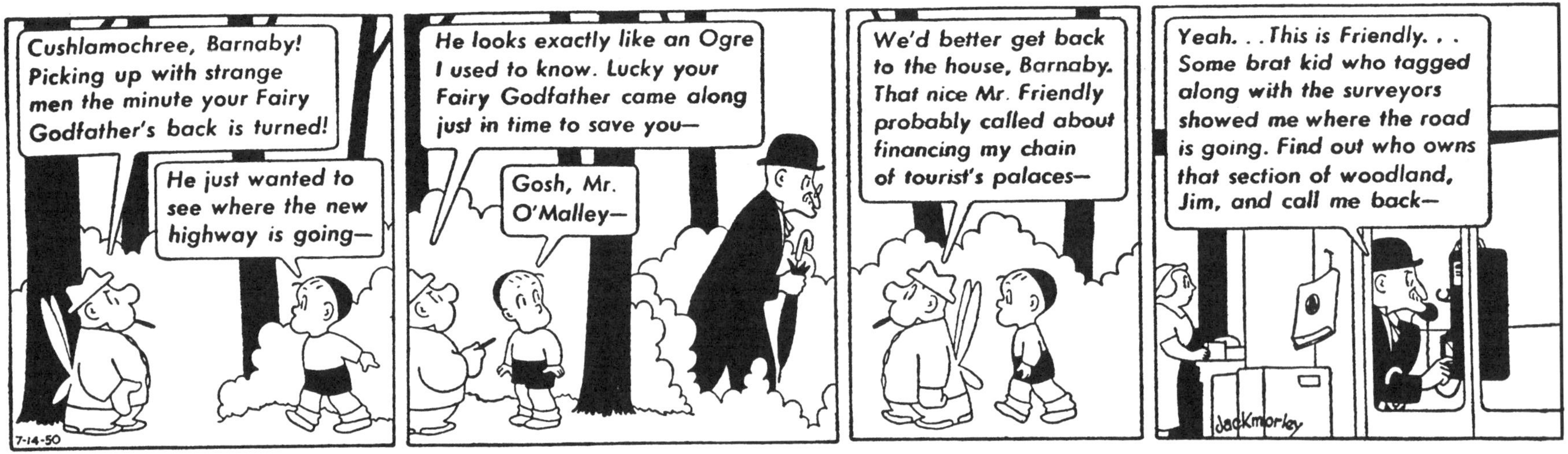
Cushlamochree, Barnaby! Picking up with strange men the minute your Fairy Godfather's back is turned!
He just wanted to see where the new highway is going—
7-14-50
He looks exactly like an Ogre I used to know. Lucky your Fairy Godfather came along just in time to save you—
Gosh, Mr. O'Malley—
We'd better get back to the house, Barnaby. That nice Mr. Friendly probably called about financing my chain of tourist's palaces—
Yeah. . . This is Friendly. . . Some brat kid who tagged along with the surveyors showed me where the road is going. Find out who owns that section of woodland, Jim, and call me back—
JackMorley

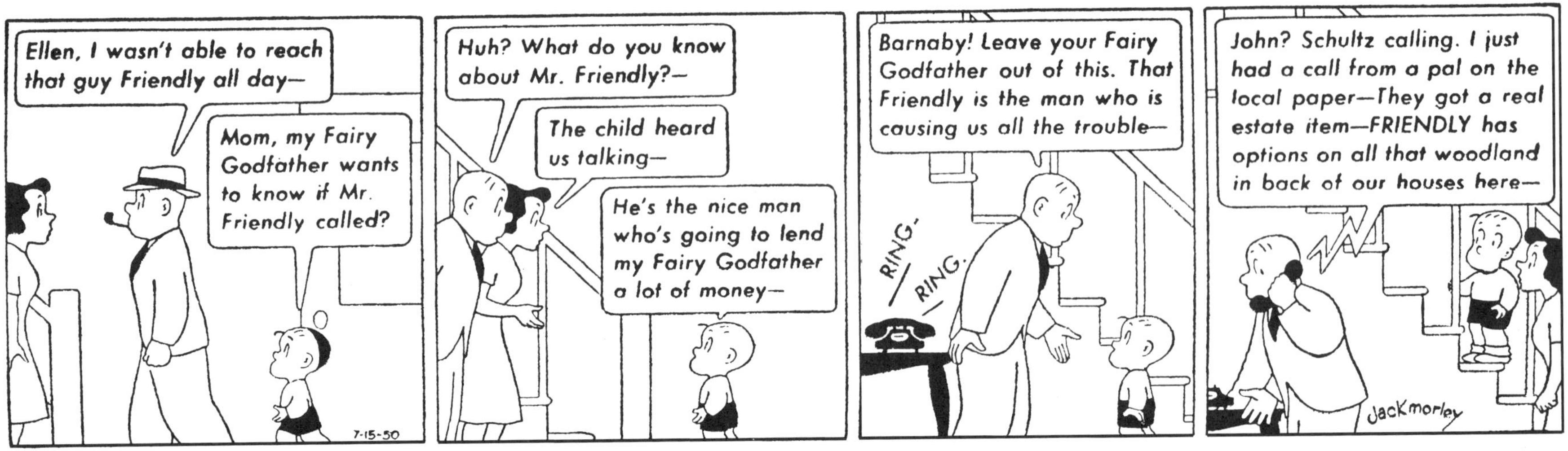
Ellen, I wasn't able to reach that guy Friendly all day—
Mom, my Fairy Godfather wants to know if Mr. Friendly called?
7-15-50
Huh? What do you know about Mr. Friendly?—
The child heard us talking—
He's the nice man who's going to lend my Fairy Godfather a lot of money—
Barnaby! Leave your Fairy Godfather out of this. That Friendly is the man who is causing us all the trouble—
RING-
RING.
John? Schultz calling. I just had a call from a pal on the local paper—They got a real estate item—FRIENDLY has options on all that woodland in back of our houses here—
JackMorley

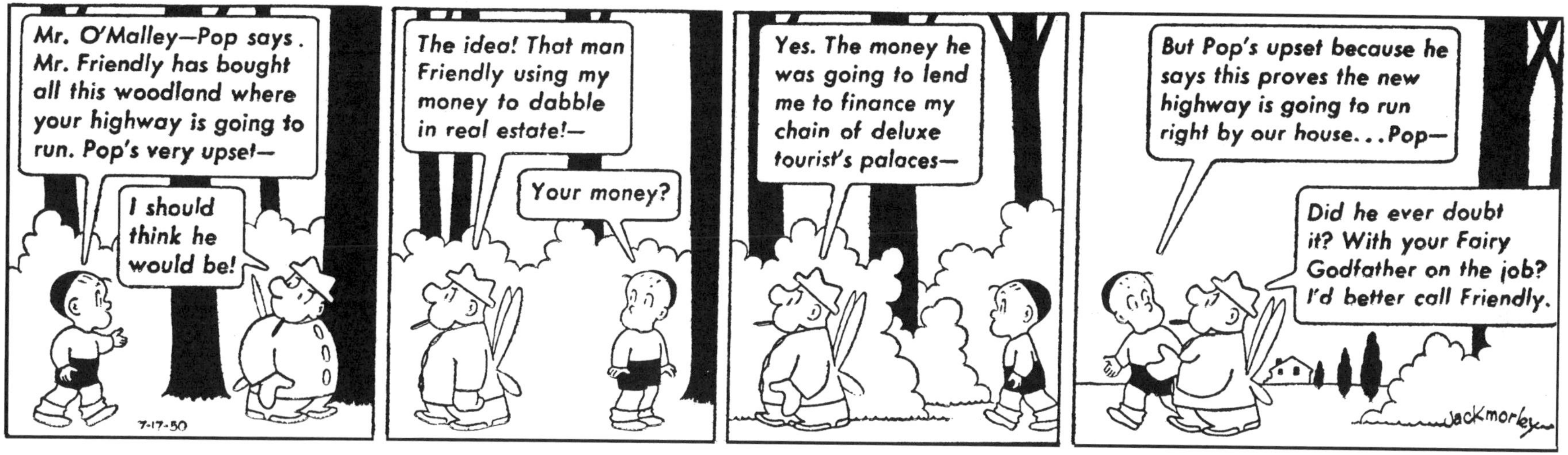
Mr. O'Malley—Pop says. Mr. Friendly has bought all this woodland where your highway is going to run. Pop's very upset—
I should think he would be!
7-17-50
The idea! That man Friendly using my money to dabble in real estate!—
Your money?
Yes. The money he was going to lend me to finance my chain of deluxe tourist's palaces—
But Pop's upset because he says this proves the new highway is going to run right by our house...Pop—
Did he ever doubt it? With your Fairy Godfather on the job? I'd better call Friendly.
Jack morley

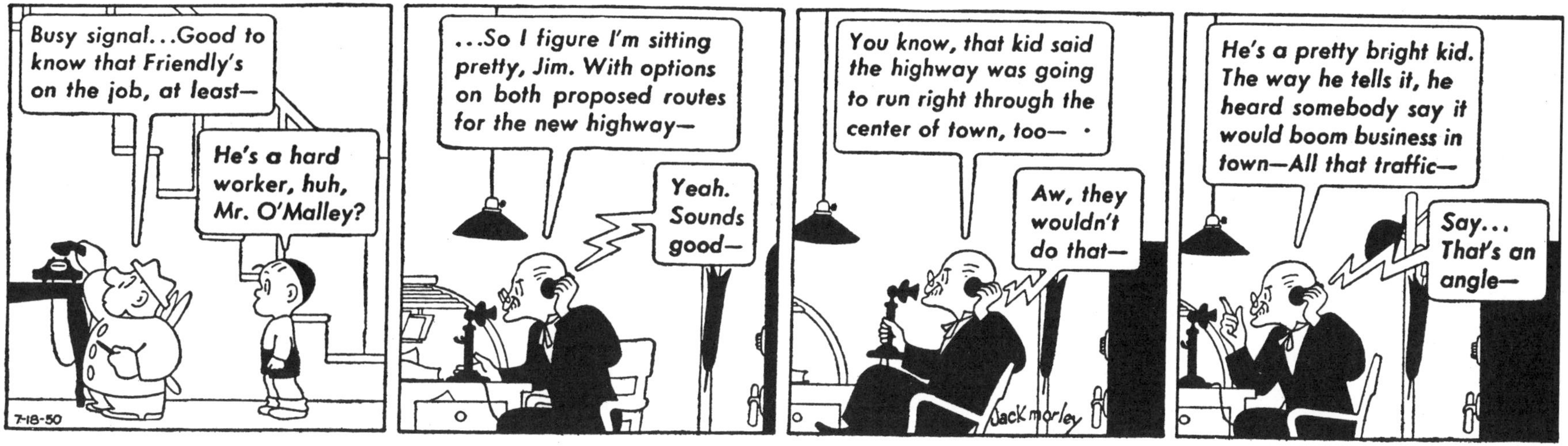
Busy signal...Good to know that Friendly's on the job, at least—
He's a hard worker, huh, Mr. O'Malley?
7-18-50
...So I figure I'm sitting pretty, Jim. With options on both proposed routes for the new highway—
Yeah. Sounds good—
You know, that kid said the highway was going to run right through the center of town, too—
Aw, they wouldn't do that—
Jack morley
He's a pretty bright kid. The way he tells it, he heard somebody say it would boom business in town—All that traffic—
Say... That's an angle—

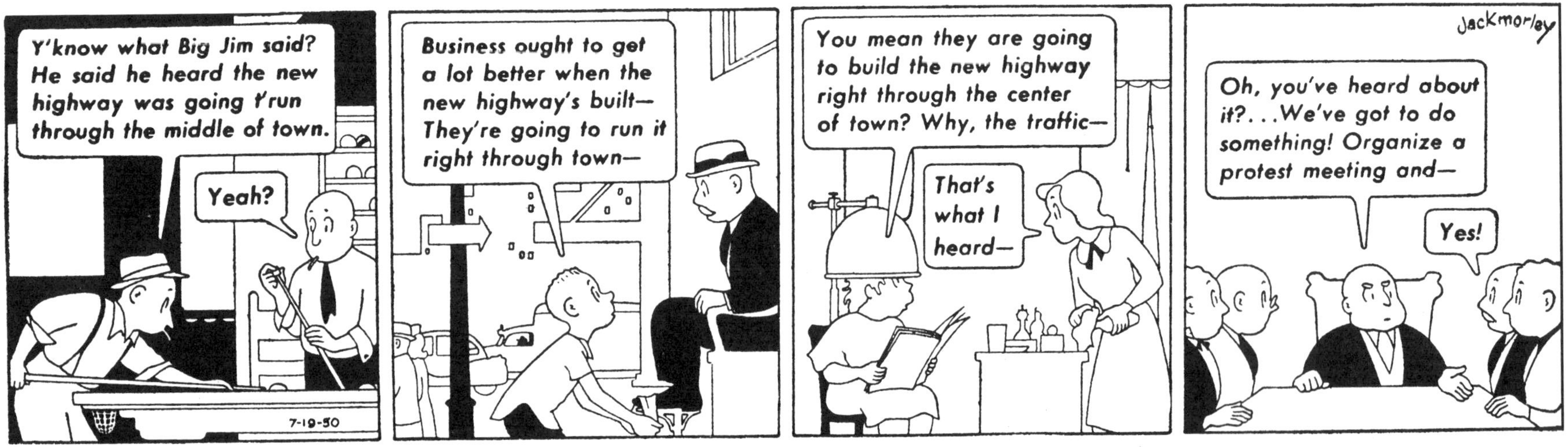
Y'know what Big Jim said? He said he heard the new highway was going t'run through the middle of town.
Yeah?
7-19-50
Business ought to get a lot better when the new highway's built—They're going to run it right through town—
You mean they are going to build the new highway right through the center of town? Why, the traffic—
That's what I heard—
JackMorley
Oh, you've heard about it?...We've got to do something! Organize a protest meeting and—
Yes!

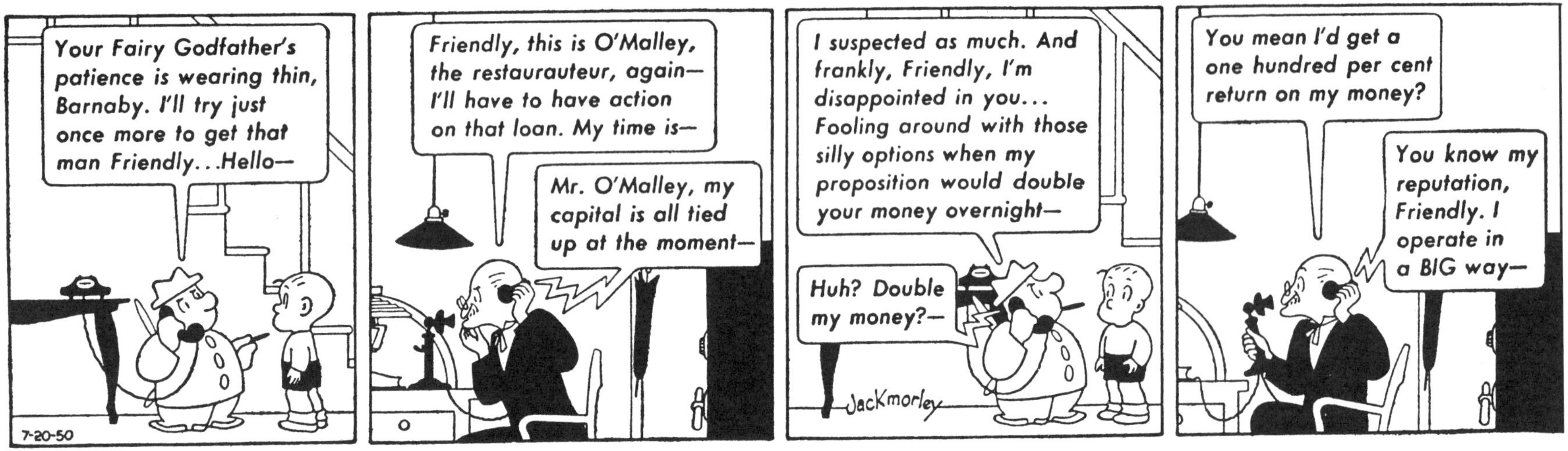
Your Fairy Godfather's patience is wearing thin, Barnaby. I'll try just once more to get that man Friendly...Hello—
7-20-50
Friendly, this is O'Malley, the restaurauteur, again—I'll have to have action on that loan. My time is—
Mr. O'Malley, my capital is all tied up at the moment—
I suspected as much. And frankly, Friendly, I'm disappointed in you... Fooling around with those silly options when my proposition would double your money overnight—
Huh? Double my money?—
JackMorley
You mean I'd get a one hundred per cent return on my money?
You know my reputation, Friendly. I operate in a BIG way—

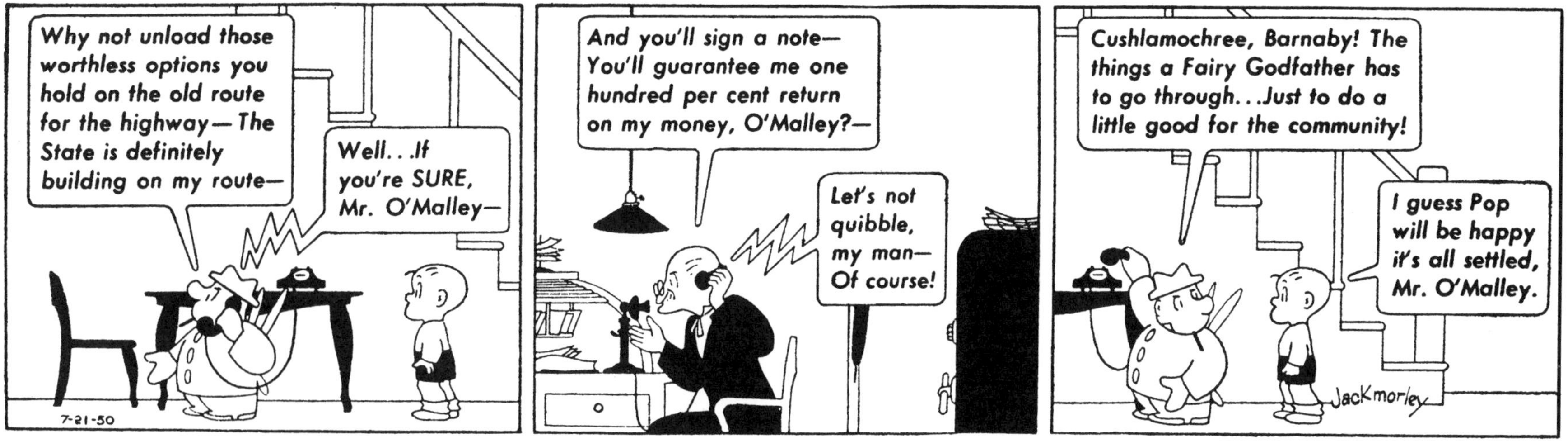
Why not unload those worthless options you hold on the old route for the highway—The State is definitely building on my route—
Well. . .If you're SURE, Mr. O'Malley—
7-21-50
And you'll sign a note—You'll guarantee me one hundred per cent return on my money, O'Malley?—
Let's not quibble, my man—Of course!
Cushlamochree, Barnaby! The things a Fairy Godfather has to go through. . .Just to do a little good for the community!
I guess Pop will be happy it's all settled, Mr. O'Malley.
JackMorley

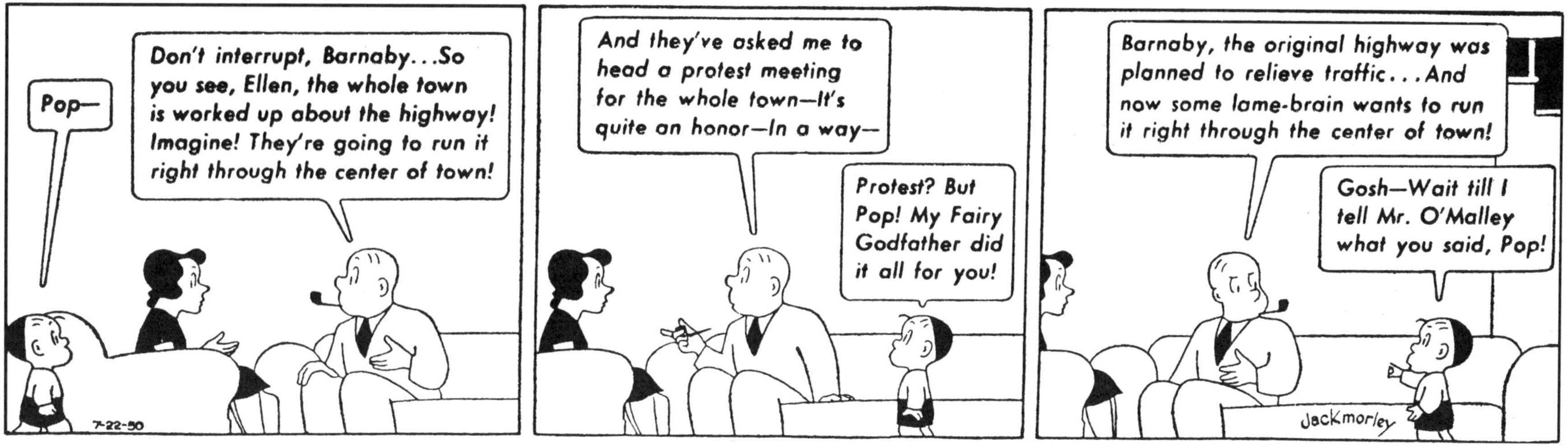
Pop—
Don't interrupt, Barnaby. . .So you see, Ellen, the whole town is worked up about the highway! Imagine! They're going to run it right through the center of town!
7-22-50
And they've asked me to head a protest meeting for the whole town—It's quite an honor—In a way—
Protest? But Pop! My Fairy Godfather did it all for you!
Barnaby, the original highway was planned to relieve traffic. . .And now some lame-brain wants to run it right through the center of town!
Gosh—Wait till I tell Mr. O'Malley what you said, Pop!
JackMorley

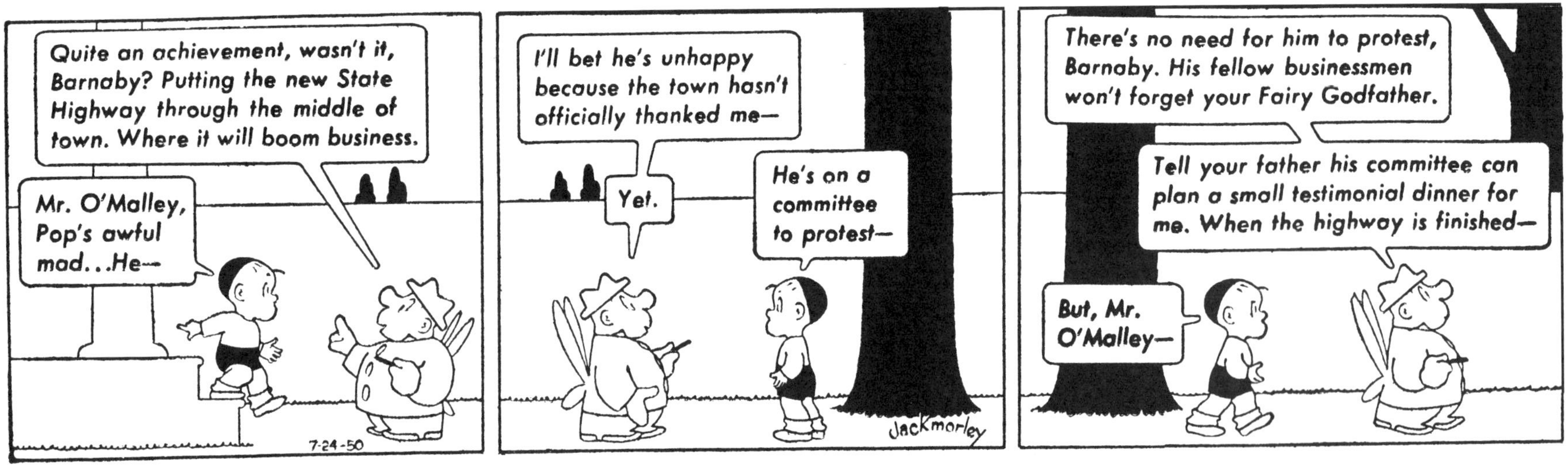
Quite an achievement, wasn't it, Barnaby? Putting the new State Highway through the middle of town. Where it will boom business.
Mr. O'Malley, Pop's awful mad...He—
7-24-50
I'll bet he's unhappy because the town hasn't officially thanked me—
Yet.
He's on a committee to protest—
JACKmorley
There's no need for him to protest, Barnaby. His fellow businessmen won't forget your Fairy Godfather.
Tell your father his committee can plan a small testimonial dinner for me. When the highway is finished—
But, Mr. O'Malley—

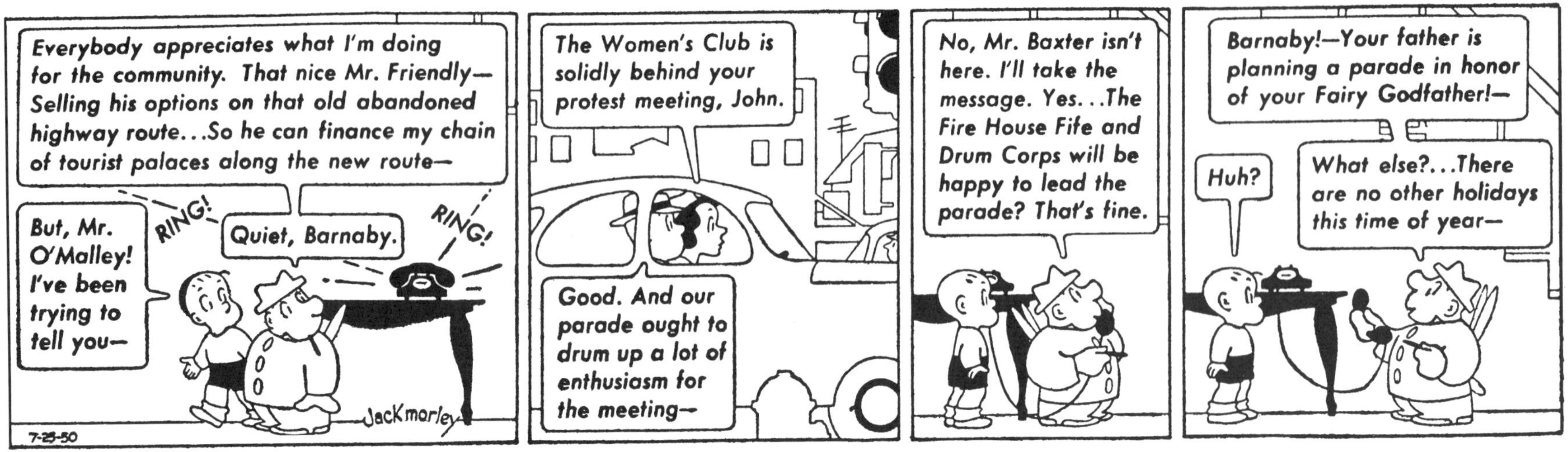
Everybody appreciates what I'm doing for the community. That nice Mr. Friendly—Selling his options on that old abandoned highway route...So he can finance my chain of tourist palaces along the new route—
But, Mr. O'Malley! I've been trying to tell you—
RING!
Quiet, Barnaby.
RING!
JACKmorley
7-25-50
The Women's Club is solidly behind your protest meeting, John.
Good. And our parade ought to drum up a lot of enthusiasm for the meeting—
No, Mr. Baxter isn't here. I'll take the message. Yes...The Fire House Fife and Drum Corps will be happy to lead the parade? That's fine.
Barnaby!—Your father is planning a parade in honor of your Fairy Godfather!—
Huh?
What else?...There are no other holidays this time of year—

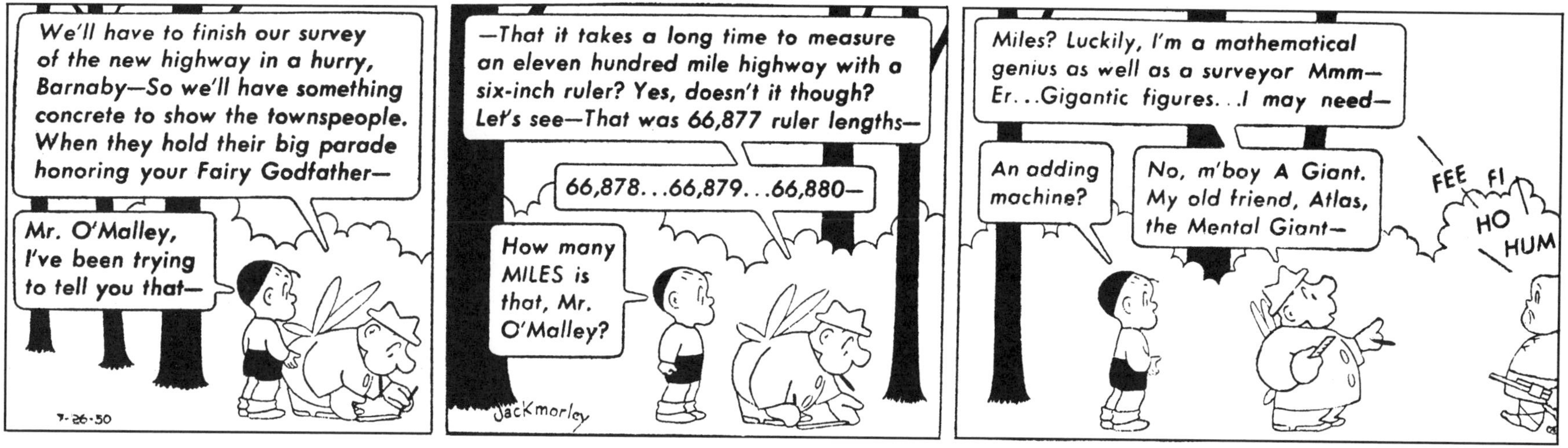
We'll have to finish our survey of the new highway in a hurry, Barnaby—So we'll have something concrete to show the townspeople. When they hold their big parade honoring your Fairy Godfather—
Mr. O'Malley, I've been trying to tell you that—
—That it takes a long time to measure an eleven hundred mile highway with a six-inch ruler? Yes, doesn't it though? Let's see—That was 66,877 ruler lengths—
66,878...66,879...66,880—
How many MILES is that, Mr. O'Malley?
Miles? Luckily, I'm a mathematical genius as well as a surveyor Mmm—Er...Gigantic figures...I may need—
An adding machine?
No, m'boy A Giant. My old friend, Atlas, the Mental Giant—
FEE FI
HO HUM

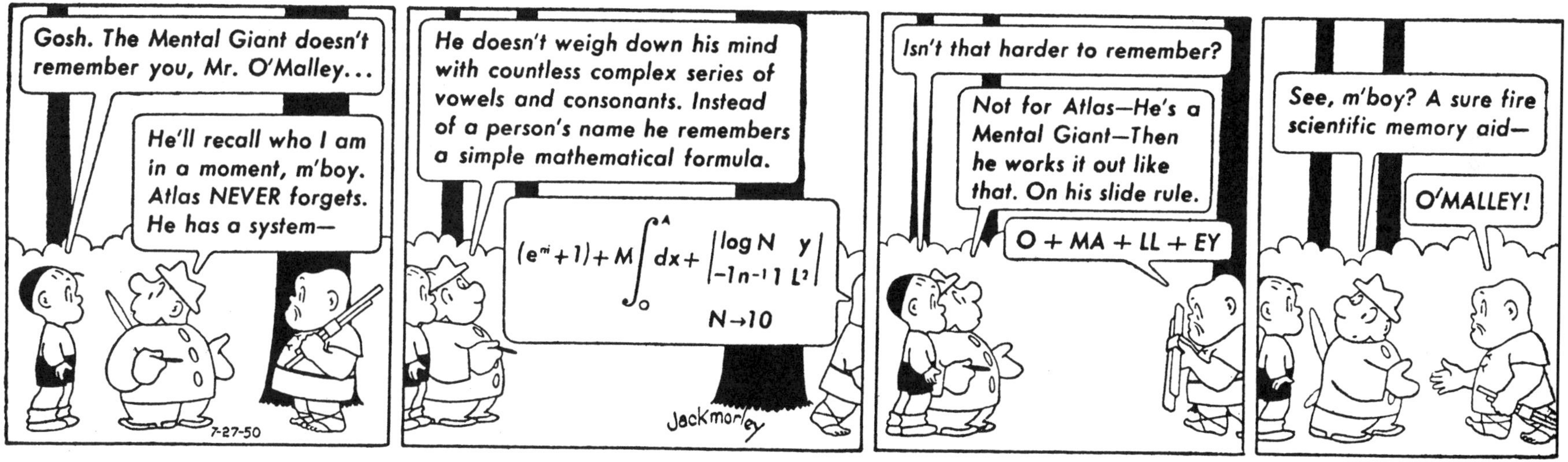
Gosh. The Mental Giant doesn't remember you, Mr. O'Malley...
He'll recall who I am in a moment, m'boy. Atlas NEVER forgets. He has a system—
He doesn't weigh down his mind with countless complex series of vowels and consonants. Instead of a person's name he remembers a simple mathematical formula.
$(e^{\pi i}+1)+M\int_0^A dx+\begin{vmatrix}\log N & y\\ -1n^{-1}1 & L^2\end{vmatrix}$ N→10
Isn't that harder to remember?
Not for Atlas—He's a Mental Giant—Then he works it out like that. On his slide rule.
O + MA + LL + EY
See, m'boy? A sure fire scientific memory aid—
O'MALLEY!

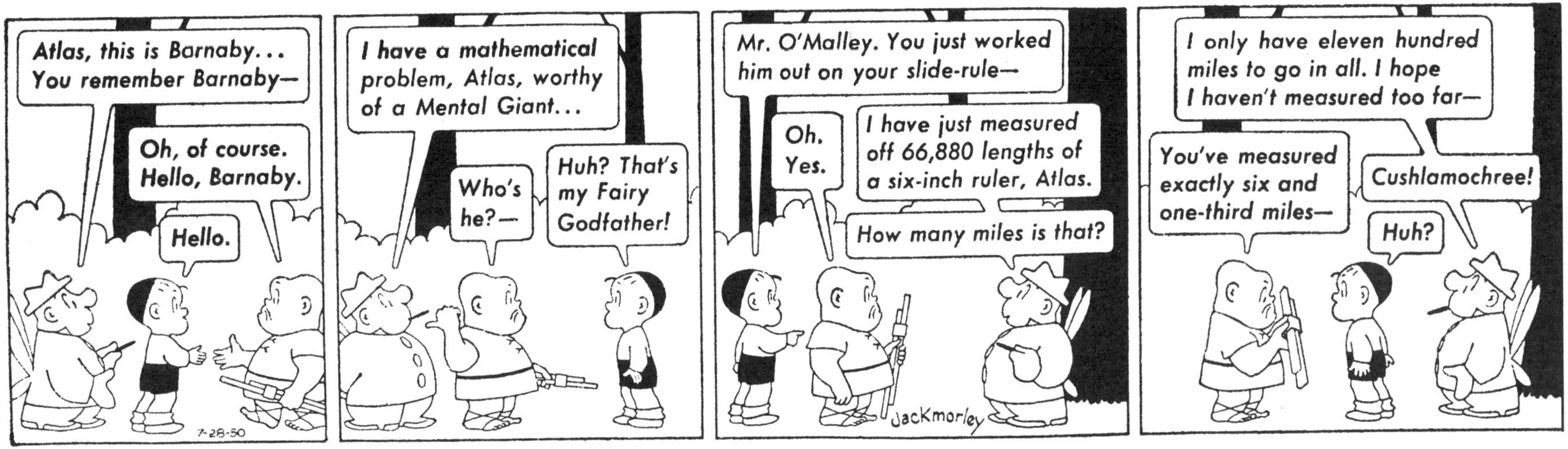
Atlas, this is Barnaby... You remember Barnaby—
Oh, of course. Hello, Barnaby.
Hello.
7-28-50
I have a mathematical problem, Atlas, worthy of a Mental Giant...
Who's he?—
Huh? That's my Fairy Godfather!
Mr. O'Malley. You just worked him out on your slide-rule—
Oh. Yes.
I have just measured off 66,880 lengths of a six-inch ruler, Atlas.
How many miles is that?
JackMorley
I only have eleven hundred miles to go in all. I hope I haven't measured too far—
You've measured exactly six and one-third miles—
Cushlamochree!
Huh?

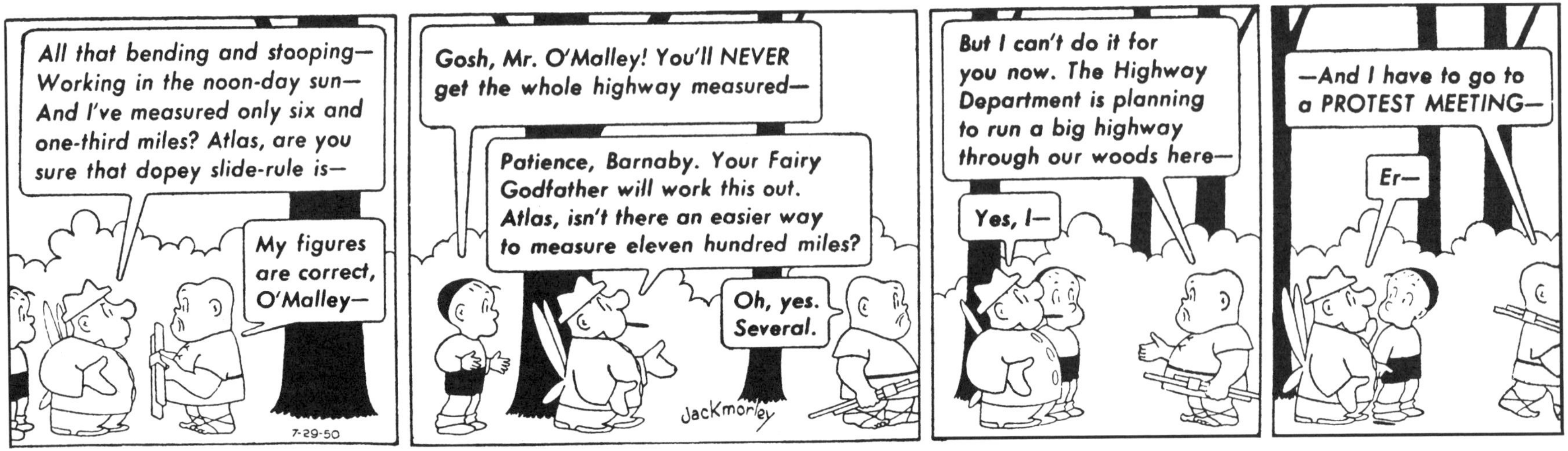
All that bending and stooping— Working in the noon-day sun— And I've measured only six and one-third miles? Atlas, are you sure that dopey slide-rule is—
My figures are correct, O'Malley—
7-29-50
Gosh, Mr. O'Malley! You'll NEVER get the whole highway measured—
Patience, Barnaby. Your Fairy Godfather will work this out. Atlas, isn't there an easier way to measure eleven hundred miles?
Oh, yes. Several.
JackMorley
But I can't do it for you now. The Highway Department is planning to run a big highway through our woods here—
Yes, I—
—And I have to go to a PROTEST MEETING—
Er—

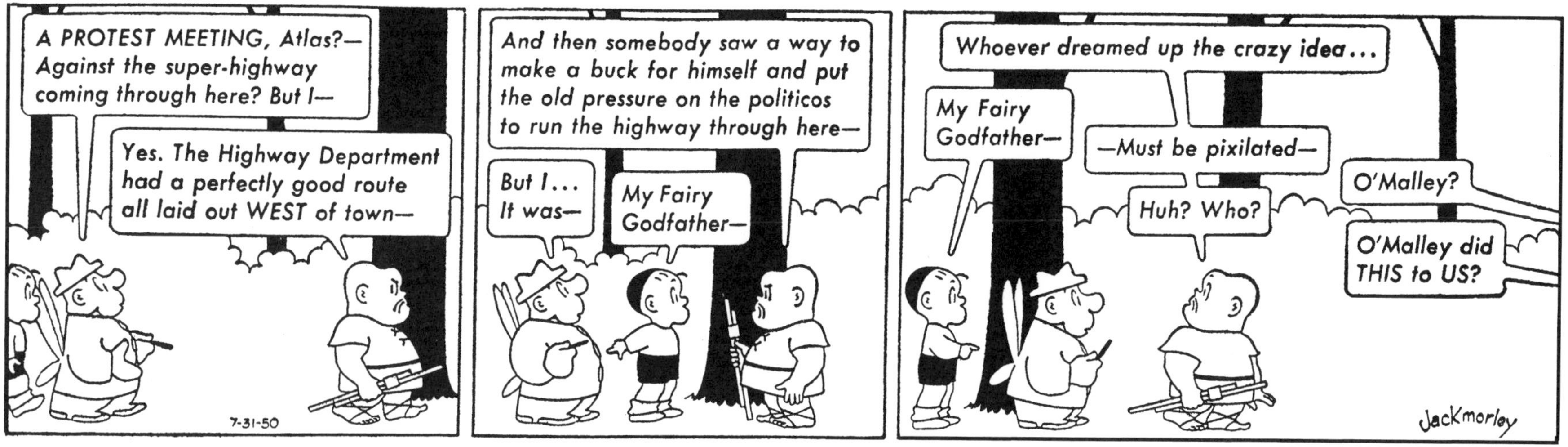
A PROTEST MEETING, Atlas?—Against the super-highway coming through here? But I—
Yes. The Highway Department had a perfectly good route all laid out WEST of town—
7-31-50
And then somebody saw a way to make a buck for himself and put the old pressure on the politicos to run the highway through here—
But I… It was—
My Fairy Godfather—
Whoever dreamed up the crazy idea…
My Fairy Godfather—
—Must be pixilated—
Huh? Who?
O'Malley?
O'Malley did THIS to US?
JackMorley

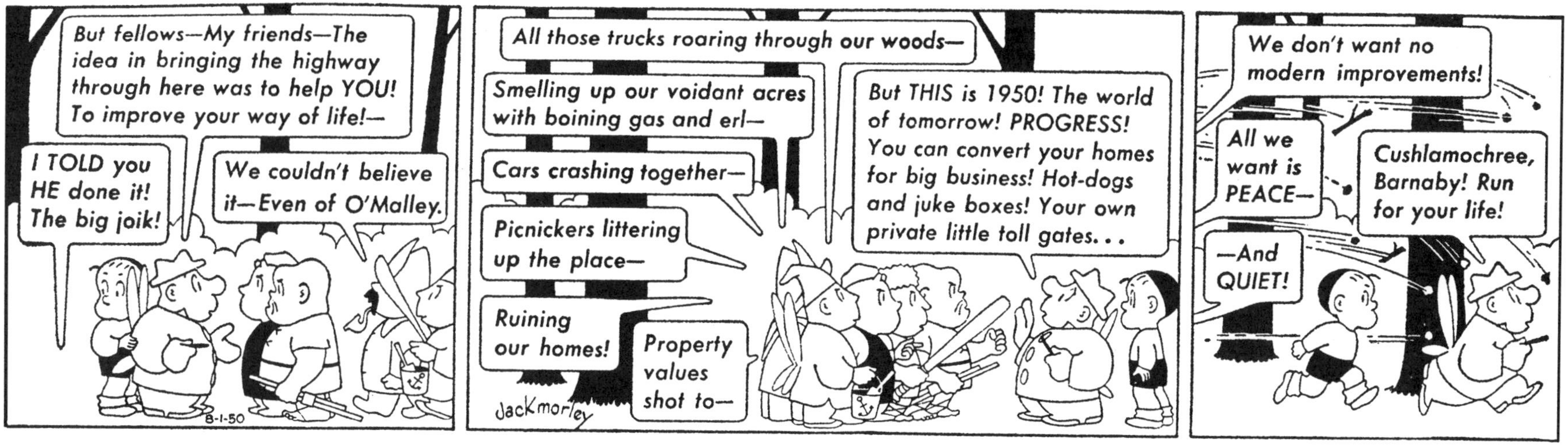
But fellows—My friends—The idea in bringing the highway through here was to help YOU! To improve your way of life!—
I TOLD you HE done it! The big joik!
We couldn't believe it—Even of O'Malley.
8-1-50
All those trucks roaring through our woods—
Smelling up our voidant acres with boining gas and erl—
Cars crashing together—
Picnickers littering up the place—
Ruining our homes!
Property values shot to—
But THIS is 1950! The world of tomorrow! PROGRESS! You can convert your homes for big business! Hot-dogs and juke boxes! Your own private little toll gates…
JackMorley
We don't want no modern improvements!
All we want is PEACE—
—And QUIET!
Cushlamochree, Barnaby! Run for your life!

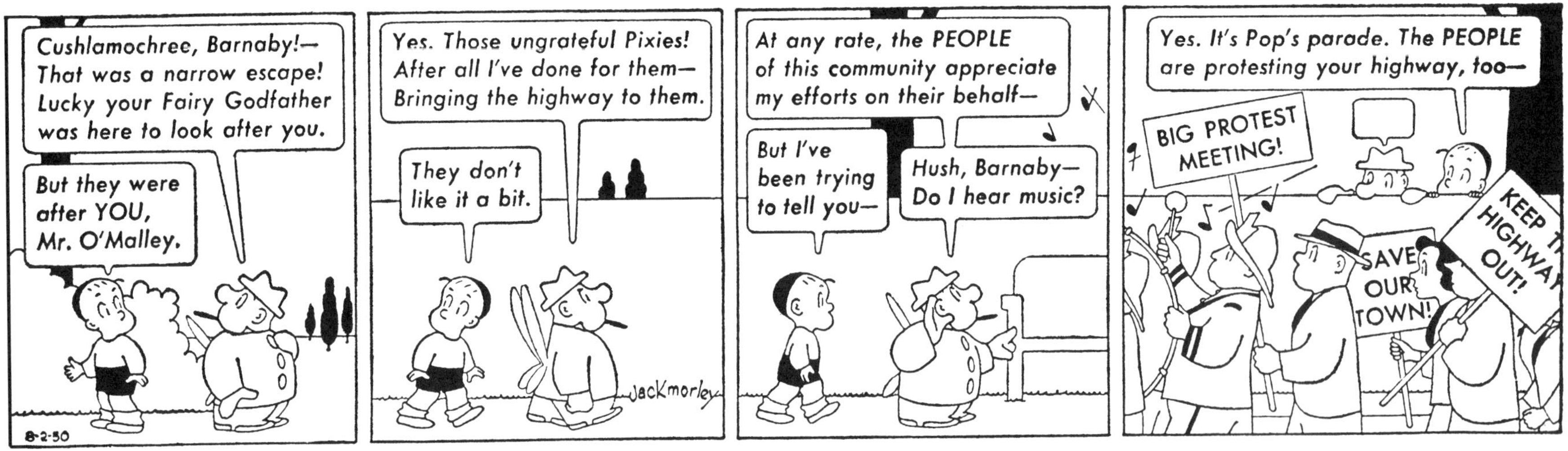
Cushlamochree, Barnaby!—
That was a narrow escape!
Lucky your Fairy Godfather
was here to look after you.
But they were
after YOU,
Mr. O'Malley.
8-2-50
Yes. Those ungrateful Pixies!
After all I've done for them—
Bringing the highway to them.
They don't
like it a bit.
Jackmorley
At any rate, the PEOPLE
of this community appreciate
my efforts on their behalf—
But I've
been trying
to tell you—
Hush, Barnaby—
Do I hear music?
Yes. It's Pop's parade. The PEOPLE
are protesting your highway, too—
BIG PROTEST
MEETING!
SAVE
OUR
TOWN!
KEEP T
HIGHWA
OUT!

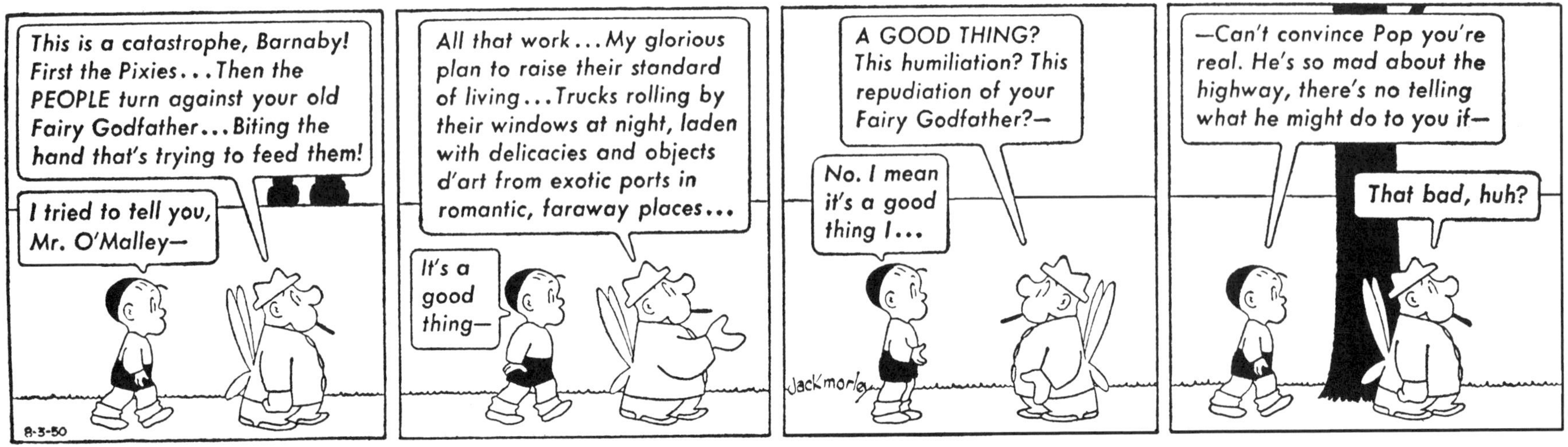
This is a catastrophe, Barnaby!
First the Pixies...Then the
PEOPLE turn against your old
Fairy Godfather...Biting the
hand that's trying to feed them!
I tried to tell you,
Mr. O'Malley—
8-3-50
All that work...My glorious
plan to raise their standard
of living...Trucks rolling by
their windows at night, laden
with delicacies and objects
d'art from exotic ports in
romantic, faraway places...
It's a
good
thing—
A GOOD THING?
This humiliation? This
repudiation of your
Fairy Godfather?—
No. I mean
it's a good
thing I...
Jackmorley
—Can't convince Pop you're
real. He's so mad about the
highway, there's no telling
what he might do to you if—
That bad, huh?

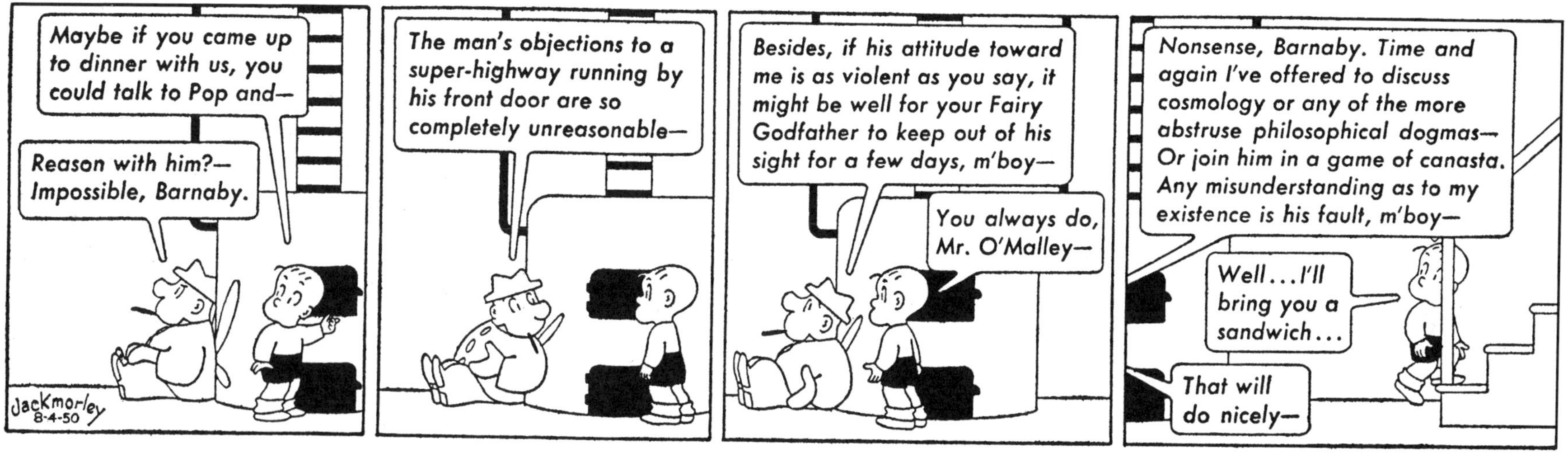
Maybe if you came up to dinner with us, you could talk to Pop and—
Reason with him?— Impossible, Barnaby.
Jackmorley 8-4-50
The man's objections to a super-highway running by his front door are so completely unreasonable—
Besides, if his attitude toward me is as violent as you say, it might be well for your Fairy Godfather to keep out of his sight for a few days, m'boy—
You always do, Mr. O'Malley—
Nonsense, Barnaby. Time and again I've offered to discuss cosmology or any of the more abstruse philosophical dogmas— Or join him in a game of canasta. Any misunderstanding as to my existence is his fault, m'boy—
Well...I'll bring you a sandwich...
That will do nicely—

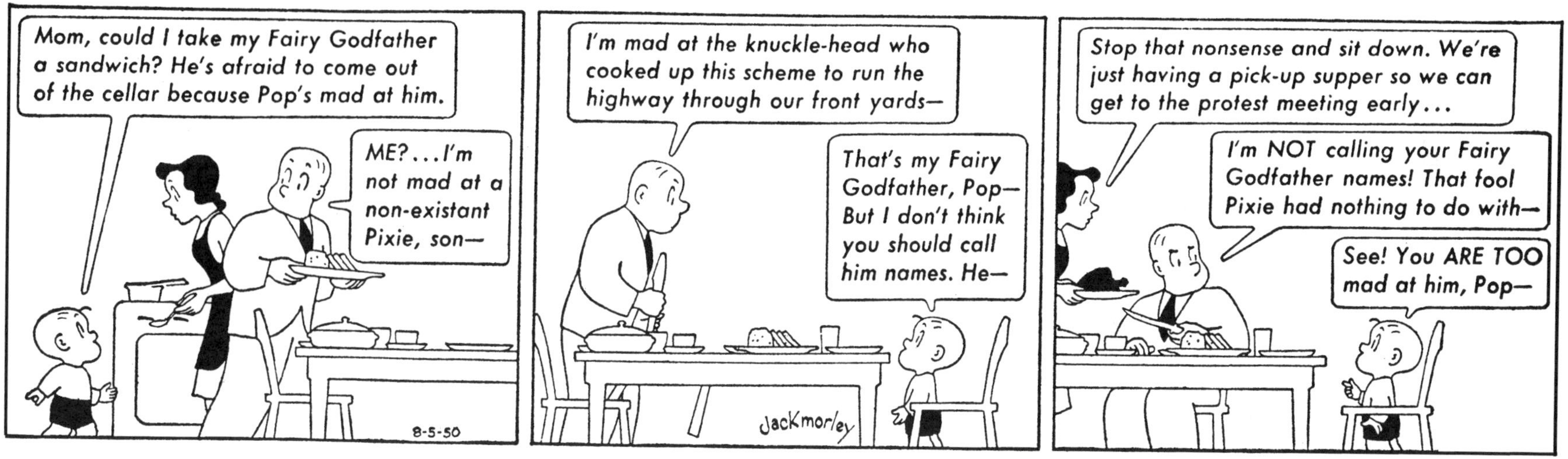
Mom, could I take my Fairy Godfather a sandwich? He's afraid to come out of the cellar because Pop's mad at him.
ME?...I'm not mad at a non-existant Pixie, son—
8-5-50
I'm mad at the knuckle-head who cooked up this scheme to run the highway through our front yards—
That's my Fairy Godfather, Pop— But I don't think you should call him names. He—
Jackmorley
Stop that nonsense and sit down. We're just having a pick-up supper so we can get to the protest meeting early...
I'm NOT calling your Fairy Godfather names! That fool Pixie had nothing to do with—
See! You ARE TOO mad at him, Pop—

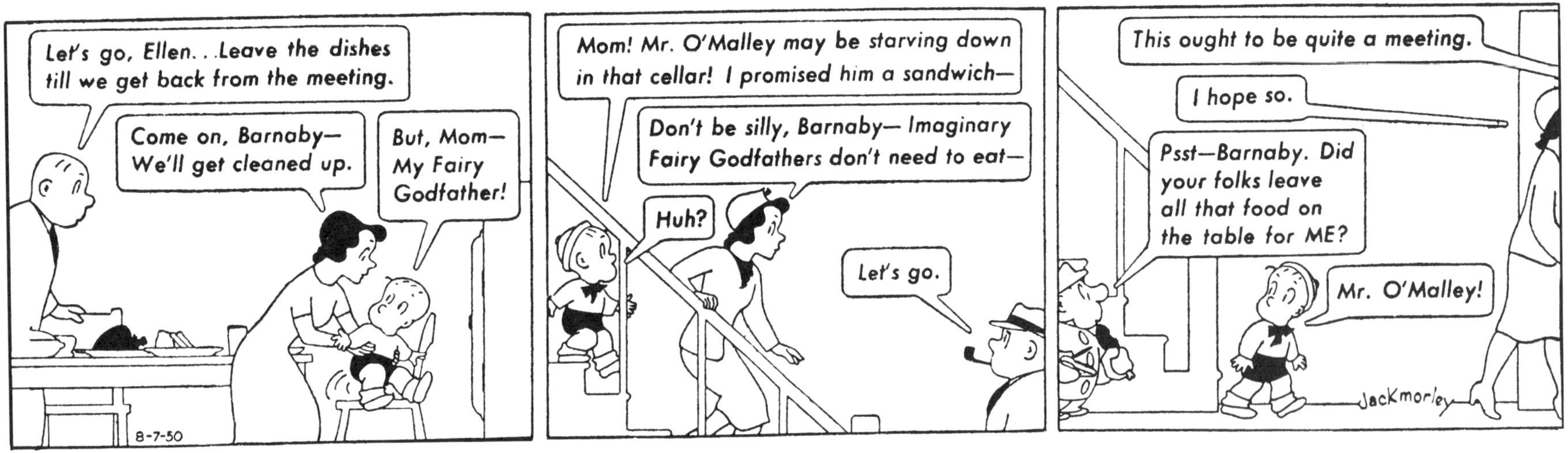
Let's go, Ellen. . .Leave the dishes till we get back from the meeting.
Come on, Barnaby— We'll get cleaned up.
But, Mom— My Fairy Godfather!
8-7-50
Mom! Mr. O'Malley may be starving down in that cellar! I promised him a sandwich—
Don't be silly, Barnaby— Imaginary Fairy Godfathers don't need to eat—
Huh?
Let's go.
This ought to be quite a meeting.
I hope so.
Psst—Barnaby. Did your folks leave all that food on the table for ME?
Mr. O'Malley!
JackMorley

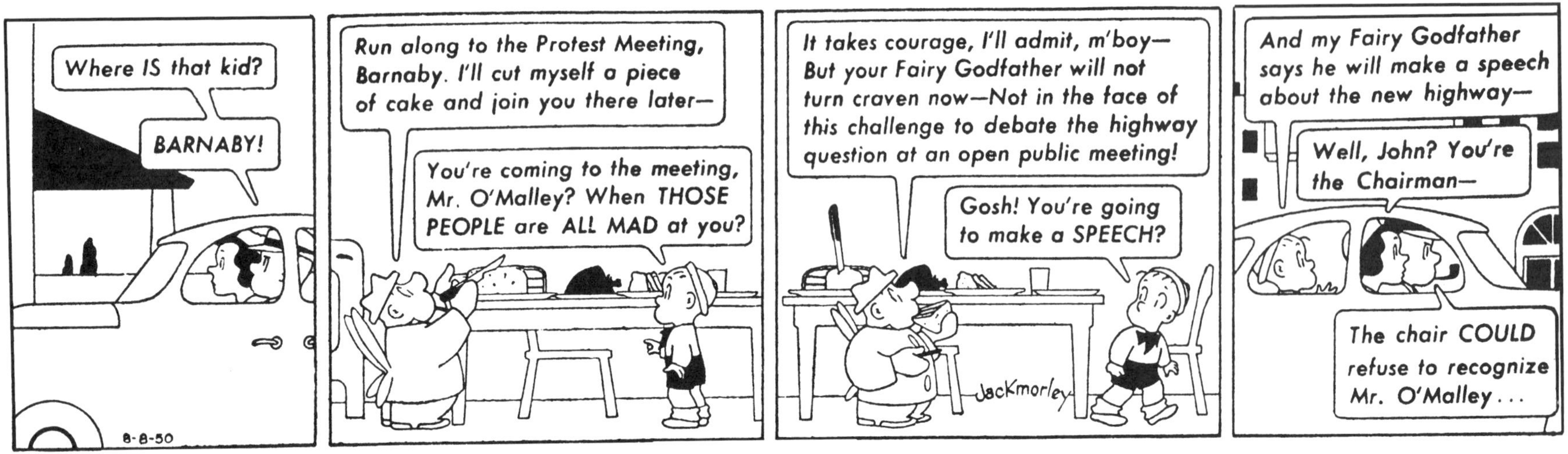
Where IS that kid?
BARNABY!
8-8-50
Run along to the Protest Meeting, Barnaby. I'll cut myself a piece of cake and join you there later—
You're coming to the meeting, Mr. O'Malley? When THOSE PEOPLE are ALL MAD at you?
It takes courage, I'll admit, m'boy— But your Fairy Godfather will not turn craven now—Not in the face of this challenge to debate the highway question at an open public meeting!
Gosh! You're going to make a SPEECH?
JackMorley
And my Fairy Godfather says he will make a speech about the new highway—
Well, John? You're the Chairman—
The chair COULD refuse to recognize Mr. O'Malley . . .

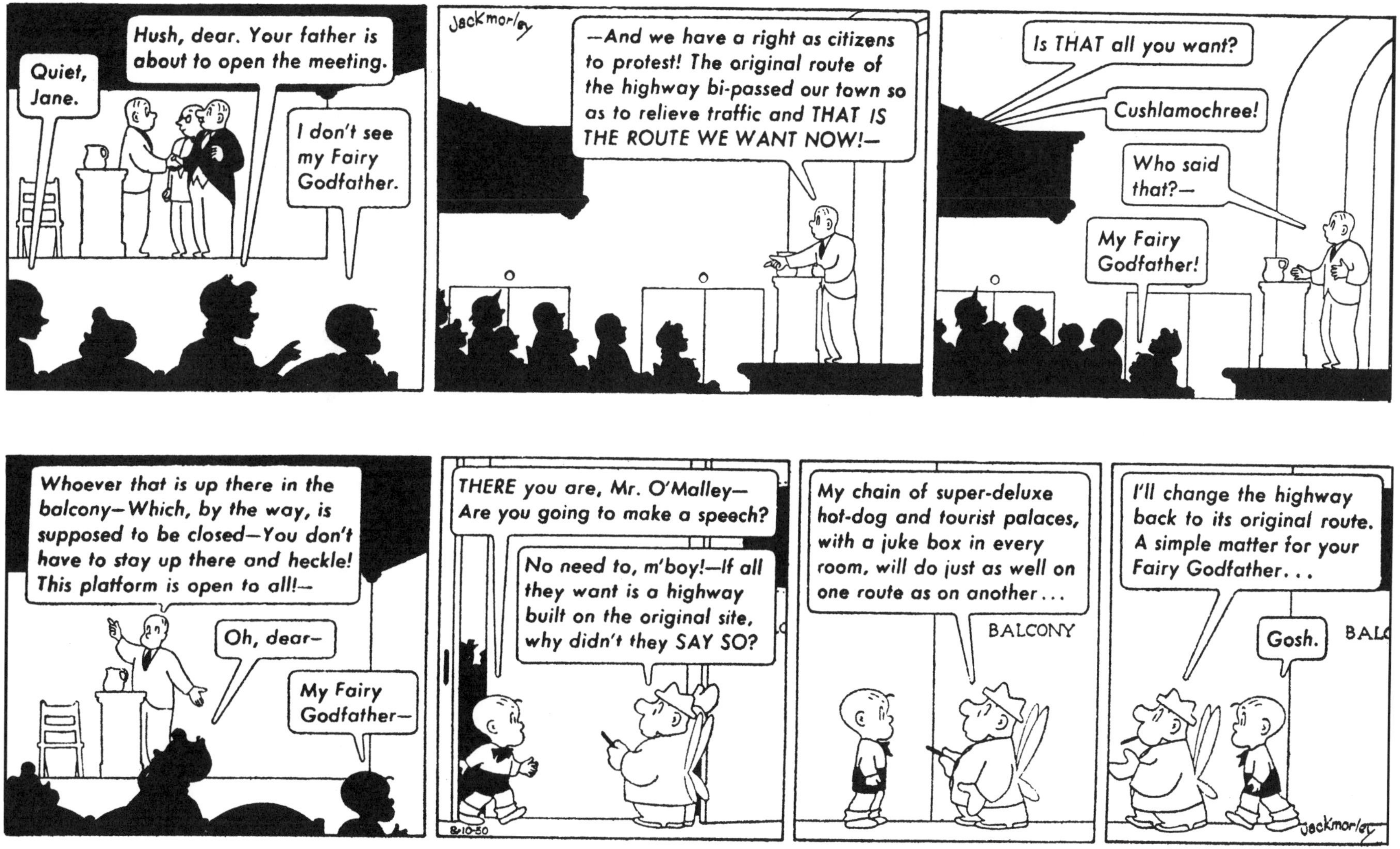
Quiet, Jane.
Hush, dear. Your father is about to open the meeting.
I don't see my Fairy Godfather.
Jackmorley
—And we have a right as citizens to protest! The original route of the highway bi-passed our town so as to relieve traffic and THAT IS THE ROUTE WE WANT NOW!—
Is THAT all you want?
Cushlamochree!
Who said that?—
My Fairy Godfather!
Whoever that is up there in the balcony—Which, by the way, is supposed to be closed—You don't have to stay up there and heckle! This platform is open to all!—
Oh, dear—
My Fairy Godfather—
THERE you are, Mr. O'Malley—Are you going to make a speech?
No need to, m'boy!—If all they want is a highway built on the original site, why didn't they SAY SO?
8-10-50
My chain of super-deluxe hot-dog and tourist palaces, with a juke box in every room, will do just as well on one route as on another . . .
BALCONY
I'll change the highway back to its original route. A simple matter for your Fairy Godfather . . .
Gosh.
BAL
Jackmorley

August 9 – 10

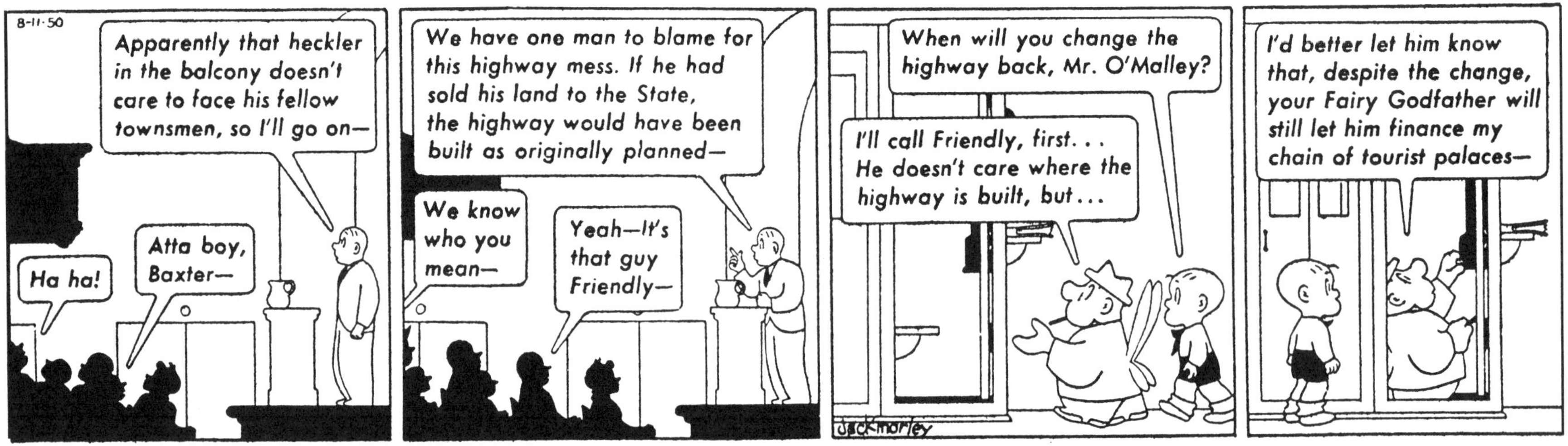
8-11-50
Apparently that heckler in the balcony doesn't care to face his fellow townsmen, so I'll go on—
Atta boy, Baxter—
Ha ha!
We have one man to blame for this highway mess. If he had sold his land to the State, the highway would have been built as originally planned—
We know who you mean—
Yeah—It's that guy Friendly—
When will you change the highway back, Mr. O'Malley?
I'll call Friendly, first. . . He doesn't care where the highway is built, but . . .
jackmorley
I'd better let him know that, despite the change, your Fairy Godfather will still let him finance my chain of tourist palaces—

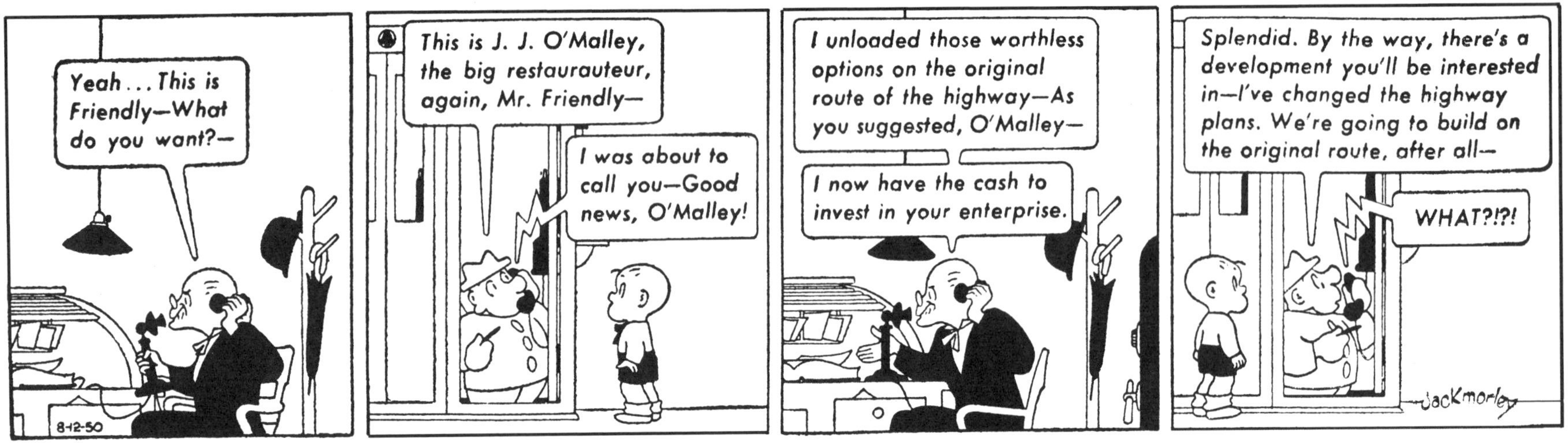
Yeah . . . This is Friendly—What do you want?—
8-12-50
This is J. J. O'Malley, the big restaurauteur, again, Mr. Friendly—
I was about to call you—Good news, O'Malley!
I unloaded those worthless options on the original route of the highway—As you suggested, O'Malley—
I now have the cash to invest in your enterprise.
Splendid. By the way, there's a development you'll be interested in—I've changed the highway plans. We're going to build on the original route, after all—
WHAT?!?!
jackmorley

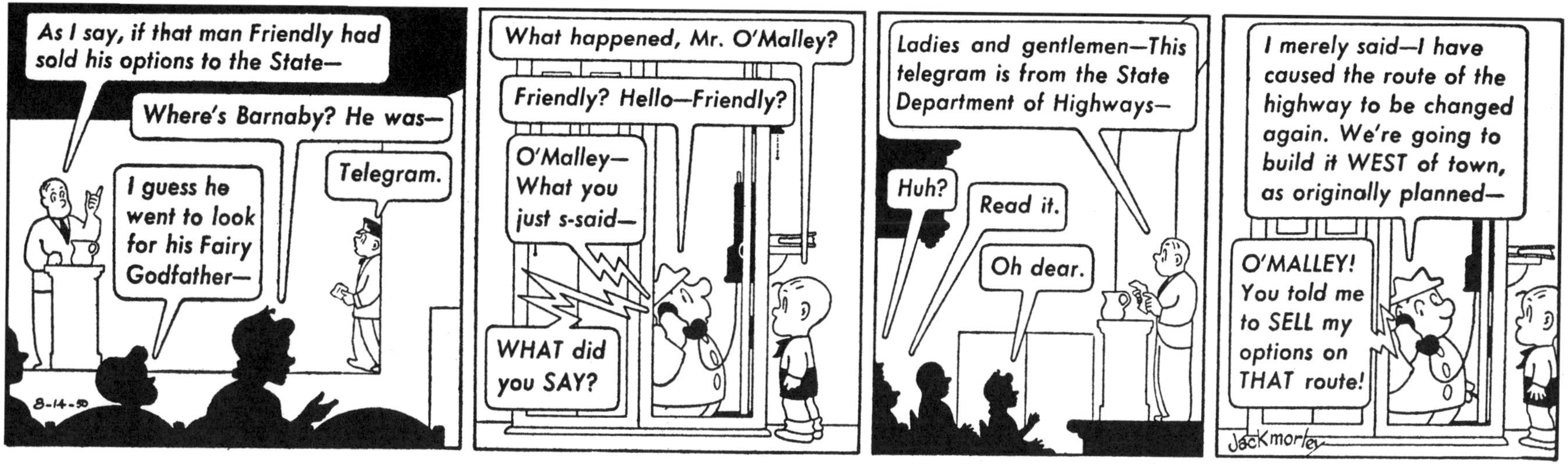
As I say, if that man Friendly had sold his options to the State—
Where's Barnaby? He was—
I guess he went to look for his Fairy Godfather—
Telegram.
8-14-50
What happened, Mr. O'Malley?
Friendly? Hello—Friendly?
O'Malley— What you just s-said—
WHAT did you SAY?
Ladies and gentlemen—This telegram is from the State Department of Highways—
Huh?
Read it.
Oh dear.
I merely said—I have caused the route of the highway to be changed again. We're going to build it WEST of town, as originally planned—
O'MALLEY! You told me to SELL my options on THAT route!
Jackmorley

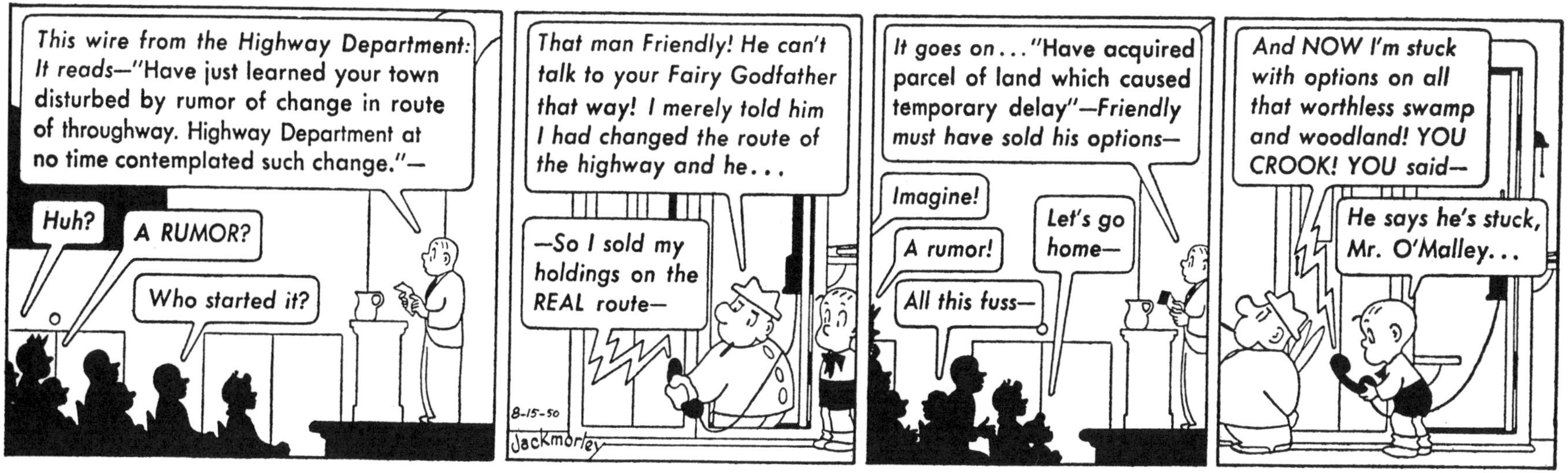
This wire from the Highway Department: It reads—"Have just learned your town disturbed by rumor of change in route of throughway. Highway Department at no time contemplated such change."—
Huh?
A RUMOR?
Who started it?
That man Friendly! He can't talk to your Fairy Godfather that way! I merely told him I had changed the route of the highway and he . . .
—So I sold my holdings on the REAL route—
8-15-50
Jackmorley
It goes on . . . "Have acquired parcel of land which caused temporary delay"—Friendly must have sold his options—
Imagine!
A rumor!
All this fuss—
Let's go home—
And NOW I'm stuck with options on all that worthless swamp and woodland! YOU CROOK! YOU said—
He says he's stuck, Mr. O'Malley . . .

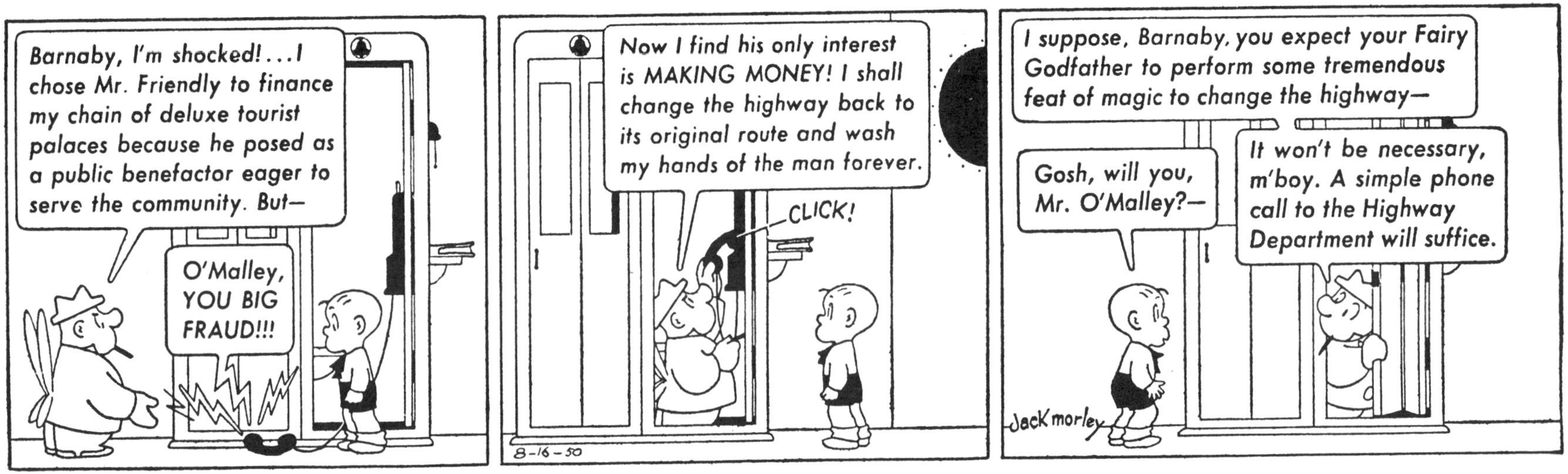
Barnaby, I'm shocked!...I chose Mr. Friendly to finance my chain of deluxe tourist palaces because he posed as a public benefactor eager to serve the community. But—
O'Malley, YOU BIG FRAUD!!!
Now I find his only interest is MAKING MONEY! I shall change the highway back to its original route and wash my hands of the man forever.
CLICK!
8-16-50
I suppose, Barnaby, you expect your Fairy Godfather to perform some tremendous feat of magic to change the highway—
Gosh, will you, Mr. O'Malley?—
It won't be necessary, m'boy. A simple phone call to the Highway Department will suffice.
Jack morley

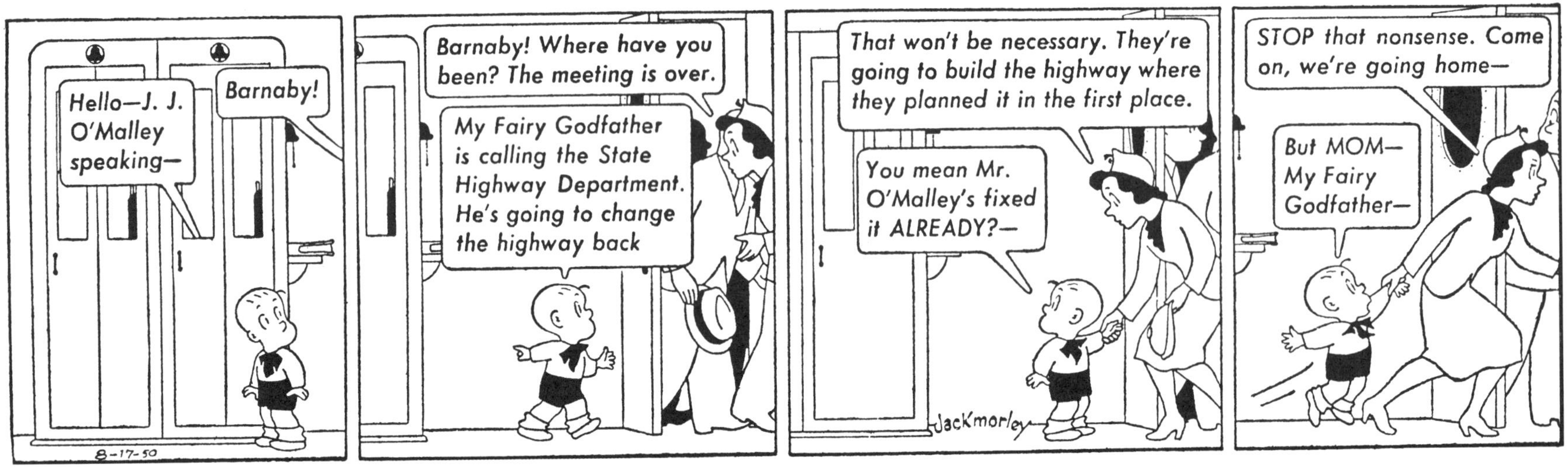
Hello—J. J. O'Malley speaking—
Barnaby!
8-17-50
Barnaby! Where have you been? The meeting is over.
My Fairy Godfather is calling the State Highway Department. He's going to change the highway back
That won't be necessary. They're going to build the highway where they planned it in the first place.
You mean Mr. O'Malley's fixed it ALREADY?—
Jack morley
STOP that nonsense. Come on, we're going home—
But MOM— My Fairy Godfather—

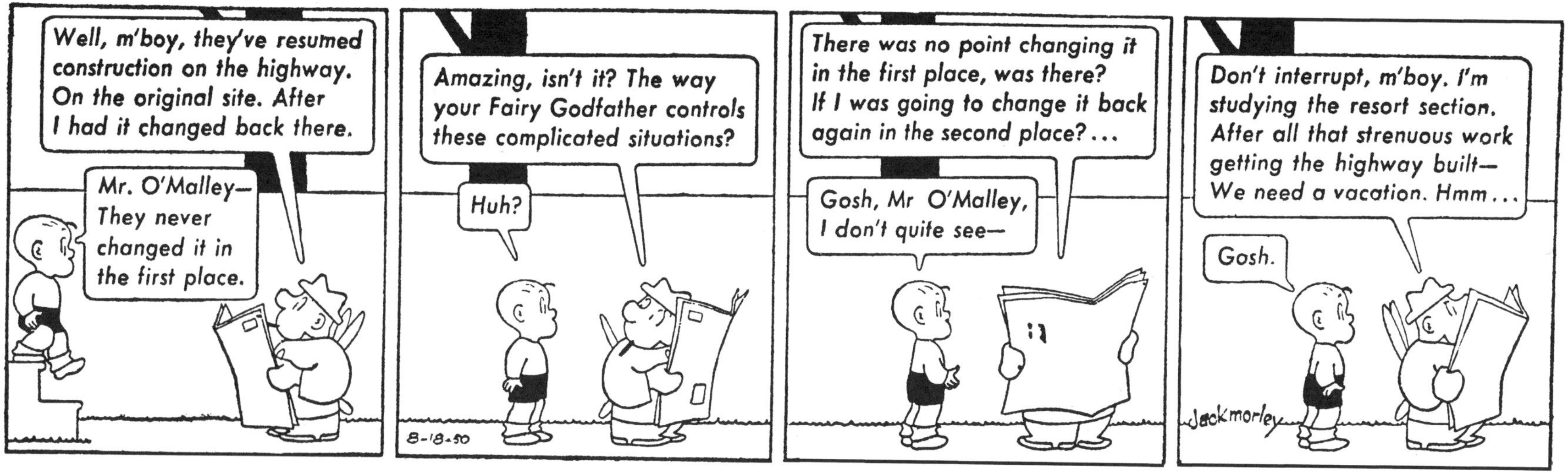
Well, m'boy, they've resumed construction on the highway. On the original site. After I had it changed back there.
Mr. O'Malley— They never changed it in the first place.
Amazing, isn't it? The way your Fairy Godfather controls these complicated situations?
Huh?
8-18-50
There was no point changing it in the first place, was there? If I was going to change it back again in the second place?...
Gosh, Mr O'Malley, I don't quite see—
Don't interrupt, m'boy. I'm studying the resort section. After all that strenuous work getting the highway built— We need a vacation. Hmm...
Gosh.
Jackmorley

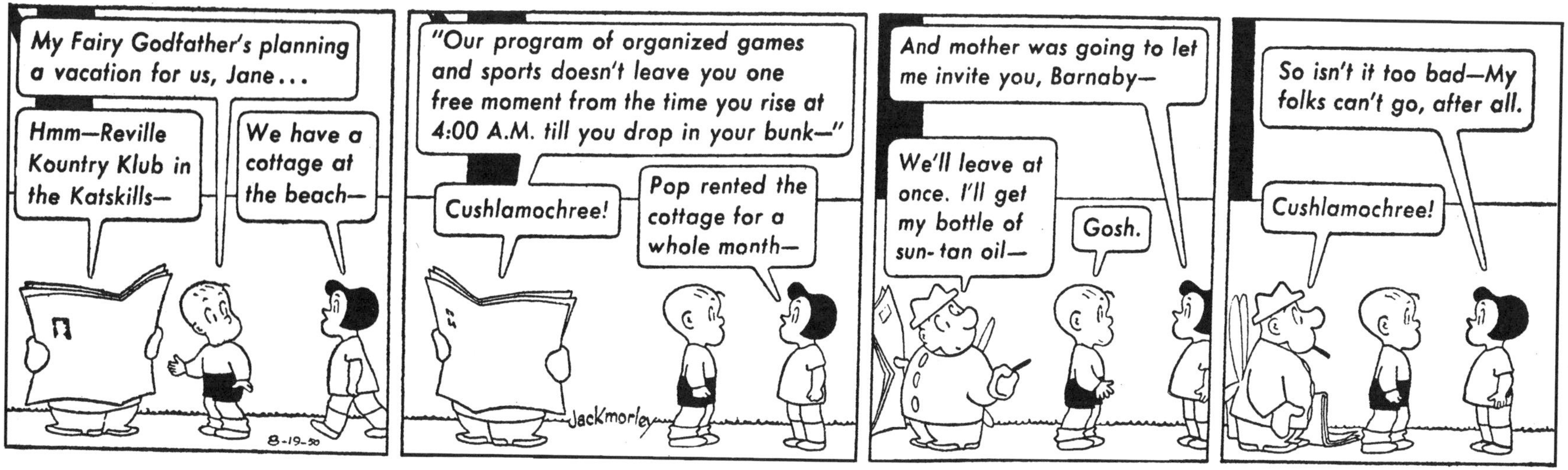
My Fairy Godfather's planning a vacation for us, Jane...
Hmm—Reville Kountry Klub in the Katskills—
We have a cottage at the beach—
8-19-50
"Our program of organized games and sports doesn't leave you one free moment from the time you rise at 4:00 A.M. till you drop in your bunk—"
Cushlamochree!
Pop rented the cottage for a whole month—
Jackmorley
And mother was going to let me invite you, Barnaby—
We'll leave at once. I'll get my bottle of sun-tan oil—
Gosh.
So isn't it too bad—My folks can't go, after all.
Cushlamochree!

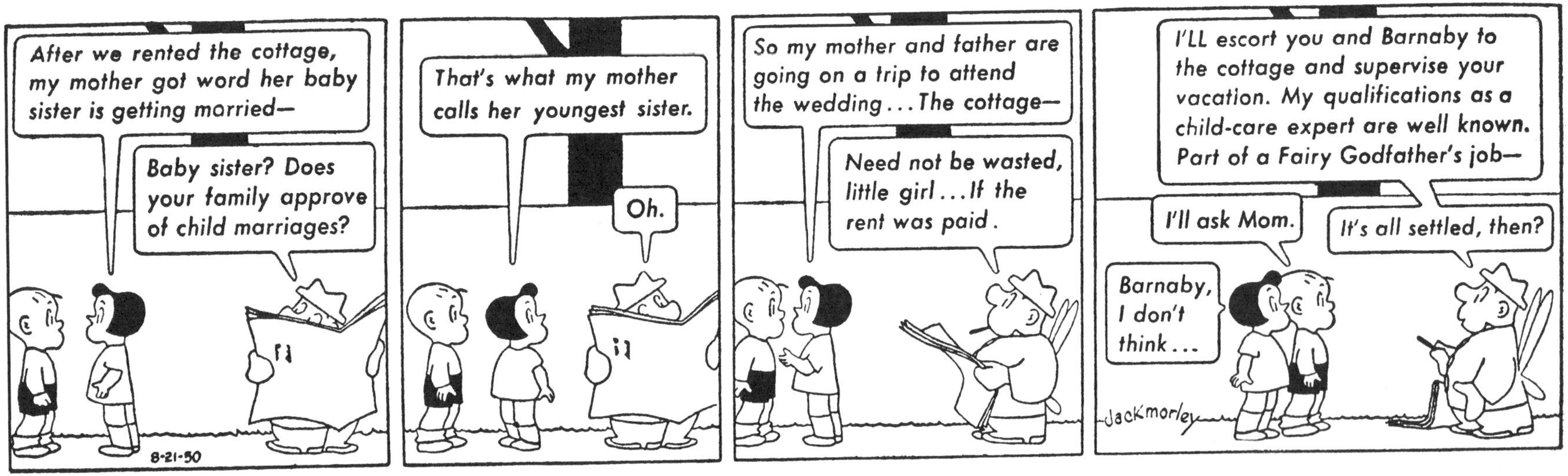
After we rented the cottage, my mother got word her baby sister is getting married—
Baby sister? Does your family approve of child marriages?
8-21-50
That's what my mother calls her youngest sister.
Oh.
So my mother and father are going on a trip to attend the wedding... The cottage—
Need not be wasted, little girl... If the rent was paid.
I'LL escort you and Barnaby to the cottage and supervise your vacation. My qualifications as a child-care expert are well known. Part of a Fairy Godfather's job—
I'll ask Mom.
It's all settled, then?
Barnaby, I don't think...
Jack Morley

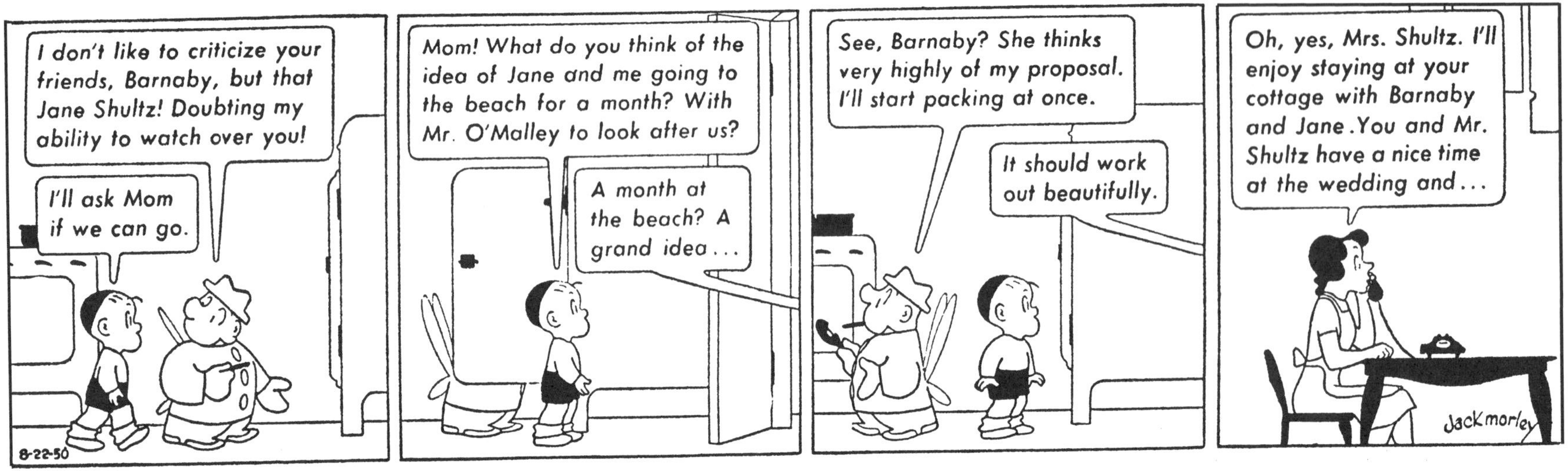
I don't like to criticize your friends, Barnaby, but that Jane Shultz! Doubting my ability to watch over you!
I'll ask Mom if we can go.
8-22-50
Mom! What do you think of the idea of Jane and me going to the beach for a month? With Mr. O'Malley to look after us?
A month at the beach? A grand idea...
See, Barnaby? She thinks very highly of my proposal. I'll start packing at once.
It should work out beautifully.
Oh, yes, Mrs. Shultz. I'll enjoy staying at your cottage with Barnaby and Jane. You and Mr. Shultz have a nice time at the wedding and...
Jack Morley

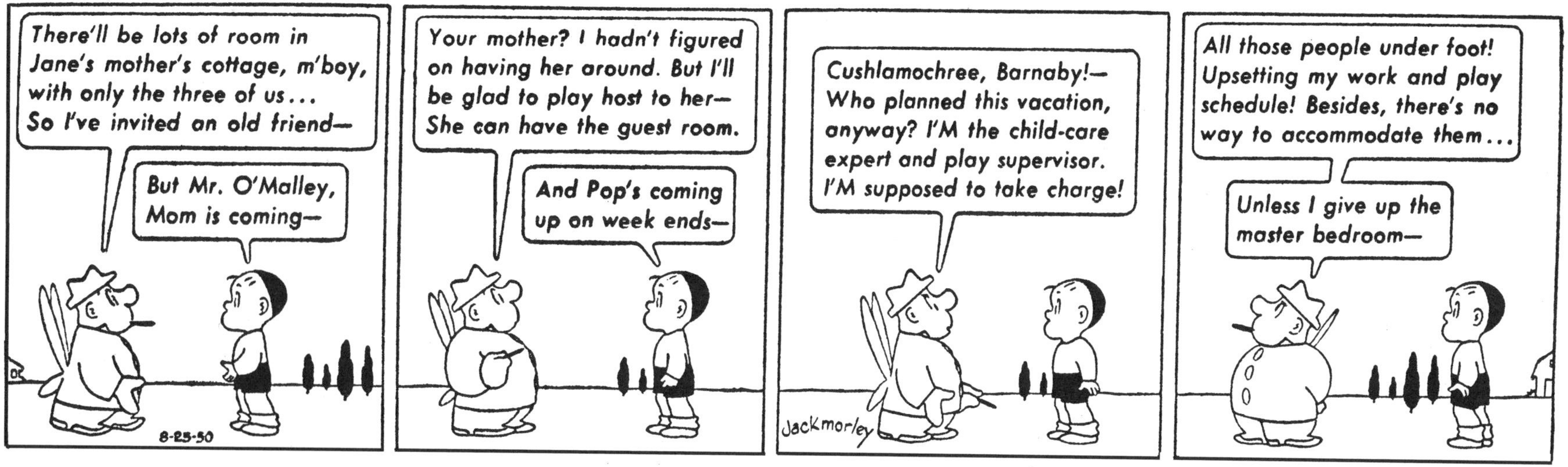
There'll be lots of room in Jane's mother's cottage, m'boy, with only the three of us... So I've invited an old friend—
But Mr. O'Malley, Mom is coming—
8-25-50
Your mother? I hadn't figured on having her around. But I'll be glad to play host to her— She can have the guest room.
And Pop's coming up on week ends—
Cushlamochree, Barnaby!— Who planned this vacation, anyway? I'M the child-care expert and play supervisor. I'M supposed to take charge!
Jackmorley
All those people under foot! Upsetting my work and play schedule! Besides, there's no way to accommodate them...
Unless I give up the master bedroom—

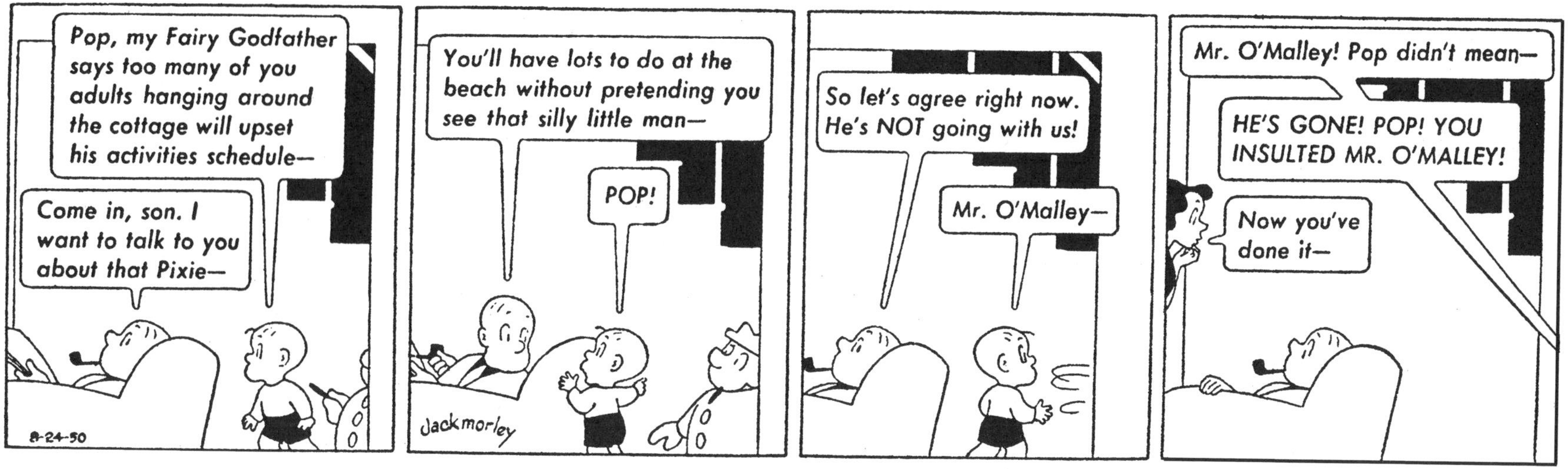
Pop, my Fairy Godfather says too many of you adults hanging around the cottage will upset his activities schedule—
Come in, son. I want to talk to you about that Pixie—
8-24-50
You'll have lots to do at the beach without pretending you see that silly little man—
POP!
Jackmorley
So let's agree right now. He's NOT going with us!
Mr. O'Malley—
Mr. O'Malley! Pop didn't mean—
HE'S GONE! POP! YOU INSULTED MR. O'MALLEY!
Now you've done it—

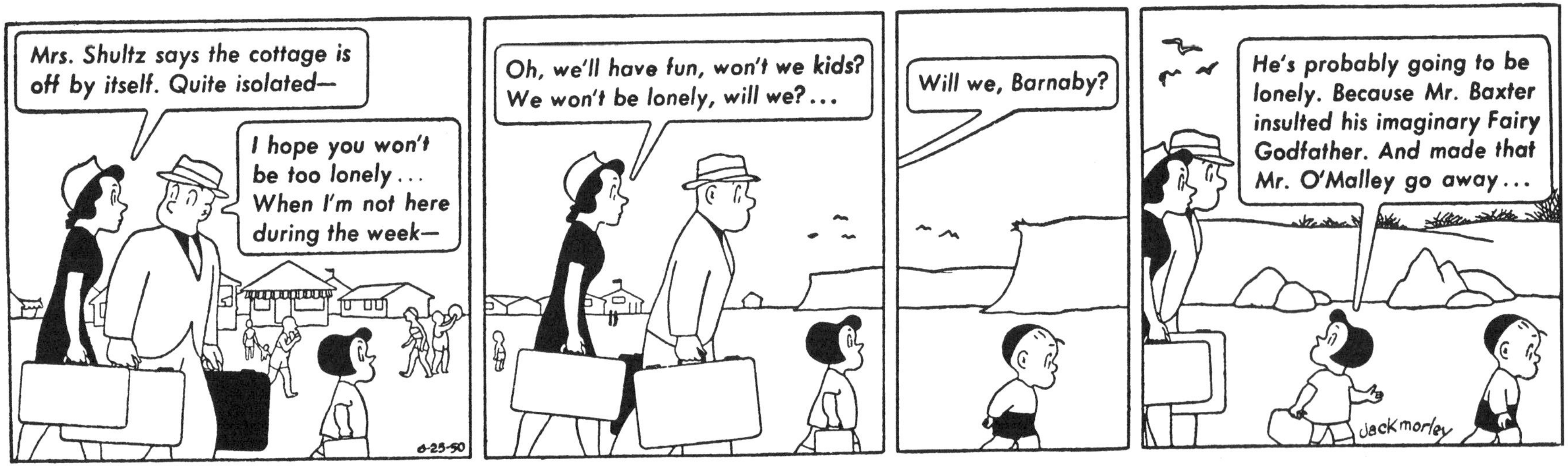
Mrs. Shultz says the cottage is off by itself. Quite isolated—
I hope you won't be too lonely... When I'm not here during the week—
6-25-50
Oh, we'll have fun, won't we kids? We won't be lonely, will we?...
Will we, Barnaby?
He's probably going to be lonely. Because Mr. Baxter insulted his imaginary Fairy Godfather. And made that Mr. O'Malley go away...
Jack Morley

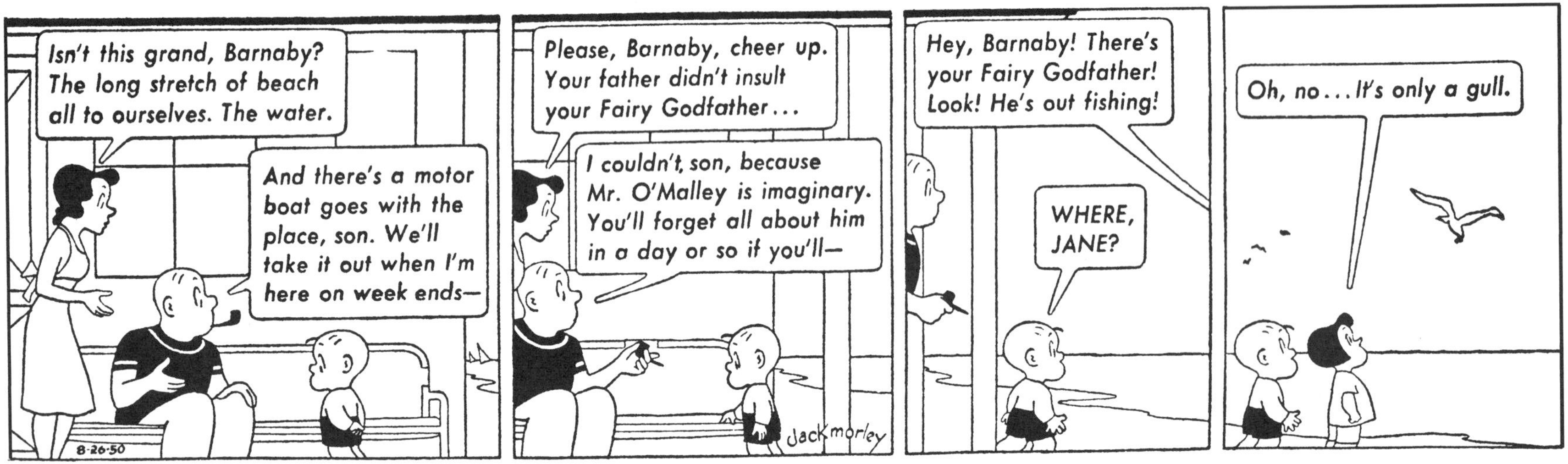
Isn't this grand, Barnaby? The long stretch of beach all to ourselves. The water.
And there's a motor boat goes with the place, son. We'll take it out when I'm here on week ends—
8-26-50
Please, Barnaby, cheer up. Your father didn't insult your Fairy Godfather...
I couldn't, son, because Mr. O'Malley is imaginary. You'll forget all about him in a day or so if you'll—
Jack Morley
Hey, Barnaby! There's your Fairy Godfather! Look! He's out fishing!
WHERE, JANE?
Oh, no... It's only a gull.

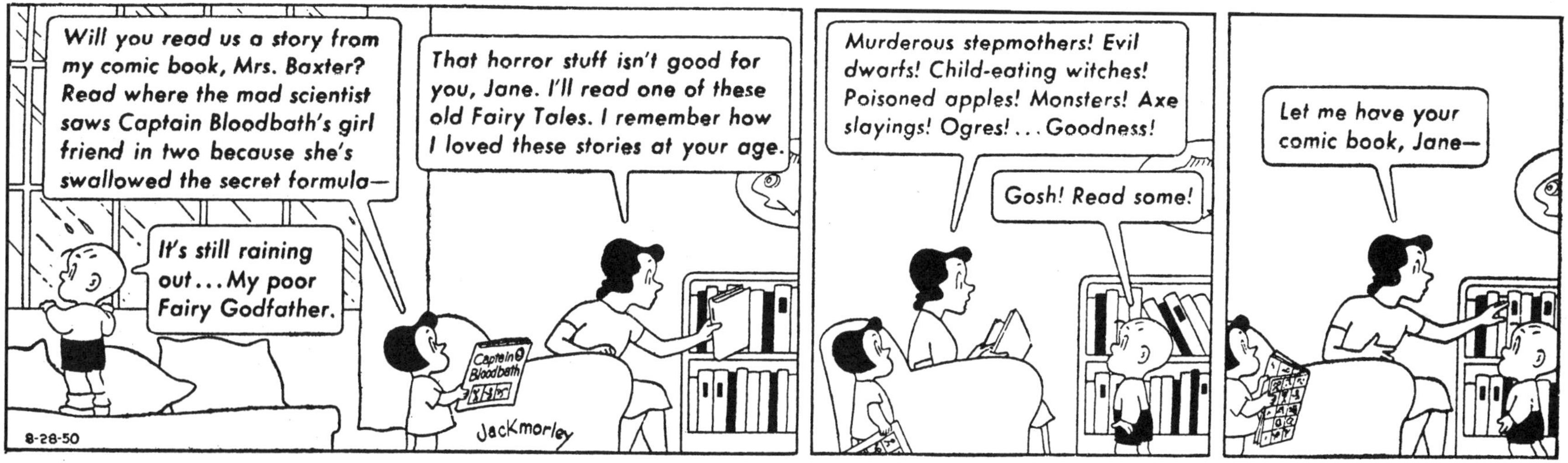
Will you read us a story from my comic book, Mrs. Baxter? Read where the mad scientist saws Captain Bloodbath's girl friend in two because she's swallowed the secret formula—
It's still raining out . . . My poor Fairy Godfather.
That horror stuff isn't good for you, Jane. I'll read one of these old Fairy Tales. I remember how I loved these stories at your age.
Captain Bloodbath
8-28-50
JacKmorley
Murderous stepmothers! Evil dwarfs! Child-eating witches! Poisoned apples! Monsters! Axe slayings! Ogres! . . . Goodness!
Gosh! Read some!
Let me have your comic book, Jane—

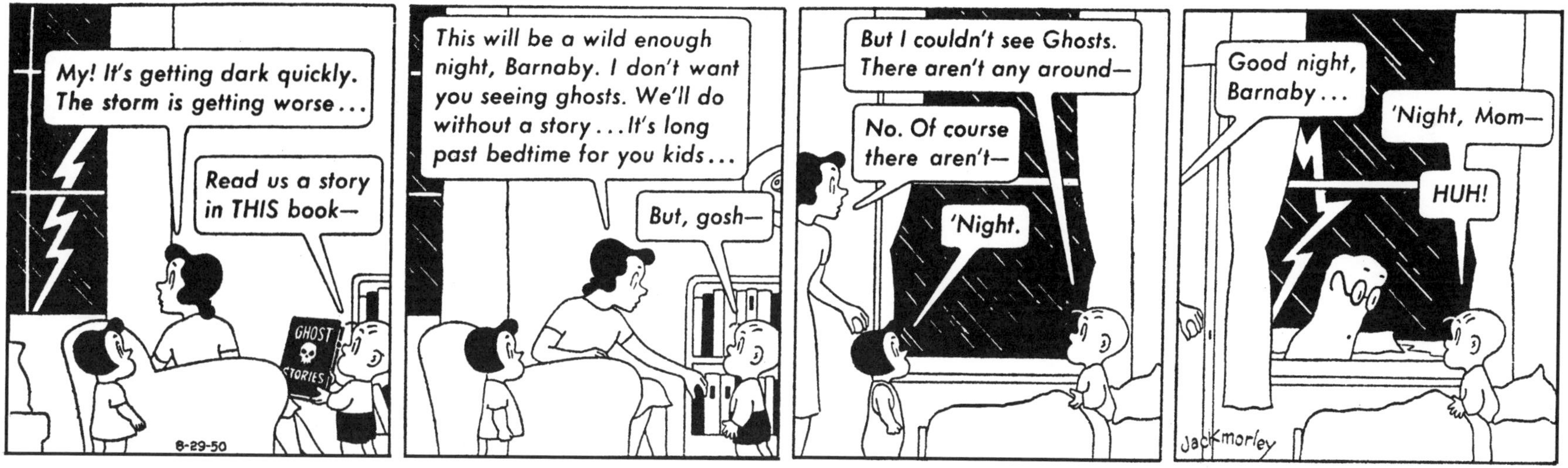
My! It's getting dark quickly. The storm is getting worse . . .
Read us a story in THIS book—
GHOST STORIES
8-29-50
This will be a wild enough night, Barnaby. I don't want you seeing ghosts. We'll do without a story . . . It's long past bedtime for you kids . . .
But, gosh—
But I couldn't see Ghosts. There aren't any around—
No. Of course there aren't—
'Night.
Good night, Barnaby . . .
'Night, Mom—
HUH!
JacKmorley

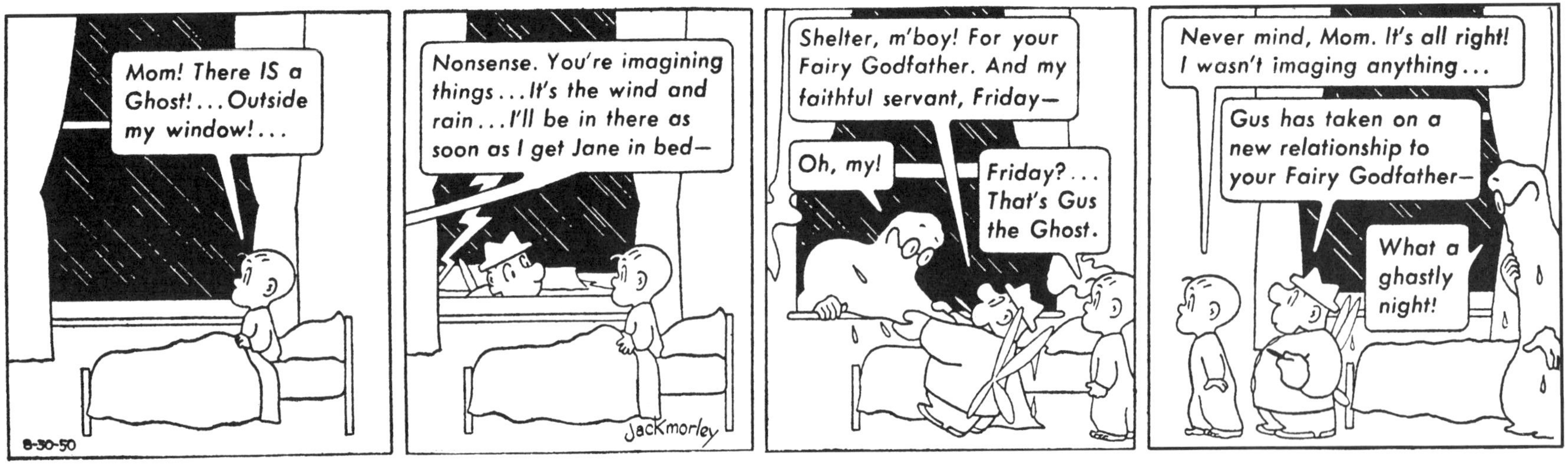
Mom! There IS a Ghost!...Outside my window!...
Nonsense. You're imagining things...It's the wind and rain...I'll be in there as soon as I get Jane in bed—
Jackmorley
Shelter, m'boy! For your Fairy Godfather. And my faithful servant, Friday—
Oh, my!
Friday?... That's Gus the Ghost.
Never mind, Mom. It's all right! I wasn't imaging anything...
Gus has taken on a new relationship to your Fairy Godfather—
What a ghastly night!
8-30-50

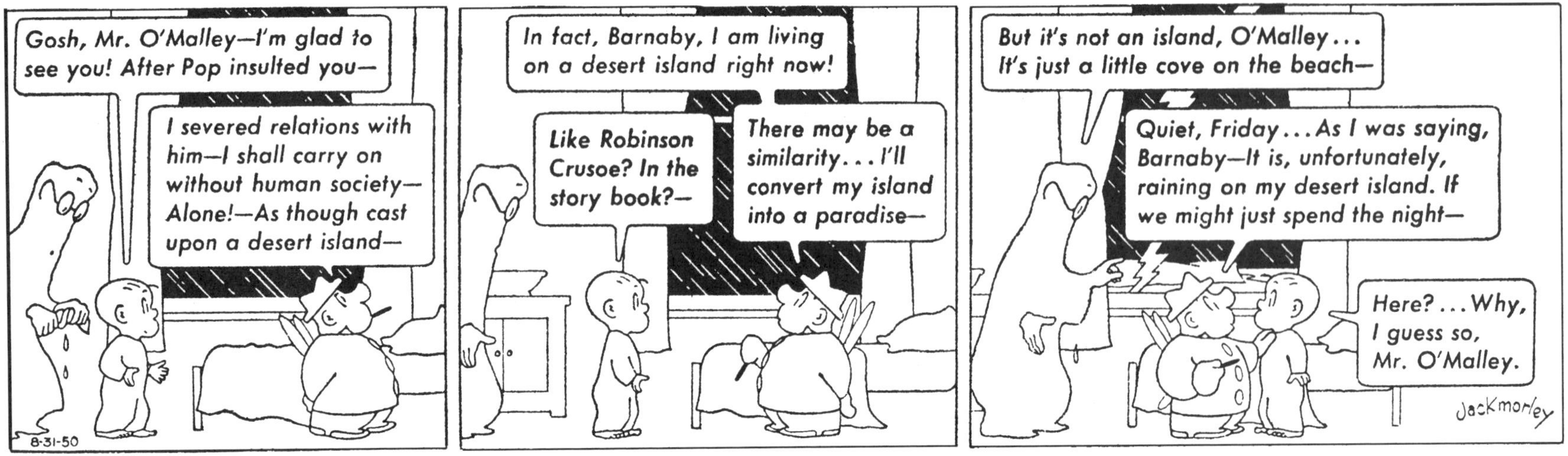
Gosh, Mr. O'Malley—I'm glad to see you! After Pop insulted you—
I severed relations with him—I shall carry on without human society—Alone!—As though cast upon a desert island—
In fact, Barnaby, I am living on a desert island right now!
Like Robinson Crusoe? In the story book?—
There may be a similarity...I'll convert my island into a paradise—
But it's not an island, O'Malley... It's just a little cove on the beach—
Quiet, Friday...As I was saying, Barnaby—It is, unfortunately, raining on my desert island. If we might just spend the night—
Here?...Why, I guess so, Mr. O'Malley.
Jackmorley
8-31-50

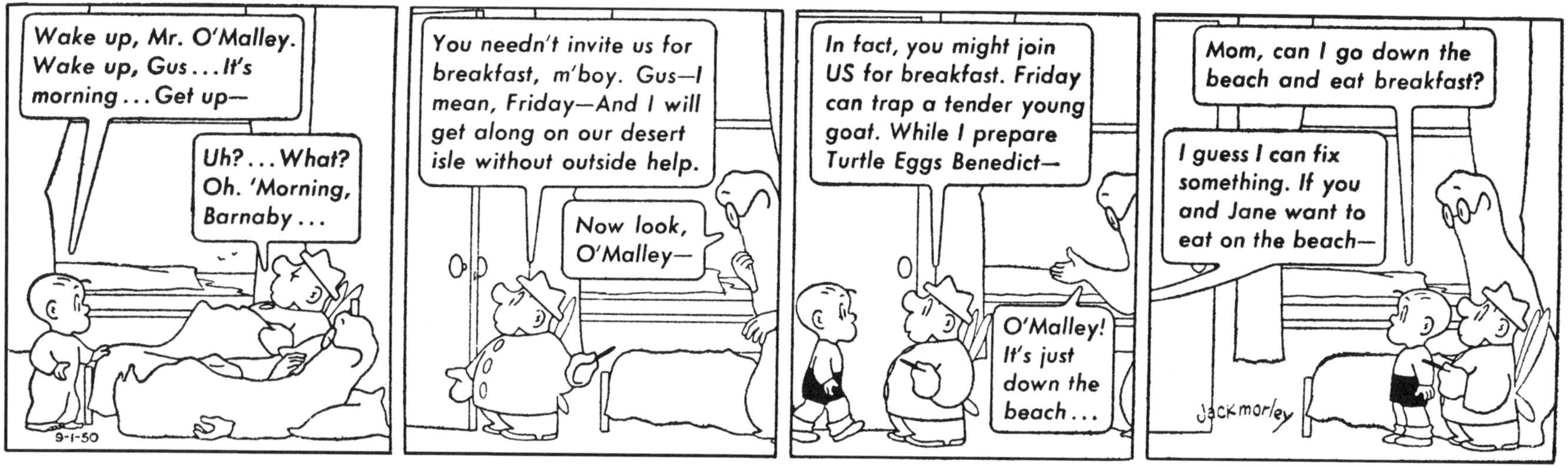

Wake up, Mr. O'Malley. Wake up, Gus . . . It's morning . . . Get up—
Uh? . . . What? Oh. 'Morning, Barnaby . . .
9-1-50
You needn't invite us for breakfast, m'boy. Gus—I mean, Friday—And I will get along on our desert isle without outside help.
Now look, O'Malley—
In fact, you might join US for breakfast. Friday can trap a tender young goat. While I prepare Turtle Eggs Benedict—
O'Malley! It's just down the beach . . .
Mom, can I go down the beach and eat breakfast?
I guess I can fix something. If you and Jane want to eat on the beach—
Jackmorley

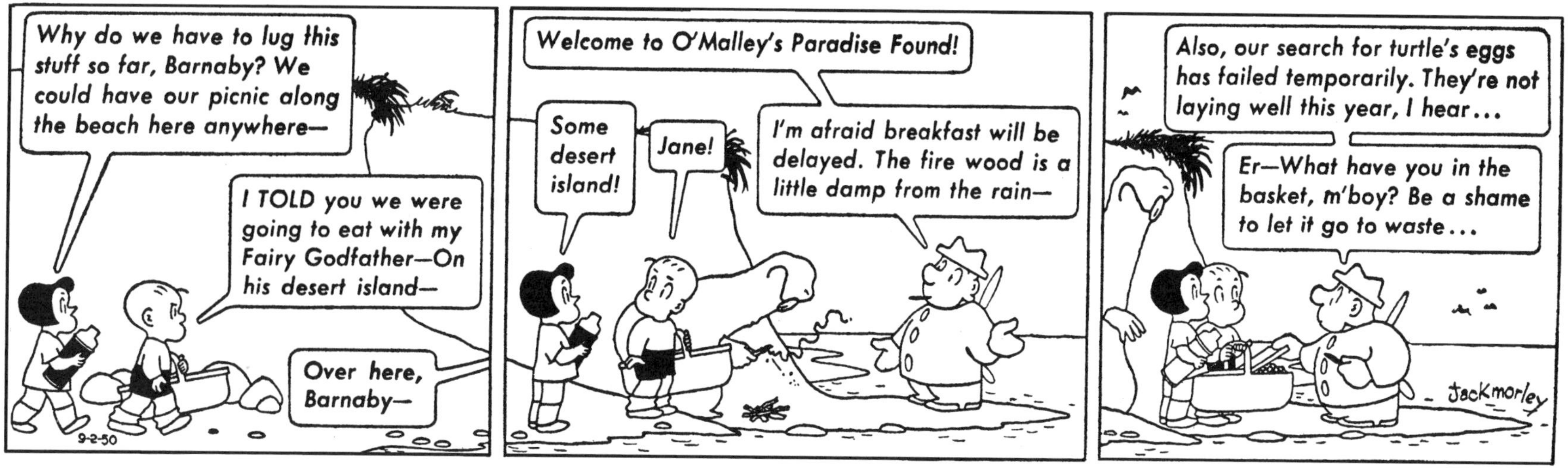

Why do we have to lug this stuff so far, Barnaby? We could have our picnic along the beach here anywhere—
I TOLD you we were going to eat with my Fairy Godfather—On his desert island—
Over here, Barnaby—
9-2-50
Welcome to O'Malley's Paradise Found!
Some desert island!
Jane!
I'm afraid breakfast will be delayed. The fire wood is a little damp from the rain—
Also, our search for turtle's eggs has failed temporarily. They're not laying well this year, I hear . . .
Er—What have you in the basket, m'boy? Be a shame to let it go to waste . . .
Jackmorley

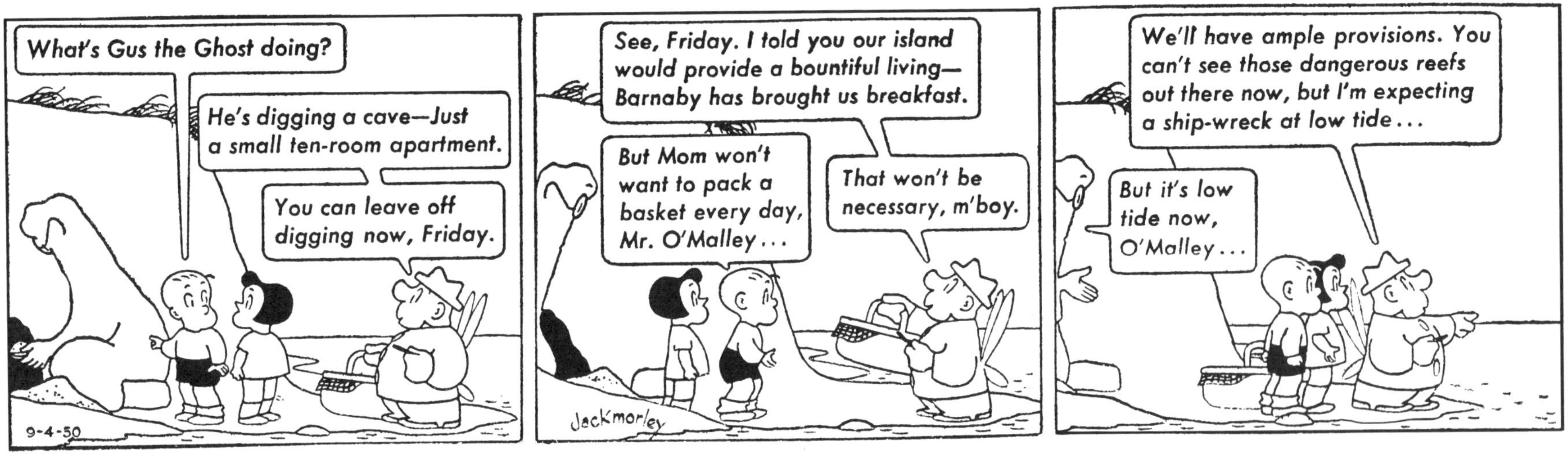
What's Gus the Ghost doing?
He's digging a cave—Just a small ten-room apartment.
You can leave off digging now, Friday.
9-4-50
See, Friday. I told you our island would provide a bountiful living—Barnaby has brought us breakfast.
But Mom won't want to pack a basket every day, Mr. O'Malley...
That won't be necessary, m'boy.
JackMorley
We'll have ample provisions. You can't see those dangerous reefs out there now, but I'm expecting a ship-wreck at low tide...
But it's low tide now, O'Malley...

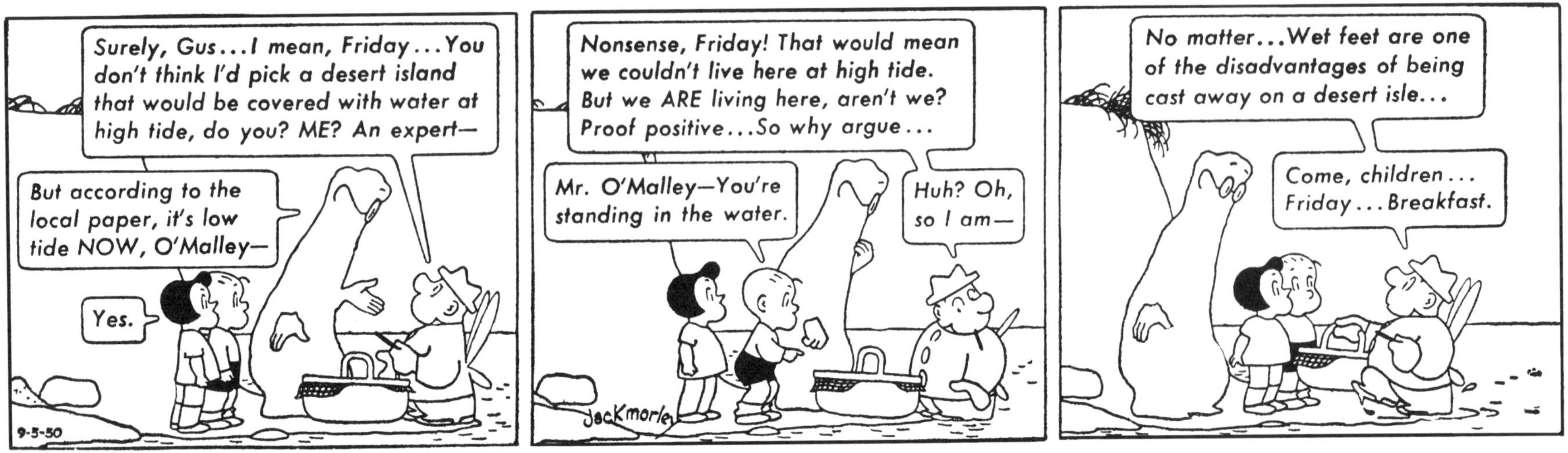
Surely, Gus...I mean, Friday...You don't think I'd pick a desert island that would be covered with water at high tide, do you? ME? An expert—
But according to the local paper, it's low tide NOW, O'Malley—
Yes.
9-5-50
Nonsense, Friday! That would mean we couldn't live here at high tide. But we ARE living here, aren't we? Proof positive...So why argue...
Mr. O'Malley—You're standing in the water.
Huh? Oh, so I am—
JackMorley
No matter...Wet feet are one of the disadvantages of being cast away on a desert isle...
Come, children... Friday...Breakfast.

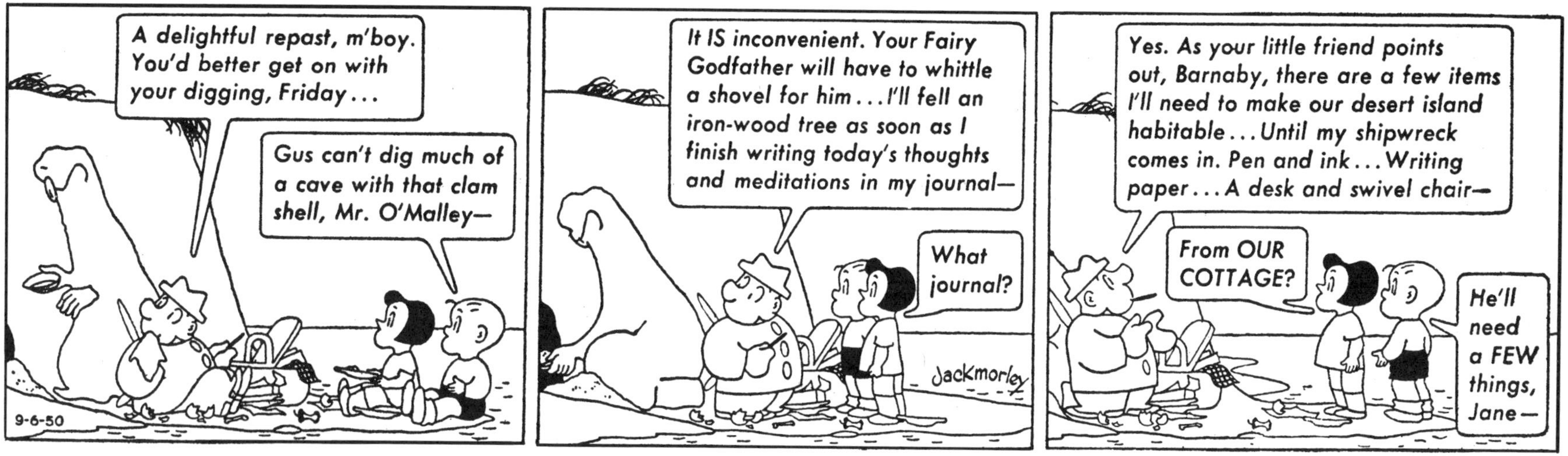
A delightful repast, m'boy. You'd better get on with your digging, Friday...
Gus can't dig much of a cave with that clam shell, Mr. O'Malley—
9-6-50
It IS inconvenient. Your Fairy Godfather will have to whittle a shovel for him...I'll fell an iron-wood tree as soon as I finish writing today's thoughts and meditations in my journal—
What journal?
Jackmorley
Yes. As your little friend points out, Barnaby, there are a few items I'll need to make our desert island habitable...Until my shipwreck comes in. Pen and ink...Writing paper...A desk and swivel chair—
From OUR COTTAGE?
He'll need a FEW things, Jane—

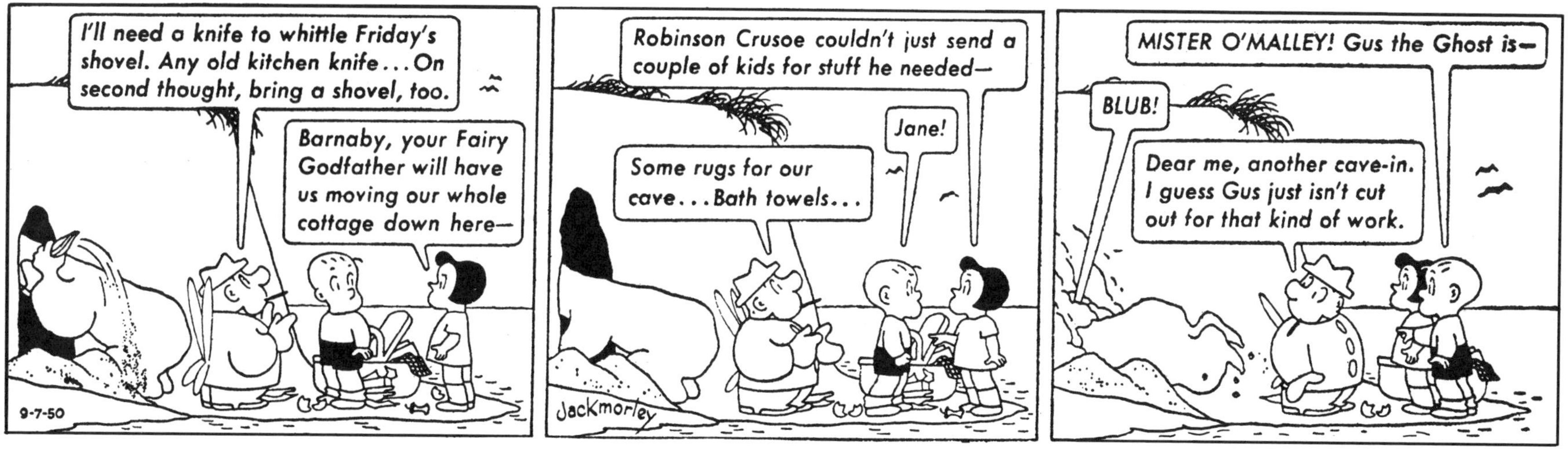
I'll need a knife to whittle Friday's shovel. Any old kitchen knife...On second thought, bring a shovel, too.
Barnaby, your Fairy Godfather will have us moving our whole cottage down here—
9-7-50
Robinson Crusoe couldn't just send a couple of kids for stuff he needed—
Some rugs for our cave...Bath towels...
Jane!
Jackmorley
MISTER O'MALLEY! Gus the Ghost is—
BLUB!
Dear me, another cave-in. I guess Gus just isn't cut out for that kind of work.

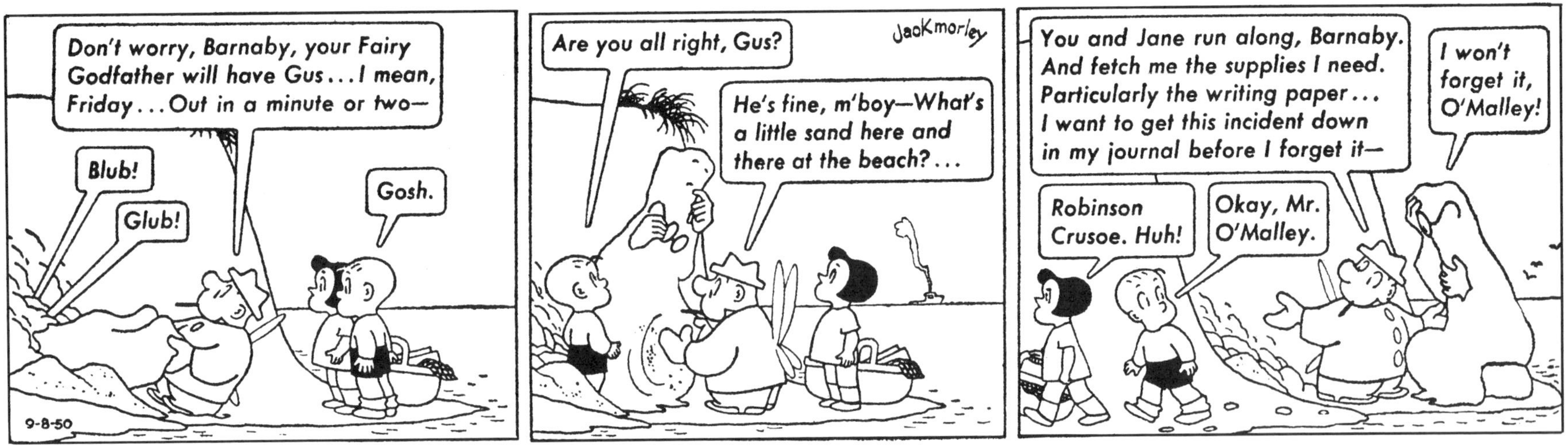
Don't worry, Barnaby, your Fairy Godfather will have Gus...I mean, Friday...Out in a minute or two—
Blub!
Glub!
Gosh.
9-8-50
Are you all right, Gus?
He's fine, m'boy—What's a little sand here and there at the beach?...
You and Jane run along, Barnaby. And fetch me the supplies I need. Particularly the writing paper... I want to get this incident down in my journal before I forget it—
I won't forget it, O'Malley!
Robinson Crusoe. Huh!
Okay, Mr. O'Malley.

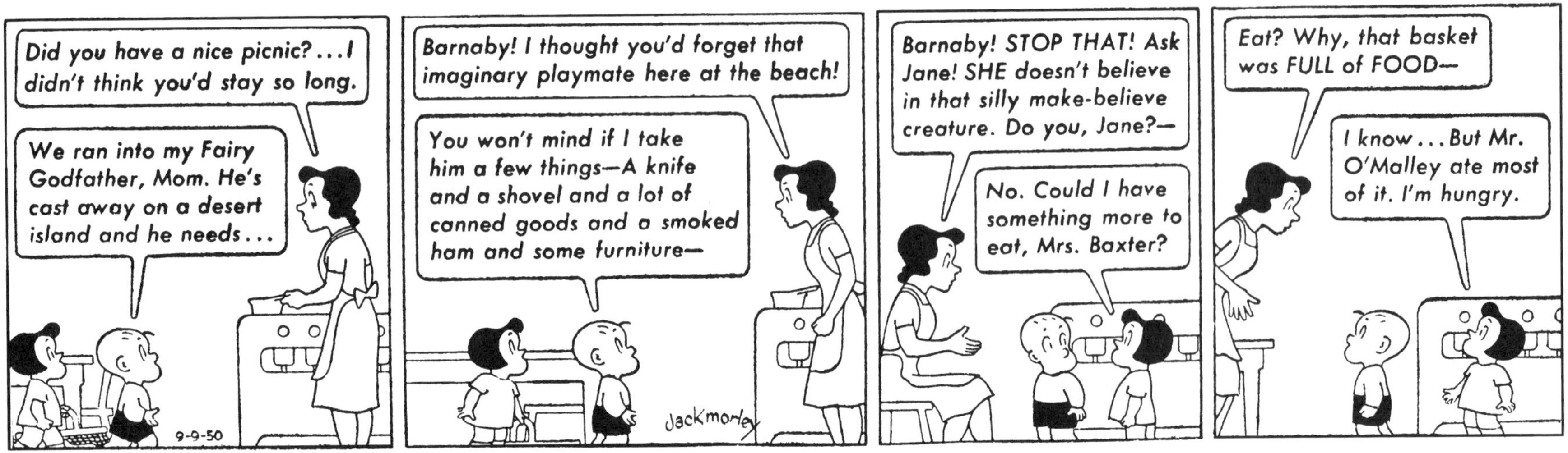
Did you have a nice picnic?...I didn't think you'd stay so long.
We ran into my Fairy Godfather, Mom. He's cast away on a desert island and he needs...
9-9-50
Barnaby! I thought you'd forget that imaginary playmate here at the beach!
You won't mind if I take him a few things—A knife and a shovel and a lot of canned goods and a smoked ham and some furniture—
Barnaby! STOP THAT! Ask Jane! SHE doesn't believe in that silly make-believe creature. Do you, Jane?—
No. Could I have something more to eat, Mrs. Baxter?
Eat? Why, that basket was FULL of FOOD—
I know...But Mr. O'Malley ate most of it. I'm hungry.

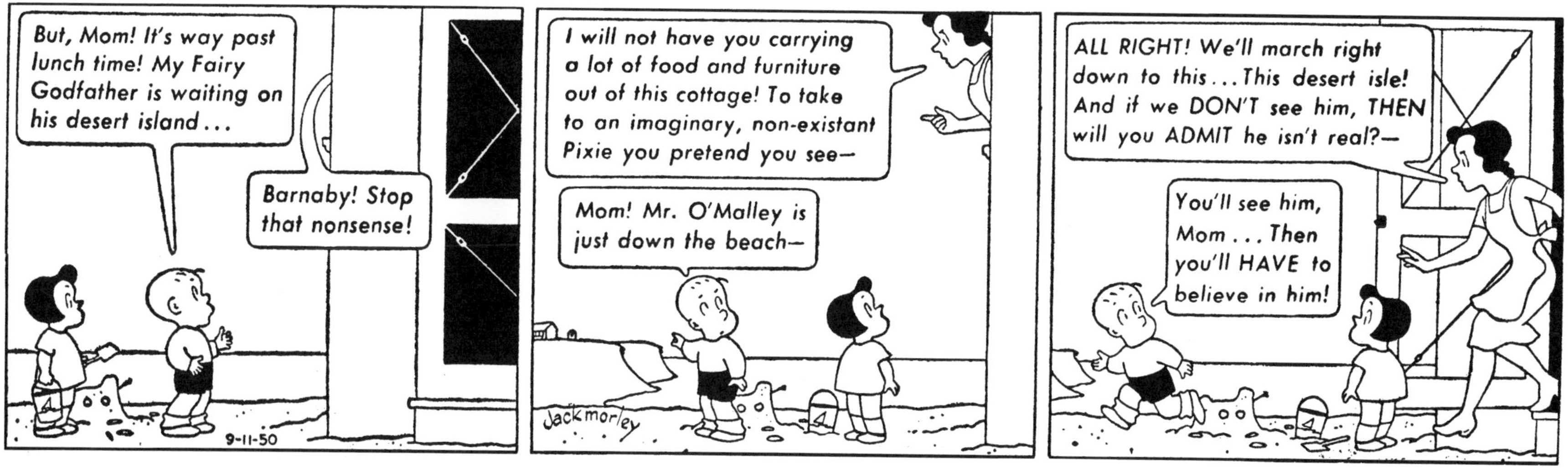
But, Mom! It's way past lunch time! My Fairy Godfather is waiting on his desert island...
Barnaby! Stop that nonsense!
9-11-50
I will not have you carrying a lot of food and furniture out of this cottage! To take to an imaginary, non-existant Pixie you pretend you see—
Mom! Mr. O'Malley is just down the beach—
Jackmorley
ALL RIGHT! We'll march right down to this...This desert isle! And if we DON'T see him, THEN will you ADMIT he isn't real?—
You'll see him, Mom...Then you'll HAVE to believe in him!

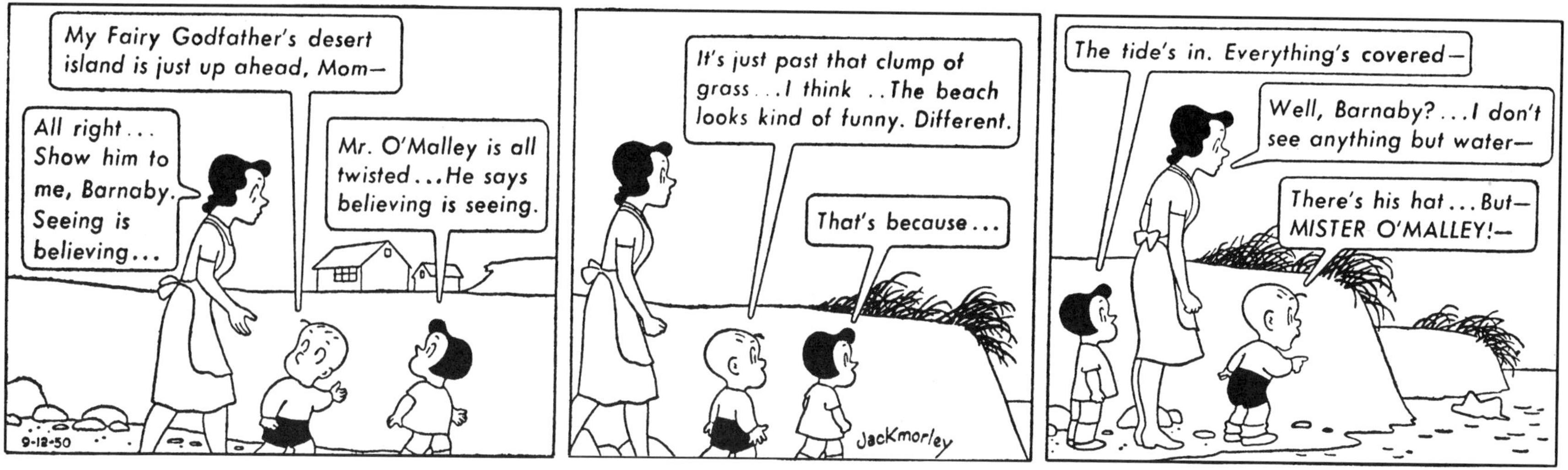
My Fairy Godfather's desert island is just up ahead, Mom—
All right... Show him to me, Barnaby. Seeing is believing...
Mr. O'Malley is all twisted...He says believing is seeing.
9-12-50
It's just past that clump of grass...I think ..The beach looks kind of funny. Different.
That's because...
Jackmorley
The tide's in. Everything's covered—
Well, Barnaby?...I don't see anything but water—
There's his hat...But— MISTER O'MALLEY!—

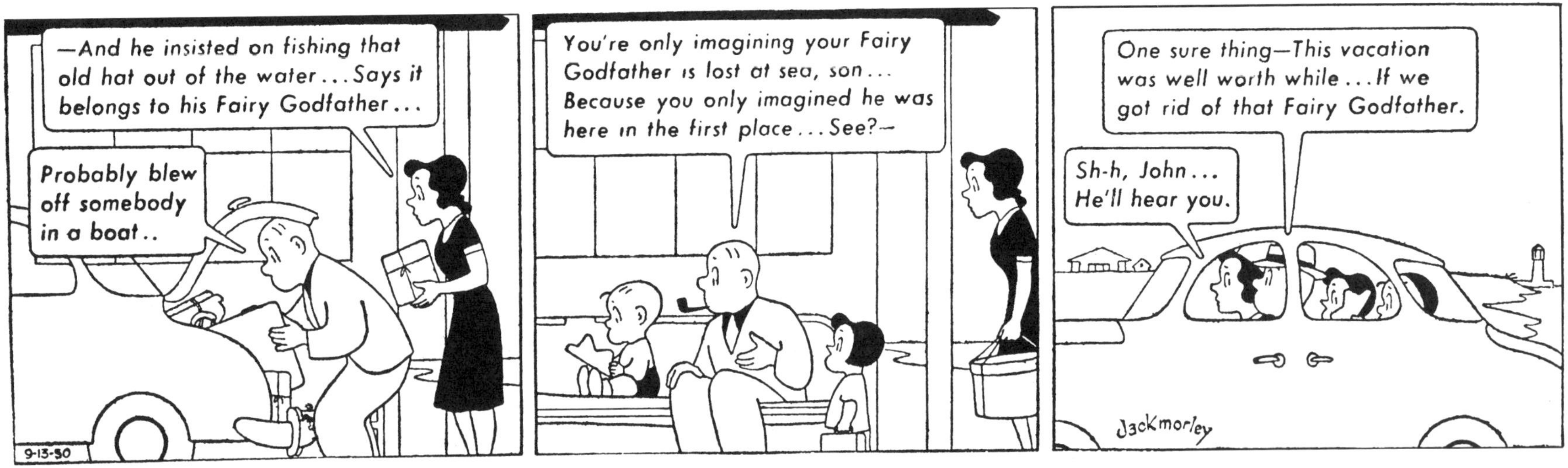
—And he insisted on fishing that old hat out of the water . . . Says it belongs to his Fairy Godfather . . .
Probably blew off somebody in a boat . .
9-13-50
You're only imagining your Fairy Godfather is lost at sea, son . . . Because you only imagined he was here in the first place . . . See?—
One sure thing—This vacation was well worth while . . . If we got rid of that Fairy Godfather.
Sh-h, John . . . He'll hear you.
Jackmorley

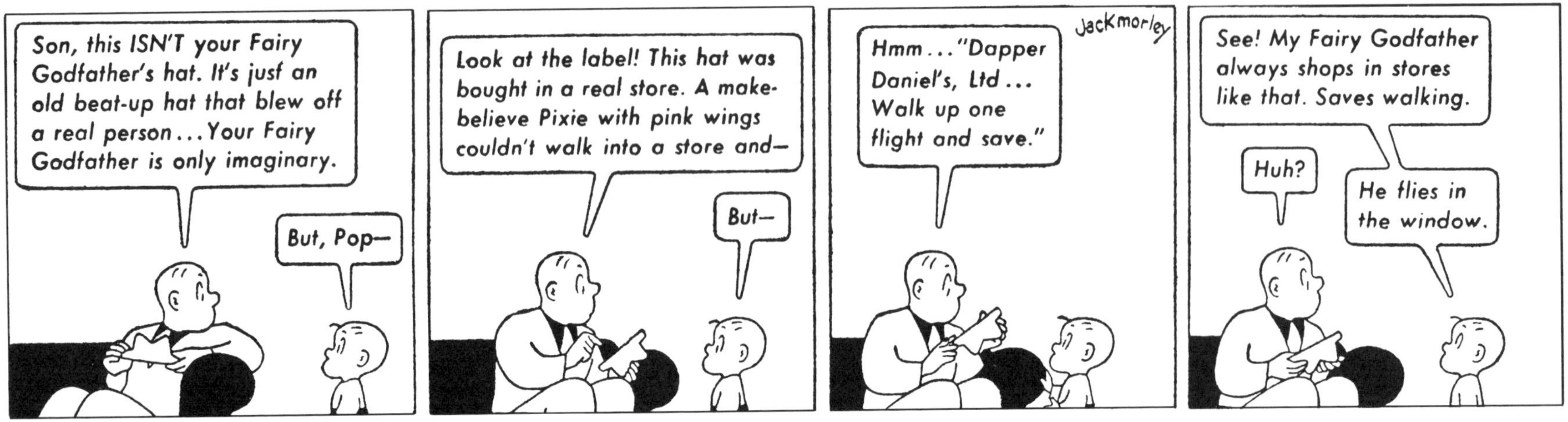
Son, this ISN'T your Fairy Godfather's hat. It's just an old beat-up hat that blew off a real person . . . Your Fairy Godfather is only imaginary.
But, Pop—
Look at the label! This hat was bought in a real store. A make-believe Pixie with pink wings couldn't walk into a store and—
But—
Jackmorley
Hmm . . . "Dapper Daniel's, Ltd . . . Walk up one flight and save."
See! My Fairy Godfather always shops in stores like that. Saves walking.
Huh?
He flies in the window.

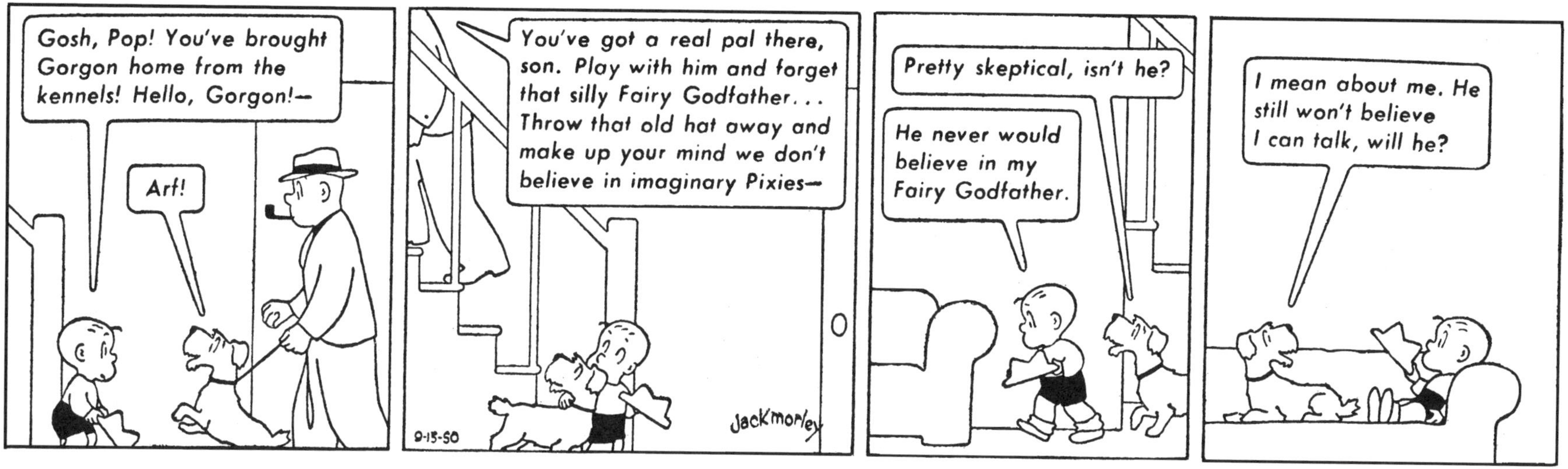
Gosh, Pop! You've brought Gorgon home from the kennels! Hello, Gorgon!—
Arf!
You've got a real pal there, son. Play with him and forget that silly Fairy Godfather... Throw that old hat away and make up your mind we don't believe in imaginary Pixies—
9-15-50
Jack Morley
Pretty skeptical, isn't he?
He never would believe in my Fairy Godfather.
I mean about me. He still won't believe I can talk, will he?

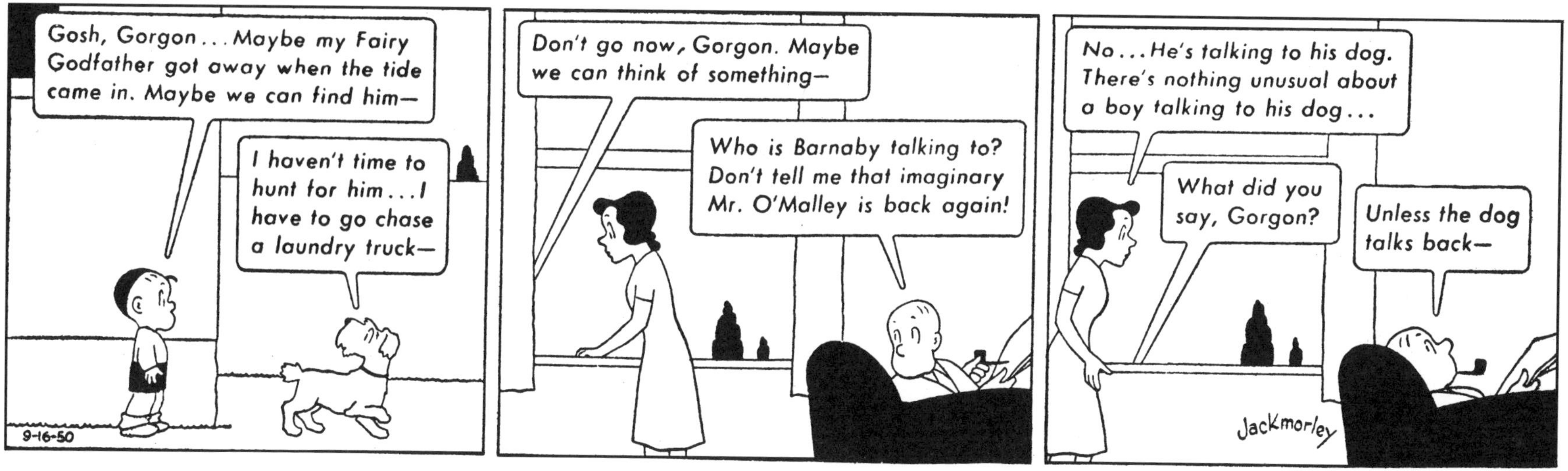
Gosh, Gorgon... Maybe my Fairy Godfather got away when the tide came in. Maybe we can find him—
I haven't time to hunt for him... I have to go chase a laundry truck—
9-16-50
Don't go now, Gorgon. Maybe we can think of something—
Who is Barnaby talking to? Don't tell me that imaginary Mr. O'Malley is back again!
No... He's talking to his dog. There's nothing unusual about a boy talking to his dog...
What did you say, Gorgon?
Unless the dog talks back—
Jack Morley

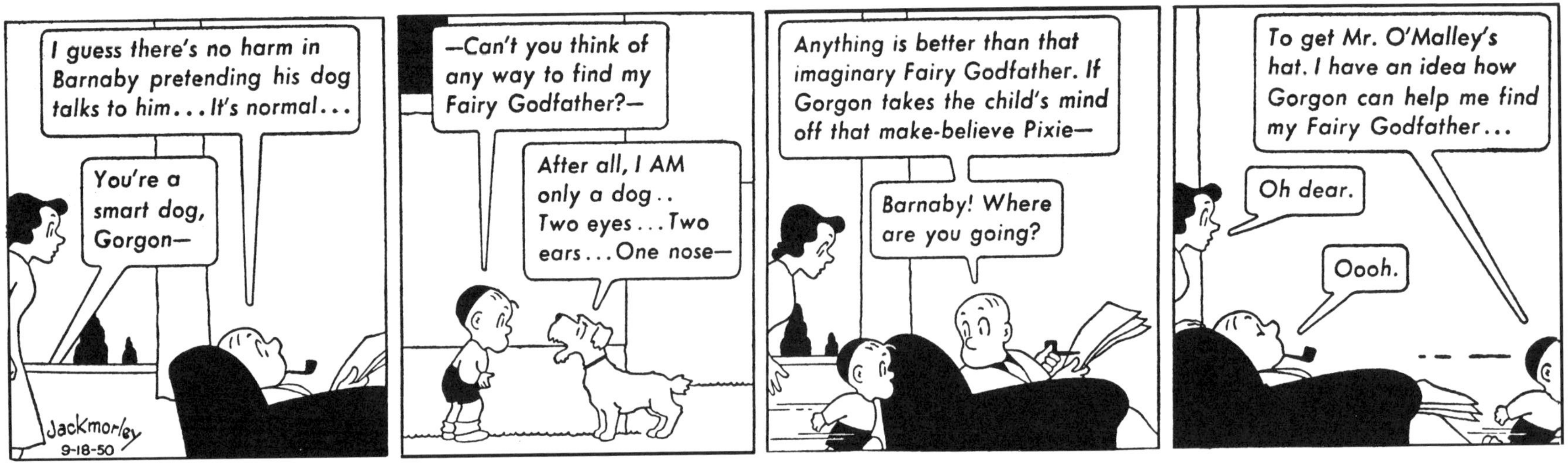
I guess there's no harm in Barnaby pretending his dog talks to him . . . It's normal . . .
You're a smart dog, Gorgon—
Jackmorley
9-18-50
—Can't you think of any way to find my Fairy Godfather?—
After all, I AM only a dog . . Two eyes . . . Two ears . . . One nose—
Anything is better than that imaginary Fairy Godfather. If Gorgon takes the child's mind off that make-believe Pixie—
Barnaby! Where are you going?
To get Mr. O'Malley's hat. I have an idea how Gorgon can help me find my Fairy Godfather . . .
Oh dear.
Oooh.

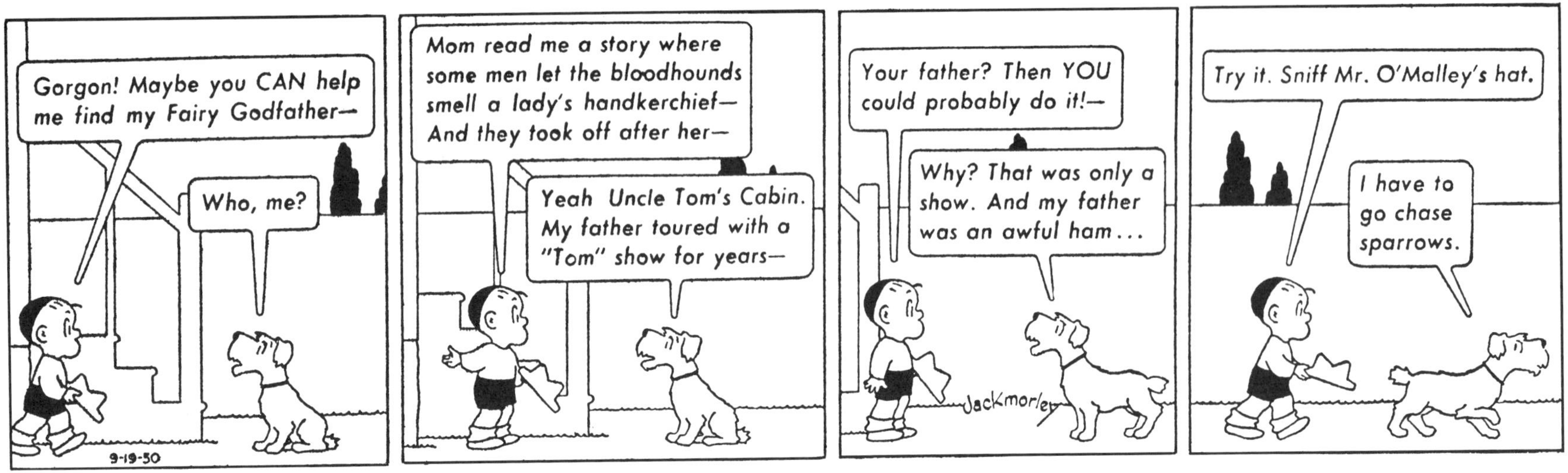
Gorgon! Maybe you CAN help me find my Fairy Godfather—
Who, me?
9-19-50
Mom read me a story where some men let the bloodhounds smell a lady's handkerchief— And they took off after her—
Yeah Uncle Tom's Cabin. My father toured with a "Tom" show for years—
Your father? Then YOU could probably do it!—
Why? That was only a show. And my father was an awful ham . . .
Jackmorley
Try it. Sniff Mr. O'Malley's hat.
I have to go chase sparrows.

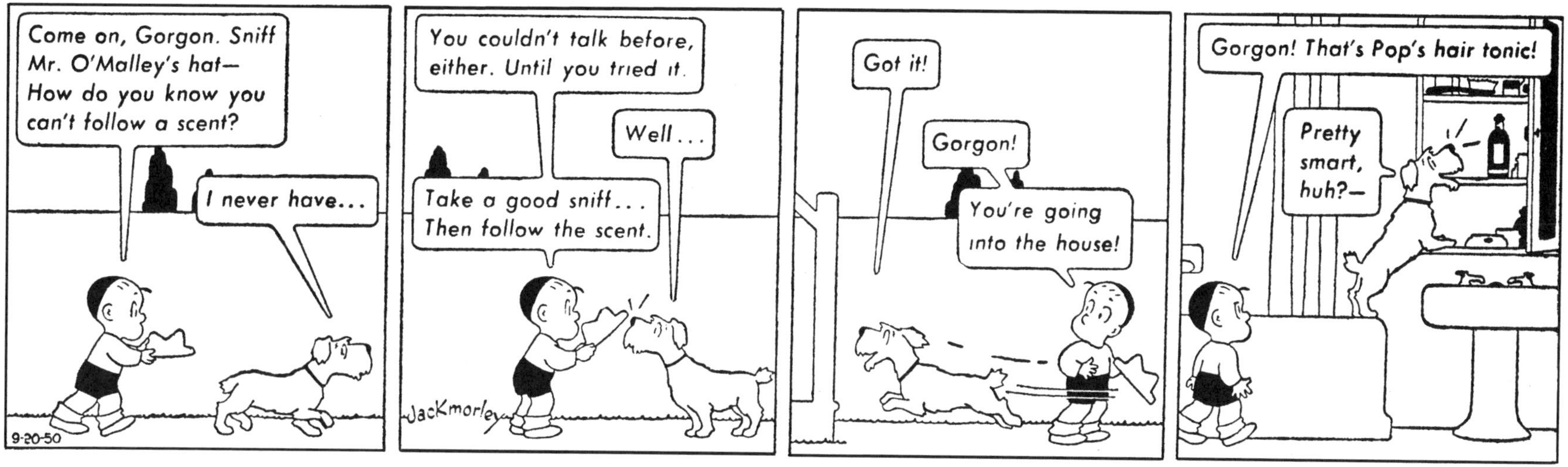
Come on, Gorgon. Sniff Mr. O'Malley's hat— How do you know you can't follow a scent?
I never have...
You couldn't talk before, either. Until you tried it.
Take a good sniff... Then follow the scent.
Well...
Got it!
Gorgon!
You're going into the house!
Gorgon! That's Pop's hair tonic!
Pretty smart, huh?—
9-20-50
JacKmorley

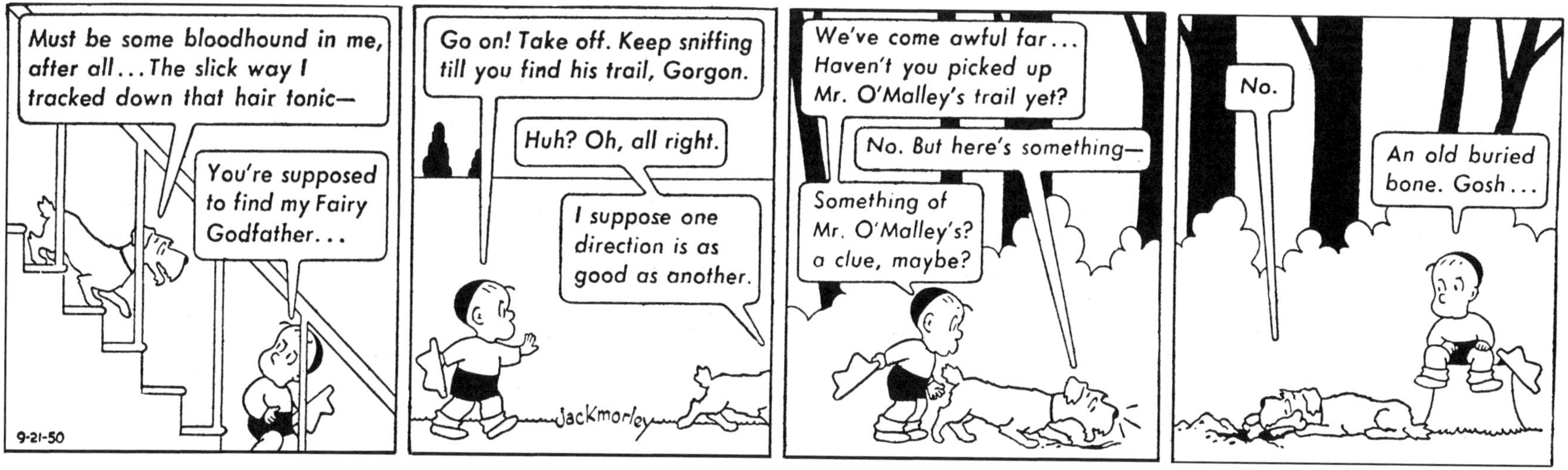
Must be some bloodhound in me, after all... The slick way I tracked down that hair tonic—
You're supposed to find my Fairy Godfather...
Go on! Take off. Keep sniffing till you find his trail, Gorgon.
Huh? Oh, all right.
I suppose one direction is as good as another.
We've come awful far... Haven't you picked up Mr. O'Malley's trail yet?
No. But here's something—
Something of Mr. O'Malley's? a clue, maybe?
No.
An old buried bone. Gosh...
9-21-50
JacKmorley

September 20 – 21

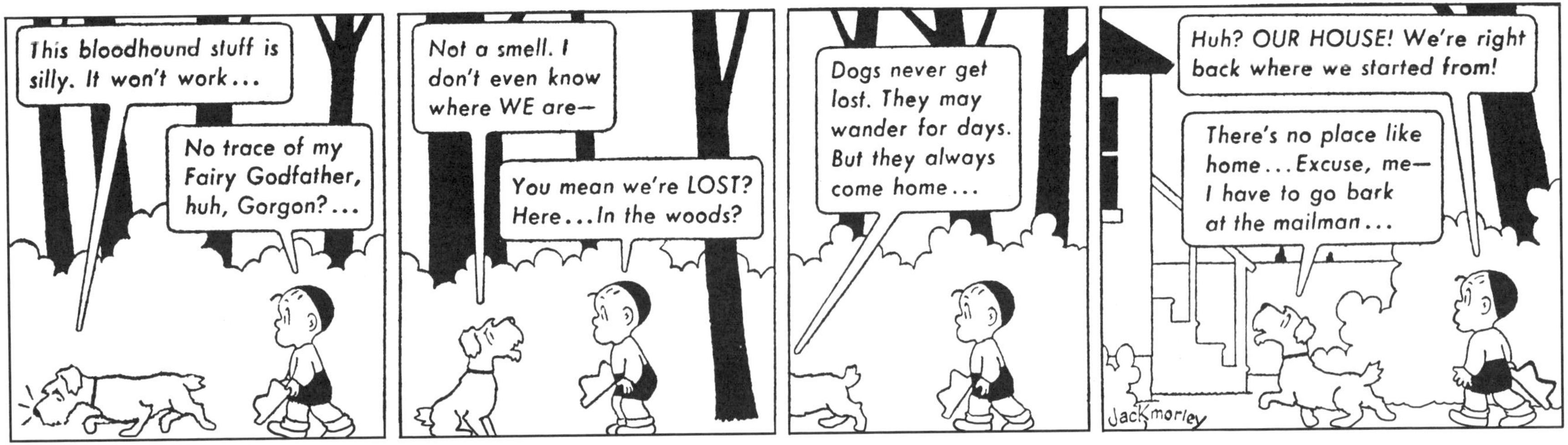
This bloodhound stuff is silly. It won't work...
No trace of my Fairy Godfather, huh, Gorgon?...
Not a smell. I don't even know where WE are—
You mean we're LOST? Here...In the woods?
Dogs never get lost. They may wander for days. But they always come home...
Huh? OUR HOUSE! We're right back where we started from!
There's no place like home...Excuse, me— I have to go bark at the mailman...
JacKmorley

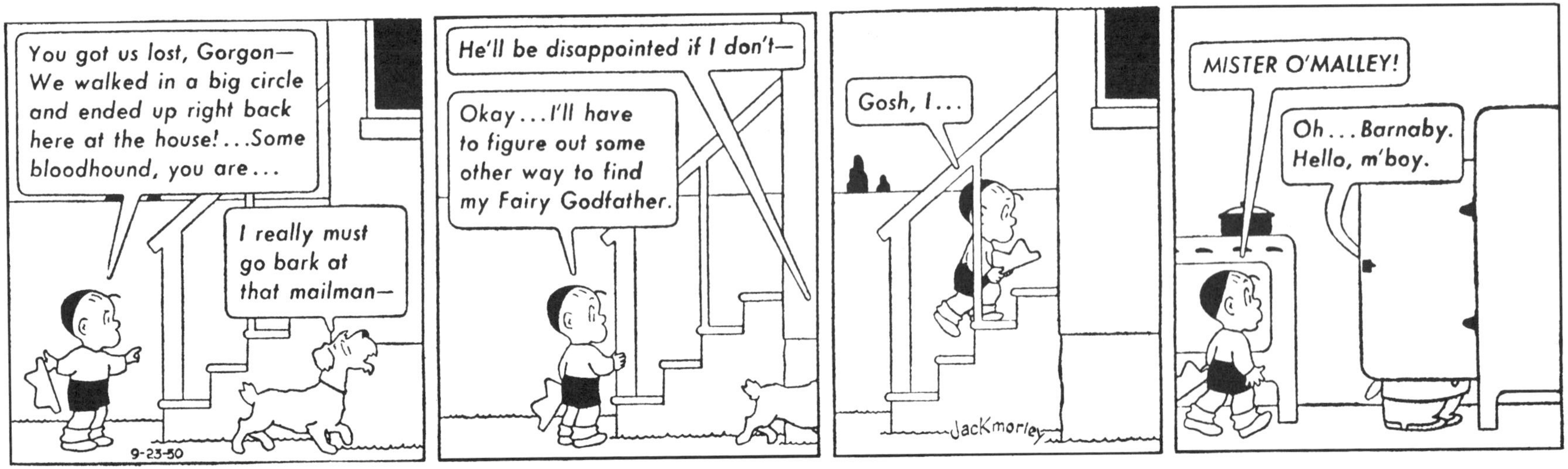
You got us lost, Gorgon— We walked in a big circle and ended up right back here at the house!...Some bloodhound, you are...
I really must go bark at that mailman—
9-23-50
He'll be disappointed if I don't—
Okay...I'll have to figure out some other way to find my Fairy Godfather.
Gosh, I...
JacKmorley
MISTER O'MALLEY!
Oh...Barnaby. Hello, m'boy.

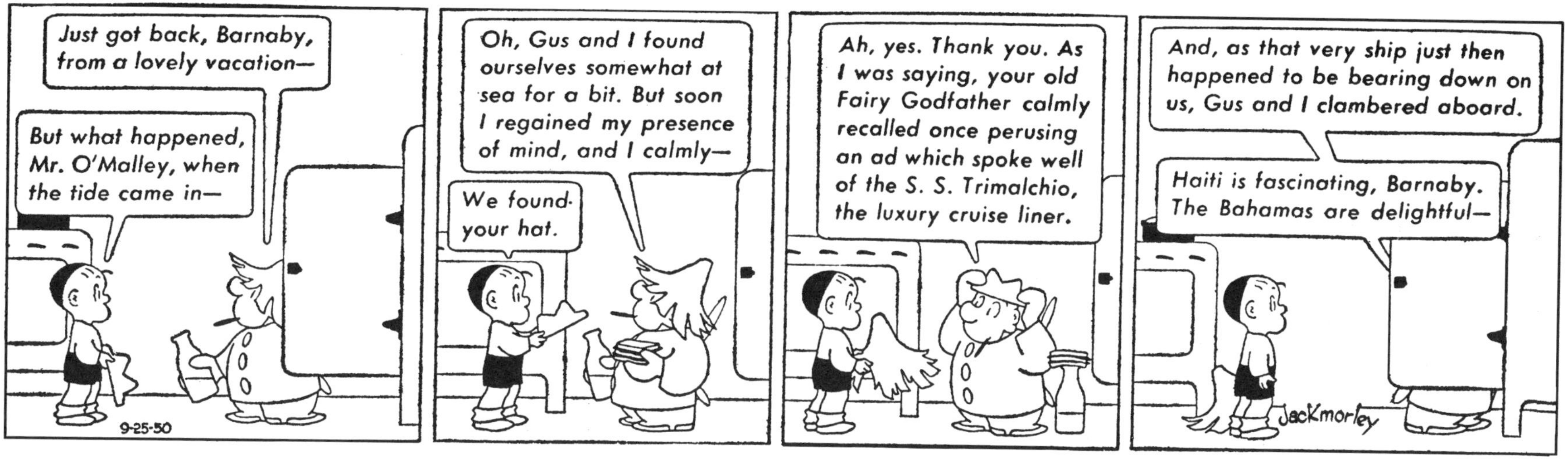
Just got back, Barnaby, from a lovely vacation—
But what happened, Mr. O'Malley, when the tide came in—
9-25-50
Oh, Gus and I found ourselves somewhat at sea for a bit. But soon I regained my presence of mind, and I calmly—
We found your hat.
Ah, yes. Thank you. As I was saying, your old Fairy Godfather calmly recalled once perusing an ad which spoke well of the S. S. Trimalchio, the luxury cruise liner.
And, as that very ship just then happened to be bearing down on us, Gus and I clambered aboard.
Haiti is fascinating, Barnaby. The Bahamas are delightful—
JacKmorley

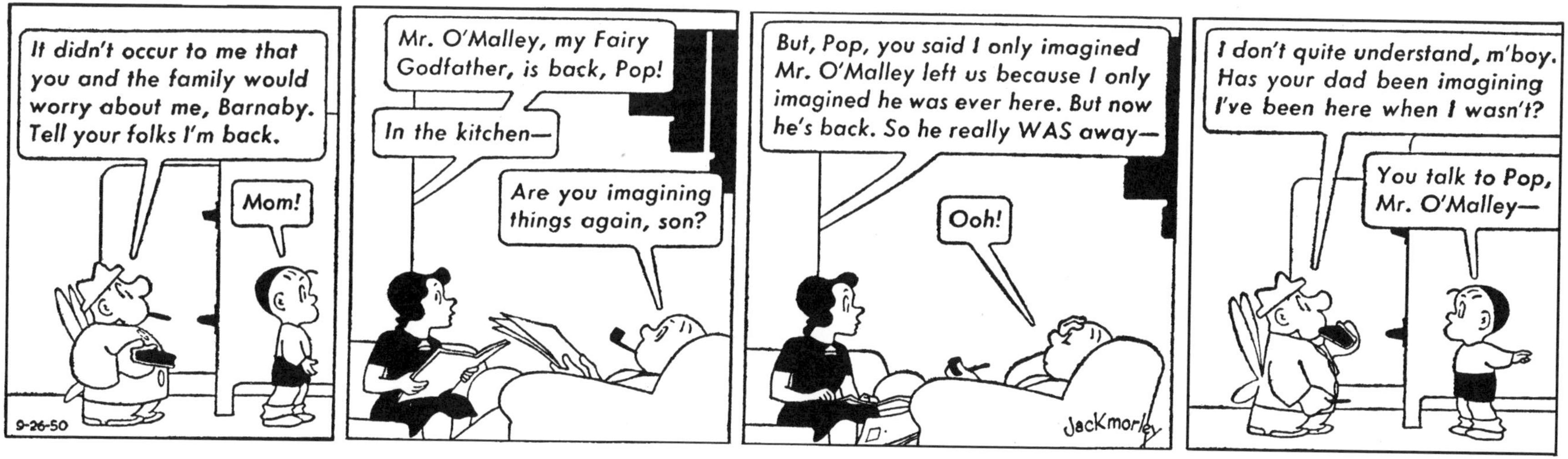
It didn't occur to me that you and the family would worry about me, Barnaby. Tell your folks I'm back.
Mom!
9-26-50
Mr. O'Malley, my Fairy Godfather, is back, Pop!
In the kitchen—
Are you imagining things again, son?
But, Pop, you said I only imagined Mr. O'Malley left us because I only imagined he was ever here. But now he's back. So he really WAS away—
Ooh!
JacKmorley
I don't quite understand, m'boy. Has your dad been imagining I've been here when I wasn't?
You talk to Pop, Mr. O'Malley—

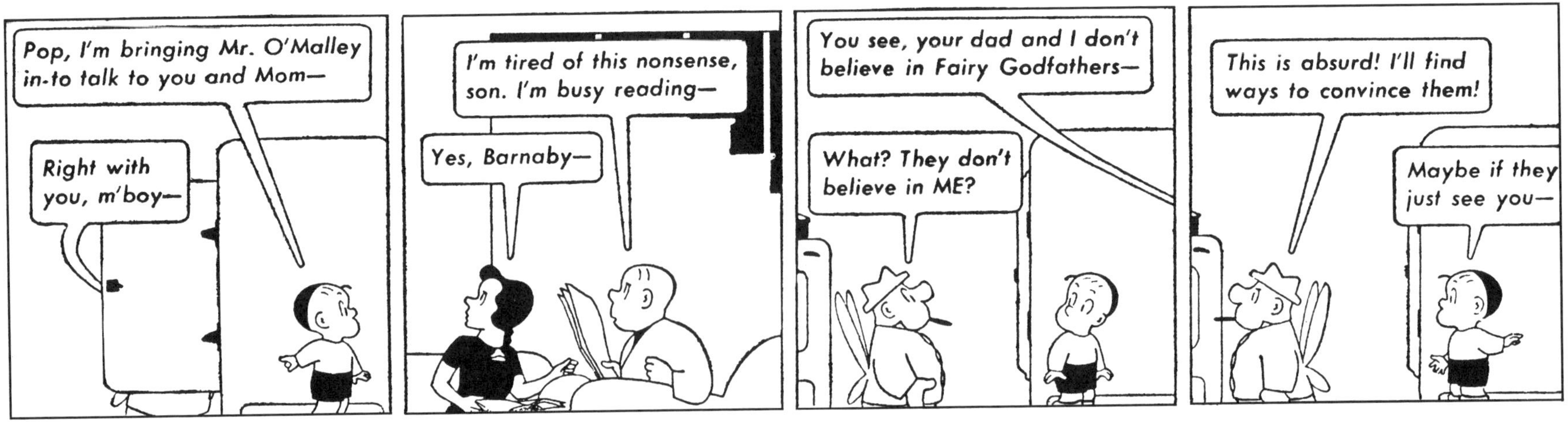
Pop, I'm bringing Mr. O'Malley in-to talk to you and Mom—
Right with you, m'boy—
I'm tired of this nonsense, son. I'm busy reading—
Yes, Barnaby—
You see, your dad and I don't believe in Fairy Godfathers—
What? They don't believe in ME?
This is absurd! I'll find ways to convince them!
Maybe if they just see you—

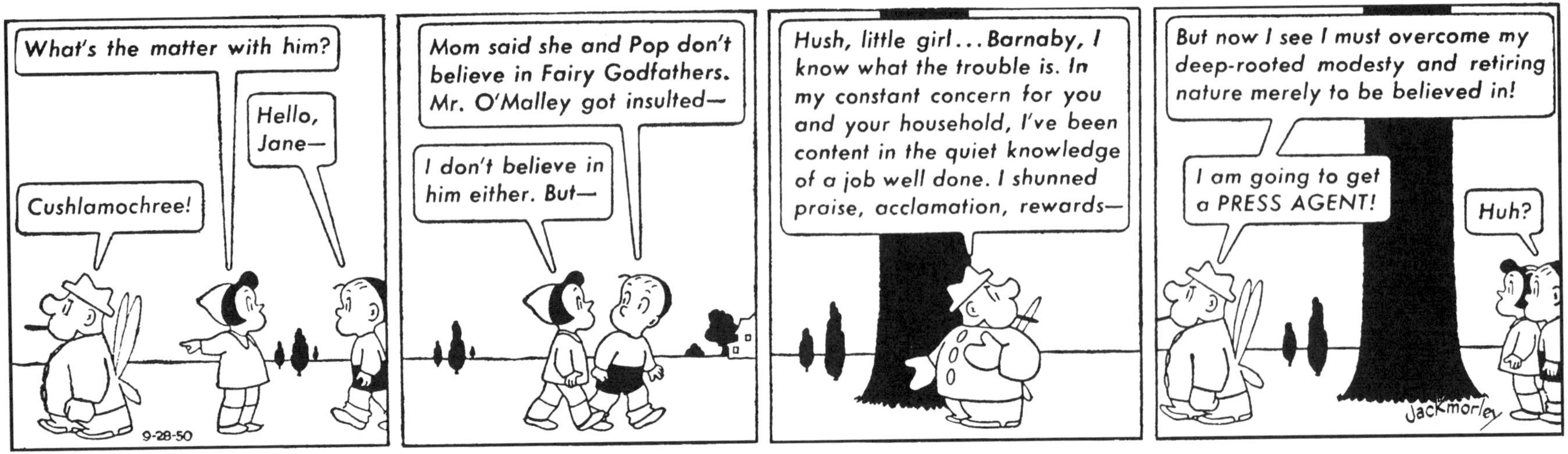
What's the matter with him?
Hello, Jane—
Cushlamochree!
9-28-50
Mom said she and Pop don't believe in Fairy Godfathers. Mr. O'Malley got insulted—
I don't believe in him either. But—
Hush, little girl... Barnaby, I know what the trouble is. In my constant concern for you and your household, I've been content in the quiet knowledge of a job well done. I shunned praise, acclamation, rewards—
But now I see I must overcome my deep-rooted modesty and retiring nature merely to be believed in!
I am going to get a PRESS AGENT!
Huh?
Jackmorley

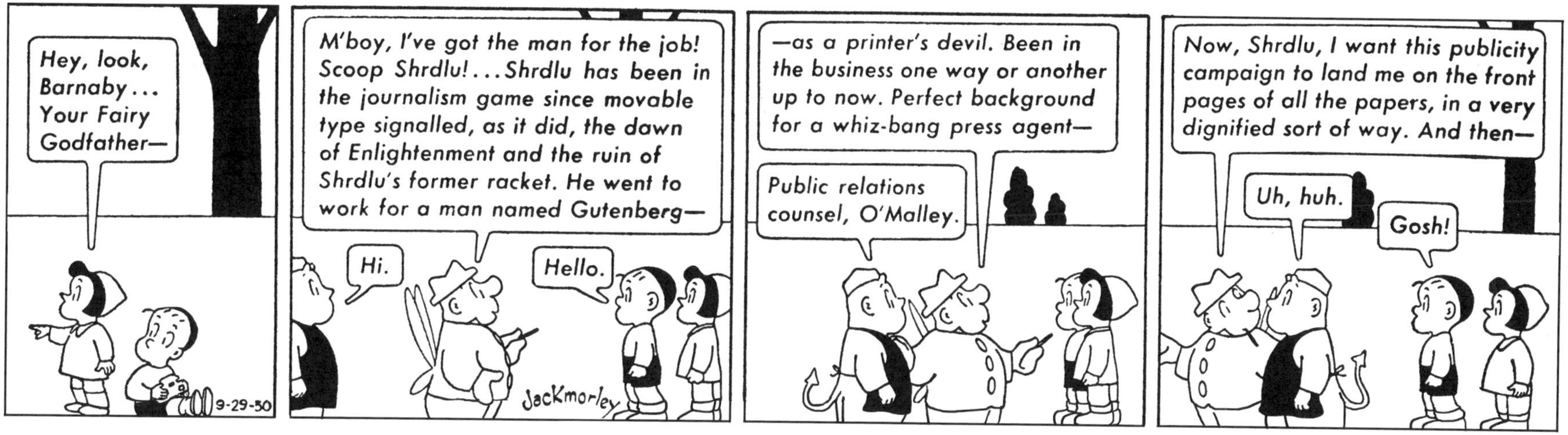
Hey, look, Barnaby... Your Fairy Godfather—
9-29-50
M'boy, I've got the man for the job! Scoop Shrdlu!...Shrdlu has been in the journalism game since movable type signalled, as it did, the dawn of Enlightenment and the ruin of Shrdlu's former racket. He went to work for a man named Gutenberg—
Hi.
Hello.
JacKmorley
—as a printer's devil. Been in the business one way or another up to now. Perfect background for a whiz-bang press agent—
Public relations counsel, O'Malley.
Now, Shrdlu, I want this publicity campaign to land me on the front pages of all the papers, in a very dignified sort of way. And then—
Uh, huh.
Gosh!

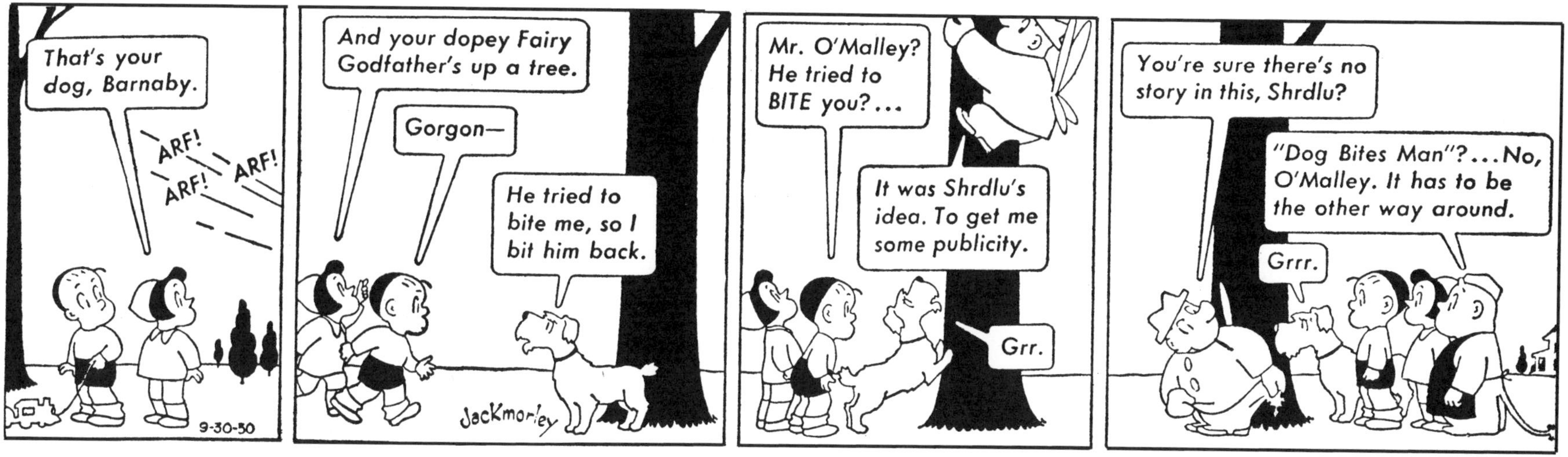
That's your dog, Barnaby.
ARF!
ARF!
ARF!
9-30-50
And your dopey Fairy Godfather's up a tree.
Gorgon—
He tried to bite me, so I bit him back.
JacKmorley
Mr. O'Malley? He tried to BITE you?...
It was Shrdlu's idea. To get me some publicity.
Grr.
You're sure there's no story in this, Shrdlu?
"Dog Bites Man"?...No, O'Malley. It has to be the other way around.
Grrr.

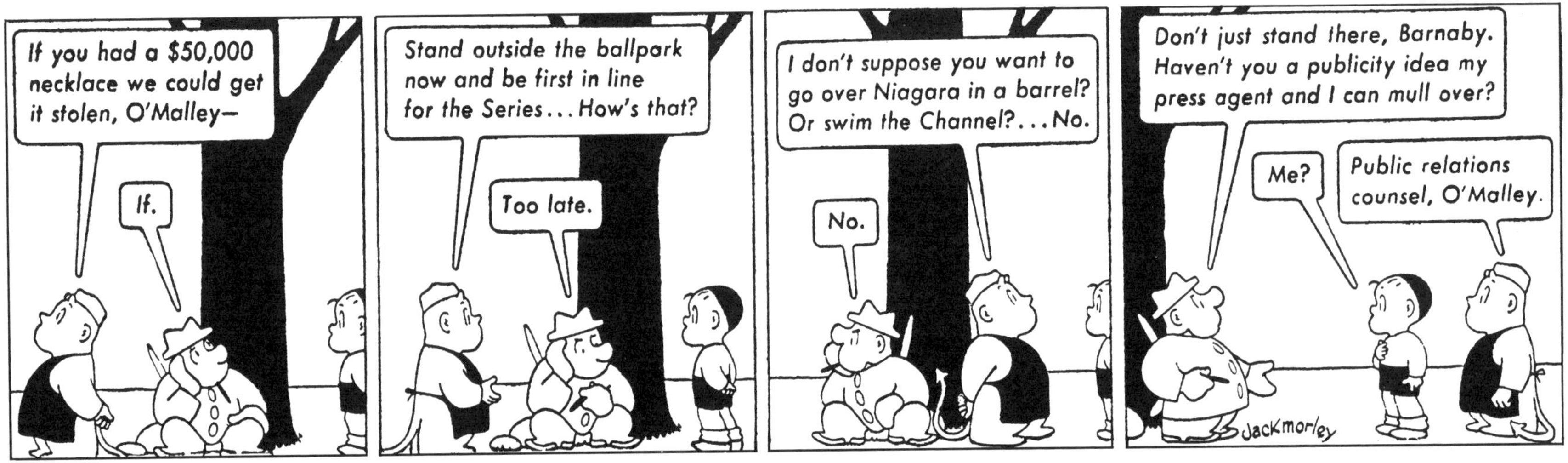

If you had a $50,000 necklace we could get it stolen, O'Malley—
If.
Stand outside the ballpark now and be first in line for the Series... How's that?
Too late.
I don't suppose you want to go over Niagara in a barrel? Or swim the Channel?... No.
No.
Don't just stand there, Barnaby. Haven't you a publicity idea my press agent and I can mull over?
Me?
Public relations counsel, O'Malley.
JACKmorley

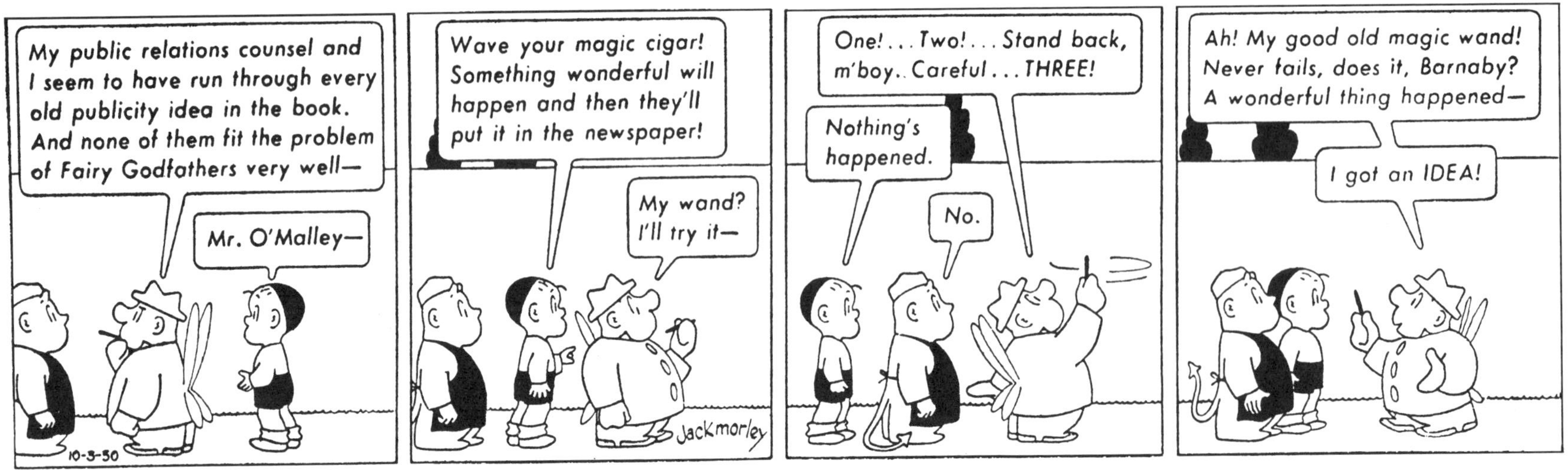

My public relations counsel and I seem to have run through every old publicity idea in the book. And none of them fit the problem of Fairy Godfathers very well—
Mr. O'Malley—
10-3-50
Wave your magic cigar! Something wonderful will happen and then they'll put it in the newspaper!
My wand? I'll try it—
JACKmorley
One!... Two!... Stand back, m'boy.. Careful... THREE!
Nothing's happened.
No.
Ah! My good old magic wand! Never fails, does it, Barnaby? A wonderful thing happened—
I got an IDEA!

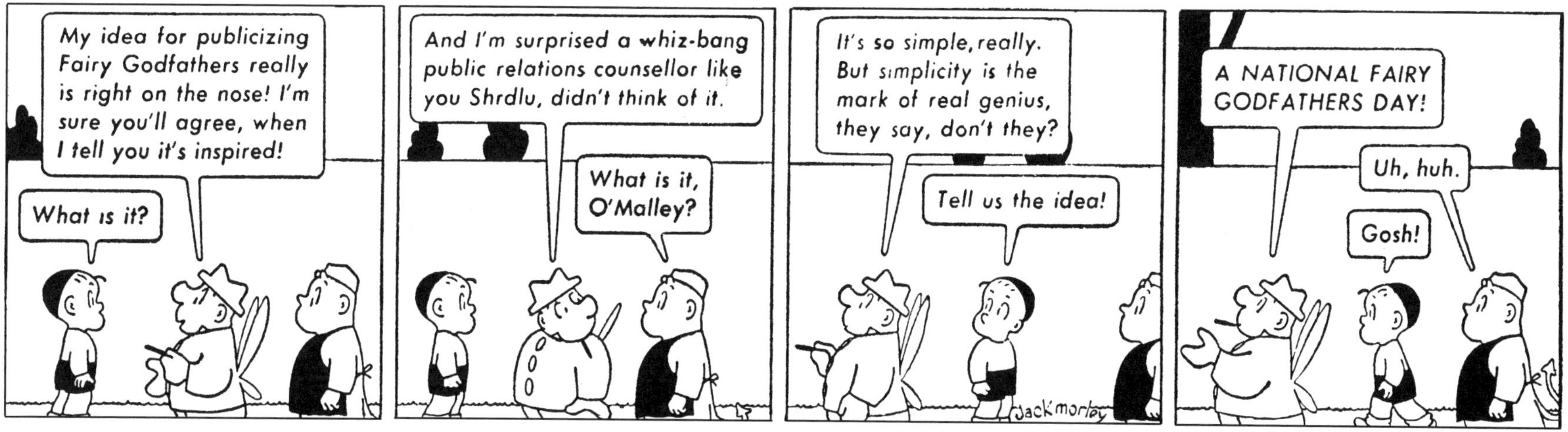
What is it?
My idea for publicizing Fairy Godfathers really is right on the nose! I'm sure you'll agree, when I tell you it's inspired!
And I'm surprised a whiz-bang public relations counsellor like you Shrdlu, didn't think of it.
What is it, O'Malley?
It's so simple, really. But simplicity is the mark of real genius, they say, don't they?
Tell us the idea!
A NATIONAL FAIRY GODFATHERS DAY!
Gosh!
Uh, huh.
JACKMORLEY

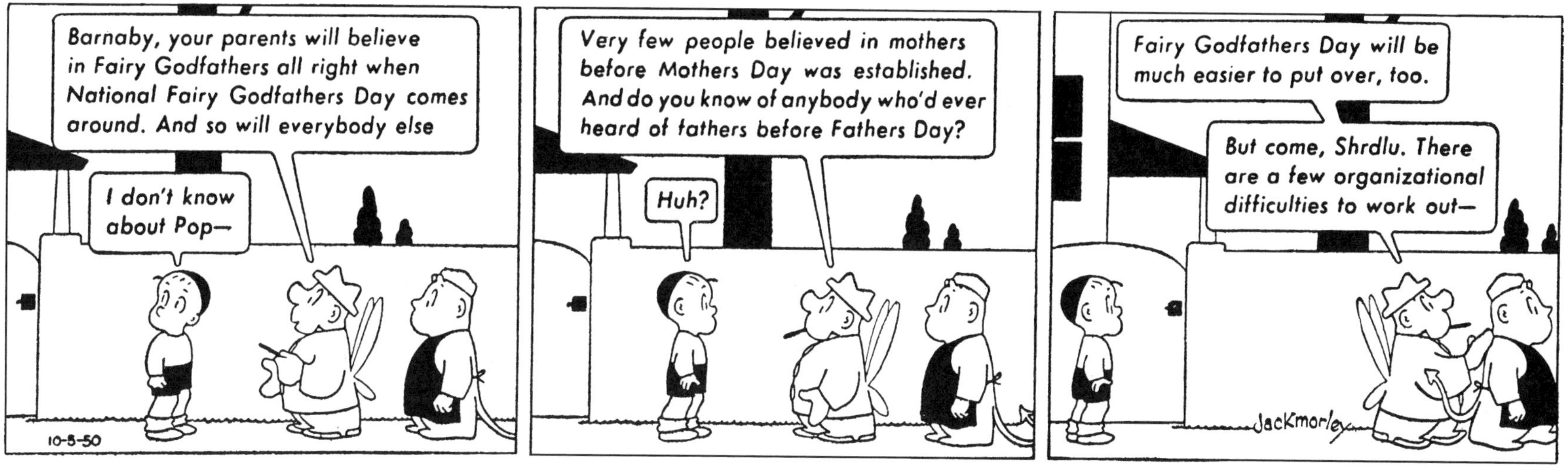
I don't know about Pop—
Barnaby, your parents will believe in Fairy Godfathers all right when National Fairy Godfathers Day comes around. And so will everybody else
10-5-50
Huh?
Very few people believed in mothers before Mothers Day was established. And do you know of anybody who'd ever heard of fathers before Fathers Day?
Fairy Godfathers Day will be much easier to put over, too.
But come, Shrdlu. There are a few organizational difficulties to work out—
JACKMORLEY

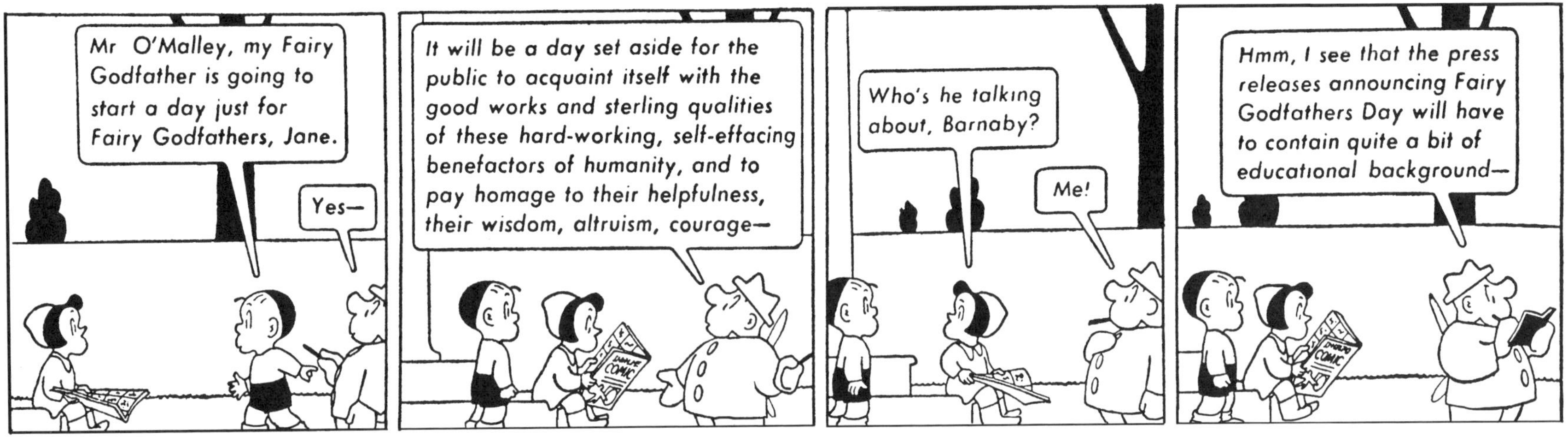
Mr O'Malley, my Fairy Godfather is going to start a day just for Fairy Godfathers, Jane.
Yes—
It will be a day set aside for the public to acquaint itself with the good works and sterling qualities of these hard-working, self-effacing benefactors of humanity, and to pay homage to their helpfulness, their wisdom, altruism, courage—
Who's he talking about, Barnaby?
Me!
Hmm, I see that the press releases announcing Fairy Godfathers Day will have to contain quite a bit of educational background—

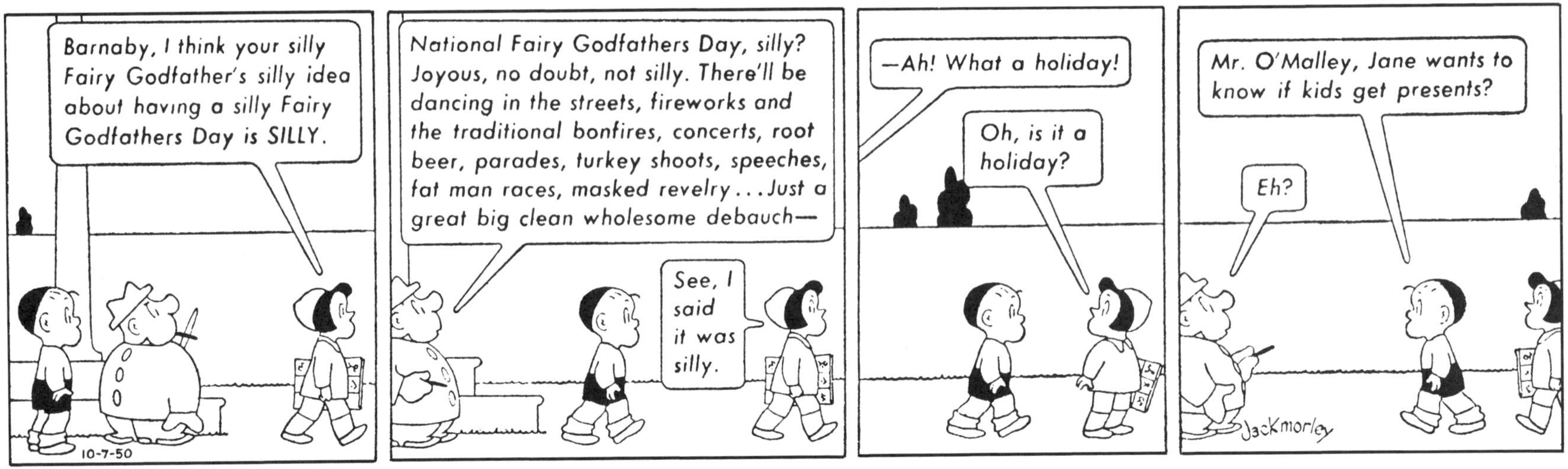
Barnaby, I think your silly Fairy Godfather's silly idea about having a silly Fairy Godfathers Day is SILLY.
10-7-50
National Fairy Godfathers Day, silly? Joyous, no doubt, not silly. There'll be dancing in the streets, fireworks and the traditional bonfires, concerts, root beer, parades, turkey shoots, speeches, fat man races, masked revelry . . . Just a great big clean wholesome debauch—
See, I said it was silly.
—Ah! What a holiday!
Oh, is it a holiday?
Mr. O'Malley, Jane wants to know if kids get presents?
Eh?
Jackmorley

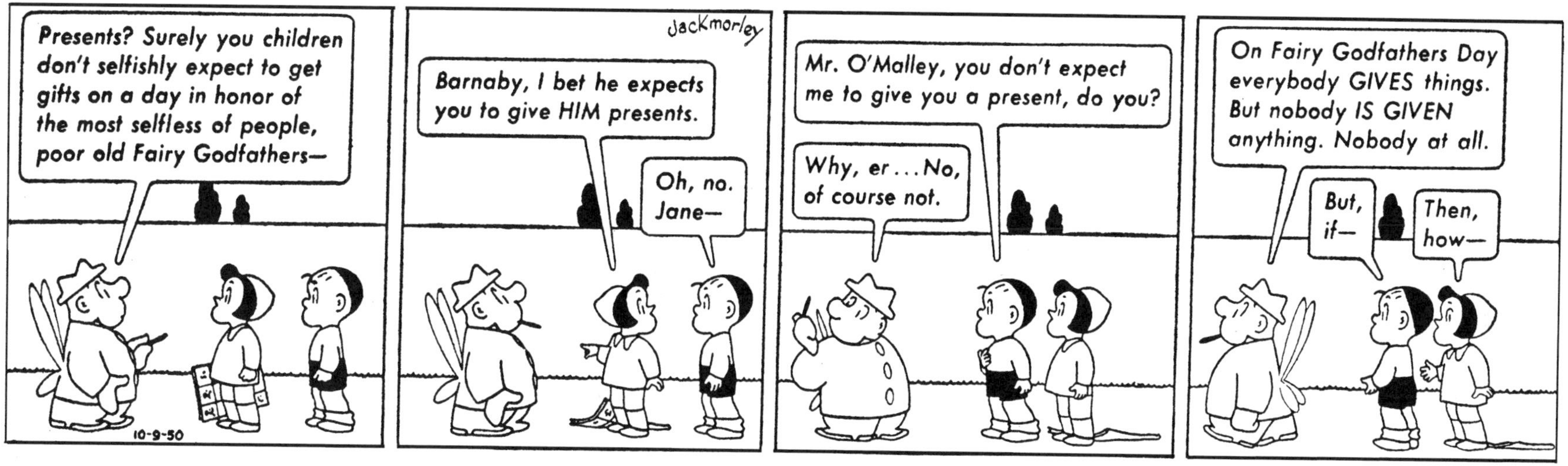
Presents? Surely you children don't selfishly expect to get gifts on a day in honor of the most selfless of people, poor old Fairy Godfathers—
10-9-50
Jackmorley
Barnaby, I bet he expects you to give HIM presents.
Oh, no. Jane—
Mr. O'Malley, you don't expect me to give you a present, do you?
Why, er . . . No, of course not.
On Fairy Godfathers Day everybody GIVES things. But nobody IS GIVEN anything. Nobody at all.
But, if—
Then, how—

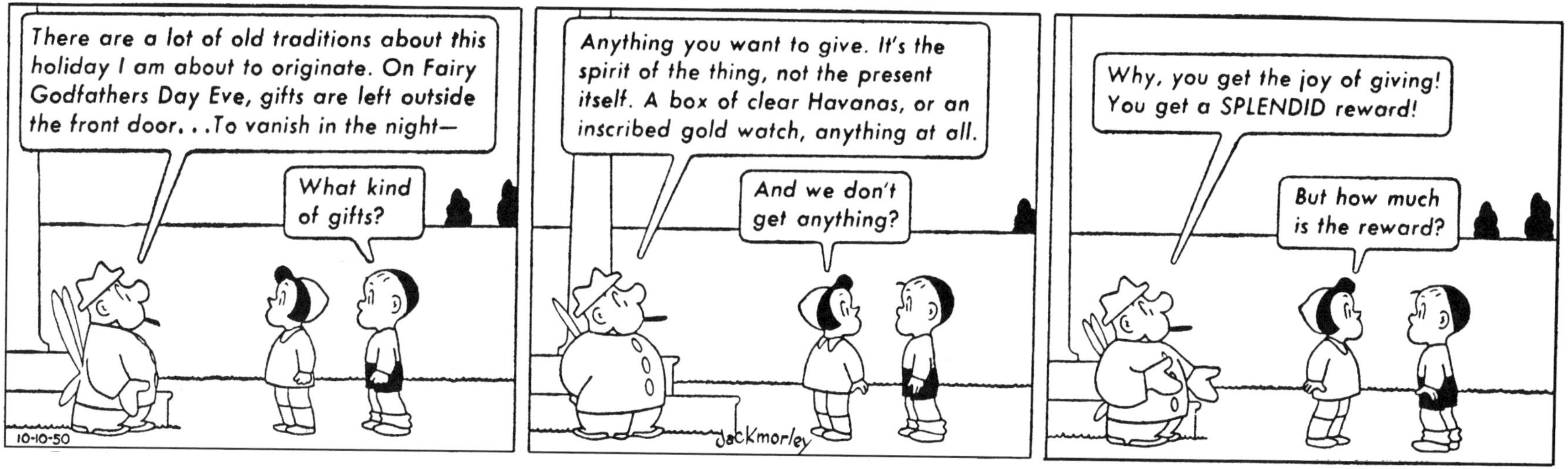
There are a lot of old traditions about this holiday I am about to originate. On Fairy Godfathers Day Eve, gifts are left outside the front door. . .To vanish in the night—
What kind of gifts?
10-10-50
Anything you want to give. It's the spirit of the thing, not the present itself. A box of clear Havanas, or an inscribed gold watch, anything at all.
And we don't get anything?
Jackmorley
Why, you get the joy of giving! You get a SPLENDID reward!
But how much is the reward?

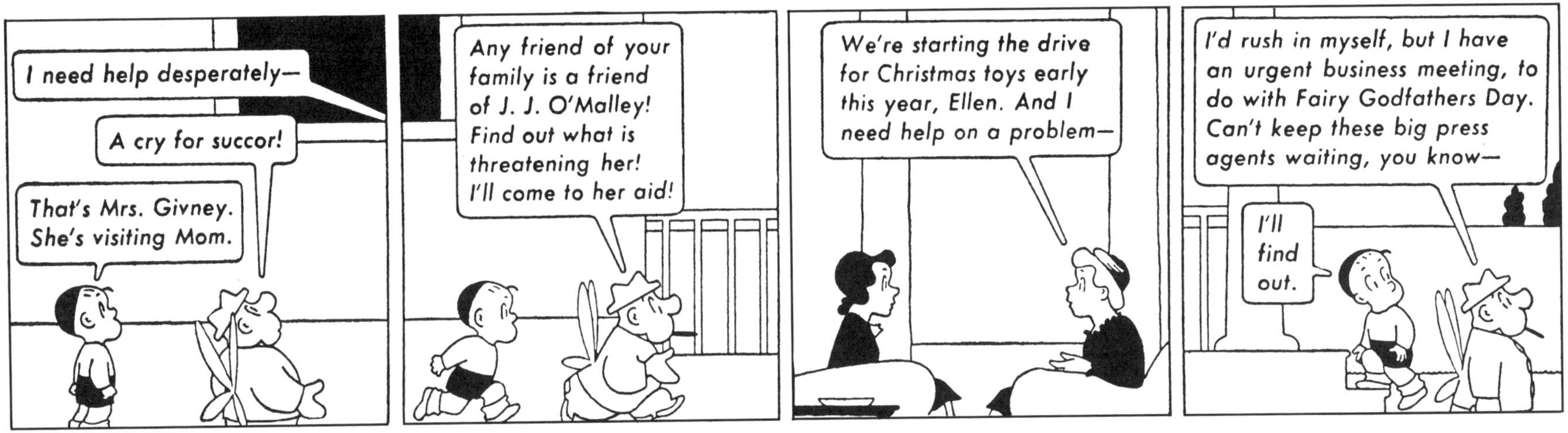
I need help desperately—
A cry for succor!
That's Mrs. Givney. She's visiting Mom.
Any friend of your family is a friend of J. J. O'Malley! Find out what is threatening her! I'll come to her aid!
We're starting the drive for Christmas toys early this year, Ellen. And I need help on a problem—
I'd rush in myself, but I have an urgent business meeting, to do with Fairy Godfathers Day. Can't keep these big press agents waiting, you know—
I'll find out.

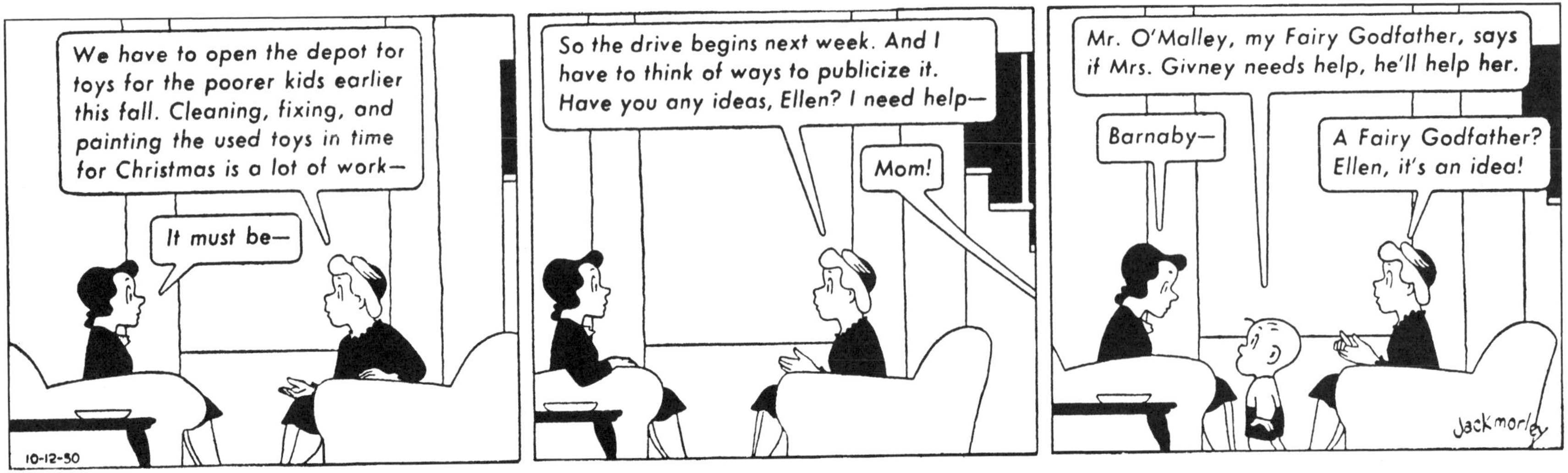
We have to open the depot for toys for the poorer kids earlier this fall. Cleaning, fixing, and painting the used toys in time for Christmas is a lot of work—
It must be—
So the drive begins next week. And I have to think of ways to publicize it. Have you any ideas, Ellen? I need help—
Mom!
Mr. O'Malley, my Fairy Godfather, says if Mrs. Givney needs help, he'll help her.
Barnaby—
A Fairy Godfather? Ellen, it's an idea!
10-12-50
Jackmorley

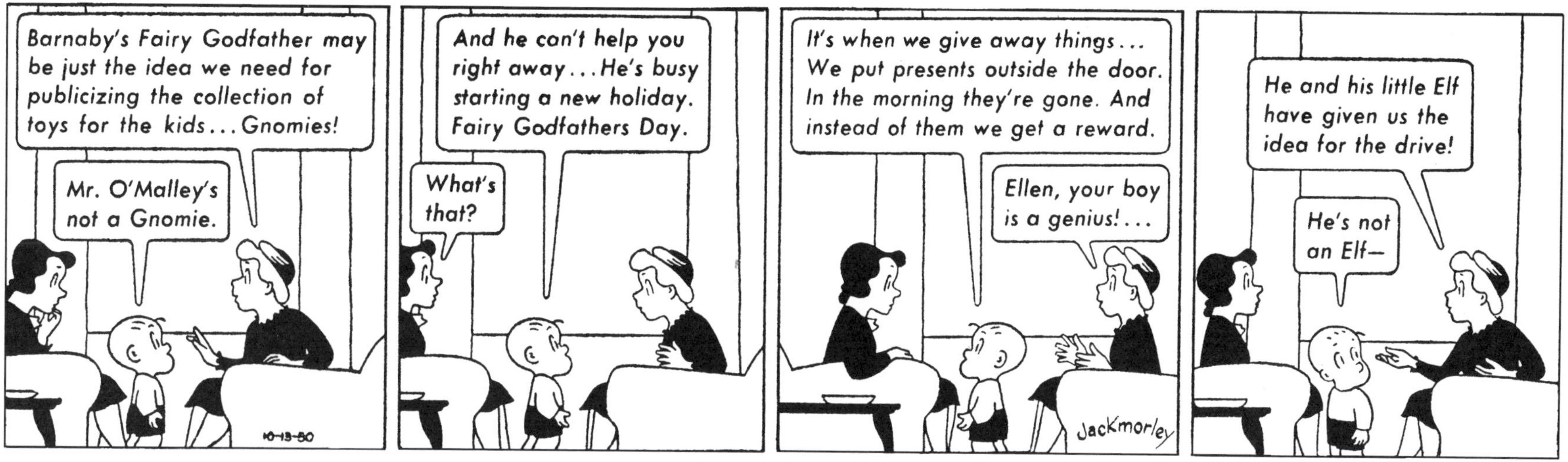
Barnaby's Fairy Godfather may be just the idea we need for publicizing the collection of toys for the kids... Gnomies!
Mr. O'Malley's not a Gnomie.
10-13-50
And he can't help you right away... He's busy starting a new holiday. Fairy Godfathers Day.
What's that?
It's when we give away things... We put presents outside the door. In the morning they're gone. And instead of them we get a reward.
Ellen, your boy is a genius!...
JackMorley
He and his little Elf have given us the idea for the drive!
He's not an Elf—

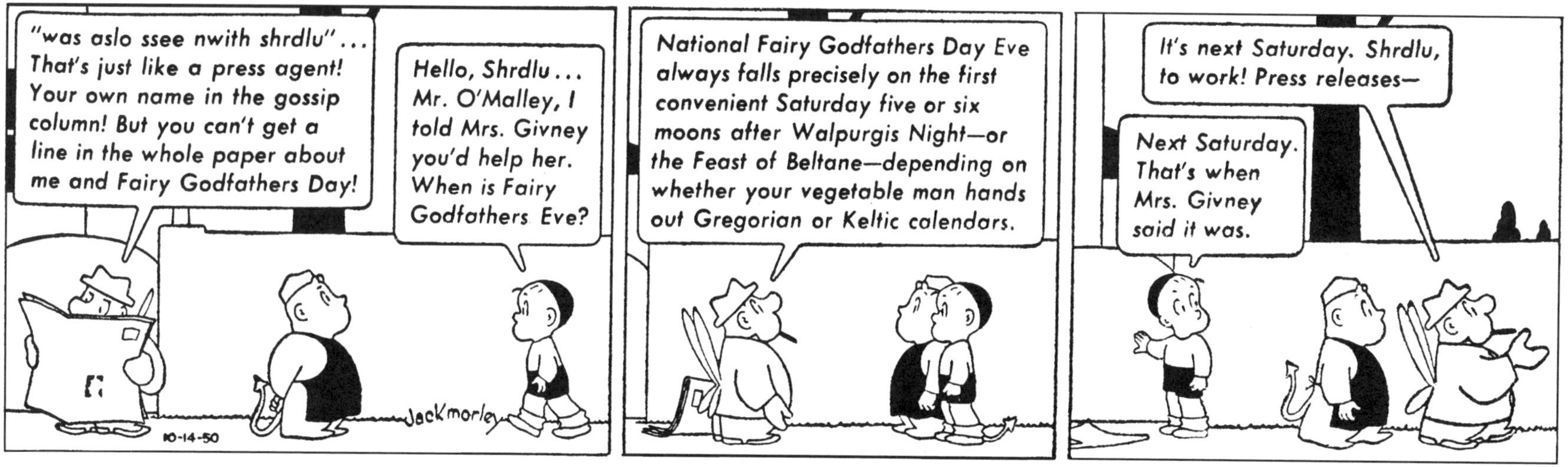
"was aslo ssee nwith shrdlu"... That's just like a press agent! Your own name in the gossip column! But you can't get a line in the whole paper about me and Fairy Godfathers Day!
Hello, Shrdlu... Mr. O'Malley, I told Mrs. Givney you'd help her. When is Fairy Godfathers Eve?
JackMorley
10-14-50
National Fairy Godfathers Day Eve always falls precisely on the first convenient Saturday five or six moons after Walpurgis Night—or the Feast of Beltane—depending on whether your vegetable man hands out Gregorian or Keltic calendars.
It's next Saturday. Shrdlu, to work! Press releases—
Next Saturday. That's when Mrs. Givney said it was.

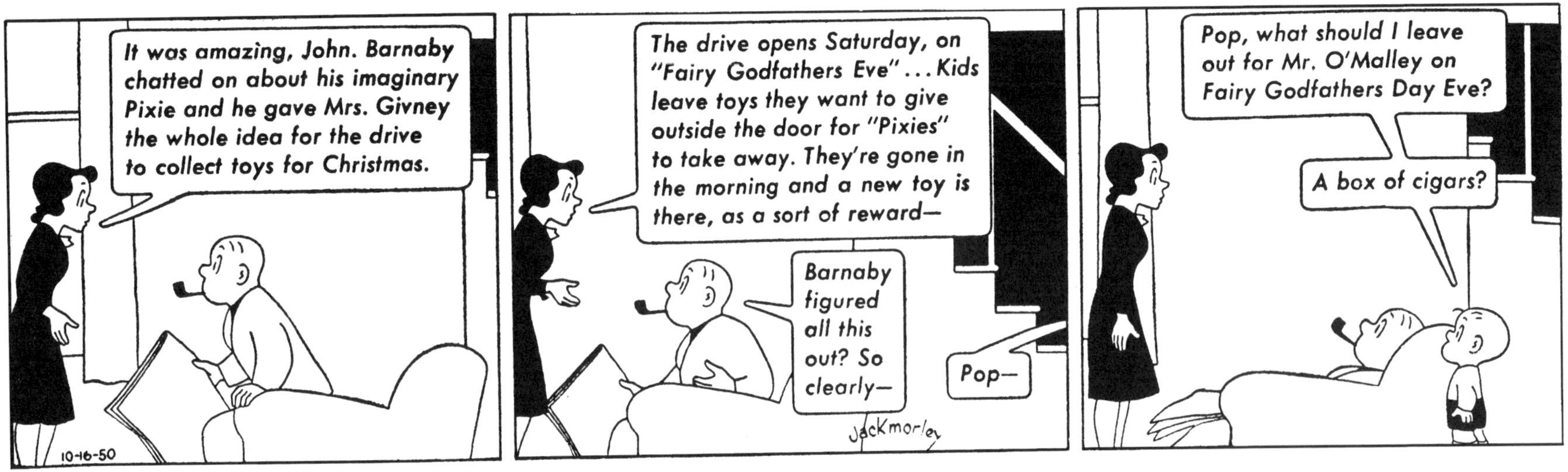
It was amazing, John. Barnaby chatted on about his imaginary Pixie and he gave Mrs. Givney the whole idea for the drive to collect toys for Christmas.
10-16-50
The drive opens Saturday, on "Fairy Godfathers Eve"... Kids leave toys they want to give outside the door for "Pixies" to take away. They're gone in the morning and a new toy is there, as a sort of reward—
Barnaby figured all this out? So clearly—
Pop—
JackMorley
Pop, what should I leave out for Mr. O'Malley on Fairy Godfathers Day Eve?
A box of cigars?

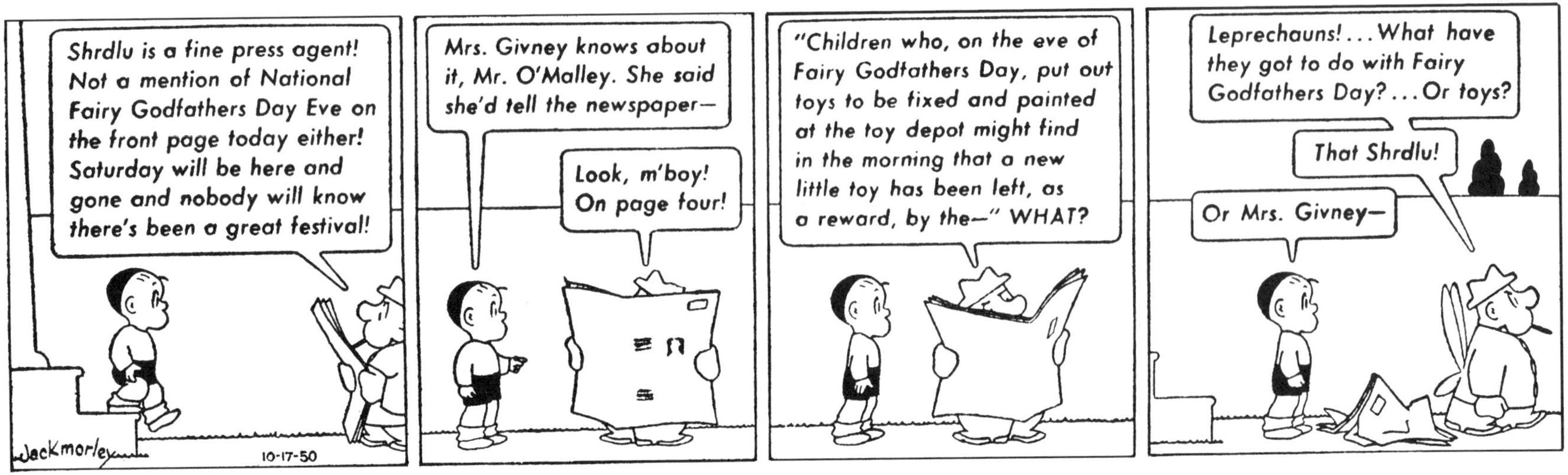
Shrdlu is a fine press agent! Not a mention of National Fairy Godfathers Day Eve on the front page today either! Saturday will be here and gone and nobody will know there's been a great festival!
JackMorley
10-17-50
Mrs. Givney knows about it, Mr. O'Malley. She said she'd tell the newspaper—
Look, m'boy! On page four!
"Children who, on the eve of Fairy Godfathers Day, put out toys to be fixed and painted at the toy depot might find in the morning that a new little toy has been left, as a reward, by the—" WHAT?
Leprechauns!...What have they got to do with Fairy Godfathers Day?...Or toys?
That Shrdlu!
Or Mrs. Givney—

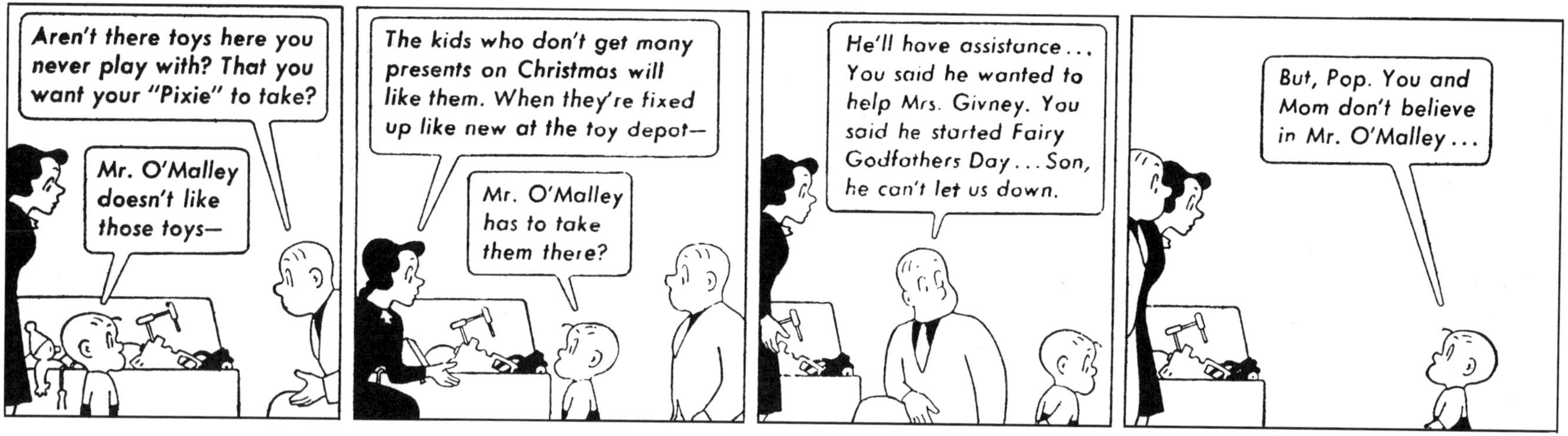
Aren't there toys here you never play with? That you want your "Pixie" to take?
Mr. O'Malley doesn't like those toys—
The kids who don't get many presents on Christmas will like them. When they're fixed up like new at the toy depot—
Mr. O'Malley has to take them there?
He'll have assistance... You said he wanted to help Mrs. Givney. You said he started Fairy Godfathers Day... Son, he can't let us down.
But, Pop. You and Mom don't believe in Mr. O'Malley...

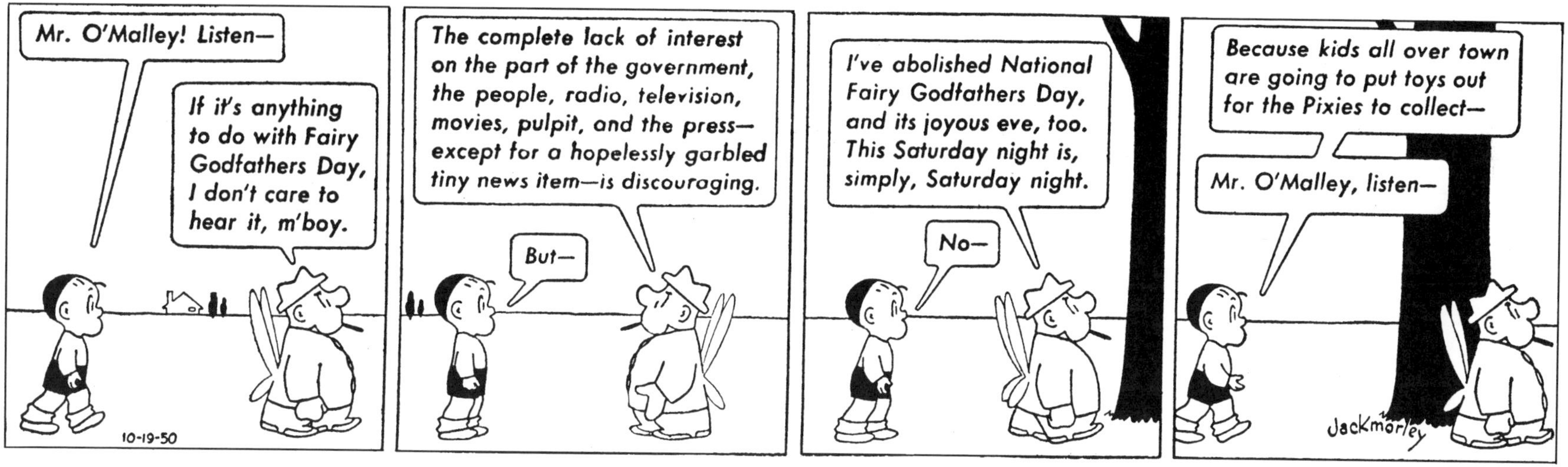
Mr. O'Malley! Listen—
If it's anything to do with Fairy Godfathers Day, I don't care to hear it, m'boy.
10-19-50
The complete lack of interest on the part of the government, the people, radio, television, movies, pulpit, and the press—except for a hopelessly garbled tiny news item—is discouraging.
But—
I've abolished National Fairy Godfathers Day, and its joyous eve, too. This Saturday night is, simply, Saturday night.
No—
Because kids all over town are going to put toys out for the Pixies to collect—
Mr. O'Malley, listen—
Jackmorley

October 18 – 19

Panel 1: Certainly, the collection of toys to be rehabilitated and distributed among children who don't get many gifts at Christmas is a nice little community effort, Barnaby.

But—

Panel 2: But I conceived of Fairy Godfathers Day as a time of such universal homage to Fairy Godfathers as to even sway your parents in their reluctance to trust in me and my capabilities—

But—

Panel 3: That's what I've been trying to tell you, Mr. O'Malley. Pop says he DOES believe in you! So does Mom! And even Jane!

They DO?

Panel 4: Because you're going to collect the toys. On Fairy Godfathers Day Eve.

M'boy...Tomorrow night, O'Malley will be on the job!

Panel 5: Just leave your toys outside for your Pixie, son. They'll be at the toy depot by morning.

Panel 6: Mr. O'Malley is getting the Elves and Gnomes at the Little Men's Club to help. Even Leprechauns.

Yes? Good for Mr. O'Malley.. Goodnight...

Panel 7: Mrs. Givney said the drive is going great. All over town.

I guess it's safe to take care of everything now.

Jackmorley

Panel 8: Ellen!...The toys are already gone!

10-21-50

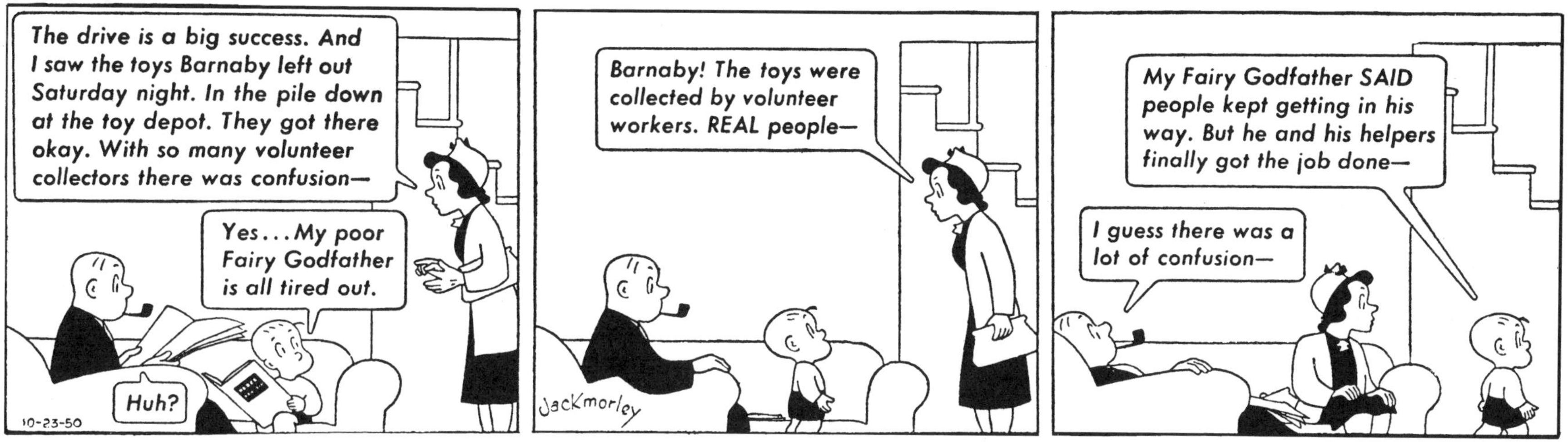
The drive is a big success. And I saw the toys Barnaby left out Saturday night. In the pile down at the toy depot. They got there okay. With so many volunteer collectors there was confusion—
Yes... My poor Fairy Godfather is all tired out.
Huh?
10-23-50
Barnaby! The toys were collected by volunteer workers. REAL people—
JacKmorley
My Fairy Godfather SAID people kept getting in his way. But he and his helpers finally got the job done—
I guess there was a lot of confusion—

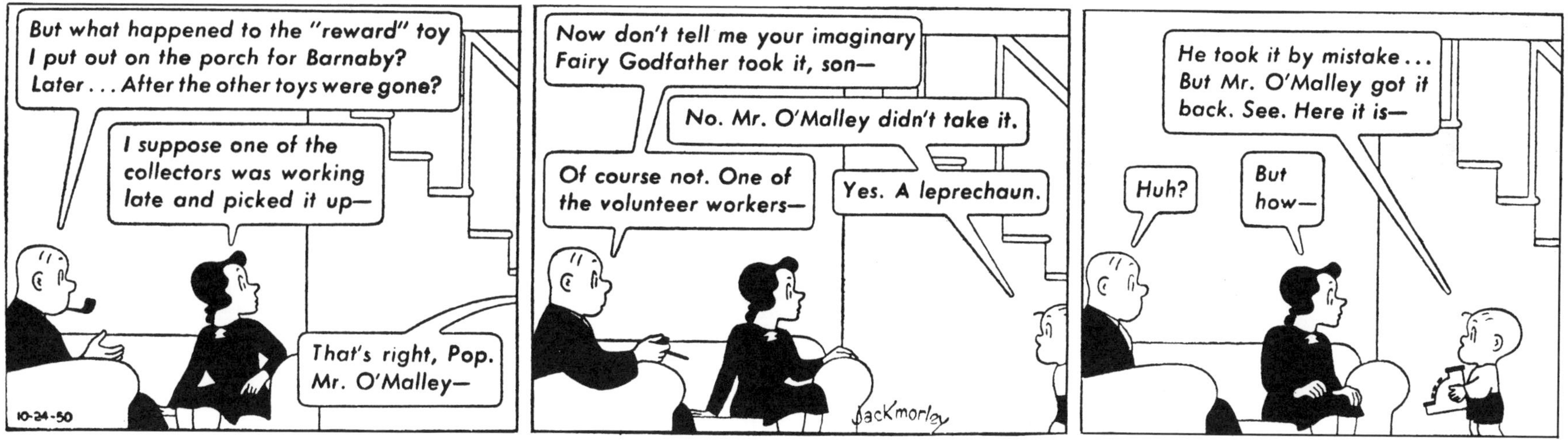
But what happened to the "reward" toy I put out on the porch for Barnaby? Later... After the other toys were gone?
I suppose one of the collectors was working late and picked it up—
That's right, Pop. Mr. O'Malley—
10-24-50
Now don't tell me your imaginary Fairy Godfather took it, son—
No. Mr. O'Malley didn't take it.
Of course not. One of the volunteer workers—
Yes. A leprechaun.
JacKmorley
He took it by mistake... But Mr. O'Malley got it back. See. Here it is—
Huh?
But how—

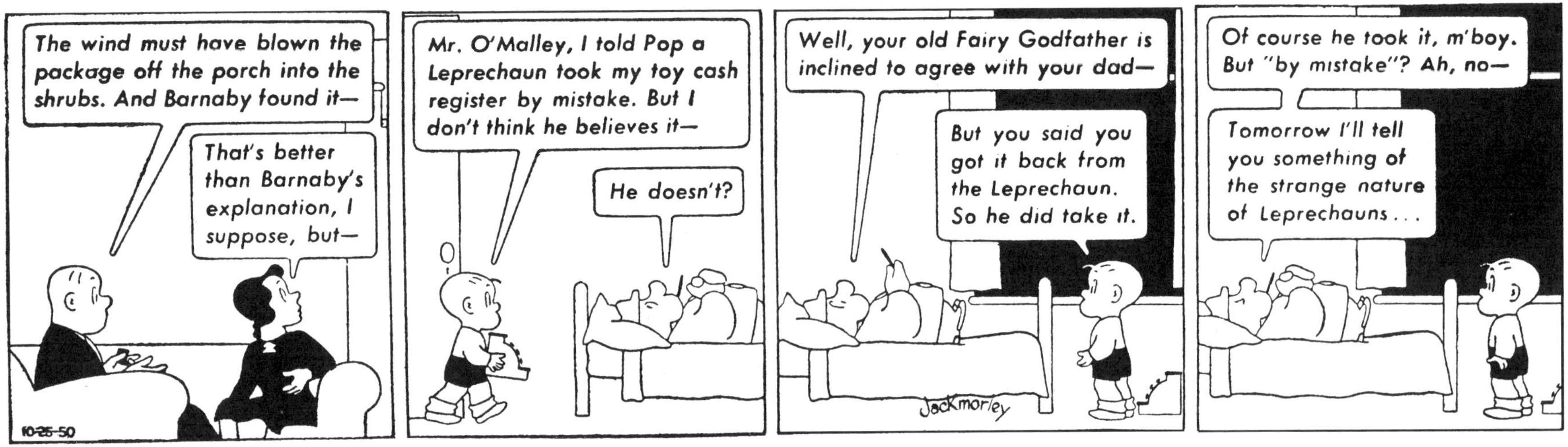
The wind must have blown the package off the porch into the shrubs. And Barnaby found it—
That's better than Barnaby's explanation, I suppose, but—
10-25-50
Mr. O'Malley, I told Pop a Leprechaun took my toy cash register by mistake. But I don't think he believes it—
He doesn't?
Well, your old Fairy Godfather is inclined to agree with your dad—
But you said you got it back from the Leprechaun. So he did take it.
JackMorley
Of course he took it, m'boy. But "by mistake"? Ah, no—
Tomorrow I'll tell you something of the strange nature of Leprechauns . . .

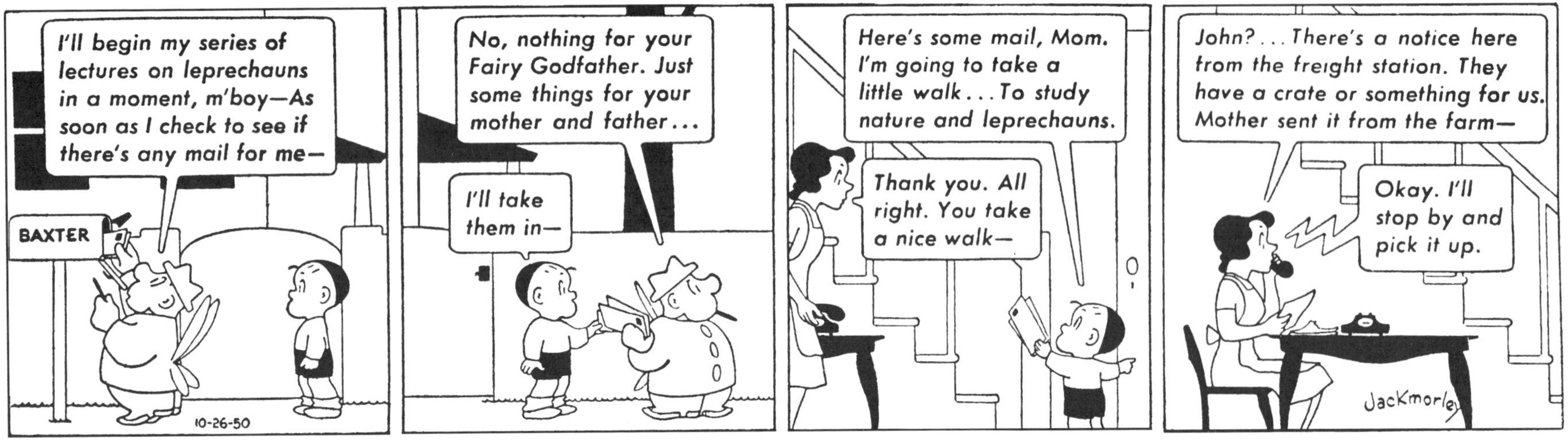
I'll begin my series of lectures on leprechauns in a moment, m'boy—As soon as I check to see if there's any mail for me—
BAXTER
10-26-50
No, nothing for your Fairy Godfather. Just some things for your mother and father . . .
I'll take them in—
Here's some mail, Mom. I'm going to take a little walk . . . To study nature and leprechauns.
Thank you. All right. You take a nice walk—
John? . . . There's a notice here from the freight station. They have a crate or something for us. Mother sent it from the farm—
Okay. I'll stop by and pick it up.
JackMorley

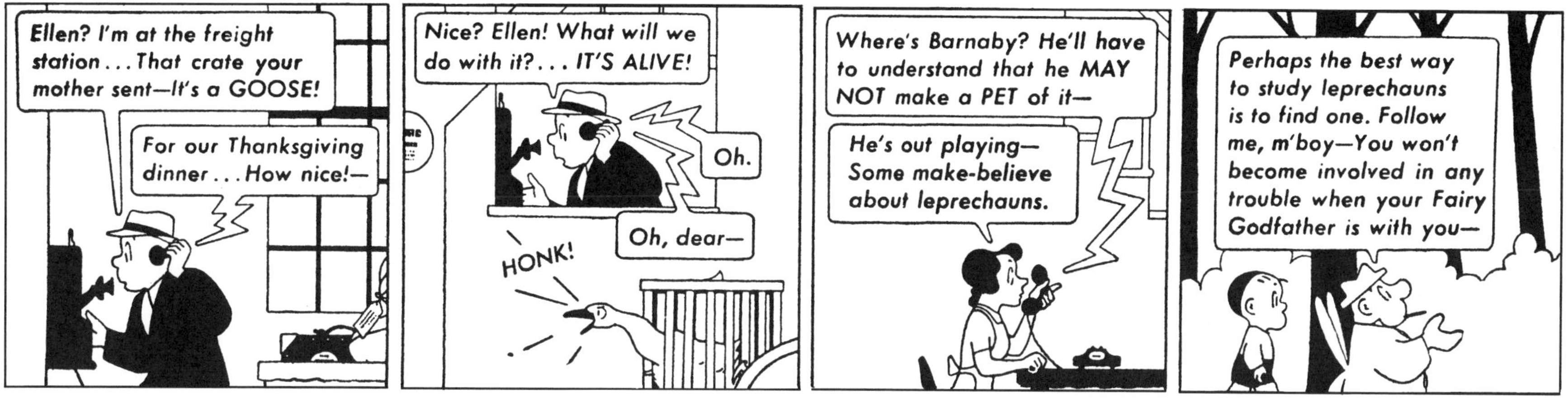
Ellen? I'm at the freight station . . . That crate your mother sent—It's a GOOSE!
For our Thanksgiving dinner . . . How nice!—
Nice? Ellen! What will we do with it? . . . IT'S ALIVE!
Oh.
Oh, dear—
HONK!
Where's Barnaby? He'll have to understand that he MAY NOT make a PET of it—
He's out playing—Some make-believe about leprechauns.
Perhaps the best way to study leprechauns is to find one. Follow me, m'boy—You won't become involved in any trouble when your Fairy Godfather is with you—

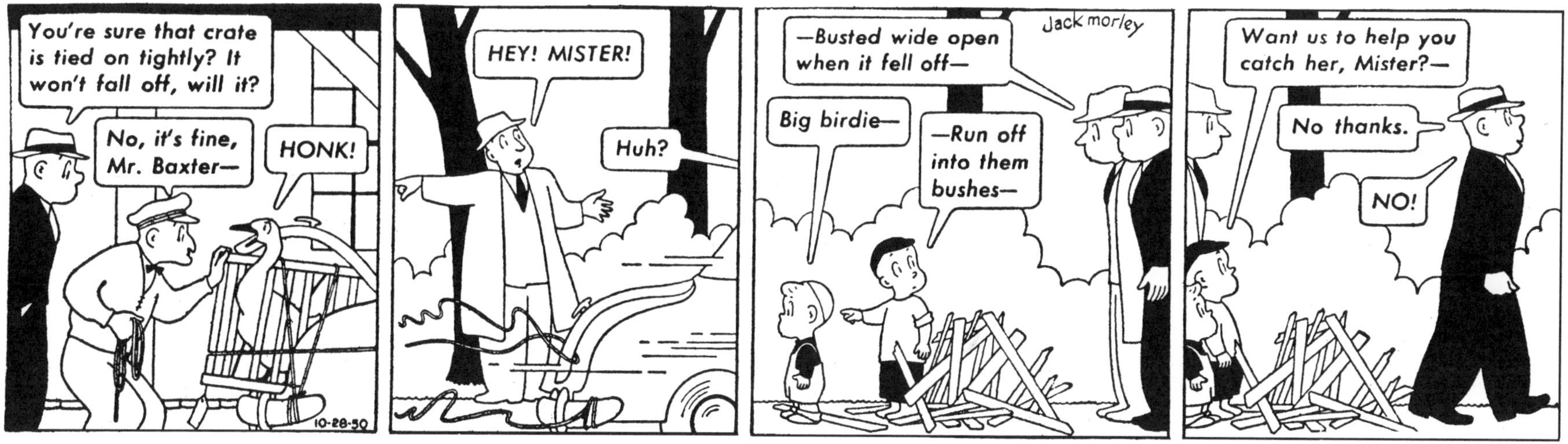
You're sure that crate is tied on tightly? It won't fall off, will it?
No, it's fine, Mr. Baxter—
HONK!
10-28-50
HEY! MISTER!
Huh?
Jack morley
—Busted wide open when it fell off—
Big birdie—
—Run off into them bushes—
Want us to help you catch her, Mister?—
No thanks.
NO!

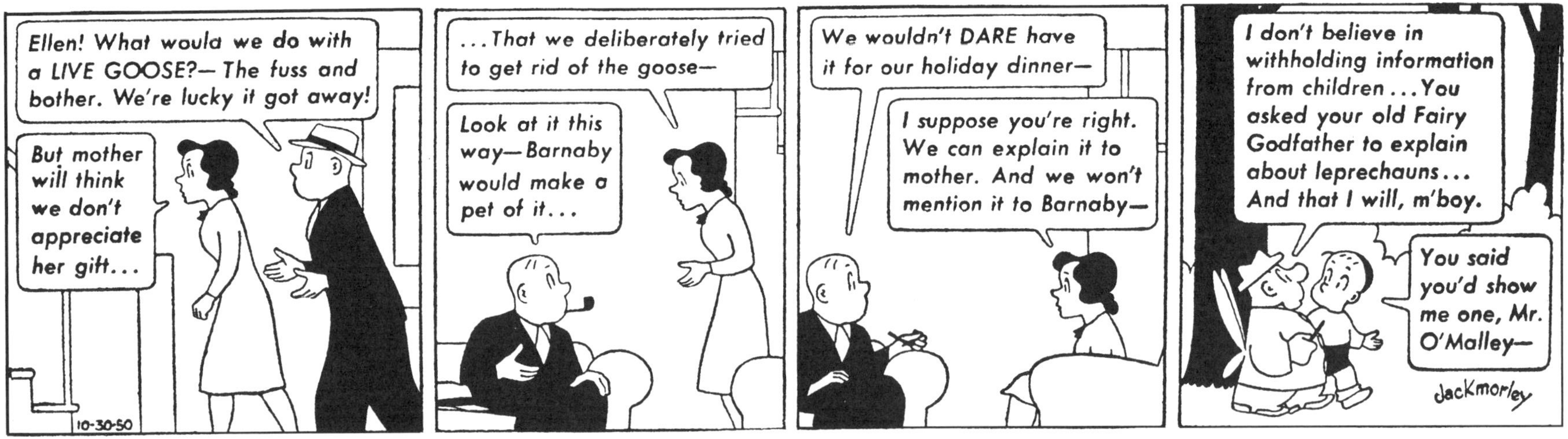
Ellen! What would we do with a LIVE GOOSE?— The fuss and bother. We're lucky it got away!
But mother will think we don't appreciate her gift...
10-30-50
...That we deliberately tried to get rid of the goose—
Look at it this way—Barnaby would make a pet of it...
We wouldn't DARE have it for our holiday dinner—
I suppose you're right. We can explain it to mother. And we won't mention it to Barnaby—
I don't believe in withholding information from children...You asked your old Fairy Godfather to explain about leprechauns... And that I will, m'boy.
You said you'd show me one, Mr. O'Malley—
JacKmorley

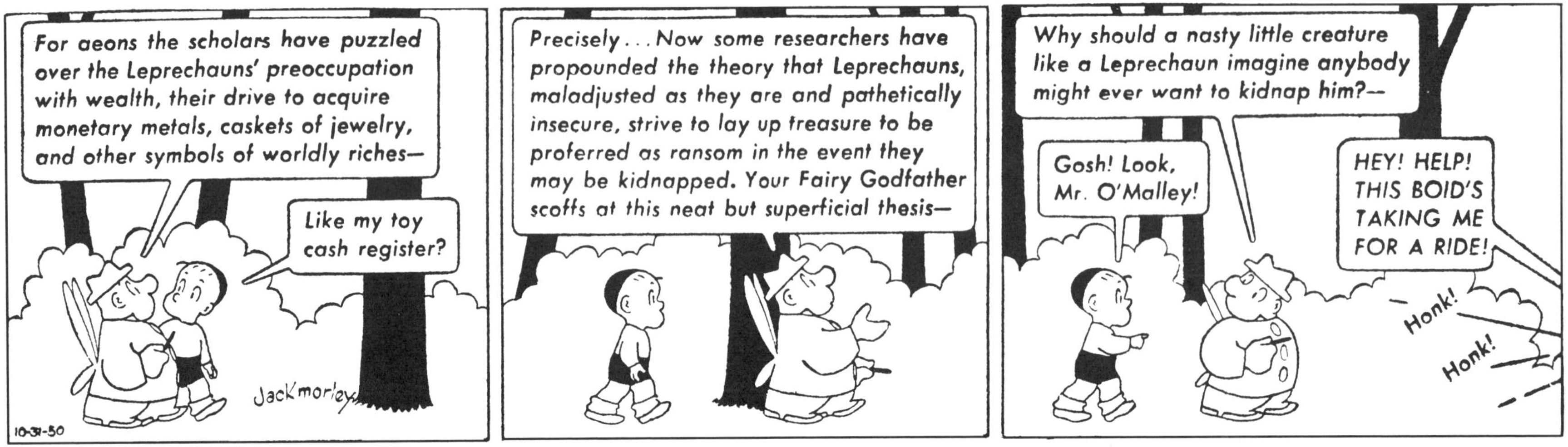
For aeons the scholars have puzzled over the Leprechauns' preoccupation with wealth, their drive to acquire monetary metals, caskets of jewelry, and other symbols of worldly riches—
Like my toy cash register?
JacKmorley
10-31-50
Precisely...Now some researchers have propounded the theory that Leprechauns, maladjusted as they are and pathetically insecure, strive to lay up treasure to be proferred as ransom in the event they may be kidnapped. Your Fairy Godfather scoffs at this neat but superficial thesis—
Why should a nasty little creature like a Leprechaun imagine anybody might ever want to kidnap him?—
Gosh! Look, Mr. O'Malley!
HEY! HELP! THIS BOID'S TAKING ME FOR A RIDE!
Honk!
Honk!

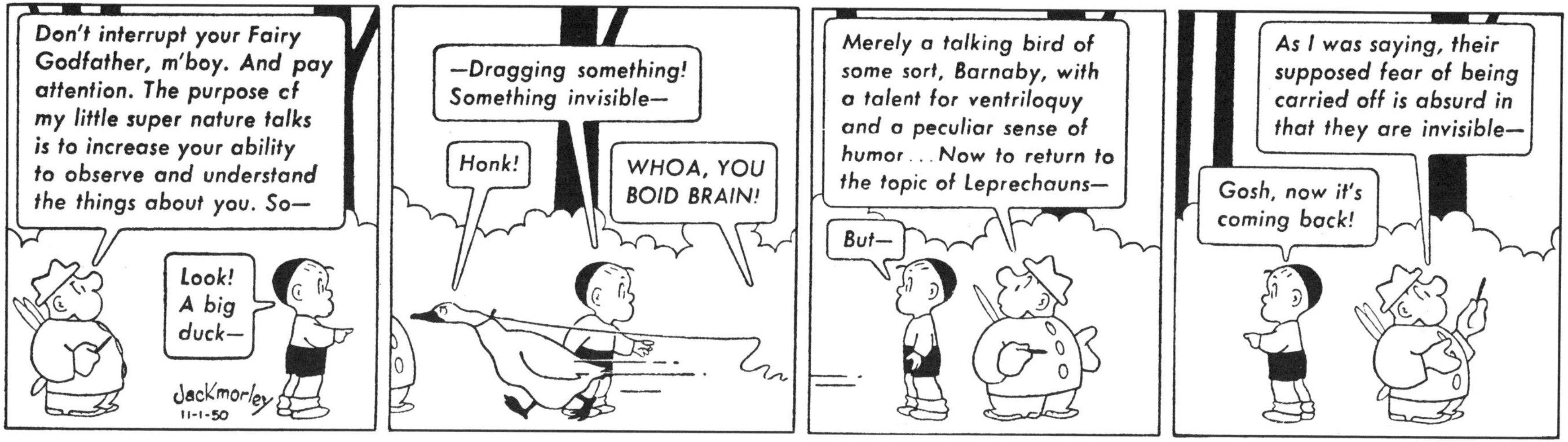
Don't interrupt your Fairy Godfather, m'boy. And pay attention. The purpose of my little super nature talks is to increase your ability to observe and understand the things about you. So—
Look! A big duck—
Jackmorley
11-1-50
—Dragging something! Something invisible—
Honk!
WHOA, YOU BOID BRAIN!
Merely a talking bird of some sort, Barnaby, with a talent for ventriloquy and a peculiar sense of humor . . . Now to return to the topic of Leprechauns—
But—
As I was saying, their supposed fear of being carried off is absurd in that they are invisible—
Gosh, now it's coming back!

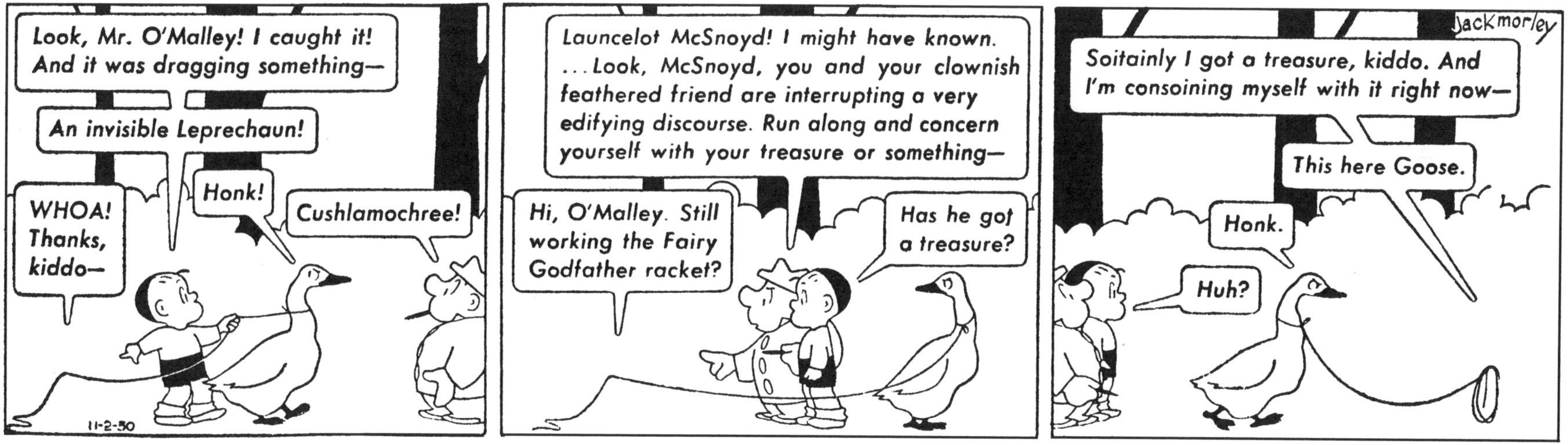
Look, Mr. O'Malley! I caught it! And it was dragging something—
An invisible Leprechaun!
WHOA! Thanks, kiddo—
Honk!
Cushlamochree!
11-2-50
Launcelot McSnoyd! I might have known. . . . Look, McSnoyd, you and your clownish feathered friend are interrupting a very edifying discourse. Run along and concern yourself with your treasure or something—
Hi, O'Malley. Still working the Fairy Godfather racket?
Has he got a treasure?
Jackmorley
Soitainly I got a treasure, kiddo. And I'm consoining myself with it right now—
This here Goose.
Honk.
Huh?

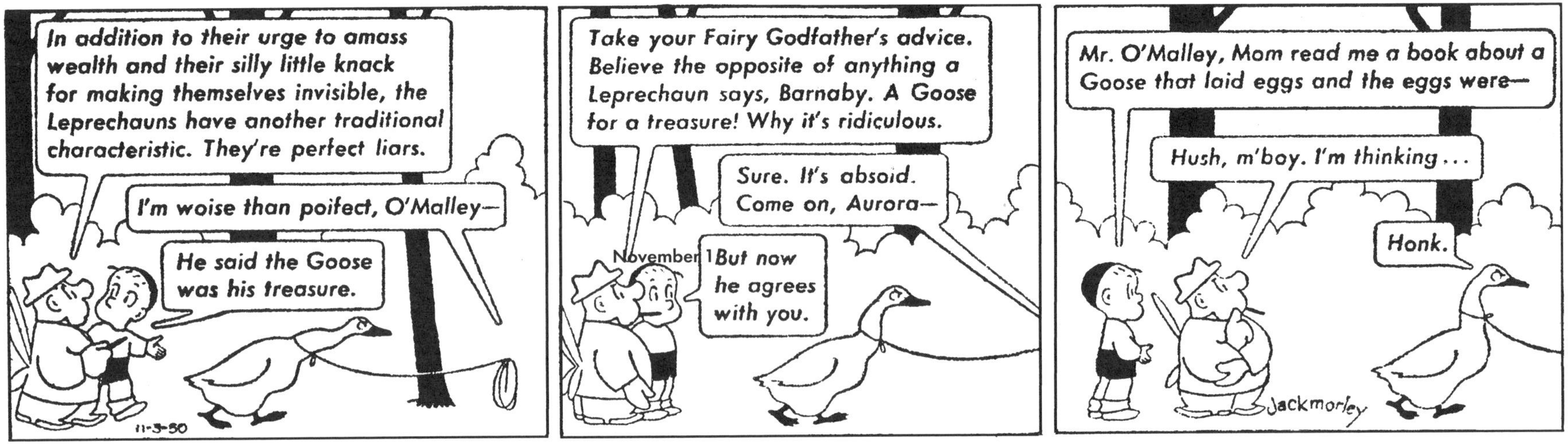
In addition to their urge to amass wealth and their silly little knack for making themselves invisible, the Leprechauns have another traditional characteristic. They're perfect liars.
I'm woise than poifect, O'Malley—
He said the Goose was his treasure.
11-3-50
Take your Fairy Godfather's advice. Believe the opposite of anything a Leprechaun says, Barnaby. A Goose for a treasure! Why it's ridiculous.
Sure. It's absoid. Come on, Aurora—
November 1
But now he agrees with you.
Mr. O'Malley, Mom read me a book about a Goose that laid eggs and the eggs were—
Hush, m'boy. I'm thinking . . .
Honk.
Jackmorley

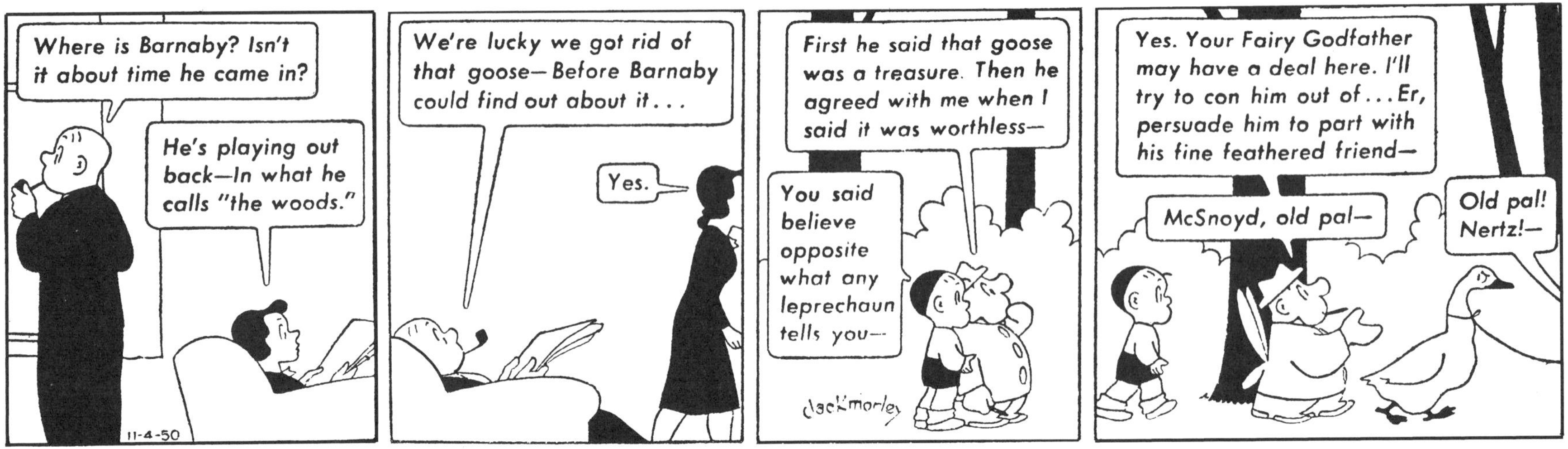
Where is Barnaby? Isn't it about time he came in?
He's playing out back—In what he calls "the woods."
11-4-50
We're lucky we got rid of that goose—Before Barnaby could find out about it . . .
Yes.
First he said that goose was a treasure. Then he agreed with me when I said it was worthless—
You said believe opposite what any leprechaun tells you—
Jackmorley
Yes. Your Fairy Godfather may have a deal here. I'll try to con him out of . . . Er, persuade him to part with his fine feathered friend—
McSnoyd, old pal—
Old pal! Nertz!—

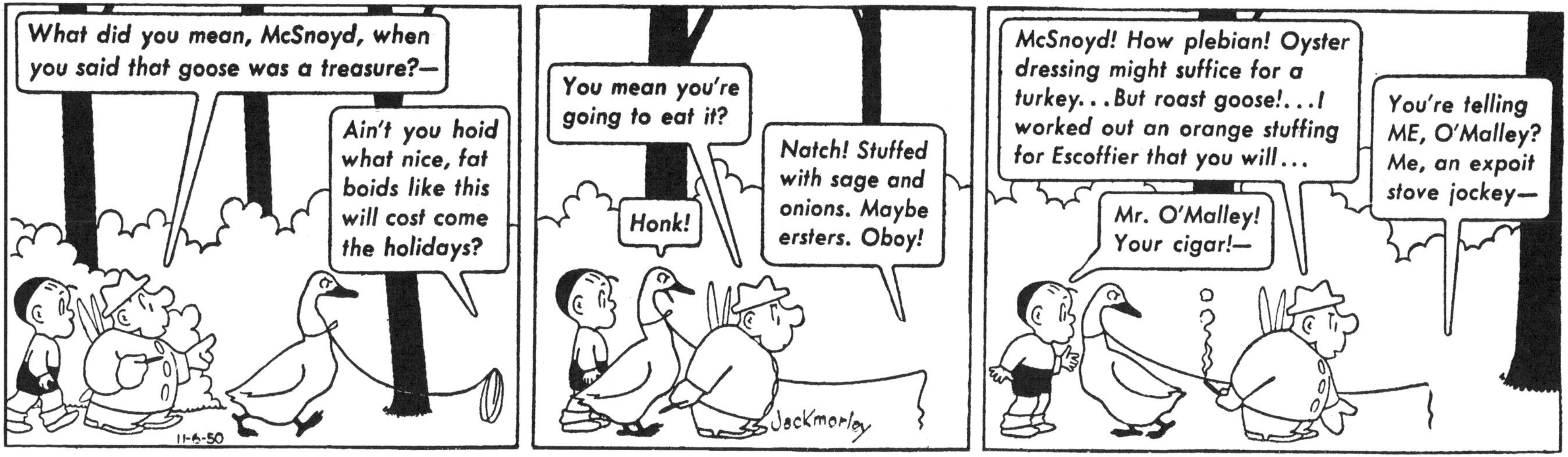
What did you mean, McSnoyd, when you said that goose was a treasure?—
Ain't you hoid what nice, fat boids like this will cost come the holidays?
11-6-50
You mean you're going to eat it?
Honk!
Natch! Stuffed with sage and onions. Maybe ersters. Oboy!
Jackmorley
McSnoyd! How plebian! Oyster dressing might suffice for a turkey. . . But roast goose!. . . I worked out an orange stuffing for Escoffier that you will . . .
You're telling ME, O'Malley? Me, an expoit stove jockey—
Mr. O'Malley! Your cigar!—

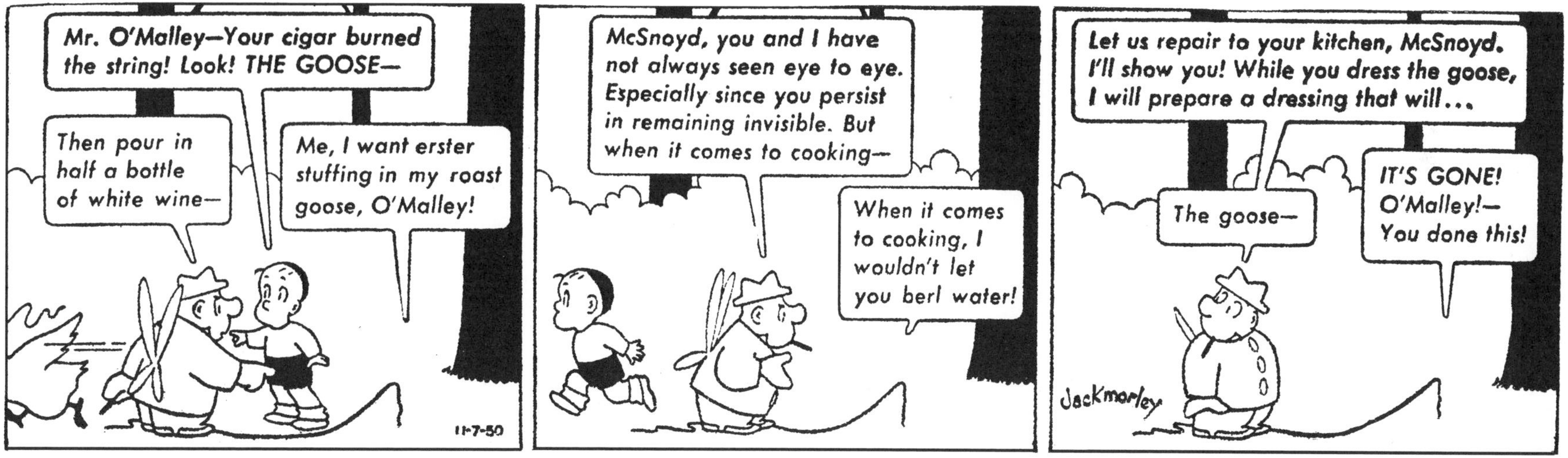
Mr. O'Malley—Your cigar burned the string! Look! THE GOOSE—
Then pour in half a bottle of white wine—
Me, I want erster stuffing in my roast goose, O'Malley!
11-7-50
McSnoyd, you and I have not always seen eye to eye. Especially since you persist in remaining invisible. But when it comes to cooking—
When it comes to cooking, I wouldn't let you berl water!
Let us repair to your kitchen, McSnoyd. I'll show you! While you dress the goose, I will prepare a dressing that will . . .
The goose—
IT'S GONE! O'Malley!— You done this!
Jackmorley

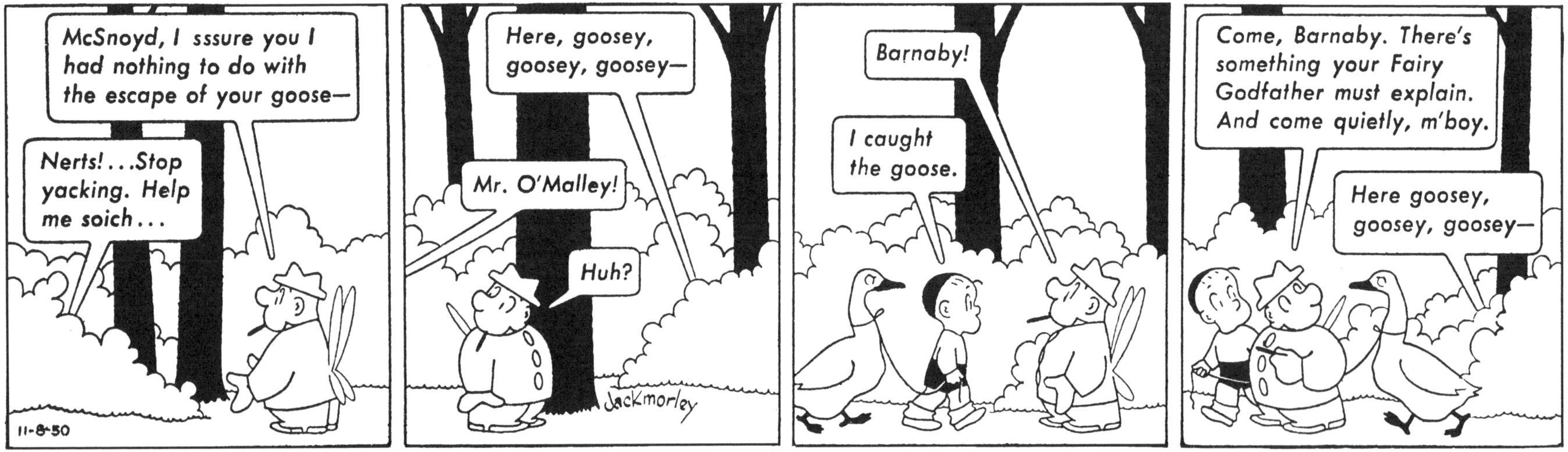
McSnoyd, I sssure you I had nothing to do with the escape of your goose—
Nerts!...Stop yacking. Help me soich...
Here, goosey, goosey, goosey—
Mr. O'Malley!
Huh?
Jackmorley
Barnaby!
I caught the goose.
Come, Barnaby. There's something your Fairy Godfather must explain. And come quietly, m'boy.
Here goosey, goosey, goosey—
11-8-50

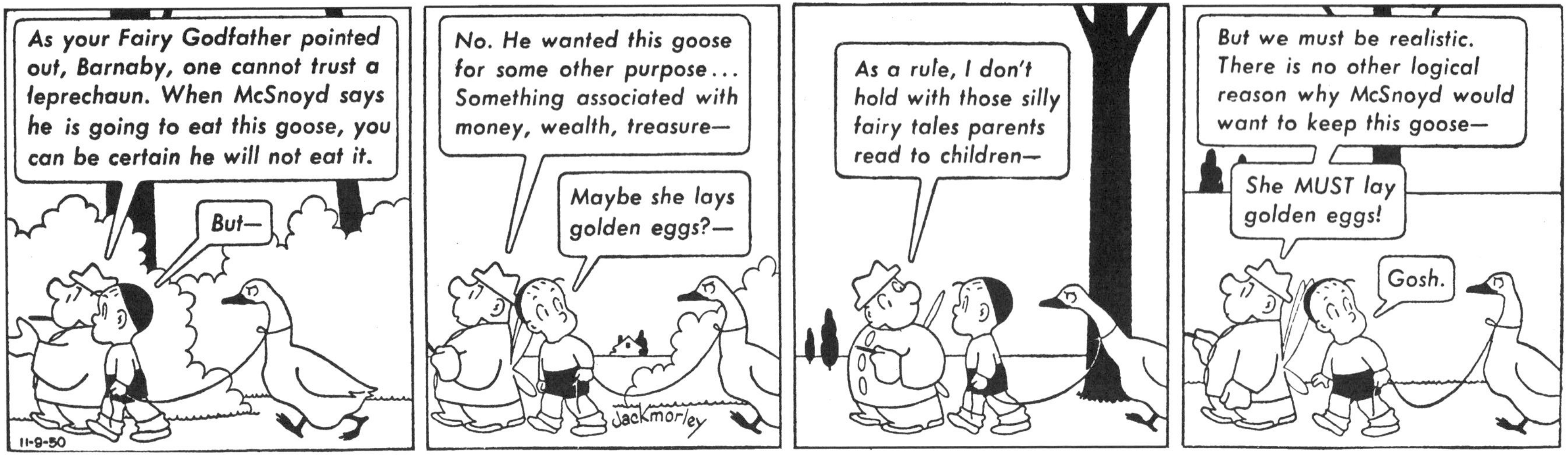
As your Fairy Godfather pointed out, Barnaby, one cannot trust a leprechaun. When McSnoyd says he is going to eat this goose, you can be certain he will not eat it.
But—
11-9-50
No. He wanted this goose for some other purpose... Something associated with money, wealth, treasure—
Maybe she lays golden eggs?—
Jackmorley
As a rule, I don't hold with those silly fairy tales parents read to children—
But we must be realistic. There is no other logical reason why McSnoyd would want to keep this goose—
She MUST lay golden eggs!
Gosh.

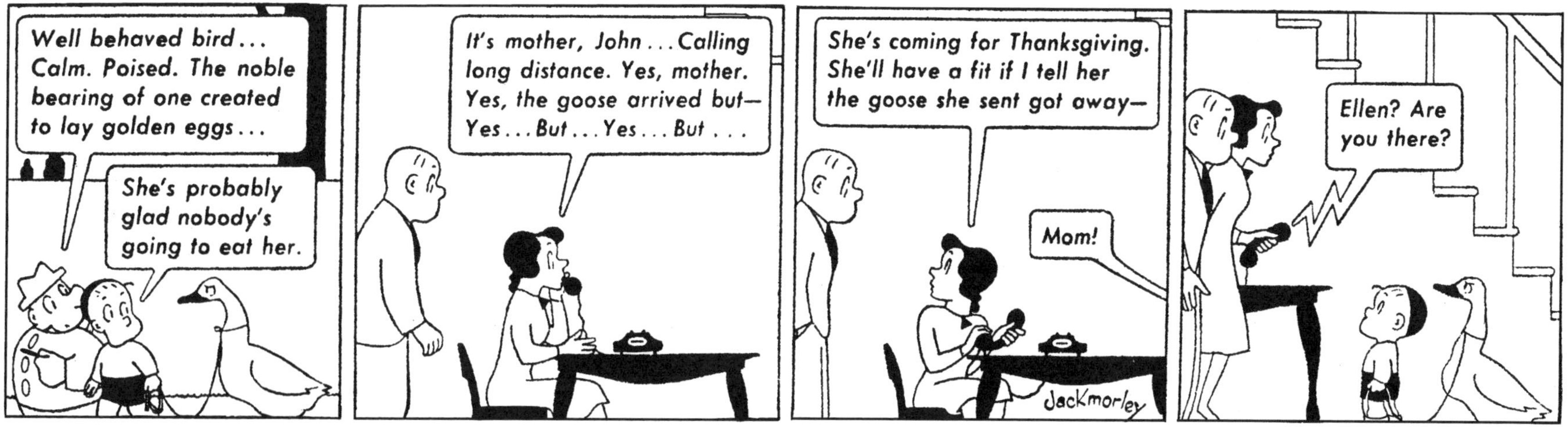
Well behaved bird... Calm. Poised. The noble bearing of one created to lay golden eggs...
She's probably glad nobody's going to eat her.
It's mother, John...Calling long distance. Yes, mother. Yes, the goose arrived but— Yes...But...Yes...But...
She's coming for Thanksgiving. She'll have a fit if I tell her the goose she sent got away—
Mom!
JackMorley
Ellen? Are you there?

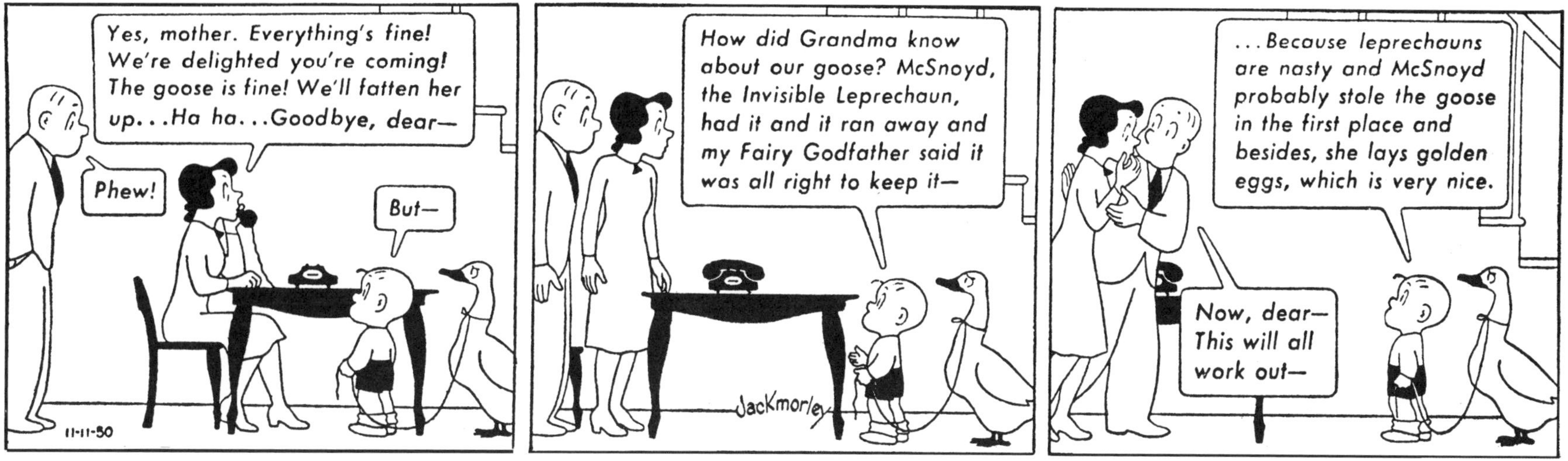
Yes, mother. Everything's fine! We're delighted you're coming! The goose is fine! We'll fatten her up...Ha ha...Goodbye, dear—
Phew!
But—
11-11-50
How did Grandma know about our goose? McSnoyd, the Invisible Leprechaun, had it and it ran away and my Fairy Godfather said it was all right to keep it—
JackMorley
...Because leprechauns are nasty and McSnoyd probably stole the goose in the first place and besides, she lays golden eggs, which is very nice.
Now, dear— This will all work out—

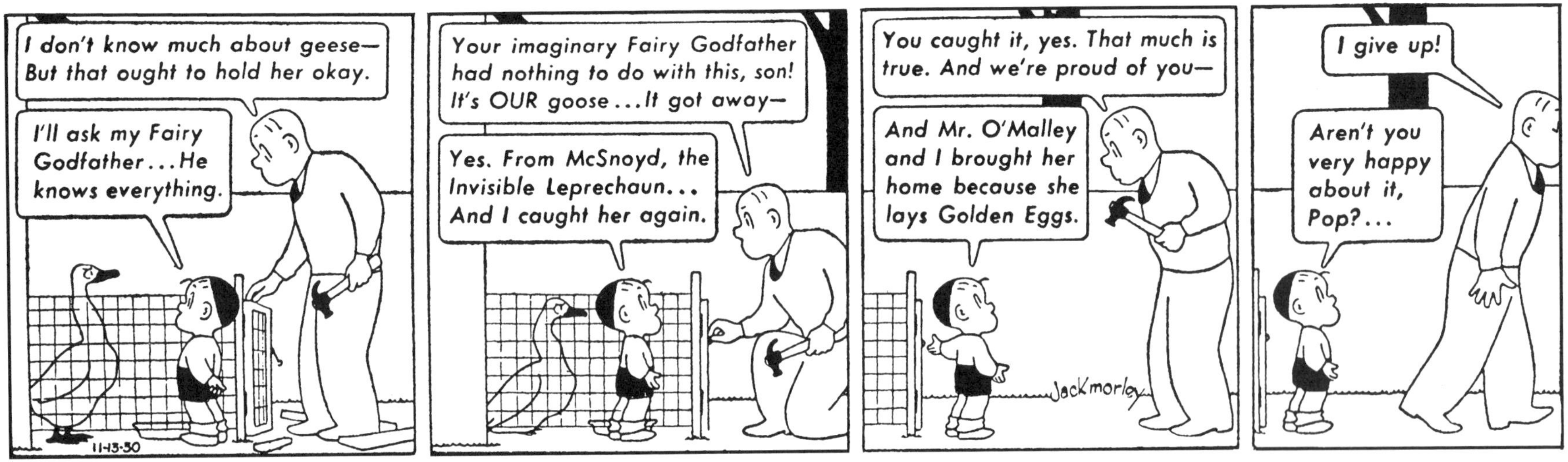

I don't know much about geese—
But that ought to hold her okay.
I'll ask my Fairy Godfather . . . He knows everything.
11-13-50
Your imaginary Fairy Godfather had nothing to do with this, son! It's OUR goose . . . It got away—
Yes. From McSnoyd, the Invisible Leprechaun . . . And I caught her again.
You caught it, yes. That much is true. And we're proud of you—
And Mr. O'Malley and I brought her home because she lays Golden Eggs.
Jackmorley
I give up!
Aren't you very happy about it, Pop? . . .

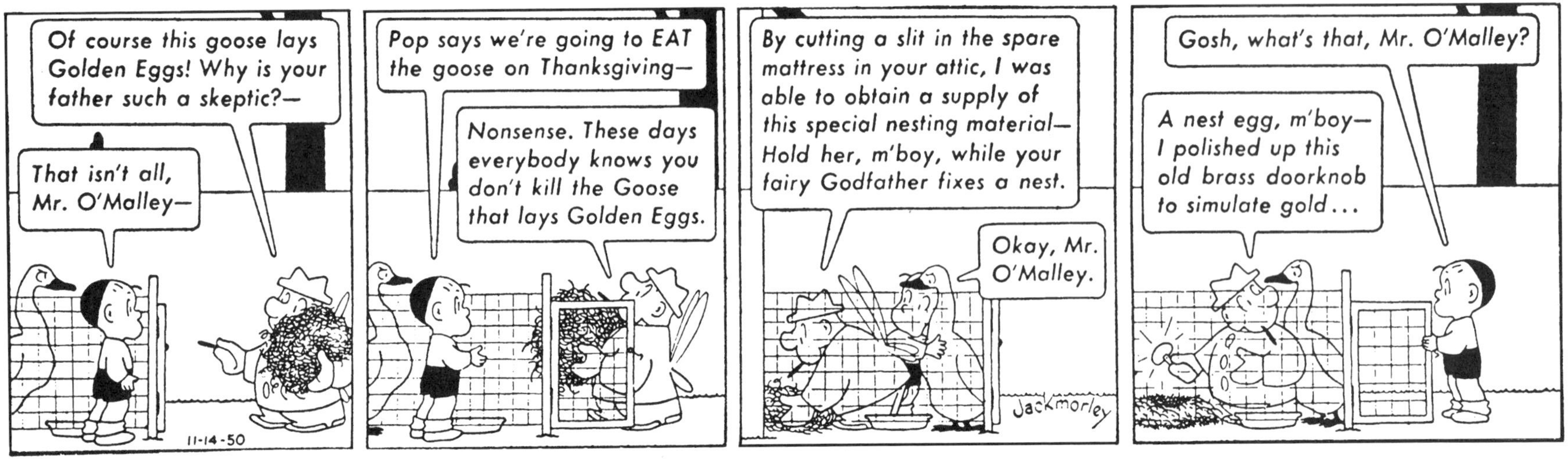

Of course this goose lays Golden Eggs! Why is your father such a skeptic?—
That isn't all, Mr. O'Malley—
11-14-50
Pop says we're going to EAT the goose on Thanksgiving—
Nonsense. These days everybody knows you don't kill the Goose that lays Golden Eggs.
By cutting a slit in the spare mattress in your attic, I was able to obtain a supply of this special nesting material— Hold her, m'boy, while your fairy Godfather fixes a nest.
Okay, Mr. O'Malley.
Jackmorley
Gosh, what's that, Mr. O'Malley?
A nest egg, m'boy— I polished up this old brass doorknob to simulate gold . . .

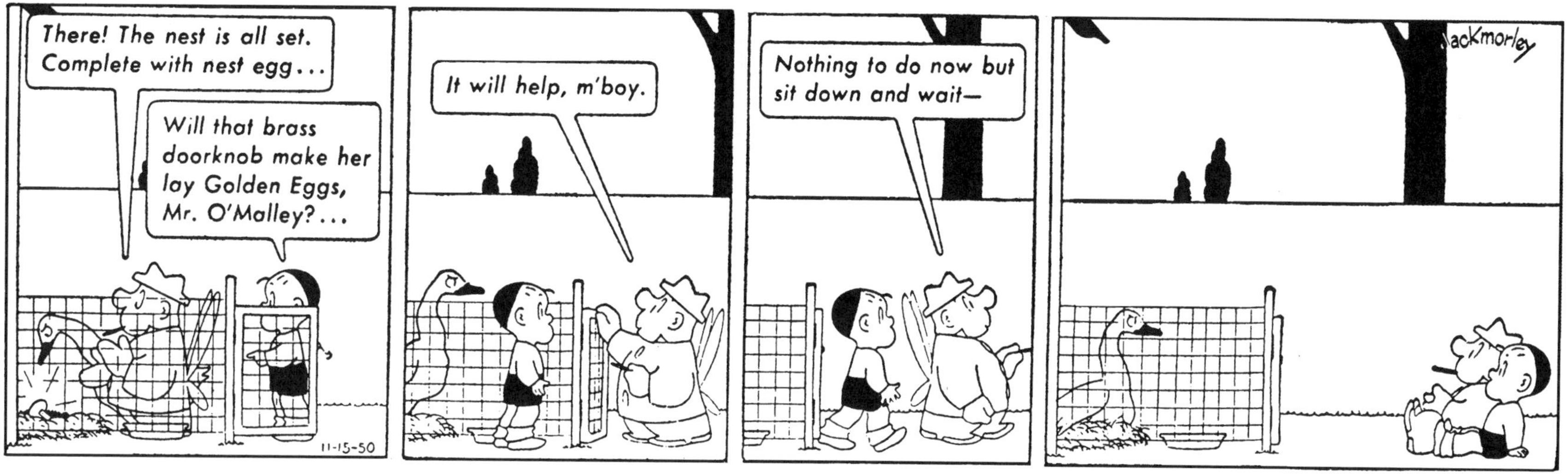
There! The nest is all set. Complete with nest egg...
Will that brass doorknob make her lay Golden Eggs, Mr. O'Malley?...
11-15-50
It will help, m'boy.
Nothing to do now but sit down and wait—
JackMorley

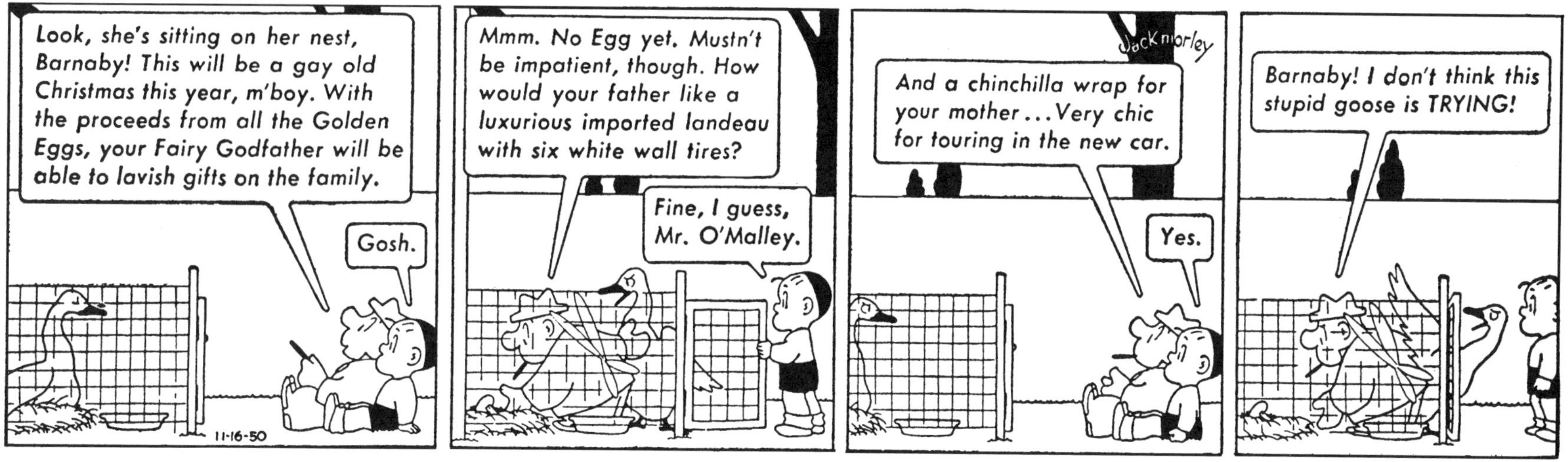
Look, she's sitting on her nest, Barnaby! This will be a gay old Christmas this year, m'boy. With the proceeds from all the Golden Eggs, your Fairy Godfather will be able to lavish gifts on the family.
Gosh.
11-16-50
Mmm. No Egg yet. Mustn't be impatient, though. How would your father like a luxurious imported landeau with six white wall tires?
Fine, I guess, Mr. O'Malley.
JackMorley
And a chinchilla wrap for your mother...Very chic for touring in the new car.
Yes.
Barnaby! I don't think this stupid goose is TRYING!

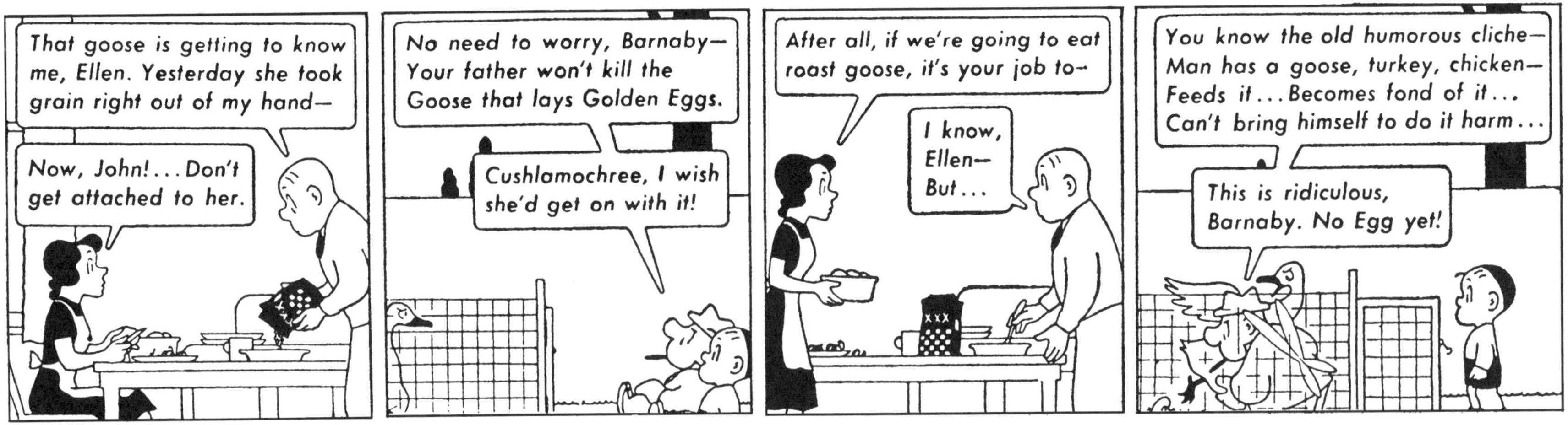
That goose is getting to know me, Ellen. Yesterday she took grain right out of my hand—
Now, John!... Don't get attached to her.
No need to worry, Barnaby— Your father won't kill the Goose that lays Golden Eggs.
Cushlamochree, I wish she'd get on with it!
After all, if we're going to eat roast goose, it's your job to—
I know, Ellen— But...
You know the old humorous cliche— Man has a goose, turkey, chicken— Feeds it... Becomes fond of it... Can't bring himself to do it harm...
This is ridiculous, Barnaby. No Egg yet!

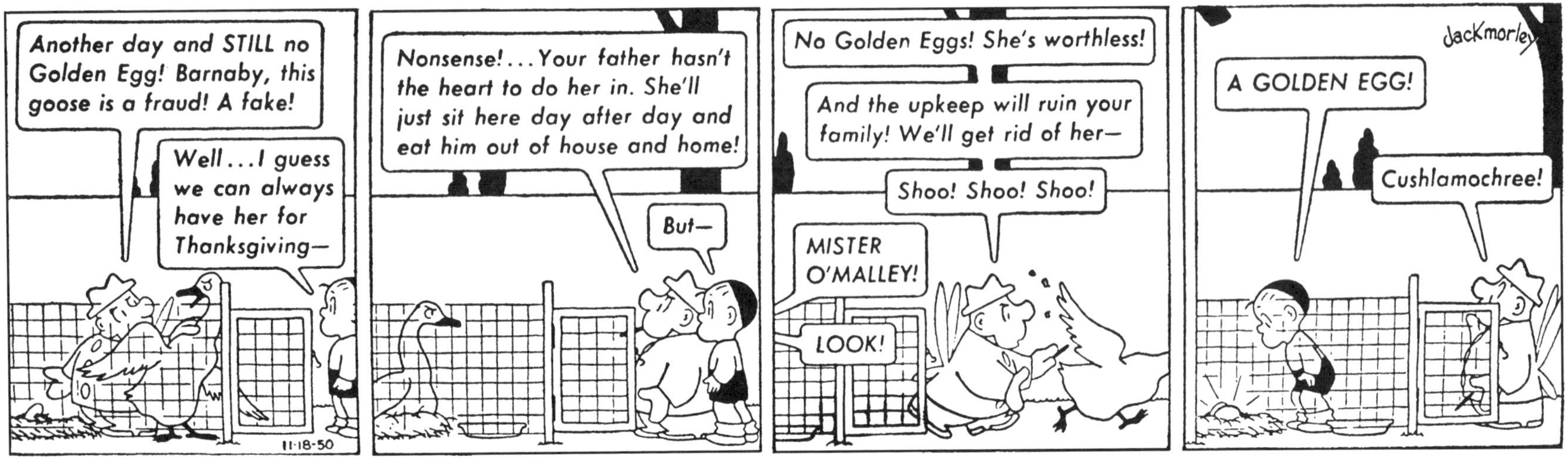
Another day and STILL no Golden Egg! Barnaby, this goose is a fraud! A fake!
Well... I guess we can always have her for Thanksgiving—
11-18-50
Nonsense!... Your father hasn't the heart to do her in. She'll just sit here day after day and eat him out of house and home!
But—
No Golden Eggs! She's worthless!
And the upkeep will ruin your family! We'll get rid of her—
Shoo! Shoo! Shoo!
MISTER O'MALLEY!
LOOK!
JacKmorley
A GOLDEN EGG!
Cushlamochree!

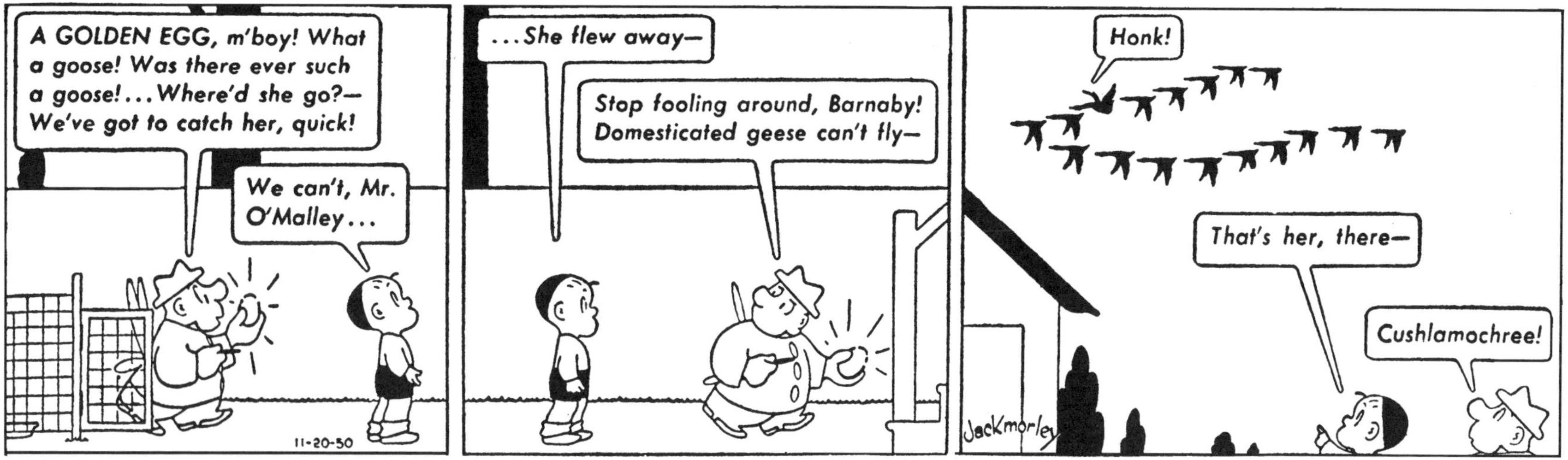
A GOLDEN EGG, m'boy! What a goose! Was there ever such a goose!... Where'd she go?— We've got to catch her, quick!
We can't, Mr. O'Malley...
11-20-50
...She flew away—
Stop fooling around, Barnaby! Domesticated geese can't fly—
Honk!
That's her, there—
Cushlamochree!
Jackmorley

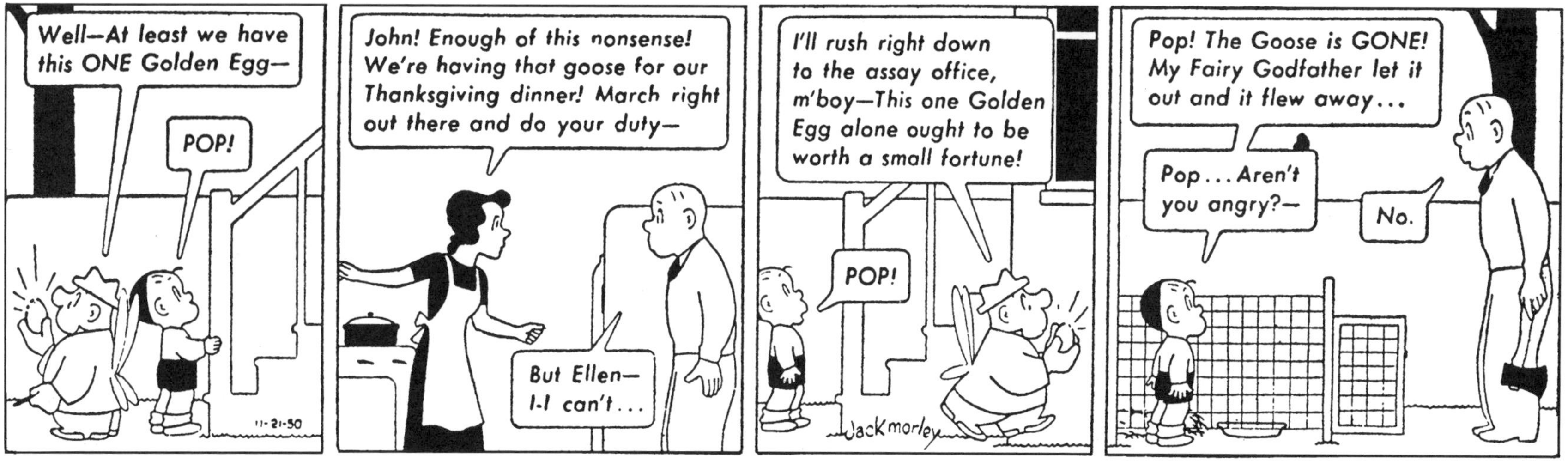
Well—At least we have this ONE Golden Egg—
POP!
11-21-50
John! Enough of this nonsense! We're having that goose for our Thanksgiving dinner! March right out there and do your duty—
But Ellen— I-I can't...
I'll rush right down to the assay office, m'boy—This one Golden Egg alone ought to be worth a small fortune!
POP!
Jackmorley
Pop! The Goose is GONE! My Fairy Godfather let it out and it flew away...
Pop... Aren't you angry?—
No.

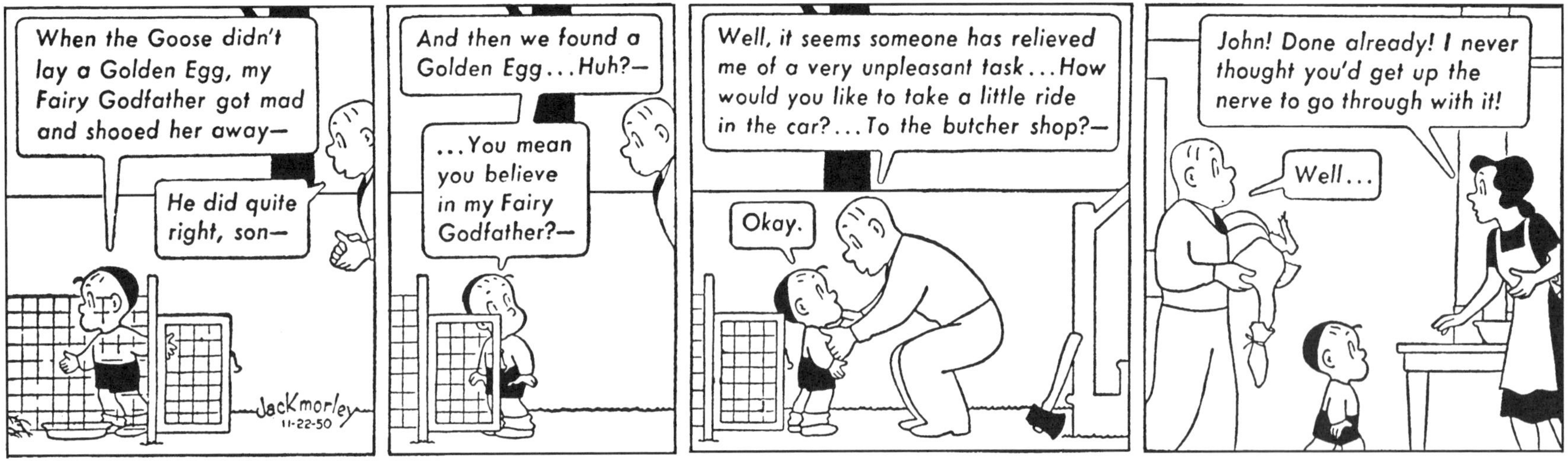
When the Goose didn't lay a Golden Egg, my Fairy Godfather got mad and shooed her away—
He did quite right, son—
Jack Morley
11-22-50
And then we found a Golden Egg...Huh?—
...You mean you believe in my Fairy Godfather?—
Well, it seems someone has relieved me of a very unpleasant task...How would you like to take a little ride in the car?...To the butcher shop?—
Okay.
John! Done already! I never thought you'd get up the nerve to go through with it!
Well...

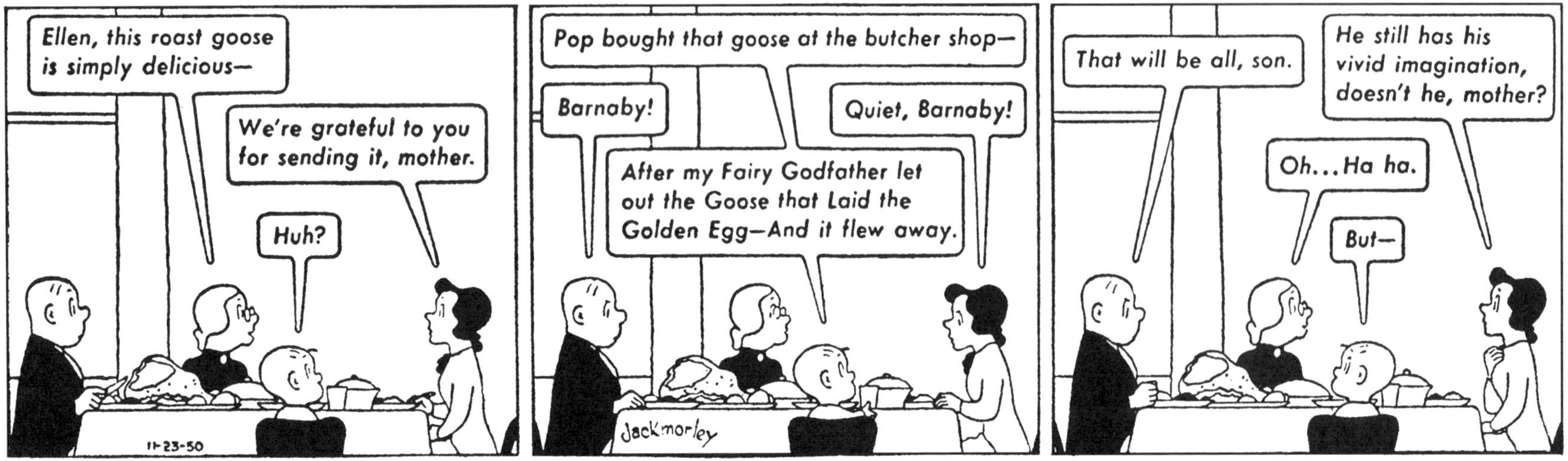
Ellen, this roast goose is simply delicious—
We're grateful to you for sending it, mother.
Huh?
11-23-50
Pop bought that goose at the butcher shop—
Barnaby!
Quiet, Barnaby!
After my Fairy Godfather let out the Goose that Laid the Golden Egg—And it flew away.
Jack Morley
That will be all, son.
He still has his vivid imagination, doesn't he, mother?
Oh...Ha ha.
But—

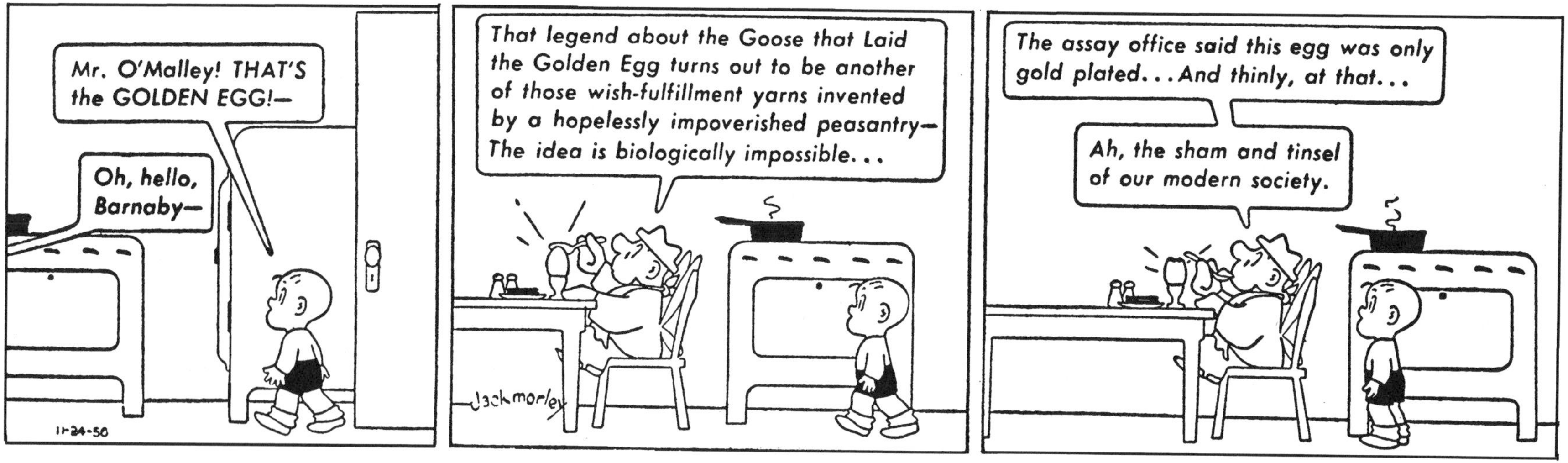
Mr. O'Malley! THAT'S the GOLDEN EGG!—
Oh, hello, Barnaby—
That legend about the Goose that Laid the Golden Egg turns out to be another of those wish-fulfillment yarns invented by a hopelessly impoverished peasantry—The idea is biologically impossible...
The assay office said this egg was only gold plated...And thinly, at that...
Ah, the sham and tinsel of our modern society.
11-24-50
Jack morley

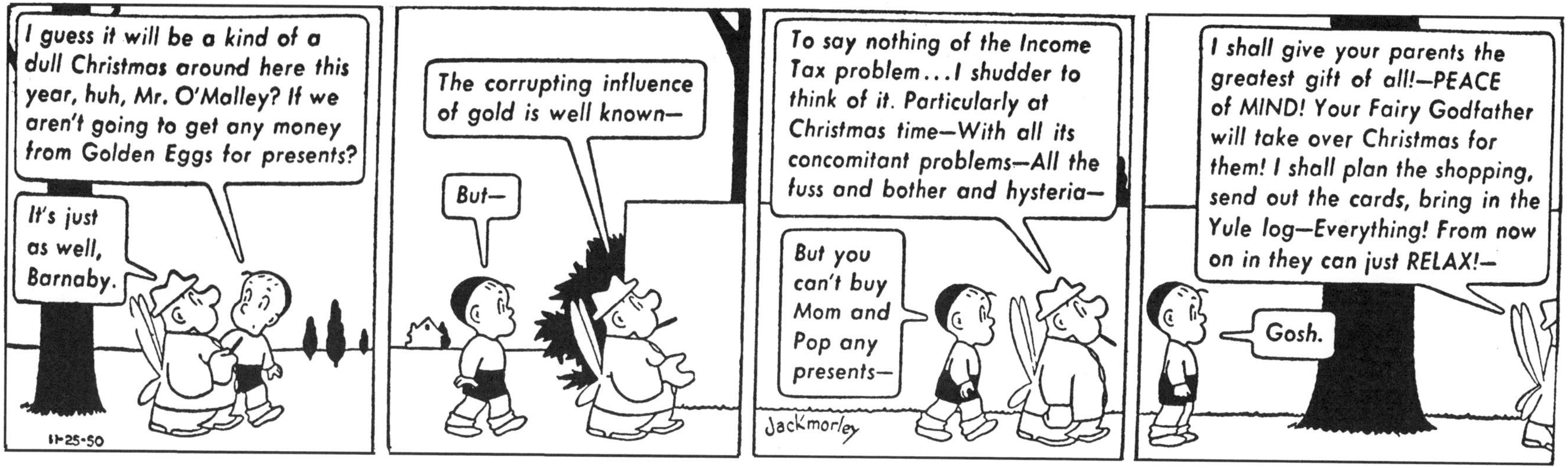
I guess it will be a kind of a dull Christmas around here this year, huh, Mr. O'Malley? If we aren't going to get any money from Golden Eggs for presents?
It's just as well, Barnaby.
The corrupting influence of gold is well known—
But—
To say nothing of the Income Tax problem...I shudder to think of it. Particularly at Christmas time—With all its concomitant problems—All the fuss and bother and hysteria—
But you can't buy Mom and Pop any presents—
I shall give your parents the greatest gift of all!—PEACE of MIND! Your Fairy Godfather will take over Christmas for them! I shall plan the shopping, send out the cards, bring in the Yule log—Everything! From now on in they can just RELAX!—
Gosh.
11-25-50
Jack morley

November 24 – 25

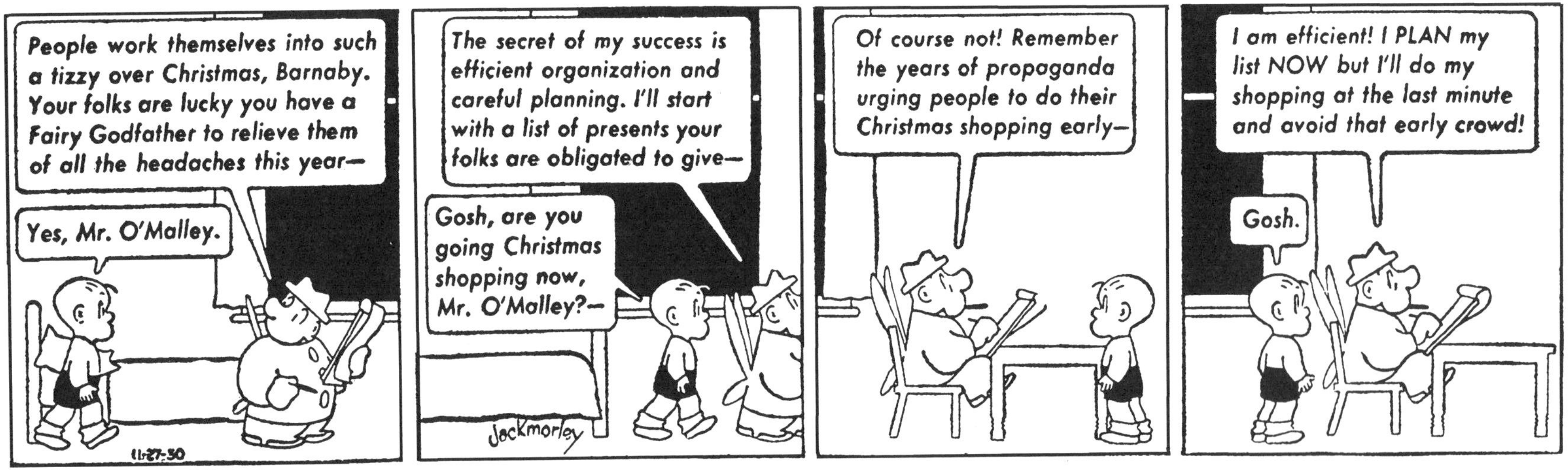
People work themselves into such a tizzy over Christmas, Barnaby. Your folks are lucky you have a Fairy Godfather to relieve them of all the headaches this year—
Yes, Mr. O'Malley.
11-27-50
The secret of my success is efficient organization and careful planning. I'll start with a list of presents your folks are obligated to give—
Gosh, are you going Christmas shopping now, Mr. O'Malley?—
Jackmorley
Of course not! Remember the years of propaganda urging people to do their Christmas shopping early—
I am efficient! I PLAN my list NOW but I'll do my shopping at the last minute and avoid that early crowd!
Gosh.

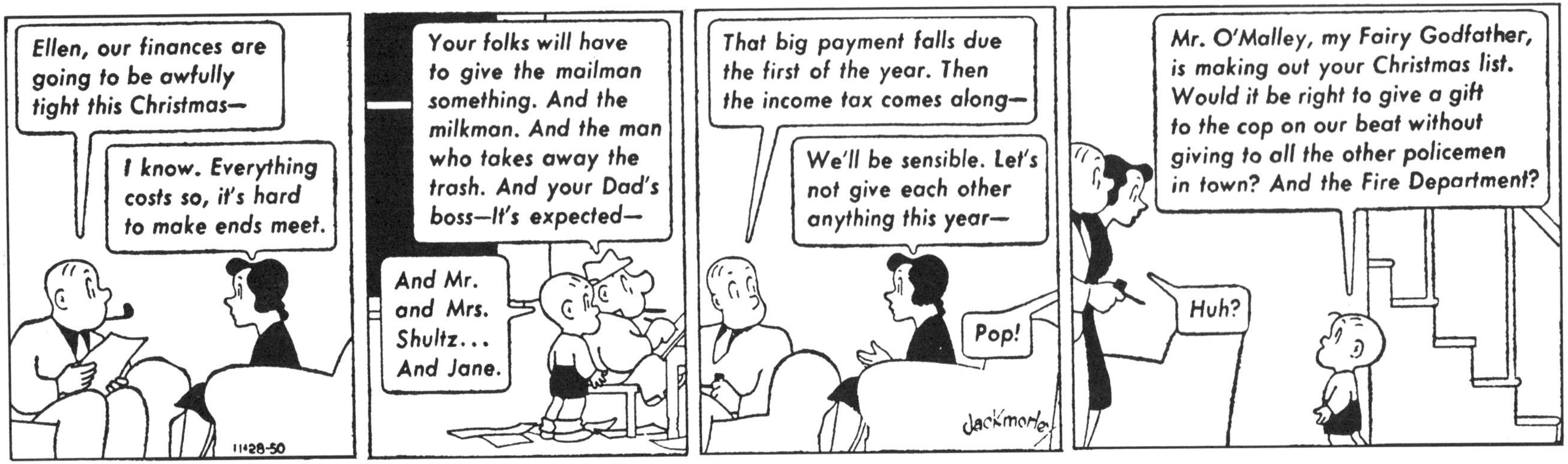
Ellen, our finances are going to be awfully tight this Christmas—
I know. Everything costs so, it's hard to make ends meet.
11-28-50
Your folks will have to give the mailman something. And the milkman. And the man who takes away the trash. And your Dad's boss—It's expected—
And Mr. and Mrs. Shultz... And Jane.
That big payment falls due the first of the year. Then the income tax comes along—
We'll be sensible. Let's not give each other anything this year—
Pop!
Jackmorley
Mr. O'Malley, my Fairy Godfather, is making out your Christmas list. Would it be right to give a gift to the cop on our beat without giving to all the other policemen in town? And the Fire Department?
Huh?

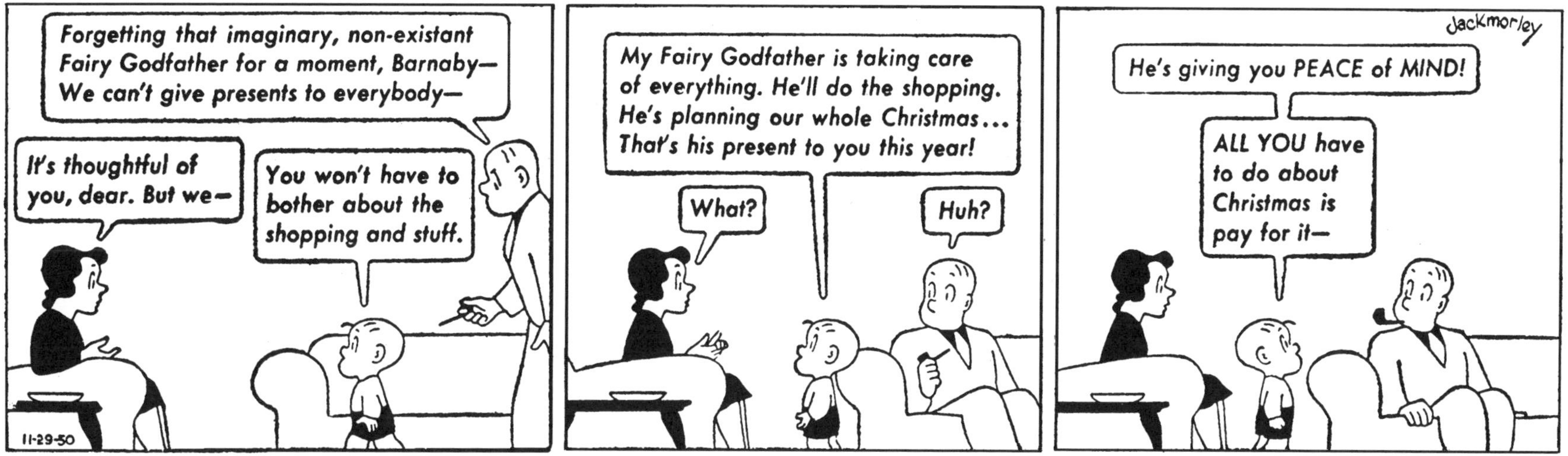
Forgetting that imaginary, non-existant Fairy Godfather for a moment, Barnaby—We can't give presents to everybody—
It's thoughtful of you, dear. But we—
You won't have to bother about the shopping and stuff.
11-29-50
My Fairy Godfather is taking care of everything. He'll do the shopping. He's planning our whole Christmas... That's his present to you this year!
What?
Huh?
Jackmorley
He's giving you PEACE of MIND!
ALL YOU have to do about Christmas is pay for it—

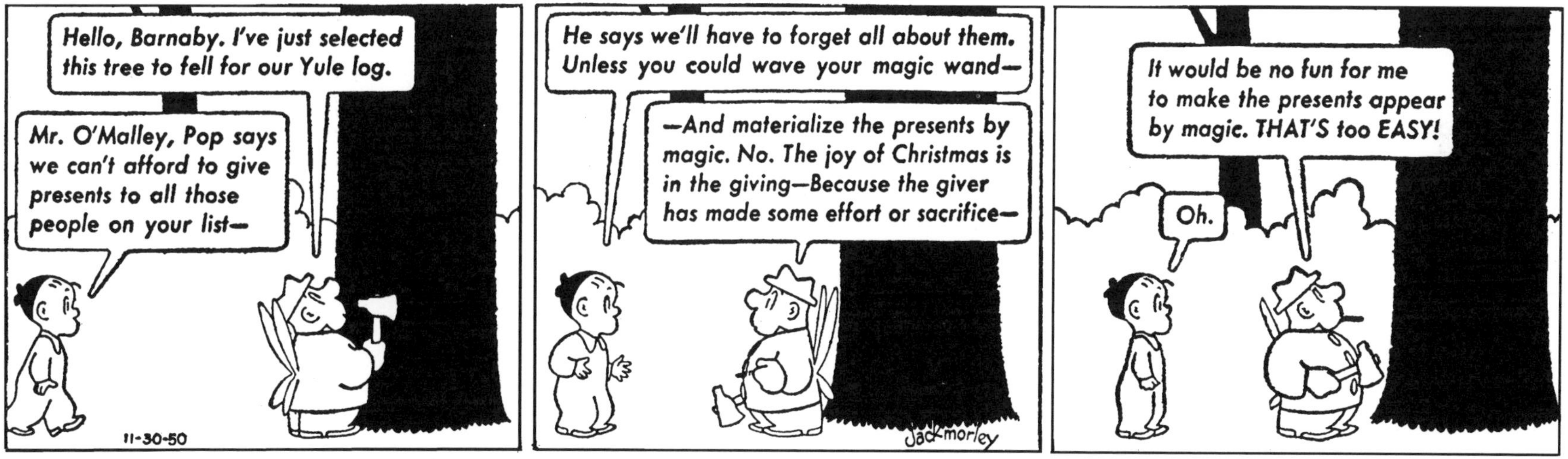
Hello, Barnaby. I've just selected this tree to fell for our Yule log.
Mr. O'Malley, Pop says we can't afford to give presents to all those people on your list—
11-30-50
He says we'll have to forget all about them. Unless you could wave your magic wand—
—And materialize the presents by magic. No. The joy of Christmas is in the giving—Because the giver has made some effort or sacrifice—
Jackmorley
It would be no fun for me to make the presents appear by magic. THAT'S too EASY!
Oh.

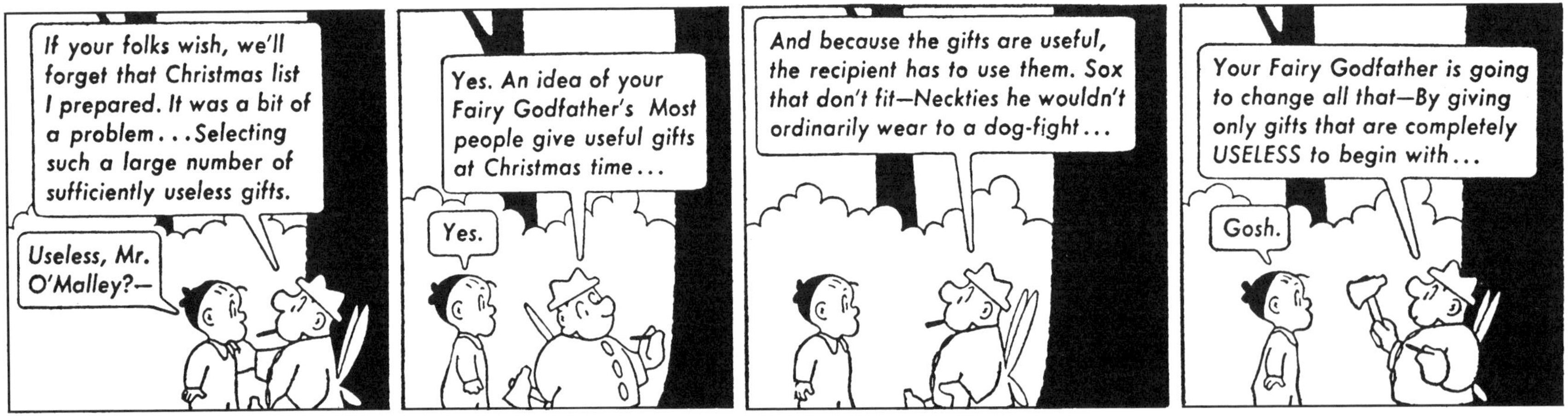
If your folks wish, we'll forget that Christmas list I prepared. It was a bit of a problem...Selecting such a large number of sufficiently useless gifts.
Useless, Mr. O'Malley?—
Yes. An idea of your Fairy Godfather's Most people give useful gifts at Christmas time...
Yes.
And because the gifts are useful, the recipient has to use them. Sox that don't fit—Neckties he wouldn't ordinarily wear to a dog-fight...
Your Fairy Godfather is going to change all that—By giving only gifts that are completely USELESS to begin with...
Gosh.

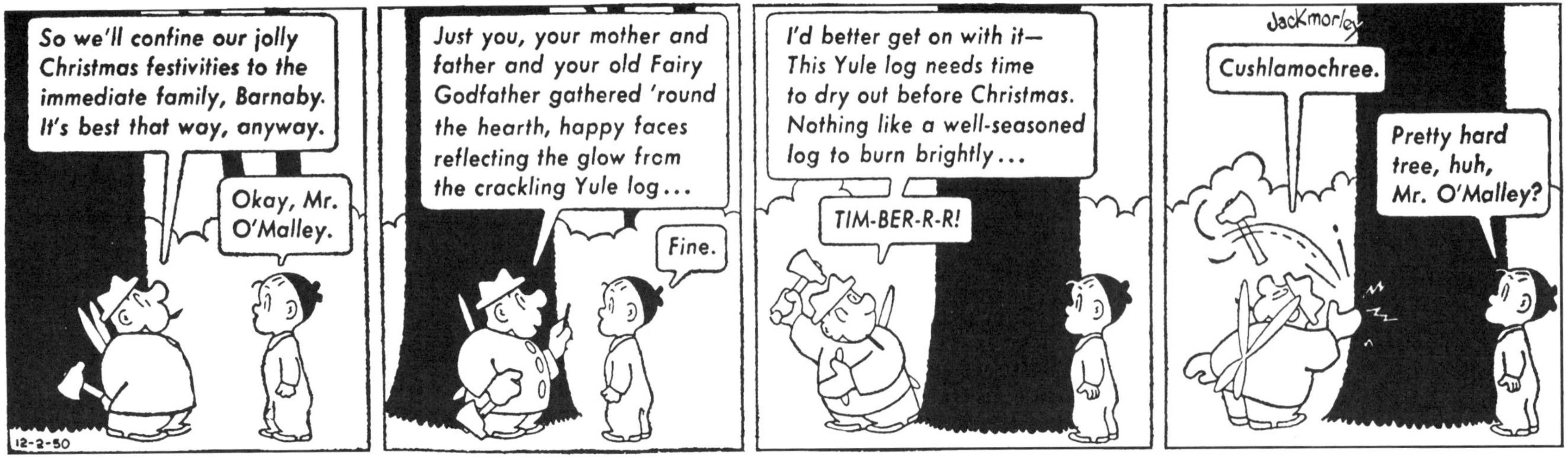
So we'll confine our jolly Christmas festivities to the immediate family, Barnaby. It's best that way, anyway.
Okay, Mr. O'Malley.
Just you, your mother and father and your old Fairy Godfather gathered 'round the hearth, happy faces reflecting the glow from the crackling Yule log...
Fine.
I'd better get on with it—This Yule log needs time to dry out before Christmas. Nothing like a well-seasoned log to burn brightly...
TIM-BER-R-R!
Jackmorley
Cushlamochree.
Pretty hard tree, huh, Mr. O'Malley?
12-2-50

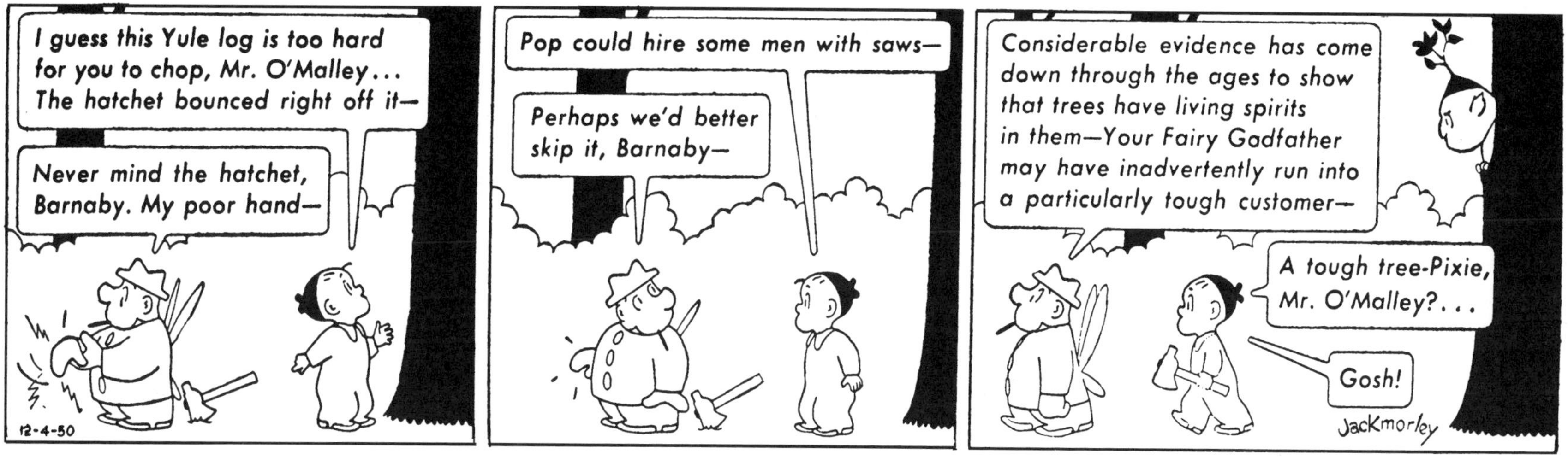
I guess this Yule log is too hard for you to chop, Mr. O'Malley... The hatchet bounced right off it—
Never mind the hatchet, Barnaby. My poor hand—
12-4-50
Pop could hire some men with saws—
Perhaps we'd better skip it, Barnaby—
Considerable evidence has come down through the ages to show that trees have living spirits in them—Your Fairy Godfather may have inadvertently run into a particularly tough customer—
A tough tree-Pixie, Mr. O'Malley?...
Gosh!
Jackmorley

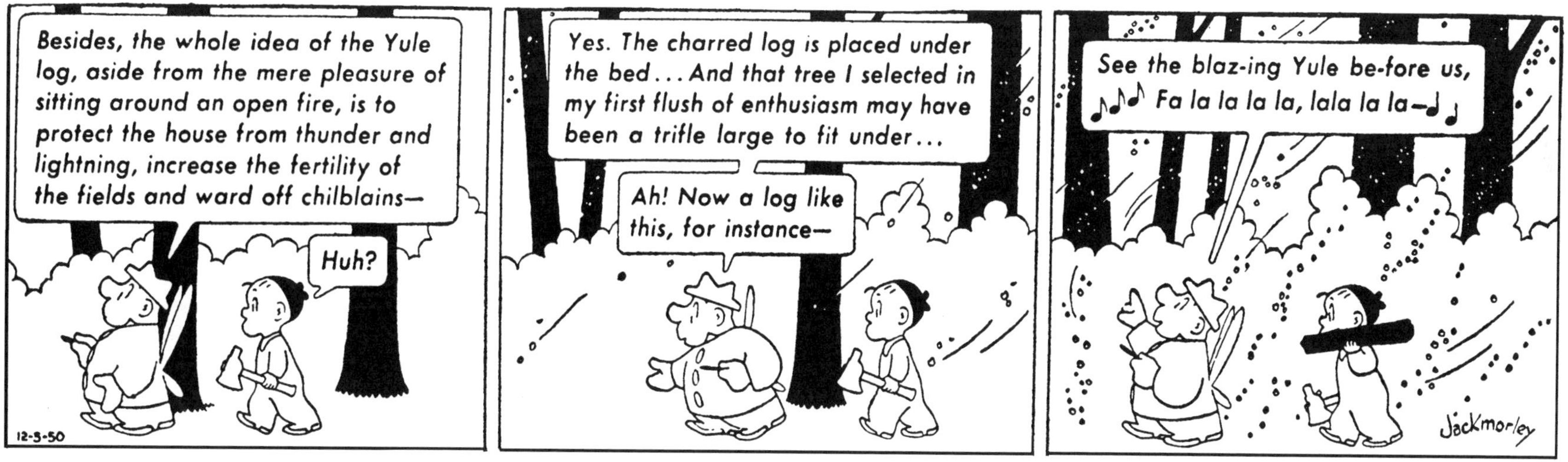
Besides, the whole idea of the Yule log, aside from the mere pleasure of sitting around an open fire, is to protect the house from thunder and lightning, increase the fertility of the fields and ward off chilblains—
Huh?
12-5-50
Yes. The charred log is placed under the bed... And that tree I selected in my first flush of enthusiasm may have been a trifle large to fit under...
Ah! Now a log like this, for instance—
See the blaz-ing Yule be-fore us, Fa la la la la, lala la la—
Jackmorley

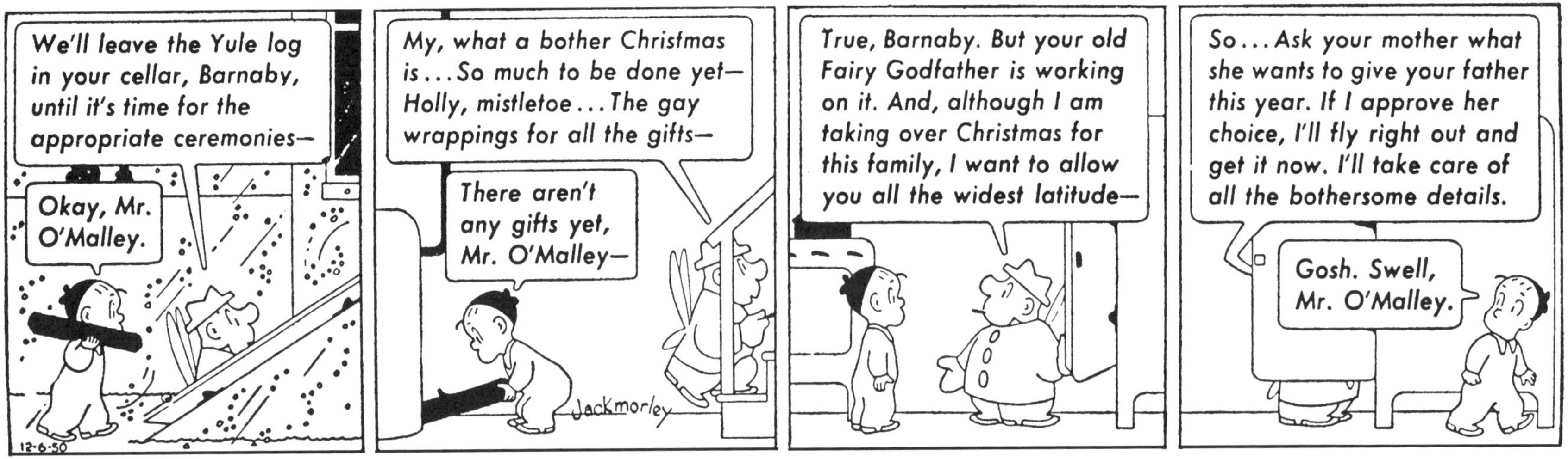
We'll leave the Yule log in your cellar, Barnaby, until it's time for the appropriate ceremonies—
Okay, Mr. O'Malley.
My, what a bother Christmas is...So much to be done yet—Holly, mistletoe...The gay wrappings for all the gifts—
There aren't any gifts yet, Mr. O'Malley—
True, Barnaby. But your old Fairy Godfather is working on it. And, although I am taking over Christmas for this family, I want to allow you all the widest latitude—
So...Ask your mother what she wants to give your father this year. If I approve her choice, I'll fly right out and get it now. I'll take care of all the bothersome details.
Gosh. Swell, Mr. O'Malley.
12-6-50
Jackmorley

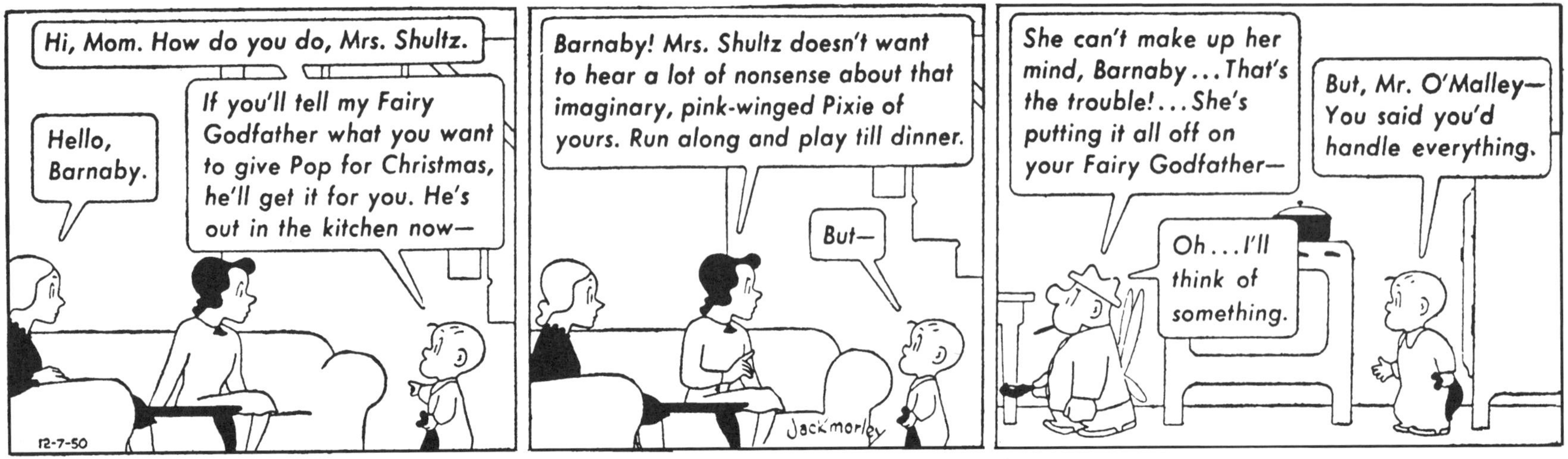
Hi, Mom. How do you do, Mrs. Shultz.
Hello, Barnaby.
If you'll tell my Fairy Godfather what you want to give Pop for Christmas, he'll get it for you. He's out in the kitchen now—
Barnaby! Mrs. Shultz doesn't want to hear a lot of nonsense about that imaginary, pink-winged Pixie of yours. Run along and play till dinner.
But—
She can't make up her mind, Barnaby...That's the trouble!...She's putting it all off on your Fairy Godfather—
Oh...I'll think of something.
But, Mr. O'Malley—You said you'd handle everything.
12-7-50
Jackmorley

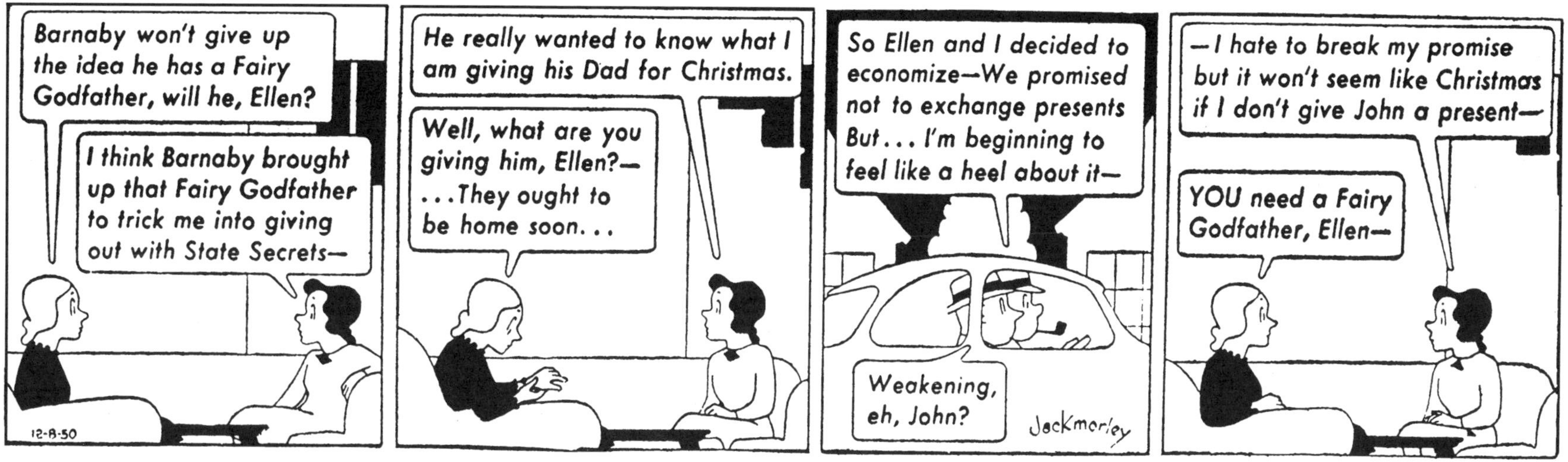
Barnaby won't give up the idea he has a Fairy Godfather, will he, Ellen?
I think Barnaby brought up that Fairy Godfather to trick me into giving out with State Secrets—
12-8-50
He really wanted to know what I am giving his Dad for Christmas.
Well, what are you giving him, Ellen?— ...They ought to be home soon...
So Ellen and I decided to economize—We promised not to exchange presents But... I'm beginning to feel like a heel about it—
Weakening, eh, John?
Jackmorley
—I hate to break my promise but it won't seem like Christmas if I don't give John a present—
YOU need a Fairy Godfather, Ellen—

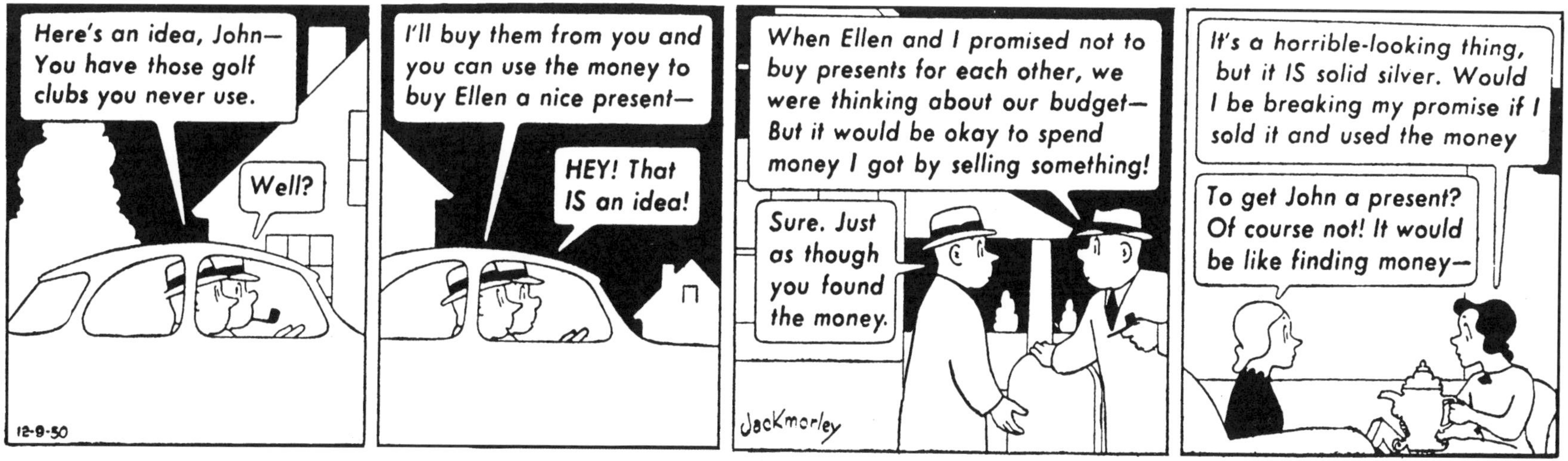
Here's an idea, John— You have those golf clubs you never use.
Well?
12-9-50
I'll buy them from you and you can use the money to buy Ellen a nice present—
HEY! That IS an idea!
When Ellen and I promised not to buy presents for each other, we were thinking about our budget— But it would be okay to spend money I got by selling something!
Sure. Just as though you found the money.
Jackmorley
It's a horrible-looking thing, but it IS solid silver. Would I be breaking my promise if I sold it and used the money
To get John a present? Of course not! It would be like finding money—

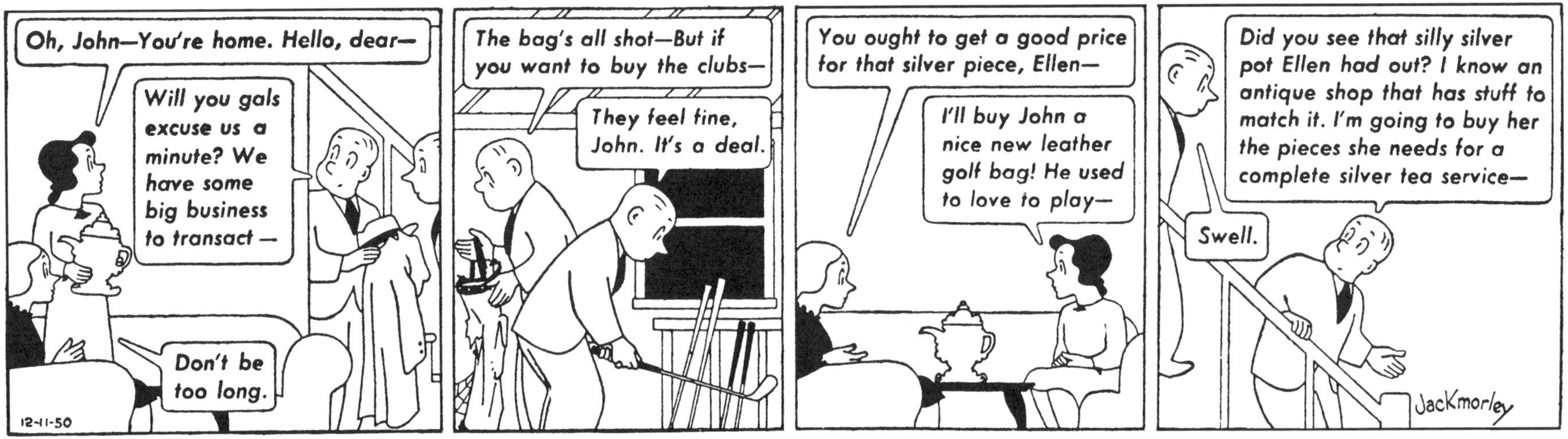

Oh, John—You're home. Hello, dear—
Will you gals excuse us a minute? We have some big business to transact —
Don't be too long.
12-11-50
The bag's all shot—But if you want to buy the clubs—
They feel fine, John. It's a deal.
You ought to get a good price for that silver piece, Ellen—
I'll buy John a nice new leather golf bag! He used to love to play—
Did you see that silly silver pot Ellen had out? I know an antique shop that has stuff to match it. I'm going to buy her the pieces she needs for a complete silver tea service—
Swell.
JacKmorley

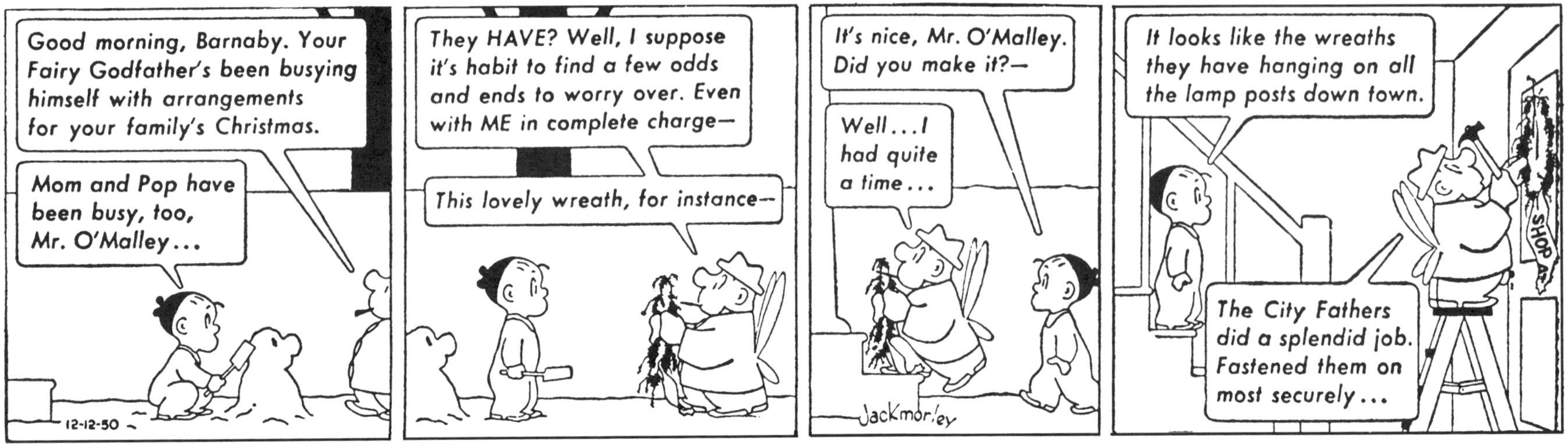

Good morning, Barnaby. Your Fairy Godfather's been busying himself with arrangements for your family's Christmas.
Mom and Pop have been busy, too, Mr. O'Malley...
12-12-50
They HAVE? Well, I suppose it's habit to find a few odds and ends to worry over. Even with ME in complete charge—
This lovely wreath, for instance—
It's nice, Mr. O'Malley. Did you make it?—
Well...I had quite a time...
JacKmorley
It looks like the wreaths they have hanging on all the lamp posts down town.
The City Fathers did a splendid job. Fastened them on most securely...
SHOP

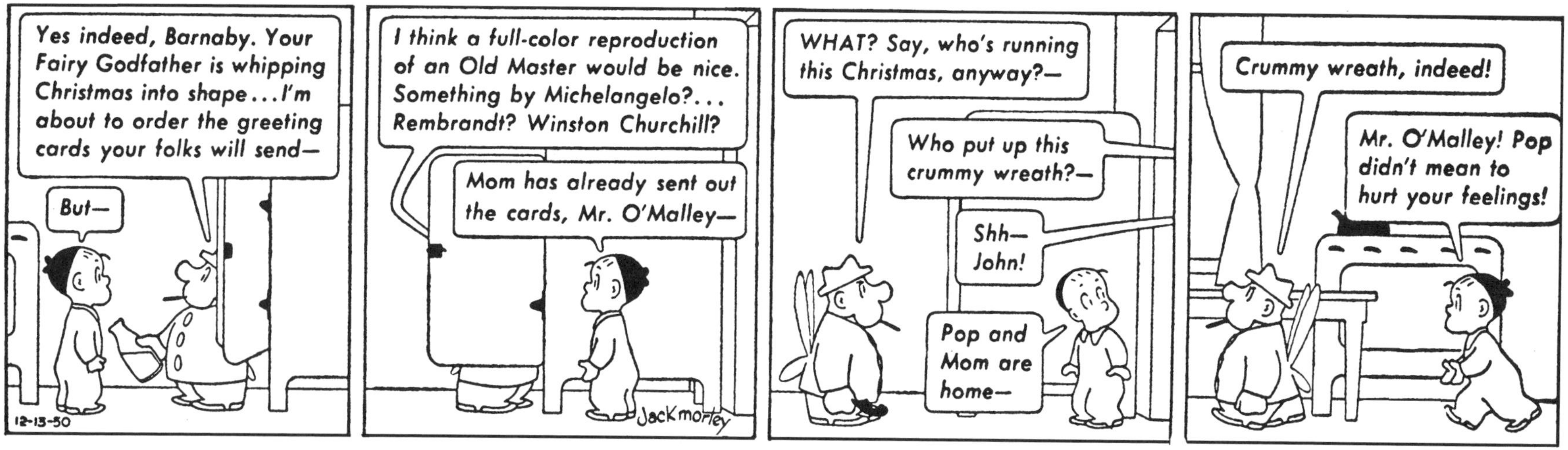
Yes indeed, Barnaby. Your Fairy Godfather is whipping Christmas into shape...I'm about to order the greeting cards your folks will send—
But—
12-13-50
I think a full-color reproduction of an Old Master would be nice. Something by Michelangelo?... Rembrandt? Winston Churchill?
Mom has already sent out the cards, Mr. O'Malley—
Jackmorley
WHAT? Say, who's running this Christmas, anyway?—
Who put up this crummy wreath?—
Shh— John!
Pop and Mom are home—
Crummy wreath, indeed!
Mr. O'Malley! Pop didn't mean to hurt your feelings!

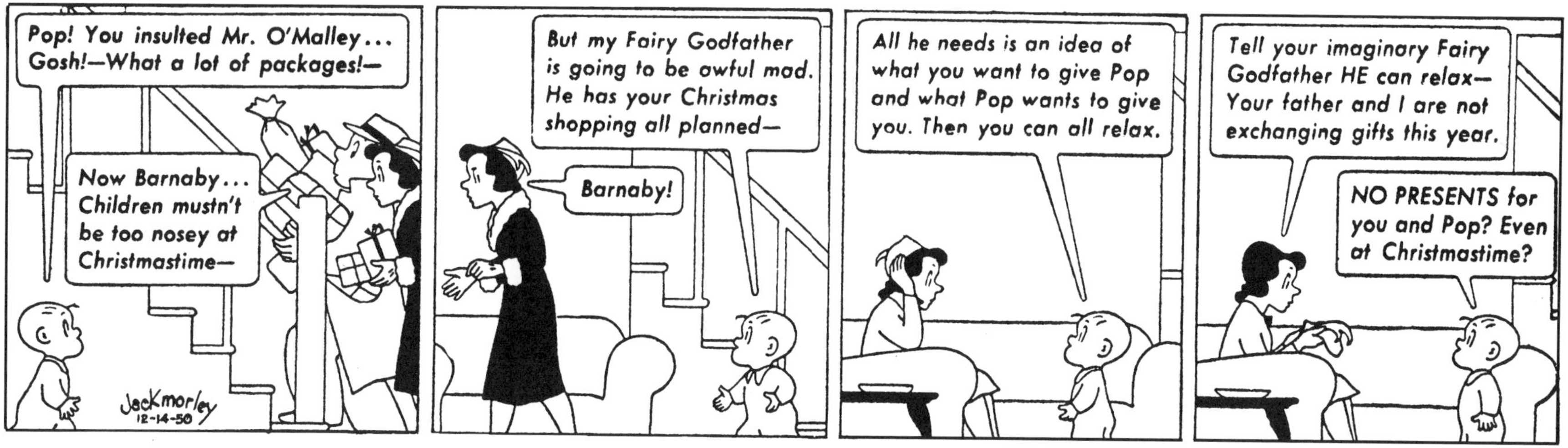
Pop! You insulted Mr. O'Malley... Gosh!—What a lot of packages!—
Now Barnaby... Children mustn't be too nosey at Christmastime—
Jackmorley
12-14-50
But my Fairy Godfather is going to be awful mad. He has your Christmas shopping all planned—
Barnaby!
All he needs is an idea of what you want to give Pop and what Pop wants to give you. Then you can all relax.
Tell your imaginary Fairy Godfather HE can relax— Your father and I are not exchanging gifts this year.
NO PRESENTS for you and Pop? Even at Christmastime?

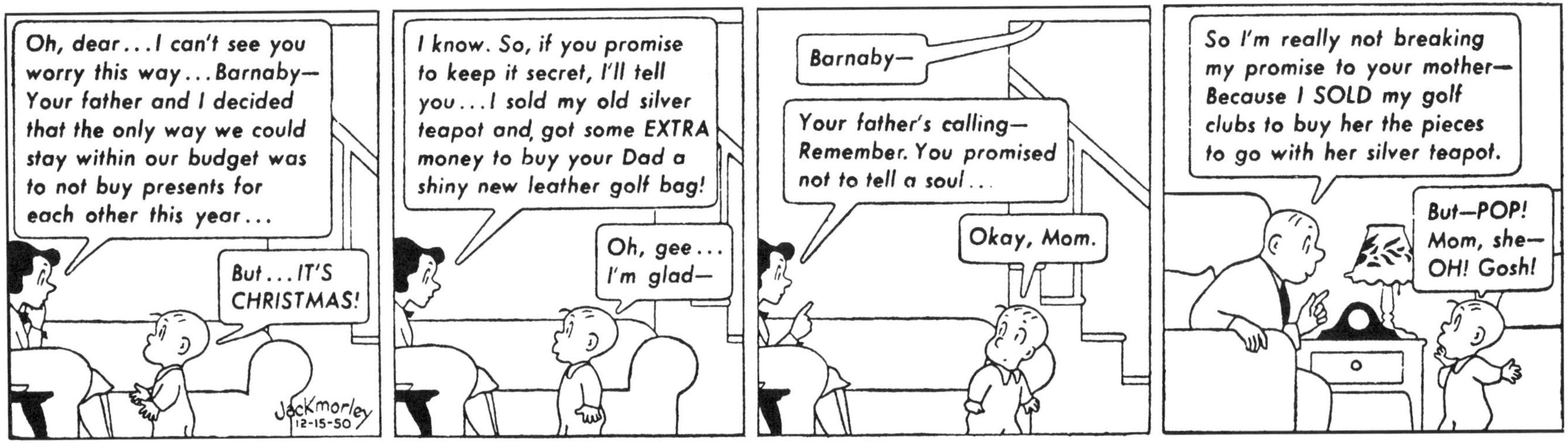
Oh, dear... I can't see you worry this way... Barnaby— Your father and I decided that the only way we could stay within our budget was to not buy presents for each other this year...
But... IT'S CHRISTMAS!
JackMorley 12-15-50
I know. So, if you promise to keep it secret, I'll tell you... I sold my old silver teapot and got some EXTRA money to buy your Dad a shiny new leather golf bag!
Oh, gee... I'm glad—
Barnaby—
Your father's calling— Remember. You promised not to tell a soul...
Okay, Mom.
So I'm really not breaking my promise to your mother— Because I SOLD my golf clubs to buy her the pieces to go with her silver teapot.
But—POP! Mom, she— OH! Gosh!

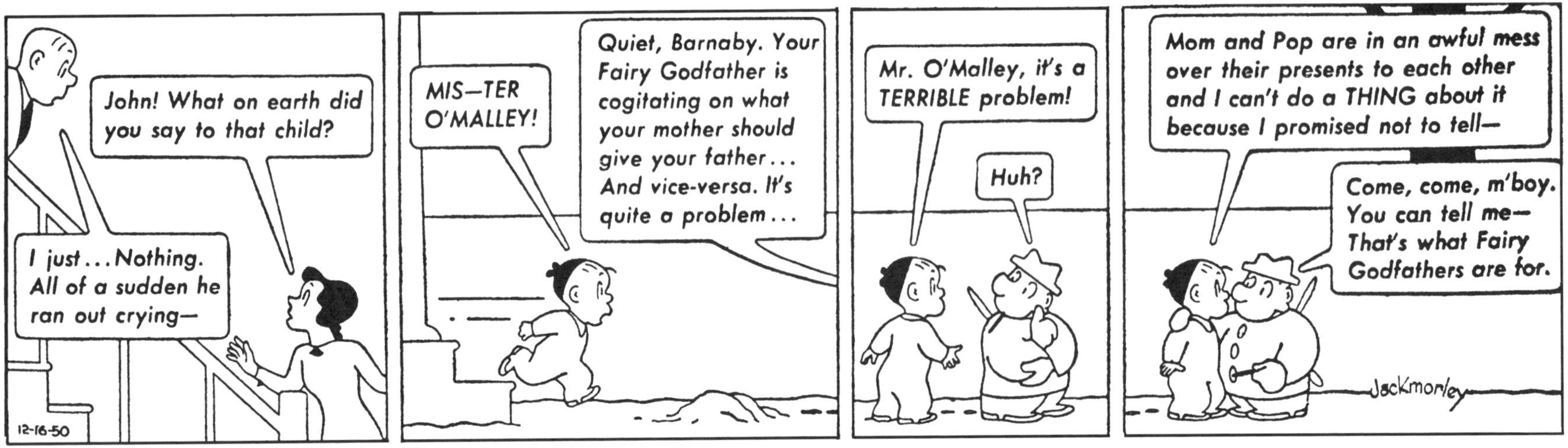
John! What on earth did you say to that child?
I just... Nothing. All of a sudden he ran out crying—
12-16-50
MIS—TER O'MALLEY!
Quiet, Barnaby. Your Fairy Godfather is cogitating on what your mother should give your father... And vice-versa. It's quite a problem...
Mr. O'Malley, it's a TERRIBLE problem!
Huh?
Mom and Pop are in an awful mess over their presents to each other and I can't do a THING about it because I promised not to tell—
Come, come, m'boy. You can tell me— That's what Fairy Godfathers are for.
JackMorley

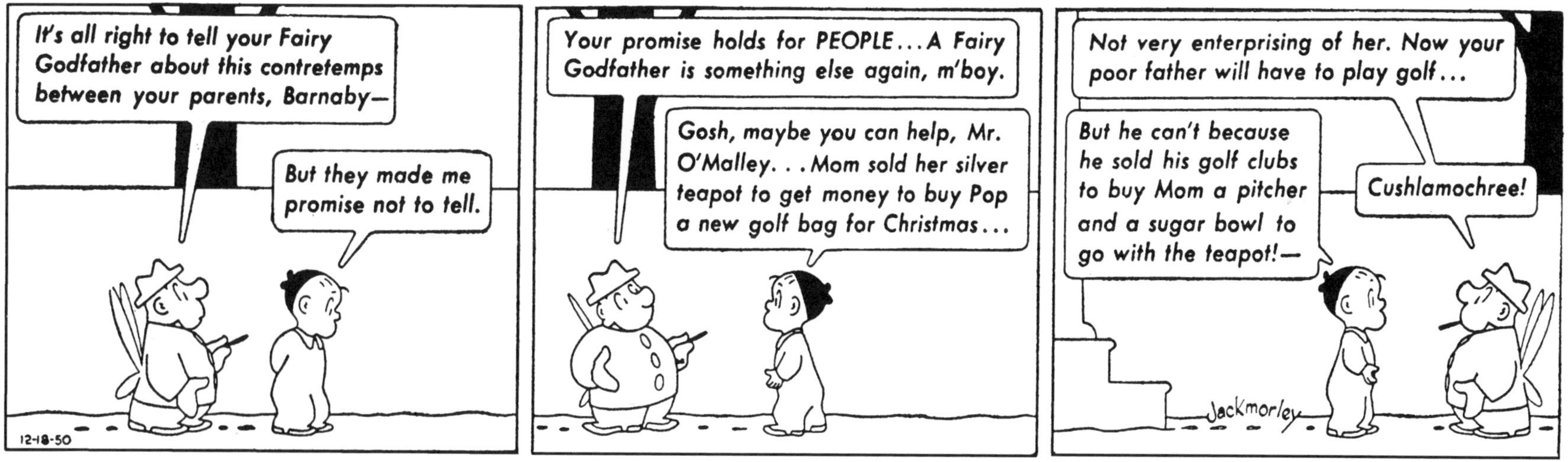
It's all right to tell your Fairy Godfather about this contretemps between your parents, Barnaby—
But they made me promise not to tell.
12-18-50
Your promise holds for PEOPLE...A Fairy Godfather is something else again, m'boy.
Gosh, maybe you can help, Mr. O'Malley. . .Mom sold her silver teapot to get money to buy Pop a new golf bag for Christmas...
Not very enterprising of her. Now your poor father will have to play golf...
But he can't because he sold his golf clubs to buy Mom a pitcher and a sugar bowl to go with the teapot!—
Cushlamochree!
Jackmorley

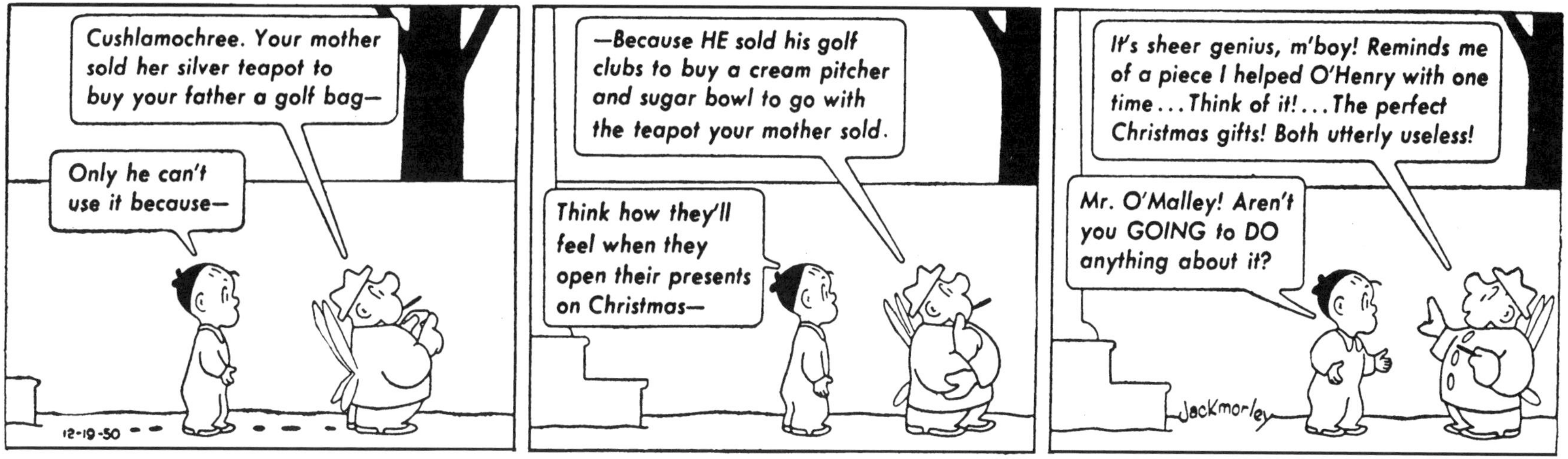
Cushlamochree. Your mother sold her silver teapot to buy your father a golf bag—
Only he can't use it because—
12-19-50
—Because HE sold his golf clubs to buy a cream pitcher and sugar bowl to go with the teapot your mother sold.
Think how they'll feel when they open their presents on Christmas—
It's sheer genius, m'boy! Reminds me of a piece I helped O'Henry with one time...Think of it!...The perfect Christmas gifts! Both utterly useless!
Mr. O'Malley! Aren't you GOING to DO anything about it?
Jackmorley

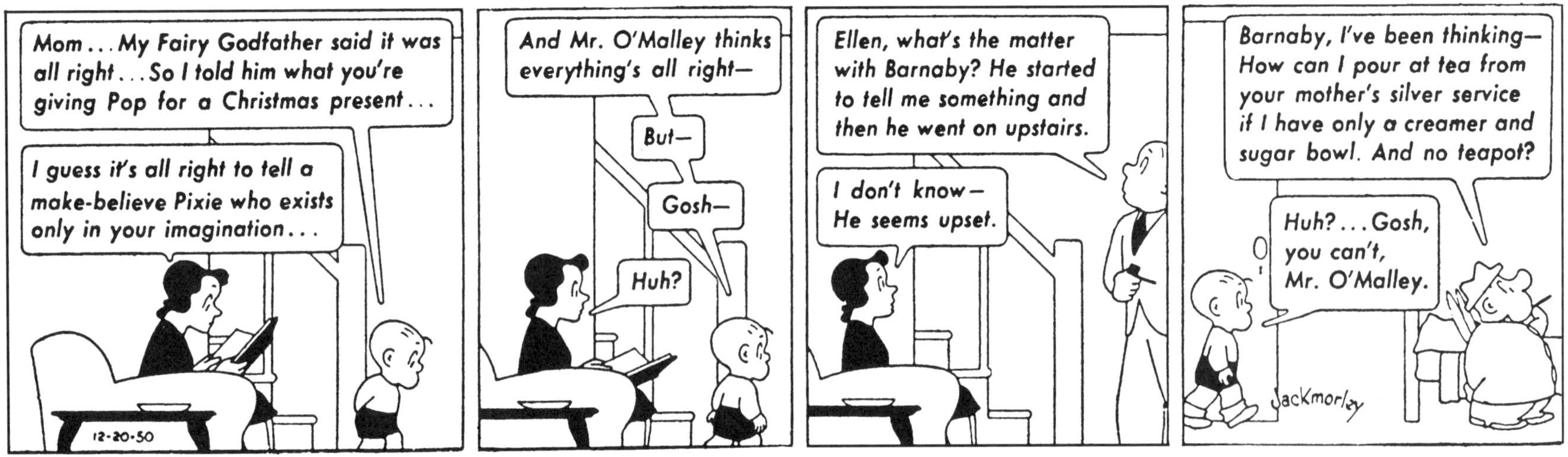
Mom . . . My Fairy Godfather said it was all right . . . So I told him what you're giving Pop for a Christmas present . . .
I guess it's all right to tell a make-believe Pixie who exists only in your imagination . . .
12-20-50
And Mr. O'Malley thinks everything's all right—
But—
Gosh—
Huh?
Ellen, what's the matter with Barnaby? He started to tell me something and then he went on upstairs.
I don't know— He seems upset.
Barnaby, I've been thinking— How can I pour at tea from your mother's silver service if I have only a creamer and sugar bowl. And no teapot?
Huh? . . . Gosh, you can't, Mr. O'Malley.
JackMorley

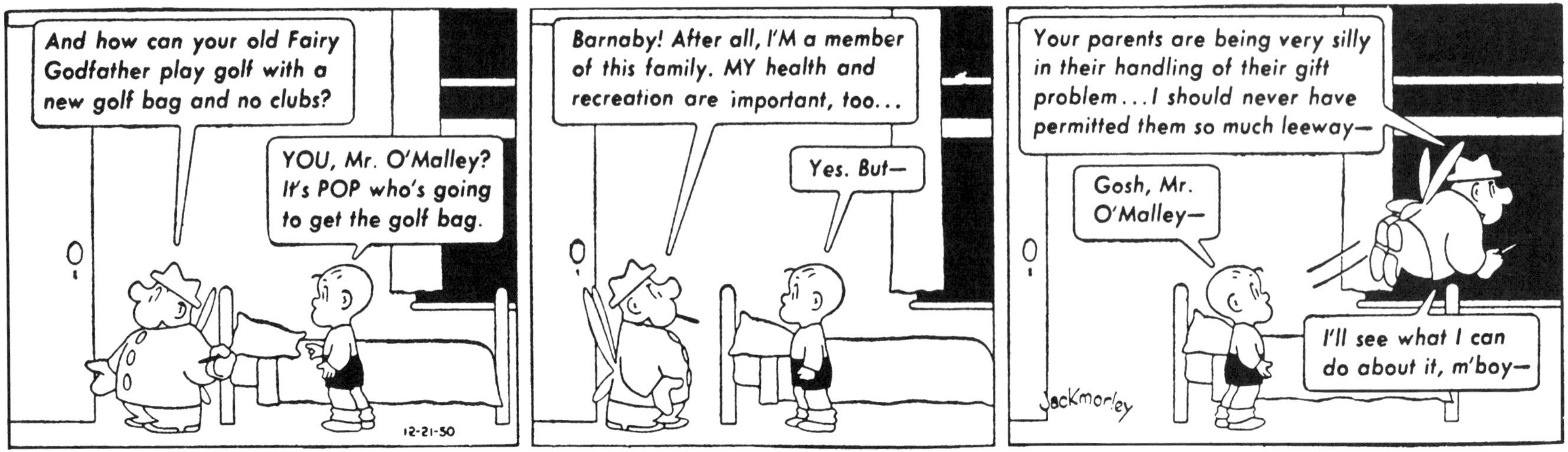
And how can your old Fairy Godfather play golf with a new golf bag and no clubs?
YOU, Mr. O'Malley? It's POP who's going to get the golf bag.
12-21-50
Barnaby! After all, I'M a member of this family. MY health and recreation are important, too . . .
Yes. But—
Your parents are being very silly in their handling of their gift problem . . . I should never have permitted them so much leeway—
Gosh, Mr. O'Malley—
I'll see what I can do about it, m'boy—
JackMorley

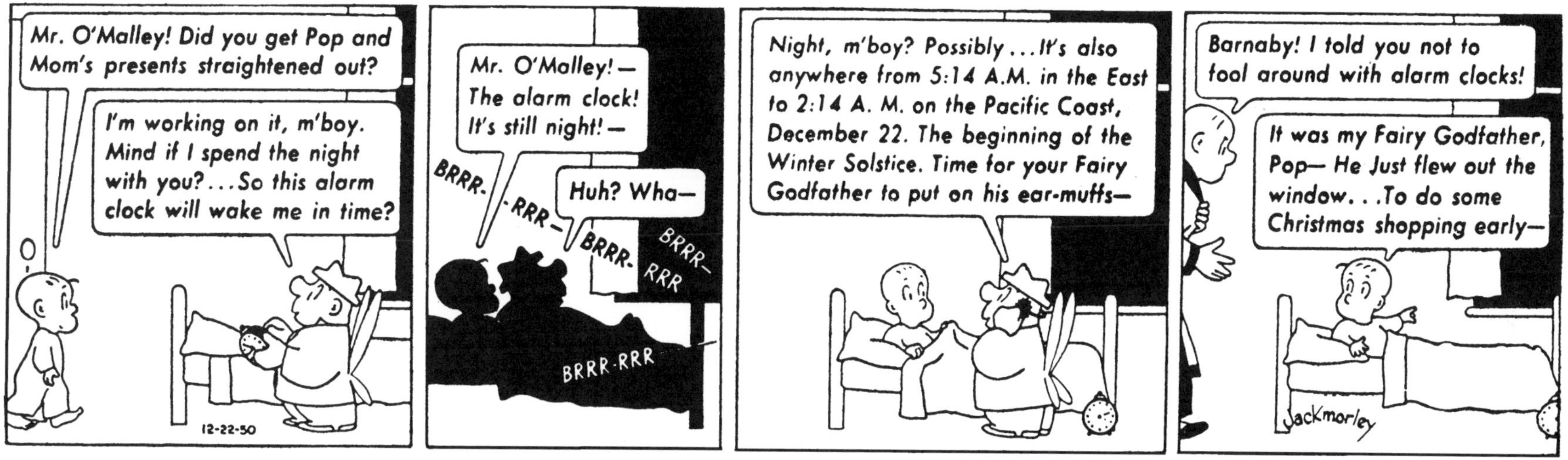
Mr. O'Malley! Did you get Pop and Mom's presents straightened out?
I'm working on it, m'boy. Mind if I spend the night with you?...So this alarm clock will wake me in time?
12-22-50
Mr. O'Malley!— The alarm clock! It's still night!—
BRRR- -RRR—
Huh? Wha—
BRRR- BRRR— RRR
BRRR-RRR
Night, m'boy? Possibly...It's also anywhere from 5:14 A.M. in the East to 2:14 A. M. on the Pacific Coast, December 22. The beginning of the Winter Solstice. Time for your Fairy Godfather to put on his ear-muffs—
Barnaby! I told you not to fool around with alarm clocks!
It was my Fairy Godfather, Pop— He Just flew out the window. . .To do some Christmas shopping early—
Jackmorley

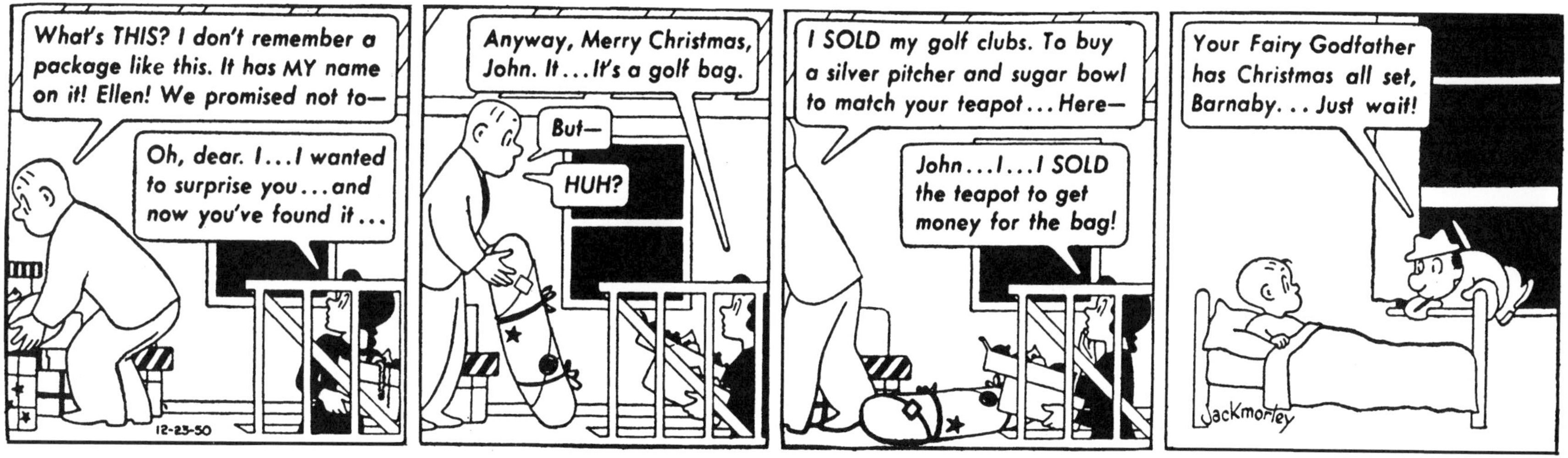
What's THIS? I don't remember a package like this. It has MY name on it! Ellen! We promised not to—
Oh, dear. I...I wanted to surprise you...and now you've found it...
12-23-50
Anyway, Merry Christmas, John. It...It's a golf bag.
But—
HUH?
I SOLD my golf clubs. To buy a silver pitcher and sugar bowl to match your teapot...Here—
John...I...I SOLD the teapot to get money for the bag!
Your Fairy Godfather has Christmas all set, Barnaby... Just wait!
Jackmorley

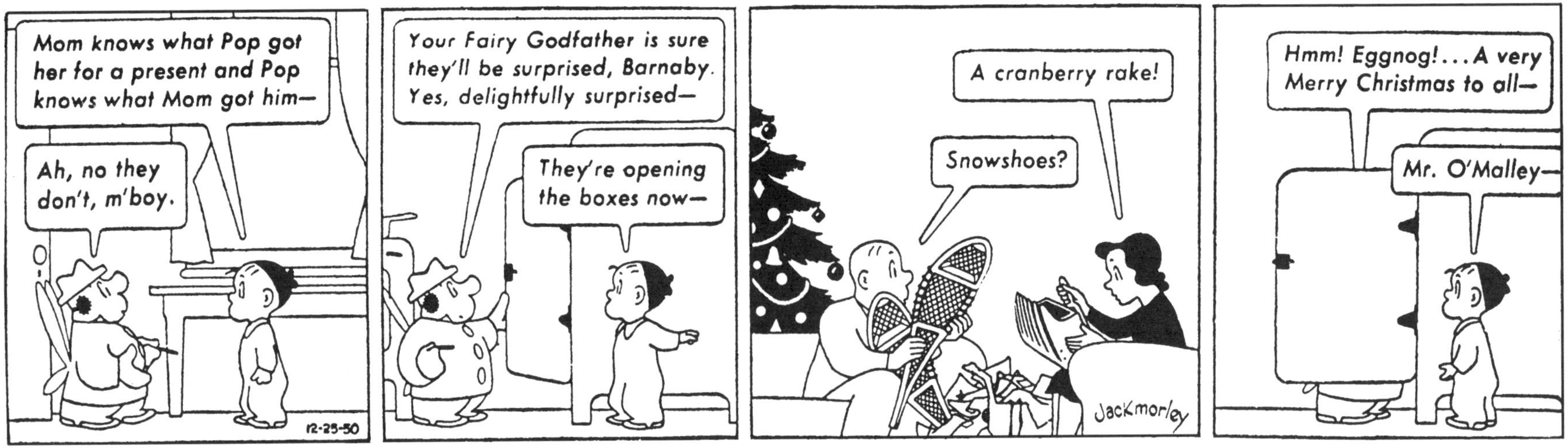
Mom knows what Pop got her for a present and Pop knows what Mom got him—
Ah, no they don't, m'boy.
12-25-50
Your Fairy Godfather is sure they'll be surprised, Barnaby. Yes, delightfully surprised—
They're opening the boxes now—
A cranberry rake!
Snowshoes?
JackMorley
Hmm! Eggnog!...A very Merry Christmas to all—
Mr. O'Malley—

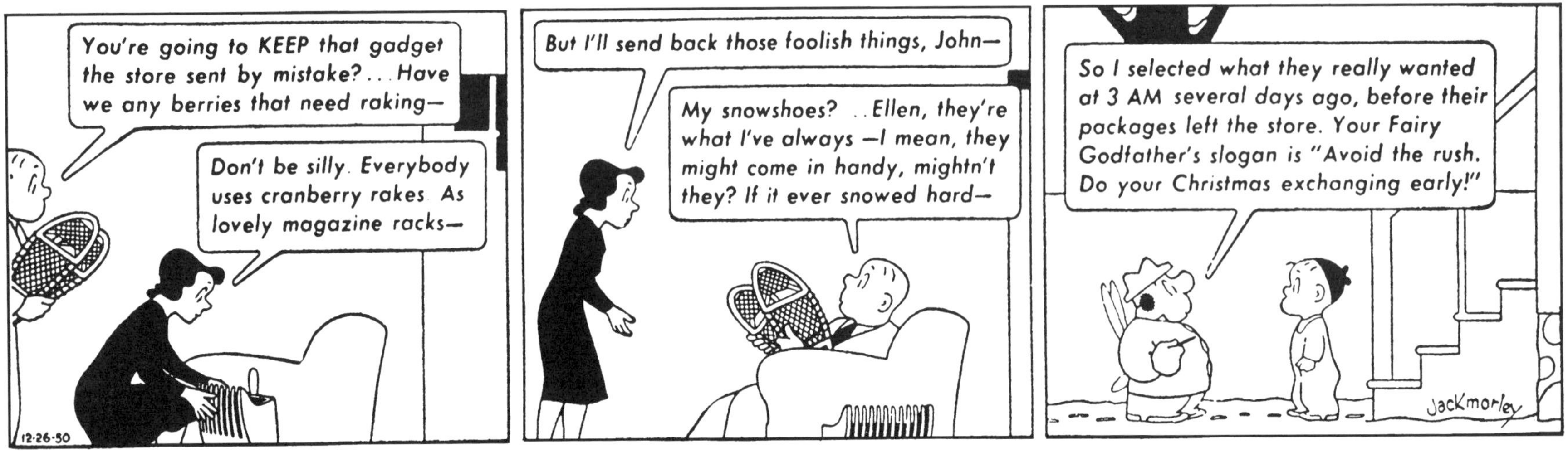
You're going to KEEP that gadget the store sent by mistake?... Have we any berries that need raking—
Don't be silly. Everybody uses cranberry rakes. As lovely magazine racks—
12-26-50
But I'll send back those foolish things, John—
My snowshoes? ..Ellen, they're what I've always —I mean, they might come in handy, mightn't they? If it ever snowed hard—
So I selected what they really wanted at 3 AM several days ago, before their packages left the store. Your Fairy Godfather's slogan is "Avoid the rush. Do your Christmas exchanging early!"
JackMorley

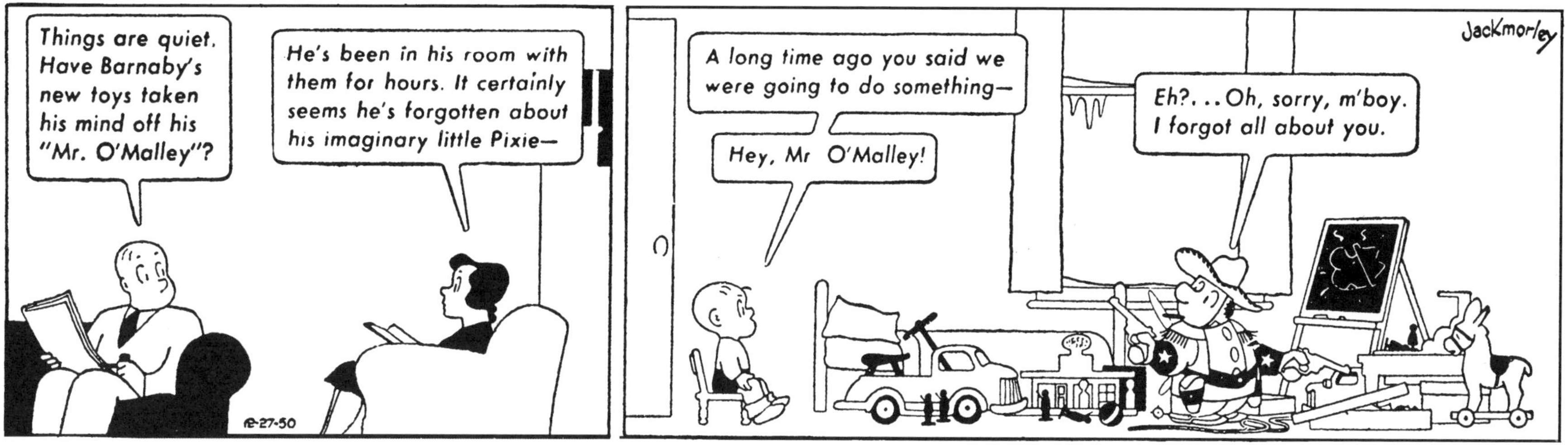
Things are quiet. Have Barnaby's new toys taken his mind off his "Mr. O'Malley"?
He's been in his room with them for hours. It certainly seems he's forgotten about his imaginary little Pixie—
A long time ago you said we were going to do something—
Hey, Mr O'Malley!
Eh?. . .Oh, sorry, m'boy. I forgot all about you.

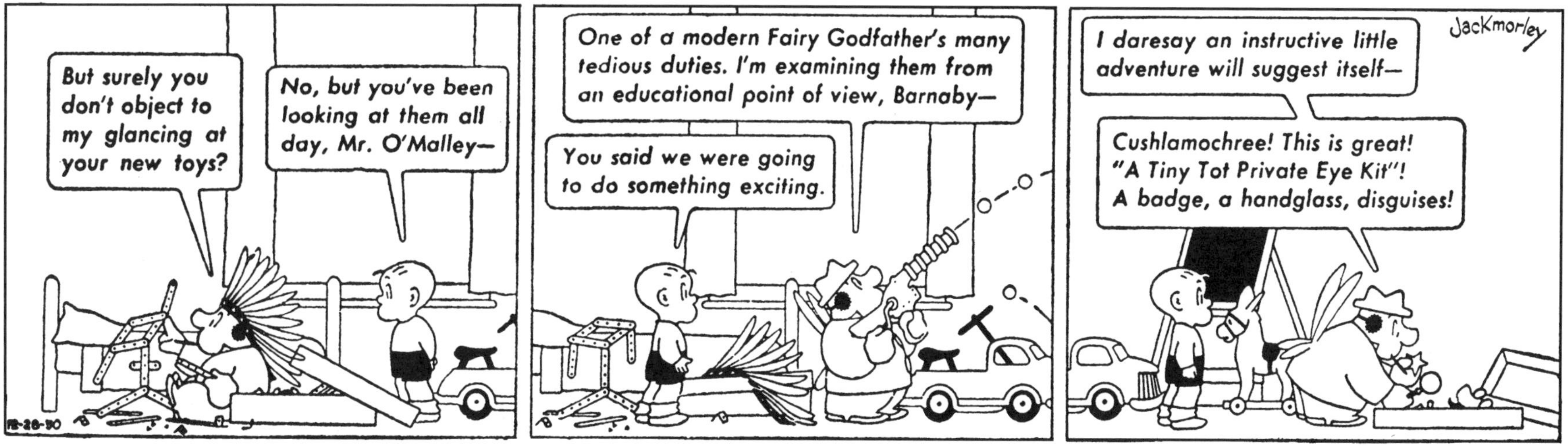
But surely you don't object to my glancing at your new toys?
No, but you've been looking at them all day, Mr. O'Malley—
One of a modern Fairy Godfather's many tedious duties. I'm examining them from an educational point of view, Barnaby—
You said we were going to do something exciting.
I daresay an instructive little adventure will suggest itself—
Cushlamochree! This is great! "A Tiny Tot Private Eye Kit"! A badge, a handglass, disguises!

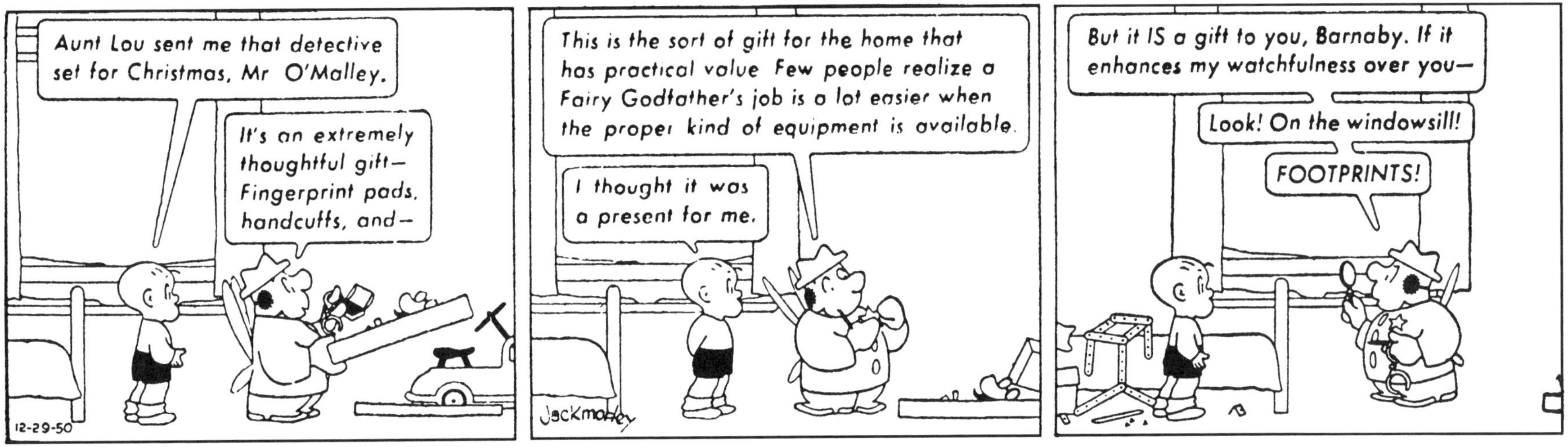
Aunt Lou sent me that detective set for Christmas, Mr O'Malley.
It's an extremely thoughtful gift— Fingerprint pads, handcuffs, and—
12-29-50
This is the sort of gift for the home that has practical value Few people realize a Fairy Godfather's job is a lot easier when the proper kind of equipment is available.
I thought it was a present for me.
JackMorley
But it IS a gift to you, Barnaby. If it enhances my watchfulness over you—
Look! On the windowsill!
FOOTPRINTS!

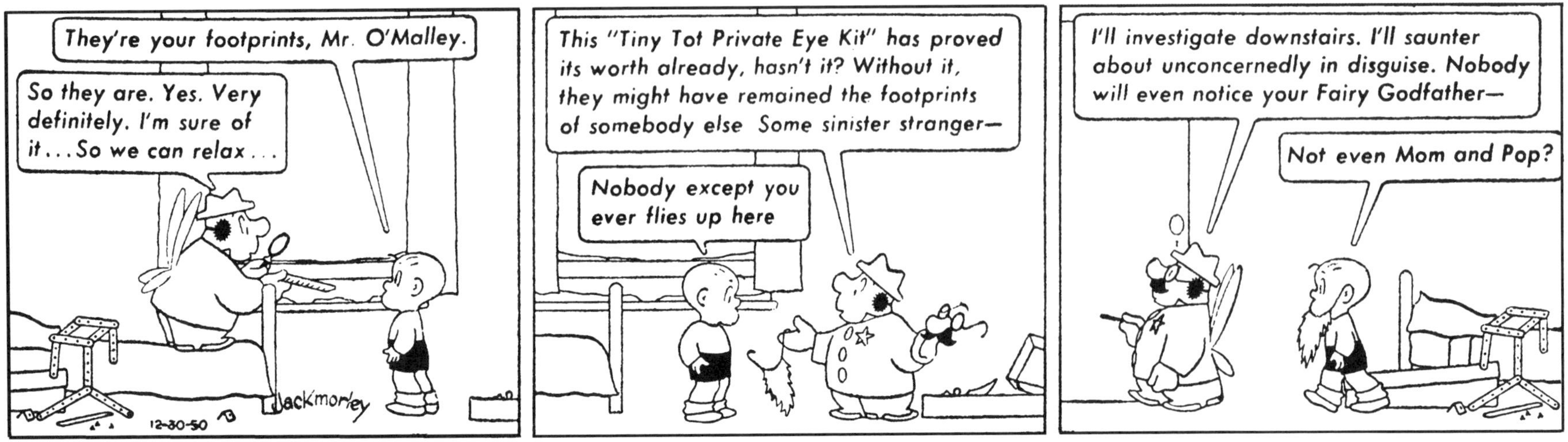
They're your footprints, Mr. O'Malley.
So they are. Yes. Very definitely. I'm sure of it . . . So we can relax . . .
JackMorley
12-30-50
This "Tiny Tot Private Eye Kit" has proved its worth already, hasn't it? Without it, they might have remained the footprints of somebody else Some sinister stranger—
Nobody except you ever flies up here
I'll investigate downstairs. I'll saunter about unconcernedly in disguise. Nobody will even notice your Fairy Godfather—
Not even Mom and Pop?

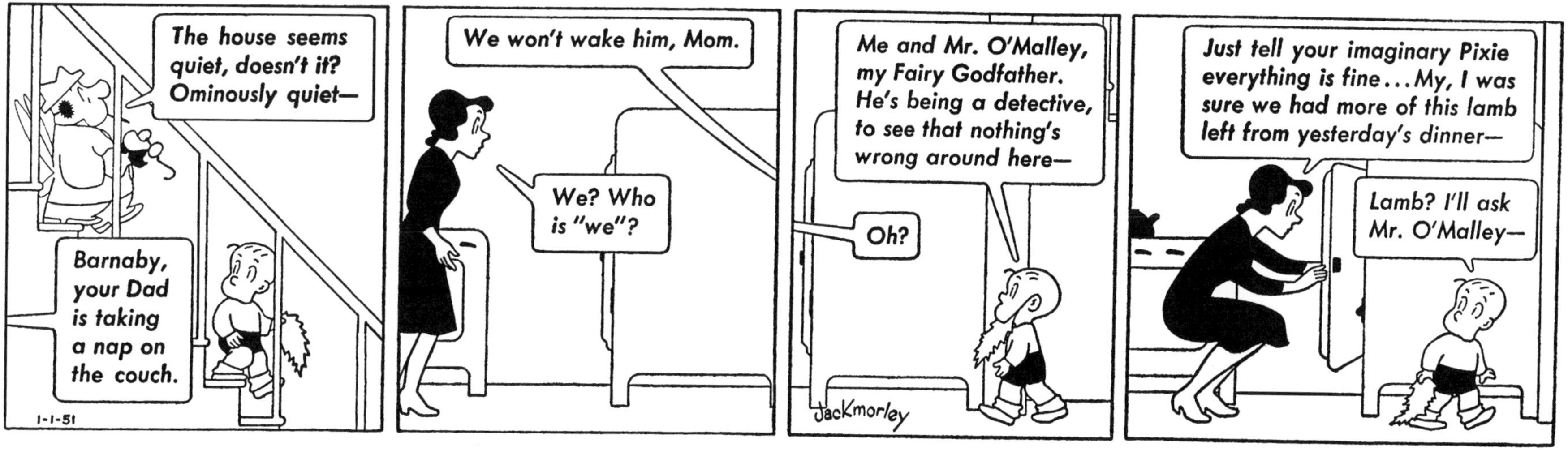
The house seems quiet, doesn't it? Ominously quiet—
Barnaby, your Dad is taking a nap on the couch.
1-1-51
We won't wake him, Mom.
We? Who is "we"?
Me and Mr. O'Malley, my Fairy Godfather. He's being a detective, to see that nothing's wrong around here—
Oh?
JacKmorley
Just tell your imaginary Pixie everything is fine... My, I was sure we had more of this lamb left from yesterday's dinner—
Lamb? I'll ask Mr. O'Malley—

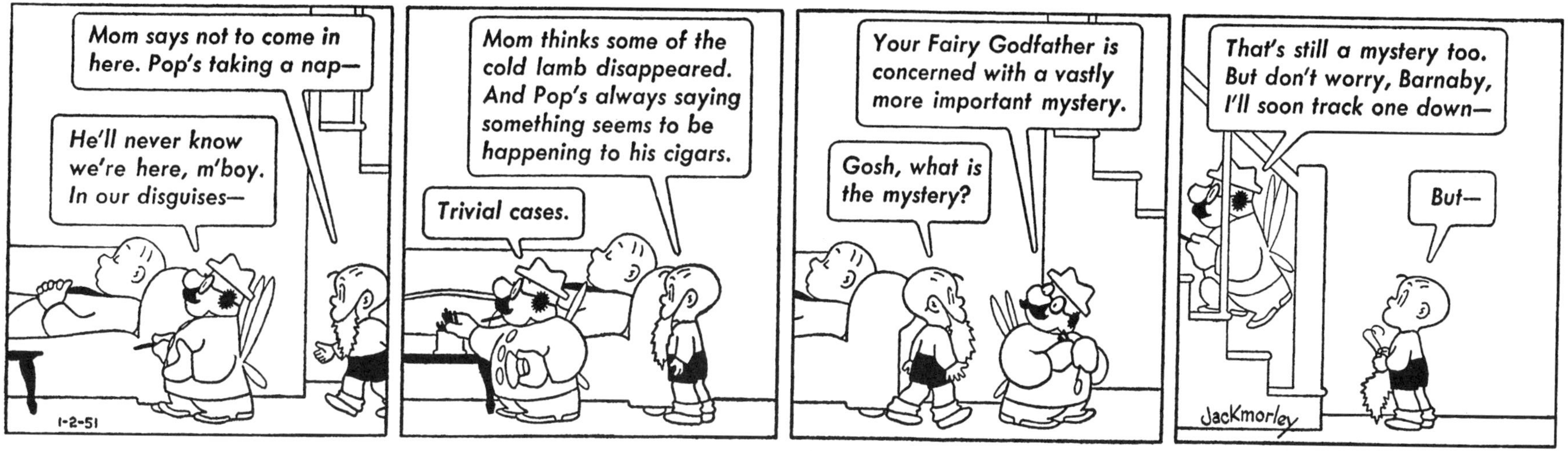
Mom says not to come in here. Pop's taking a nap—
He'll never know we're here, m'boy. In our disguises—
1-2-51
Mom thinks some of the cold lamb disappeared. And Pop's always saying something seems to be happening to his cigars.
Trivial cases.
Your Fairy Godfather is concerned with a vastly more important mystery.
Gosh, what is the mystery?
That's still a mystery too. But don't worry, Barnaby, I'll soon track one down—
But—
JacKmorley

January 1 – 2

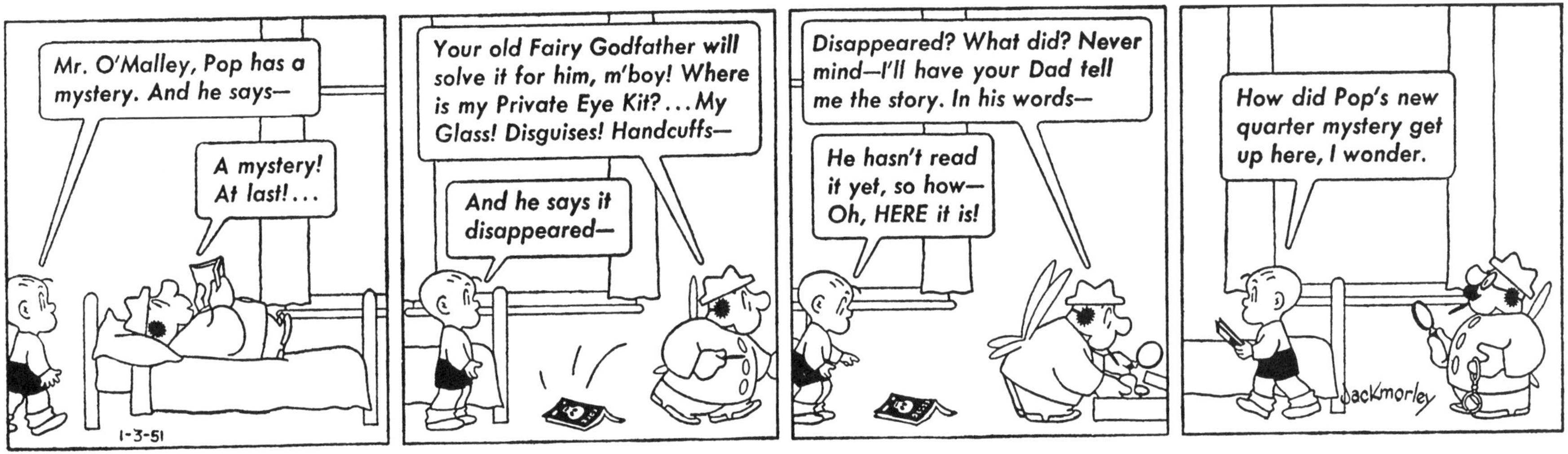
Mr. O'Malley, Pop has a mystery. And he says—
A mystery! At last! . . .
1-3-51
Your old Fairy Godfather will solve it for him, m'boy! Where is my Private Eye Kit? . . . My Glass! Disguises! Handcuffs—
And he says it disappeared—
Disappeared? What did? Never mind—I'll have your Dad tell me the story. In his words—
He hasn't read it yet, so how— Oh, HERE it is!
How did Pop's new quarter mystery get up here, I wonder.
Jackmorley

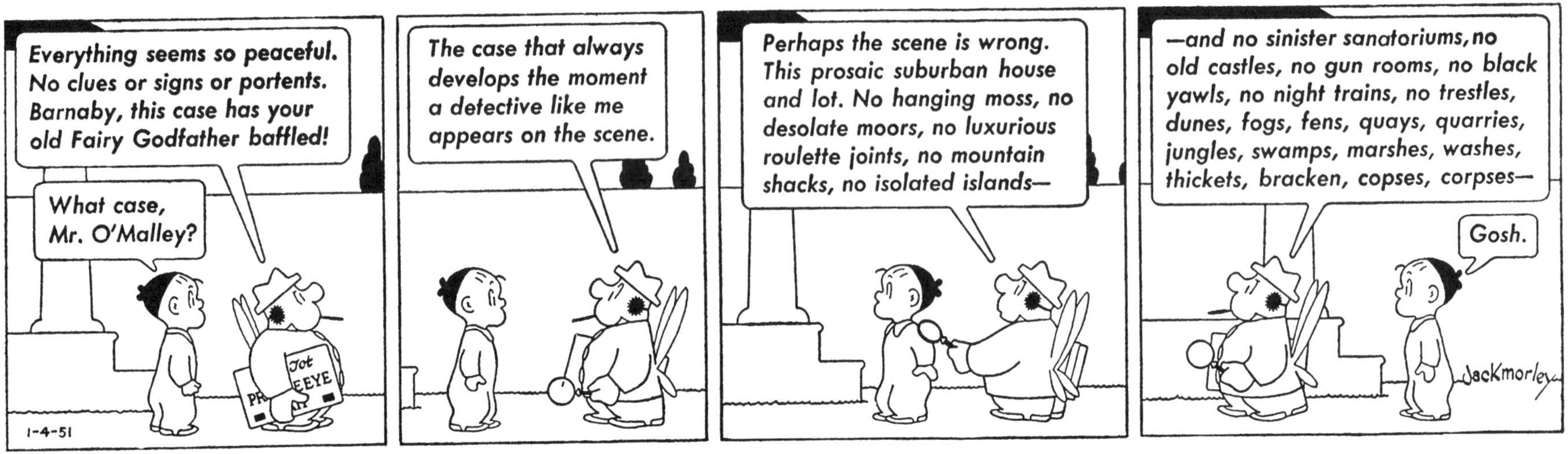
Everything seems so peaceful. No clues or signs or portents. Barnaby, this case has your old Fairy Godfather baffled!
What case, Mr. O'Malley?
EYE
1-4-51
The case that always develops the moment a detective like me appears on the scene.
Perhaps the scene is wrong. This prosaic suburban house and lot. No hanging moss, no desolate moors, no luxurious roulette joints, no mountain shacks, no isolated islands—
—and no sinister sanatoriums, no old castles, no gun rooms, no black yawls, no night trains, no trestles, dunes, fogs, fens, quays, quarries, jungles, swamps, marshes, washes, thickets, bracken, copses, corpses—
Gosh.
Jackmorley

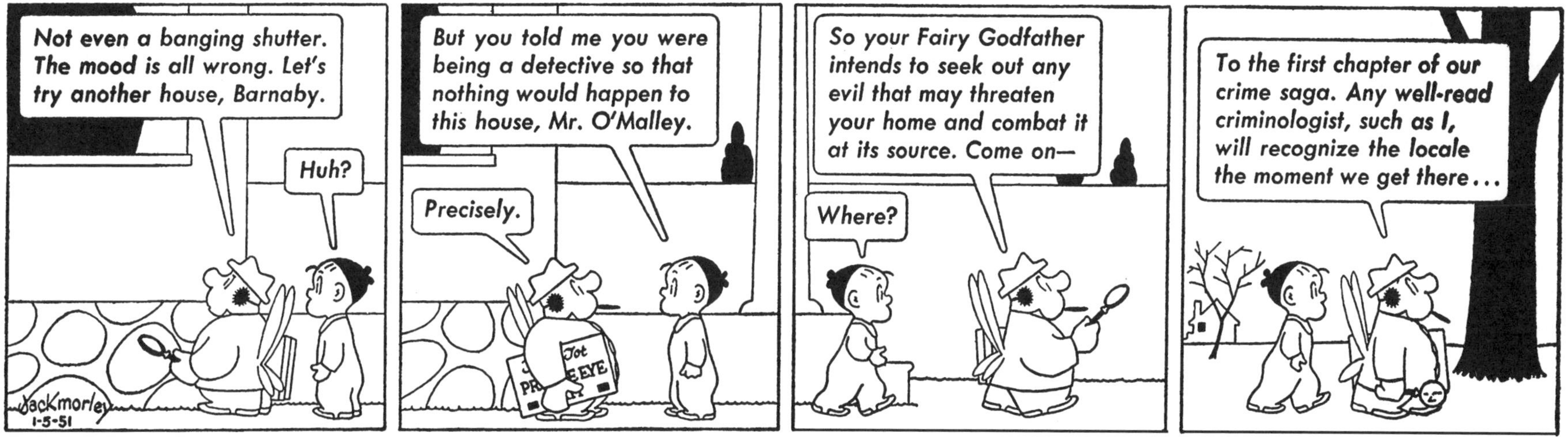
Not even a banging shutter. The mood is all wrong. Let's try another house, Barnaby.
Huh?
Jackmorley
1-5-51
But you told me you were being a detective so that nothing would happen to this house, Mr. O'Malley.
Precisely.
So your Fairy Godfather intends to seek out any evil that may threaten your home and combat it at its source. Come on—
Where?
To the first chapter of our crime saga. Any well-read criminologist, such as I, will recognize the locale the moment we get there...

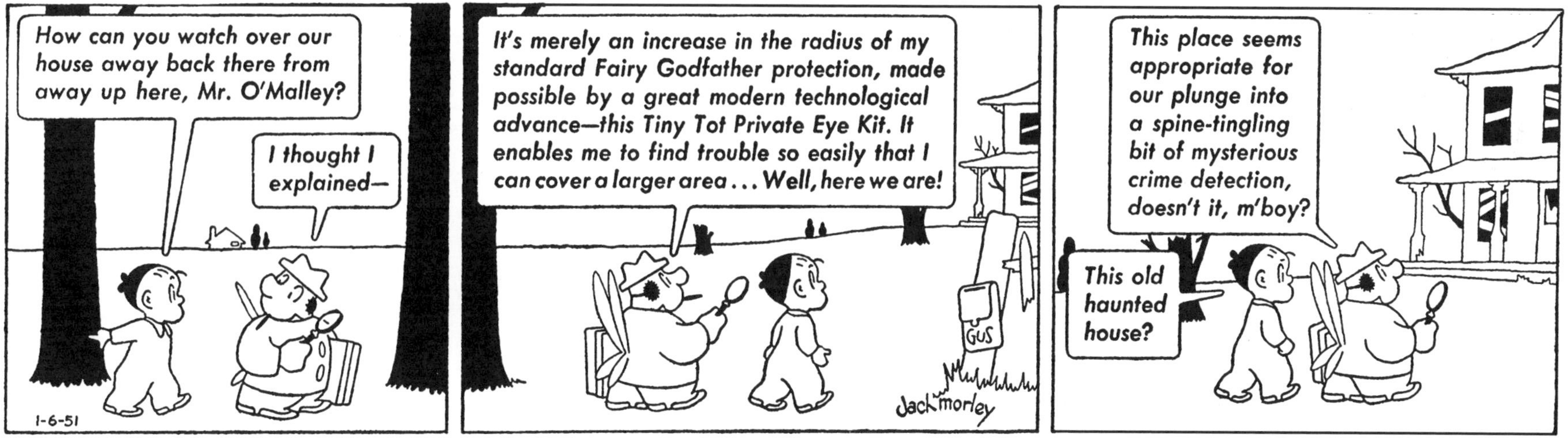
How can you watch over our house away back there from away up here, Mr. O'Malley?
I thought I explained—
1-6-51
It's merely an increase in the radius of my standard Fairy Godfather protection, made possible by a great modern technological advance—this Tiny Tot Private Eye Kit. It enables me to find trouble so easily that I can cover a larger area... Well, here we are!
GUS
Jack morley
This place seems appropriate for our plunge into a spine-tingling bit of mysterious crime detection, doesn't it, m'boy?
This old haunted house?

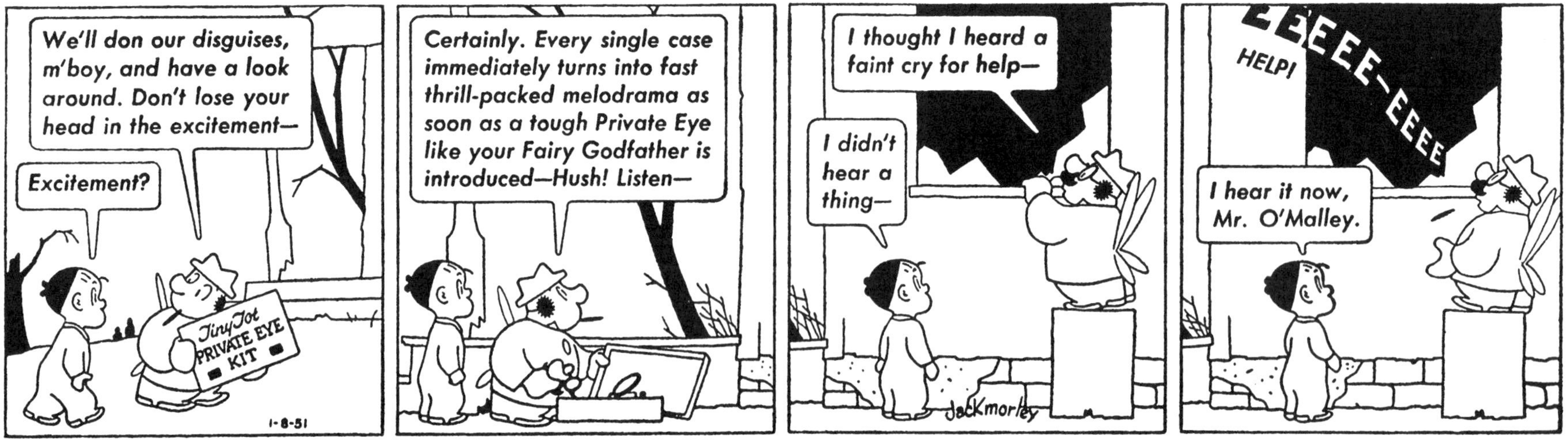
We'll don our disguises, m'boy, and have a look around. Don't lose your head in the excitement—
Excitement?
Tiny Tot PRIVATE EYE KIT
1-8-51
Certainly. Every single case immediately turns into fast thrill-packed melodrama as soon as a tough Private Eye like your Fairy Godfather is introduced—Hush! Listen—
I thought I heard a faint cry for help—
I didn't hear a thing—
Jackmorley
EEEEE-EEEE
HELP!
I hear it now, Mr. O'Malley.

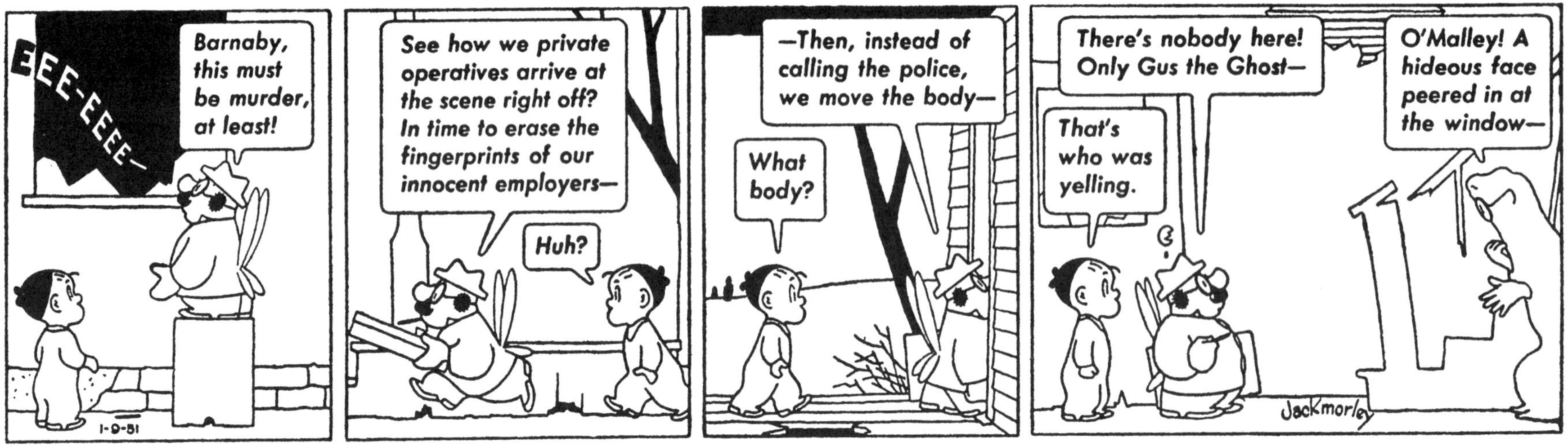
EEE-EEEE-
Barnaby, this must be murder, at least!
1-9-51
See how we private operatives arrive at the scene right off? In time to erase the fingerprints of our innocent employers—
Huh?
—Then, instead of calling the police, we move the body—
What body?
There's nobody here! Only Gus the Ghost—
That's who was yelling.
O'Malley! A hideous face peered in at the window—
Jackmorley

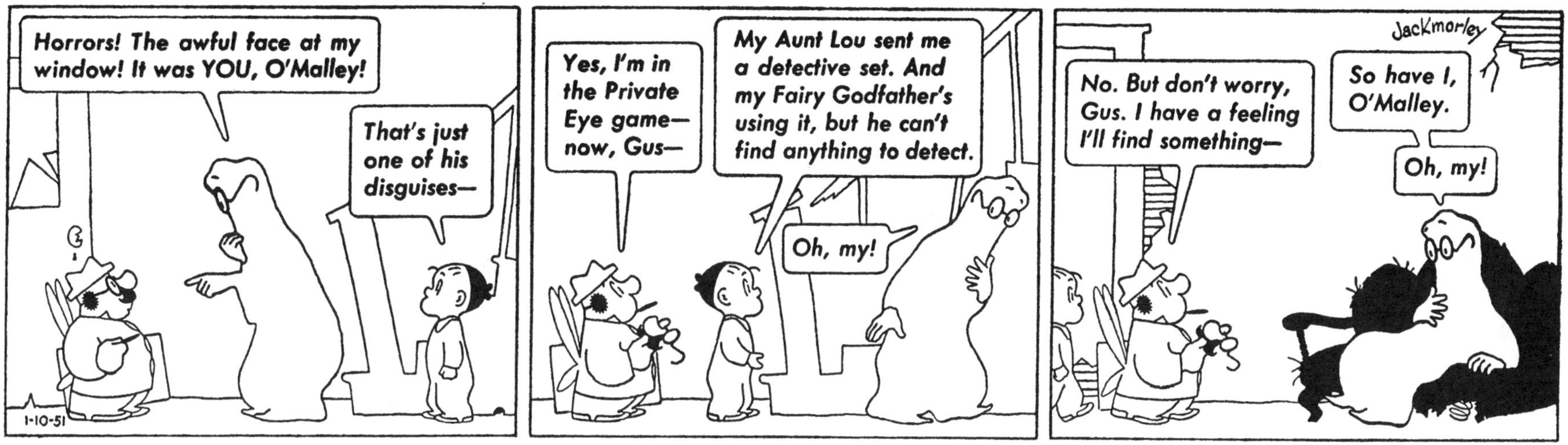
Horrors! The awful face at my window! It was YOU, O'Malley!
That's just one of his disguises—
Yes, I'm in the Private Eye game—now, Gus—
My Aunt Lou sent me a detective set. And my Fairy Godfather's using it, but he can't find anything to detect.
Oh, my!
No. But don't worry, Gus. I have a feeling I'll find something—
So have I, O'Malley.
Oh, my!
1-10-51
Jackmorley

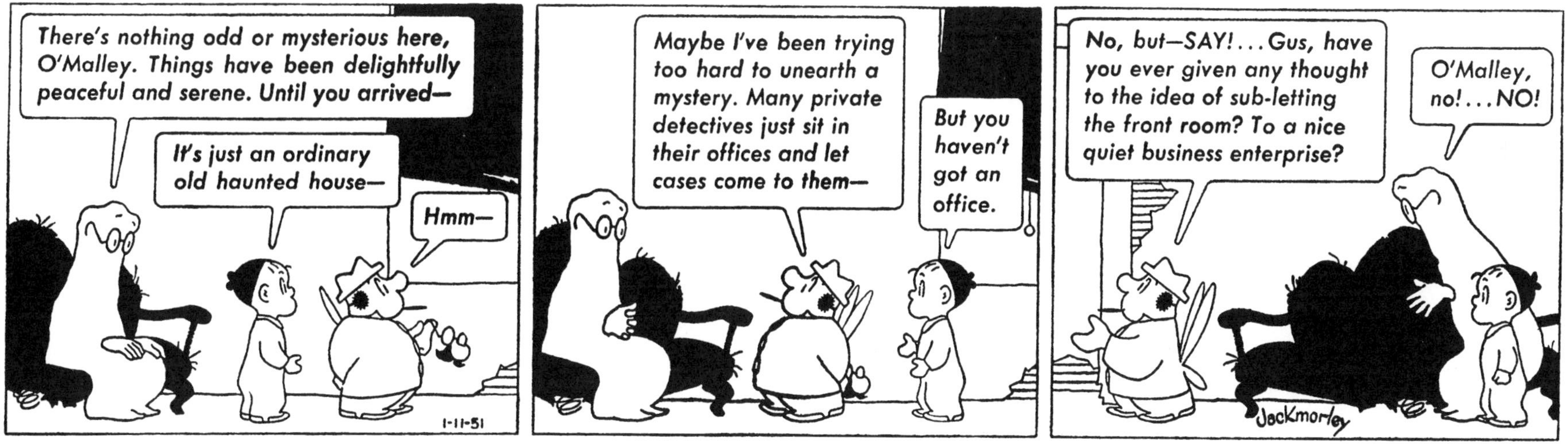
There's nothing odd or mysterious here, O'Malley. Things have been delightfully peaceful and serene. Until you arrived—
It's just an ordinary old haunted house—
Hmm—
Maybe I've been trying too hard to unearth a mystery. Many private detectives just sit in their offices and let cases come to them—
But you haven't got an office.
No, but—SAY!...Gus, have you ever given any thought to the idea of sub-letting the front room? To a nice quiet business enterprise?
O'Malley, no!...NO!
1-11-51
Jackmorley

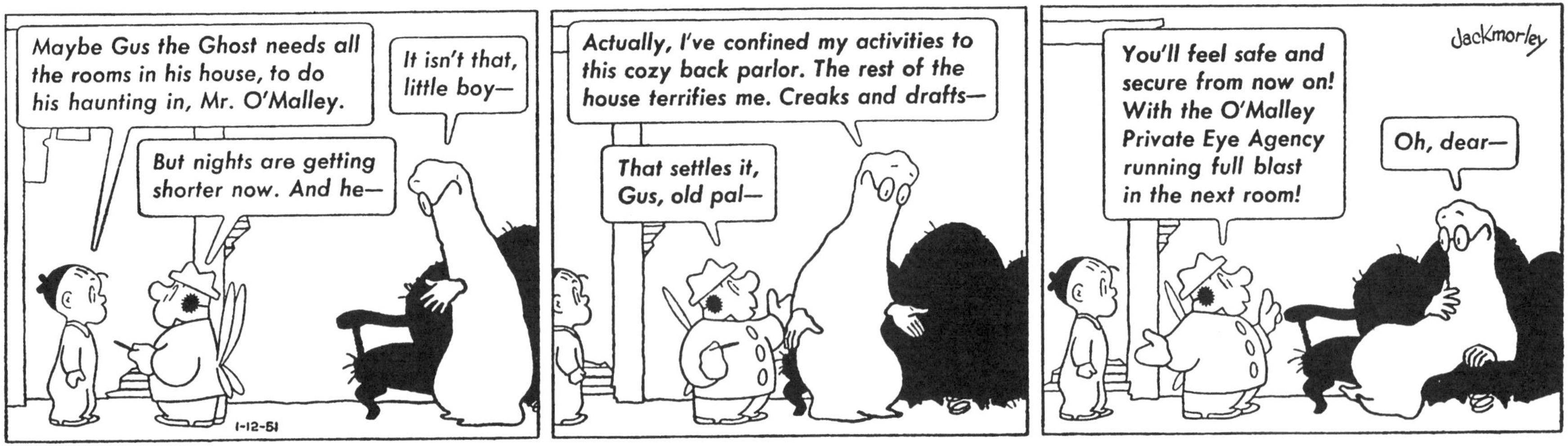
Maybe Gus the Ghost needs all the rooms in his house, to do his haunting in, Mr. O'Malley.
It isn't that, little boy—
But nights are getting shorter now. And he—
1-12-51
Actually, I've confined my activities to this cozy back parlor. The rest of the house terrifies me. Creaks and drafts—
That settles it, Gus, old pal—
JackMorley
You'll feel safe and secure from now on! With the O'Malley Private Eye Agency running full blast in the next room!
Oh, dear—

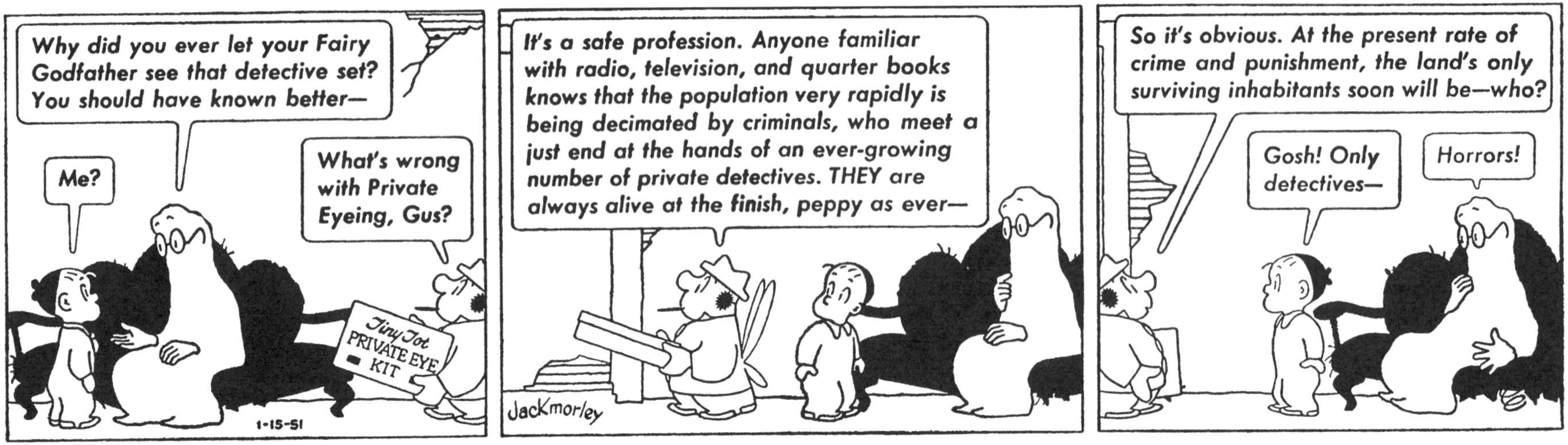
Why did you ever let your Fairy Godfather see that detective set? You should have known better—
Me?
What's wrong with Private Eyeing, Gus?
Tiny Tot PRIVATE EYE KIT
1-15-51
It's a safe profession. Anyone familiar with radio, television, and quarter books knows that the population very rapidly is being decimated by criminals, who meet a just end at the hands of an ever-growing number of private detectives. THEY are always alive at the finish, peppy as ever—
JackMorley
So it's obvious. At the present rate of crime and punishment, the land's only surviving inhabitants soon will be—who?
Gosh! Only detectives—
Horrors!

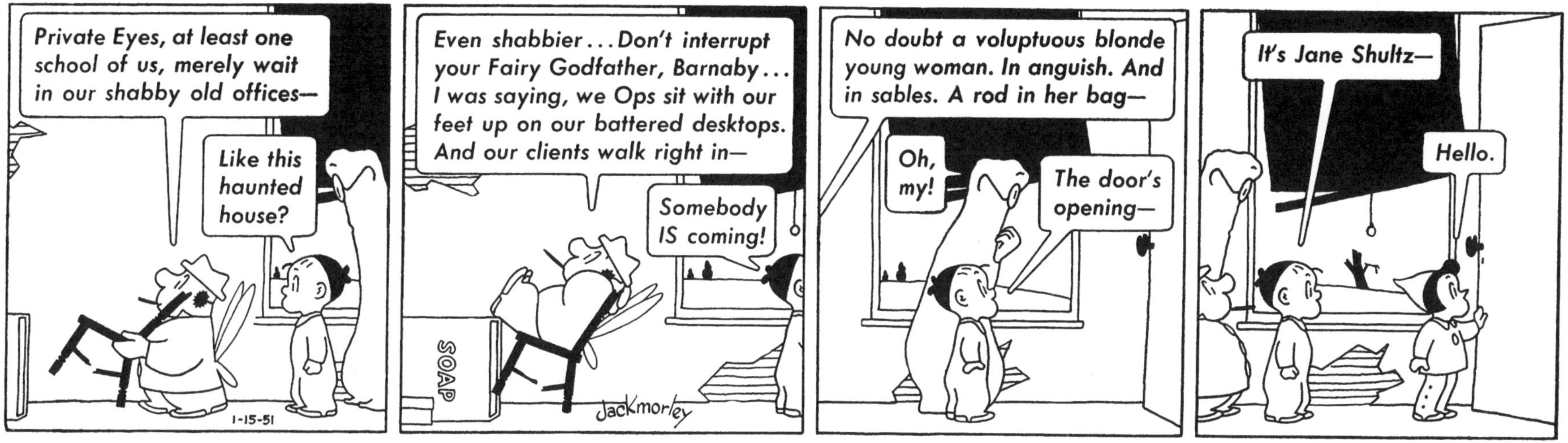
Private Eyes, at least one school of us, merely wait in our shabby old offices—
Like this haunted house?
1-15-51
Even shabbier . . . Don't interrupt your Fairy Godfather, Barnaby . . . I was saying, we Ops sit with our feet up on our battered desktops. And our clients walk right in—
Somebody IS coming!
SOAP
Jackmorley
No doubt a voluptuous blonde young woman. In anguish. And in sables. A rod in her bag—
Oh, my!
The door's opening—
It's Jane Shultz—
Hello.

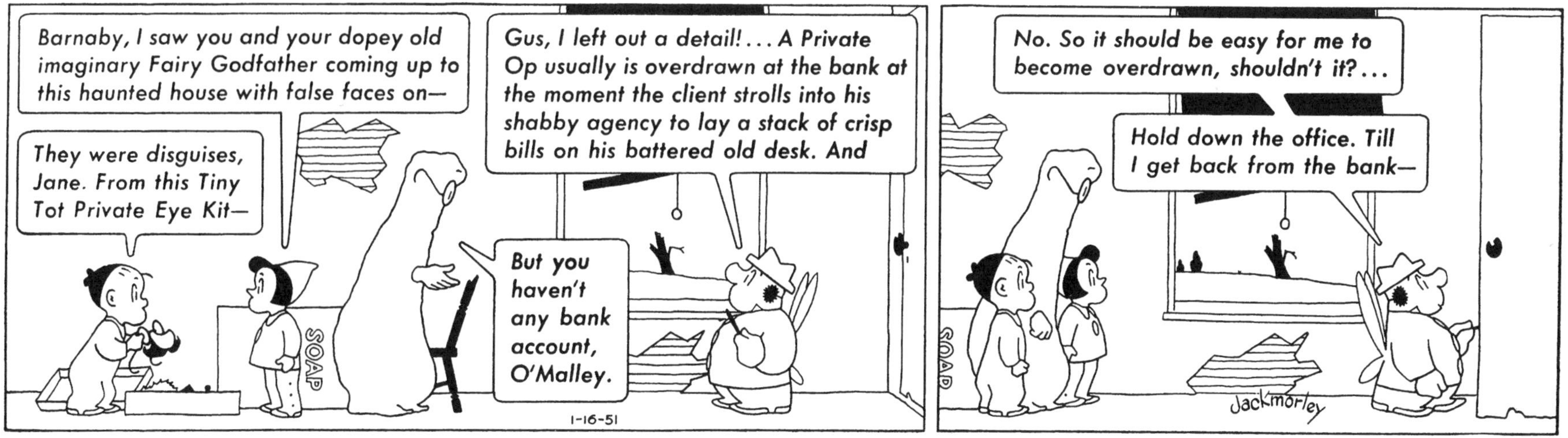
Barnaby, I saw you and your dopey old imaginary Fairy Godfather coming up to this haunted house with false faces on—
They were disguises, Jane. From this Tiny Tot Private Eye Kit—
SOAP
Gus, I left out a detail! . . . A Private Op usually is overdrawn at the bank at the moment the client strolls into his shabby agency to lay a stack of crisp bills on his battered old desk. And
But you haven't any bank account, O'Malley.
1-16-51
No. So it should be easy for me to become overdrawn, shouldn't it? . . .
Hold down the office. Till I get back from the bank—
SOAP
Jackmorley

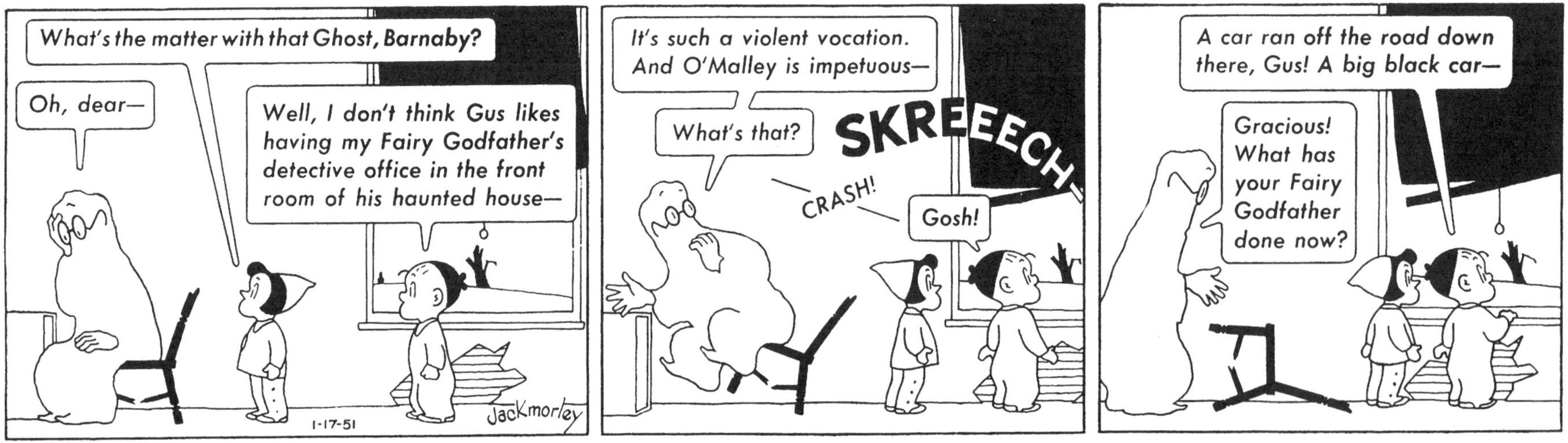
What's the matter with that Ghost, Barnaby?
Oh, dear—
Well, I don't think Gus likes having my Fairy Godfather's detective office in the front room of his haunted house—
1-17-51
Jackmorley
It's such a violent vocation. And O'Malley is impetuous—
What's that?
SKREEECH—
CRASH!
Gosh!
A car ran off the road down there, Gus! A big black car—
Gracious! What has your Fairy Godfather done now?

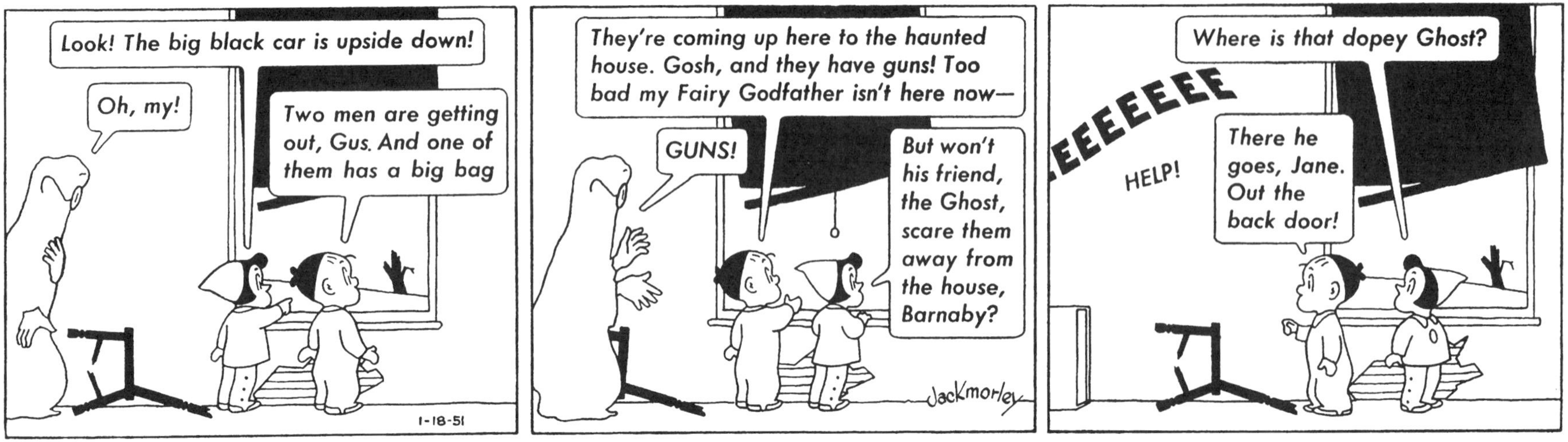
Look! The big black car is upside down!
Oh, my!
Two men are getting out, Gus. And one of them has a big bag
1-18-51
They're coming up here to the haunted house. Gosh, and they have guns! Too bad my Fairy Godfather isn't here now—
GUNS!
But won't his friend, the Ghost, scare them away from the house, Barnaby?
Jackmorley
Where is that dopey Ghost?
EEEEEEEEE
HELP!
There he goes, Jane. Out the back door!

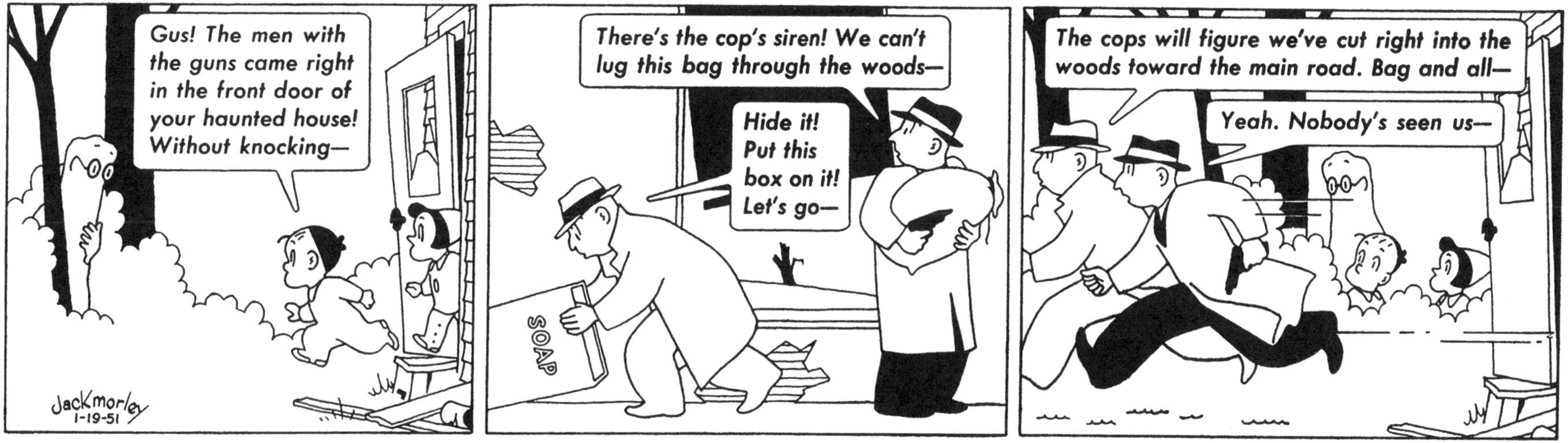
Gus! The men with the guns came right in the front door of your haunted house! Without knocking—
JacKmorley 1-19-51
There's the cop's siren! We can't lug this bag through the woods—
Hide it! Put this box on it! Let's go—
SOAP
The cops will figure we've cut right into the woods toward the main road. Bag and all—
Yeah. Nobody's seen us—

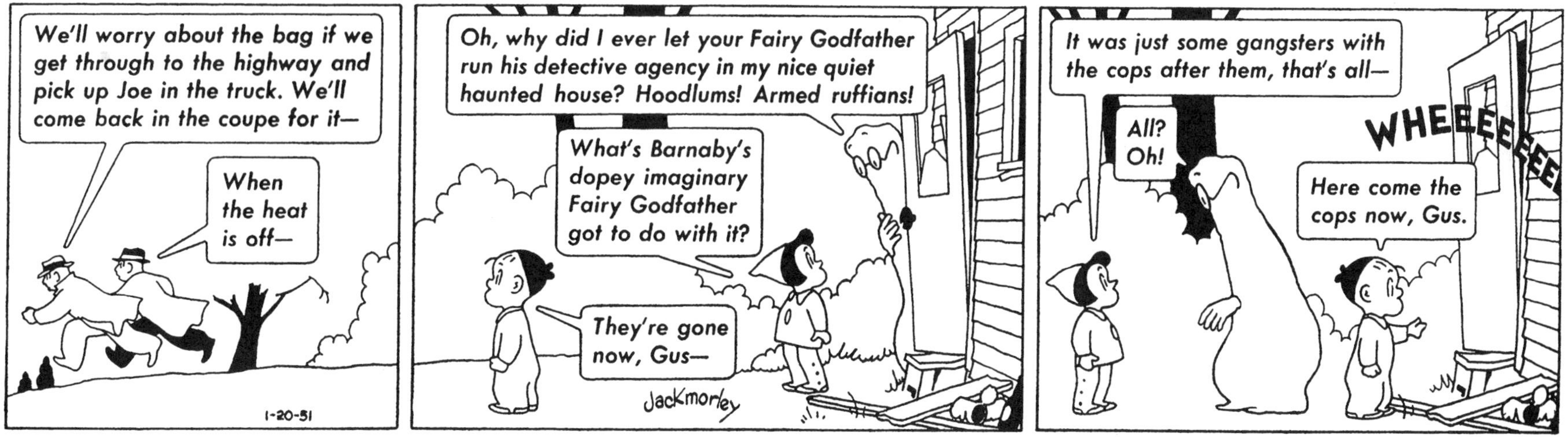
We'll worry about the bag if we get through to the highway and pick up Joe in the truck. We'll come back in the coupe for it—
When the heat is off—
1-20-51
Oh, why did I ever let your Fairy Godfather run his detective agency in my nice quiet haunted house? Hoodlums! Armed ruffians!
What's Barnaby's dopey imaginary Fairy Godfather got to do with it?
They're gone now, Gus—
JacKmorley
It was just some gangsters with the cops after them, that's all—
All? Oh!
WHEEEEEEE
Here come the cops now, Gus.

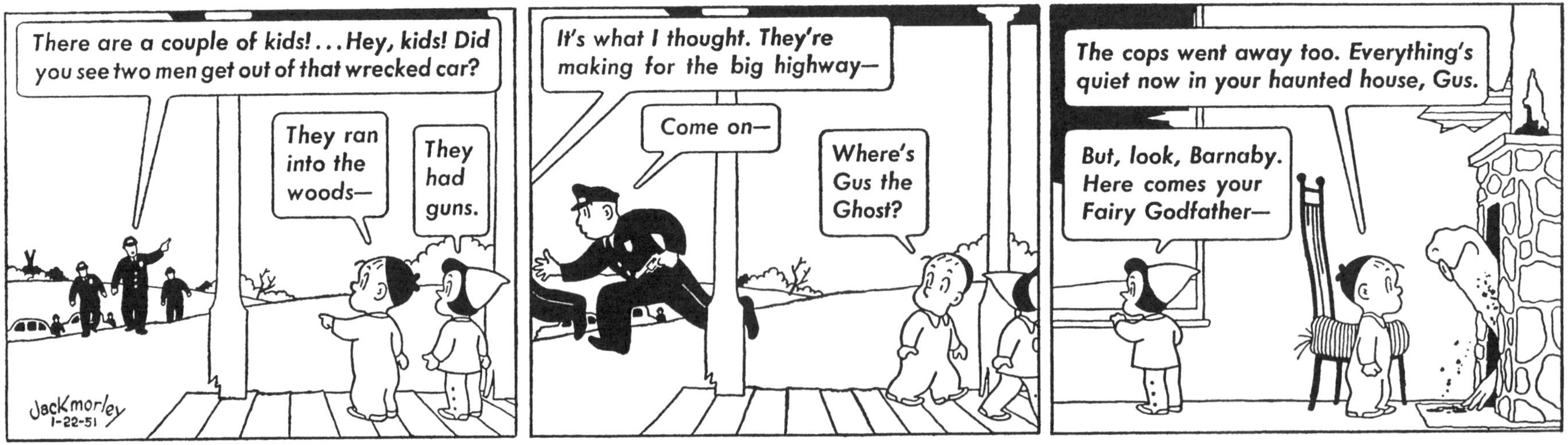
There are a couple of kids! . . . Hey, kids! Did you see two men get out of that wrecked car?
They ran into the woods—
They had guns.
Jackmorley 1-22-51
It's what I thought. They're making for the big highway—
Come on—
Where's Gus the Ghost?
The cops went away too. Everything's quiet now in your haunted house, Gus.
But, look, Barnaby. Here comes your Fairy Godfather—

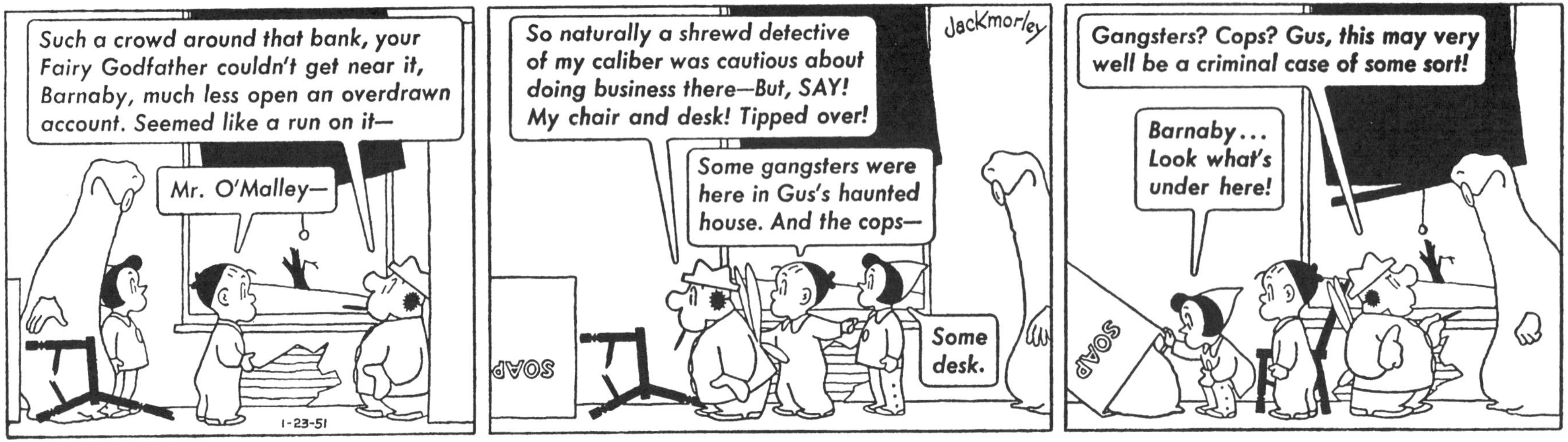
Such a crowd around that bank, your Fairy Godfather couldn't get near it, Barnaby, much less open an overdrawn account. Seemed like a run on it—
Mr. O'Malley—
1-23-51
So naturally a shrewd detective of my caliber was cautious about doing business there—But, SAY! My chair and desk! Tipped over!
Jackmorley
Some gangsters were here in Gus's haunted house. And the cops—
Some desk.
SOAP
Gangsters? Cops? Gus, this may very well be a criminal case of some sort!
Barnaby . . . Look what's under here!
SOAP

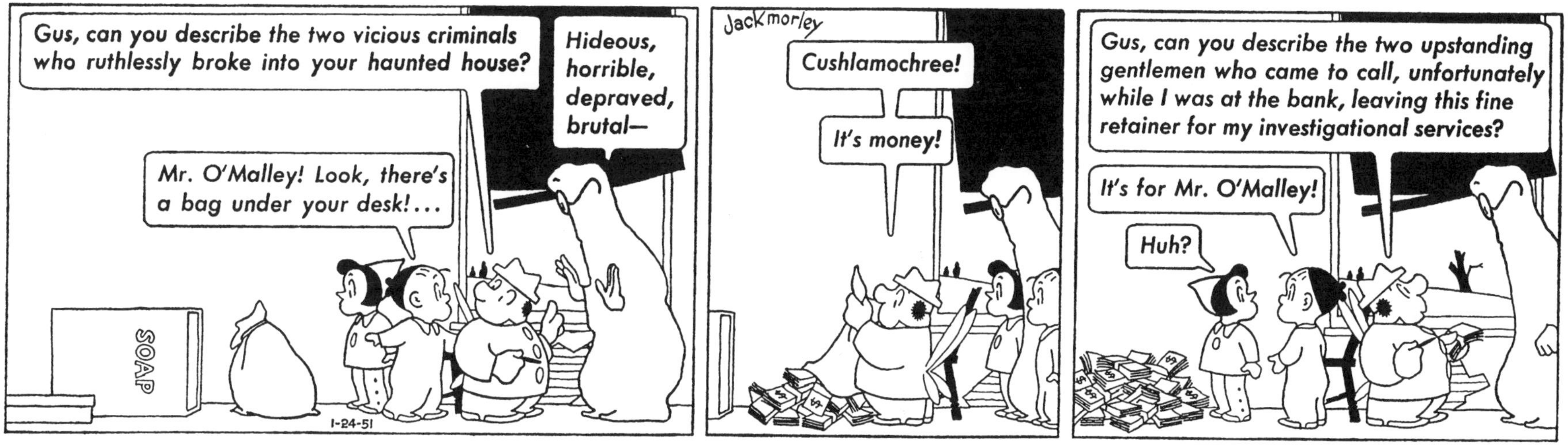
Gus, can you describe the two vicious criminals who ruthlessly broke into your haunted house?
Hideous, horrible, depraved, brutal—
Mr. O'Malley! Look, there's a bag under your desk!...
SOAP
1-24-51
Jack morley
Cushlamochree!
It's money!
Gus, can you describe the two upstanding gentlemen who came to call, unfortunately while I was at the bank, leaving this fine retainer for my investigational services?
It's for Mr. O'Malley!
Huh?

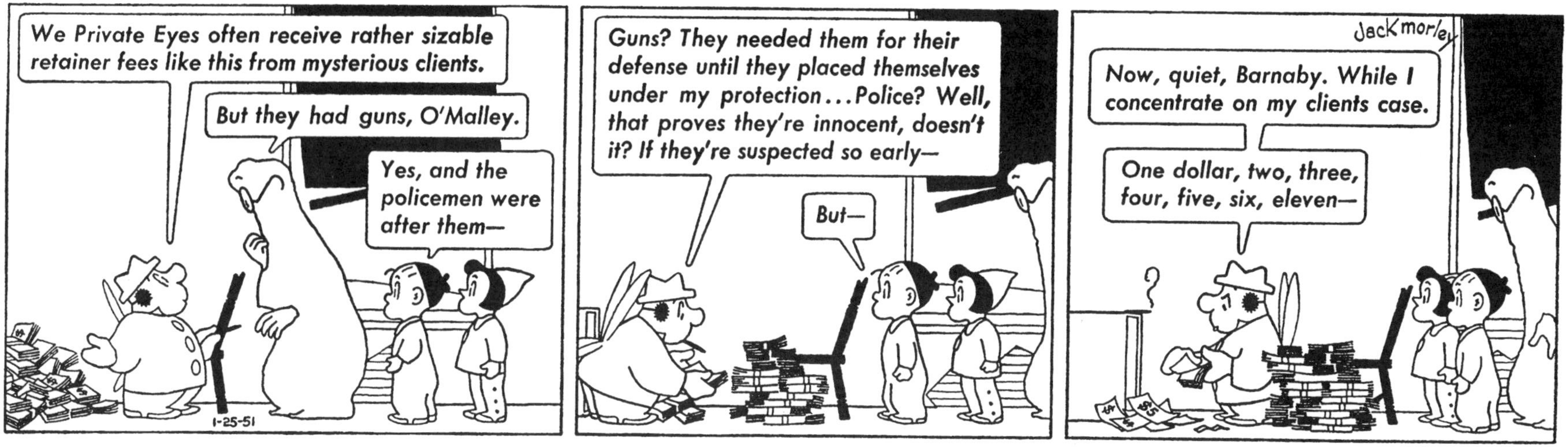
We Private Eyes often receive rather sizable retainer fees like this from mysterious clients.
But they had guns, O'Malley.
Yes, and the policemen were after them—
1-25-51
Guns? They needed them for their defense until they placed themselves under my protection...Police? Well, that proves they're innocent, doesn't it? If they're suspected so early—
But—
Jack morley
Now, quiet, Barnaby. While I concentrate on my clients case.
One dollar, two, three, four, five, six, eleven—

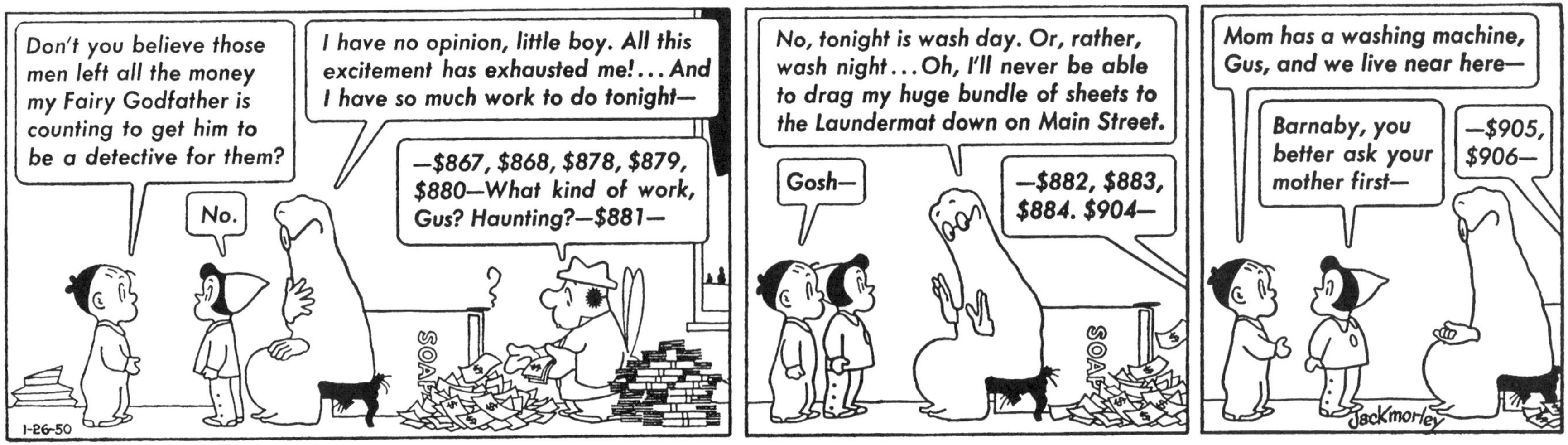
Don't you believe those men left all the money my Fairy Godfather is counting to get him to be a detective for them?
No.
I have no opinion, little boy. All this excitement has exhausted me!... And I have so much work to do tonight—
—$867, $868, $878, $879, $880—What kind of work, Gus? Haunting?—$881—
SOAP
1-26-50
No, tonight is wash day. Or, rather, wash night... Oh, I'll never be able to drag my huge bundle of sheets to the Laundermat down on Main Street.
Gosh—
—$882, $883, $884. $904—
SOAP
Mom has a washing machine, Gus, and we live near here—
Barnaby, you better ask your mother first—
—$905, $906—
JackMorley

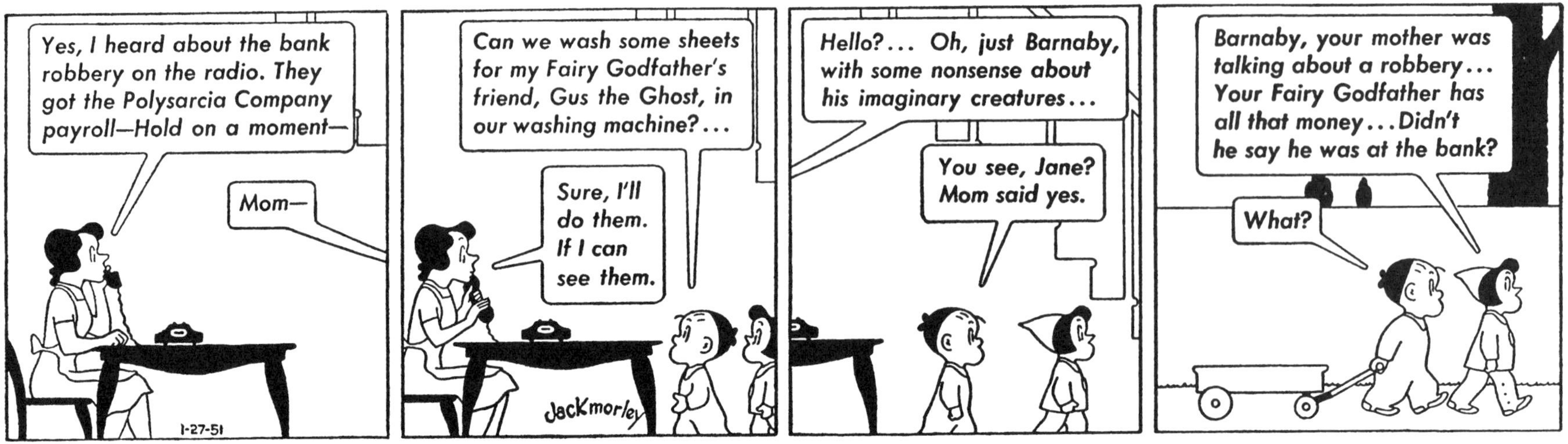
Yes, I heard about the bank robbery on the radio. They got the Polysarcia Company payroll—Hold on a moment—
Mom—
1-27-51
Can we wash some sheets for my Fairy Godfather's friend, Gus the Ghost, in our washing machine?...
Sure, I'll do them. If I can see them.
JackMorley
Hello?... Oh, just Barnaby, with some nonsense about his imaginary creatures...
You see, Jane? Mom said yes.
Barnaby, your mother was talking about a robbery... Your Fairy Godfather has all that money... Didn't he say he was at the bank?
What?

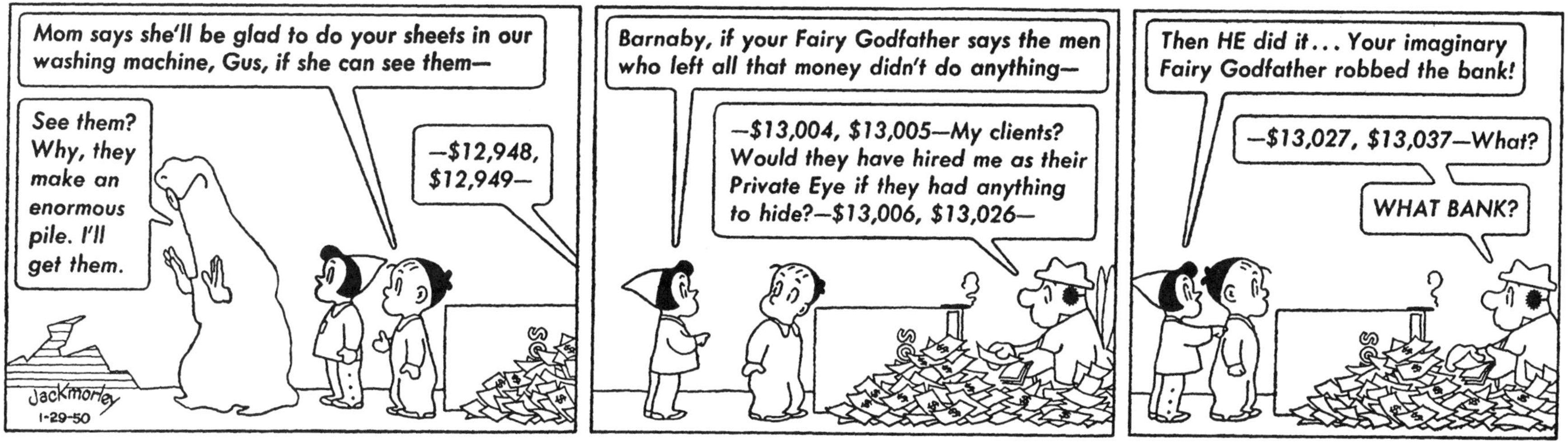
Mom says she'll be glad to do your sheets in our washing machine, Gus, if she can see them—
See them? Why, they make an enormous pile. I'll get them.
—$12,948, $12,949—
Jackmorley
1-29-50
Barnaby, if your Fairy Godfather says the men who left all that money didn't do anything—
—$13,004, $13,005—My clients? Would they have hired me as their Private Eye if they had anything to hide?—$13,006, $13,026—
Then HE did it... Your imaginary Fairy Godfather robbed the bank!
—$13,027, $13,037—What?
WHAT BANK?

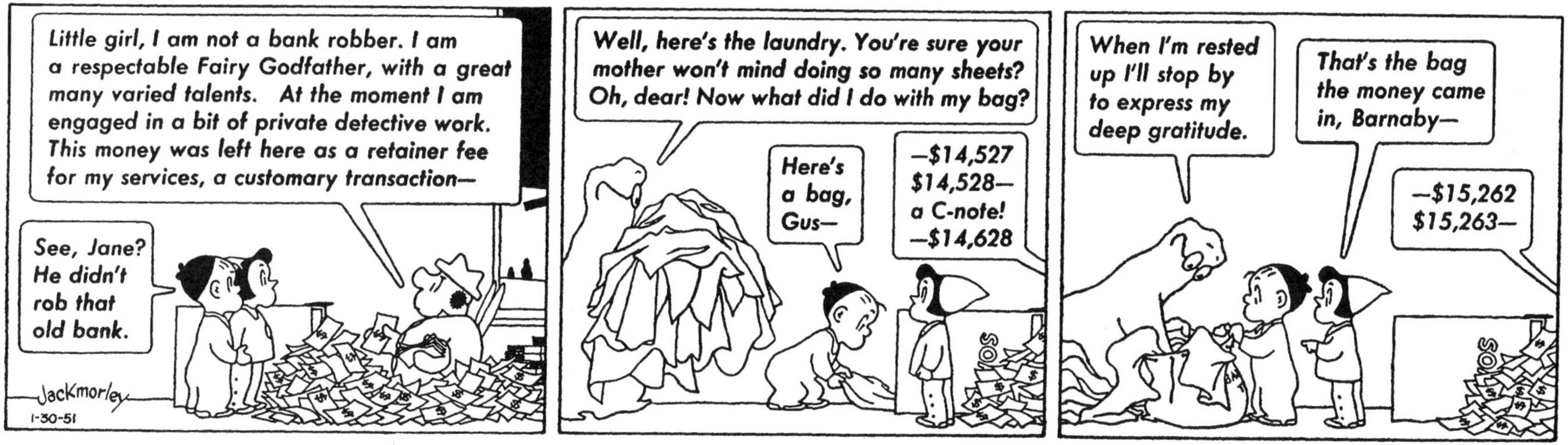
Little girl, I am not a bank robber. I am a respectable Fairy Godfather, with a great many varied talents. At the moment I am engaged in a bit of private detective work. This money was left here as a retainer fee for my services, a customary transaction—
See, Jane? He didn't rob that old bank.
Jackmorley
1-30-51
Well, here's the laundry. You're sure your mother won't mind doing so many sheets? Oh, dear! Now what did I do with my bag?
Here's a bag, Gus—
—$14,527 $14,528— a C-note! —$14,628
When I'm rested up I'll stop by to express my deep gratitude.
That's the bag the money came in, Barnaby—
—$15,262 $15,263—

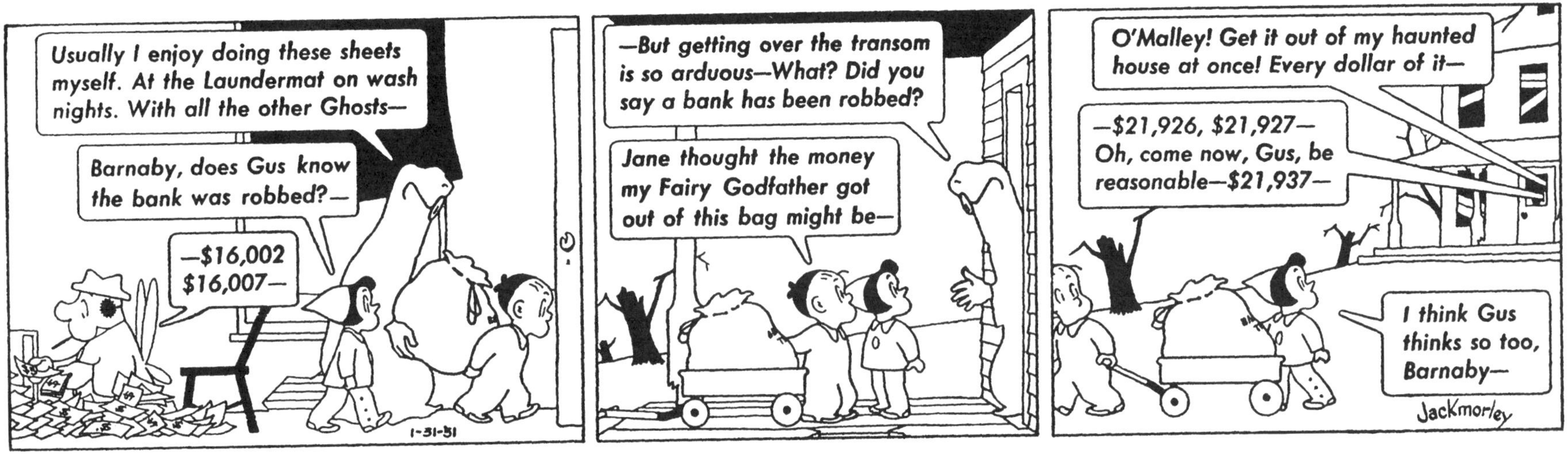
Usually I enjoy doing these sheets myself. At the Laundermat on wash nights. With all the other Ghosts—
Barnaby, does Gus know the bank was robbed?—
—$16,002 $16,007—
1-31-51
—But getting over the transom is so arduous—What? Did you say a bank has been robbed?
Jane thought the money my Fairy Godfather got out of this bag might be—
O'Malley! Get it out of my haunted house at once! Every dollar of it—
—$21,926, $21,927— Oh, come now, Gus, be reasonable—$21,937—
I think Gus thinks so too, Barnaby—
Jackmorley

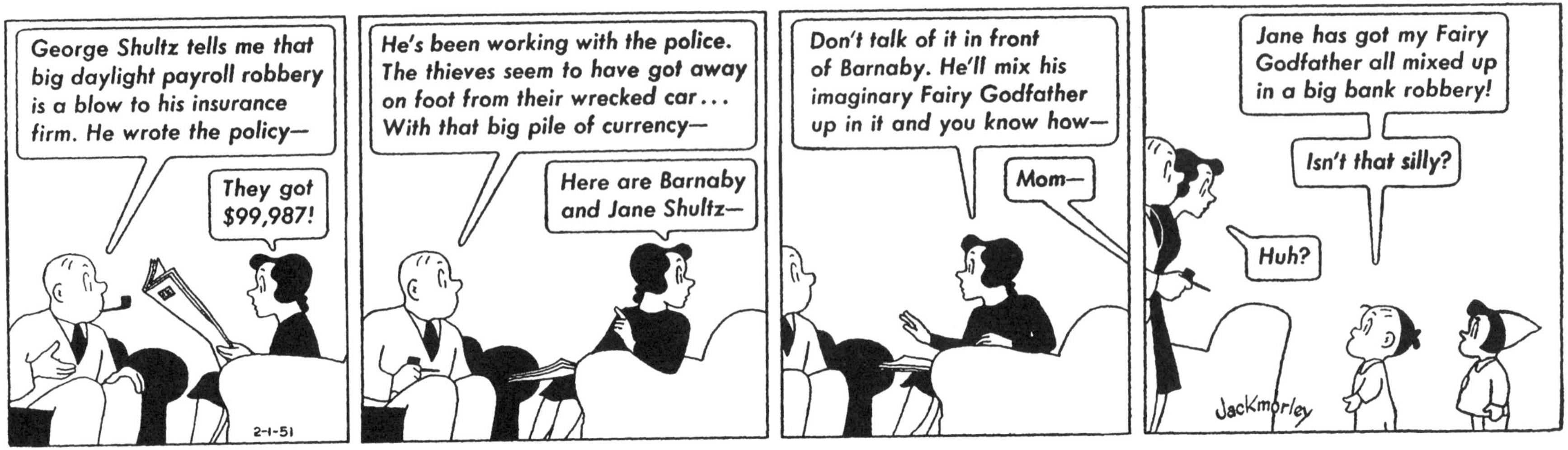
George Shultz tells me that big daylight payroll robbery is a blow to his insurance firm. He wrote the policy—
They got $99,987!
2-1-51
He's been working with the police. The thieves seem to have got away on foot from their wrecked car... With that big pile of currency—
Here are Barnaby and Jane Shultz—
Don't talk of it in front of Barnaby. He'll mix his imaginary Fairy Godfather up in it and you know how—
Mom—
Jane has got my Fairy Godfather all mixed up in a big bank robbery!
Isn't that silly?
Huh?
Jackmorley

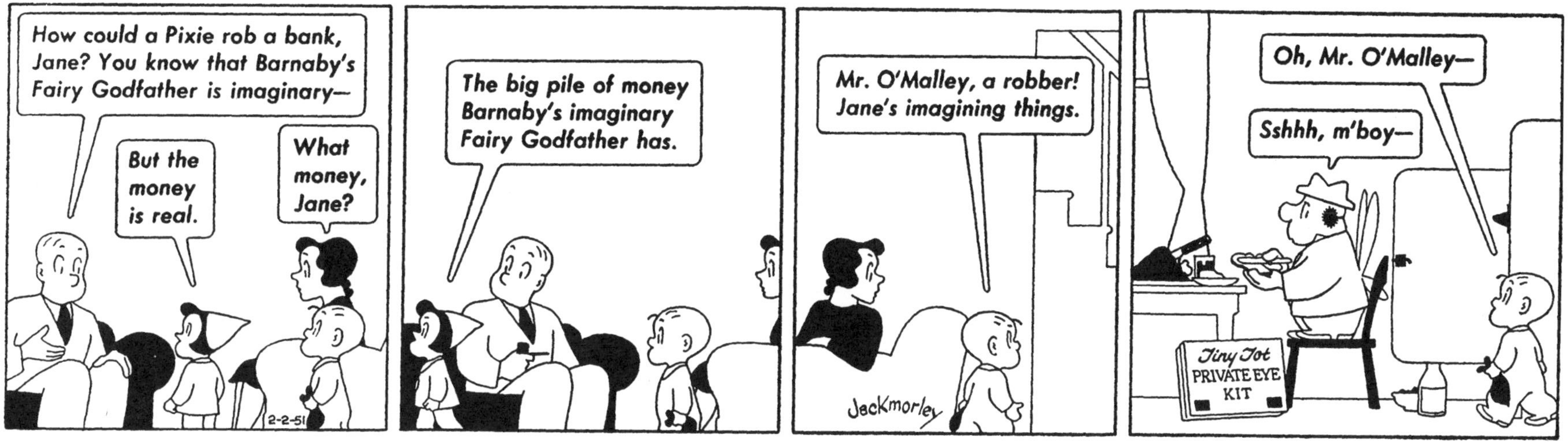
How could a Pixie rob a bank, Jane? You know that Barnaby's Fairy Godfather is imaginary—
But the money is real.
What money, Jane?
2-2-51
The big pile of money Barnaby's imaginary Fairy Godfather has.
Mr. O'Malley, a robber! Jane's imagining things.
Jackmorley
Oh, Mr. O'Malley—
Sshhh, m'boy—
Tiny Tot PRIVATE EYE KIT

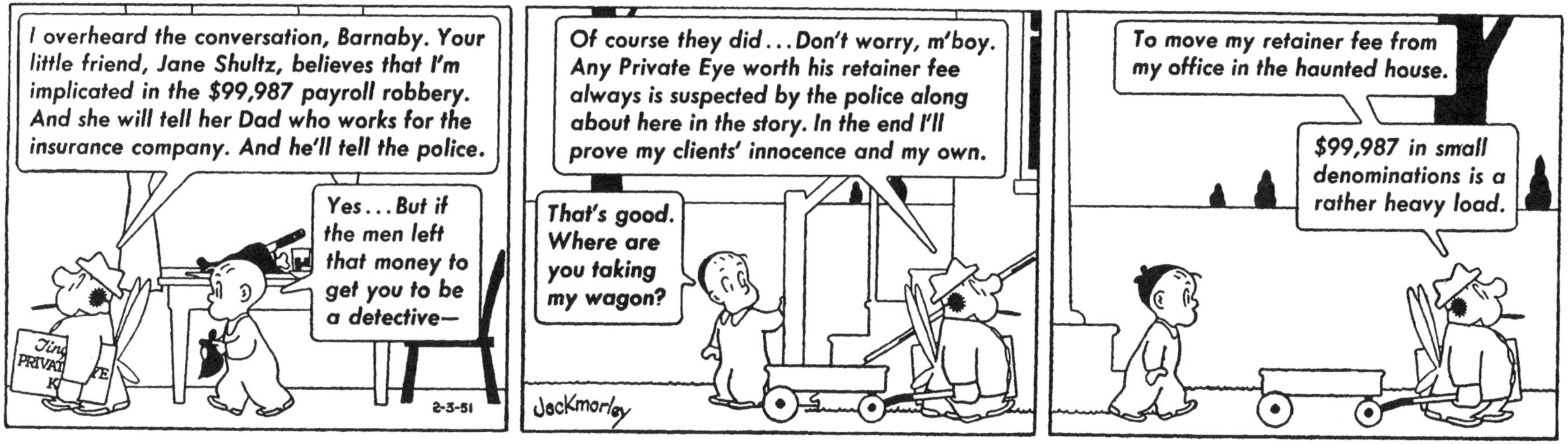
I overheard the conversation, Barnaby. Your little friend, Jane Shultz, believes that I'm implicated in the $99,987 payroll robbery. And she will tell her Dad who works for the insurance company. And he'll tell the police.
Yes... But if the men left that money to get you to be a detective—
2-3-51
Of course they did... Don't worry, m'boy. Any Private Eye worth his retainer fee always is suspected by the police along about here in the story. In the end I'll prove my clients' innocence and my own.
That's good. Where are you taking my wagon?
Jackmorley
To move my retainer fee from my office in the haunted house.
$99,987 in small denominations is a rather heavy load.

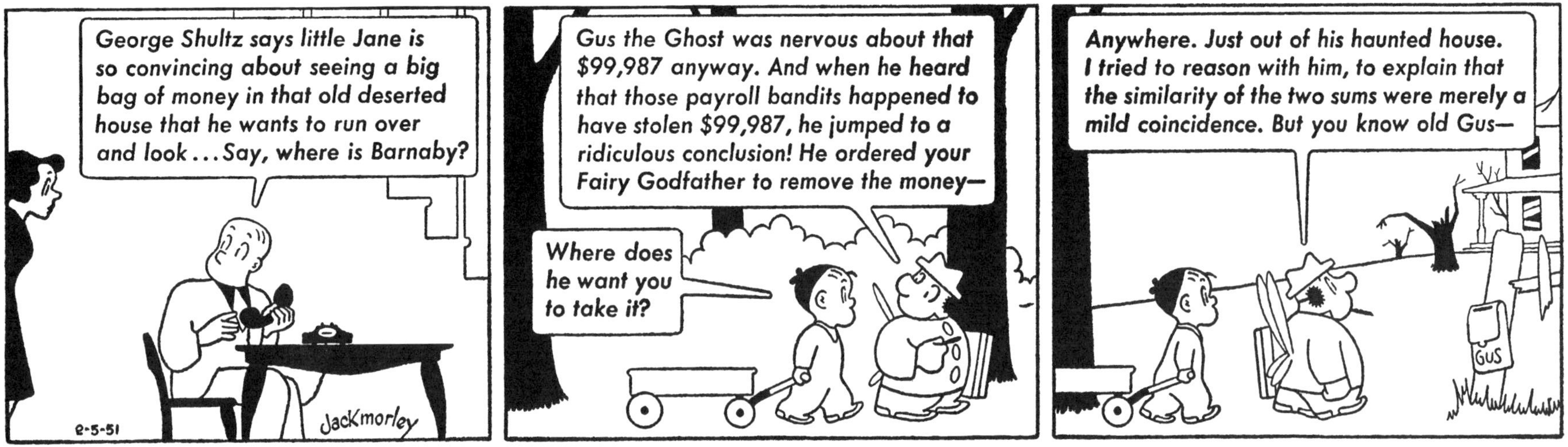
George Shultz says little Jane is so convincing about seeing a big bag of money in that old deserted house that he wants to run over and look . . . Say, where is Barnaby?
2-5-51
Jackmorley
Gus the Ghost was nervous about that $99,987 anyway. And when he heard that those payroll bandits happened to have stolen $99,987, he jumped to a ridiculous conclusion! He ordered your Fairy Godfather to remove the money—
Where does he want you to take it?
Anywhere. Just out of his haunted house. I tried to reason with him, to explain that the similarity of the two sums were merely a mild coincidence. But you know old Gus—
GUS

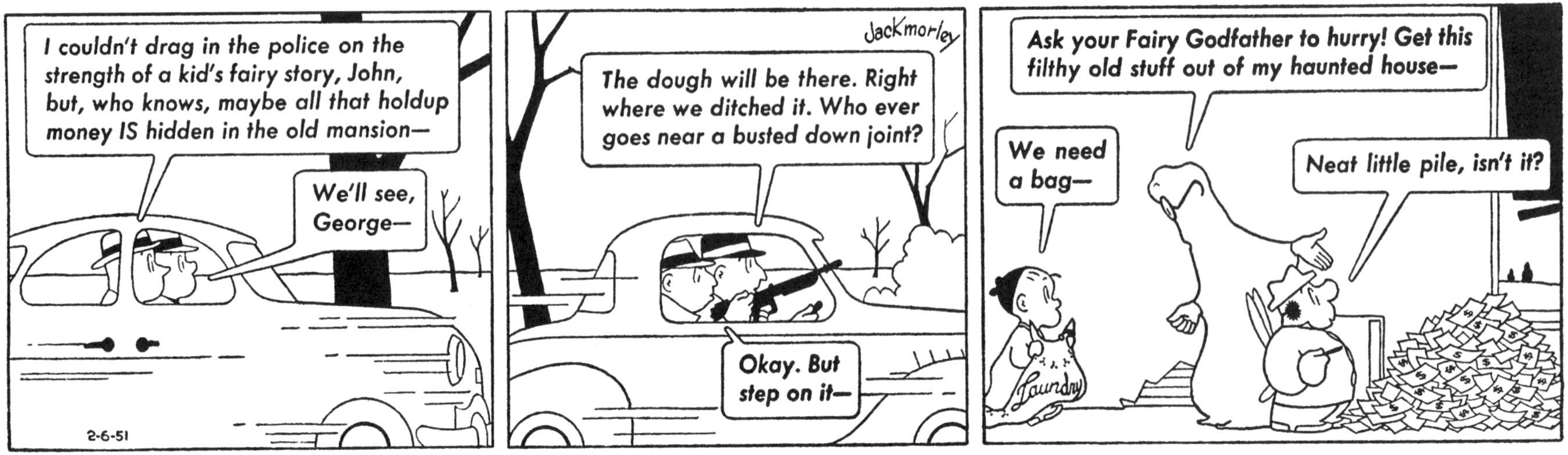
I couldn't drag in the police on the strength of a kid's fairy story, John, but, who knows, maybe all that holdup money IS hidden in the old mansion—
We'll see, George—
2-6-51
Jackmorley
The dough will be there. Right where we ditched it. Who ever goes near a busted down joint?
Okay. But step on it—
Ask your Fairy Godfather to hurry! Get this filthy old stuff out of my haunted house—
We need a bag—
Neat little pile, isn't it?
Laundry

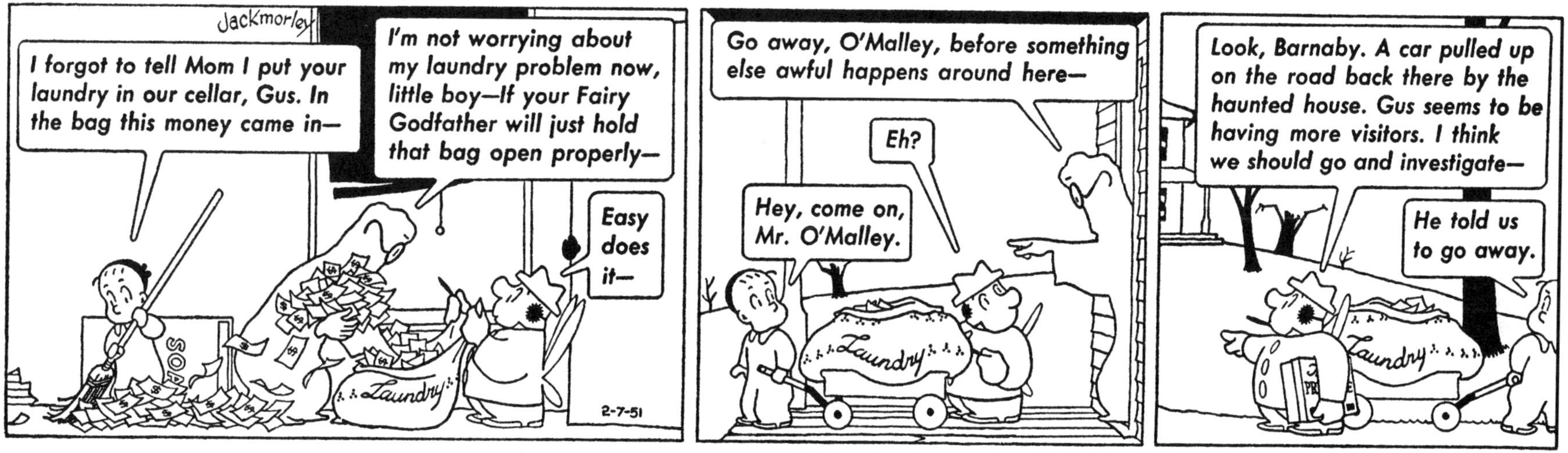
Jackmorley
I forgot to tell Mom I put your laundry in our cellar, Gus. In the bag this money came in—
I'm not worrying about my laundry problem now, little boy—If your Fairy Godfather will just hold that bag open properly—
Easy does it—
SOAP
Laundry
2-7-51
Go away, O'Malley, before something else awful happens around here—
Eh?
Hey, come on, Mr. O'Malley.
Laundry
Look, Barnaby. A car pulled up on the road back there by the haunted house. Gus seems to be having more visitors. I think we should go and investigate—
He told us to go away.
Laundry

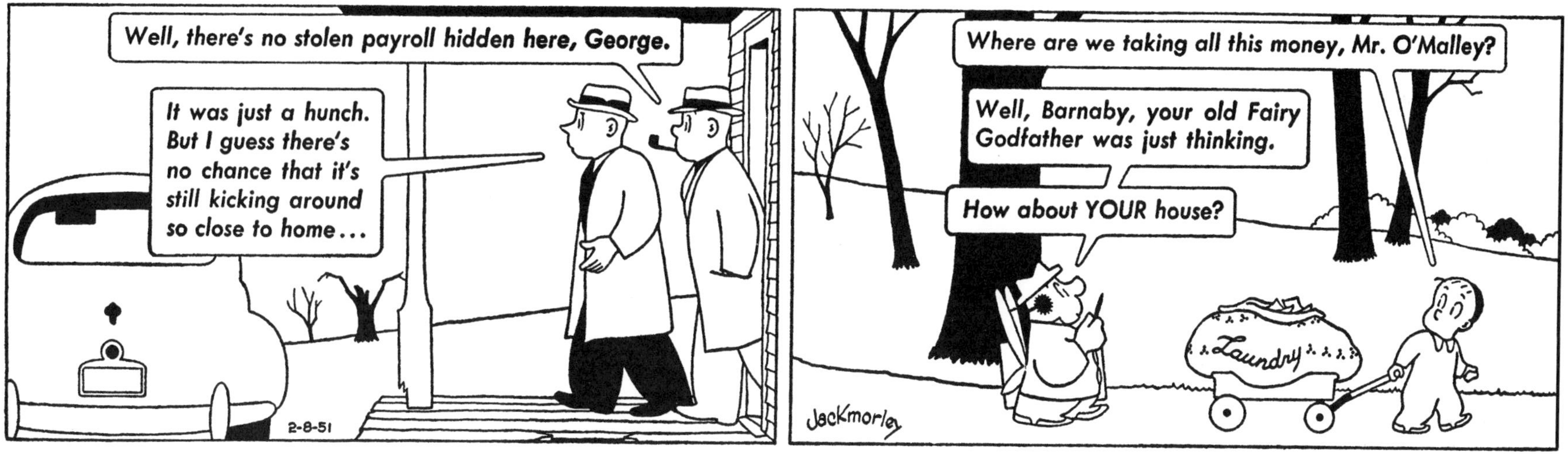
Well, there's no stolen payroll hidden here, George.
It was just a hunch. But I guess there's no chance that it's still kicking around so close to home...
2-8-51
Where are we taking all this money, Mr. O'Malley?
Well, Barnaby, your old Fairy Godfather was just thinking.
How about YOUR house?
Laundry
Jackmorley

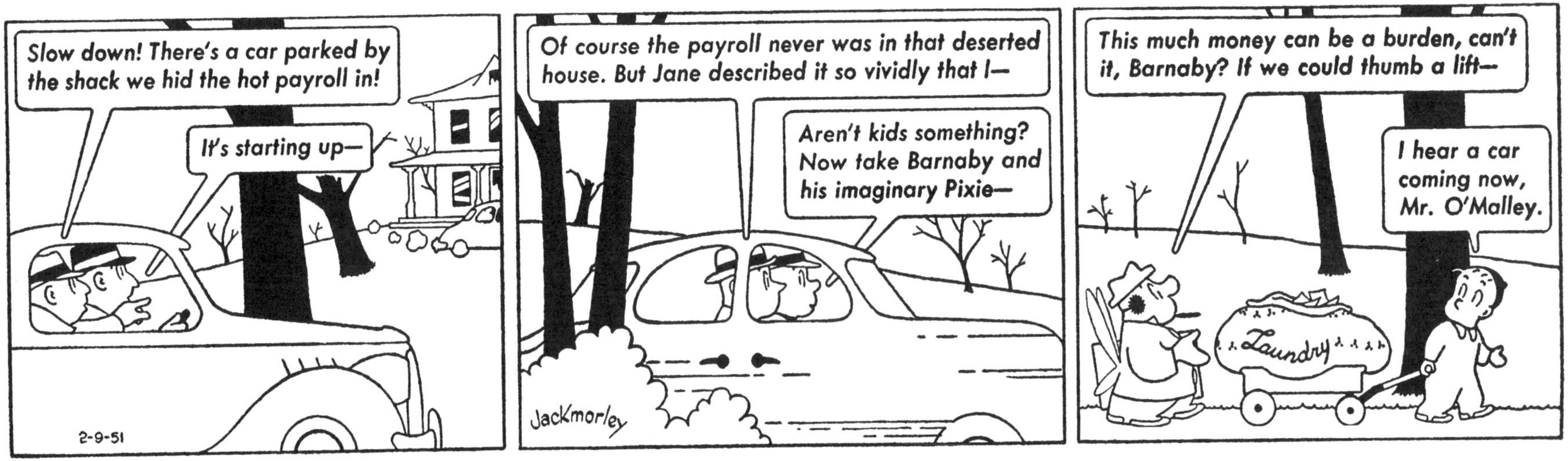
Slow down! There's a car parked by the shack we hid the hot payroll in!
It's starting up—
2-9-51
Of course the payroll never was in that deserted house. But Jane described it so vividly that I—
Aren't kids something? Now take Barnaby and his imaginary Pixie—
Jackmorley
This much money can be a burden, can't it, Barnaby? If we could thumb a lift—
I hear a car coming now, Mr. O'Malley.
Laundry

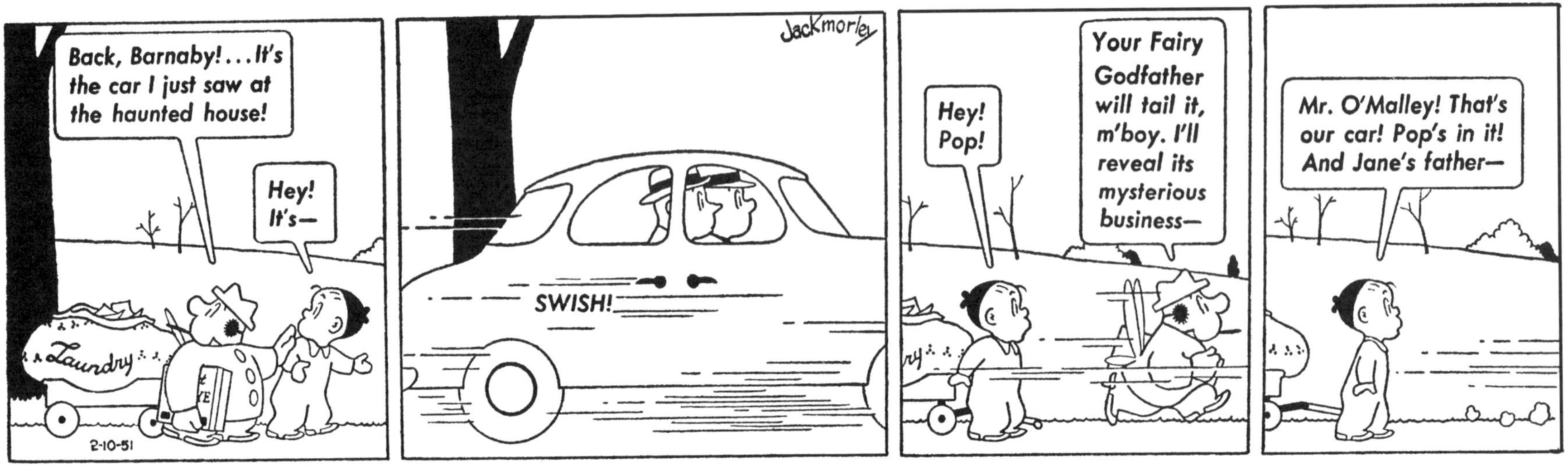
Back, Barnaby!... It's the car I just saw at the haunted house!
Hey! It's—
Laundry
2-10-51
Jackmorley
SWISH!
Hey! Pop!
Your Fairy Godfather will tail it, m'boy. I'll reveal its mysterious business—
Mr. O'Malley! That's our car! Pop's in it! And Jane's father—

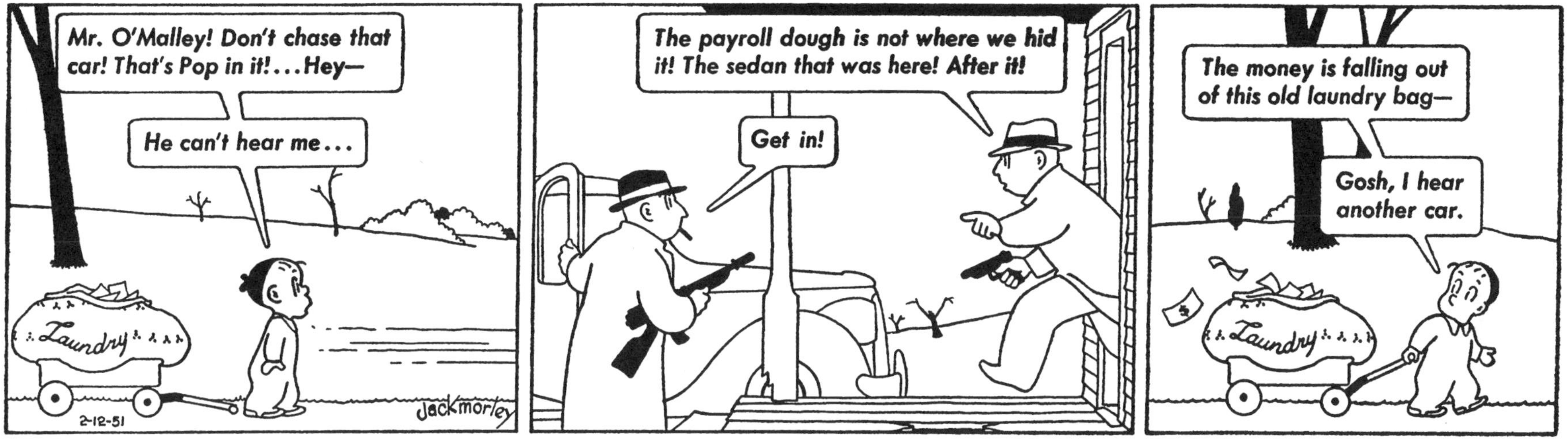
Mr. O'Malley! Don't chase that car! That's Pop in it!...Hey—
He can't hear me...
2-12-51
jackmorley
The payroll dough is not where we hid it! The sedan that was here! After it!
Get in!
The money is falling out of this old laundry bag—
Gosh, I hear another car.
Laundry

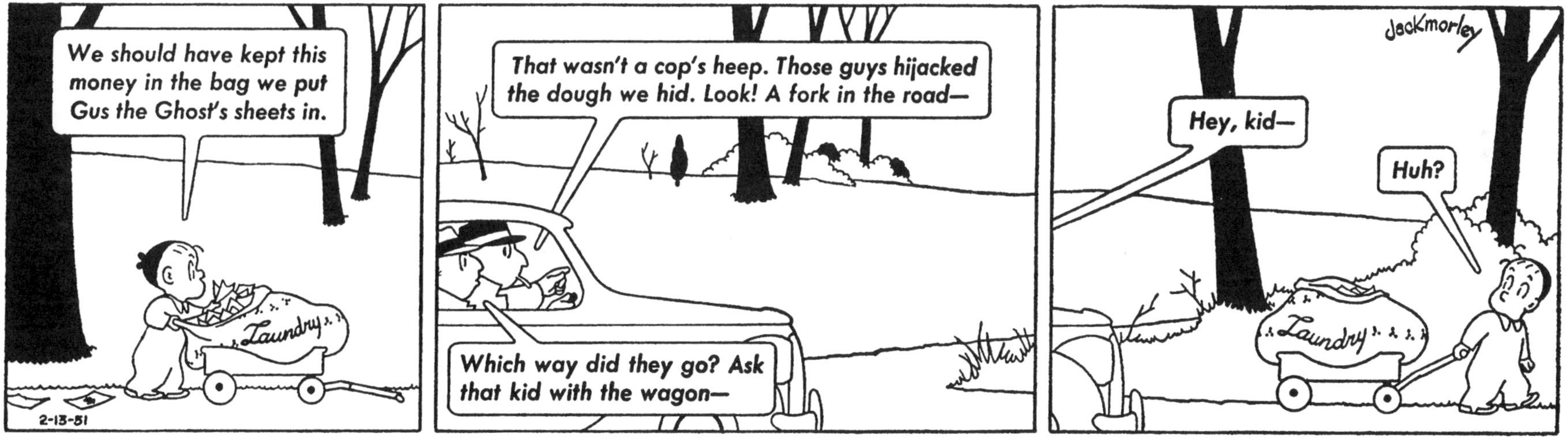
We should have kept this money in the bag we put Gus the Ghost's sheets in.
Laundry
2-13-51
That wasn't a cop's heep. Those guys hijacked the dough we hid. Look! A fork in the road—
Which way did they go? Ask that kid with the wagon—
jackmorley
Hey, kid—
Huh?
Laundry

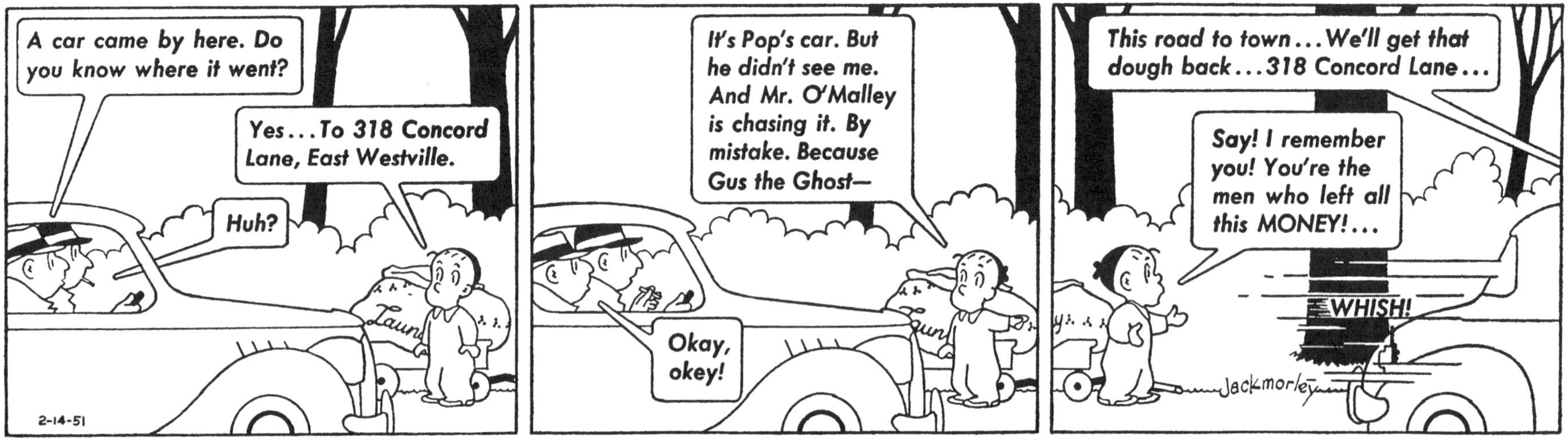
A car came by here. Do you know where it went?
Yes...To 318 Concord Lane, East Westville.
Huh?
2-14-51
It's Pop's car. But he didn't see me. And Mr. O'Malley is chasing it. By mistake. Because Gus the Ghost—
Okay, okey!
This road to town...We'll get that dough back...318 Concord Lane...
Say! I remember you! You're the men who left all this MONEY!...
WHISH!
Jackmorley

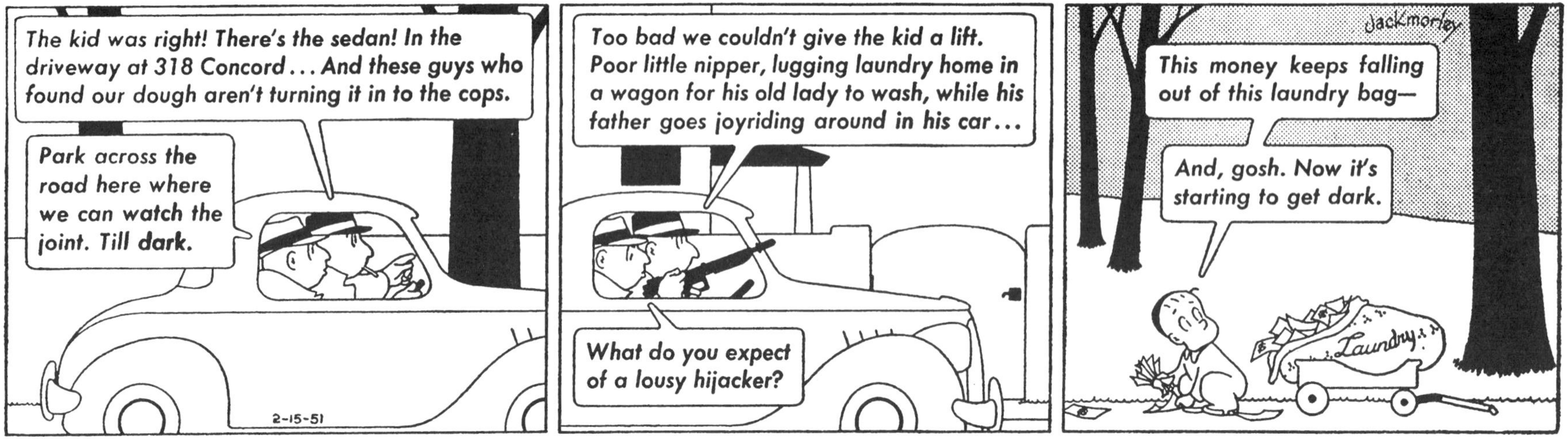
The kid was right! There's the sedan! In the driveway at 318 Concord...And these guys who found our dough aren't turning it in to the cops.
Park across the road here where we can watch the joint. Till dark.
2-15-51
Too bad we couldn't give the kid a lift. Poor little nipper, lugging laundry home in a wagon for his old lady to wash, while his father goes joyriding around in his car...
What do you expect of a lousy hijacker?
Jackmorley
This money keeps falling out of this laundry bag—
And, gosh. Now it's starting to get dark.
Laundry

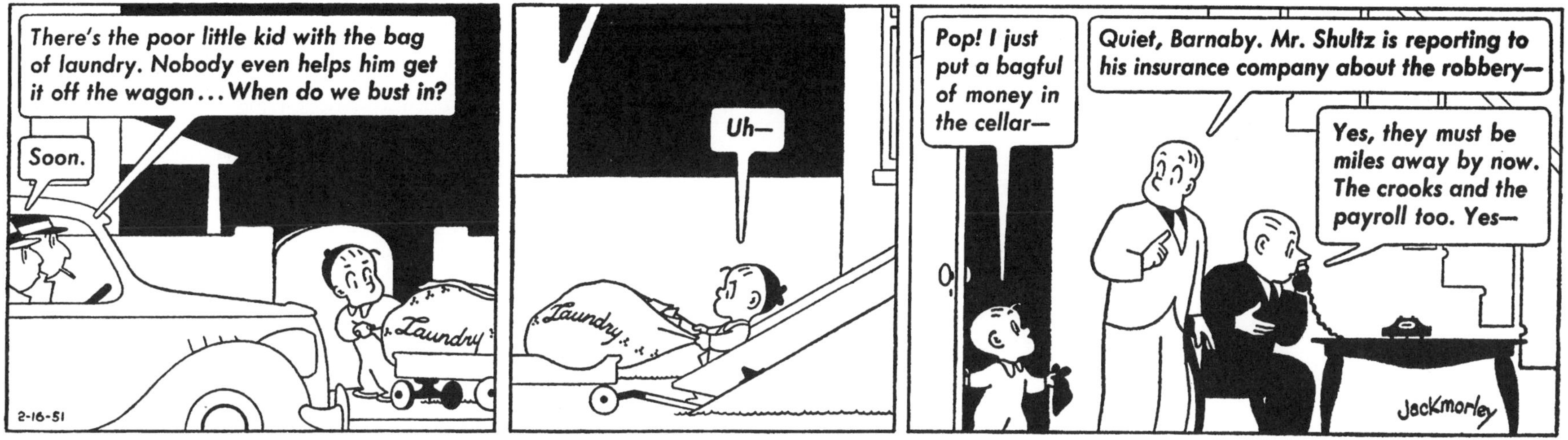
There's the poor little kid with the bag of laundry. Nobody even helps him get it off the wagon...When do we bust in?
Soon.
Laundry
2-16-51
Uh—
Laundry
Pop! I just put a bagful of money in the cellar—
Quiet, Barnaby. Mr. Shultz is reporting to his insurance company about the robbery—
Yes, they must be miles away by now. The crooks and the payroll too. Yes—
JackMorley

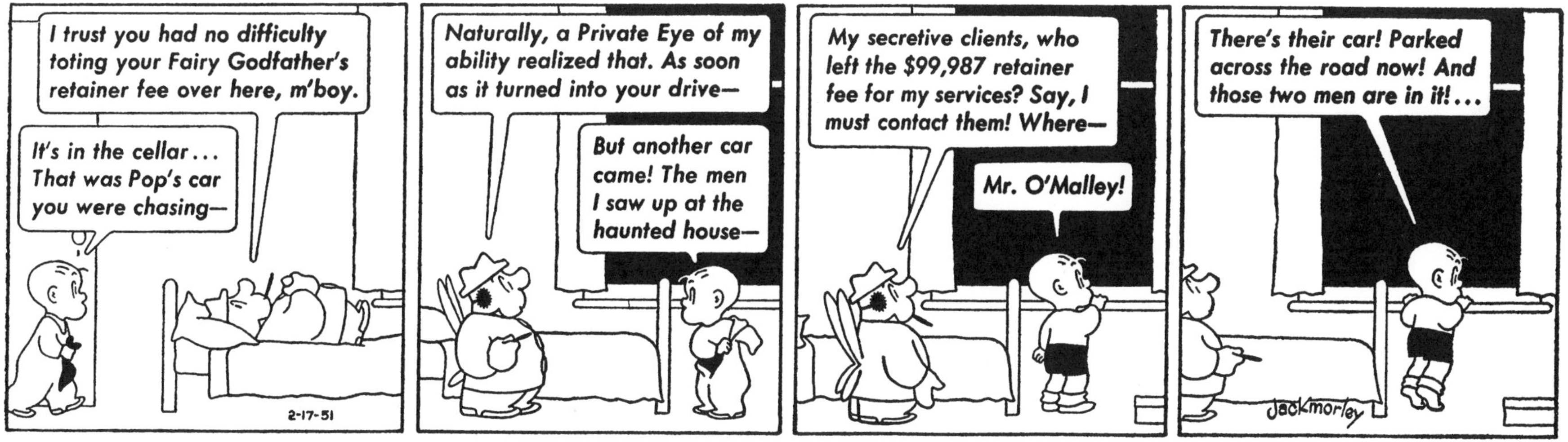
I trust you had no difficulty toting your Fairy Godfather's retainer fee over here, m'boy.
It's in the cellar... That was Pop's car you were chasing—
2-17-51
Naturally, a Private Eye of my ability realized that. As soon as it turned into your drive—
But another car came! The men I saw up at the haunted house—
My secretive clients, who left the $99,987 retainer fee for my services? Say, I must contact them! Where—
Mr. O'Malley!
There's their car! Parked across the road now! And those two men are in it!...
JackMorley

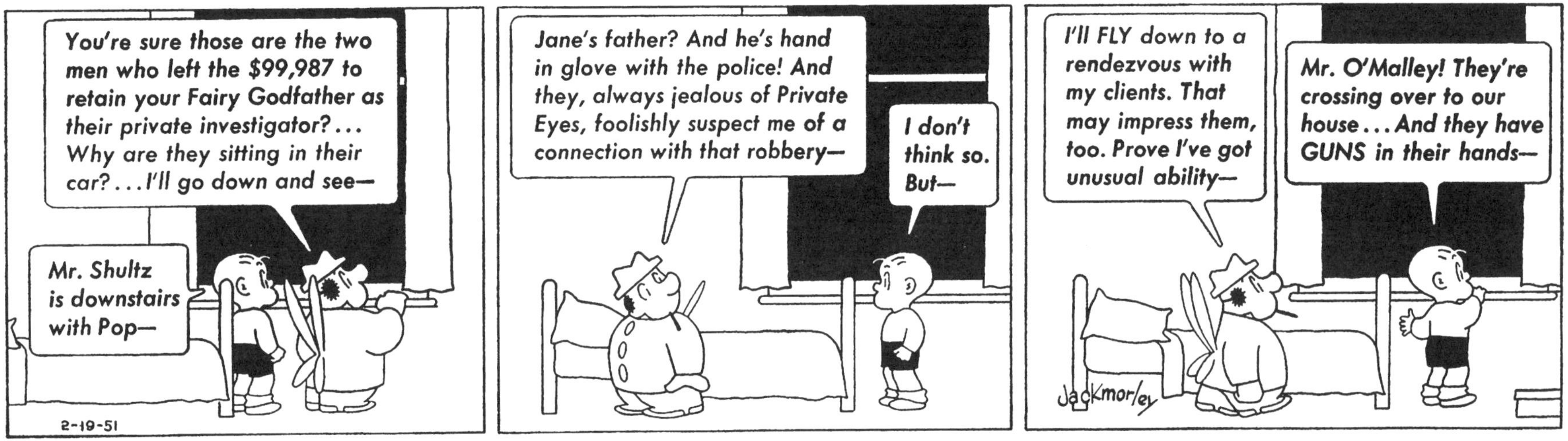
You're sure those are the two men who left the $99,987 to retain your Fairy Godfather as their private investigator? . . . Why are they sitting in their car? . . . I'll go down and see—
Mr. Shultz is downstairs with Pop—
2-19-51
Jane's father? And he's hand in glove with the police! And they, always jealous of Private Eyes, foolishly suspect me of a connection with that robbery—
I don't think so. But—
I'll FLY down to a rendezvous with my clients. That may impress them, too. Prove I've got unusual ability—
Mr. O'Malley! They're crossing over to our house . . . And they have GUNS in their hands—
Jackmorley

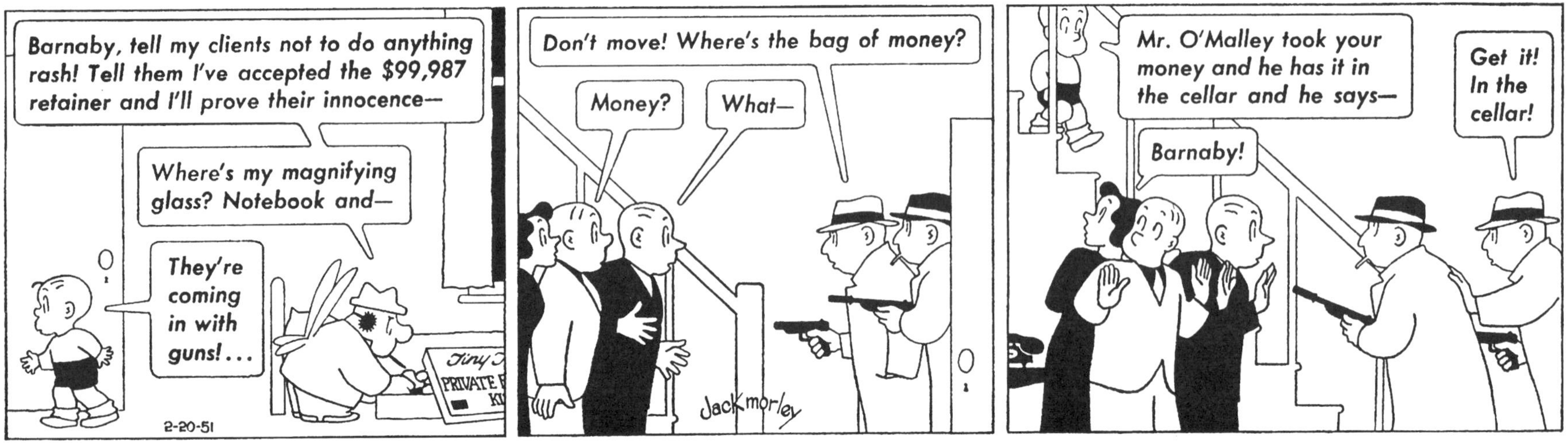
Barnaby, tell my clients not to do anything rash! Tell them I've accepted the $99,987 retainer and I'll prove their innocence—
Where's my magnifying glass? Notebook and—
They're coming in with guns! . . .
2-20-51
Don't move! Where's the bag of money?
Money?
What—
Jackmorley
Mr. O'Malley took your money and he has it in the cellar and he says—
Barnaby!
Get it! In the cellar!

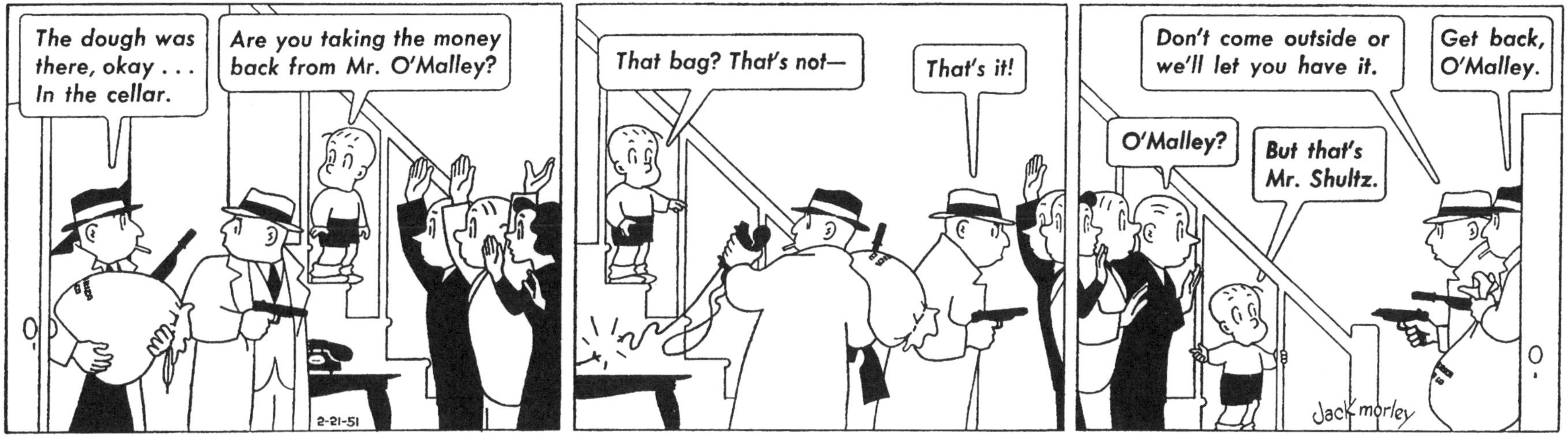
The dough was there, okay . . . In the cellar.
Are you taking the money back from Mr. O'Malley?
2-21-51
That bag? That's not—
That's it!
Don't come outside or we'll let you have it.
Get back, O'Malley.
O'Malley?
But that's Mr. Shultz.
Jack Morley

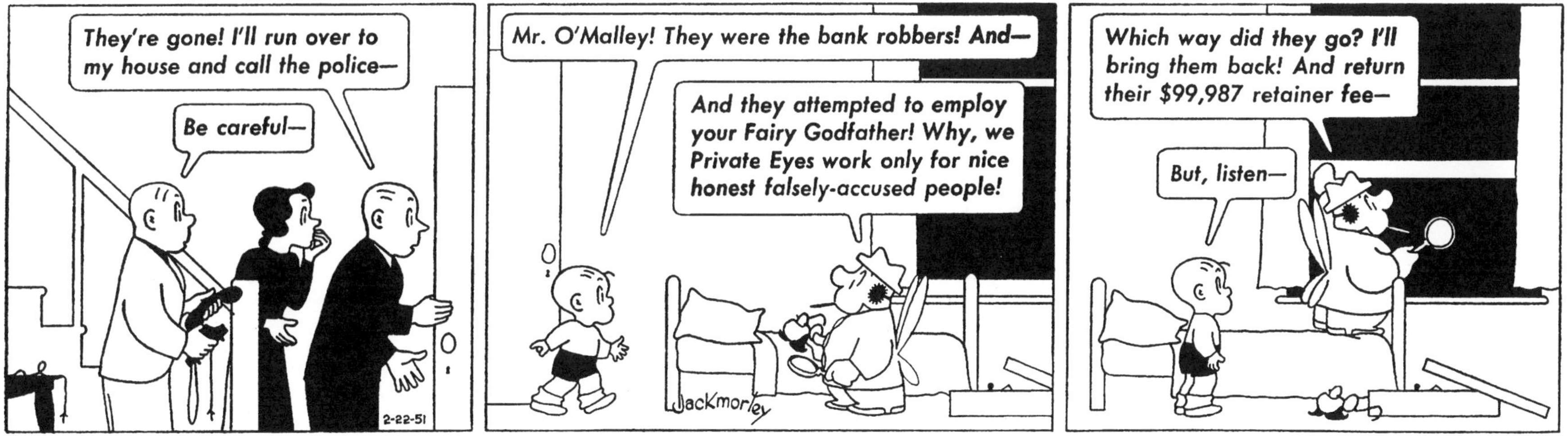
They're gone! I'll run over to my house and call the police—
Be careful—
2-22-51
Mr. O'Malley! They were the bank robbers! And—
And they attempted to employ your Fairy Godfather! Why, we Private Eyes work only for nice honest falsely-accused people!
Jack Morley
Which way did they go? I'll bring them back! And return their $99,987 retainer fee—
But, listen—

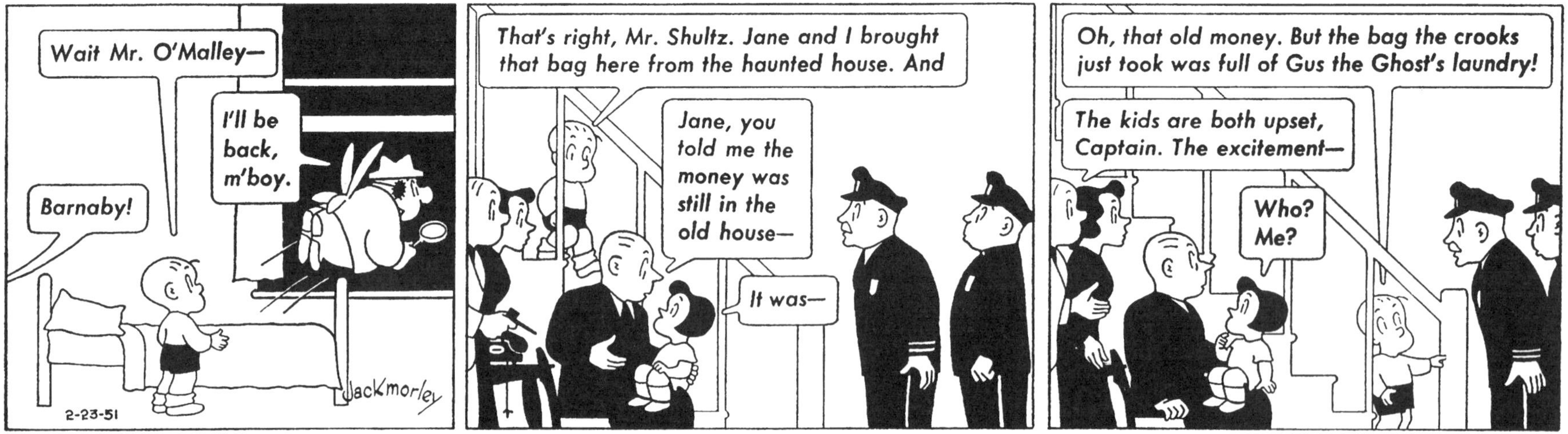
Wait Mr. O'Malley—
I'll be back, m'boy.
Barnaby!
2-23-51
That's right, Mr. Shultz. Jane and I brought that bag here from the haunted house. And
Jane, you told me the money was still in the old house—
It was—
Oh, that old money. But the bag the crooks just took was full of Gus the Ghost's laundry!
The kids are both upset, Captain. The excitement—
Who? Me?

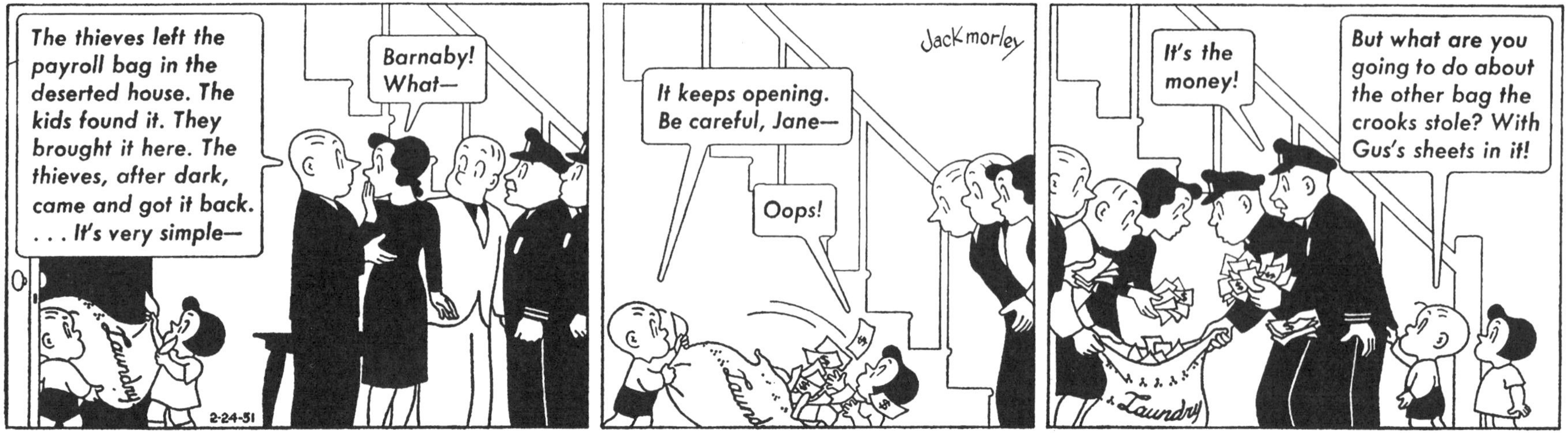
The thieves left the payroll bag in the deserted house. The kids found it. They brought it here. The thieves, after dark, came and got it back. . . . It's very simple—
Barnaby! What—
2-24-51
It keeps opening. Be careful, Jane—
Oops!
It's the money!
But what are you going to do about the other bag the crooks stole? With Gus's sheets in it!

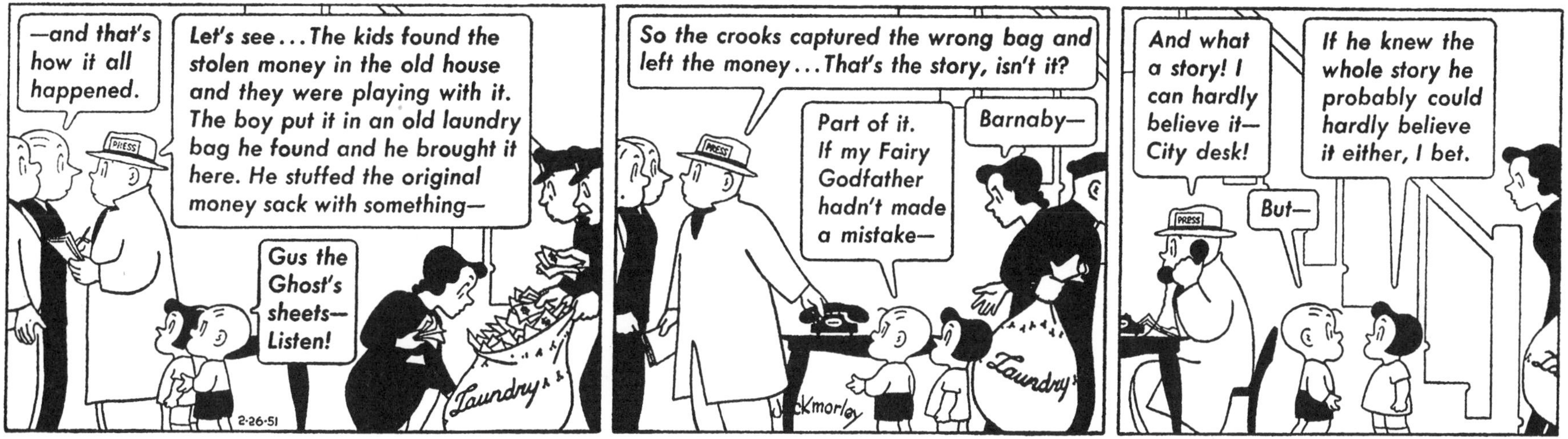
—and that's how it all happened.
Let's see...The kids found the stolen money in the old house and they were playing with it. The boy put it in an old laundry bag he found and he brought it here. He stuffed the original money sack with something—
Gus the Ghost's sheets— Listen!
Laundry
2-26-51
So the crooks captured the wrong bag and left the money...That's the story, isn't it?
Part of it. If my Fairy Godfather hadn't made a mistake—
Barnaby—
Laundry
Jackmorley
And what a story! I can hardly believe it— City desk!
But—
If he knew the whole story he probably could hardly believe it either, I bet.

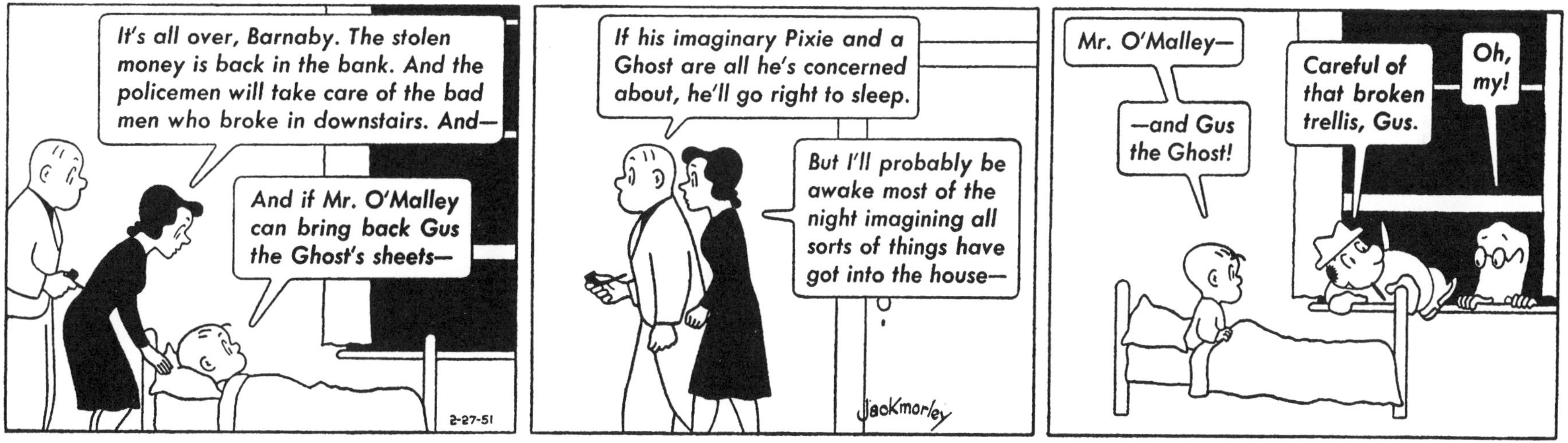
It's all over, Barnaby. The stolen money is back in the bank. And the policemen will take care of the bad men who broke in downstairs. And—
And if Mr. O'Malley can bring back Gus the Ghost's sheets—
2-27-51
If his imaginary Pixie and a Ghost are all he's concerned about, he'll go right to sleep.
But I'll probably be awake most of the night imagining all sorts of things have got into the house—
Jackmorley
Mr. O'Malley—
—and Gus the Ghost!
Careful of that broken trellis, Gus.
Oh, my!

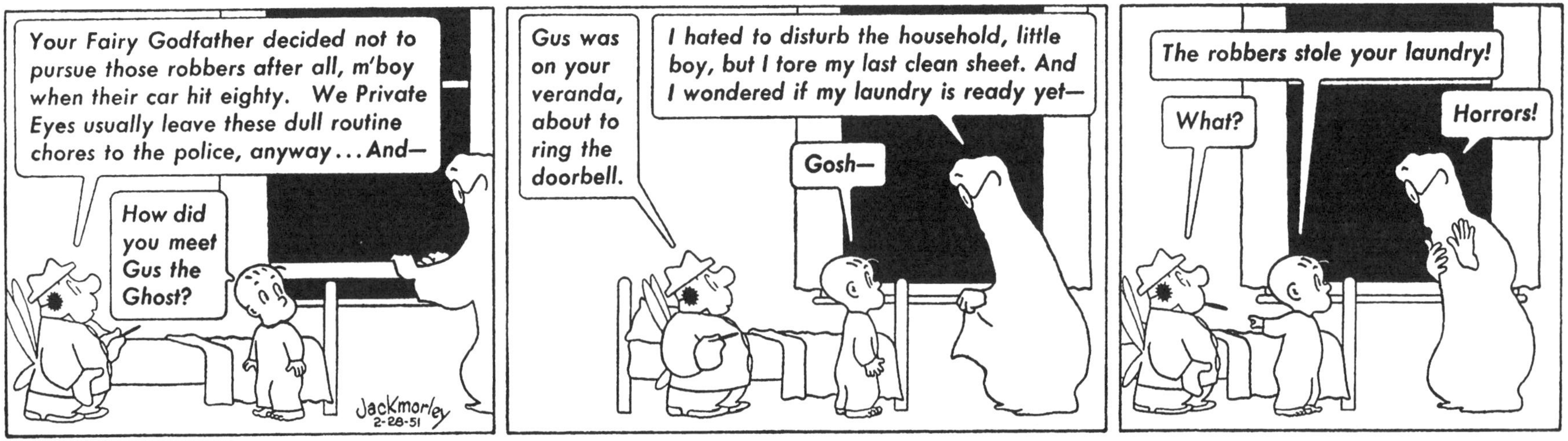
Your Fairy Godfather decided not to pursue those robbers after all, m'boy when their car hit eighty. We Private Eyes usually leave these dull routine chores to the police, anyway... And—
How did you meet Gus the Ghost?
JackMorley 2-28-51
Gus was on your veranda, about to ring the doorbell.
I hated to disturb the household, little boy, but I tore my last clean sheet. And I wondered if my laundry is ready yet—
Gosh—
The robbers stole your laundry!
What?
Horrors!

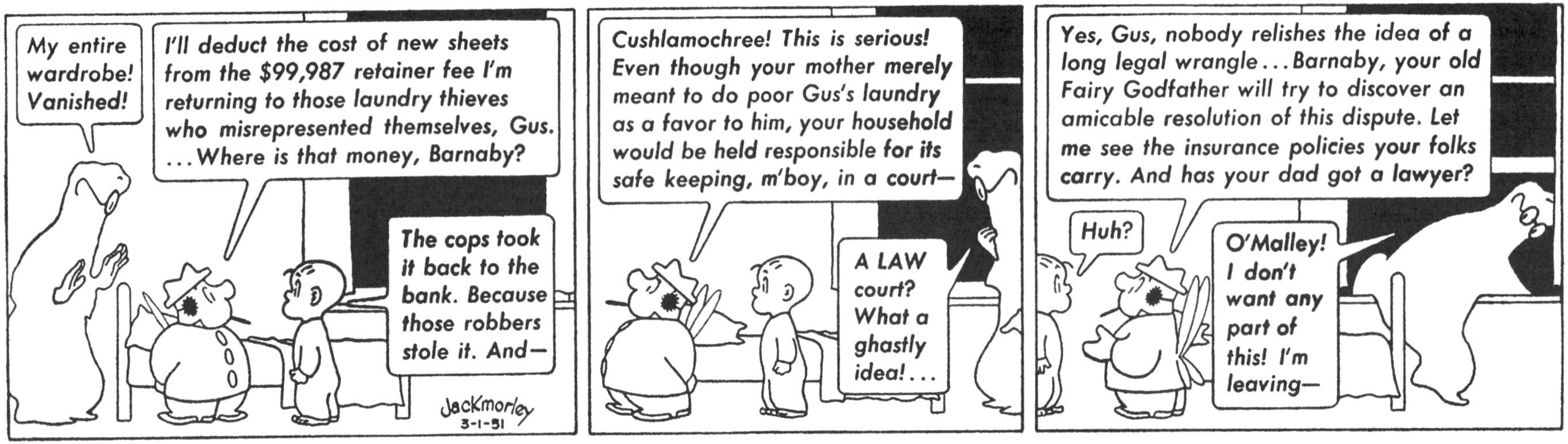
My entire wardrobe! Vanished!
I'll deduct the cost of new sheets from the $99,987 retainer fee I'm returning to those laundry thieves who misrepresented themselves, Gus. ...Where is that money, Barnaby?
The cops took it back to the bank. Because those robbers stole it. And—
JackMorley 3-1-51
Cushlamochree! This is serious! Even though your mother merely meant to do poor Gus's laundry as a favor to him, your household would be held responsible for its safe keeping, m'boy, in a court—
A LAW court? What a ghastly idea!...
Yes, Gus, nobody relishes the idea of a long legal wrangle...Barnaby, your old Fairy Godfather will try to discover an amicable resolution of this dispute. Let me see the insurance policies your folks carry. And has your dad got a lawyer?
Huh?
O'Malley! I don't want any part of this! I'm leaving—

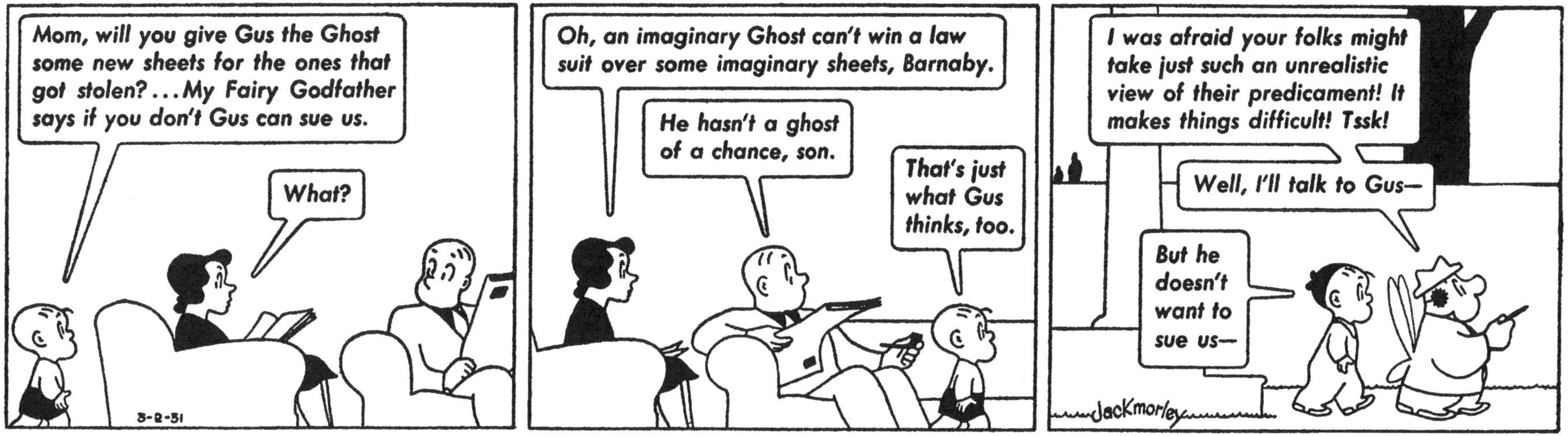
Mom, will you give Gus the Ghost some new sheets for the ones that got stolen? . . . My Fairy Godfather says if you don't Gus can sue us.
What?
3-2-51
Oh, an imaginary Ghost can't win a law suit over some imaginary sheets, Barnaby.
He hasn't a ghost of a chance, son.
That's just what Gus thinks, too.
I was afraid your folks might take just such an unrealistic view of their predicament! It makes things difficult! Tssk!
Well, I'll talk to Gus—
But he doesn't want to sue us—
JackMorley

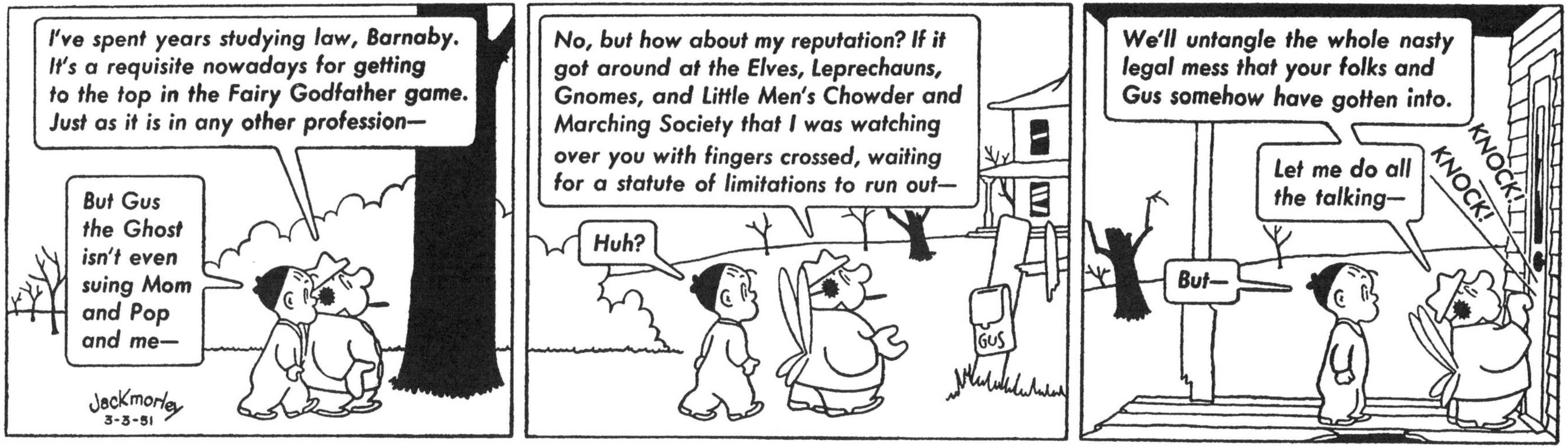
I've spent years studying law, Barnaby. It's a requisite nowadays for getting to the top in the Fairy Godfather game. Just as it is in any other profession—
But Gus the Ghost isn't even suing Mom and Pop and me—
JackMorley
3-3-51
No, but how about my reputation? If it got around at the Elves, Leprechauns, Gnomes, and Little Men's Chowder and Marching Society that I was watching over you with fingers crossed, waiting for a statute of limitations to run out—
Huh?
GUS
We'll untangle the whole nasty legal mess that your folks and Gus somehow have gotten into.
Let me do all the talking—
KNOCK! KNOCK!
But—

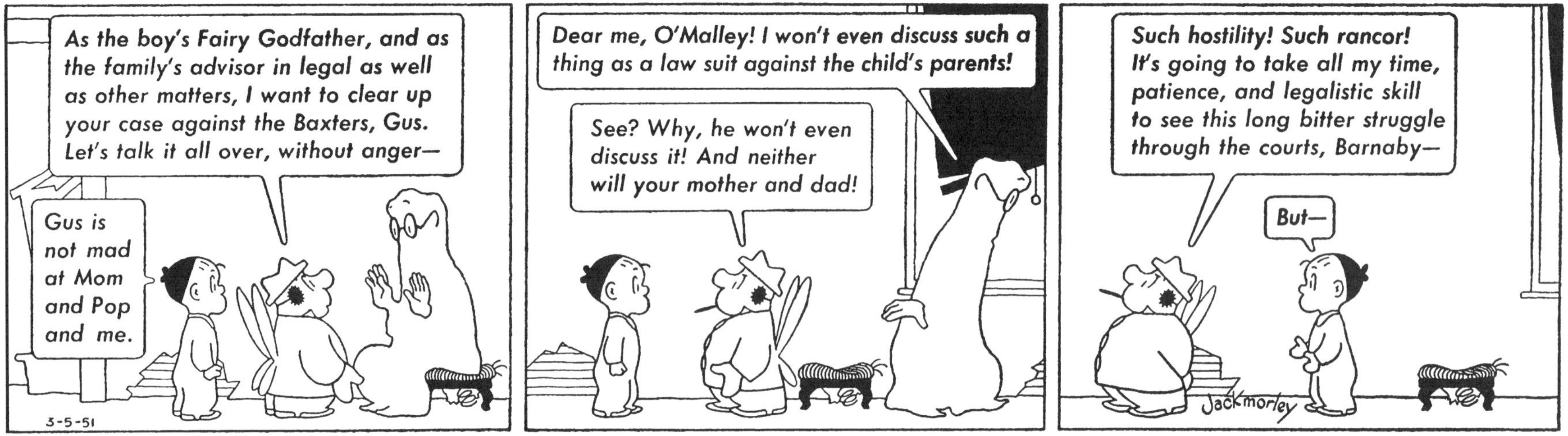
As the boy's Fairy Godfather, and as the family's advisor in legal as well as other matters, I want to clear up your case against the Baxters, Gus. Let's talk it all over, without anger—
Gus is not mad at Mom and Pop and me.
3-5-51
Dear me, O'Malley! I won't even discuss such a thing as a law suit against the child's parents!
See? Why, he won't even discuss it! And neither will your mother and dad!
Such hostility! Such rancor! It's going to take all my time, patience, and legalistic skill to see this long bitter struggle through the courts, Barnaby—
But—
Jackmorley

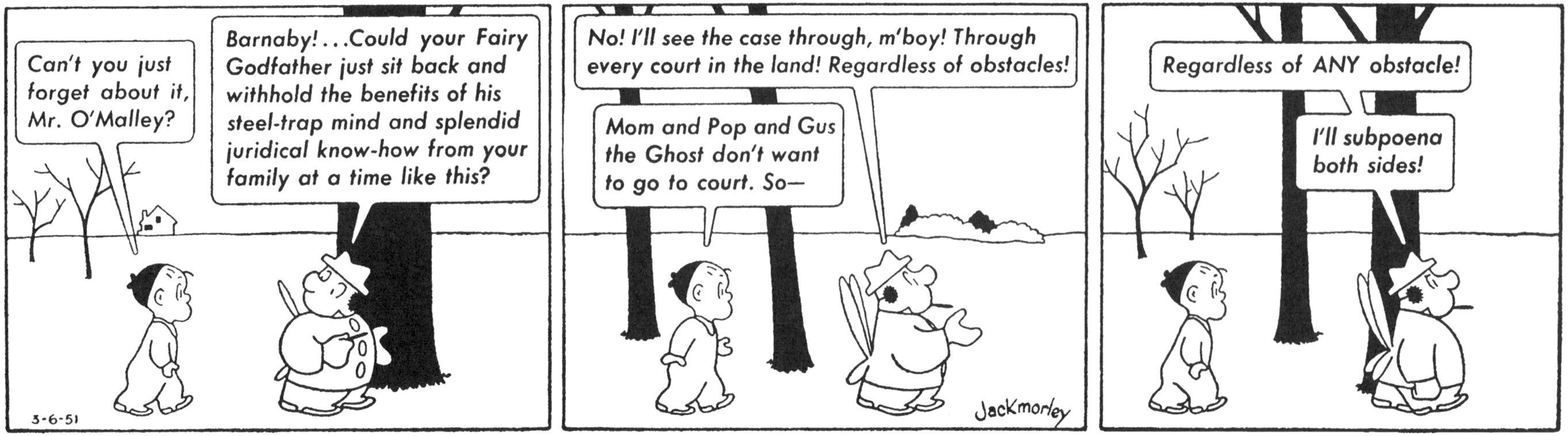
Can't you just forget about it, Mr. O'Malley?
Barnaby!...Could your Fairy Godfather just sit back and withhold the benefits of his steel-trap mind and splendid juridical know-how from your family at a time like this?
3-6-51
No! I'll see the case through, m'boy! Through every court in the land! Regardless of obstacles!
Mom and Pop and Gus the Ghost don't want to go to court. So—
Jackmorley
Regardless of ANY obstacle!
I'll subpoena both sides!

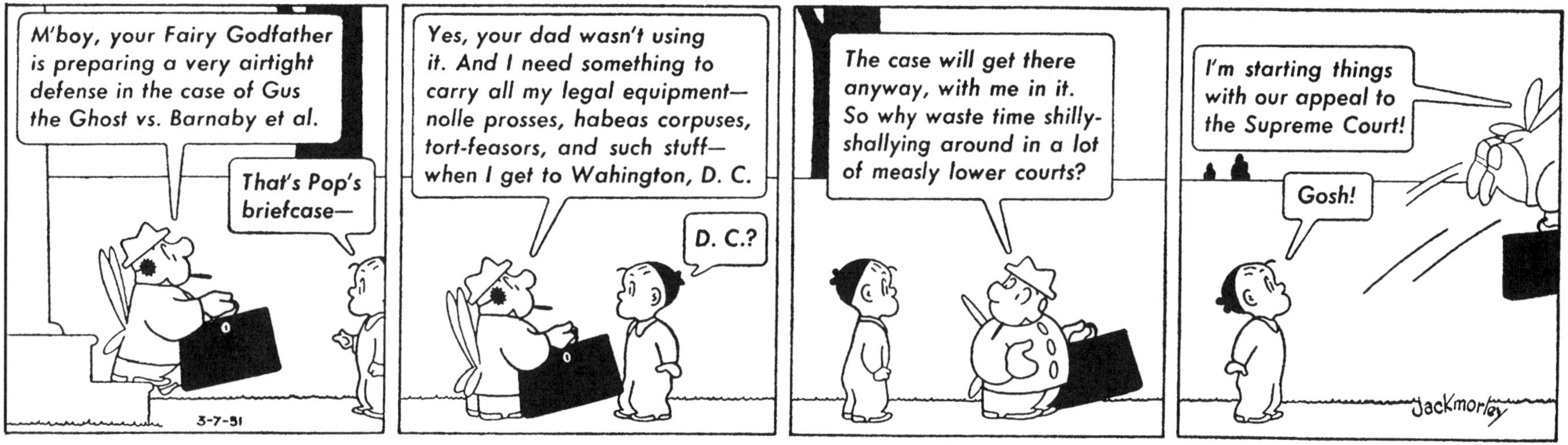
M'boy, your Fairy Godfather is preparing a very airtight defense in the case of Gus the Ghost vs. Barnaby et al.
That's Pop's briefcase—
3-7-51
Yes, your dad wasn't using it. And I need something to carry all my legal equipment—nolle prosses, habeas corpuses, tort-feasors, and such stuff—when I get to Wahington, D. C.
D. C.?
The case will get there anyway, with me in it. So why waste time shilly-shallying around in a lot of measly lower courts?
I'm starting things with our appeal to the Supreme Court!
Gosh!
JackMorley

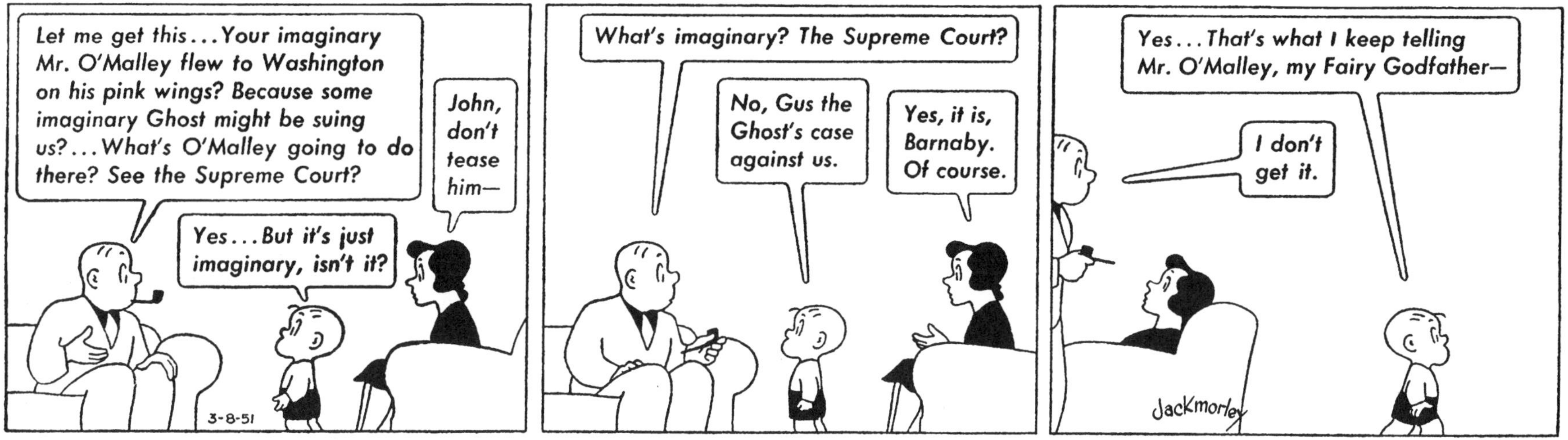
Let me get this...Your imaginary Mr. O'Malley flew to Washington on his pink wings? Because some imaginary Ghost might be suing us?...What's O'Malley going to do there? See the Supreme Court?
John, don't tease him—
Yes...But it's just imaginary, isn't it?
3-8-51
What's imaginary? The Supreme Court?
No, Gus the Ghost's case against us.
Yes, it is, Barnaby. Of course.
Yes...That's what I keep telling Mr. O'Malley, my Fairy Godfather—
I don't get it.
JackMorley

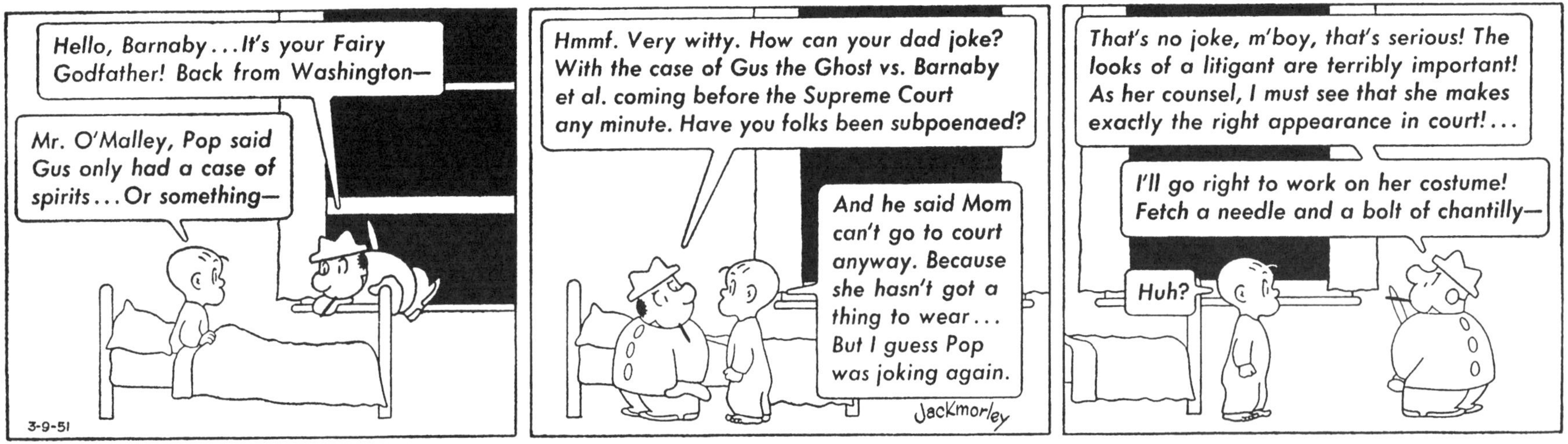
Hello, Barnaby...It's your Fairy Godfather! Back from Washington—
Mr. O'Malley, Pop said Gus only had a case of spirits...Or something—
3-9-51
Hmmf. Very witty. How can your dad joke? With the case of Gus the Ghost vs. Barnaby et al. coming before the Supreme Court any minute. Have you folks been subpoenaed?
And he said Mom can't go to court anyway. Because she hasn't got a thing to wear... But I guess Pop was joking again.
Jackmorley
That's no joke, m'boy, that's serious! The looks of a litigant are terribly important! As her counsel, I must see that she makes exactly the right appearance in court!...
I'll go right to work on her costume! Fetch a needle and a bolt of chantilly—
Huh?

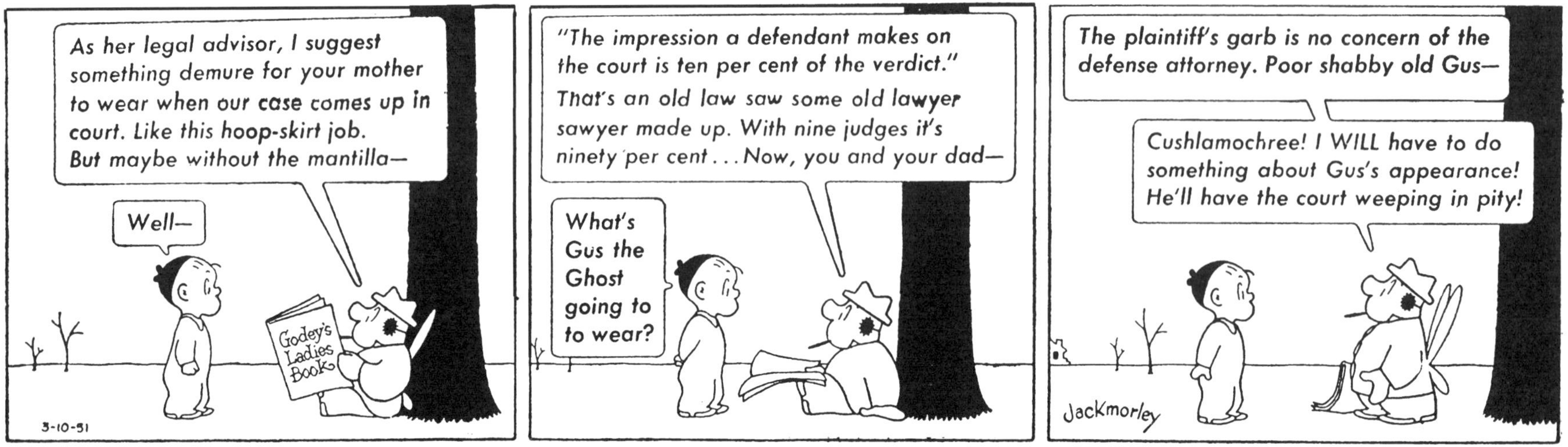
As her legal advisor, I suggest something demure for your mother to wear when our case comes up in court. Like this hoop-skirt job. But maybe without the mantilla—
Well—
Godey's Ladies Book
3-10-51
"The impression a defendant makes on the court is ten per cent of the verdict." That's an old law saw some old lawyer sawyer made up. With nine judges it's ninety per cent...Now, you and your dad—
What's Gus the Ghost going to to wear?
The plaintiff's garb is no concern of the defense attorney. Poor shabby old Gus—
Cushlamochree! I WILL have to do something about Gus's appearance! He'll have the court weeping in pity!
Jackmorley

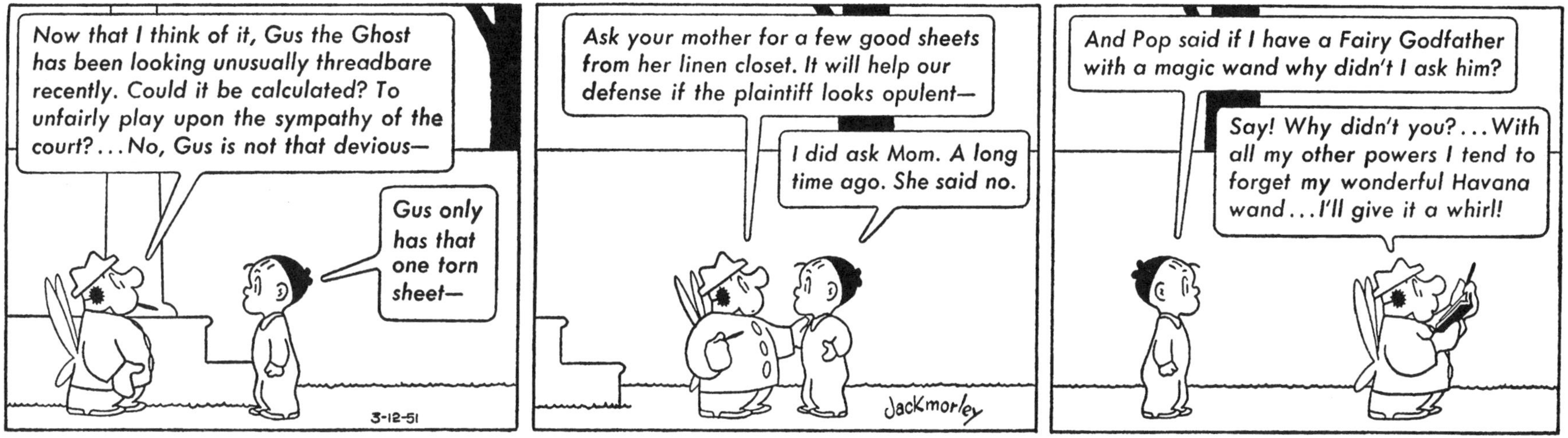
Now that I think of it, Gus the Ghost has been looking unusually threadbare recently. Could it be calculated? To unfairly play upon the sympathy of the court?...No, Gus is not that devious—
Gus only has that one torn sheet—
3-12-51
Ask your mother for a few good sheets from her linen closet. It will help our defense if the plaintiff looks opulent—
I did ask Mom. A long time ago. She said no.
Jackmorley
And Pop said if I have a Fairy Godfather with a magic wand why didn't I ask him?
Say! Why didn't you?...With all my other powers I tend to forget my wonderful Havana wand...I'll give it a whirl!

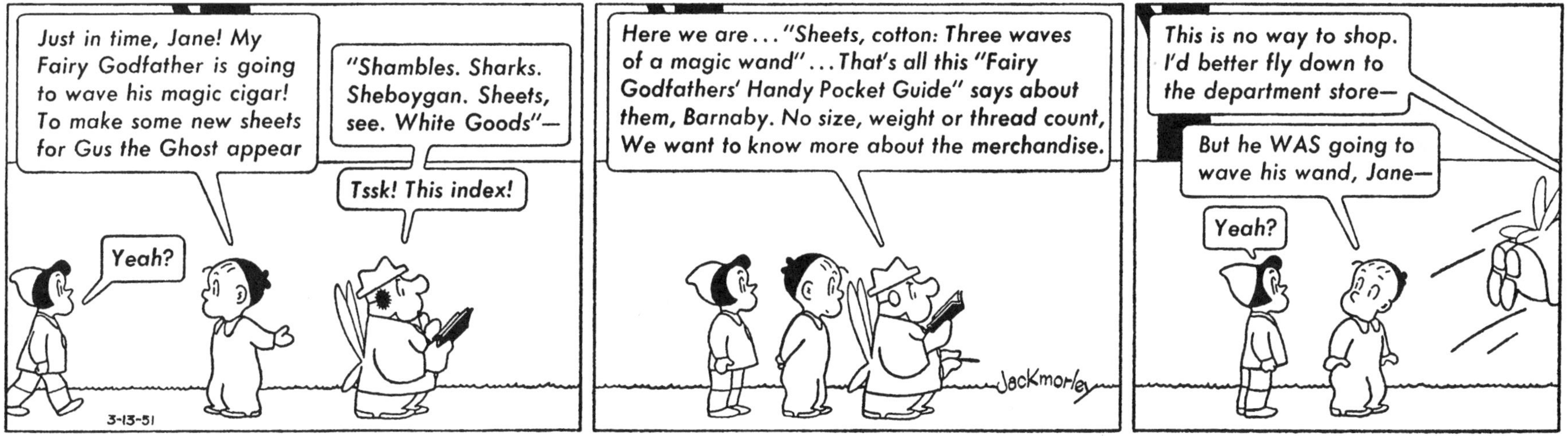
Just in time, Jane! My Fairy Godfather is going to wave his magic cigar! To make some new sheets for Gus the Ghost appear
Yeah?
"Shambles. Sharks. Sheboygan. Sheets, see. White Goods"—
Tssk! This index!
3-13-51
Here we are..."Sheets, cotton: Three waves of a magic wand"...That's all this "Fairy Godfathers' Handy Pocket Guide" says about them, Barnaby. No size, weight or thread count, We want to know more about the merchandise.
Jackmorley
This is no way to shop. I'd better fly down to the department store—
But he WAS going to wave his wand, Jane—
Yeah?

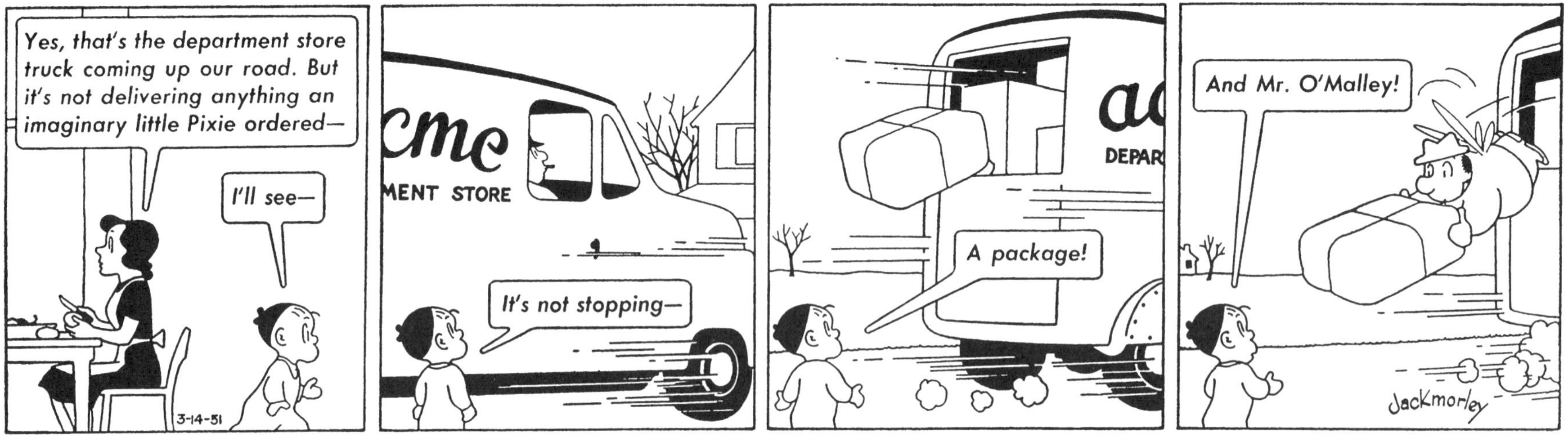
Yes, that's the department store truck coming up our road. But it's not delivering anything an imaginary little Pixie ordered—
I'll see—
3-14-51
It's not stopping—
A package!
And Mr. O'Malley!
Jackmorley

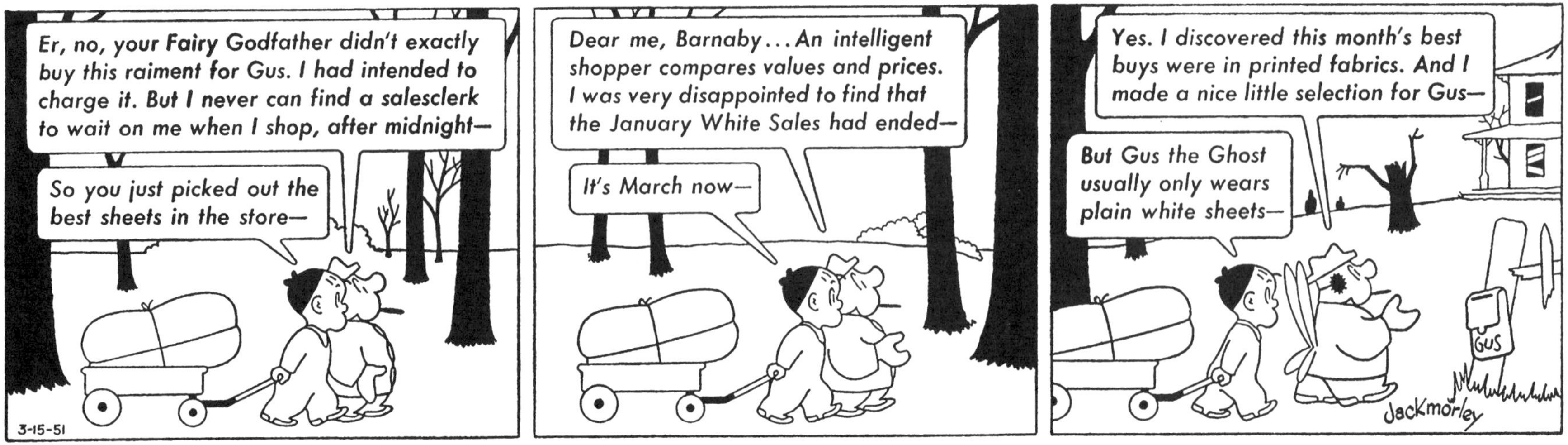
Er, no, your **Fairy** Godfather didn't exactly buy this raiment for Gus. I had intended to charge it. But I never can find a salesclerk to wait on me when I shop, after midnight—
So you just picked out the best sheets in the store—
3-15-51
Dear me, Barnaby... An intelligent shopper compares values and prices. I was very disappointed to find that the January White Sales had ended—
It's March now—
Yes. I discovered this month's best buys were in printed fabrics. And I made a nice little selection for Gus—
But Gus the Ghost usually only wears plain white sheets—
GUS
Jackmorley

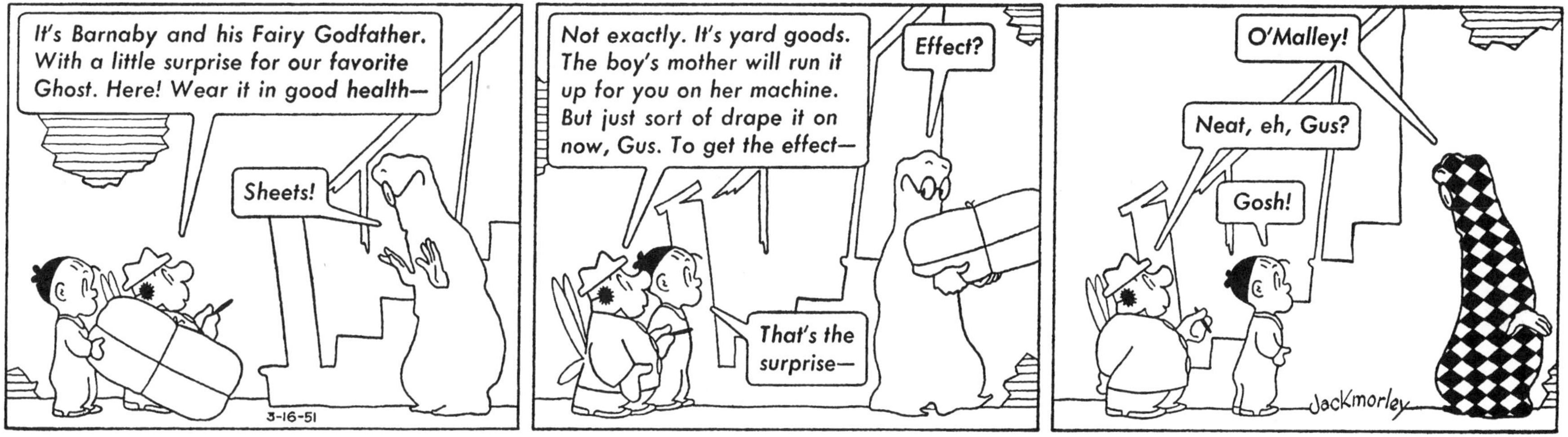
It's Barnaby and his Fairy Godfather. With a little surprise for our favorite Ghost. Here! Wear it in good health—
Sheets!
3-16-51
Not exactly. It's yard goods. The boy's mother will run it up for you on her machine. But just sort of drape it on now, Gus. To get the effect—
Effect?
That's the surprise—
O'Malley!
Neat, eh, Gus?
Gosh!
JACKMORLEY

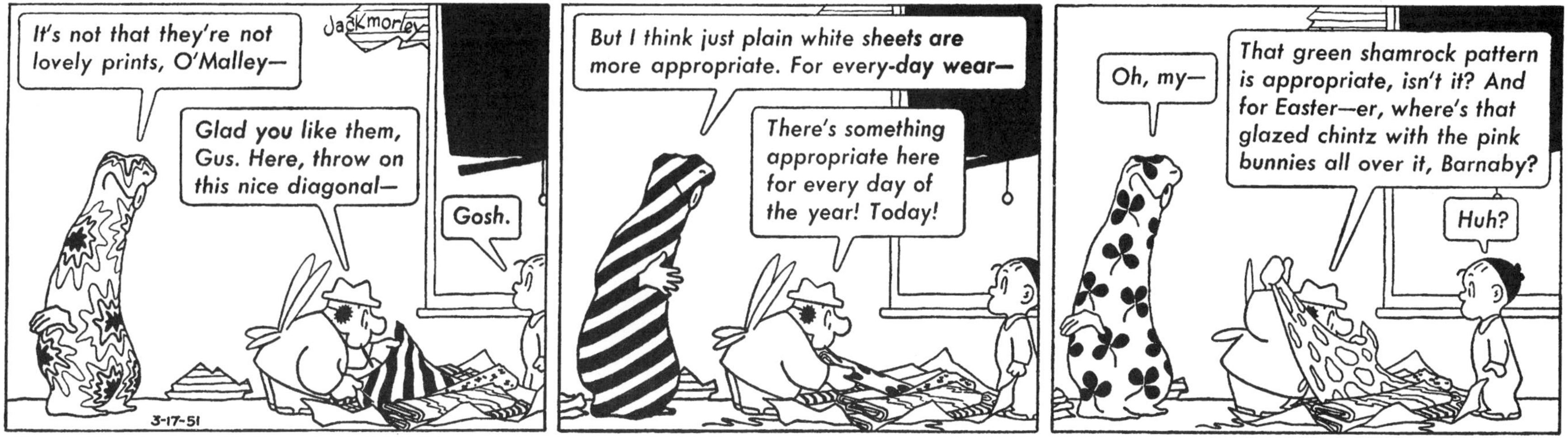
It's not that they're not lovely prints, O'Malley—
JACKMORLEY
Glad you like them, Gus. Here, throw on this nice diagonal—
Gosh.
3-17-51
But I think just plain white sheets are more appropriate. For every-day wear—
There's something appropriate here for every day of the year! Today!
Oh, my—
That green shamrock pattern is appropriate, isn't it? And for Easter—er, where's that glazed chintz with the pink bunnies all over it, Barnaby?
Huh?

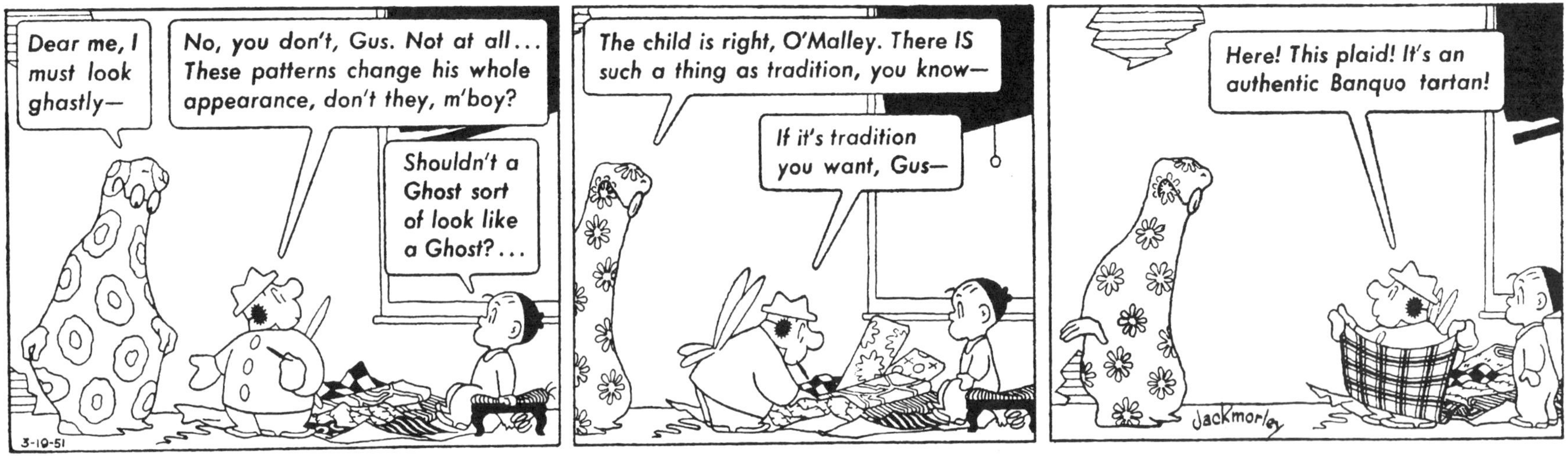
Dear me, I must look ghastly—
No, you don't, Gus. Not at all... These patterns change his whole appearance, don't they, m'boy?
Shouldn't a Ghost sort of look like a Ghost?...
The child is right, O'Malley. There IS such a thing as tradition, you know—
If it's tradition you want, Gus—
Here! This plaid! It's an authentic Banquo tartan!
Jackmorley
3-19-51

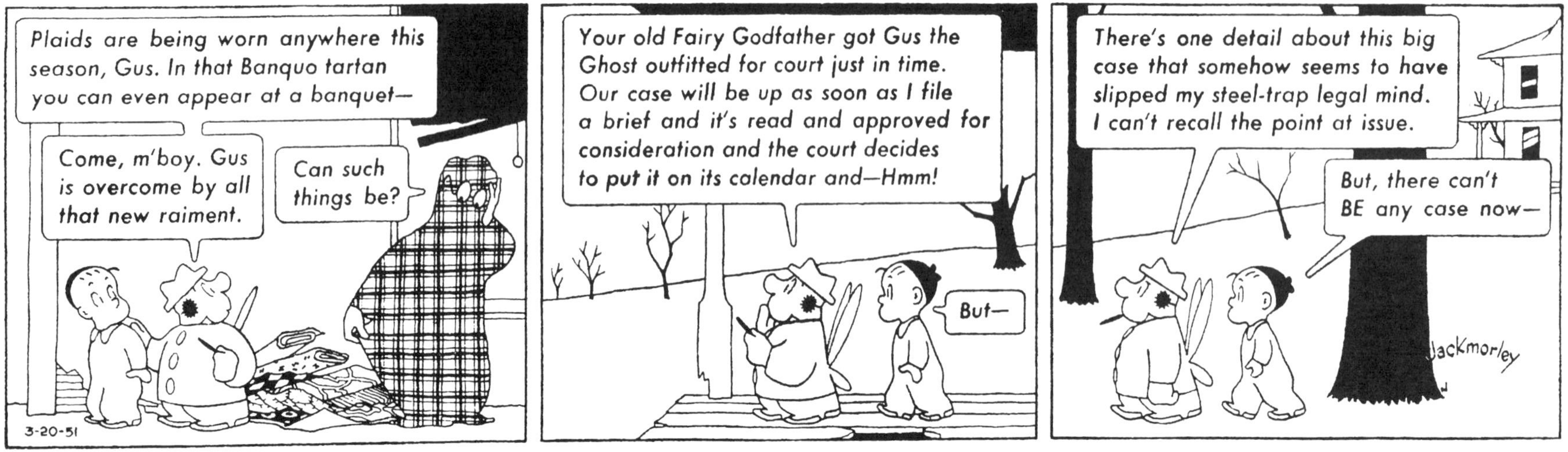
Plaids are being worn anywhere this season, Gus. In that Banquo tartan you can even appear at a banquet—
Come, m'boy. Gus is overcome by all that new raiment.
Can such things be?
Your old Fairy Godfather got Gus the Ghost outfitted for court just in time. Our case will be up as soon as I file a brief and it's read and approved for consideration and the court decides to put it on its calendar and—Hmm!
But—
There's one detail about this big case that somehow seems to have slipped my steel-trap legal mind. I can't recall the point at issue.
But, there can't BE any case now—
Jackmorley
3-20-51

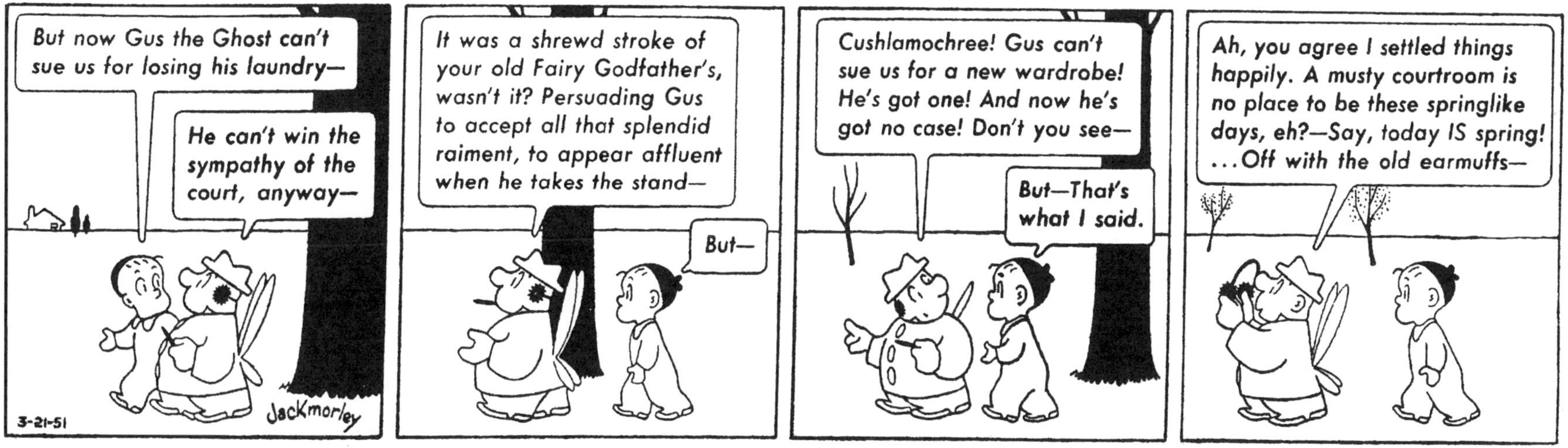
But now Gus the Ghost can't sue us for losing his laundry—
He can't win the sympathy of the court, anyway—
3-21-51
Jackmorley
It was a shrewd stroke of your old Fairy Godfather's, wasn't it? Persuading Gus to accept all that splendid raiment, to appear affluent when he takes the stand—
But—
Cushlamochree! Gus can't sue us for a new wardrobe! He's got one! And now he's got no case! Don't you see—
But—That's what I said.
Ah, you agree I settled things happily. A musty courtroom is no place to be these springlike days, eh?—Say, today IS spring! ...Off with the old earmuffs—

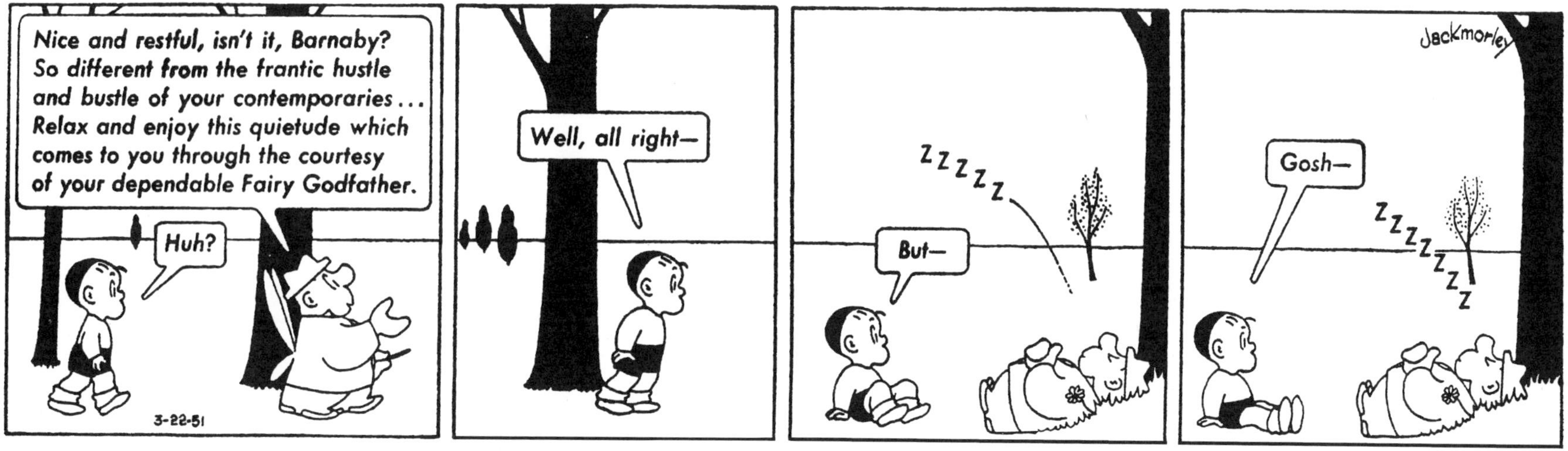
Nice and restful, isn't it, Barnaby? So different from the frantic hustle and bustle of your contemporaries... Relax and enjoy this quietude which comes to you through the courtesy of your dependable Fairy Godfather.
Huh?
3-22-51
Well, all right—
Z Z Z Z Z
But—
Jackmorley
Gosh—
Z Z Z Z Z Z Z

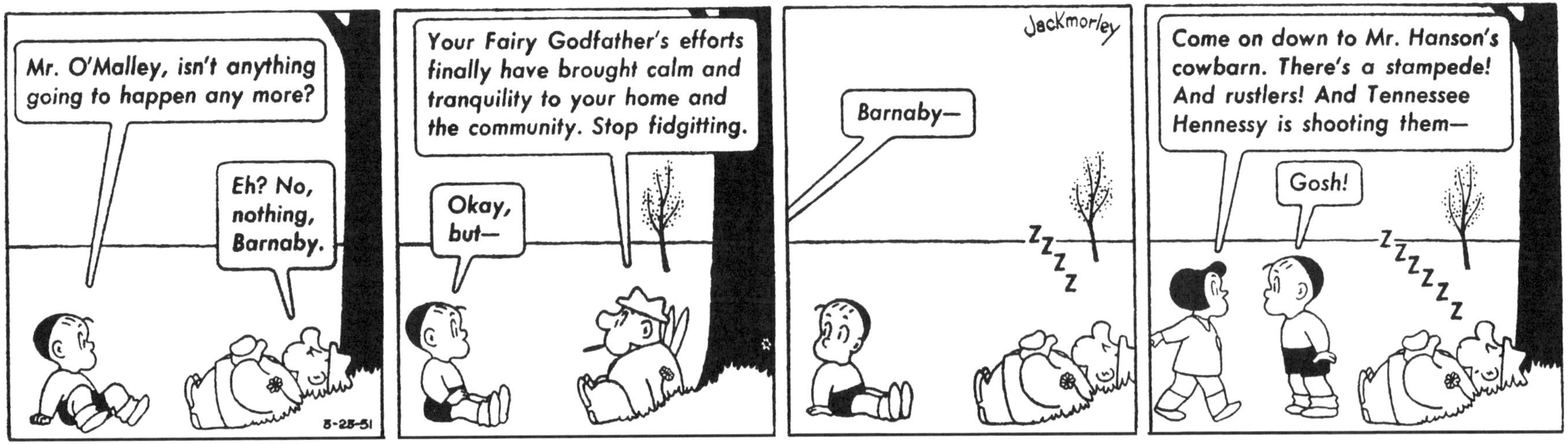
Mr. O'Malley, isn't anything going to happen any more?
Eh? No, nothing, Barnaby.
3-23-51
Your Fairy Godfather's efforts finally have brought calm and tranquility to your home and the community. Stop fidgitting.
Okay, but—
Jackmorley
Barnaby—
ZZZZ
Come on down to Mr. Hanson's cowbarn. There's a stampede! And rustlers! And Tennessee Hennessy is shooting them—
Gosh!
ZZZZZZ

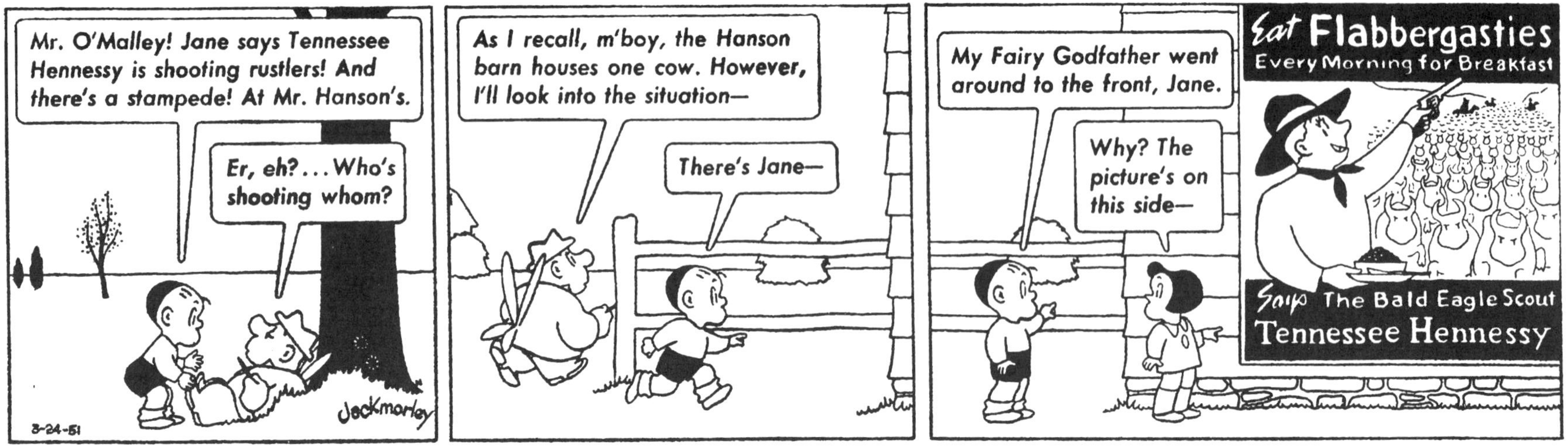
Mr. O'Malley! Jane says Tennessee Hennessy is shooting rustlers! And there's a stampede! At Mr. Hanson's.
Er, eh?... Who's shooting whom?
3-24-51
Jackmorley
As I recall, m'boy, the Hanson barn houses one cow. However, I'll look into the situation—
There's Jane—
My Fairy Godfather went around to the front, Jane.
Why? The picture's on this side—
Eat Flabbergasties
Every Morning for Breakfast
Says The Bald Eagle Scout
Tennessee Hennessy

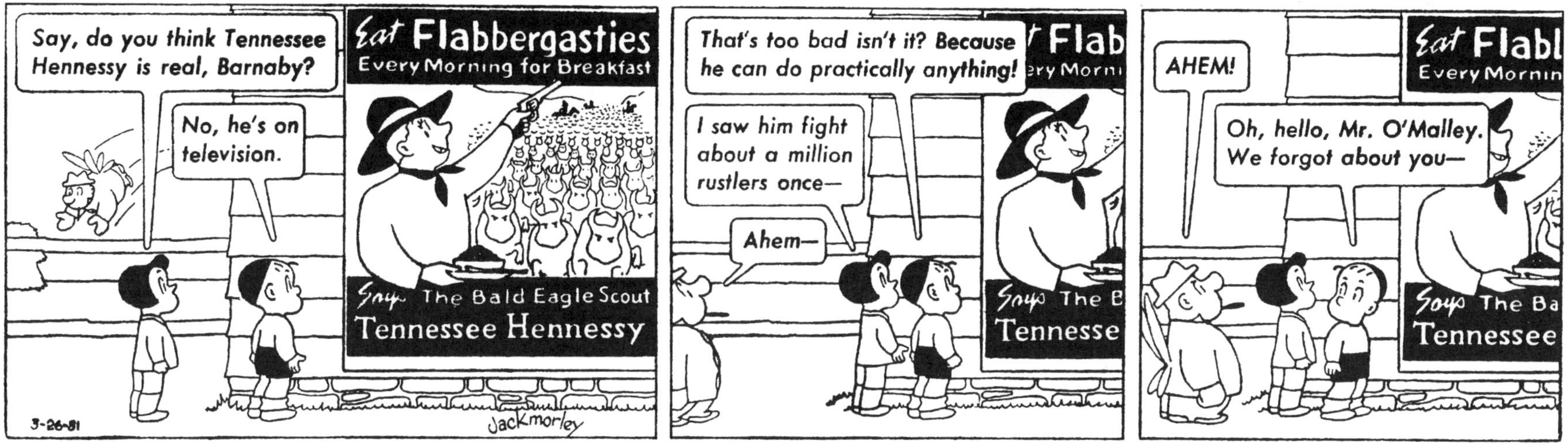
Say, do you think Tennessee Hennessy is real, Barnaby?
No, he's on television.
Eat Flabbergasties Every Morning for Breakfast
Says The Bald Eagle Scout Tennessee Hennessy
3-26-51
Jackmorley
That's too bad isn't it? Because he can do practically anything!
I saw him fight about a million rustlers once—
Ahem—
AHEM!
Oh, hello, Mr. O'Malley. We forgot about you—

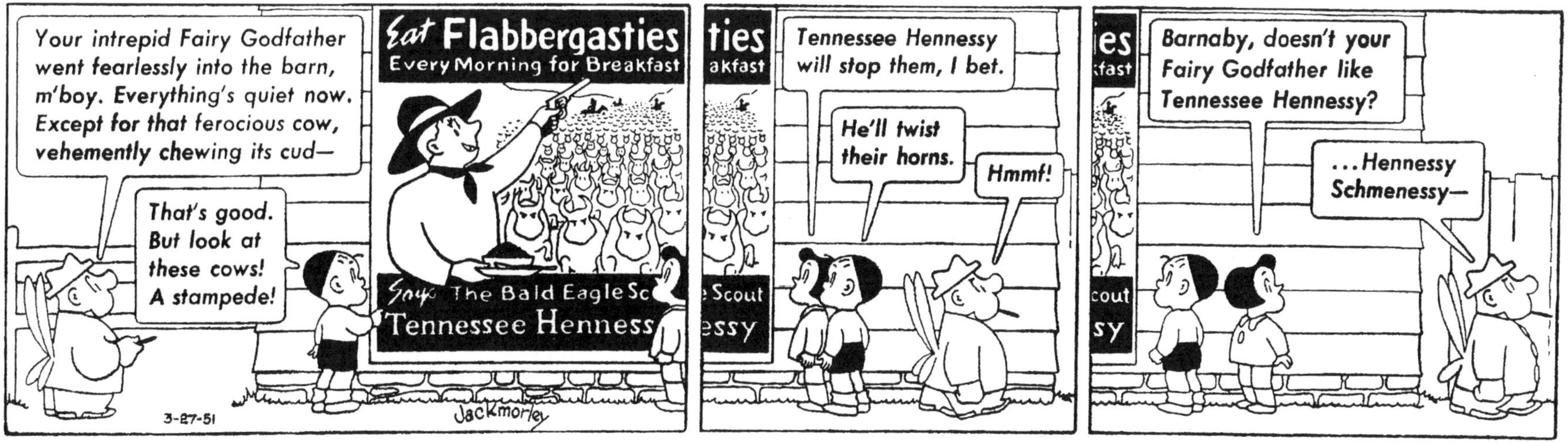
Your intrepid Fairy Godfather went fearlessly into the barn, m'boy. Everything's quiet now. Except for that ferocious cow, vehemently chewing its cud—
That's good. But look at these cows! A stampede!
Eat Flabbergasties Every Morning for Breakfast
Says The Bald Eagle Scout Tennessee Hennessy
3-27-51
Jackmorley
Tennessee Hennessy will stop them, I bet.
He'll twist their horns.
Hmmf!
Barnaby, doesn't your Fairy Godfather like Tennessee Hennessy?
...Hennessy Schmenessy—

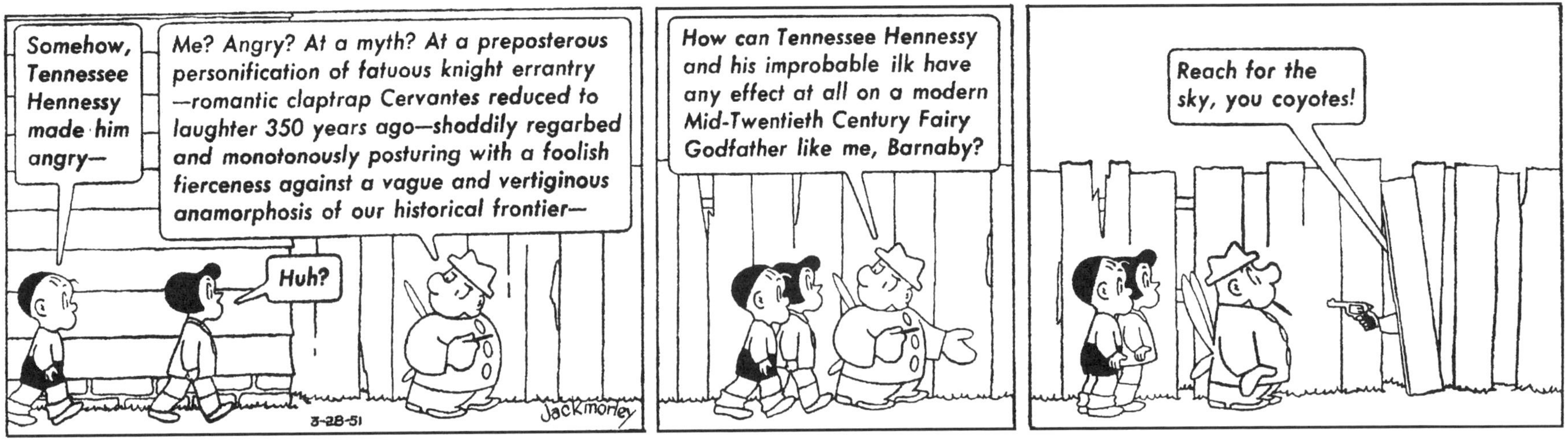
Somehow, Tennessee Hennessy made him angry—
Me? Angry? At a myth? At a preposterous personification of fatuous knight errantry —romantic claptrap Cervantes reduced to laughter 350 years ago—shoddily regarbed and monotonously posturing with a foolish fierceness against a vague and vertiginous anamorphosis of our historical frontier—
Huh?
3-28-51
Jackmorley
How can Tennessee Hennessy and his improbable ilk have any effect at all on a modern Mid-Twentieth Century Fairy Godfather like me, Barnaby?
Reach for the sky, you coyotes!

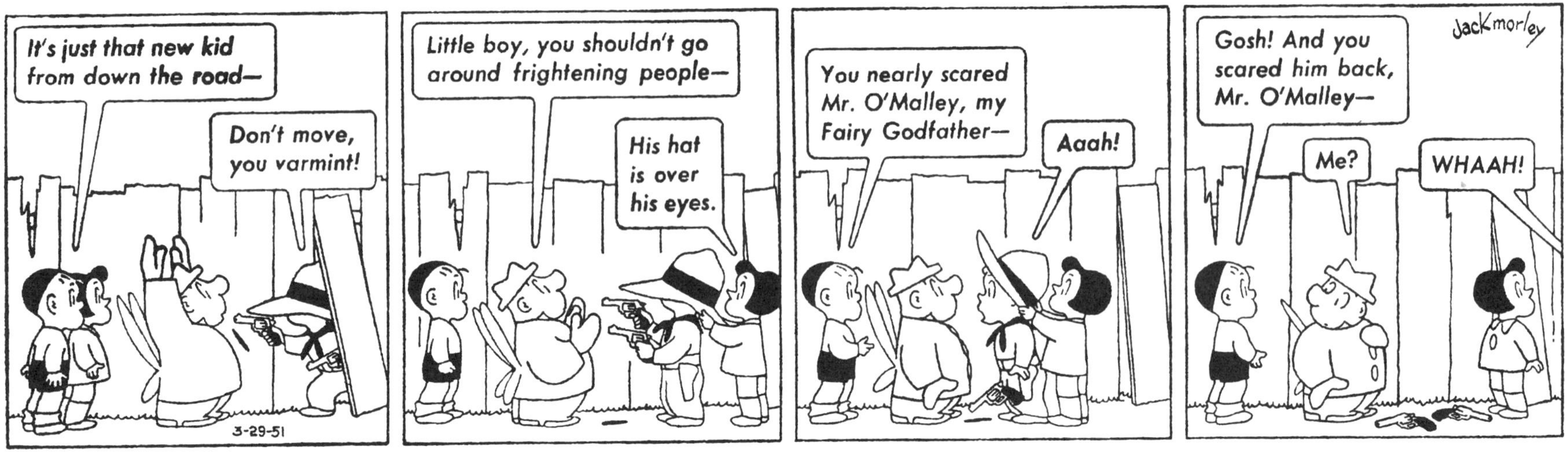
It's just that new kid from down the road—
Don't move, you varmint!
3-29-51
Little boy, you shouldn't go around frightening people—
His hat is over his eyes.
You nearly scared Mr. O'Malley, my Fairy Godfather—
Aaah!
Jackmorley
Gosh! And you scared him back, Mr. O'Malley—
Me?
WHAAH!

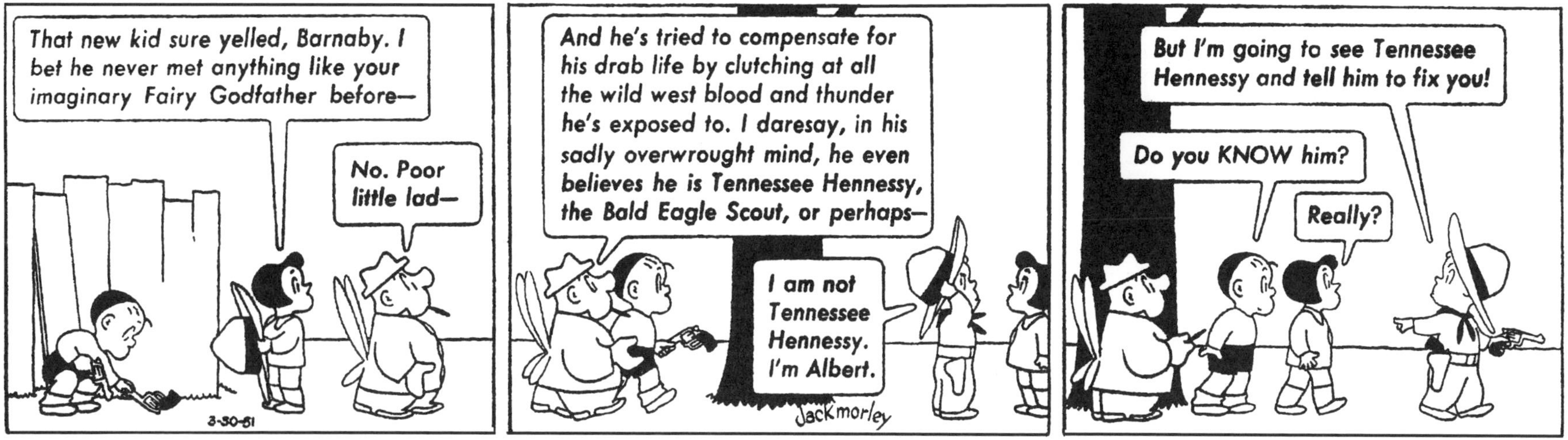
That new kid sure yelled, Barnaby. I bet he never met anything like your imaginary Fairy Godfather before—
No. Poor little lad—
3-30-51
And he's tried to compensate for his drab life by clutching at all the wild west blood and thunder he's exposed to. I daresay, in his sadly overwrought mind, he even believes he is Tennessee Hennessy, the Bald Eagle Scout, or perhaps—
I am not Tennessee Hennessy. I'm Albert.
Jackmorley
But I'm going to see Tennessee Hennessy and tell him to fix you!
Do you KNOW him?
Really?

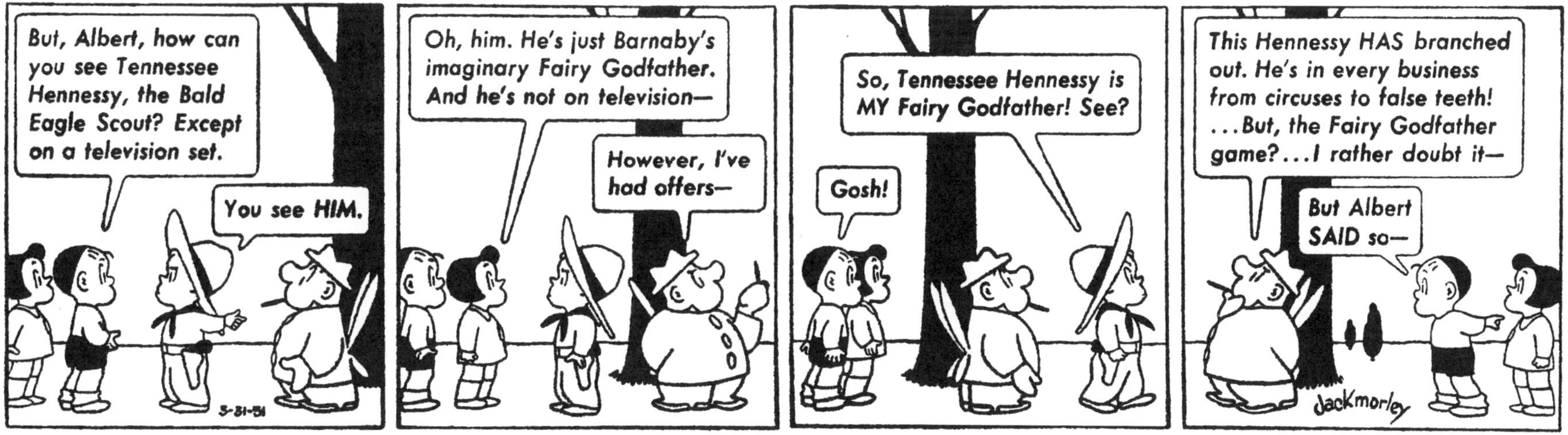
But, Albert, how can you see Tennessee Hennessy, the Bald Eagle Scout? Except on a television set.
You see HIM.
3-31-51
Oh, him. He's just Barnaby's imaginary Fairy Godfather. And he's not on television—
However, I've had offers—
So, Tennessee Hennessy is MY Fairy Godfather! See?
Gosh!
This Hennessy HAS branched out. He's in every business from circuses to false teeth! ...But, the Fairy Godfather game?...I rather doubt it—
But Albert SAID so—
Jackmorley

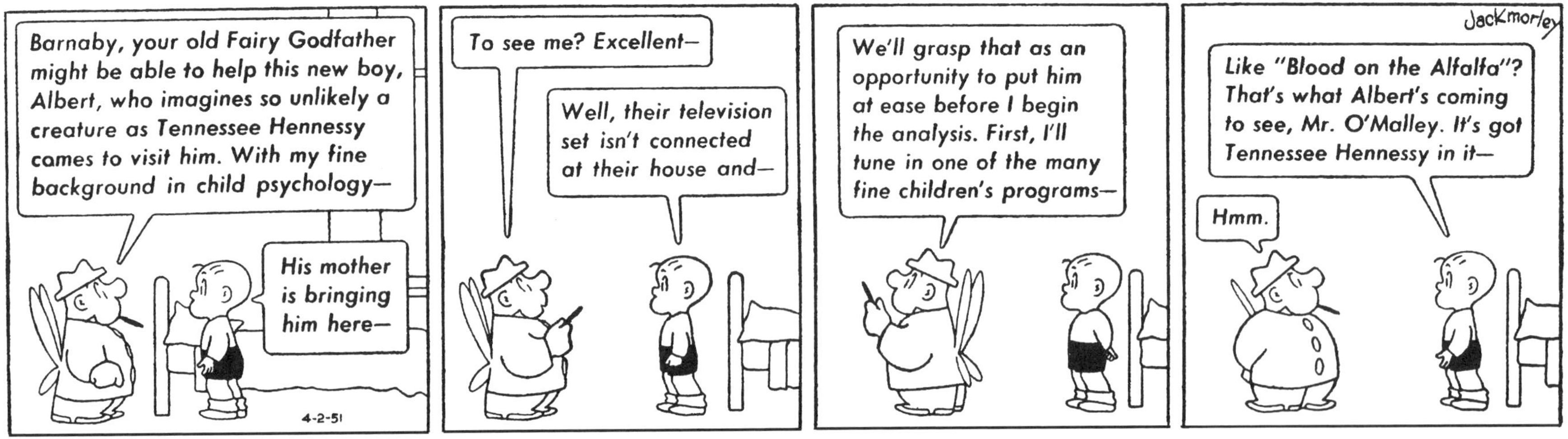
Barnaby, your old Fairy Godfather might be able to help this new boy, Albert, who imagines so unlikely a creature as Tennessee Hennessy comes to visit him. With my fine background in child psychology—
His mother is bringing him here—
4-2-51
To see me? Excellent—
Well, their television set isn't connected at their house and—
We'll grasp that as an opportunity to put him at ease before I begin the analysis. First, I'll tune in one of the many fine children's programs—
Jackmorley
Like "Blood on the Alfalfa"? That's what Albert's coming to see, Mr. O'Malley. It's got Tennessee Hennessy in it—
Hmm.

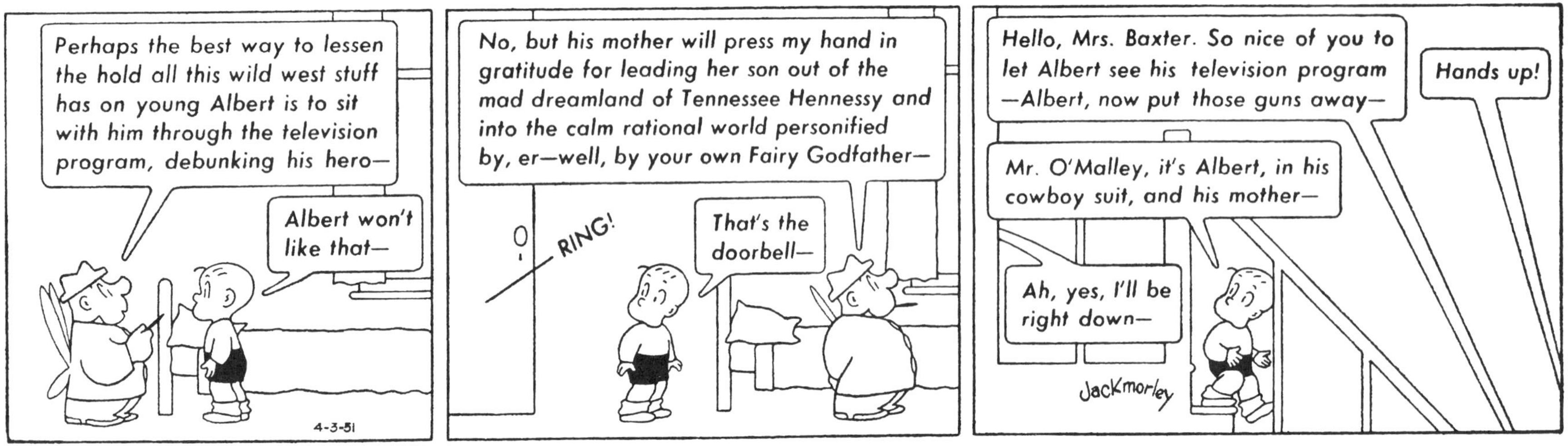
Perhaps the best way to lessen the hold all this wild west stuff has on young Albert is to sit with him through the television program, debunking his hero—
Albert won't like that—
4-3-51
No, but his mother will press my hand in gratitude for leading her son out of the mad dreamland of Tennessee Hennessy and into the calm rational world personified by, er—well, by your own Fairy Godfather—
RING!
That's the doorbell—
Hello, Mrs. Baxter. So nice of you to let Albert see his television program —Albert, now put those guns away—
Hands up!
Mr. O'Malley, it's Albert, in his cowboy suit, and his mother—
Ah, yes, I'll be right down—
Jackmorley

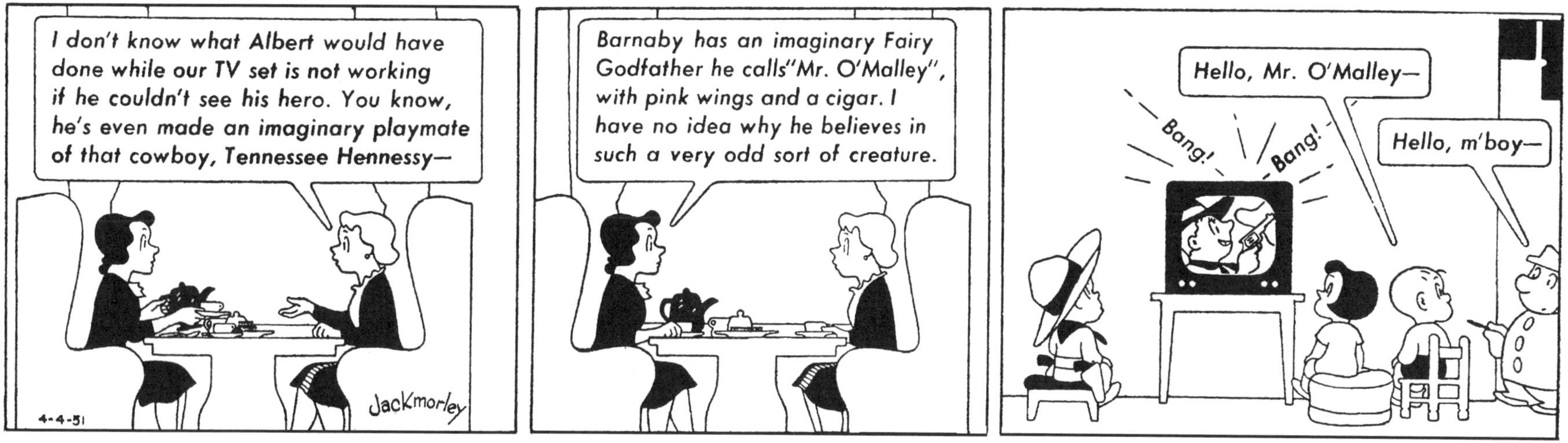
I don't know what Albert would have done while our TV set is not working if he couldn't see his hero. You know, he's even made an imaginary playmate of that cowboy, Tennessee Hennessy—
4-4-51
JackMorley
Barnaby has an imaginary Fairy Godfather he calls "Mr. O'Malley", with pink wings and a cigar. I have no idea why he believes in such a very odd sort of creature.
Hello, Mr. O'Malley—
Bang!
Bang!
Hello, m'boy—

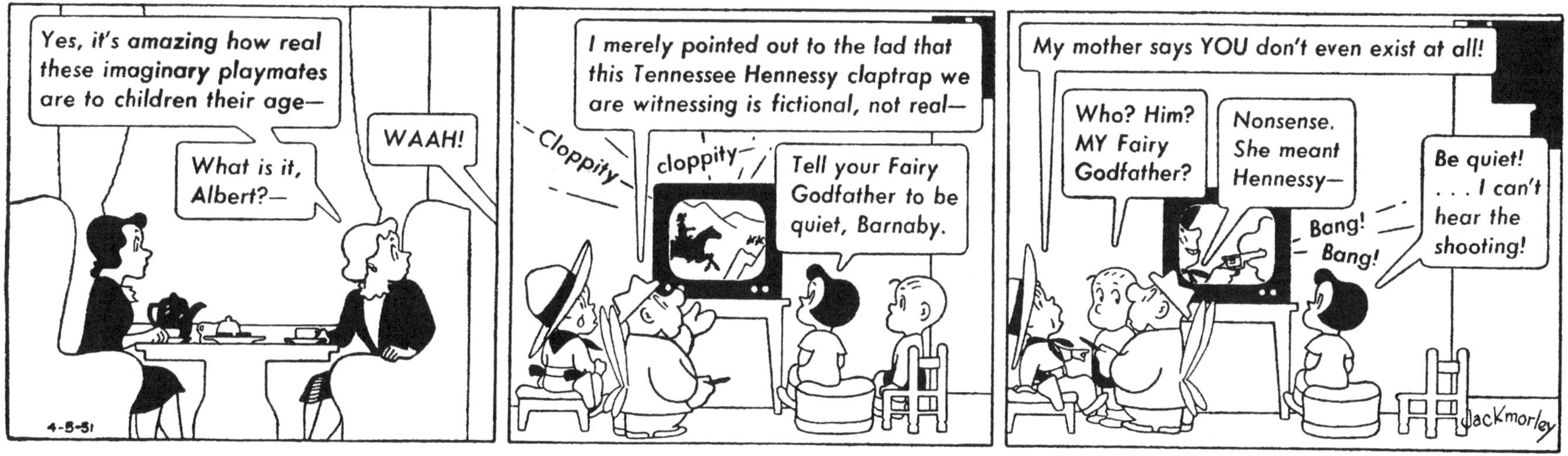
Yes, it's amazing how real these imaginary playmates are to children their age—
What is it, Albert?—
WAAH!
4-5-51
I merely pointed out to the lad that this Tennessee Hennessy claptrap we are witnessing is fictional, not real—
Cloppity
cloppity
Tell your Fairy Godfather to be quiet, Barnaby.
My mother says YOU don't even exist at all!
Who? Him? MY Fairy Godfather?
Nonsense. She meant Hennessy—
Bang!
Bang!
Be quiet! . . . I can't hear the shooting!
JackMorley

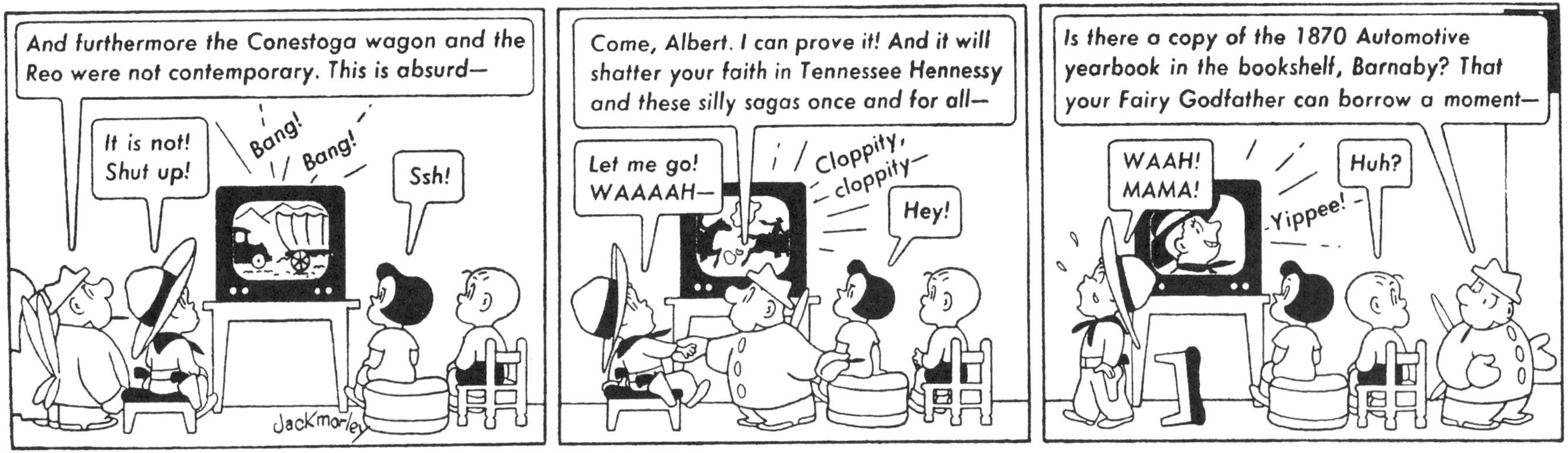
And furthermore the Conestoga wagon and the Reo were not contemporary. This is absurd—
It is not! Shut up!
Bang!
Bang!
Ssh!
JackMorley
Come, Albert. I can prove it! And it will shatter your faith in Tennessee Hennessy and these silly sagas once and for all—
Let me go! WAAAAH—
Cloppity, cloppity—
Hey!
Is there a copy of the 1870 Automotive yearbook in the bookshelf, Barnaby? That your Fairy Godfather can borrow a moment—
WAAH! MAMA!
Yippee!
Huh?

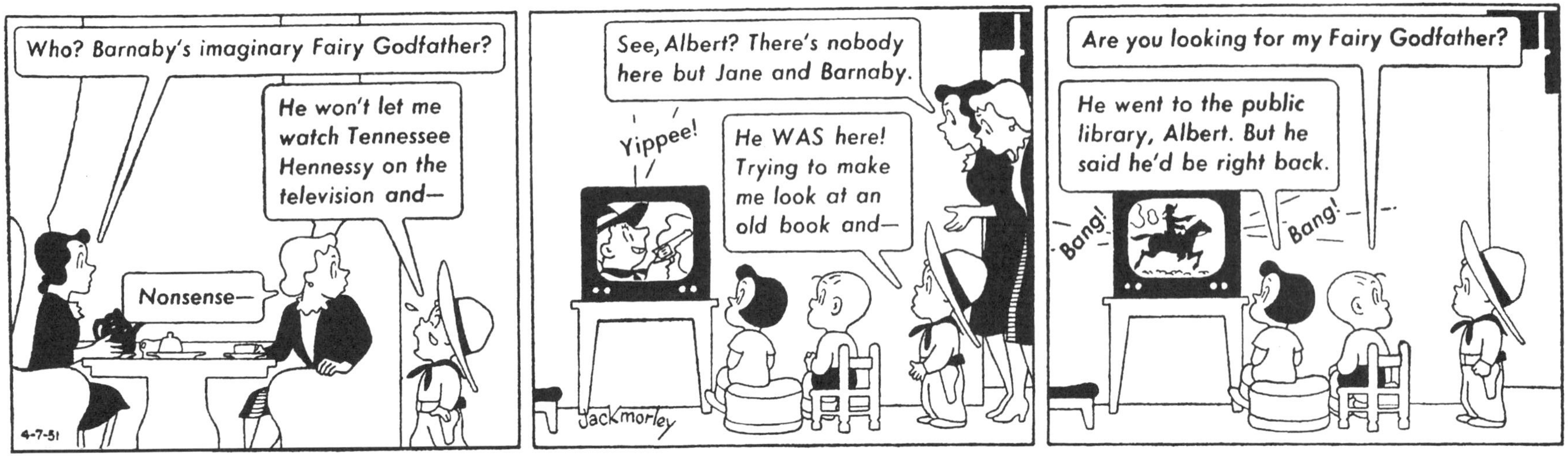
Who? Barnaby's imaginary Fairy Godfather?
He won't let me watch Tennessee Hennessy on the television and—
Nonsense—
4-7-51
See, Albert? There's nobody here but Jane and Barnaby.
Yippee!
He WAS here! Trying to make me look at an old book and—
JackMorley
Are you looking for my Fairy Godfather?
He went to the public library, Albert. But he said he'd be right back.
Bang!
Bang!

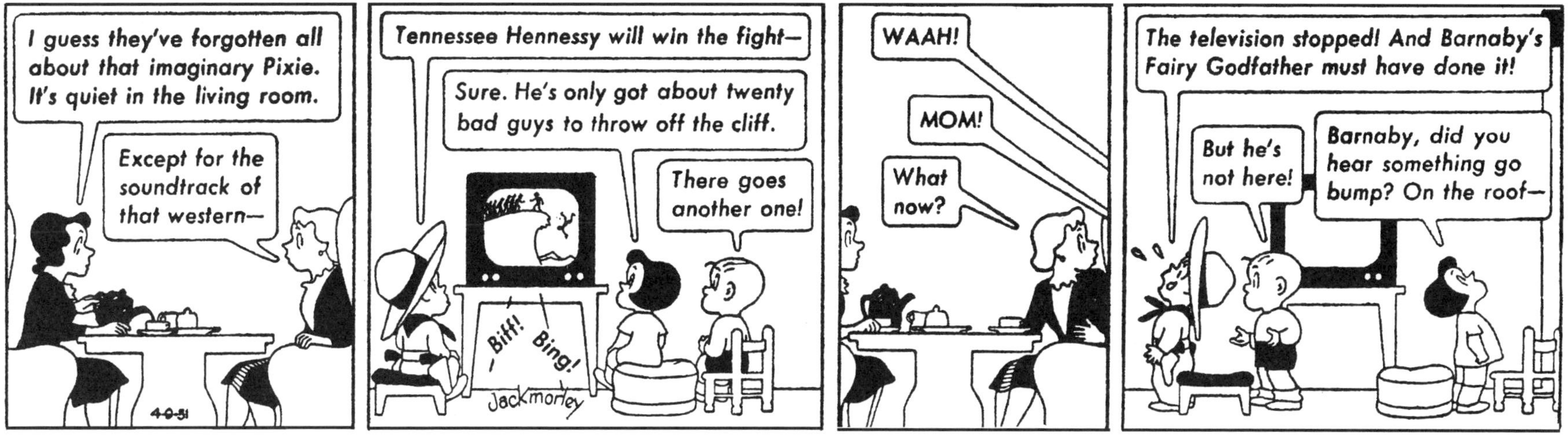
I guess they've forgotten all about that imaginary Pixie. It's quiet in the living room.
Except for the soundtrack of that western—
4-9-51
Tennessee Hennessy will win the fight—
Sure. He's only got about twenty bad guys to throw off the cliff.
There goes another one!
Biff!
Bing!
Jackmorley
WAAH!
MOM!
What now?
The television stopped! And Barnaby's Fairy Godfather must have done it!
But he's not here!
Barnaby, did you hear something go bump? On the roof—

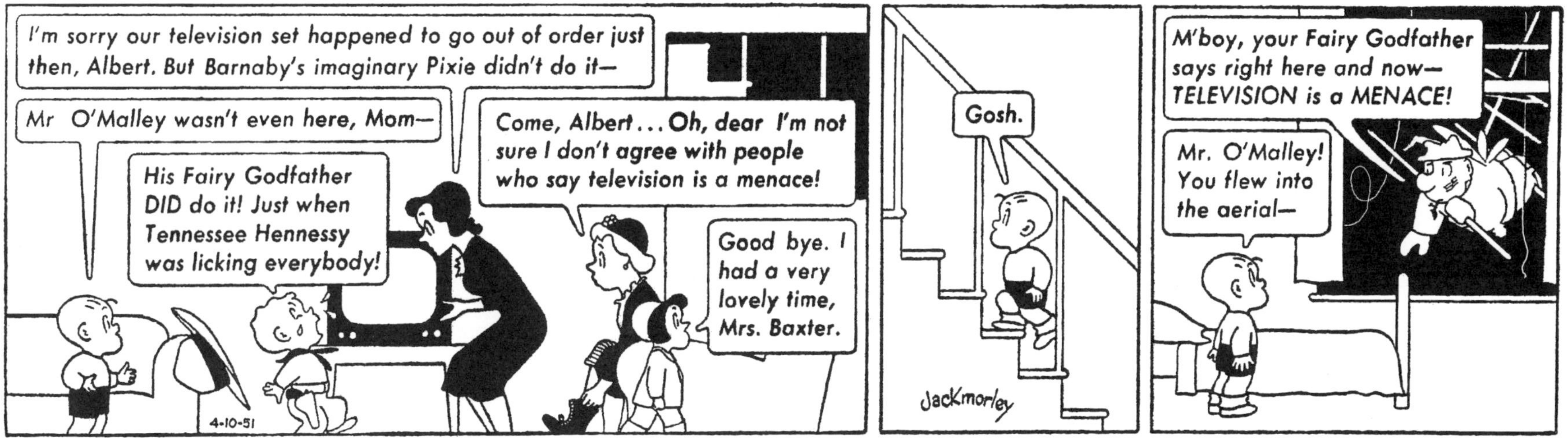
I'm sorry our television set happened to go out of order just then, Albert. But Barnaby's imaginary Pixie didn't do it—
Mr O'Malley wasn't even here, Mom—
His Fairy Godfather DID do it! Just when Tennessee Hennessy was licking everybody!
Come, Albert... Oh, dear I'm not sure I don't agree with people who say television is a menace!
Good bye. I had a very lovely time, Mrs. Baxter.
4-10-51
Gosh.
Jackmorley
M'boy, your Fairy Godfather says right here and now— TELEVISION is a MENACE!
Mr. O'Malley! You flew into the aerial—

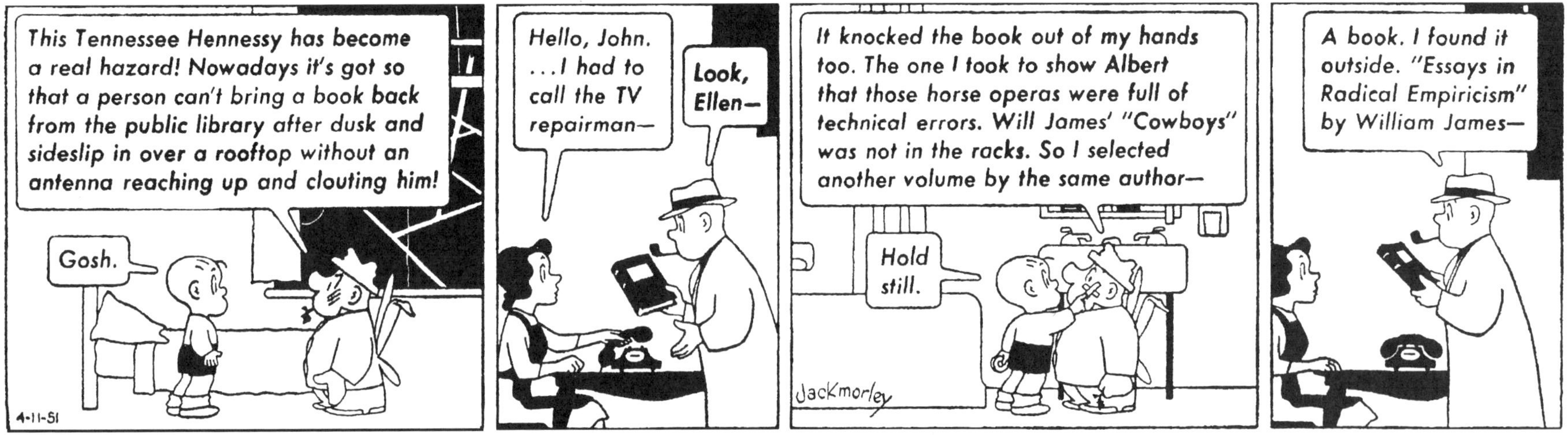
This Tennessee Hennessy has become a real hazard! Nowadays it's got so that a person can't bring a book back from the public library after dusk and sideslip in over a rooftop without an antenna reaching up and clouting him!
Gosh.
4-11-51
Hello, John. ...I had to call the TV repairman—
Look, Ellen—
It knocked the book out of my hands too. The one I took to show Albert that those horse operas were full of technical errors. Will James' "Cowboys" was not in the racks. So I selected another volume by the same author—
Hold still.
Jackmorley
A book. I found it outside. "Essays in Radical Empiricism" by William James—

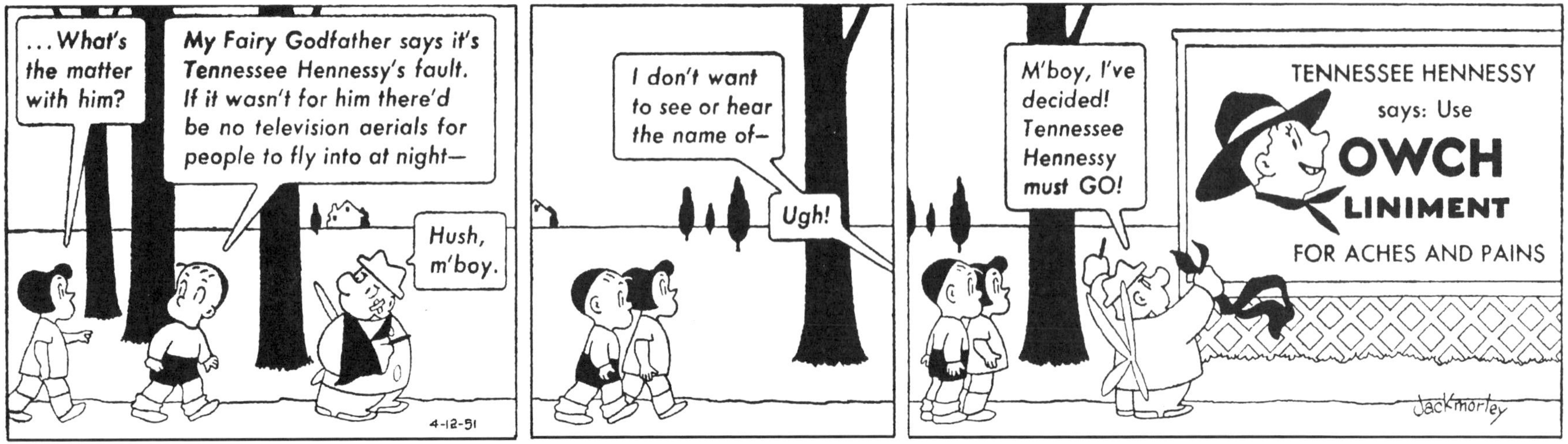
...What's the matter with him?
My Fairy Godfather says it's Tennessee Hennessy's fault. If it wasn't for him there'd be no television aerials for people to fly into at night—
Hush, m'boy.
4-12-51
I don't want to see or hear the name of—
Ugh!
M'boy, I've decided! Tennessee Hennessy must GO!
TENNESSEE HENNESSY
says: Use
OWCH
LINIMENT
FOR ACHES AND PAINS
Jackmorley

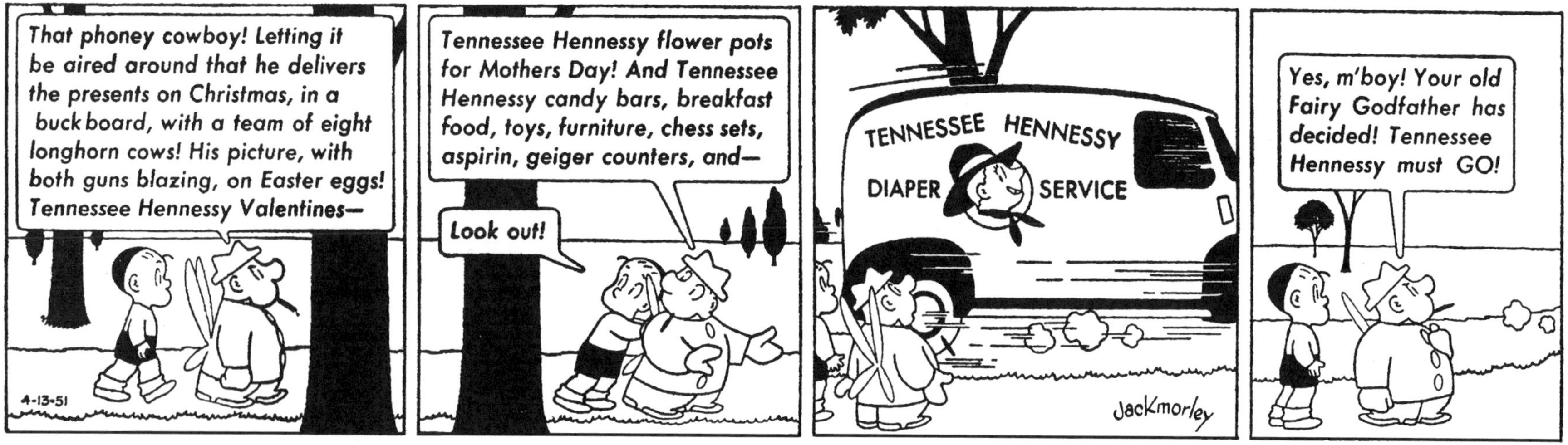
That phoney cowboy! Letting it be aired around that he delivers the presents on Christmas, in a buckboard, with a team of eight longhorn cows! His picture, with both guns blazing, on Easter eggs! Tennessee Hennessy Valentines—
4-13-51
Tennessee Hennessy flower pots for Mothers Day! And Tennessee Hennessy candy bars, breakfast food, toys, furniture, chess sets, aspirin, geiger counters, and—
Look out!
TENNESSEE HENNESSY
DIAPER SERVICE
Jackmorley
Yes, m'boy! Your old Fairy Godfather has decided! Tennessee Hennessy must GO!

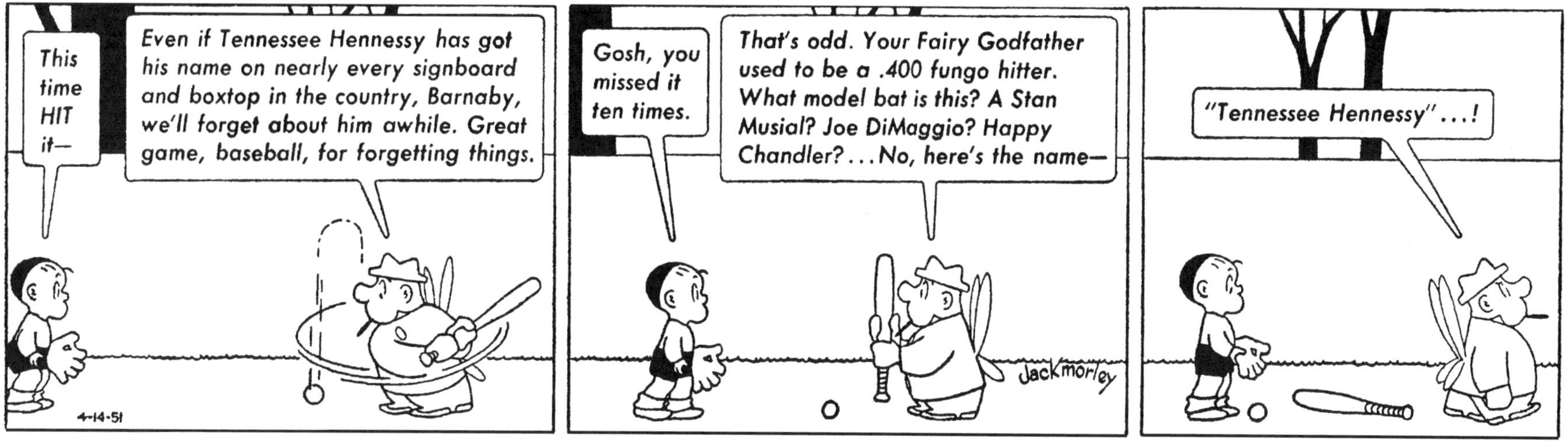
This time HIT it—
Even if Tennessee Hennessy has got his name on nearly every signboard and boxtop in the country, Barnaby, we'll forget about him awhile. Great game, baseball, for forgetting things.
4-14-51
Gosh, you missed it ten times.
That's odd. Your Fairy Godfather used to be a .400 fungo hitter. What model bat is this? A Stan Musial? Joe DiMaggio? Happy Chandler? . . . No, here's the name—
Jackmorley
"Tennessee Hennessy" . . . !

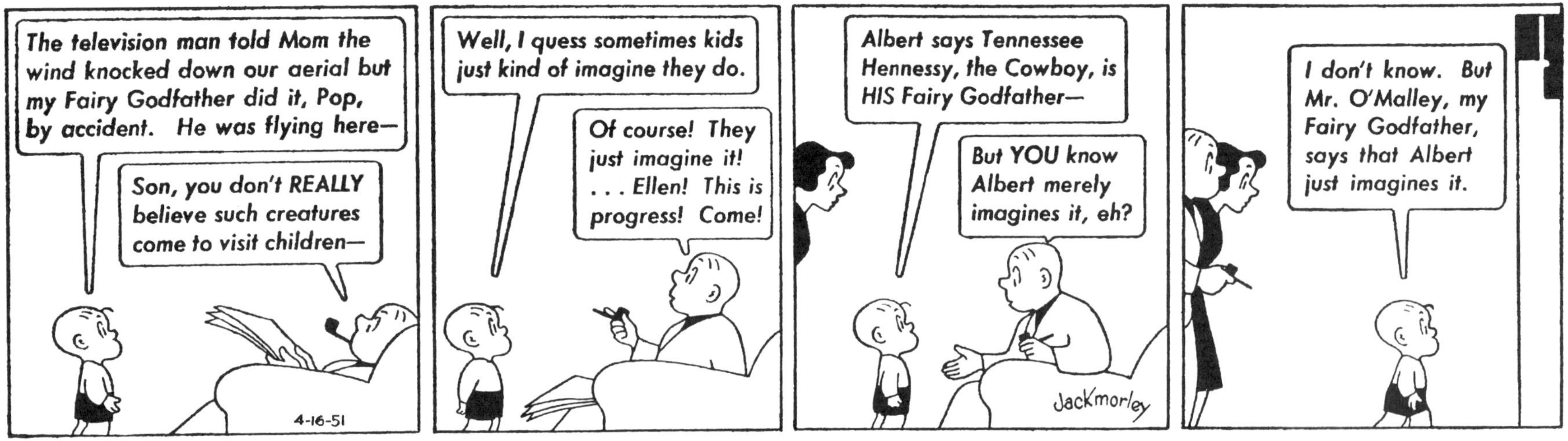
The television man told Mom the wind knocked down our aerial but my Fairy Godfather did it, Pop, by accident. He was flying here—
Son, you don't REALLY believe such creatures come to visit children—
4-16-51
Well, I guess sometimes kids just kind of imagine they do.
Of course! They just imagine it! . . . Ellen! This is progress! Come!
Albert says Tennessee Hennessy, the Cowboy, is HIS Fairy Godfather—
But YOU know Albert merely imagines it, eh?
JackMorley
I don't know. But Mr. O'Malley, my Fairy Godfather, says that Albert just imagines it.

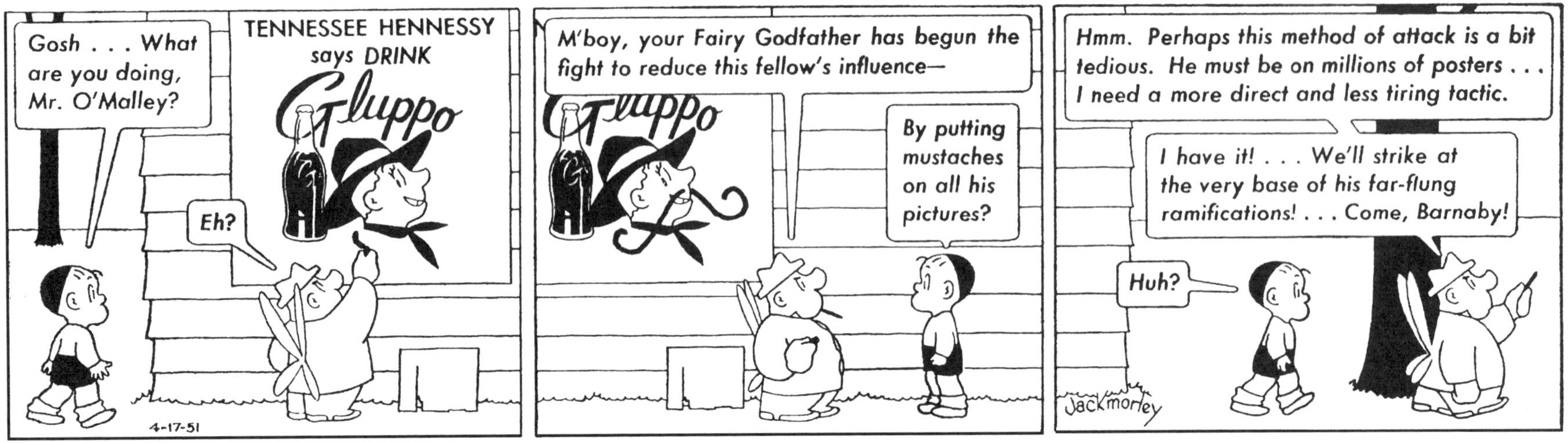
Gosh . . . What are you doing, Mr. O'Malley?
TENNESSEE HENNESSY says DRINK
Gluppo
Eh?
4-17-51
M'boy, your Fairy Godfather has begun the fight to reduce this fellow's influence—
Gluppo
By putting mustaches on all his pictures?
Hmm. Perhaps this method of attack is a bit tedious. He must be on millions of posters . . . I need a more direct and less tiring tactic.
I have it! . . . We'll strike at the very base of his far-flung ramifications! . . . Come, Barnaby!
Huh?
JackMorley

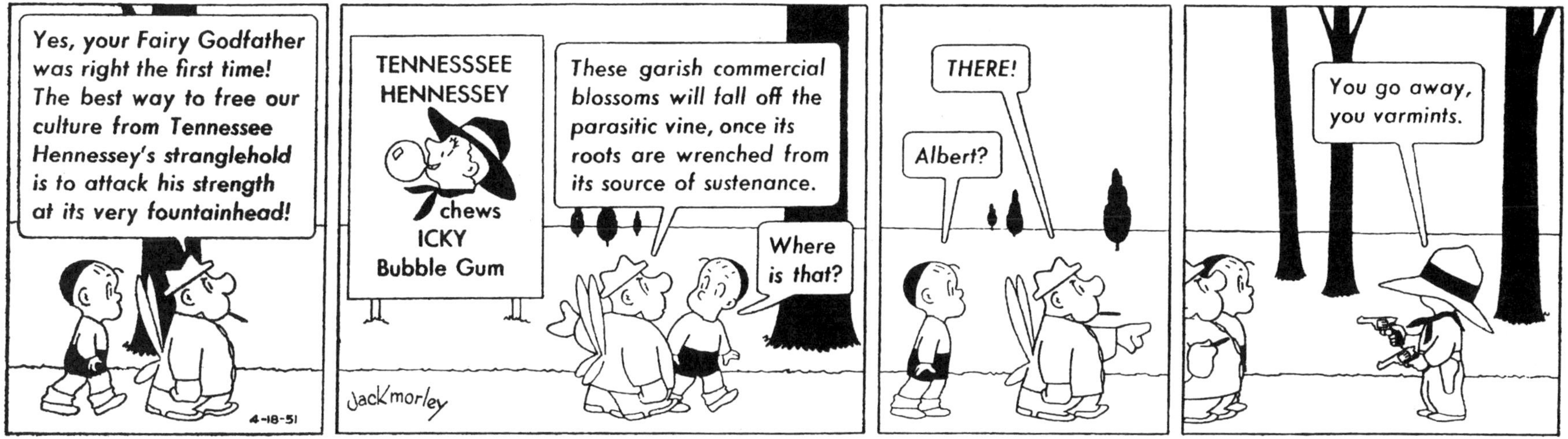
Yes, your Fairy Godfather was right the first time! The best way to free our culture from Tennessee Hennessey's stranglehold is to attack his strength at its very fountainhead!
4-18-51
TENNESSSEE HENNESSEY chews ICKY Bubble Gum
These garish commercial blossoms will fall off the parasitic vine, once its roots are wrenched from its source of sustenance.
Where is that?
JackMorley
THERE!
Albert?
You go away, you varmints.

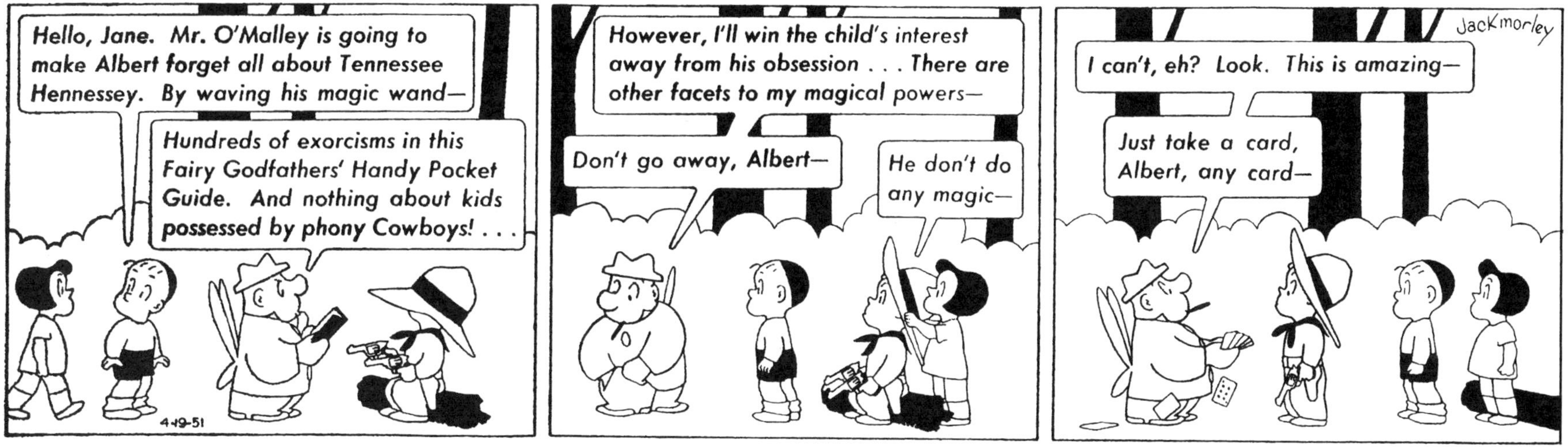
Hello, Jane. Mr. O'Malley is going to make Albert forget all about Tennessee Hennessey. By waving his magic wand—
Hundreds of exorcisms in this Fairy Godfathers' Handy Pocket Guide. And nothing about kids possessed by phony Cowboys! . . .
4-19-51
However, I'll win the child's interest away from his obsession . . . There are other facets to my magical powers—
Don't go away, Albert—
He don't do any magic—
JackMorley
I can't, eh? Look. This is amazing—
Just take a card, Albert, any card—

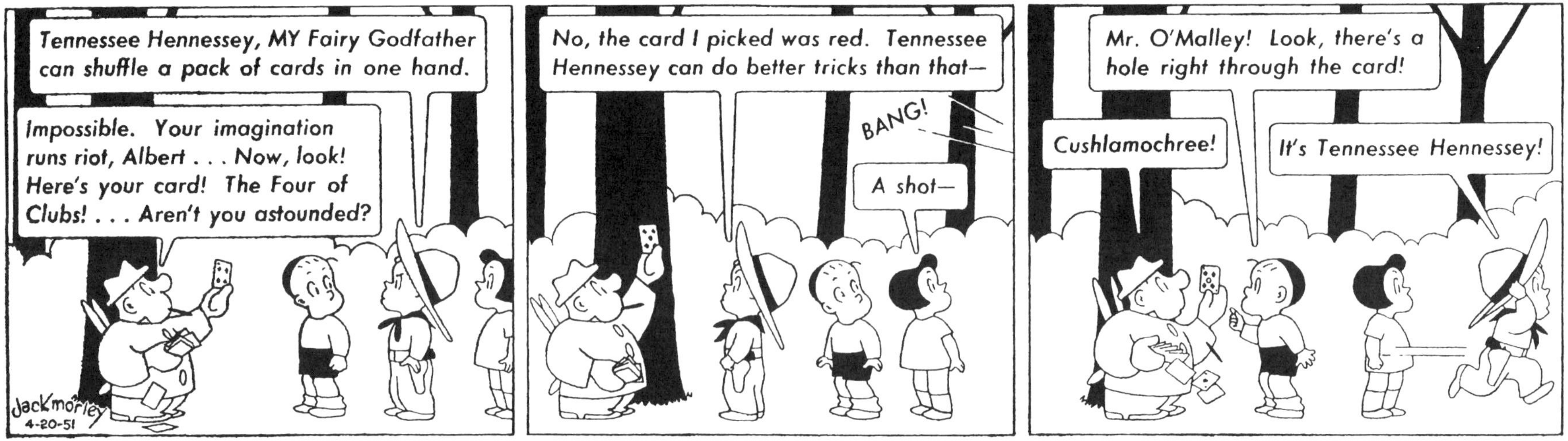
Tennessee Hennessey, MY Fairy Godfather can shuffle a pack of cards in one hand.
Impossible. Your imagination runs riot, Albert . . . Now, look! Here's your card! The Four of Clubs! . . . Aren't you astounded?
Jack morley
4-20-51
No, the card I picked was red. Tennessee Hennessey can do better tricks than that—
BANG!
A shot—
Mr. O'Malley! Look, there's a hole right through the card!
Cushlamochree!
It's Tennessee Hennessey!

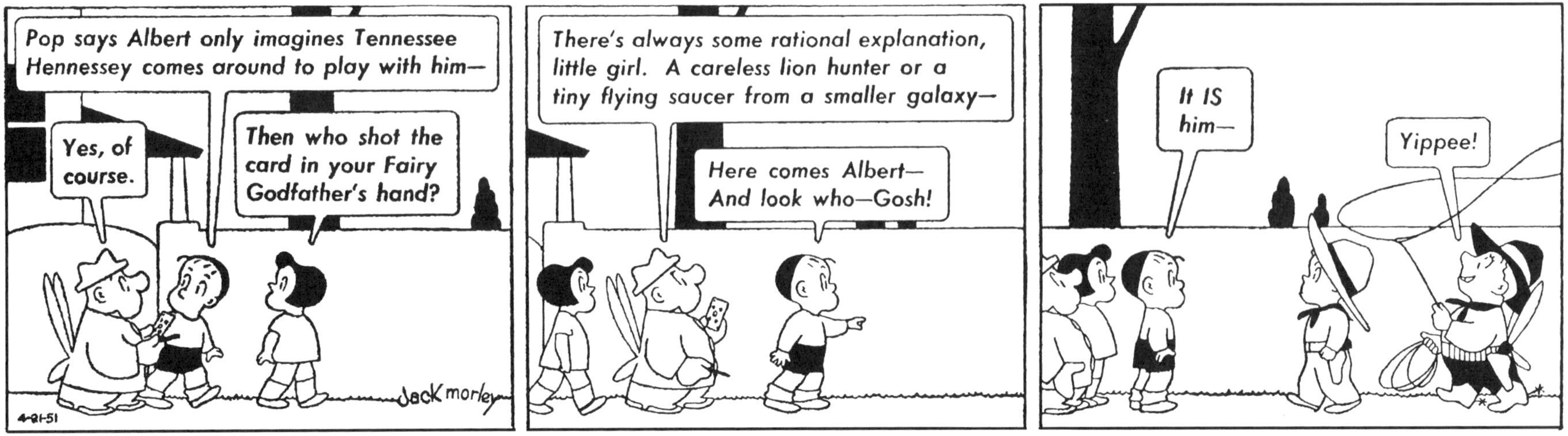
Pop says Albert only imagines Tennessee Hennessey comes around to play with him—
Yes, of course.
Then who shot the card in your Fairy Godfather's hand?
Jack morley
4-21-51
There's always some rational explanation, little girl. A careless lion hunter or a tiny flying saucer from a smaller galaxy—
Here comes Albert— And look who—Gosh!
It IS him—
Yippee!

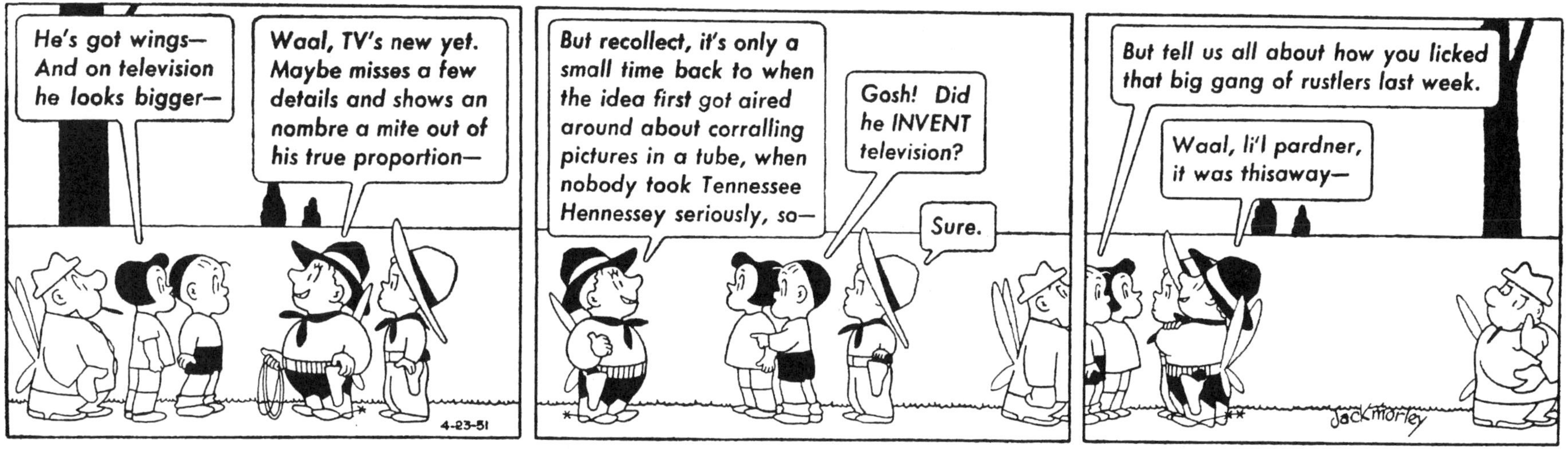
He's got wings—
And on television he looks bigger—
Waal, TV's new yet. Maybe misses a few details and shows an nombre a mite out of his true proportion—
4-23-51
But recollect, it's only a small time back to when the idea first got aired around about corralling pictures in a tube, when nobody took Tennessee Hennessey seriously, so—
Gosh! Did he INVENT television?
Sure.
But tell us all about how you licked that big gang of rustlers last week.
Waal, li'l pardner, it was thisaway—
JackMorley

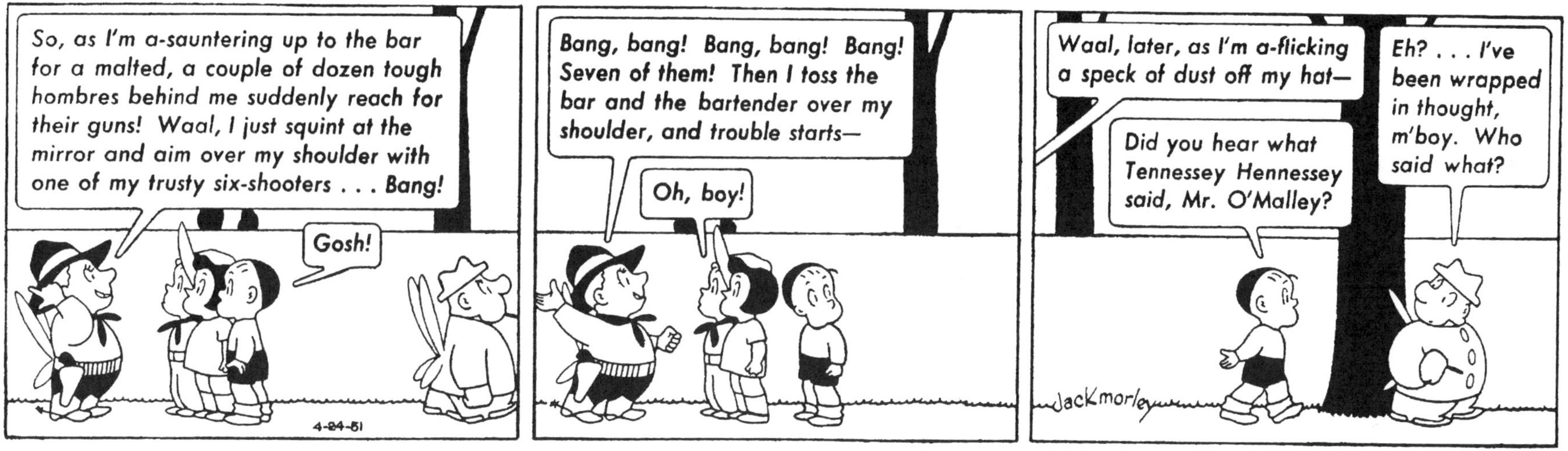
So, as I'm a-sauntering up to the bar for a malted, a couple of dozen tough hombres behind me suddenly reach for their guns! Waal, I just squint at the mirror and aim over my shoulder with one of my trusty six-shooters . . . Bang!
Gosh!
4-24-51
Bang, bang! Bang, bang! Bang! Seven of them! Then I toss the bar and the bartender over my shoulder, and trouble starts—
Oh, boy!
Waal, later, as I'm a-flicking a speck of dust off my hat—
Did you hear what Tennessey Hennessey said, Mr. O'Malley?
Eh? . . . I've been wrapped in thought, m'boy. Who said what?
JackMorley

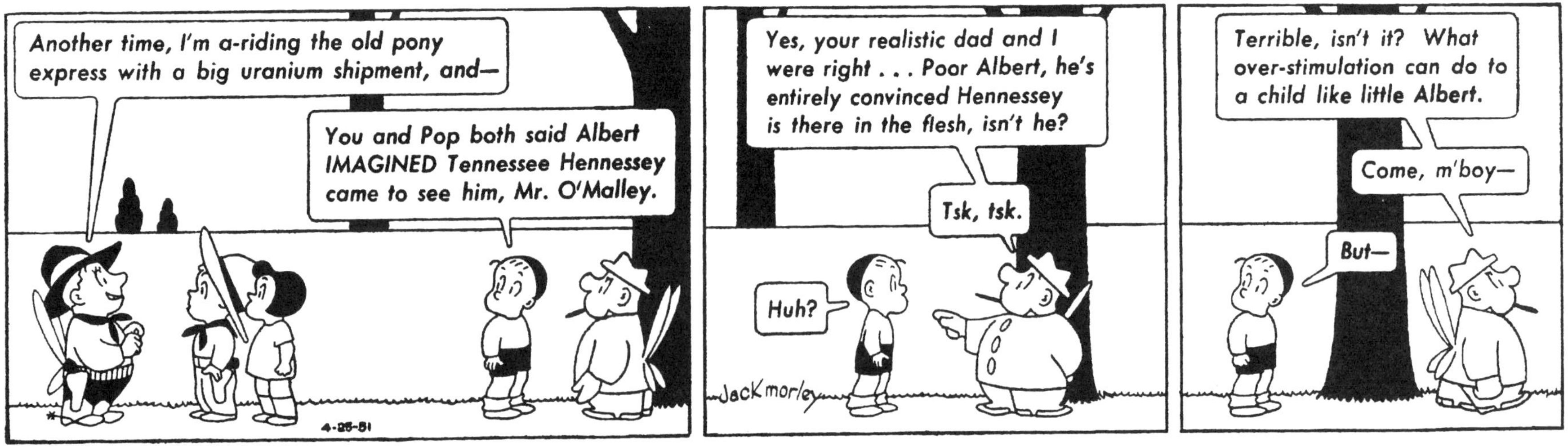
Another time, I'm a-riding the old pony express with a big uranium shipment, and—
You and Pop both said Albert IMAGINED Tennessee Hennessey came to see him, Mr. O'Malley.
4-25-51
Yes, your realistic dad and I were right . . . Poor Albert, he's entirely convinced Hennessey is there in the flesh, isn't he?
Tsk, tsk.
Huh?
Jack morley
Terrible, isn't it? What over-stimulation can do to a child like little Albert.
Come, m'boy—
But—

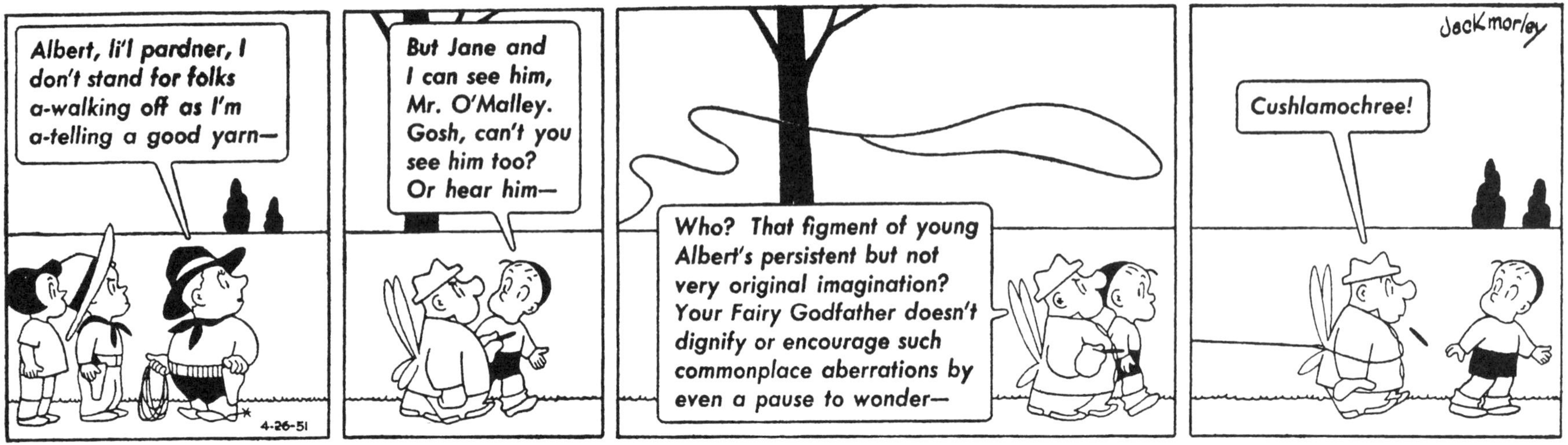
Albert, li'l pardner, I don't stand for folks a-walking off as I'm a-telling a good yarn—
4-26-51
But Jane and I can see him, Mr. O'Malley. Gosh, can't you see him too? Or hear him—
Who? That figment of young Albert's persistent but not very original imagination? Your Fairy Godfather doesn't dignify or encourage such commonplace aberrations by even a pause to wonder—
Jack morley
Cushlamochree!

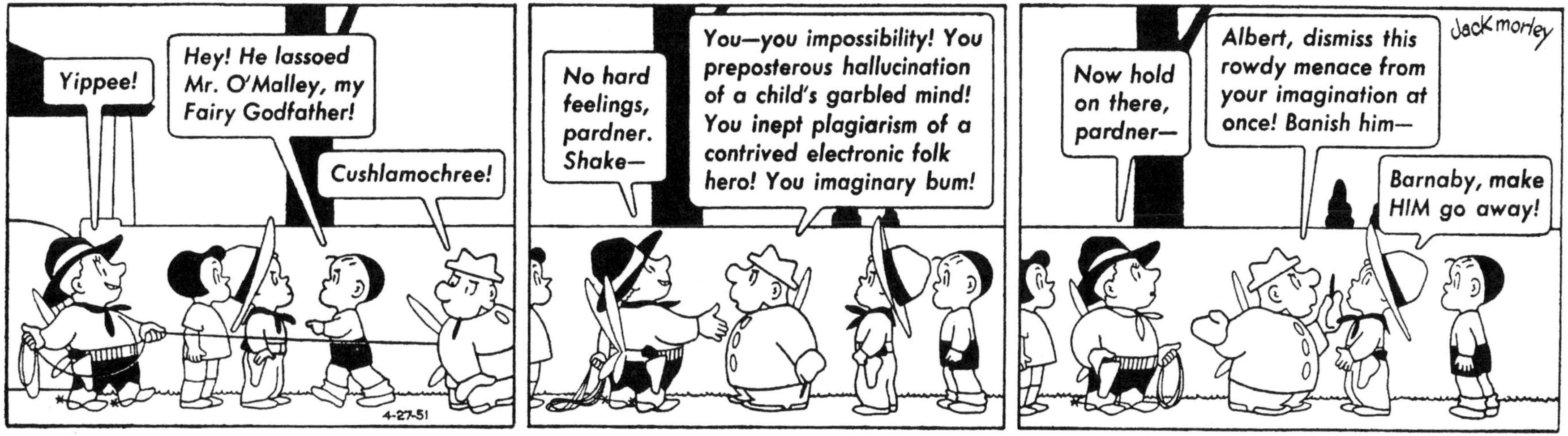

Yippee!
Hey! He lassoed Mr. O'Malley, my Fairy Godfather!
Cushlamochree!
4-27-51
No hard feelings, pardner. Shake—
You—you impossibility! You preposterous hallucination of a child's garbled mind! You inept plagiarism of a contrived electronic folk hero! You imaginary bum!
Jack morley
Now hold on there, pardner—
Albert, dismiss this rowdy menace from your imagination at once! Banish him—
Barnaby, make HIM go away!

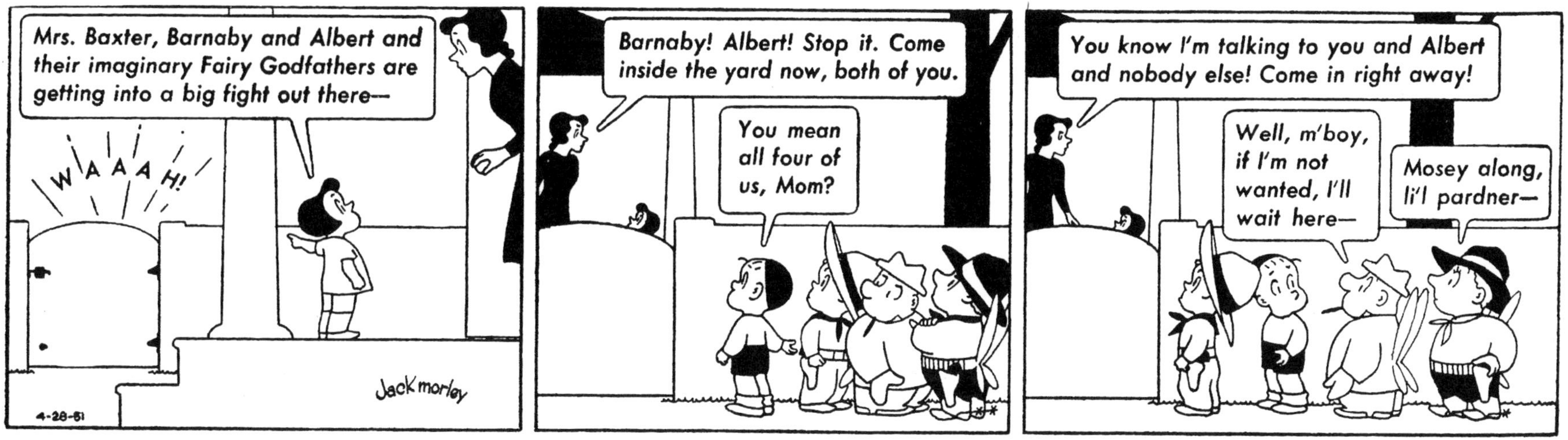

Mrs. Baxter, Barnaby and Albert and their imaginary Fairy Godfathers are getting into a big fight out there—
WAAAH!
Jack morley
4-28-51
Barnaby! Albert! Stop it. Come inside the yard now, both of you.
You mean all four of us, Mom?
You know I'm talking to you and Albert and nobody else! Come in right away!
Well, m'boy, if I'm not wanted, I'll wait here—
Mosey along, li'l pardner—

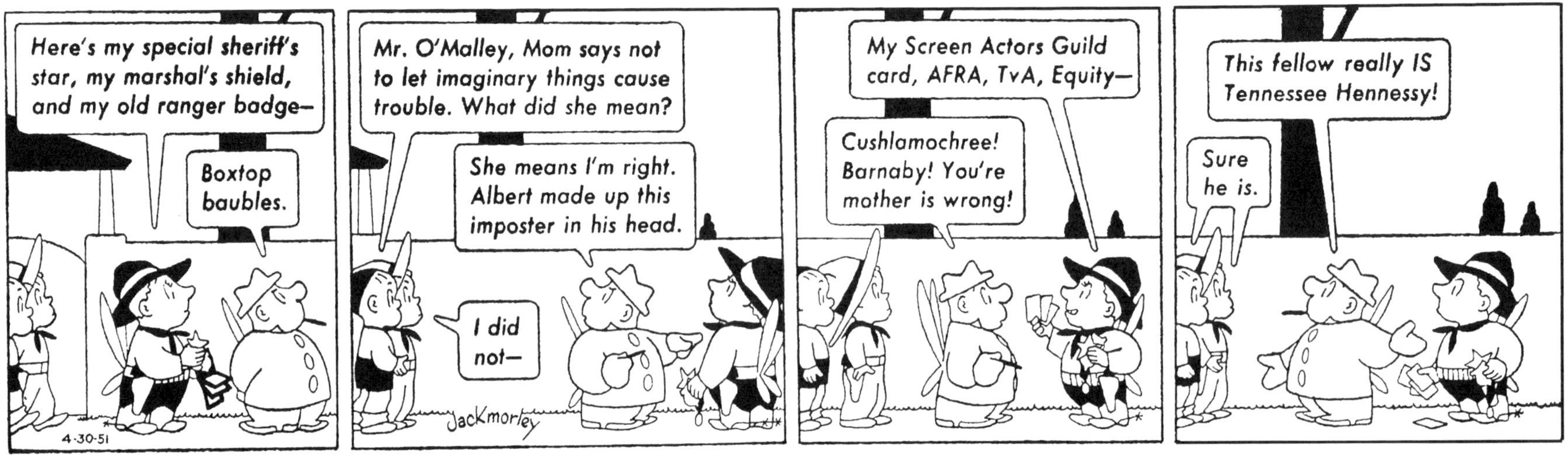
Here's my special sheriff's star, my marshal's shield, and my old ranger badge—
Boxtop baubles.
4-30-51
Mr. O'Malley, Mom says not to let imaginary things cause trouble. What did she mean?
She means I'm right. Albert made up this imposter in his head.
I did not—
JackMorley
My Screen Actors Guild card, AFRA, TvA, Equity—
Cushlamochree! Barnaby! You're mother is wrong!
This fellow really IS Tennessee Hennessy!
Sure he is.

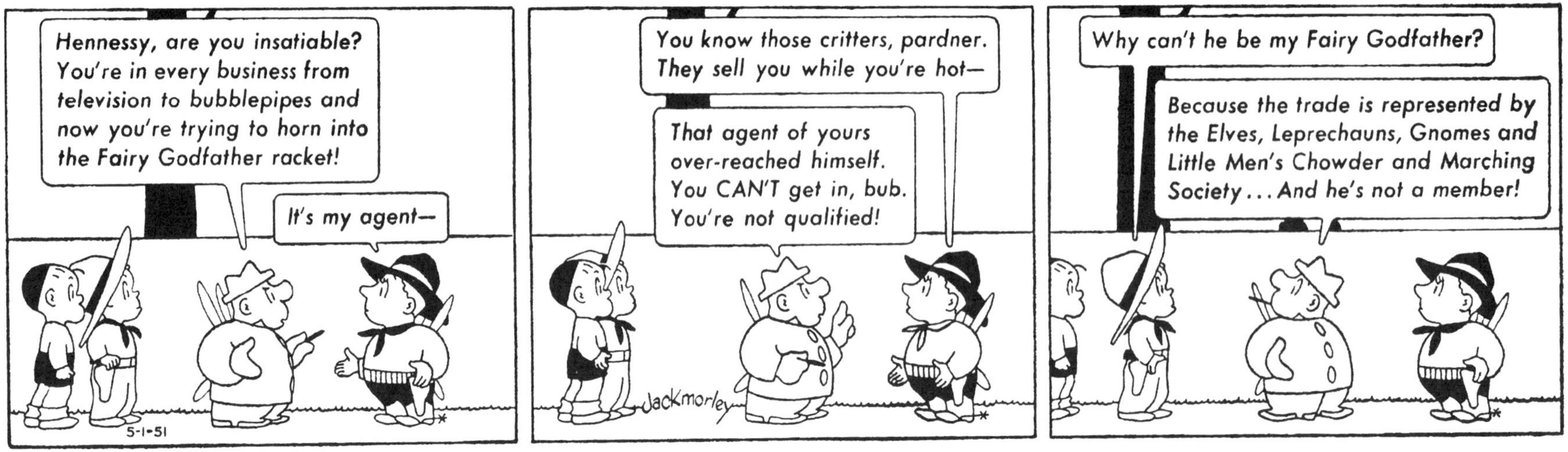
Hennessy, are you insatiable? You're in every business from television to bubblepipes and now you're trying to horn into the Fairy Godfather racket!
It's my agent—
5-1-51
You know those critters, pardner. They sell you while you're hot—
That agent of yours over-reached himself. You CAN'T get in, bub. You're not qualified!
JackMorley
Why can't he be my Fairy Godfather?
Because the trade is represented by the Elves, Leprechauns, Gnomes and Little Men's Chowder and Marching Society... And he's not a member!

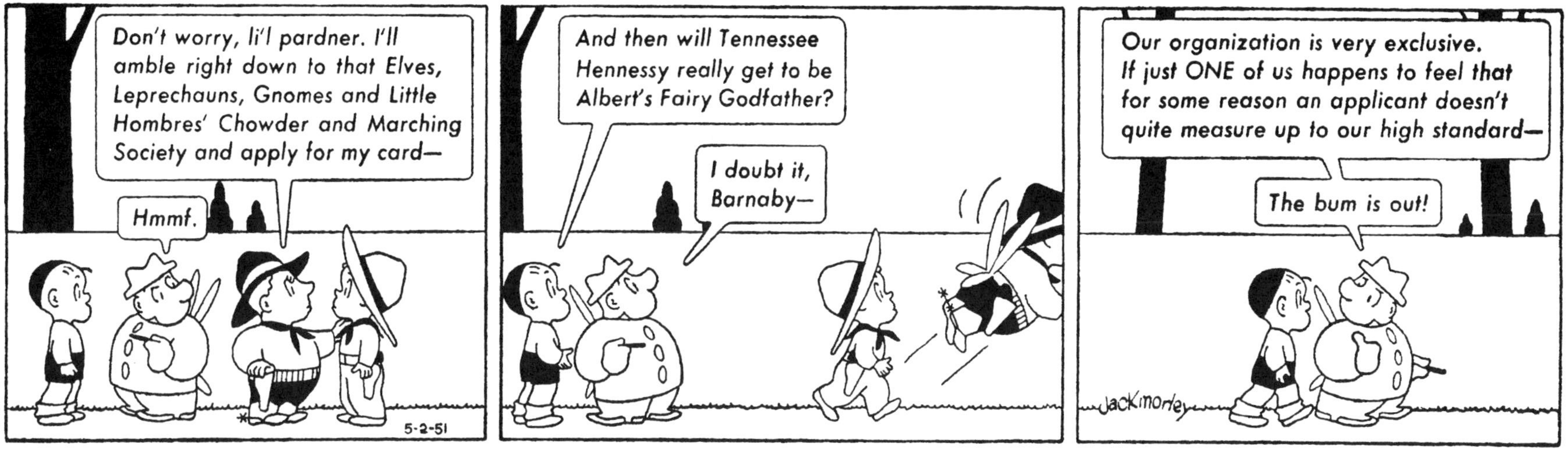
Don't worry, li'l pardner. I'll amble right down to that Elves, Leprechauns, Gnomes and Little Hombres' Chowder and Marching Society and apply for my card—
Hmmf.
5-2-51
And then will Tennessee Hennessy really get to be Albert's Fairy Godfather?
I doubt it, Barnaby—
Our organization is very exclusive. If just ONE of us happens to feel that for some reason an applicant doesn't quite measure up to our high standard—
The bum is out!
JACK MORLEY

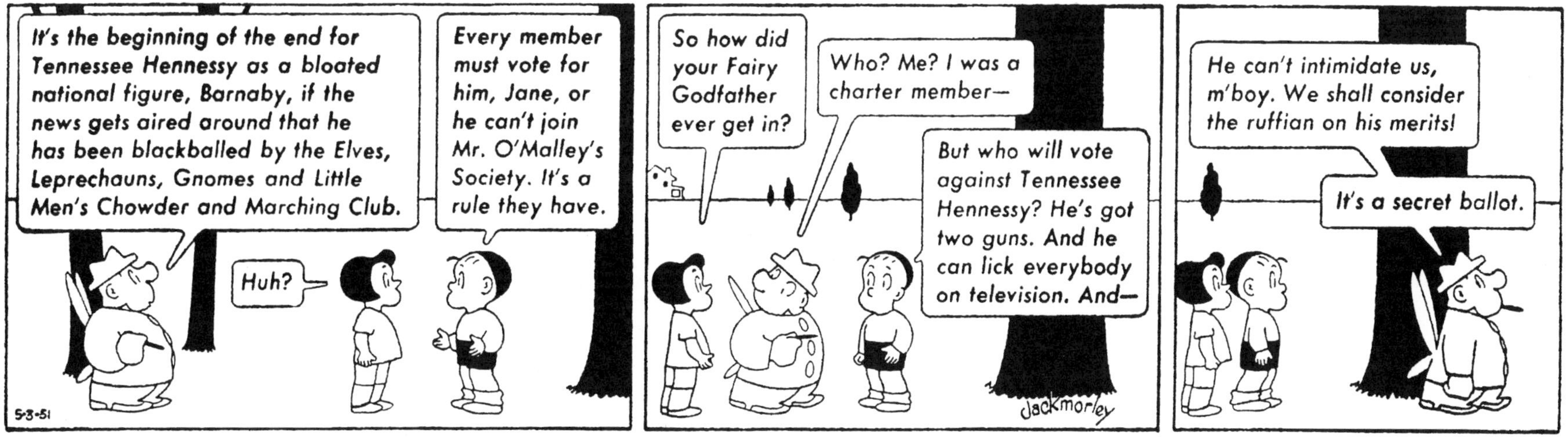
It's the beginning of the end for Tennessee Hennessy as a bloated national figure, Barnaby, if the news gets aired around that he has been blackballed by the Elves, Leprechauns, Gnomes and Little Men's Chowder and Marching Club.
Huh?
Every member must vote for him, Jane, or he can't join Mr. O'Malley's Society. It's a rule they have.
5-3-51
So how did your Fairy Godfather ever get in?
Who? Me? I was a charter member—
But who will vote against Tennessee Hennessy? He's got two guns. And he can lick everybody on television. And—
Jack Morley
He can't intimidate us, m'boy. We shall consider the ruffian on his merits!
It's a secret ballot.

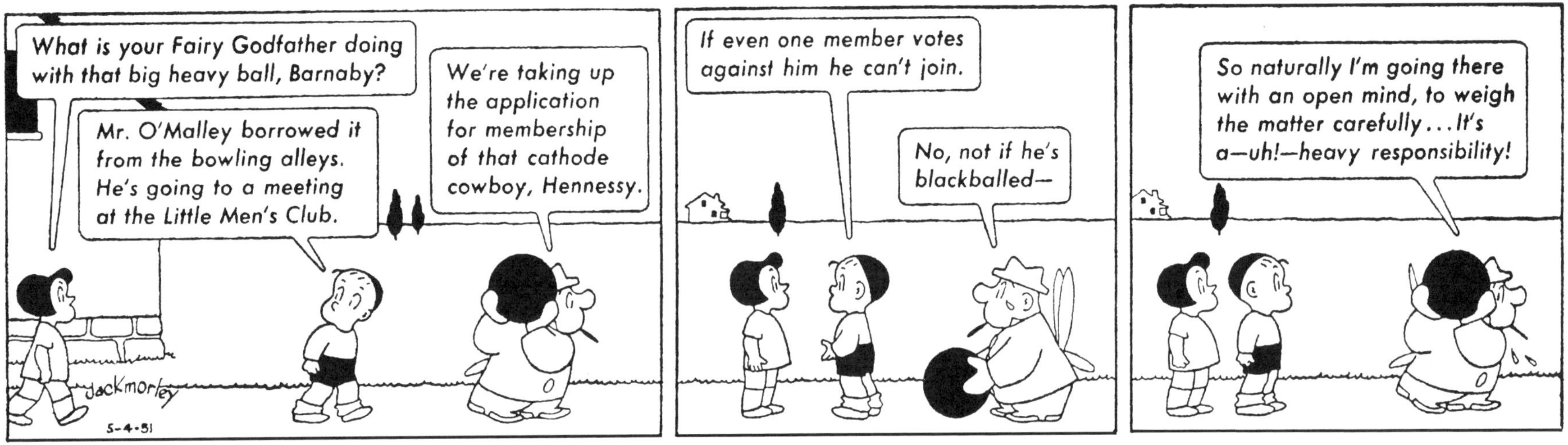
What is your Fairy Godfather doing with that big heavy ball, Barnaby?
Mr. O'Malley borrowed it from the bowling alleys. He's going to a meeting at the Little Men's Club.
We're taking up the application for membership of that cathode cowboy, Hennessy.
Jackmorley
5-4-51
If even one member votes against him he can't join.
No, not if he's blackballed—
So naturally I'm going there with an open mind, to weigh the matter carefully... It's a—uh!—heavy responsibility!

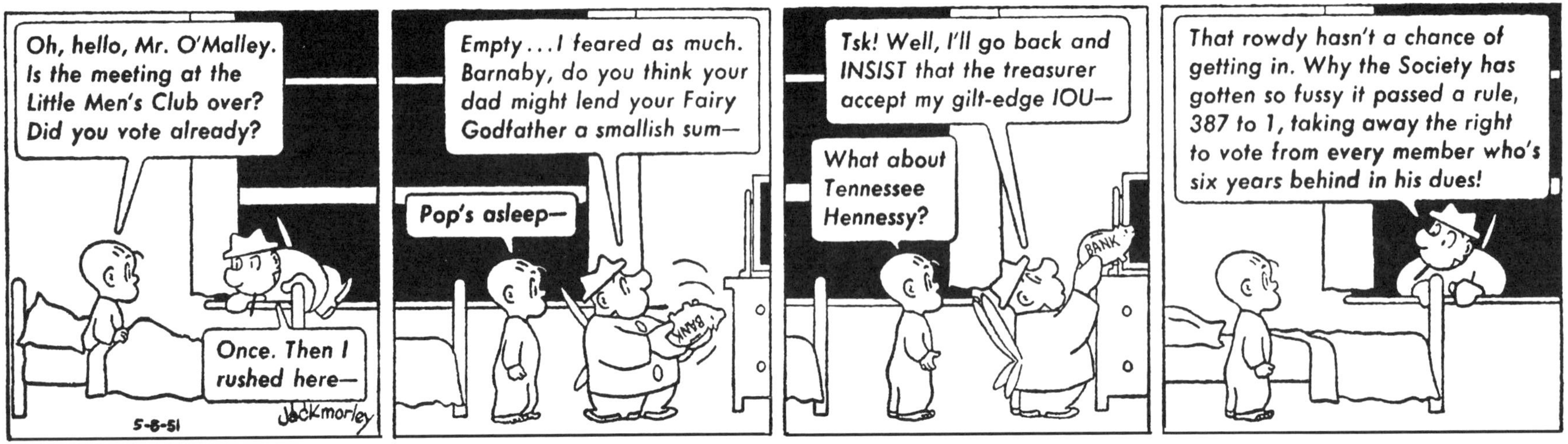
Oh, hello, Mr. O'Malley. Is the meeting at the Little Men's Club over? Did you vote already?
Once. Then I rushed here—
Jackmorley
Pop's asleep—
Empty... I feared as much. Barnaby, do you think your dad might lend your Fairy Godfather a smallish sum—
BANK
What about Tennessee Hennessy?
Tsk! Well, I'll go back and INSIST that the treasurer accept my gilt-edge IOU—
BANK
That rowdy hasn't a chance of getting in. Why the Society has gotten so fussy it passed a rule, 387 to 1, taking away the right to vote from every member who's six years behind in his dues!

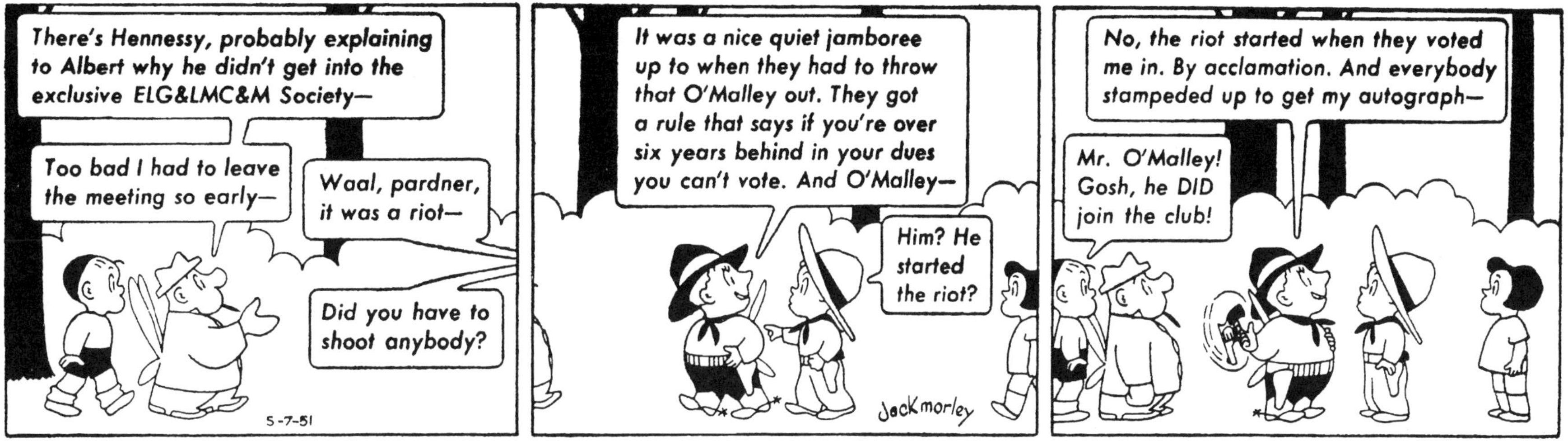
There's Hennessy, probably explaining to Albert why he didn't get into the exclusive ELG&LMC&M Society—
Too bad I had to leave the meeting so early—
Waal, pardner, it was a riot—
Did you have to shoot anybody?
5-7-51
It was a nice quiet jamboree up to when they had to throw that O'Malley out. They got a rule that says if you're over six years behind in your dues you can't vote. And O'Malley—
Him? He started the riot?
Jackmorley
No, the riot started when they voted me in. By acclamation. And everybody stampeded up to get my autograph—
Mr. O'Malley! Gosh, he DID join the club!

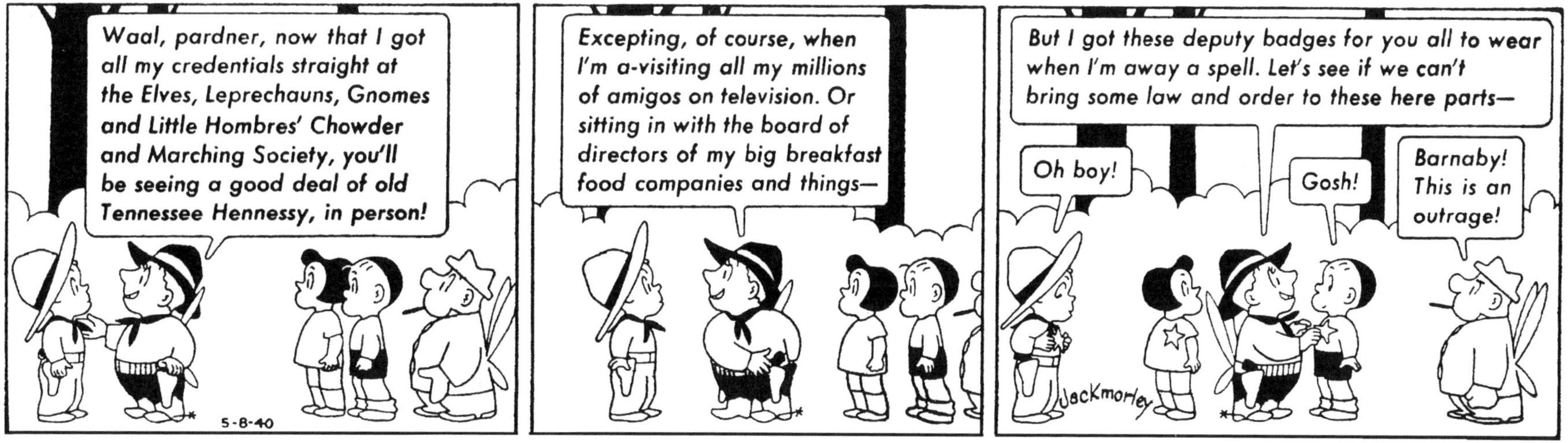
Waal, pardner, now that I got all my credentials straight at the Elves, Leprechauns, Gnomes and Little Hombres' Chowder and Marching Society, you'll be seeing a good deal of old Tennessee Hennessy, in person!
5-8-40
Excepting, of course, when I'm a-visiting all my millions of amigos on television. Or sitting in with the board of directors of my big breakfast food companies and things—
But I got these deputy badges for you all to wear when I'm away a spell. Let's see if we can't bring some law and order to these here parts—
Oh boy!
Gosh!
Barnaby! This is an outrage!
Jackmorley

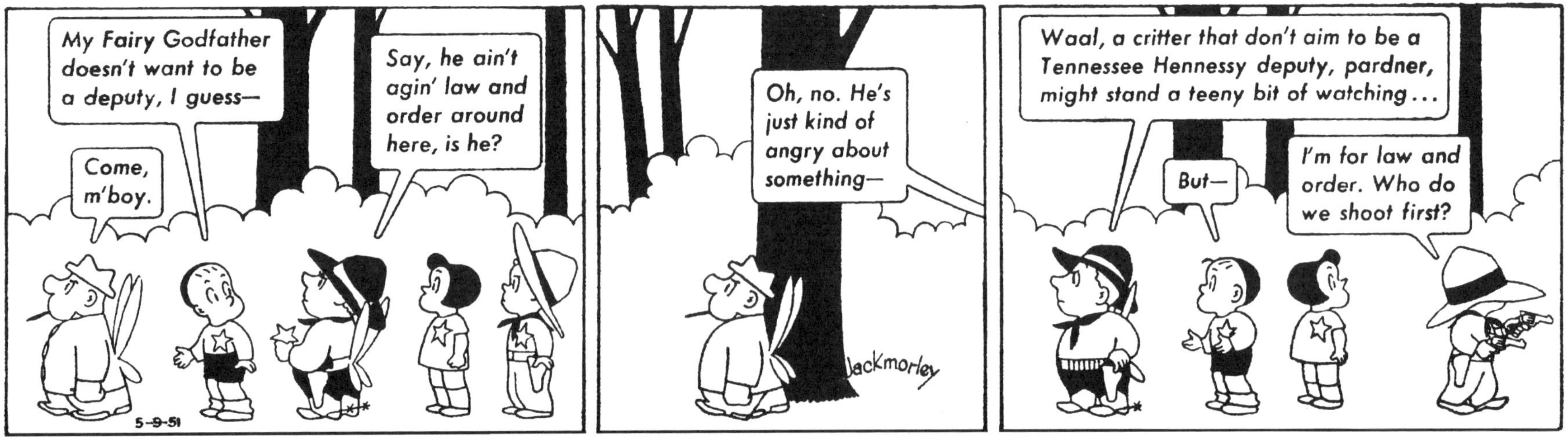
My Fairy Godfather doesn't want to be a deputy, I guess—
Come, m'boy.
Say, he ain't agin' law and order around here, is he?
5-9-51
Oh, no. He's just kind of angry about something—
Jackmorley
Waal, a critter that don't aim to be a Tennessee Hennessy deputy, pardner, might stand a teeny bit of watching...
But—
I'm for law and order. Who do we shoot first?

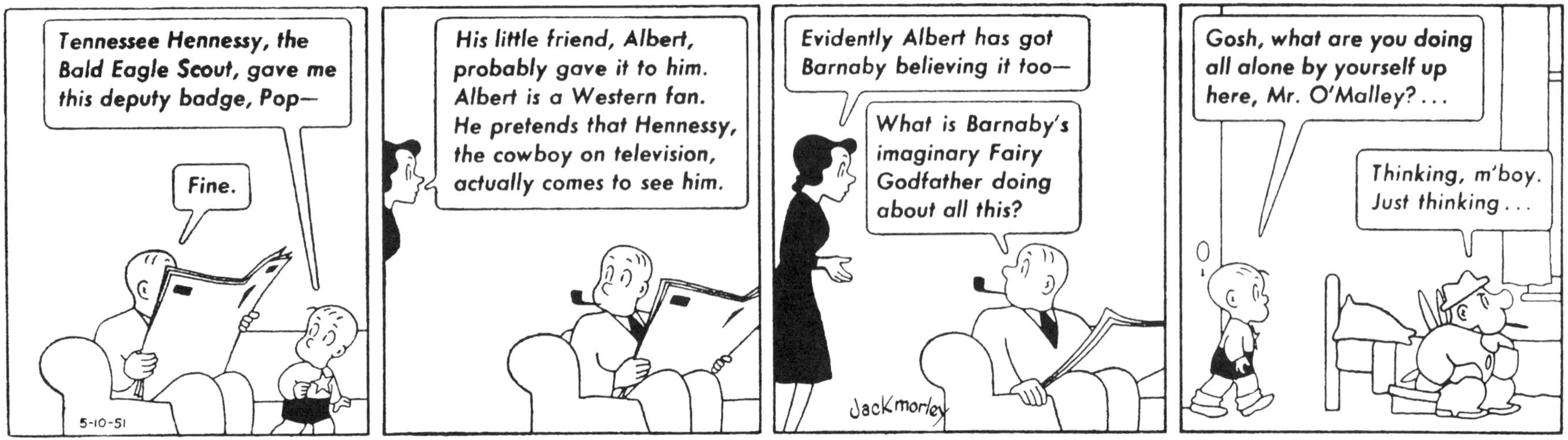
Tennessee Hennessy, the Bald Eagle Scout, gave me this deputy badge, Pop—
Fine.
5-10-51
His little friend, Albert, probably gave it to him. Albert is a Western fan. He pretends that Hennessy, the cowboy on television, actually comes to see him.
Evidently Albert has got Barnaby believing it too—
What is Barnaby's imaginary Fairy Godfather doing about all this?
Jackmorley
Gosh, what are you doing all alone by yourself up here, Mr. O'Malley?...
Thinking, m'boy. Just thinking...

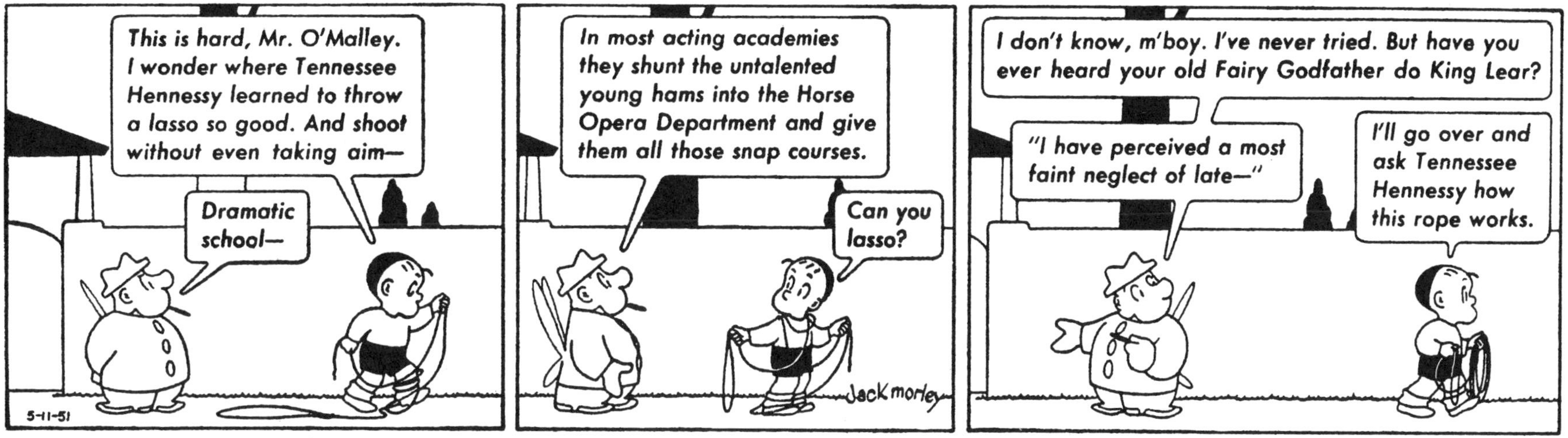
This is hard, Mr. O'Malley. I wonder where Tennessee Hennessy learned to throw a lasso so good. And shoot without even taking aim—
Dramatic school—
5-11-51
In most acting academies they shunt the untalented young hams into the Horse Opera Department and give them all those snap courses.
Can you lasso?
Jack morley
I don't know, m'boy. I've never tried. But have you ever heard your old Fairy Godfather do King Lear?
"I have perceived a most faint neglect of late—"
I'll go over and ask Tennessee Hennessy how this rope works.

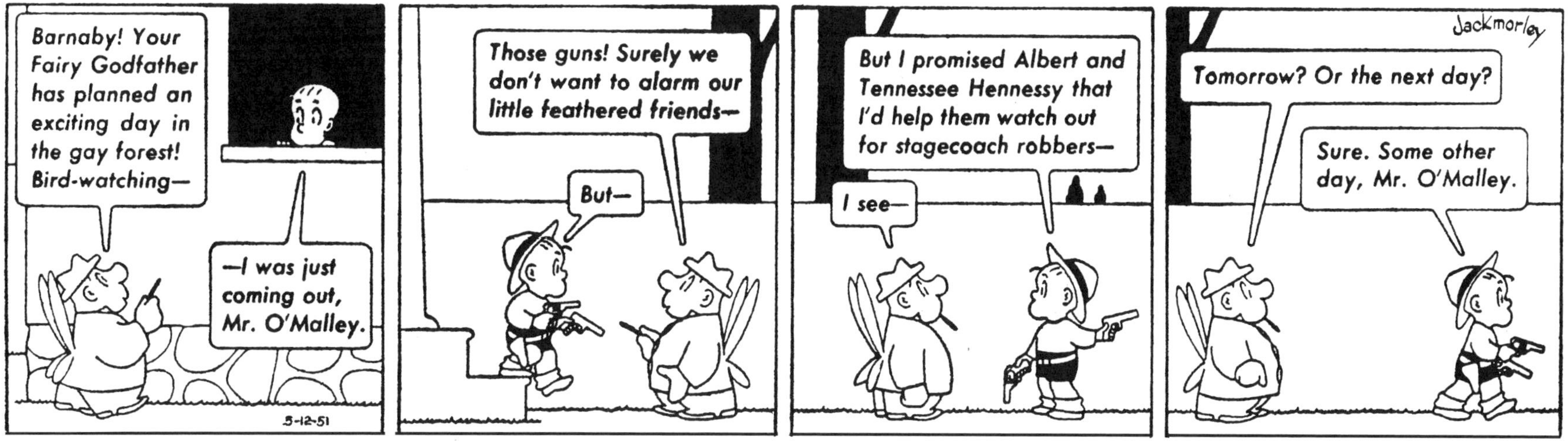
Barnaby! Your Fairy Godfather has planned an exciting day in the gay forest! Bird-watching—
—I was just coming out, Mr. O'Malley.
5-12-51
Those guns! Surely we don't want to alarm our little feathered friends—
But—
But I promised Albert and Tennessee Hennessy that I'd help them watch out for stagecoach robbers—
I see—
Jack morley
Tomorrow? Or the next day?
Sure. Some other day, Mr. O'Malley.

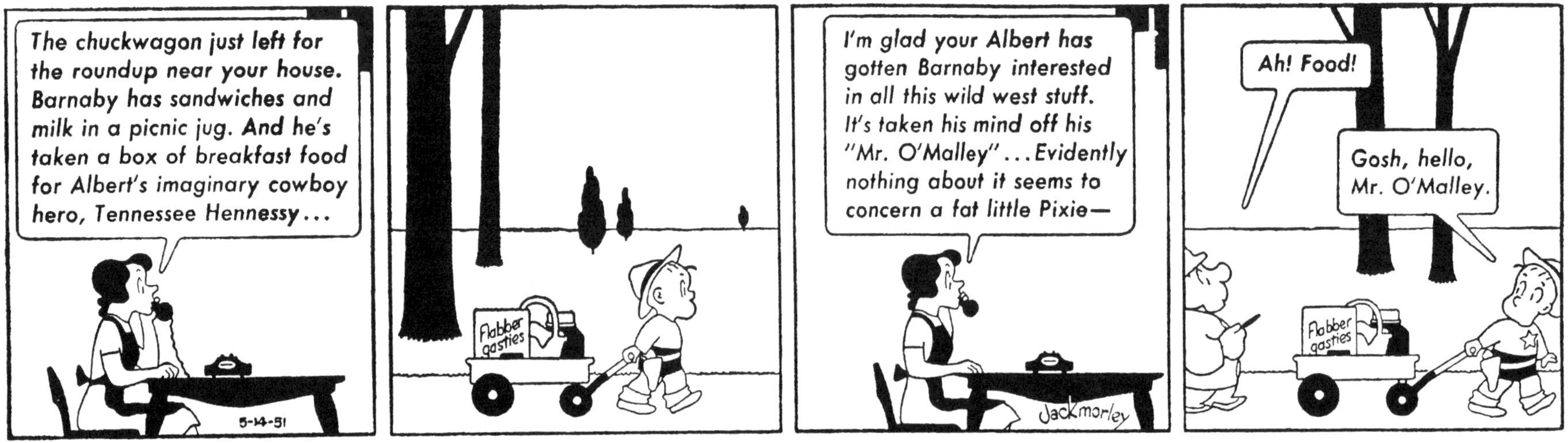
The chuckwagon just left for the roundup near your house. Barnaby has sandwiches and milk in a picnic jug. And he's taken a box of breakfast food for Albert's imaginary cowboy hero, Tennessee Hennessy...
5-14-51
Flabber gasties
I'm glad your Albert has gotten Barnaby interested in all this wild west stuff. It's taken his mind off his "Mr. O'Malley"... Evidently nothing about it seems to concern a fat little Pixie—
JackMorley
Ah! Food!
Gosh, hello, Mr. O'Malley.
Flabber gasties

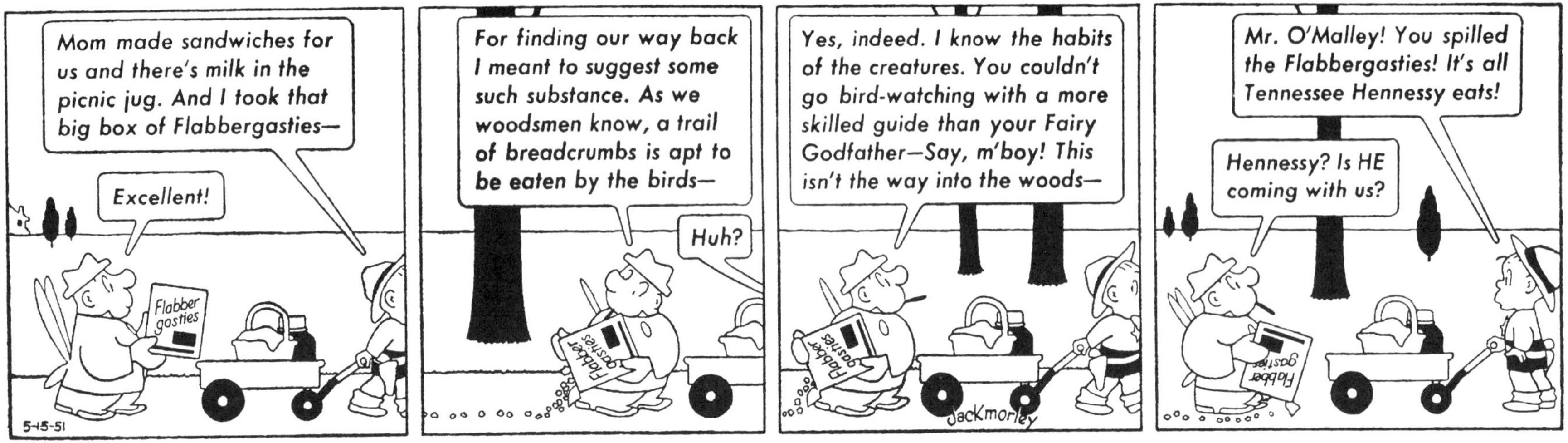
Mom made sandwiches for us and there's milk in the picnic jug. And I took that big box of Flabbergasties—
Excellent!
Flabber gasties
5-15-51
For finding our way back I meant to suggest some such substance. As we woodsmen know, a trail of breadcrumbs is apt to be eaten by the birds—
Huh?
Flabber gasties
Yes, indeed. I know the habits of the creatures. You couldn't go bird-watching with a more skilled guide than your Fairy Godfather—Say, m'boy! This isn't the way into the woods—
Flabber gasties
JackMorley
Mr. O'Malley! You spilled the Flabbergasties! It's all Tennessee Hennessy eats!
Hennessy? Is HE coming with us?
Flabber gasties

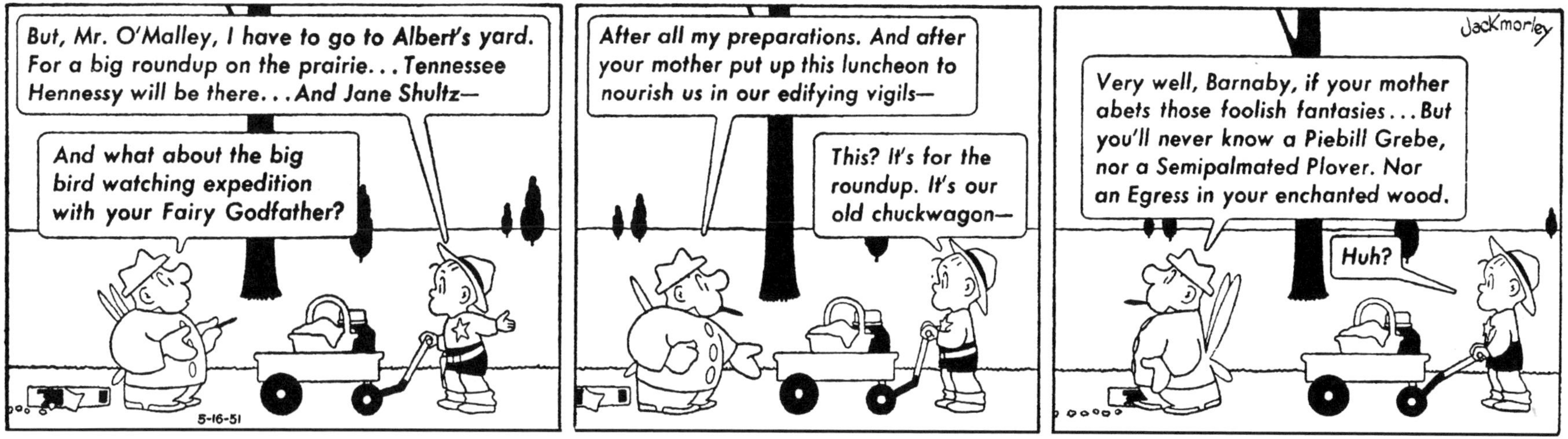

But, Mr. O'Malley, I have to go to Albert's yard. For a big roundup on the prairie... Tennessee Hennessy will be there... And Jane Shultz—
And what about the big bird watching expedition with your Fairy Godfather?
5-16-51
After all my preparations. And after your mother put up this luncheon to nourish us in our edifying vigils—
This? It's for the roundup. It's our old chuckwagon—
Jackmorley
Very well, Barnaby, if your mother abets those foolish fantasies... But you'll never know a Piebill Grebe, nor a Semipalmated Plover. Nor an Egress in your enchanted wood.
Huh?

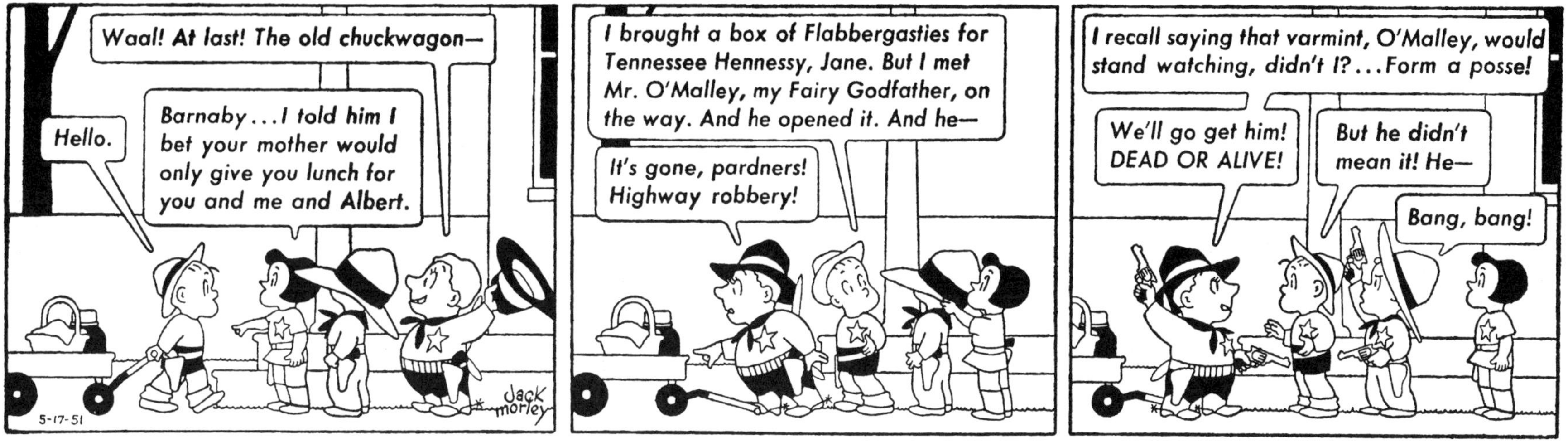

Waal! At last! The old chuckwagon—
Hello.
Barnaby... I told him I bet your mother would only give you lunch for you and me and Albert.
5-17-51
Jack morley
I brought a box of Flabbergasties for Tennessee Hennessy, Jane. But I met Mr. O'Malley, my Fairy Godfather, on the way. And he opened it. And he—
It's gone, pardners! Highway robbery!
I recall saying that varmint, O'Malley, would stand watching, didn't I?... Form a posse!
We'll go get him! DEAD OR ALIVE!
But he didn't mean it! He—
Bang, bang!

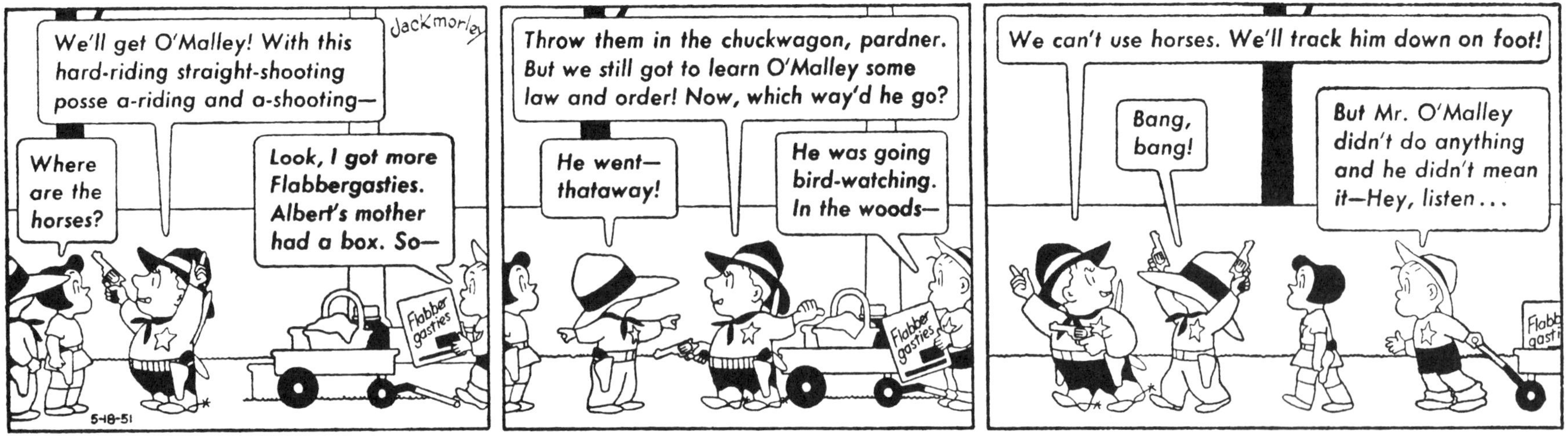
JackMorley
We'll get O'Malley! With this hard-riding straight-shooting posse a-riding and a-shooting—
Where are the horses?
Look, I got more Flabbergasties. Albert's mother had a box. So—
Flabber gasties
5-18-51
Throw them in the chuckwagon, pardner. But we still got to learn O'Malley some law and order! Now, which way'd he go?
He went— thataway!
He was going bird-watching. In the woods—
Flabber gasties
We can't use horses. We'll track him down on foot!
Bang, bang!
But Mr. O'Malley didn't do anything and he didn't mean it—Hey, listen . . .

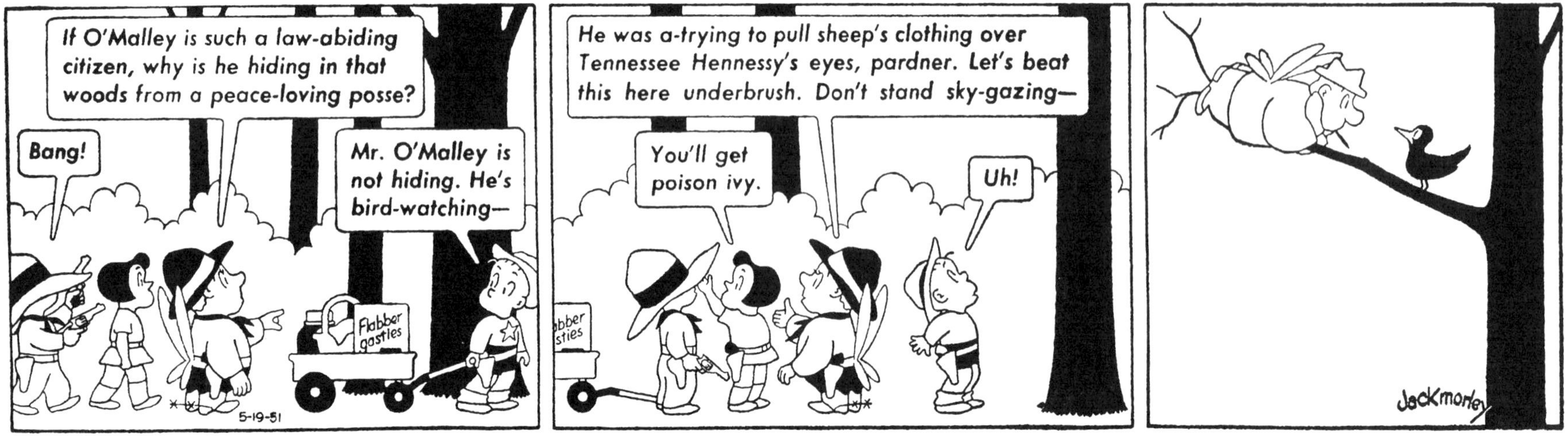
If O'Malley is such a law-abiding citizen, why is he hiding in that woods from a peace-loving posse?
Bang!
Mr. O'Malley is not hiding. He's bird-watching—
Flabber gasties
5-19-51
He was a-trying to pull sheep's clothing over Tennessee Hennessy's eyes, pardner. Let's beat this here underbrush. Don't stand sky-gazing—
You'll get poison ivy.
Uh!
JackMorley

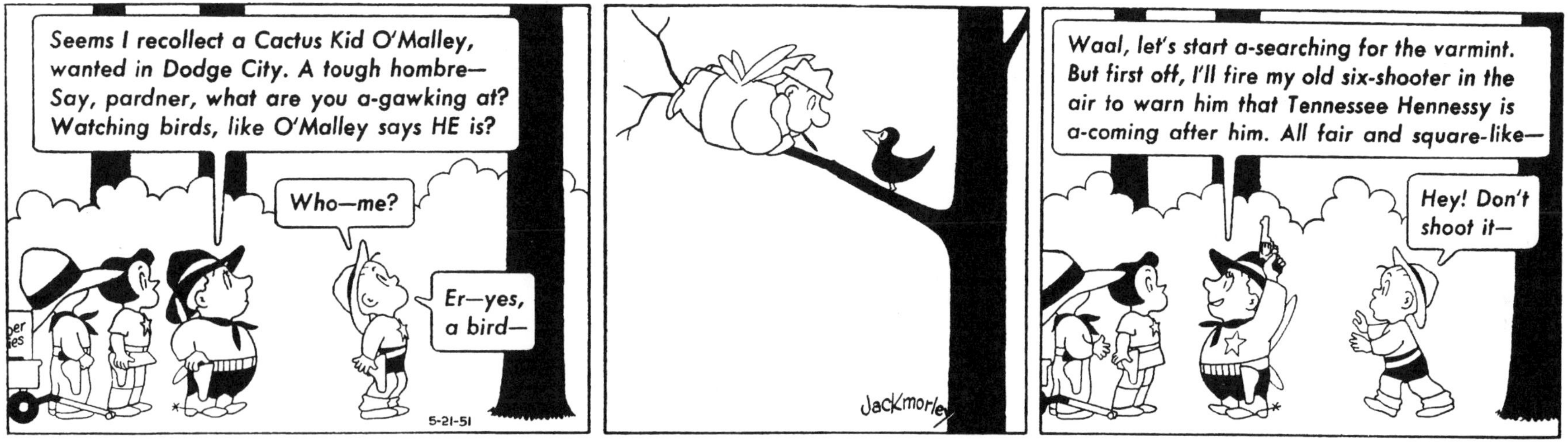

Seems I recollect a Cactus Kid O'Malley, wanted in Dodge City. A tough hombre—Say, pardner, what are you a-gawking at? Watching birds, like O'Malley says HE is?
Who—me?
Er—yes, a bird—
5-21-51
Jackmorley
Waal, let's start a-searching for the varmint. But first off, I'll fire my old six-shooter in the air to warn him that Tennessee Hennessy is a-coming after him. All fair and square-like—
Hey! Don't shoot it—

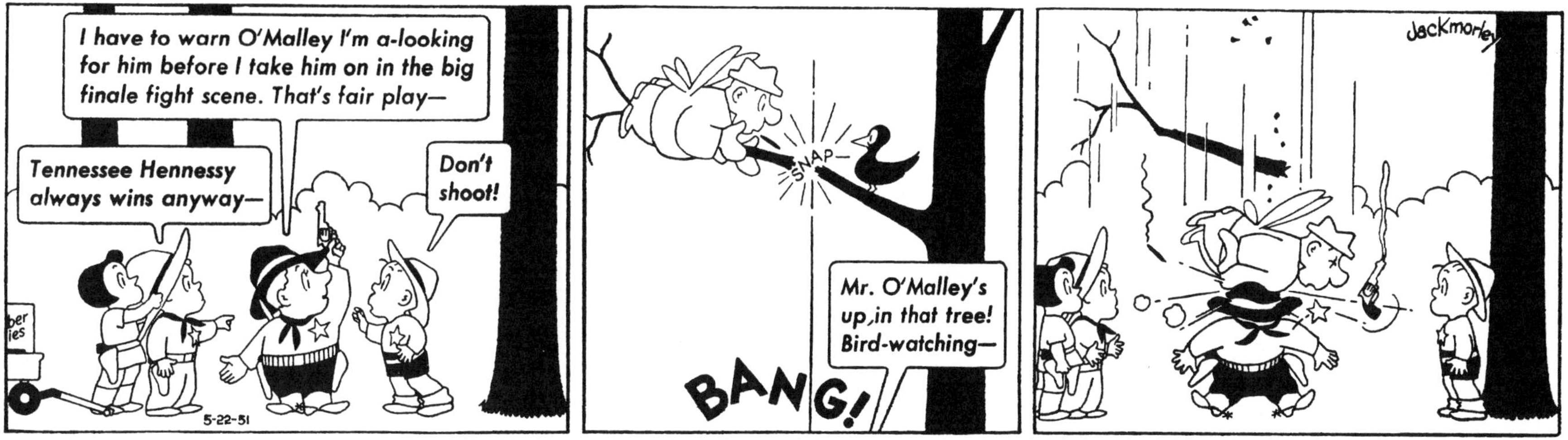

I have to warn O'Malley I'm a-looking for him before I take him on in the big finale fight scene. That's fair play—
Tennessee Hennessy always wins anyway—
Don't shoot!
5-22-51
SNAP
Mr. O'Malley's up, in that tree! Bird-watching—
BANG!
Jackmorley

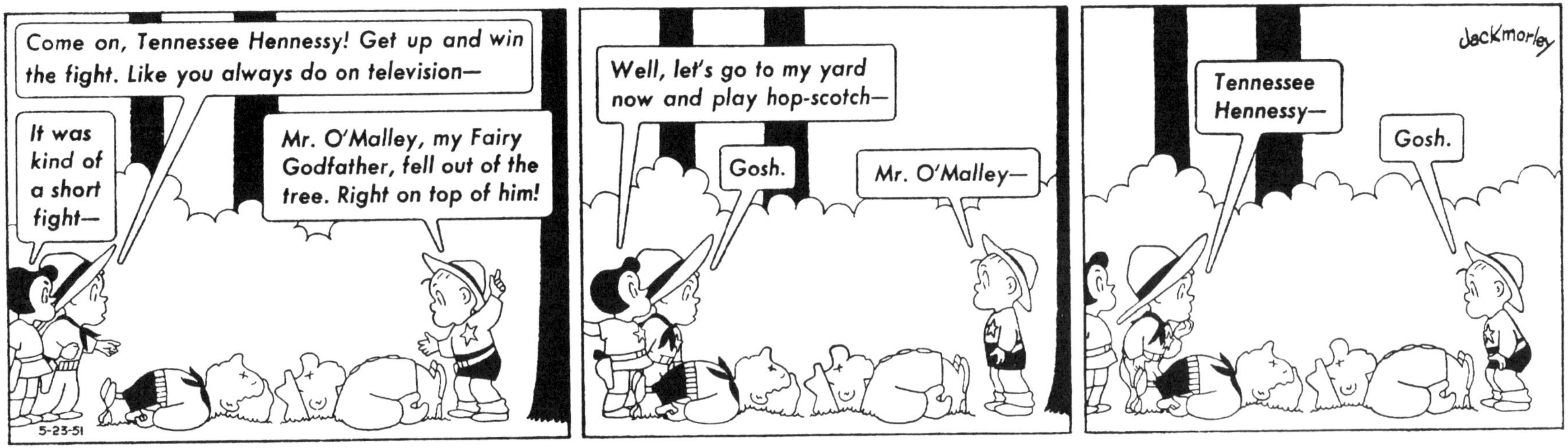

Come on, Tennessee Hennessy! Get up and win the fight. Like you always do on television—
It was kind of a short fight—
Mr. O'Malley, my Fairy Godfather, fell out of the tree. Right on top of him!
5-23-51
Well, let's go to my yard now and play hop-scotch—
Gosh.
Mr. O'Malley—
JackMorley
Tennessee Hennessy—
Gosh.

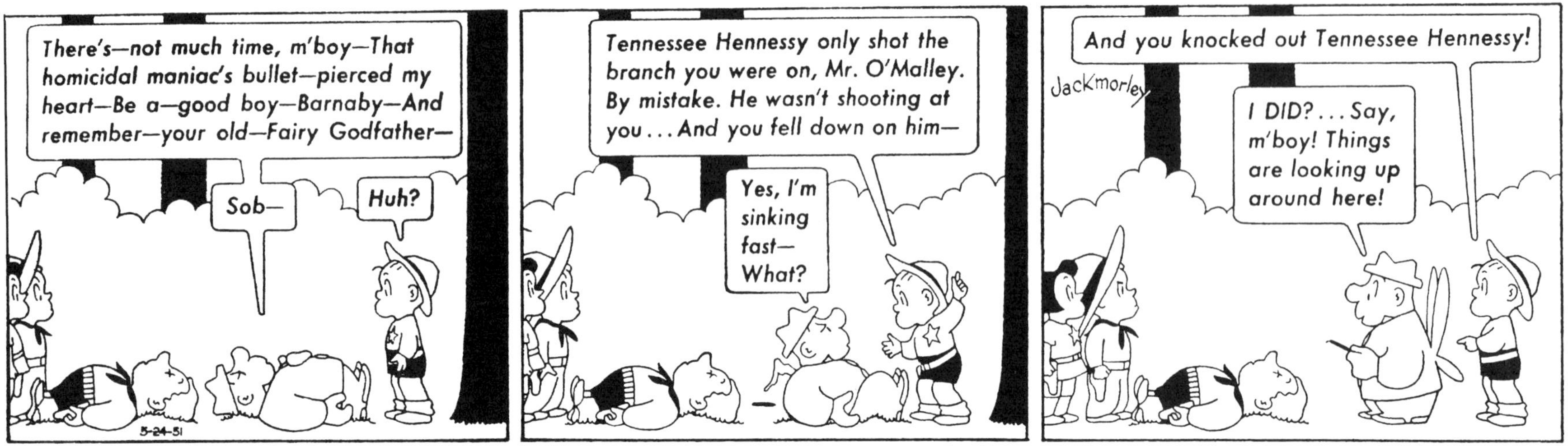

There's—not much time, m'boy—That homicidal maniac's bullet—pierced my heart—Be a—good boy—Barnaby—And remember—your old—Fairy Godfather—
Sob—
Huh?
5-24-51
Tennessee Hennessy only shot the branch you were on, Mr. O'Malley. By mistake. He wasn't shooting at you... And you fell down on him—
Yes, I'm sinking fast— What?
And you knocked out Tennessee Hennessy!
JackMorley
I DID?... Say, m'boy! Things are looking up around here!

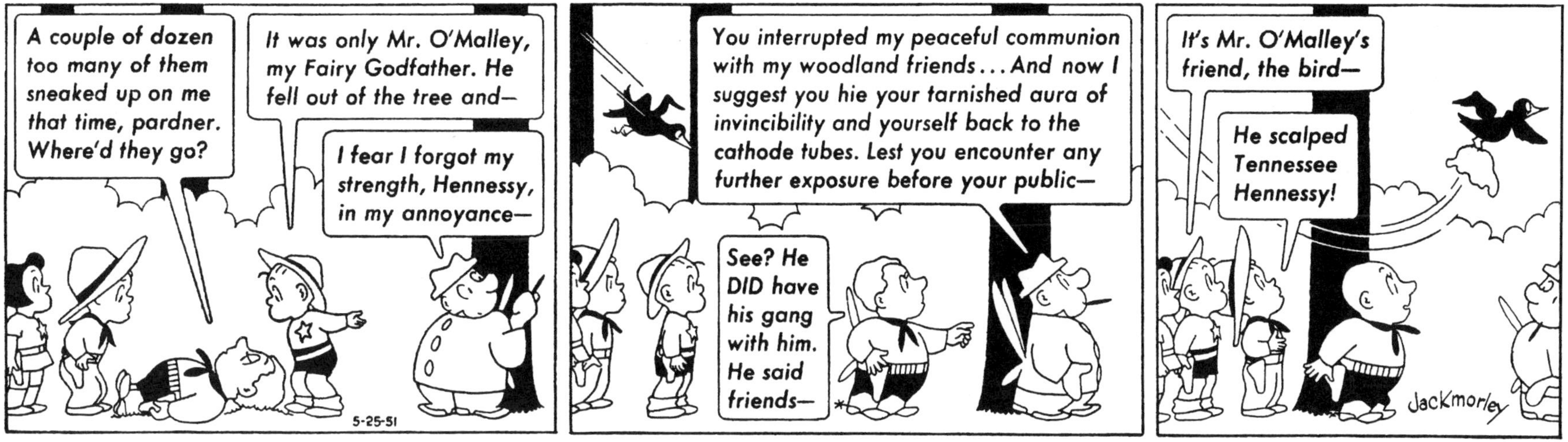
A couple of dozen too many of them sneaked up on me that time, pardner. Where'd they go?
It was only Mr. O'Malley, my Fairy Godfather. He fell out of the tree and—
I fear I forgot my strength, Hennessy, in my annoyance—
5-25-51
You interrupted my peaceful communion with my woodland friends... And now I suggest you hie your tarnished aura of invincibility and yourself back to the cathode tubes. Lest you encounter any further exposure before your public—
See? He DID have his gang with him. He said friends—
It's Mr. O'Malley's friend, the bird—
He scalped Tennessee Hennessy!
Jackmorley

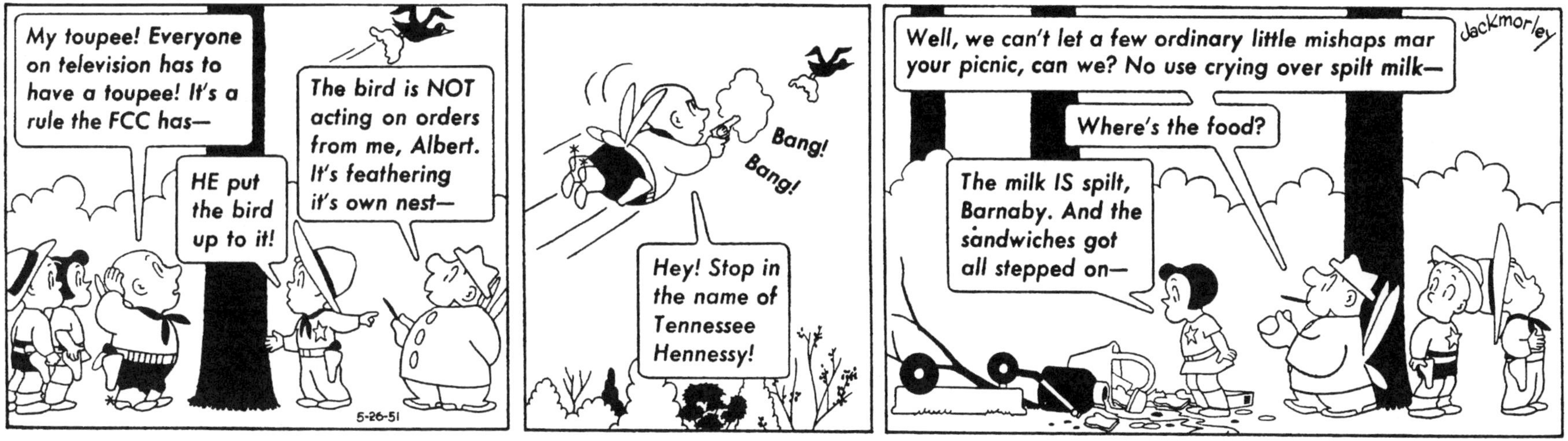
My toupee! Everyone on television has to have a toupee! It's a rule the FCC has—
HE put the bird up to it!
The bird is NOT acting on orders from me, Albert. It's feathering it's own nest—
5-26-51
Bang!
Bang!
Hey! Stop in the name of Tennessee Hennessy!
Well, we can't let a few ordinary little mishaps mar your picnic, can we? No use crying over spilt milk—
Where's the food?
The milk IS spilt, Barnaby. And the sandwiches got all stepped on—
Jackmorley

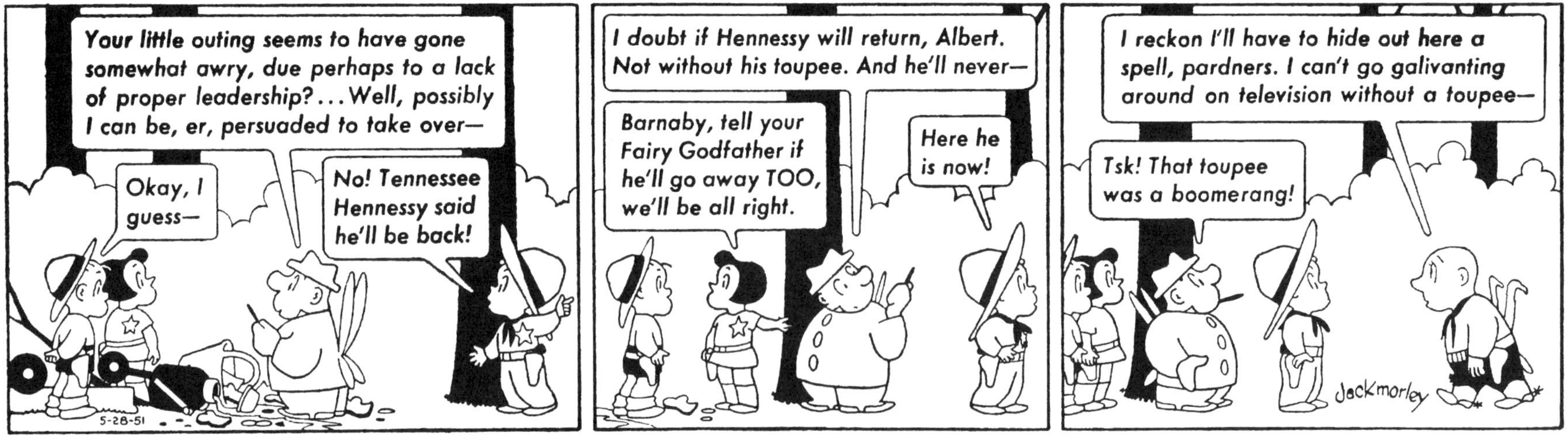
Your little outing seems to have gone somewhat awry, due perhaps to a lack of proper leadership? . . . Well, possibly I can be, er, persuaded to take over—
Okay, I guess—
No! Tennessee Hennessy said he'll be back!
5-28-51
I doubt if Hennessy will return, Albert. Not without his toupee. And he'll never—
Barnaby, tell your Fairy Godfather if he'll go away TOO, we'll be all right.
Here he is now!
I reckon I'll have to hide out here a spell, pardners. I can't go galivanting around on television without a toupee—
Tsk! That toupee was a boomerang!
Jackmorley

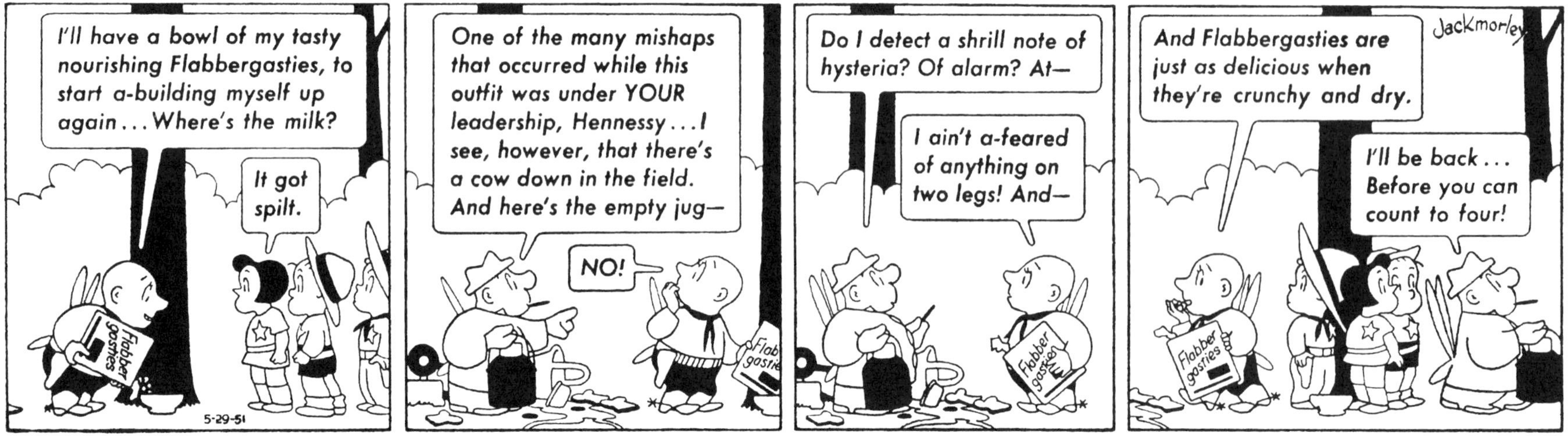
I'll have a bowl of my tasty nourishing Flabbergasties, to start a-building myself up again . . . Where's the milk?
It got spilt.
Flabbergasties
5-29-51
One of the many mishaps that occurred while this outfit was under YOUR leadership, Hennessy . . . I see, however, that there's a cow down in the field. And here's the empty jug—
NO!
Do I detect a shrill note of hysteria? Of alarm? At—
I ain't a-feared of anything on two legs! And—
Flabbergasties
Jackmorley
And Flabbergasties are just as delicious when they're crunchy and dry.
I'll be back . . . Before you can count to four!
Flabbergasties

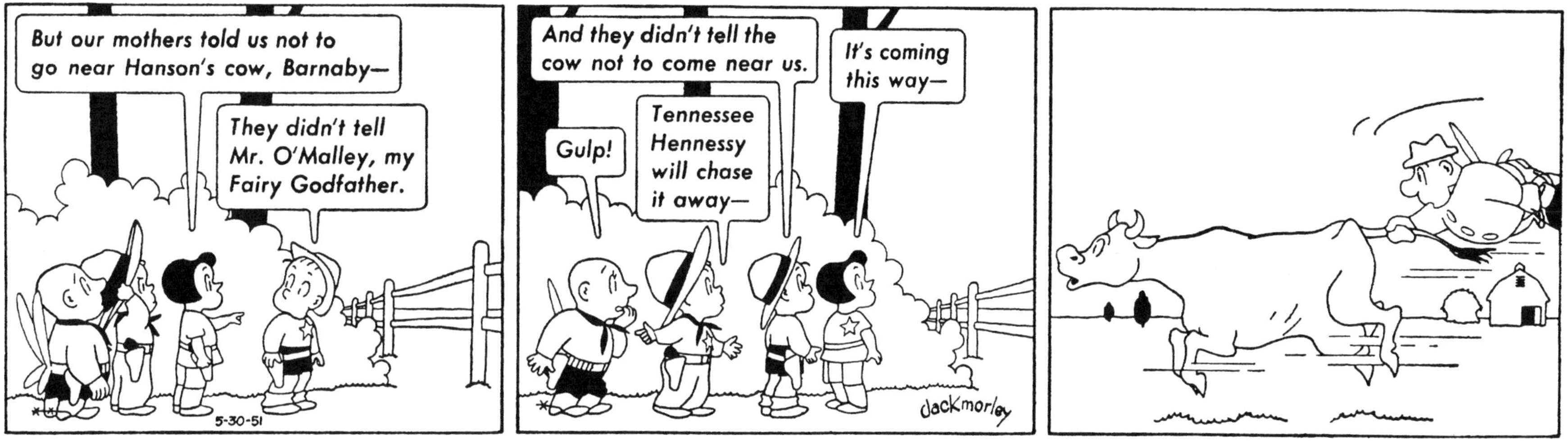
But our mothers told us not to go near Hanson's cow, Barnaby—
They didn't tell Mr. O'Malley, my Fairy Godfather.
5-30-51
And they didn't tell the cow not to come near us.
Gulp!
Tennessee Hennessy will chase it away—
It's coming this way—
Jack morley

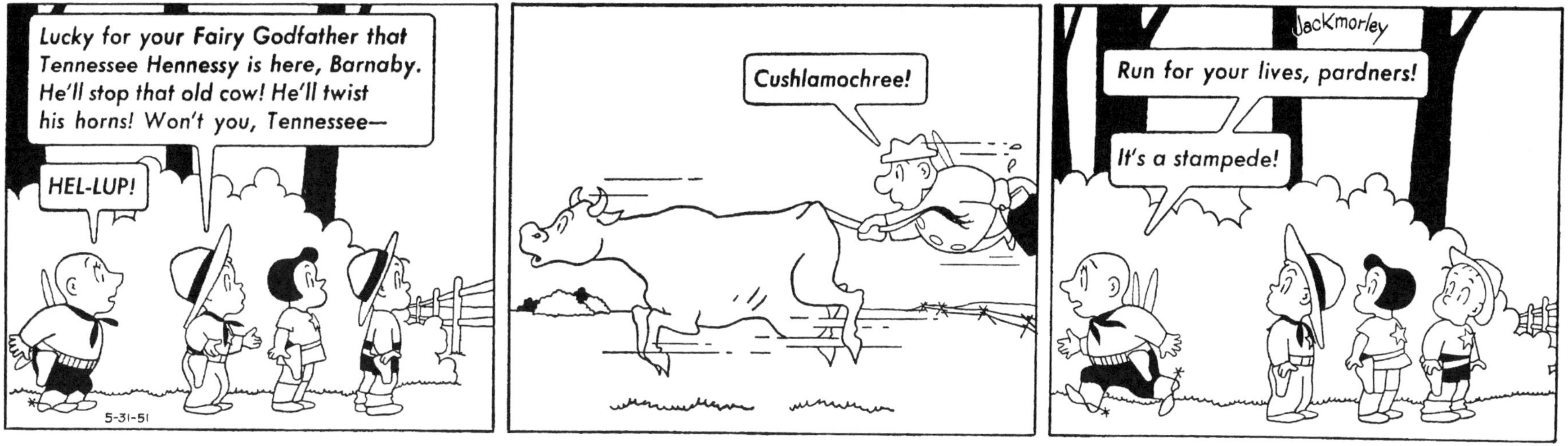
Lucky for your Fairy Godfather that Tennessee Hennessy is here, Barnaby. He'll stop that old cow! He'll twist his horns! Won't you, Tennessee—
HEL-LUP!
5-31-51
Cushlamochree!
Jack morley
Run for your lives, pardners!
It's a stampede!

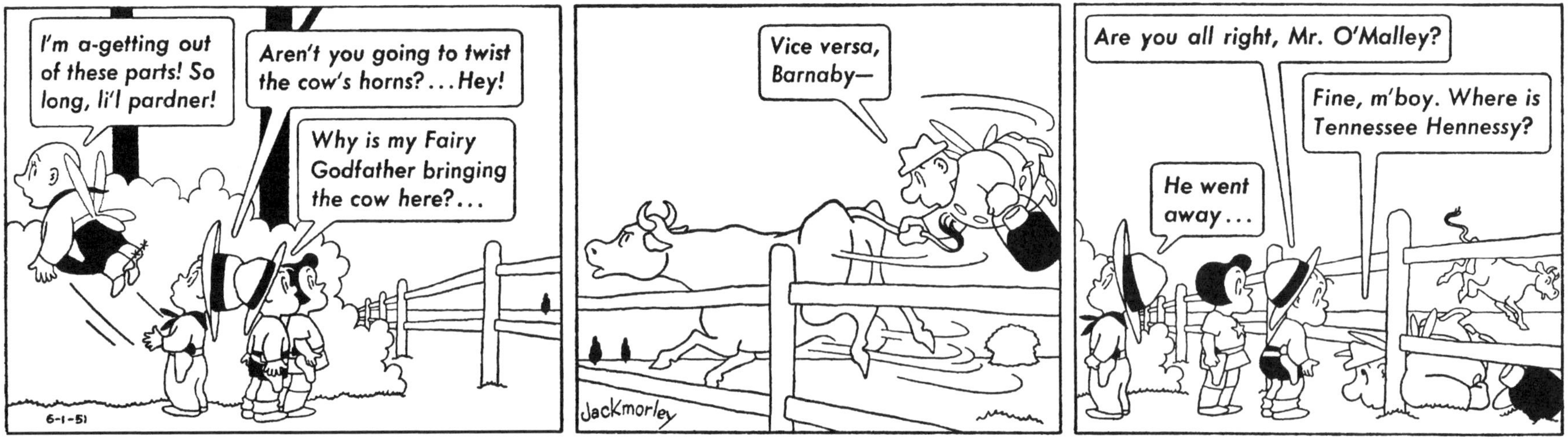
I'm a-getting out of these parts! So long, li'l pardner!
Aren't you going to twist the cow's horns?...Hey!
Why is my Fairy Godfather bringing the cow here?...
6-1-51
Vice versa, Barnaby—
JacKmorley
Are you all right, Mr. O'Malley?
He went away...
Fine, m'boy. Where is Tennessee Hennessy?

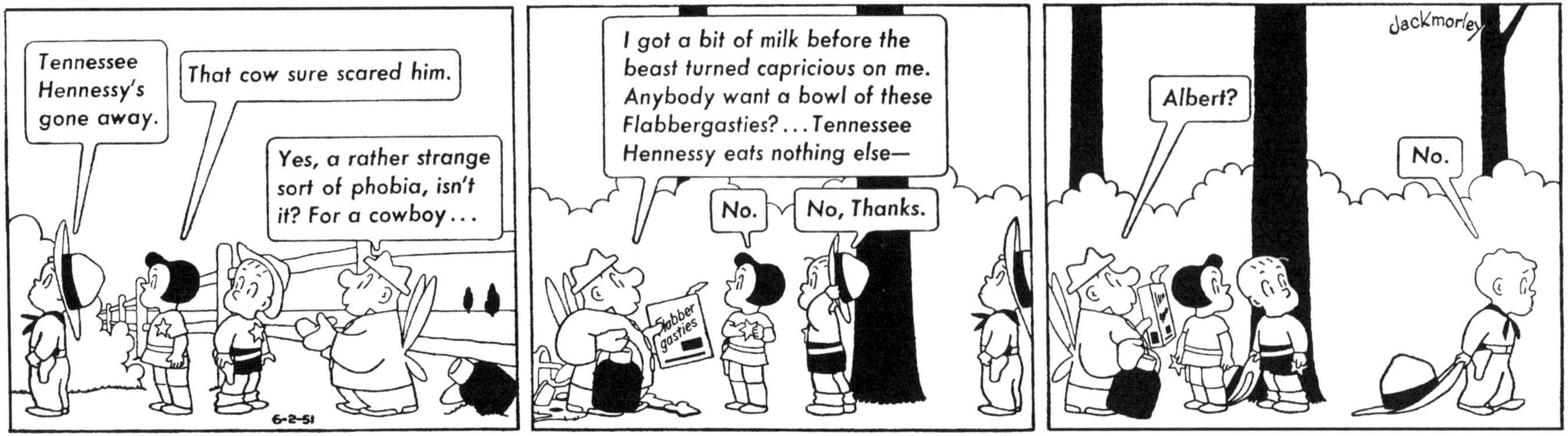
Tennessee Hennessy's gone away.
That cow sure scared him.
Yes, a rather strange sort of phobia, isn't it? For a cowboy...
6-2-51
I got a bit of milk before the beast turned capricious on me. Anybody want a bowl of these Flabbergasties?...Tennessee Hennessy eats nothing else—
Flabbergasties
No.
No, Thanks.
JacKmorley
Albert?
No.

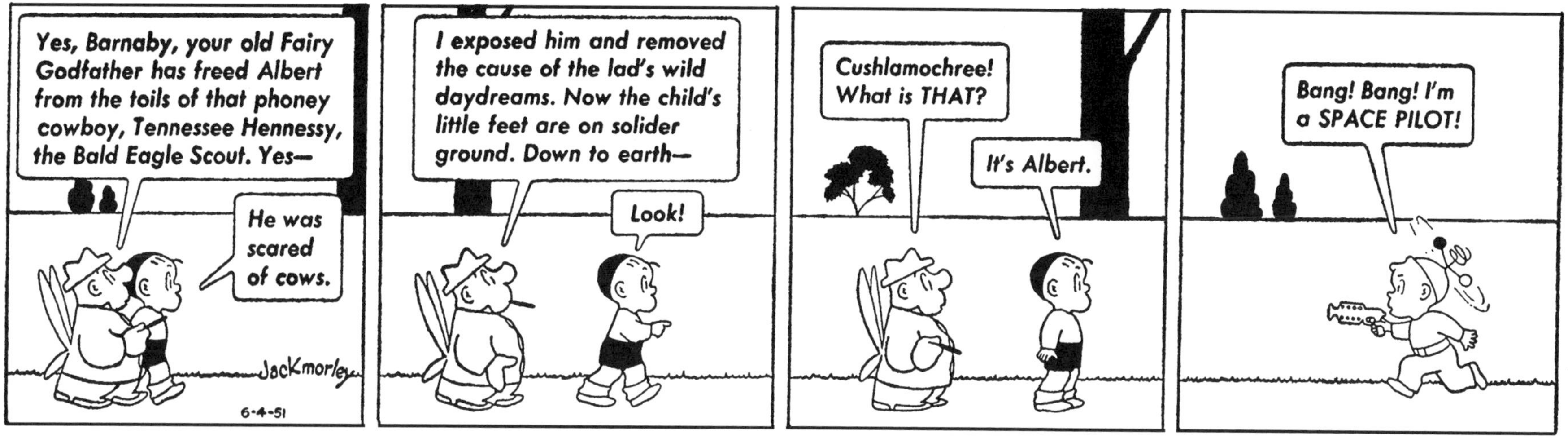
Yes, Barnaby, your old Fairy Godfather has freed Albert from the toils of that phoney cowboy, Tennessee Hennessy, the Bald Eagle Scout. Yes—
He was scared of cows.
JackMorley
6-4-51
I exposed him and removed the cause of the lad's wild daydreams. Now the child's little feet are on solider ground. Down to earth—
Look!
Cushlamochree! What is THAT?
It's Albert.
Bang! Bang! I'm a SPACE PILOT!

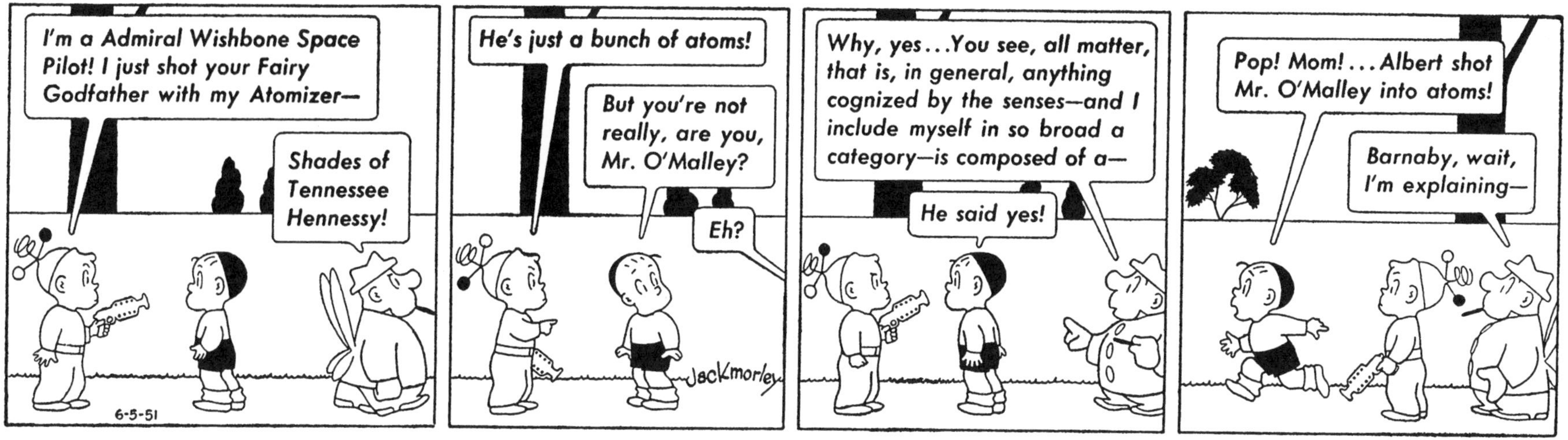
I'm a Admiral Wishbone Space Pilot! I just shot your Fairy Godfather with my Atomizer—
Shades of Tennessee Hennessy!
6-5-51
He's just a bunch of atoms!
But you're not really, are you, Mr. O'Malley?
Eh?
JackMorley
Why, yes...You see, all matter, that is, in general, anything cognized by the senses—and I include myself in so broad a category—is composed of a—
He said yes!
Pop! Mom!...Albert shot Mr. O'Malley into atoms!
Barnaby, wait, I'm explaining—

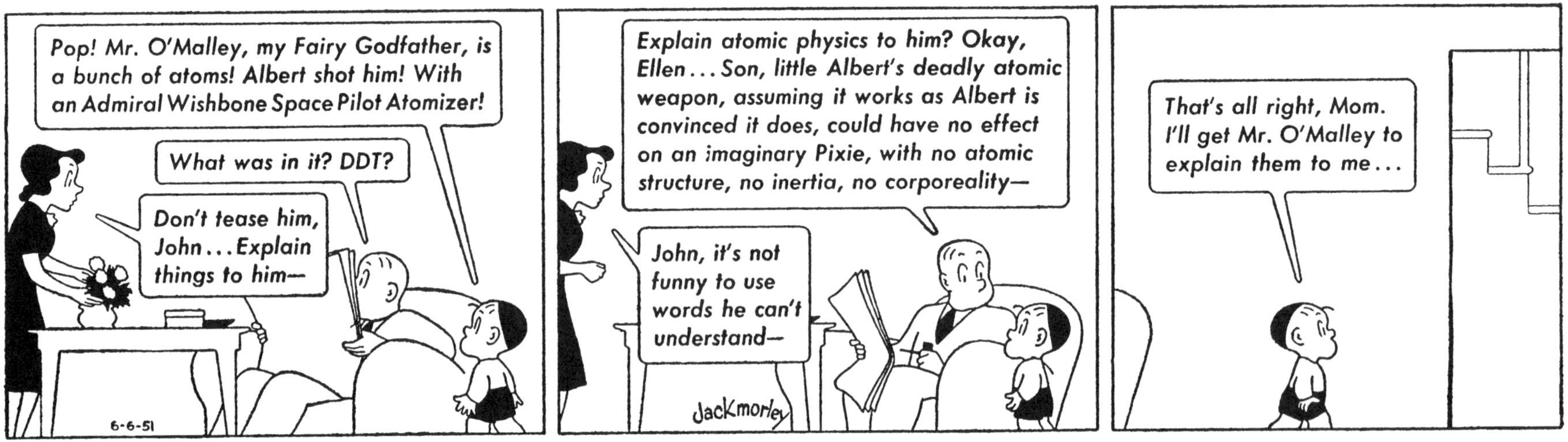
Pop! Mr. O'Malley, my Fairy Godfather, is a bunch of atoms! Albert shot him! With an Admiral Wishbone Space Pilot Atomizer!
What was in it? DDT?
Don't tease him, John... Explain things to him—
6-6-51
Explain atomic physics to him? Okay, Ellen... Son, little Albert's deadly atomic weapon, assuming it works as Albert is convinced it does, could have no effect on an imaginary Pixie, with no atomic structure, no inertia, no corporeality—
John, it's not funny to use words he can't understand—
JacKmorley
That's all right, Mom. I'll get Mr. O'Malley to explain them to me...

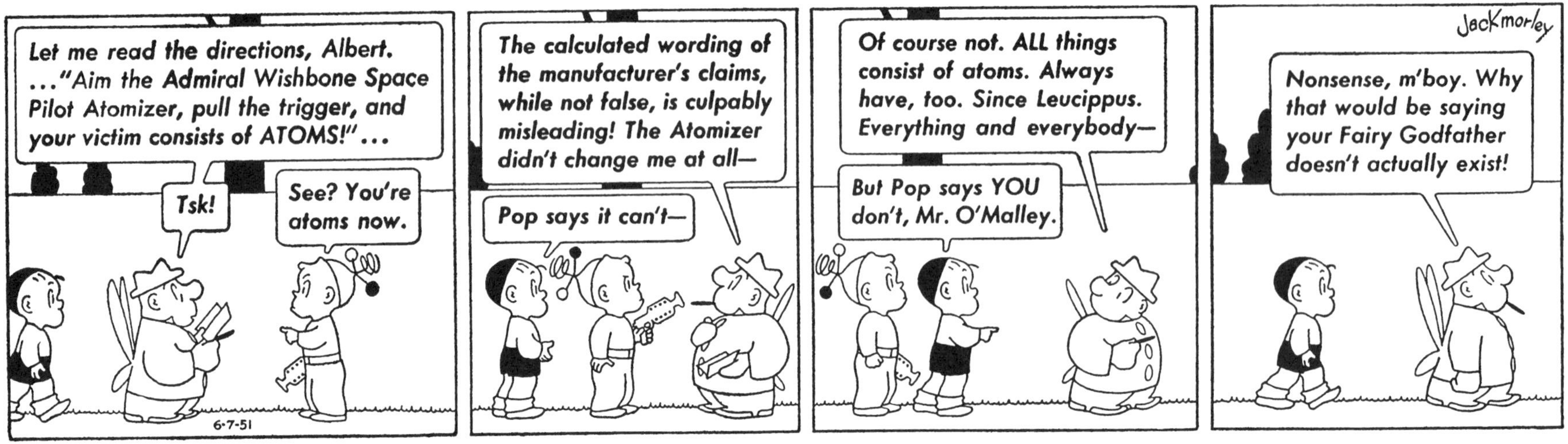
Let me read the directions, Albert. ..."Aim the Admiral Wishbone Space Pilot Atomizer, pull the trigger, and your victim consists of ATOMS!"...
Tsk!
See? You're atoms now.
6-7-51
The calculated wording of the manufacturer's claims, while not false, is culpably misleading! The Atomizer didn't change me at all—
Pop says it can't—
Of course not. ALL things consist of atoms. Always have, too. Since Leucippus. Everything and everybody—
But Pop says YOU don't, Mr. O'Malley.
JacKmorley
Nonsense, m'boy. Why that would be saying your Fairy Godfather doesn't actually exist!

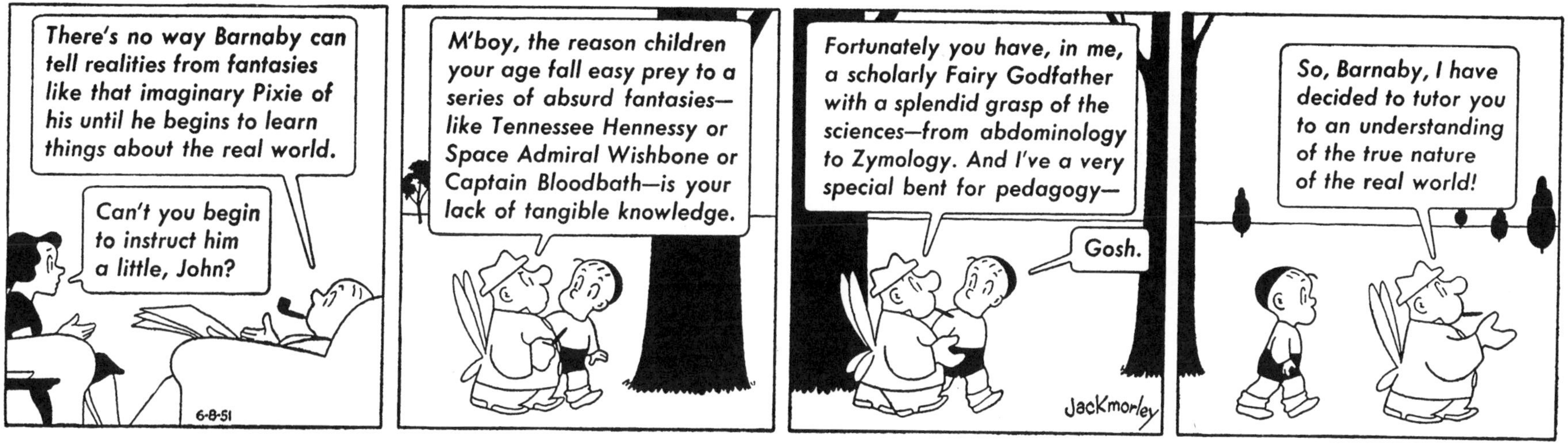
There's no way Barnaby can tell realities from fantasies like that imaginary Pixie of his until he begins to learn things about the real world.
Can't you begin to instruct him a little, John?
6-8-51
M'boy, the reason children your age fall easy prey to a series of absurd fantasies—like Tennessee Hennessy or Space Admiral Wishbone or Captain Bloodbath—is your lack of tangible knowledge.
Fortunately you have, in me, a scholarly Fairy Godfather with a splendid grasp of the sciences—from abdominology to Zymology. And I've a very special bent for pedagogy—
Gosh.
JackMorley
So, Barnaby, I have decided to tutor you to an understanding of the true nature of the real world!

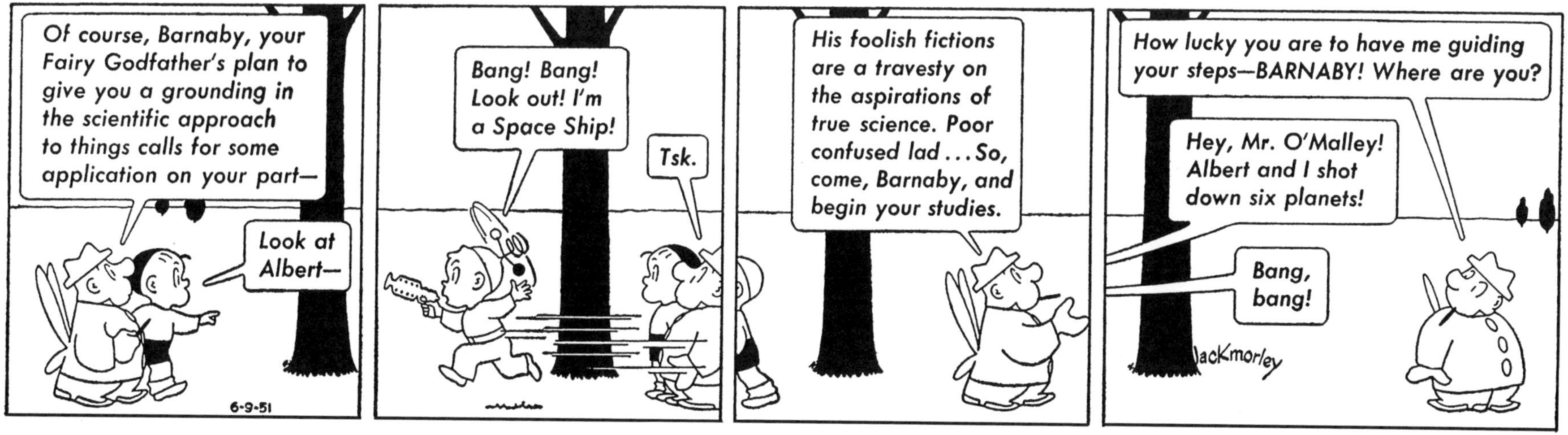
Of course, Barnaby, your Fairy Godfather's plan to give you a grounding in the scientific approach to things calls for some application on your part—
Look at Albert—
6-9-51
Bang! Bang! Look out! I'm a Space Ship!
Tsk.
His foolish fictions are a travesty on the aspirations of true science. Poor confused lad . . . So, come, Barnaby, and begin your studies.
How lucky you are to have me guiding your steps—BARNABY! Where are you?
Hey, Mr. O'Malley! Albert and I shot down six planets!
Bang, bang!
JackMorley

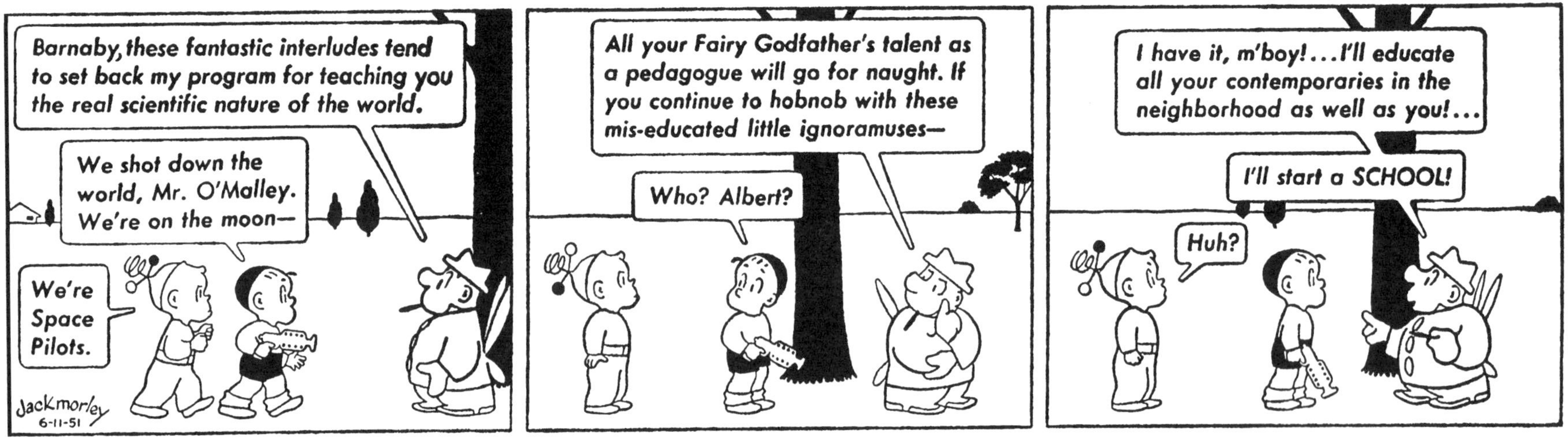
Barnaby, these fantastic interludes tend to set back my program for teaching you the real scientific nature of the world.
We shot down the world, Mr. O'Malley. We're on the moon—
We're Space Pilots.
Jackmorley
6-11-51
All your Fairy Godfather's talent as a pedagogue will go for naught. If you continue to hobnob with these mis-educated little ignoramuses—
Who? Albert?
I have it, m'boy!...I'll educate all your contemporaries in the neighborhood as well as you!...
I'll start a SCHOOL!
Huh?

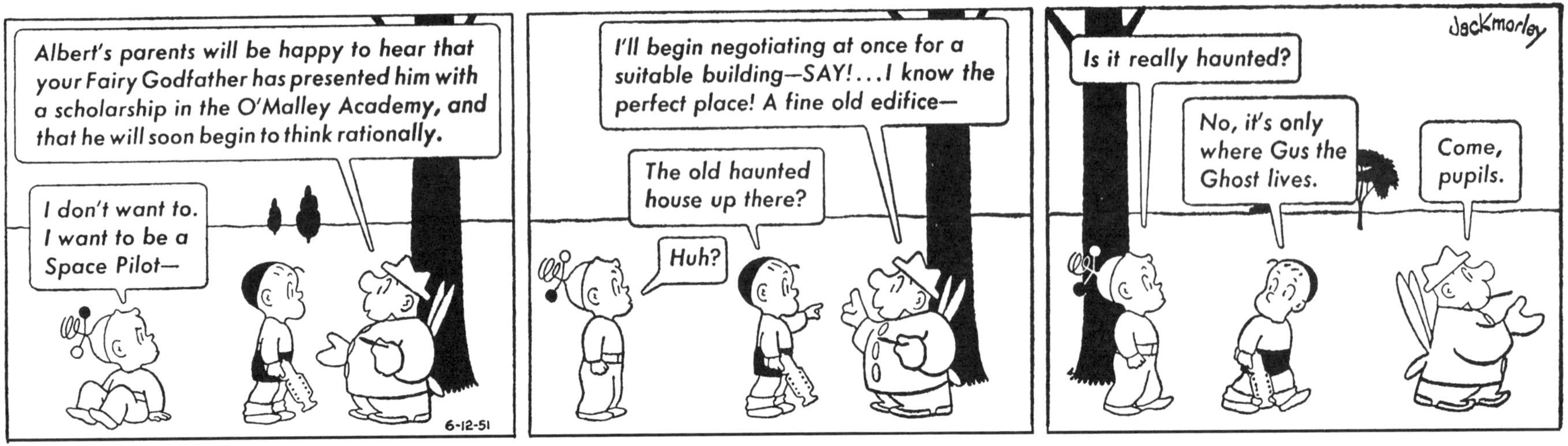
Albert's parents will be happy to hear that your Fairy Godfather has presented him with a scholarship in the O'Malley Academy, and that he will soon begin to think rationally.
I don't want to. I want to be a Space Pilot—
6-12-51
I'll begin negotiating at once for a suitable building—SAY!...I know the perfect place! A fine old edifice—
The old haunted house up there?
Huh?
Jackmorley
Is it really haunted?
No, it's only where Gus the Ghost lives.
Come, pupils.

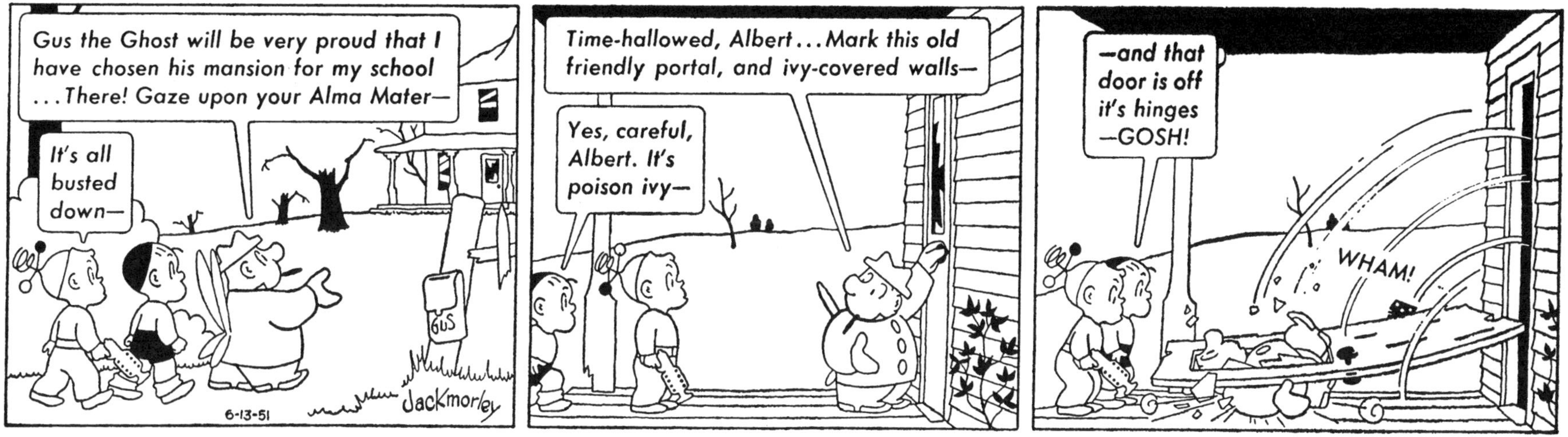
Gus the Ghost will be very proud that I have chosen his mansion for my school ...There! Gaze upon your Alma Mater—
It's all busted down—
GUS
6-13-51
Jackmorley
Time-hallowed, Albert...Mark this old friendly portal, and ivy-covered walls—
Yes, careful, Albert. It's poison ivy—
—and that door is off it's hinges —GOSH!
WHAM!

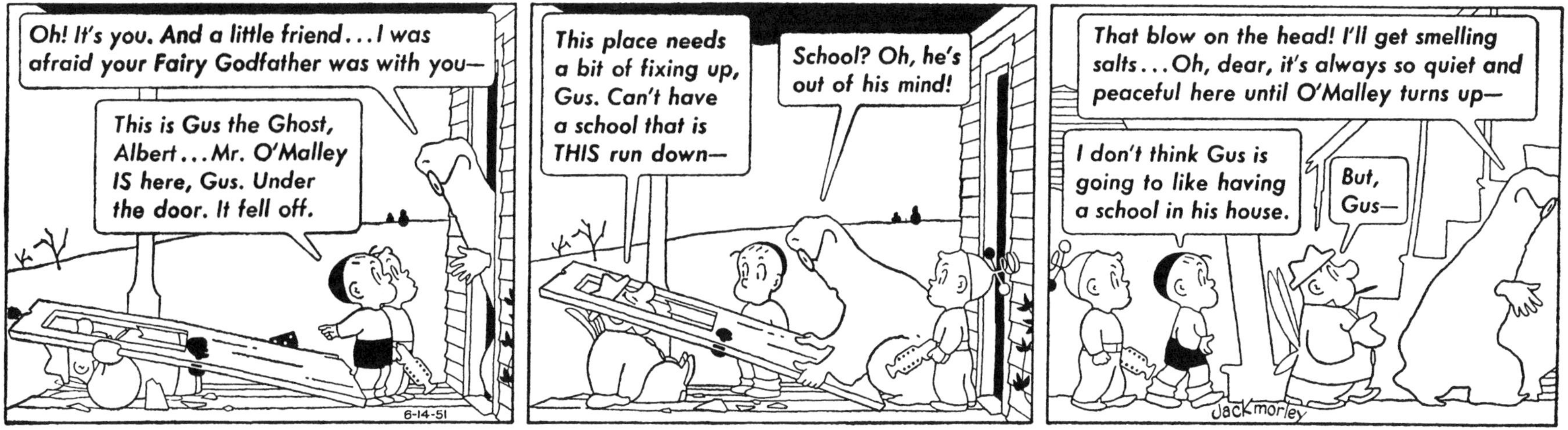
Oh! It's you. And a little friend...I was afraid your Fairy Godfather was with you—
This is Gus the Ghost, Albert...Mr. O'Malley IS here, Gus. Under the door. It fell off.
6-14-51
This place needs a bit of fixing up, Gus. Can't have a school that is THIS run down—
School? Oh, he's out of his mind!
That blow on the head! I'll get smelling salts...Oh, dear, it's always so quiet and peaceful here until O'Malley turns up—
I don't think Gus is going to like having a school in his house.
But, Gus—
Jackmorley

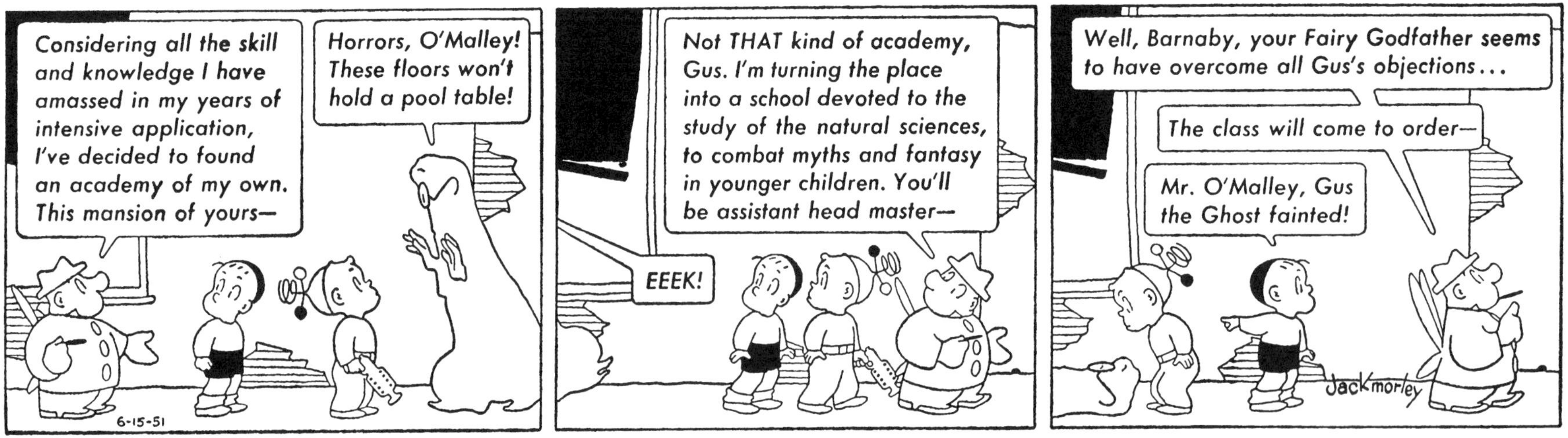
Considering all the skill and knowledge I have amassed in my years of intensive application, I've decided to found an academy of my own. This mansion of yours—
Horrors, O'Malley! These floors won't hold a pool table!
6-15-51
Not THAT kind of academy, Gus. I'm turning the place into a school devoted to the study of the natural sciences, to combat myths and fantasy in younger children. You'll be assistant head master—
EEEK!
Well, Barnaby, your Fairy Godfather seems to have overcome all Gus's objections...
The class will come to order—
Mr. O'Malley, Gus the Ghost fainted!
Jackmorley

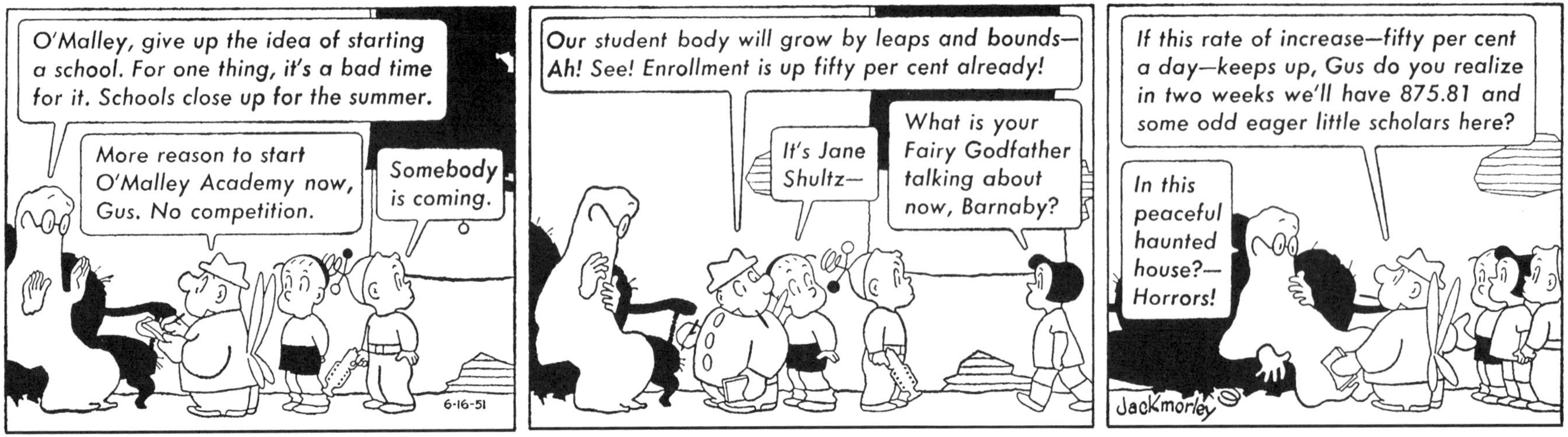
O'Malley, give up the idea of starting a school. For one thing, it's a bad time for it. Schools close up for the summer.
More reason to start O'Malley Academy now, Gus. No competition.
Somebody is coming.
6-16-51
Our student body will grow by leaps and bounds— Ah! See! Enrollment is up fifty per cent already!
It's Jane Shultz—
What is your Fairy Godfather talking about now, Barnaby?
If this rate of increase—fifty per cent a day—keeps up, Gus do you realize in two weeks we'll have 875.81 and some odd eager little scholars here?
In this peaceful haunted house?— Horrors!
Jackmorley

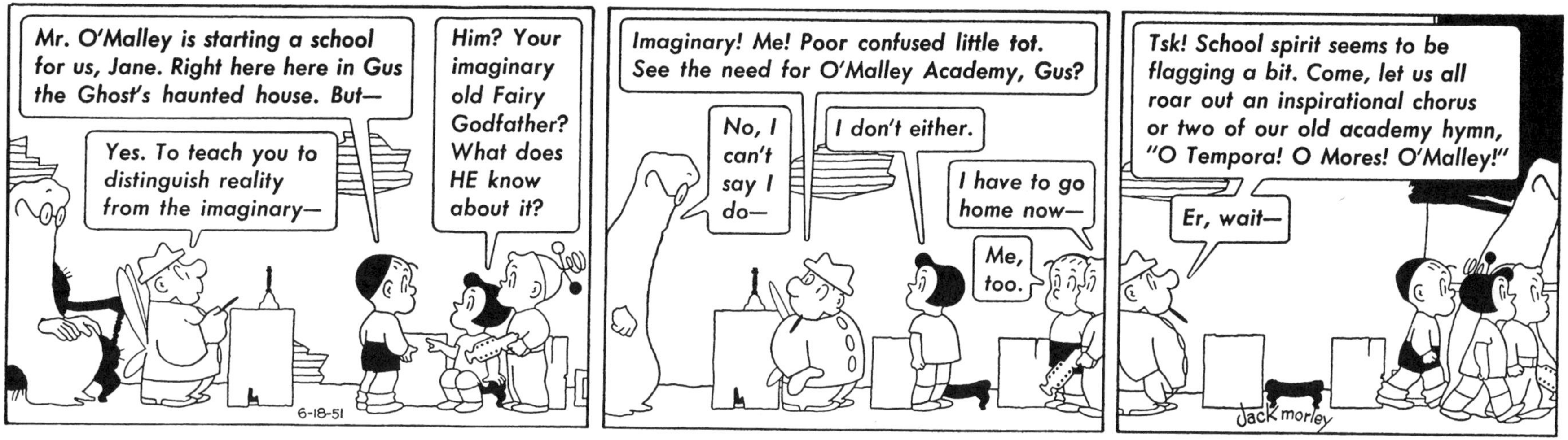
Mr. O'Malley is starting a school for us, Jane. Right here here in Gus the Ghost's haunted house. But—
Yes. To teach you to distinguish reality from the imaginary—
Him? Your imaginary old Fairy Godfather? What does HE know about it?
6-18-51
Imaginary! Me! Poor confused little tot. See the need for O'Malley Academy, Gus?
No, I can't say I do—
I don't either.
I have to go home now—
Me, too.
Tsk! School spirit seems to be flagging a bit. Come, let us all roar out an inspirational chorus or two of our old academy hymn, "O Tempora! O Mores! O'Malley!"
Er, wait—
Jack Morley

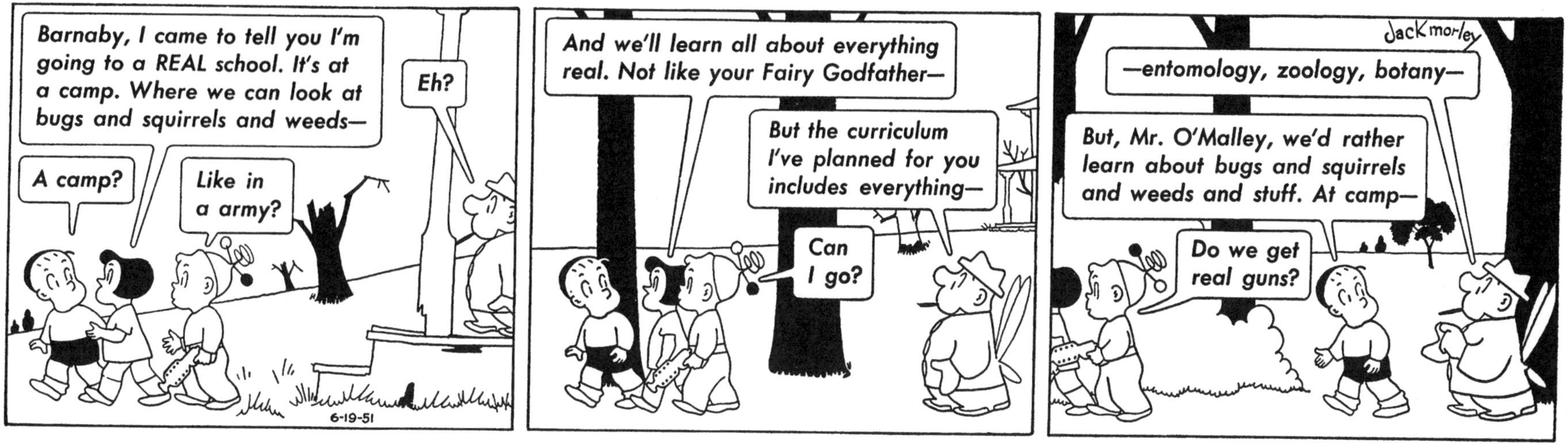
Barnaby, I came to tell you I'm going to a REAL school. It's at a camp. Where we can look at bugs and squirrels and weeds—
Eh?
A camp?
Like in a army?
6-19-51
And we'll learn all about everything real. Not like your Fairy Godfather—
But the curriculum I've planned for you includes everything—
Can I go?
Jack Morley
—entomology, zoology, botany—
But, Mr. O'Malley, we'd rather learn about bugs and squirrels and weeds and stuff. At camp—
Do we get real guns?

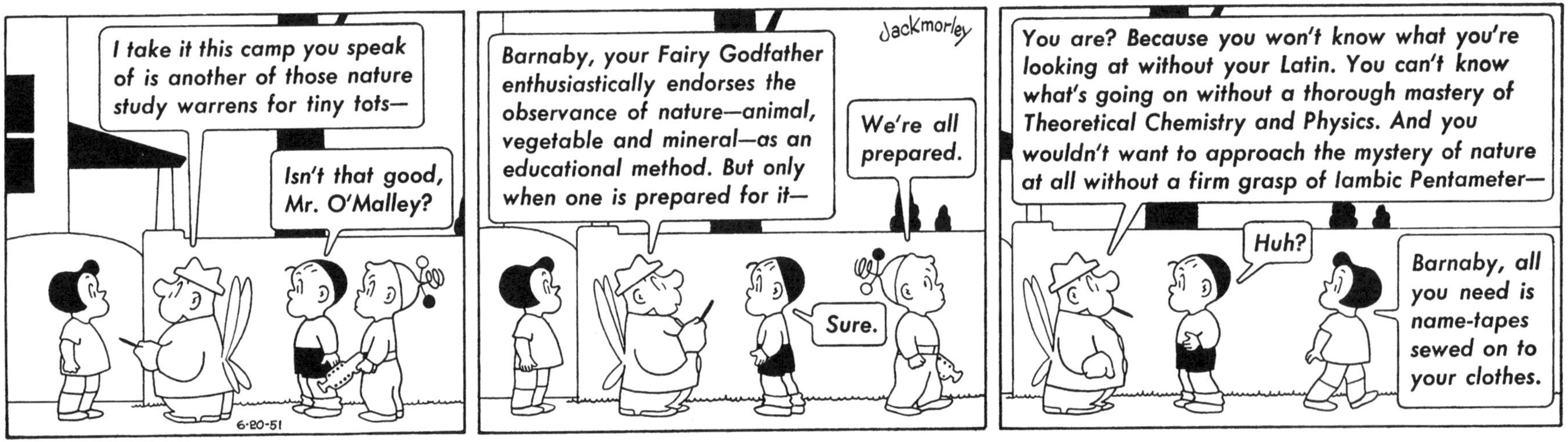
I take it this camp you speak of is another of those nature study warrens for tiny tots—
Isn't that good, Mr. O'Malley?
6-20-51
Jackmorley
Barnaby, your Fairy Godfather enthusiastically endorses the observance of nature—animal, vegetable and mineral—as an educational method. But only when one is prepared for it—
We're all prepared.
Sure.
You are? Because you won't know what you're looking at without your Latin. You can't know what's going on without a thorough mastery of Theoretical Chemistry and Physics. And you wouldn't want to approach the mystery of nature at all without a firm grasp of Iambic Pentameter—
Huh?
Barnaby, all you need is name-tapes sewed on to your clothes.

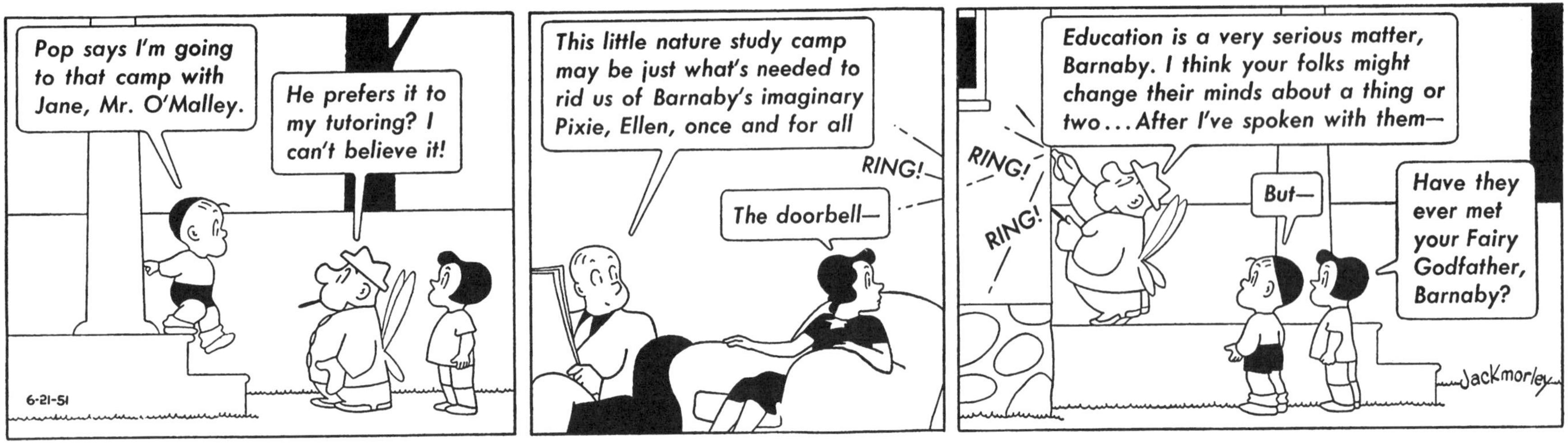
Pop says I'm going to that camp with Jane, Mr. O'Malley.
He prefers it to my tutoring? I can't believe it!
6-21-51
This little nature study camp may be just what's needed to rid us of Barnaby's imaginary Pixie, Ellen, once and for all
RING!
The doorbell—
Education is a very serious matter, Barnaby. I think your folks might change their minds about a thing or two . . . After I've spoken with them—
RING!
RING!
But—
Have they ever met your Fairy Godfather, Barnaby?
Jackmorley

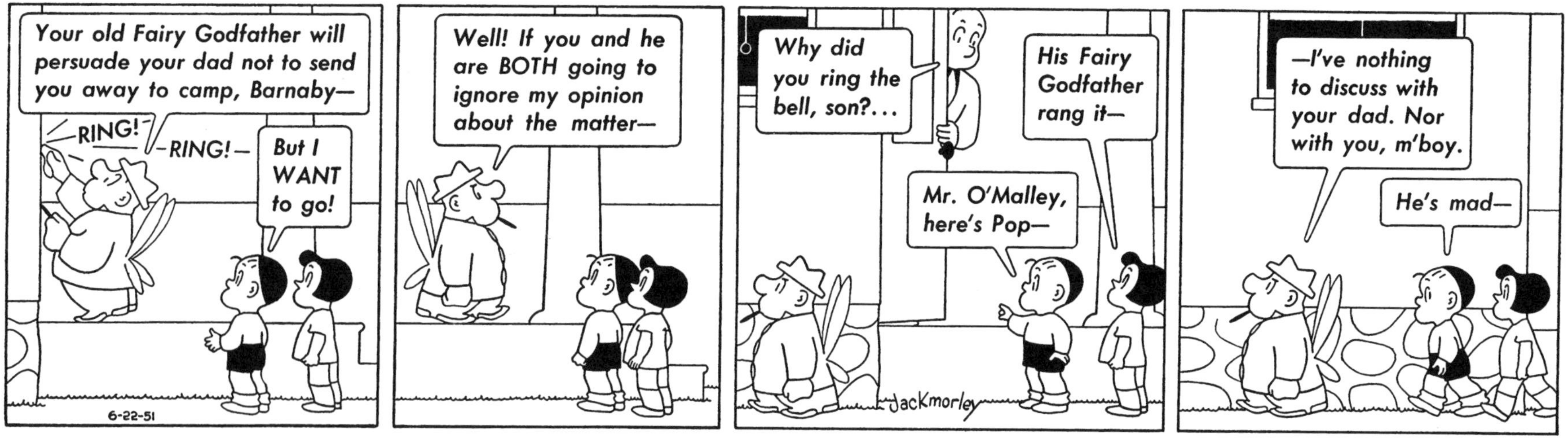
Your old Fairy Godfather will persuade your dad not to send you away to camp, Barnaby—
RING!
—RING!—
But I WANT to go!
6-22-51
Well! If you and he are BOTH going to ignore my opinion about the matter—
Why did you ring the bell, son?...
His Fairy Godfather rang it—
Mr. O'Malley, here's Pop—
JACKmorley
—I've nothing to discuss with your dad. Nor with you, m'boy.
He's mad—

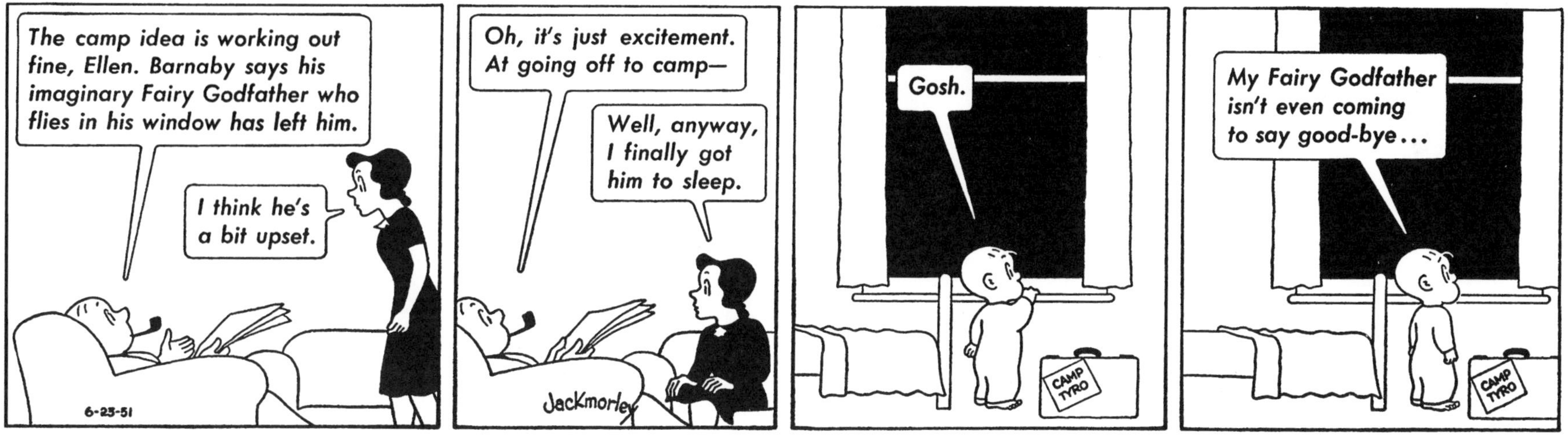
The camp idea is working out fine, Ellen. Barnaby says his imaginary Fairy Godfather who flies in his window has left him.
I think he's a bit upset.
6-23-51
Oh, it's just excitement. At going off to camp—
Well, anyway, I finally got him to sleep.
JACKmorley
Gosh.
CAMP TYRO
My Fairy Godfather isn't even coming to say good-bye...
CAMP TYRO

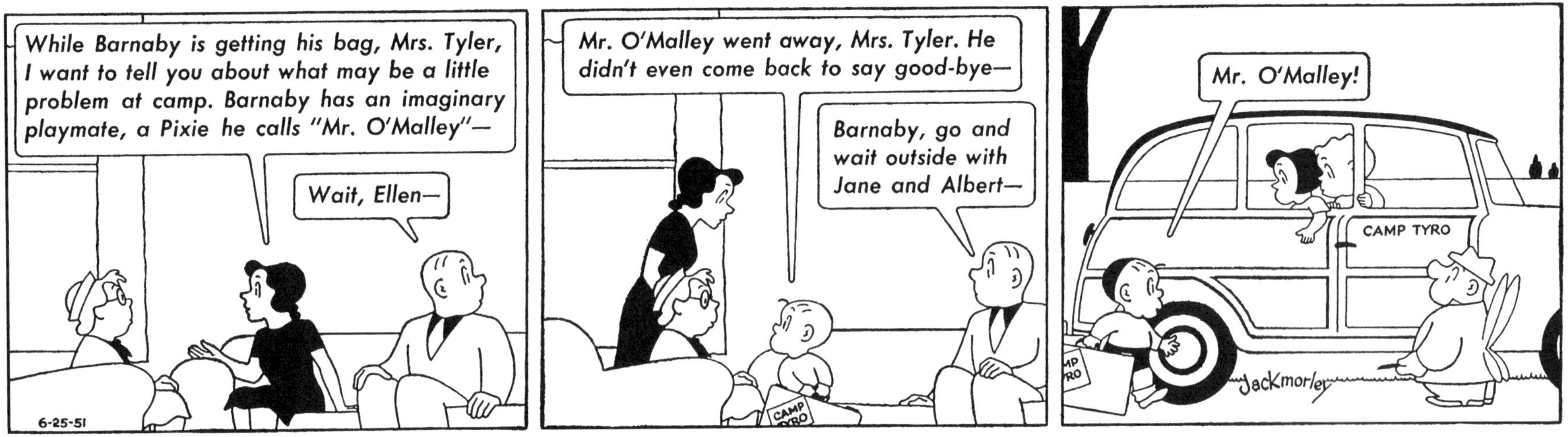
While Barnaby is getting his bag, Mrs. Tyler, I want to tell you about what may be a little problem at camp. Barnaby has an imaginary playmate, a Pixie he calls "Mr. O'Malley"—
Wait, Ellen—
6-25-51
Mr. O'Malley went away, Mrs. Tyler. He didn't even come back to say good-bye—
Barnaby, go and wait outside with Jane and Albert—
Mr. O'Malley!
CAMP TYRO
JackMorley

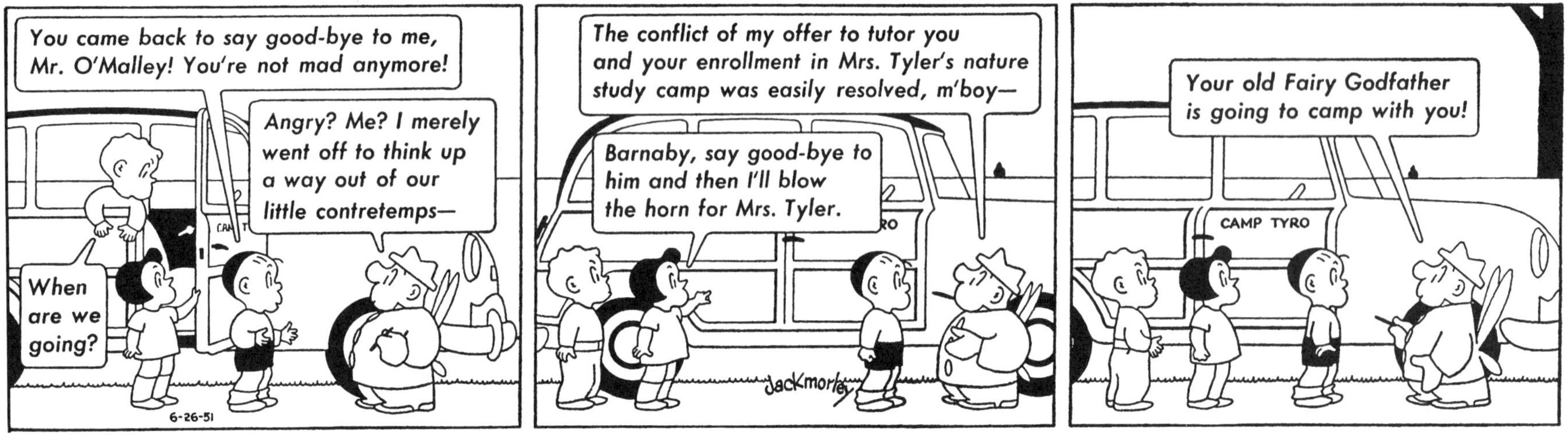
You came back to say good-bye to me, Mr. O'Malley! You're not mad anymore!
Angry? Me? I merely went off to think up a way out of our little contretemps—
When are we going?
6-26-51
The conflict of my offer to tutor you and your enrollment in Mrs. Tyler's nature study camp was easily resolved, m'boy—
Barnaby, say good-bye to him and then I'll blow the horn for Mrs. Tyler.
JackMorley
Your old Fairy Godfather is going to camp with you!
CAMP TYRO

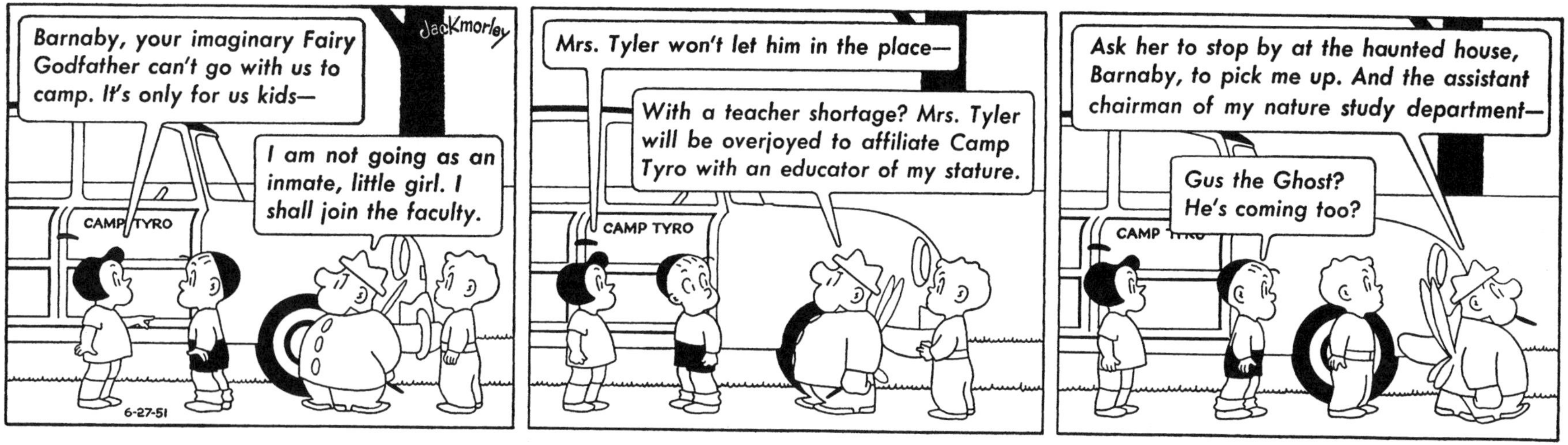
Jackmorley
Barnaby, your imaginary Fairy Godfather can't go with us to camp. It's only for us kids—
I am not going as an inmate, little girl. I shall join the faculty.
CAMP TYRO
6-27-51
Mrs. Tyler won't let him in the place—
With a teacher shortage? Mrs. Tyler will be overjoyed to affiliate Camp Tyro with an educator of my stature.
CAMP TYRO
Ask her to stop by at the haunted house, Barnaby, to pick me up. And the assistant chairman of my nature study department—
Gus the Ghost? He's coming too?

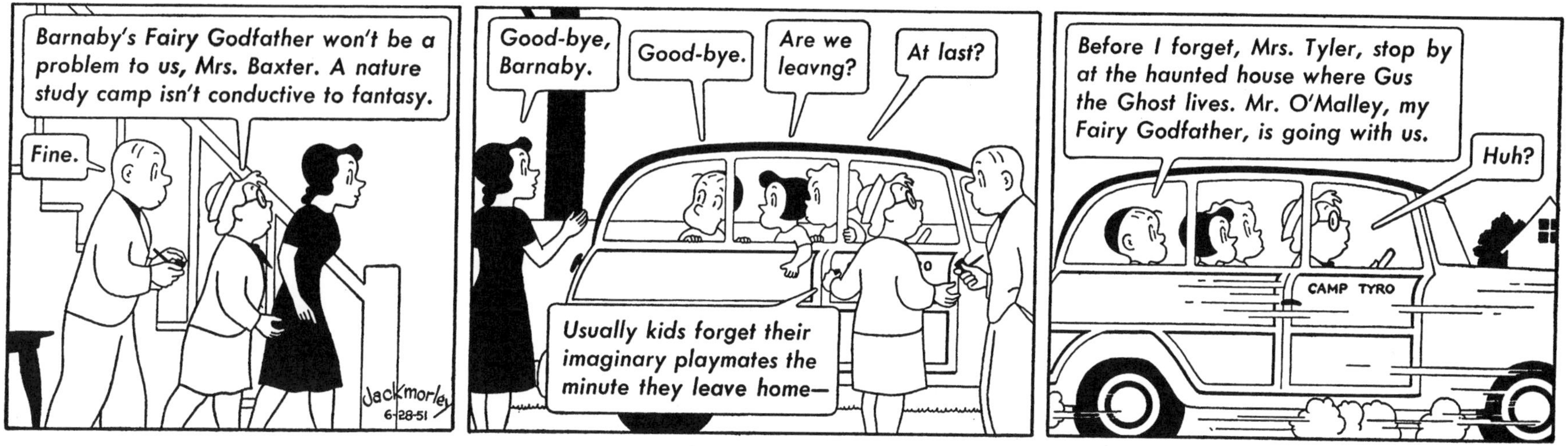
Barnaby's Fairy Godfather won't be a problem to us, Mrs. Baxter. A nature study camp isn't conductive to fantasy.
Fine.
Jackmorley
6-28-51
Good-bye, Barnaby.
Good-bye.
Are we leavng?
At last?
Usually kids forget their imaginary playmates the minute they leave home—
Before I forget, Mrs. Tyler, stop by at the haunted house where Gus the Ghost lives. Mr. O'Malley, my Fairy Godfather, is going with us.
Huh?
CAMP TYRO

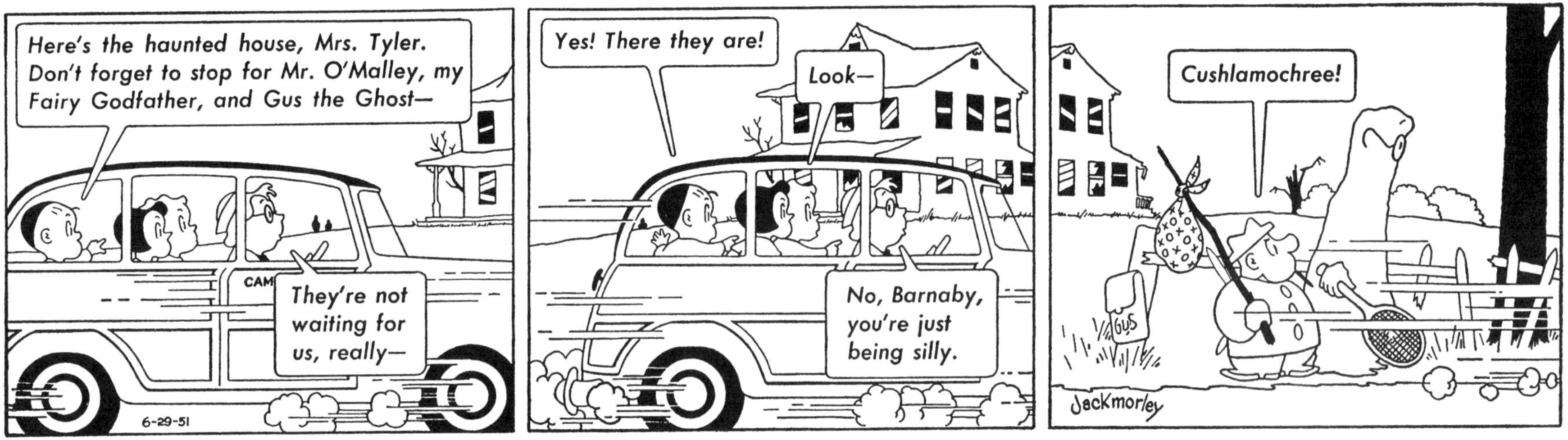
Here's the haunted house, Mrs. Tyler. Don't forget to stop for Mr. O'Malley, my Fairy Godfather, and Gus the Ghost—
They're not waiting for us, really—
6-29-51
Yes! There they are!
Look—
No, Barnaby, you're just being silly.
Cushlamochree!
GUS
JACKMORLEY

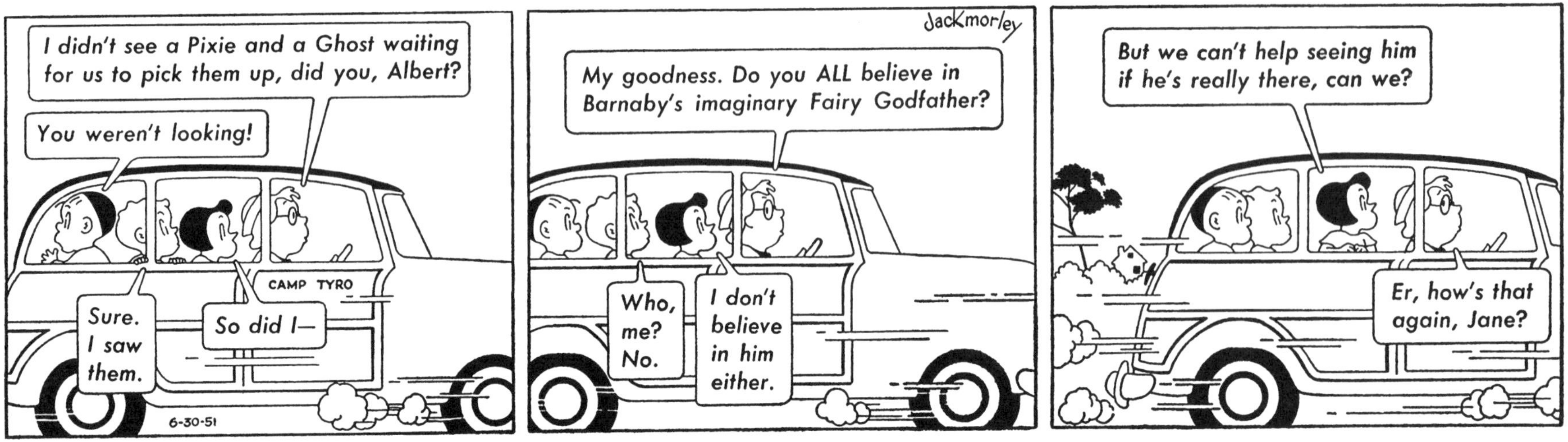
I didn't see a Pixie and a Ghost waiting for us to pick them up, did you, Albert?
You weren't looking!
Sure. I saw them.
So did I—
CAMP TYRO
6-30-51
JACKMORLEY
My goodness. Do you ALL believe in Barnaby's imaginary Fairy Godfather?
Who, me? No.
I don't believe in him either.
But we can't help seeing him if he's really there, can we?
Er, how's that again, Jane?

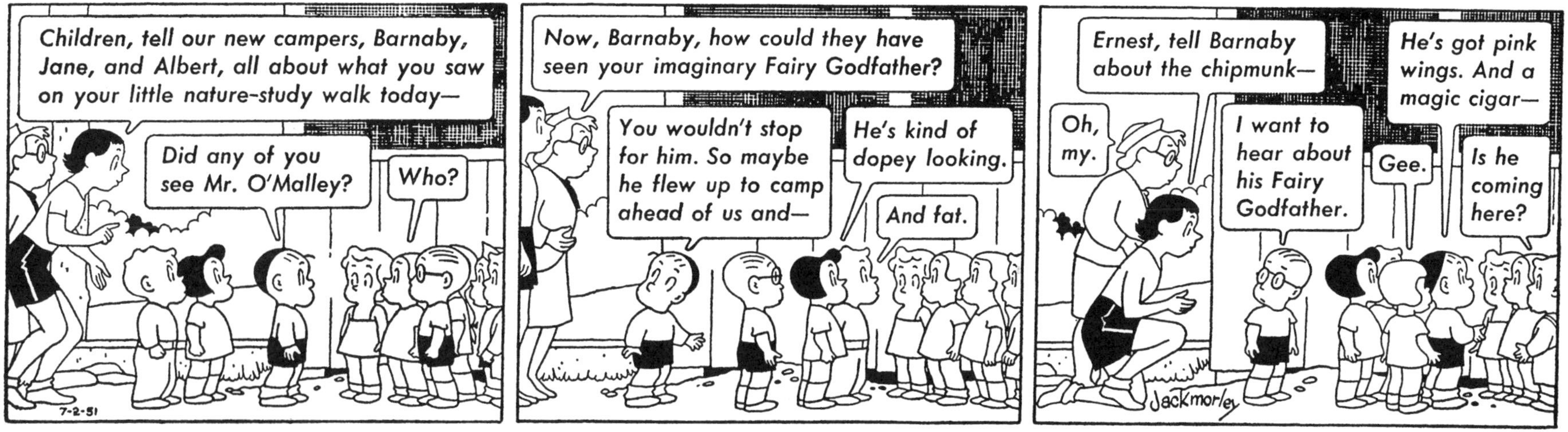
Children, tell our new campers, Barnaby, Jane, and Albert, all about what you saw on your little nature-study walk today—
Did any of you see Mr. O'Malley?
Who?
7-2-51
Now, Barnaby, how could they have seen your imaginary Fairy Godfather?
You wouldn't stop for him. So maybe he flew up to camp ahead of us and—
He's kind of dopey looking.
And fat.
Ernest, tell Barnaby about the chipmunk—
Oh, my.
I want to hear about his Fairy Godfather.
He's got pink wings. And a magic cigar—
Gee.
Is he coming here?
Jackmorley

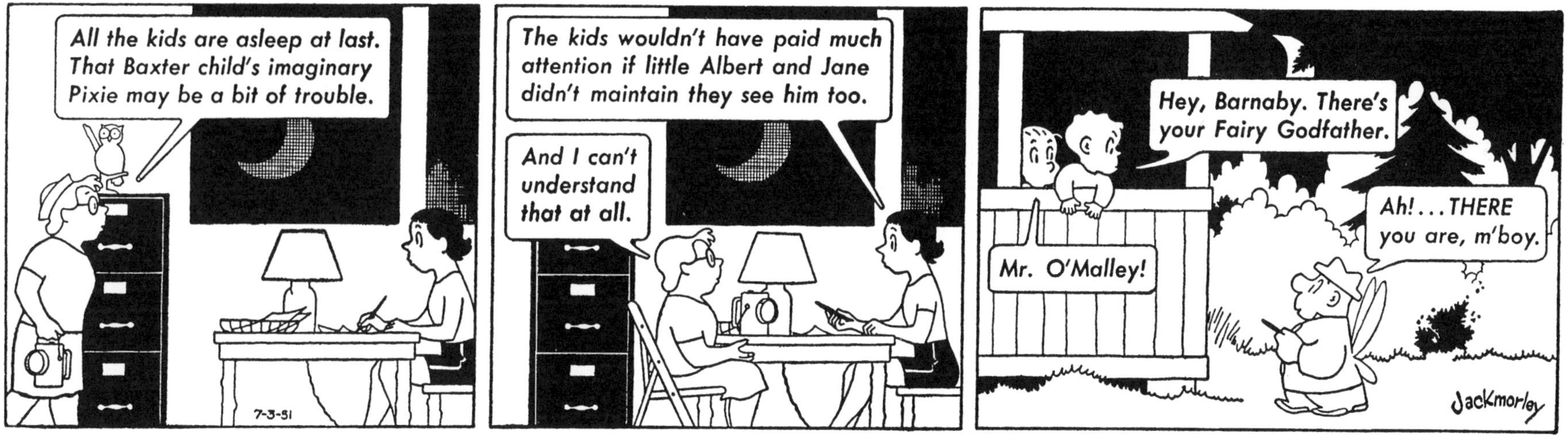
All the kids are asleep at last. That Baxter child's imaginary Pixie may be a bit of trouble.
7-3-51
The kids wouldn't have paid much attention if little Albert and Jane didn't maintain they see him too.
And I can't understand that at all.
Hey, Barnaby. There's your Fairy Godfather.
Mr. O'Malley!
Ah!...THERE you are, m'boy.
Jackmorley

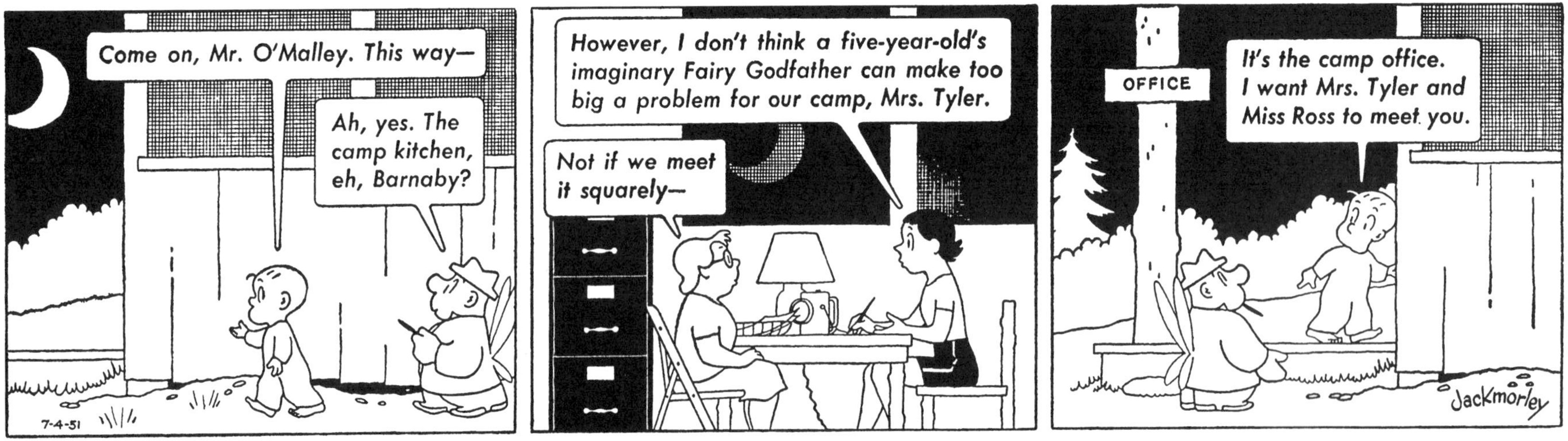
Come on, Mr. O'Malley. This way—
Ah, yes. The camp kitchen, eh, Barnaby?
7-4-51
However, I don't think a five-year-old's imaginary Fairy Godfather can make too big a problem for our camp, Mrs. Tyler.
Not if we meet it squarely—
OFFICE
It's the camp office. I want Mrs. Tyler and Miss Ross to meet you.
Jackmorley

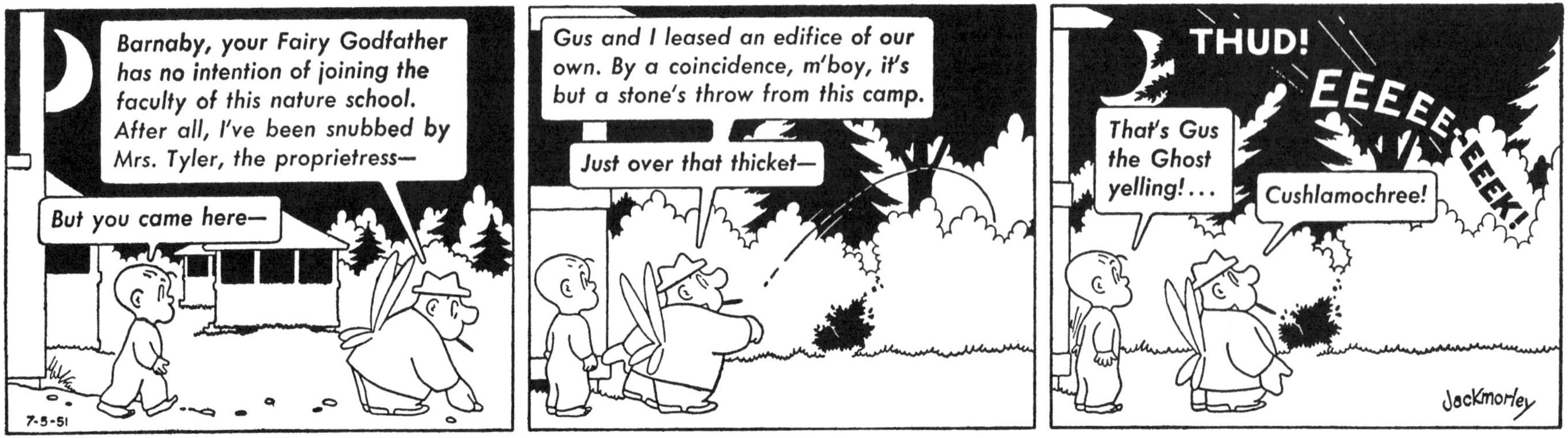
Barnaby, your Fairy Godfather has no intention of joining the faculty of this nature school. After all, I've been snubbed by Mrs. Tyler, the proprietress—
But you came here—
7-5-51
Gus and I leased an edifice of our own. By a coincidence, m'boy, it's but a stone's throw from this camp.
Just over that thicket—
THUD!
EEEEEE-EEEK!
That's Gus the Ghost yelling!...
Cushlamochree!
Jackmorley

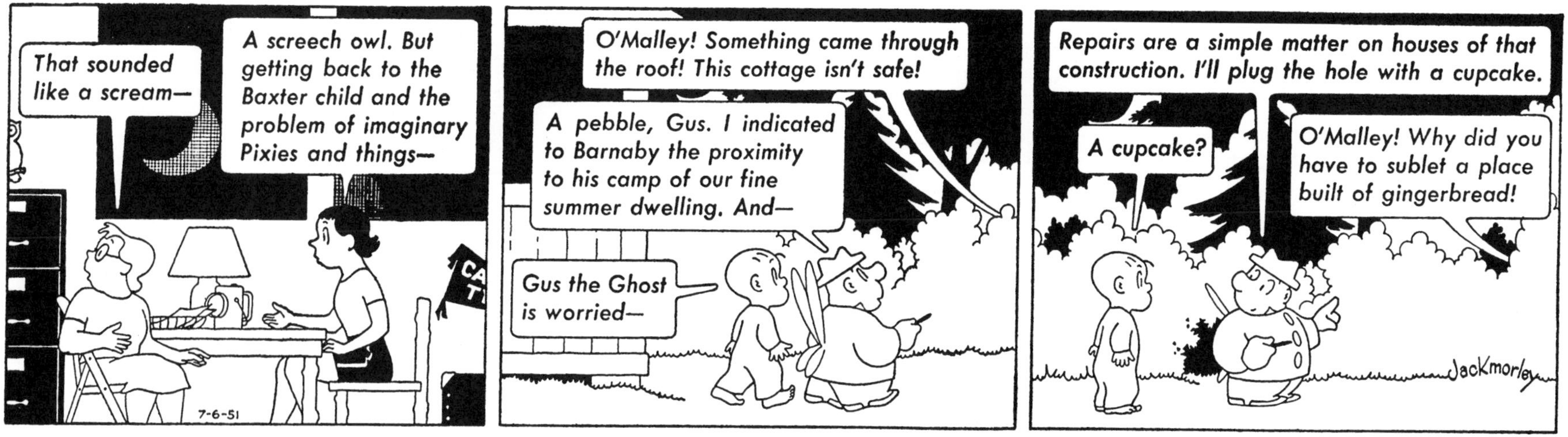
That sounded like a scream—
A screech owl. But getting back to the Baxter child and the problem of imaginary Pixies and things—
7-6-51
O'Malley! Something came through the roof! This cottage isn't safe!
A pebble, Gus. I indicated to Barnaby the proximity to his camp of our fine summer dwelling. And—
Gus the Ghost is worried—
Repairs are a simple matter on houses of that construction. I'll plug the hole with a cupcake.
A cupcake?
O'Malley! Why did you have to sublet a place built of gingerbread!
Jackmorley

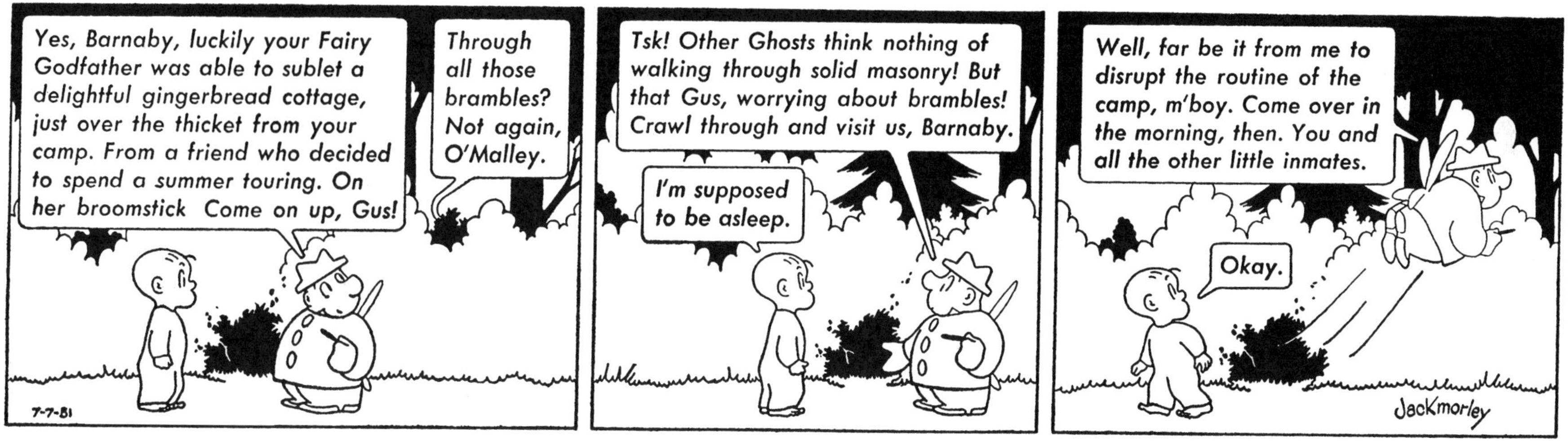
Yes, Barnaby, luckily your Fairy Godfather was able to sublet a delightful gingerbread cottage, just over the thicket from your camp. From a friend who decided to spend a summer touring. On her broomstick Come on up, Gus!
Through all those brambles? Not again, O'Malley.
7-7-51
Tsk! Other Ghosts think nothing of walking through solid masonry! But that Gus, worrying about brambles! Crawl through and visit us, Barnaby.
I'm supposed to be asleep.
Well, far be it from me to disrupt the routine of the camp, m'boy. Come over in the morning, then. You and all the other little inmates.
Okay.
Jackmorley

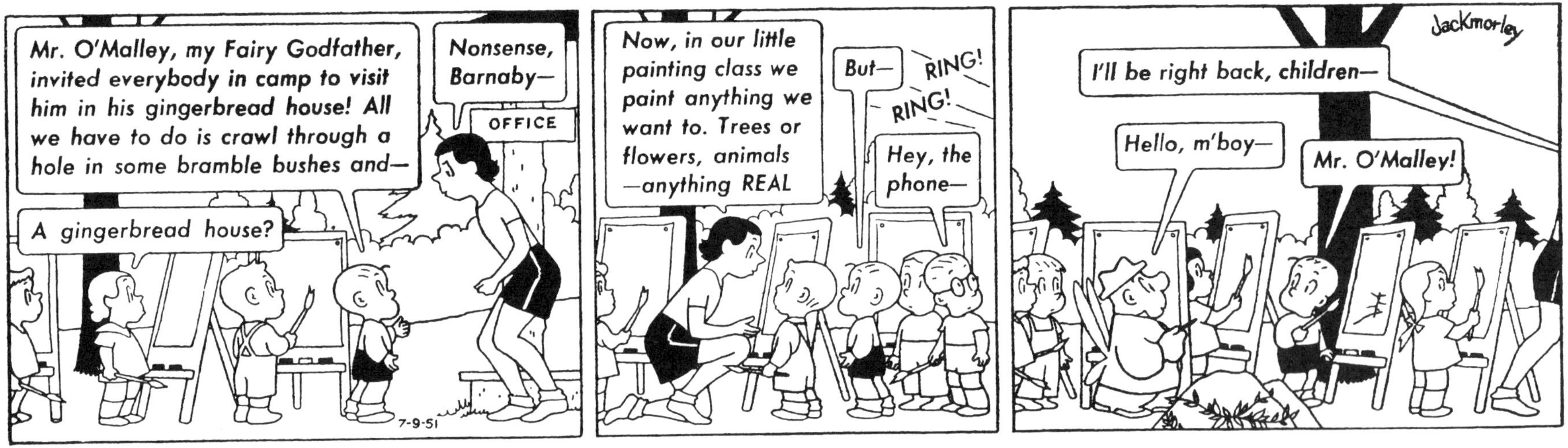
Mr. O'Malley, my Fairy Godfather, invited everybody in camp to visit him in his gingerbread house! All we have to do is crawl through a hole in some bramble bushes and—
Nonsense, Barnaby—
OFFICE
A gingerbread house?
7-9-51
Now, in our little painting class we paint anything we want to. Trees or flowers, animals —anything REAL
But—
RING!
RING!
Hey, the phone—
Jackmorley
I'll be right back, children—
Hello, m'boy—
Mr. O'Malley!

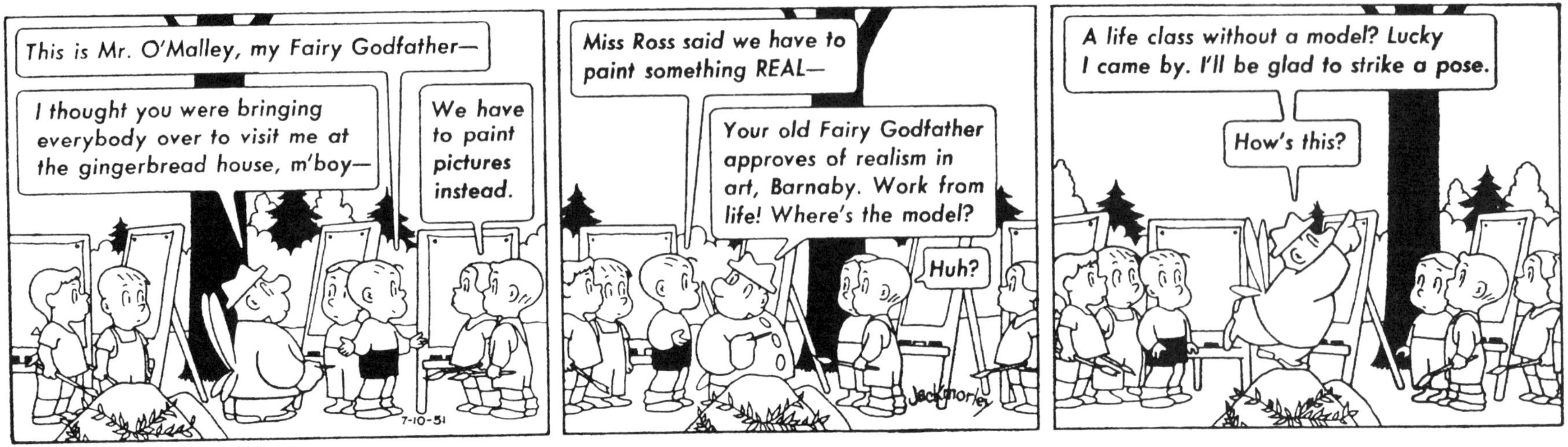
This is Mr. O'Malley, my Fairy Godfather—
I thought you were bringing everybody over to visit me at the gingerbread house, m'boy—
We have to paint pictures instead.
7-10-51
Miss Ross said we have to paint something REAL—
Your old Fairy Godfather approves of realism in art, Barnaby. Work from life! Where's the model?
Huh?
Jackmorley
A life class without a model? Lucky I came by. I'll be glad to strike a pose.
How's this?

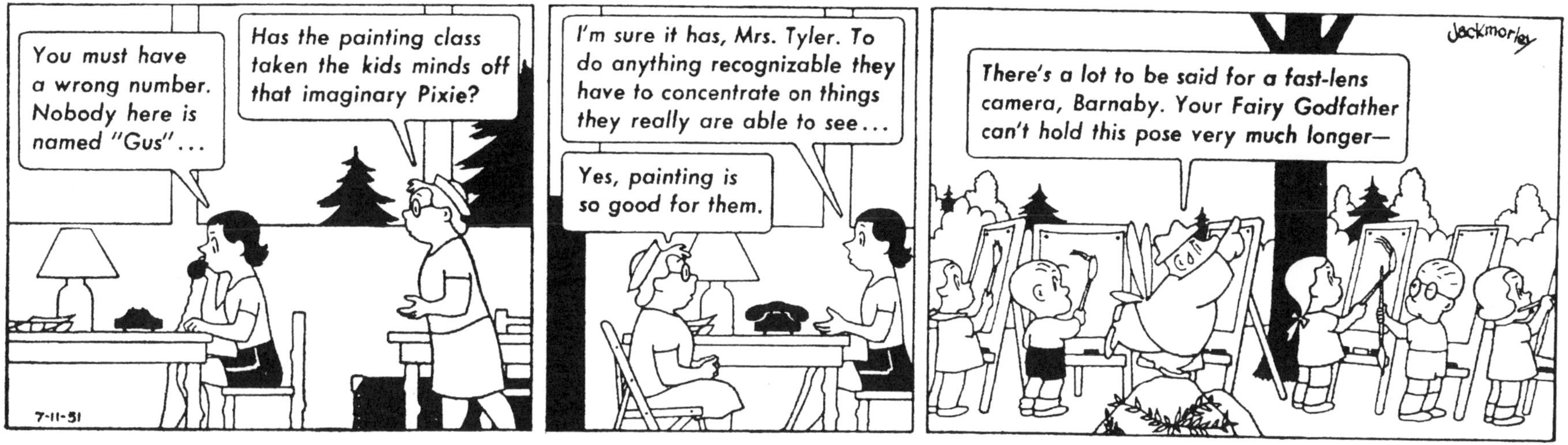
You must have a wrong number. Nobody here is named "Gus"...
Has the painting class taken the kids minds off that imaginary Pixie?
7-11-51
I'm sure it has, Mrs. Tyler. To do anything recognizable they have to concentrate on things they really are able to see...
Yes, painting is so good for them.
Jackmorley
There's a lot to be said for a fast-lens camera, Barnaby. Your Fairy Godfather can't hold this pose very much longer—

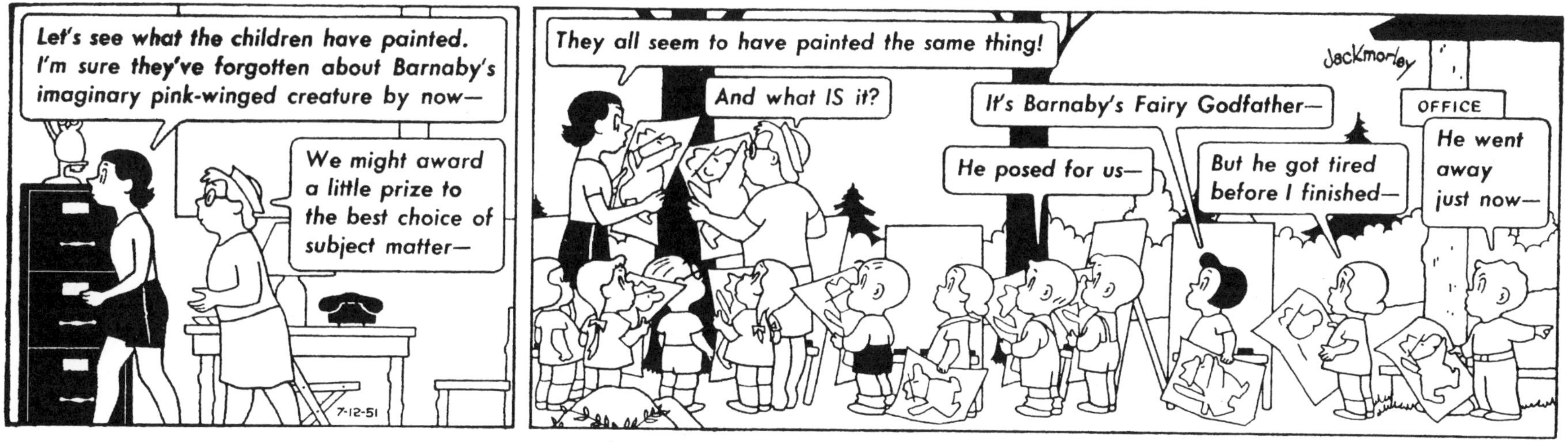
Let's see what the children have painted. I'm sure they've forgotten about Barnaby's imaginary pink-winged creature by now—
We might award a little prize to the best choice of subject matter—
7-12-51
They all seem to have painted the same thing!
And what IS it?
It's Barnaby's Fairy Godfather—
He posed for us—
But he got tired before I finished—
He went away just now—
Jackmorley
OFFICE

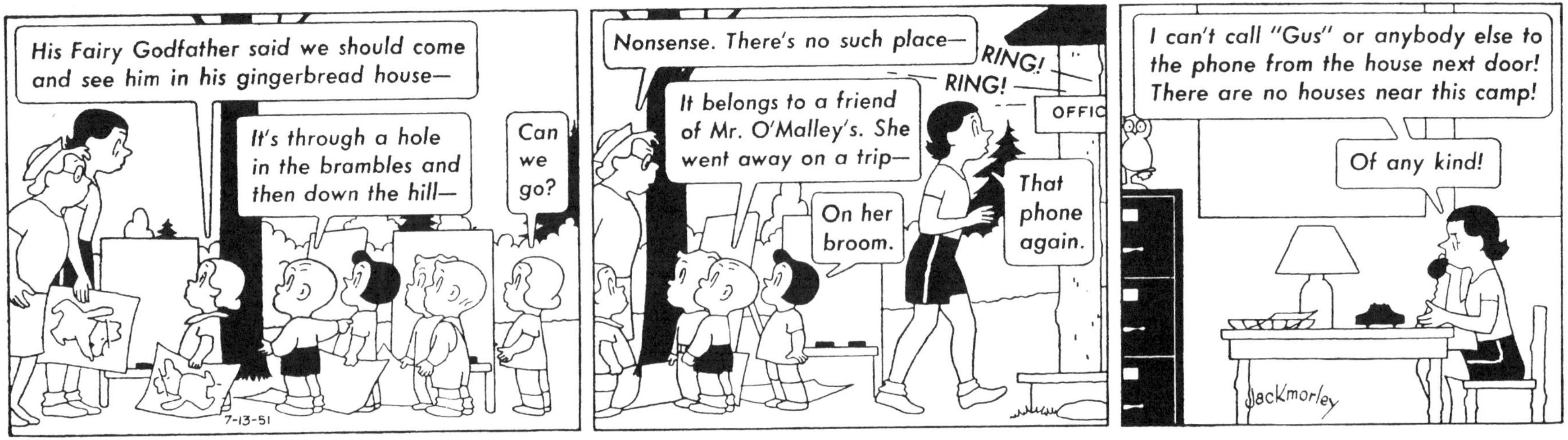
His Fairy Godfather said we should come and see him in his gingerbread house—
It's through a hole in the brambles and then down the hill—
Can we go?
7-13-51
Nonsense. There's no such place—
RING!
RING!
OFFIC
It belongs to a friend of Mr. O'Malley's. She went away on a trip—
On her broom.
That phone again.
I can't call "Gus" or anybody else to the phone from the house next door! There are no houses near this camp!
Of any kind!
Jackmorley

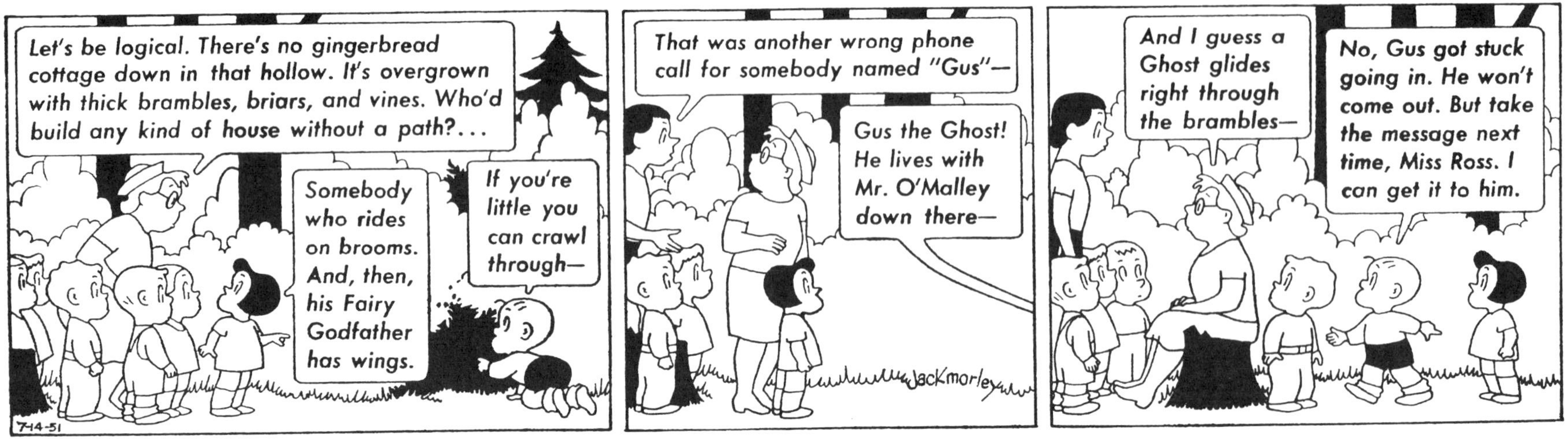
Let's be logical. There's no gingerbread cottage down in that hollow. It's overgrown with thick brambles, briars, and vines. Who'd build any kind of house without a path?...
Somebody who rides on brooms. And, then, his Fairy Godfather has wings.
If you're little you can crawl through—
7-14-51
That was another wrong phone call for somebody named "Gus"—
Gus the Ghost! He lives with Mr. O'Malley down there—
Jackmorley
And I guess a Ghost glides right through the brambles—
No, Gus got stuck going in. He won't come out. But take the message next time, Miss Ross. I can get it to him.

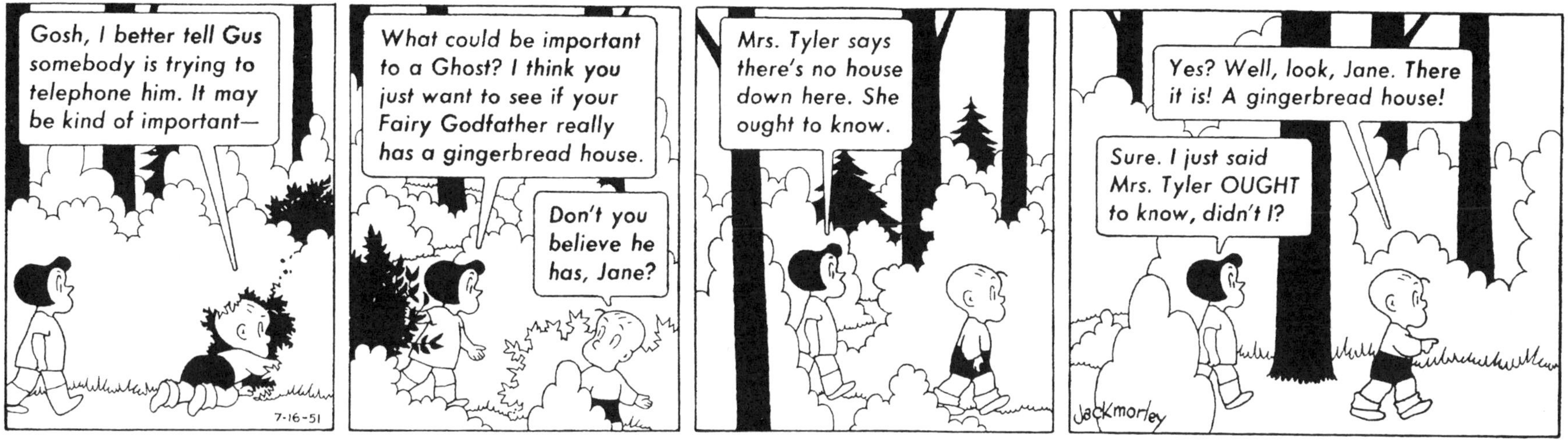
Gosh, I better tell Gus somebody is trying to telephone him. It may be kind of important—
What could be important to a Ghost? I think you just want to see if your Fairy Godfather really has a gingerbread house.
Don't you believe he has, Jane?
Mrs. Tyler says there's no house down here. She ought to know.
Yes? Well, look, Jane. There it is! A gingerbread house!
Sure. I just said Mrs. Tyler OUGHT to know, didn't I?
7-16-51
Jackmorley

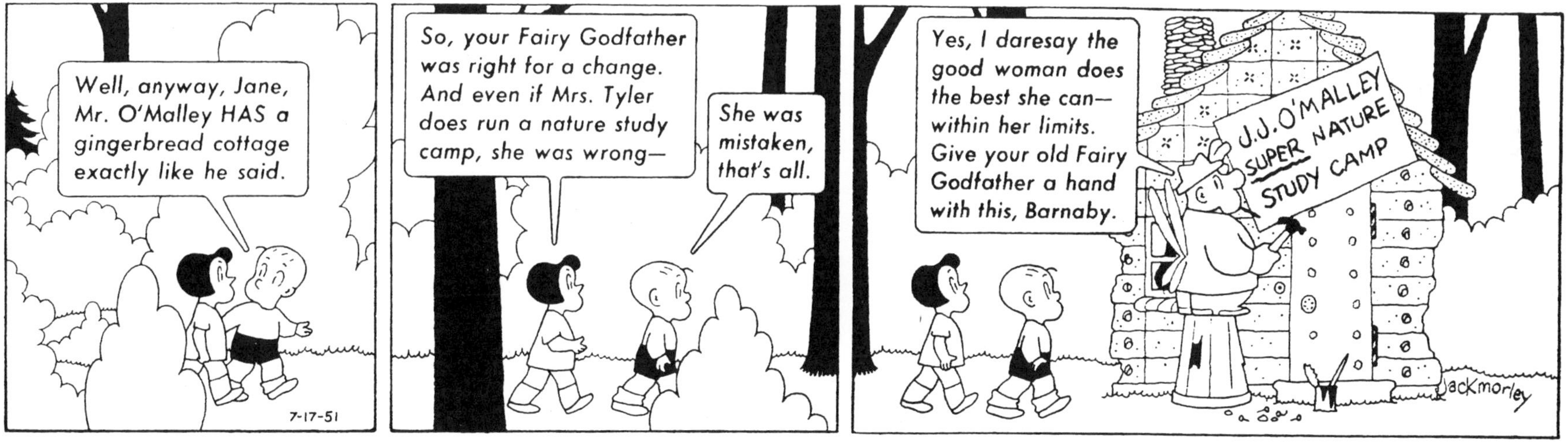
Well, anyway, Jane, Mr. O'Malley HAS a gingerbread cottage exactly like he said.
7-17-51
So, your Fairy Godfather was right for a change. And even if Mrs. Tyler does run a nature study camp, she was wrong—
She was mistaken, that's all.
Yes, I daresay the good woman does the best she can— within her limits. Give your old Fairy Godfather a hand with this, Barnaby.
J.J. O'MALLEY SUPER NATURE STUDY CAMP
Jackmorley

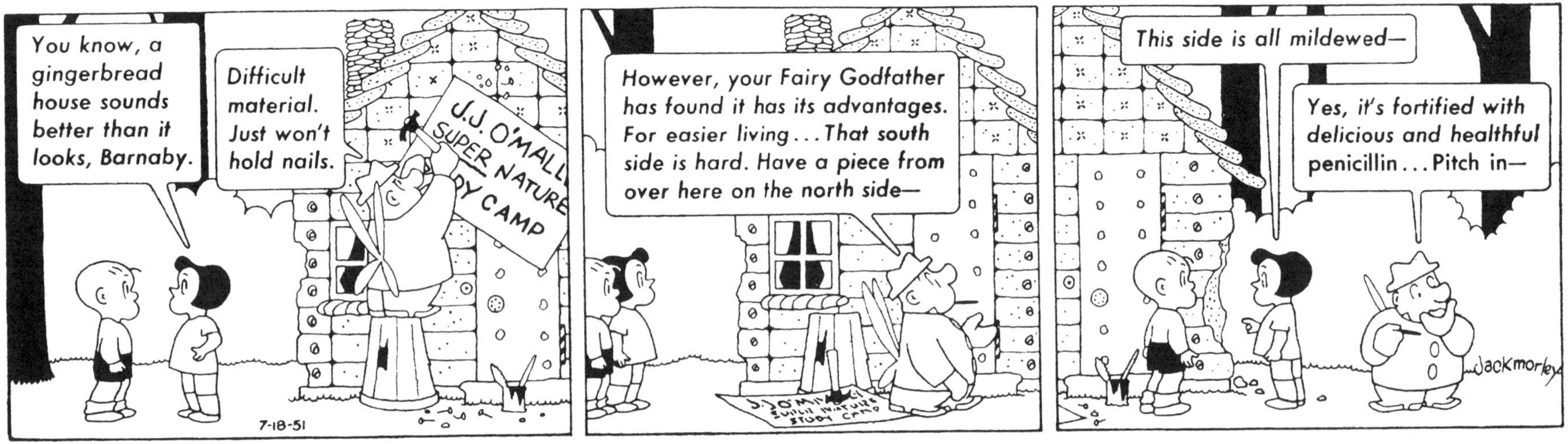
You know, a gingerbread house sounds better than it looks, Barnaby.
Difficult material. Just won't hold nails.
7-18-51
However, your Fairy Godfather has found it has its advantages. For easier living... That south side is hard. Have a piece from over here on the north side—
This side is all mildewed—
Yes, it's fortified with delicious and healthful penicillin... Pitch in—
Jackmorley

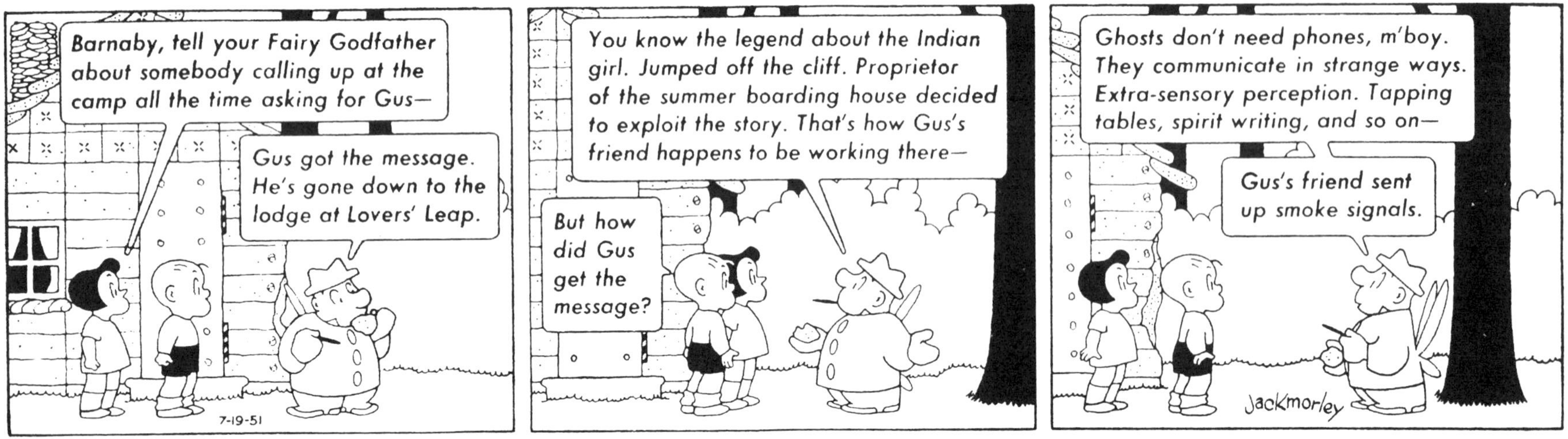
Barnaby, tell your Fairy Godfather about somebody calling up at the camp all the time asking for Gus—
Gus got the message. He's gone down to the lodge at Lovers' Leap.
7-19-51
But how did Gus get the message?
You know the legend about the Indian girl. Jumped off the cliff. Proprietor of the summer boarding house decided to exploit the story. That's how Gus's friend happens to be working there—
Ghosts don't need phones, m'boy. They communicate in strange ways. Extra-sensory perception. Tapping tables, spirit writing, and so on—
Gus's friend sent up smoke signals.
Jackmorley

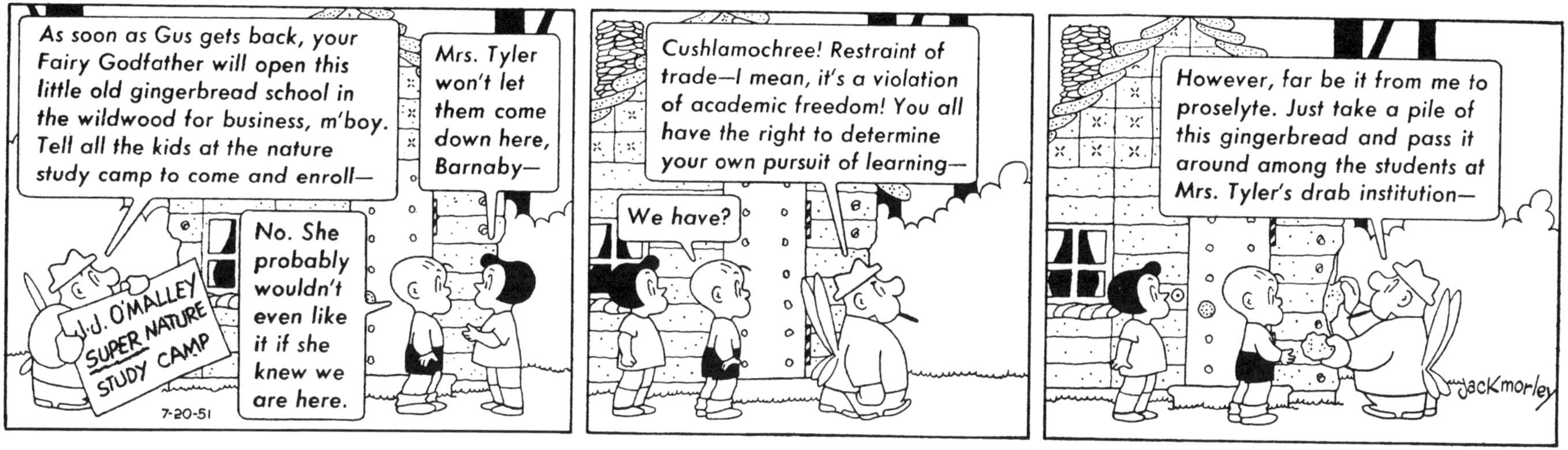
As soon as Gus gets back, your Fairy Godfather will open this little old gingerbread school in the wildwood for business, m'boy. Tell all the kids at the nature study camp to come and enroll—
Mrs. Tyler won't let them come down here, Barnaby—
J.J. O'MALLEY SUPER NATURE STUDY CAMP
No. She probably wouldn't even like it if she knew we are here.
7-20-51
Cushlamochree! Restraint of trade—I mean, it's a violation of academic freedom! You all have the right to determine your own pursuit of learning—
We have?
However, far be it from me to proselyte. Just take a pile of this gingerbread and pass it around among the students at Mrs. Tyler's drab institution—
JackMorley

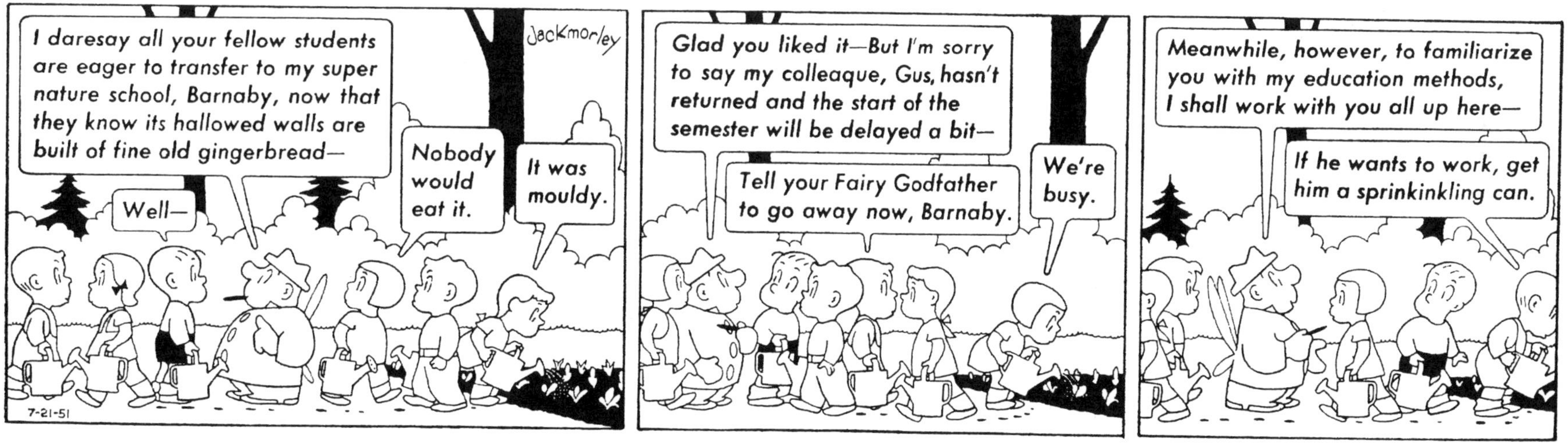
I daresay all your fellow students are eager to transfer to my super nature school, Barnaby, now that they know its hallowed walls are built of fine old gingerbread—
JackMorley
Well—
Nobody would eat it.
It was mouldy.
7-21-51
Glad you liked it—But I'm sorry to say my colleaque, Gus, hasn't returned and the start of the semester will be delayed a bit—
Tell your Fairy Godfather to go away now, Barnaby.
We're busy.
Meanwhile, however, to familiarize you with my education methods, I shall work with you all up here—
If he wants to work, get him a sprinkinkling can.

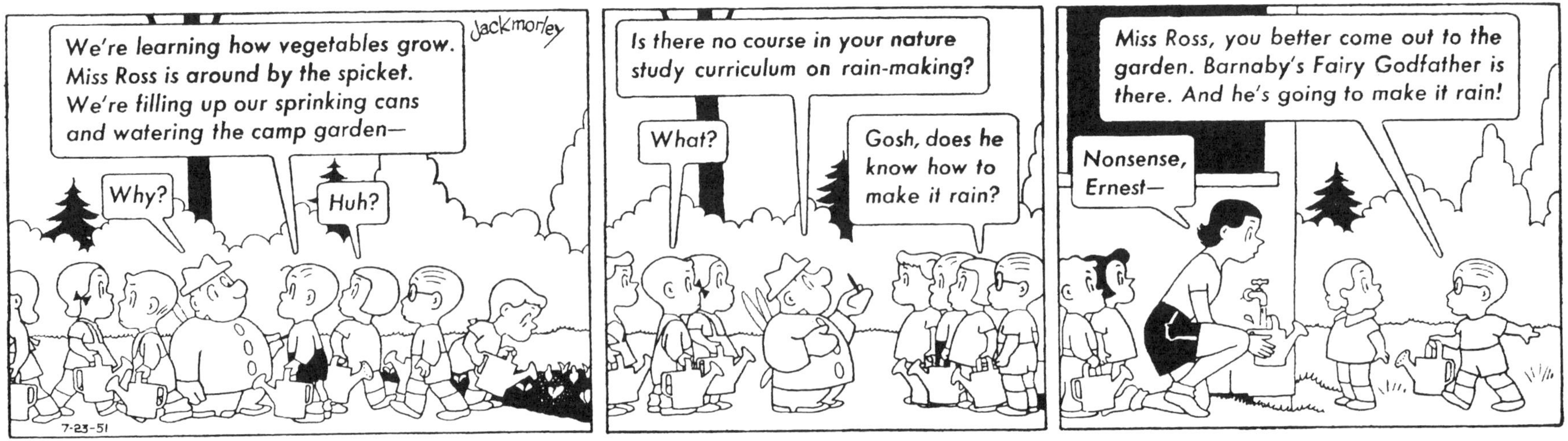
Jackmorley
We're learning how vegetables grow. Miss Ross is around by the spicket. We're filling up our sprinking cans and watering the camp garden—
Why?
Huh?
7-23-51
Is there no course in your nature study curriculum on rain-making?
What?
Gosh, does he know how to make it rain?
Miss Ross, you better come out to the garden. Barnaby's Fairy Godfather is there. And he's going to make it rain!
Nonsense, Ernest—

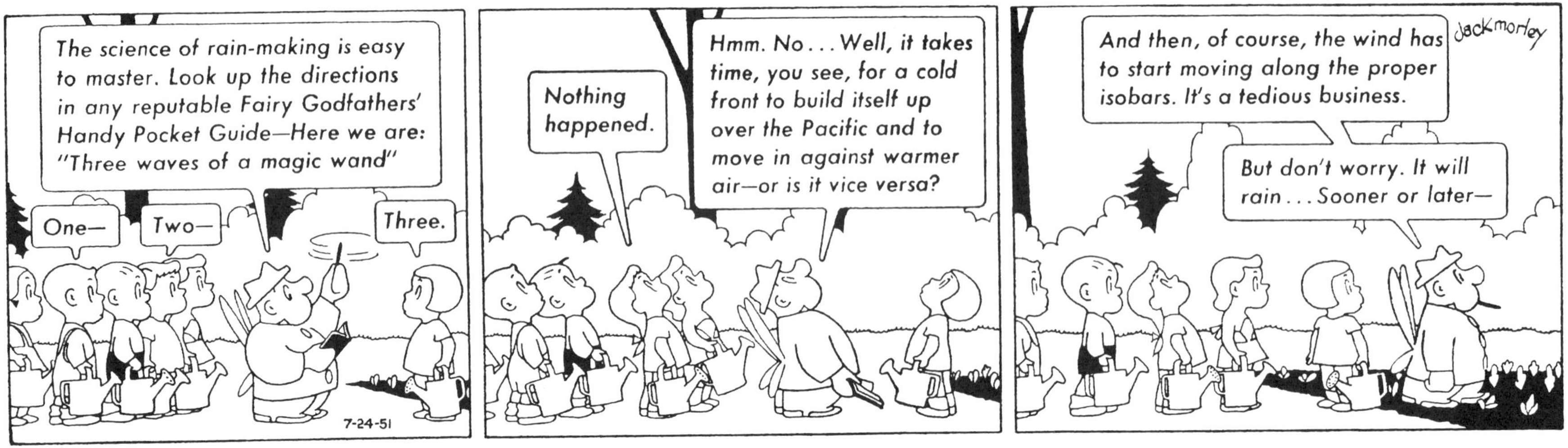
The science of rain-making is easy to master. Look up the directions in any reputable Fairy Godfathers' Handy Pocket Guide—Here we are: "Three waves of a magic wand"
One—
Two—
Three.
7-24-51
Nothing happened.
Hmm. No . . . Well, it takes time, you see, for a cold front to build itself up over the Pacific and to move in against warmer air—or is it vice versa?
Jackmorley
And then, of course, the wind has to start moving along the proper isobars. It's a tedious business.
But don't worry. It will rain . . . Sooner or later—

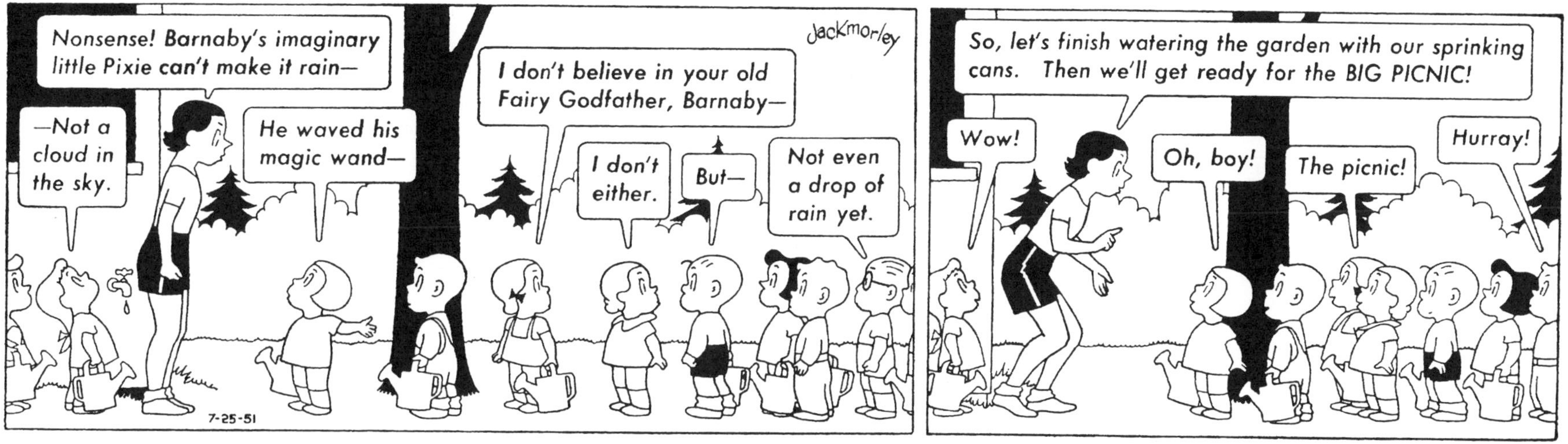

Nonsense! Barnaby's imaginary little Pixie can't make it rain—
—Not a cloud in the sky.
He waved his magic wand—
I don't believe in your old Fairy Godfather, Barnaby—
I don't either.
But—
Not even a drop of rain yet.
Jackmorley
7-25-51
So, let's finish watering the garden with our sprinkling cans. Then we'll get ready for the BIG PICNIC!
Wow!
Oh, boy!
The picnic!
Hurray!

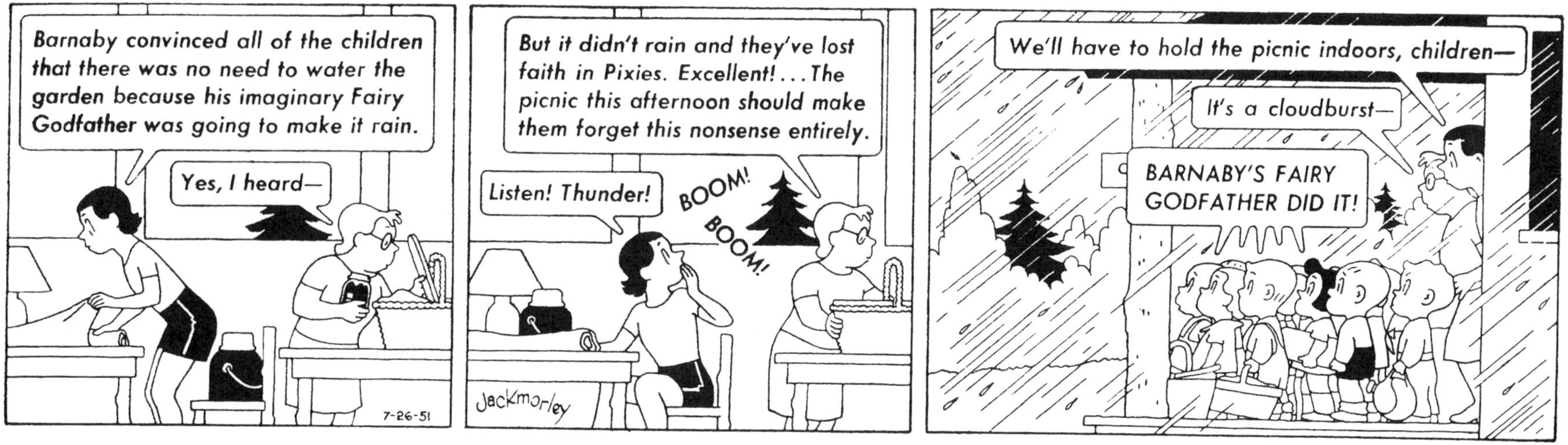

Barnaby convinced all of the children that there was no need to water the garden because his imaginary Fairy Godfather was going to make it rain.
Yes, I heard—
7-26-51
But it didn't rain and they've lost faith in Pixies. Excellent!...The picnic this afternoon should make them forget this nonsense entirely.
Listen! Thunder!
BOOM!
BOOM!
Jackmorley
We'll have to hold the picnic indoors, children—
It's a cloudburst—
BARNABY'S FAIRY GODFATHER DID IT!

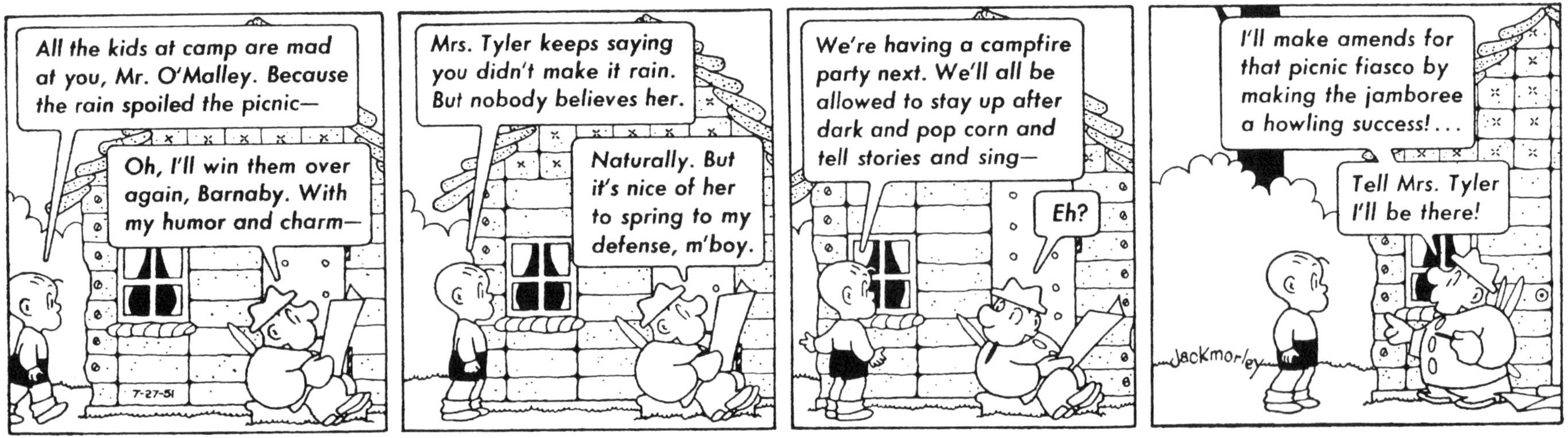
All the kids at camp are mad at you, Mr. O'Malley. Because the rain spoiled the picnic—
Oh, I'll win them over again, Barnaby. With my humor and charm—
7-27-51
Mrs. Tyler keeps saying you didn't make it rain. But nobody believes her.
Naturally. But it's nice of her to spring to my defense, m'boy.
We're having a campfire party next. We'll all be allowed to stay up after dark and pop corn and tell stories and sing—
Eh?
I'll make amends for that picnic fiasco by making the jamboree a howling success!...
Tell Mrs. Tyler I'll be there!
JACKMORLEY

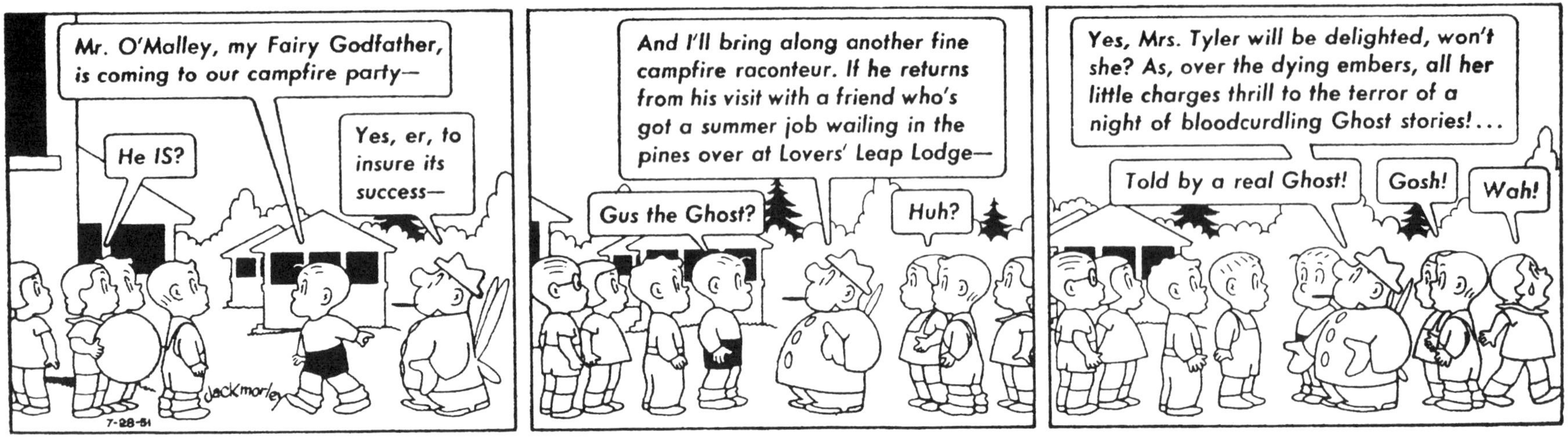
Mr. O'Malley, my Fairy Godfather, is coming to our campfire party—
He IS?
Yes, er, to insure its success—
jackmorley
7-28-51
And I'll bring along another fine campfire raconteur. If he returns from his visit with a friend who's got a summer job wailing in the pines over at Lovers' Leap Lodge—
Gus the Ghost?
Huh?
Yes, Mrs. Tyler will be delighted, won't she? As, over the dying embers, all her little charges thrill to the terror of a night of bloodcurdling Ghost stories!...
Told by a real Ghost!
Gosh!
Wah!

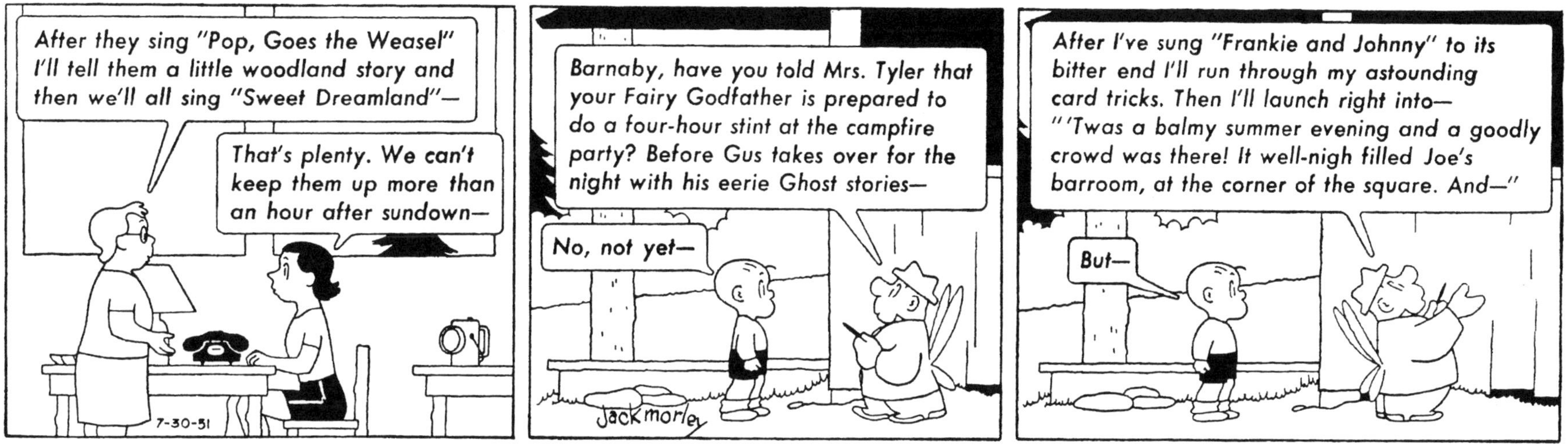
After they sing "Pop, Goes the Weasel" I'll tell them a little woodland story and then we'll all sing "Sweet Dreamland"—
That's plenty. We can't keep them up more than an hour after sundown—
7-30-51
Barnaby, have you told Mrs. Tyler that your Fairy Godfather is prepared to do a four-hour stint at the campfire party? Before Gus takes over for the night with his eerie Ghost stories—
No, not yet—
Jack Morley
After I've sung "Frankie and Johnny" to its bitter end I'll run through my astounding card tricks. Then I'll launch right into— "'Twas a balmy summer evening and a goodly crowd was there! It well-nigh filled Joe's barroom, at the corner of the square. And—"
But—

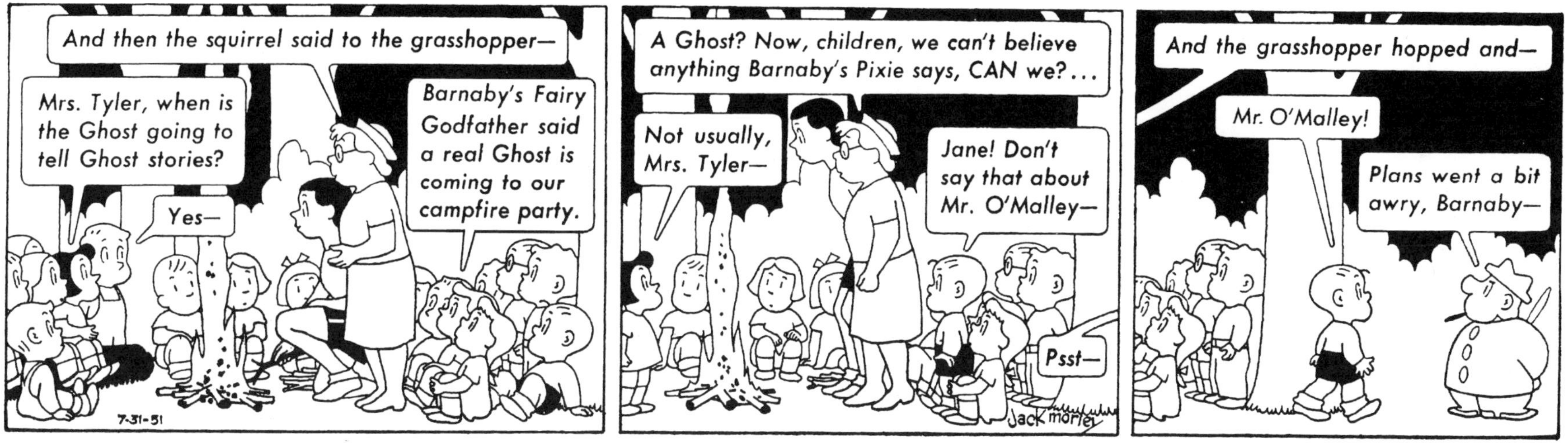
And then the squirrel said to the grasshopper—
Mrs. Tyler, when is the Ghost going to tell Ghost stories?
Yes—
Barnaby's Fairy Godfather said a real Ghost is coming to our campfire party.
7-31-51
A Ghost? Now, children, we can't believe anything Barnaby's Pixie says, CAN we?...
Not usually, Mrs. Tyler—
Jane! Don't say that about Mr. O'Malley—
Psst—
Jack Morley
And the grasshopper hopped and—
Mr. O'Malley!
Plans went a bit awry, Barnaby—

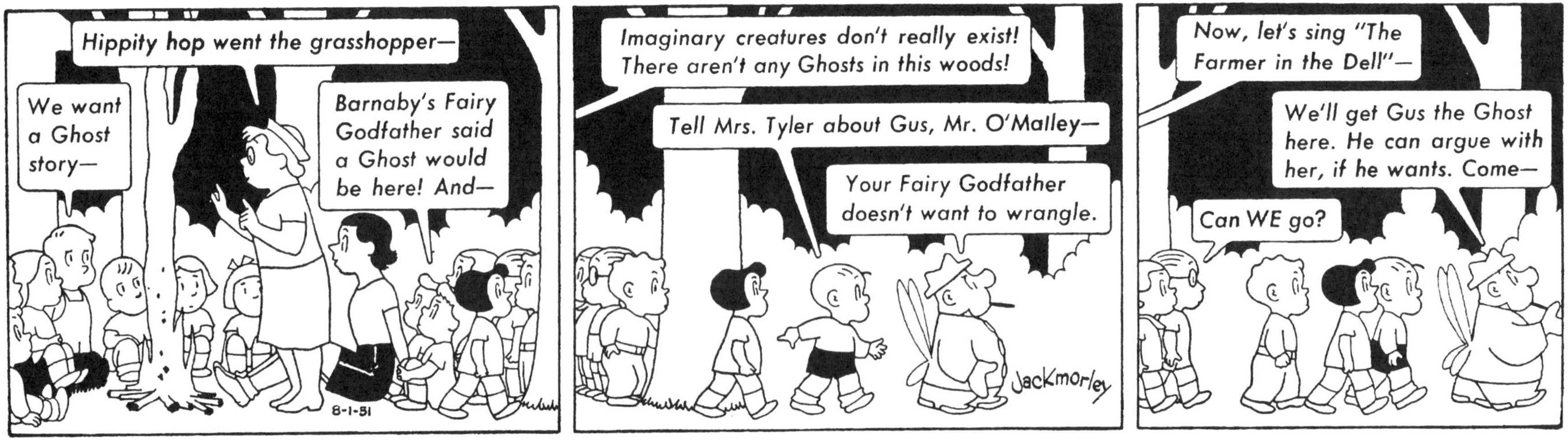
Hippity hop went the grasshopper—
We want a Ghost story—
Barnaby's Fairy Godfather said a Ghost would be here! And—
8-1-51
Imaginary creatures don't really exist! There aren't any Ghosts in this woods!
Tell Mrs. Tyler about Gus, Mr. O'Malley—
Your Fairy Godfather doesn't want to wrangle.
Jackmorley
Now, let's sing "The Farmer in the Dell"—
We'll get Gus the Ghost here. He can argue with her, if he wants. Come—
Can WE go?

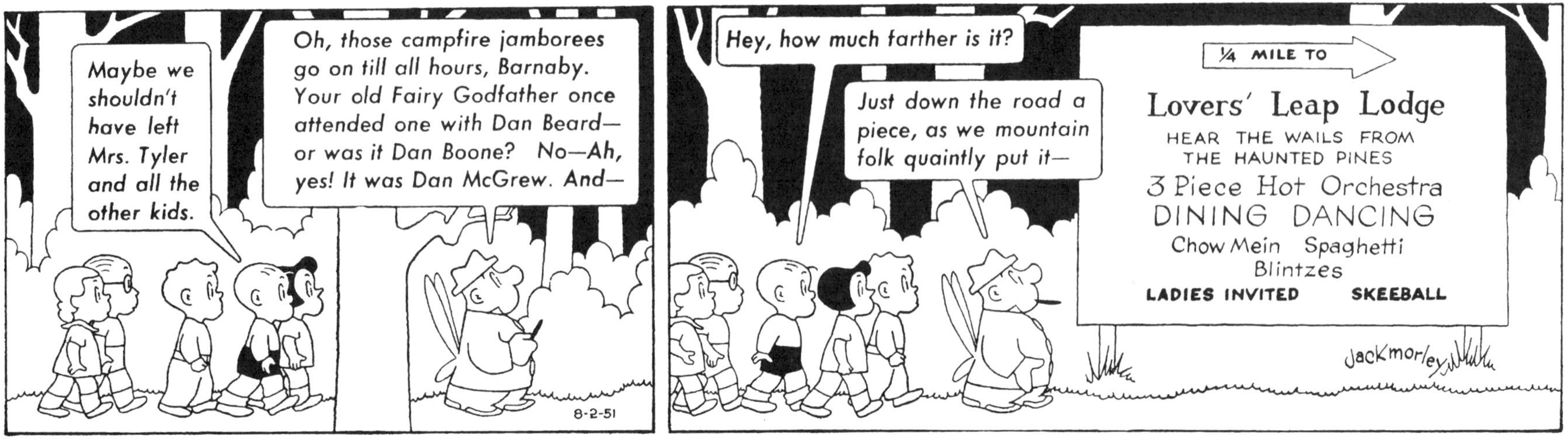
Maybe we shouldn't have left Mrs. Tyler and all the other kids.
Oh, those campfire jamborees go on till all hours, Barnaby. Your old Fairy Godfather once attended one with Dan Beard— or was it Dan Boone? No—Ah, yes! It was Dan McGrew. And—
8-2-51
Hey, how much farther is it?
Just down the road a piece, as we mountain folk quaintly put it—
¼ MILE TO
Lovers' Leap Lodge
HEAR THE WAILS FROM THE HAUNTED PINES
3 Piece Hot Orchestra
DINING DANCING
Chow Mein Spaghetti
Blintzes
LADIES INVITED SKEEBALL
Jackmorley

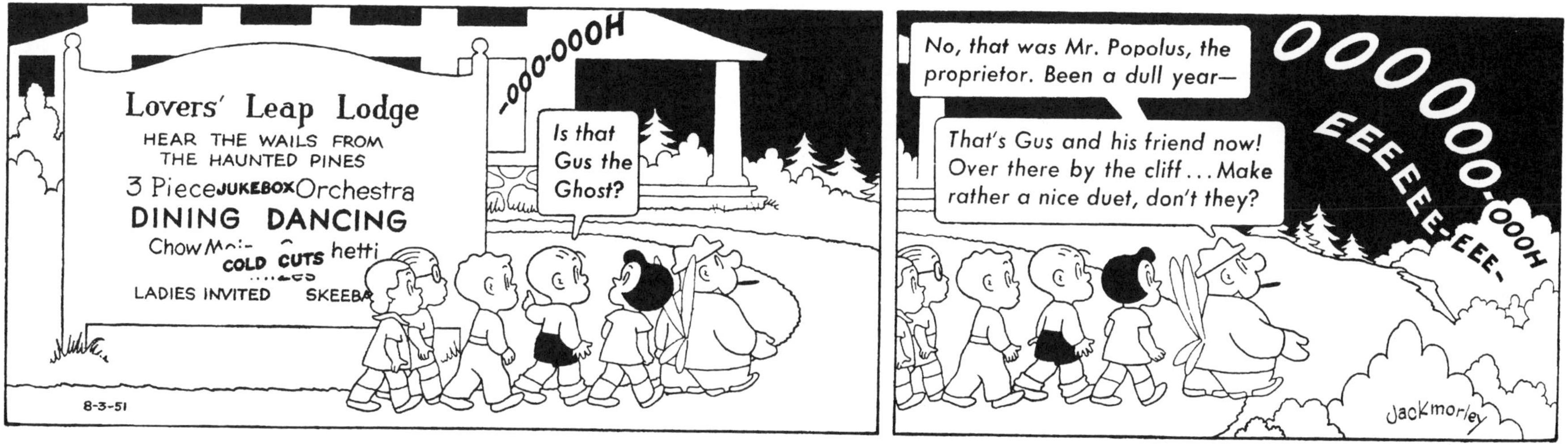
Lovers' Leap Lodge
HEAR THE WAILS FROM THE HAUNTED PINES
3 Piece JUKEBOX Orchestra
DINING DANCING
COLD CUTS
LADIES INVITED
-000-000H
Is that Gus the Ghost?
8-3-51
No, that was Mr. Popolus, the proprietor. Been a dull year—
That's Gus and his friend now! Over there by the cliff . . . Make rather a nice duet, don't they?
OOOOOO-OOOH
EEEEEE-EEE-
jackmorley

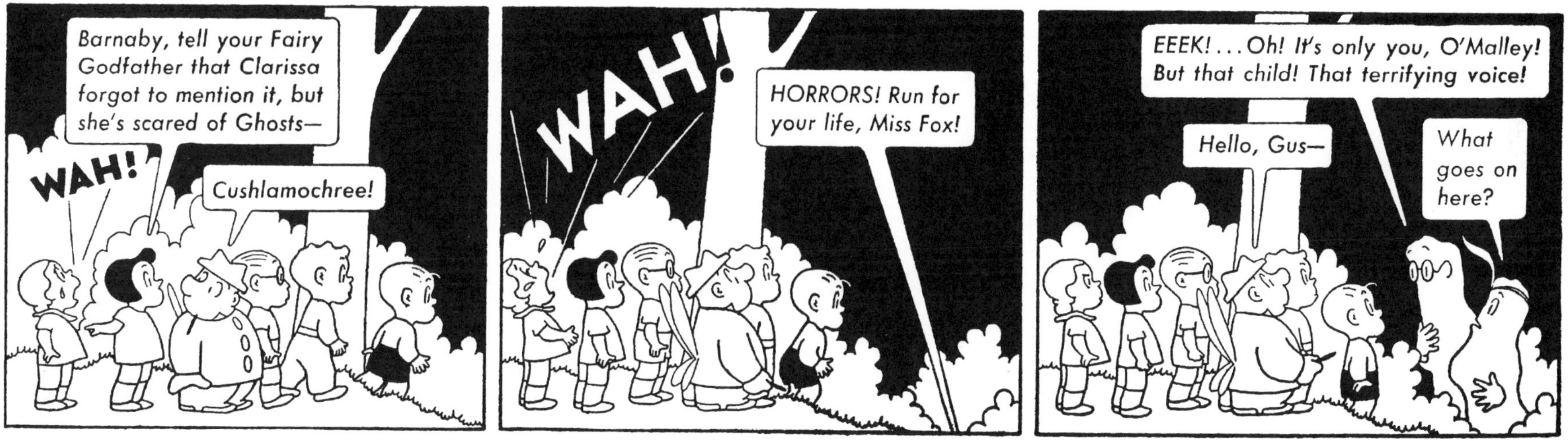
Barnaby, tell your Fairy Godfather that Clarissa forgot to mention it, but she's scared of Ghosts—
WAH!
Cushlamochree!
WAH!
HORRORS! Run for your life, Miss Fox!
EEEK! . . . Oh! It's only you, O'Malley! But that child! That terrifying voice!
Hello, Gus—
What goes on here?

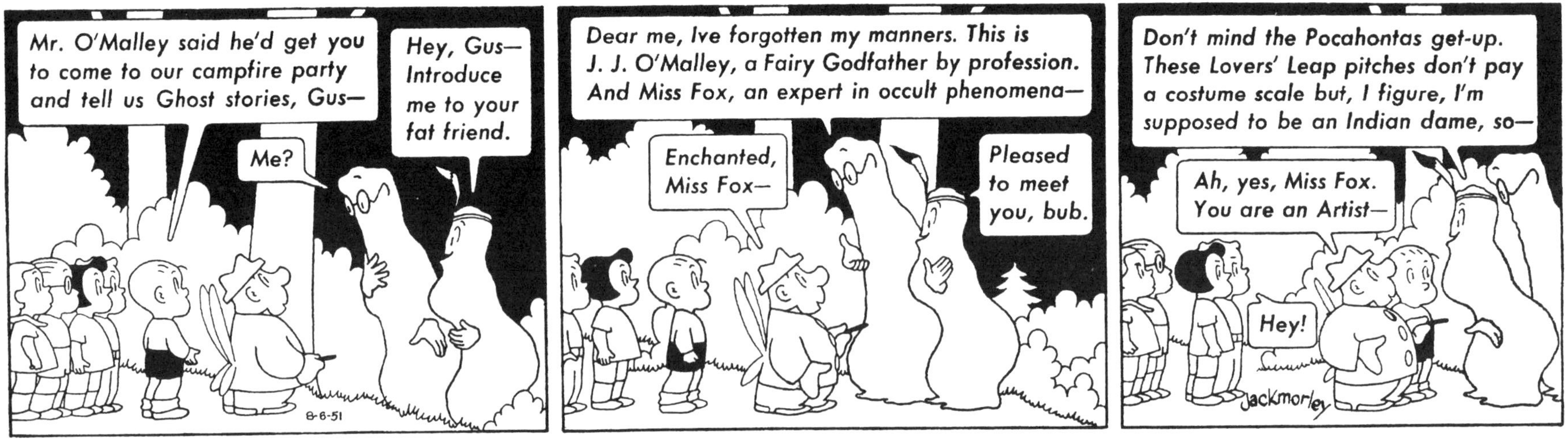
Mr. O'Malley said he'd get you to come to our campfire party and tell us Ghost stories, Gus—
Hey, Gus— Introduce me to your fat friend.
Me?
8-6-51
Dear me, Ive forgotten my manners. This is J. J. O'Malley, a Fairy Godfather by profession. And Miss Fox, an expert in occult phenomena—
Enchanted, Miss Fox—
Pleased to meet you, bub.
Don't mind the Pocahontas get-up. These Lovers' Leap pitches don't pay a costume scale but, I figure, I'm supposed to be an Indian dame, so—
Ah, yes, Miss Fox. You are an Artist—
Hey!
Jackmorley

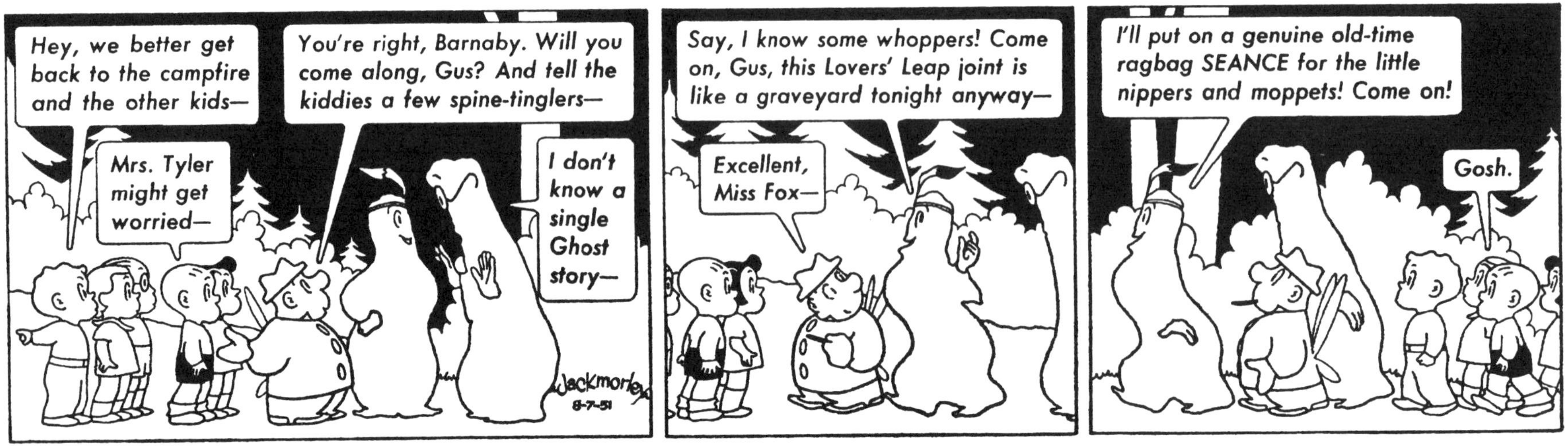
Hey, we better get back to the campfire and the other kids—
Mrs. Tyler might get worried—
You're right, Barnaby. Will you come along, Gus? And tell the kiddies a few spine-tinglers—
I don't know a single Ghost story—
Jackmorley
8-7-51
Say, I know some whoppers! Come on, Gus, this Lovers' Leap joint is like a graveyard tonight anyway—
Excellent, Miss Fox—
I'll put on a genuine old-time ragbag SEANCE for the little nippers and moppets! Come on!
Gosh.

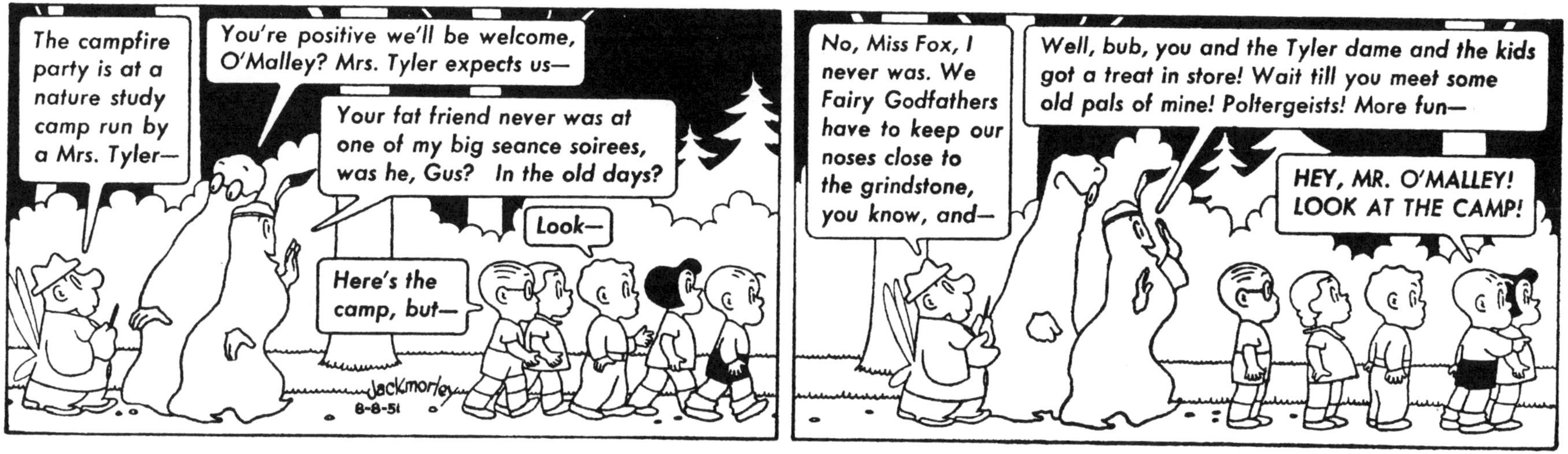
The campfire party is at a nature study camp run by a Mrs. Tyler—
You're positive we'll be welcome, O'Malley? Mrs. Tyler expects us—
Your fat friend never was at one of my big seance soirees, was he, Gus? In the old days?
Look—
Here's the camp, but—
Jackmorley
8-8-51
No, Miss Fox, I never was. We Fairy Godfathers have to keep our noses close to the grindstone, you know, and—
Well, bub, you and the Tyler dame and the kids got a treat in store! Wait till you meet some old pals of mine! Poltergeists! More fun—
HEY, MR. O'MALLEY! LOOK AT THE CAMP!

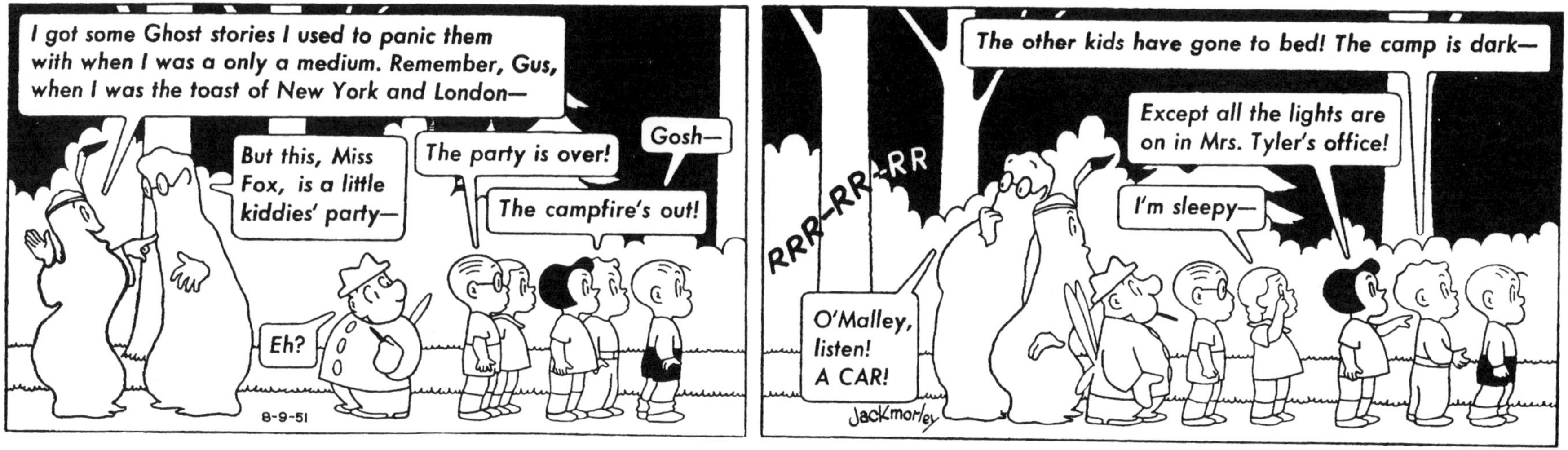
I got some Ghost stories I used to panic them with when I was a only a medium. Remember, Gus, when I was the toast of New York and London—
But this, Miss Fox, is a little kiddies' party—
The party is over!
Gosh—
The campfire's out!
Eh?
8-9-51
The other kids have gone to bed! The camp is dark—
Except all the lights are on in Mrs. Tyler's office!
I'm sleepy—
RRR-RR-RR
O'Malley, listen! A CAR!
Jackmorley

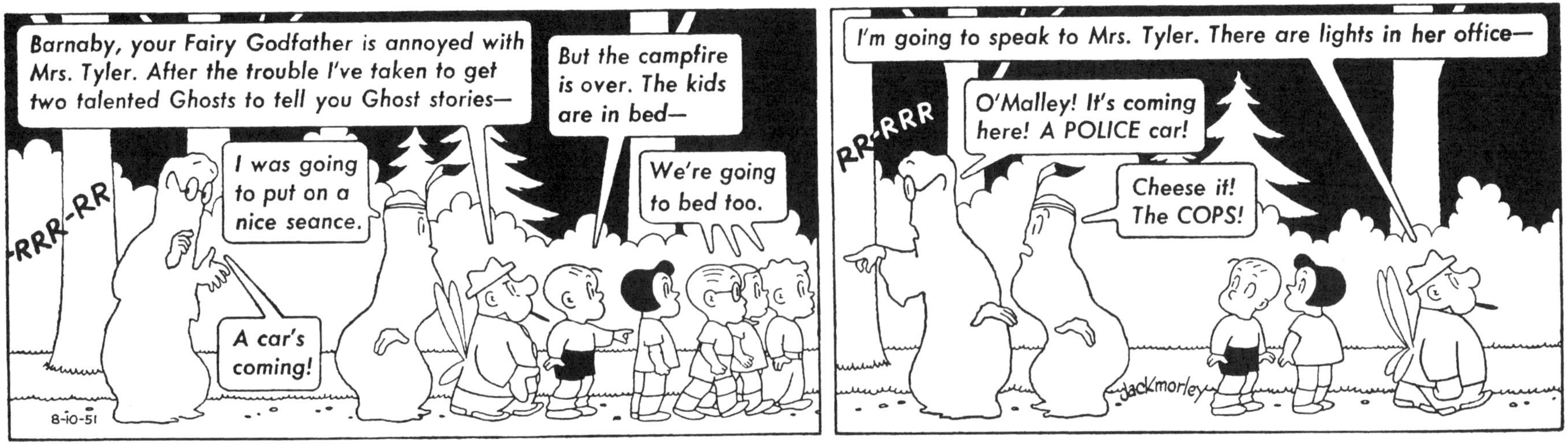
Barnaby, your Fairy Godfather is annoyed with Mrs. Tyler. After the trouble I've taken to get two talented Ghosts to tell you Ghost stories—
But the campfire is over. The kids are in bed—
I was going to put on a nice seance.
We're going to bed too.
RRR-RR
A car's coming!
8-10-51
I'm going to speak to Mrs. Tyler. There are lights in her office—
RR-RRR
O'Malley! It's coming here! A POLICE car!
Cheese it! The COPS!
Jackmorley

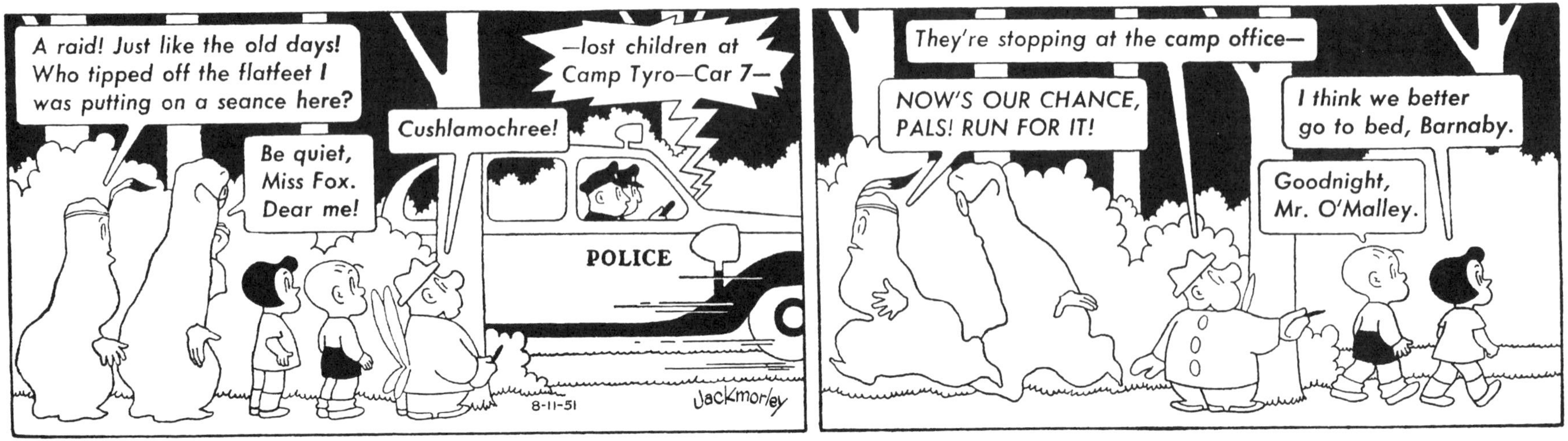
A raid! Just like the old days! Who tipped off the flatfeet I was putting on a seance here?
—lost children at Camp Tyro—Car 7—
Be quiet, Miss Fox. Dear me!
Cushlamochree!
POLICE
8-11-51
Jackmorley
They're stopping at the camp office—
NOW'S OUR CHANCE, PALS! RUN FOR IT!
I think we better go to bed, Barnaby.
Goodnight, Mr. O'Malley.

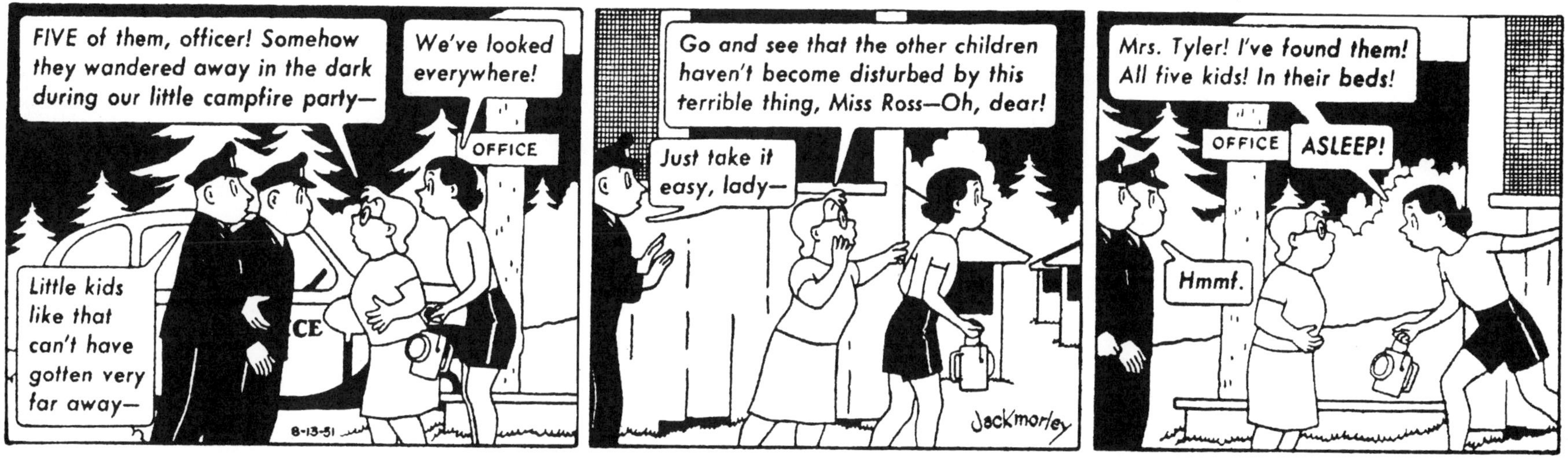
FIVE of them, officer! Somehow they wandered away in the dark during our little campfire party—
We've looked everywhere!
OFFICE
Little kids like that can't have gotten very far away—
8-13-51
Go and see that the other children haven't become disturbed by this terrible thing, Miss Ross—Oh, dear!
Just take it easy, lady—
Mrs. Tyler! I've found them! All five kids! In their beds!
OFFICE
ASLEEP!
Hmmf.

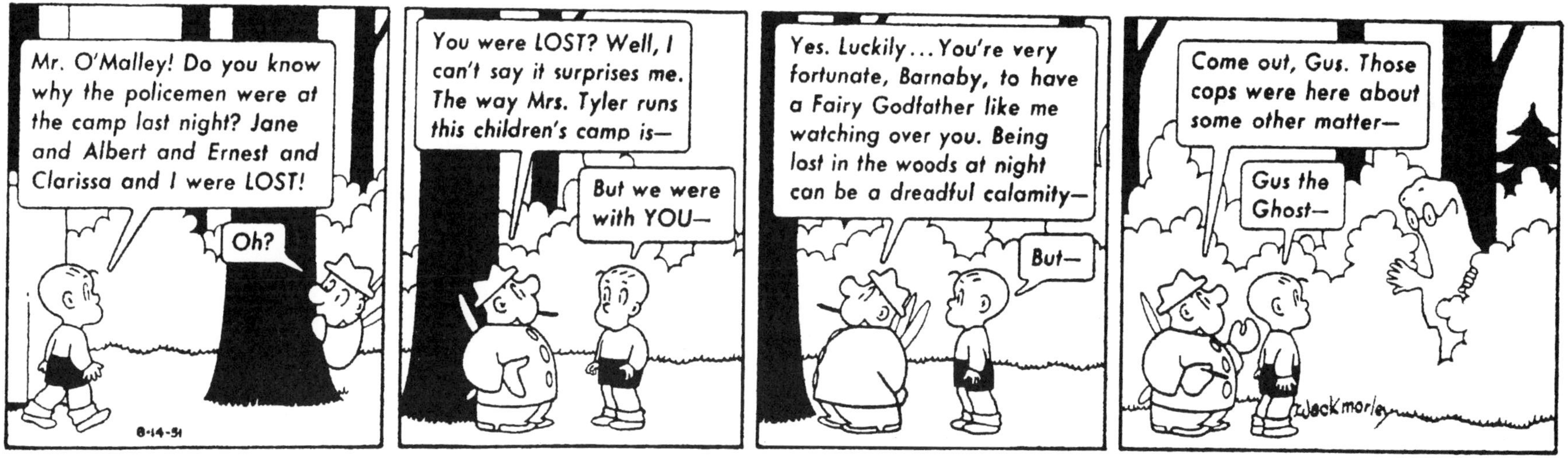
Mr. O'Malley! Do you know why the policemen were at the camp last night? Jane and Albert and Ernest and Clarissa and I were LOST!
Oh?
8-14-51
You were LOST? Well, I can't say it surprises me. The way Mrs. Tyler runs this children's camp is—
But we were with YOU—
Yes. Luckily...You're very fortunate, Barnaby, to have a Fairy Godfather like me watching over you. Being lost in the woods at night can be a dreadful calamity—
But—
Come out, Gus. Those cops were here about some other matter—
Gus the Ghost—

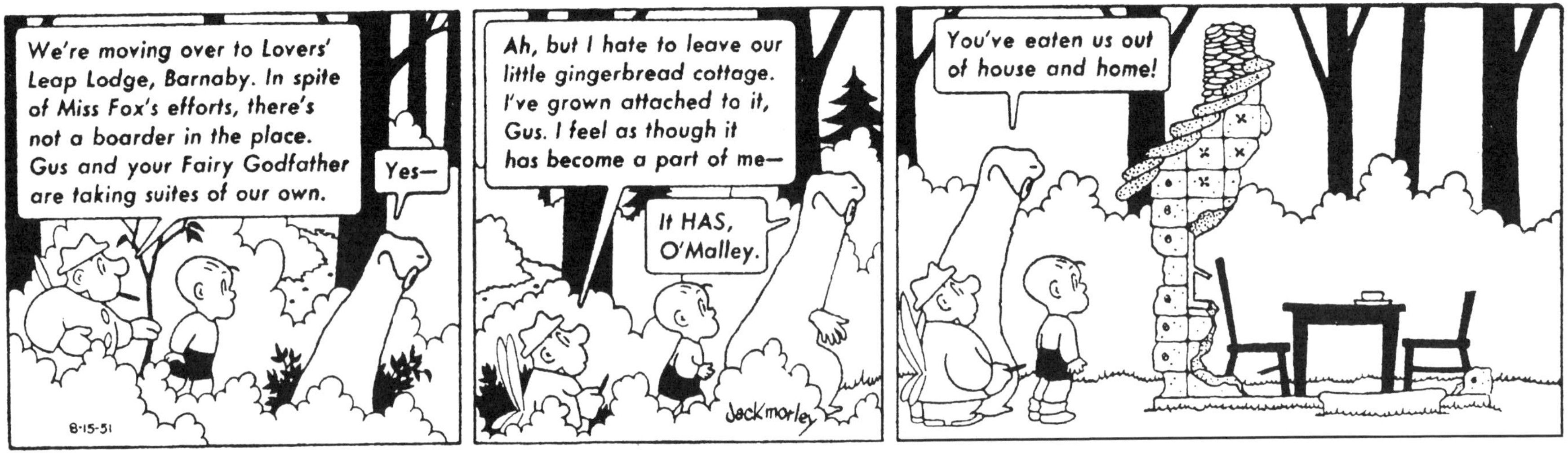
We're moving over to Lovers' Leap Lodge, Barnaby. In spite of Miss Fox's efforts, there's not a boarder in the place. Gus and your Fairy Godfather are taking suites of our own.
Yes—
8-15-51
Ah, but I hate to leave our little gingerbread cottage. I've grown attached to it, Gus. I feel as though it has become a part of me—
It HAS, O'Malley.
Jackmorley
You've eaten us out of house and home!

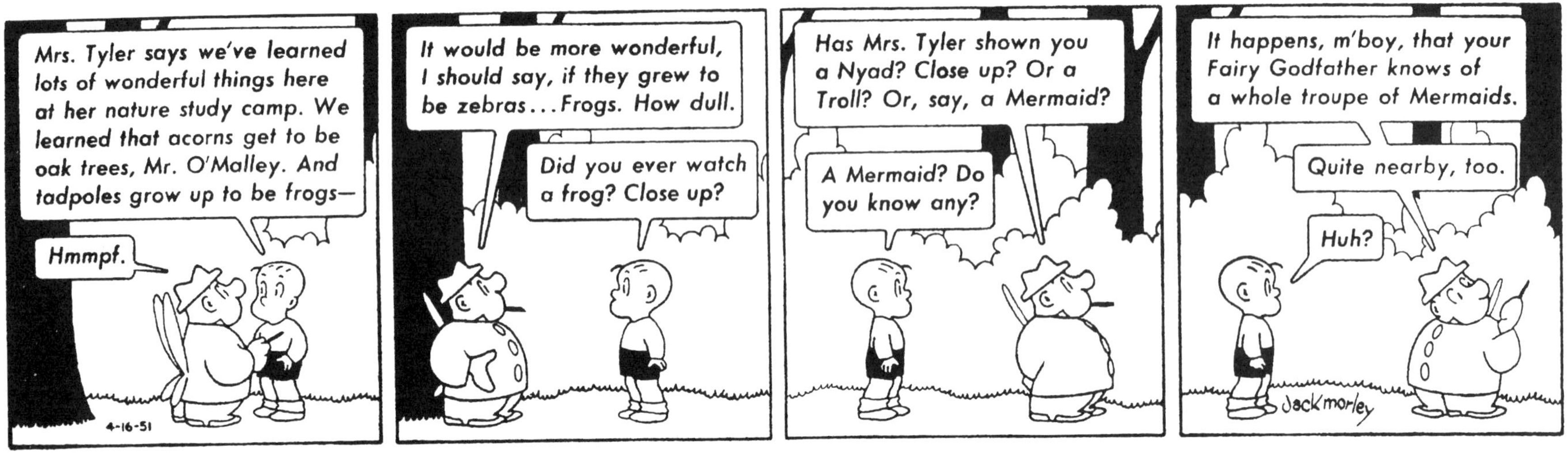
Mrs. Tyler says we've learned lots of wonderful things here at her nature study camp. We learned that acorns get to be oak trees, Mr. O'Malley. And tadpoles grow up to be frogs—
Hmmpf.
4-16-51
It would be more wonderful, I should say, if they grew to be zebras...Frogs. How dull.
Did you ever watch a frog? Close up?
Has Mrs. Tyler shown you a Nyad? Close up? Or a Troll? Or, say, a Mermaid?
A Mermaid? Do you know any?
It happens, m'boy, that your Fairy Godfather knows of a whole troupe of Mermaids.
Quite nearby, too.
Huh?
Jackmorley

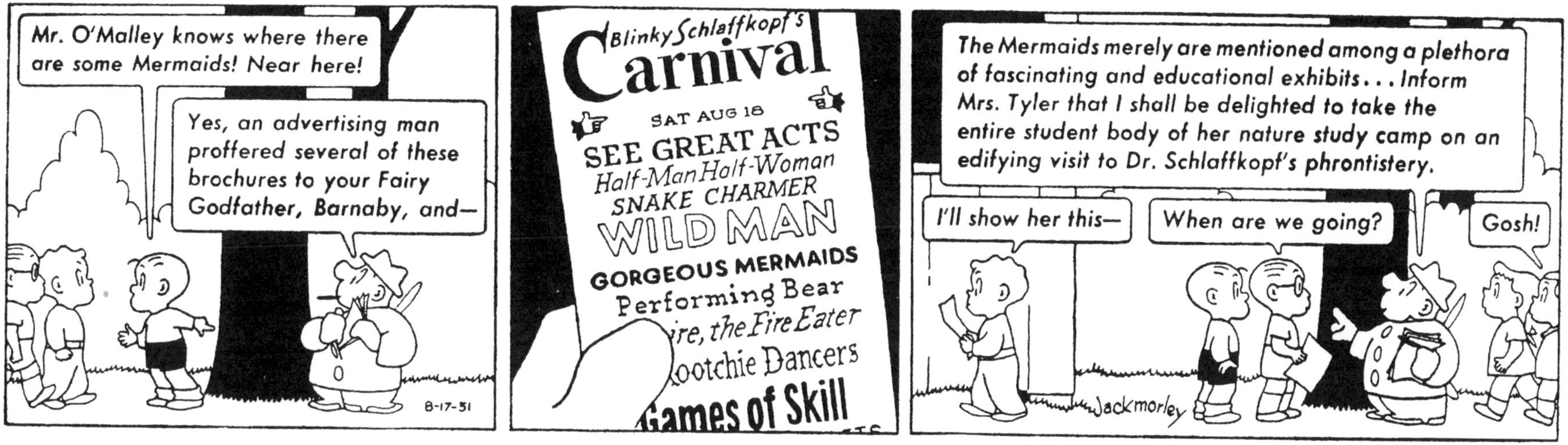
Mr. O'Malley knows where there are some Mermaids! Near here!
Yes, an advertising man proffered several of these brochures to your Fairy Godfather, Barnaby, and—
8-17-51
Blinky Schlaffkopf's
Carnival
SAT AUG 18
SEE GREAT ACTS
Half-Man Half-Woman
SNAKE CHARMER
WILD MAN
GORGEOUS MERMAIDS
Performing Bear
ire, the Fire Eater
ootchie Dancers
Games of Skill
The Mermaids merely are mentioned among a plethora of fascinating and educational exhibits . . . Inform Mrs. Tyler that I shall be delighted to take the entire student body of her nature study camp on an edifying visit to Dr. Schlaffkopf's phrontistery.
I'll show her this—
When are we going?
Gosh!
Jackmorley

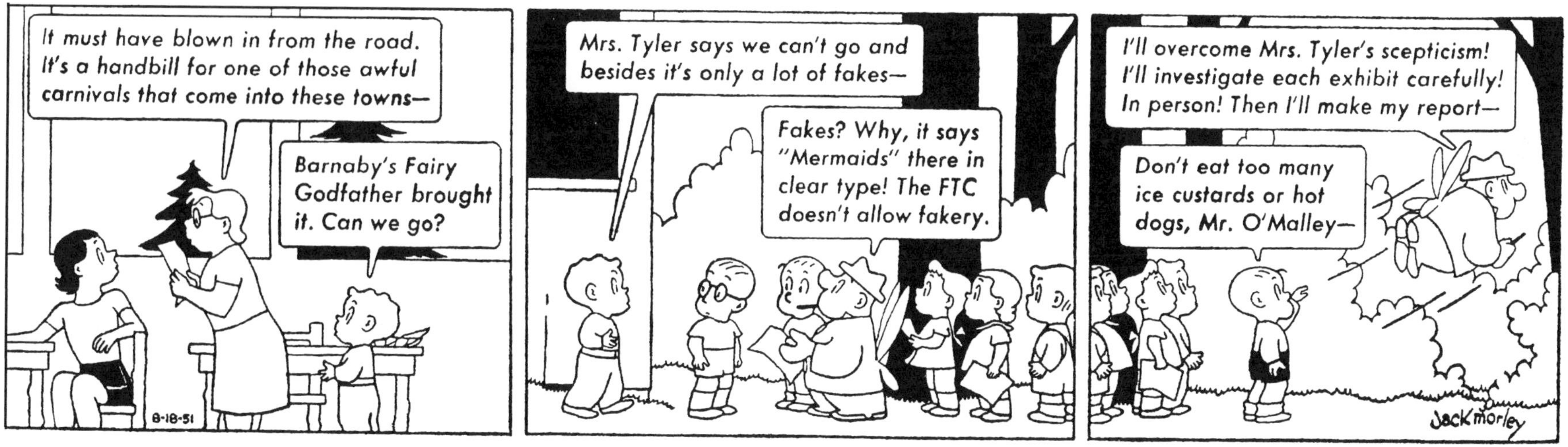
It must have blown in from the road. It's a handbill for one of those awful carnivals that come into these towns—
Barnaby's Fairy Godfather brought it. Can we go?
8-18-51
Mrs. Tyler says we can't go and besides it's only a lot of fakes—
Fakes? Why, it says "Mermaids" there in clear type! The FTC doesn't allow fakery.
I'll overcome Mrs. Tyler's scepticism! I'll investigate each exhibit carefully! In person! Then I'll make my report—
Don't eat too many ice custards or hot dogs, Mr. O'Malley—
Jackmorley

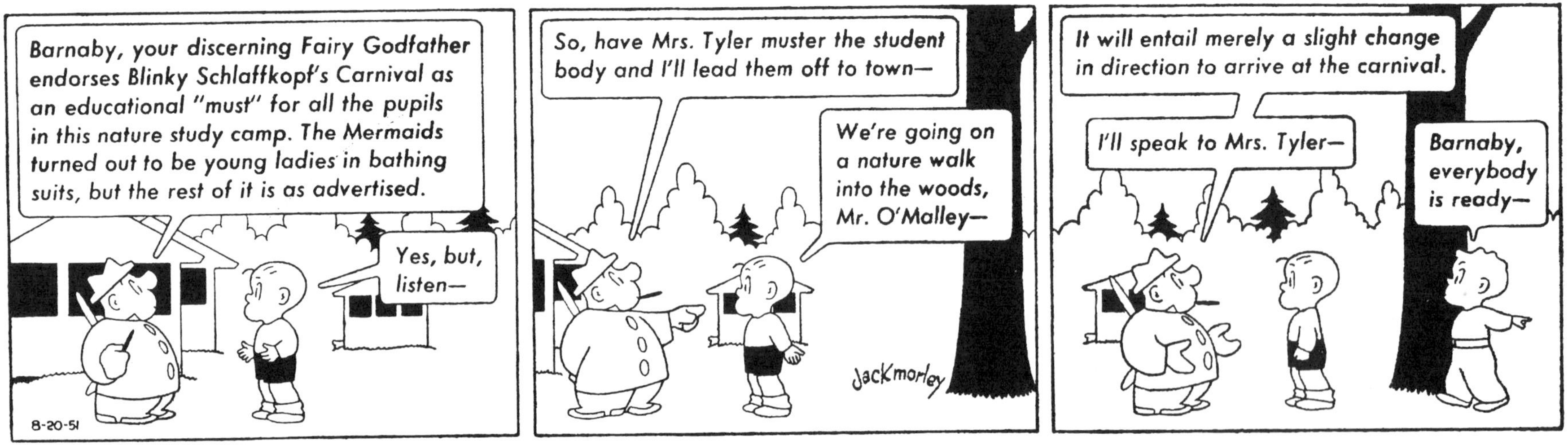
Barnaby, your discerning Fairy Godfather endorses Blinky Schlaffkopf's Carnival as an educational "must" for all the pupils in this nature study camp. The Mermaids turned out to be young ladies in bathing suits, but the rest of it is as advertised.
Yes, but, listen—
8-20-51
So, have Mrs. Tyler muster the student body and I'll lead them off to town—
We're going on a nature walk into the woods, Mr. O'Malley—
Jackmorley
It will entail merely a slight change in direction to arrive at the carnival.
I'll speak to Mrs. Tyler—
Barnaby, everybody is ready—

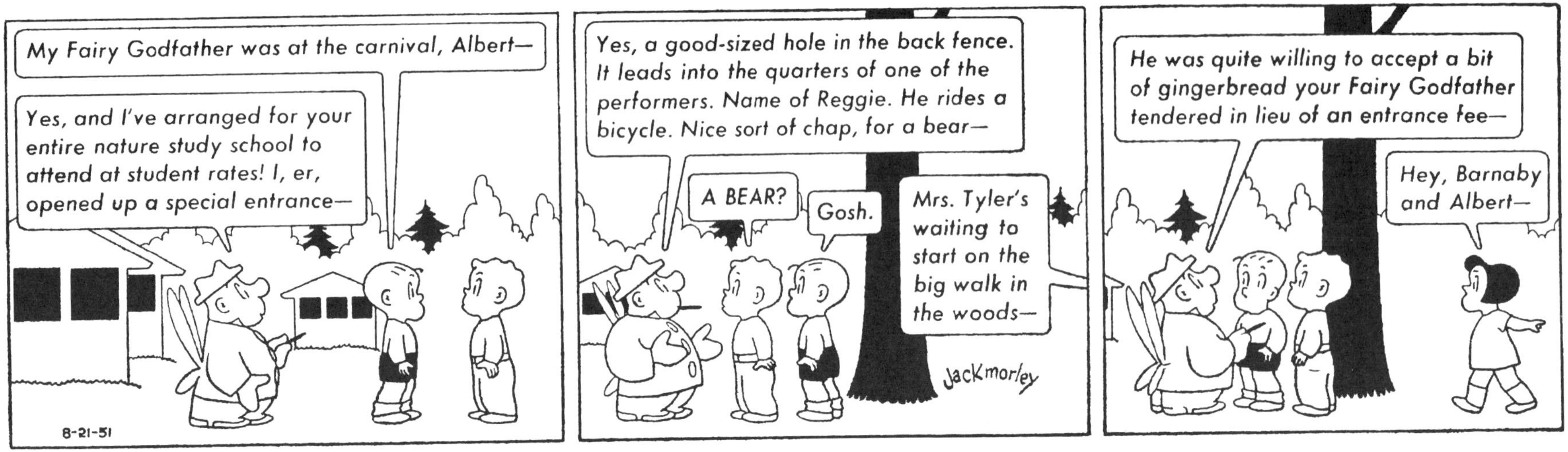
My Fairy Godfather was at the carnival, Albert—
Yes, and I've arranged for your entire nature study school to attend at student rates! I, er, opened up a special entrance—
8-21-51
Yes, a good-sized hole in the back fence. It leads into the quarters of one of the performers. Name of Reggie. He rides a bicycle. Nice sort of chap, for a bear—
A BEAR?
Gosh.
Mrs. Tyler's waiting to start on the big walk in the woods—
Jackmorley
He was quite willing to accept a bit of gingerbread your Fairy Godfather tendered in lieu of an entrance fee—
Hey, Barnaby and Albert—

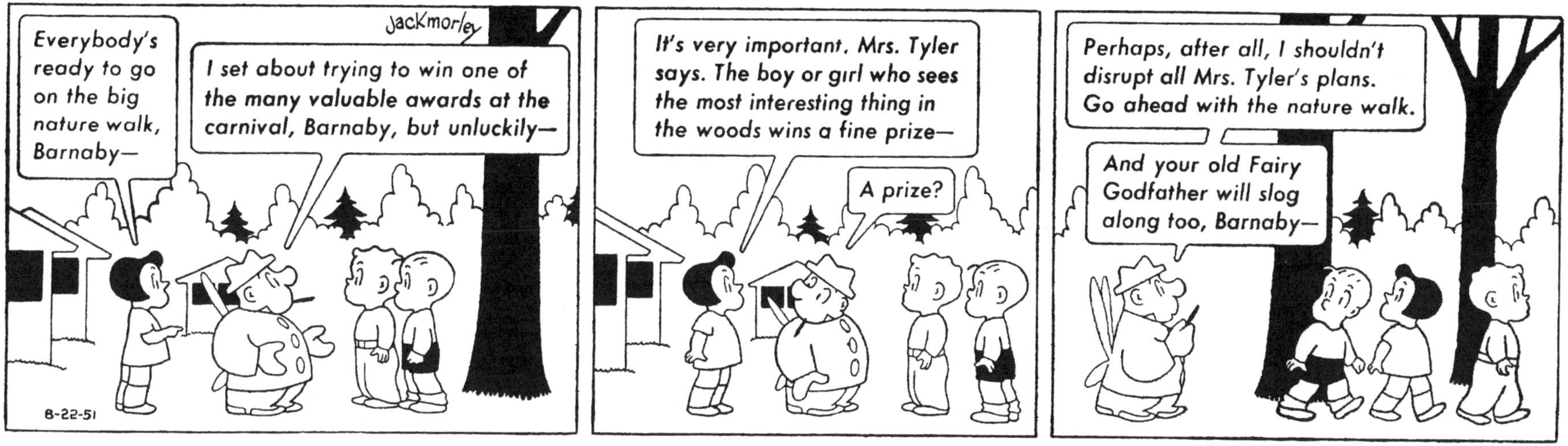
JACKMORLEY
Everybody's ready to go on the big nature walk, Barnaby—
I set about trying to win one of the many valuable awards at the carnival, Barnaby, but unluckily—
It's very important. Mrs. Tyler says. The boy or girl who sees the most interesting thing in the woods wins a fine prize—
A prize?
Perhaps, after all, I shouldn't disrupt all Mrs. Tyler's plans. Go ahead with the nature walk.
And your old Fairy Godfather will slog along too, Barnaby—
8-22-51

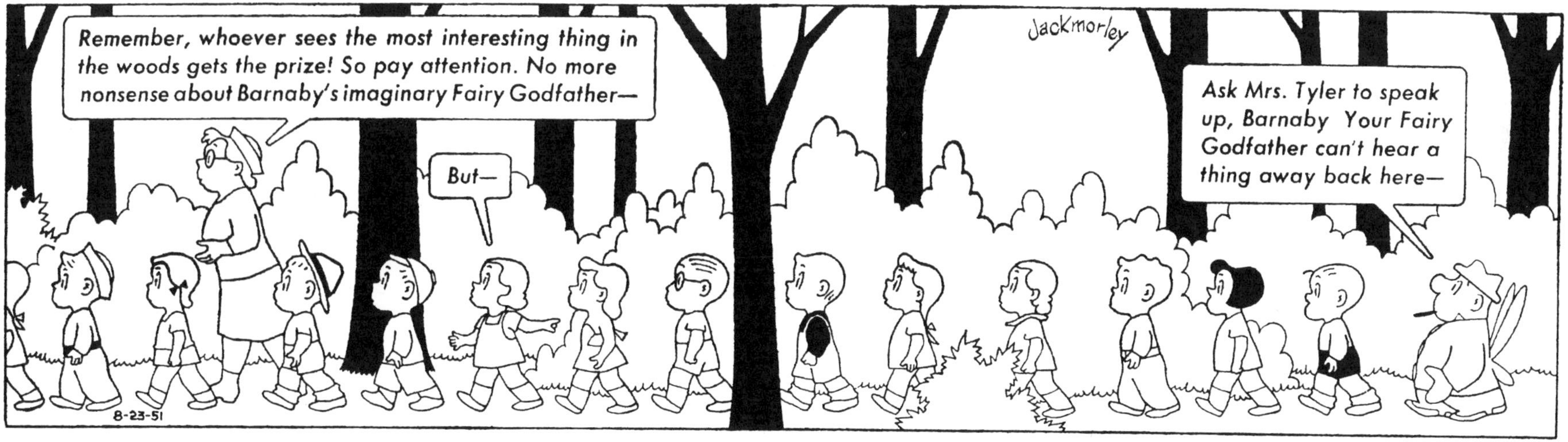
Remember, whoever sees the most interesting thing in the woods gets the prize! So pay attention. No more nonsense about Barnaby's imaginary Fairy Godfather—
But—
JACKMORLEY
Ask Mrs. Tyler to speak up, Barnaby Your Fairy Godfather can't hear a thing away back here—
8-23-51

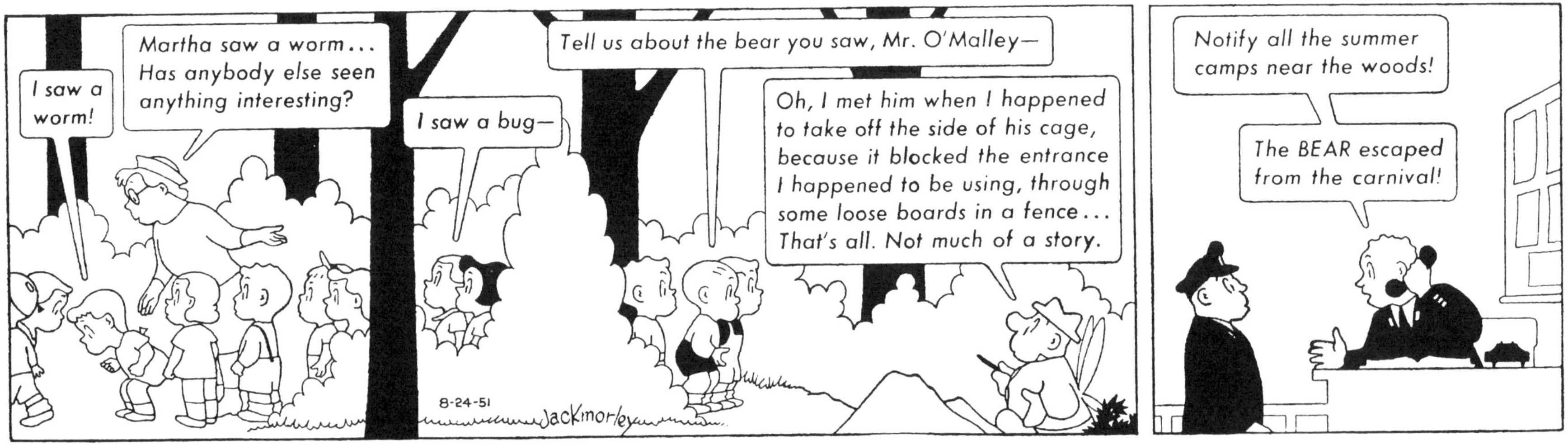
I saw a worm!
Martha saw a worm... Has anybody else seen anything interesting?
I saw a bug—
Tell us about the bear you saw, Mr. O'Malley—
Oh, I met him when I happened to take off the side of his cage, because it blocked the entrance I happened to be using, through some loose boards in a fence... That's all. Not much of a story.
8-24-51
Jackmorley
Notify all the summer camps near the woods!
The BEAR escaped from the carnival!

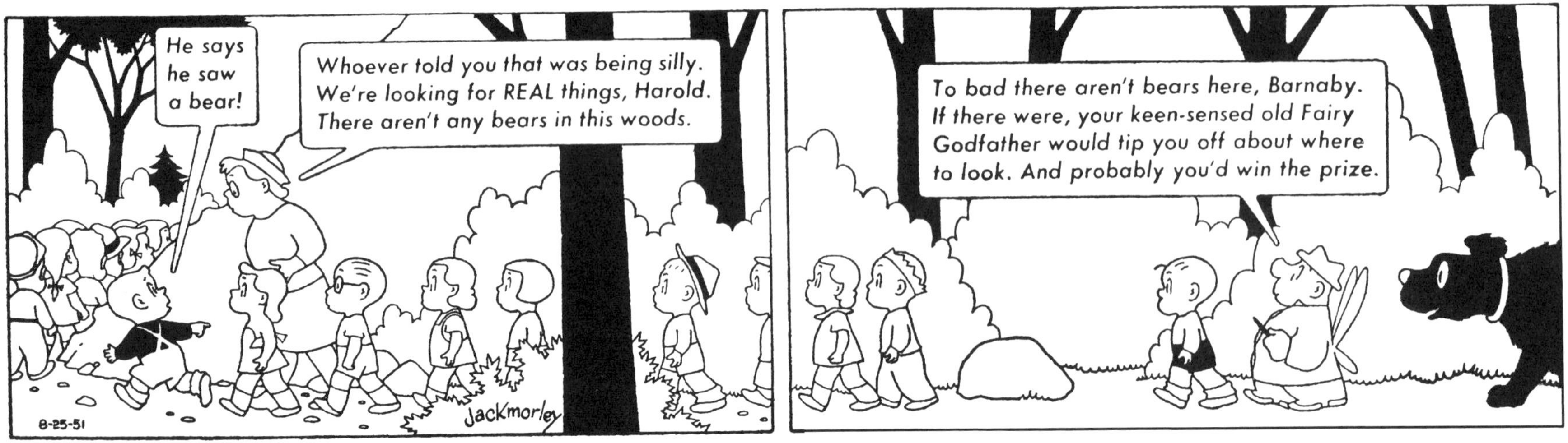
He says he saw a bear!
Whoever told you that was being silly. We're looking for REAL things, Harold. There aren't any bears in this woods.
8-25-51
Jackmorley
To bad there aren't bears here, Barnaby. If there were, your keen-sensed old Fairy Godfather would tip you off about where to look. And probably you'd win the prize.

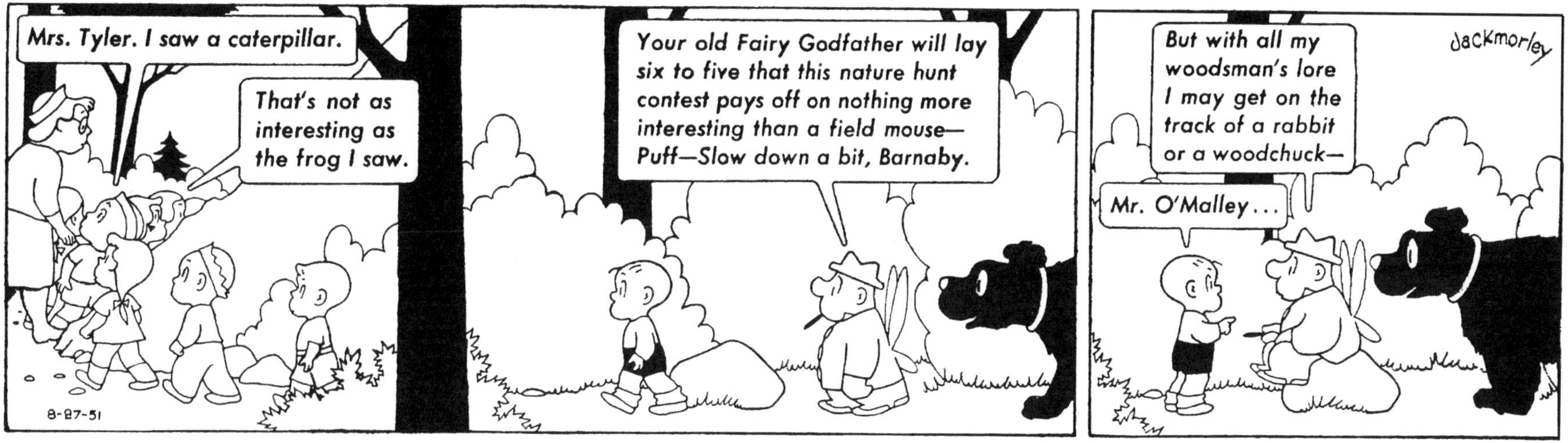
Mrs. Tyler. I saw a caterpillar.
That's not as interesting as the frog I saw.
8-27-51
Your old Fairy Godfather will lay six to five that this nature hunt contest pays off on nothing more interesting than a field mouse— Puff—Slow down a bit, Barnaby.
But with all my woodsman's lore I may get on the track of a rabbit or a woodchuck—
Mr. O'Malley . . .
Jackmorley

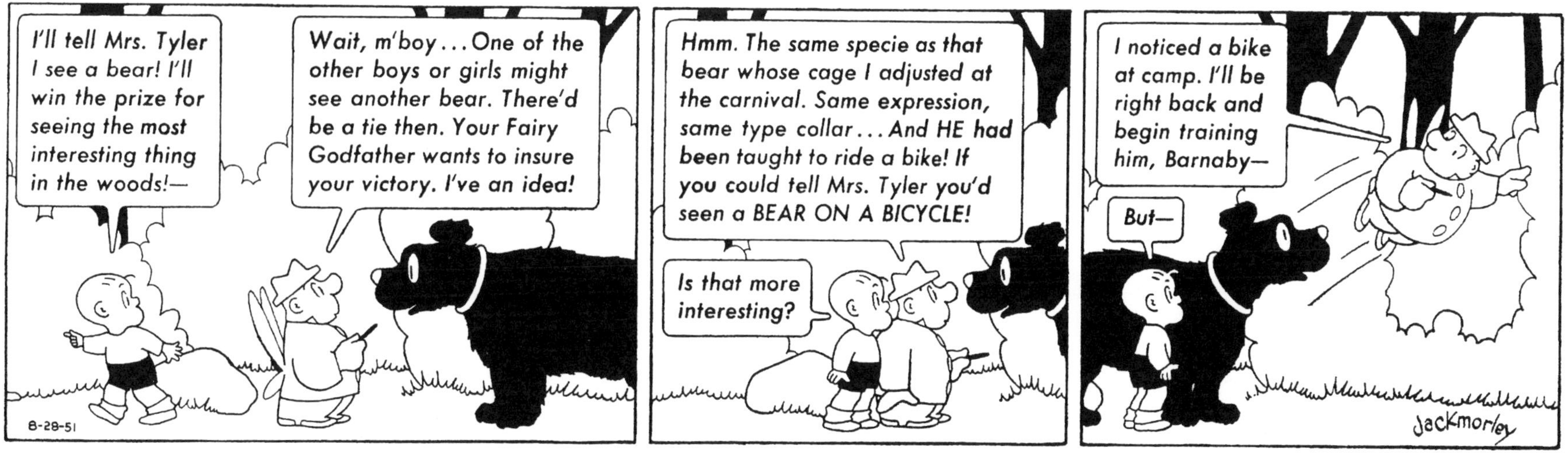
I'll tell Mrs. Tyler I see a bear! I'll win the prize for seeing the most interesting thing in the woods!—
Wait, m'boy . . . One of the other boys or girls might see another bear. There'd be a tie then. Your Fairy Godfather wants to insure your victory. I've an idea!
8-28-51
Hmm. The same specie as that bear whose cage I adjusted at the carnival. Same expression, same type collar . . . And HE had been taught to ride a bike! If you could tell Mrs. Tyler you'd seen a BEAR ON A BICYCLE!
Is that more interesting?
I noticed a bike at camp. I'll be right back and begin training him, Barnaby—
But—
Jackmorley

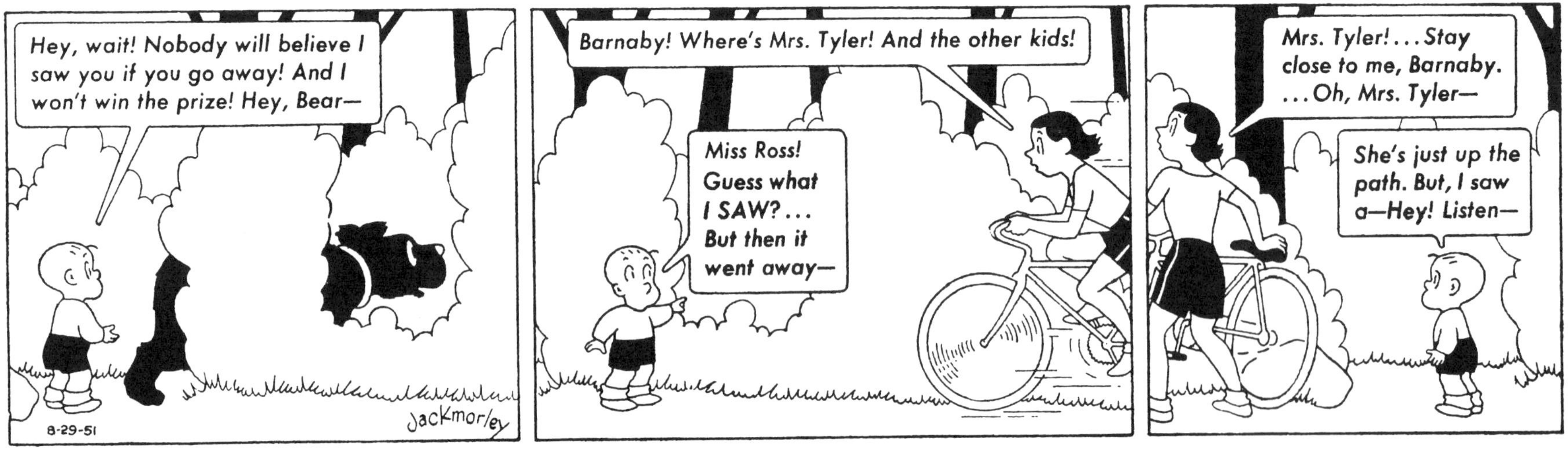
Hey, wait! Nobody will believe I saw you if you go away! And I won't win the prize! Hey, Bear—
8-29-51
Jackmorley
Barnaby! Where's Mrs. Tyler! And the other kids!
Miss Ross! Guess what I SAW? . . . But then it went away—
Mrs. Tyler! . . . Stay close to me, Barnaby. . . . Oh, Mrs. Tyler—
She's just up the path. But, I saw a—Hey! Listen—

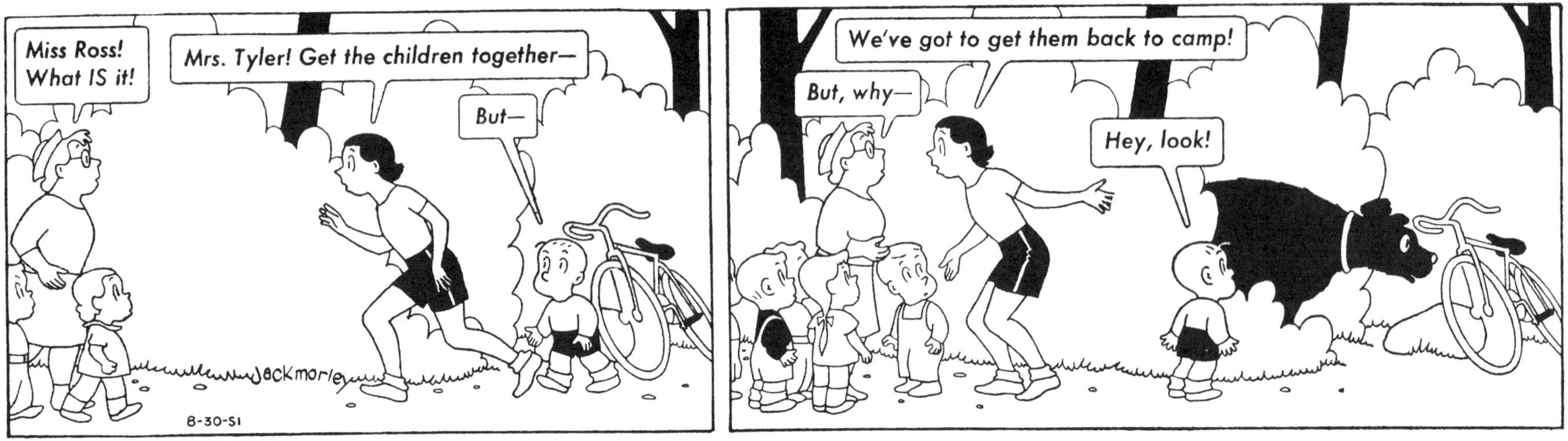
Miss Ross! What IS it!
Mrs. Tyler! Get the children together—
But—
Jackmorley
8-30-51
We've got to get them back to camp!
But, why—
Hey, look!

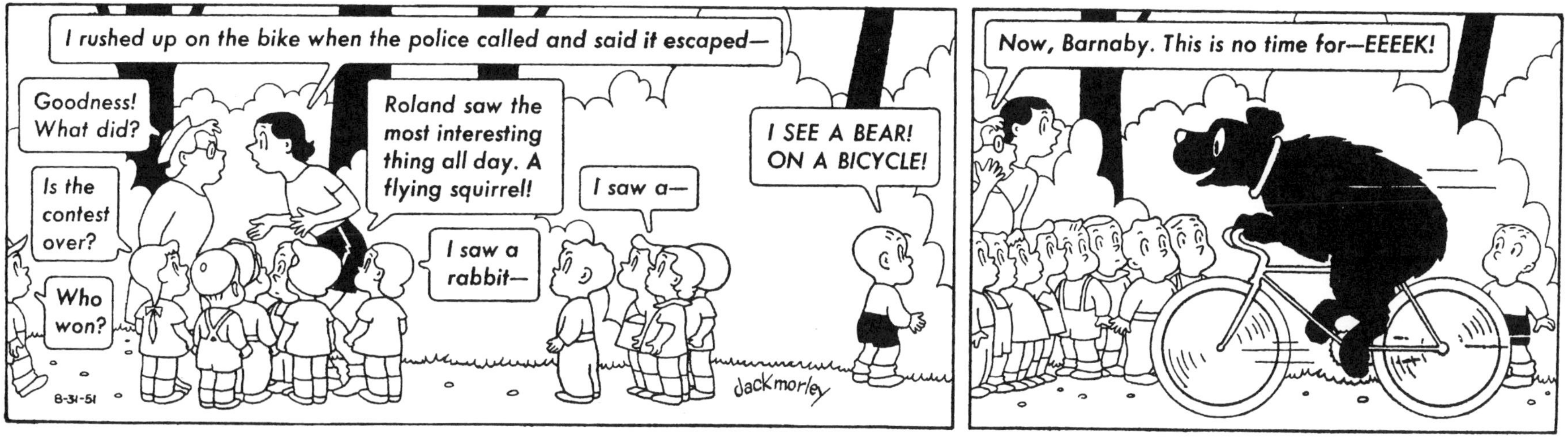
I rushed up on the bike when the police called and said it escaped—
Goodness! What did?
Roland saw the most interesting thing all day. A flying squirrel!
Is the contest over?
Who won?
I saw a rabbit—
I saw a—
I SEE A BEAR! ON A BICYCLE!
8-31-51
jackmorley
Now, Barnaby. This is no time for—EEEEK!

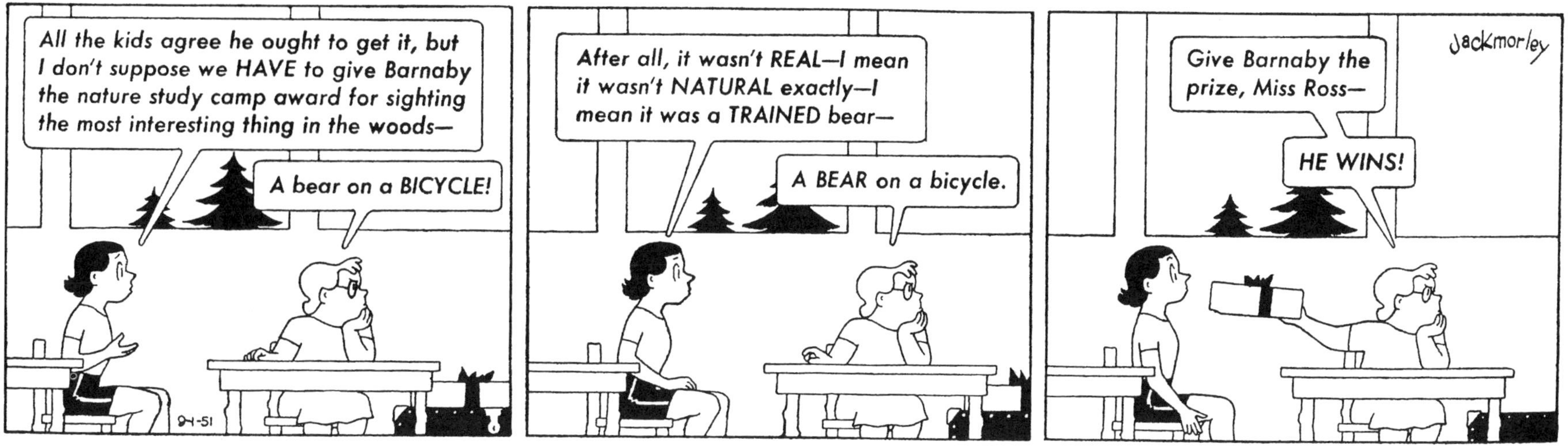
All the kids agree he ought to get it, but I don't suppose we HAVE to give Barnaby the nature study camp award for sighting the most interesting thing in the woods—
A bear on a BICYCLE!
9-1-51
After all, it wasn't REAL—I mean it wasn't NATURAL exactly—I mean it was a TRAINED bear—
A BEAR on a bicycle.
jackmorley
Give Barnaby the prize, Miss Ross—
HE WINS!

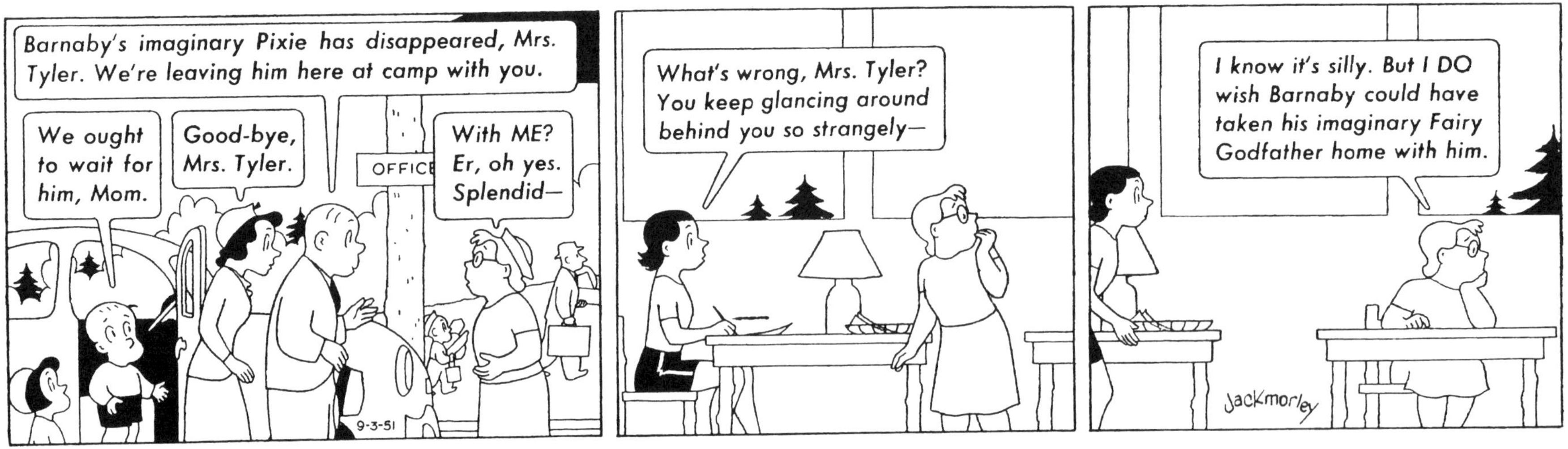

Barnaby's imaginary Pixie has disappeared, Mrs. Tyler. We're leaving him here at camp with you.
We ought to wait for him, Mom.
Good-bye, Mrs. Tyler.
OFFICE
With ME? Er, oh yes. Splendid—
9-3-51
What's wrong, Mrs. Tyler? You keep glancing around behind you so strangely—
I know it's silly. But I DO wish Barnaby could have taken his imaginary Fairy Godfather home with him.
JACKMORLEY

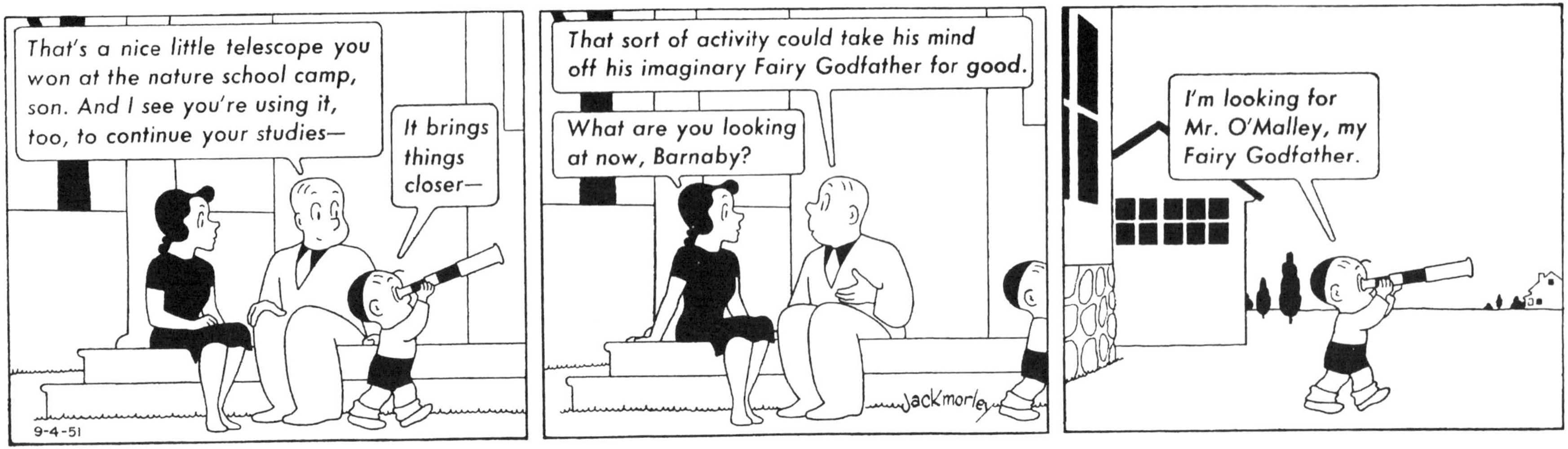

That's a nice little telescope you won at the nature school camp, son. And I see you're using it, too, to continue your studies—
It brings things closer—
9-4-51
That sort of activity could take his mind off his imaginary Fairy Godfather for good.
What are you looking at now, Barnaby?
JACKMORLEY
I'm looking for Mr. O'Malley, my Fairy Godfather.

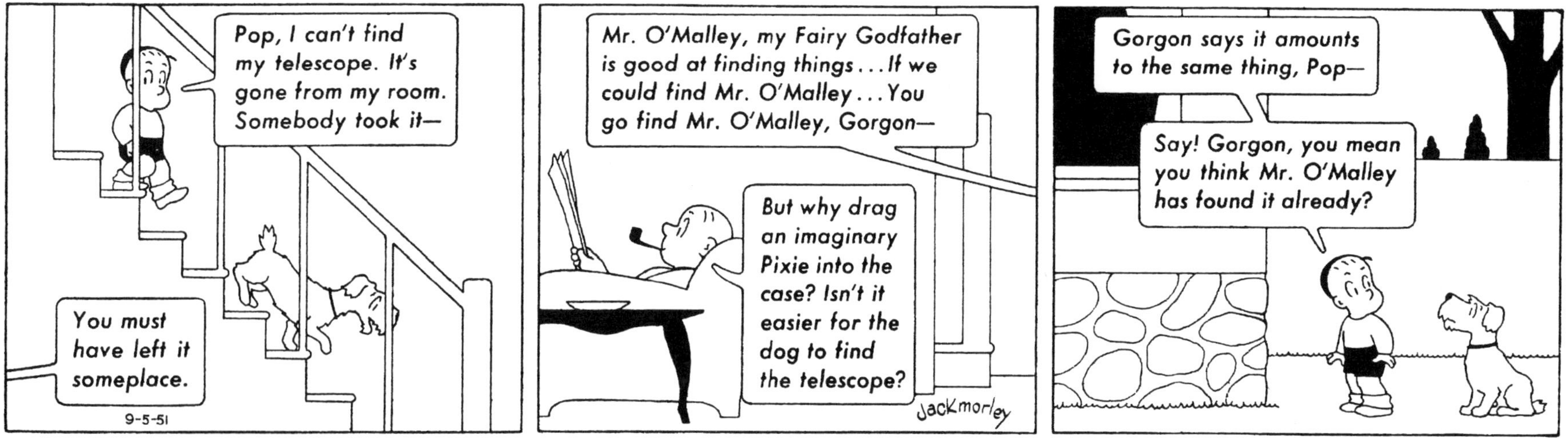
Pop, I can't find my telescope. It's gone from my room. Somebody took it—
You must have left it someplace.
9-5-51
Mr. O'Malley, my Fairy Godfather is good at finding things... If we could find Mr. O'Malley... You go find Mr. O'Malley, Gorgon—
But why drag an imaginary Pixie into the case? Isn't it easier for the dog to find the telescope?
Jackmorley
Gorgon says it amounts to the same thing, Pop—
Say! Gorgon, you mean you think Mr. O'Malley has found it already?

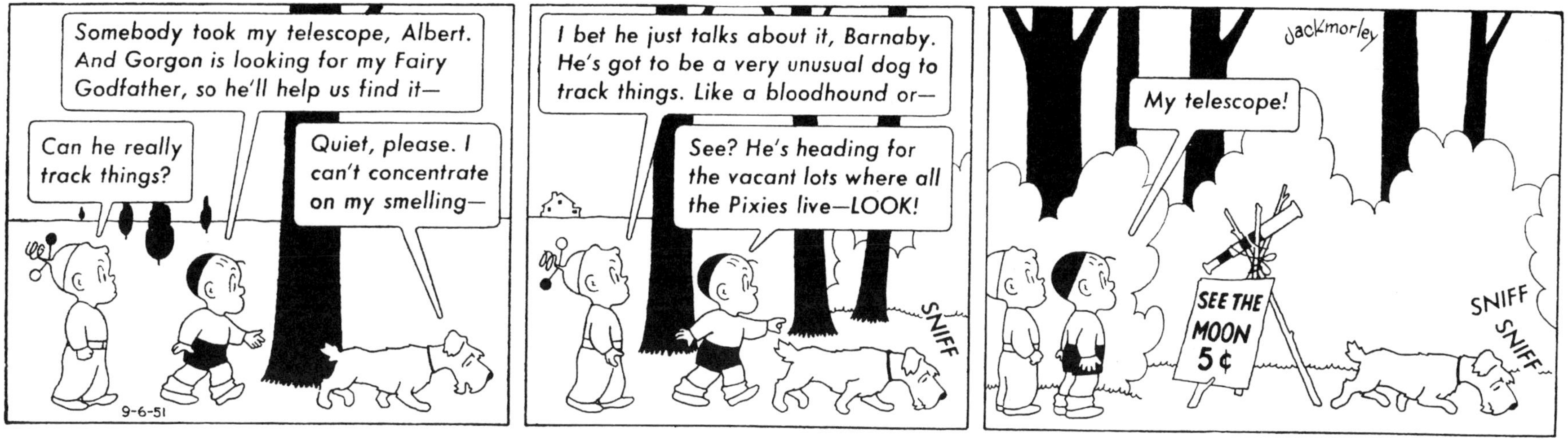
Somebody took my telescope, Albert. And Gorgon is looking for my Fairy Godfather, so he'll help us find it—
Can he really track things?
Quiet, please. I can't concentrate on my smelling—
9-6-51
I bet he just talks about it, Barnaby. He's got to be a very unusual dog to track things. Like a bloodhound or—
See? He's heading for the vacant lots where all the Pixies live—LOOK!
SNIFF
Jackmorley
My telescope!
SEE THE MOON 5¢
SNIFF
SNIFF

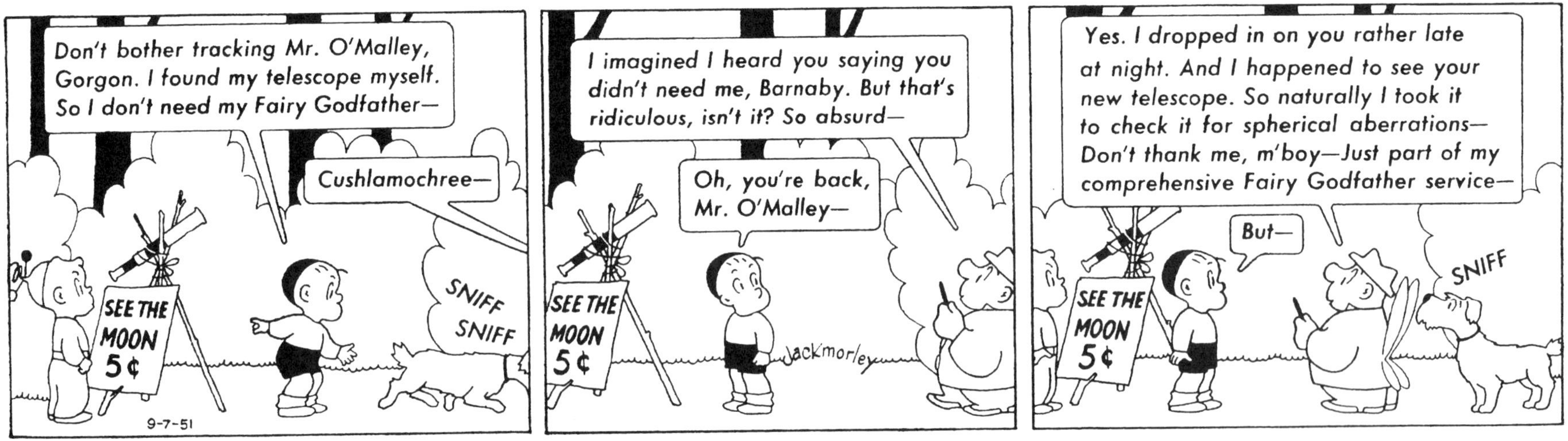
Don't bother tracking Mr. O'Malley, Gorgon. I found my telescope myself. So I don't need my Fairy Godfather—
Cushlamochree—
SEE THE MOON 5¢
SNIFF SNIFF
I imagined I heard you saying you didn't need me, Barnaby. But that's ridiculous, isn't it? So absurd—
Oh, you're back, Mr. O'Malley—
SEE THE MOON 5¢
Jackmorley
Yes. I dropped in on you rather late at night. And I happened to see your new telescope. So naturally I took it to check it for spherical aberrations— Don't thank me, m'boy—Just part of my comprehensive Fairy Godfather service—
But—
SNIFF
SEE THE MOON 5¢

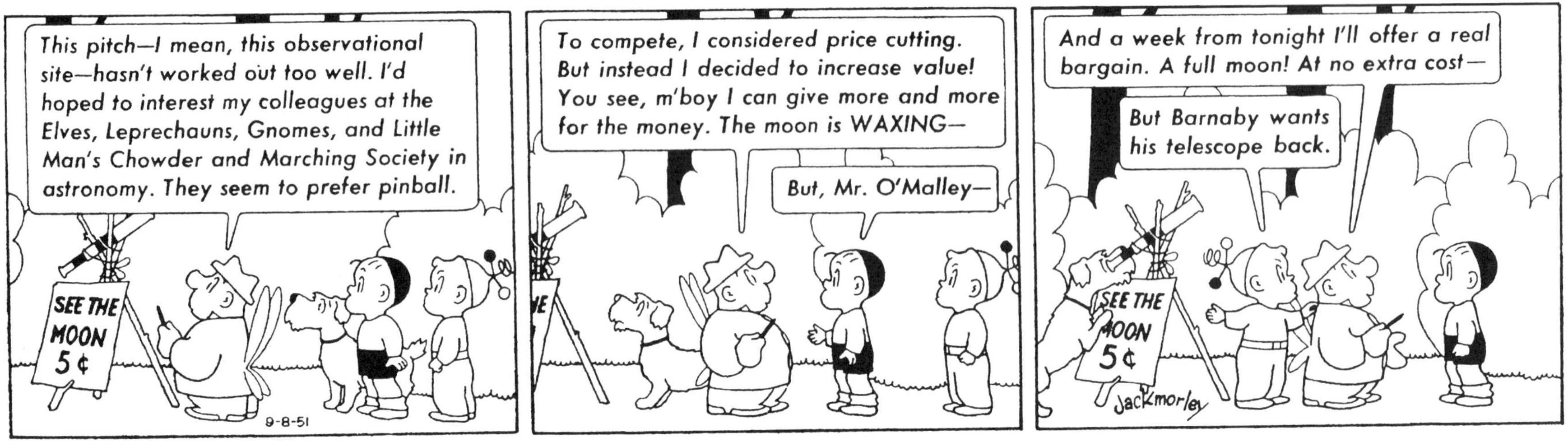
This pitch—I mean, this observational site—hasn't worked out too well. I'd hoped to interest my colleagues at the Elves, Leprechauns, Gnomes, and Little Man's Chowder and Marching Society in astronomy. They seem to prefer pinball.
SEE THE MOON 5¢
To compete, I considered price cutting. But instead I decided to increase value! You see, m'boy I can give more and more for the money. The moon is WAXING—
But, Mr. O'Malley—
And a week from tonight I'll offer a real bargain. A full moon! At no extra cost—
But Barnaby wants his telescope back.
SEE THE MOON 5¢
Jackmorley

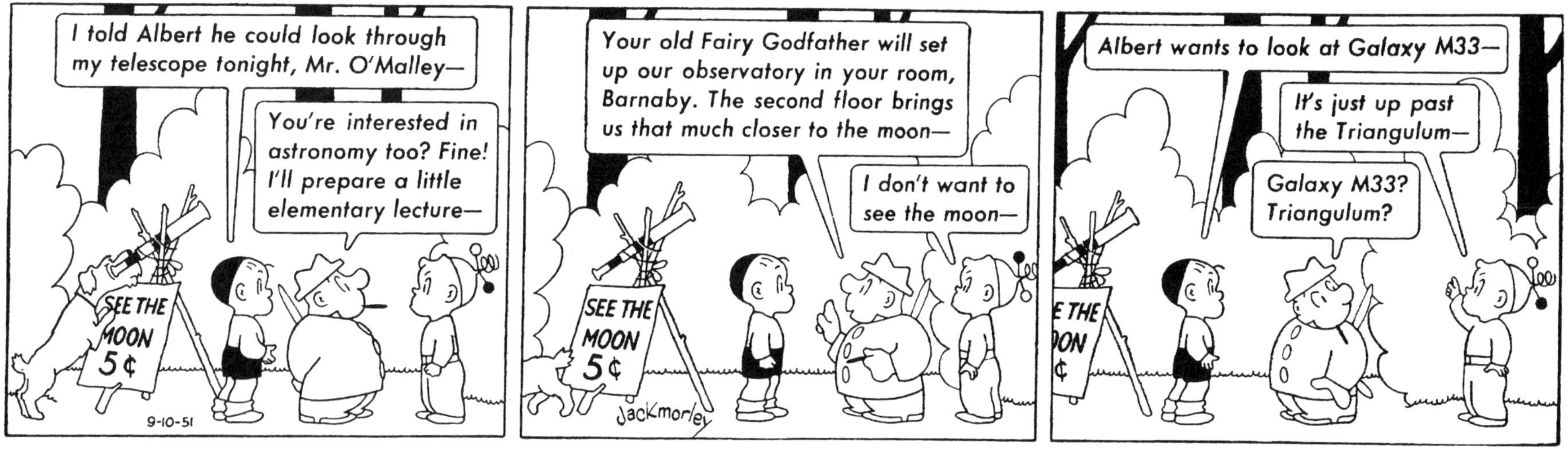
I told Albert he could look through my telescope tonight, Mr. O'Malley—
You're interested in astronomy too? Fine! I'll prepare a little elementary lecture—
SEE THE MOON 5¢
9-10-51
Your old Fairy Godfather will set up our observatory in your room, Barnaby. The second floor brings us that much closer to the moon—
I don't want to see the moon—
SEE THE MOON 5¢
Jackmorley
Albert wants to look at Galaxy M33—
It's just up past the Triangulum—
Galaxy M33? Triangulum?

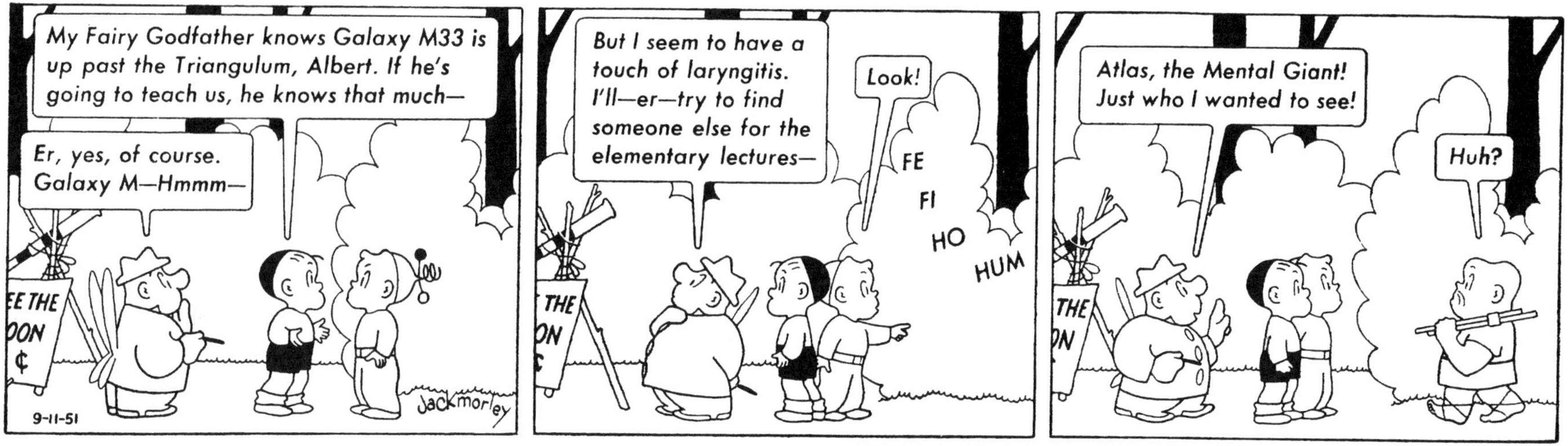
My Fairy Godfather knows Galaxy M33 is up past the Triangulum, Albert. If he's going to teach us, he knows that much—
Er, yes, of course. Galaxy M—Hmmm—
9-11-51
Jackmorley
But I seem to have a touch of laryngitis. I'll—er—try to find someone else for the elementary lectures—
Look!
FE
FI
HO
HUM
Atlas, the Mental Giant! Just who I wanted to see!
Huh?

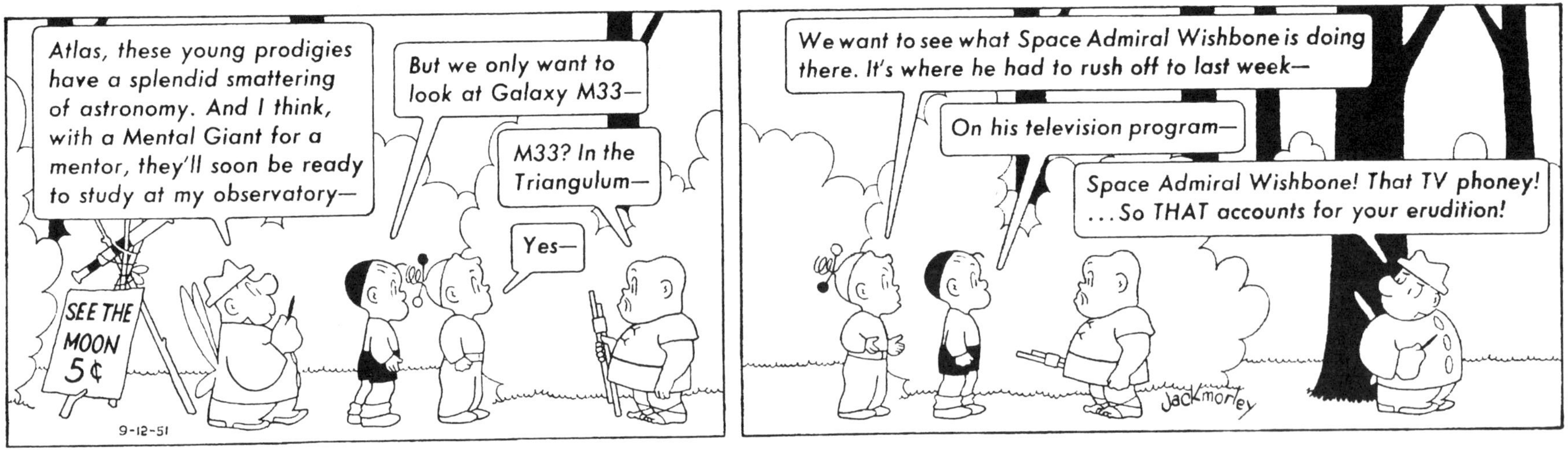
Atlas, these young prodigies have a splendid smattering of astronomy. And I think, with a Mental Giant for a mentor, they'll soon be ready to study at my observatory—
But we only want to look at Galaxy M33—
M33? In the Triangulum—
Yes—
SEE THE MOON 5¢
9-12-51
We want to see what Space Admiral Wishbone is doing there. It's where he had to rush off to last week—
On his television program—
Space Admiral Wishbone! That TV phoney! . . . So THAT accounts for your erudition!
Jackmorley

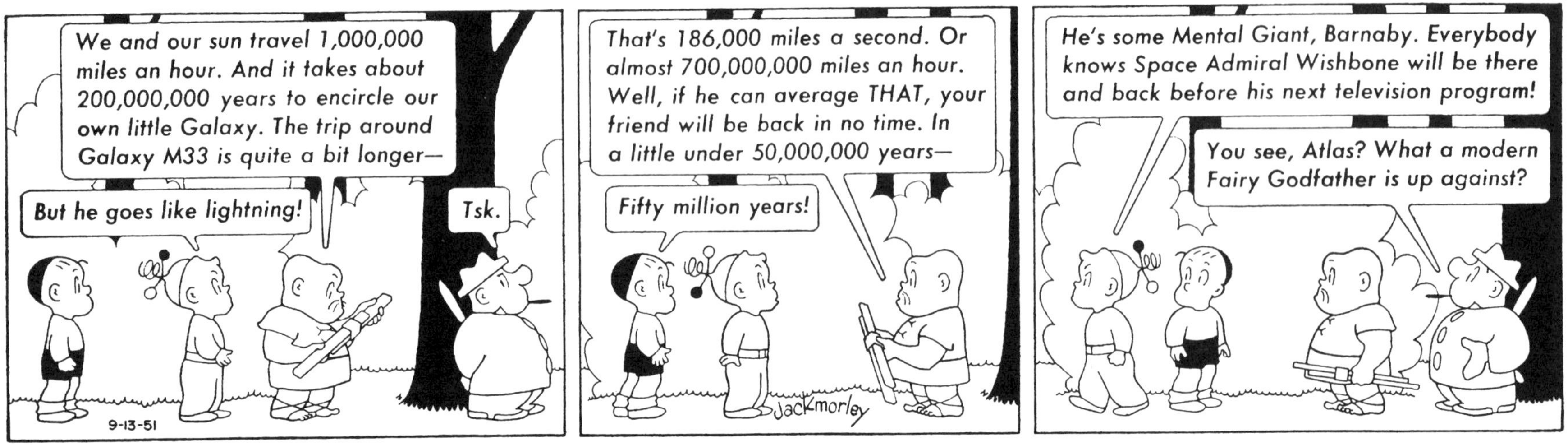
We and our sun travel 1,000,000 miles an hour. And it takes about 200,000,000 years to encircle our own little Galaxy. The trip around Galaxy M33 is quite a bit longer—
But he goes like lightning!
Tsk.
9-13-51
That's 186,000 miles a second. Or almost 700,000,000 miles an hour. Well, if he can average THAT, your friend will be back in no time. In a little under 50,000,000 years—
Fifty million years!
Jackmorley
He's some Mental Giant, Barnaby. Everybody knows Space Admiral Wishbone will be there and back before his next television program!
You see, Atlas? What a modern Fairy Godfather is up against?

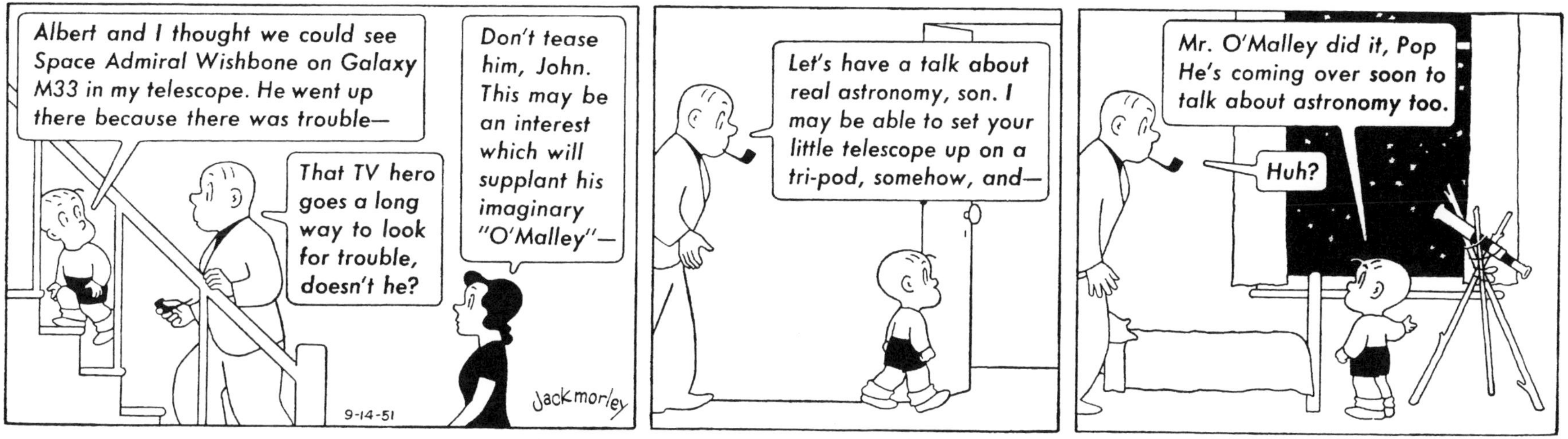
Albert and I thought we could see Space Admiral Wishbone on Galaxy M33 in my telescope. He went up there because there was trouble—
That TV hero goes a long way to look for trouble, doesn't he?
Don't tease him, John. This may be an interest which will supplant his imaginary "O'Malley"—
9-14-51
Jackmorley
Let's have a talk about real astronomy, son. I may be able to set your little telescope up on a tri-pod, somehow, and—
Mr. O'Malley did it, Pop He's coming over soon to talk about astronomy too.
Huh?

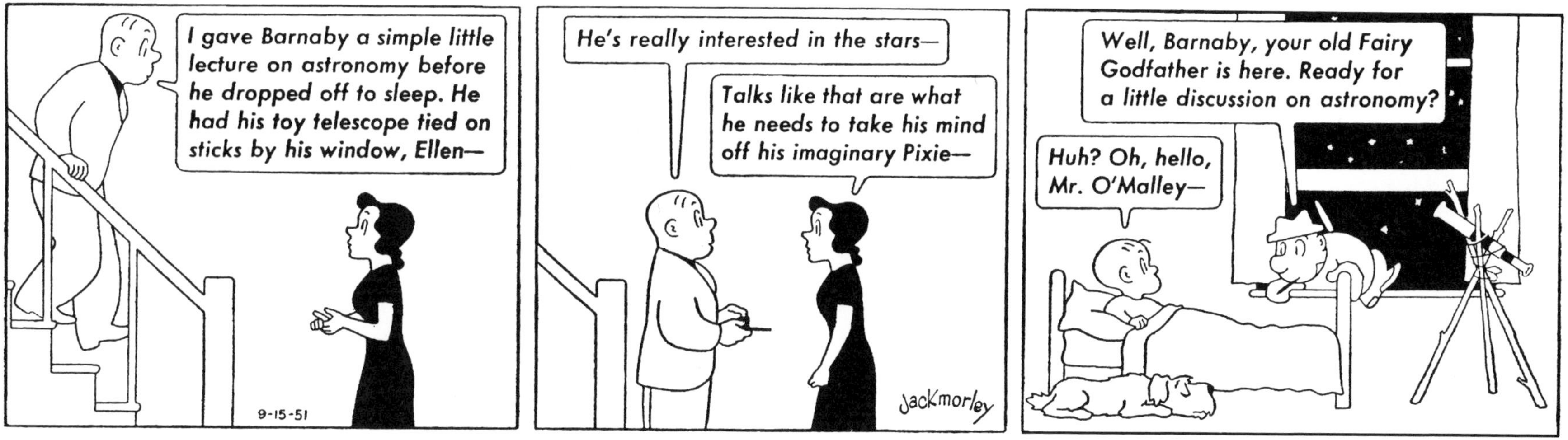
I gave Barnaby a simple little lecture on astronomy before he dropped off to sleep. He had his toy telescope tied on sticks by his window, Ellen—
9-15-51
He's really interested in the stars—
Talks like that are what he needs to take his mind off his imaginary Pixie—
Jackmorley
Well, Barnaby, your old Fairy Godfather is here. Ready for a little discussion on astronomy?
Huh? Oh, hello, Mr. O'Malley—

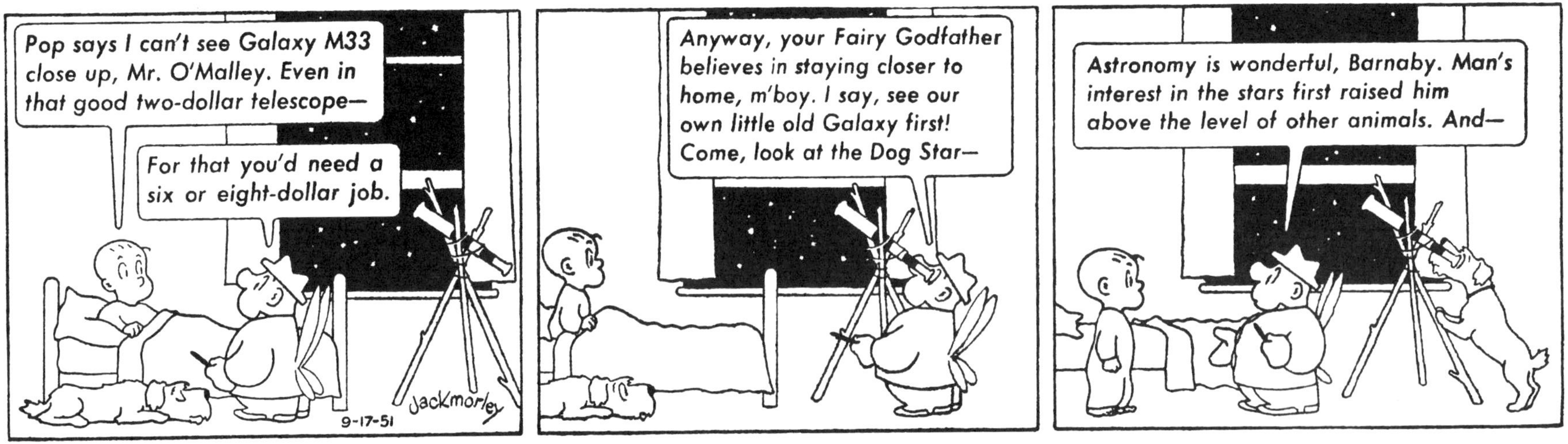
Pop says I can't see Galaxy M33 close up, Mr. O'Malley. Even in that good two-dollar telescope—
For that you'd need a six or eight-dollar job.
9-17-51
Jackmorley
Anyway, your Fairy Godfather believes in staying closer to home, m'boy. I say, see our own little old Galaxy first! Come, look at the Dog Star—
Astronomy is wonderful, Barnaby. Man's interest in the stars first raised him above the level of other animals. And—

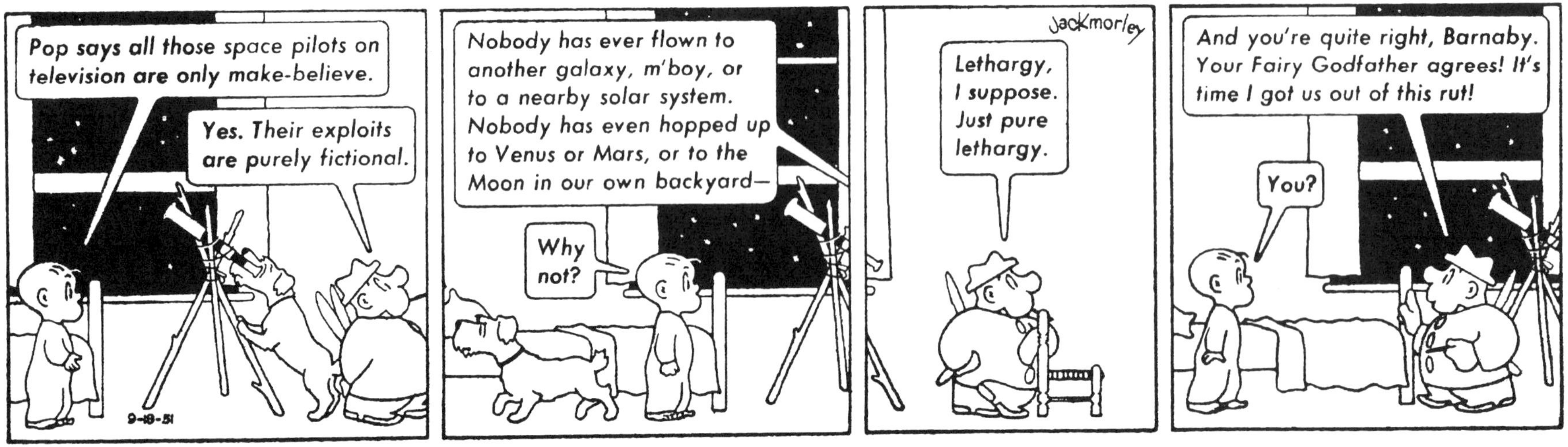
Pop says all those space pilots on television are only make-believe.
Yes. Their exploits are purely fictional.
9-18-51
Nobody has ever flown to another galaxy, m'boy, or to a nearby solar system. Nobody has even hopped up to Venus or Mars, or to the Moon in our own backyard—
Why not?
Jackmorley
Lethargy, I suppose. Just pure lethargy.
And you're quite right, Barnaby. Your Fairy Godfather agrees! It's time I got us out of this rut!
You?

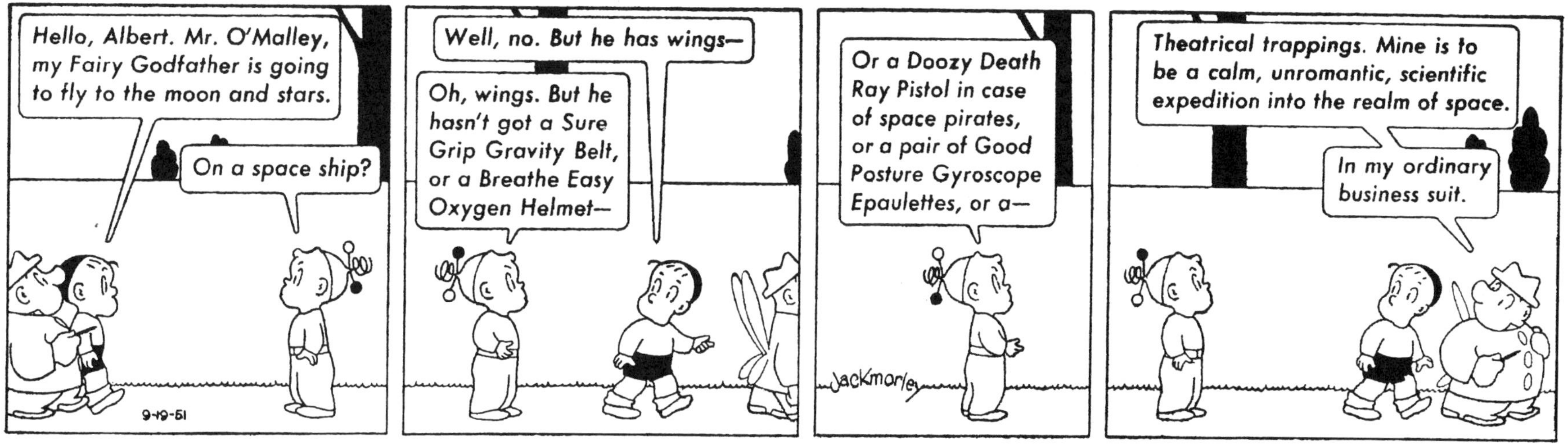
Hello, Albert. Mr. O'Malley, my Fairy Godfather is going to fly to the moon and stars.
On a space ship?
9-19-51
Well, no. But he has wings—
Oh, wings. But he hasn't got a Sure Grip Gravity Belt, or a Breathe Easy Oxygen Helmet—
Or a Doozy Death Ray Pistol in case of space pirates, or a pair of Good Posture Gyroscope Epaulettes, or a—
Jackmorley
Theatrical trappings. Mine is to be a calm, unromantic, scientific expedition into the realm of space.
In my ordinary business suit.

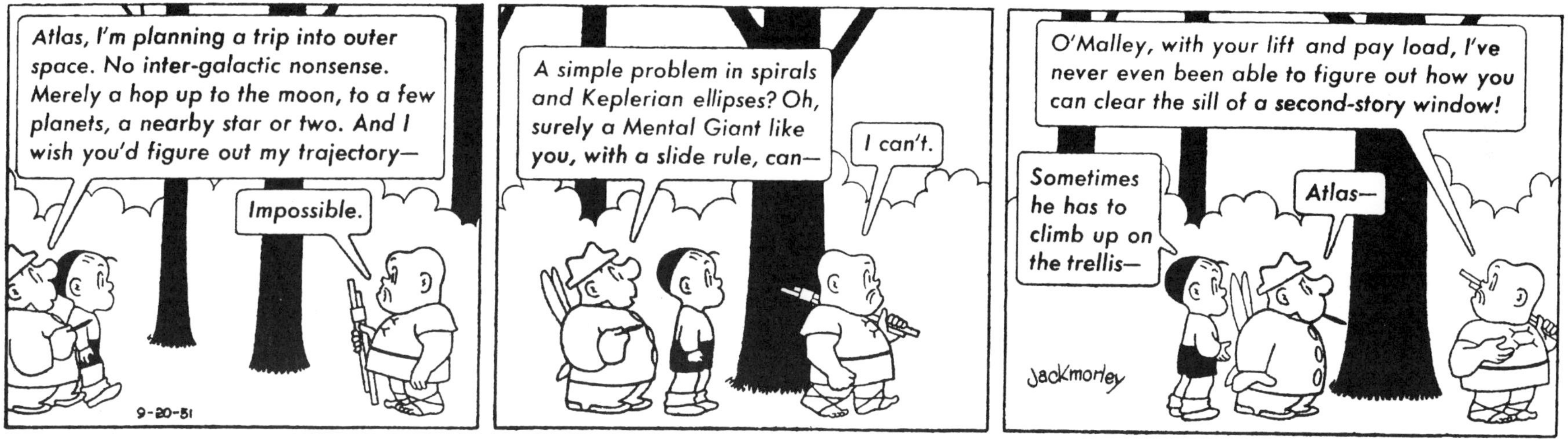
Atlas, I'm planning a trip into outer space. No inter-galactic nonsense. Merely a hop up to the moon, to a few planets, a nearby star or two. And I wish you'd figure out my trajectory—
Impossible.
9-20-51
A simple problem in spirals and Keplerian ellipses? Oh, surely a Mental Giant like you, with a slide rule, can—
I can't.
O'Malley, with your lift and pay load, I've never even been able to figure out how you can clear the sill of a second-story window!
Sometimes he has to climb up on the trellis—
Atlas—
Jackmorley

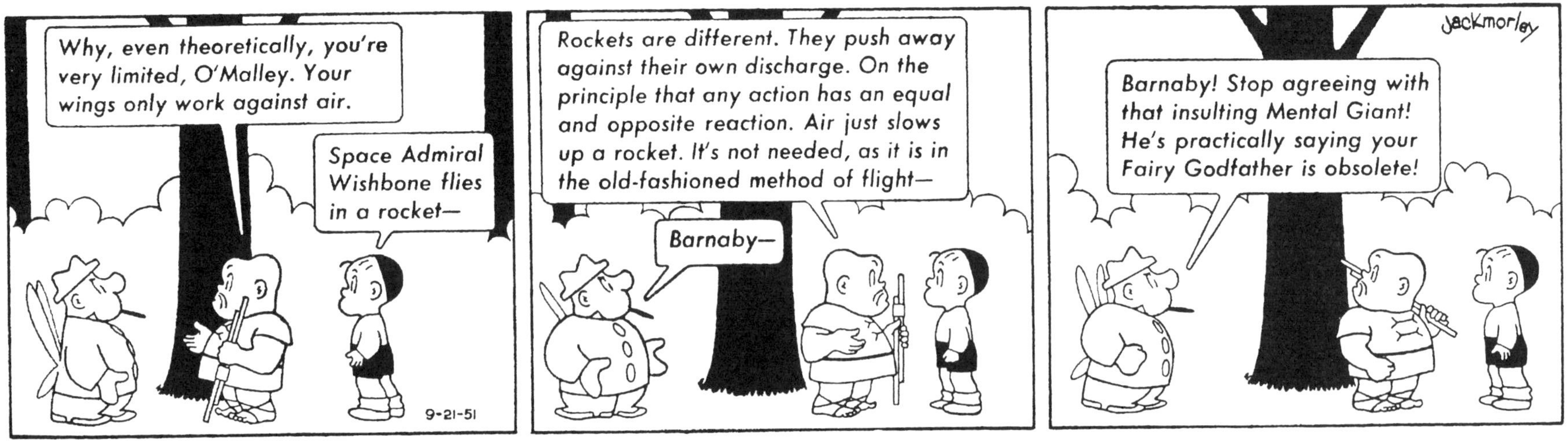
Why, even theoretically, you're very limited, O'Malley. Your wings only work against air.
Space Admiral Wishbone flies in a rocket—
9-21-51
Rockets are different. They push away against their own discharge. On the principle that any action has an equal and opposite reaction. Air just slows up a rocket. It's not needed, as it is in the old-fashioned method of flight—
Barnaby—
JACKMORLEY
Barnaby! Stop agreeing with that insulting Mental Giant! He's practically saying your Fairy Godfather is obsolete!

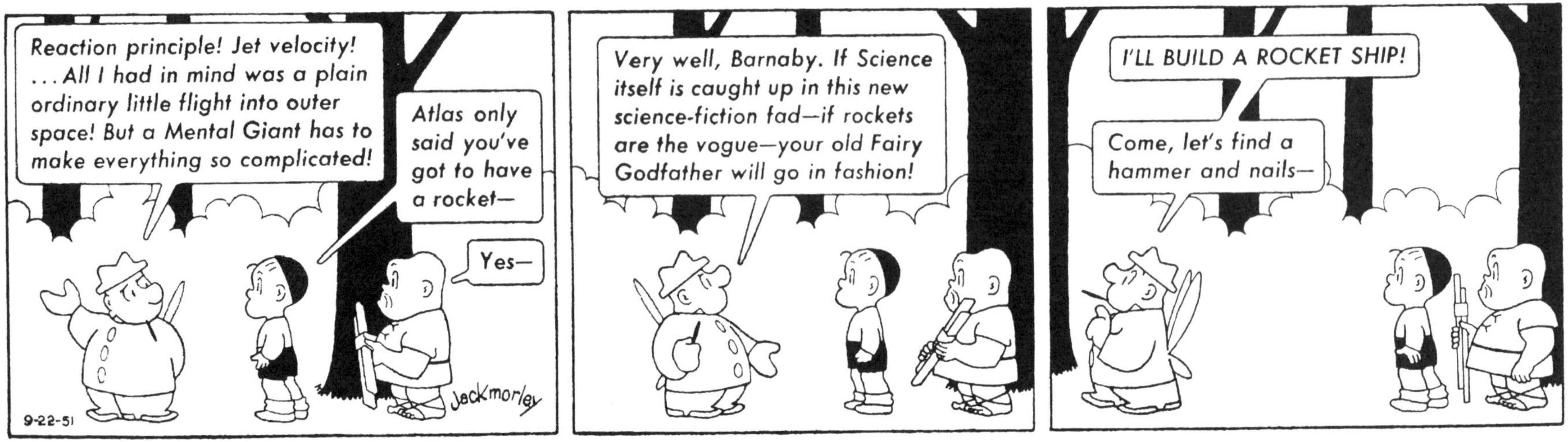
Reaction principle! Jet velocity! . . . All I had in mind was a plain ordinary little flight into outer space! But a Mental Giant has to make everything so complicated!
Atlas only said you've got to have a rocket—
Yes—
Jackmorley
9-22-51
Very well, Barnaby. If Science itself is caught up in this new science-fiction fad—if rockets are the vogue—your old Fairy Godfather will go in fashion!
I'LL BUILD A ROCKET SHIP!
Come, let's find a hammer and nails—

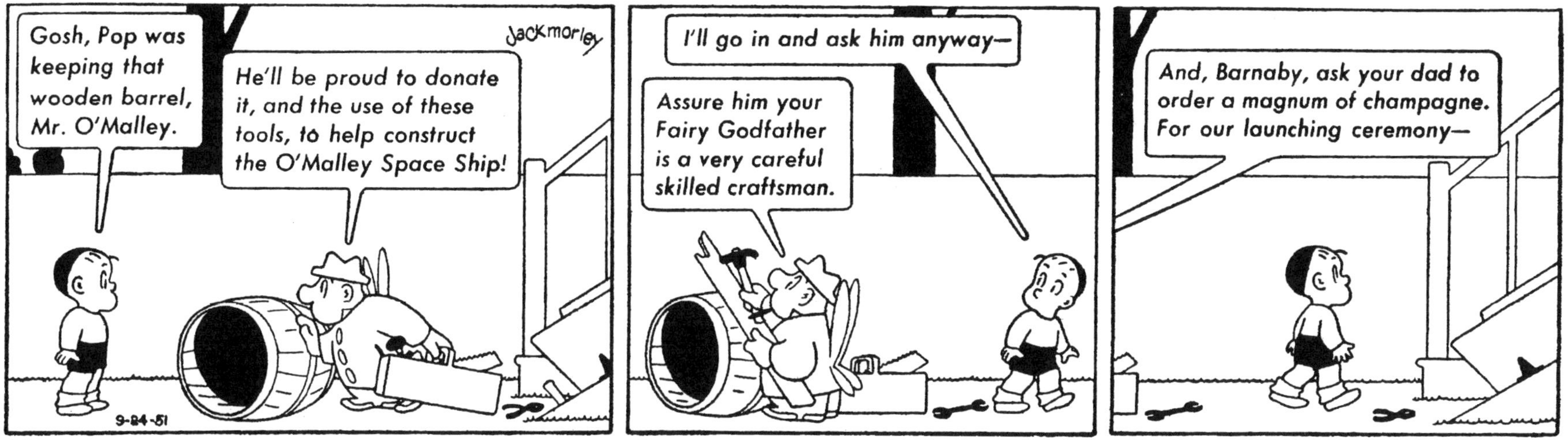
Gosh, Pop was keeping that wooden barrel, Mr. O'Malley.
He'll be proud to donate it, and the use of these tools, to help construct the O'Malley Space Ship!
Jackmorley
9-24-51
I'll go in and ask him anyway—
Assure him your Fairy Godfather is a very careful skilled craftsman.
And, Barnaby, ask your dad to order a magnum of champagne. For our launching ceremony—

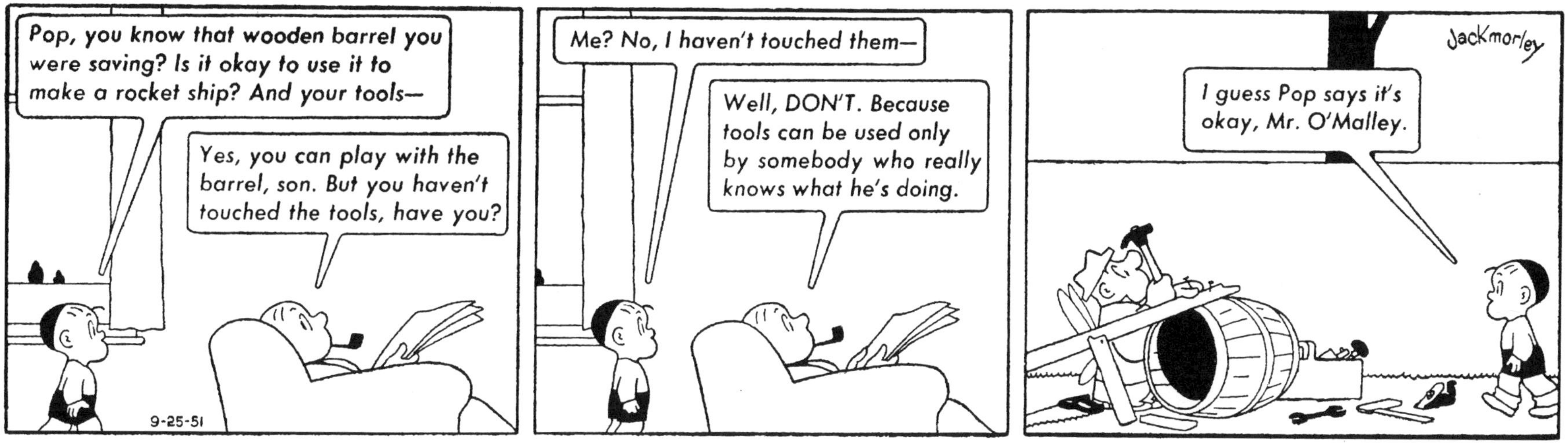
Pop, you know that wooden barrel you were saving? Is it okay to use it to make a rocket ship? And your tools—
Yes, you can play with the barrel, son. But you haven't touched the tools, have you?
9-25-51
Me? No, I haven't touched them—
Well, DON'T. Because tools can be used only by somebody who really knows what he's doing.
Jackmorley
I guess Pop says it's okay, Mr. O'Malley.

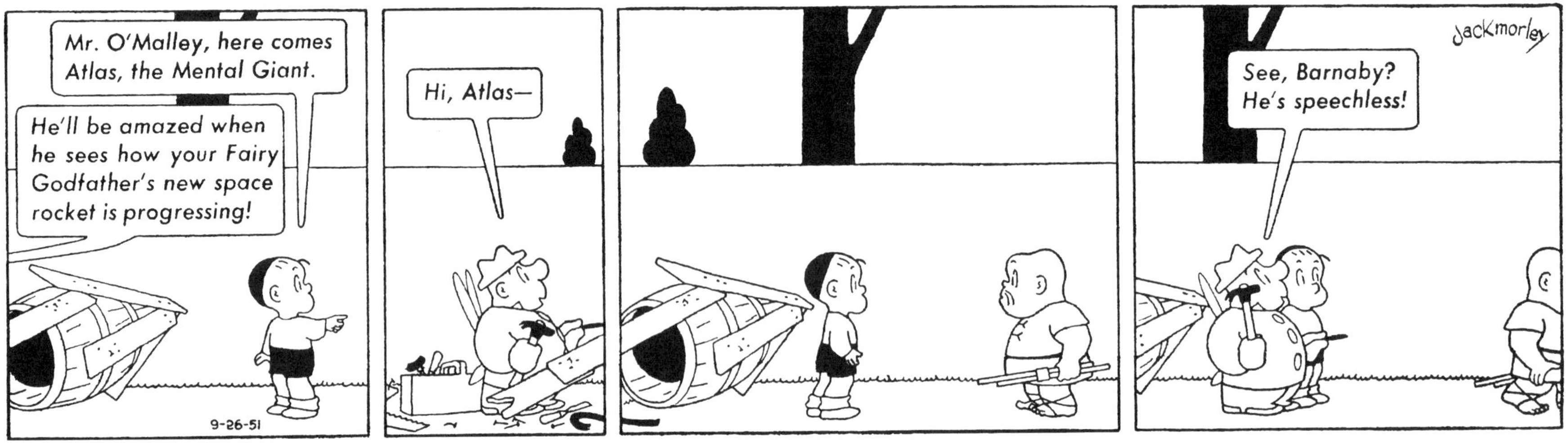
Mr. O'Malley, here comes Atlas, the Mental Giant.
He'll be amazed when he sees how your Fairy Godfather's new space rocket is progressing!
9-26-51
Hi, Atlas—
Jackmorley
See, Barnaby? He's speechless!

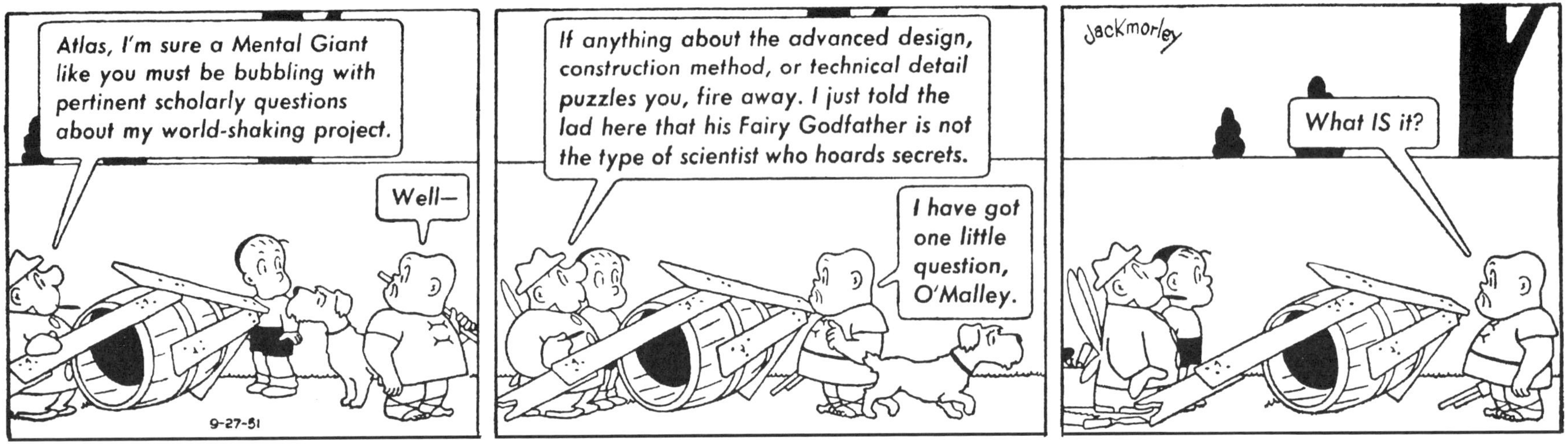
Atlas, I'm sure a Mental Giant like you must be bubbling with pertinent scholarly questions about my world-shaking project.
Well—
9-27-51
If anything about the advanced design, construction method, or technical detail puzzles you, fire away. I just told the lad here that his Fairy Godfather is not the type of scientist who hoards secrets.
I have got one little question, O'Malley.
Jackmorley
What IS it?

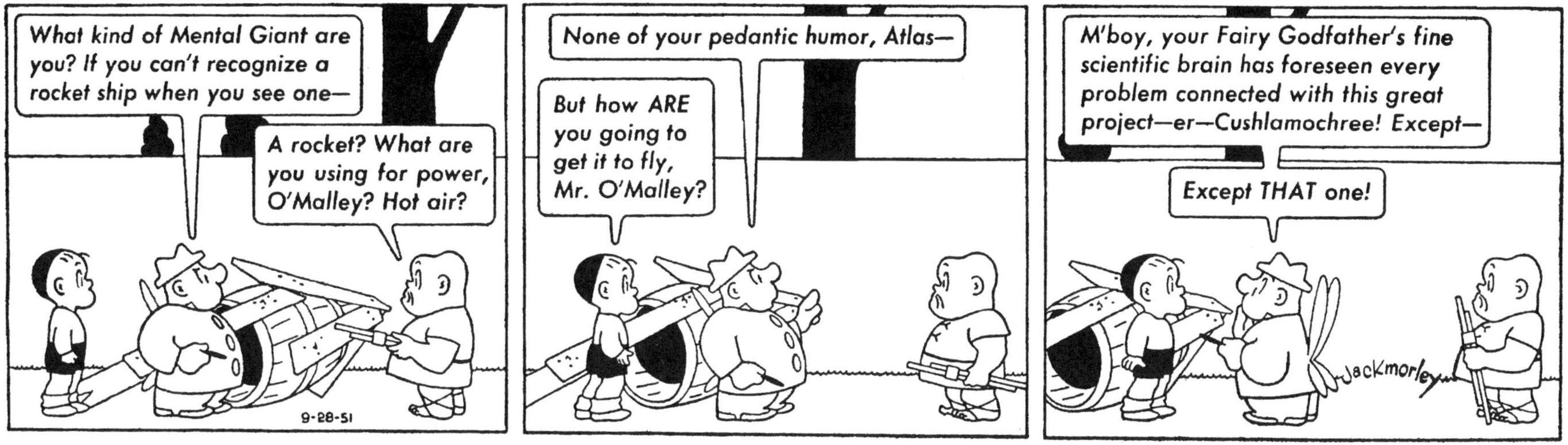
What kind of Mental Giant are you? If you can't recognize a rocket ship when you see one—
A rocket? What are you using for power, O'Malley? Hot air?
9-28-51
None of your pedantic humor, Atlas—
But how ARE you going to get it to fly, Mr. O'Malley?
M'boy, your Fairy Godfather's fine scientific brain has foreseen every problem connected with this great project—er—Cushlamochree! Except—
Except THAT one!
Jackmorley

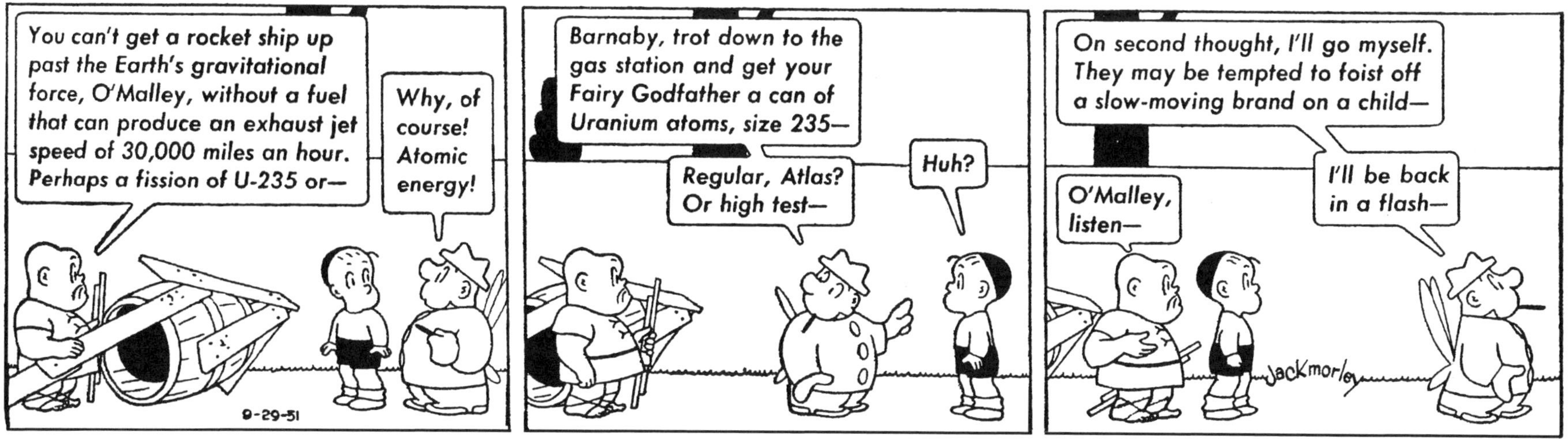
You can't get a rocket ship up past the Earth's gravitational force, O'Malley, without a fuel that can produce an exhaust jet speed of 30,000 miles an hour. Perhaps a fission of U-235 or—
Why, of course! Atomic energy!
9-29-51
Barnaby, trot down to the gas station and get your Fairy Godfather a can of Uranium atoms, size 235—
Regular, Atlas? Or high test—
Huh?
On second thought, I'll go myself. They may be tempted to foist off a slow-moving brand on a child—
O'Malley, listen—
I'll be back in a flash—
Jackmorley

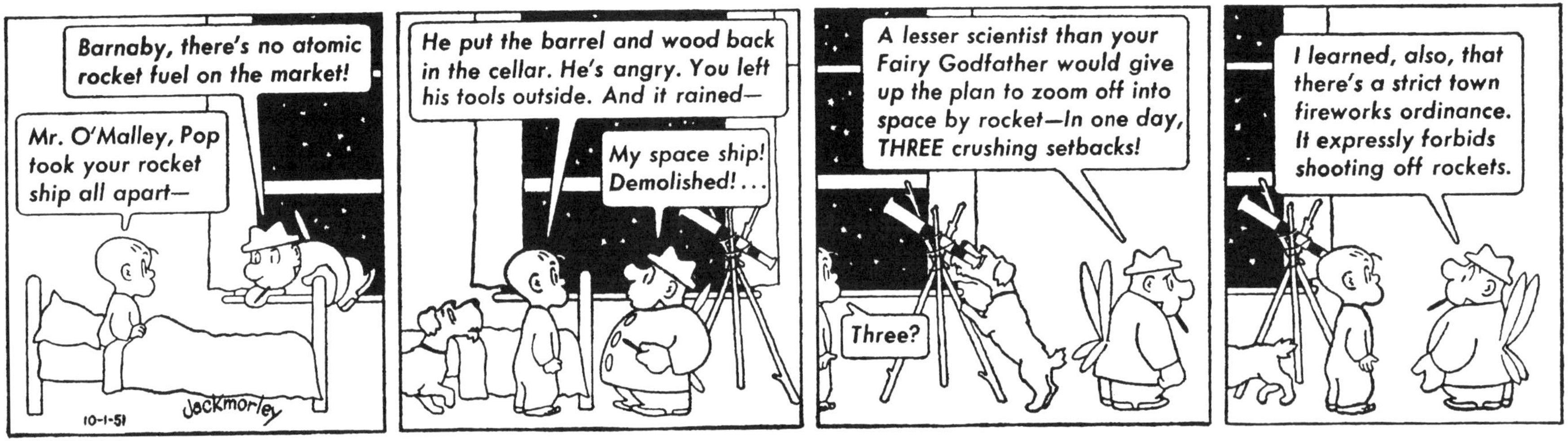
Barnaby, there's no atomic rocket fuel on the market!
Mr. O'Malley, Pop took your rocket ship all apart—
10-1-51
Jackmorley
He put the barrel and wood back in the cellar. He's angry. You left his tools outside. And it rained—
My space ship! Demolished!...
A lesser scientist than your Fairy Godfather would give up the plan to zoom off into space by rocket—In one day, THREE crushing setbacks!
Three?
I learned, also, that there's a strict town fireworks ordinance. It expressly forbids shooting off rockets.

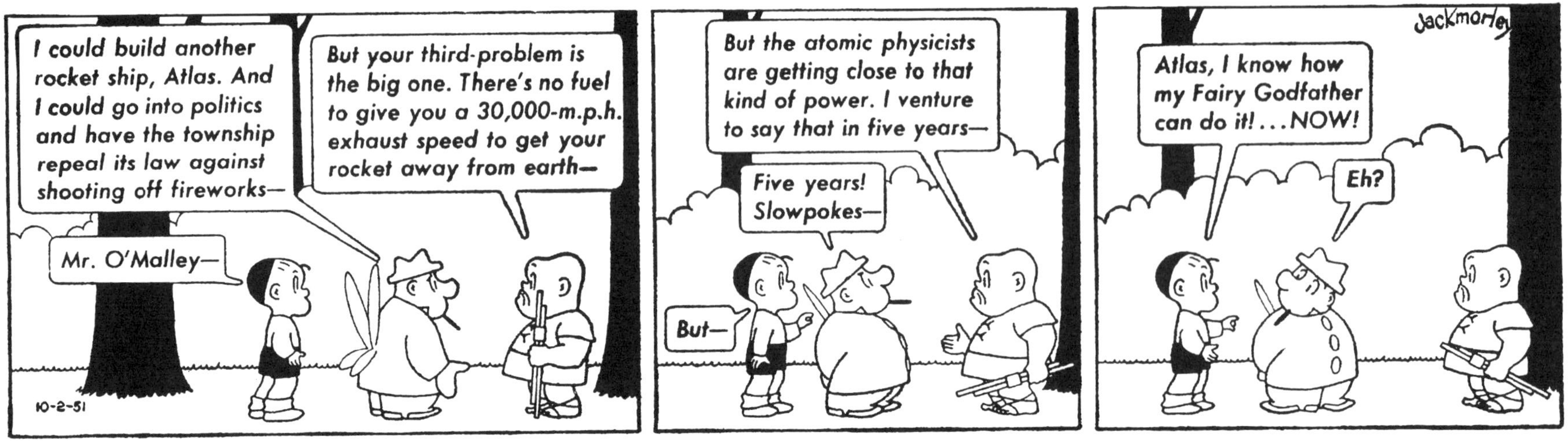
I could build another rocket ship, Atlas. And I could go into politics and have the township repeal its law against shooting off fireworks—
But your third-problem is the big one. There's no fuel to give you a 30,000-m.p.h. exhaust speed to get your rocket away from earth—
Mr. O'Malley—
10-2-51
But the atomic physicists are getting close to that kind of power. I venture to say that in five years—
Five years! Slowpokes—
But—
Jackmorley
Atlas, I know how my Fairy Godfather can do it!...NOW!
Eh?

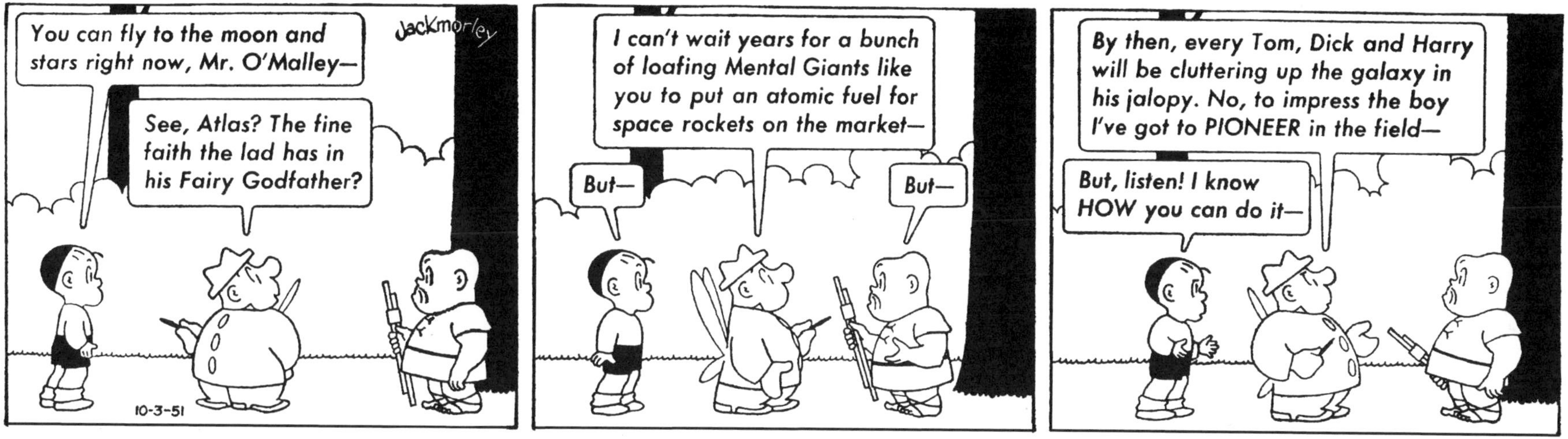

Jackmorley
You can fly to the moon and stars right now, Mr. O'Malley—
See, Atlas? The fine faith the lad has in his Fairy Godfather?
10-3-51
I can't wait years for a bunch of loafing Mental Giants like you to put an atomic fuel for space rockets on the market—
But—
But—
By then, every Tom, Dick and Harry will be cluttering up the galaxy in his jalopy. No, to impress the boy I've got to PIONEER in the field—
But, listen! I know HOW you can do it—

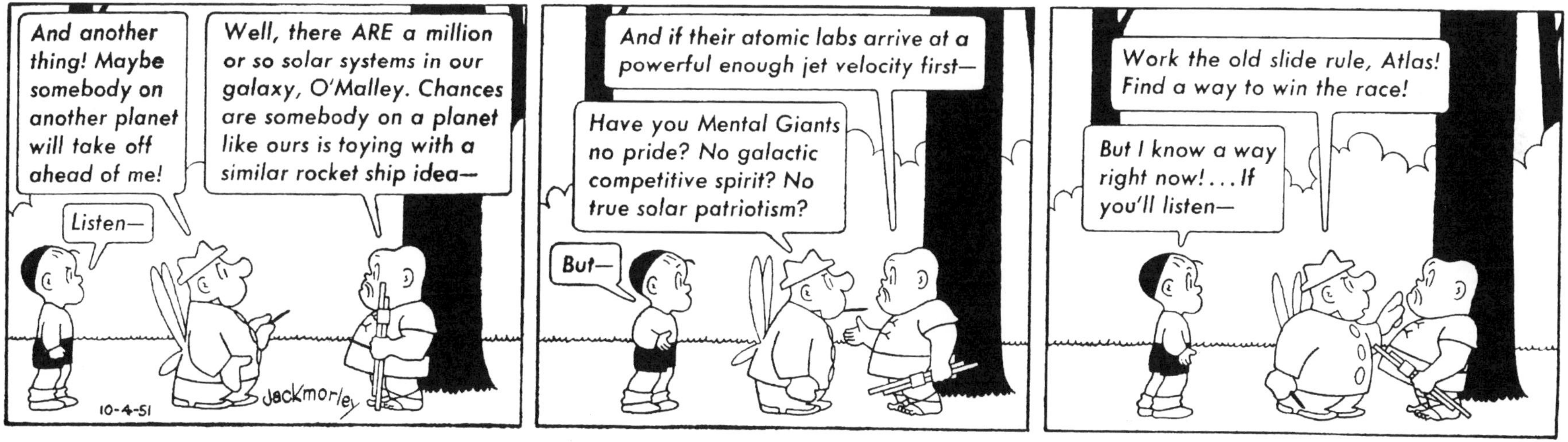

And another thing! Maybe somebody on another planet will take off ahead of me!
Well, there ARE a million or so solar systems in our galaxy, O'Malley. Chances are somebody on a planet like ours is toying with a similar rocket ship idea—
Listen—
10-4-51
Jackmorley
And if their atomic labs arrive at a powerful enough jet velocity first—
Have you Mental Giants no pride? No galactic competitive spirit? No true solar patriotism?
But—
Work the old slide rule, Atlas! Find a way to win the race!
But I know a way right now! . . . If you'll listen—

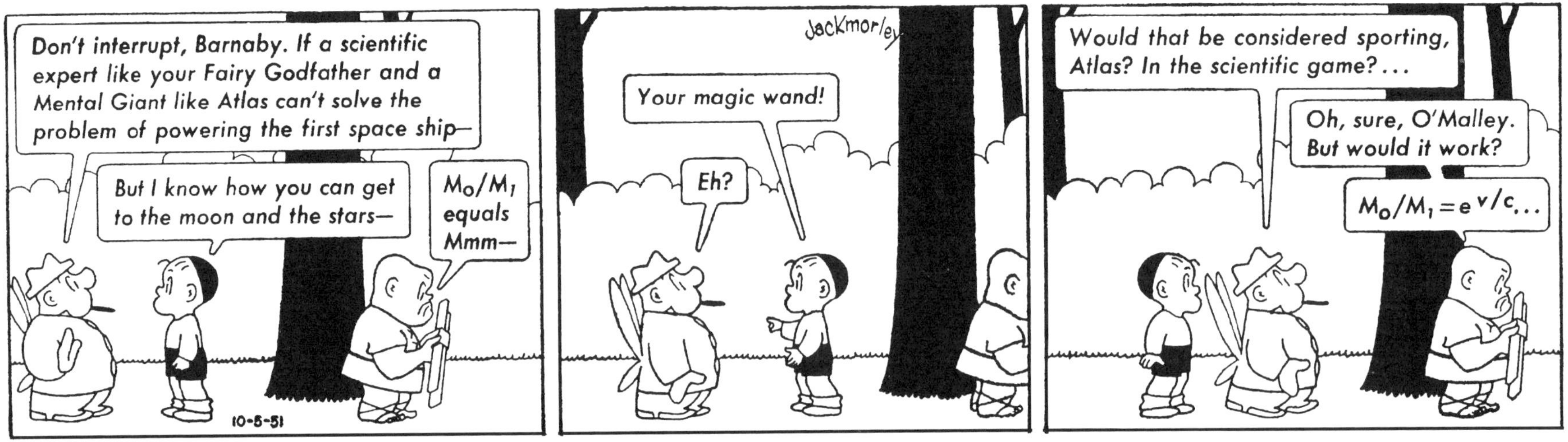
Don't interrupt, Barnaby. If a scientific expert like your Fairy Godfather and a Mental Giant like Atlas can't solve the problem of powering the first space ship—
But I know how you can get to the moon and the stars—
M_0/M_1 equals Mmm—
10-5-51
Your magic wand!
Eh?
Jackmorley
Would that be considered sporting, Atlas? In the scientific game?...
Oh, sure, O'Malley. But would it work?
$M_0/M_1 = e^{v/c}$...

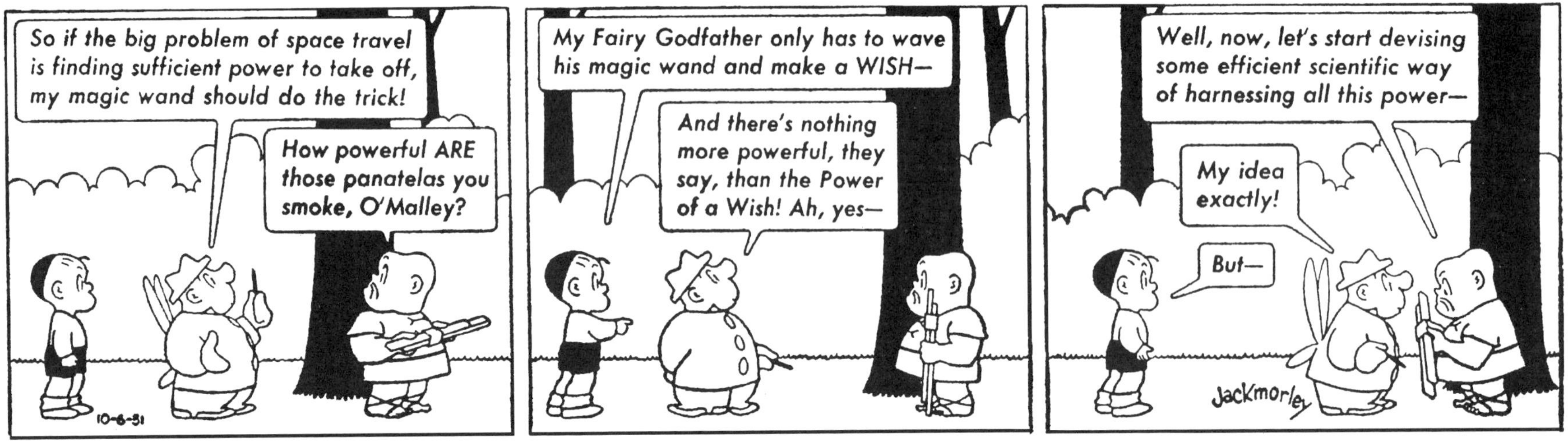
So if the big problem of space travel is finding sufficient power to take off, my magic wand should do the trick!
How powerful ARE those panatelas you smoke, O'Malley?
10-6-51
My Fairy Godfather only has to wave his magic wand and make a WISH—
And there's nothing more powerful, they say, than the Power of a Wish! Ah, yes—
Well, now, let's start devising some efficient scientific way of harnessing all this power—
My idea exactly!
But—
Jackmorley

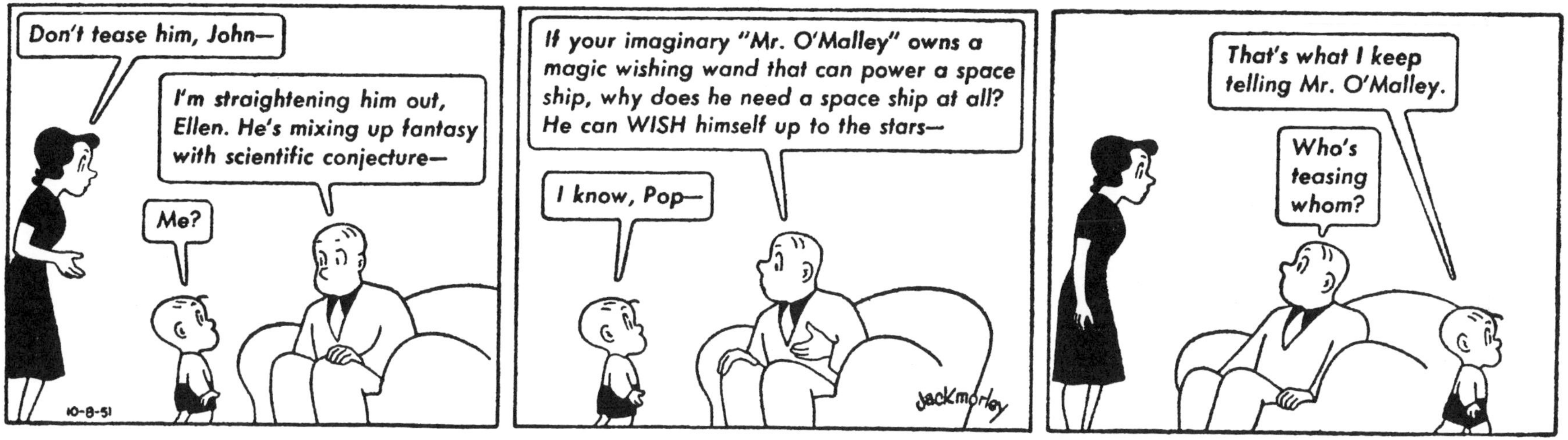
Don't tease him, John—
I'm straightening him out, Ellen. He's mixing up fantasy with scientific conjecture—
Me?
10-8-51
If your imaginary "Mr. O'Malley" owns a magic wishing wand that can power a space ship, why does he need a space ship at all? He can WISH himself up to the stars—
I know, Pop—
Jackmorley
That's what I keep telling Mr. O'Malley.
Who's teasing whom?

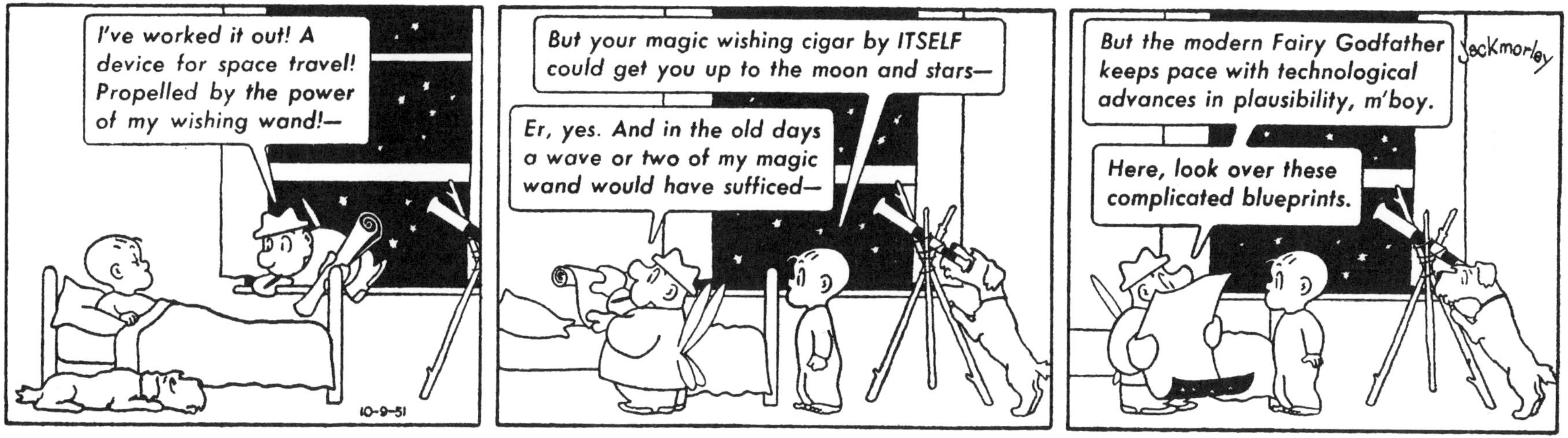
I've worked it out! A device for space travel! Propelled by the power of my wishing wand!—
10-9-51
But your magic wishing cigar by ITSELF could get you up to the moon and stars—
Er, yes. And in the old days a wave or two of my magic wand would have sufficed—
But the modern Fairy Godfather keeps pace with technological advances in plausibility, m'boy.
Here, look over these complicated blueprints.
Jackmorley

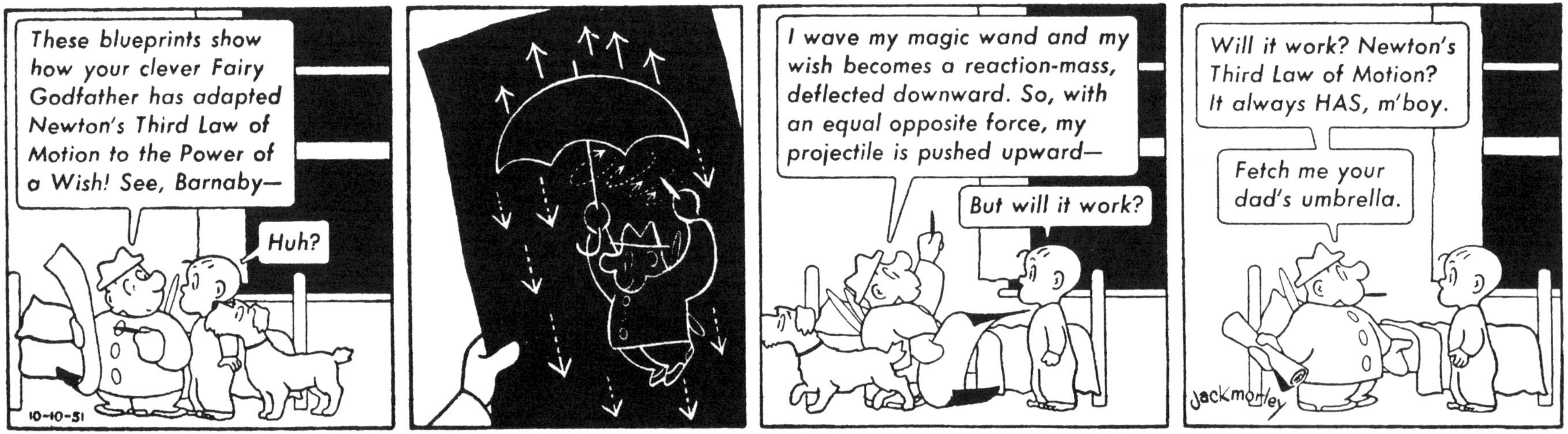
These blueprints show how your clever Fairy Godfather has adapted Newton's Third Law of Motion to the Power of a Wish! See, Barnaby—
Huh?
10-10-51
I wave my magic wand and my wish becomes a reaction-mass, deflected downward. So, with an equal opposite force, my projectile is pushed upward—
But will it work?
Will it work? Newton's Third Law of Motion? It always HAS, m'boy.
Fetch me your dad's umbrella.
Jackmorley

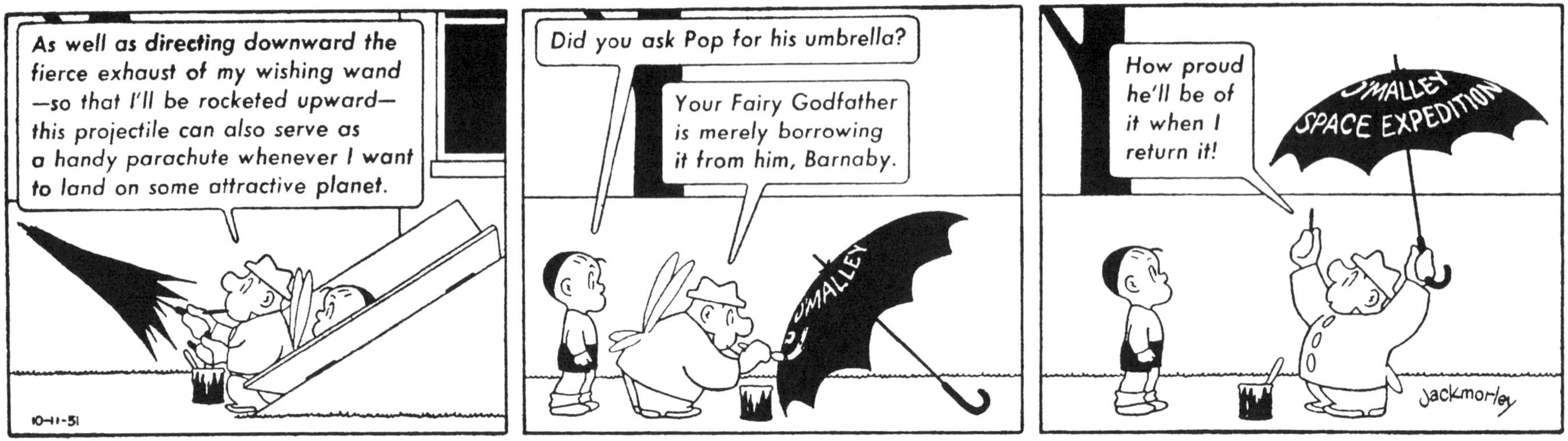
As well as directing downward the fierce exhaust of my wishing wand —so that I'll be rocketed upward— this projectile can also serve as a handy parachute whenever I want to land on some attractive planet.
10-11-51
Did you ask Pop for his umbrella?
Your Fairy Godfather is merely borrowing it from him, Barnaby.
O'MALLEY
How proud he'll be of it when I return it!
O'MALLEY SPACE EXPEDITION
Jackmorley

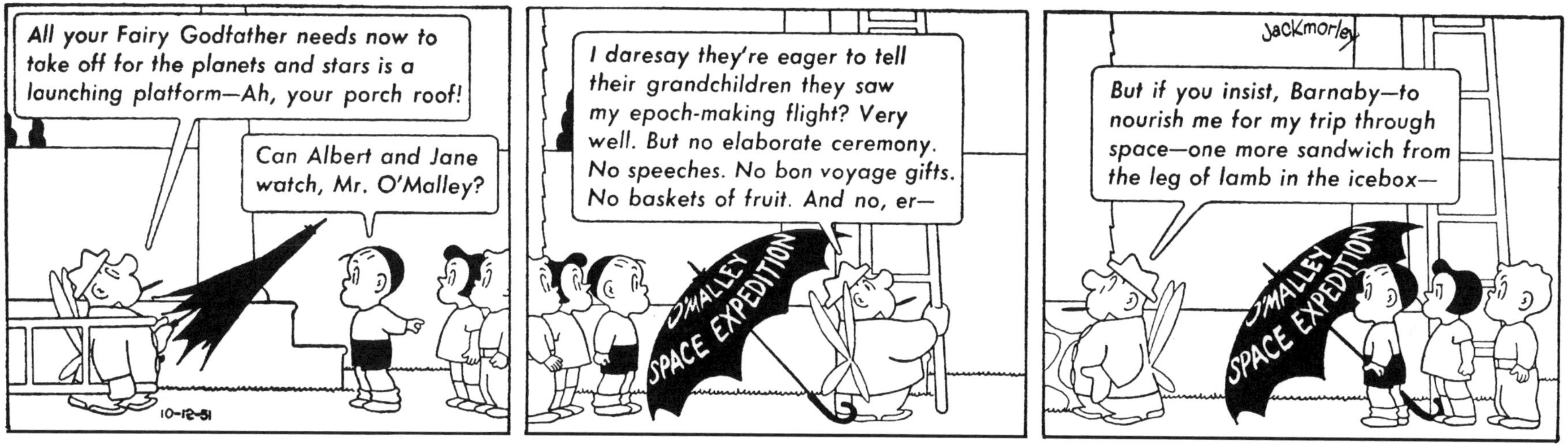
All your Fairy Godfather needs now to take off for the planets and stars is a launching platform—Ah, your porch roof!
Can Albert and Jane watch, Mr. O'Malley?
10-12-51
I daresay they're eager to tell their grandchildren they saw my epoch-making flight? Very well. But no elaborate ceremony. No speeches. No bon voyage gifts. No baskets of fruit. And no, er—
O'MALLEY SPACE EXPEDITION
JACKMORLEY
But if you insist, Barnaby—to nourish me for my trip through space—one more sandwich from the leg of lamb in the icebox—
O'MALLEY SPACE EXPEDITION

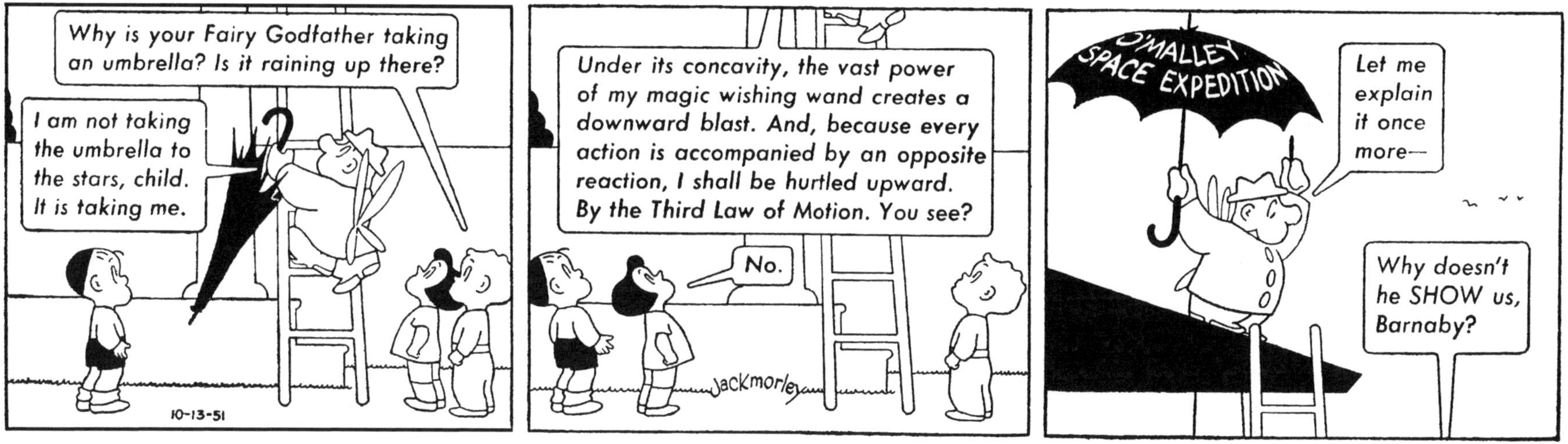
Why is your Fairy Godfather taking an umbrella? Is it raining up there?
I am not taking the umbrella to the stars, child. It is taking me.
10-13-51
Under its concavity, the vast power of my magic wishing wand creates a downward blast. And, because every action is accompanied by an opposite reaction, I shall be hurtled upward. By the Third Law of Motion. You see?
No.
JACKMORLEY
O'MALLEY SPACE EXPEDITION
Let me explain it once more—
Why doesn't he SHOW us, Barnaby?

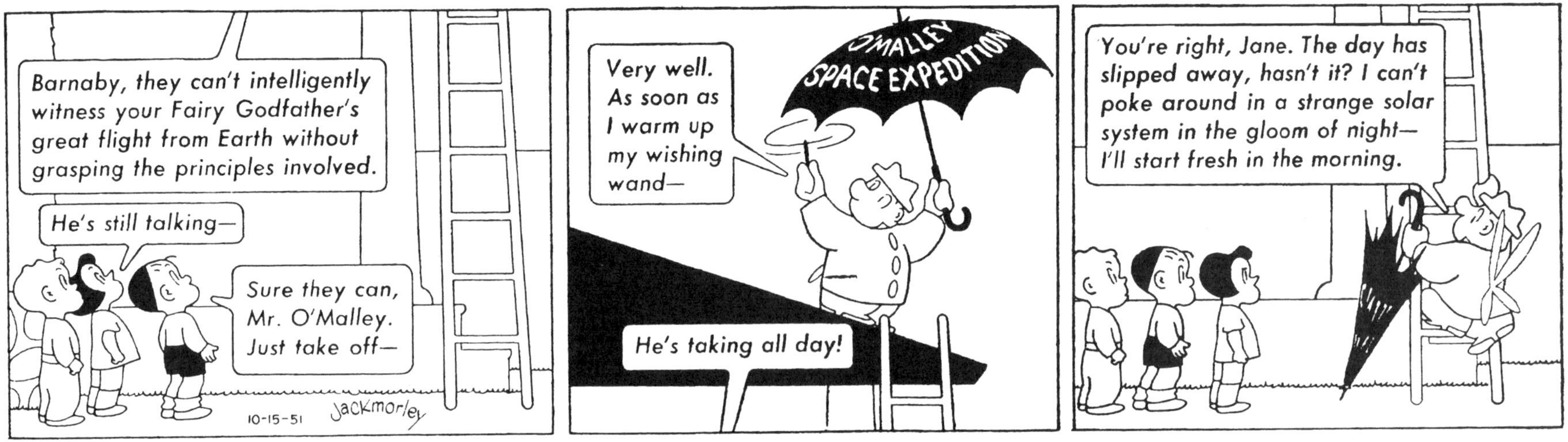
Barnaby, they can't intelligently witness your Fairy Godfather's great flight from Earth without grasping the principles involved.
He's still talking—
Sure they can, Mr. O'Malley. Just take off—
10-15-51
Jackmorley
Very well. As soon as I warm up my wishing wand—
O'MALLEY SPACE EXPEDITION
He's taking all day!
You're right, Jane. The day has slipped away, hasn't it? I can't poke around in a strange solar system in the gloom of night— I'll start fresh in the morning.

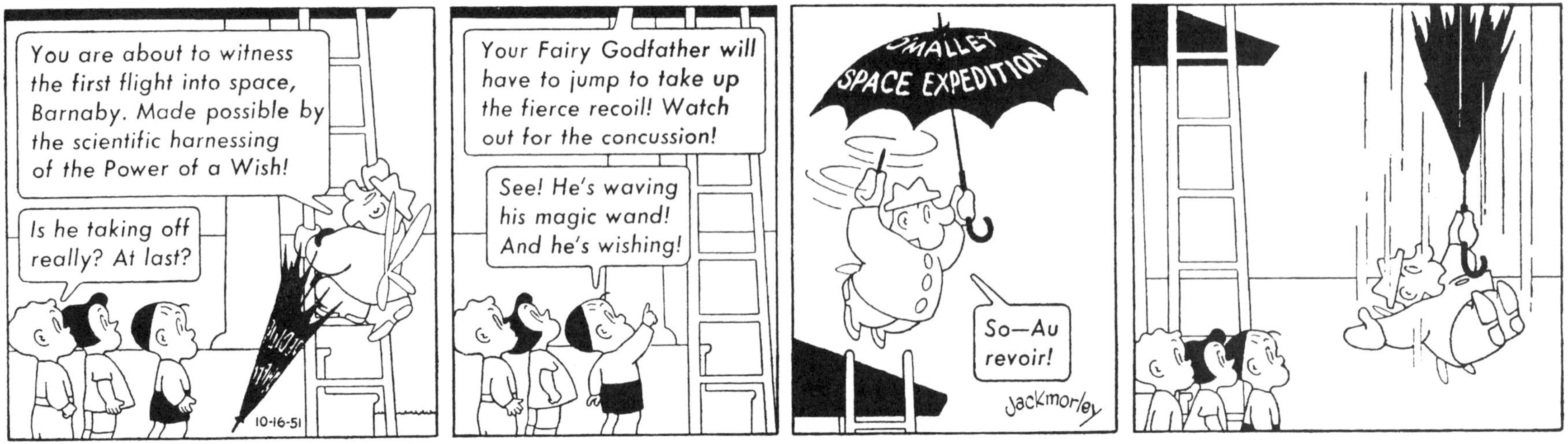
You are about to witness the first flight into space, Barnaby. Made possible by the scientific harnessing of the Power of a Wish!
Is he taking off really? At last?
10-16-51
Your Fairy Godfather will have to jump to take up the fierce recoil! Watch out for the concussion!
See! He's waving his magic wand! And he's wishing!
O'MALLEY SPACE EXPEDITION
So—Au revoir!
Jackmorley

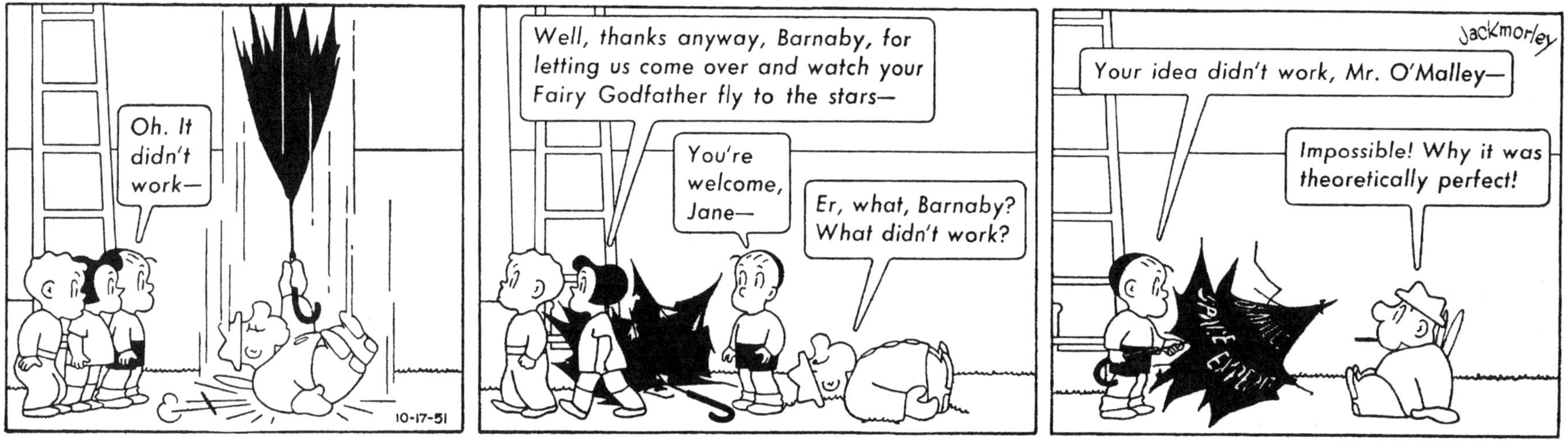
Oh. It didn't work—
10-17-51
Well, thanks anyway, Barnaby, for letting us come over and watch your Fairy Godfather fly to the stars—
You're welcome, Jane—
Er, what, Barnaby? What didn't work?
Jackmorley
Your idea didn't work, Mr. O'Malley—
Impossible! Why it was theoretically perfect!

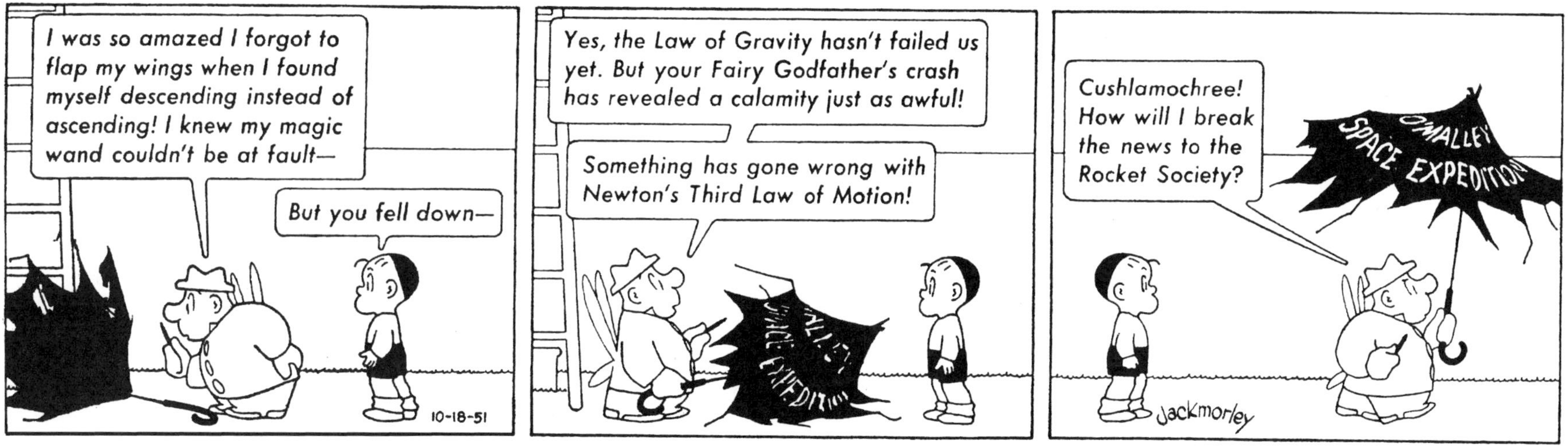
I was so amazed I forgot to flap my wings when I found myself descending instead of ascending! I knew my magic wand couldn't be at fault—
But you fell down—
10-18-51
Yes, the Law of Gravity hasn't failed us yet. But your Fairy Godfather's crash has revealed a calamity just as awful!
Something has gone wrong with Newton's Third Law of Motion!
Cushlamochree! How will I break the news to the Rocket Society?
O'MALLEY SPACE EXPEDITION
Jackmorley

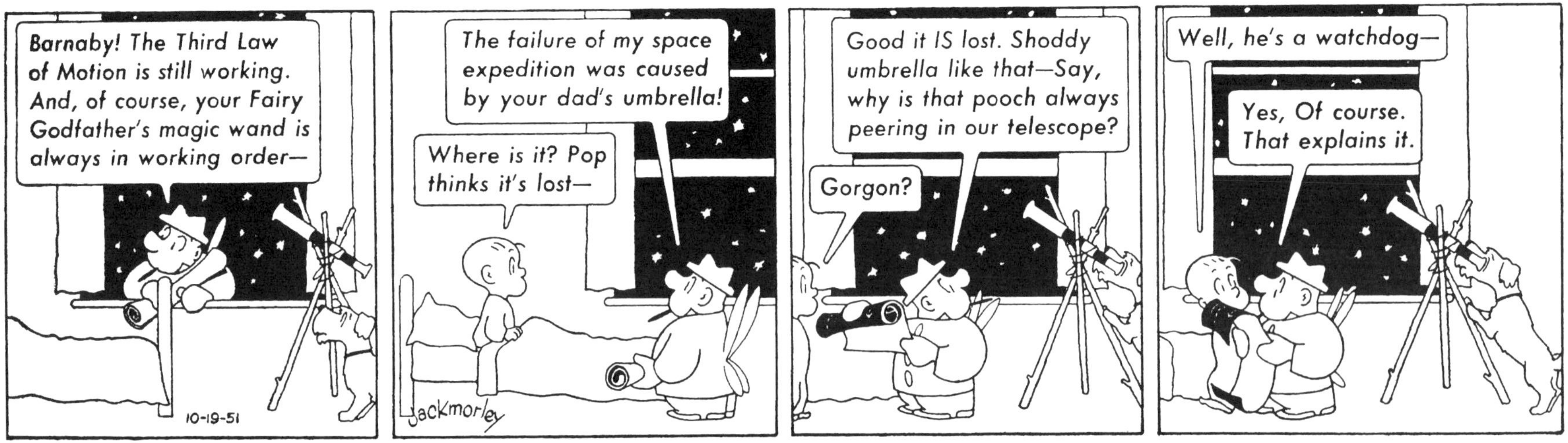

Barnaby! The Third Law of Motion is still working. And, of course, your Fairy Godfather's magic wand is always in working order—
10-19-51
The failure of my space expedition was caused by your dad's umbrella!
Where is it? Pop thinks it's lost—
Jackmorley
Good it IS lost. Shoddy umbrella like that—Say, why is that pooch always peering in our telescope?
Gorgon?
Well, he's a watchdog—
Yes, Of course. That explains it.

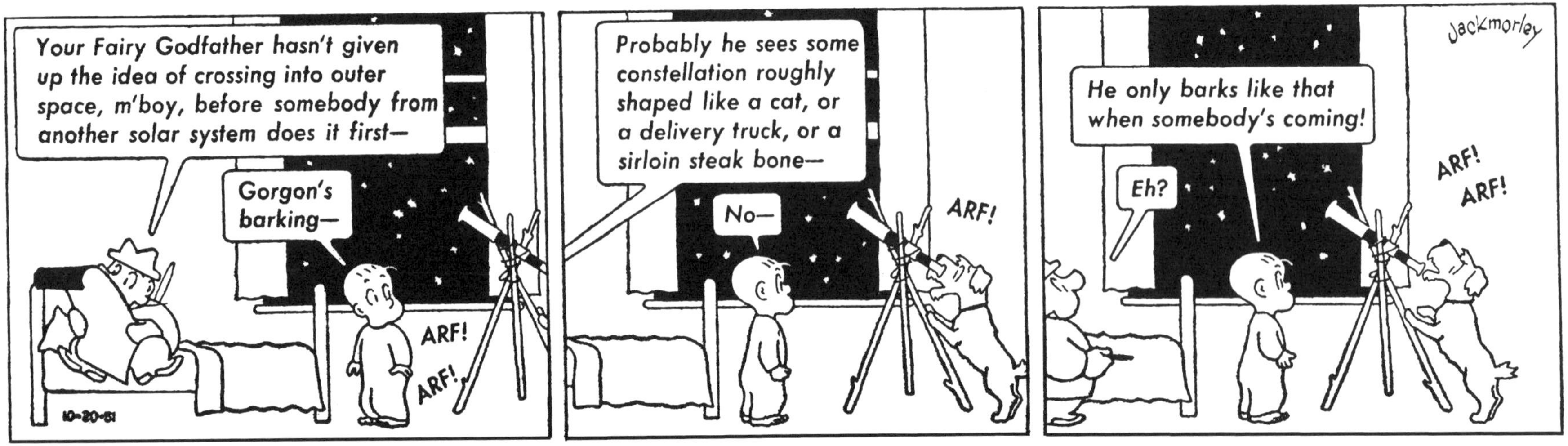

Your Fairy Godfather hasn't given up the idea of crossing into outer space, m'boy, before somebody from another solar system does it first—
Gorgon's barking—
ARF!
ARF!
10-20-51
Probably he sees some constellation roughly shaped like a cat, or a delivery truck, or a sirloin steak bone—
No—
ARF!
Jackmorley
He only barks like that when somebody's coming!
Eh?
ARF!
ARF!

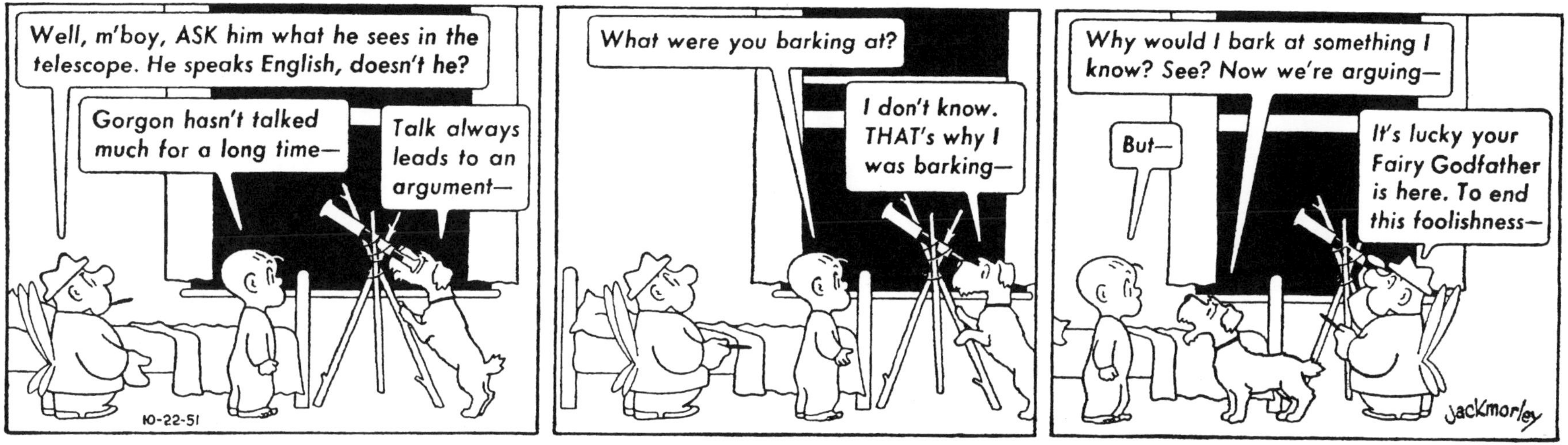
Well, m'boy, ASK him what he sees in the telescope. He speaks English, doesn't he?
Gorgon hasn't talked much for a long time—
Talk always leads to an argument—
10-22-51
What were you barking at?
I don't know. THAT's why I was barking—
Why would I bark at something I know? See? Now we're arguing—
But—
It's lucky your Fairy Godfather is here. To end this foolishness—
JACKMORLEY

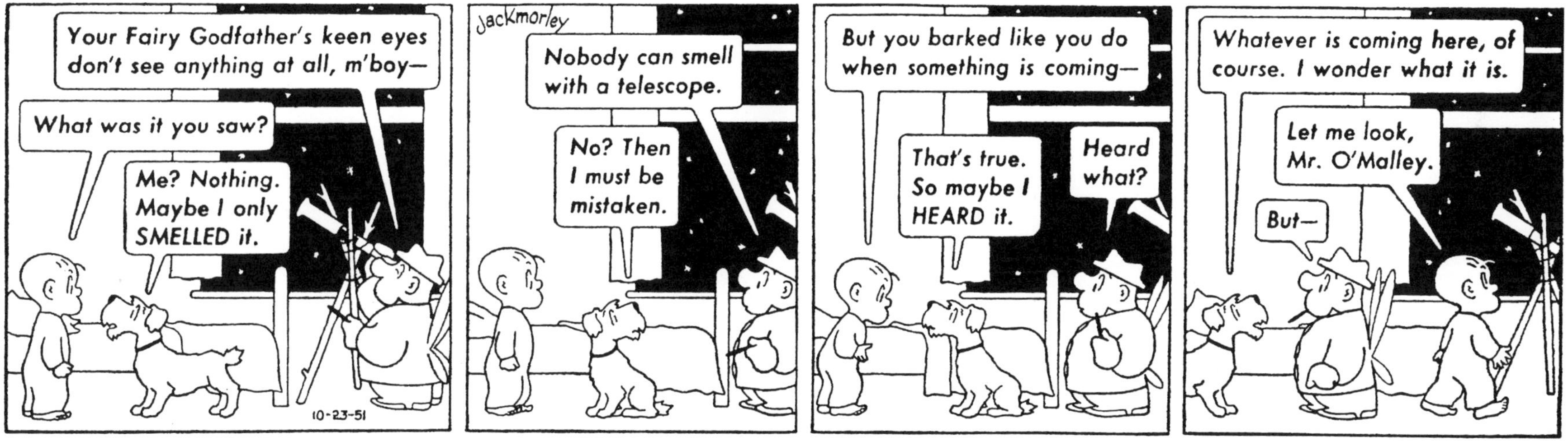
Your Fairy Godfather's keen eyes don't see anything at all, m'boy—
What was it you saw?
Me? Nothing. Maybe I only SMELLED it.
10-23-51
JACKMORLEY
Nobody can smell with a telescope.
No? Then I must be mistaken.
But you barked like you do when something is coming—
That's true. So maybe I HEARD it.
Heard what?
Whatever is coming here, of course. I wonder what it is.
Let me look, Mr. O'Malley.
But—

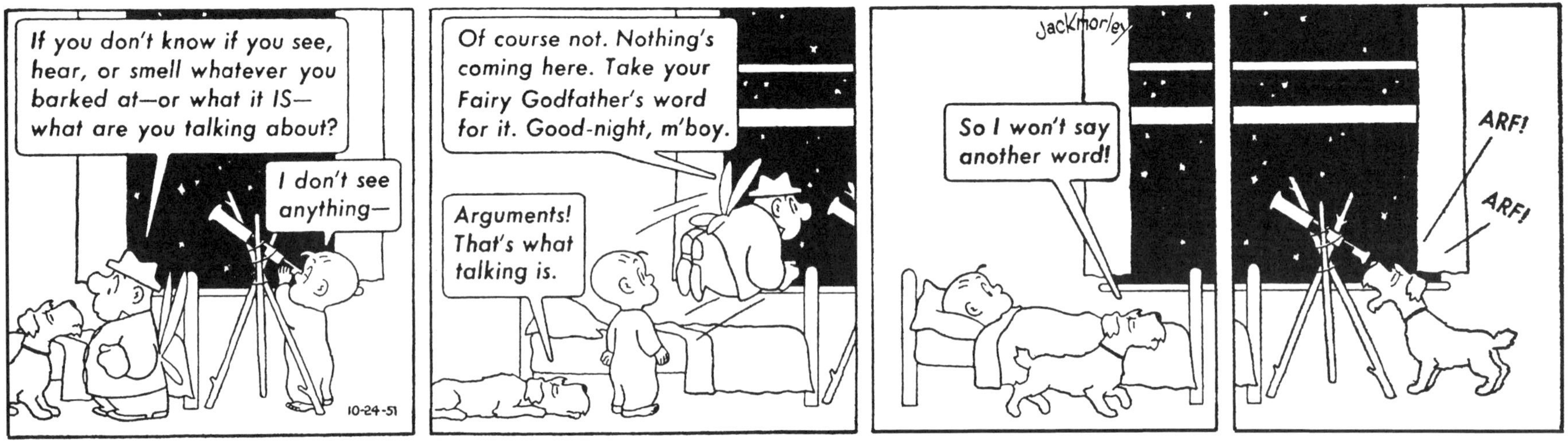
If you don't know if you see, hear, or smell whatever you barked at—or what it IS—what are you talking about?
I don't see anything—
10-24-51
Of course not. Nothing's coming here. Take your Fairy Godfather's word for it. Good-night, m'boy.
Arguments! That's what talking is.
Jackmorley
So I won't say another word!
ARF!
ARF!

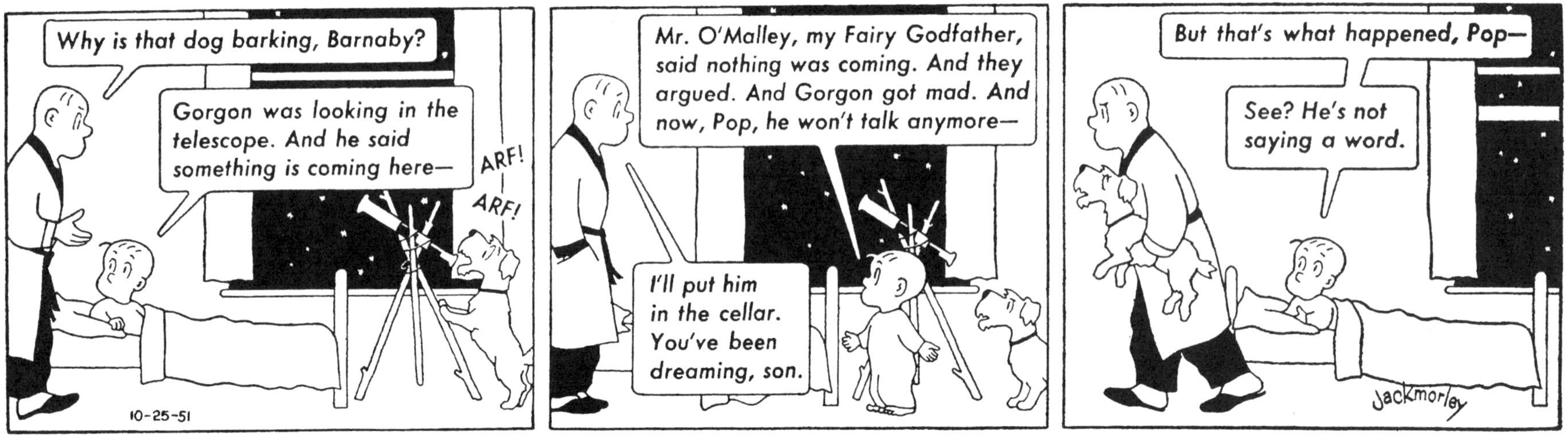
Why is that dog barking, Barnaby?
Gorgon was looking in the telescope. And he said something is coming here—
ARF!
ARF!
10-25-51
Mr. O'Malley, my Fairy Godfather, said nothing was coming. And they argued. And Gorgon got mad. And now, Pop, he won't talk anymore—
I'll put him in the cellar. You've been dreaming, son.
But that's what happened, Pop—
See? He's not saying a word.
Jackmorley

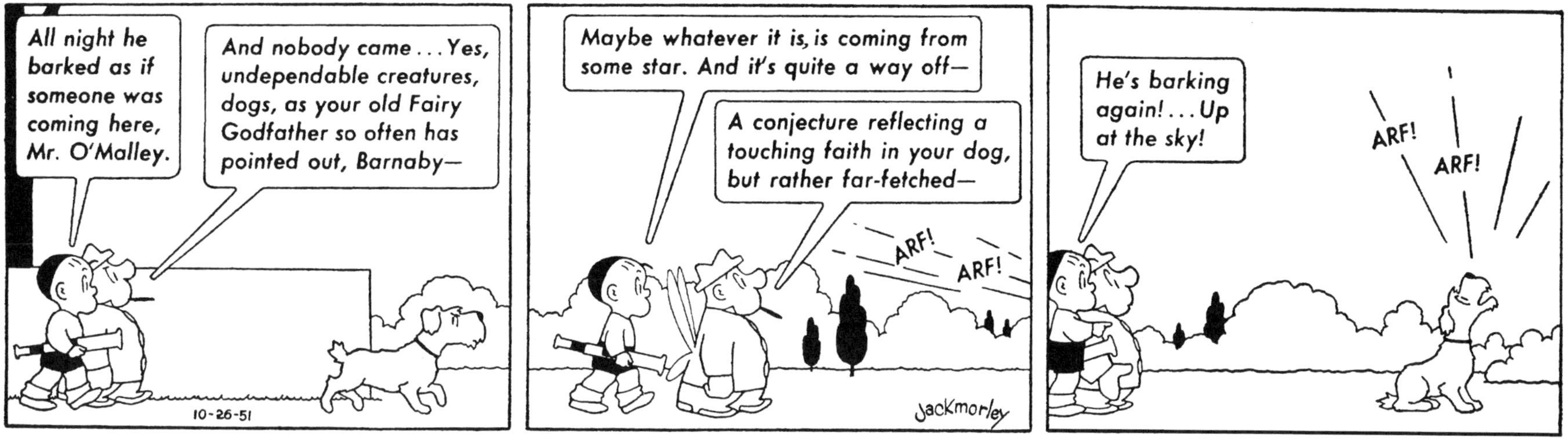
All night he barked as if someone was coming here, Mr. O'Malley.
And nobody came . . . Yes, undependable creatures, dogs, as your old Fairy Godfather so often has pointed out, Barnaby—
10-26-51
Maybe whatever it is, is coming from some star. And it's quite a way off—
A conjecture reflecting a touching faith in your dog, but rather far-fetched—
ARF!
ARF!
Jackmorley
He's barking again! . . . Up at the sky!
ARF!
ARF!

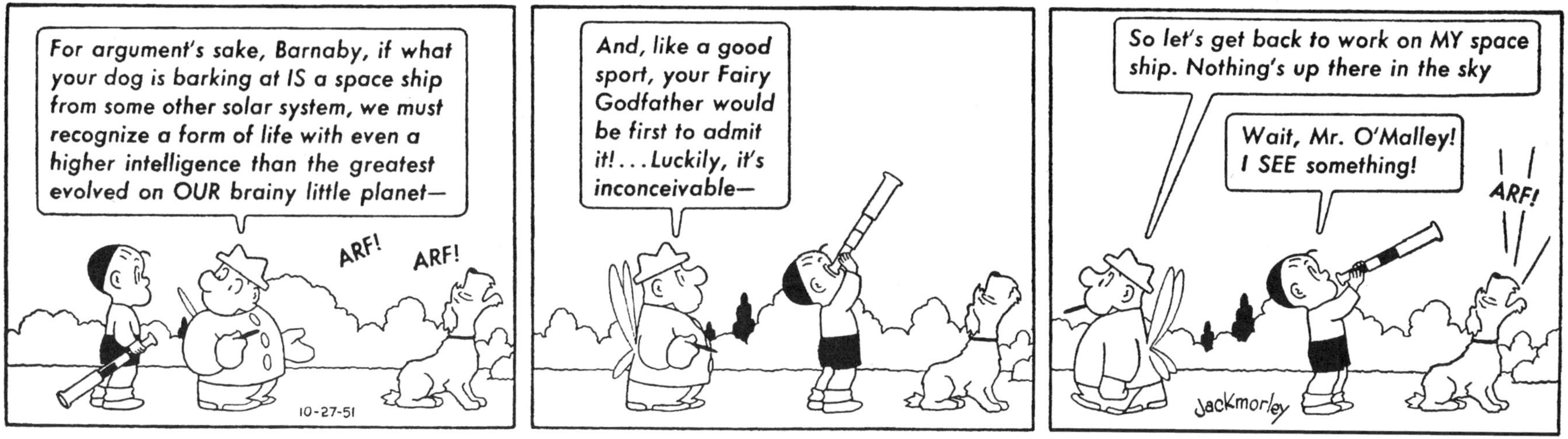
For argument's sake, Barnaby, if what your dog is barking at IS a space ship from some other solar system, we must recognize a form of life with even a higher intelligence than the greatest evolved on OUR brainy little planet—
ARF!
ARF!
10-27-51
And, like a good sport, your Fairy Godfather would be first to admit it! . . . Luckily, it's inconceivable—
So let's get back to work on MY space ship. Nothing's up there in the sky
Wait, Mr. O'Malley! I SEE something!
ARF!
Jackmorley

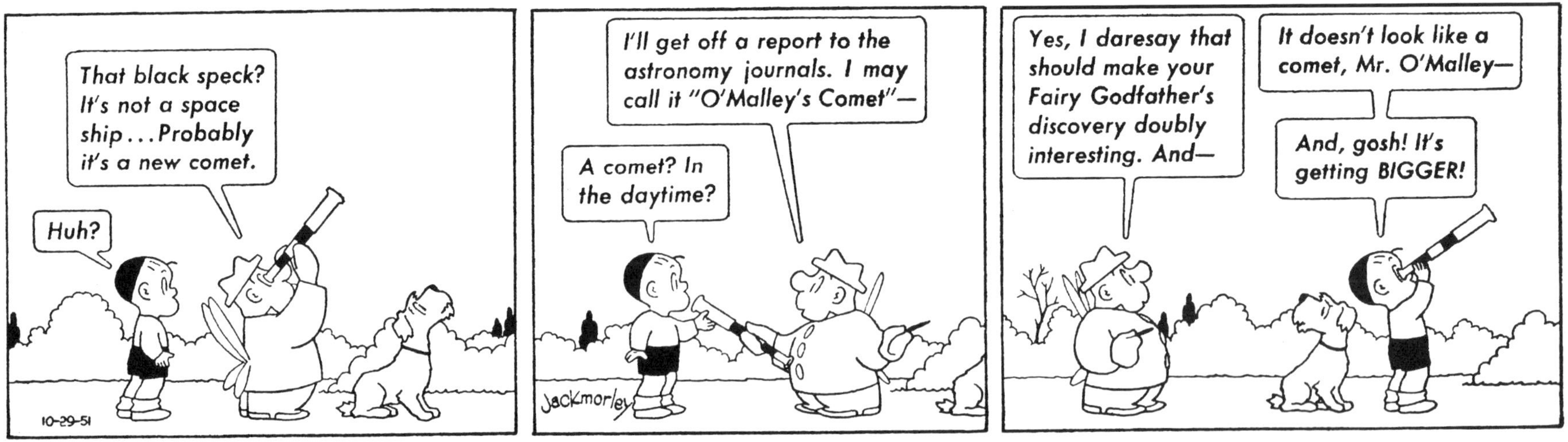
That black speck? It's not a space ship . . . Probably it's a new comet.
Huh?
10-29-51
A comet? In the daytime?
I'll get off a report to the astronomy journals. I may call it "O'Malley's Comet"—
Jackmorley
Yes, I daresay that should make your Fairy Godfather's discovery doubly interesting. And—
It doesn't look like a comet, Mr. O'Malley—
And, gosh! It's getting BIGGER!

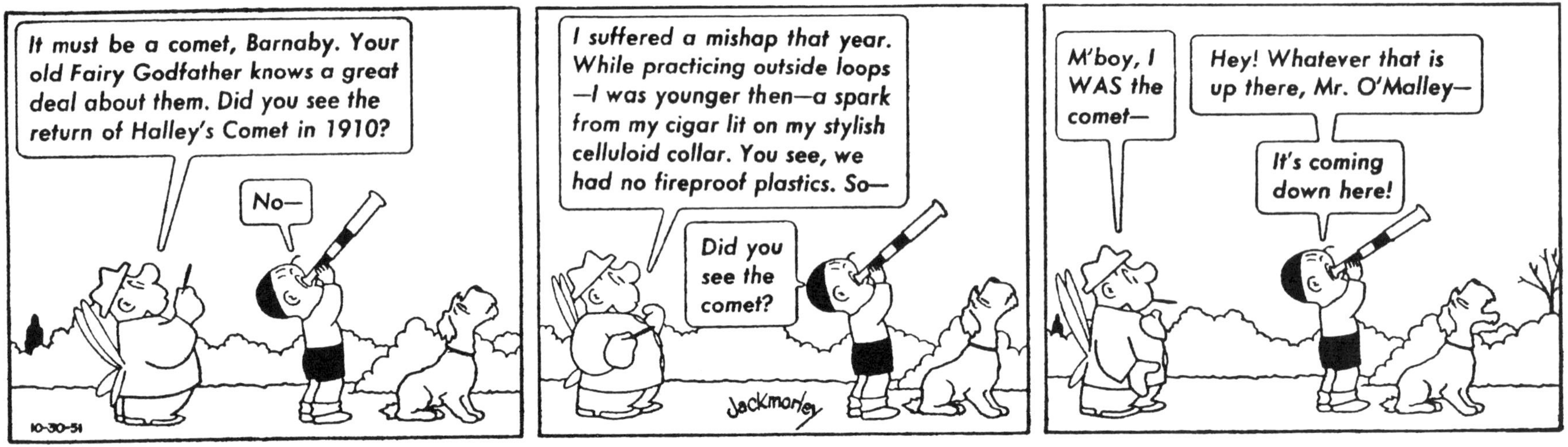
It must be a comet, Barnaby. Your old Fairy Godfather knows a great deal about them. Did you see the return of Halley's Comet in 1910?
No—
10-30-51
I suffered a mishap that year. While practicing outside loops —I was younger then—a spark from my cigar lit on my stylish celluloid collar. You see, we had no fireproof plastics. So—
Did you see the comet?
Jackmorley
M'boy, I WAS the comet—
Hey! Whatever that is up there, Mr. O'Malley—
It's coming down here!

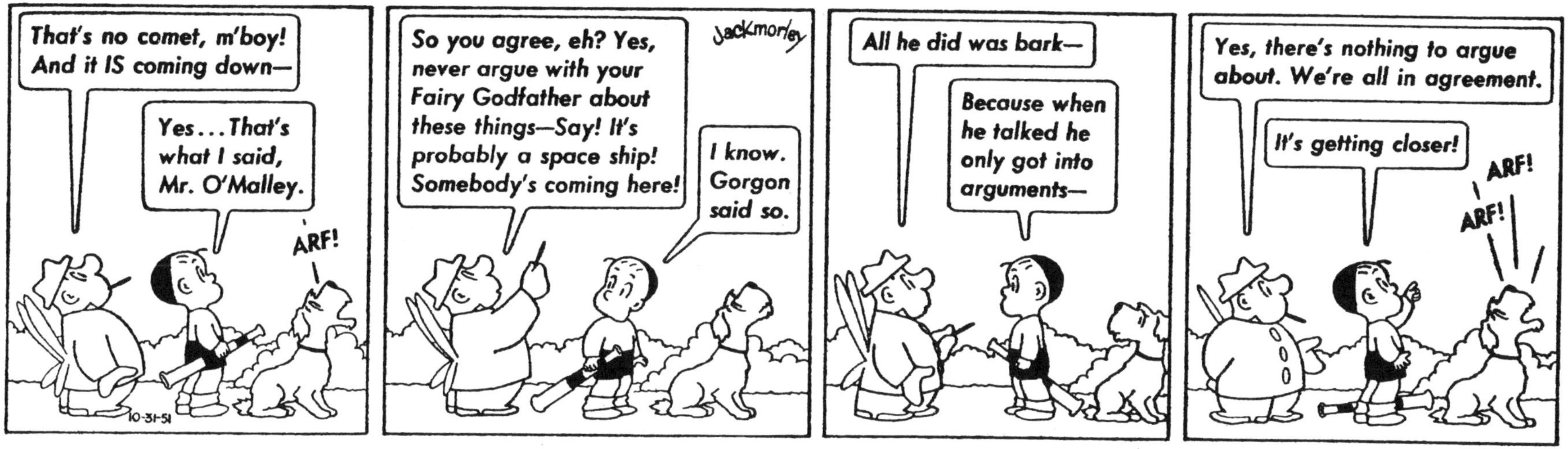
That's no comet, m'boy! And it IS coming down—
Yes... That's what I said, Mr. O'Malley.
ARF!
10-31-51
So you agree, eh? Yes, never argue with your Fairy Godfather about these things—Say! It's probably a space ship! Somebody's coming here!
Jackmorley
I know. Gorgon said so.
All he did was bark—
Because when he talked he only got into arguments—
Yes, there's nothing to argue about. We're all in agreement.
It's getting closer!
ARF!
ARF!

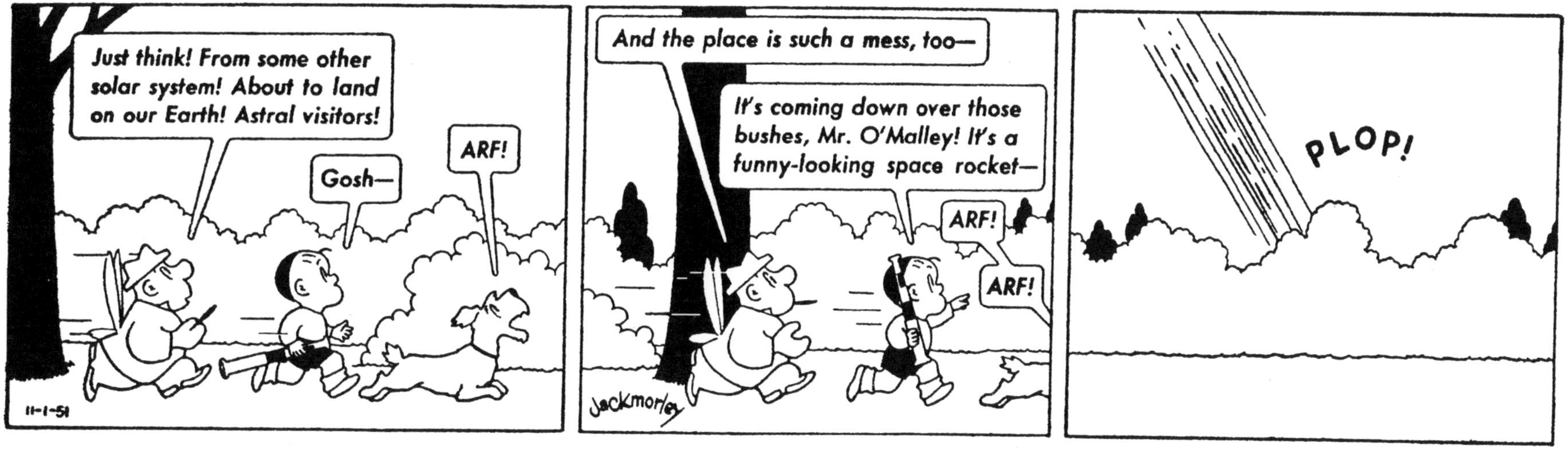
Just think! From some other solar system! About to land on our Earth! Astral visitors!
Gosh—
ARF!
11-1-51
And the place is such a mess, too—
It's coming down over those bushes, Mr. O'Malley! It's a funny-looking space rocket—
ARF!
ARF!
Jackmorley
PLOP!

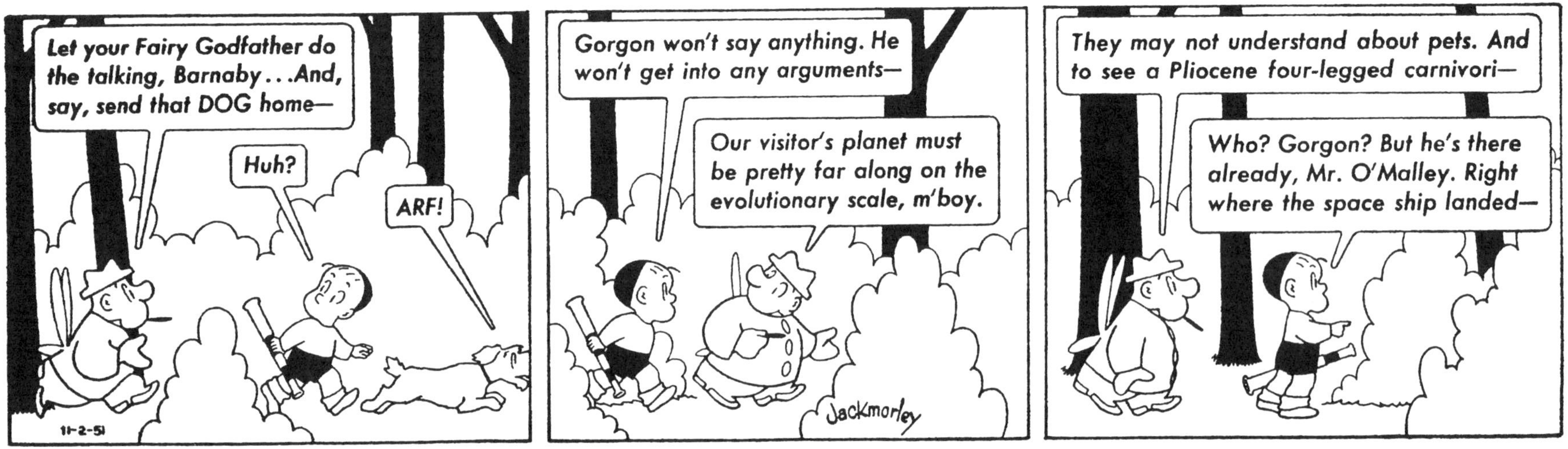
Let your Fairy Godfather do the talking, Barnaby...And, say, send that DOG home—
Huh?
ARF!
11-2-51
Gorgon won't say anything. He won't get into any arguments—
Our visitor's planet must be pretty far along on the evolutionary scale, m'boy.
Jackmorley
They may not understand about pets. And to see a Pliocene four-legged carnivori—
Who? Gorgon? But he's there already, Mr. O'Malley. Right where the space ship landed—

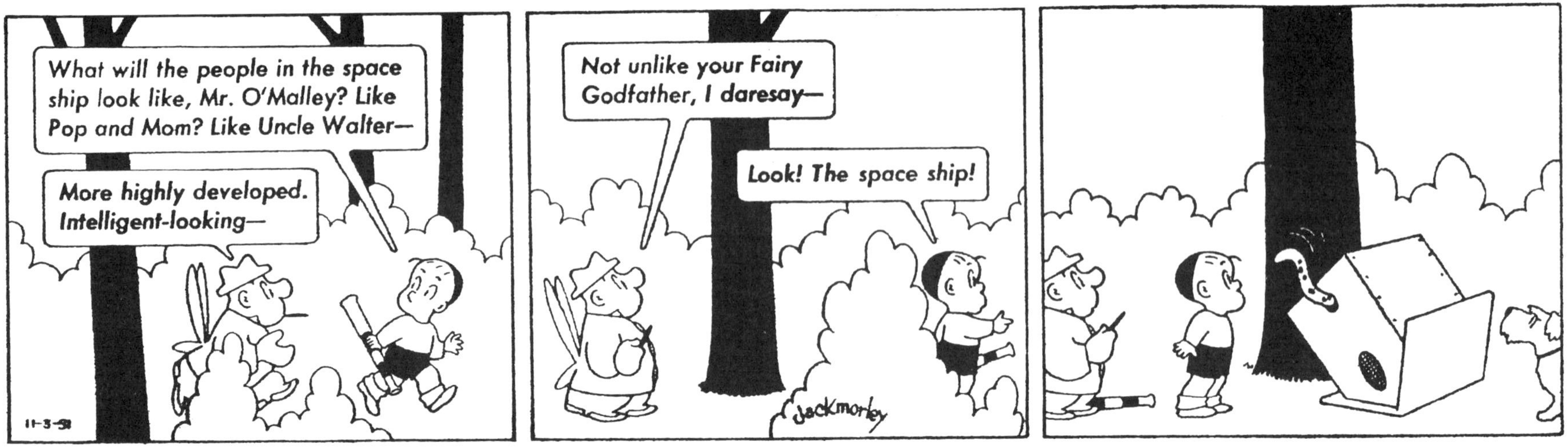
What will the people in the space ship look like, Mr. O'Malley? Like Pop and Mom? Like Uncle Walter—
More highly developed. Intelligent-looking—
11-3-51
Not unlike your Fairy Godfather, I daresay—
Look! The space ship!
Jackmorley

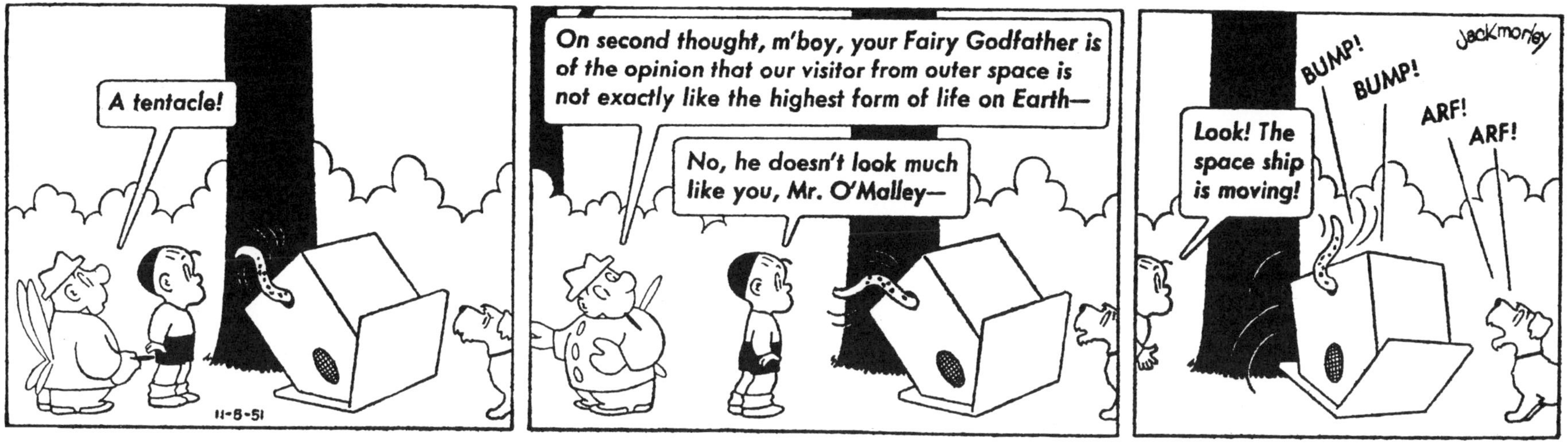
A tentacle!
11-5-51
On second thought, m'boy, your Fairy Godfather is of the opinion that our visitor from outer space is not exactly like the highest form of life on Earth—
No, he doesn't look much like you, Mr. O'Malley—
Jackmorley
BUMP!
BUMP!
ARF!
ARF!
Look! The space ship is moving!

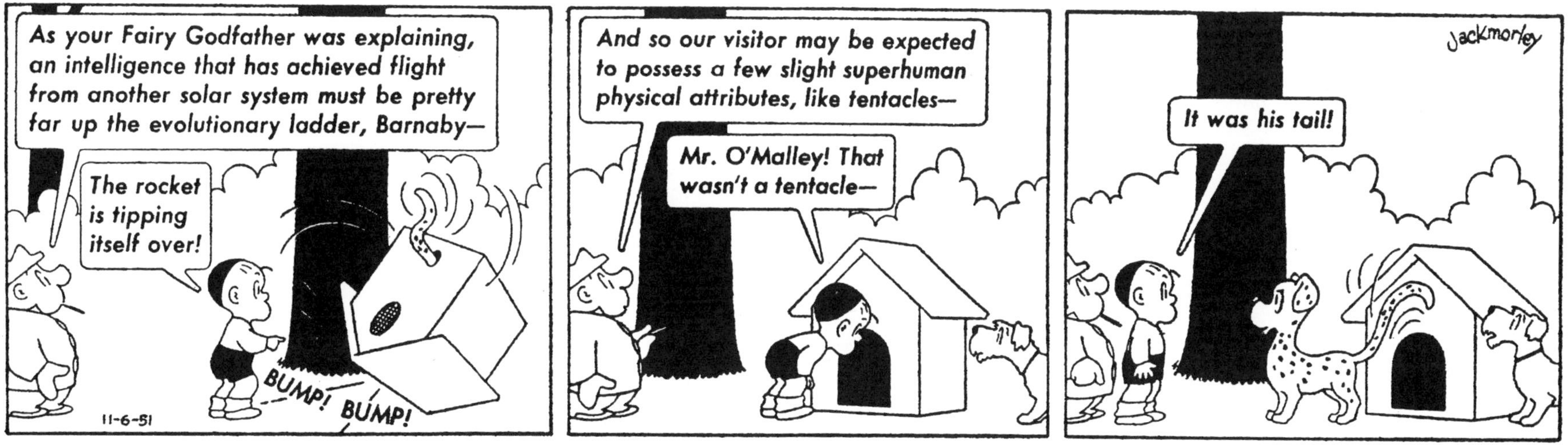
As your Fairy Godfather was explaining, an intelligence that has achieved flight from another solar system must be pretty far up the evolutionary ladder, Barnaby—
The rocket is tipping itself over!
BUMP! BUMP!
11-6-51
And so our visitor may be expected to possess a few slight superhuman physical attributes, like tentacles—
Mr. O'Malley! That wasn't a tentacle—
Jackmorley
It was his tail!

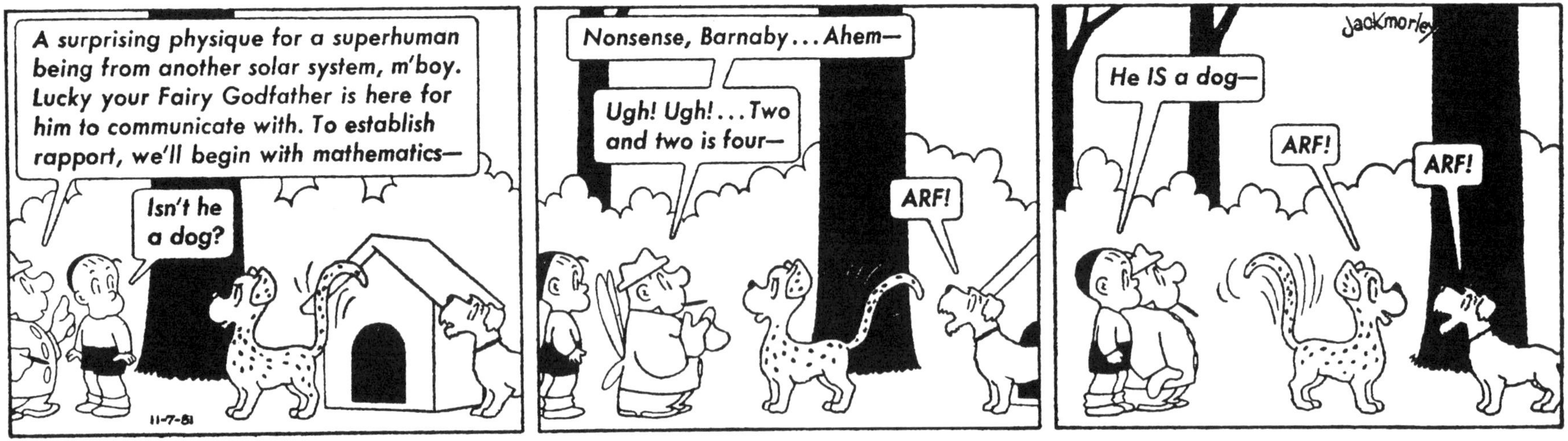
A surprising physique for a superhuman being from another solar system, m'boy. Lucky your Fairy Godfather is here for him to communicate with. To establish rapport, we'll begin with mathematics—
Isn't he a dog?
11-7-51
Nonsense, Barnaby... Ahem—
Ugh! Ugh!... Two and two is four—
ARF!
Jackmorley
He IS a dog—
ARF!
ARF!

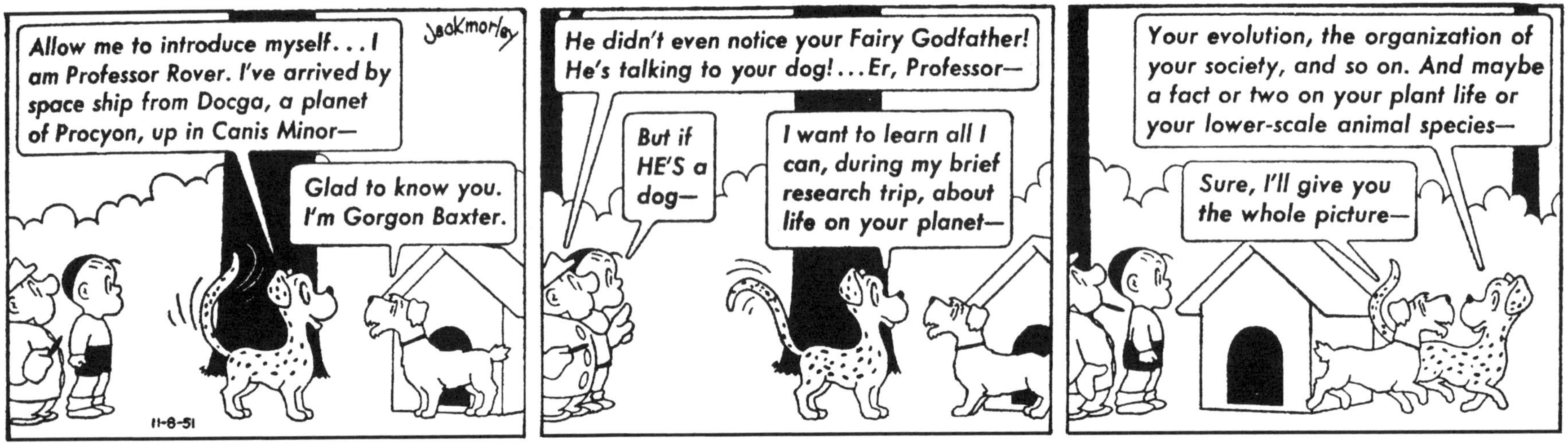
Jackmorley
Allow me to introduce myself... I am Professor Rover. I've arrived by space ship from Docga, a planet of Procyon, up in Canis Minor—
Glad to know you. I'm Gorgon Baxter.
11-8-51
He didn't even notice your Fairy Godfather! He's talking to your dog!... Er, Professor—
But if HE'S a dog—
I want to learn all I can, during my brief research trip, about life on your planet—
Your evolution, the organization of your society, and so on. And maybe a fact or two on your plant life or your lower-scale animal species—
Sure, I'll give you the whole picture—

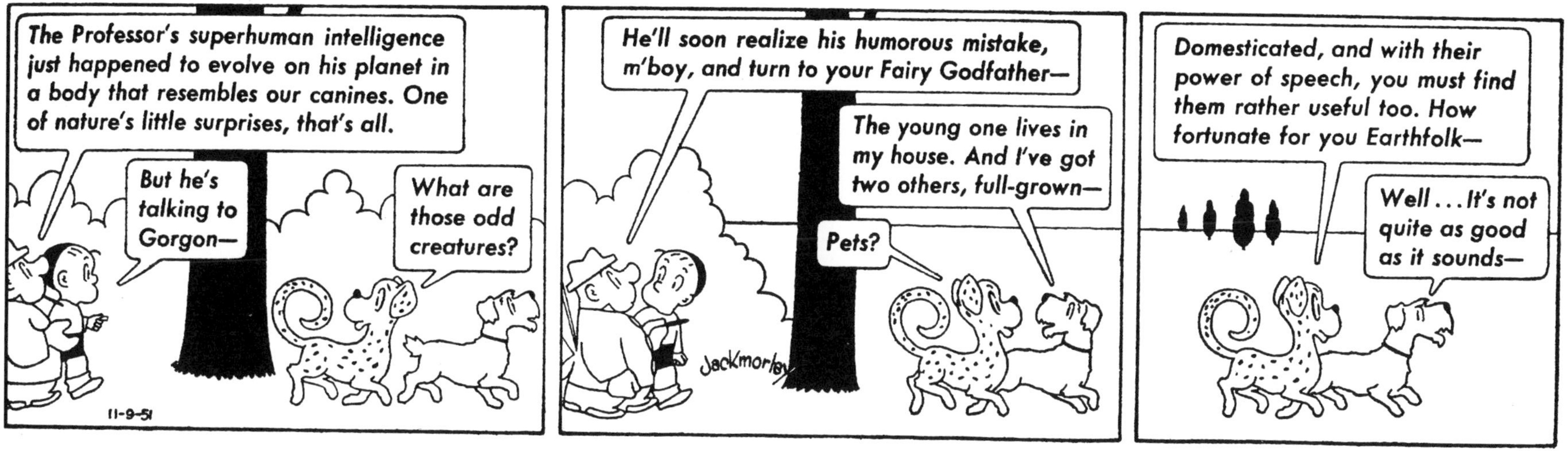
The Professor's superhuman intelligence just happened to evolve on his planet in a body that resembles our canines. One of nature's little surprises, that's all.
But he's talking to Gorgon—
What are those odd creatures?
11-9-51
He'll soon realize his humorous mistake, m'boy, and turn to your Fairy Godfather—
The young one lives in my house. And I've got two others, full-grown—
Pets?
Jackmorley
Domesticated, and with their power of speech, you must find them rather useful too. How fortunate for you Earthfolk—
Well . . . It's not quite as good as it sounds—

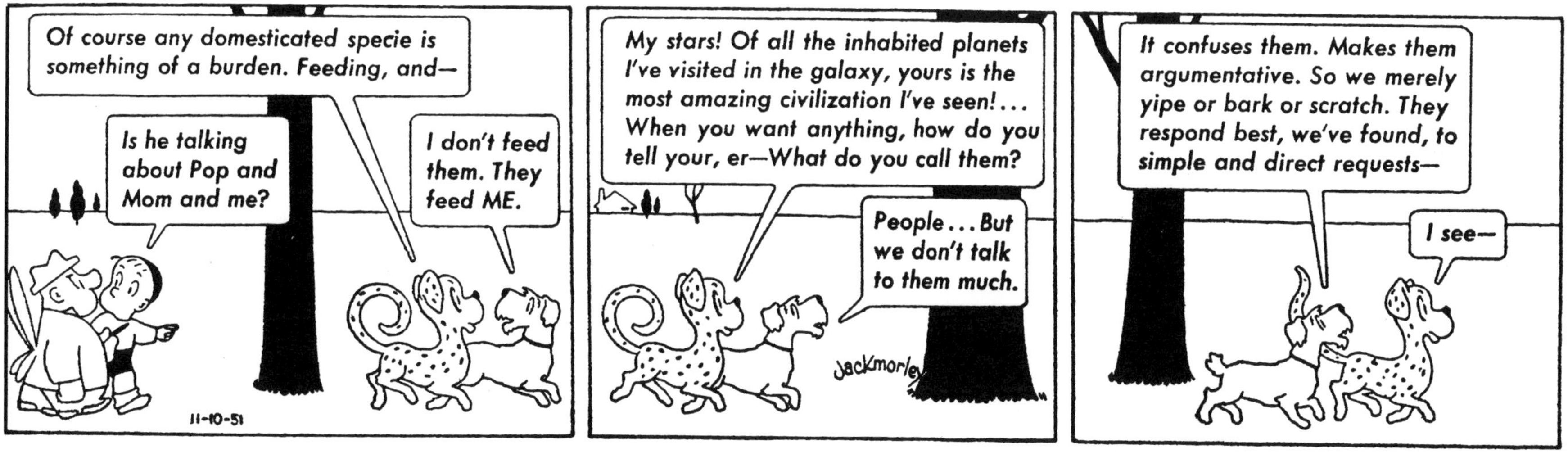
Of course any domesticated specie is something of a burden. Feeding, and—
Is he talking about Pop and Mom and me?
I don't feed them. They feed ME.
11-10-51
My stars! Of all the inhabited planets I've visited in the galaxy, yours is the most amazing civilization I've seen! . . . When you want anything, how do you tell your, er—What do you call them?
People . . . But we don't talk to them much.
Jackmorley
It confuses them. Makes them argumentative. So we merely yipe or bark or scratch. They respond best, we've found, to simple and direct requests—
I see—

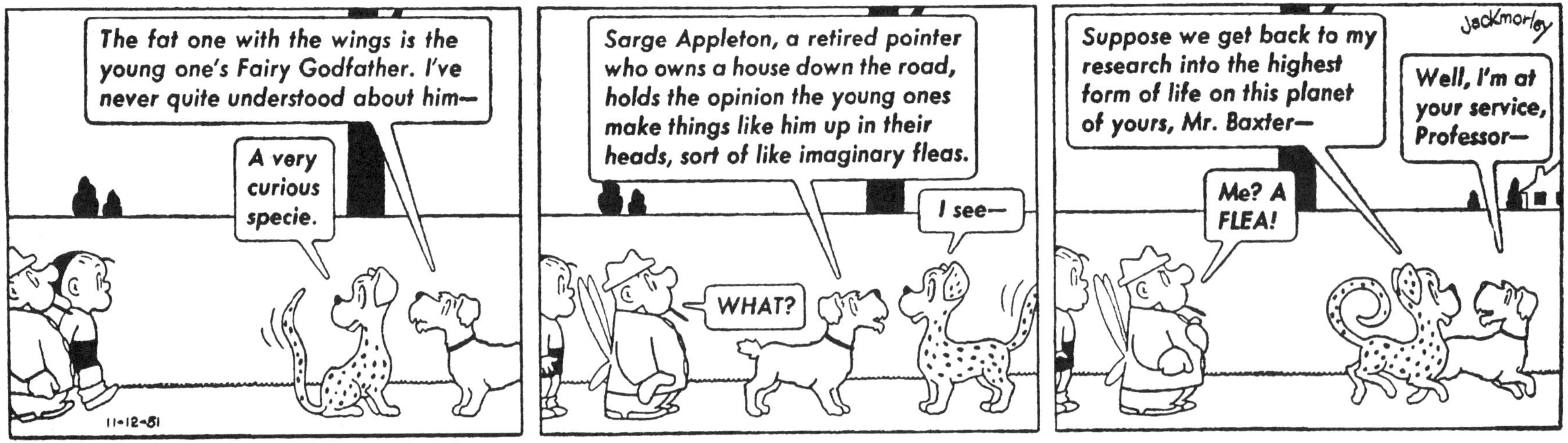
The fat one with the wings is the young one's Fairy Godfather. I've never quite understood about him—
A very curious specie.
11-12-51
Sarge Appleton, a retired pointer who owns a house down the road, holds the opinion the young ones make things like him up in their heads, sort of like imaginary fleas.
WHAT?
I see—
Jackmorley
Suppose we get back to my research into the highest form of life on this planet of yours, Mr. Baxter—
Well, I'm at your service, Professor—
Me? A FLEA!

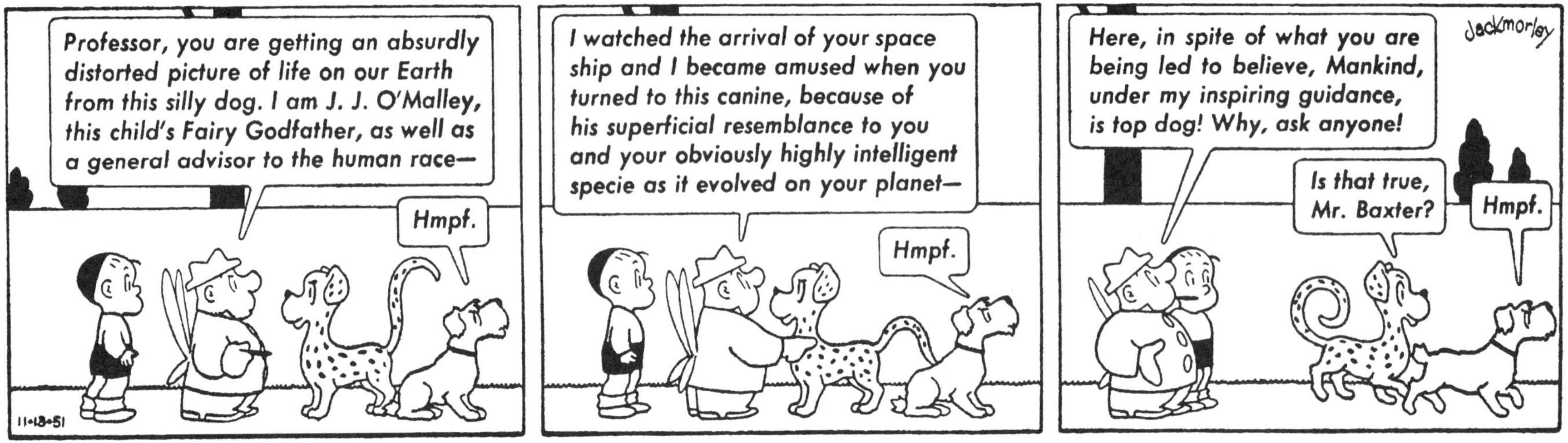
Professor, you are getting an absurdly distorted picture of life on our Earth from this silly dog. I am J. J. O'Malley, this child's Fairy Godfather, as well as a general advisor to the human race—
Hmpf.
11-13-51
I watched the arrival of your space ship and I became amused when you turned to this canine, because of his superficial resemblance to you and your obviously highly intelligent specie as it evolved on your planet—
Hmpf.
Jackmorley
Here, in spite of what you are being led to believe, Mankind, under my inspiring guidance, is top dog! Why, ask anyone!
Is that true, Mr. Baxter?
Hmpf.

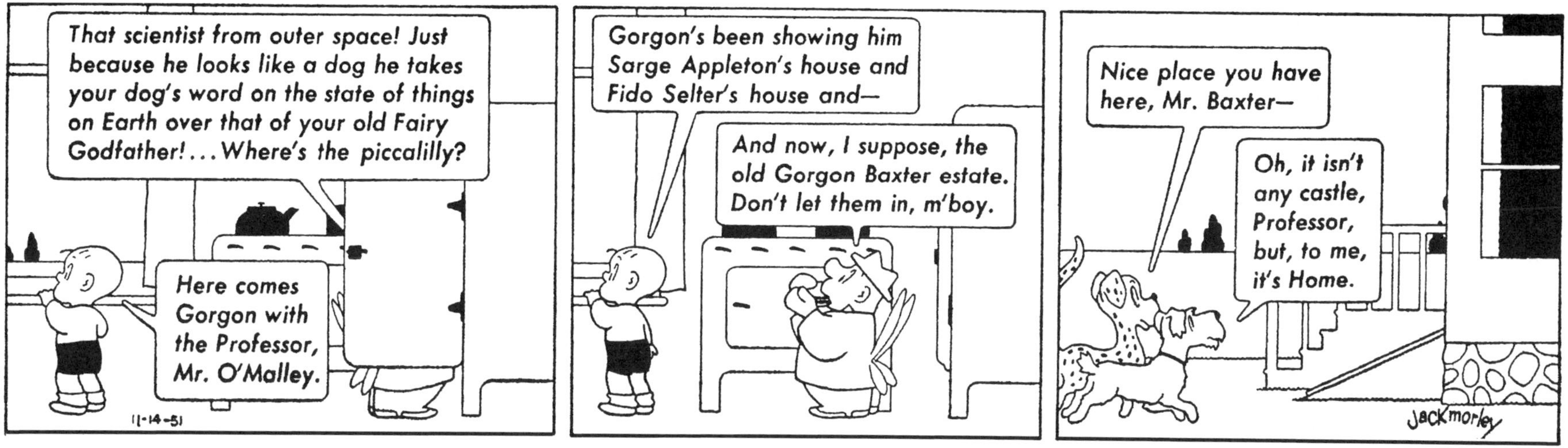
That scientist from outer space! Just because he looks like a dog he takes your dog's word on the state of things on Earth over that of your old Fairy Godfather!...Where's the piccalilly?
Here comes Gorgon with the Professor, Mr. O'Malley.
11-14-51
Gorgon's been showing him Sarge Appleton's house and Fido Selter's house and—
And now, I suppose, the old Gorgon Baxter estate. Don't let them in, m'boy.
Nice place you have here, Mr. Baxter—
Oh, it isn't any castle, Professor, but, to me, it's Home.
JACKmorley

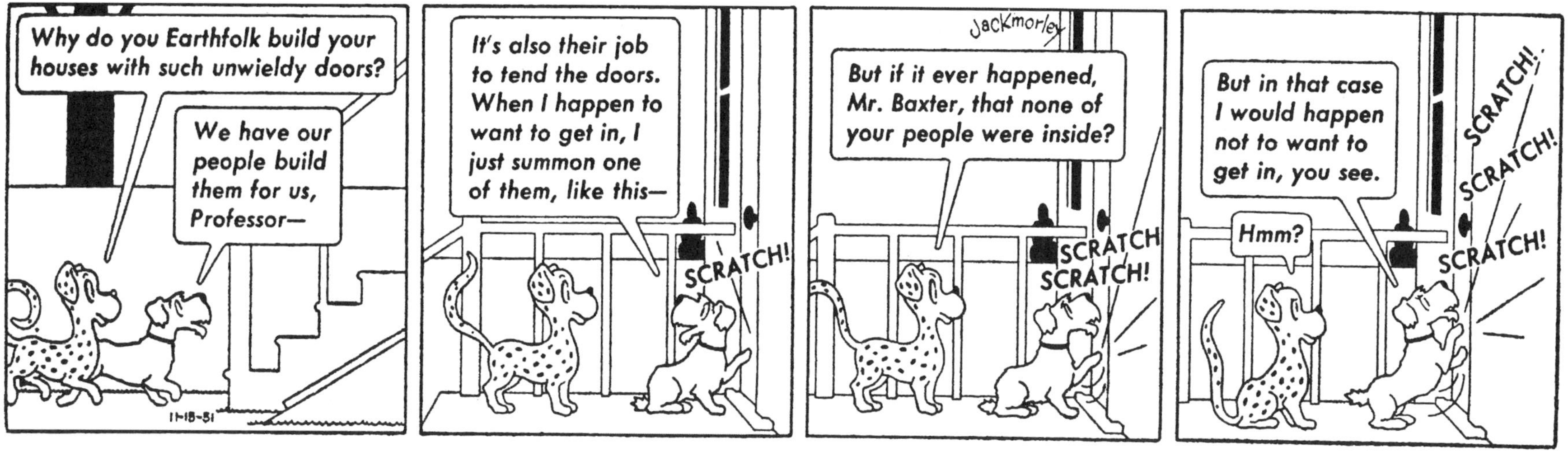
Why do you Earthfolk build your houses with such unwieldy doors?
We have our people build them for us, Professor—
11-15-51
It's also their job to tend the doors. When I happen to want to get in, I just summon one of them, like this—
SCRATCH!
JACKmorley
But if it ever happened, Mr. Baxter, that none of your people were inside?
SCRATCH
SCRATCH!
But in that case I would happen not to want to get in, you see.
Hmm?
SCRATCH!
SCRATCH!
SCRATCH!

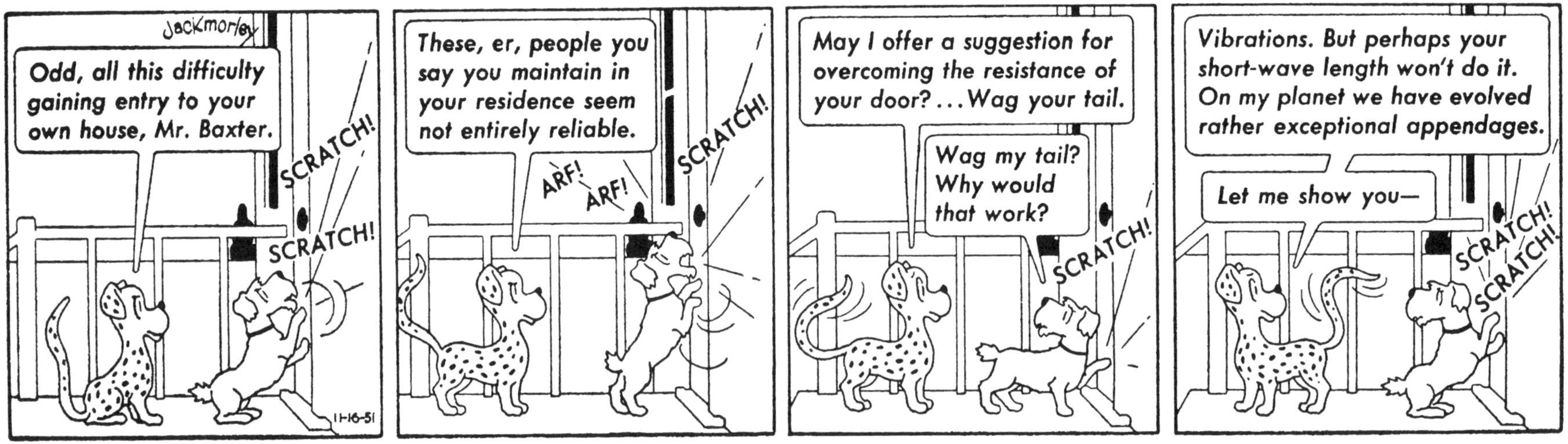
JACKMORLEY
Odd, all this difficulty gaining entry to your own house, Mr. Baxter.
SCRATCH!
SCRATCH!
11-16-51
These, er, people you say you maintain in your residence seem not entirely reliable.
ARF!
ARF!
SCRATCH!
May I offer a suggestion for overcoming the resistance of your door?...Wag your tail.
Wag my tail? Why would that work?
SCRATCH!
Vibrations. But perhaps your short-wave length won't do it. On my planet we have evolved rather exceptional appendages.
Let me show you—
SCRATCH!
SCRATCH!

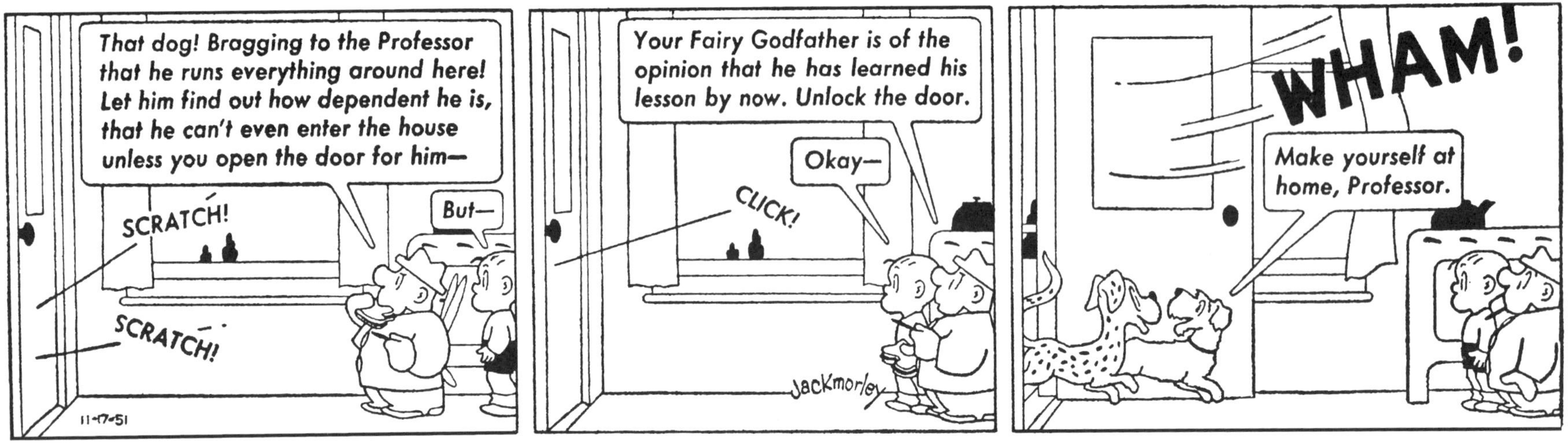
That dog! Bragging to the Professor that he runs everything around here! Let him find out how dependent he is, that he can't even enter the house unless you open the door for him—
But—
SCRATCH!
SCRATCH!
11-17-51
Your Fairy Godfather is of the opinion that he has learned his lesson by now. Unlock the door.
Okay—
CLICK!
JACKMORLEY
WHAM!
Make yourself at home, Professor.

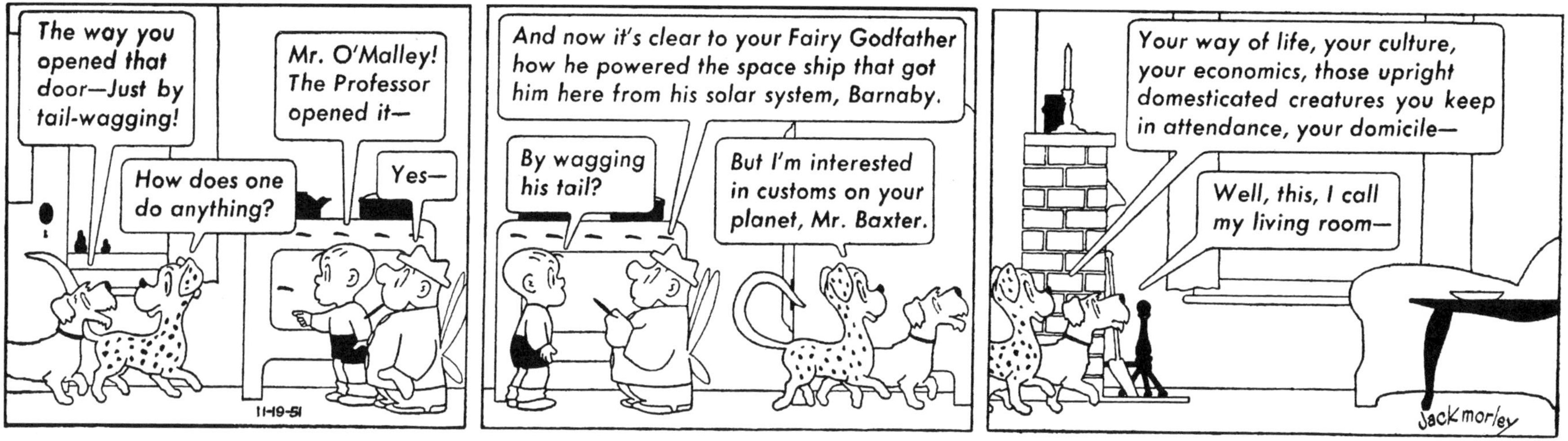
The way you opened that door—Just by tail-wagging!
How does one do anything?
Mr. O'Malley! The Professor opened it—
Yes—
11-19-51
And now it's clear to your Fairy Godfather how he powered the space ship that got him here from his solar system, Barnaby.
By wagging his tail?
But I'm interested in customs on your planet, Mr. Baxter.
Your way of life, your culture, your economics, those upright domesticated creatures you keep in attendance, your domicile—
Well, this, I call my living room—
Jack Morley

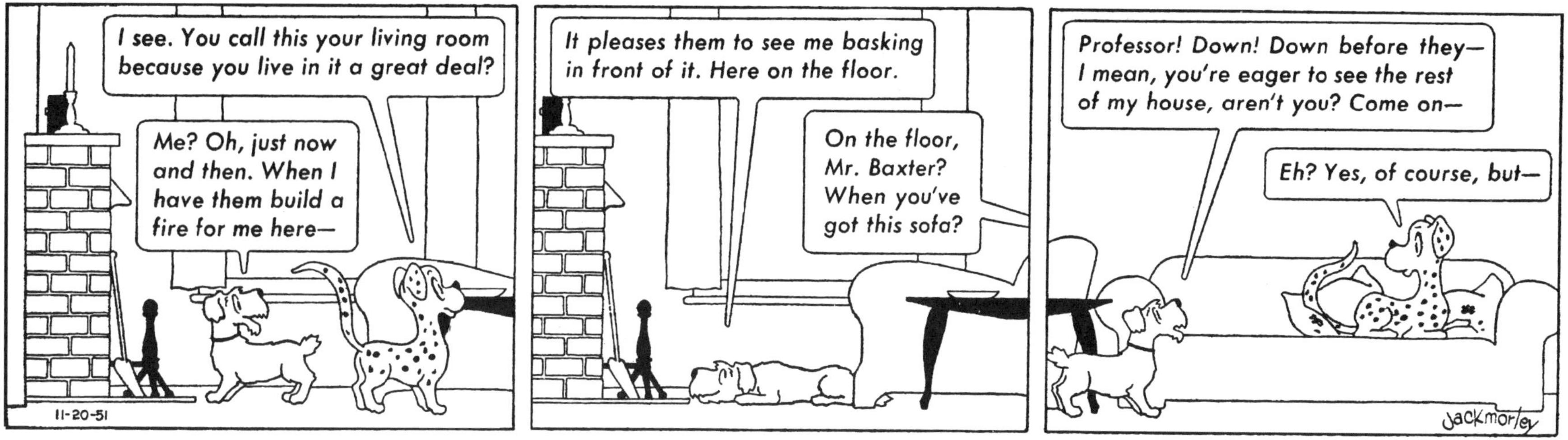
I see. You call this your living room because you live in it a great deal?
Me? Oh, just now and then. When I have them build a fire for me here—
11-20-51
It pleases them to see me basking in front of it. Here on the floor.
On the floor, Mr. Baxter? When you've got this sofa?
Professor! Down! Down before they—I mean, you're eager to see the rest of my house, aren't you? Come on—
Eh? Yes, of course, but—
Jack Morley

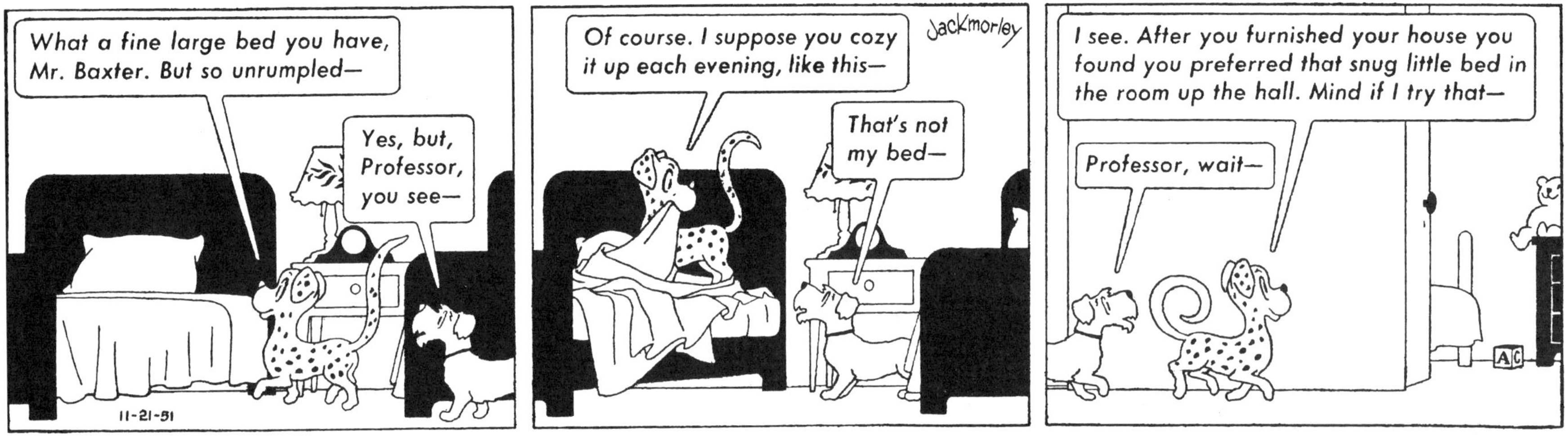
What a fine large bed you have, Mr. Baxter. But so unrumpled—
Yes, but, Professor, you see—
11-21-51
Jackmorley
Of course. I suppose you cozy it up each evening, like this—
That's not my bed—
I see. After you furnished your house you found you preferred that snug little bed in the room up the hall. Mind if I try that—
Professor, wait—
AC

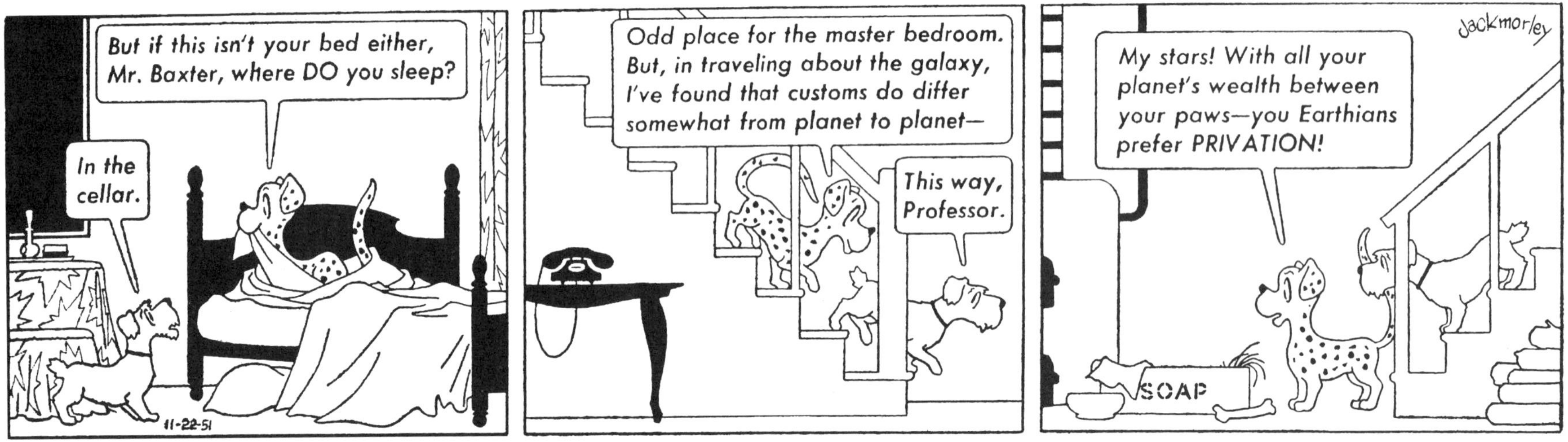
But if this isn't your bed either, Mr. Baxter, where DO you sleep?
In the cellar.
11-22-51
Odd place for the master bedroom. But, in traveling about the galaxy, I've found that customs do differ somewhat from planet to planet—
This way, Professor.
Jackmorley
My stars! With all your planet's wealth between your paws—you Earthians prefer PRIVATION!
SOAP

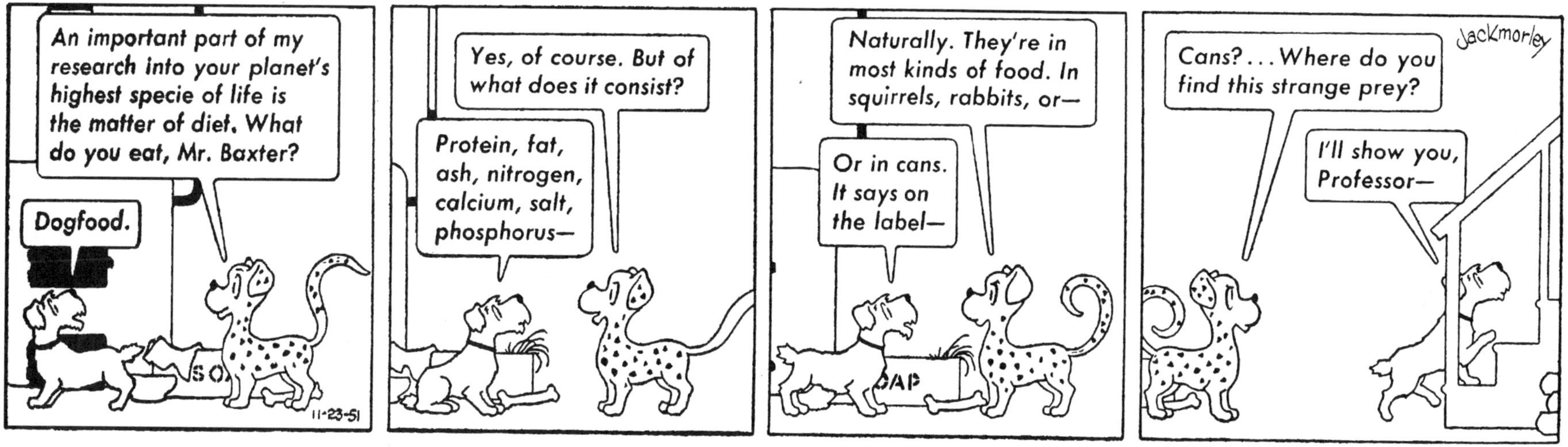
An important part of my research into your planet's highest specie of life is the matter of diet. What do you eat, Mr. Baxter?
Dogfood.
11-23-51
Yes, of course. But of what does it consist?
Protein, fat, ash, nitrogen, calcium, salt, phosphorus—
Naturally. They're in most kinds of food. In squirrels, rabbits, or—
Or in cans. It says on the label—
Jackmorley
Cans? . . . Where do you find this strange prey?
I'll show you, Professor—

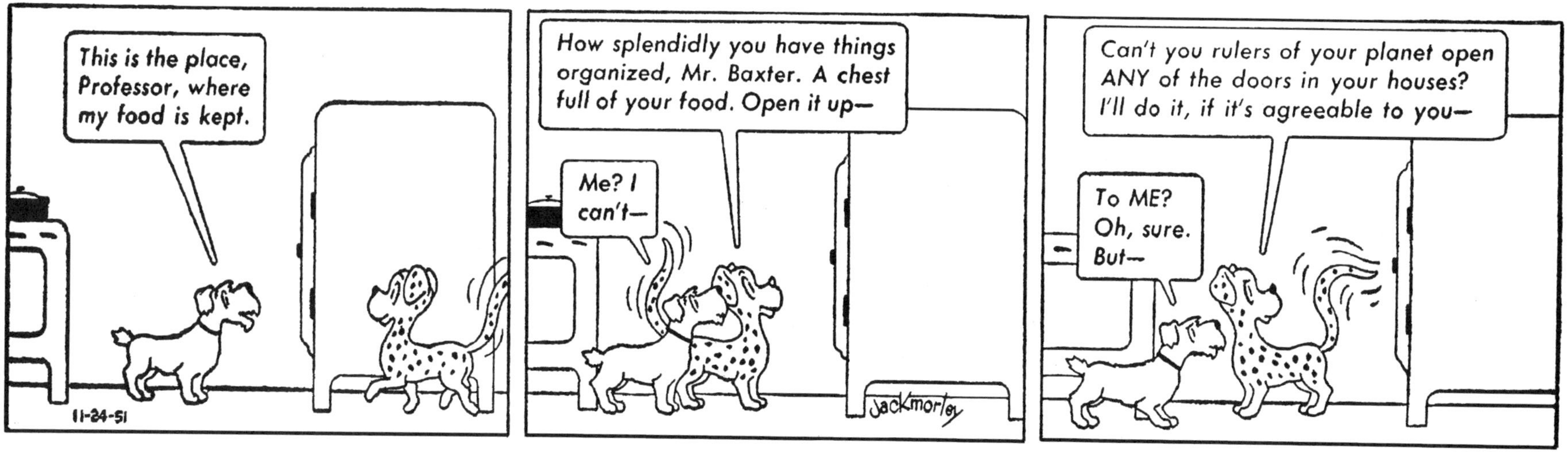
This is the place, Professor, where my food is kept.
11-24-51
How splendidly you have things organized, Mr. Baxter. A chest full of your food. Open it up—
Me? I can't—
Jackmorley
Can't you rulers of your planet open ANY of the doors in your houses? I'll do it, if it's agreeable to you—
To ME? Oh, sure. But—

November 23 – 24

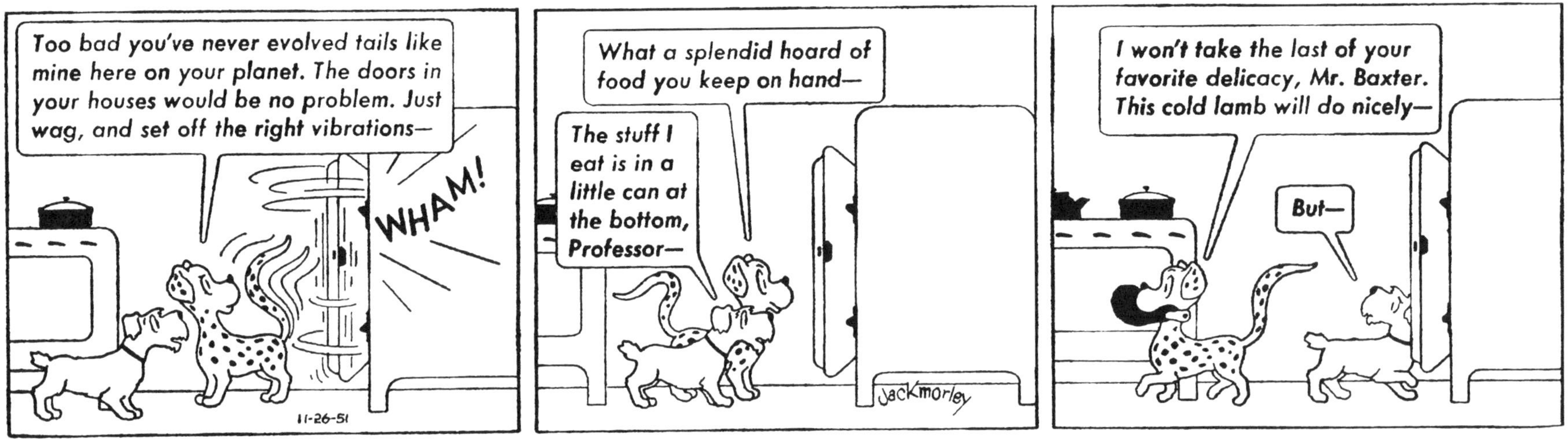
Too bad you've never evolved tails like mine here on your planet. The doors in your houses would be no problem. Just wag, and set off the right vibrations—
WHAM!
11-26-51
What a splendid hoard of food you keep on hand—
The stuff I eat is in a little can at the bottom, Professor—
JackMorley
I won't take the last of your favorite delicacy, Mr. Baxter. This cold lamb will do nicely—
But—

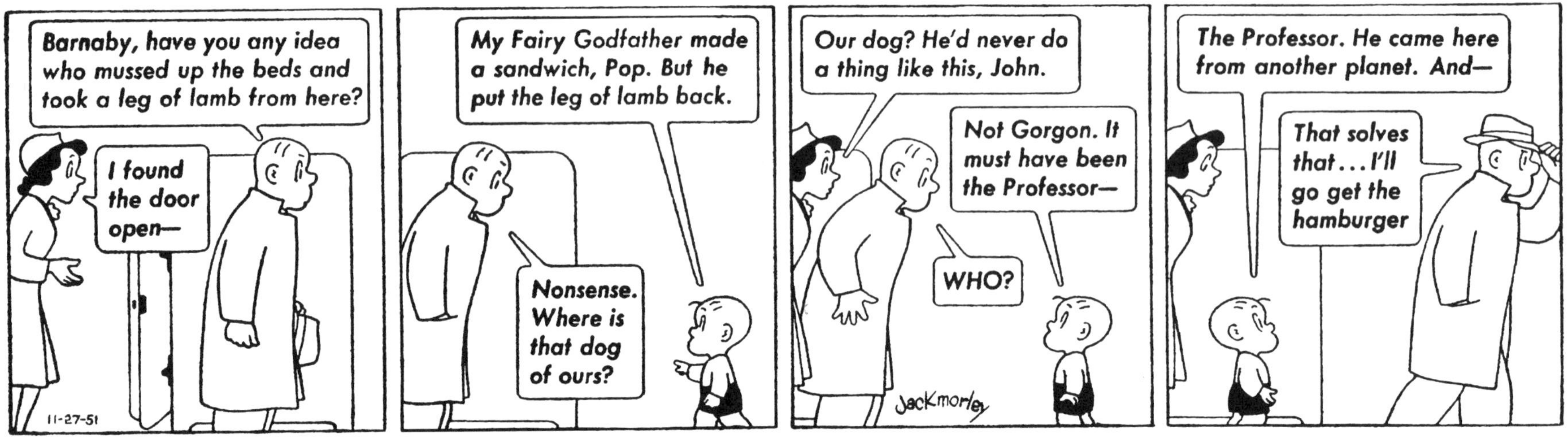
Barnaby, have you any idea who mussed up the beds and took a leg of lamb from here?
I found the door open—
11-27-51
My Fairy Godfather made a sandwich, Pop. But he put the leg of lamb back.
Nonsense. Where is that dog of ours?
Our dog? He'd never do a thing like this, John.
Not Gorgon. It must have been the Professor—
WHO?
JackMorley
The Professor. He came here from another planet. And—
That solves that . . . I'll go get the hamburger

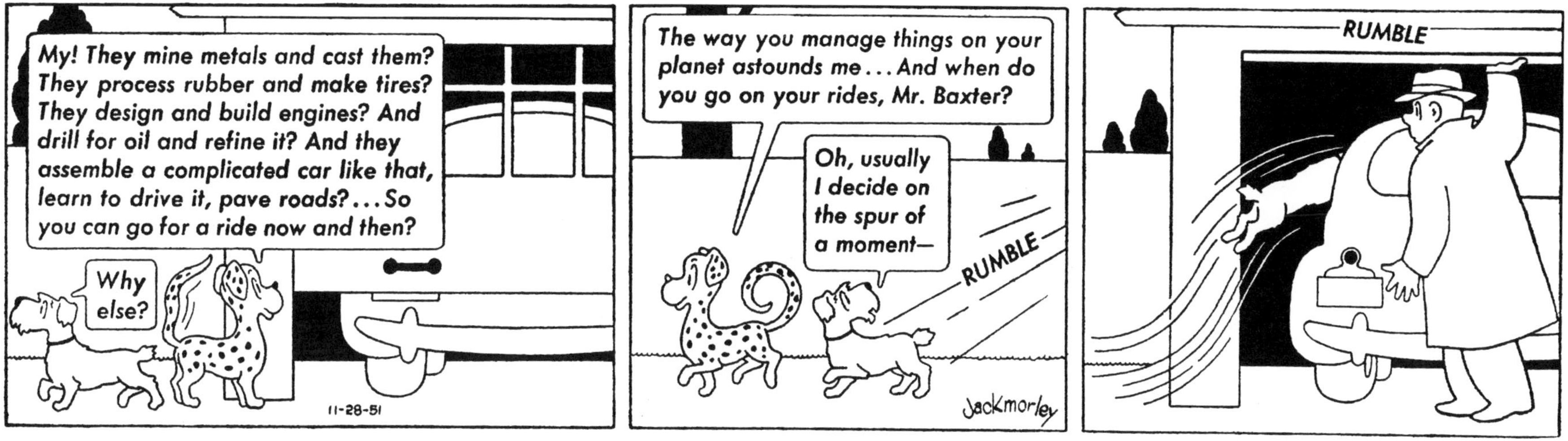
My! They mine metals and cast them? They process rubber and make tires? They design and build engines? And drill for oil and refine it? And they assemble a complicated car like that, learn to drive it, pave roads?... So you can go for a ride now and then?
Why else?
11-28-51
The way you manage things on your planet astounds me... And when do you go on your rides, Mr. Baxter?
Oh, usually I decide on the spur of a moment—
RUMBLE
Jackmorley
RUMBLE

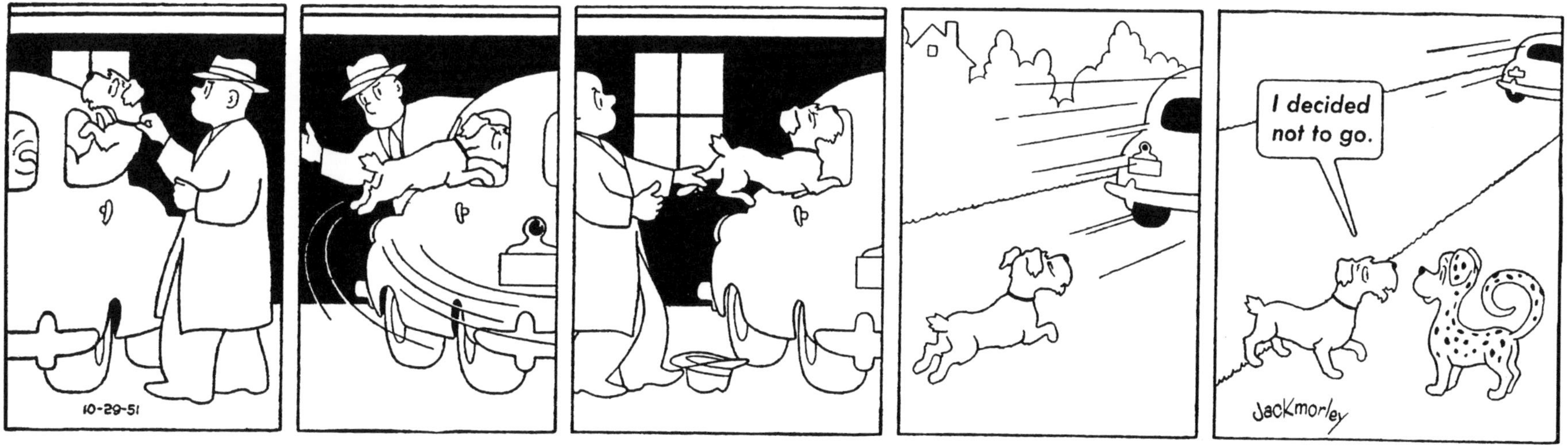
10-29-51
I decided not to go.
Jackmorley

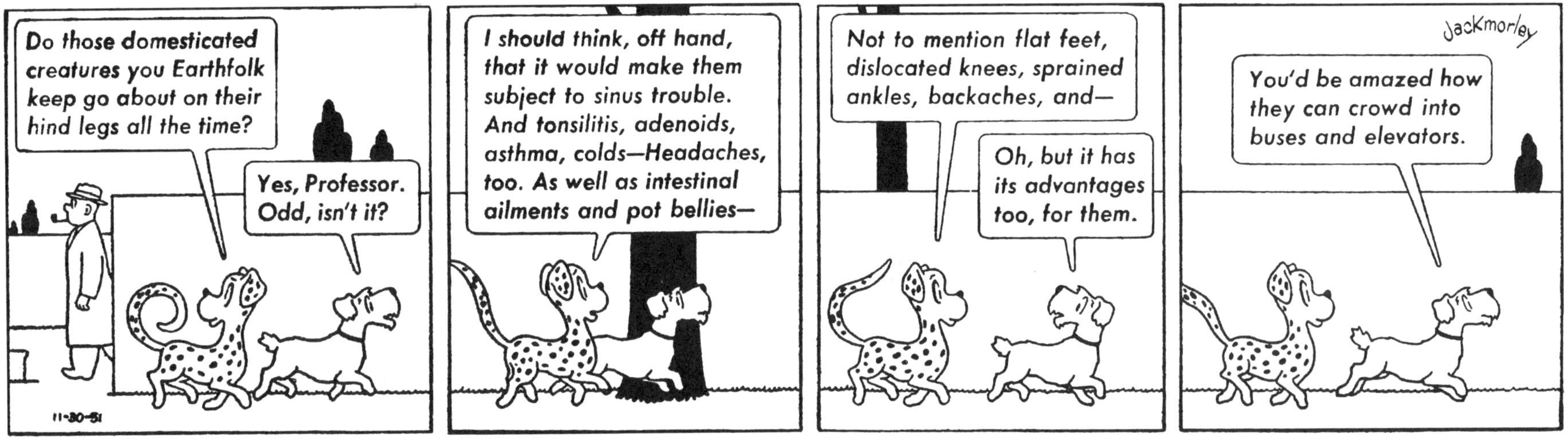
Do those domesticated creatures you Earthfolk keep go about on their hind legs all the time?
Yes, Professor. Odd, isn't it?
11-30-51
I should think, off hand, that it would make them subject to sinus trouble. And tonsilitis, adenoids, asthma, colds—Headaches, too. As well as intestinal ailments and pot bellies—
Not to mention flat feet, dislocated knees, sprained ankles, backaches, and—
Oh, but it has its advantages too, for them.
Jackmorley
You'd be amazed how they can crowd into buses and elevators.

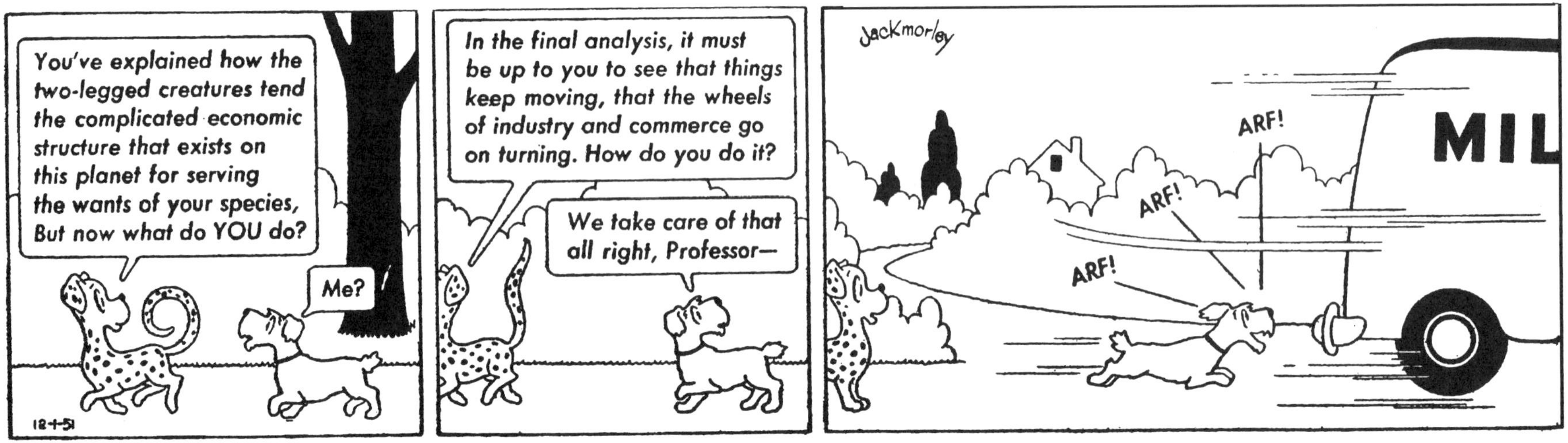
You've explained how the two-legged creatures tend the complicated economic structure that exists on this planet for serving the wants of your species, But now what do YOU do?
Me?
12-1-51
In the final analysis, it must be up to you to see that things keep moving, that the wheels of industry and commerce go on turning. How do you do it?
We take care of that all right, Professor—
Jackmorley
MIL
ARF!
ARF!
ARF!

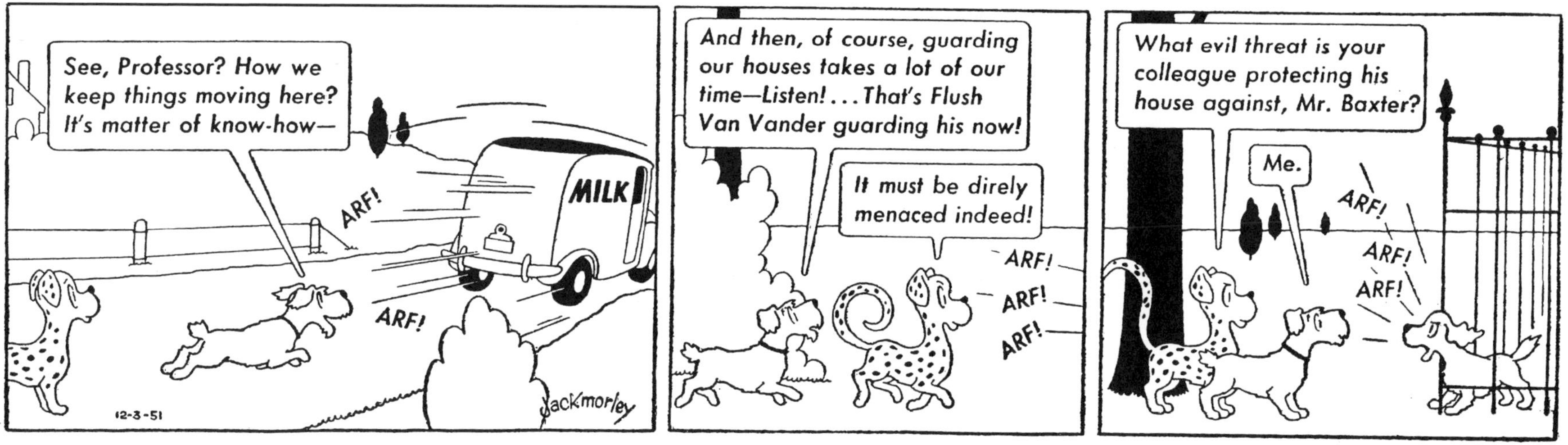
See, Professor? How we keep things moving here? It's matter of know-how—
ARF!
ARF!
MILK
12-3-51
Jackmorley
And then, of course, guarding our houses takes a lot of our time—Listen! . . . That's Flush Van Vander guarding his now!
It must be direly menaced indeed!
ARF!
ARF!
ARF!
What evil threat is your colleague protecting his house against, Mr. Baxter?
Me.
ARF!
ARF!
ARF!

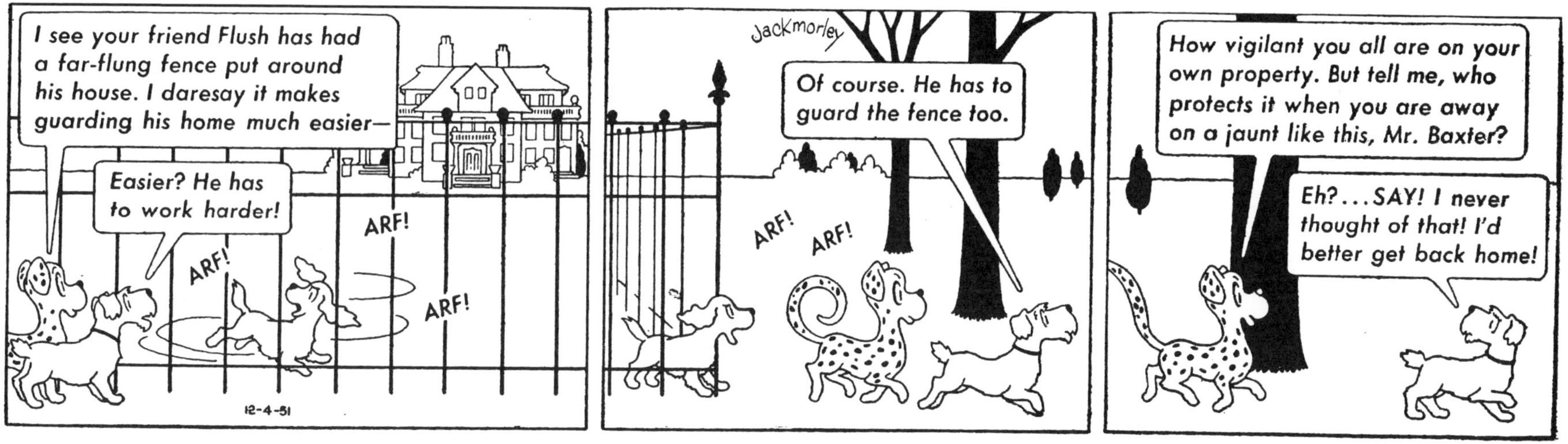
I see your friend Flush has had a far-flung fence put around his house. I daresay it makes guarding his home much easier—
Easier? He has to work harder!
ARF!
ARF!
ARF!
12-4-51
Jackmorley
Of course. He has to guard the fence too.
ARF!
ARF!
How vigilant you all are on your own property. But tell me, who protects it when you are away on a jaunt like this, Mr. Baxter?
Eh? . . . SAY! I never thought of that! I'd better get back home!

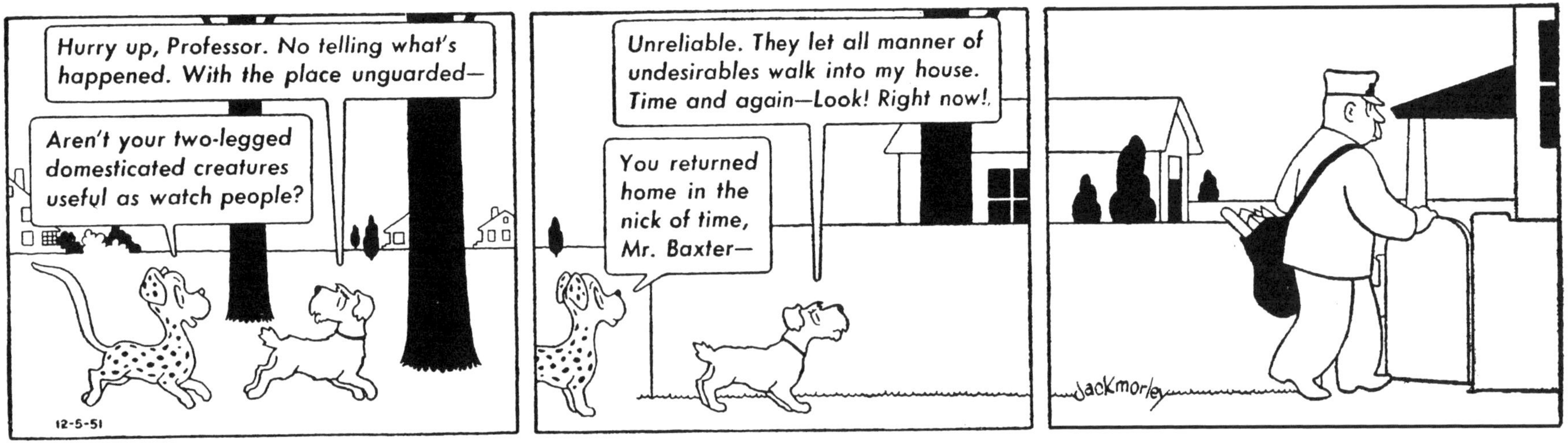
Hurry up, Professor. No telling what's happened. With the place unguarded—
Aren't your two-legged domesticated creatures useful as watch people?
12-5-51
Unreliable. They let all manner of undesirables walk into my house. Time and again—Look! Right now!
You returned home in the nick of time, Mr. Baxter—
Jackmorley

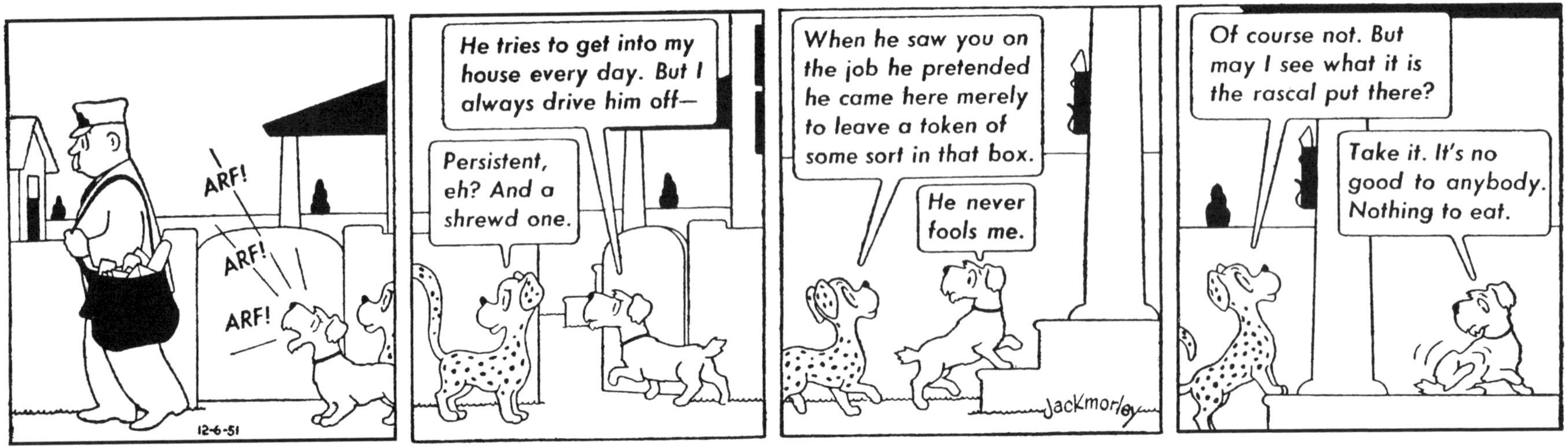
ARF!
ARF!
ARF!
12-6-51
He tries to get into my house every day. But I always drive him off—
Persistent, eh? And a shrewd one.
When he saw you on the job he pretended he came here merely to leave a token of some sort in that box.
He never fools me.
Jackmorley
Of course not. But may I see what it is the rascal put there?
Take it. It's no good to anybody. Nothing to eat.

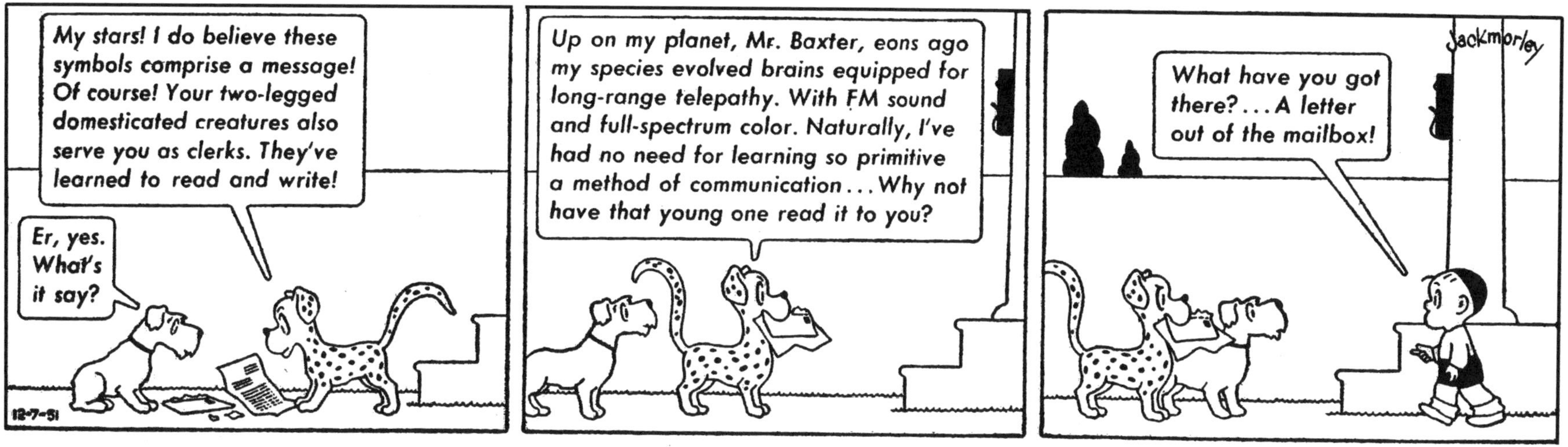
My stars! I do believe these symbols comprise a message! Of course! Your two-legged domesticated creatures also serve you as clerks. They've learned to read and write!
Er, yes. What's it say?
12-7-51
Up on my planet, Mr. Baxter, eons ago my species evolved brains equipped for long-range telepathy. With FM sound and full-spectrum color. Naturally, I've had no need for learning so primitive a method of communication . . . Why not have that young one read it to you?
Jackmorley
What have you got there? . . . A letter out of the mailbox!

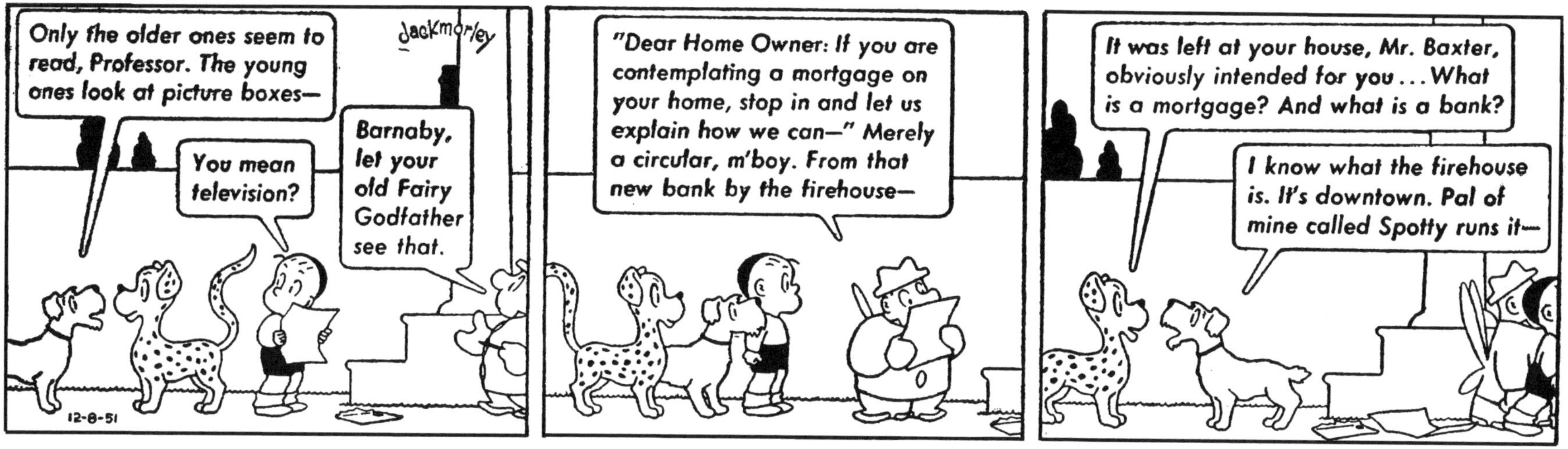
Only the older ones seem to read, Professor. The young ones look at picture boxes—
Jackmorley
You mean television?
Barnaby, let your old Fairy Godfather see that.
12-8-51
"Dear Home Owner: If you are contemplating a mortgage on your home, stop in and let us explain how we can—" Merely a circular, m'boy. From that new bank by the firehouse—
It was left at your house, Mr. Baxter, obviously intended for you . . . What is a mortgage? And what is a bank?
I know what the firehouse is. It's downtown. Pal of mine called Spotty runs it—

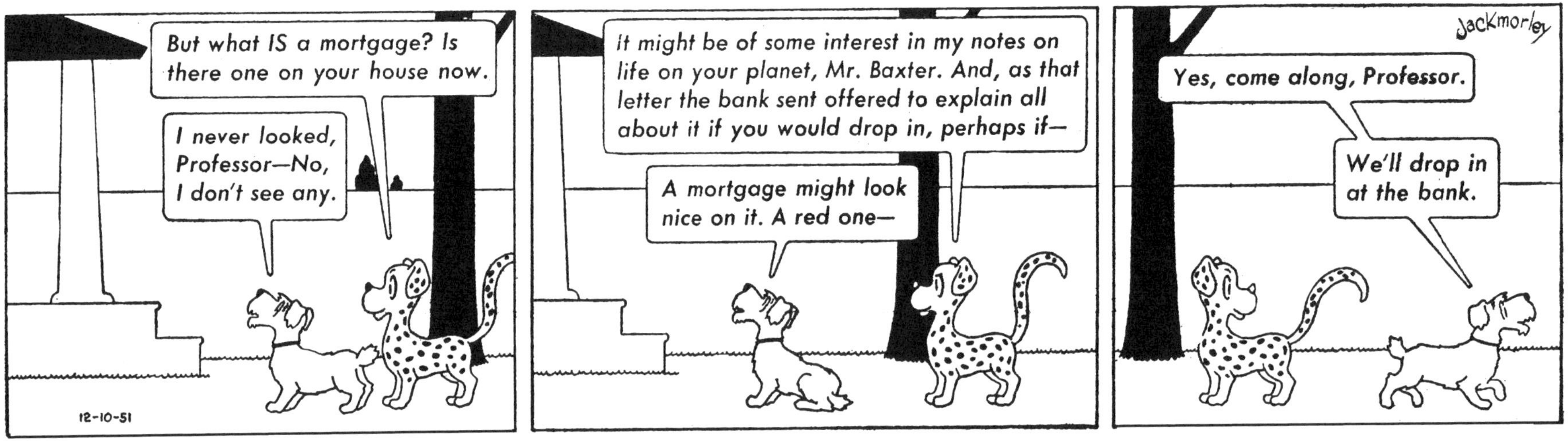
But what IS a mortgage? Is there one on your house now.
I never looked, Professor—No, I don't see any.
12-10-51
It might be of some interest in my notes on life on your planet, Mr. Baxter. And, as that letter the bank sent offered to explain all about it if you would drop in, perhaps if—
A mortgage might look nice on it. A red one—
Jackmorley
Yes, come along, Professor.
We'll drop in at the bank.

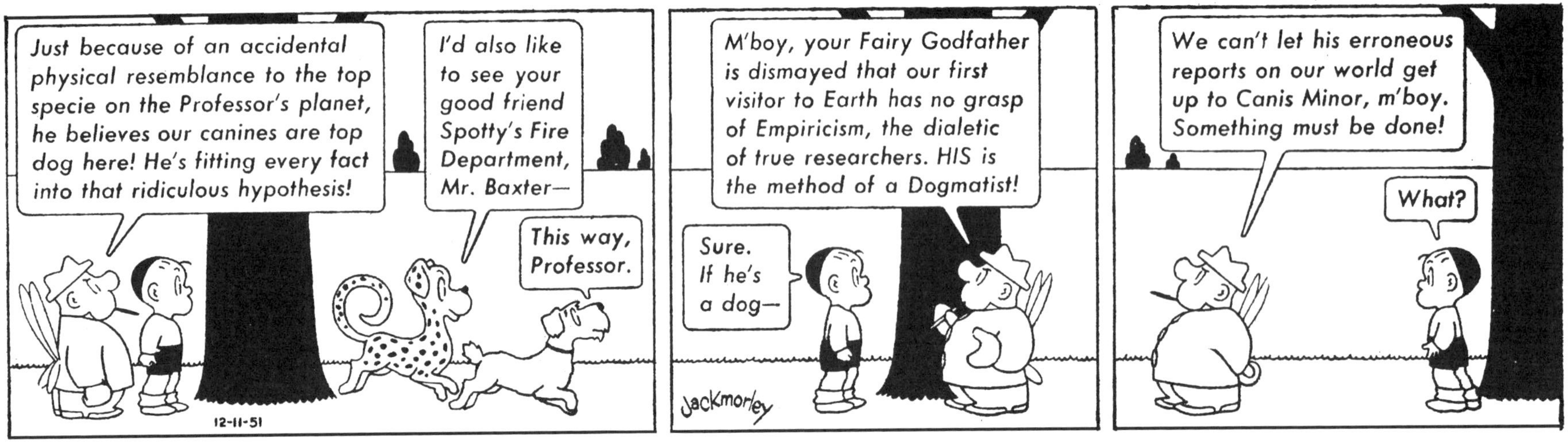
Just because of an accidental physical resemblance to the top specie on the Professor's planet, he believes our canines are top dog here! He's fitting every fact into that ridiculous hypothesis!
I'd also like to see your good friend Spotty's Fire Department, Mr. Baxter—
This way, Professor.
12-11-51
M'boy, your Fairy Godfather is dismayed that our first visitor to Earth has no grasp of Empiricism, the dialetic of true researchers. HIS is the method of a Dogmatist!
Sure. If he's a dog—
Jackmorley
We can't let his erroneous reports on our world get up to Canis Minor, m'boy. Something must be done!
What?

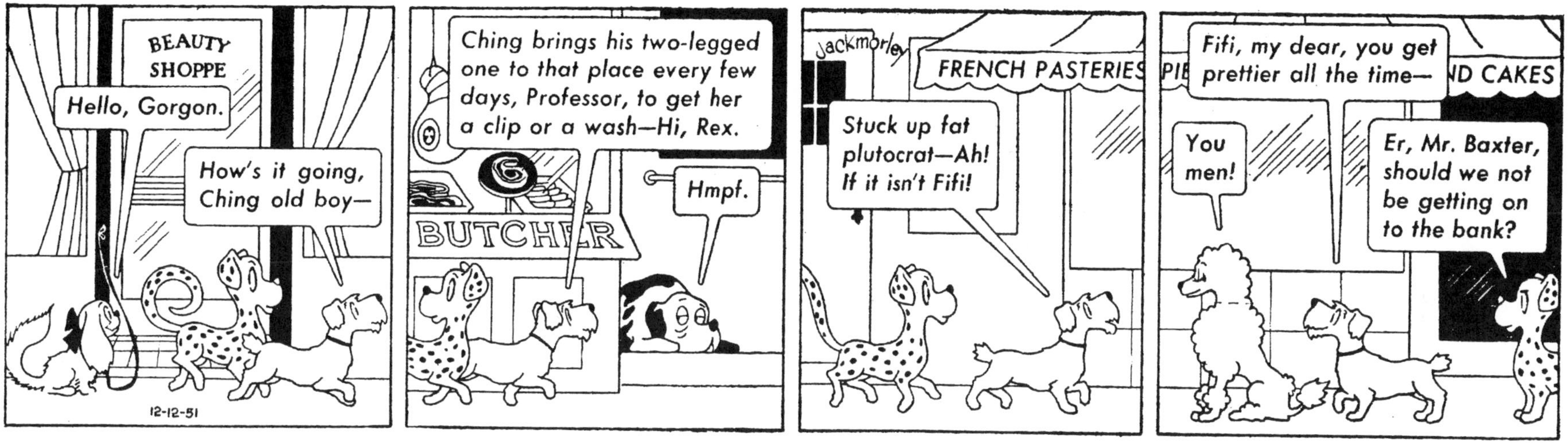
BEAUTY SHOPPE
Hello, Gorgon.
How's it going, Ching old boy—
12-12-51
Ching brings his two-legged one to that place every few days, Professor, to get her a clip or a wash—Hi, Rex.
BUTCHER
Hmpf.
Jackmorley
FRENCH PASTERIES
Stuck up fat plutocrat—Ah! If it isn't Fifi!
Fifi, my dear, you get prettier all the time—
You men!
ND CAKES
Er, Mr. Baxter, should we not be getting on to the bank?

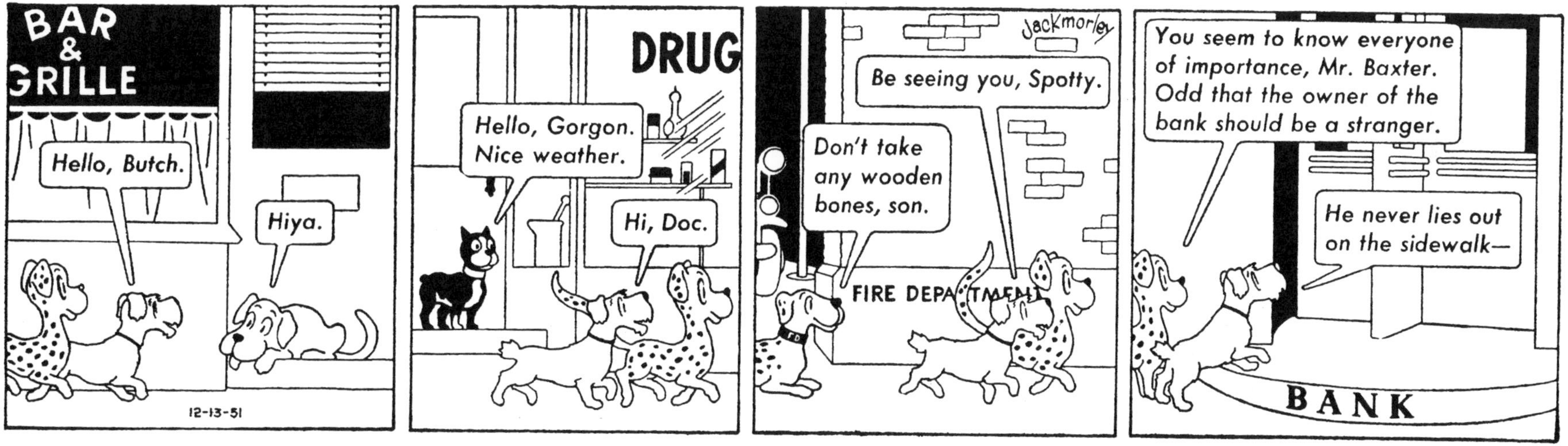
BAR & GRILLE
Hello, Butch.
Hiya.
12-13-51
DRUG
Hello, Gorgon. Nice weather.
Hi, Doc.
Jackmorley
Be seeing you, Spotty.
Don't take any wooden bones, son.
FIRE DEPA
You seem to know everyone of importance, Mr. Baxter. Odd that the owner of the bank should be a stranger.
He never lies out on the sidewalk—
BANK

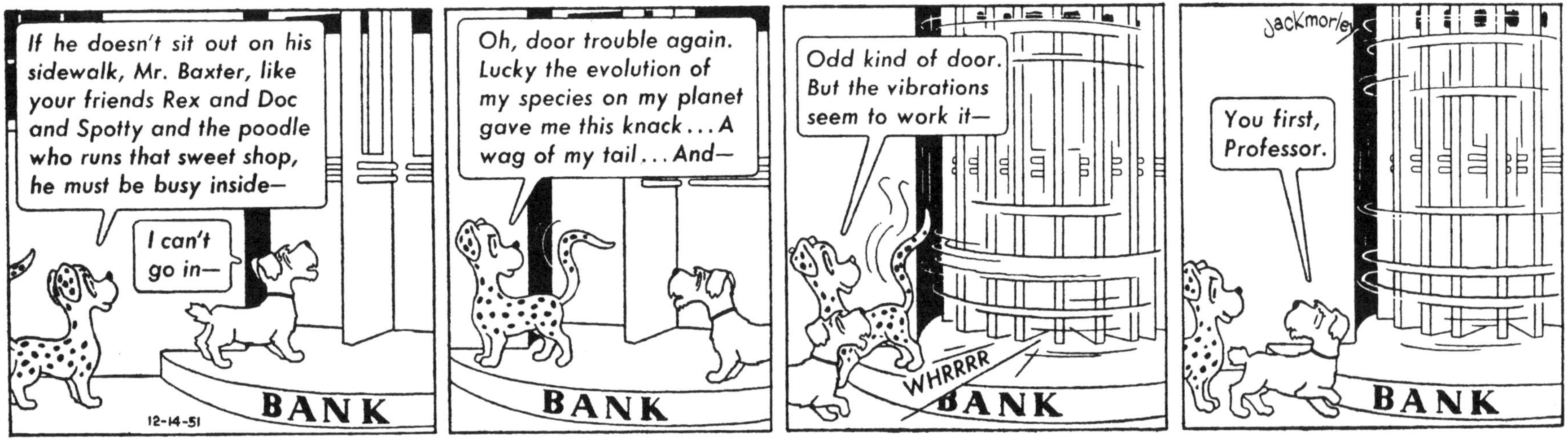
If he doesn't sit out on his sidewalk, Mr. Baxter, like your friends Rex and Doc and Spotty and the poodle who runs that sweet shop, he must be busy inside—
I can't go in—
BANK
12-14-51
Oh, door trouble again. Lucky the evolution of my species on my planet gave me this knack . . . A wag of my tail . . . And—
BANK
Odd kind of door. But the vibrations seem to work it—
WHRRRR
BANK
JACKmorley
You first, Professor.
BANK

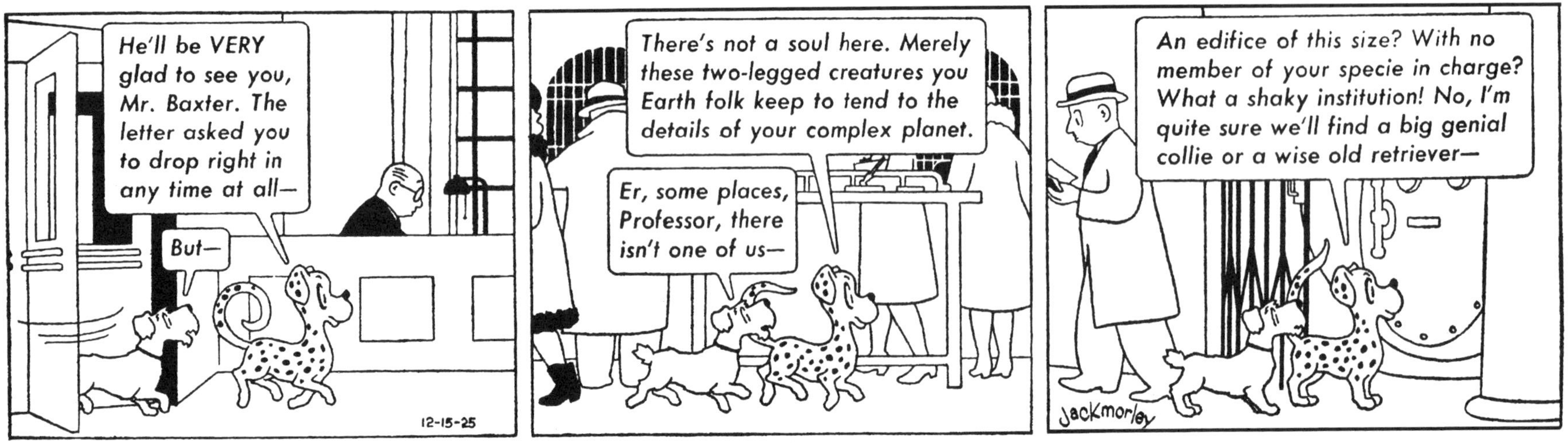
He'll be VERY glad to see you, Mr. Baxter. The letter asked you to drop right in any time at all—
But—
12-15-25
There's not a soul here. Merely these two-legged creatures you Earth folk keep to tend to the details of your complex planet.
Er, some places, Professor, there isn't one of us—
An edifice of this size? With no member of your specie in charge? What a shaky institution! No, I'm quite sure we'll find a big genial collie or a wise old retriever—
JACKmorley

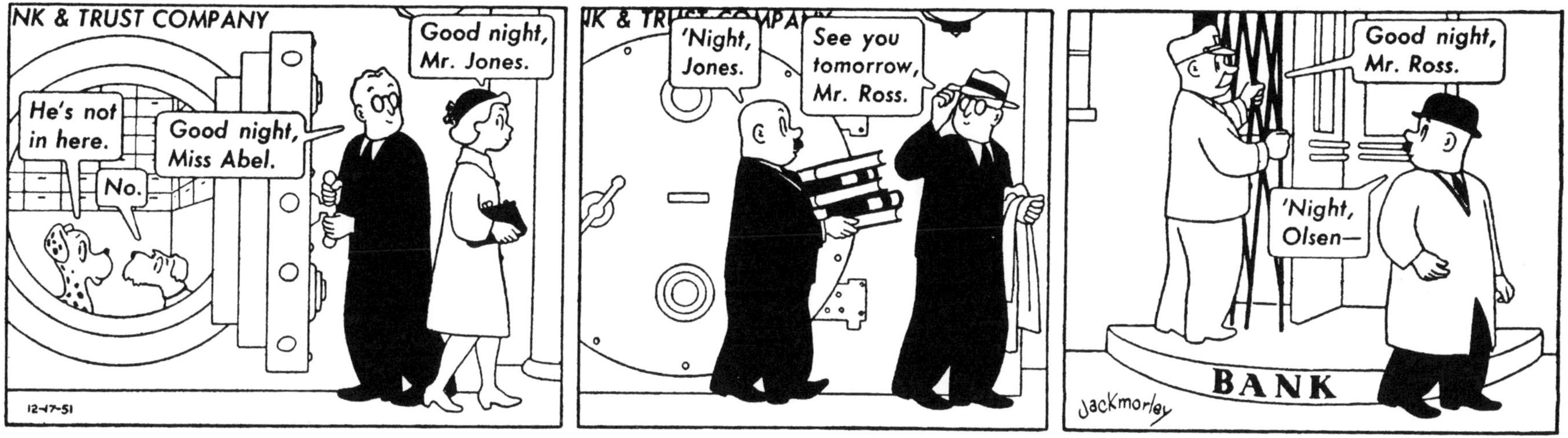
NK & TRUST COMPANY
Good night, Mr. Jones.
He's not in here.
Good night, Miss Abel.
No.
12-17-51
'Night, Jones.
See you tomorrow, Mr. Ross.
Good night, Mr. Ross.
'Night, Olsen—
BANK
jackmorley

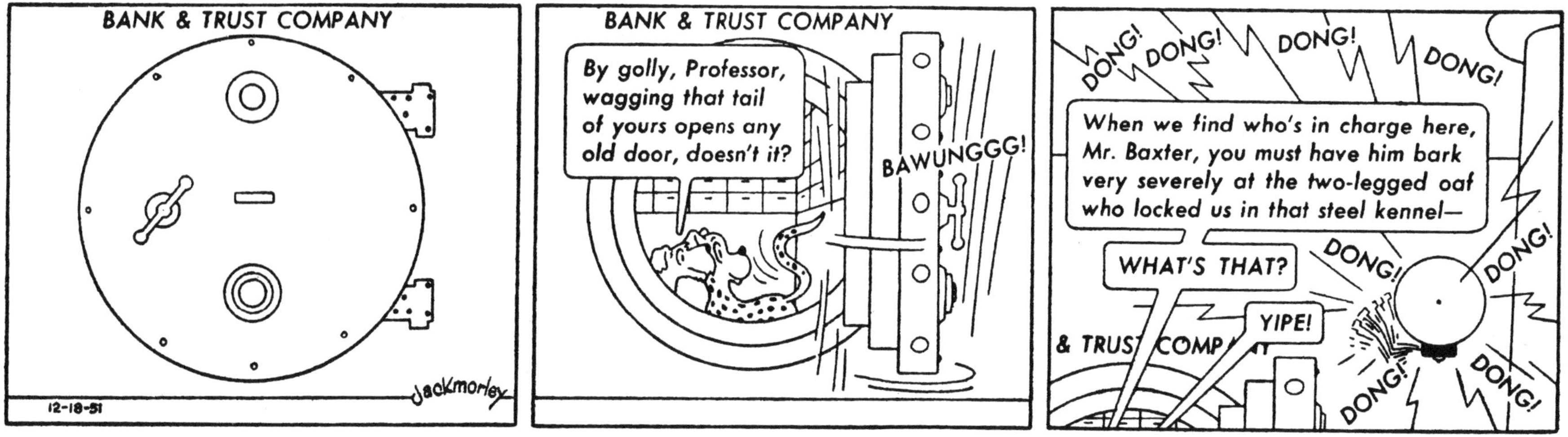
BANK & TRUST COMPANY
12-18-51
jackmorley
BANK & TRUST COMPANY
By golly, Professor, wagging that tail of yours opens any old door, doesn't it?
BAWUNGGG!
DONG! DONG! DONG! DONG!
When we find who's in charge here, Mr. Baxter, you must have him bark very severely at the two-legged oaf who locked us in that steel kennel—
WHAT'S THAT?
YIPE!
DONG! DONG! DONG! DONG!

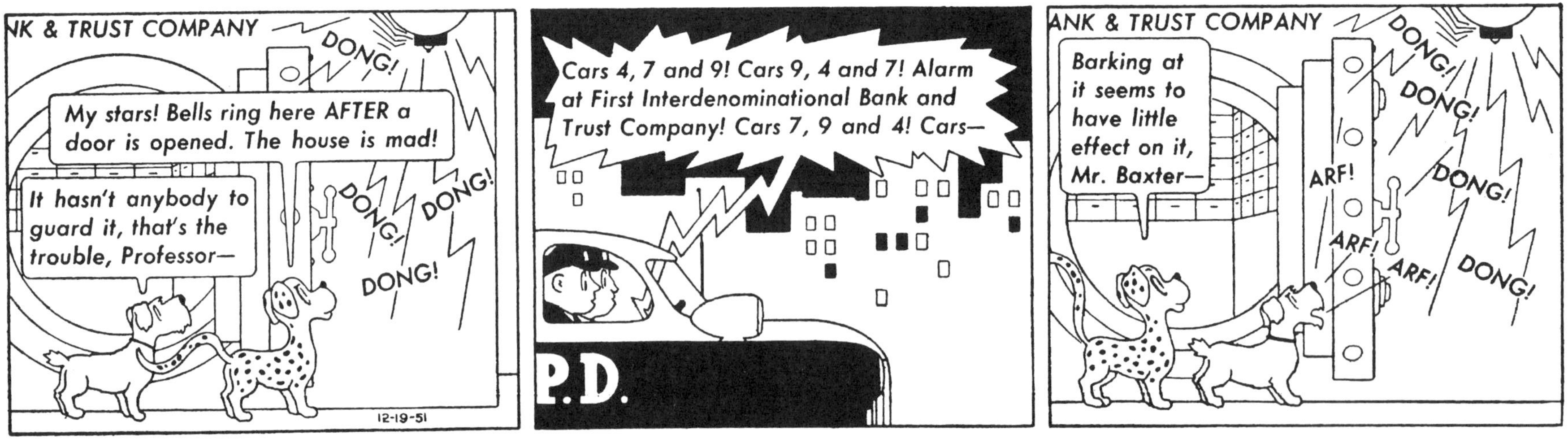
NK & TRUST COMPANY
DONG!
My stars! Bells ring here AFTER a door is opened. The house is mad!
It hasn't anybody to guard it, that's the trouble, Professor—
DONG!
DONG!
DONG!
12-19-51
Cars 4, 7 and 9! Cars 9, 4 and 7! Alarm at First Interdenominational Bank and Trust Company! Cars 7, 9 and 4! Cars—
P.D.
ANK & TRUST COMPANY
DONG!
DONG!
Barking at it seems to have little effect on it, Mr. Baxter—
ARF!
DONG!
ARF!
ARF!
DONG!

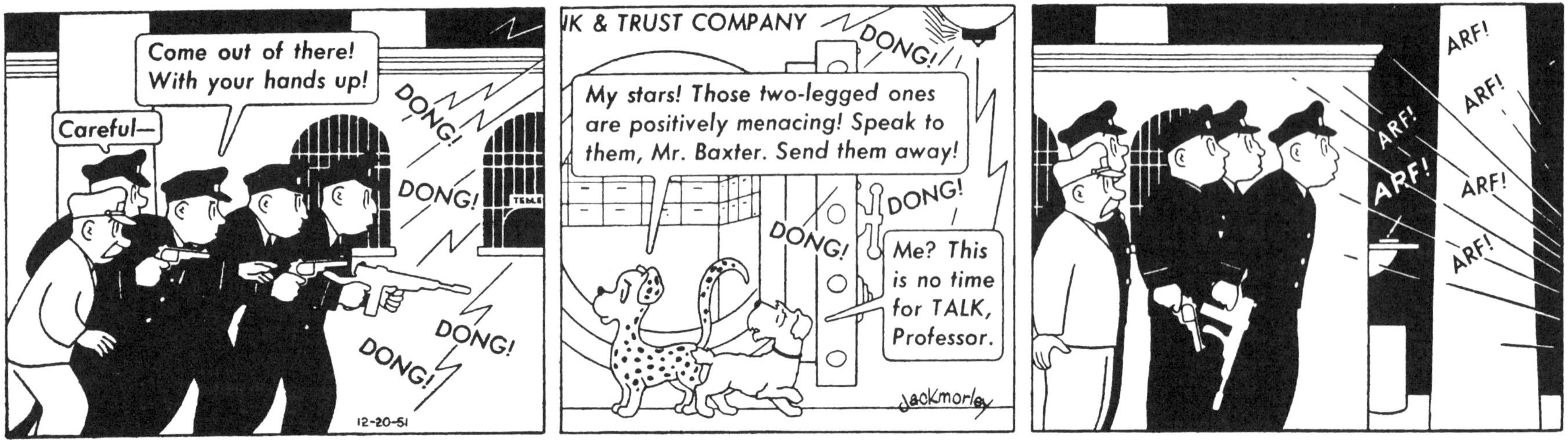
Careful—
Come out of there! With your hands up!
DONG!
DONG!
DONG!
DONG!
12-20-51
NK & TRUST COMPANY
DONG!
My stars! Those two-legged ones are positively menacing! Speak to them, Mr. Baxter. Send them away!
DONG!
DONG!
Me? This is no time for TALK, Professor.
jackmorley
ARF!
ARF!
ARF!
ARF!
ARF!
ARF!

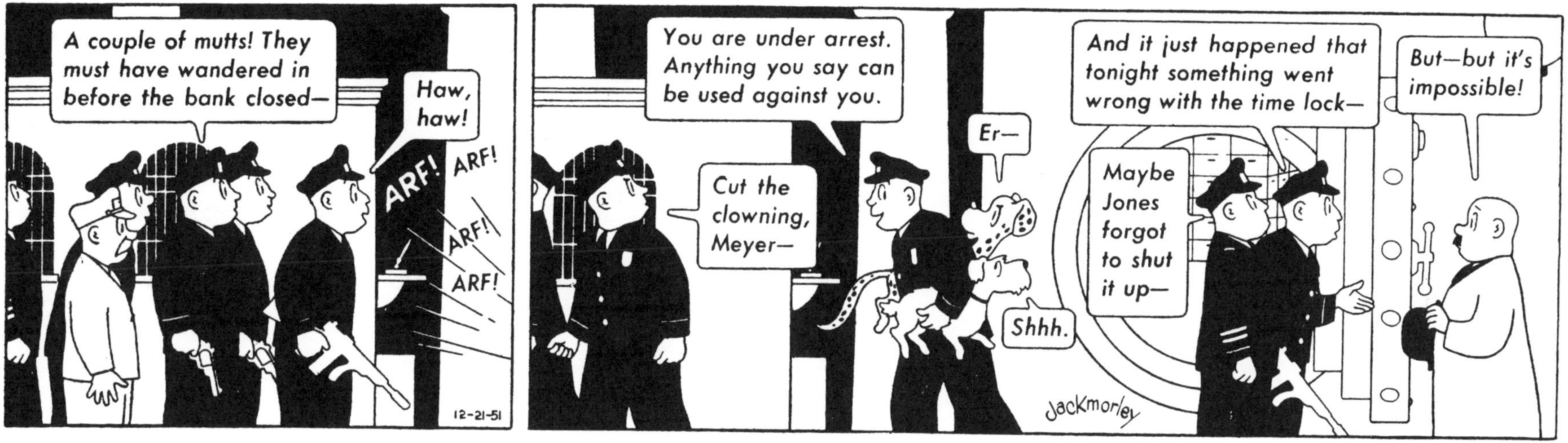
A couple of mutts! They must have wandered in before the bank closed—
Haw, haw!
ARF! ARF!
ARF!
ARF!
12-21-51
You are under arrest. Anything you say can be used against you.
Cut the clowning, Meyer—
Er—
Shhh.
And it just happened that tonight something went wrong with the time lock—
Maybe Jones forgot to shut it up—
But—but it's impossible!
Jackmorley

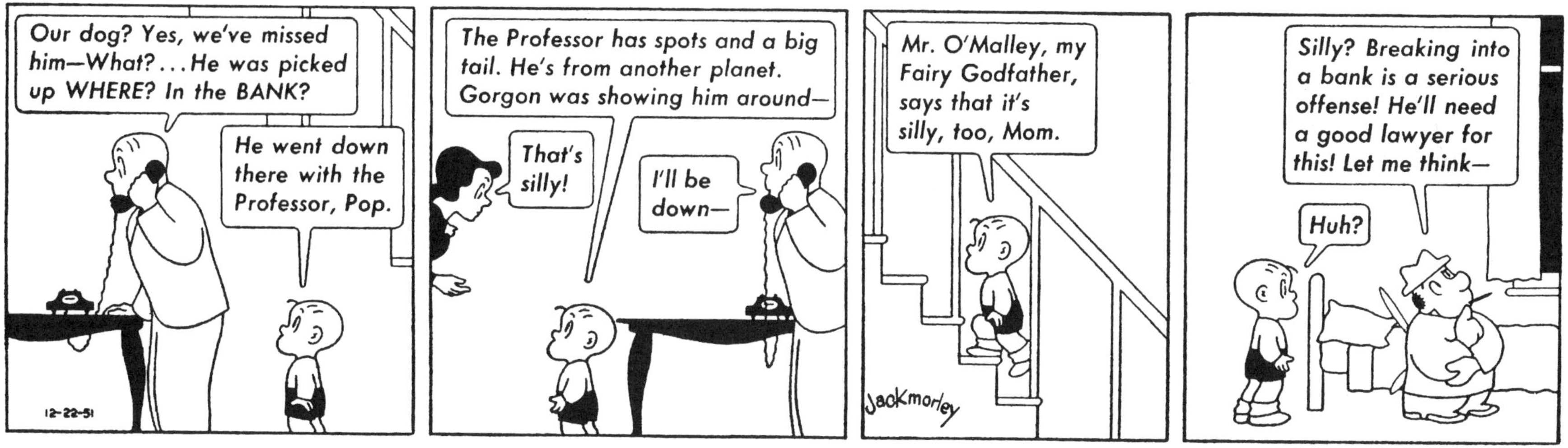
Our dog? Yes, we've missed him—What?...He was picked up WHERE? In the BANK?
He went down there with the Professor, Pop.
12-22-51
The Professor has spots and a big tail. He's from another planet. Gorgon was showing him around—
That's silly!
I'll be down—
Mr. O'Malley, my Fairy Godfather, says that it's silly, too, Mom.
Jackmorley
Silly? Breaking into a bank is a serious offense! He'll need a good lawyer for this! Let me think—
Huh?

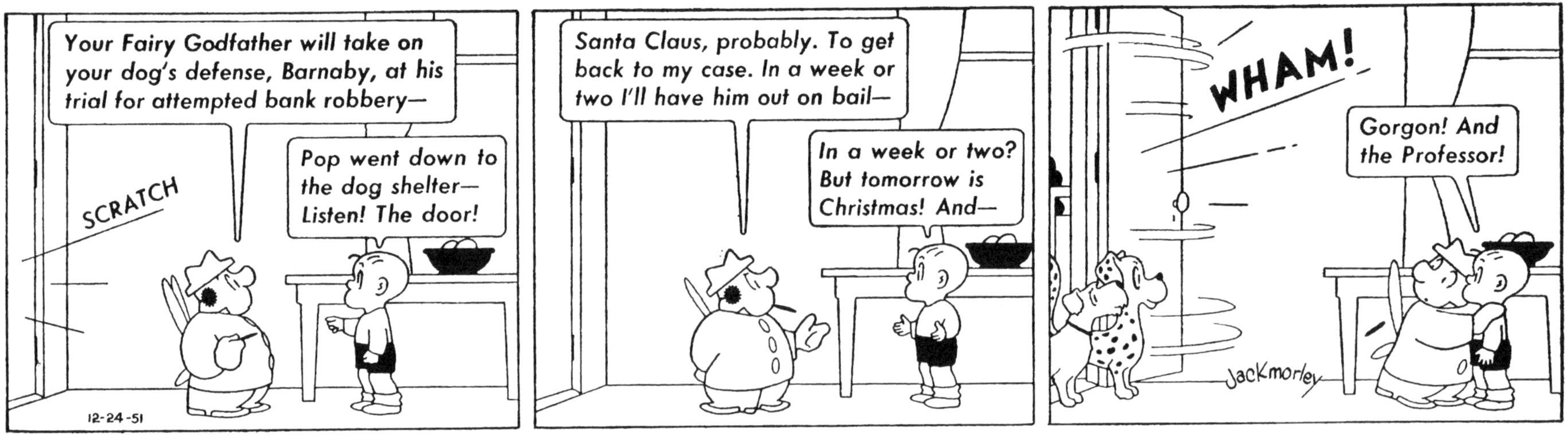
Your Fairy Godfather will take on your dog's defense, Barnaby, at his trial for attempted bank robbery—
SCRATCH
Pop went down to the dog shelter— Listen! The door!
12-24-51
Santa Claus, probably. To get back to my case. In a week or two I'll have him out on bail—
In a week or two? But tomorrow is Christmas! And—
WHAM!
Gorgon! And the Professor!
JackMorley

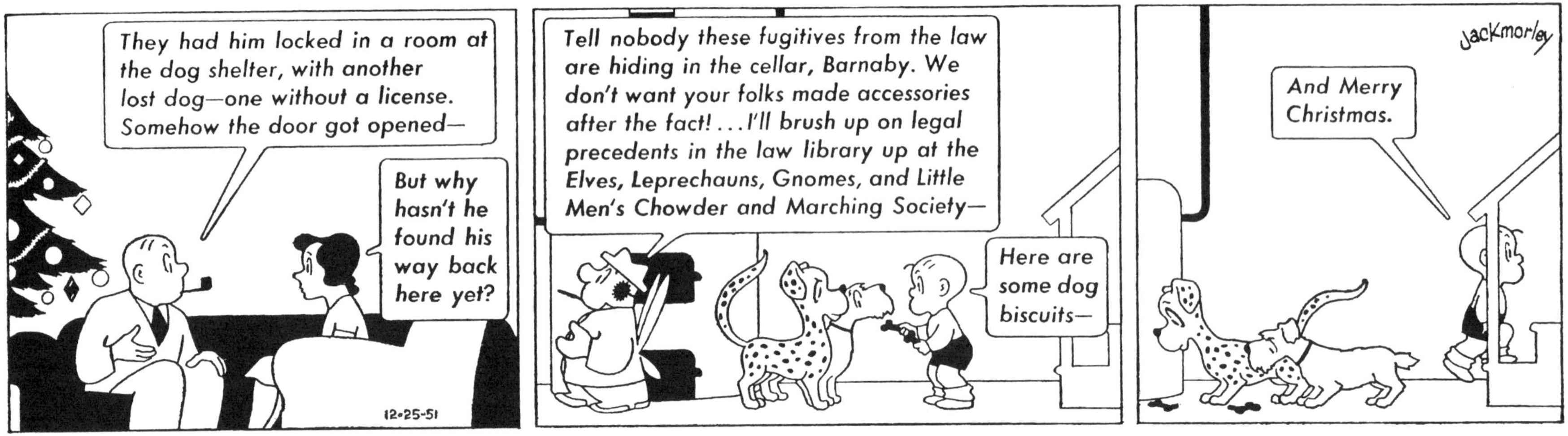
They had him locked in a room at the dog shelter, with another lost dog—one without a license. Somehow the door got opened—
But why hasn't he found his way back here yet?
12-25-51
Tell nobody these fugitives from the law are hiding in the cellar, Barnaby. We don't want your folks made accessories after the fact! . . . I'll brush up on legal precedents in the law library up at the Elves, Leprechauns, Gnomes, and Little Men's Chowder and Marching Society—
Here are some dog biscuits—
JackMorley
And Merry Christmas.

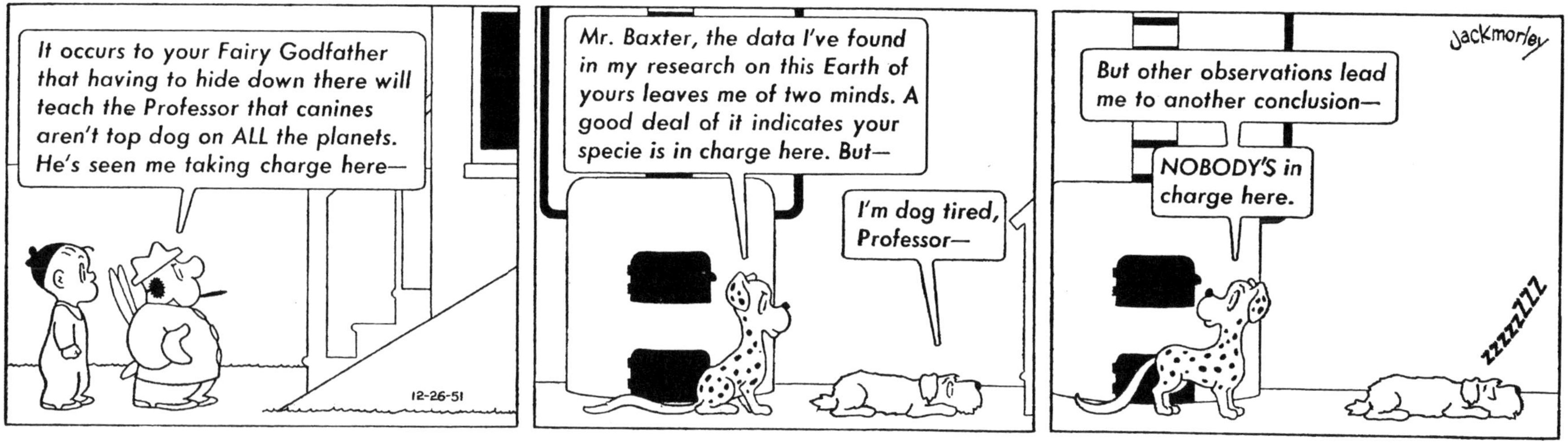
It occurs to your Fairy Godfather that having to hide down there will teach the Professor that canines aren't top dog on ALL the planets. He's seen me taking charge here—
12-26-51
Mr. Baxter, the data I've found in my research on this Earth of yours leaves me of two minds. A good deal of it indicates your specie is in charge here. But—
I'm dog tired, Professor—
Jackmorley
But other observations lead me to another conclusion—
NOBODY'S in charge here.
zzzzzZZZ

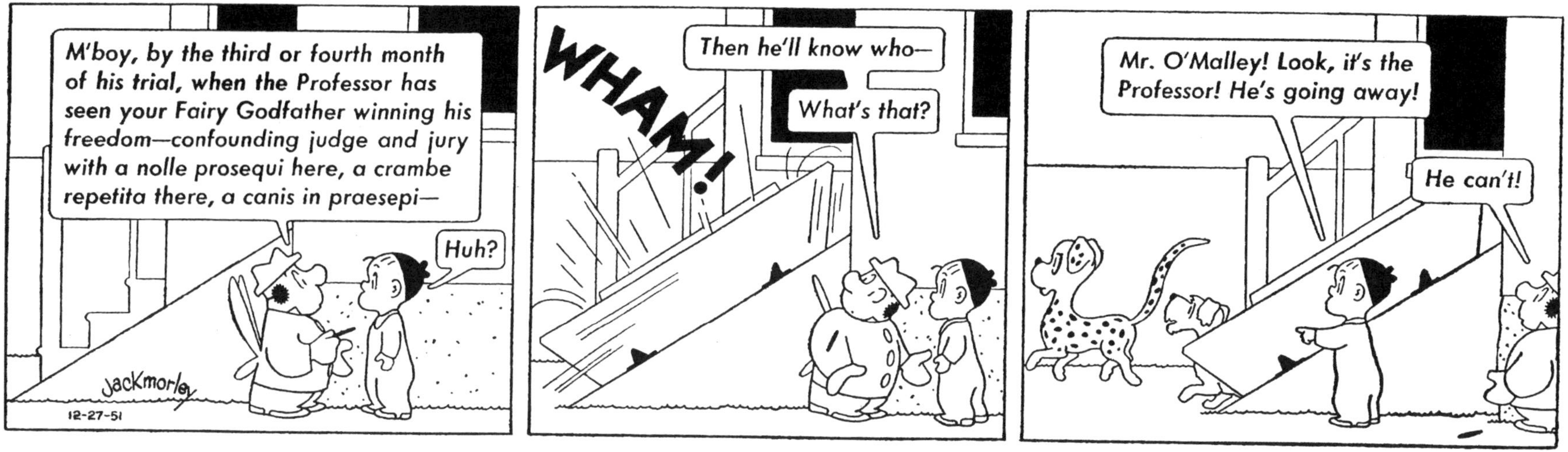
M'boy, by the third or fourth month of his trial, when the Professor has seen your Fairy Godfather winning his freedom—confounding judge and jury with a nolle prosequi here, a crambe repetita there, a canis in praesepi—
Huh?
Jackmorley
12-27-51
WHAM!
Then he'll know who—
What's that?
Mr. O'Malley! Look, it's the Professor! He's going away!
He can't!

December 26 – 27

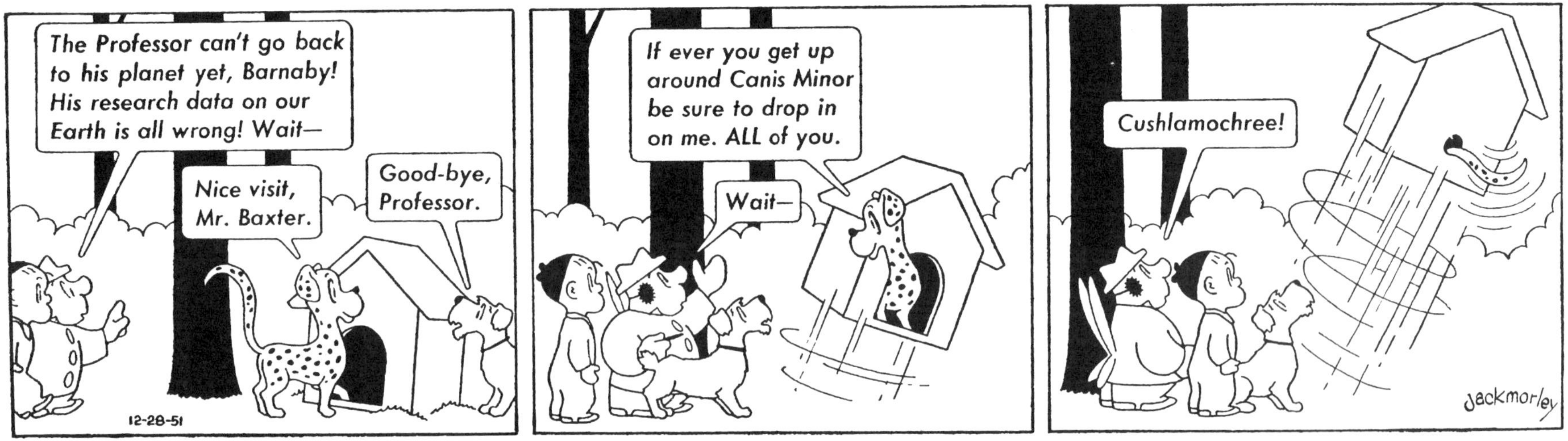
The Professor can't go back to his planet yet, Barnaby! His research data on our Earth is all wrong! Wait—
Nice visit, Mr. Baxter.
Good-bye, Professor.
12-28-51
If ever you get up around Canis Minor be sure to drop in on me. ALL of you.
Wait—
Cushlamochree!
Jackmorley

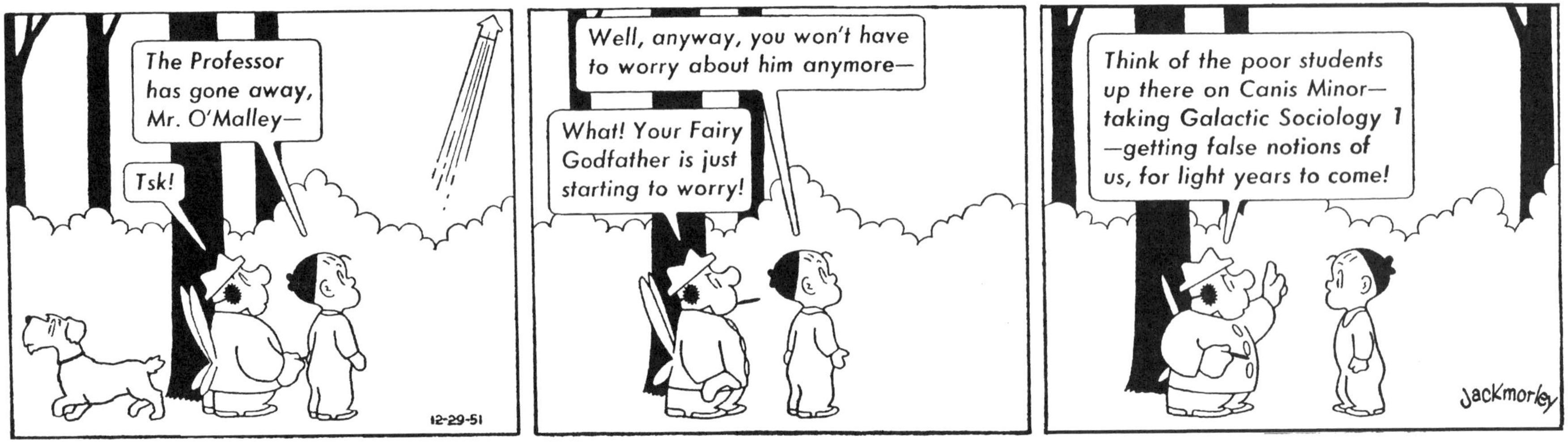
The Professor has gone away, Mr. O'Malley—
Tsk!
12-29-51
Well, anyway, you won't have to worry about him anymore—
What! Your Fairy Godfather is just starting to worry!
Think of the poor students up there on Canis Minor—taking Galactic Sociology 1—getting false notions of us, for light years to come!
Jackmorley

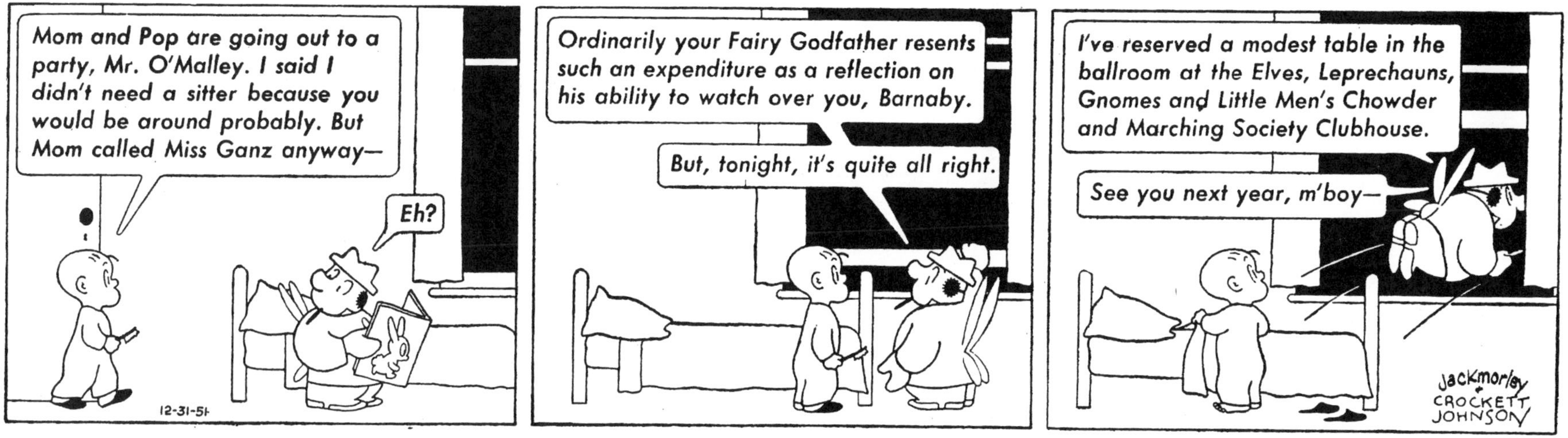
Mom and Pop are going out to a party, Mr. O'Malley. I said I didn't need a sitter because you would be around probably. But Mom called Miss Ganz anyway—
Eh?
12-31-51
Ordinarily your Fairy Godfather resents such an expenditure as a reflection on his ability to watch over you, Barnaby.
But, tonight, it's quite all right.
I've reserved a modest table in the ballroom at the Elves, Leprechauns, Gnomes and Little Men's Chowder and Marching Society Clubhouse.
See you next year, m'boy—
Jackmorley + CROCKETT JOHNSON

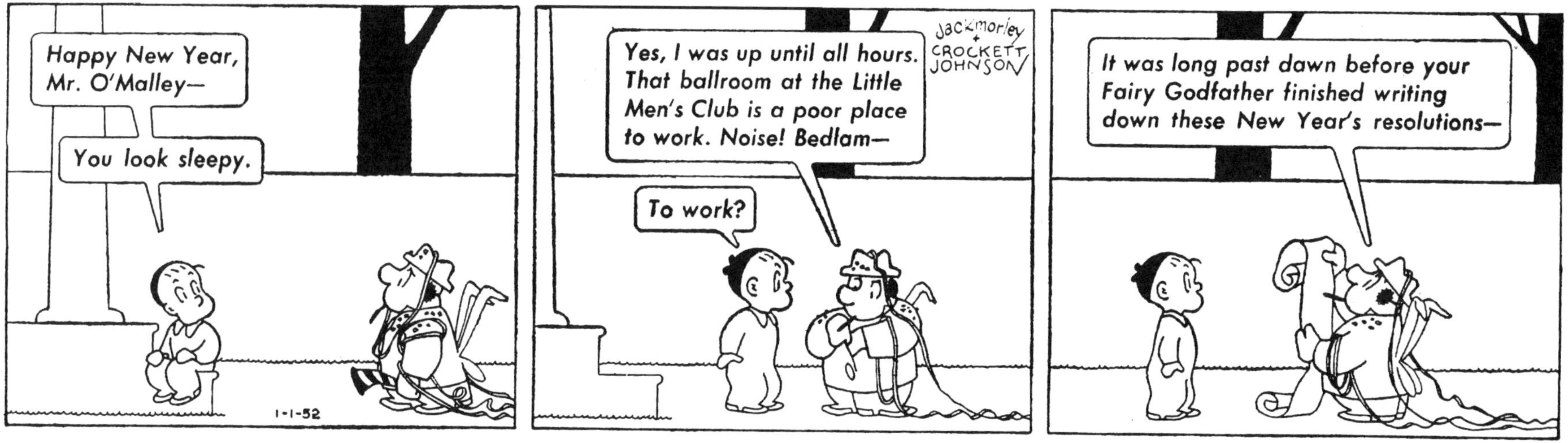
Happy New Year, Mr. O'Malley—
You look sleepy.
1-1-52
Yes, I was up until all hours. That ballroom at the Little Men's Club is a poor place to work. Noise! Bedlam—
Jackmorley + CROCKETT JOHNSON
To work?
It was long past dawn before your Fairy Godfather finished writing down these New Year's resolutions—

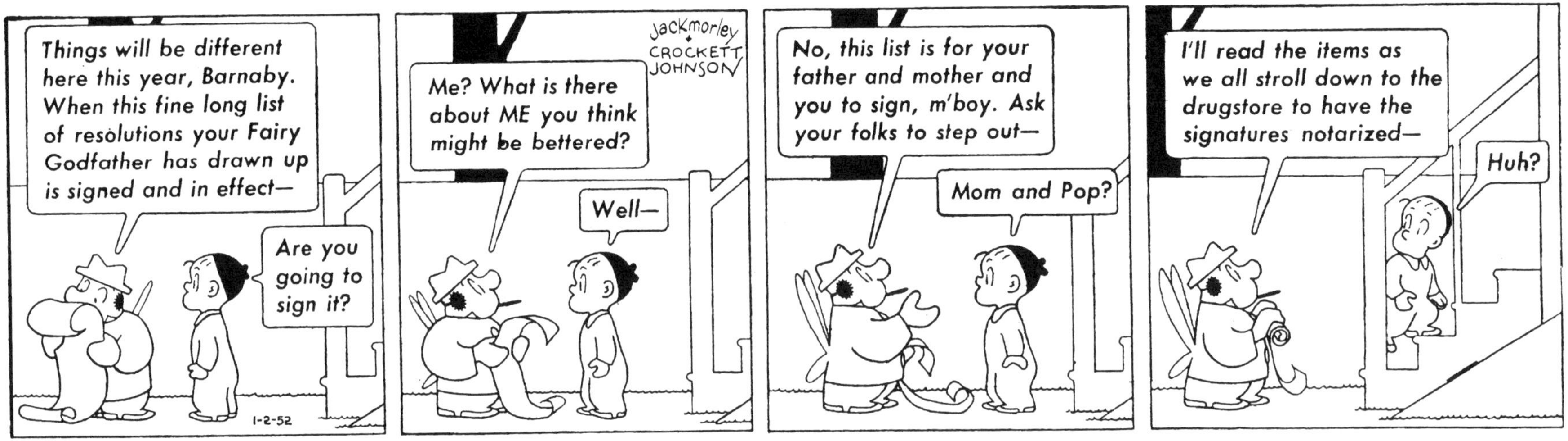
Things will be different here this year, Barnaby. When this fine long list of resolutions your Fairy Godfather has drawn up is signed and in effect—
Are you going to sign it?
1-2-52
Me? What is there about ME you think might be bettered?
Well—
JACKMORLEY + CROCKETT JOHNSON
No, this list is for your father and mother and you to sign, m'boy. Ask your folks to step out—
Mom and Pop?
I'll read the items as we all stroll down to the drugstore to have the signatures notarized—
Huh?

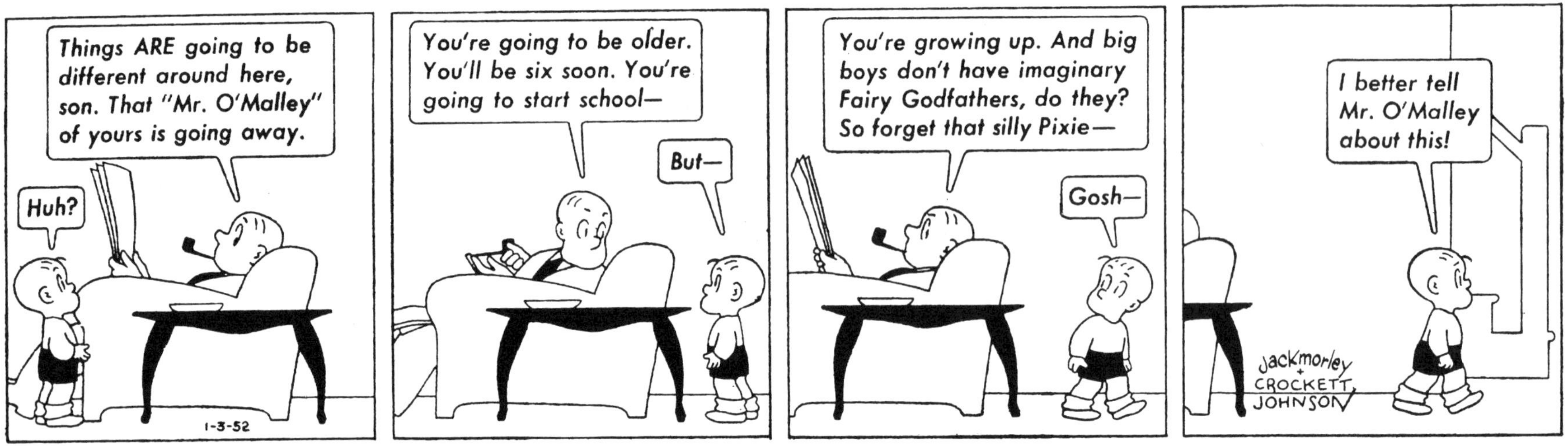
Things ARE going to be different around here, son. That "Mr. O'Malley" of yours is going away.
Huh?
1-3-52
You're going to be older. You'll be six soon. You're going to start school—
But—
You're growing up. And big boys don't have imaginary Fairy Godfathers, do they? So forget that silly Pixie—
Gosh—
I better tell Mr. O'Malley about this!
JACKMORLEY + CROCKETT JOHNSON

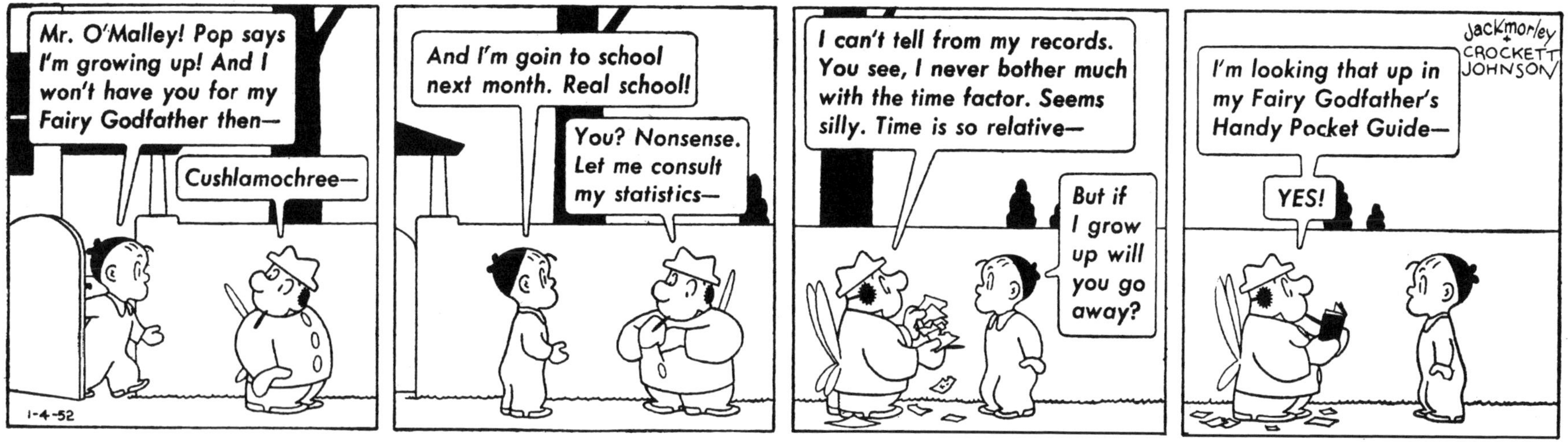
Mr. O'Malley! Pop says I'm growing up! And I won't have you for my Fairy Godfather then—
Cushlamochree—
1-4-52
And I'm goin to school next month. Real school!
You? Nonsense. Let me consult my statistics—
I can't tell from my records. You see, I never bother much with the time factor. Seems silly. Time is so relative—
But if I grow up will you go away?
I'm looking that up in my Fairy Godfather's Handy Pocket Guide—
YES!
JACKMORLEY + CROCKETT JOHNSON

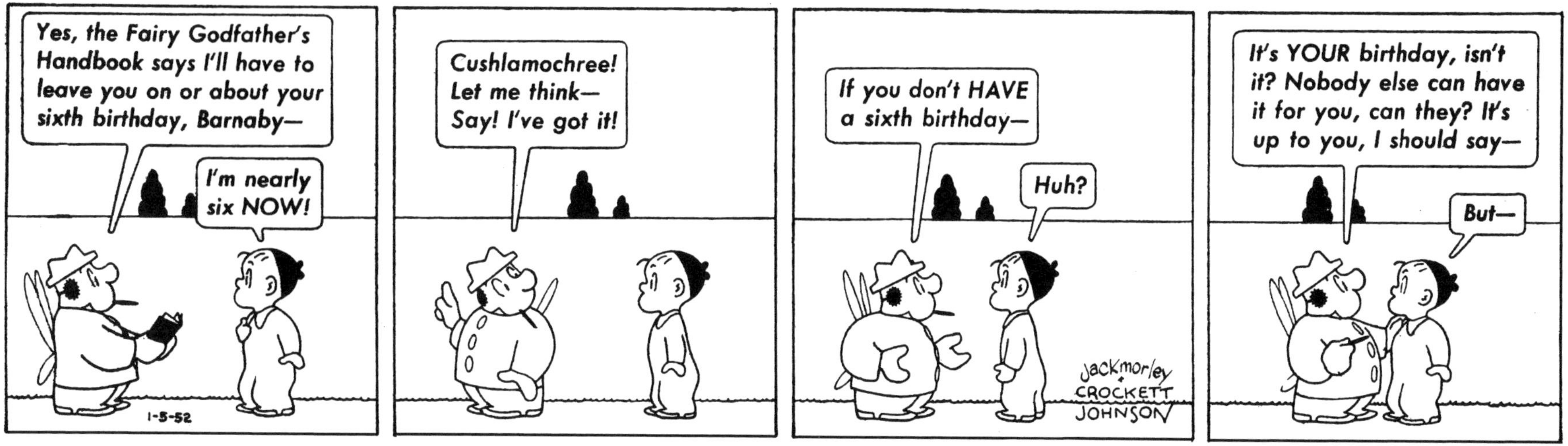
Yes, the Fairy Godfather's Handbook says I'll have to leave you on or about your sixth birthday, Barnaby—
I'm nearly six NOW!
1-5-52
Cushlamochree! Let me think— Say! I've got it!
If you don't HAVE a sixth birthday—
Huh?
JACKMORLEY + CROCKETT JOHNSON
It's YOUR birthday, isn't it? Nobody else can have it for you, can they? It's up to you, I should say—
But—

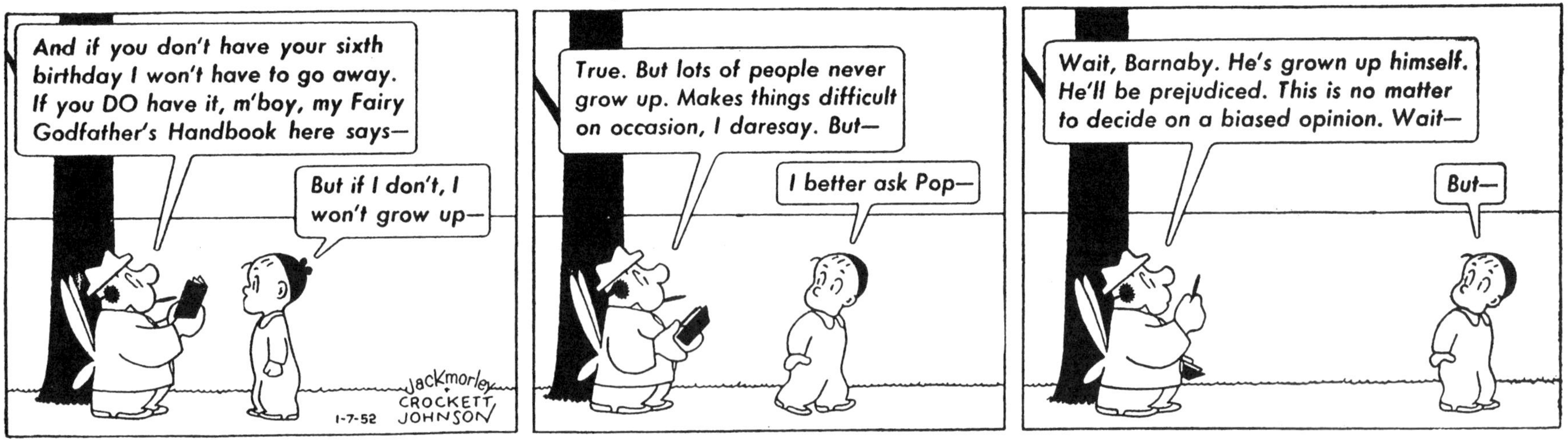
And if you don't have your sixth birthday I won't have to go away. If you DO have it, m'boy, my Fairy Godfather's Handbook here says—
But if I don't, I won't grow up—
Jackmorley • CROCKETT JOHNSON
1-7-52
True. But lots of people never grow up. Makes things difficult on occasion, I daresay. But—
I better ask Pop—
Wait, Barnaby. He's grown up himself. He'll be prejudiced. This is no matter to decide on a biased opinion. Wait—
But—

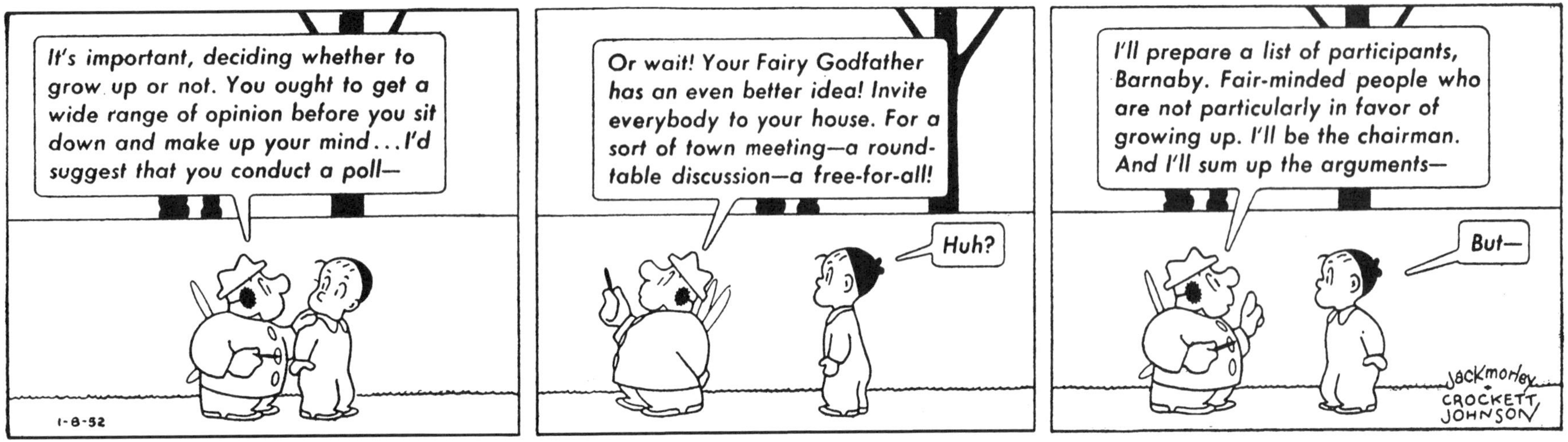
It's important, deciding whether to grow up or not. You ought to get a wide range of opinion before you sit down and make up your mind . . . I'd suggest that you conduct a poll—
1-8-52
Or wait! Your Fairy Godfather has an even better idea! Invite everybody to your house. For a sort of town meeting—a round-table discussion—a free-for-all!
Huh?
I'll prepare a list of participants, Barnaby. Fair-minded people who are not particularly in favor of growing up. I'll be the chairman. And I'll sum up the arguments—
But—
Jackmorley • CROCKETT JOHNSON

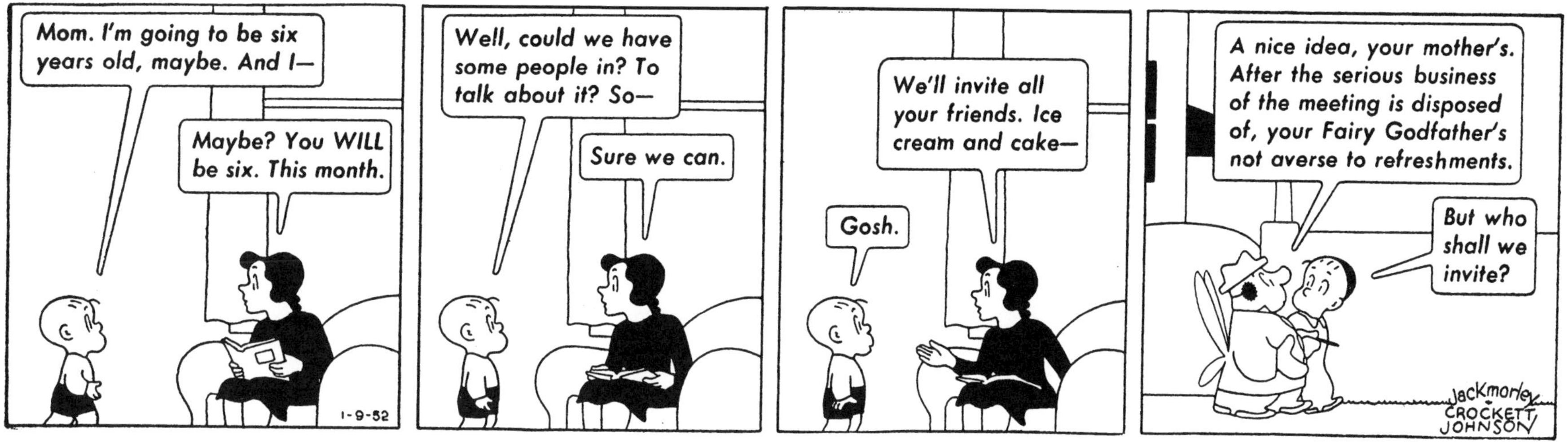
Mom. I'm going to be six years old, maybe. And I—
Maybe? You WILL be six. This month.
1-9-52
Well, could we have some people in? To talk about it? So—
Sure we can.
Gosh.
We'll invite all your friends. Ice cream and cake—
A nice idea, your mother's. After the serious business of the meeting is disposed of, your Fairy Godfather's not averse to refreshments.
But who shall we invite?
JacKmorley
CROCKETT JOHNSON

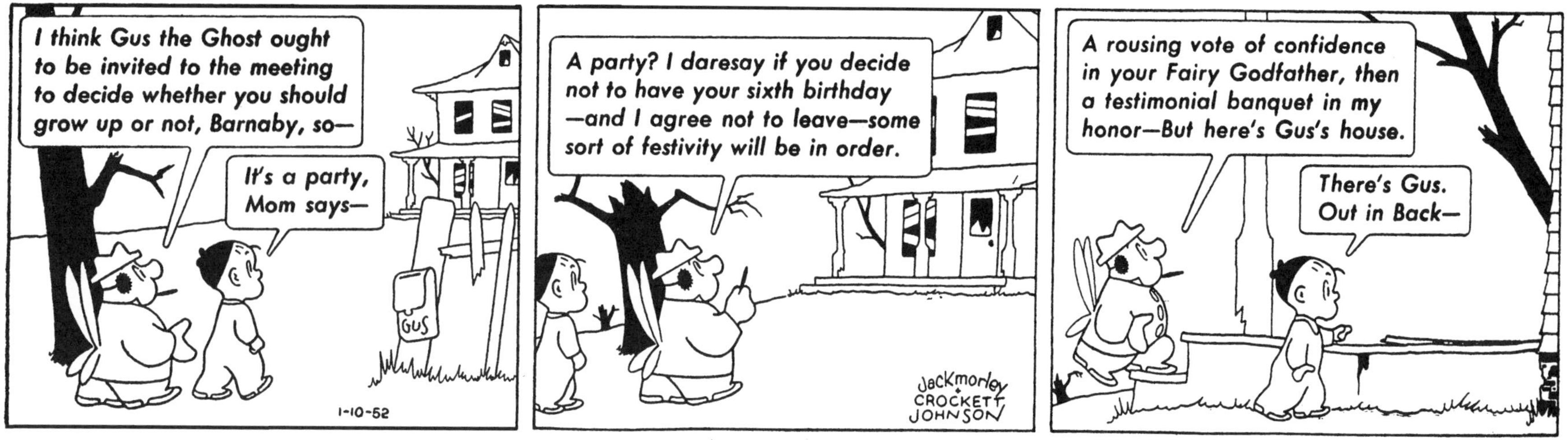
I think Gus the Ghost ought to be invited to the meeting to decide whether you should grow up or not, Barnaby, so—
It's a party, Mom says—
GUS
1-10-52
A party? I daresay if you decide not to have your sixth birthday—and I agree not to leave—some sort of festivity will be in order.
JacKmorley
CROCKETT JOHNSON
A rousing vote of confidence in your Fairy Godfather, then a testimonial banquet in my honor—But here's Gus's house.
There's Gus. Out in Back—

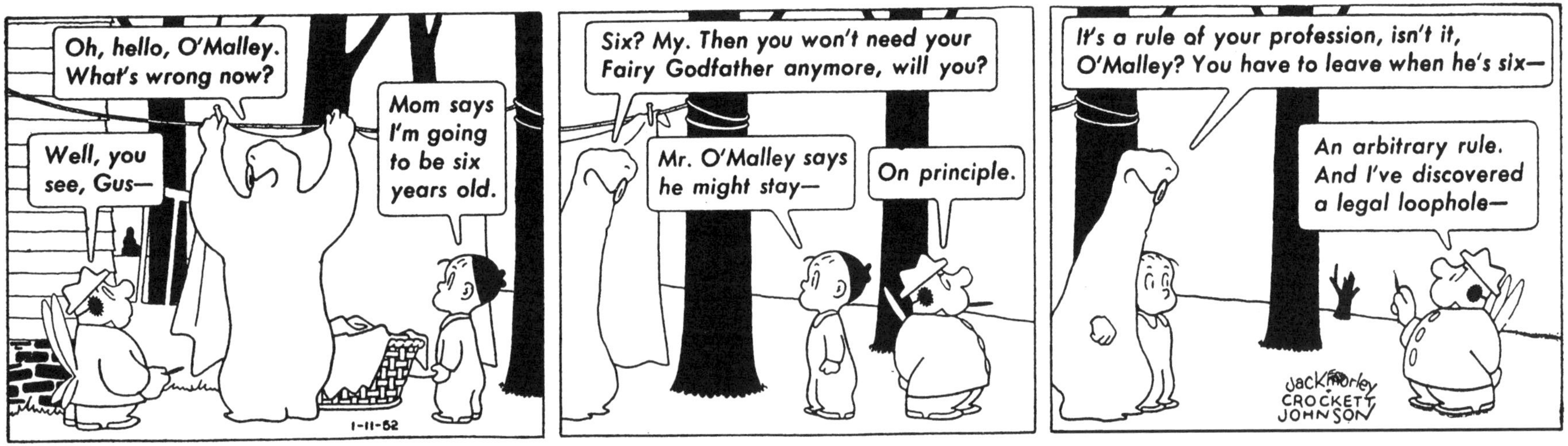
Oh, hello, O'Malley. What's wrong now?
Well, you see, Gus—
Mom says I'm going to be six years old.
1-11-52
Six? My. Then you won't need your Fairy Godfather anymore, will you?
Mr. O'Malley says he might stay—
On principle.
It's a rule of your profession, isn't it, O'Malley? You have to leave when he's six—
An arbitrary rule. And I've discovered a legal loophole—
Jack Morley
CROCKETT JOHNSON

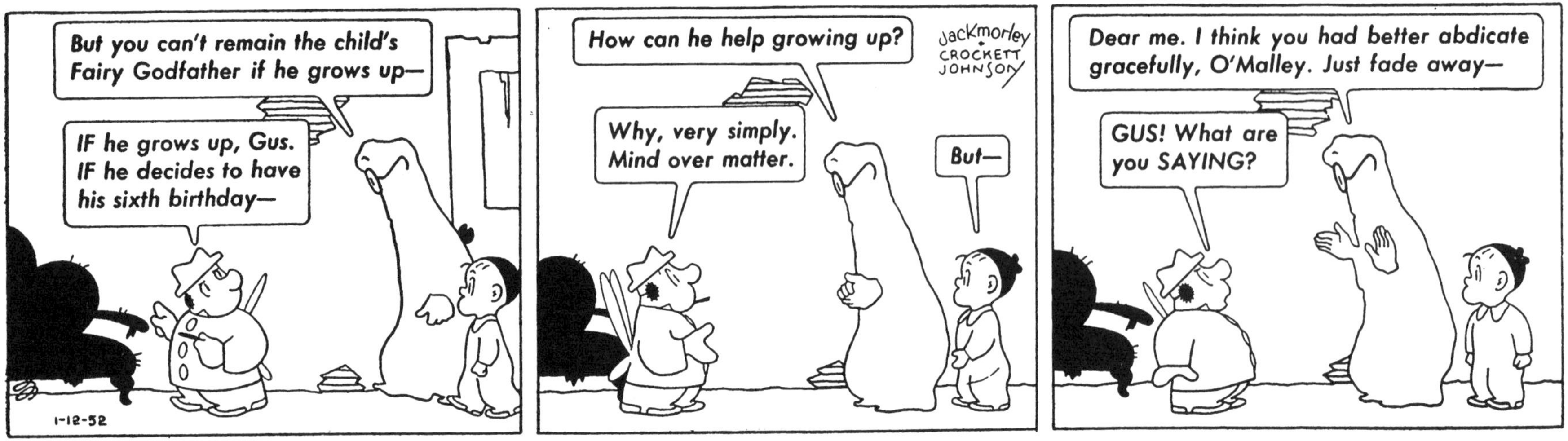
But you can't remain the child's Fairy Godfather if he grows up—
IF he grows up, Gus. IF he decides to have his sixth birthday—
1-12-52
How can he help growing up?
Jack morley
CROCKETT JOHNSON
Why, very simply. Mind over matter.
But—
Dear me. I think you had better abdicate gracefully, O'Malley. Just fade away—
GUS! What are you SAYING?

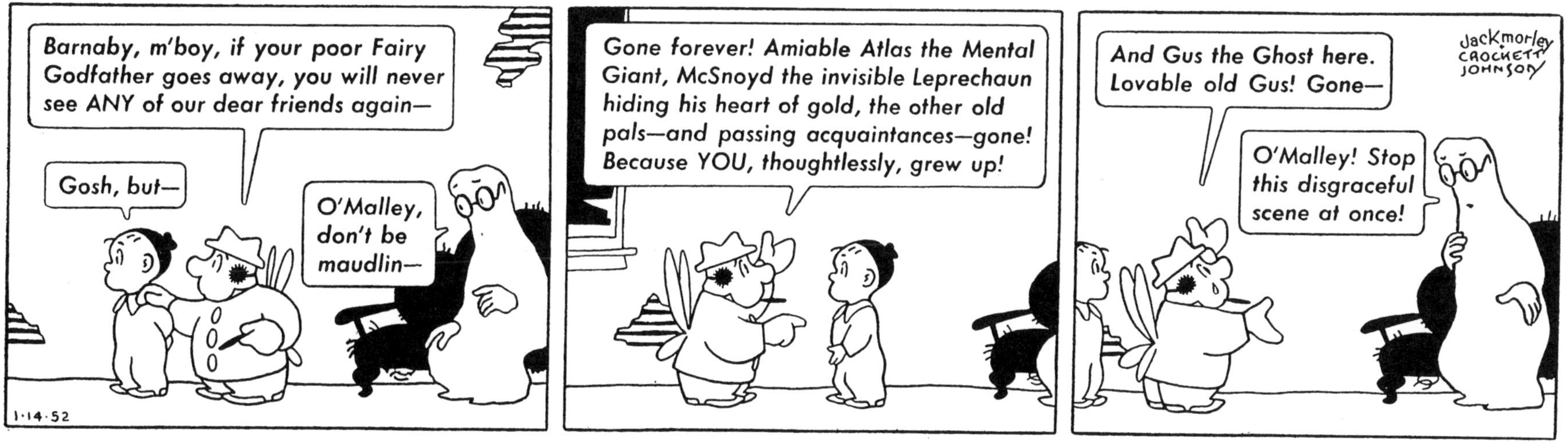
Barnaby, m'boy, if your poor Fairy Godfather goes away, you will never see ANY of our dear friends again—
Gosh, but—
O'Malley, don't be maudlin—
1·14·52
Gone forever! Amiable Atlas the Mental Giant, McSnoyd the invisible Leprechaun hiding his heart of gold, the other old pals—and passing acquaintances—gone! Because YOU, thoughtlessly, grew up!
JacKmorley CROCKETT JOHNSON
And Gus the Ghost here. Lovable old Gus! Gone—
O'Malley! Stop this disgraceful scene at once!

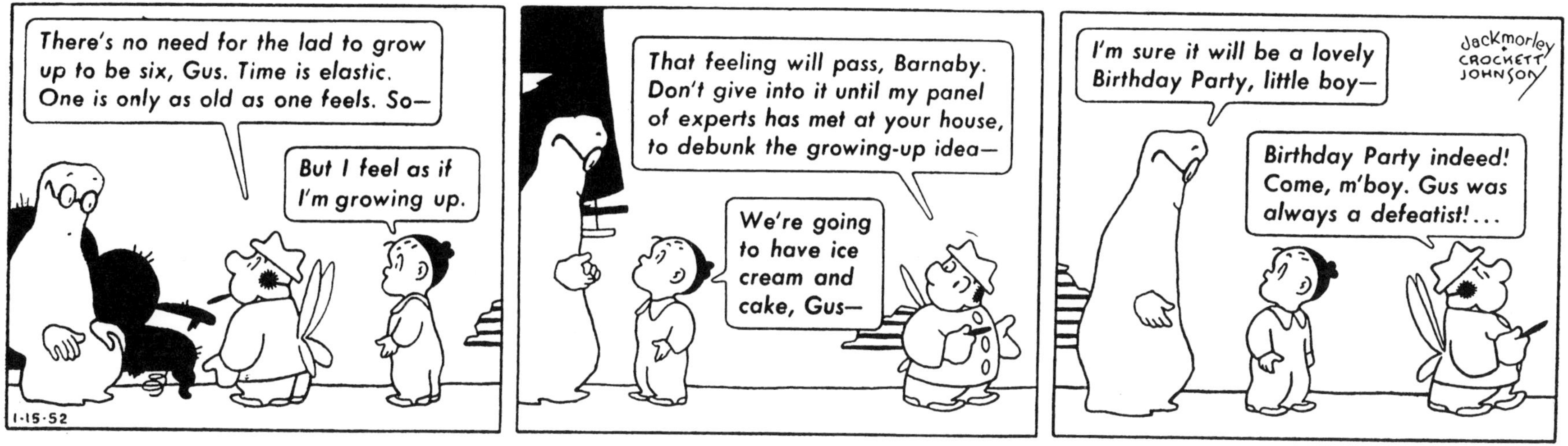
There's no need for the lad to grow up to be six, Gus. Time is elastic. One is only as old as one feels. So—
But I feel as if I'm growing up.
1·15·52
That feeling will pass, Barnaby. Don't give into it until my panel of experts has met at your house, to debunk the growing-up idea—
We're going to have ice cream and cake, Gus—
JacKmorley CROCKETT JOHNSON
I'm sure it will be a lovely Birthday Party, little boy—
Birthday Party indeed! Come, m'boy. Gus was always a defeatist!...

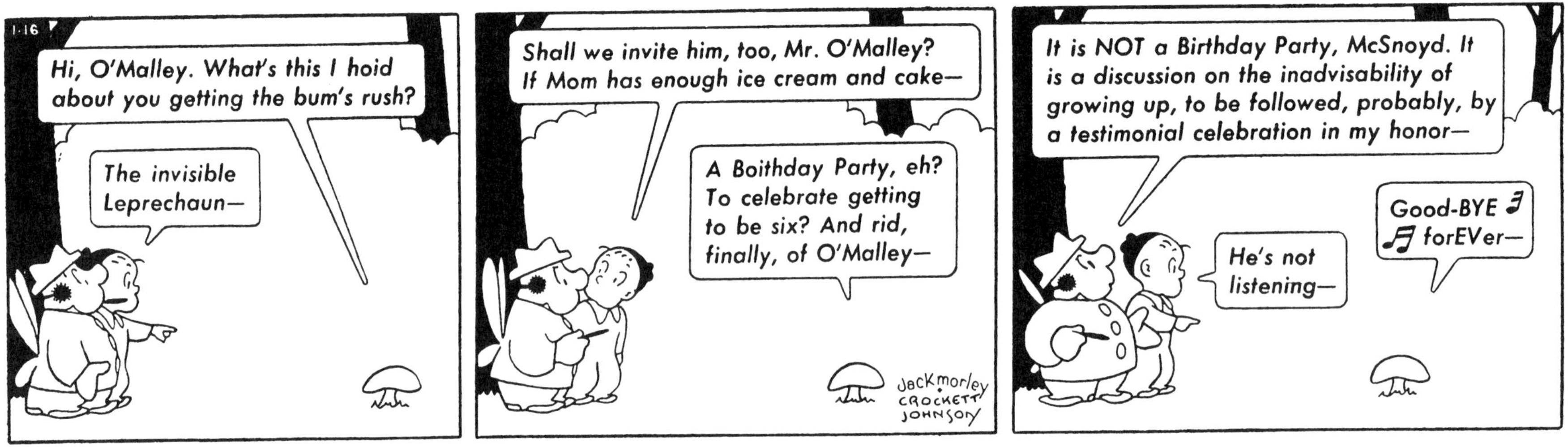
1·16
Hi, O'Malley. What's this I hoid about you getting the bum's rush?
The invisible Leprechaun—
Shall we invite him, too, Mr. O'Malley? If Mom has enough ice cream and cake—
A Boithday Party, eh? To celebrate getting to be six? And rid, finally, of O'Malley—
Jack morley
CROCKETT JOHNSON
It is NOT a Birthday Party, McSnoyd. It is a discussion on the inadvisability of growing up, to be followed, probably, by a testimonial celebration in my honor—
He's not listening—
Good-BYE forEVer—

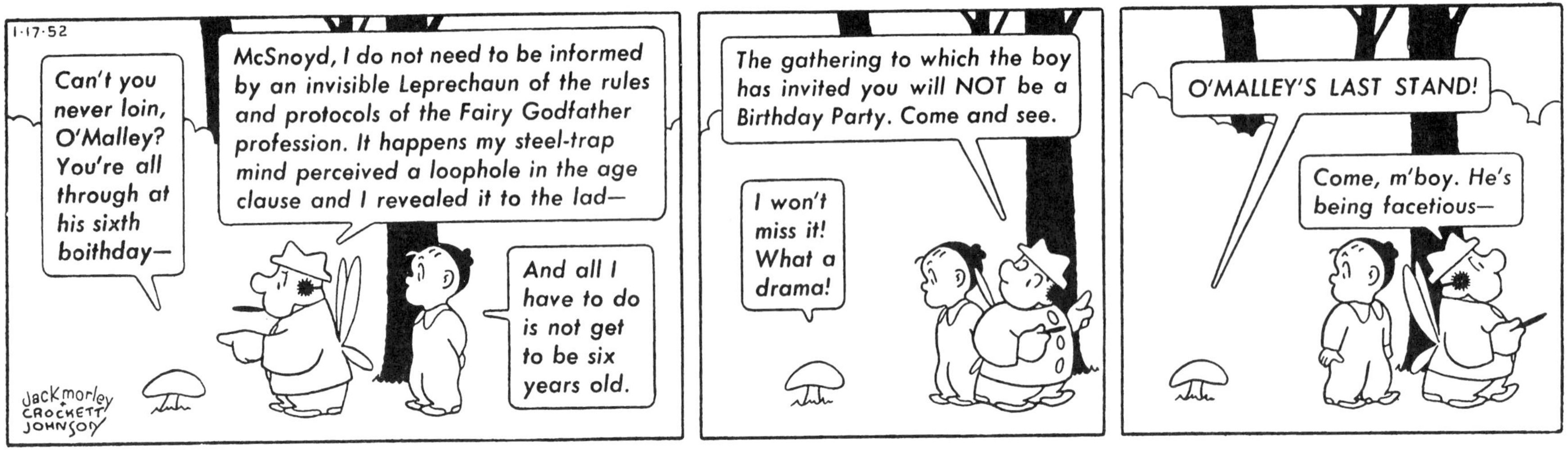
1·17·52
Can't you never loin, O'Malley? You're all through at his sixth boithday—
McSnoyd, I do not need to be informed by an invisible Leprechaun of the rules and protocols of the Fairy Godfather profession. It happens my steel-trap mind perceived a loophole in the age clause and I revealed it to the lad—
And all I have to do is not get to be six years old.
Jack morley
CROCKETT JOHNSON
The gathering to which the boy has invited you will NOT be a Birthday Party. Come and see.
I won't miss it! What a drama!
O'MALLEY'S LAST STAND!
Come, m'boy. He's being facetious—

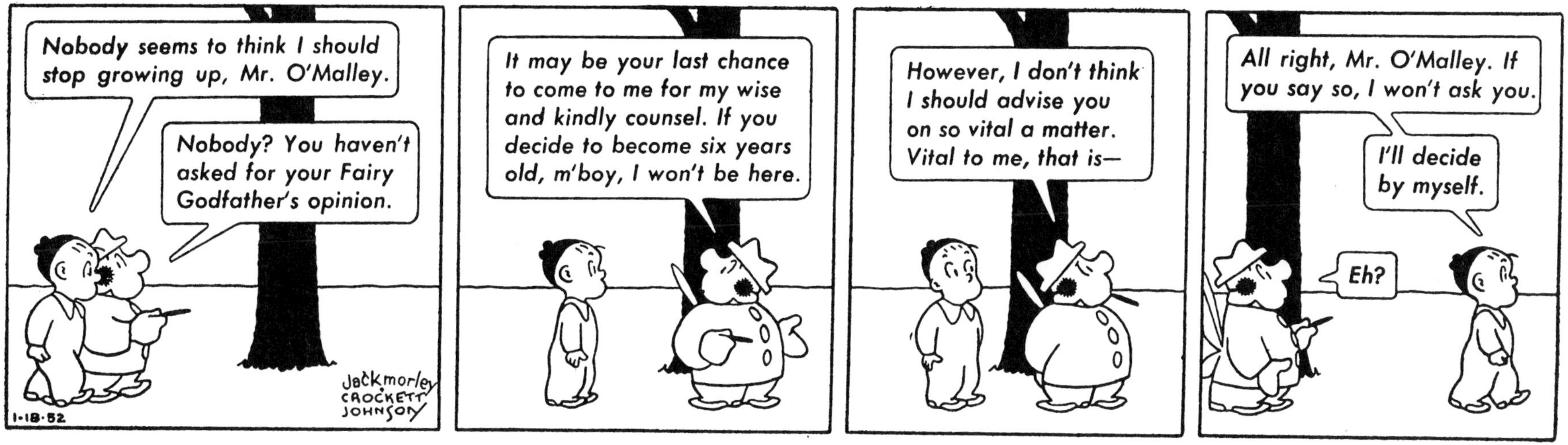
Nobody seems to think I should stop growing up, Mr. O'Malley.
Nobody? You haven't asked for your Fairy Godfather's opinion.
Jackmorley CROCKETT JOHNSON
1-18-52
It may be your last chance to come to me for my wise and kindly counsel. If you decide to become six years old, m'boy, I won't be here.
However, I don't think I should advise you on so vital a matter. Vital to me, that is—
All right, Mr. O'Malley. If you say so, I won't ask you.
I'll decide by myself.
Eh?

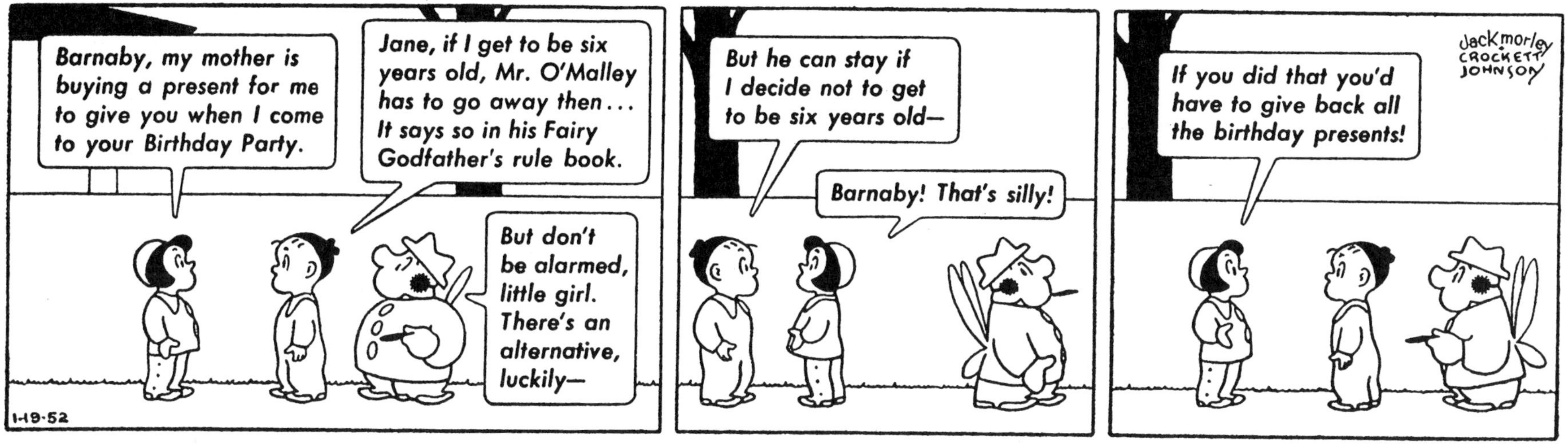
Barnaby, my mother is buying a present for me to give you when I come to your Birthday Party.
Jane, if I get to be six years old, Mr. O'Malley has to go away then... It says so in his Fairy Godfather's rule book.
But don't be alarmed, little girl. There's an alternative, luckily—
1-19-52
But he can stay if I decide not to get to be six years old—
Barnaby! That's silly!
Jackmorley CROCKETT JOHNSON
If you did that you'd have to give back all the birthday presents!

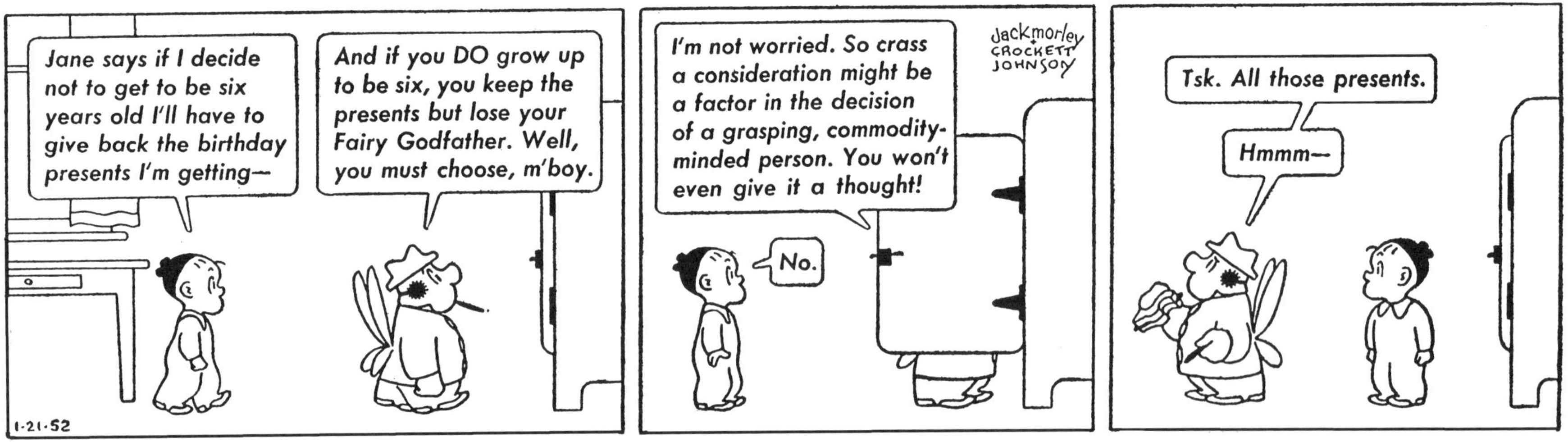
Jane says if I decide not to get to be six years old I'll have to give back the birthday presents I'm getting—
And if you DO grow up to be six, you keep the presents but lose your Fairy Godfather. Well, you must choose, m'boy.
1-21-52
I'm not worried. So crass a consideration might be a factor in the decision of a grasping, commodity-minded person. You won't even give it a thought!
No.
Jackmorley + CROCKETT JOHNSON
Tsk. All those presents.
Hmmm—

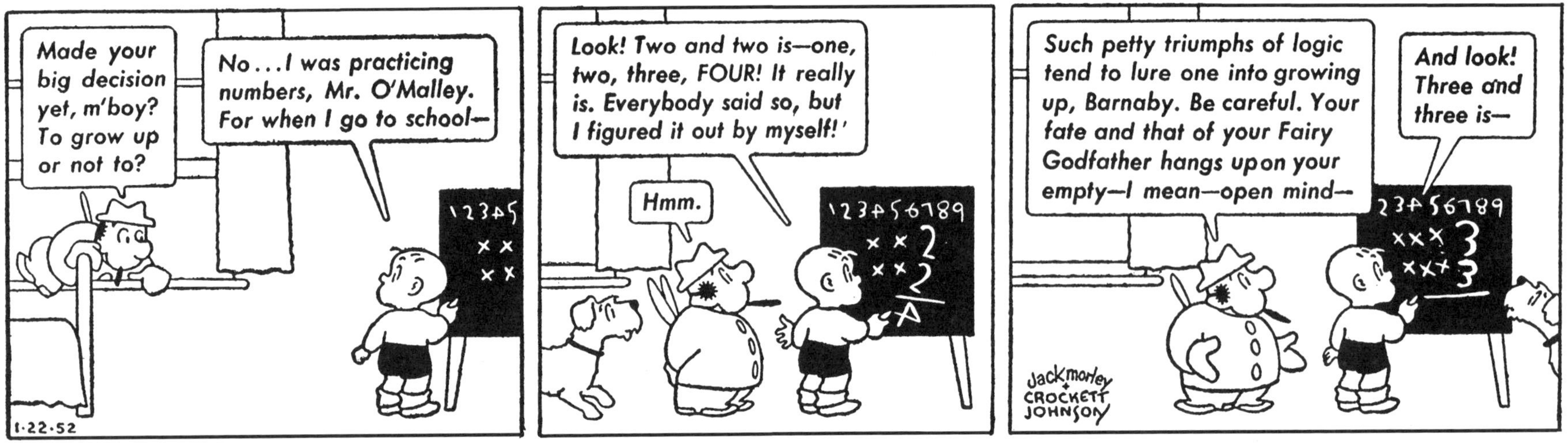
Made your big decision yet, m'boy? To grow up or not to?
No . . . I was practicing numbers, Mr. O'Malley. For when I go to school—
1 2 3 4 5
1-22-52
Look! Two and two is—one, two, three, FOUR! It really is. Everybody said so, but I figured it out by myself!'
Hmm.
1 2 3 4 5 6 7 8 9
Such petty triumphs of logic tend to lure one into growing up, Barnaby. Be careful. Your fate and that of your Fairy Godfather hangs upon your empty—I mean—open mind—
And look! Three and three is—
Jackmorley + CROCKETT JOHNSON

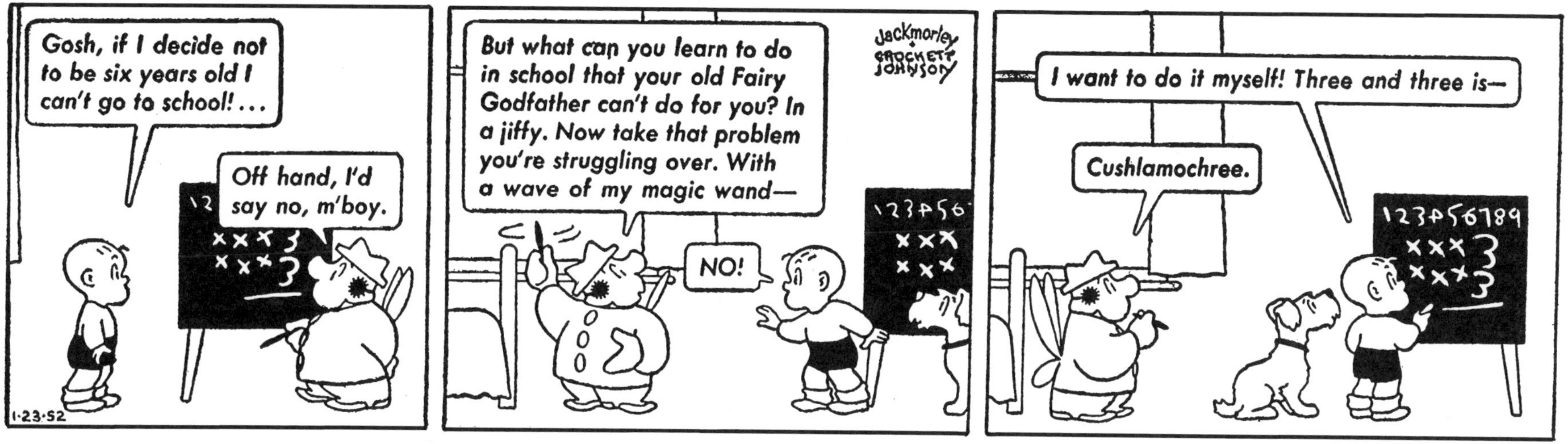
Gosh, if I decide not to be six years old I can't go to school! . . .
Off hand, I'd say no, m'boy.
1·23·52
But what can you learn to do in school that your old Fairy Godfather can't do for you? In a jiffy. Now take that problem you're struggling over. With a wave of my magic wand—
NO!
JACKMORLEY + CROCKETT JOHNSON
I want to do it myself! Three and three is—
Cushlamochree.

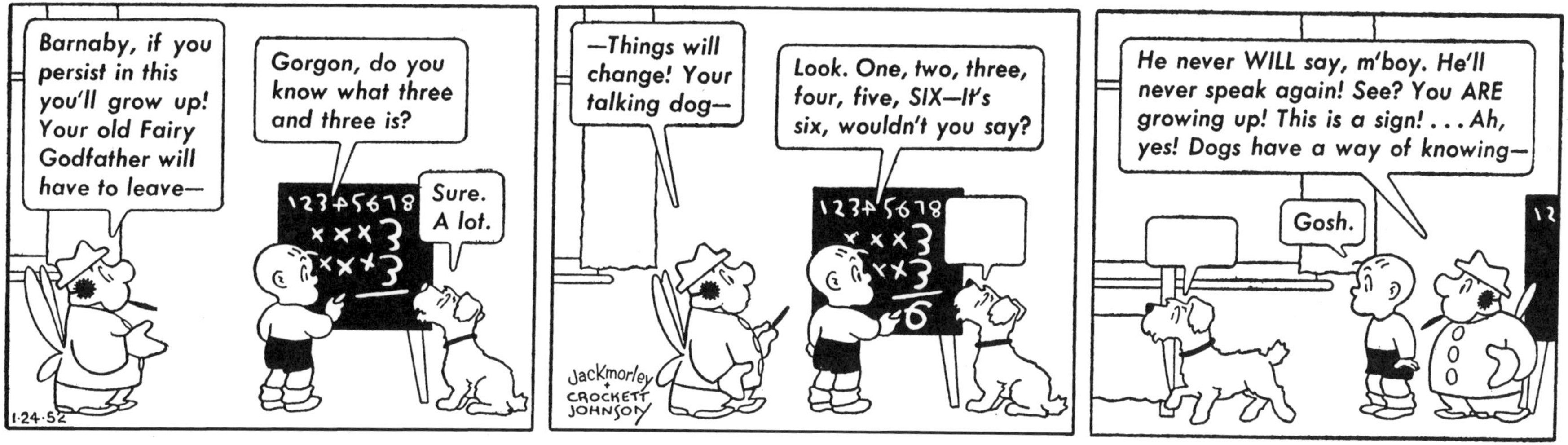
Barnaby, if you persist in this you'll grow up! Your old Fairy Godfather will have to leave—
Gorgon, do you know what three and three is?
Sure. A lot.
1·24·52
—Things will change! Your talking dog—
Look. One, two, three, four, five, SIX—It's six, wouldn't you say?
JACKMORLEY + CROCKETT JOHNSON
He never WILL say, m'boy. He'll never speak again! See? You ARE growing up! This is a sign! . . . Ah, yes! Dogs have a way of knowing—
Gosh.

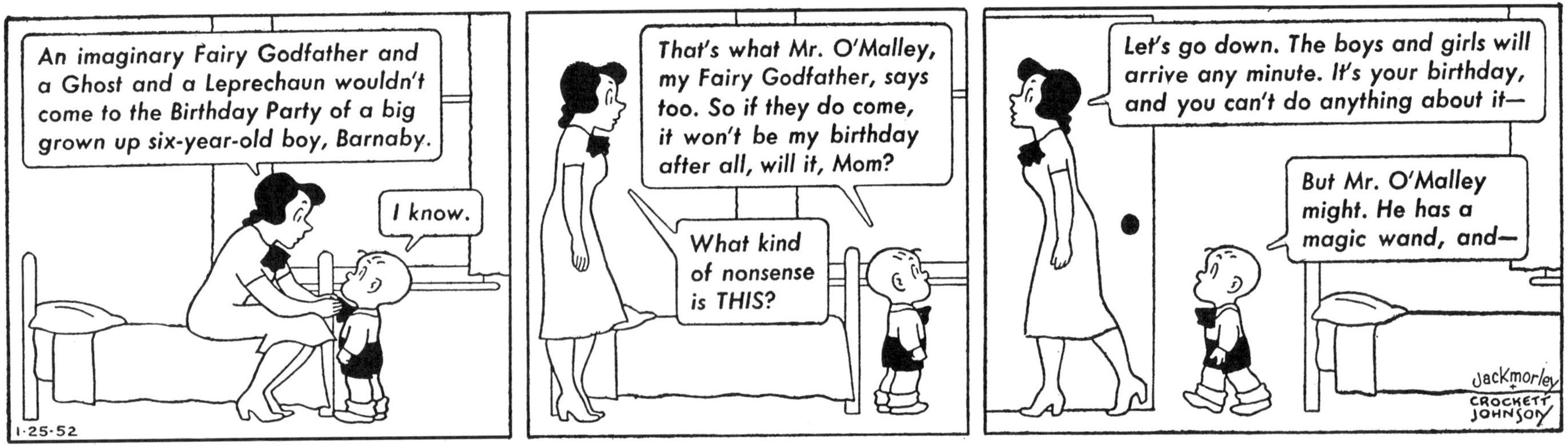
An imaginary Fairy Godfather and a Ghost and a Leprechaun wouldn't come to the Birthday Party of a big grown up six-year-old boy, Barnaby.
I know.
That's what Mr. O'Malley, my Fairy Godfather, says too. So if they do come, it won't be my birthday after all, will it, Mom?
What kind of nonsense is THIS?
Let's go down. The boys and girls will arrive any minute. It's your birthday, and you can't do anything about it—
But Mr. O'Malley might. He has a magic wand, and—
JackMorley + CROCKETT JOHNSON
1·25·52

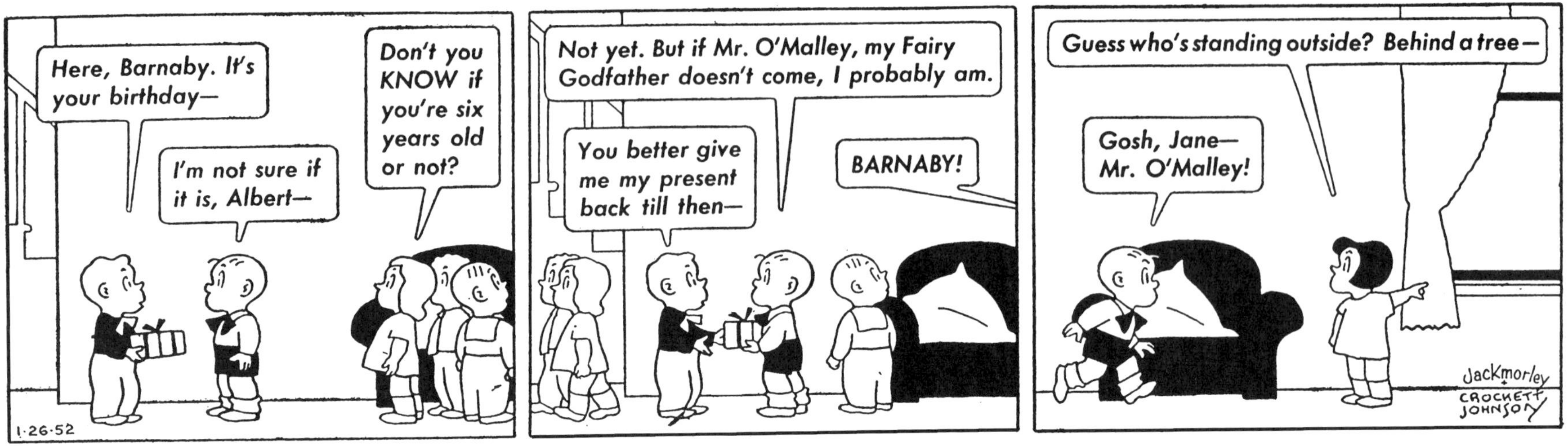
Here, Barnaby. It's your birthday—
I'm not sure if it is, Albert—
Don't you KNOW if you're six years old or not?
Not yet. But if Mr. O'Malley, my Fairy Godfather doesn't come, I probably am.
You better give me my present back till then—
BARNABY!
Guess who's standing outside? Behind a tree—
Gosh, Jane— Mr. O'Malley!
JackMorley + CROCKETT JOHNSON
1·26·52

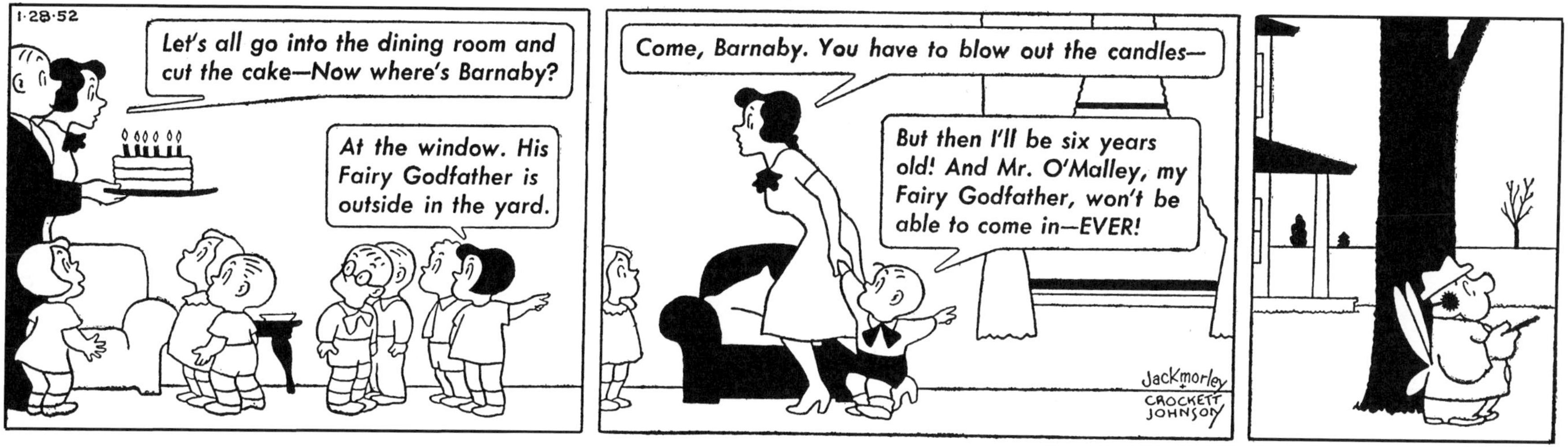
1·28·52
Let's all go into the dining room and cut the cake—Now where's Barnaby?
At the window. His Fairy Godfather is outside in the yard.
Come, Barnaby. You have to blow out the candles—
But then I'll be six years old! And Mr. O'Malley, my Fairy Godfather, won't be able to come in—EVER!
Jackmorley
CROCKETT JOHNSON

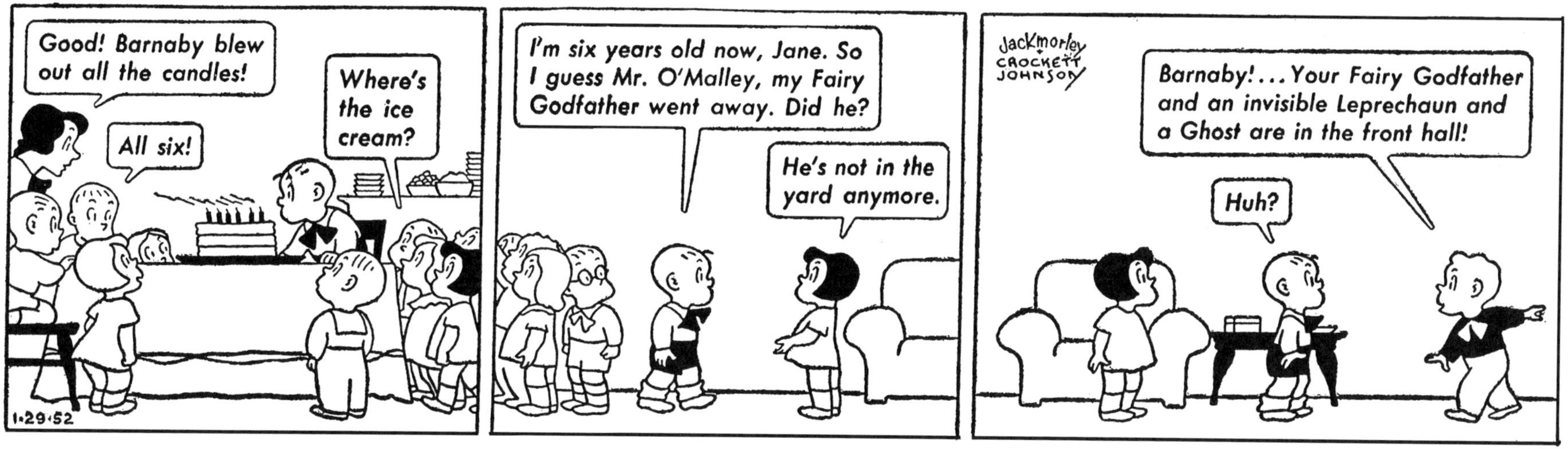
Good! Barnaby blew out all the candles!
All six!
Where's the ice cream?
1·29·52
I'm six years old now, Jane. So I guess Mr. O'Malley, my Fairy Godfather went away. Did he?
He's not in the yard anymore.
Jackmorley
CROCKETT JOHNSON
Barnaby!... Your Fairy Godfather and an invisible Leprechaun and a Ghost are in the front hall!
Huh?

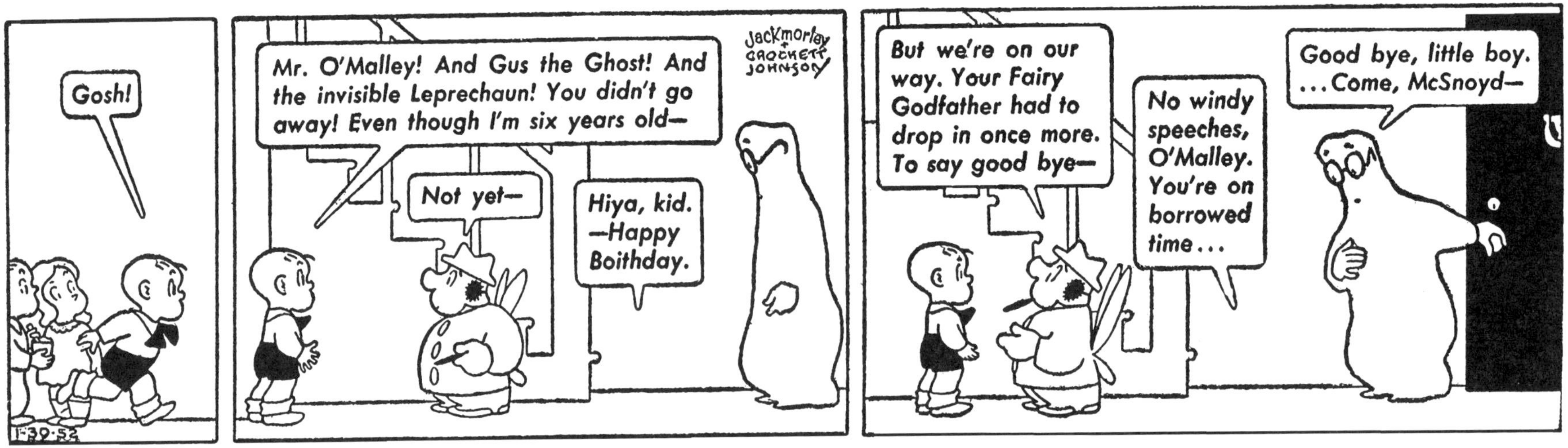
Gosh!
Mr. O'Malley! And Gus the Ghost! And the invisible Leprechaun! You didn't go away! Even though I'm six years old—
Not yet—
Hiya, kid. —Happy Boithday.
Jackmorley + Crockett Johnson
But we're on our way. Your Fairy Godfather had to drop in once more. To say good bye—
No windy speeches, O'Malley. You're on borrowed time...
Good bye, little boy. ...Come, McSnoyd—
1·30·52

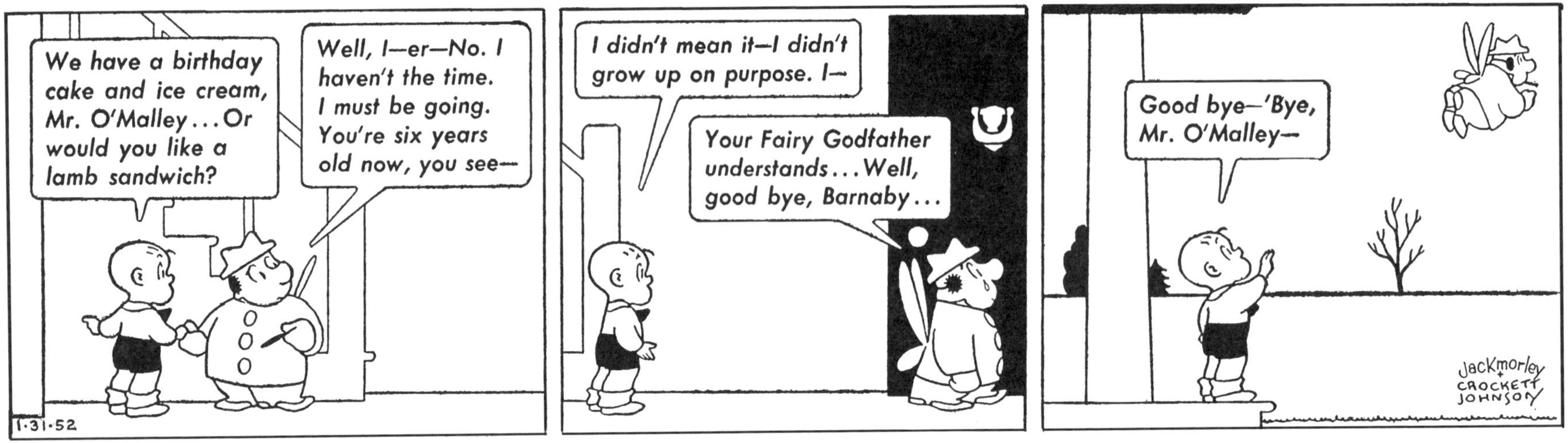
We have a birthday cake and ice cream, Mr. O'Malley...Or would you like a lamb sandwich?
Well, I—er—No. I haven't the time. I must be going. You're six years old now, you see—
1·31·52
I didn't mean it—I didn't grow up on purpose. I—
Your Fairy Godfather understands...Well, good bye, Barnaby...
Good bye—'Bye, Mr. O'Malley—
Jackmorley + Crockett Johnson

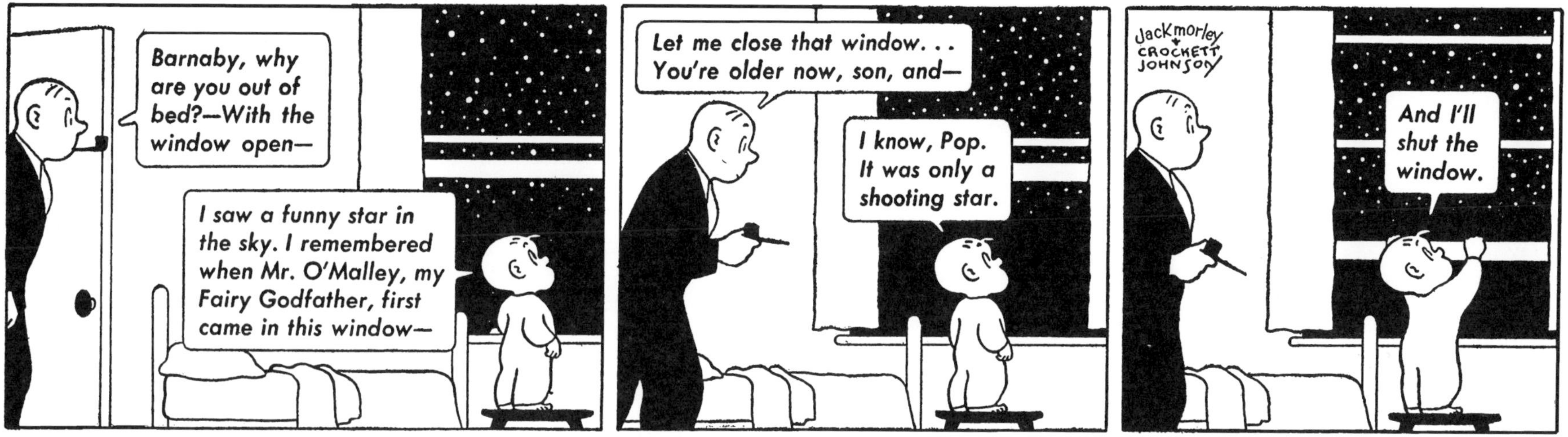

Barnaby, why are you out of bed?—With the window open—
I saw a funny star in the sky. I remembered when Mr. O'Malley, my Fairy Godfather, first came in this window—
Let me close that window. . . You're older now, son, and—
I know, Pop. It was only a shooting star.
JACKMORLEY + CROCKETT JOHNSON
And I'll shut the window.

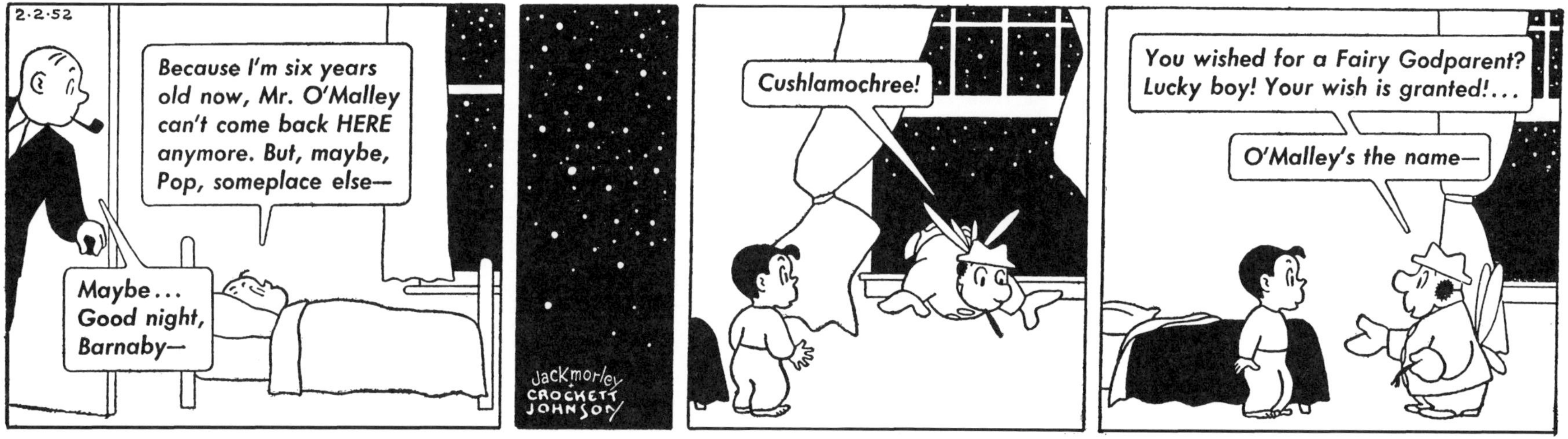

2·2·52
Because I'm six years old now, Mr. O'Malley can't come back HERE anymore. But, maybe, Pop, someplace else—
Maybe... Good night, Barnaby—
JACKMORLEY + CROCKETT JOHNSON
Cushlamochree!
You wished for a Fairy Godparent? Lucky boy! Your wish is granted!...
O'Malley's the name—

FANTASTIC COMPANIONS

By Crockett Johnson

I once did a comic strip about a small boy who was visited in his suburban home by an unlikely fairy godfather named Mr. O'Malley — a purely fictional creation. Almost from the start it brought me letters from parents telling me of astonishing creatures that visited *their* homes. These writers were not inventing. They were reporting fact.

Not only is there scientific verification of the existence of these fantastic "companions" — as the child-study books call them — but they exist in disturbingly vast numbers. Authorities estimate that half of our pre-school youngsters enjoy (if that is the word) the exclusive attentions of one or more of the monsters. In the United States alone, then, there must be over *ten million* of them going daily, about their odd affairs.

Despite their prevalence, shockingly little is known about them. Indeed, I have found nothing in the way of collated material on the species that compares with even my own casual collection of individual dossiers. Several of these are appended here, in the hope that they may help stimulate interest in a thorough and comprehensive fact-finding study.

MRS. BIRDFEATHER

In her playroom at Hicksville, New York, Glenda D. has been observing almost daily for six months a "Mrs. Birdfeather" energetically "making things." Glenda states that all the furnishings of the room are the work of Mrs. Birdfeather and that they were made with nothing but a needle and a bit of thread. "The thread is worsted thread," Glenda points out with a significance that so far has eluded investigators. Skeptical, naturally, when apprised of the fact that no other tools or raw materials were used in production, several qualified experts have examined carefully every article in the room. Admitting amazement, all have testified that the maple chairs and table, the metal bed, the plastic toys, and everything else is not only substantial but of perfectly sound quality. Glenda, the only member of the household who has studied Mrs. Birdfeather's method of work, describes it very simply. "She just makes things, that's all." Like most busy people, Mrs. Birdfeather talks very little. Because of this, almost nothing has been learned about the industrious creature's personal life except that she lives with her parents in a lovely house the family constructed together; that her mother, too, is known as Mrs. Birdfeather; and that her father also goes by the name of Mrs. Birdfeather.

THE GREAT YAFTY

"Yafty is the funniest thing I ever saw in my whole life," declares thirty-nine-months-old Walter P. from his Philadelphia home, where the comedian is being held over for his twelfth week. Walter's unequivocal statement is borne out by the gales of laughter that emanate from any room of the house in which the strolling player has happened to find Walter alone. Yafty prefers a very small audience, probably because his sensitive humor and delicate timing require an immediate sympathetic reception and complete rapport. "As soon as Yafty comes in I laugh at him," is the way Walter puts it. He describes the performer's physical appearance in a way that leaves nothing to be desired in a comic, "He looks funny." However, Yafty does not

rely on his appearance alone. He is hard-working and versatile. "He does every kind of funny thing," Walter testifies, with an encompassing gesture. Asked for an example of any kind from the talented mime's repertoire, Walter chuckles as his mind flicks back through Yafty's hilarious routines and he selects his favorite, the mere memory of which reduces him to a state of collapse. "Once Yafty put a flower pot on his head!" When he recovers enough to speak again, Walter adds, "Too bad you couldn't see him."

A MOUSE WHO WARNS PEOPLE

With Mary McH. in her home in Davenport, Iowa, lives a mouse whose apparent concern for the welfare of human beings makes him worthy of mention. "He's a good mouse because he goes around warning people about things," Mary says. Actually, Mary is the only person in the household he has succeeded in warning about anything, but this is understandable because the weak voice of a mouse does not carry far and "the bell he rings with his [evidently prehensile] tail" necessarily must be too small an instrument to raise vibrations to the ears of people who have grown over thirty-six months tall. The alarms of the mouse are sounded in fine dramatic fashion but his warnings, while undeniably sensible, are usually somewhat anti-climactic in nature. Also they are often oddly timed. Mary, breathlessly heeding the sudden clanging of the tiny bell at three o'clock of an afternoon, is likely to receive the news that "everybody should eat all of their breakfast!" The mouse has rushed out to exhort her, with an urgency that seems questionable in Iowa, to "watch out not to fall in the ocean because there's a big fish in it!" Another warning, and one that for a time led Mary's relatives toward the belief that the mouse was developing a kind of perverse humor, occurred one day just as Mary donned a freshly laundered frock with starched collar and cuffs. She flung herself on the floor, her customary position for listening to the zealous mouse's excited monitions, to hear that "people shouldn't get their clean dresses mussed!"

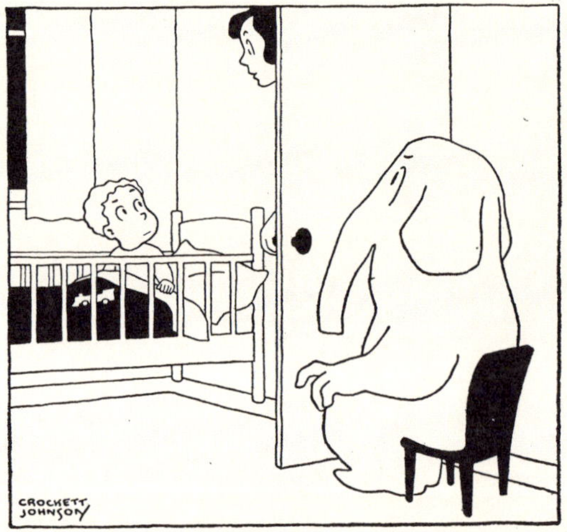
CROCKETT JOHNSON

GUMGAW WHO COMES TO CHAT

Gumgaw is a friend of Henry M. of New York City and he drops in at the twenty-nine-month-old host's nursery nearly every night at bedtime for no other reason than the pleasure of a good chat. Knowing Henry to be normally a person of few words, his relatives were puzzled one night a few months ago to hear what they believed to be his voice carrying on an animated and seemingly endless monologue in his room. Their confusion was cleared up when they learned about Gumgaw, who is "big, with a face like an elephant" and who "talks all the time" in a voice that surprisingly, considering his bulk, is pitched high enough to be mistaken through a closed door for Henry's own. Henry says, "He talks about everything!" Evidently he does, fascinatingly, sometimes till all hours. People have asked Henry why a raconteur of such genius is not given to making public appearances, envisioning sure-fire success for him on the dais at association banquets and perhaps in politics. The answer seems to lie in Gumgaw's shyness. Probably because of a deep self-consciousness about his unusual appearance he is ill at ease with strangers. An interruption even by a member of his friend Henry's immediate family will silence him in the middle of a sentence and, if indeed he does not leave at once, he is apt to sit quietly for some time after the withdrawal of the offending person, tapping his knee in annoyance, before resuming his discourse.

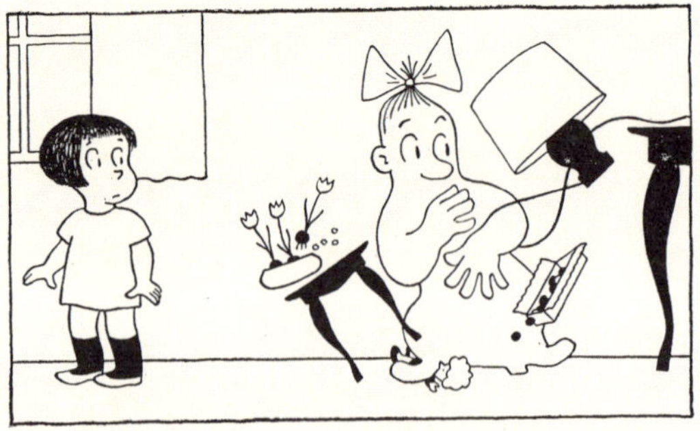

BIVVY WHO BREAKS THINGS

Bivvy, a frequent visitor at the residence of Mildred K. in Pasadena, California, is described as wearing "a beautiful big hair ribbon on top of her head," an effort at adornment that suggests an eagerness on Bivvy's part to make herself a charming and ornamental guest. But unfortunately her desire to please, as well as any other admirable qualities she may possess, is obscured by one serious social handicap. "Bivvy knocks things over and breaks things," says Mildred sadly. "But she can't help it and she's sorry." The sorry creature is "always very ashamed" too, as well she might be, judging by the mishaps that plague her. Once she reached daintily for a caramel on the library table, dropped the box and, in a laudably quick move to avert that calamity, pulled over a table lamp, backed into a taboret holding a bowl of tulip bulbs, and stepped on her hostess's newest doll. "Because she is so embarrassed" when that sort of thing happens, Bivvy flees immediately. This fact is attested to by other members of the household, who, no matter how quickly they arrive on the scene of disaster, find Bivvy gone and Mildred by herself amidst the debris. Rather reluctantly Mildred admits there seldom are any mitigating circumstances, that these recurring catastrophes must be attributed to her ill-starred friend's shocking ineptness, and that when they occur Mildred herself usually is "away over on the other side of the room."

BEARS WITH WOTS ON THEM

An unusual species of bear has been discovered in New Haven, Connecticut, by Michael S., a four-year-old resident, who is making a study of the pair of beasts. Understandably reluctant to have any conclusions drawn until he has all his data in hand, the young naturalist has released very little information about the animals to date. The picture below, therefore, does not pretend to photographic exactness and is in fact merely an "artist's conception" based on what few remarks Michael has made to neighbors and members of his own household about the "bears with wots on them." After wearily denying that "wots" are in any precise way like "spots" or "dots," Michael did say as he ended one particular interview, "The wots are on their fur, of course!" This leads to a reasonable speculation that the animals merely have markings on their coats that can be said to be somewhat more or less wot-shaped. Generally pleasant-tempered, the bears seem to make fairly good companions at games of the simpler sort. However, should any controversial situation arise, they are apt to turn ferocious without warning and at such times can be driven off only by having marbles rolled at them by a steady hand. Also, they speak a kind of basic English, but so poorly that the accomplishment, Michael has intimated, scarcely deserves attention.

Published in the June 1955 issue of Harper's Magazine.

Barnaby, if you persist in this you'll grow up! Your old Fairy Godfather will have to leave—

— Mr. O'Malley, 24 Jan. 1952

AFTERWORD:
The End?

By Philip Nel

Stories end.

But comics typically exist in a perpetual present. True, there are exceptions: characters grow older in Frank King's *Gasoline Alley*, Lynn Johnston's *For Better or for Worse*, Tom Batiuk's *Funky Winkerbean*, and Garry Trudeau's *Doonesbury*. However, comic-strip characters usually move through time without succumbing to its effects. Days pass and seasons change. But the characters remain as they have always been.

That was true of *Barnaby* until its final month. From April 20, 1942 to January 2, 1952, Barnaby was always 5 years old. On January 3, 1952, Mr. Baxter tells his son that Mr. O'Malley "is going away" because "You'll be six soon. You're going to start school" and "big boys don't have imaginary Fairy Godfathers, do they?" Since O'Malley has foiled Mr. Baxter's previous attempts to expel him from the household, readers might at first wonder *How will O'Malley prevail this time?* However, within the next month (or a few days, within the internal timeline of the strip itself), O'Malley will learn that he cannot defeat time. And readers will discover that Crockett Johnson has made the highly unusual choice of writing a narrative conclusion to *Barnaby*.

> Made your big decision yet, m'boy?
>
> — Mr. O'Malley, 22 Jan. 1952

Why did Johnson end the strip? In a February 1952 letter to Johnson, journalist Charles Fisher (who had profiled Johnson back in November 1943) lamented *Barnaby*'s conclusion: "I don't know what the hell is wrong with a world where Barnaby had to go down the spout." He continued, "What Barnaby is going to do without Mr. O'Malley, I don't know. I don't know what I'm going to do without him either, the old bum. I felt sad as a son of a bitch to see him fly away."

Offering his most complete answer to the question of why he concluded *Barnaby*, Johnson responded immediately and candidly, citing three reasons for why he "had to let the strip go." First, he notes that "I think the last year or so hit a peak for quality but sales continued to slough off steadily." At the height of its popularity, *Barnaby* was syndicated in 52 newspapers — which, to put that in

Philadelphia · New York · Chicago · Detroit
Boston · San Francisco · Hollywood · Honolulu

N·W·AYER & SON INC.

West Washington Square, Philadelphia 6

February 5th

Dear Dave:

I don't know what the hell is wrong with a world
where Barnaby had to go down the spout. Anyway, the almost-last
sequence about the dog from outer space was magnificent and showed
that there wasn't any diminuition in your and Mr. Morley's
inventiveness.

What Barnaby is going to do without Mr. O'Malley,
I don't know. I don't know what I'm going to do without him
either, the old bum. I felt sad as a son of a bitch to see him
fly away. He took so much charm with him, and there's so little
of it around. And Barnaby, the poor little bugger, growing up and
probably winding up in the advertising business...

The hell with it. That strip was a very important
piece of work. Perhaps you remember that I wrote about it in the
dead Record years ago, when it was new. I stayed with it with
reasonable consistency. Today when I called the Inquirer to get
Bell's address, without giving my name, I said I was sorry to
see Barnaby go and the girl on the 'phone said sadly "We all were,
too," and seemed to mean it.

best regards

Charlie Fisher

CROCKETT JOHNSON
74 ROWAYTON AVENUE, ROWAYTON, CONN.

February 11, 1952

Dear Charlie,

It was very nice to hear from you. I have wondered about
you and what you were doing. Things would be better in every way
if your column was appearing daily in newspapers from coast to
coast. But the press seems to have come full cycle from the days
when Thomas Jefferson said the only believable items in newspapers
were their advertisements. A grownup Barnaby is better off in an
agency than a city room at the moment. Speaking of agencies, I
have the feeling that Ayer is an exceptionally civilized outfit of
its kind; in my dealings there from time to time I have experienced
a high degree of decency and personal consideration.

I had to let the strip go. I think the last year or so hit
a peak for quality but sales continued to slough off steadily. I
decided that while I continued writing it I would never be able
to start anything else. Now I have to. However, before I get it
out of my hair altogether, I think I will put the basic story and
most of the better sequences in text form in a book. There also
is some interest in it as a television series and I am going through
the necessary motions toward that end for a west coast producing
organization. By the way, the last strip was somewhat better than
it appeared in the Inquirer (where it was changed so "that we would
not be deluged with letters and calls," as E.B.Thompson, perhaps a
bit too sanguinely, thought they might be). On the chance that you
saw it in no other paper I am enclosing a release proof.

Maybe we can get together again sometime. If business ever
brings you to New York, I am only an hour away. Meanwhile, thanks
for the charming letter and for your appreciation and great help in
the past.

Sincerely,

Dave

1. *Letter from Charles Fisher to Crockett Johnson, 5 Feb. 1952. Image courtesy of the Smithsonian Institution.*

2. *Letter from Crockett Johnson to Charles Fisher, 11 Feb. 1952. Image courtesy of Christopher Wheeler.*

context, is but 1/17th of the circulation of a massively popular strip like *Blondie*. I don't know its precise circulation in December 1951, when Johnson announced his decision to end *Barnaby*. But when he saw its circulation declining from small to smaller, Johnson likely realized that if he did not end the strip soon, then he might not be able to do so on his own terms.

Second, Johnson explains, "I decided that while I continued writing it I would never be able to start anything else." Then 45 years old, he was doubtless more conscious of the tension between his many interests and the diminishing time left to explore them. He was already considering three other professions, one of which was creating books for children. In the 1940s, he illustrated two children's books, and the author of one of those books — his wife Ruth Krauss — often sought his advice on hers. By the summer of 1951, 23-year-old Maurice Sendak was spending weekends at the Johnson-Krauss home, in Rowayton, Connecticut. Together, he and Krauss were working on *A Hole Is to Dig*, the success of which would allow Sendak to leave his job as window-display artist for FAO Schwarz, and become a full-time illustrator of books for children. As Sendak recalled, Johnson "would referee" the arguments between writer and artist, and offer suggestions on book design: "His name should be on all our books for the technical savvy and cool consideration he brought to them" (qtd. in Nel, *Crockett Johnson and Ruth Krauss*, p. 124).

In 1951, Johnson created his first book as both author and artist — *Who's Upside Down?*, published the following year. A kangaroo picks up a book titled *MAPS*, sees an illustration depicting two children standing on "top" of the globe in North America and a kangaroo standing on the "bottom" of the globe in Australia. Unable to read, she feels upside down. Assisted by her little kangaroo, she learns that she is not. And children learn about gravity. In the next fourteen years, Johnson would create another eighteen children's books, and co-create (usually as artist) six children's books.

In 1951 and 1952, Johnson was also inventing a four-way adjustable mattress. Inspired by Krauss's intermittent back trouble and his own poor nights' sleep on soft mattresses (especially when traveling), Johnson designed a mattress with

3

Who's Upside Down?
by Crockett Johnson
by Crockett Johnson
Who's Upside Down?

4

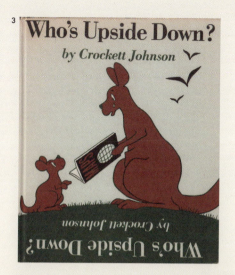

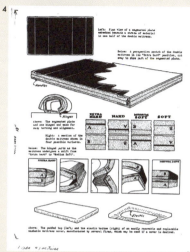

adjustable firmness. He submitted a patent application in 1952, received a patent in 1955, and in 1956 met with hotel magnate Conrad Hilton to see if he might want to purchase it for his chain of hotels. Though his attempts to market this idea would fail, it was a live option in 1951.

Johnson's other possible future was a return to advertising work. In the 1940s, Johnson used his earlier strip "The Little Man with the Eyes" as the basis of a well-regarded campaign for Ford. He also created political ads supporting unions, President Roosevelt's 1944 re-election campaign, and national health insurance. Johnson may allude to the possibility of designing ads when — referring to the fact that Fisher has left journalism for advertising — he says "the press seems to

3. *Crockett Johnson, cover of Who's Upside Down? (William R. Scott, 1952). Image courtesy of Philip Nel.*

4. *Crockett Johnson, diagram from patent #2,721,339 (for 4-way adjustable mattress), granted 25 Oct 1955.*

5

(Advertisement)

CROCKETT JOHNSON

"Have you considered using Kimberly-Clark coated papers?"

Kimberly-Clark Enamels and Coated Printing Papers add crisp freshness and sparkling new eye-appeal to reports, advertising pieces, brochures and house organs — often at remarkable savings in cost. Today—ask your buyer or printer to see new Hifect* Enamel, Trufect*, Lithofect* Offset Enamel and Multifect*—and compare them with the paper he is now using.

have come full circle from the days when Thomas Jefferson said the only believable items in newspapers were their advertisements. A grown-up Barnaby is better off in an agency than in a city room at the moment."

The third reason for ending the strip that Johnson cites is (paradoxically?) ongoing interest in *Barnaby* itself. He proposes putting "the basic story and some of the better sequences in text form in a book" — a project that he would work on and ultimately abandon later in the decade. He also mentions interest in *Barnaby* "as a television series" via a "west coast producing organization." That would result in the most successful adaptation of his comic strip to date.

Five days before Christmas 1959, CBS' *General Electric Theater* aired the full-color pilot episode "as a special Christmas presentation." Introduced by Ronald Reagan as "a magical story based on the cartoons and books by Crockett Johnson," the half-hour show starred Bert Lahr (aka the Cowardly Lion in *The Wizard of Oz*) as Mr. O'Malley, 5-year-old Ronny Howard as Barnaby, and Mel Blanc as the voice of McSnoyd. (As Howard recounts in his foreword to this volume, meeting the voice of Bugs Bunny and Daffy Duck was a highlight for him.) The broadcast received

excellent reviews, with *Variety* predicting that Howard's agent would find his phone ringing "with enough offers to keep him busy until next Yule time." *Variety* was right. In 1960, Howard won the role that launched his career: Opie Taylor on the *Andy Griffith Show*. But no other episodes of this *Barnaby* TV program were made.

> *I recall saying that varmint, O'Malley, would stand watching, didn't I? . . . Form a posse!*
>
> — Tennessee Hennessey, 17 May 1951

A possible cause for *Barnaby*'s conclusion not mentioned by Johnson is his rising profile as a suspected Communist. In April 1950, the FBI identified Johnson as a "concealed Communist" and opened a file on him. The agency began monitoring his bank account and noting the names of anyone who phoned or corresponded with him. That August, when one agent knocked on his front door, Johnson opened it and chatted, while a second agent covertly took his photograph. In April 1951, the second HUAC report to name Johnson cited him a half-dozen times — a fact picked up by local newspapers. In the early 1950s, it was even rumored that, if Johnson and Krauss held a party, the FBI would be outside writing down the license plate numbers of those attending.

Though these allegations against him were public, Crockett Johnson was not on any official blacklist that I know of. (He is not named in *Red Channels*, for example.) As Julia Mickenberg has documented, many on the political left found

5. *Crockett Johnson, advertisement for Kimberly-Clark, 1953.*

6. *First page of FBI file for David Johnson Leisk. Image courtesy of Freedom of Information Act and the Federal Bureau of Investigation.*

7. *Another page of FBI file for David Johnson Leisk. Image courtesy of Freedom of Information Act and the Federal Bureau of Investigation.*

6

STANDARD FORM NO. 64

Office Memorandum • UNITED STATES GOVERNMENT

TO : DIRECTOR, FBI DATE: June 2, 1950

FROM : SAC, NEW HAVEN

SUBJECT: DAVID JOHNSON LEISK alias Crockett Johnson
SECURITY MATTER - C

For the information of the Bureau, by letter dated May 8, 1950, the New York Division advised that on April 21, 1950, [redacted] reported that CROCKETT JOHNSON is one of "400 concealed Communists".

b7D

Subject JOHNSON is a cartoonist who is presently residing with his wife at 74 Rowayton Avenue, Rowayton, Connecticut. The Darien and Norwalk, Connecticut, voting records indicate that subject's correct name is DAVID JOHNSON LEISK. Subject's wife, RUTH I. KRAUSS LEISK, reportedly writes children's books under the name of RUTH KRAUSS.

The New Haven indices contain numerous references to subject under his pen name relating to subject's association with the ICCASP in Connecticut. Subject reportedly is a former editor of the "New Masses" and is the creator of a cartoon strip entitled "Barnaby" which is now written by JACK MORLEY.

The New York Division is requested to furnish the New Haven office in report form any information contained in the New York files relating to subject.

2 cc New York

100-12659
FXM/clb

ALL INFORMATION CONTAINED
HEREIN IS UNCLASSIFIED
DATE 10-13-2004 BY 60290AUC/BCE/DG/CE

RECORDED - 84
INDEXED - 84

100-369616

EX-32

52 JUN 14 1950

7

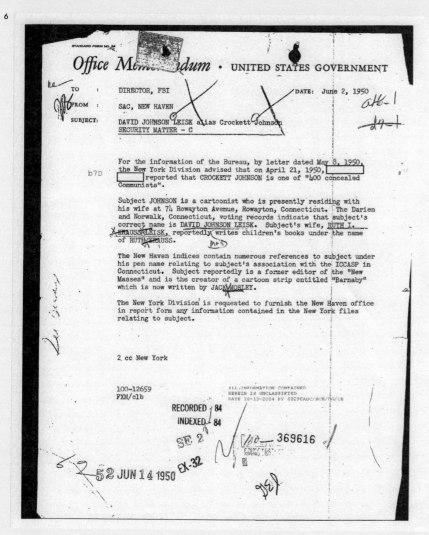

NH 100-12659

for the Defense of Peace, World Peace Congress, was held in Paris, France, from April 20 through April 25, 1949.

Informants [redacted] and [redacted] have pointed out that the above mentioned Congress was organized as part of a world wide Communist inspired "peace" propaganda campaign and that the "peace" movement originated in the Executive Committee of the Cominform.

b2

b7D

Confidential Informant [redacted] identified subject CROCKETT JOHNSON of South Norwalk, Connecticut, as one of the many prominent Americans endorsing the World Peace Appeal.

The following is a description of the subject as obtained by observation, supplemented by information obtained from the records of the identification section of the FBI:

Name and alias:	DAVID JOHNSON LEISK, wa CROCKETT JOHNSON
Born:	October 20, 1906
Place:	New York City
Height:	5'11
Weight:	220
Eyes:	Blue
Hair:	Dark brown, center bald spot, receding forehead
Build:	Heavy
Complexion:	Fair
Race:	White
Sex:	Male
Scars:	Mole on left thigh
Occupation:	Cartoonist and writer
Marital Status:	Married
Wife:	RUTH I. KRAUSS LEISK
Residence:	74 Rowayton Avenue, Rowayton, Conn.
Characteristics:	Round, chubby face
Glasses:	Wears glasses for reading and working
FBI No:	526 198 A

Under date of October 12, 1950, the following identification record relating to subject was received from the files of the FBI:

-2-

work as children's authors or illustrators because anti-Communist zealots deemed children's books — most of which were written by women — less important, and so did not monitor the field closely.

But, as Johnson well knew, blacklisting can also operate more stealthily. He and Krauss lived in Rowayton, the section of Norwalk adjacent to Village Creek, a planned, fully integrated community. They had many friends there, and — had it been established a few years earlier — may well have moved there themselves. Suspicious Norwalk residents called it "Commie Creek," claiming that the houses' modern roofs, viewed from above, were designed to lead Soviet bombers directly to New York City. Norma Simon — a friend of both Johnson and Krauss — established Village Creek's Community Cooperative Nursery School, which local conservatives dubbed "the Little Red Schoolhouse." Simon, whose first children's book was published in 1954, soon discovered that her association with the Little Red Schoolhouse led to an unofficial blacklist: a PTA would invite her to speak, discover that she was director of the school, and, instead of accusing her directly, would then phone up to say, sorry, but the meeting had been cancelled, no need to come.

Since blacklisting does not require an actual list of names, it is impossible to prove or to disprove that blacklisting prompted newspapers to drop *Barnaby*. That said, Johnson likely wondered whether he would become a target. He was a former art editor for the weekly Communist magazine *New Masses*. It didn't matter that he left the publication over a decade earlier. Nor that he was not a member of the Communist Party. In the 1940s, he had publicly advocated for racial justice, championed workers' rights, and campaigned for Progressive Party candidates — all causes that made him suspect in the eyes of Red-hunters. As noted in the Afterword to *Barnaby Volume Four*, the U.S. government was then targeting people Johnson supported or knew personally, and had succeeded in jailing several.

Suggesting that anti-Communist persecution may have curtailed Johnson's satirical impulses, *Barnaby* in 1950–1952 makes only a very few allusions to the FBI, HUAC, and Senator McCarthy. In contrast, *Barnaby* in 1943 actively mocks the Dies Committee (as HUAC was then known) for a full month. In the early 1950s,

when McCarthyism was in the ascendant, the strip avoids sustained satire of the national hysteria surrounding alleged Reds. True, Johnson might be challenging the credibility of the FBI in the May 1950 strip where O'Malley's "G-man badge" is a novelty item won by sending in breakfast-cereal box-tops. Or he may just be inviting laughter at O'Malley's attempt to use a toy as a badge. The object of satire is ambiguous. In counting those who are invisible to most adults, O'Malley's pixie census (the reason he's wearing that badge) does resonate thematically with a paranoid way of seeing. But readers know that these pixies *are* real; they're not mere projections of a paranoiac. The object of this satire is ambiguous, too.

In its final two years, *Barnaby* comes closest to mocking McCarthyism and affiliated activities when it lampoons the authoritarian mindset of TV cowboy Tennessee Hennessey and his number-one fan, Albert. On May 9, when Hennessey says of O'Malley that "a critter that don't aim to be a Tennessee Hennessey deputy, pardner, might stand a teeny bit of watching," his claim shares the illogic of anti-Communists who allege that if you don't join their crusade, then you should be under surveillance yourself. On May 19, Hennessey deploys the same fallacious reasoning when he says "If O'Malley is such a law-abiding citizen, why is he hiding in that woods from a peace-loving posse?" Exemplifying the authoritarian disposition of McCarthy's followers, *Barnaby*'s friend Albert has been ready to join the posse since at least May 9, when he proclaims: "I'm for law and order. Who do we shoot first?" But these moments are as near as Johnson gets to spoofing the "patriotic" paranoia of the early 1950s.

His relative reticence on this subject is especially notable in light of his much bolder satire, in the February–March 1950 storyline, of right-wing charlatans who simultaneously want to exploit labor and (falsely) insist that capitalist managers could run things better. This culminates in the strip's stand-off between management and labor in March 1950, and O'Malley's apparent advocacy for a general strike. As O'Malley says on March 13, "This strike is more than a mere struggle between management and labor — It becomes a national emergency when the public begins to suffer." But, then, Johnson dreamed up these strips before McCarthy's demagoguery had gone mainstream — the Wisconsin Senator gave his first speeches alleging Communist infiltration of the State Department in February 1950.

Whether wary of persecution, weary of writing the strip, or simply eager to pursue other ventures, Johnson in 1951 announced the end of *Barnaby*. Rather than merely stop, he devised a final episode which offers an unequivocal conclusion to the story of Barnaby and Mr. O'Malley.

> *O'MALLEY'S LAST STAND!*
>
> — McSnoyd, 17 Jan. 1952

As Frank Kermode's *The Sense of an Ending* points out, "In a novel the beginning implies the end" (p. 148). But the same is not true of a comic strip.

Narrative conclusions to newspaper strips are rare.

These comics may cease publication due to a decline in popularity, or the retirement (or death) of the creator. Often, though, when a creator of a strip departs, other writers step in, creating new material — and generating income for themselves, the syndicate, and the creator (or the estate).

There are a few exceptions, each significantly different from *Barnaby*.

Focusing on those few, here is *Barnaby*'s location in an admittedly speculative, idiosyncratic map of American newspaper comic-strip endings. (If a unified field theory of comic-strip finales is not of interest, feel free to skip ahead to the next section.) When concluding a mainstream newspaper strip, its creator typically offers at least one of these four concluding gestures: (1) delivering meta-commentary on the medium of comics, (2) launching a new strip from the old one, (3) noting that the characters' adventures continue unchronicled, or (4) announcing the death or retirement of the creator.

In the early twentieth-century, Sydney Smith and Milt Gross each end a strip by ejecting its characters and introducing the successor strip. Offering sly commentary on the fungibility of the comics, Sydney Smith has a landlord evict the title character of his *Old Doc Yak* (1912–1917), making explicit reference to the newspaper page on which it is printed. In a Monday 1917 strip, addressing Old Doc Yak's son, the landlord says, "I want you to tell that father of yours if he doesn't pay the rent for this space by Saturday I'm gonna throw you both off this page." The next day, the landlord returns to say that "The advertising rates are too steep and the price of white paper is too high to let you stay here if you don't come through." Old Doc Yak — an anthropomorphic yak who is a cosmetic surgeon — fails to raise the money by week's end. On Monday, the Gump family move into the same house vacated by Yak and his son Yutch, and Smith's new strip *The Gumps* begins. When, two years later, Smith ends the Sunday *Old Doc Yak* to replace it with a Sunday *Gumps*, Old Doc Yak sells his car to Andy Gump.

But that isn't quite the end of *Old Doc Yak*. In December 1930, Smith revives the strip at the bottom of each *Gumps* Sunday page. It continues there until his death in 1935.

Offering his take on the comic-strip switcheroo, Milt Gross ends *Hitz and Mrs* (1923) when he begins adding a new concluding panel that comments upon the preceding ones. He initially uses the word "Applesauce!" — then a common

8

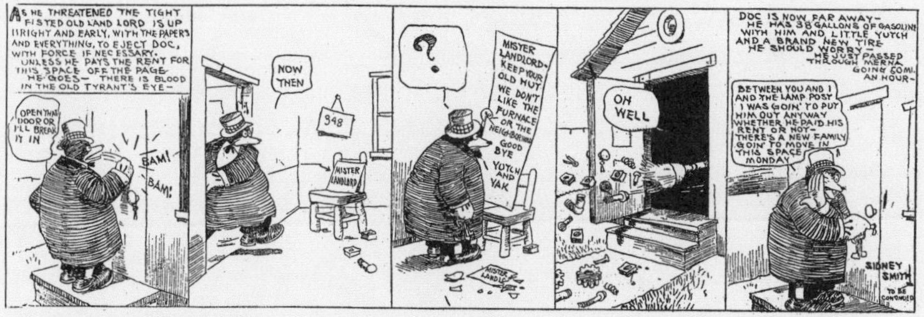

AS HE THREATENED THE TIGHT FISTED OLD LAND LORD IS UP BRIGHT AND EARLY, WITH THE PAPERS AND EVERYTHING, TO EJECT DOC, WITH FORCE IF NECESSARY. UNLESS HE PAYS THE RENT FOR THIS SPACE OFF THE PAGE HE GOES— THERE IS BLOOD IN THE OLD TYRANT'S EYE—
OPEN THAT DOOR OR I'LL BREAK IT IN
BAM!
BAM!
NOW THEN
948
MISTER LANDLORD
?
MISYER LANDLORD- KEEP YOUR OLD HUT WE DON'T LIKE THE FURNACE OR THE NEIGHBORHOOD GOOD BYE YUTCH AND YAK
OH WELL
DOC IS NOW FAR AWAY— HE HAS 38 GALLONS OF GASOLINE WITH HIM AND LITTLE YUTCH AND A BRAND NEW TIRE HE SHOULD WORRY— HE JUST PASSED THROUGH MERNA GOING 50 MI. AN HOUR—
BETWEEN YOU AND I AND THE LAMP POST I WAS GOIN' TO PUT HIM OUT ANYWAY WHETHER HE PAID HIS RENT OR NOT— THERE'S A NEW FAMILY GOIN' TO MOVE IN THIS SPACE MONDAY
SIDNEY SMITH
TO BE CONTINUED

8. *Sidney Smith, final daily* Old Doc Yak *strip, 1919. Image courtesy of* The Smithsonian Collection of Newspaper Comics, *edited by Bill Blackbeard and Martin Williams (Abrams, 1977).*

expression of incredulity. But by November 1923, he is adding a phrase of his own invention: "Banana Oil!" As comics scholar Allan Holtz writes, each day of the final week (December 1923) of *Hitz and Mrs*, "Mr. Hitz keeps getting handed a piece of paper that says 'Banana Oil' on it." The recurrence of this phrase proved too much for the title characters. To quote comics creator and scholar Mark Newgarden, "Hitz and Mrs were literally driven from their own strip (if not bananas) by the vexing catchphrase, which finally replaced the couple's antics in January 1924 and became Gross's first true hit" (7). As Smith had done with *Old Doc Yak*, Gross used the end of *Hitz and Mrs* to launch a newer, more successful strip — *Banana Oil* (1924–1925). Though the ending of *Barnaby* shares the finality of both *Hitz and Mrs* and the original run of *Old Doc Yak* (in each case, the title characters' stories are over), Johnson offers a much more fully developed narrative, lingering in the emotional consequences for his characters.

In its 1989 absurdist and ambivalent "ending," Berke Breathed's *Bloom County* leans into its gonzo conclusion, offers meta-humor on the medium, and promises that its characters live on — in other comic strips. Killed by his yacht's anchor, Donald Trump survives via transplanting his brain into Bill the Cat's body. Bill the Cat/Trump moves to Bloom County, gradually regains power, buys the *Bloom County* strip, and fires all the characters. All seek work in other comic strips, except for Ronald-Ann and Opus. In the strip's final days, both step into Outland. But the story doesn't quite end because Breathed brings many Bloom County denizens back in his sequel strips *Outland* (1989–1995) and *Opus* (2003–2008), as well as in his revival of *Bloom County* (2015–). In each, he creates new stories for his characters. In contrast, Johnson's 1960–1962 revival of *Barnaby* — inspired by the success of the 1959 TV pilot — updates old plotlines and has new art by Warren Sattler. The Hot Coffee Ring of 1943 becomes the Credit Card Ring of 1961. The revised *Barnaby* concludes with the same 1952 ending because the story really ended in 1952; the 1960s *Barnaby* was a re-run, not a continuation. Johnson's imaginative investment in *Barnaby* mostly ends in 1952. Breathed, on the other hand, keeps returning to the Bloom County multiverse.

9

IT'S OVER ? FINI ?
I FEEL POSITIVELY NAUSEOUS.
SOMEONE BOUGHT US ?... LIKE A PIECE OF JUNK REAL ESTATE ?!
WHAT EVIL BONEHEAD DORK IS BEHIND THIS ?!
TRUMP THE STRI
GUESS WHAT, EVERY-BODY ?...
7-14
YOU ALL WILL BE HAPPY TO KNOW THAT "TRUMP, THE STRIP" WILL REMAIN THE SAME AS "BLOOM COUNTY"...
..EXCEPT THE CHARACTERS. I'VE FIRED THEM ALL.
ESPECIALLY THE LITTLE FAT-NOSED TOAD THING—.
SPLAT!
TRUMP PASTED IN PUSS WITH PIE
SHORT, AGITATED MAN WITH FLARING NOSTRILS ARRESTED
Today, a short, toad-like man attacked billionaire comic-strip developer Donald Trump
7-15

Both conveying continuity and suggesting denouement, Bill Watterson's ending for *Calvin and Hobbes* is more subtle than *Barnaby*, *Bloom County*, *Hitz and Mrs*, and *Old Doc Yak*. On November 9, 1995, Watterson announced that he would stop drawing *Calvin and Hobbes*. For the final seven weeks of *Calvin and Hobbes*, readers' knowledge of the ending might have supplied some anticipatory melancholy to Calvin's reminiscences on photos of himself at ages 2 and 3 (in the strips of November 17–18). However, unlike Johnson, Watterson does not otherwise create a clear end. Calvin does not grow up. Hobbes does not become a mere stuffed tiger.

9. *Berkeley Breathed,* Bloom County *strips of 14 and 15 July 1989. (These strips begin the narrative that ends on 5 August 1989.) Image courtesy of Breathed's* The Real Classy Complete Bloom County 1980-1989 *(IDW Publishing, 2017).*

Watterson's final Sunday strip both is a beautiful finale and refuses the finality of a definitive conclusion. Carrying a sled under his arm, Hobbes says the snow-covered landscape is "like having a big white sheet of paper to draw on," and Calvin agrees that the day is "full of possibilities!" Only Calvin, Hobbes, and the sled are in color; the rest is in black-and-white. In an understated gesture to the medium, Hobbes' comparison and the whiteness of the page alludes to blank sheets upon which Watterson will no longer draw an imaginative boy and his tiger pal. The strip is ending. But the scene also hews closely to the strip's central themes of creativity and wonder, and (if readers did not know better) could be just another Sunday *Calvin and Hobbes* strip. In the penultimate panel, Calvin tells Hobbes, "It's a magical world, ol' buddy," and, sledding off to the right edge of the final panel, adds, "Let's go exploring!" Its open-endedness affirms comics' perpetual present. That's the last new *Calvin and Hobbes*, but their adventures continue, even though Watterson has stopped chronicling them. We might imagine these new stories ourselves, or go back to the strip's beginning and savor the pleasures of re-reading and remembering.

Before Lynn Johnston's *For Better or for Worse* slips into its "remembering" mode and ultimately into reruns, in August 2008 it presents a fully developed narrative conclusion that — in its detail and specific references to the story's end — is closer to the conclusion of Johnson's *Barnaby*. Given that Johnston's characters age in almost-real time, her ending aptly includes three major life events. Marriage is its central focus, but the possibility of death figures prominently, and birth appears in the final strip. On Monday the 25th, Elizabeth Patterson — who first appeared in the strip as a toddler nearly three decades earlier — marries Anthony Caine, a high-school boyfriend she resumed dating the year before. Realizing that her Grandpa Jim was too ill to attend, Elizabeth and her new husband drive straight from the ceremony to the hospital, visiting him in the strips of the 27th through the 30th. The final character to speak in the daily strip, Iris — Grandpa Jim's wife — concludes her affirmation of marriage with "For better or for worse, my dears... for better or for worse." At strip's bottom, Lynn Johnston announces: "This concludes my story — with grateful thanks to everyone who has made this all possible." The following day, in the final Sunday strip, Johnston writes a longer epilogue, giving glimpses into the futures of many characters, including this: "Grandpa Jim lived to welcome Anthony and Elizabeth's first child, James Allen. Jim passed away at the age of 89, with his wife, Iris, at his side."

Though her epilogue does offer a very traditional ending, Johnston also rejects endings as artificial, and states what *Calvin and Hobbes'* last strip merely implies: the characters' lives go on even when their creator stops drawing them. In the penultimate panel of her final strip, Johnston writes, "The extended families, friends and acquaintances of the Pattersons continue to live and grow, love and laugh and experience life as we do... as if part of a complex novel, whose pages are carefully crafted and then turned by another hand." In the final panel, Johnston draws herself at her drawing board, offers a thank-you, and announces that she will re-draw the strip from the beginning, updating it as she goes. Ultimately, however, she did not become the comics' Henry James (who, in later life, issued a 24-volume revised edition of most of his fiction) or Taylor Swift (who, in 2021, began releasing re-recordings of her first six albums, to gain ownership of the masters). Instead, Johnston revised 22 months of *For Better or for Worse* and in July 2010 the strip shifted into straight reruns.

Milt Caniff's *Steve Canyon* and Charles M. Schulz's *Peanuts* also pursue the announcement route, and not via storytelling (as *Barnaby* and *For Better or For Worse* do). In April 1988, after Caniff died, his assistants — artist Dick Rockwell and letterer Shel Dorf — wrapped up the current story, but offered no indication of it being the final *Steve Canyon* tale. Canyon does not retire, die, or change profession. Posing as a researcher updating a "book on the U.S. in the Persian Gulf Command in WWII (while actually looking for Soviet missile bases)," Steve helps rescue a group of "outcast children" (whose grandfathers were American G.I.s) and a Belgian hostage. The last plot-driven strip finds the entire group going onboard a U.S. navy ship, en route to safety. Then, two additional concluding strips make clear that the comic strip has ended. For the final daily, Rockwell included one of Caniff's self-portraits, followed by his dates, and a prose tribute to his boss. The next day is a Bill Mauldin panel in which his everyman soldier character Willie plants a rifle-sized pen, nib-end down, in the ground. Standing nearby and wearing a helmet labeled "Canyon," Steve Canyon places a helmet labeled "Caniff" atop the pen. 78 admirers (most of them cartoonists) signed the page, including G.B. Trudeau, Charles Schulz, Will Eisner, Mort Walker, Pat Oliphant, Hank Ketcham, Jeff MacNelly, and Bil Keane. *Steve Canyon's* conclusion eulogizes Caniff, while suggesting that Canyon may yet be the hero of other undrawn adventures.

On February 13, 2000, the day *after* Charles M. Schulz died, *Peanuts* ends with a letter from Schulz, which — in the strip — is typed by Snoopy. In the first panel, Charlie Brown answers the phone, "No, I think he's writing." In the second, Snoopy — seated atop his doghouse — starts typing, "Dear Friends..." The large third panel, placed below the top two, features the full letter, framed by a montage of eleven scenes from the strip and Snoopy looking up from his typewriter. In the letter, Schulz explains that he is "no longer able to maintain the schedule demanded by a daily comic strip," that his "family does not wish *Peanuts* to be continued by anyone else," and that he is therefore retiring. He expresses his gratitude to his editors and fans, and concludes with "Charlie Brown, Snoopy, Linus, Lucy... how can I ever forget them..." — followed by his signature.

In its posthumous finale, *Peanuts* recalls the end of another classic strip. Though not a planned conclusion, George Herriman's final *Krazy Kat* strips (June 1944) are eerily prescient. In the penultimate Sunday, Offisa Pupp and Ignatz Mouse dive into a pond and save Krazy from drowning. In the final Sunday strip, Offisa Pupp thinks the bubbles emerging from the pond are Ignatz trying to trick him. Too late, he realizes that it is in fact Krazy. Pupp dives in to save Krazy. In the concluding narrative panel, Pupp — eyes wide in worry — carries the dripping, silent Krazy, whose eyes are closed, and who may be dead. Ignatz looks on, a dark squiggle over his head, and a large tear falling from his eye. That's the last strip Herriman finished. He died two months before it ran.

Barnaby takes a fifth course. Having used the meta-ending for the Sunday *Barnaby* back in 1948 (see Volume Four), Johnson does not take that route again. While Old Doc Yak, Hitz, Mrs, and the residents of Bloom County leave the page to make way for a new strip, *Barnaby* has no successor. Where *Peanuts* simply stops when Charles Schulz signs off, *Barnaby's* use of narrative to conclude the adventures of its titular character also marks it as different. The histories of Steve Canyon, Calvin, Hobbes, the Pattersons, and the Bloom County gang continue. Mostly. In the Pattersons' case, some main characters will die — as had already happened in *For Better or for Worse*. But their stories do not conclude. In contrast, *Barnaby's* adventures are over.

That said, the finale of *Barnaby's* does contain elements of two of these strips' conclusions. As in *For Better or For Worse*, some characters' stories go on. O'Malley's escapades continue, even as the Baxter household is restored to its "normal," pre-Fairy-Godfather state. And, if we read Herriman's unplanned ending as announcing the demise of Krazy Kat, then *Barnaby's* ending shares the common feature of the title character departing. Though death does not claim Barnaby, the strip's namesake will no longer go adventuring with O'Malley and friends.

In many respects, *Barnaby's* conclusion most closely resembles the endings to the serialized narratives of nineteenth-century novels and twentieth-century graphic novels — all finite tales published on newsprint. Charles Dickens' *The Pickwick Papers* (1836–1837), Wilkie Collins' *The Woman in White* (1859–1860), Alexandre Dumas' *Les Trois Mousquetaires* (*The Three Musketeers*, 1844) and *Le Comte de Monte-Cristo* (*The Count of Monte Cristo*, 1844–1846) first appeared in newspapers before being collected into books. Likewise, Gary Panter's *Dal Tokyo* (1983–1984, 1996–2007), Chris Ware's *Jimmy Corrigan* (1992–1999), and Charles Burns' *Black Hole* (1995–2005) also ran serially prior to their publication as stand-alone graphic novels. While *Barnaby* (1943, divided into 13 chapters) and *Barnaby and Mr. O'Malley* (1944, 8 chapters) are all long-form narratives told via the comics medium, they're less self-contained as *narratives* than the other works mentioned in this paragraph. Both of the 1940s

10

PEANUTS
Schulz
NO, I THINK HE'S WRITING..
Dear Friends...
BONK!
RAINING..
AAUGH!
CREDIT ON A D-MINUS?
UNCOMMONLY WEIRD, MARCIE!
PLANS FOR MY WORK..
CLOMP!
GOOD GRIEF!
PSYCHIATRIC HELP 5¢
THE DOCTOR IS IN
Dear Friends,
I have been fortunate to draw Charlie Brown and his friends for almost 50 years. It has been the fulfillment of my childhood ambition.
Unfortunately, I am no longer able to maintain the schedule demanded by a daily comic strip. My family does not wish Peanuts to be continued by anyone else, therefore I am announcing my retirement.
I have been grateful over the years for the loyalty of our editors and the wonderful support and love expressed to me by fans of the comic strip.
Charlie Brown, Snoopy, Linus, Lucy...how can I ever forget them...
Charles M. Schulz
2-13-00

11

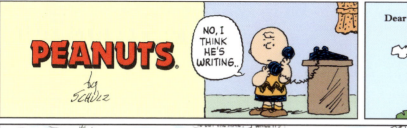

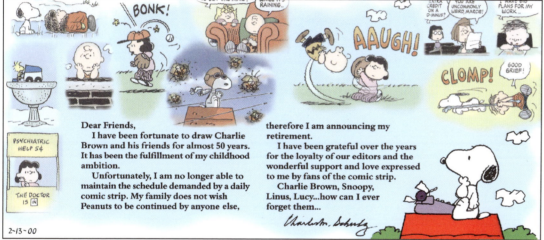

10. *Charles M. Schulz, final* Peanuts *strip, 13 February 2000.*

11. *George Herriman, panel from final Sunday* Krazy Kat*, 25 June 1944.*

12

BARNABY THUR JAN 31

We have a birthday
cake and ice cream,
Mr. O'Malley...Or
~~mayhaps~~ ~~you~~
~~would~~ you like a
lamb sandwich? ( ) B

Hall
Barnaby (pointing
off left)
O'Malley

Well, I--er--No. I
haven't the time.
I must be going.
You're six years
old now, you see-- OM

I didn't mean it--I didn't
grow up on purpose. I-- B

Your Fairy Godfather
understands...Well,
goodbye, Barnaby... OM

Hall (pan to right)
Barnaby following
O'Malley (facing
right) walking
stolidly out the
open door - one tear

Front of porch

~~Goodbye~~

Goodbye--'Bye,
Mr. O'Malley-- B

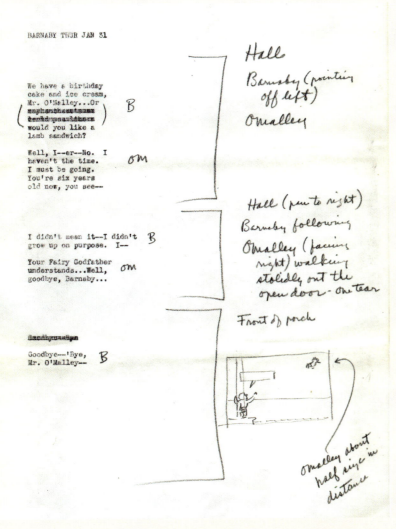

O'Malley about
half size in
distance

13

BARNABY FRI FEB 1

Barnaby, why
are you out of
bed?--With the
window open-- P

Barnaby's bedroom, night
Pop partly in at left
Barnaby, back to Pop, looking
quietly out the open window
(cut feet for space if necessary
but show chair or footstool
near window)

I saw a funny star in
the sky. I remembered
when Mr. O'Malley, my
Fairy Godfather, first
came in this window-- B

Let me close that ~~the~~ window.
You're older now, son, and-- P
I know, ~~Pop,~~ Pop.
It was only a
shooting star. B

Same
Pop closer to window
Barnaby turned to face him,
not glib, very thoughtful

And I'll
shut the
window. B

Same
Barnaby, standing on
chair, shutting window,
resolutely, seriously.

12. Crockett Johnson, script for Barnaby of 31 January 1952. Image courtesy of the Smithsonian Institution.
13. Crockett Johnson, script for Barnaby of 1 February 1952. Image courtesy of the Smithsonian Institution.
14. Crockett Johnson, script for Barnaby of 2 February 1952. Image courtesy of the Smithsonian Institution.

14

BARNABY SAT FEB 2

[illegible]

Because I'm six years old now, Mr. O'Malley can't come back HERE anymore. But, maybe, Pop, someplace else-- B

Maybe... Goodnight, Barnaby-- P

Narrow panel of night sky, Stars

Strange child's bedroom

Cushlamochree! OM

Boy with dark hair

You wished for a Fairy Godparent? Lucky boy! Your wish is granted! OM

O'Malley's the name-- OM

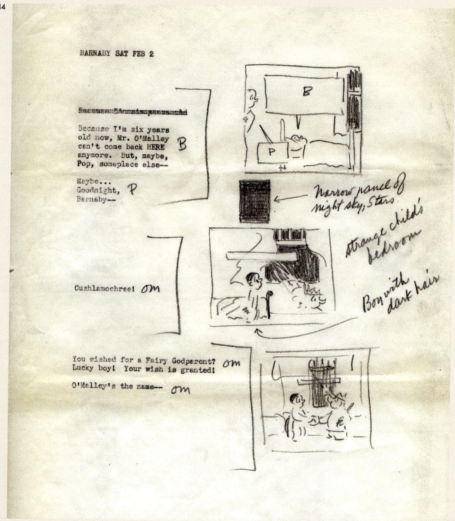

Barnaby books conclude with the suggestion of more adventures in a future volume — unlike the strip's 1952 finale.

The rarity of *Barnaby*'s narrative ending likely influenced the *Philadelphia Inquirer*'s decision to run an alternate ending (reproduced in Susan Kirtley's introduction), telling readers they're reading the final *Barnaby* strip. Indeed, the shock of this end may explain some of the distraught readers' mail. Of the strip's conclusion, one *Barnaby* fan wrote: "I should not have believed the extent of the deprivation I feel; there have been deaths in my family that have hurt me much less" (Armstrong). Another called it a "dire loss" (Lord). Yet another said that as Barnaby grows older, "he will need more and more a J.J. O'Malley to guide him through these hazards. And now to see this poor, innocent child deprived of his fairy godfather when he needs him most! It is too much! My heart bleeds!" (Frank).

> *Such petty triumphs of logic tend to lure one into growing up, Barnaby. Be careful. Your fate and that of your Fairy Godfather hangs upon your empty—I mean—open mind—*
>
> — Mr. O'Malley, 22 Jan. 1952

In sending O'Malley to a different child's bedroom, *Barnaby* — as *Calvin and Hobbes* would do four decades later — glances towards the comics' continuous present. *Barnaby*'s final two panels offer a slight abridgement of the April 21 1942 *Barnaby* strip's final two panels, but with another 5-year-old boy. In another household, the narrative continues. O'Malley and this unnamed child have new adventures.

However, since the adventures of the Barnaby-O'Malley duo cease, this is but a *glance* towards the ongoing "now" of comic-strip time. As Kirtley notes, *Barnaby* spends its final month in farewells and reminders that Fairy Godfathers must leave when their charges turn six. So must all their pixie associates. Even Barnaby's dog stops speaking in words.

And yet I don't think Johnson is suggesting that growing up requires that we relinquish the richly imaginative life of childhood. Instead, he reminds us that only extraordinary people age without abandoning a child's flexibility of mind — people like Mr. Dormant, the unusual adult who chats with Mr. O'Malley in the strips of March 2 through 6, 1945. Or Mr. O'Malley, who, in the strip of January 7, 1952, reminds Barnaby that "lots of people never grow up. Makes things difficult on occasion, I daresay." And Crockett Johnson, an artist who never wrote down to children because he remembered his own childhood so well. As he told Charles Fisher in 1943, "when it comes to knowing about children, it's a terribly old thing to say, but everyone was once a child himself."

To put this another way, the comic strip *Barnaby* ends because O'Malley leaves Barnaby. Though named for Barnaby, Mr. O'Malley is the strip's *sine qua non*. Without him, there's no satire, no whimsy, and no story. As noted in the afterword for *Barnaby Volume One*, Johnson first thought that his strip's comic tension would be between a precocious five-year-old and his parents. After drawing a few episodes, he realized that was not enough to sustain the strip. Then, in came O'Malley, and the strip suddenly had the catalyst it needed.

O'Malley is the strip's imaginative force. Barnaby is always more of a realist. Mr. and Mrs. Baxter think their son's tales of O'Malley and friends are fanciful, the products of a little boy's vivid imagination. However, Barnaby is merely providing factual reports of events the grown-ups have not seen — or, in some cases, have chosen not to notice. In the strips without O'Malley, *Barnaby* becomes an ordinary domestic-comedy strip: Gorgon creates some narrative interest during O'Malley's longest absence (May 24 to July 1, 1947), but he cannot replace the spark reliably generated by an irrepressible Fairy Godfather. In the first panel of the O'Malley-less strip of May 22, 1948, Barnaby observes, "It's quiet around here since Mr. O'Malley, my Fairy Godfather, went away, isn't it, Pop?" Mr. Baxter agrees: "Yes, it is, son." The remaining three panels are silent.

Seated behind his father's high-backed chair, Barnaby plays with his blocks. His father reads a book. Nothing else happens.

Or nothing with the narrative interest to sustain a daily strip.

Because Barnaby's play is something. Play — with blocks or a fairy godparent — is an immersive, absorbing experience. It's one reason that time in childhood can seem to pass more slowly than it does in adulthood. Another is that our earlier years are often more potent, richer with new experiences, than our later years. As Alan Burdick writes in his excellent *Why Time Flies*, "When we're young virtually every experience is new, so it remains vivid years later. But as we age, habit and routine become the norm; novel experiences are fewer (we've done everything already) and we barely take notice of the time we currently inhabit."

The change in ratio of one's age to a unit of time is another reason that the experience of childhood, as it happens, feels longer than the experience of adulthood, as it happens. A year is one fifth of a 5-year-old's life, but only one forty-fifth of a 45-year-old's life. As Burdick reports, philosopher Paul Janet even came up with a formula: "the apparent length of a given span of time varies inversely in proportion to your age. One year seems five times shorter to a fifty-year-old man than to a ten-year-old boy, because a year is one-fiftieth of the man's life and only one-tenth of the boy's."

In this sense, ten years of a comic strip devoted to Barnaby's fifth year are proportionally appropriate. If we return to Janet's formula, time for Crockett Johnson was then passing ninefold as quickly as it was for Barnaby. (According to that formula, a year for a 5-year-old would be nine years for a 45-year old — Johnson's age when he ended the strip.) I don't know whether Johnson knew that particular formula, though I am sure that — as an amateur mathematician himself — he would have enjoyed it. It's no coincidence that the pivotal scene in Barnaby's decision to grow up centers on his desire to solve math problems by himself. In the strip of January 22, he is delighted to confirm that two and two is four: "Everybody said so, but I figured it out by myself!" In the next day's strip, when O'Malley offers to solve 3+3 with a wave of his wand, Barnaby becomes unusually assertive. He turns and says, "NO! I want to do it myself!"

Though *Barnaby*'s conclusion figures reason and imagination as opposites, Johnson himself knew better. In the last ten years of his life, he painted solutions to mathematical theorems. He explored the problems spatially, on large canvases, and then corresponded with mathematicians to refine the algebraic expression of what he'd worked out geometrically. His creative approach led Johnson to publish two original theorems in mathematical journals, in 1970 and 1975. In his own mind, imagining and reasoning were not opposites. But in order to pursue other interests, Johnson needed time. This conclusion gave him a way out.

Like all elements of fiction, endings are contrivances that we accept. In providing the form that life lacks, they grant us perspective — a vantage point from which we can view the entire structure, interpret, and understand. As Kierkegaard observed, though it "must be lived forward," life "must be understood backwards" (p. 179). Or, as Kermode writes, "For us to make sense of our lives from where we are ... stranded in the middle, we need fictions of beginnings and fictions of ends,

15

16

15. *Crockett Johnson with one version of his Squared Circle, c. 1972. Photo by Jackie Curtis. Image courtesy of Jackie Curtis.*

16. *Crockett Johnson, another version of Squared Circle, c. 1969. Photo by Dane Webster. Image courtesy of Philip Nel.*

fictions which unite beginning and end and endow the interval between them with meaning" (p. 190).

I think that's why Johnson figures O'Malley as a metaphorical Halley's Comet. According to the October 30 1951 strip, O'Malley was mistaken for Halley's Comet in 1910. Underscoring his connection to this celestial firework, a "shooting star" heralds his arrival to the bedrooms of both Barnaby in 1942 and the unnamed boy in the final 1952 strip. Though a shooting star is a meteor (rock that burns up upon entering Earth's atmosphere) and not a comet (ball of ice and dirt orbiting the sun), Johnson is invoking the famous comet figuratively, not literally. He knows more than his characters — that the comet appears every 75–76 years, for instance, and that a child might not distinguish between comet and meteor (in the penultimate strip, Barnaby also refers to it via the even less precise term "funny star").

The comet — and O'Malley's identification with it — both zooms out beyond human perspective and hones in on the human experience of time passing. Halley's Comet is the sole comet visible to the naked eye that can appear twice in a person's life. It famously framed the life of Mark Twain, referenced in the December 8 1948 strip, when O'Malley notes that Twain resolved narrative challenges by killing off his characters. Born in November 1835 when Halley's Comet was in the sky, Twain died in April 1910, the day after the comet reached its perihelion (moment when it is closest to the sun). People remember this because Twain himself made the connection in 1909, telling his biographer that, since Halley's Comet arrived the year of his birth and would return the following year, "The Almighty has said, no doubt, 'Now here are these two unaccountable freaks; they came in together, they must go out together.'" The appearance of this "funny star" at both beginning and end of *Barnaby* not only marks the boundaries of the strip, but gestures to the boundaries of human life — the fact that, as Nabokov observes, "our existence is but a brief crack of light between two eternities of darkness" (p. 19).

Johnson's own father died at the age of 60, when Johnson was still 18. He then dropped out of college to support his mother and sister, and was launched into his working life before having the chance to contemplate career options. He leveraged his skills in drawing and typography to get jobs in magazine design, and finally became a professional cartoonist. Twenty-seven years after his father's death, 45-year-old Johnson now had more yesterdays than he did tomorrows, and knew his time to explore other vocations was fast disappearing. And so, as O'Malley does, Johnson has to say goodbye to Barnaby.

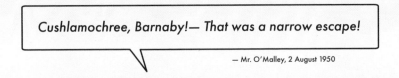

Cushlamochree, Barnaby!— That was a narrow escape!

— Mr. O'Malley, 2 August 1950

Well, Johnson *mostly* says goodbye. Since it was the work for which he was then best-known, Crockett Johnson could never fully leave Barnaby or Mr. O'Malley behind. They make him an authority on children's "Fantastic Companions," his illustrated mock-scholarly essay published in *Harper's Magazine* in June 1955 (and reproduced in this volume). O'Malley makes a cameo appearance in *Is This You?* (1955), a children's book Johnson illustrated and co-wrote with Krauss. Gus the Ghost shows up at a housewarming (or attic-warming) party for the title character of *The Saga of Quilby: A Ghost Story Especially Devised for Advertisers Who Stay Up Late*, an advertising pamphlet created for *This Week* magazine in the mid-1950s. Johnson includes O'Malley, Barnaby, and Harold in a self-promotional brochure, likely devised in 1966, when there were plans to create an animated *Barnaby* TV series.

Though Johnson never got around to collecting the unpublished strips in books, there is evidence that he hoped to do so. At the Smithsonian, in his papers, are four scrapbooks of uncollected *Barnaby* strips. He has carefully pasted three to a page, and given each volume a title in neat block capital letters. Most of the 1951 strips in this volume come from the one labeled "BARNABY SEQUENCE 4." On the first page, in Johnson's tidy cursive, are instructions for photographing them.

17

Is this your friend?
Is this?
Is this?
Is this your friend?
This?

18

The next evening, a delegation of ghosts from nearby expansion attics dropped in to welcome Quilby to the neighborhood.
After the introductions, Quilby singled out an elderly ghost and asked: "What has happened in America? Who are these young families we're living with?"

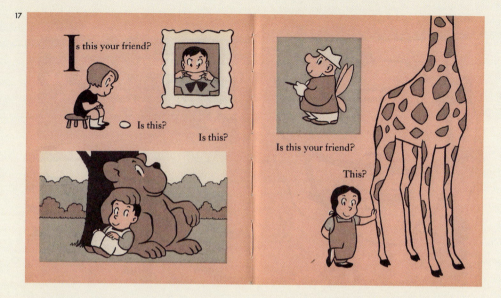

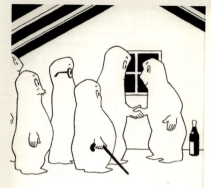

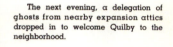

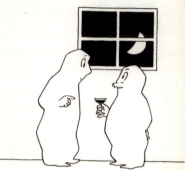

Johnson comes closest to writing a new O'Malley story in his children's book *Time for Spring* (1957). If you imagine O'Malley as a snowman assigned to play with Jane instead of Barnaby, that's the central dynamic of the book. Buds have begun to appear on the trees, the grass is turning green, and Irene is ready to take her tricycle out for a ride. "And then," Johnson's narrator reports, "as it so often does when it is time for spring, it snowed." Reluctantly, Irene makes a snowman. He comes to life, delights in playing in the snow, and promises that "Spring won't come, while I'm here." His size, hat, irrepressible personality, and tendency to devise plans that benefit himself all recall Barnaby's Fairy Godfather. Yet, unlike a *Barnaby* narrative, *Time for Spring* has a melancholic undercurrent. Though she wishes spring would arrive, Irene also worries that, for his own safety, the snowman needs to go somewhere colder soon. On the spring day of the final pages, Irene finds the snowman's hat and, assuming he went to the North Pole, she vows to "save it for him till next year." Despite her optimism, the story's conclusion also gestures to loss, leaving open the possibility that this hat is all that remains of a melted snowman.

Apart from these moments, Johnson's creative energy gravitated toward other subjects. Before making children's books his primary focus, Johnson first tried advertising and even considered creating a new comic strip. In the 1950s, he drew ads for Kimberly-Clark paper, *Ladies Home Journal*, and the American

17. *Ruth Krauss and Crockett Johnson, two-page spread from* Is This You? *(William R. Scott, 1955). Image courtesy of Philip Nel.*

18. *Crockett Johnson, two-page spread from* The Saga of Quilby *(c. 1955). Image courtesy of the Northeast Children's Literature Collection, Dodd Research Center, University of Connecticut, Storrs.*

19

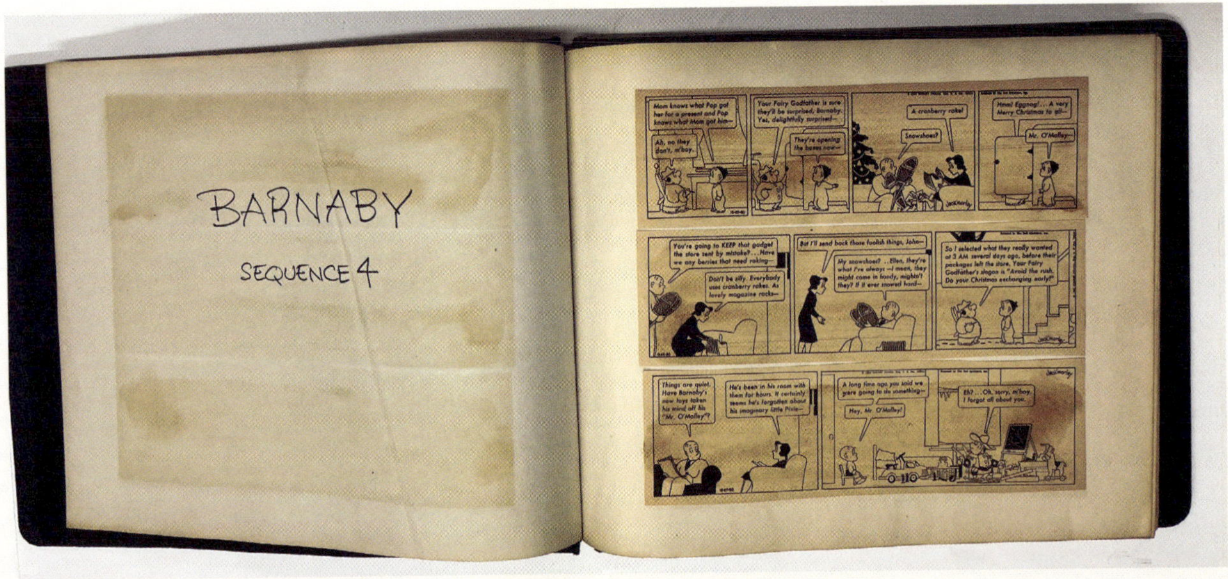
BARNABY
SEQUENCE 4
Mom knows what Pop got her for a present and Pop knows what Mom got him—
Ah, no they don't, m'boy.
Your Fairy Godfather is sure they'll be surprised, Barnaby. Yes, delightfully surprised—
They're opening the boxes now—
Snowshoes?
A cranberry rake!
Hmm! Eggnog!... A very Merry Christmas to all—
Mr. O'Malley—
You're going to KEEP that gadget the store sent by mistake?...Have we any berries that need raking—
Don't be silly. Everybody uses cranberry rakes. As lovely magazine racks—
But I'll send back those foolish things, John—
My snowshoes? ..Ellen, they're what I've always —I mean, they might come in handy, mightn't they? If it ever snowed hard—
So I selected what they really wanted at 3 AM several days ago, before their packages left the store. Your Fairy Godfather's slogan is "Avoid the rush. Do your Christmas exchanging early!"
Things are quiet. Have Barnaby's new toys taken his mind off his "Mr. O'Malley"?
He's been in his room with them for hours. It certainly seems he's forgotten about his imaginary little Pixie—
A long time ago you said we were going to do something—
Hey, Mr. O'Malley!
Eh?...Oh, sorry, m'boy. I forgot all about you.

20

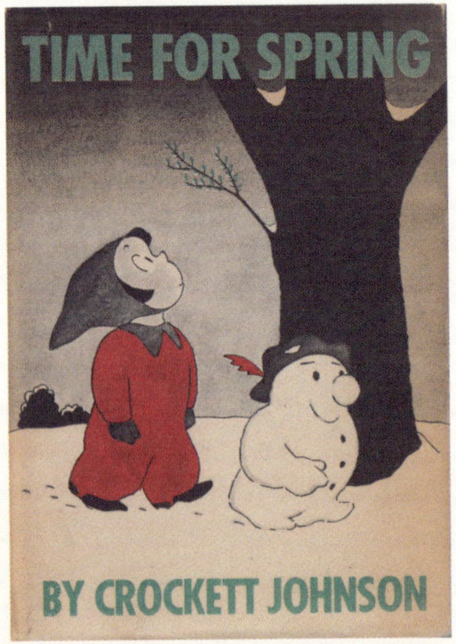
TIME FOR SPRING
BY CROCKETT JOHNSON

21

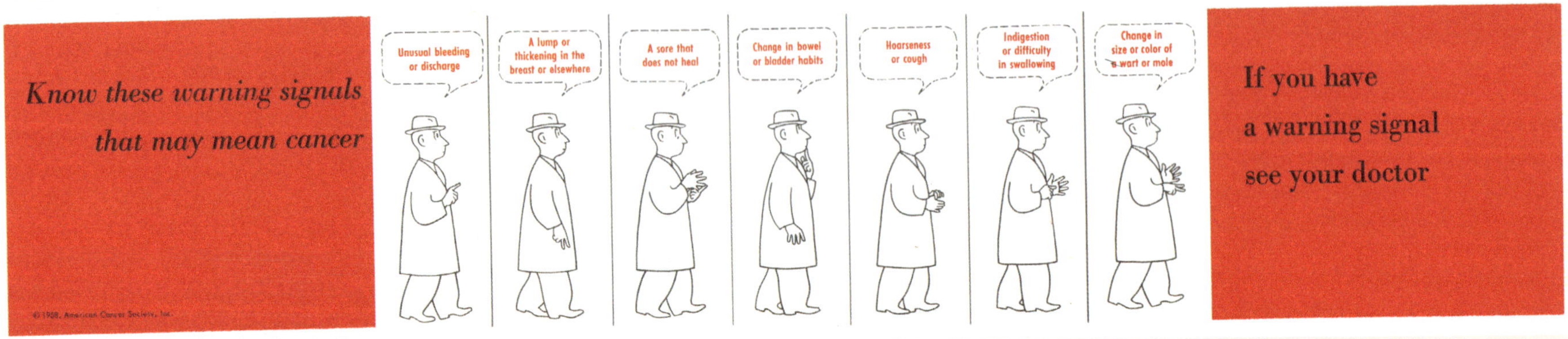
Know these warning signals
that may mean cancer
© 1958, American Cancer Society, Inc.
Unusual bleeding or discharge
A lump or thickening in the breast or elsewhere
A sore that does not heal
Change in bowel or bladder habits
Hoarseness or cough
Indigestion or difficulty in swallowing
Change in size or color of a wart or mole
If you have
a warning signal
see your doctor

The comic strip panels contain the following dialogue:

Panel 1: "I GLANCED UP FROM THE CRIME NEWS AT MY ASSISTANT INVESTIGATOR, IDLY TOYING WITH HIS ATOMIC RAY PISTOL--" / "Careful where you point that gat, Matson."

Panel 2: "MATSON WAS IN ONE OF HIS MOODS. HE HAD WANTED US TO BECOME SPACE PILOTS INSTEAD OF RELENTLESS SUPER SLEUTHS." / "We've been private eyes for an hour, Mr. Herkimer... Where's all that crime you said us private eyes were going to fight against?"

Panel 3: "Here in the paper... pages and pages of them. I'm analyzing each carefully." / "Read me some... The good ones."

Panel 4: "MY ASSISTANT AND I QUICKLY ANALYZED THE PROBLEM OF THE CITY'S CRIME AND ARRIVED AT A PLAN TO WIPE IT OUT--" / "These varied crimes have one thing in common. They're all bad!" / "Probably because they're all done by somebody bad..."

Panel 5: "Yes, or as we criminologists put it, every crime is the conception of a warped brain!" / "Come on! Let's go down there and catch him, Mr. Herkimer."

Panel 6: "Go down where? Get whom?" / "Let's go down to the Underworld of course... and catch The Brain!"

19. Crockett Johnson's scrapbook, collecting the final 58 weeks of Barnaby. Image courtesy of the Smithsonian Institution.

20. Crockett Johnson, cover of Time for Spring (Heinemann, 1957). Image courtesy of Philip Nel.

21. Crockett Johnson, booklet for American Cancer Society, 1958. Image courtesy of Mark Newgarden.

22. Jules Feiffer and Crockett Johnson, first two strips of untitled comic strip, 1953. Image courtesy of the Smithsonian Institution.

Cancer Society. In 1953, Maurice Sendak introduced him to Jules Feiffer, then fresh out of the U.S. Army. With Johnson writing the dialogue and Feiffer making the art, they created two weeks of a strip about a private eye named Herkimer and his assistant, a small boy named Matson. No syndicate picked that up, but in May 1955, a syndicate did pick up *Barkis*, Johnson's single-panel comic that translated a terrier's barks into the ideas he was trying to express. Unfortunately, *Barkis* launched a year after Brad Anderson's highly successful *Marmaduke* made its debut. The comics pages didn't have room for a second single-panel dog comic, and the syndicate dropped *Barkis* after six months.

Fortunately, *Harold and the Purple Crayon* was an immediate hit. Published in October 1955, its first print run of ten thousand sold so well that Harper was already ordering a new print run of seventy-five hundred in November. The story of a small boy and his world-making crayon — which has since been translated into fourteen languages — launched a seven-book series (1955–63), three animated shorts (1959, 1971, 1974), an Emmy-winning animated HBO series (2001–02), board game (2001), two stage plays (1990, 2009), a live-action film (2024), and a Broadway musical in development (2024). Today, the *Harold* books are Crockett Johnson's best-known works. Though *Barnaby* is one of the classic comic strips, I would wager that more readers of this five-volume series arrived here via Harold than via Mr. O'Malley.

But we cannot choose how we are remembered or, indeed, if we are remembered at all. During Johnson's lifetime, *Barnaby* was his most famous creation. In 1948, the engineers of the St. Paul Minnesota firm Engineering Research Associates named their computer "Atlas" after Crockett Johnson's mental giant. The first Atlas Computer, a UNIVAC 1101, was delivered to the National Security Agency in Washington, in

Let's see what the weather's like out the BACK door.

December 1950. The NSA relied so heavily on the computer's code-breaking and code-making that it ordered a second Atlas in 1951 (Gray).

In addition to the six adaptations of *Barnaby* already mentioned in these Afterwords (feature film [unrealized], two radio dramas, two stage plays, one live action TV pilot, one cartoon TV series [unrealized]), an animated version won first prize at the Venice Film Festival in 1967. Before he produced *All in the Family* or *Maude* and the other groundbreaking sitcoms for which he is known, Norman Lear in 1966 co-produced a TV pilot for *Barnaby*, starring Sorrell Booke — the actor who would portray Boss Hogg on the *Dukes of Hazzard* — as Mr. O'Malley. When lung cancer claimed Johnson in July 1975, the *New York Times* devoted most of its obituary to *Barnaby*. Its headline read "Crockett Johnson, Cartoonist, Creator of 'Barnaby,' Is Dead."

Even as Harold and his purple crayon became Johnson's most recognized creations, Barnaby and his Fairy Godfather continued to reappear. In 1985 and 1986, Ballantine's Del Rey imprint published six paperbacks of *Barnaby*, the first time the original strip had appeared in book form. (For the Henry Holt collections of 1943 and 1944, Johnson redrew his favorite episodes.) Ballantine had planned a twelve-volume *Barnaby* series, but Judy-Lynn Del Rey — the editor who initiated the reprint — died in February 1986. So, it never got beyond those first six books.

In 2012, Swedish journalist Paul Frigyes suggested Mr. O'Malley as an inspiration for the title character of Astrid Lindgren's *Karlson on the Roof* (*Karlsson på taket*, 1955), who appears in that book and its two sequels. I don't know whether Johnson's comics influenced Lindgren's novels, but Frigyes is right to note parallels between O'Malley and Karlson. In Sarah Death's English-language translation, Karlson is "a very small, round, determined gentleman, and he can fly" (2). Where O'Malley has wings, Karlson has a propeller on his back. As O'Malley does, Karlson uses the window to enter the home of his young charge — a seven-year-old boy who turns eight at the end of the first book. Karlson loves food (especially toffees), and is a figure of mischief, initially unseen by any but seven-year-old Lillebror — "Little Brother" in Swedish,

23. *Crockett Johnson, panel (1955) from* Barkis: Some precise and some speculative interpretations of the meaning of a dog's bark at certain times and in certain [illustrated] circumstances *(Simon and Schuster, 1956). Image courtesy of Philip Nel.*

24. *Crockett Johnson, cover drawing for* Harold and the Purple Crayon, *1955. Image courtesy of the Smithsonian Institution.*

25. *Crockett Johnson, cover of Italian translation of* Barnaby *(Oscar Monadori, 1970). Image courtesy of Philip Nel.*

26. *Crockett Johnson, drawing of Mr. O'Malley done for fan Frank Paccassi, Jr. in 1962. This may be Johnson's last drawing of O'Malley. Image courtesy of Philip Nel.*

25

BARNABY
Il mondo come verità e immaginazione nella più singolare storia a fumetti dei nostri tempi
di Crockett Johnson
Prefazione di Oreste del Buono
OSCAR MONDADORI

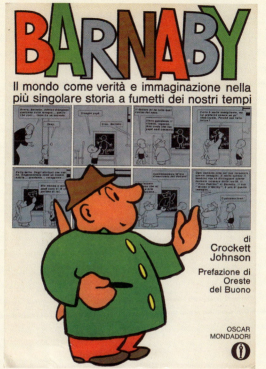

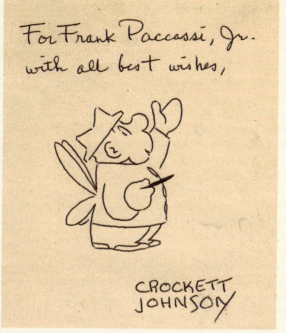

and "Smidge" in the translation I read. However, Karlson's visibility to others is also a difference: by the end of the first book, Lillebror's friends, older brother and older sister, and even his parents see Karlson. They vow not to tell anyone because either no one would believe them, or, if they did, "we wouldn't get a minute's peace for the rest of our lives" (162). In Lindgren's Karlson stories, the visibility of allegedly "imaginary" childhood companions does not have an age limit. That said, it is of course possible that Lindgren came across copies of *Barnaby* (1943) or *Barnaby and Mr. O'Malley* (1944), either when she visited the United States in 1948 or in her role as children's-book editor for Rabén & Sjögren from 1946 to 1970. The possibility of Johnson inspiring Lindgren is an intriguing hypothesis.

Many have assumed that *Barnaby* influenced *Calvin and Hobbes*. Both strips' central characters are a young boy and a companion assumed (by adults) to be imaginary. Both comics also combine fantasy and satire. In 2003, *Washington Post* columnist Gene Weingarten even sent Watterson a first edition of Johnson's *Barnaby* (1943), and a letter declaring that he would wait in a nearby hotel room for "as long as it took for Watterson to contact him" (Martell, p. 6). The next morning, Lee Salem — Watterson's editor at Universal Press Syndicate — phoned Weingarten to tell him that no, Watterson would neither arrive nor respond. Given Watterson's famous disinterest in talking to the press, I doubt that sending him first editions of a Walt Kelly *Pogo* or a Charles Schulz *Peanuts* would have worked either. However, as collections of strips that Watterson has genuine affection for, both *Pogo* and *Peanuts* would have been a better choice than *Barnaby*. Despite the similarities between the strips, when Watterson began writing *Calvin and Hobbes*, he had only ever seen *Barnaby* in anthologies, and had "never seen the work at any length." As he told Andrew Christie in 1987, since a few people had made the comparison between his strip and Johnson's, "I should look it up just to see what the fuss is about."

For Frank Paccassi, Jr.
with all best wishes,
CROCKETT JOHNSON

26

I hope that Fantagraphics' *Barnaby* series has shown more readers what the fuss is about. It's one thing to read the words of the strip's many fans — to note that, for instance, Charles Schulz considered *Barnaby* "one of the great comic strips of all time." Or that comics historian Richard Marschall deemed *Barnaby* "an artistic masterpiece" containing "some of the cleverest and most literate writing in comics." It's another thing to read a few selected strips in *The Smithsonian Collection of*

Newspaper Comics (1977) or the second volume of Art Spiegelman and François Mouly's *Little Lit* (2001). However, it's still another to be able to immerse yourself in ten years of Barnaby and Mr. O'Malley, to read Crockett Johnson's masterpiece from start to finish. Unless you had the full Ballantine/Del Rey run *and* collected all the individual strips from June 1946 on, reading *Barnaby* in its entirety has been impossible until the publication of this volume.

As the biographer of Crockett Johnson, I'm grateful to Eric Reynolds and Fantagraphics for inviting me to co-edit this labor of love, and for sticking with it until Volume Five — especially because, as was true in the strip's heyday, these editions of *Barnaby* have won more critical praise than sales. But just as Mr. O'Malley believes that his schemes will succeed, I continue to have faith that Crockett Johnson's strip will find the larger audience that it deserves. Of *Barnaby*, we might repeat what Bill Watterson said of *Krazy Kat*: it "was not very successful as a commercial venture, but it was something better. It was art" (p. 10).

WORKS CITED

The main source for the Afterword is my *Crockett Johnson and Ruth Krauss: How an Unlikely Couple Found Love, Dodged the FBI, and Transformed Children's Literature* (University Press of Mississippi, 2012) and the decade of research behind it. But here are a few additional sources.

Andersen, Jens. *Astrid Lindgren: The Woman Behind Pippi Longstocking.* Translated by Caroline Waight. New Haven and London: Yale UP, 2018.

Armstrong, Ray. Letter to Crockett Johnson. 11 Feb. 1952. "Barnaby Fan Mail II," Box 14, Crockett Johnson Papers, Smithsonian Institution.

Burdick, Alan. *Why Time Flies: A Mostly Scientific Investigation.* New York: Simon & Schuster 2017.

Christie, Andrew. "Bill Watterson." *Honk!* magazine, issue 2, Jan. 1987, pp. 28–33.

Committee on Un-American Activities, "Report on the Communist 'Peace' Offensive: A Campaign to Disarm and Defeat the United States." Issued by 82nd Congress, 1st session, House Report No. 378. Washington, DC: Committee on Un-American Activities, House of Representatives, April 25, 1951.

Frank, Nancy. Letter to Crockett Johnson and Jack Morley. 9 Feb. 1952. "Barnaby Fan Mail II," Box 14, Crockett Johnson Papers, Smithsonian Institution.

Frigyes, Paul. "Astrid Lindgren hade förebild i U.S.A." *Dagens Nyheter.* 15 Jan. 2012. <https://www.dn.se/kultur-noje/astrid-lindgren-hade-forebild-i-usa/>.

Gray, George. "Engineering Research Associates and the Atlas Computer (UNIVAC 1101)." *Unisys History Newsletter,* vol. 3, no. 3, June 1999. <http://www.cc.gatech.edu/gvu/people/randy.carpenter/folklore/v3n3.html>. Date of access: 3 Jan. 2003.

Glover, James W. *United States Life Tables: 1890, 1901, 1910, and 1901–1910.* Department of Commerce, Bureau of the Census. Washington: Government Printing Office, 1921. <https://www.cdc.gov/nchs/data/lifetables/life1890–1910.pdf>

Holtz, Allan. "Obscurity of the Day: Hitz and Mrs." *Stripper's Guide.* 27 Nov. 2017. <http://strippersguide.blogspot.com/2017/11/obscurity-of-day-hitz-and-mrs.html>. Date of access: 16 Sept. 2021.

Kierkegaard, Søren. *Kierkegaard's Journals and Notebooks, Volume 2: Journals EE-KK.* Edited by Niels Jørgen Cappelorn, Alastair Hannay, Vanessa Rumble, and George Pattison. Princeton University Press, 2008.

Lindgren, Astrid. *Karlson on the Roof.* Translated by Sarah Death. Oxford UP, 2008.

Lord, Mary. "Laments Barnaby." Letter to the editor. Press clipping in "Barnaby Fan Mail II," Box 14, Crockett Johnson Papers, Smithsonian Institution.

Martell, Nevin. *Looking for Calvin and Hobbes: The Unconventional Story of Bill Watterson and His Revolutionary Comic Strip.* New York: Continuum International Publishing Group, 2009.

Mickenberg, Julia L. *Learning from the Left: Children's Literature, the Cold War, and Radical Politics in the United States.* New York: Oxford UP, 2006.

Nabokov, Vladimir. *Speak, Memory: An Autobiography Revisited.* 1967. New York: Vintage, 1989.

Nel, Philip. Telephone interview with Norma Simon. 20 June 2002.

Newgarden, Mark. "Gross, Milt, 1895–1953 (see: 20th Century, School of American Wacky)." *Gross Exaggerations: The Meshuga Comic Strips of Milt Gross, 1926–1934.* Edited by Peter Maresca. Sunday Press, 2020. pp. 5–10.

Watterson, Bill. "An Appreciation: A Few Thoughts on *Krazy Kat.*" *George Herriman: A Celebration.* Ed. Craig Yoe. New York: Abrams Comics Arts, 2011. 9–10.

Crockett Johnson, illustration from The Saga of Quilby (c. 1955). Image courtesy of the Northeast Children's Literature Collection, Dodd Research Center, University of Connecticut, Storrs.

I don't believe in withholding information from children...You asked your old Fairy Godfather to explain about leprechauns... And that I will, m'boy.

— Mr. O'Malley, 30 Oct. 1950

The Elves, Leprechauns, Gnomes, and Little Men's Chowder and Marching Society: A Handy Pocket Guide

By Philip Nel

Some of *Barnaby*'s allusions may elude modern readers and certainly eluded some of Johnson's contemporaries. Enjoying *Barnaby* doesn't require these notes, but since you're among the few whose curiosity has led you here, I hope that this additional context enriches your reading experience. Also, I should let you know that, though written in the spirit of the chapter titles in *Barnaby* (1943) and *Barnaby and Mr. O'Malley* (1944), the chapter titles here are my invention.

A GUIDE TO HOUSEHOLD PIXIES • 25 NOV. 1949 – 25 MAR. 1950

... and on the unimpeachable authority of a cab driver who carried him as a passenger in 1941 ... (21 Jan. 1950). Johnson pokes fun at the lazy journalistic adjective "unimpeachable," often used to assert credibility for an unnamed source.

my "O'Malley Speed-up Plan" swept the country. Captains of industry talked of little else. (30 Jan.) Johnson is having O'Malley take credit for the Taylor Speed-up Plan — created by Frederick "Speedy" Taylor (1856–1915), which was a dominant school of thought among those in management. Johnson gestures to labor unions' critique of Taylorism: in making labor more efficient,

this plan increases productivity by decreasing workers' autonomy, and makes automation easier, which in turn leads to unemployment. O'Malley's comment that "they were debating my theories on street corners. Over little piles of apples" posits a connection between Taylorism and the Great Depression. O'Malley's scheme of household management also affords Johnson an opportunity to mock the application of Taylorism to domestic labor — running a home as a business. The practice became sufficiently popular to inspire household management classes (for women) and articles in women's magazines promoting efficiency schedules — "Business Ideals at Home," to quote the title of a 1923 article from *The Woman's Journal* (Whiting, p. 12).

an idle Pixie is a non-producing Pixie (31 Jan.) Further mockery of Taylorism.

I'm the original captive audience (4 Feb.) Johnson is punning on "captive audience," which in 1950 operates in two divergent contexts. One, still in use today, is an "audience that cannot escape a particular form of entertainment or instruction" (*OED*). December 1949 protests against Grand Central Station's use of commercial-sponsored Muzak broadcasts — that inspired news coverage and even a satirical cartoon in the *New Yorker* — led to the cessation of that practice. Summarizing the opposition, the *New York Times* noted that "a surprisingly voluble commuting element [...] insisted that the public had an inalienable right to privacy, a right not to listen, upon which the broadcasts infringed. They warned that this would be only the beginning, not the end, and that if 'captive audiences' could be forced to listen to commercials in a radio station, soon they would have them dinned into their ears on the trains themselves" (Moscow, p. 38). Johnson also would have known the term's use in U.S. labor law as a "situation in which an employer gives speeches that discourage workers from joining a union or that are in some way anti-union. These speeches may be given to employees on company time and company property and only if they are not coercive" ("Captive Audience"). This second use was more common in 1950, and the radio pixie's use of the word "original" points at this then-dominant context for the term.

Tennessee Hennessey, the Bald Eagle Scout (4 Feb). This character, who becomes a major narrative focus in April 1951, is first mentioned in the strip of 27 Jan. 1948. See the note for that strip in *Barnaby, Volume Four*, p. 362.

Pmub is bump spelled backwards, little boy. In radio, all key words are... (6 Feb.) I'm stumped by this reference. In radio, key words are not backwards. Nor are they backwards in telegraphic communication. Is this a reference to cryptography? The source of O'Malley's misinformation eludes me.

a large economy-size jar of Glozoon, the miracle ointment containing soothing lanolin for my head (6 Feb.). Lanolin — sometimes called "wool grease" because it is "cholesterin-fatty matter extracted from sheep's wool" (*OED*) — is a popular ingredient for ointments, and (as a search for the term in the *New York Times* archive for 1949 reveals) is named in lots of ads as a key ingredient. Williams Shaving Cream broadcasts its use of "this wonderful substance called EXTRACT OF LANOLIN, which is *25% more concentrated than the well-known skin conditioner, Lanolin!*" ("New discovery gives BETTER SHAVES!"). John Wanamaker's department store advertised "LANOLIN

PLUS" a "New Liquid Beauty Agent" that promises to "Help keep your skin soft and smooth" ("LANOLIN PLUS").

young Doctor Malone (7 Feb.). *Young Doctor Malone* was a popular American soap opera that ran on radio (1939–1960) and television (1958–1963). In its radio version, several different actors starred in the title role — small-town physician Jerry Malone.

twenty-three field goals and ten free-throws (15 Feb.). O'Malley is mixing up his sports: you get field goals in football and free-throws in basketball.

POP VS. O'MALLEY REDUX • 27 MAR. – 1 MAY 1950

Pony Boy (26 Apr.). With music by Charlie O'Donnell and lyrics by Bobbie Heath, "My Pony Boy" is a popular song featured in the Broadway musical *Miss Innocence* (1909). It was later frequently used in Western movies and, by the 1950s, had become a popular song for children. O'Malley holds the sheet music in the strip of 15 March 1943 (*Barnaby, Volume One*, p. 15).

The Civil Aeronautics Board (1 May). Established in 1938, the CAB regulated air safety (until the Federal Aviation Administration took that over in 1958), investigated airline accidents (until the National Transportation Safety Board took on that job in 1967), and regulated the commercial airline industry (until the CAB was abolished in 1985).

THE O'MALLEY CENSUS • 2 – 20 MAY 1950

So businessmen can make up their sucker lists — (8 May). The term "sucker list" emerges in the early 1900s as a roster of people who can be easily defrauded by unscrupulous businessmen, stockbrokers, bankers, politicians, etc.

G-man (11 & 15 May). Though an abbreviation for "Government man," the term often refers to an FBI agent. By the end of April 1950, the FBI's New York Division had begun compiling a file on Johnson. As explored in greater detail in the Afterword, Johnson — though he likely did not yet know of their activities

— likely suspected that his politics would make him a target. In suggesting that a "G-man badge" can be acquired by sending in breakfast-cereal box-tops, Johnson may be mocking the legitimacy of FBI inquiries. Or it could be simply another feature of O'Malley's inept con-artistry.

Flabbergasties (15 May). See note for 28 Dec. 1948 in *Barnaby, Volume Four*, p. 374.

THE O'MALLEY EXPRESS HIGHWAY • 22 MAY – 18 AUG. 1950

Pop says our mayor ACTS like a Pixie sometimes — (22 May). O'Malley's response — "That's merely a figure of speech people use, Barnaby" — is true. During this period, people do use the simile "like a pixie." It's also possible that Johnson is alluding to one of the inspirations for Mr. O'Malley — the diminutive (5'2") Fiorello La Guardia, mayor of New York from 1934 to 1945.

I see the Highway Department is finally going ahead with the new express highway (23 May). Though the Federal-Aid Highway Act of 1952 authorized the first funding specifically for the National System of Interstate Highways, its authorization began with the Federal-Aid Highway Act of 1944 (without funding). Following the lead of New York and Connecticut (where Johnson lived), Pennsylvania, Ohio, and New Jersey in 1949 all authorized the construction of toll highways, under public instead of private auspices. Similar plans for toll roads were taking shape in seven other states (Heffernan). The postwar highway boom was underway.

A transit. And a Y-level. An azimuth compass. High lace boots. (6 June). A *Y-level* is a spirit-level (device for assessing whether a surface is horizontal), used with a telescope and placed upon a Y-shaped support (*OED*). Also used by mariners for navigation, an *azimuth compass* is "designed to observe the value of the local magnetic variation," and displays directions in degrees: 0º is north, 90 is east, 180º is south, and 270º is west. Tall boots, laced at the front, were a key feature of the classic surveyor's outfit. (For *transit*, see note for 3 Feb. 1944, *Barnaby, Volume Two*, p. 355.)

No leveling-rod. No surveyor's chain — (7 June). Typical surveying equipment of the period and earlier. *Merriam-Webster* defines a leveling rod as "a graduated rod used in measuring the vertical distance between a point on the ground and the line of sight of a surveyor's level," and identifies 1855 as the first year the term was used. The Surveyor's chain, also called Gunter's chain (after mathematician Edmund Gunter, who invented it in the early seventeenth century), is a 22-yard chain divided into 100 links. It is still in use today ("Surveyor's chain").

According to the Chadleans, four thousand camel steps make one mile. (7 June). For the purposes of the joke, Johnson is invoking an ancient civilization, and imagining their methods of measurement to be less precise. *Chadleans* could refer to the people from Chadlea — as a country, Chadlea existed in the early 9th and mid-6th century BCE. Or *Chadleans* might refer to the people of the Chadlean Empire, aka the Neo-Babylonian Empire, which lasted from 626 BCE to 539 BCE.

The BENDS! (22 June). O'Malley is bent but does not have the bends. Today known as decompression sickness, the bends are most commonly a result of resurfacing from a dive too quickly or without proper depressurization.

Juke joints (28 June). Typically found at the roadside, a juke joint is "any establishment where patrons can dance to the music of a juke box" to borrow the phrasing of J. E. Lighter's *Random House Historical Dictionary of American Slang*, Volume II.

He looks exactly like an Ogre I used to know (14 July). Mr. Friendly does bear a resemblance to Bilharzia Ogre/Mr. Jones, a central character in the *Barnaby* narrative of July–August 1942. See *Barnaby, Volume One*.

$$(e^{\pi i}+1) + M \int_0^A dx + \left| \begin{matrix} \log N & y \\ -\ln^{-1} 1 & L^2 \end{matrix} \right|_{N \to 10}$$

(27 July). This formula spells "O'MALLEY." See note for 27 Jan. 1944, *Barnaby, Volume Two*, p. 354.

CASTAWAY O'MALLEY • 19 AUG. – 13 SEPT. 1950

Captain Bloodbath (28 Aug.) Johnson again pokes fun at the debate over whether comic books were suitable fare for children, noting (in panel three) that fairy tales contain far more of that "horror stuff." See also the notes for 27 Aug. 1943 (*Barnaby, Volume One*, p. 311), 25 April 1944 (*Volume Two*, p. 357), 29 May 1945 (*Volume Two*, p. 367–368), and 15 Oct. 1949 (*Volume Four*, p. 380).

my faithful servant, Friday (30 Aug.), **Robinson Crusoe** (31 Aug.) For the next ten days, Daniel Defoe's *Robinson Crusoe* (1719–1720) serves as Johnson's comic foil. Twenty-five years after being shipwrecked on an island, Crusoe rescues a man from "Savages," and — rather than ask his name — simply re-names him *Friday* after the day on which he saved the man's life. Defoe depicts this "tawny" Friday as naturally docile, subservient, and glad to be Crusoe's "Slave for ever" (172). In summary: via an engaging narrative, Defoe's novel serves up a racist fantasy of colonialism.

Turtle Eggs Benedict (1 Sept.) Though I can find no record of an actual "Turtle Eggs Benedict," the choice of "turtle" signals that this dish is exotic, a delicacy, and thus *very* unlikely to be prepared on a beach. By the mid-eighteenth century, "turtle soup was *haute cuisine*" and remained so as late as the mid-twentieth-century (Wills). Perhaps indicative of the turtle's continued status as fancy cuisine, a 1950 *New York Times* article on gourmet dining in the Caribbean mentions both "turtle steaks" and "turtleburgers" (Candee).

will have to whittle a shovel for him . . . I'll fell an iron-wood tree (6 Sept.) O'Malley makes another allusion to Defoe's *Robinson Crusoe*. Shipwrecked and wanting tools, Crusoe decides to make them. He uses his axe to "cut a Piece" of an "Iron Tree" (so-called for "its exceeding Hardness"), and then "work'd it effectually by little and little into the Form of a Shovel or Spade" (63). In having O'Malley write "thought and meditations" in a journal, Johnson is poking fun at the fact that, despite the challenges of surviving on an island, Crusoe somehow manages to find time to keep a journal.

LOOKING FOR MR. O'MALLEY • 14 SEPT. – 25 SEPT. 1950

Dapper Daniel's, Ltd. (14 Sept.) See note for 27 April 1945 in *Barnaby, Volume Two*, p. 367.

Mom read me a story where some men let the bloodhounds smell a lady's handkerchief — And they took off after her — (19 Sept.) As Gorgon says in his response, this sounds like a reference to an *Uncle Tom's Cabin* stage show, perhaps slave-catchers in pursuit of Eliza, an enslaved woman who escapes.

Yeah. Uncle Tom's Cabin. My father toured with a "Tom" show for years — (19 Sept.) Gorgon also mentions this in the strip of 14 June 1943 (*Barnaby, Volume One*, p. 197). As Robin Bernstein notes, "Tom shows" are "staged performances of *Uncle Tom's Cabin*," the first of which "thundered through popular culture in the fall and winter of 1852 and which remained continuously on the boards, staged simultaneously by as many five hundred Tom companies, until the 1930s" (p. 113). Tom shows were so popular that they "ultimately eclipsed [Harriet Beecher] Stowe's novel, replacing Stowe's counterparts in the popular imagination" (p. 113). For an extraordinary look at how Tom shows shaped the cultures of childhood, check out Bernstein's *Racial Innocence*.

FAIRY GODFATHER'S DAY • 26 SEPT. – 24 OCT. 1950

S. S. Trimalchio, the luxury cruise liner (25 Sept.) The central character of Petronius' *Satyricon*, Trimalchio is a rich former slave who throws lavish, gaudy parties. His wealth brings him economic class but not social class. He aspires to be accepted among the elite, but he is rude, crude, and vain. So "a luxury cruise liner" named for Trimalchio would be gilded and ugly — desperately trying to prove its classiness, but in extremely poor taste. Imagine what the decor of a Donald Trump cruise ship would look like, and you'll have the general idea.

Shrdlu has been in the journalism game since movable type signaled, as it did, the dawn of Enlightenment and the ruin of Shrdlu's former racket (29 Sept.) As explained in the 3 Sept. 1945 strip (*Barnaby, Volume Two*), Shrdlu is an ex-devil who became a printer's devil. See also the notes for that day (*Volume Two*, pp. 369–370).

Gutenberg (29 Sept.) O'Malley alleges that Shrdlu worked for Johannes Gutenberg (1400–1468), inventor of the printing press.

"Dog Bites Man"? . . . No, O'Malley. It has to be the other way around. (30 Sept.) Shrdlu is correct: "Man bites dog" is the expression. It conveys the media's preference for novelty. The idea is attributed to John B. Bogart, city editor of the New York *Sun*, who said: "When a dog bites a man, that is not news, because it happens so often. But if a man bites a dog, that is news" (Kaplan, p. 554).

Public relations counsel (2 Oct.) Shrdlu corrects O'Malley because this (in 1950) is a contemporary term for "press agent."

NATIONAL FAIRY GODFATHERS DAY! (4 Oct.) Establishing a national day for anything is far more difficult than O'Malley imagines. Though the U.S. officially recognized Mother's Day (proposed in 1908) as a national holiday in 1914, Father's Day (proposed in 1910) did not receive official recognition until 1972. That said, it was observed unofficially, and by 1950 retailers had discovered Father's Day promotions were very effective in increasing sales (Conroy).

dancing in the streets, fireworks and the traditional bonfires, concerts, root beer, parades, turkey shoots, speeches, fat man races, masked revelry . . . (7 Oct.) O'Malley proposes an amalgam of activities associated with a disparate array of holidays and other festive occasions: fireworks (Independence Day, U.S.A), bonfires (Guy Fawkes, UK), masked revelry (Mardi Gras, New Orleans, U.S.; also Twelfth Night, UK).

On Fairy Godfathers Day Eve, gifts are left outside the front door. . . To vanish in the night — (10 Oct.) O'Malley might be extrapolating from the Christmas Eve tradition of leaving food for Santa Claus/Saint Nicholas/ Father Christmas. In North America, the food is often milk and cookies; in England, it's beer and mince pies.

Gnomie (13 Oct.) This is either a diminutive of the word *gnome* or an etymological throwback to the word's root, the Latin *Gnomi*, used by Paracelsus to describe beings that "have earth as their element,... through which they move unobstructed as fish do through water, or birds and land animals through air" (*OED*). More generally, a *gnome* is "One of a race of diminutive spirits fabled to inhabit the interior of the earth and to be the guardians of its treasures" (*OED*). And, of course, gnomes are among the beings admitted to the Elves, Leprechauns, Gnomes and Little Men's Chowder and Marching Society. (Fairy Godfathers belong to the *Little Men* part of that taxonomy.)

"was aslo ssee nwith shrdlu" (14 Oct.) Typos are intentional. As Shrdlu explains on 4 Sept. 1945, he is "responsible for all omissions, typographical errors, pied lines, switched captions, and misspelled names" (*Barnaby, Volume Two*, p. 281).

always falls precisely on the first convenient Saturday five or six moons after Walpurgis Night — or the Feast of Beltane — depending on whether your vegetable man hands out Gregorian or Keltic Calendars (14 Oct.). If you want to celebrate Fairy Godfather's Day (and why wouldn't you?), here's how to calculate when. Walpurgis Night is celebrated on April 30; the Feast of Beltane falls on May 1. On average, a lunar month is 29 days, 12 hours, and 44 minutes. However, in this context ("five or six moons"), the word "moon" generally refers to a calendar month. So, Fairy Godfather's Day would happen around October 1 (five moons after May 1) or November 1 (6 moons after May 1) or — if no "convenient" Saturday has occurred — any time after that point.

Celebrated in northern Europe, Walpurgis Night commemorates the canonization of St. Walpurga, famous for her reputed ability to oppose witchcraft and evil spirits. An ancient Celtic festival, the Feast of Beltane included rituals to ward off evil, and to protect crops, animals, and people.

O'MALLEY AND THE GOOSE • 25 OCT. – 24 NOV. 1950

But "by mistake"? Ah, no — Tomorrow I'll tell you something of the strange nature of Leprechauns (25 Oct.) and **Leprechauns' preoccupation with wealth, their drive to acquire monetary metals, caskets of jewelry, and other symbols of worldly riches** (31 Oct.) Originating in Irish folklore, leprechauns are indeed noted for harboring a hidden crock of gold. Via McSnoyd (the invisible leprechaun), Johnson returns to this idea throughout *Barnaby*.

Mom read me a book about a Goose that laid eggs and the eggs were — (3 Nov.) In Aesop's tale of "The Goose that Laid the Golden Eggs," the couple that owns the goose, assuming that the fowl must have a lump of gold inside it, kill the bird to remove the treasure. After killing it, they instead discover that the goose is otherwise ordinary, and thus — in their greed — lose the source of their golden eggs. The fable is the source of the saying "Don't kill the goose that lays the golden eggs" — to which subsequent *Barnaby* strips (6–7 & 9–20 Nov.) allude.

luxurious imported landeau with six white wall tires (16 Nov.) If by *landeau*, O'Malley means a horse-drawn carriage the back of which can be open or closed, then his addition of white wall tires is anachronistic (those are found on automobiles). On the other hand, if O'Malley means *landaulet*, then he is describing an automobile with a convertible top for the rear passengers. It's a fancy car that, by the 1950s, was rare — likely to be transporting a head of state through a parade, but unlikely for a middle-class family such as the Baxters.

Domesticated geese can't fly (20 Nov.) O'Malley is correct: domesticated geese can't fly. But this goose appears not to be domesticated.

the sham and tinsel of our modern society (24 Nov.) An indicator of falsity, the phrase "sham and tinsel" first shows up in the popular press in around 1859, and continued to be a regular expression until the mid twentieth-century — used by people of all backgrounds and politics.

THE GIFTS OF THE BAXTERS • 25 NOV. – 26 DEC. 1950

the whole idea of the Yule log, aside from the mere pleasure of sitting around an open fire, is to protect the house from thunder and lightning, increase the fertility of the fields and ward off chilblains (5 Dec.) Many beliefs circulate around the Yule log, the tradition of which dates to the 17th century. Jacqueline Simpson's *Dictionary of English Folklore* reports that "it was generally believed that it would be very unlucky if the log was allowed to go out on Christmas Day." Chilblains — an archaic term by 1950 — are "an inflammatory swelling produced by exposure to cold, affecting the hands and feet" (*OED*).

I'll buy John a nice new leather golf bag! He used to love to play — (11 Dec.) Johnson is here retelling O. Henry's short story, "The Gift of the Magi" (1905), in which a husband and wife sell their most prized possessions to give the other a gift, the utility of which depends upon the recently sold possession. Della sells her hair to buy Jim a watch chain; Jim sells his watch to buy Della a set of expensive combs.

Winston Churchill? (13 Dec.) While not an "Old Master," Churchill took up painting in 1915, and continued throughout his life. Though he only managed to paint one picture while British Prime Minister during the Second World War, he found more time for painting after the Conservative Party lost power in 1945. Framing the first page of a November 26, 1950 *New York Times Magazine* profile on Churchill were five photos, each labeled with one of the roles he was then filling: "STATESMAN," "POLITICIAN," "AUTHOR," "SUNDAY PAINTER," and "SPORTSMAN." The article's title and subtitle conveys its thesis: "Churchill's Way: 2-Days-in-1: The wartime Prime Minister at 76 thus carries on his work as party leader and author and has time for his hobbies" (Hailey, p. 7).

Reminds me of a piece I helped O'Henry with one time . . . Think of it! . . . The perfect Christmas gifts! Both utterly useless! (19 Dec.) Johnson makes a direct reference to O'Henry's "The Gift of the Magi" (see note for 11

Dec.), which concludes as follows: "I have lamely related to you the uneventful chronicle of two foolish children in a flat who most unwisely sacrificed for each other the greatest treasures of their house. But in a last word to the wise of these days let it be said that of all who give gifts these two were the wisest. Of all who give and receive gifts, such as they are wisest. Everywhere they are wisest. They are the magi."

J.J. O'MALLEY, PRIVATE EYE • 27 DEC. 1950 – 28 FEB. 1951

Pop's new quarter mystery (3 Jan.) Likely a paperback mystery novel sold for a quarter — twenty-five cents.

No hanging moss, no desolate moors, no luxurious roulette joints, no mountain shacks, no isolated islands — and no sinister sanitoriums, no old castles, no gun rooms, no black yawls, no night trains, no trestles, dunes, fogs, fens, quays, quarries, jungles, swamps, marshes, washes, thickets, bracken, copses, corpses — (4 Jan.) Johnson was an avid mystery reader and here invokes a range of tropes from books and films. This strip also appears in (what we now consider) the classic film noir era. In the years immediately prior to this strip, these hit films would have been playing at his local cinema: *The Big Sleep* (1946, starring Humphrey Bogart and Lauren Bacall), *Out of the Past* (1947, Robert Mitchum), *Key Largo* (1948, Bogart and Bacall), *In a Lonely Place* (1950, Bogart and Gloria Grahame), and *Gun Crazy* (1950).

Many private detectives just sit in their offices and let cases come to them — (11 Jan.) Famously, Sam Spade (Humphrey Bogart) in the film adaptation of Dashiell Hammett's *The Maltese Falcon* (1941).

Polysarcia Company payroll (27 Jan.). *Polysarcia* is an archaic medical term for "excessive accumulation of fat; corpulence; obesity" (*OED*). Johnson is playing with the trope, common in political cartoons, of the "fat capitalist" — typically represented as an obese human, a fat cat, a big pig, or even just a personified bag of money.

C-note (30 Jan.) A $100-dollar bill.

318 Concord Lane, East Westville. (14 Feb.) In the strips of 23 November 1943, 23 September 1947, and 17 February 1948, *Barnaby* identifies East Westville as the town where the Baxters live. The 1943 strip gives this same street address, but the 1947 strip gives 238 Poplar Street. For the possible location of the town, see *Barnaby, Volume Four*, p. 363.

J.J. O'MALLEY, ATTORNEY AT LAW • 1 MAR. – 23 MAR. 1951

nolle prosses, habeas corpuses, tort-feasors (7 Mar.) These are all legal terms. A *nolle pros* (abbreviated from the Latin *nolle prosequi*) is a "procedure by which the Attorney General may terminate criminal proceedings" or "proceeding in which a plaintiff or prosecutor relinquishes part or all of a suit or prosecution against a defendant" (*OED*). From Latin for "thou (shalt) have the body (in court)," *habeas corpus* is a "writ issuing out of a court of justice, or awarded by a judge in vacation, requiring the body of a person to be brought before the judge or into the court for the purpose specified in the writ"; specifically, it requires "the body of a person restrained of liberty to be brought before the judge or into court, that the lawfulness of the restraint may be investigated and determined" (*OED*). A *tortfeasor* is a person "who is guilty of a tort; a wrongdoer, trespasser" (*OED*).

a bolt of chantilly (9 Mar.) Chantilly is "a type of delicate bobbin lace originally made at Chantilly in the 17th cent., characterized by its high quality and fine detail, and often made of silk" (*OED*). Presumably, an outfit featuring delicate lace would convey the impression that its wearer were refined, higher-class. It's also *not* a contemporary look in 1951.

Like this hoop-skirt job. But maybe without the mantilla — (10 Mar.) & **Godey's Ladies Book** (10 Mar.) O'Malley's sense of women's fashion is eighty or so years out of date. Hoop skirts went out of style in the 1860s. The mantilla (a small cape or mantle) was not commonly worn after the 1870s, though — in certain communities — was still worn for formal occasions. *Godey's Lady's*

Book was a popular and influential women's magazine in the nineteenth century. In 1898, the magazine — then called *Godey's Magazine* — ceased publication.

Sheboygan (13 Mar.) A city in Wisconsin.

It's an authentic Banquo tartan! Alludes to Shakespeare's *Macbeth* (set in Scotland), in which the title character murders Banquo — who then returns as a ghost.

TENNESSEE HENNESSY • 24 MAR. – 4 JUNE 1951

Flabbergasties (24 Mar.). Johnson pokes fun at the tendency of breakfast cereals to end in "ies" or a variant thereof. See note for 28 Dec. 1948 in *Barnaby, Volume Four*, p. 374.

preposterous personification of fatuous knight errantry — romantic claptrap Cervantes reduced to laughter 350 years ago — (28 Mar.) Miguel de Cervantes' *Don Quixote* (1605 & 1615) famously mocks chivalric romances via its title character who has read so many of them that he imagines himself a knight-errant.

"Blood on the Alfalfa" (2 Apr.). Johnson's parodic title may be a riff on the western noir *Blood on the Moon* (1948, starring Robert Mitchum)

Conestoga wagon and the Reo were not contemporary (6 Apr.) O'Malley is correct. The Conestoga wagon dates to the early eighteenth century, and was widely used well into the mid-nineteenth century. However, the REO Speed Wagon is a flatbed truck made by the REO Motor Company from 1915 to 1953. And there is of course no "1870 Automotive yearbook…"

people who say television is a menace! (10 Apr.) In the recurring references to *Captain Bloodbath* (Jane's favorite comic), Johnson mocks anti-comics hysteria. Though these *Barnaby* strips display his delight in skewering TV westerns, he did not think the medium a menace: in fact, he especially loved watching broadcasts of sports. So, O'Malley's hysterical tone in the third panel (echoing Albert's mother in panel one) is indicative of Johnson's distance from this sentiment — a prominent one in the early 1950s.

Will James' "Cowboys" (11 Apr.). Will James (1892–1942) was a Canadian-born artist and writer of stories about cowboys, including *Cowboys North and South* (1924), *Smoky the Cowhorse* (1927, winner of the Newbery Medal), *Lone Cowboy* (1930, James' fictionalized autobiography), and *The American Cowboy* (1942). O'Malley might be referring to *The Will James Cowboy Book* (1938), a collection of stories for young readers. Several of James' works were adapted as films, but are unreliable as sources of history (contrary to what O'Malley alleges).

"Essays in Radical Empiricism" by William James (11 Apr.). O'Malley has confused a popular writer of cowboy tales with William James (1842–1910), the eminent American philosopher and psychologist. *Essays in Radical Empiricism* (1912), a posthumous collection comprised of pieces written over the course of 30 years, shows the development of his idea of radical empiricism — a concept which does have some bearing on a fairy godfather alleged to be purely imaginary. According to James, "The relations between things, conjunctive as well as disjunctive, are just as much matters of direct particular experience, neither more so nor less so, than the things themselves." And: "The parts of experience hold together from next to next by relations that are themselves parts of experience. The directly apprehended universe needs, in short, no extraneous transempirical connective support, but possesses in its own right a concatenated or continuous structure" ("Radical empiricism"). The notion that "relations between things" are as real as "the things themselves," and that all comprise "parts of experience" is James' effort at reconciling the gap between thoughts and things, human consciousness and the content of the world. It's an apt choice for a fairy godfather who is simultaneously regarded as a product of Barnaby's consciousness and yet is an observable presence in the world of the strip.

That phoney cowboy! Letting it be aired around that he delivers the presents on Christmas, in a buckboard, with a team of eight longhorn cows! His picture, with both guns blazing, on Easter eggs!

Tennessee Hennessy Valentines — Tennessee Hennessy flower pots for Mothers Day! And Tennessee Hennessee candy bars, breakfast food, toys, furniture, chess sets, aspirin, geiger counters, and — (13 Apr.) Johnson is spoofing the craze for TV westerns. In 1949, two shows debuted: *Hopalong Cassidy* (1949–1954) and *The Lone Ranger* (1949–1957). 1950 saw the debuts of twice as many programs, including *The Cisco Kid* (1950–1956) and *The Gene Autry Show* (1950–1956). 1951 would see another half-dozen westerns arrive on the small screen.

What model bat is this? A Stan Musial? Joe DiMaggio? Happy Chandler? (14 Apr.) Stan Musial (1920–2013), first baseman for St. Louis Cardinals from 1941 to 1944 and 1946 to 1963 (in 1945, he served in the U.S. Navy), was one of baseball's great hitters. During the integration of Major League Baseball in the 1940s, Musial notably did not participate in racist taunts of Black players. As the Dodgers' Don Newcombe (the third Black pitcher in the Major Leagues) said, "The man [Musial's nickname was Stan the Man] went about his job and did it damn well and never had the need to sit in the dugout and call a black guy a bunch of names, because he was trying to change the game and make it what it should have been in the first place, a game for all people" (Goldstein). An even greater hitter, Joe DiMaggio (1914–1999) played for The New York Yankees from 1936 to 1942 and 1946 to 1951 (from 1943 to 1945, he served in the U.S. Air Force). He famously had a 56-game hitting streak in 1941. When he retired in December 1951, DiMaggio ranked fifth in career home runs. For Happy Chandler, see the note for 28 May 1946 in *Barnaby, Volume Three*, p. 361.

I'm a-riding the old pony express with a big uranium shipment (25 Apr.) Another of the anachronisms that O'Malley complains of in the strip of April 6.

My Screen Actors Guild card, AFRA, TvA, Equity — (30 Apr.) O'Malley offers a list of entertainment industry unions, starting with the Screen Actors Guild, founded in 1933. AFRA is the American Federation of Radio Artists, a union founded in 1937. The TvA is the Television Authority, the union that would merge with the AFRA in 1952, forming AFTRA. After merging with the Screen Actors Guild in 2012, this would become SAG-AFTRA. Equity is Actors Equity, a union founded by theatre actors in 1913.

Horse Opera (11 May). Western movie or TV series.

"I have perceived a most faint neglect of late —" (11 May). Lear is a very challenging dramatic role, and it is unlikely that O'Malley could do it justice. In this particular speech from Act I, Scene 4, Lear is agreeing that, though he had wondered if he were simply imagining it, people *have* been unkind to him lately: "I have perceiv'd a most faint neglect of late, which I have rather blam'd as mine own jealous curiosity than as a very pretense and purpose of unkindness. I will look further into it." In fact, Lear has been the unkind one, banishing his loyal daughter (Cordelia) and earl (Kent). This speech and Shakespeare's *King Lear* are an unlikely choice for an audience of five-year-olds.

But you'll never know a Piebill Grebe, nor a Semipalmated Plover. Nor an Egress in your enchanted wood. (16 May) Barnaby's response ("Huh?") is apt. Though O'Malley is trying to sound impressive, his knowledge of birds is a bit muddled. Though "far less sociable than most grebes" (according to the Audubon Society), the Piebill Grebe (also spelled *Pied-billed Grebe*) lives mostly in ponds in North America and so might be found in Barnaby's neighborhood. However, the Semipalmated Plover lives mostly in Alaska and northern Canada. *Egress* means "exit," but O'Malley might mean *Egret*, a bird found in the northeastern U.S. (where the strip takes place).

THE O'MALLEY ACADEMY • 5 JUNE – 18 JUNE 1951

What was in it? DDT? (6 June). Mr. Baxter is comparing O'Malley to an insect. Developed in the 1940s, DDT (dichloro-diphenyl-trichloroethane) is an insecticide, initially used to fight insect-borne human diseases like malaria, and later used to protect crops, and to keep the mosquito population under control. Rachel Carson's *Silent Spring* (1962) called attention to the pesticide's other (unintended) effects, including poisoning birds (and other wildlife) and causing cancer in humans. In 1972, the Environmental Protection Agency banned its use in the U.S. But in 1951, DDT was merely an effective, modern insecticide.

could have no effect on an imaginary Pixie, with no atomic structure, no inertia, no corporeality — (6 June). O'Malley's reality, as expressed in two sides of a scientific-philosophical debate. In the previous day's strip, O'Malley affirms that he *is* "just a bunch of atoms," and so Albert's claim is technically correct. Since "all matter" (as O'Malley explains) is made of atoms, so a Fairy Godfather is also a collection of atoms. So, contrary to Albert's assumption, the "Atomizer" gun has not disintegrated O'Malley: turning him into atoms would not change him because he is already atoms. However, from Mr. Baxter's perspective, an atomic weapon would have no effect on Mr. O'Malley because Mr. O'Malley does not exist: he is non-corporeal, and thus lacks any atoms to be "atomized" by Albert's Atomizer.

ALL things consist of atoms. Always have, too. Since Leucippus (7 June). O'Malley refers to Leucippus, a Greek philosopher from the fifth century BCE who is believed to be the first to develop the theory of atomism (that everything in the world is made up of atoms).

a splendid grasp of the sciences — from abdominology to Zymology (8 June). Zymology is the science of fermentation, but O'Malley seems to have invented "abdominology" — which presumably names the study of the abdomen.

If this rate of increase — fifty per cent a day — keeps up, Gus do you realize in two weeks we'll have 875.81 and some odd eager little scholars here? (16 June) O'Malley's assumption that his student body will grow by 50% daily is false, but his math is essentially correct — and is a reminder of Johnson's interest in mathematics. If we let x = the current number of pupils, r = the rate of daily increase, n = the number of days, and y = the number of expected students after n days (presuming a constant rate of daily increase), then we could calculate that increase as follows: $x \times r^n = y$. Let x =3 (the number of pupils today, according to O'Malley), r=1.5 (if 50% more

students each day, then your daily total number of students is 150% of the previous day's total), and n = 14 days (two weeks). Thus:

$$x \times r^n = y$$
$$3 \times 1.5^{14} = y$$
$$3 \times 291.92926025390625 = y$$
$$3 \times 291.92926025390625 = 875.78778076171875$$

The small (two hundredths) discrepancy between my 875.79 (if we round up) and his 875.81 can likely be explained by the fact that I'm using a calculator, and Crockett Johnson was using a slide rule. It would be more work for him to calculate 1.5^{14} out to the 14th decimal point. (His 875.81 would be accurate for a result of 3×291.93 — which is close enough for the purposes of the joke!)

"O Tempora! O Mores! O'Malley!" (18 June). "O Tempora! O Mores!" ("Oh the times! Oh the customs!" in Latin) was first spoken by Cicero, as a *criticism* of the times and the customs. So, pairing these two with "O'Malley" does not have the effect Barnaby's Fairy Godfather intends — which he realizes when he adds, "Er, wait —."

CAMP TYRO • 19 JUNE – 3 SEPT. 1951

Iambic Pentameter (20 June). The meter favored by Shakespeare — five iambs (each of which is an unstressed syllable followed by stressed syllable) per line.

Camp Tyro (25 June). "Tyro" is likely a reference to the Tyrol, a region of the Alps in southern Austria and northern Italy.

delicious and healthful penicillin (18 July). An allusion to Alexander Fleming's discovery of penicillin. Noticing that a culture of *Staphylococcus aureus* had been contaminated by the fungus *penicillium*, Fleming realized also that the penicillium — or "mould juice," as he called it — was also killing any bacteria in the vicinity (Green 82; Tan and Tatsumura 366–367). Hence O'Malley's claim that the "mildewed" side of the house is "fortified with delicious and healthful penicillin."

You know the legend about the Indian girl. Jumped off the cliff. Proprietor of the summer boarding house decided to exploit the story (19 July). There are many legends of Native American girls alleged to have jumped off cliffs (or bridges or waterfalls) to avoid marriage to suitors they did not love. In *Life on the Mississippi* (1883), Mark Twain writes satirically of this recurring story and notes its frequent connection to tourism. Another reference to these tales, "Lovers' Leap Lodge" (28 July) has a slightly more specific connection to Twain's book, which observes that "There are fifty Lover's Leaps along the Mississippi from whose summit disappointed Indian girls have jumped." I say "slightly" because even readers unfamiliar with Twain would know "Lover's Leap" as a popular name for such summits. The *Barnaby* strip of 12 August 1943 also makes reference to this tale (*Barnaby, Volume One*, p. 222).

Restraint of trade — I mean, it's a violation of academic freedom! (20 July). O'Malley is flailing here. *Restraint of trade* covers a range of practices that interfere with business, including "interference with free-market conditions" (*OED*), price-fixing, "creating a monopoly, coercing another party to stop competing with your business, or unlawfully interfering with a business deal" ("Restraint of trade"). In contrast, *academic freedom* refers to a scholar's right to participate in an open exchange of ideas and to pursue inquiry where it may lead without fear of reprisal. As representatives of the American Association of University Professors and of the Association of American Colleges wrote in their "Statement of Principles on Academic Freedom and Tenure" (1940), "The common good depends upon the free search for truth and its free exposition." And "Freedom in research is fundamental to the advancement of truth. Academic freedom in its teaching aspect is fundamental for the protection of the rights of the teacher in teaching and of the student to freedom in learning."

it takes time, you see, for a cold front to build itself up over the Pacific and to move in against warmer air — or is it vice-versa? (24 July). O'Malley's understanding of weather systems is basically accurate: when a cold front meets warm air, *if that air has sufficient moisture*, then rain may be the result.

"Pop Goes the Weasel" (30 July). Nineteenth-century English singing game and nursery rhyme popular in the U.S.

"Sweet Dreamland" (30 July). There are two candidates for this song, the most likely of which is "Sweet Dreamland," a lullaby with lyrics by Nannie H. Barrett and music by J. L. Drummond (published in 1884). The chorus invites listeners into "Sweet dreamland, sweet dreamland, in the fair sweet dreamland." Another possibility is "Meet Me Tonight in Dreamland," a waltz with lyric by Beth Slater Whitson and music by Leo Friedman. Though first published in 1909, the song was popular in the early twentieth century and a featured tune performed by Judy Garland in the hit film *In the Good Old Summertime* (1949), the musical adaptation of *The Shop Around the Corner* (1940). In contrast with O'Malley's choices in the third panel, both songs are gentle and suitable for bedtime.

"Frankie and Johnny" (30 July). A popular murder ballad, the first published version of which dates to 1904, and which — like many of O'Malley's choices — is not typically performed for children. In the song, Johnny and Frankie promise to be faithful to each other. When Frankie finds Johnny with another woman, she shoots him dead because he "was doing her wrong" (a repeated lyric). By song's end, Frankie is being sent to the electric chair.

"'Twas a balmy summer evening and a goodly crowd was there! It well-nigh villed Joe's barroom, at the corner of the square. And —" (30 July). O'Malley is reciting "The Face Upon the Barroom Floor" (1887) by Hugh Antoine d'Arcy (1843–1925). In this long-winded narrative poem, a "vagabond" arrives at a bar, and, after patrons buy him drinks, tells them how he became "came to be the dirty sot" they see before them: he was a famous artist, but took to drink after his beloved left him for another man. For another whiskey, he offers to draw her portrait on the barroom floor. In the midst of adding one more lock of hair to her "shapely" face, he shrieks, and "leaped and fell across the picture — dead!"

"The Farmer in the Dell" (1 Aug.) Popular children's rhyme beginning, "The farmer in the dell, / The farmer in the dell, / Hi-ho, the derry-o, / The farmer in the dell." According to Iona and Peter Opie's *The Singing Game* (1985), it originates in Germany in 1826, migrates to the U.S. by 1883, and appears in Scotland (where Johnson's father was born) by 1898.

Your old Fairy Godfather once attended one with Dan Beard — or was it Dan Boone? No — Ah, yes! It was Dan McGrew (2 Aug.) For Dan Beard and Daniel Boone, see the note for 18 May 1944 in *Barnaby, Volume Two*, p. 358. Appropriately perhaps, O'Malley settles on the one fictional Dan of this group — Dan McGrew, the subject of Robert W. Service's narrative poem "The Shooting of Dan McGrew" (1907). So popular was the poem that it inspired the song "Dangerous Dan McGrew," recorded by Guy Lombardo and His Royal Canadians in 1949. Robert Service's verse begins like this:

> A bunch of the boys were whooping it up in the Malamute saloon;
> The kid that handles the music-box was hitting a jag-time tune;
> Back of the bar, in a solo game, sat Dangerous Dan McGrew,
> And watching his luck was his light-o'-love, the lady that's known as Lou.
> When out of the night, which was fifty below, and into the din and the glare,
> There stumbled a miner fresh from the creeks, dog-dirty, and loaded for bear.
> He looked like a man with a foot in the grave and scarcely the strength of a louse,
> Yet he tilted a poke of dust on the bar, and he called for drinks for the house.
> There was none could place the stranger's face, though we searched ourselves for a clue;
> But we drank his health, and the last to drink was Dangerous Dan McGrew.

Over the course of the poem, we learn that the stranger, McGrew and Lou have a history. McGrew seems to have "stolen the woman [the stranger] loved" — she is Lou, and the stranger is there for vengeance. He and McGrew shoot each other, with the stranger dying while "clutched to the breast of the lady that's known as Lou." In the final line, the narrator reveals that Lou "pinched his [the stranger's] poke" of gold.

Mr. Popolus, the proprietor. Been a dull year — (3 Aug.) If this is a misspelling of *populus*, then Johnson is making a tree pun. A lodge with "haunted pines" on its sign has a proprietor named for is a genus of tree that includes the poplar, the aspen, and the cottonwood.

Miss Fox (4 & 6 Aug.) The ghost of one of the Fox sisters, nineteenth-century Spiritualists and mediums. See the note for 15 Sept. 1944 in *Barnaby, Volume Two*, p. 361.

Pocahontas (6 Aug.) A member of the Powhatan people, Pocahontas (1596-1617) is perhaps the most famous and most misrepresented Native American woman. The "Lover's Leap" context suggests a reference to the myth that she and Captain John Smith were in love with each other (they weren't). Given that Miss Fox was a fraud, Johnson's decision to give this "Pocahontas" line to her may indicate that he's knowingly referring to the legend.

Cheese it! The COPS! (10 Aug.) In this context, "cheese" is a verb meaning "stop (what one is saying or doing) instantly, esp. (now solely) at the approach of authority," according to the first volume of J.E. Lighter's *Random House Dictionary of American Slang*.

Flatfoot (11 Aug.) In this context, a police officer or detective.

Nyad (16 Aug.) More commonly spelled as "naiad," this creature from Greek mythology is a "nymph of fresh water, thought to inhabit a river, spring, etc., as its tutelary spirit" or "a young woman likened to a naiad, esp. through some association with water" (*OED*).

Kootchie Dancers (17 Aug.) An abbreviation of *hootchy-kootchy dancers*. This can also be spelled *hootchie-cootchie* dancers, and is often abbreviated as *hootchie cootchie* — as it is in the lyric from "Meet Me in St. Louis" ("We will dance the hoochie coochie / I will be your tootsie wootsie"). According to the second volume of Lighter's *Random House Dictionary of American Slang*, the term *hootchy-kootchy* dates to the 1890s and refers to "a sinuous, suggestive dance, usu. in crude imitation of a belly dance, performed by a woman, esp. as a carnival attraction" (pp. 149–150).

Dr. Schlaffkopf (17 Aug.) A joke that depends upon basic knowledge of German: *Kopf* means head or mind, and *schlaff* is limp, slack, sagging, or droopy. So, this might translate to *Dr. Slack-brained*.

phrontistery (17 Aug.) A "place for thinking or studying; a school, college, or other educational institution," from "Aristophanes' representation of the school of Socrates," and thus a term that is sometimes used ironically (*OED*). O'Malley isn't being ironic here, but Johnson certainly is.

FTC (18 Aug.) The Federal Trade Commission, a U.S. government agency, is supposed to protect consumers from fraud. See note for 3 April 1947 in *Barnaby Volume Four*, p. 365.

Name of Reggie. Rides a bicycle. Nice sort of chap, for a bear (21 Aug.) If this is an allusion to any particular person or animal, I could not discover who.

We're looking for REAL things, Harold. (25 Aug.) Yes, I also wanted to see some foreshadowing (or irony) in a child named Harold rebuked for allegedly veering from the real. But the title character of *Harold and the Purple Crayon* (1955) is named for Johnson's nephew, Harold Frank, born in 1953. And there are other, stronger, parallels with that book elsewhere in *Barnaby* — such as the "Lively Arts" narrative of March 1949 (collected in *Barnaby, Volume Four*).

J.J. O'MALLEY, ROCKET SCIENTIST • 4 SEPT. – 19 OCT. 1951

Galaxy M33? Triangulum? (10 Sept.) M33 — named for Charles Messier, who discovered it in 1764 — is a spiral galaxy, located in the Triangulum constellation, three million light years from Earth (Garner).

Dog Star (17 Sept.) Easily visible via Barnaby's telescope, the Dog Star — also known as Sirius and Alpha Canis Major — is the brightest star in the night sky. It's located in the constellation Canis Major.

A simple problem in spirals and Keplerian ellipses? (20 Sept.) The *Keplerian ellipse* refers to the first law of planetary motion proposed by German mathematician and astronomer Johannes Kepler (1571–1630) — that the "orbit of every planet is an ellipse with the sun at a focus."

O'Malley, with your lift and pay load, I've never even been able to figure out how you can clear the sill of a second-story window! (20 Sept.) In aeronautics, *lift* is the upward force that keeps an airplane aloft. When a wing moves horizontally through the air, it creates lift. However, O'Malley's payload — a term which Atlas is using euphemistically to refer to O'Malley's weight — would require far greater lift than his small wings could realistically provide. Via Atlas, Johnson is winking at the impossibility of someone of O'Malley's shape gaining flight at all.

Rockets are different. They push away against their own discharge. On the principle that every action has an equal and opposite reaction. Air just slows up a rocket. (21 Sept.) Newton's Third Law of Motion (which O'Malley names in the strip of October 10) states that "when two bodies interact, they apply forces to one another that are equal in magnitude and opposite in direction" ("Newton's laws of motion"). Also known as the law of action and reaction, it is often summarized as "every action has an equal and opposite reaction." Atlas is correct that rocket flight and winged flight work differently. A rocket pushes against the gases inside it, but wings push against the air.

You can't get a rocket ship up past the Earth's gravitational force, O'Malley, without a fuel that can produce an exhaust jet speed of 30,000 miles an hour. Perhaps a fission of U-235 or — (29 Sept.) Johnson has clearly been reading about rockets and space travel. According to current estimates, a spacecraft needs to be traveling at speeds of over 25,000 miles per hour to break free of earth's gravity and enter orbit. O'Malley's response — "Why, of course! Atomic energy!" — signals Johnson's awareness that rocket scientists had been studying the possibility of nuclear-powered rockets. As O'Malley discovers in the strip of October 1, Uranium 235 was not available for purchase.

$M_0/M_1 = e^{v/c}$ (5 Oct.) Though most of the formulae in *Barnaby* are accurate, this one is not. As physicist Chris Sorensen explains, the M likely represents mass, and "the left hand side of the formula is a ratio of masses of the same object at different speeds v." On the right hand side, e = 2.718, "the base of the natural logarithms," and "v/c is very likely the ratio of a velocity of some mass to the speed of light." So, Sorensen says, "the formula looks like Einstein's Special Relativity, but only looks like." This is his reasoning:

> Application of the formula for v = 0 yields $M_0 = M_1$. This is reasonable because it implies that if there is no velocity, the mass doesn't change; this is true. On the other hand, the largest v an object can have according to relativity law is v = c. Then the formula predicts $M_0 = eM_1 = 2.717M_1$. This is wrong. At v = c, all M = infinity ala relativity.

As Sorensen puts it, "I think whoever wrote the formula knew a little bit about the, especially then, mysterious theory of relativity and the superhuman genius Einstein, and then fabricated something that looked like a relativity formula."

Newton's Third Law of Motion (10 Oct.) See note for 21 Sept. 1951.

Your Fairy Godfather will have to jump to take up the fierce recoil! Watch out for the concussion! (16 Oct.) In this context, the *recoil* is the "rebound or kick of a gun or firearm when discharged" (O'Malley imagines his wish will have a comparably explosive power) and *concussion* refers to "the shock of impact" (*OED*).

THE DOG FROM ANOTHER PLANET • 21 OCT. – 31 DEC. 1951

the return of Halley's Comet in 1910? (30 Oct.) As noted in the Afterword, since it appears every 75 years, Halley's Comet is the sole comet visible to the naked eye that can appear twice in a human lifetime. At the time of this strip, it had last appeared in April 1910, when Crockett Johnson was three and a half years old. The comet is named for Edmond Halley (1656–1742), who saw the comet in 1682, and who correctly predicted its return in 1758–59. It appeared again in 1835, 1910, and 1986.

Pliocene four-legged carnivori — (2 Nov.) Dogs emerge in the Pliocene era (5.333 million to 2.58 years ago); their ancestor is an extinct wolf from that era.

Docga, a planet of Procyon up in Canis Minor — (8 Nov.) The *other* and less bright dog star, Procyon is indeed in the constellation Canis Minor.

With FM sound and full-spectrum color (7 Dec.) These sound like advertisements for the latest models of television sets. Johnson was what we would today call an "early adopter" of television: he bought his first set in 1947, and was likely attentive to new developments in the technology. By 1950, ads were heralding "FM sound" as the latest in audio. In New York City, in November 1950, CBS and Gimbels Department store began offering public demonstrations of color television ("New Yorkers See Color"). In September 1951, the first color TV sets reached the American market (Rothman).

Empiricism, the dialectic of true researchers. HIS is the method of a Dogmatist (11 Dec.) Johnson is punning on the "dog" in "dogmatism," though O'Malley is using the term to cast doubt on the Professor's capacity to reason well. In his sense, dogmatism is "a way of thinking based upon principles which have not been tested by reflection," nor confirmed by experience (*OED*). In contrast, empiricism "emphasizes or privileges the role of experience in knowledge, esp. claiming that sense experience or direct observation rather than abstract reasoning is the foundation of all knowledge of reality" (*OED*).

Don't take any wooden bones, son. (13 Dec.) The canine version of "Don't take any wooden nickels."

Spotty. (13 Dec.) This seems to be Gorgon's father, who we first meet in June 1943. Then, Barnaby calls him "Rover," but that is also a generic dog name — and, in the strip, is never confirmed as his real name.

confounding judge and jury with a nolle prosequi here, a crambe repetita there, a canis in praesepi — (27 Dec.) For *nolle prosequi*, see note for 7 Mar. 1951. The other two are *not* legal terms. *Crambe repetita* means "cabbage repeated" (translated, variously, as "warmed-over cabbage," "cabbage boiled twice," "cabbage reheated") and comes from Juvenal's *Satires*: "Occidit miseros crambe repetita magistros," which the *Oxford Dictionary of Quotations* translates (idiomatically) as "That cabbage hashed up again and again proves the death of the wretched teachers" (287) — in other words, a criticism of stale school curriculum. *Canis in praesepi* is Latin for "the dog in the manger," and derives from a fable of Aesop's, in which a dog prevents a hungry ox from eating hay, even though the dog has no use for the hay. The phrase is now associated with the moral "One who selfishly refuses to allow others to use that for which he has no use" (Dickenson, p. 40).

GROWING UP • 1 JAN. – 2 FEB. 1952

Mind over matter (12 Jan. 1952). Another of Johnson's references to O'Malley's ambiguous status, this one is especially apt given the link that the strip posits between Barnaby's cognitive development (his ability to solve math problems on his own, in the strips of 22-24 January) and increasing doubt towards his Fairy Godfather's continued presence. The idea originates in antiquity but this particular phrasing gained prominence via Charles Lyell's observation, in *The Geological Evidences of the Antiquity of Man* (1863): "It may be said that, so far from having a materialistic tendency, the supposed introduction into the earth at successive geological periods of life — sensation, instinct, the intelligence of the higher mammalia bordering on reason, and lastly, the improvable reason of Man himself — presents us with a picture of the ever-increasing dominion of mind over matter" (Kaplan, p. 420). Where Lyell suggests a correlation between mental capacity and evolutionary advancement, Johnson's *Barnaby* correlates improved reason with maturation and the education that accompanies it.

Johnson's strip also invokes the phrase's colloquial meaning, which is somewhat at odds with Lyell's use. In ordinary speech, the phrase also means "mental and psychical control over, or influence on, physical phenomena," especially as pertaining to "the mind's curative effect on bodily illness" (*OED*). In giving this line to Barnaby's Fairy Godfather, Johnson is both expressing O'Malley's belief and reminding readers of its fundamental fallacy: unless they die in childhood, all children grow up. And so will Barnaby, whether O'Malley likes it or not.

WORKS CITED

In addition to the works listed below, I also made extensive use of ProQuest's historical *New York Times* database, the *Oxford English Dictionary*, and *Wikipedia*.

"1940 Statement of Principles on Academic Freedom and Tenure." *American Association of University Professors.* <https://www.aaup.org/report/1940-statement-principles-academic-freedom-and-tenure>. Date of access: 14 Sept. 2021.

"azimuth compass." *Oxford Reference.* Originally in *The Oxford Companion to Ships and the Sea.* <https://www.oxfordreference.com/view/10.1093/oi/authority.20110803095438313>. Date of access: 12 Aug. 2021.

Barrett, Nannie H., and J. L. Drummond. "Sweet Dreamland." sheet music. San Francisco: I. L. A. Brodersen, 1884. Library of Congress. <https://www.loc.gov/item/sm1884.14041/>. Date of access: 13 Aug. 2021.

Bernstein, Robin. *Racial Innocence: Performing American Childhood from Slavery to Civil Rights.* New York and London: New York University Press, 2011.

Candee, Marjorie Dent. "Gourmet's Guide Along the Old Spanish Main." *New York Times* 16 April 1950. p. xx3.

"Captive Audience." Legal Information Institute. Cornell Law School. <https://www.law.cornell.edu/wex/captive_audience>. Date of access 26 July 2021.

Conroy, Thomas F. "Father's Day Aids Many Trade Lines." *New York Times.* 11 June 1950. pp. 1, 6.

Defoe, Daniel. *Robinson Crusoe.* 1719–1720. Edited with an Introduction by Thomas Keymer. Oxford and New York: Oxford UP, 2008.

Dickenson, H.J. *Juta's Phrase & Idiom.* Second Edition. Twelfth Impression. Cape Town & Johannesburg: Juta & Co., 1944.

Garner, Rob. "Messier 33 (The Triangulum Galaxy)." *Hubble's Messier Catalog.* NASA. 20 Feb. 2019. <https://www.nasa.gov/feature/goddard/2019/messier-33-the-triangulum-galaxy>. Date of access: 16 July 2021.

Goldstein, Richard. "Stan Musial, Gentlemanly Slugger and Cardinals' Stan the Man, Dies at 92." *New York Times.* 19 Jan. 2013, p. A25.

Green, John. "Staphylococcus aureus." *The Anthropocene Reviewed.* New York: Dutton/Penguin, 2021. pp. 79–84.

Hailey, Foster. "Churchill's Way: 2-Days-in-1." *New York Times Magazine.* 26 Nov. 1950. pp. 7, 52, 53.

Heffernan, Paul. "New Impetus Given to Toll Highways." *New York Times.* 2 Oct. 1949. pp. 1, 2.

Kaplan, Justin, General Editor. *Bartlett's Familiar Quotations.* Sixteenth Edition. Boston, Toronto, and London: Little, Brown and Company, 1992.

"LANOLIN PLUS." advertisement. *New York Times.* 17 July 1949. p. 38.

Lighter, J.E. *Random House Historical Dictionary of American Slang, Volume I: A-G.* New York: Random House, 1994.

Lighter, J.E. *Random House Historical Dictionary of American Slang, Volume II: H-O.* New York: Random House, 1997.

Moscow, Warren. "Protests Cause End Tonight Of Grand Central Broadcasts." *New York Times.* 2 Jan. 1950, pp. 1, 38.

"Newton's laws of motion." *Encyclopedia Britannica.* <https://www.britannica.com/science/Newtons-laws-of-motion>. Date of access: 14 Sept. 2021.

"New discovery gives BETTER SHAVES!" advertisement. *New York Times.* 4 Dec. 1949. p. SM8.

"New Yorkers See Color." *New York Times* 15 Nov. 1950. pp. 33, 45.

Opie, Iona, and Peter Opie. *The Singing Game.* Oxford UP, 1985.

The Oxford Dictionary of Quotations. Third Edition, reprinted with corrections. New York: Oxford UP, 1980.

Panati, Charles. *The Extraordinary Origin of Everyday Things.* New York: Harper & Row, 1987.

"Radical empiricism." *Encyclopedia Britannica.* 13 Sept. 2019. <https://www.britannica.com/topic/radical-empiricism>. Date of access: 13 July 2021.

"Restraint of trade." *FindLaw.* 20 June 2016. <https://www.findlaw.com/smallbusiness/business-laws-and-regulations/restraint-of-trade.html>. Date of access: 14 Sept. 2021.

Rothman, Lily. "How the Supreme Court Made Color Television Possible." *Time.* 28 Sept. 2015: <https://time.com/4043328/supreme-court-color-television/>. Date of access: 13 Sept. 2021.

Service, Robert W. "The Shooting of Dan McGrew." *Poetry Foundation.* <https://www.poetryfoundation.org/poems/45082/the-shooting-of-dan-mcgrew>. Date of access: 12 July 2021.

Simpson, Jacqueline. *A Dictionary of English Folklore.* Oxford and New York: Oxford UP, 2000.

"Surveyor's chain." *Encyclopedia Britannica.* <https://www.britannica.com/technology/surveyors-chain>. Date of access: 13 Sept. 2021.

Tan, Siang Yong, and Yvonne Tatsumura. "Alexander Fleming (1881–1955): Discoverer of penicillin." *Singapore Medical Journal* vol. 56, no. 7, July 2015. pp. 366–367.

Whiting, Isabel Kimball. "Business Ideals at Home." *The Woman's Journal.* 10 Mar. 1923. pp. 12, 29.

Wills, Matthew. "Turtle Soup: From Class to Mass to Aghast." *JSTOR Daily.* 4 Dec. 2020. <https://daily.jstor.org/turtle-soup-from-class-to-mass-to-aghast/>. Date of access: 15 Sept. 2021.

CREDITS

Unless otherwise indicated, strips and other images reprinted with the permission of The Ruth Krauss Foundation, Stewart I. Edelstein, President. *Barnaby* strips reproduced courtesy of Crockett Johnson Papers, Division of Medicine and Science, National Museum of American History, Smithsonian Institution; and the Billy Ireland Cartoon Library and Museum, Ohio State University.

Additional images courtesy of Crockett Johnson Papers, Division of Medicine and Science, National Museum of American History, Smithsonian Institution: scripts for the final *Barnaby* strips, *The Philadelphia Inquirer*'s version of the final *Barnaby* strip, E.B. Thompson's 4 Feb. 1952 letter to Johnson, Charles Fisher's 5 Feb. 1952 letter to Johnson, Johnson's *Barnaby* scrapbook, Jules Feiffer and Crockett Johnson's untitled strip, cover drawing for *Harold and the Purple Crayon*. Courtesy of the Everett Collection: photos of the 1959 General Electric Theater production of *Barnaby and Mr. O'Malley*. Thanks to the Howard family for the still from the 1959 *Barnaby & Mr. O'Malley*. From Christopher Wheeler: Johnson's 11 Feb. 1952 letter to Charles Fisher. From Philip Nel: the cover for Johnson's *Who's Upside Down?*, 1953 Kimberly-Clark advertisement, Dane Webster's photo of Johnson's *Squared Circle*, 2-page spread from Krauss and Johnson's *Is This You?*, cover for Johnson's *Time for Spring*, *Barkis* panel, cover from Italian edition of *Barnaby* (1970), O'Malley drawing done for Frank Paccassi Jr. From *The Smithsonian Collection of Newspaper Comics*: Sidney Smith's final daily *Old Doc Yak* strip. From IDW Publishing: the *Bloom County* strips. From Jackie Curtis: photo of Johnson with his *Squared Circle*. From the Northeast Children's Literature Collection, Dodd Center, University of Connecticut: two-page spread from Johnson's *The Saga of Quilby*. Thanks to Mark Newgarden: Johnson's American Cancer Society booklet.

THANK YOU

An all-caps THANKS to Peggy Kidwell and Drew Robarge (Division of Medicine & Science, National Museum of American History, Smithsonian Institution), Jenny Robb and Marilyn Scott (Billy Ireland Cartoon Library & Museum, Ohio State University), and Stewart Edelstein (President of The Ruth Krauss Foundation, Inc.) for their ongoing support of this series.

For putting us in touch with Ron Howard's agent, thanks to Stephen Barbara of InkWell Management. Thanks to Mr. Howard and HarperCollins for allowing us to run an excerpt from *The Boys: A Memoir of Hollywood and Family* (HarperCollins, 2021). Thanks to Ron Howard and to the late Rance Howard for sharing the TV pilot of *Barnaby and Mr. O'Malley*.

For research assistance on Johnson's allusions, special thanks to Natasha Muhametzyanova. For excellent sleuthing on one allusion we would have otherwise misidentified, thanks to Robert W. Harwood. For helping us get a better grasp on narrative endings in newspaper comic strips, thanks to Jared Gardner, R.C. Harvey, Susan Kirtley, Mark Newgarden, Michael O'Connor, and Chris Ware. For sharing his expertise in physics, thanks to Chris Sorensen. Finally, thanks to Vicki Smith for sending the original drawing of Mr. O'Malley (done for Frank Paccassi, Jr.).

For helping us track down and obtain scans of the 1951 (and a few 1952) *Barnaby* strips, hearty thanks to Charles Cohen, Daniel Clowes, Sara Willett Duke (Library of Congress), Karen Green (Columbia University), Sara Kearns (Kansas State University), Peggy Kidwell (again!), Tim Noakes (Stanford), and Rick Norwood.

ERRATA FOR BARNABY VOLUMES ONE THROUGH FOUR

BY PHILIP NEL

Any typographical errors in the *Barnaby* series are of course the work of Shrdlu. But these omissions and mistakes are mine. I'm glad to have the opportunity to correct them here.

Corrections for *Volume One*
We should have included this note:
flahoolagh (15 July 1942) is an Irish word meaning "'generous, good-hearted', sometimes to an overly-generous degree." Source: page 34 of Jeffrey L. Kallen, "The English Language in Ireland: An Introduction," *International Journal of Language, Translation, and Intercultural Communication* 2012 1 (1) 25-41.

The narrative title on page 304 has the wrong date: "O'Malley vs. Ogre" ends on 31 August 1942, not 31 October 1942.

A correction for *Volume Two*
Sigahstaw (27 Oct. 1945). The first sentence is correct: This is a purely imaginary tribe. But strike the rest of the note and replace with this: Pronounced "Cigar Store," as in "Cigar Store Indian" — an advertisement in the form of a wooden statue purportedly representing an American Indian. Once commonly found in front of a tobacconist's store, these caricatures of Native Americans can range in size from that of a child (as Howard is here) to adult.

Thanks to those who pointed this out, but especially to Paolo Polesello — the first who alerted us to the error.

ABOUT THE AUTHOR

Crockett Johnson was the pen name of cartoonist and children's book illustrator David Johnson Leisk (October 20, 1906 – July 11, 1975). He is best known for the comic strip *Barnaby* (1942–1952) and the *Harold* series of books begun with *Harold and the Purple Crayon* (1955). Born in New York City, Johnson grew up in Corona, Queens, studying art at Cooper Union in 1924. On his choice of pseudonym, Johnson explained: "Crockett is my childhood nickname. My real name is David Johnson Leisk. Leisk was too hard to pronounce — so — I am now Crockett Johnson!" Johnson also collaborated on four children's books with his wife, the writer Ruth Krauss, including *The Carrot Seed* (1945).

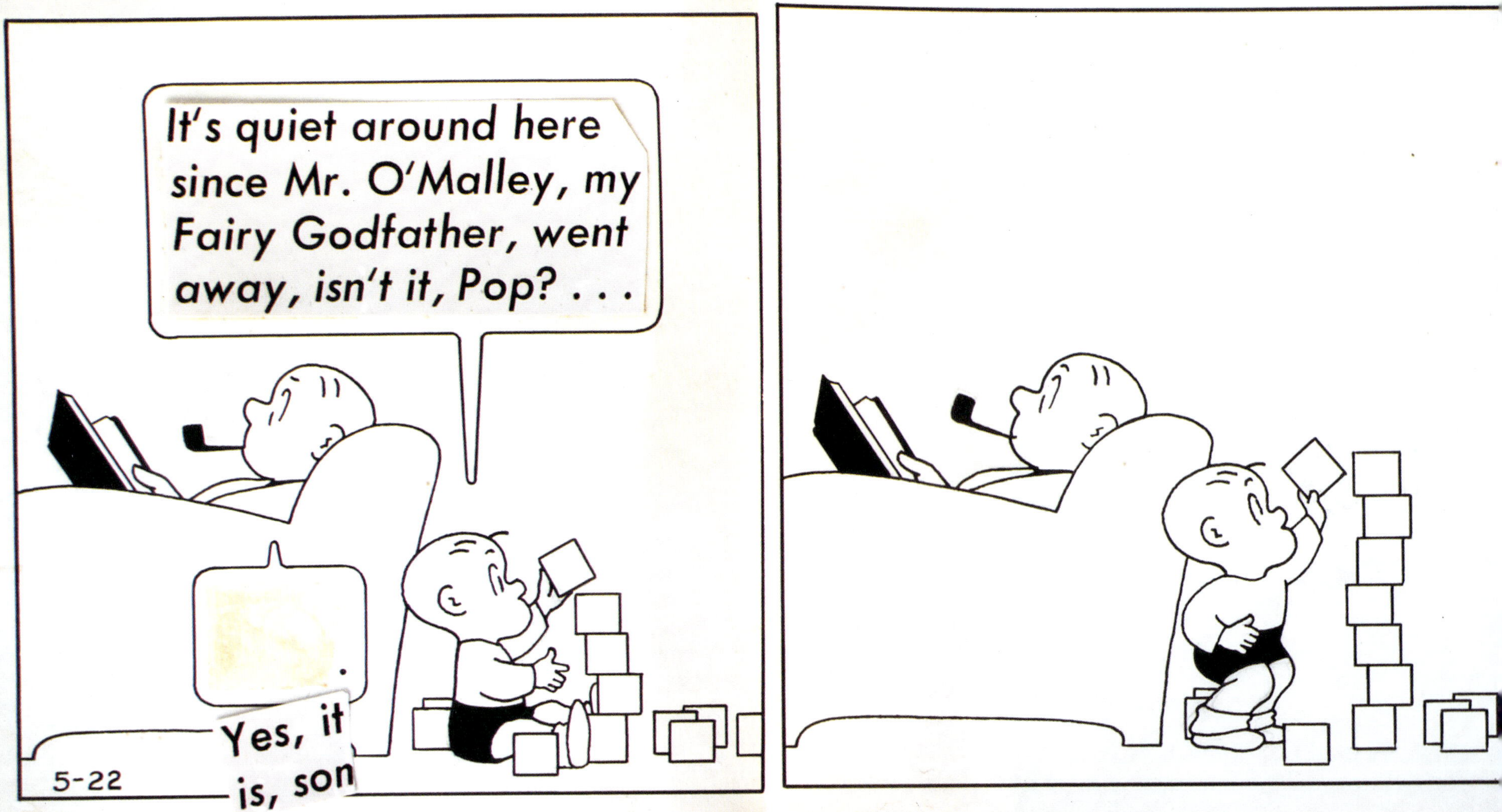
It's quiet around here since Mr. O'Malley, my Fairy Godfather, went away, isn't it, Pop? . . .
Yes, it is, son
5-22